Commonly Used Notat

b	Retention or plowback ratio
C	Call option value
CF	Cash flow
D	Duration
E	Exchange rate
$E(x)$	Expected value of random variable x
F	Futures price
e	2.718, the base for the natural logarithm, used for continuous compounding
e_{it}	The firm-specific return, also called the residual return, of security i in period t
f	Forward rate of interest
g	Growth rate of dividends
H	Hedge ratio for an option, sometimes called the option's delta
i	Inflation rate
k	Market capitalization rate, the required rate of return on a firm's stock
ln	Natural logarithm function
M	The market portfolio
$N(d)$	Cumulative normal function, the probability that a standard normal random variable will have value less than d
p	Probability
P	Put value
PV	Present value
P/E	Price-to-earnings multiple
r	Rate of return on a security; for fixed-income securities, r may denote the rate of interest for a particular period

r_f	The risk-free rate of interest
r_M	The rate of return on the market portfolio
ROE	Return on equity, incremental economic earnings per dollar reinvested in the firm
S_p	Reward-to-volatility ratio of a portfolio, also called Sharpe's measure; the excess expected return divided by the standard deviation
t	Time
T_p	Treynor's measure for a portfolio, excess expected return divided by beta
V	Intrinsic value of a firm, the present value of future dividends per share
X	Exercise price of an option
y	Yield to maturity
α	Rate of return beyond the value that would be forecast from the market's return and the systematic risk of the security
β	Systematic or market risk of a security
ρ_{ij}	Correlation coefficient between returns on securities i and j
σ	Standard deviation
σ^2	Variance
$\text{Cov}(r_i, r_j)$	Covariance between returns on securities i and j

INVESTMENTS

The McGraw-Hill/Irwin Series in Finance, Insurance and Real Estate

Stephen A. Ross, Franco Modigliani Professor of Finance and Economics, Sloan School of Management, Massachusetts Institute of Technology, Consulting Editor

Financial Management

Adair
Excel Applications for Corporate Finance
First Edition

Block, Hirt, and Danielsen
Foundations of Financial Management
Thirteenth Edition

Brealey, Myers, and Allen
Principles of Corporate Finance
Ninth Edition

Brealey, Myers, and Allen
Principles of Corporate Finance, Concise Edition
First Edition

Brealey, Myers, and Marcus
Fundamentals of Corporate Finance
Sixth Edition

Brooks
FinGame Online 5.0

Bruner
Case Studies in Finance: Managing for Corporate Value Creation
Fifth Edition

Chew
The New Corporate Finance: Where Theory Meets Practice
Third Edition

Cornett, Adair, and Nofsinger
Finance: Applications and Theory
First Edition

DeMello
Cases in Finance
Second Edition

Grinblatt (editor)
Stephen A. Ross, Mentor: Influence through Generations

Grinblatt and Titman
Financial Markets and Corporate Strategy
Second Edition

Higgins
Analysis for Financial Management
Ninth Edition

Kellison
Theory of Interest
Third Edition

Kester, Ruback, and Tufano
Case Problems in Finance
Twelfth Edition

Ross, Westerfield, and Jaffe
Corporate Finance
Eighth Edition

Ross, Westerfield, Jaffe, and Jordan
Corporate Finance: Core Principles and Applications
Second Edition

Ross, Westerfield, and Jordan
Essentials of Corporate Finance
Sixth Edition

Ross, Westerfield and Jordan
Fundamentals of Corporate Finance
Eighth Edition

Shefrin
Behavioral Corporate Finance: Decisions that Create Value
First Edition

White
Financial Analysis with an Electronic Calculator
Sixth Edition

Investments

Bodie, Kane, and Marcus
Essentials of Investments
Seventh Edition

Bodie, Kane, and Marcus
Investments
Eighth Edition

Hirt and Block
Fundamentals of Investment Management
Ninth Edition

Hirschey and Nofsinger
Investments: Analysis and Behavior
First Edition

Jordan and Miller
Fundamentals of Investments: Valuation and Management
Fifth Edition

Financial Institutions and Markets

Rose and Hudgins
Bank Management and Financial Services
Seventh Edition

Rose and Marquis
Money and Capital Markets: Financial Institutions and Instruments in a Global Marketplace
Tenth Edition

Saunders and Cornett
Financial Institutions Management: A Risk Management Approach
Sixth Edition

Saunders and Cornett
Financial Markets and Institutions: An Introduction to the Risk Management Approach
Fourth Edition

International Finance

Eun and Resnick
International Financial Management
Fifth Edition

Kuemmerle
Case Studies in International Entrepreneurship: Managing and Financing Ventures in the Global Economy
First Edition

Real Estate

Brueggeman and Fisher
Real Estate Finance and Investments
Thirteenth Edition

Ling and Archer
Real Estate Principles: A Value Approach
Second Edition

Financial Planning and Insurance

Allen, Melone, Rosenbloom, and Mahoney
Retirement Plans: 401(k)s, IRAs, and Other Deferred Compensation Approaches
Tenth Edition

Altfest
Personal Financial Planning
First Edition

Harrington and Niehaus
Risk Management and Insurance
Second Edition

Kapoor, Dlabay, and Hughes
Focus on Personal Finance: An Active Approach to Help You Develop Successful Financial Skills
Second Edition

Kapoor, Dlabay, and Hughes
Personal Finance
Ninth Edition

INVESTMENTS

EIGHTH EDITION

ZVI BODIE

Boston University

ALEX KANE

University of California, San Diego

ALAN J. MARCUS

Boston College

Boston   Burr Ridge, IL   Dubuque, IA   New York   San Francisco   St. Louis
Bangkok   Bogotá   Caracas   Kuala Lumpur   Lisbon   London   Madrid   Mexico City
Milan   Montreal   New Delhi   Santiago   Seoul   Singapore   Sydney   Taipei   Toronto

ABOUT THE AUTHORS

ZVI BODIE
Boston University

Zvi Bodie is the Norman and Adele Barron Professor of Management at Boston University. He holds a PhD from the Massachusetts Institute of Technology and has served on the finance faculty at the Harvard Business School and MIT's Sloan School of Management. Professor Bodie has published widely on pension finance and investment strategy in leading professional journals. In cooperation with the Research Foundation of the CFA Institute, he has recently produced a series of Webcasts and a monograph entitled *The Future of Life Cycle Saving and Investing.*

ALEX KANE
University of California, San Diego

Alex Kane is professor of finance and economics at the Graduate School of International Relations and Pacific Studies at the University of California, San Diego. He has been visiting professor at the Faculty of Economics, University of Tokyo; Graduate School of Business, Harvard; Kennedy School of Government, Harvard; and research associate, National Bureau of Economic Research. An author of many articles in finance and management journals, Professor Kane's research is mainly in corporate finance, portfolio management, and capital markets, most recently in the measurement of market volatility and pricing of options.

ALAN J. MARCUS
Boston College

Alan Marcus is professor of finance in the Wallace E. Carroll School of Management at Boston College. He received his PhD in economics from MIT. Professor Marcus has been a visiting professor at the Athens Laboratory of Business Administration and at MIT's Sloan School of Management and has served as a research associate at the National Bureau of Economic Research. Professor Marcus has published widely in the fields of capital markets and portfolio management. His consulting work has ranged from new product development to provision of expert testimony in utility rate proceedings. He also spent 2 years at the Federal Home Loan Mortgage Corporation (Freddie Mac), where he developed models of mortgage pricing and credit risk. He currently serves on the Research Foundation Advisory Board of the CFA Institute.

BRIEF CONTENTS

BRIEF CONTENTS

CONTENTS

CONTENTS

CONTENTS

CONTENTS

CONTENTS

CONTENTS

CONTENTS

CONTENTS

PREFACE

We wrote the first edition of this textbook two decades ago. The intervening years have been a period of rapid, profound, and ongoing change in the investments industry. This is due in part to an abundance of newly designed securities, in part to the creation of new trading strategies that would have been impossible without concurrent advances in computer technology, and in part to rapid advances in the theory of investments that have come out of the academic community. In no other field, perhaps, is the transmission of theory to real-world practice as rapid as is now commonplace in the financial industry. These developments place new burdens on practitioners and teachers of investments far beyond what was required only a short while ago. Of necessity, our text has evolved along with financial markets.

Investments, Eighth Edition, is intended primarily as a textbook for courses in investment analysis. Our guiding principle has been to present the material in a framework that is organized by a central core of consistent fundamental principles. We make every attempt to strip away unnecessary mathematical and technical detail, and we have concentrated on providing the intuition that may guide students and practitioners as they confront new ideas and challenges in their professional lives.

This text will introduce you to major issues currently of concern to all investors. It can give you the skills to conduct a sophisticated assessment of current issues and debates covered by both the popular media as well as more-specialized finance journals. Whether you plan to become an investment professional, or simply a sophisticated individual investor, you will find these skills essential.

Our primary goal is to present material of practical value, but all three of us are active researchers in the science of financial economics and find virtually all of the material in this book to be of great intellectual interest. Fortunately, we think, there is no contradiction in the field of investments between the pursuit of truth and the pursuit of money. Quite the opposite. The capital asset pricing model, the arbitrage pricing model, the efficient markets hypothesis, the option-pricing model, and the other centerpieces of modern financial research are as much intellectually satisfying subjects of scientific inquiry as they are of immense practical importance for the sophisticated investor.

In our effort to link theory to practice, we also have attempted to make our approach consistent with that of the CFA Institute. In addition to fostering research in finance, the CFA Institute administers an education and certification program to candidates seeking the designation of Chartered Financial Analyst (CFA). The CFA curriculum represents the consensus of a committee of distinguished scholars and practitioners regarding the core of knowledge required by the investment professional. This text also is used in many certification programs for the Financial Planning Association and by the Society of Actuaries.

There are many features of this text that make it consistent with and relevant to the CFA curriculum. Questions from past CFA exams appear at the end of nearly every chapter, and, for students who will be taking the exam, those same questions and the exam from which they've been taken, are listed at the end of the book. Chapter 3 includes excerpts from the "Code of Ethics and Standards of Professional Conduct" of the CFA Institute. Chapter 28, which discusses investors and the investment process, presents the CFA Institute's framework for systematically relating investor objectives and constraints to ultimate investment policy.

In the Eighth Edition, we have further extended our systematic collection of Excel spreadsheets that give tools to explore concepts more deeply than was previously possible. These spreadsheets are available on the Web site for this text (**www.mhhe.com/bkm**), and provide a taste of the sophisticated analytic tools available to professional investors.

UNDERLYING PHILOSOPHY

In the Eighth Edition, we address many of the changes in the investment environment.

At the same time, many basic *principles* remain important. We believe that attention to these few important principles can simplify the study of otherwise difficult material and that fundamental principles should organize and motivate all study. These principles are crucial to understanding the securities already traded in financial markets and in understanding new securities that will be introduced in the future. For this reason, we have made this book thematic, meaning we never offer rules of thumb without reference to the central tenets of the modern approach to finance.

The common theme unifying this book is that *security markets are nearly efficient,* meaning most securities are usually priced appropriately given their risk and return attributes. There are few free lunches found in markets as competitive as the financial market. This simple observation is, nevertheless, remarkably powerful in its implications for the design of investment strategies; as a result, our discussions of strategy are always guided by the implications of the efficient markets hypothesis. While the degree of market efficiency is, and always will be, a matter of debate (and in fact, in this edition, we devote a full chapter to the behavioral challenge to the efficient market hypothesis), we hope our discussions throughout the book convey a good dose of healthy criticism concerning much conventional wisdom.

Distinctive Themes

Investments is organized around several important themes:

1. **The central theme** is the near-informational-efficiency of well-developed security markets, such as those in the United States, and the general awareness that competitive markets do not offer "free lunches" to participants.

   A second theme is the risk–return trade-off. This too is a no-free-lunch notion, holding that in competitive security markets, higher expected returns come only at a price: the need to bear greater investment risk. However, this notion leaves several questions unanswered. How should one measure the risk of an asset? What should be the quantitative trade-off between risk (properly measured) and expected return? The approach we present to these issues is known as *modern portfolio theory,* which is another organizing principle of this book. Modern portfolio theory focuses on the techniques and implications of *efficient diversification,* and we devote considerable attention to the effect of diversification on portfolio risk as well as the implications of efficient diversification for the proper measurement of risk and the risk–return relationship.

2. **This text places** greater emphasis on asset allocation than most of its competitors. We prefer this emphasis for two important reasons. First, it corresponds to the procedure that most individuals actually follow. Typically, you start with all of your money in a bank account, only then considering how much to invest in something riskier that might offer a higher expected return. The logical step at this point is to consider other risky asset classes, such as stock, bonds, or real estate. This is an asset allocation decision. Second, in most cases, the asset allocation choice is far more important in determining overall investment performance than is the set of security selection decisions. Asset allocation is the primary determinant of the risk–return profile of the investment portfolio, and so it deserves primary attention in a study of investment policy.

3. **This text offers** a much broader and deeper treatment of futures, options, and other derivative security markets than most investments texts. These markets have become both crucial and integral to the financial universe and are the major sources of innovation in that universe. Your only choice is to become conversant in these markets—whether you are to be a finance professional or simply a sophisticated individual investor.

NEW IN THE EIGHTH EDITION

The following is a guide to changes in the Eighth Edition. This is not an exhaustive road map, but instead is meant to provide an overview of substantial additions and changes to coverage from the last edition of the text.

Chapter 3 How Securities Are Traded

This chapter has been largely rewritten to reflect the ongoing transformation of trading practices, the growing dominance of electronic trading, the accelerating consolidation of securities markets, and continuing regulatory reform, in particular the response to the Sarbanes-Oxley Act.

Chapter 7 Optimal Risky Portfolios

This chapter contains additional material on the "art" of selecting reasonable parameter values for portfolio construction, and a discussion of what can go wrong when inputs are derived solely from recent historical experience.

Chapter 9 The Capital Asset Pricing Model

We introduce new material generalizing the intuition of the simple CAPM to more sophisticated treatments of risk, for example, consumption risk. We have also updated the material on liquidity and asset pricing throughout the set of chapters dealing with portfolio theory.

Chapter 11 The Efficient Market Hypothesis

We critically evaluate recent suggestions for "fundamental indexing" as a response to market errors in security valuation. We show that these strategies are nothing more than variations on the value-tilted portfolio strategies discussed earlier in the chapter.

Chapter 13 Empirical Evidence on Security Returns

We add considerable new material on the interpretation of risk premiums. For example, we examine new evidence on the relation between the Fama-French risk factors and more fundamental measures of security risk.

Chapter 14 Bond Prices and Yields

The chapter has new material explaining collateralized debt obligations (CDOs) as well as the role of credit rating agencies in the recent credit market crisis.

Chapter 19 Financial Statement Analysis

The chapter has been updated to address current issues in fair value accounting. It also contains additional discussion of the proper interpretation of market-to-book ratios.

Chapter 20 Options Markets

We have added a discussion of options backdating to this chapter.

Chapter 23 Futures, Swaps, and Risk Management

We have added new material on credit default swaps to this chapter. We show how these securities are constructed, and how they are used to transfer credit risk.

Chapter 26 Hedge Funds

This new chapter covers various hedge fund strategies; market-neutral investing and portable alpha; performance evaluation for hedge funds with changing risk exposures; selection bias in hedge fund performance; tail risk in hedge fund portfolios; and hedge fund fees.

Chapter 28 Investment Policy and the Framework of the CFA Institute

This chapter has been updated to reflect the CFA Institute's expanded rubric for constructing a statement of investment policy.

ORGANIZATION AND CONTENT

The text is composed of seven sections that are fairly independent and may be studied in a variety of sequences. Because there is enough material in the book for a two-semester course, clearly a one-semester course will require the instructor to decide which parts to include.

Part One is introductory and contains important institutional material focusing on the financial environment. We discuss the major players in the financial markets, provide an overview of the types of securities traded in those markets, and explain how and where securities are traded. We also discuss in depth mutual funds and other investment companies, which have become an increasingly important means of investing for individual investors.

The material presented in Part One should make it possible for instructors to assign term projects early in the course. These projects might require the student to analyze in detail a particular group of securities. Many instructors like to involve their students in some sort of investment game, and the material in these chapters will facilitate this process.

Parts Two and Three contain the core of modern portfolio theory. Chapter 5 is a general discussion of risk and return, making the general point that historical returns on broad asset classes are consistent with a risk–return trade-off, and examining the distribution of stock returns. We focus more closely in Chapter 6 on how to describe investors' risk preferences and how they bear on asset allocation. In the next two chapters, we turn to to portfolio optimization (Chapter 7) and its implementation using index models (Chapter 8).

After our treatment of modern portfolio theory in Part Two, we investigate in Part Three the implications of that theory for the equilibrium structure of expected rates of return on risky assets. Chapter 9 treats the capital asset pricing model and Chapter 10 covers multifactor descriptions of risk and the arbitrage pricing theory. Chapter 11 covers the efficient market hypothesis, including its rationale as well as evidence that supports the hypothesis and challenges it. Chapter 12 is devoted to the behavioral critique of market rationality. Finally, we conclude Part Three with Chapter 13 on empirical evidence on security pricing. This chapter contains evidence concerning the risk–return relationship, as well as liquidity effects on asset pricing.

Part Four is the first of three parts on security valuation. This part treats fixed-income securities—bond pricing (Chapter 14), term structure relationships (Chapter 15), and interest-rate risk management (Chapter 16). **Parts Five and Six** deal with equity securities and derivative securities. For a course emphasizing security analysis and excluding portfolio theory, one may proceed directly from Part One to Part Four with no loss in continuity.

Finally, **Part Seven** considers several topics important for portfolio managers, including performance evaluation, international diversification, active management, and practical issues in the process of portfolio management. This part also contains a new chapter on hedge funds.

This book contains several features designed to make it easy for the student to understand, absorb, and apply the concepts and techniques presented.

New and Enhanced Pedagogy

CHAPTER OPENING VIGNETTES

SERVE TO OUTLINE the upcoming material in the chapter and provide students with a road map of what they will learn.

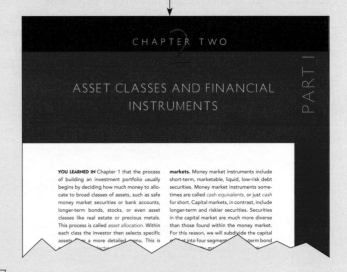

CHAPTER TWO

2

ASSET CLASSES AND FINANCIAL INSTRUMENTS

PART I

YOU LEARNED IN Chapter 1 that the process of building an investment portfolio usually begins by deciding how much money to allocate to broad classes of assets, such as safe money market securities or bank accounts, longer-term bonds, stocks, or even asset classes like real estate or precious metals. This process is called *asset allocation*. Within each class the investor then selects specific assets from a more detailed menu. This is

markets. Money market instruments include short-term, marketable, liquid, low-risk debt securities. Money market instruments sometimes are called *cash equivalents*, or just *cash* for short. Capital markets, in contrast, include longer-term and riskier securities. Securities in the capital market are much more diverse than those found within the money market. For this reason, we will subdivide the capital market into four segments: term bond

CONCEPT CHECKS

A UNIQUE FEATURE of this book! These self-test questions and problems found in the body of the text enable the students to determine whether they've understood the preceding material. Detailed solutions are provided at the end of each chapter.

heterogeneous beliefs is for Paul and Mary to "merge their information," that is, for each party to verify that he or she possesses all relevant information and processes the information properly. Of course, the acquisition of information and the extensive communication that is required to eliminate all heterogeneity in expectations is costly, and thus up to a point heterogeneous expectations cannot be taken as irrational. If, however, Paul and Mary enter such contracts frequently, they would recognize the information problem in one of two ways: Either they will realize that they are creating gambles when each wins half of the bets, or the consistent loser will admit that he or she has been betting on the basis of inferior forecasts.

 CONCEPT CHECK 1

Assume that dollar-denominated T-bills in the United States and pound-denominated bills in the United Kingdom offer equal yields to maturity. Both are short-term assets, and both are free of default risk. Neither offers investors a risk premium. However, a U.S. investor who holds U.K. bills is subject to exchange rate risk, because the pounds earned on the U.K. bills eventually will be exchanged for dollars at the future exchange rate. Is the U.S. investor engaging in speculation or gambling?

NUMBERED EXAMPLES

NUMBERED AND TITLED examples are integrated throughout chapters. Using the worked-out solutions to these examples as models, students can learn how to solve specific problems step-by-step as well as gain insight into general principles by seeing how they are applied to answer concrete questions.

EXAMPLE 5.1   Approximating the Real Rate

If the nominal interest rate on a 1-year CD is 8%, and you expect inflation to be 5% over the coming year, then using the approximation formula, you expect the real rate of interest to be $r = 8\% - 5\% = 3\%$. Using the exact formula, the real rate is $r = \dfrac{.08 - .05}{1 + .05} = .0286$, or 2.86%. Therefore, the approximation rule overstates the expected real rate by only .14% (14 basis points). The approximation rule is more exact for small inflation rates and is perfectly exact for continuously compounded rates. We discuss further details in the next section.

Before the decision to invest, you should realize that conventional certificates of deposit

GOOGLING FOR GOLD

With the news that shares of online search giant Google Inc. (**GOOG**) had crossed the lofty $400-per-share mark in November 2005, the world may have witnessed something akin to the birth of a new financial planetary system. Given its market cap of $120 billion, double that of its nearest competitor, Yahoo!, Google now has the gravitational pull to draw in a host of institutions and company matchmakers unable to resist the potential profit opportunities. Google stock, with a price–earnings ratio of 70, represents one of the richest dealmaking currencies anywhere. That heft has attracted a growing galaxy of entrepreneurs, venture capitalists, and investment bankers, all of whom are orbiting Google in the hopes of selling it something—a new service, a start-up company, even a new strategy—anything to get their hands on a little of the Google gold.

The Google effect is already changing the delicate balance in Silicon Valley between venture capitalists

(VCs) and start-up companies. Instead of nurturing the most promising start-ups with an eye toward taking the fledgling businesses public, a growing number of VCs now scour the landscape for anyone with a technology or service that might fill a gap in Google's portfolio. Google itself and not the larger market has become the exit strategy as VCs plan for the day they can take their money out of their start-ups. Business founders have felt the tug as well. "You're hearing about a lot of entrepreneurs pitching VCs with their end goal to be acquired by Google," says Daniel Primack, editor of *PE Week Wire*, a dealmaking digest popular in VC circles. "It's a complete 180 [degree turn] from the IPO craze of five years ago; now Google is looked at like NASDAQ was then." Other entrepreneurs, meanwhile, are skipping the VC stage altogether, hoping to sell directly to Google.

Source: *BusinessWeek Online*, **www.businessweek.com/magazine.** Reprinted from the December 5, 2005, issue of *BusinessWeek* by special permission. © 2005 McGraw-Hill Companies, Inc.

Allocation of Risk

Virtually all real assets involve some risk. When GM builds its auto plants, for example, it

WORDS FROM THE STREET BOXES

SHORT ARTICLES FROM business periodicals, such as *The Wall Street Journal*, are included in boxes throughout the text. The articles are chosen for real-world relevance and clarity of presentation.

EXCEL APPLICATIONS

THE EIGHTH EDITION has expanded the boxes featuring Excel Spreadsheet Applications. A sample spreadsheet is presented in the Investments text with an interactive version available on the book's Web site at **www.mhhe.com/bkm.**

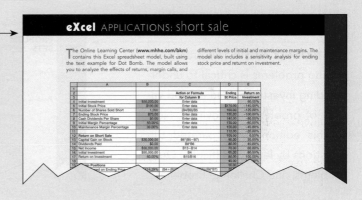

eXcel APPLICATIONS: short sale

The Online Learning Center (**www.mhhe.com/bkm**) contains this Excel spreadsheet model, built using the text example for Dot Bomb. The model allows you to analyze the effects of returns, margin calls, and different levels of initial and maintenance margins. The model also includes a sensitivity analysis for ending stock price and return on investment.

EXCEL EXHIBITS

SELECTED EXHIBITS ARE set as Excel spreadsheets and are denoted by an icon. They are also available on the book's Web site at **www.mhhe.com/bkm.**

	A	B	C	D	E	F	G	H
1								
2								
3	Rates of return expressed as decimals							
4	Purchase Price =		$100		T-bill Rate =	0.06		
5								
6						Squared		Squared
7	State of the		Year-end	Cash		Deviations	Excess	Deviations
8	Economy	Probability	Price	Dividends	HPR	from Mean	Returns	from Mean
9	Boom	0.3	129.50	4.50	0.34	0.040	0.28	0.040
10	Normal growth	0.5	110.00	4.00	0.14	0.000	0.08	0.000
11	Recession	0.2	80.50	3.50	−0.16	0.090	−0.22	0.090
12	Expected value (mean)	SUMPRODUCT(B9:B11, E9:E11) =			0.14			
13	Standard deviation of HPR		SUMPRODUCT(B9:B11, F9:F11)^.5 =		0.1732			
14	Risk premium		SUMPRODUCT(B9:B11, G9:G11) =			0.08		
15	Standard deviation of excess return			SUMPRODUCT(B9:B11, H9:H11)^0.5 = 0.1732				

SPREADSHEET 5.1

Distribution of HPR on the stock-index fund

eXcel
Please visit us at
www.mhhe.com/bkm

END OF CHAPTER FEATURES . . .

SUMMARY

AT THE END of each chapter, a detailed summary outlines the most important concepts presented. A listing of related Web sites for each chapter can also be found on the book's Web site at **www.mhhe.com/bkm.** These sites make it easy for students to research topics further and retrieve financial data and information.

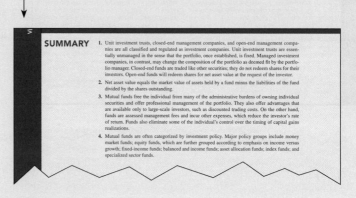

PROBLEM SETS

WE STRONGLY BELIEVE that practice in solving problems is critical to understanding investments, so a good variety of problems is provided. New to this edition, we separated the questions by level of difficulty: Quiz, Problems, and Challenge Problems.

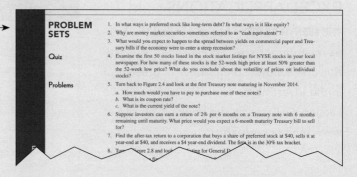

CFA PROBLEMS

WE PROVIDE SEVERAL questions from recent CFA examination in applicable chapters. These questions represent the kinds of questions that professionals in the field believe are relevant to the "real world." Located at the back of the book is a listing of each CFA question and the level and year of the CFA exam it was included in for easy reference when studying for the exam.

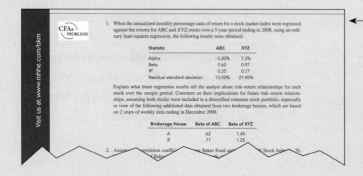

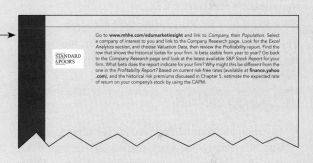

eXcel

Please visit us at
www.mhhe.com/bkm

stock?

9. You are bullish on Telecom stock. The current market price is $50 per share, and you have $5,000 of your own to invest. You borrow an additional $5,000 from your broker at an interest rate of 8% per year and invest $10,000 in the stock.

   a. What will be your rate of return if the price of Telecom stock goes up by 10% during the next year? (Ignore the expected dividend.)
   b. How far does the price of Telecom stock have to fall for you to get a margin call if the maintenance margin is 30%? Assume the price fall happens immediately.

10. You are bearish on Telecom and decide to sell short 100 shares at the current market price of $50 per share.

    a. How much in cash or securities must you put into your brokerage account if the broker's initial margin requirement is 50% of the value of the short position?
    b. How high can the price of the stock go before you get a margin call if the maintenance margin is 30% of the value of the short position?

11. Suppose that Intel currently is selling at $40 per share. You buy 500 shares using $15,000 of your own money, borrowing the remainder of the purchase price from your broker. The rate on the margin loan is 8%.

    a. What is the percentage increase in the net worth of your brokerage account if the price of Intel *immediately* changes to: (i) $44; (ii) $40; (iii) $36? What is the relationship between your percentage return and the percentage change in the price of Intel?

EXCEL PROBLEMS

SELECTED CHAPTERS CONTAIN problems, denoted by an icon, specifically linked to Excel templates that are available on the book's Web site at **www.mhhe.com/bkm**.

STANDARD & POOR'S PROBLEMS

SELECTED CHAPTERS CONTAIN problems directly incorporating the Educational Version of Market Insight, a service based on Standard & Poor's renowned Compustat database. Problems are based in market data provided by 1,000 real companies to gain better understanding of practical business situations. The site is updated daily to ensure the most current information is available.

STANDARD
&POOR'S

Go to **www.mhhe.com/edumarketinsight** and link to *Company*, then *Population*. Select a company of interest to you and link to the Company Research page. Look for the *Excel Analytics* section, and choose *Valuation Data*, then review the *Profitability* report. Find the row that shows the historical betas for your firm. Is beta stable from year to year? Go back to the *Company Research* page and look at the latest available *S&P Stock Report* for your firm. What beta does the report indicate for your firm? Why might this be different from the one in the *Profitability Report*? Based on current risk-free rates (available at **finance.yahoo .com**), and the historical risk premiums discussed in Chapter 5, estimate the expected rate of return on your company's stock by using the CAPM.

E-INVESTMENTS BOXES

THESE EXERCISES PROVIDE students with simple activities to enhance their experience using the Internet. Easy-to-follow instructions and questions are presented so students can utilize what they have learned in class and apply it to today's Web-driven world.

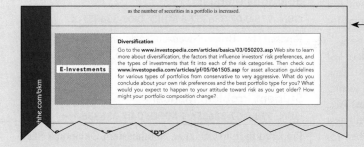

as the number of securities in a portfolio is increased.

E-Investments

Diversification

Go to the **www.investopedia.com/articles/basics/03/050203.asp** Web site to learn more about diversification, the factors that influence investors' risk preferences, and the types of investments that fit into each of the risk categories. Then check out **www.investopedia.com/articles/pf/05/061505.asp** for asset allocation guidelines for various types of portfolios from conservative to very aggressive. What do you conclude about your own risk preferences and the best portfolio type for you? What would you expect to happen to your attitude toward risk as you get older? How might your portfolio composition change?

SUPPLEMENTS

FOR THE INSTRUCTOR

Instructor's Resource CD
ISBN: 978-0-07-3365353-0 MHID: 0-07-336354-5

This comprehensive CD contains all of the following instructor supplements. We have compiled them in electronic format for easier access and convenience. Print copies are available through your McGraw-Hill representative.

- **Instructor's Manual** Prepared by Sue Hine, Colorado State University, has been revised and improved for this edition. Each chapter includes a Chapter Overview, Learning Objectives, and Presentation of Material, which outlines and organizes the material around the PowerPoint Presentation.

- **Test Bank** Prepared by Larry Prather, Southeastern Oklahoma State University, has been revised to increase the quantity and variety of questions. Each question is ranked by level of difficulty, which allows greater flexibility in creating a test and also provides a rationale for the solution. A computerized format for Windows is also available.

- **Computerized Test Bank** A comprehensive bank of test questions is provided within a computerized test bank powered by McGraw-Hill's flexible electronic testing program EZ Test Online (**www.eztestonline.com**). You can select questions from multiple McGraw-Hill test banks or author your own, and then print the test for paper distribution or give it online. This user-friendly program allows you to sort questions by format; edit existing questions or add new ones; and scramble questions for multiple versions of the same test. You can export your tests for use in WebCT, Blackboard, PageOut, and Apple's iQuiz. Sharing tests with colleagues, adjuncts, TAs is easy! Instant scoring and feedback is provided and EZ Test's grade book is designed to export to your grade book.

- **PowerPoint Presentation System** These presentation slides, also developed by Sue Hine, contain figures and tables from the text, key points, and summaries in a visually stimulating collection of slides. These slides follow the order of the chapters, but if you have PowerPoint software, you can customize the program to fit your lecture.

- **Solutions Manual** Prepared by Bruce Swensen, Adelphi University, provides detailed solutions to the end-of-chapter problem sets. This supplement is also available for purchase by your students or can be packaged with your text at a discount.

FOR THE STUDENT

Solutions Manual
ISBN: 978-0-07-336357-8 MHID: 0-07-336357-X

Revised by Bruce Swensen, Adelphi University, this manual provides detailed solutions to the end-of-chapter problems.

Student Problem Manual
ISBN: 978-0-07-336356-1 MHID: 0-07-336356-1

Prepared by Larry Prather, Southeastern Oklahoma State University, this useful supplement contains problems created to specifically relate to the concepts discussed in each chapter. Solutions are provided at the end of each chapter in the manual. Perfect for additional practice in working through problems!

ONLINE SUPPORT

Online Learning Center www.mhhe.com/bkm

Find a wealth of information online! At this book's Web site instructors have access to teaching supports such as electronic files of the ancillary materials. Students have access to study materials created specifically for this text and much more. All Excel spreadsheets, denoted by an icon in the text are located at this site. Links to the additional support material, are also included. See below for a description of some of the exciting assets available to you!

- **Standard & Poor's Educational Version of Market Insight** McGraw-Hill/Irwin has partnered exclusively with Standard and Poor's to bring you the Educational Version of Market Insight. This rich online resource provides 6 years of financial data for 1,000 companies in the renowned COMPUSTAT® database. S&P problems can be found at the end of relevant chapters of the text.

- **Excel Templates** Revised by Pete Crabb, Northwest Nazarene University, templates are available for selected spreadsheets featured within the text, as well as those featured among the Excel Applications boxes. Selected end-of-chapter problems have also been designated as Excel problems, for which the available template allows students to solve the problem and gain experience using spreadsheets. Each template can also be found on the book's Web site **www.mhhe. com/bkm.**

- **Related Web Sites** A list of suggested Web sites is provided for each chapter. To keep Web addresses up-to-date, the suggested sites as well as their links are provided online. Each chapter summary contains a reference to its related sites.

- **Online Quizzes** These multiple-choice questions are provided as an additional testing and reinforcement tool for students. Each quiz is organized by chapter to test the specific concepts presented in that particular chapter. Immediate scoring of the quiz occurs upon submission and the correct answers are provided.

PACKAGING OPTIONS

Please contact your McGraw-Hill/Irwin sales representative to find out more about these exciting packaging options now available for your class.

- *BusinessWeek* **Package** Your students can subscribe to *BusinessWeek* for a special rate of $8.25 in addition to the price of the text. Students will receive a pass code card shrink-wrapped with their new text that refers them to a registration site to receive their subscription. Subscriptions are available in print copy or digital format.

- *Financial Times* **Package** Your students can subscribe to the *Financial Times* for 15 weeks at a specially priced rate of $10 in addition to the price of the text. Students will receive a subscription card shrink-wrapped with their new text that activates their subscriptions once they complete and submit the card. The subscription also provides access to FT.com.

ACKNOWLEDGMENTS

Throughout the development of this text, experienced instructors have provided critical feedback and suggestions for improvement. These individuals deserve a special thanks for their valuable insights and contributions. The following instructors played a vital role in the development of this and previous editions of *Investments:*

J. Amanda Addkisson
Texas A&M University

Tor-Erik Bakke
University of Wisconsin

Richard J. Bauer Jr.
St. Mary's University

Scott Besley
University of Florida

John Binder
University of Illinois at Chicago

Paul Bolster
Northwestern University

Phillip Braun
Northeastern University

Leo Chan
Delaware State University

Charles Chang
Cornell University

Kee Chaung
SUNY Buffalo

Ludwig Chincarini
Pomona College

Stephen Ciccone
University of New Hampshire

James Cotter
Wake Forest University

L. Michael Couvillion
Plymouth State University

Anna Craig
Emory University

Elton Daal
University of New Orleans

David C. Distad
University of California at Berkeley

Craig Dunbar
University of Western Ontario

David Durr
Murray State University

Bjorn Eaker
Duke University

John Earl
University of Richmond

Michael C. Ehrhardt
University of Tennessee at Knoxville

Venkat Eleswarapu
Southern Methodist University

David Ellis
Babson College

Andrew Ellul
Indiana University

Greg Filbeck
University of Toledo

Jeremy Goh
Washington University

Richard Grayson
Loyola College

John M. Griffin
Arizona State University

Weiyu Guo
University of Nebraska at Omaha

Mahmoud Haddad
Wayne State University

Greg Hallman
University of Texas at Austin

Robert G. Hansen
Dartmouth College

Joel Hasbrouck
New York University

Andrea Heuson
University of Miami

Eric Higgins
Drexel University

Shalom J. Hochman
University of Houston

Eric Hughson
University of Colorado

Delroy Hunter
University of South Florida

A. James Ifflander
A. James Ifflander and Associates

Robert Jennings
Indiana University

George Jiang
University of Arizona

Richard D. Johnson
Colorado State University

Susan D. Jordan
University of Kentucky

G. Andrew Karolyi
Ohio State University

Ajay Khorana
Georgia Institute of Technology

Josef Lakonishok
University of Illinois at Champaign/Urbana

ACKNOWLEDGMENTS

Malek Lashgari
University of Hartford

Dennis Lasser
Binghamton University

Hongbok Lee
Western Illinois University

Bruce Lehmann
University of California at San Diego

Jack Li
Northeastern University

Larry Lockwood
Texas Christian University

Christopher K. Ma
Texas Tech University

Anil K. Makhija
University of Pittsburgh

Davinder Malhotra
Philadelphia University

Steven Mann
University of South Carolina

Deryl W. Martin
Tennessee Technical University

Jean Masson
University of Ottawa

Ronald May
St. John's University

Rick Meyer
University of South Florida

Mbodja Mougoue
Wayne State University

Kyung-Chun (Andrew) Mun
Truman State University

Carol Osler
Brandeis University

Gurupdesh Pandner
DePaul University

Don B. Panton
University of Texas at Arlington

Dilip Patro
Rutgers University

Robert Pavlik
Southwest Texas State

Eileen St. Pierre
University of Northern Colorado

Marianne Plunkert
University of Colorado at Denver

Andrew Prevost
Ohio University

Herbert Quigley
University of the District of Columbia

Murli Rajan
University of Scranton

Speima Rao
University of Southwestern Louisiana

Rathin Rathinasamy
Ball State University

William Reese
Tulane University

Craig Rennie
University of Arkansas

Maurico Rodriquez
Texas Christian University

Leonard Rosenthal
Bentley College

Anthony Sanders
Ohio State University

Gary Sanger
Louisiana State University

Don Seeley
University of Arizona

John Settle
Portland State University

Edward C. Sims
Western Illinois University

Robert Skena
Carnegie Mellon University

Steve L. Slezak
University of North Carolina at Chapel Hill

Keith V. Smith
Purdue University

Patricia B. Smith
University of New Hampshire

Laura T. Starks
University of Texas

Mick Swartz
University of Southern California

Manuel Tarrazo
University of San Francisco

Steve Thorley
Brigham Young University

Jack Treynor
Treynor Capital Management

Charles A. Trzincka
SUNY Buffalo

Yiuman Tse
SUNY Binghampton

Joe Ueng
University of St. Thomas

Gopala Vasuderan
Suffolk University

Joseph Vu
DePaul University

Richard Warr
North Carolina State University

Simon Wheatley
University of Chicago

Marilyn K. Wiley
Florida Atlantic University

James Williams
California State University at Northridge

Tony R. Wingler
University of North Carolina at Greensboro

Guojun Wu
University of Michigan

Hsiu-Kwang Wu
University of Alabama

Geungu Yu
Jackson State University

Thomas J. Zwirlein
University of Colorado at Colorado Springs

Edward Zychowicz
Hofstra University

For granting us permission to include many of their examination questions in the text, we are grateful to the CFA Institute.

Much credit is due to the development and production team at McGraw-Hill/Irwin: our special thanks go to Michele Janicek, Executive Editor; Christina Kouvelis, Senior Developmental Editor; Lori Koetters, Managing Editor; Ashley Smith, Marketing Manager; Jennifer Jelinski, Marketing Specialist; Michael McCormick, Senior Production Supervisor; Matthew Baldwin, Designer; and Lynn Bluhm, Media Project Manager.

Finally, we thank Judy, Hava, and Sheryl, who contribute to the book with their support and understanding.

Zvi Bodie
Alex Kane
Alan J. Marcus

CHAPTER ONE

THE INVESTMENT ENVIRONMENT

AN INVESTMENT IS the *current* commitment of money or other resources in the expectation of reaping *future* benefits. For example, an individual might purchase shares of stock anticipating that the future proceeds from the shares will justify both the time that her money is tied up as well as the risk of the investment. The time you will spend studying this text (not to mention its cost) also is an investment. You are forgoing either current leisure or the income you could be earning at a job in the expectation that your future career will be sufficiently enhanced to justify this commitment of time and effort. While these two investments differ in many ways, they share one key attribute that is central to all investments: You sacrifice something of value now, expecting to benefit from that sacrifice later.

This text can help you become an informed practitioner of investments. We will focus on investments in securities such as stocks, bonds, or options and futures contracts, but much of what we discuss will be useful in the analysis of any type of investment. The text will provide you with background in the organization of various securities markets; will survey

the valuation and risk-management principles useful in particular markets, such as those for bonds or stocks; and will introduce you to the principles of portfolio construction.

Broadly speaking, this chapter addresses three topics that will provide a useful perspective for the material that is to come later. First, before delving into the topic of "investments," we consider the role of financial assets in the economy. We discuss the relationship between securities and the "real" assets that actually produce goods and services for consumers, and we consider why financial assets are important to the functioning of a developed economy. Given this background, we then take a first look at the types of decisions that confront investors as they assemble a portfolio of assets. These investment decisions are made in an environment where higher returns usually can be obtained only at the price of greater risk and in which it is rare to find assets that are so mispriced as to be obvious bargains. These themes—the risk–return trade-off and the efficient pricing of financial assets—are central to the investment process, so it is worth pausing for a brief discussion of their implications as we begin the text. These implications will be fleshed out in much greater detail in later chapters.

Finally, we conclude with an introduction to the organization of security markets, the various players that participate in those markets, and a brief overview of some of the more important changes in those markets in recent years. Together, these various topics should give you a feel for who the major participants are in the securities markets as well as the setting in which they act. We close with an overview of the remainder of the text.

1.1 REAL ASSETS VERSUS FINANCIAL ASSETS

The material wealth of a society is ultimately determined by the productive capacity of its economy, that is, the goods and services its members can create. This capacity is a function of the **real assets** of the economy: the land, buildings, machines, and knowledge that can be used to produce goods and services.

In contrast to such real assets are **financial assets** such as stocks and bonds. Such securities are no more than sheets of paper or, more likely, computer entries and do not contribute directly to the productive capacity of the economy. Instead, these assets are the means by which individuals in well-developed economies hold their claims on real assets. Financial assets are claims to the income generated by real assets (or claims on income from the government). If we cannot own our own auto plant (a real asset), we can still buy shares in General Motors or Toyota (financial assets) and, thereby, share in the income derived from the production of automobiles.

While real assets generate net income to the economy, financial assets simply define the allocation of income or wealth among investors. Individuals can choose between consuming their wealth today or investing for the future. If they choose to invest, they may place their wealth in financial assets by purchasing various securities. When investors buy these securities from companies, the firms use the money so raised to pay for real assets, such as plant, equipment, technology, or inventory. So investors' returns on securities ultimately come from the income produced by the real assets that were financed by the issuance of those securities.

The distinction between real and financial assets is apparent when we compare the balance sheet of U.S. households, shown in Table 1.1, with the composition of national wealth in the United States, shown in Table 1.2. Household wealth includes financial assets such as bank accounts, corporate stock, or bonds. However, these securities, which are financial assets of households, are *liabilities* of the issuers of the securities. For example, a bond that you treat as an asset because it gives you a claim on interest income and repayment of principal from General Motors is a liability of General Motors, which is obligated to make these payments to you. Your asset is GM's liability. Therefore, when we aggregate over all balance sheets, these claims cancel out, leaving only real assets as the net wealth of the economy. National wealth consists of structures, equipment, inventories of goods, and land.[1]

[1]You might wonder why real assets held by households in Table 1.1 amount to $27,086 billion, while total real assets in the domestic economy (Table 1.2) are far larger, at $48,038 billion. One major reason is that real assets held by firms, for example, property, plant, and equipment, are included as *financial* assets of the household sector, specifically through the value of corporate equity and other stock market investments. Another reason is that equity and stock investments in Table 1.1 are measured by market value, whereas plant and equipment in Table 1.2 are valued at replacement cost.

Assets	$ Billion	% Total	Liabilities and Net Worth	$ Billion	% Total
Real assets					
Real estate	$22,874	32.9%	Mortgages	$10,070	14.5%
Consumer durables	3,966	5.7	Consumer credit	2,413	3.5
Other	247	0.4	Bank and other loans	222	0.3
Total real assets	$27,086	38.9%	Security credit	310	0.4
			Other	418	0.6
			Total liabilities	$13,432	19.3%
Financial assets					
Deposits	$ 6,629	9.5%			
Life insurance reserves	1,174	1.7			
Pension reserves	12,188	17.5			
Corporate equity	5,391	7.7			
Equity in noncorp. business	7,553	10.9			
Mutual fund shares	5,123	7.4			
Debt securities	3,160	4.5			
Other	1,305	1.9			
Total financial assets	42,522	61.1	Net worth	56,176	80.7
Total	$69,608	100.0%		$69,608	100.0%

TABLE 1.1

Balance sheet of U.S. households, 2007

Note: Column sums may differ from total because of rounding error.
Source: *Flow of Funds Accounts of the United States,* Board of Governors of the Federal Reserve System, June 2007.

TABLE 1.2

Domestic net worth

Assets	$ Billion
Nonresidential real estate	$ 9,549
Residential real estate	28,265
Equipment and software	4,498
Inventories	1,759
Consumer durables	3,966
Total	$ 48,038

Note: Column sums may differ from total because of rounding error.
Source: *Flow of Funds Accounts of the United States,* Board of Governors of the Federal Reserve System, June 2007.

We will focus almost exclusively on financial assets. But you shouldn't lose sight of the fact that the successes or failures of the financial assets we choose to purchase ultimately depend on the performance of the underlying real assets.

CONCEPT CHECK 1

Are the following assets real or financial?

a. Patents
b. Lease obligations
c. Customer goodwill
d. A college education
e. A $5 bill

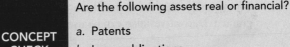

1.2   A TAXONOMY OF FINANCIAL ASSETS

It is common to distinguish among three broad types of financial assets: fixed income, equity, and derivatives. **Fixed-income** or **debt securities** promise either a fixed stream of income or a stream of income that is determined according to a specified formula. For example, a corporate bond typically would promise that the bondholder will receive a fixed amount of interest each year. Other so-called floating-rate bonds promise payments that depend on current interest rates. For example, a bond may pay an interest rate that is fixed at 2 percentage points above the rate paid on U.S. Treasury bills. Unless the borrower is declared bankrupt, the payments on these securities are either fixed or determined by formula. For this reason, the investment performance of debt securities typically is least closely tied to the financial condition of the issuer.

Nevertheless, fixed-income securities come in a tremendous variety of maturities and payment provisions. At one extreme, the *money market* refers to debt securities that are short term, highly marketable, and generally of very low risk. Examples of money market securities are U.S. Treasury bills or bank certificates of deposit (CDs). In contrast, the fixed-income *capital market* includes long-term securities such as Treasury bonds, as well as bonds issued by federal agencies, state and local municipalities, and corporations. These bonds range from very safe in terms of default risk (for example, Treasury securities) to relatively risky (for example, high yield or "junk" bonds). They also are designed with extremely diverse provisions regarding payments provided to the investor and protection against the bankruptcy of the issuer. We will take a first look at these securities in Chapter 2 and undertake a more detailed analysis of the debt market in Part Four.

Unlike debt securities, common stock, or **equity,** in a firm represents an ownership share in the corporation. Equityholders are not promised any particular payment. They receive any dividends the firm may pay and have prorated ownership in the real assets of the firm. If the firm is successful, the value of equity will increase; if not, it will decrease. The performance of equity investments, therefore, is tied directly to the success of the firm and its real assets. For this reason, equity investments tend to be riskier than investments in debt securities. Equity markets and equity valuation are the topics of Part Five.

Finally, **derivative securities** such as options and futures contracts provide payoffs that are determined by the prices of *other* assets such as bond or stock prices. For example, a call option on a share of Intel stock might turn out to be worthless if Intel's share price remains below a threshold or "exercise" price such as $30 a share, but it can be quite valuable if the stock price rises above that level.[2] Derivative securities are so named because their values derive from the prices of other assets. For example, the value of the call option will depend on the price of Intel stock. Other important derivative securities are futures and swap contracts. We will treat these in Part Six.

Derivatives have become an integral part of the investment environment. One use of derivatives, perhaps the primary use, is to hedge risks or transfer them to other parties. This is done successfully every day, and the use of these securities for risk management is so commonplace that the multitrillion-dollar market in derivative assets is routinely taken for granted. Derivatives also can be used to take highly speculative positions, however. Every

---

[2]A call option is the right to buy a share of stock at a given exercise price on or before the option's expiration date. If the market price of Intel remains below $30 a share, the right to buy for $30 will turn out to be valueless. If the share price rises above $30 before the option expires, however, the option can be exercised to obtain the share for only $30.

so often, one of these positions blows up, resulting in well-publicized losses of hundreds of millions of dollars. While these losses attract considerable attention, they are in fact the exception to the more common use of such securities as risk management tools. Derivatives will continue to play an important role in portfolio construction and the financial system. We will return to this topic later in the text.

In addition to these financial assets, individuals might invest directly in some real assets. For example, real estate or commodities such as precious metals or agricultural products are real assets that might form part of an investment portfolio.

1.3   FINANCIAL MARKETS AND THE ECONOMY

We stated earlier that real assets determine the wealth of an economy, while financial assets merely represent claims on real assets. Nevertheless, financial assets and the markets in which they trade play several crucial roles in developed economies. Financial assets allow us to make the most of the economy's real assets.

The Informational Role of Financial Markets

In a capitalist system, financial markets play a central role in the allocation of capital resources. Investors in the stock market ultimately decide which companies will live and which will die. If a corporation seems to have good prospects for future profitability, investors will bid up its stock price. The company's management will find it easy to issue new shares or borrow funds to finance research and development, build new production facilities, and expand its operations. The nearby box provides an illustration of this process. As Google's stock price has surged, it has been able to expand and initiate many new business prospects. If, on the other hand, a company's prospects seem poor, investors will bid down its stock price. The company will have to downsize and may eventually disappear.

The process by which capital is allocated through the stock market sometimes seems wasteful. Some companies can be "hot" for a short period of time, attract a large flow of investor capital, and then fail after only a few years. But that is an unavoidable implication of uncertainty. It is impossible to predict with certainty which ventures will succeed and which will fail. But the stock market encourages allocation of capital to those firms that appear *at the time* to have the best prospects. Many smart, well-trained, and well-paid professionals analyze the prospects of firms whose shares trade on the stock market. Stock prices reflect their collective judgment.

Consumption Timing

Some individuals in an economy are earning more than they currently wish to spend. Others, for example, retirees, spend more than they currently earn. How can you shift your purchasing power from high-earnings periods to low-earnings periods of life? One way is to "store" your wealth in financial assets. In high-earnings periods, you can invest your savings in financial assets such as stocks and bonds. In low-earnings periods, you can sell these assets to provide funds for your consumption needs. By so doing, you can "shift" your consumption over the course of your lifetime, thereby allocating your consumption to periods that provide the greatest satisfaction. Thus, financial markets allow individuals to separate decisions concerning current consumption from constraints that otherwise would be imposed by current earnings.

GOOGLING FOR GOLD

With the news that shares of online search giant Google Inc. (**GOOG**) had crossed the lofty $400-per-share mark in November 2005, the world may have witnessed something akin to the birth of a new financial planetary system. Given its market cap of $120 billion, double that of its nearest competitor, Yahoo!, Google now has the gravitational pull to draw in a host of institutions and company matchmakers unable to resist the potential profit opportunities. Google stock, with a price–earnings ratio of 70, represents one of the richest dealmaking currencies anywhere. That heft has attracted a growing galaxy of entrepreneurs, venture capitalists, and investment bankers, all of whom are orbiting Google in the hopes of selling it something—a new service, a start-up company, even a new strategy—anything to get their hands on a little of the Google gold.

The Google effect is already changing the delicate balance in Silicon Valley between venture capitalists

(VCs) and start-up companies. Instead of nurturing the most promising start-ups with an eye toward taking the fledgling businesses public, a growing number of VCs now scour the landscape for anyone with a technology or service that might fill a gap in Google's portfolio. Google itself and not the larger market has become the exit strategy as VCs plan for the day they can take their money out of their start-ups. Business founders have felt the tug as well. "You're hearing about a lot of entrepreneurs pitching VCs with their end goal to be acquired by Google," says Daniel Primack, editor of *PE Week Wire*, a dealmaking digest popular in VC circles. "It's a complete 180 [degree turn] from the IPO craze of five years ago; now Google is looked at like NASDAQ was then." Other entrepreneurs, meanwhile, are skipping the VC stage altogether, hoping to sell directly to Google.

Source: *BusinessWeek Online*, **www.businessweek.com/magazine**. Reprinted from the December 5, 2005, issue of *BusinessWeek* by special permission. © 2005 McGraw-Hill Companies, Inc.

Allocation of Risk

Virtually all real assets involve some risk. When GM builds its auto plants, for example, it cannot know for sure what cash flows those plants will generate. Financial markets and the diverse financial instruments traded in those markets allow investors with the greatest taste for risk to bear that risk, while other, less risk-tolerant individuals can, to a greater extent, stay on the sidelines. For example, if GM raises the funds to build its auto plant by selling both stocks and bonds to the public, the more optimistic or risk-tolerant investors can buy shares of stock in GM, while the more conservative ones can buy GM bonds. Because the bonds promise to provide a fixed payment, the stockholders bear most of the business risk but reap potentially higher rewards. Thus, capital markets allow the risk that is inherent to all investments to be borne by the investors most willing to bear that risk.

This allocation of risk also benefits the firms that need to raise capital to finance their investments. When investors are able to select security types with the risk–return characteristics that best suit their preferences, each security can be sold for the best possible price. This facilitates the process of building the economy's stock of real assets.

Separation of Ownership and Management

Many businesses are owned and managed by the same individual. This simple organization is well suited to small businesses and, in fact, was the most common form of business organization before the Industrial Revolution. Today, however, with global markets and large-scale production, the size and capital requirements of firms have skyrocketed. For example, at the end of 2006 General Electric listed on its balance sheet about $75 billion of property, plant, and equipment, and total assets of nearly $700 billion. Corporations of such size simply cannot exist as owner-operated firms. GE actually has about 625,000 stockholders with an ownership stake in the firm proportional to their holdings of shares.

Such a large group of individuals obviously cannot actively participate in the day-to-day management of the firm. Instead, they elect a board of directors that in turn hires and supervises the management of the firm. This structure means that the owners and managers of the firm are different parties. This gives the firm a stability that the owner-managed firm cannot achieve. For example, if some stockholders decide they no longer wish to hold shares in the firm, they can sell their shares to other investors, with no impact on the management of the firm. Thus, financial assets and the ability to buy and sell those assets in the financial markets allow for easy separation of ownership and management.

How can all of the disparate owners of the firm, ranging from large pension funds holding hundreds of thousands of shares to small investors who may hold only a single share, agree on the objectives of the firm? Again, the financial markets provide some guidance. All may agree that the firm's management should pursue strategies that enhance the value of their shares. Such policies will make all shareholders wealthier and allow them all to better pursue their personal goals, whatever those goals might be.

Do managers really attempt to maximize firm value? It is easy to see how they might be tempted to engage in activities not in the best interest of shareholders. For example, they might engage in empire building or avoid risky projects to protect their own jobs or overconsume luxuries such as corporate jets, reasoning that the cost of such perquisites is largely borne by the shareholders. These potential conflicts of interest are called **agency problems** because managers, who are hired as agents of the shareholders, may pursue their own interests instead.

Several mechanisms have evolved to mitigate potential agency problems. First, compensation plans tie the income of managers to the success of the firm. A major part of the total compensation of top executives is often in the form of stock options, which means that the managers will not do well unless the stock price increases, benefiting shareholders. (Of course, we've learned more recently that overuse of options can create its own agency problem. Options can create an incentive for managers to manipulate information to prop up a stock price temporarily, giving them a chance to cash out before the price returns to a level reflective of the firm's true prospects. More on this shortly.) Second, while boards of directors are sometimes portrayed as defenders of top management, they can, and increasingly do, force out management teams that are underperforming. Third, outsiders such as security analysts and large institutional investors such as pension funds monitor the firm closely and make the life of poor performers at the least uncomfortable.

Finally, bad performers are subject to the threat of takeover. If the board of directors is lax in monitoring management, unhappy shareholders in principle can elect a different board. They can do this by launching a *proxy contest* in which they seek to obtain enough proxies (i.e., rights to vote the shares of other shareholders) to take control of the firm and vote in another board. However, this threat is usually minimal. Shareholders who attempt such a fight have to use their own funds, while management can defend itself using corporate coffers. Most proxy fights fail. The real takeover threat is from other firms. If one firm observes another underperforming, it can acquire the underperforming business and replace management with its own team. The stock price should rise to reflect the prospects of improved performance, which provides incentive for firms to engage in such takeover activity.

EXAMPLE 1.1   The Hewlett-Packard/Compaq Proxy Fight

When Carly Fiorina, then the CEO of Hewlett-Packard, proposed a merger with Compaq Computer in 2001, Walter Hewlett, son of the company's founder and member of the HP board of directors, dissented. The merger had to be approved by shareholders, and Hewlett engaged in a proxy fight to block the deal. One estimate is that HP spent $150 million to lobby shareholders to support the merger; even small shareholders of HP reported receiving 20 or more phone calls from the company in support of the deal.[3] The merger ultimately was approved in an uncharacteristically close vote. No surprise that less than 1% of public companies face proxy contests in any particular year.

Corporate Governance and Corporate Ethics

We've argued that securities markets can play an important role in facilitating the deployment of capital resources to their most productive uses. But for markets to effectively serve this purpose, there must be an acceptable level of transparency that allows investors to make well-informed decisions. If firms can mislead the public about their prospects, then much can go wrong.

Despite the many mechanisms to align incentives of shareholders and managers, the 3 years between 2000 and 2002 were filled with a seemingly unending series of scandals that collectively signaled a crisis in corporate governance and ethics. For example, the telecom firm WorldCom overstated its profits by at least $3.8 billion by improperly classifying expenses as investments. When the true picture emerged, it resulted in the largest bankruptcy in U.S. history. The second-largest U.S. bankruptcy was Enron, which used its now-notorious "special-purpose entities" to move debt off its own books and similarly present a misleading picture of its financial status. Unfortunately, these firms had plenty of company. Other firms such as Rite Aid, HealthSouth, Global Crossing, and Qwest Communications also manipulated and misstated their accounts to the tune of billions of dollars. And the scandals were hardly limited to the United States. Parmalat, the Italian dairy firm, claimed to have a $4.8 billion bank account that turned out not to exist. These episodes suggest that agency and incentive problems are far from solved.

Other scandals of that period included systematically misleading and overly optimistic research reports put out by stock market analysts. (Their favorable analysis was traded for the promise of future investment banking business, and analysts were commonly compensated not for their accuracy or insight, but for their role in garnering investment banking business for their firms.) Additionally, initial public offerings were allocated to corporate executives as a quid pro quo for personal favors or the promise to direct future business back to the manager of the IPO.

What about the auditors who were supposed to be the watchdogs of the firms? Here too, incentives were skewed. Recent changes in business practice had made the consulting businesses of these firms more lucrative than the auditing function. For example, Enron's (now-defunct) auditor Arthur Andersen earned more money consulting for Enron than by auditing it; given Arthur Andersen's incentive to protect its consulting profits, we should not be surprised that it, and other auditors, were overly lenient in their auditing work.

In 2002, in response to the spate of ethics scandals, Congress passed the Sarbanes-Oxley Act to tighten the rules of corporate governance. For example, the act requires corporations to have more independent directors, that is, more directors who are not themselves managers (or affiliated with managers). The act also requires each CFO to personally vouch for the corporation's accounting statements, created an oversight board to oversee the auditing of public companies, and prohibits auditors from providing various other services to clients.

In the wake of these scandals, Wall Street belatedly recognized that markets require trust to function. The value of reputation is better appreciated, and reliance on more straightforward incentive structures has increased. As one Wall Street insider put it, "This is an industry of trust; it's one of its key assets . . . [Wall Street] is going to have to invest in getting [that trust] back . . . without that trust, there's nothing."[4] Ultimately, a firm's

[3]See "Designed by Committee," *The Economist*, June 13, 2002.

[4]"How Corrupt Is Wall Street?" *BusinessWeek*, May 13, 2002.

reputation for integrity is key to building long-term relationships with its customers and is therefore one of its most valuable assets. Indeed, the motto of the London Stock Exchange is "My word is my bond." Every so often firms forget this lesson but, in the end, investments in reputation are in fact good business practice.

1.4 THE INVESTMENT PROCESS

Saving, Investing, and Safe Investing

Saving means not spending all of your current income on consumption. Investing, on the other hand, is choosing what assets to hold. You may choose to invest in safe assets, risky assets, or a combination of both. In common usage, however, the term *saving* is often taken to mean investing in safe assets such as an insured bank account. It is easy to confuse saving with safe investing. To avoid confusion remember this example. Suppose you earn $100,000 a year from your job, and you spend $80,000 of it on consumption. You are saving $20,000. Suppose you decide to invest all $20,000 in risky assets. You are still saving $20,000, but you are not investing it safely.

An investor's *portfolio* is simply his collection of investment assets. Once the portfolio is established, it is updated or "rebalanced" by selling existing securities and using the proceeds to buy new securities, by investing additional funds to increase the overall size of the portfolio, or by selling securities to decrease the size of the portfolio.

Investment assets can be categorized into broad asset classes, such as stocks, bonds, real estate, commodities, and so on. Investors make two types of decisions in constructing their portfolios. The **asset allocation** decision is the choice among these broad asset classes, while the **security selection** decision is the choice of which particular securities to hold *within* each asset class.

"Top-down" portfolio construction starts with asset allocation. For example, an individual who currently holds all of his money in a bank account would first decide what proportion of the overall portfolio ought to be moved into stocks, bonds, and so on. In this way, the broad features of the portfolio are established. For example, while the average annual return on the common stock of large firms since 1926 has been about 12% per year, the average return on U.S. Treasury bills has been less than 4%. On the other hand, stocks are far riskier, with annual returns (as measured by the Standard & Poor's 500 index) that have ranged as low as –46% and as high as 55%. In contrast, T-bills are effectively risk-free: you know what interest rate you will earn when you buy them. Therefore, the decision to allocate your investments to the stock market or to the money market where Treasury bills are traded will have great ramifications for both the risk and the return of your portfolio. A top-down investor first makes this and other crucial asset allocation decisions before turning to the decision of the particular securities to be held in each asset class.

Security analysis involves the valuation of particular securities that might be included in the portfolio. For example, an investor might ask whether Merck or Pfizer is more attractively priced. Both bonds and stocks must be evaluated for investment attractiveness, but valuation is far more difficult for stocks because a stock's performance usually is far more sensitive to the condition of the issuing firm.

In contrast to top-down portfolio management is the "bottom-up" strategy. In this process, the portfolio is constructed from the securities that seem attractively priced without as much concern for the resultant asset allocation. Such a technique can result in unintended bets on one or another sector of the economy. For example, it might turn out that the portfolio ends up with a very heavy representation of firms in one industry, from one part of the country, or with exposure to one source of uncertainty. However, a bottom-up strategy does focus the portfolio on the assets that seem to offer the most attractive investment opportunities.

1.5   MARKETS ARE COMPETITIVE

Financial markets are highly competitive. Thousands of intelligent and well-backed analysts constantly scour securities markets searching for the best buys. This competition means that we should expect to find few, if any, "free lunches," securities that are so underpriced that they represent obvious bargains. There are several implications of this no-free-lunch proposition. Let's examine two.

The Risk–Return Trade-Off

Investors invest for anticipated future returns, but those returns rarely can be predicted precisely. There will almost always be risk associated with investments. Actual or realized returns will almost always deviate from the expected return anticipated at the start of the investment period. For example, in 1931 (the worst calendar year for the market since 1926), the S&P 500 index fell by 46%. In 1933 (the best year), the index gained 55%. You can be sure that investors did not anticipate such extreme performance at the start of either of these years.

Naturally, if all else could be held equal, investors would prefer investments with the highest expected return.[5] However, the no-free-lunch rule tells us that all else cannot be held equal. If you want higher expected returns, you will have to pay a price in terms of accepting higher investment risk. If higher expected return can be achieved without bearing extra risk, there will be a rush to buy the high-return assets, with the result that their prices will be driven up. Individuals considering investing in the asset at the now-higher price will find the investment less attractive: If you buy at a higher price, your expected rate of return (that is, profit per dollar invested) is lower. The asset will be considered attractive and its price will continue to rise until its expected return is no more than commensurate with risk. At this point, investors can anticipate a "fair" return relative to the asset's risk, but no more. Similarly, if returns were independent of risk, there would be a rush to sell high-risk assets. Their prices would fall (and their expected future rates of return rise) until they eventually were attractive enough to be included again in investor portfolios. We conclude that there should be a **risk–return trade-off** in the securities markets, with higher-risk assets priced to offer higher expected returns than lower-risk assets.

Of course, this discussion leaves several important questions unanswered. How should one measure the risk of an asset? What should be the quantitative trade-off between risk (properly measured) and expected return? One would think that risk would have something to do with the volatility of an asset's returns, but this guess turns out to be only partly correct. When we mix assets into diversified portfolios, we need to consider the interplay among assets and the effect of diversification on the risk of the entire portfolio.

---

[5]The "expected" return is not the return investors believe they necessarily will earn, or even their most likely return. It is instead the result of averaging across all possible outcomes, recognizing that some outcomes are more likely than others. It is the average rate of return across possible economic scenarios.

Diversification means that many assets are held in the portfolio so that the exposure to any particular asset is limited. The effect of diversification on portfolio risk, the implications for the proper measurement of risk, and the risk–return relationship are the topics of Part Two. These topics are the subject of what has come to be known as *modern portfolio theory*. The development of this theory brought two of its pioneers, Harry Markowitz and William Sharpe, Nobel Prizes.

Efficient Markets

Another implication of the no-free-lunch proposition is that we should rarely expect to find bargains in the security markets. We will spend all of Chapter 11 examining the theory and evidence concerning the hypothesis that financial markets process all relevant information about securities quickly and efficiently, that is, that the security price usually reflects all the information available to investors concerning the value of the security. According to this hypothesis, as new information about a security becomes available, the price of the security quickly adjusts so that at any time, the security price equals the market consensus estimate of the value of the security. If this were so, there would be neither underpriced nor overpriced securities.

One interesting implication of this "efficient market hypothesis" concerns the choice between active and passive investment-management strategies. **Passive management** calls for holding highly diversified portfolios without spending effort or other resources attempting to improve investment performance through security analysis. **Active management** is the attempt to improve performance either by identifying mispriced securities or by timing the performance of broad asset classes—for example, increasing one's commitment to stocks when one is bullish on the stock market. If markets are efficient and prices reflect all relevant information, perhaps it is better to follow passive strategies instead of spending resources in a futile attempt to outguess your competitors in the financial markets.

If the efficient market hypothesis were taken to the extreme, there would be no point in active security analysis; only fools would commit resources to actively analyze securities. Without ongoing security analysis, however, prices eventually would depart from "correct" values, creating new incentives for experts to move in. Therefore, even in environments as competitive as the financial markets, we may observe only *near*-efficiency, and profit opportunities may exist for especially diligent and creative investors. In Chapter 12, we examine such challenges to the efficient market hypothesis, and this motivates our discussion of active portfolio management in Part Seven. More important, our discussions of security analysis and portfolio construction generally must account for the likelihood of nearly efficient markets.

1.6 THE PLAYERS

From a bird's-eye view, there would appear to be three major players in the financial markets:

1. Firms are net borrowers. They raise capital now to pay for investments in plant and equipment. The income generated by those real assets provides the returns to investors who purchase the securities issued by the firm.
2. Households typically are net savers. They purchase the securities issued by firms that need to raise funds.
3. Governments can be borrowers or lenders, depending on the relationship between tax revenue and government expenditures. Since World War II, the U.S.

government typically has run budget deficits, meaning that its tax receipts have been less than its expenditures. The government, therefore, has had to borrow funds to cover its budget deficit. Issuance of Treasury bills, notes, and bonds is the major way that the government borrows funds from the public. In contrast, in the latter part of the 1990s, the government enjoyed a budget surplus and was able to retire some outstanding debt.

Corporations and governments do not sell all or even most of their securities directly to individuals. For example, about half of all stock is held by large financial institutions such as pension funds, mutual funds, insurance companies, and banks. These financial institutions stand between the security issuer (the firm) and the ultimate owner of the security (the individual investor). For this reason, they are called *financial intermediaries*. Similarly, corporations do not market their own securities to the public. Instead, they hire agents, called investment bankers, to represent them to the investing public. Let's examine the roles of these intermediaries.

Financial Intermediaries

Households want desirable investments for their savings, yet the small (financial) size of most households makes direct investment difficult. A small investor seeking to lend money to businesses that need to finance investments doesn't advertise in the local newspaper to find a willing and desirable borrower. Moreover, an individual lender would not be able to diversify across borrowers to reduce risk. Finally, an individual lender is not equipped to assess and monitor the credit risk of borrowers.

For these reasons, **financial intermediaries** have evolved to bring lenders and borrowers together. These financial intermediaries include banks, investment companies, insurance companies, and credit unions. Financial intermediaries issue their own securities to raise funds to purchase the securities of other corporations.

For example, a bank raises funds by borrowing (taking deposits) and lending that money to other borrowers. The spread between the interest rates paid to depositors and the rates charged to borrowers is the source of the bank's profit. In this way, lenders and borrowers do not need to contact each other directly. Instead, each goes to the bank, which acts as an intermediary between the two. The problem of matching lenders with borrowers is solved when each comes independently to the common intermediary.

Financial intermediaries are distinguished from other businesses in that both their assets and their liabilities are overwhelmingly financial. Table 1.3 presents the aggregated balance sheet of commercial banks, one of the largest sectors of financial intermediaries. Notice that the balance sheet includes only very small amounts of real assets. Compare Table 1.3 to the aggregated balance sheet of the nonfinancial corporate sector in Table 1.4 for which real assets are about half of all assets. The contrast arises because intermediaries simply move funds from one sector to another. In fact, the primary social function of such intermediaries is to channel household savings to the business sector.

Other examples of financial intermediaries are investment companies, insurance companies, and credit unions. All these firms offer similar advantages in their intermediary role. First, by pooling the resources of many small investors, they are able to lend considerable sums to large borrowers. Second, by lending to many borrowers, intermediaries achieve significant diversification, so they can accept loans that individually might be too risky. Third, intermediaries build expertise through the volume of business they do and can use economies of scale and scope to assess and monitor risk.

Investment companies, which pool and manage the money of many investors, also arise out of economies of scale. Here, the problem is that most household portfolios are not large enough to be spread among a wide variety of securities. It is very expensive in terms

Assets	$ Billion	% Total	Liabilities and Net Worth	$ Billion	% Total
Real assets			**Liabilities**		
Equipment and premises	$ 100.7	1.0%	Deposits	$ 6,865.3	65.9%
Other real estate	6.8	0.1	Borrowed funds	1,242.5	11.9
Total real assets	$ 107.5	1.0%	Subordinated debt	161.3	1.5
			Federal funds and repurchase agreements	771.4	7.4
			Other	320.8	3.1
			Total liabilities	$ 9,361.3	89.9%
Financial assets					
Cash	$ 457.5	4.4%			
Investment securities	2,180.0	20.9			
Loans and leases	6,089.3	58.5			
Other financial assets	822.3	7.9			
Total financial assets	$ 9,549.1	91.7%			
Other assets					
Intangible assets	$ 379.2	3.6%			
Other	375.1	3.6			
Total other assets	$ 754.3	7.2%	Net worth	$ 1,049.6	10.1%
Total	$ 10,410.9	100.0%		$10,410.9	100.0%

TABLE 1.3

Balance sheet of commercial banks, 2007

Note: Column sums may differ from total because of rounding error.
Source: Federal Deposit Insurance Corporation, **www.fdic.gov,** September 2007.

Assets	$ Billion	% Total	Liabilities and Net Worth	$ Billion	% Total
Real assets			**Liabilities**		
Equipment and software	$ 3,764	15.0%	Bonds and mortgages	$ 4,397	17.5%
Real estate	7,861	31.2	Bank loans	707	2.8
Inventories	1,671	6.6	Other loans	745	3.0
Total real assets	$13,295	52.8%	Trade debt	1,651	6.6
			Other	3,319	13.2
Financial assets			Total liabilities	$10,818	43.0%
Deposits and cash	$ 608	2.4%			
Marketable securities	953	3.8			
Trade and consumer credit	2,200	8.7			
Other	8,108	32.2			
Total financial assets	$11,868	47.2%			
Total	$25,164	100.0%	Net worth	$14,346	57.0%
				$25,164	100.0%

TABLE 1.4

Balance sheet of nonfinancial U.S. business, 2007

Note: Column sums may differ from total because of rounding error.
Source: *Flow of Funds Accounts of the United States,* Board of Governors of the Federal Reserve System, June 2007.

of brokerage fees and research costs to purchase one or two shares of many different firms. Mutual funds have the advantage of large-scale trading and portfolio management, while participating investors are assigned a prorated share of the total funds according to the size of their investment. This system gives small investors advantages they are willing to pay for via a management fee to the mutual fund operator.

Investment companies also can design portfolios specifically for large investors with particular goals. In contrast, mutual funds are sold in the retail market, and their investment philosophies are differentiated mainly by strategies that are likely to attract a large number of clients.

Economies of scale also explain the proliferation of analytic services available to investors. Newsletters, databases, and brokerage house research services all engage in research to be sold to a large client base. This setup arises naturally. Investors clearly want information, but with small portfolios to manage, they do not find it economical to personally gather all of it. Hence, a profit opportunity emerges: A firm can perform this service for many clients and charge for it.

CONCEPT CHECK 2	Computer networks have made it much cheaper and easier for small investors to trade for their own accounts and perform their own security analysis. What will be the likely effect on financial intermediation?

Investment Bankers

Just as economies of scale and specialization create profit opportunities for financial intermediaries, so do these economies create niches for firms that perform specialized services for businesses. Firms raise much of their capital by selling securities such as stocks and bonds to the public. Because these firms do not do so frequently, however, investment banking firms that specialize in such activities can offer their services at a cost below that of maintaining an in-house security issuance division.

Investment bankers such as Goldman, Sachs or Merrill Lynch or Citigroup advise the issuing corporation on the prices it can charge for the securities issued, appropriate interest rates, and so forth. Ultimately, the investment banking firm handles the marketing of the security in the **primary market,** where new issues of securities are offered to the public. Later, investors can trade previously issued securities among themselves in the so-called **secondary market.**

Investment bankers can provide more than just expertise to security issuers. Because investment bankers are constantly in the market, assisting one firm or another in issuing securities, it is in their own interest to protect and maintain their reputation for honesty. Their investment in reputation is another type of scale economy that arises from frequent participation in the capital markets. An investment banker will suffer along with investors if the securities it underwrites are marketed to the public with overly optimistic or exaggerated claims; the public will not be so trusting the next time that investment banker participates in a security sale. As we have seen, this lesson was relearned with considerable pain in the boom years of the late 1990s and the subsequent high-tech crash of 2000–2002. Too many investment bankers got caught up in the flood of money that could be made by pushing stock issues to an overly eager public. The failure of many of these offerings soured the public on both the stock market and the firms managing the IPOs. At least some on Wall Street recognized that they had squandered a valuable asset—reputational capital—and that the conflicts of interest that engendered these deals were not only wrong but bad for business as well. An investment banker's effectiveness and ability to command future business depend on the reputation it has established over time.

1.7   RECENT TRENDS

Four important trends have changed the contemporary investment environment: (1) globalization, (2) securitization, (3) financial engineering, and (4) information and computer networks.

Globalization

If a wider range of investment choices can benefit investors, why should we limit ourselves to purely domestic assets? Increasingly efficient communication technology and the dismantling of regulatory constraints have encouraged **globalization** in recent years.

U.S. investors commonly can participate in foreign investment opportunities in several ways: (1) purchase foreign securities using American Depository Receipts (ADRs), which are domestically traded securities that represent claims to shares of foreign stocks; (2) purchase foreign securities that are offered in dollars; (3) buy mutual funds that invest internationally; and (4) buy derivative securities with payoffs that depend on prices in foreign security markets.

Brokers who act as intermediaries for American Depository Receipts purchase an inventory of stock from some foreign issuer. The broker then issues an American Depository Receipt that represents a claim to some number of those foreign shares held in inventory. The ADR is denominated in dollars and can be traded on U.S. stock exchanges but is in essence no more than a claim on a foreign stock. Thus, from the investor's point of view, there is no more difference between buying a British versus a U.S. stock than there is in holding a Massachusetts-based company compared with a California-based one. Of course, the investment implication may differ: ADRs still expose investors to exchange-rate risk.

Exchange-traded funds, or ETFs, are a variation on ADRs. ETFs also use a depository structure but buy entire portfolios of stocks. While ETFs may specialize in sectors as diverse as commodities or individual industries, others buy shares of firms of one particular country. These funds thus enable U.S. investors to obtain and trade diversified portfolios of foreign stocks in one fell swoop. Popular ETF brands are iShares (marketed by Barclays) or WEBS (World Equity Benchmark Shares), which are designed to replicate the investment performance of Morgan Stanley Capital International (MSCI) country indexes.

A giant step toward globalization took place in 1999 when 11 European countries replaced their existing currencies with a new currency called the *euro*.[6] The idea behind the euro is that a common currency will facilitate trade and encourage integration of markets across national boundaries. Figure 1.1 is an announcement of a debt offering in

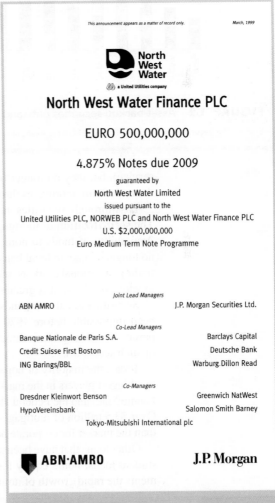

This announcement appears as a matter of record only.   *March, 1999*

North West Water
a United Utilities company

North West Water Finance PLC

EURO 500,000,000

4.875% Notes due 2009

guaranteed by
North West Water Limited
issued pursuant to the
United Utilities PLC, NORWEB PLC and North West Water Finance PLC
U.S. $2,000,000,000
Euro Medium Term Note Programme

Joint Lead Managers

ABN AMRO   J.P. Morgan Securities Ltd.

Co-Lead Managers

Banque Nationale de Paris S.A.   Barclays Capital
Credit Suisse First Boston   Deutsche Bank
ING Barings/BBL   Warburg.Dillon Read

Co-Managers

Dresdner Kleinwort Benson   Greenwich NatWest
HypoVereinsbank   Salomon Smith Barney
Tokyo-Mitsubishi International plc

ABN·AMRO   **J.P. Morgan**

FIGURE 1.1 Globalization: A debt issue denominated in euros

Source: North West Water Finance PLC, April 1999.

---

[6]The 11 countries are Belgium, Germany, Spain, France, Ireland, Italy, Luxembourg, Netherlands, Austria, Portugal, and Finland. Greece and Slovenia later adopted the common currency. Several other countries, primarily in middle and eastern Europe, have joined the European Union and are likely to adopt the euro in the next few years.

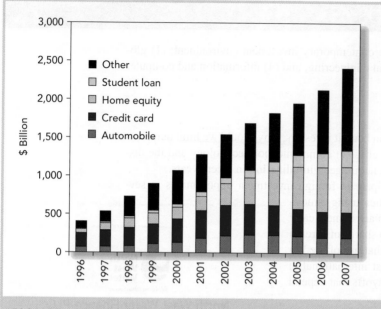

FIGURE 1.2   Asset-backed securities outstanding

Source: The Securities Industry and Financial Markets Association, **www.sifma.org**

the amount of 500 million euros. (In early 2008, the euro was worth about $1.45; the symbol for the euro is €.)

Securitization

In 1970, mortgage **pass-through securities** were introduced by the Government National Mortgage Association (GNMA, or Ginnie Mae). These securities aggregate individual home mortgages into relatively homogeneous pools. Each pool acts as backing for a GNMA pass-through security. Investors who buy GNMA securities receive prorated shares of all the principal and interest payments made on the underlying mortgage pool.

For example, the pool might total $100 million of 8%, 30-year conventional mortgages. The banks that originated the mortgages continue to service them (receiving fee-for-service), but they no longer own the mortgage investment; they pass the cash flows from the underlying mortgages through to the GNMA security holders.

Pass-through securities represented a tremendous innovation in mortgage markets. The **securitization** of mortgages means mortgages can be traded just like other securities. Availability of funds to homebuyers no longer depends on local credit conditions and is no longer subject to local banks' potential monopoly powers; with mortgage pass-throughs trading in national markets, mortgage funds can flow from any region (literally worldwide) to wherever demand is greatest.

Securitization also expands the menu of choices for the investor. Whereas it would have been impossible before 1970 for investors to invest in mortgages directly, they now can purchase mortgage pass-through securities or invest in mutual funds that offer portfolios of such securities.

Today, the majority of home mortgages are pooled into mortgage-backed securities. The two biggest players in the market are the Federal National Mortgage Association (FNMA, or Fannie Mae) and the Federal Home Loan Mortgage Corporation (FHLMC, or Freddie Mac). Over $3.5 trillion of mortgage-backed securities are outstanding, making this market larger than the market for corporate bonds.

Other loans that have been securitized into pass-through arrangements include car loans, student loans, home equity loans, credit card loans, and debts of firms. Figure 1.2 documents the rapid growth of nonmortgage asset–backed securities since 1996.

CONCEPT CHECK 3

When mortgages are pooled into securities, the pass-through agencies (Freddie Mac and Fannie Mae) typically guarantee the underlying mortgage loans. If the homeowner defaults on the loan, the pass-through agency makes good on the loan; the investor in the mortgage-backed security does not bear the credit risk. Why does the allocation of risk to the pass-through agency rather than the security holder make economic sense?

Financial Engineering

Financial engineering is the use of mathematical models and computer-based trading technology to synthesize new financial products. A good example of a financially engineered investment product is the *principal-protected equity-linked note.* These are securities issued by financial intermediaries that guarantee a minimum fixed return plus an additional amount that depends on the performance of some specified stock index, such as the S&P 500.

Financial engineering often involves **unbundling** securities—breaking up and allocating the cash flows from one security to create several new securities—or **bundling**—combining more than one security into a composite security. Such creative engineering of new investment products allows one to design securities with custom-tailored risk attributes. An example of bundling appears in Figure 1.3.

Boise Cascade, with the assistance of Goldman, Sachs and other underwriters, has issued a hybrid security with features of preferred stock combined with various call and put option contracts. The security is structured as preferred stock for 4 years, at which time it is converted into common stock of the company. However, the number of shares of common stock into which the security can be converted depends on the price of the stock in 4 years, which means that the security holders are exposed to risk similar to the risk they would bear if they held option positions on the firm.

Often, creating a security that appears to be attractive requires the unbundling of an asset. An example is given in Figure 1.4. There, a mortgage pass-through certificate is

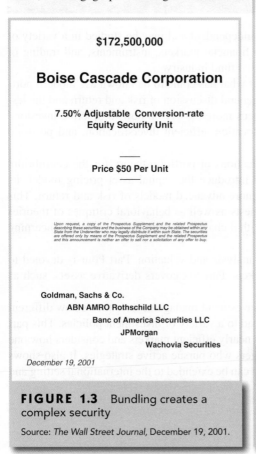

FIGURE 1.3   Bundling creates a complex security

Source: *The Wall Street Journal,* December 19, 2001.

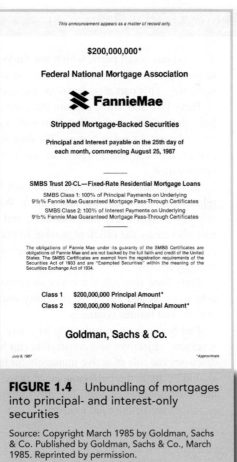

FIGURE 1.4   Unbundling of mortgages into principal- and interest-only securities

Source: Copyright March 1985 by Goldman, Sachs & Co. Published by Goldman, Sachs & Co., March 1985. Reprinted by permission.

unbundled into classes. Class 1 receives only principal payments from the mortgage pool, whereas Class 2 receives only interest payments.

Computer Networks

The Internet and other advances in computer networking have transformed many sectors of the economy, and few more so than the financial sector. These advances will be treated in greater detail in Chapter 3, but for now we can mention a few important innovations: online trading, online information dissemination, and automated trade crossing.

Online trading connects a customer directly to a brokerage firm. Online brokerage firms can process trades more cheaply and therefore can charge lower commissions. The average commission for an online trade is below $20, compared to more than $100 at full-service brokers.

The Internet has also allowed vast amounts of information to be made cheaply and widely available to the public. Individual investors today can obtain data, investment tools, and even analyst reports that just a decade ago would have been available only to professionals.

Electronic communication networks that allow direct trading among investors have exploded in recent years. These networks allow members to post buy or sell orders and to have those orders automatically matched up or "crossed" with orders of other traders in the system without benefit of an intermediary such as a securities dealer.

1.8   OUTLINE OF THE TEXT

The text has seven parts, which are fairly independent and may be studied in a variety of sequences. Part One is an introduction to financial markets, instruments, and trading of securities. This part also describes the mutual fund industry.

Parts Two and Three contain the core of what has come to be known as "modern portfolio theory." We start in Part Two with a general discussion of risk and return and the lessons of capital market history. We then focus more closely on how to describe investors' risk preferences and progress to asset allocation, efficient diversification, and portfolio optimization.

In Part Three, we investigate the implications of portfolio theory for the equilibrium relationship between risk and return. We introduce the capital asset pricing model, its implementation using index models, and more advanced models of risk and return. This part also treats the efficient market hypothesis as well as behavioral critiques of theories based on investor rationality and closes with a chapter on empirical evidence concerning security returns.

Parts Four through Six cover security analysis and valuation. Part Four is devoted to debt markets and Part Five to equity markets. Part Six covers derivative assets, such as options and futures contracts.

Part Seven is an introduction to active investment management. It shows how different investors' objectives and constraints can lead to a variety of investment policies. This part discusses the role of active management in nearly efficient markets and considers how one should evaluate the performance of managers who pursue active strategies. It also shows how the principles of portfolio construction can be extended to the international setting and examines the hedge fund industry.

1. Real assets create wealth. Financial assets represent claims to parts or all of that wealth. Financial assets determine how the ownership of real assets is distributed among investors.

2. Financial assets can be categorized as fixed income, equity, or derivative instruments. Top-down portfolio construction techniques start with the asset allocation decision—the allocation of funds across broad asset classes—and then progress to more specific security-selection decisions.

3. Competition in financial markets leads to a risk–return trade-off, in which securities that offer higher expected rates of return also impose greater risks on investors. The presence of risk, however, implies that actual returns can differ considerably from expected returns at the beginning of the investment period. Competition among security analysts also promotes financial markets that are nearly informationally efficient, meaning that prices reflect all available information concerning the value of the security. Passive investment strategies may make sense in nearly efficient markets.

4. Financial intermediaries pool investor funds and invest them. Their services are in demand because small investors cannot efficiently gather information, diversify, and monitor portfolios. The financial intermediary sells its own securities to the small investors. The intermediary invests the funds thus raised, uses the proceeds to pay back the small investors, and profits from the difference (the spread).

5. Investment banking brings efficiency to corporate fund-raising. Investment bankers develop expertise in pricing new issues and in marketing them to investors.

Related Web sites for this chapter are available at **www.mhhe.com/bkm**

6. Recent trends in financial markets include globalization, securitization, financial engineering of assets, and growth of information and computer networks.

investment	security selection	primary market
real assets	security analysis	secondary market
financial assets	risk–return trade-off	globalization
fixed-income (debt) securities	passive management	pass-through securities
equity	active management	securitization
derivative securities	financial intermediaries	financial engineering
agency problem	investment companies	bundling
asset allocation	investment bankers	unbundling

1. Financial engineering has been disparaged as nothing more than paper shuffling. Critics argue that resources used for *rearranging* wealth (that is, bundling and unbundling financial assets) might be better spent on *creating* wealth (that is, creating real assets). Evaluate this criticism. Are any benefits realized by creating an array of derivative securities from various primary securities?

2. Why would you expect securitization to take place only in highly developed capital markets?

3. What is the relationship between securitization and the role of financial intermediaries in the economy? What happens to financial intermediaries as securitization progresses?

4. Although we stated that real assets comprise the true productive capacity of an economy, it is hard to conceive of a modern economy without well-developed financial markets and security types. How would the productive capacity of the U.S. economy be affected if there were no markets in which one could trade financial assets?

5. Firms raise capital from investors by issuing shares in the primary markets. Does this imply that corporate financial managers can ignore trading of previously issued shares in the secondary market?

Visit us at www.mhhe.com/bkm

Problems

6. Suppose you discover a treasure chest of $10 billion in cash.

    a. Is this a real or financial asset?
    b. Is society any richer for the discovery?
    c. Are you wealthier?
    d. Can you reconcile your answers to (*b*) and (*c*)? Is anyone worse off as a result of the discovery?

7. Lanni Products is a start-up computer software development firm. It currently owns computer equipment worth $30,000 and has cash on hand of $20,000 contributed by Lanni's owners. For each of the following transactions, identify the real and/or financial assets that trade hands. Are any financial assets created or destroyed in the transaction?

    a. Lanni takes out a bank loan. It receives $50,000 in cash and signs a note promising to pay back the loan over 3 years.
    b. Lanni uses the cash from the bank plus $20,000 of its own funds to finance the development of new financial planning software.
    c. Lanni sells the software product to Microsoft, which will market it to the public under the Microsoft name. Lanni accepts payment in the form of 1,500 shares of Microsoft stock.
    d. Lanni sells the shares of stock for $80 per share and uses part of the proceeds to pay off the bank loan.

8. Reconsider Lanni Products from Problem 7.

    a. Prepare its balance sheet just after it gets the bank loan. What is the ratio of real assets to total assets?
    b. Prepare the balance sheet after Lanni spends the $70,000 to develop its software product. What is the ratio of real assets to total assets?
    c. Prepare the balance sheet after Lanni accepts the payment of shares from Microsoft. What is the ratio of real assets to total assets?

9. Examine the balance sheet of commercial banks in Table 1.3. What is the ratio of real assets to total assets? What is that ratio for nonfinancial firms (Table 1.4)? Why should this difference be expected?

10. Consider Figure 1.5, which describes an issue of American gold certificates.

    a. Is this issue a primary or secondary market transaction?
    b. Are the certificates primitive or derivative assets?
    c. What market niche is filled by this offering?

11. Discuss the advantages and disadvantages of the following forms of managerial compensation in terms of mitigating agency problems, that is, potential conflicts of interest between managers and shareholders.

    a. A fixed salary.
    b. Stock in the firm.
    c. Call options on shares of the firm.

12. We noted that oversight by large institutional investors or creditors is one mechanism to reduce agency problems. Why don't individual investors in the firm have the same incentive to keep an eye on management?

13. Give an example of three financial intermediaries and explain how they act as a bridge between small investors and large capital markets or corporations.

14. The average rate of return on investments in large stocks has outpaced that on investments in Treasury bills by about 8% since 1926. Why, then, does anyone invest in Treasury bills?

15. What are some advantages and disadvantages of top-down versus bottom-up investing styles?

This announcement is neither an offer to sell nor a solicitation of an offer to buy any of these Certificates.
This offer is made only by the Offering Memorandum.

NEW ISSUE

$100,000,000

July 7, 1987

AMERICAN GOLD CERTIFICATES

Due July 1, 1991

• *American Gold Certificates represent physical allocated gold bullion
insured and held in safekeeping at Bank of Delaware.*
• *Anytime during the four-year period, the certificate holder
may request physical delivery of the gold.*

*Copies of the Offering Memorandum may be obtained in any State from only such of the undersigned
as may legally offer these certificates in such State*

J. W. KORTH CAPITAL MARKETS, INC.

THE CHICAGO CORPORATION	COWEN & CO.	DOMINICK & DOMINICK INCORPORATED
FIRST ALBANY CORPORATION	GRIFFIN, KUBIK, STEPHENS & THOMPSON, INC.	
INTERSTATE SECURITIES CORPORATION	JANNEY MONTGOMERY SCOTT INC.	
McDONALD & COMPANY SECURITIES, INC.	PACIFIC SECURITIES, INC.	
RONEY & CO.	STEPHENS INC.	UMIC, INC.
VINING-SPARKS SECURITIES, INC.	WESTCAP SECURITIES, INC.	
BAKER, WATTS & CO.	BARCLAY INVESTMENTS, INC.	
BIRR, WILSON SECURITIES, INC.	D. A. DAVIDSON & CO. INCORPORATED	
INDEPENDENCE SECURITIES, INC.	JESUP & LAMONT SECURITIES CO., INC.	
EMMETT A. LARKIN CO., INC.	SCOTT & STRINGFELLOW, INC.	
SEIDLER AMDEC SECURITIES INC.	UNDERWOOD, NEUHAUS & CO. INCORPORATED	

FIGURE 1.5 A gold-backed security

16. You see an advertisement for a book that claims to show how you can make $1 million with no risk and with no money down. Will you buy the book?

17. Below is an excerpt from the investor education Web site of the SEC.

    a. How does the excerpt define the difference between saving and investing?

    b. In what ways does this differ from the economist's definition given in this chapter?

    Your "savings" are usually put into the safest places or products that allow you access to your money at any time. Examples include savings accounts, checking accounts, and certificates of deposit. At some banks and savings and loan associations your deposits may be insured by the Federal Deposit Insurance Corporation (FDIC). But there's a tradeoff for getting that security and ready availability. Your money is paid a low wage as it works for you.

    When you "invest," you have a greater chance of losing your money than when you "save." Unlike FDIC-insured deposits, the money you invest in securities, mutual funds, and other similar investments are not federally insured. You could lose your "principal," which is the amount you've invested. That's true even if you purchase your investments through a bank. But when you invest, you also have the opportunity to earn more money than when you save.

18. Here is another quote on savings and investment from the Securities Industry Association (**www.pathtoinvesting.org**). Critique and correct this statement in light of the definitions of saving and investment contained in the chapter.

    Saving and investing aren't the same—although they both play a role in your financial plan. While they both involve setting aside some of your income for the future, saving often refers to putting money in the bank—in savings and money market accounts—while investing means buying stocks, bonds, mutual funds, or other uninsured assets . . . While investing can help you achieve your long-term goals, saving is an effective way of managing your money to meet short-term needs and to provide a safety net for emergency expenses.

---

1. Go to the Market Insight Web site at **www.mhhe.com/edumarketinsight.** Select the *Company* tab and enter ticker symbol WB. Click on *Company Profile* in the Compustat Reports section. What kind of firm is Wachovia?

2. In the EDGAR section, locate Wachovia's most recent balance sheet. This may be annual (10-K) or quarterly (10-Q). When you click on the link, the entire filing will appear. Scroll down until you find the Balance Sheet.

3. Calculate the common-size percentage for Wachovia's net worth, which equals total stockholders' equity divided by total assets. How does this percentage compare to the net worth of commercial banks from Table 1.3 in the text? Repeat the process for Bank of America (BAC) and US Bancorp (USB) and compare your answers.

STANDARD &POOR'S

E-Investments

Market Regulators

1. Go to the Securities and Exchange Commission Web site, **www.sec.gov.** What is the mission of the SEC? What information and advice does the SEC offer to beginning investors?

2. Go to the NASD Web site, **www.finra.org** What is its mission? What information and advice does it offer to beginners?

3. Go to the IOSCO Web site, **www.iosco.org.** What is its mission? What information and advice does it offer to beginners?

Visit us at www.mhhe.com/bkm

SOLUTIONS TO CONCEPT CHECKS

1. *a.* Real
   b. Financial
   c. Real
   d. Real
   e. Financial

2. If the new technology enables investors to trade and perform research for themselves, the need for financial intermediaries will decline. Part of the service intermediaries now offer is a lower-cost method for individuals to participate in securities markets. This part of the intermediaries' service would be less sought after.

3. The pass-through agencies are far better equipped to evaluate the credit risk associated with the pool of mortgages. They are constantly in the market, have ongoing relationships with the originators of the loans, and find it economical to set up "quality control" departments to monitor the credit risk of the mortgage pools. Therefore, the pass-through agencies are better able to incur the risk; they charge for this "service" via a "guarantee fee." Investors might not find it worthwhile to purchase these securities if they must assess the credit risk of these loans for themselves. It is far cheaper for them to allow the agencies to collect the guarantee fee.

CHAPTER TWO

ASSET CLASSES AND FINANCIAL INSTRUMENTS

YOU LEARNED IN Chapter 1 that the process of building an investment portfolio usually begins by deciding how much money to allocate to broad classes of assets, such as safe money market securities or bank accounts, longer-term bonds, stocks, or even asset classes like real estate or precious metals. This process is called *asset allocation.* Within each class the investor then selects specific assets from a more detailed menu. This is called *security selection.*

Each broad asset class contains many specific security types, and the many variations on a theme can be overwhelming. Our goal in this chapter is to introduce you to the important features of broad classes of securities. Toward this end, we organize our tour of financial instruments according to asset class.

Financial markets are traditionally segmented into **money markets** and **capital markets.** Money market instruments include short-term, marketable, liquid, low-risk debt securities. Money market instruments sometimes are called *cash equivalents,* or just *cash* for short. Capital markets, in contrast, include longer-term and riskier securities. Securities in the capital market are much more diverse than those found within the money market. For this reason, we will subdivide the capital market into four segments: longer-term bond markets, equity markets, and the derivative markets for options and futures.

We first describe money market instruments. We then move on to debt and equity securities. We explain the structure of various stock market indexes in this chapter because market benchmark portfolios play an important role in portfolio construction and evaluation. Finally, we survey the derivative security markets for options and futures contracts.

2.1   THE MONEY MARKET

The money market is a subsector of the fixed-income market. It consists of very short-term debt securities that usually are highly marketable. Many of these securities trade in large denominations, and so are out of the reach of individual investors. Money market funds, however, are easily accessible to small investors. These mutual funds pool the resources of many investors and purchase a wide variety of money market securities on their behalf.

Figure 2.1 is a reprint of a money rates listing from *The Wall Street Journal.* It includes the various instruments of the money market that we will describe in detail. Table 2.1 provides the outstanding volume of the major instruments of the money market.

Treasury Bills

U.S. *Treasury bills* (T-bills, or just bills, for short) are the most marketable of all money market instruments. T-bills represent the simplest form of borrowing: The government raises money by selling bills to the public. Investors buy the bills at a discount from the stated maturity value. At the bill's maturity, the holder receives from the government a payment equal to the face value of the bill. The difference between the purchase price and ultimate maturity value constitutes the investor's earnings.

T-bills are issued with initial maturities of 28, 91, or 182 days. Individuals can purchase T-bills directly, at auction, or on the secondary market from a government securities dealer. T-bills are highly liquid; that is, they are easily converted to cash and sold at low transaction cost and with not much price risk. Unlike most other money market instruments, which sell in minimum denominations of $100,000, T-bills sell in minimum denominations of only $100. The income earned on T-bills is exempt from all state and local taxes, another characteristic distinguishing bills from other money market instruments.

Figure 2.2 is a listing of T-bill rates. Rather than providing prices of each bill, the financial press reports

Money Rates

January 4, 2007

International rates

Prime rates	Latest	Week ago	52-WEEK High	Low
U.S.	8.25	8.25	8.25	7.25
Canada	6.00	6.00	6.00	5.00
Euro zone	3.50	3.50	3.50	2.25
Japan	1.625	1.625	1.625	1.375
Britain	5.00	5.00	5.00	4.50

Overnight repurchase				
U.S.	5.22	5.19	5.28	4.13
U.K. (BBA)	5.080	5.047	5.150	4.100
Euro zone	3.60	3.77	3.77	2.26

U.S. government rates

Federal funds				
Effective rate	5.24	5.25	5.37	4.21

Treasury bill auction				
4 weeks	4.760	4.660	5.170	3.950
13 weeks	4.930	4.875	4.990	4.070
26 weeks	4.900	4.900	5.110	4.250

Secondary market

Freddie Mac 30-year mortgage yields				
30 days	5.92	6.06	6.71	5.81
60 days	5.93	6.07	6.75	5.82
One-year ARM	3.375	3.375	3.375	3.375

Fannie Mae 30-year mortgage yields				
30 days	6.066	6.107	6.792	5.913
60 days	6.089	6.125	6.821	5.924

Bankers acceptances				
30 days	5.29	5.31	5.38	4.35
60 days	5.30	5.31	5.43	4.44
90 days	5.31	5.31	5.49	4.49

Other short-term rates

Commercial paper	Latest	Week ago	52-WEEK High	Low
30 to 60 days	5.23	...	...	...
61 to 90 days	5.22	...	...	...
91 to 120 days	5.20	...	...	...

Dealer commercial paper				
30 days	5.26	5.27	5.36	4.32
60 days	5.26	5.28	5.41	4.42
90 days	5.25	5.30	5.46	4.46

Euro commercial paper				
30 day	3.58	3.58	3.62	2.00
Two month	3.62	3.62	3.63	2.39
Three month	3.69	3.68	3.69	2.45

London interbank offered rate, or Libor				
One month	5.32000	5.3256	5.4200	4.4188
Three month	5.36000	5.3600	5.5200	4.5500

Euro Libor				
One month	3.628	3.634	3.713	2.386
Three month	3.733	3.724	3.733	2.488

Euro interbank offered rate (Euribor)				
One month	3.625	3.634	3.672	2.384
Three month	3.734	3.723	3.734	2.490

Asian dollars				
One month	5.335	5.337	5.425	4.418
Three month	5.363	5.370	5.525	3.570

Eurodollars (mid rates)	LATEST Offer	Bid	Week ago	52-WEEK High	Low
One month	5.28	5.30	5.32	5.39	4.36
Two month	5.29	5.31	5.32	5.44	4.45
Three month	5.30	5.32	5.34	5.51	4.51

FIGURE 2.1   Rates on money market securities

	$ Billion
Repurchase agreements	$1,150.2
Small-denomination time deposits*	1,164.4
Large-denomination time deposits*	2,155.7
Eurodollars	530.3
Treasury bills	911.5
Commercial paper	2,252.5
Savings deposits	3,874.8
Money market mutual funds	2,390.0

TABLE 2.1

Major components of
the money market

*Small denominations are less than $100,000.
Sources: *Economic Report of the President*, U.S. Government Printing
Office, 2007; *Flow of Funds Accounts of the United States*, Board of Governors of the Federal Reserve System, June 2007.

yields based on those prices. You will see yields corresponding to both bid and asked prices. The **asked price** is the price you would have to pay to buy a T-bill from a securities dealer. The **bid price** is the slightly lower price you would receive if you wanted to sell a bill to a dealer. The **bid–asked spread** is the difference in these prices, which is the dealer's source of profit. (Notice in Figure 2.2 that the bid *yield* is higher than the ask yield. This is because prices and yields are inversely related.)

The first two yields in Figure 2.2 are reported using the *bank-discount method*. This means that the bill's discount from par value is "annualized" based on a 360-day year, and then reported as a percentage of par value. For example, for the highlighted bill maturing on April 5, days to maturity are 90 and the yield under the column labeled "Asked" is given as 4.90%. This means that a dealer was willing to sell the bill at a discount from par value of $4.90\% \times (90/360) = 1.225\%$. So a bill with $10,000 par value could be purchased for $10,000 $\times (1 - .01225) = \$9,877.50$. Similarly, based on the bid yield of 4.91%, a dealer would be willing to *purchase* the bill for $10,000 $\times [1 - .0491 \times (90/360)] = \$9,877.25$.

The bank discount method for computing yields has a long tradition, but it is flawed for at least two reasons. First, it assumes that the year has only 360 days. Second, it computes the yield as a fraction of par value rather than of the price the investor paid to acquire the bill.[1] An investor who buys the bill for the asked price and holds it until maturity will see her investment grow over 90 days by a multiple of $10,000/$9,877.50 = 1.01240, or 1.240%. Annualizing this return using a 365-day year results in a yield of $1.240\% \times 365/90 = 5.03\%$,

Treasury Bills

MATURITY	DAYS TO MAT	BID	ASKED	CHG	ASK YLD
Jan 11 07	6	4.50	4.49	−0.11	4.56
Jan 18 07	13	4.57	4.56	−0.09	4.63
Jan 25 07	20	4.61	4.60	−0.01	4.68
Feb 01 07	27	4.70	4.69	−0.06	4.77
Feb 08 07	34	4.70	4.69	+0.01	4.78
Feb 15 07	41	4.73	4.72	−0.08	4.81
Feb 22 07	48	4.79	4.78	−0.04	4.88
Mar 01 07	55	4.83	4.82	−0.02	4.92
Mar 08 07	62	4.86	4.85	+0.01	4.96
Mar 15 07	69	4.85	4.84	−0.01	4.95
Mar 22 07	76	4.88	4.87	−0.02	4.99
Mar 29 07	83	4.88	4.87	−0.02	4.99
Apr 05 07	90	4.91	4.90	−0.01	5.03
Apr 12 07	97	4.90	4.89	−0.01	5.02
Apr 19 07	104	4.90	4.89	−0.01	5.03
Apr 26 07	111	4.90	4.89	−0.01	5.03

FIGURE 2.2   Treasury bill yields

Source: Compiled from data obtained from *The Wall Street Journal Online*, January 4, 2007.

---

[1]Both of these "errors" were dictated by computational simplicity in precomputer days. It is easier to compute percentage discounts from a round number such as par value rather than purchase price. It is also easier to annualize using a 360-day year, because 360 is an even multiple of so many numbers.

which is the value reported in the last column under "Ask Yld." This last value is called the Treasury-bill's *bond-equivalent yield.*

Certificates of Deposit

A **certificate of deposit,** or CD, is a time deposit with a bank. Time deposits may not be withdrawn on demand. The bank pays interest and principal to the depositor only at the end of the fixed term of the CD. CDs issued in denominations greater than $100,000 are usually negotiable, however; that is, they can be sold to another investor if the owner needs to cash in the certificate before its maturity date. Short-term CDs are highly marketable, although the market significantly thins out for maturities of 3 months or more. CDs are treated as bank deposits by the Federal Deposit Insurance Corporation, so they are insured for up to $100,000 in the event of a bank insolvency.

Commercial Paper

Large, well-known companies often issue their own short-term unsecured debt notes rather than borrow directly from banks. These notes are called **commercial paper.** Very often, commercial paper is backed by a bank line of credit, which gives the borrower access to cash that can be used (if needed) to pay off the paper at maturity.

Commercial paper maturities range up to 270 days; longer maturities would require registration with the Securities and Exchange Commission and so are almost never issued. Most often, commercial paper is issued with maturities of less than 1 or 2 months. Usually, it is issued in multiples of $100,000. Therefore, small investors can invest in commercial paper only indirectly, via money market mutual funds.

Commercial paper is considered to be a fairly safe asset, because a firm's condition presumably can be monitored and predicted over a term as short as 1 month.

While most commercial paper is issued by nonfinancial firms, in recent years there has been a sharp increase in *asset-backed commercial paper* issued by financial firms such as banks. This is short-term commercial paper typically used to raise funds for the institution to invest in other assets. These assets in turn are used as collateral for the commercial paper—hence the label "asset backed." This practice led to many difficulties starting in the summer of 2007 when the subprime mortgages in which the banks invested performed poorly as default rates spiked. The banks found themselves unable to issue new commercial paper to refinance their positions as the old paper matured.

Bankers' Acceptances

A **banker's acceptance** starts as an order to a bank by a bank's customer to pay a sum of money at a future date, typically within 6 months. At this stage, it is similar to a postdated check. When the bank endorses the order for payment as "accepted," it assumes responsibility for ultimate payment to the holder of the acceptance. At this point, the acceptance may be traded in secondary markets like any other claim on the bank. Bankers' acceptances are considered very safe assets because traders can substitute the bank's credit standing for their own. They are used widely in foreign trade where the creditworthiness of one trader is unknown to the trading partner. Acceptances sell at a discount from the face value of the payment order, just as T-bills sell at a discount from par value.

Eurodollars

Eurodollars are dollar-denominated deposits at foreign banks or foreign branches of American banks. By locating outside the United States, these banks escape regulation by the Federal Reserve. Despite the tag "Euro," these accounts need not be in European banks, although that is where the practice of accepting dollar-denominated deposits outside the United States began.

Most Eurodollar deposits are for large sums, and most are time deposits of less than 6 months' maturity. A variation on the Eurodollar time deposit is the Eurodollar certificate of deposit. A Eurodollar CD resembles a domestic bank CD except that it is the liability of a non-U.S. branch of a bank, typically a London branch. The advantage of Eurodollar CDs over Eurodollar time deposits is that the holder can sell the asset to realize its cash value before maturity. Eurodollar CDs are considered less liquid and riskier than domestic CDs, however, and thus offer higher yields. Firms also issue Eurodollar bonds, which are dollar-denominated bonds outside the U.S., although bonds are not a money market investment because of their long maturities.

Repos and Reverses

Dealers in government securities use **repurchase agreements,** also called "repos" or "RPs," as a form of short-term, usually overnight, borrowing. The dealer sells government securities to an investor on an overnight basis, with an agreement to buy back those securities the next day at a slightly higher price. The increase in the price is the overnight interest. The dealer thus takes out a 1-day loan from the investor, and the securities serve as collateral.

A *term repo* is essentially an identical transaction, except that the term of the implicit loan can be 30 days or more. Repos are considered very safe in terms of credit risk because the loans are backed by the government securities. A *reverse repo* is the mirror image of a repo. Here, the dealer finds an investor holding government securities and buys them, agreeing to sell them back at a specified higher price on a future date.

Federal Funds

Just as most of us maintain deposits at banks, banks maintain deposits of their own at a Federal Reserve bank. Each member bank of the Federal Reserve System, or "the Fed," is required to maintain a minimum balance in a reserve account with the Fed. The required balance depends on the total deposits of the bank's customers. Funds in the bank's reserve account are called **federal funds,** or *fed funds.* At any time, some banks have more funds than required at the Fed. Other banks, primarily big banks in New York and other financial centers, tend to have a shortage of federal funds. In the federal funds market, banks with excess funds lend to those with a shortage. These loans, which are usually overnight transactions, are arranged at a rate of interest called the federal funds rate.

Although the fed funds market arose primarily as a way for banks to transfer balances to meet reserve requirements, today the market has evolved to the point that many large banks use federal funds in a straightforward way as one component of their total sources of funding. Therefore, the fed funds rate is simply the rate of interest on very short-term loans among financial institutions. While most investors cannot participate in this market, the fed funds rate commands great interest as a key barometer of monetary policy.

Brokers' Calls

Individuals who buy stocks on margin borrow part of the funds to pay for the stocks from their broker. The broker in turn may borrow the funds from a bank, agreeing to repay the bank immediately (on call) if the bank requests it. The rate paid on such loans is usually about 1% higher than the rate on short-term T-bills.

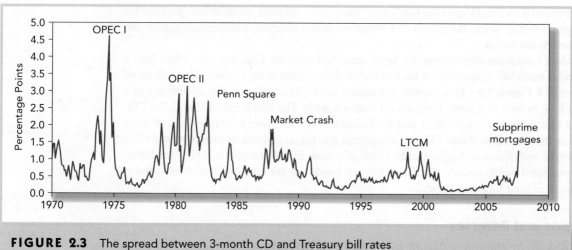

FIGURE 2.3 The spread between 3-month CD and Treasury bill rates

The LIBOR Market

The **London Interbank Offered Rate** (LIBOR) is the rate at which large banks in London are willing to lend money among themselves. This rate, which is quoted on dollar- denominated loans, has become the premier short-term interest rate quoted in the European money market, and it serves as a reference rate for a wide range of transactions. For example, a corporation might borrow at a floating rate equal to LIBOR plus 2%.

LIBOR interest rates may be tied to currencies other than the U.S. dollar. For example, LIBOR rates are widely quoted for transactions denominated in British pounds, yen, euros, and so on. There is also a similar rate called EURIBOR (European Interbank Offered Rate) at which banks in the euro zone are willing to lend euros among themselves.

Yields on Money Market Instruments

Although most money market securities are of low risk, they are not risk-free. The securities of the money market promise yields greater than those on default-free T-bills, at least in part because of greater relative riskiness. In addition, many investors require more liquidity; thus they will accept lower yields on securities such as T-bills that can be quickly and cheaply sold for cash. Figure 2.3 shows that bank CDs, for example, consistently have paid a premium over T-bills. Moreover, that premium increased with economic crises such as the energy price shocks associated with the two OPEC disturbances, the failure of Penn Square bank, the stock market crash in 1987, the collapse of Long Term Capital Management in 1998, and the virtual breakdown of the market in subprime mortgages in 2007.

2.2 THE BOND MARKET

The bond market is composed of longer-term borrowing or debt instruments than those that trade in the money market. This market includes Treasury notes and bonds, corporate bonds, municipal bonds, mortgage securities, and federal agency debt.

These instruments are sometimes said to comprise the *fixed-income capital market*, because most of them promise either a fixed stream of income or a stream of income that is determined according to a specific formula. In practice, these formulas can result in a flow of income that is far from fixed. Therefore, the term "fixed income" is probably not fully appropriate. It is simpler and more straightforward to call these securities either debt instruments or bonds.

Treasury Notes and Bonds

The U.S. government borrows funds in large part by selling **Treasury notes** and **Treasury bonds.** T-note maturities range up to 10 years, whereas bonds are issued with maturities ranging from 10 to 30 years. Both are issued in denominations of $1,000 or more. Both notes and bonds make semiannual interest payments called *coupon payments,* a name derived from precomputer days, when investors would literally clip coupons attached to the bond and present a coupon to receive the interest payment.

U.S. Government Bonds and Notes

RATE	MATURITY MO/YR	BID	ASKED	CHG	ASK YLD	RATE	MATURITY MO/YR	BID	ASKED	CHG	ASK YLD
3.375	Jan 07i	99:28	99:29	....	6.72	4.250	Nov 13n	97:29	97:30	+10	4.60
3.125	Jan 07n	99:27	99:28	....	4.62	2.000	Jan 14i	97:16	97:17	+1	2.38
2.250	Feb 07n	99:21	99:22	....	4.89	4.000	Feb 14n	96:09	96:10	+10	4.61
6.250	Feb 07n	100:04	100:05	....	4.73	4.750	May 14n	100:26	100:27	+9	4.61
3.375	Feb 07n	99:23	99:24	....	4.90	13.250	May 14	119:02	119:03	+4	4.61
3.750	Mar 07n	99:21	99:22	....	4.99	2.000	Jul 14i	97:14	97:15	....	2.37
3.875	Feb 13n	96:06	96:07	+8	4.59	4.250	Aug 14n	97:21	97:22	+10	4.61
3.625	May 13n	94:23	94:24	+8	4.58	12.500	Aug 14	119:04	119:05	+4	4.62
1.875	Jul 13i	97:00	97:01	+1	2.37	11.750	Nov 14	118:30	118:31	+6	4.59
4.250	Aug 13n	98:00	98:01	+9	4.60	4.250	Nov 14n	97:19	97:20	+9	4.61
12.000	Aug 13	111:04	111:05	+2	4.71	1.625	Jan 15i	94:18	94:19	+1	2.37

FIGURE 2.4   Listing of Treasury issues

Source: Compiled from data obtained from the online edition of *The Wall Street Journal,* January 5, 2007.

Figure 2.4 is a listing of Treasury issues. Notice the highlighted note that matures in February 2014. The coupon income, or interest, paid by the note is 4% of par value, meaning that a $1,000 face-value note pays $40 in annual interest in two semiannual installments of $20 each. The numbers to the right of the colon in the bid and asked prices represent units of $\frac{1}{32}$ of a point.

The bid price of the note is $96\frac{9}{32}$, or 96.281. The asked price is $96\frac{10}{32}$, or 96.3125. Although notes and bonds are sold in denominations of $1,000 par value, the prices are quoted as a percentage of par value. Thus the bid price of 96.281 should be interpreted as 96.281% of par, or $962.81, for the $1,000 par value security. Similarly, the note could be bought from a dealer for $963.125. The +10 change means the closing price on this day rose $\frac{10}{32}$ (as a percentage of par value) from the previous day's closing price. Finally, the yield to maturity on the note based on the asked price is 4.61%.

The **yield to maturity** reported in the financial pages is calculated by determining the semiannual yield and then doubling it, rather than compounding it for two half-year periods. This use of a simple interest technique to annualize means that the yield is quoted on an annual percentage rate (APR) basis rather than as an effective annual yield. The APR method in this context is also called the *bond equivalent yield.* We discuss the yield to maturity in more detail in Part Four.

CONCEPT CHECK 1

What were the bid price, asked price, and yield to maturity of the 4¾% May 2014 Treasury note displayed in Figure 2.4? What was its asked price the previous day?

Inflation-Protected Treasury Bonds

The best place to start building an investment portfolio is at the least risky end of the spectrum. Around the world, governments of many countries, including the United States, have issued bonds that are linked to an index of the cost of living in order to provide their citizens with an effective way to hedge inflation risk. See the E-Investments box on inflation-protected bonds around the world at the end of this chapter.

In the United States inflation-protected Treasury bonds are called TIPS (Treasury Inflation-Protected Securities). The principal amount on these bonds is adjusted in proportion to increases in the Consumer Price Index. Therefore, they provide a constant stream of income in real (inflation-adjusted) dollars. An *i* following the bond's maturity date in Figure 2.4 denotes that the bond is an inflation-indexed TIPS bond, and you will see that the reported yields on these bonds are lower than those on surrounding conventional Treasuries. Compare, for example, the reported yield on the July 14*i* bond, 2.37%, to the 4.61% yield on the August bond that follows it. The yields on TIPS bonds should be interpreted as real or inflation-adjusted interest rates. We return to TIPS bonds in more detail in Chapter 14.

Federal Agency Debt

Some government agencies issue their own securities to finance their activities. These agencies usually are formed to channel credit to a particular sector of the economy that Congress believes might not receive adequate credit through normal private sources.

The major mortgage-related agencies are the Federal Home Loan Bank (FHLB), the Federal National Mortgage Association (FNMA, or Fannie Mae), the Government National Mortgage Association (GNMA, or Ginnie Mae), and the Federal Home Loan Mortgage Corporation (FHLMC, or Freddie Mac). The FHLB borrows money by issuing securities and lends this money to savings and loan institutions to be lent in turn to individuals borrowing for home mortgages.

Freddie Mac and Ginnie Mae were organized to provide liquidity to the mortgage market. Until the pass-through securities sponsored by these agencies were established (see the discussion of mortgages and mortgage-backed securities later in this section), the lack of a secondary market in mortgages hampered the flow of investment funds into mortgages and made mortgage markets dependent on local, rather than national, credit availability.

Some of these agencies are government owned, and therefore can be viewed as branches of the U.S. government. Thus their debt is fully free of default risk. Ginnie Mae is an example of a government-owned agency. Other agencies, such as the farm credit agencies, the Federal Home Loan Bank, Fannie Mae, and Freddie Mac, are merely federally *sponsored*.

Although the debt of federally sponsored agencies is not explicitly insured by the federal government, it is widely assumed that the government would step in with assistance if an agency neared default. Thus these securities are considered extremely safe assets, and their yield spread above Treasury securities is usually small.

International Bonds

Many firms borrow abroad and many investors buy bonds from foreign issuers. In addition to national capital markets, there is a thriving international capital market, largely centered in London.

A *Eurobond* is a bond denominated in a currency other than that of the country in which it is issued. For example, a dollar-denominated bond sold in Britain would be called a Eurodollar bond. Similarly, investors might speak of Euroyen bonds, yen-denominated bonds sold outside Japan. Because the European currency is called the euro, the term Eurobond may be confusing. It is best to think of them simply as international bonds.

In contrast to bonds that are issued in foreign currencies, many firms issue bonds in foreign countries but in the currency of the investor. For example, a Yankee bond is a dollar-denominated bond sold in the United States by a non-U.S. issuer. Similarly, Samurai bonds are yen-denominated bonds sold in Japan by non-Japanese issuers.

Municipal Bonds

Municipal bonds are issued by state and local governments. They are similar to Treasury and corporate bonds except that their interest income is exempt from federal income

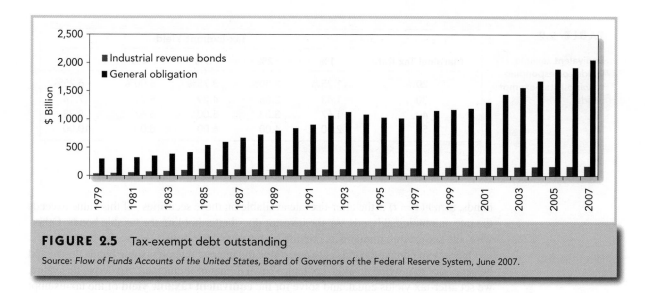

FIGURE 2.5 Tax-exempt debt outstanding

Source: *Flow of Funds Accounts of the United States*, Board of Governors of the Federal Reserve System, June 2007.

taxation. The interest income also is exempt from state and local taxation in the issuing state. Capital gains taxes, however, must be paid on "munis" when the bonds mature or if they are sold for more than the investor's purchase price.

There are basically two types of municipal bonds. *General obligation* bonds are backed by the "full faith and credit" (i.e., the taxing power) of the issuer, while *revenue bonds* are issued to finance particular projects and are backed either by the revenues from that project or by the particular municipal agency operating the project. Typical issuers of revenue bonds are airports, hospitals, and turnpike or port authorities. Obviously, revenue bonds are riskier in terms of default than general obligation bonds. Figure 2.5 plots outstanding amounts of both types of municipal securities.

An *industrial development bond* is a revenue bond that is issued to finance commercial enterprises, such as the construction of a factory that can be operated by a private firm. In effect, these private-purpose bonds give the firm access to the municipality's ability to borrow at tax-exempt rates, and the federal government limits the amount of these bonds that may be issued.[2]

Like Treasury bonds, municipal bonds vary widely in maturity. A good deal of the debt issued is in the form of short-term *tax anticipation notes,* which raise funds to pay for expenses before actual collection of taxes. Other municipal debt is long term and used to fund large capital investments. Maturities range up to 30 years.

The key feature of municipal bonds is their tax-exempt status. Because investors pay neither federal nor state taxes on the interest proceeds, they are willing to accept lower yields on these securities.

An investor choosing between taxable and tax-exempt bonds must compare after-tax returns on each bond. An exact comparison requires a computation of after-tax rates of return that explicitly accounts for taxes on income and realized capital gains. In practice, there is a simpler rule of thumb. If we let t denote the investor's combined federal plus local marginal tax bracket and r denote the total before-tax rate of return available on taxable

---

[2]A warning, however. Although interest on industrial development bonds usually is exempt from federal tax, it can be subject to the alternative minimum tax if the bonds are used to finance projects of for-profit companies.

TABLE 2.2

Equivalent taxable yields corresponding to various tax-exempt yields

			Tax-Exempt Yield		
Marginal Tax Rate	**1%**	**2%**	**3%**	**4%**	**5%**
20%	1.25%	2.50%	3.75%	5.00%	6.25%
30	1.43	2.86	4.29	5.71	7.14
40	1.67	3.33	5.00	6.67	8.33
50	2.00	4.00	6.00	8.00	10.00

bonds, then $r(1 - t)$ is the after-tax rate available on those securities.[3] If this value exceeds the rate on municipal bonds, r_m, the investor does better holding the taxable bonds. Otherwise, the tax-exempt municipals provide higher after-tax returns.

One way to compare bonds is to determine the interest rate on taxable bonds that would be necessary to provide an after-tax return equal to that of municipals. To derive this value, we set after-tax yields equal, and solve for the **equivalent taxable yield** of the tax-exempt bond. This is the rate a taxable bond must offer to match the after-tax yield on the tax-free municipal.

$$r(1 - t) = r_m \tag{2.1}$$

or

$$r = r_m/(1 - t) \tag{2.2}$$

Thus the equivalent taxable yield is simply the tax-free rate divided by $1 - t$. Table 2.2 presents equivalent taxable yields for several municipal yields and tax rates.

This table frequently appears in the marketing literature for tax-exempt mutual bond funds because it demonstrates to high-tax-bracket investors that municipal bonds offer highly attractive equivalent taxable yields. Each entry is calculated from Equation 2.2. If the equivalent taxable yield exceeds the actual yields offered on taxable bonds, the investor is better off after taxes holding municipal bonds. Notice that the equivalent taxable interest rate increases with the investor's tax bracket; the higher the bracket, the more valuable the tax-exempt feature of municipals. Thus high-tax-bracket investors tend to hold municipals.

We also can use Equation 2.1 or 2.2 to find the tax bracket at which investors are indifferent between taxable and tax-exempt bonds. The cutoff tax bracket is given by solving Equation 2.2 for the tax bracket at which after-tax yields are equal. Doing so, we find that

$$t = 1 - \frac{r_m}{r} \tag{2.3}$$

Thus the yield ratio r_m/r is a key determinant of the attractiveness of municipal bonds. The higher the yield ratio, the lower the cutoff tax bracket, and the more individuals will prefer to hold municipal debt. Figure 2.6 graphs the yield ratio since 1955.

---

[3]An approximation to the combined federal plus local tax rate is just the sum of the two rates. For example, if your federal tax rate is 28% and your state rate is 5%, your combined tax rate would be approximately 33%. A more precise approach would recognize that state taxes are deductible at the federal level. You owe federal taxes only on income net of state taxes. Therefore, for every dollar of income, your after-tax proceeds would be $(1 - t_{federal}) \times (1 - t_{state})$. In our example, your after-tax proceeds on each dollar earned would be $(1 - .28) \times (1 - .05) = .684$, which implies a combined tax rate of $1 - .684 = .316$, or 31.6%.

EXAMPLE 2.1   Taxable versus Tax-Exempt Yields

Figure 2.6 shows that in recent years, the ratio of tax-exempt to taxable yields has fluctuated around .75. What does this imply about the cutoff tax bracket above which tax-exempt bonds provide higher after-tax yields? Equation 2.3 shows that an investor whose tax bracket (federal plus local) exceeds $1 - .75 = .25$, or 25%, will derive a greater after-tax yield from municipals. Note, however, that it is difficult to control precisely for differences in the risks of these bonds, so the cutoff tax bracket must be taken as approximate.

CONCEPT
CHECK
2   Suppose your tax bracket is 30%. Would you prefer to earn a 6% taxable return or a 4% tax-free return? What is the equivalent taxable yield of the 4% tax-free yield?

Corporate Bonds

Corporate bonds are the means by which private firms borrow money directly from the public. These bonds are similar in structure to Treasury issues—they typically pay semiannual coupons over their lives and return the face value to the bondholder at maturity. They differ most importantly from Treasury bonds in degree of risk. Default risk is a real consideration in the purchase of corporate bonds, and Chapter 14 discusses this issue in considerable detail. For now, we distinguish only among *secured bonds,* which have specific collateral backing them in the event of firm bankruptcy; unsecured bonds, called *debentures,* which have no collateral; and *subordinated debentures,* which have a lower-priority claim to the firm's assets in the event of bankruptcy.

Corporate bonds sometimes come with options attached. *Callable bonds* give the firm the option to repurchase the bond from the holder at a stipulated call price. *Convertible bonds* give the bondholder the option to convert each bond into a stipulated number of shares of stock. These options are treated in more detail in Chapter 14.

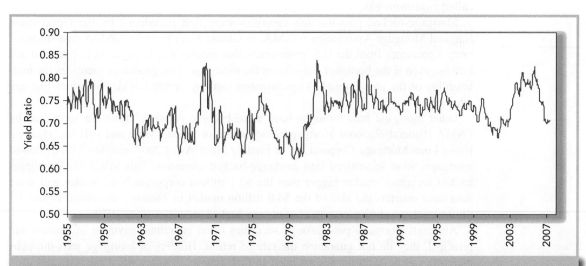

FIGURE 2.6   Ratio of yields on tax-exempt to taxable bonds

Source: Authors' calculations, using data from Moody's Investors Service and Mergent Municipal and Government Manual.

Mortgages and Mortgage-Backed Securities

An investments text of 30 years ago probably would not have included a section on mortgage loans, because investors could not invest in these loans. Now, because of the explosion in mortgage-backed securities, almost anyone can invest in a portfolio of mortgage loans, and these securities have become a major component of the fixed-income market.

Until the 1970s, almost all home mortgages were written for a long term (15- to 30-year maturity), with a fixed interest rate over the life of the loan, and with equal fixed monthly payments. These so-called conventional mortgages are still the most popular, but a diverse set of alternative mortgage designs has developed.

Fixed-rate mortgages have posed difficulties to lenders in years of increasing interest rates. Because banks and thrift institutions traditionally issued short-term liabilities (the deposits of their customers) and held long-term assets such as fixed-rate mortgages, they suffered losses when interest rates increased and the rates paid on deposits increased while mortgage income remained fixed.

The *adjustable-rate mortgage* was a response to this interest rate risk. These mortgages require the borrower to pay an interest rate that varies with some measure of the current market interest rate. For example, the interest rate might be set at 2 percentage points above the current rate on 1-year Treasury bills and might be adjusted once a year. Usually, the contract sets a limit, or cap, on the maximum size of an interest rate change within a year and over the life of the contract. The adjustable-rate contract shifts much of the risk of fluctuations in interest rates from the lender to the borrower. Because of the shifting of interest rate risk to their customers, lenders are willing to offer lower rates on adjustable-rate mortgages than on conventional fixed-rate mortgages.

A *mortgage-backed security* is either an ownership claim in a pool of mortgages or an obligation that is secured by such a pool. These claims represent securitization of mortgage loans. Mortgage lenders originate loans and then sell packages of these loans in the secondary market. Specifically, they sell their claim to the cash inflows from the mortgages as those loans are paid off. The mortgage originator continues to service the loan, collecting principal and interest payments, and passes these payments along to the purchaser of the mortgage. For this reason, these mortgage-backed securities are called *pass-throughs*.

Mortgage-backed pass-through securities were first introduced by the Government National Mortgage Association (GNMA, or Ginnie Mae) in 1970. GNMA pass-throughs carry a guarantee from the U.S. government that ensures timely payment of principal and interest, even if the borrower defaults on the mortgage. This guarantee increases the marketability of the pass-through. Thus investors can buy or sell GNMA securities like any other bond.

Other mortgage pass-throughs have since become popular. These are sponsored by FNMA (Federal National Mortgage Association, or Fannie Mae) and FHLMC (Federal Home Loan Mortgage Corporation, or Freddie Mac). As of 2007, roughly $3.8 trillion of mortgages were securitized into mortgage-backed securities. This makes the mortgage-backed securities market bigger than the $3.1 trillion corporate bond market and more than three-quarters the size of the $4.6 trillion market in Treasury securities. Figure 2.7 illustrates the explosive growth of mortgage-backed securities since 1979.

Although mortgage pass-through securities often guarantee payment of interest and principal, they do not guarantee the rate of return. Holders of mortgage pass-throughs therefore can be severely disappointed in their returns in years when interest rates drop

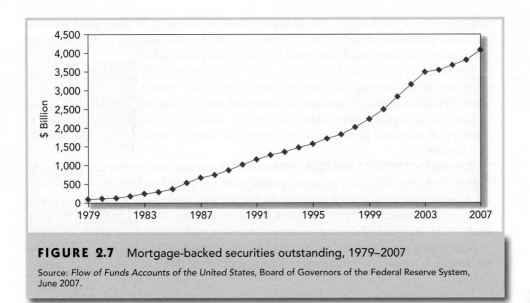

FIGURE 2.7   Mortgage-backed securities outstanding, 1979–2007

Source: *Flow of Funds Accounts of the United States,* Board of Governors of the Federal Reserve System, June 2007.

significantly. This is because homeowners usually have an option to prepay, or pay ahead of schedule, the remaining principal outstanding on their mortgages.

Most pass-throughs comprise *conforming mortgages,* which means that the loans meet underwriting guidelines required for Fannie Mae or Freddie Mac to purchase them. More recently, private banks have begun to purchase *subprime mortgages* (which do not meet these underwriting guidelines) and to sell pools of these riskier mortgages to investors. These investments turned out to be disastrous investments in the summer of 2007, with losses exceeding $100 billion spread among several investment banks, hedge funds, and other investors.

The tremendous growth in mortgage-backed pass-throughs has encouraged introduction of pass-through securities backed by other assets. Figure 1.2 of the previous chapter documented the rapid development of the market in asset-backed securities.

2.3   EQUITY SECURITIES

Common Stock as Ownership Shares

Common stocks, also known as *equity securities* or **equities,** represent ownership shares in a corporation. Each share of common stock entitles its owner to one vote on any matters of corporate governance that are put to a vote at the corporation's annual meeting and to a share in the financial benefits of ownership.[4]

The corporation is controlled by a board of directors elected by the shareholders. The board, which meets only a few times each year, selects managers who actually run the

---

[4]A corporation sometimes issues two classes of common stock, one bearing the right to vote, the other not. Because of its restricted rights, the nonvoting stock might sell for a lower price.

corporation on a day-to-day basis. Managers have the authority to make most business decisions without the board's specific approval. The board's mandate is to oversee the management to ensure that it acts in the best interests of shareholders.

The members of the board are elected at the annual meeting. Shareholders who do not attend the annual meeting can vote by *proxy,* empowering another party to vote in their name. Management usually solicits the proxies of shareholders and normally gets a vast majority of these proxy votes. Thus, management usually has considerable discretion to run the firm as it sees fit—without daily oversight from the equityholders who actually own the firm.

We noted in Chapter 1 that such separation of ownership and control can give rise to "agency problems," in which managers pursue goals not in the best interests of shareholders. However, there are several mechanisms that alleviate these agency problems. Among these are compensation schemes that link the success of the manager to that of the firm; oversight by the board of directors as well as outsiders such as security analysts, creditors, or large institutional investors; the threat of a proxy contest in which unhappy shareholders attempt to replace the current management team; or the threat of a takeover by another firm.

The common stock of most large corporations can be bought or sold freely on one or more stock exchanges. A corporation whose stock is not publicly traded is said to be closely held. In most closely held corporations, the owners of the firm also take an active role in its management. Therefore, takeovers are generally not an issue.

Characteristics of Common Stock

The two most important characteristics of common stock as an investment are its **residual claim** and **limited liability** features.

Residual claim means that stockholders are the last in line of all those who have a claim on the assets and income of the corporation. In a liquidation of the firm's assets the shareholders have a claim to what is left after all other claimants such as the tax authorities, employees, suppliers, bondholders, and other creditors have been paid. For a firm not in liquidation, shareholders have claim to the part of operating income left over after interest and taxes have been paid. Management can either pay this residual as cash dividends to shareholders or reinvest it in the business to increase the value of the shares.

Limited liability means that the most shareholders can lose in the event of failure of the corporation is their original investment. Unlike owners of unincorporated businesses, whose creditors can lay claim to the personal assets of the owner (house, car, furniture), corporate shareholders may at worst have worthless stock. They are not personally liable for the firm's obligations.

CONCEPT CHECK 3

a. If you buy 100 shares of IBM stock, to what are you entitled?

b. What is the most money you can make on this investment over the next year?

c. If you pay $80 per share, what is the most money you could lose over the year?

Stock Market Listings

Figure 2.8 presents key trading data for a small sample of stocks traded on the New York Stock Exchange. The NYSE is one of several markets in which investors may buy or sell shares of stock. We will examine these markets in detail in Chapter 3.

To interpret Figure 2.8, consider the highlighted listing for General Electric. The table provides the ticker symbol (GE), the closing price of the stock ($37.56), and its change (−$.19) from the previous trading day. About 26.9 million shares of GE traded on this day. The listing also provides the highest and lowest price at which GE has traded in the last 52 weeks. The 1.12 value in the Dividend column means that the last quarterly dividend payment was $.28 per share, which is consistent with annual dividend payments of

NAME	SYMBOL	CLOSE	NET CHG	VOLUME	52 WK HIGH	52 WK LOW	DIV	YIELD	P/E	YTD% CHG
Gencorp	GY	13.59	−0.29	491,300	20.75	12.02	....	....	dd	−3.1
Genentech	DNA	83.68	−0.35	3,986,300	94.46	75.58	....	....	49	3.1
General Cable	BGC	42.67	−1.11	679,700	45.41	20.3	....	....	23	−2.4
General Dynamics	GD	74.59	0.17	1,497,300	77.98	56.68	0.92	1.2	16	0.3
General Electric	GE	37.56	−0.19	26,907,700	38.49	32.06	1.12	3	23	0.9
General Gwth Prop	GGP	51.51	−0.8	1,308,200	56.14	41.92	1.8	3.5	215	−1.4
General Maritime	GMR	34.56	−0.83	597,400	40.64	30.34	4.8	13.9	5	−1.8
General Mills	GIS	56.97	−0.42	1,355,600	59.23	47.05	1.48	2.6	18	−1.1
General Motors	GM	30.24	0.6	10,477,600	36.56	19	1	3.3	dd	−1.6
Genesco Inc	GCO	36.75	−0.9	127,900	43.72	25.5	....	....	15	−1.5
Genesee & Wyoming	GWR	25.86	−0.5	364,500	36.75	21	....	....	9	−1.4
Genesis Lease	GLS	23.6	0.1	298,500	24.4	23	....	....		0.4
Genuine Parts co.	GPC	46.86	−0.51	384,400	48.34	40	1.35	2.9	17	−1.2
Genworth Financial	GNW	33.79	−0.32	1,414,900	36.47	31	0.36	1.1	13	−1.2
Geo Group Inc	GEO	37.57	−1.53	157,500	40.3	14.69	....	....	35	0.1
Georgia Gulf	GGC	18.69	−0.38	479,000	34.65	18.36	0.32	1.7	6	−3.2
Gerber Scientific	GRB	12.32	−0.07	243,200	16.8	9	....	....	27	−1.9
Gerdau Ameristeel	GNA	8.59	−0.04	446,200	11.02	5.85	0.08	0.9	7	−3.7
Gerdau S.A. Ads	GGB	15.57	−0.56	1,729,100	18.16	11.27	0.58	3.7	....	−2.7

FIGURE 2.8   Listing of stocks traded on the New York Stock Exchange

Source: Compiled from data from *The Wall Street Journal Online*, January 9, 2007.

$.28 × 4 = $1.12. This corresponds to an annual dividend yield (i.e., annual dividend per dollar paid for the stock) of 1.12/37.56 = .030, or 3.0%.

The dividend yield is only part of the return on a stock investment. It ignores prospective **capital gains** (i.e., price increases) or losses. Low dividend firms presumably offer greater prospects for capital gains, or investors would not be willing to hold these stocks in their portfolios. If you scan Figure 2.8, you will see that dividend yields vary widely across companies.

The P/E ratio, or **price–earnings ratio,** is the ratio of the current stock price to last year's earnings per share. The P/E ratio tells us how much stock purchasers must pay per dollar of earnings that the firm generates. For GE, the ratio of price to earnings is 23. The P/E ratio also varies widely across firms. Where the dividend yield and P/E ratio are not reported in Figure 2.8, the firms have zero dividends, or zero or negative earnings. We shall have much to say about P/E ratios in Chapter 18. Finally, we see that GE's stock price has increased by 0.9% since the beginning of the year.

Preferred Stock

Preferred stock has features similar to both equity and debt. Like a bond, it promises to pay to its holder a fixed amount of income each year. In this sense preferred stock is similar to an infinite-maturity bond, that is, a perpetuity. It also resembles a bond in that it does not convey voting power regarding the management of the firm. Preferred stock is an equity investment, however. The firm retains discretion to make the dividend payments to the preferred stockholders; it has no contractual obligation to pay those dividends. Instead, preferred dividends are usually *cumulative;* that is, unpaid dividends cumulate and must be paid in full before any dividends may be paid to holders of common stock. In contrast, the firm does have a contractual obligation to make the interest payments on the debt. Failure to make these payments sets off corporate bankruptcy proceedings.

Preferred stock also differs from bonds in terms of its tax treatment for the firm. Because preferred stock payments are treated as dividends rather than interest, they are not tax-deductible expenses for the firm. This disadvantage is somewhat offset by the fact that corporations may exclude 70% of dividends received from domestic corporations in the computation of their taxable income. Preferred stocks therefore make desirable fixed-income investments for some corporations.

Even though preferred stock ranks after bonds in terms of the priority of its claims to the assets of the firm in the event of corporate bankruptcy, preferred stock often sells at lower yields than do corporate bonds. Presumably, this reflects the value of the dividend exclusion, because the higher risk of preferred would tend to result in higher yields than those offered by bonds. Individual investors, who cannot use the 70% tax exclusion, generally will find preferred stock yields unattractive relative to those on other available assets.

Preferred stock is issued in variations similar to those of corporate bonds. It may be callable by the issuing firm, in which case it is said to be *redeemable*. It also may be convertible into common stock at some specified conversion ratio. Adjustable-rate preferred stock is another variation that, like adjustable-rate bonds, ties the dividend to current market interest rates.

Depository Receipts

American Depository Receipts, or ADRs, are certificates traded in U.S. markets that represent ownership in shares of a foreign company. Each ADR may correspond to ownership of a fraction of a foreign share, one share, or several shares of the foreign corporation. ADRs were created to make it easier for foreign firms to satisfy U.S. security registration requirements. They are the most common way for U.S. investors to invest in and trade the shares of foreign corporations.

2.4   STOCK AND BOND MARKET INDEXES

Stock Market Indexes

The daily performance of the Dow Jones Industrial Average is a staple portion of the evening news report. Although the Dow is the best-known measure of the performance of the stock market, it is only one of several indicators. Other more broadly based indexes are computed and published daily. In addition, several indexes of bond market performance are widely available.

The ever-increasing role of international trade and investments has made indexes of foreign financial markets part of the general news as well. Thus foreign stock exchange indexes such as the Nikkei Average of Tokyo and the Financial Times index of London are fast becoming household names.

Dow Jones Averages

The Dow Jones Industrial Average (DJIA) of 30 large, "blue-chip" corporations has been computed since 1896. Its long history probably accounts for its preeminence in the public mind. (The average covered only 20 stocks until 1928.)

Originally, the DJIA was calculated as the simple average of the stocks included in the index. Thus, one would add up the prices of the 30 stocks in the index and divide by 30. The percentage change in the DJIA would then be the percentage change in the average price of the 30 shares.

This procedure means that the percentage change in the DJIA measures the return (excluding dividends) on a portfolio that invests one share in each of the 30 stocks in the index. The value of such a portfolio (holding one share of each stock in the index) is the sum of the 30 prices. Because the percentage change in the *average* of the 30 prices is the same as the percentage change in the *sum* of the 30 prices, the index and the portfolio have the same percentage change each day.

Because the Dow corresponds to a portfolio that holds one share of each component stock, the investment in each company in that portfolio is proportional to the company's share price. Therefore, the Dow is called a **price-weighted average.**

EXAMPLE 2.2   Price-Weighted Average

Consider the data in Table 2.3 for a hypothetical two-stock version of the Dow Jones Average. Let's compare the changes in the value of the portfolio holding one share of each firm and the price-weighted index. Stock ABC starts at $25 a share and increases to $30. Stock XYZ starts at $100, but falls to $90.

Portfolio:	Initial value = $25 + $100 = $125
	Final value = $30 + $90 = $120
	Percentage change in portfolio value = −5/125 = −.04 = −4%
Index:	Initial index value = (25 + 100)/2 = 62.5
	Final index value = (30 + 90)/2 = 60
	Percentage change in index = −2.5/62.5 = −.04 = −4%

The portfolio and the index have identical 4% declines in value.

Notice that price-weighted averages give higher-priced shares more weight in determining performance of the index. For example, although ABC increased by 20%, while XYZ fell by only 10%, the index dropped in value. This is because the 20% increase in ABC represented a smaller price gain ($5 per share) than the 10% decrease in XYZ ($10 per share). The "Dow portfolio" has four times as much invested in XYZ as in ABC because XYZ's price is four times that of ABC. Therefore, XYZ dominates the average. We conclude that a high-price stock can dominate a price-weighted average.

TABLE 2.3

Data to construct stock price indexes

Stock	Initial Price	Final Price	Shares (million)	Initial Value of Outstanding Stock ($ million)	Final Value of Outstanding Stock ($ million)
ABC	$25	$30	20	$500	$600
XYZ	100	90	1	100	90
Total				$600	$690

You might wonder why the DJIA is now (in early 2008) at a level of about 13,000 if it is supposed to be the average price of the 30 stocks in the index. The DJIA no longer equals the average price of the 30 stocks because the averaging procedure is adjusted whenever a stock splits or pays a stock dividend of more than 10%, or when one company in the group of 30 industrial firms is replaced by another. When these events occur, the divisor used to compute the "average price" is adjusted so as to leave the index unaffected by the event.

EXAMPLE 2.3   Splits and Price-Weighted Averages

Suppose XYZ were to split two for one so that its share price fell to $50. We would not want the average to fall, as that would incorrectly indicate a fall in the general level of market prices. Following a split, the divisor must be reduced to a value that leaves the average unaffected. Table 2.4 illustrates this point. The initial share price of XYZ, which was $100 in Table 2.3, falls to $50 if the stock splits at the beginning of the period. Notice that the number of shares outstanding doubles, leaving the market value of the total shares unaffected.

We find the new divisor as follows. The index value before the stock split = 125/2 = 62.5. We must find a new divisor, d, that leaves the index unchanged after XYZ splits and its price falls to $50. Therefore, we solve for d in the following equation:

$$\frac{\text{Price of ABC} + \text{Price of XYZ}}{d} = \frac{25 + 50}{d} = 62.5$$

which implies that the divisor must fall from its original value of 2.0 to a new value of 1.20.

Because the split changes the price of stock XYZ, it also changes the relative weights of the two stocks in the price-weighted average. Therefore, the return of the index is affected by the split.

At period-end, ABC will sell for $30, while XYZ will sell for $45, representing the same negative 10% return it was assumed to earn in Table 2.3. The new value of the price-weighted average is (30 + 45)/1.20 = 62.5, the same as its value at the start of the year; therefore, the rate of return is zero, rather than the −4% return that we calculated in the absence of a split.

The split reduces the relative weight of XYZ because its initial price is lower; because XYZ is the poorer-performing stock, the performance of the average is higher. This example illustrates that the implicit weighting scheme of a price-weighted average is somewhat arbitrary, being determined by the prices rather than by the outstanding market values (price per share times number of shares) of the shares in the average.

TABLE 2.4

Data to construct stock price indexes after a stock split

Stock	Initial Price	Final Price	Shares (million)	Initial Value of Outstanding Stock ($ million)	Final Value of Outstanding Stock ($ million)
ABC	$25	$30	20	$500	$600
XYZ	50	45	2	100	90
Total				$600	$690

HOW THE 30 STOCKS IN THE DOW JONES INDUSTRIAL AVERAGE HAVE CHANGED SINCE OCT. 1, 1928

Oct. 1, 1928	1929	1930s	1940s	1950s	1960s	1970s	1980s	1990s	April 8, 2004
Wright Aeronautical	Curtiss-Wright ('29)	Hudson Motor ('30) Coca-Cola ('32) National Steel ('35)	Aluminum Co. of America ('59)					Alcoa*	Alcoa
Allied Chemical & Dye							Allied Signal* ('85)	Honeywell*	Honeywell‡
North American		Johns-Manville ('30)					Amer. Express ('82)		American Express
Victor Talking Machine	Natl Cash Register ('29)	IBM ('32) AT&T ('39)							AIG Group
International Nickel						Inco Ltd.* ('76)	Boeing ('87)		Boeing
International Harvester							Navistar* ('86)	Caterpillar ('91)	Caterpillar
Westinghouse Electric								Travelers Group ('97)	Citigroup*
Texas Gulf Sulphur		Intl. Shoe ('32) United Aircraft ('33) National Distillers ('34)		Owens-Illinois ('59)			Coca-Cola ('87)		Coca-Cola
American Sugar		Borden ('30) DuPont ('35)							DuPont
American Tobacco (B)		Eastman Kodak ('30)							Pfizer
Standard Oil (N.J.)						Exxon* ('72)		ExxonMobil*	ExxonMobil
General Electric									General Electric
General Motors									General Motors
Texas Corp.				Texaco* ('59)				Hewlett-Packard ('97)	Hewlett-Packard
Sears Roebuck								Home Depot	Home Depot
Chrysler						IBM ('79)			IBM
Atlantic Refining		Goodyear ('30)						Intel	Intel
Paramount Publix		Loew's ('32)		Intl. Paper ('56)					Verizon
Bethlehem Steel								Johnson & Johnson ('97)	Johnson & Johnson
General Railway Signal		Liggett & Myers ('30) Amer. Tobacco ('32)					McDonald's ('85)		McDonald's
Mack Trucks		Drug Inc. ('32) Corn Products ('33)		Swift & Co. ('59)		Esmark* ('73) Merck ('79)			Merck
Union Carbide								Microsoft	Microsoft
American Smelting				Anaconda ('59)		Minn. Mining ('76)			Minn. Mining (3M)
American Can							Primerica* ('87)	J.P. Morgan ('91)	J.P. Morgan
Postum Inc.	General Foods* ('29)						Philip Morris ('85)		Altria Group‡
Nash Motors		United Air Trans. ('30) Procter & Gamble ('32)							Procter & Gamble
Goodrich		Standard Oil (Calif) ('30)					Chevron* ('84)	SBC Communications	SBC Communications
Radio Corp.		Nash Motors ('32) United Aircraft ('39)				United Tech.* ('75)			United Technologies
Woolworth								Wal-Mart Stores ('97)	Wal-Mart
U.S. Steel							USX Corp.* ('86)	Walt Disney ('91)	Walt Disney

Notes: Year of change shown in (); * denotes name change, in some cases following a takeover or merger. To track changes in the components, begin in the column for 1928 and work across. For instance, American Sugar was replaced by Borden in 1930, which in turn was replaced by DuPont in 1935. ‡This table does not reflect the change in index components occurring on February 19, 2008, when Bank of America and Chevron replaced Honeywell International and Altria Group.

Source: *The Wall Street Journal,* October 27, 1999. Reprinted by permission of Dow Jones & Company, Inc. via Copyright Clearance Center, Inc. © 1999. Dow Jones & Company, Inc. All Rights Reserved Worldwide. Updated by authors.

Because the Dow Jones Averages are based on small numbers of firms, care must be taken to ensure that they are representative of the broad market. As a result, the composition of the average is changed every so often to reflect changes in the economy. The last change took place on February 19, 2008, when Bank of America and Chevron replaced Altria Group and Honeywell International in the index. The nearby box presents the history of the firms in the index since 1928. The fate of many companies once considered "the bluest of the blue chips" is striking evidence of the changes in the U.S. economy in the last eight decades.

In the same way that the divisor is updated for stock splits, if one firm is dropped from the average and another firm with a different price is added, the divisor has to be updated to leave the average unchanged by the substitution. By 2008, the divisor for the Dow Jones Industrial Average had fallen to a value of about .123.

Dow Jones & Company also computes a Transportation Average of 20 airline, trucking, and railroad stocks; a Public Utility Average of 15 electric and natural gas utilities; and a Composite Average combining the 65 firms of the three separate averages. Each is a price-weighted average, and thus overweights the performance of high-priced stocks.

CONCEPT CHECK **4**	Suppose XYZ in Table 2.3 increases in price to $110, while ABC falls to $20. Find the percentage change in the price-weighted average of these two stocks. Compare that to the percentage return of a portfolio that holds one share in each company.

Standard & Poor's Indexes

The Standard & Poor's Composite 500 (S&P 500) stock index represents an improvement over the Dow Jones Averages in two ways. First, it is a more broadly based index of 500 firms. Second, it is a **market-value-weighted index.** In the case of the firms XYZ and ABC in Example 2.2, the S&P 500 would give ABC five times the weight given to XYZ because the market value of its outstanding equity is five times larger, $500 million versus $100 million.

The S&P 500 is computed by calculating the total market value of the 500 firms in the index and the total market value of those firms on the previous day of trading. The percentage increase in the total market value from one day to the next represents the increase in the index. The rate of return of the index equals the rate of return that would be earned by an investor holding a portfolio of all 500 firms in the index in proportion to their market values, except that the index does not reflect cash dividends paid by those firms.

Actually, most indexes today use a modified version of market-value weights. Rather than weighting by total market value, they weight by the market value of *free float,* that is, by the value of shares that are freely tradable among investors. For example, this procedure does not count shares held by founding families or governments. These shares are effectively not available for investors to purchase. The distinction is more important in Japan and Europe, where a higher fraction of shares are held in such nontraded portfolios.

EXAMPLE 2.4 Value-Weighted Indexes

To illustrate how value-weighted indexes are computed, look again at Table 2.3. The final value of all outstanding stock in our two-stock universe is $690 million. The initial value was $600 million. Therefore, if the initial level of a market-value-weighted index of stocks

ABC and XYZ were set equal to an arbitrarily chosen starting value such as 100, the index value at year-end would be $100 \times (690/600) = 115$. The increase in the index reflects the 15% return earned on a portfolio consisting of those two stocks held in proportion to outstanding market values.

Unlike the price-weighted index, the value-weighted index gives more weight to ABC. Whereas the price-weighted index fell because it was dominated by higher-price XYZ, the value-weighted index rises because it gives more weight to ABC, the stock with the higher total market value.

Note also from Tables 2.3 and 2.4 that market-value-weighted indexes are unaffected by stock splits. The total market value of the outstanding XYZ stock decreases from $100 million to $90 million regardless of the stock split, thereby rendering the split irrelevant to the performance of the index.

CONCEPT CHECK 5

Reconsider companies XYZ and ABC from Concept Check 4. Calculate the percentage change in the market-value-weighted index. Compare that to the rate of return of a portfolio that holds $500 of ABC stock for every $100 of XYZ stock (i.e., an index portfolio).

A nice feature of both market-value-weighted and price-weighted indexes is that they reflect the returns to straightforward portfolio strategies. If one were to buy shares in each component firm in the index in proportion to its outstanding market value, the value-weighted index would perfectly track capital gains on the underlying portfolio. Similarly, a price-weighted index tracks the returns on a portfolio comprised of an equal number of shares of each firm.

Investors today can easily buy market indexes for their portfolios. One way is to purchase shares in mutual funds that hold shares in proportion to their representation in the S&P 500 or another index. These **index funds** yield a return equal to that of the index and so provide a low-cost passive investment strategy for equity investors. Another approach is to purchase an *exchange-traded fund* or ETF, which is a portfolio of shares that can be bought or sold as a unit, just as one can buy or sell a single share of stock. Available ETFs range from portfolios that track extremely broad global market indexes all the way to narrow industry indexes. We discuss both mutual funds and ETFs in detail in Chapter 4.

Standard & Poor's also publishes a 400-stock Industrial Index, a 20-stock Transportation Index, a 40-stock Utility Index, and a 40-stock Financial Index.

Other U.S. Market-Value Indexes

The New York Stock Exchange publishes a market-value-weighted composite index of all NYSE-listed stocks, in addition to subindexes for industrial, utility, transportation, and financial stocks. These indexes are even more broadly based than the S&P 500. The National Association of Securities Dealers publishes an index of more than 3,000 firms traded on the NASDAQ market.

The ultimate U.S. equity index so far computed is the Wilshire 5000 index of the market value of all NYSE and American Stock Exchange (Amex) stocks plus actively traded NASDAQ stocks. Despite its name, the index actually includes about 6,000 stocks. The performance of many of these indexes appears daily in *The Wall Street Journal.*

Figure 2.9 shows the performance of the S&P 500, Dow Jones Industrial Average, and NASDAQ composite over a 6-year period. Usually, the indexes move closely together, as in this figure. Occasionally though, they diverge. For example, during the Internet boom

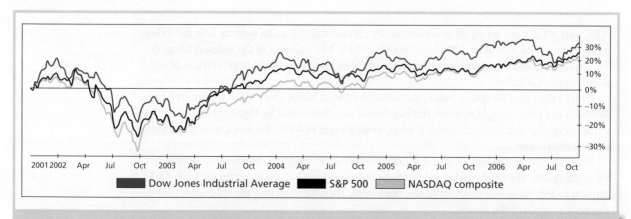

FIGURE 2.9   Comparative performance of several stock market indexes, 2001–2006

and bust of 1999–2002, the NASDAQ index, which is dominated by the technology sector, first greatly outperformed, and then underperformed, the S&P 500.

Equally Weighted Indexes

Market performance is sometimes measured by an equally weighted average of the returns of each stock in an index. Such an averaging technique, by placing equal weight on each return, corresponds to an implicit portfolio strategy that places equal dollar values on each stock. This is in contrast to both price weighting (which requires equal numbers of shares of each stock) and market value weighting (which requires investments in proportion to outstanding value).

Unlike price- or market-value-weighted indexes, equally weighted indexes do not correspond to buy-and-hold portfolio strategies. Suppose that you start with equal dollar investments in the two stocks of Table 2.3, ABC and XYZ. Because ABC increases in value by 20% over the year while XYZ decreases by 10%, your portfolio no longer is equally weighted. It is now more heavily invested in ABC. To reset the portfolio to equal weights, you would need to rebalance: sell off some ABC stock and/or purchase more XYZ stock. Such rebalancing would be necessary to align the return on your portfolio with that on the equally weighted index.

Foreign and International Stock Market Indexes

Development in financial markets worldwide includes the construction of indexes for these markets. Among these are the Nikkei (Japan), FTSE (U.K.; pronounced "footsie"), DAX (Germany), Hang Seng (Hong Kong), and TSX (Canada).

A leader in the construction of international indexes has been MSCI (Morgan Stanley Capital International), which computes over 50 country indexes and several regional indexes. Table 2.5 presents many of the indexes computed by MSCI.

Bond Market Indicators

Just as stock market indexes provide guidance concerning the performance of the overall stock market, several bond market indicators measure the performance of various categories of bonds. The three most well-known groups of indexes are those of Merrill Lynch, Lehman Brothers, and Salomon Smith Barney (now part of Citigroup). Table 2.6 lists the components of the bond market in 2007.

Regional Indexes		Countries	
Developed Markets	**Emerging Markets**	**Developed Markets**	**Emerging Markets**
EAFE (Europe, Australia, Far East)	Emerging Markets (EM)	Australia	Argentina
EASEA (EAFE excluding Japan)	EM Asia	Austria	Brazil
Europe	EM Far East	Belgium	Chile
European Monetary Union (EMU)	EM Latin America	Canada	China
Far East	EM Eastern Europe	Denmark	Colombia
Kokusai (World excluding Japan)	EM Europe	Finland	Czech Republic
Nordic Countries	EM Europe & Middle East	France	Egypt
North America		Germany	Hungary
Pacific		Greece	India
The World Index		Hong Kong	Indonesia
G7 countries		Ireland	Israel
World excluding U.S.		Italy	Jordan
		Japan	Korea
		Netherlands	Malaysia
		New Zealand	Mexico
		Norway	Morocco
		Portugal	Pakistan
		Singapore	Peru
		Spain	Philippines
		Sweden	Poland
		Switzerland	Russia
		U.K.	South Africa
		U.S.	Taiwan
			Thailand
			Turkey

TABLE 2.5

Sample of MSCI stock indexes
Source: **MSCI Barra.**

Sector	Size ($ billion)	% of Market
Treasury	$4,554.4	25.0%
Government sponsored enterprise	2,686.1	14.7
Corporate	3,111.4	17.1
Tax-exempt*	2,090.4	11.5
Mortgage-backed	3,818.3	20.9
Asset-backed	1,985.8	10.9
Total	$18,246.4	100.0%

TABLE 2.6

The U.S. bond market

*Includes private-purpose tax-exempt debt.
Source: *Flow of Funds Accounts of the United States: Flows & Outstandings,* Board of Governors of the Federal Reserve System, June 2007.

The major problem with bond market indexes is that true rates of return on many bonds are difficult to compute because the infrequency with which the bonds trade makes reliable up-to-date prices difficult to obtain. In practice, some prices must be estimated from bond-valuation models. These "matrix" prices may differ from true market values.

2.5   DERIVATIVE MARKETS

One of the most significant developments in financial markets in recent years has been the growth of futures, options, and related derivatives markets. These instruments provide payoffs that depend on the values of other assets such as commodity prices, bond and stock prices, or market index values. For this reason these instruments sometimes are called **derivative assets,** or **contingent claims.** Their values derive from or are contingent on the values of other assets.

Options

A **call option** gives its holder the right to purchase an asset for a specified price, called the **exercise** or **strike price,** on or before a specified expiration date. For example, a December call option on General Electric stock with an exercise price of $35 entitles its owner to purchase GE stock for a price of $35 at any time up to and including the expiration date in December. Each option contract is for the purchase of 100 shares. However, quotations are made on a per-share basis. The holder of the call need not exercise the option; it will be profitable to exercise only if the market value of the asset that may be purchased exceeds the exercise price.

When the market price exceeds the exercise price, the option holder may "call away" the asset for the exercise price and reap a payoff equal to the difference between the stock price and the exercise price. Otherwise, the option will be left unexercised. If not exercised before the expiration date of the contract, the option simply expires and no longer has value. Calls therefore provide greater profits when stock prices increase and thus represent bullish investment vehicles.

In contrast, a **put option** gives its holder the right to sell an asset for a specified exercise price on or before a specified expiration date. A December put on GE with an exercise price of $35 thus entitles its owner to sell GE stock to the put writer at a price of $35 at any time before expiration in December, even if the market price of GE is lower than $35. Whereas profits on call options increase when the asset increases in value, profits on put options increase when the asset value falls. The put is exercised only if its holder can deliver an asset worth less than the exercise price in return for the exercise price.

Figure 2.10 presents options quotations for GE. The price of GE shares on this date was $41.10. The first two columns give the expiration month and exercise (or strike) price for each option. We have included listings for call and put options with exercise prices ranging from $37.50 to $42.50 per share, and with expiration dates in October, November, December 2007 and March 2008.

The next columns provide the closing prices, trading volume, and open interest (out-standing contracts) of each option. For example, 4,823 contracts traded on the October 2007 expiration call with exercise price of $40. The last trade was at $1.68, meaning that an option to purchase one share of GE at an exercise price of $40 sold for $1.68. Each option *contract* (on 100 shares) therefore costs $168.

Notice that the prices of call options decrease as the exercise price increases. For example, the October expiration call with exercise price $42.50 costs only $.38. This makes

Gen El (GE)						Underlying stock price: 41.10		
		Call			**Put**			
Expiration	Strike	Last	Volume	Open Interest	Last	Volume	Open Interest
Oct 2007	37.50	3.90	110	10411	0.12	394	20014
Nov 2007	37.50	4.23	112	2	0.27	236	140
Dec 2007	37.50	4.45	257	27876	0.49	507	33731
Mar 2008	37.50	...	...	5721	1.07	272	11931
Oct 2007	40.00	1.68	4823	46175	0.45	1659	17500
Nov 2007	40.00	2.14	897	135	0.70	170	163
Dec 2007	40.00	2.49	700	136176	1.06	356	36470
Mar 2008	40.00	3.35	113	13141	1.78	49	18901
Oct 2007	42.50	0.38	4525	66631	1.64	2838	5784
Nov 2007	42.50	0.72	1439	1996	1.83	67	269
Dec 2007	42.50	1.07	540	31560	2.13	805	10872
Mar 2008	42.50	1.90	74	9767	2.98	50	4054

FIGURE 2.10 Trading data on General Electric options

Source: Compiled from data downloaded from *The Wall Street Journal Online*, September 25, 2007.

sense, because the right to purchase a share at a higher exercise price is less valuable. Conversely, put prices increase with the exercise price. The right to sell a share of GE at a price of $40 in October costs $.45 while the right to sell at $42.50 costs $1.64.

Option prices also increase with time until expiration. Clearly, one would rather have the right to buy GE for $40 at any time until December rather than at any time until October. Not surprisingly, this shows up in a higher price for the December expiration options. For example, the call with exercise price $40 expiring in December sells for $2.49, compared to only $1.68 for the October call.

CONCEPT CHECK 6
What would be the profit or loss per share of stock to an investor who bought the October expiration GE call option with exercise price $40 if the stock price at the expiration date is $42? What about a purchaser of the put option with the same exercise price and expiration?

Futures Contracts

A **futures contract** calls for delivery of an asset (or in some cases, its cash value) at a specified delivery or maturity date for an agreed-upon price, called the futures price, to be paid at contract maturity. The *long position* is held by the trader who commits to purchasing the asset on the delivery date. The trader who takes the *short position* commits to delivering the asset at contract maturity.

Figure 2.11 illustrates the listing of several futures contracts. The top line in boldface type gives the contract name, the exchange on which the futures contract is traded (in parentheses), and the contract size. Thus, the first contract listed is for corn traded on the Chicago Board of Trade (CBT). Each contract calls for delivery of 5,000 bushels of corn.

The next several rows detail prices for contracts expiring on various dates. The March maturity contract opened during the day at a futures price of $3.71 per bushel. The highest

Agriculture Futures

	OPEN	HIGH	LOW	SETTLE	CHG	OPEN INT
Corn (CBT)-5,000 bu.; cents per bu.						
March	371.00	372.50	360.50	**362.25**	–8.25	591,430
Dec	361.75	366.00	357.00	**359.00**	–3.00	311,690
Oats (CBT)-5,000 bu.; cents per bu.						
March	261.75	265.75	258.25	**261.25**	–.75	8,823
Dec	233.00	234.25	232.50	**233.75**	.75	3,907
Soybeans (CBT)-5,000 bu.; cents per bu.						
Jan	667.00	675.00	659.75	**662.75**	–6.50	9,947
March	681.00	687.75	672.50	**675.50**	–6.50	220,362

Currency Futures

Japanese Yen (CME)-¥12,500,000; $ per 100¥

March	.8456	.8485	.8447	**.8479**	.0016	275,282
June	.8561	.8579	.8545	**.8577**	.0016	5,119

British Pound (CME)-£62,500; $ per £

March	1.9516	1.9537	1.9403	**1.9448**	–.0063	136,995
June	1.9446	1.9531	1.9402	**1.9443**	–.0063	191

Index Futures

DJ Industrial Average (CBT)-$10 x index

March	12543	12575	12470	**12549**	19	64,555
June	12629	12647	12601	**12647**	18	44

S&P 500 Index (CME)-$250 x index

March	1425.20	1431.50	1417.00	**1427.50**	2.70	601,655
June	1432.00	1444.50	1430.50	**1440.10**	2.60	13,287

FIGURE 2.11   Listing of selected futures contracts

futures price during the day was $3.725, the lowest was $3.605, and the settlement price (a representative trading price during the last few minutes of trading) was $3.6225. The settlement price decreased by $.0825 from the previous trading day. Finally, open interest, or the number of outstanding contracts, was 591,430. Corresponding information is given for each maturity date.

The trader holding the long position profits from price increases. Suppose that at contract maturity, corn is selling for $3.8225 per bushel. The long position trader who entered the contract at the futures price of $3.6225 on January 4 would pay the previously agreed-upon $3.6225 for each unit of the index, which at contract maturity would be worth $3.8225.

Because each contract calls for delivery of 5,000 bushels, the profit to the long position would equal 5,000 × ($3.8225 − $3.6225) = $1,000. Conversely, the short position must deliver 5,000 bushels for the previously agreed-upon futures price. The short position's loss equals the long position's profit.

The right to purchase the asset at an agreed-upon price, as opposed to the obligation, distinguishes call options from long positions in futures contracts. A futures contract *obliges* the long position to purchase the asset at the futures price; the call option, in contrast, *conveys the right* to purchase the asset at the exercise price. The purchase will be made only if it yields a profit.

Clearly, a holder of a call has a better position than the holder of a long position on a futures contract with a futures price equal to the option's exercise price. This advantage, of course, comes only at a price. Call options must be purchased; futures contracts may be entered into without cost. The purchase price of an option is called the *premium*. It represents the compensation the purchaser of the call must pay for the ability to exercise the option only when it is profitable to do so. Similarly, the difference between a put option and a short futures position is the right, as opposed to the obligation, to sell an asset at an agreed-upon price.

SUMMARY

1. Money market securities are very short-term debt obligations. They are usually highly market-able and have relatively low credit risk. Their low maturities and low credit risk ensure minimal capital gains or losses. These securities trade in large denominations, but they may be purchased indirectly through money market funds.

2. Much of U.S. government borrowing is in the form of Treasury bonds and notes. These are coupon-paying bonds usually issued at or near par value. Treasury notes and bonds are similar in design to coupon-paying corporate bonds.

3. Municipal bonds are distinguished largely by their tax-exempt status. Interest payments (but not capital gains) on these securities are exempt from federal income taxes. The equivalent taxable yield offered by a municipal bond equals $r_m/(1 - t)$, where r_m is the municipal yield and t is the investor's tax bracket.

4. Mortgage pass-through securities are pools of mortgages sold in one package. Owners of pass-throughs receive the principal and interest payments made by the borrowers. The originator that issued the mortgage merely services it, simply "passing through" the payments to the purchasers of the mortgage. A federal agency may guarantee the payment of interest and principal on mort-gages pooled into these pass-through securities.

5. Common stock is an ownership share in a corporation. Each share entitles its owner to one vote on matters of corporate governance and to a prorated share of the dividends paid to shareholders. Stock, or equity, owners are the residual claimants on the income earned by the firm.

6. Preferred stock usually pays fixed dividends for the life of the firm; it is a perpetuity. A firm's failure to pay the dividend due on preferred stock, however, does not precipitate corporate bank-ruptcy. Instead, unpaid dividends simply cumulate. Newer varieties of preferred stock include convertible and adjustable-rate issues.

7. Many stock market indexes measure the performance of the overall market. The Dow Jones Averages, the oldest and best-known indicators, are price-weighted indexes. Today, many broad-based, market-value-weighted indexes are computed daily. These include the Standard & Poor's 500 stock index, the NYSE index, the NASDAQ index, the Wilshire 5000 index, and indexes of many non-U.S. stock markets.

8. A call option is a right to purchase an asset at a stipulated exercise price on or before an expiration date. A put option is the right to sell an asset at some exercise price. Calls increase in value while puts decrease in value as the price of the underlying asset increases.

9. A futures contract is an obligation to buy or sell an asset at a stipulated futures price on a maturity date. The long position, which commits to purchasing, gains if the asset value increases while the short position, which commits to purchasing, loses.

Related Web sites for this chapter are available at www.mhhe.com/bkm

KEY TERMS

money market	London Interbank Offered	price–earnings ratio
capital markets	Rate (LIBOR)	preferred stock
asked price	Treasury notes	price-weighted average
bid price	Treasury bonds	market-value-weighted index
bid–asked spread	yield to maturity	index funds
certificate of deposit	municipal bonds	derivative assets
commercial paper	equivalent taxable yield	contingent claims
banker's acceptance	equities	call option
Eurodollars	residual claim	exercise (strike) price
repurchase agreements	limited liability	put option
federal funds	capital gains	futures contract

PROBLEM SETS

Quiz

Problems

1. In what ways is preferred stock like long-term debt? In what ways is it like equity?

2. Why are money market securities sometimes referred to as "cash equivalents"?

3. What would you expect to happen to the spread between yields on commercial paper and Treasury bills if the economy were to enter a steep recession?

4. Examine the first 50 stocks listed in the stock market listings for NYSE stocks in your local newspaper. For how many of these stocks is the 52-week high price at least 50% greater than the 52-week low price? What do you conclude about the volatility of prices on individual stocks?

5. Turn back to Figure 2.4 and look at the first Treasury note maturing in November 2014.

   a. How much would you have to pay to purchase one of these notes?
   b. What is its coupon rate?
   c. What is the current yield of the note?

6. Suppose investors can earn a return of 2% per 6 months on a Treasury note with 6 months remaining until maturity. What price would you expect a 6-month maturity Treasury bill to sell for?

7. Find the after-tax return to a corporation that buys a share of preferred stock at $40, sells it at year-end at $40, and receives a $4 year-end dividend. The firm is in the 30% tax bracket.

8. Turn to Figure 2.8 and look at the listing for General Dynamics.

   a. What was the firm's closing price yesterday?
   b. How many shares could you buy for $5,000?
   c. What would be your annual dividend income from those shares?
   d. What must be its earnings per share?

9. Consider the three stocks in the following table. P_t represents price at time t, and Q_t represents shares outstanding at time t. Stock C splits two for one in the last period.

	P_0	Q_0	P_1	Q_1	P_2	Q_2
A	90	100	95	100	95	100
B	50	200	45	200	45	200
C	100	200	110	200	55	400

   a. Calculate the rate of return on a price-weighted index of the three stocks for the first period ($t = 0$ to $t = 1$).
   b. What must happen to the divisor for the price-weighted index in year 2?
   c. Calculate the rate of return for the second period ($t = 1$ to $t = 2$).

10. Using the data in Problem 9, calculate the first-period rates of return on the following indexes of the three stocks:

    a. A market-value-weighted index.
    b. An equally weighted index.

11. An investor is in a 30% tax bracket. If corporate bonds offer 9% yields, what must municipals offer for the investor to prefer them to corporate bonds?

12. Find the equivalent taxable yield of a short-term municipal bond currently offering yields of 4% for tax brackets of zero, 10%, 20%, and 30%.

13. Which security should sell at a greater price?

    a. A 10-year Treasury bond with a 9% coupon rate versus a 10-year T-bond with a 10% coupon.

b. A 3-month maturity call option with an exercise price of $40 versus a 3-month call on the same stock with an exercise price of $35.

c. A put option on a stock selling at $50, or a put option on another stock selling at $60 (all other relevant features of the stocks and options may be assumed to be identical).

14. Look at the futures listings for the S&P 500 index in Figure 2.11.

a. Suppose you buy one contract for March delivery. If the contract closes in March at a level of 1300, what will your profit be?

b. How many March maturity contracts are outstanding?

15. Turn back to Figure 2.10 and look at the GE options. Suppose you buy a November expiration call option with exercise price $40.

a. Suppose the stock price in November is $42. Will you exercise your call? What are the profit and rate of return on your position?

b. What if you had bought the November call with exercise price $42.50?

c. What if you had bought a November put with exercise price $42.50?

16. Why do call options with exercise prices greater than the price of the underlying stock sell for positive prices?

17. Both a call and a put currently are traded on stock XYZ; both have strike prices of $50 and expirations of 6 months. What will be the profit to an investor who buys the call for $4 in the following scenarios for stock prices in 6 months? What will be the profit in each scenario to an investor who buys the put for $6?

a. $40

b. $45

c. $50

d. $55

e. $60

18. Explain the difference between a put option and a short position in a futures contract.

19. Explain the difference between a call option and a long position in a futures contract.

Challenge Problems

---

1. A firm's preferred stock often sells at yields below its bonds because

a. Preferred stock generally carries a higher agency rating.

b. Owners of preferred stock have a prior claim on the firm's earnings.

c. Owners of preferred stock have a prior claim on a firm's assets in the event of liquidation.

d. Corporations owning stock may exclude from income taxes most of the dividend income they receive.

2. A municipal bond carries a coupon of 6¾% and is trading at par. What is the equivalent taxable yield to a taxpayer in a combined federal plus state 34% tax bracket?

3. Which is the *most risky* transaction to undertake in the stock index option markets if the stock market is expected to increase substantially after the transaction is completed?

a. Write a call option.

b. Write a put option.

c. Buy a call option.

d. Buy a put option.

4. Short-term municipal bonds currently offer yields of 4%, while comparable taxable bonds pay 5%. Which gives you the higher after-tax yield if your tax bracket is:

a. Zero

b. 10%

CFA® PROBLEMS

Visit us at www.mhhe.com/bkm

Visit us at www.mhhe.com/bkm

    c. 20%
    d. 30%

5. The coupon rate on a tax-exempt bond is 5.6%, and the rate on a taxable bond is 8%. Both bonds sell at par. At what tax bracket (marginal tax rate) would an investor be indifferent between the two bonds?

STANDARD &POOR'S

Go to **www.mhhe.com/edumarketinsight.** Select the *Company* tab and enter ticker symbol DIS. Click on the EDGAR section and find the link for Disney's most recent annual report (10-K).

When you click on the link the entire filing will appear. Use the Edit, Find (on this page) menu to search for the words "commercial paper." Repeat the search as many times as necessary to answer the following questions.

1. What is the total amount of the net change in Disney's commercial paper borrowing as of the date of this statement?
2. How does Disney plan to use its commercial paper?
3. What are the net amounts of the company's commercial paper borrowings for the last 3 years?
4. What is the effective interest rate on Disney's commercial paper during the most recent year?

Now return to the main page and look in the S&P Stock Reports section for the Wall Street Consensus report. Answer the following questions based on the information in the report.

5. What is the Wall Street Consensus Opinion on Disney stock?
6. Has the opinion changed recently?
7. How many analysts follow this stock?
8. What are the average earnings estimates for the current year and for next year?
9. What growth rate in earnings is expected?

E-Investments

Inflation-Protected Bonds around the World

Barclays maintains a Web site at **www.barcap.com/inflation/index.shtml** with information about inflation around the world and tools to help issuers and investors understand the inflation-linked asset class. Inflation-linked bonds were issued by a number of countries after 1945, including Israel, Argentina, Brazil, and Iceland. However, the modern market is generally deemed to have been born in 1981, when the first index-linked gilts were issued in the U.K. The other large markets adopted somewhat different calculations to those used by the U.K., mostly copying the more straightforward model first employed by Canada in 1991. In chronological order, the markets are the U.K. (1981), Australia (1985), Canada (1991), Sweden (1994), the United States (1997), France (1998), Italy (2003), and Japan (2004).

SOLUTIONS TO CONCEPT CHECKS

1. The bond sells for 100:26 bid which is a price of 100.813% of par, or $1008.13, and 100:27 ask, or $1,008.438. This ask price corresponds to a yield of 4.61%. The ask price rose $\frac{9}{32}$ from its level yesterday, so the ask price then must have been 100:18, or $1,005.625.

2. A 6% taxable return is equivalent to an after-tax return of 6(1 − .30) = 4.2%. Therefore, you would be better off in the taxable bond. The equivalent taxable yield of the tax-free bond is 4/(1 − .30) = 5.71%. So a taxable bond would have to pay a 5.71% yield to provide the same after-tax return as a tax-free bond offering a 4% yield.

3. *a.* You are entitled to a prorated share of IBM's dividend payments and to vote in any of IBM's stockholder meetings.

   b. Your potential gain is unlimited because IBM's stock price has no upper bound.

   c. Your outlay was $80 × 100 = $8,000. Because of limited liability, this is the most you can lose.

4. The price-weighted index increases from 62.5 [i.e., (100 + 25)/2] to 65 [i.e., (110 + 20)/2], a gain of 4%. An investment of one share in each company requires an outlay of $125 that would increase in value to $130, for a return of 4% (i.e., 5/125), which equals the return to the price-weighted index.

5. The market-value-weighted index return is calculated by computing the increase in the value of the stock portfolio. The portfolio of the two stocks starts with an initial value of $100 million + $500 million = $600 million and falls in value to $110 million + $400 million = $510 million, a loss of 90/600 = .15, or 15%. The index portfolio return is a weighted average of the returns on each stock with weights of $\frac{1}{6}$ on XYZ and $\frac{5}{6}$ on ABC (weights proportional to relative investments). Because the return on XYZ is 10%, while that on ABC is −20%, the index portfolio return is $\frac{1}{6} × 10\% + \frac{5}{6} × (−20\%) = −15\%$, equal to the return on the market-value-weighted index.

6. The payoff to the call option is $2 per share at maturity. The option cost is $1.68 per share. The dollar profit is therefore $0.32. The put option expires worthless. Therefore, the investor's loss is the cost of the put, or $.45.

PART II

HOW SECURITIES ARE TRADED

THIS CHAPTER WILL provide you with a broad introduction to the many venues and procedures available for trading securities in the United States and international markets. We will see that trading mechanisms range from direct negotiation among market participants to fully automated computer crossing of trade orders.

The first time a security trades is when it is issued to the public. Therefore, we begin with a look at how securities are first marketed to the public by investment bankers, the midwives of securities. We turn next to a broad survey of how already-issued securities may be traded among investors, focusing on the differences between dealer markets, electronic markets, and specialist markets. With this background, we then turn to specific trading arenas such as the New York Stock Exchange, NASDAQ, and several foreign security markets, examining the competition among these markets for the patronage of security traders. We consider the costs of trading in these markets, the quality of trade execution, and the ongoing quest for cross-market integration of trading.

We then turn to the essentials of some specific types of transactions, such as buying on margin and short-selling stocks. We close the chapter with a look at some important aspects of the regulations governing security trading, including insider trading laws, circuit breakers, and the role of security markets as self-regulating organizations.

3.1 HOW FIRMS ISSUE SECURITIES

When firms need to raise capital they may choose to sell or *float* securities. These new issues of stocks, bonds, or other securities typically are marketed to the public by investment bankers in what is called the **primary market.** Trading of already-issued securities among investors occurs in the **secondary market.** Trading in secondary markets does not affect the outstanding amount of securities; ownership is simply transferred from one investor to another.

There are two types of primary market issues of common stock. **Initial public offerings,** or **IPOs,** are stocks issued by a formerly privately owned company that is going public, that is, selling stock to the public for the first time. *Seasoned* equity offerings are offered by companies that already have floated equity. For example, a sale by IBM of new shares of stock would constitute a seasoned new issue.

In the case of bonds, we also distinguish between two types of primary market issues, a *public offering* and a *private placement.* The former refers to an issue of bonds sold to the general investing public that can then be traded on the secondary market. The latter refers to an issue that usually is sold to one or a few institutional investors and is generally held to maturity.

Investment Banking

Public offerings of both stocks and bonds typically are marketed by investment bankers who in this role are called **underwriters.** More than one investment banker usually markets the securities. A lead firm forms an underwriting syndicate of other investment bankers to share the responsibility for the stock issue.

Investment bankers advise the firm regarding the terms on which it should attempt to sell the securities. A preliminary registration statement must be filed with the Securities and Exchange Commission (SEC), describing the issue and the prospects of the company. This preliminary prospectus is known as a *red herring* because it includes a statement printed in red, stating that the company is not attempting to sell the security before the registration is approved. When the statement is in final form, and accepted by the SEC, it is called the **prospectus.** At this point, the price at which the securities will be offered to the public is announced.

In a typical underwriting arrangement, the investment bankers purchase the securities from the issuing company and then resell them to the public. The issuing firm sells the securities to the underwriting syndicate for the public offering price less a spread that serves as compensation to the underwriters. This procedure is called a *firm commitment.* In addition to the spread, the investment banker also may receive shares of common stock or other securities of the firm. Figure 3.1 depicts the relationships among the firm issuing the security, the lead underwriter, the underwriting syndicate, and the public.

Shelf Registration

An important innovation in the issuing of securities was introduced in 1982 when the SEC approved Rule 415, which allows firms to register securities and gradually sell them to the public for 2 years following the initial registration. Because the securities are already registered, they can be sold on short notice, with little additional paperwork. Moreover, they can be sold in small amounts without incurring substantial flotation costs. The securities are "on the shelf," ready to be issued, which has given rise to the term *shelf registration.*

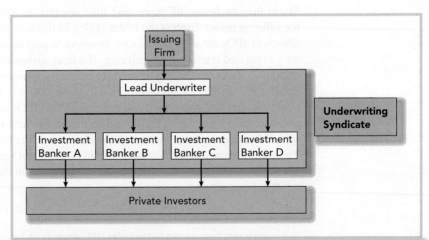

FIGURE 3.1 Relationship among a firm issuing securities, the underwriters, and the public

CONCEPT CHECK 1

Why does it make sense for shelf registration to be limited in time?

Private Placements

Primary offerings also can be sold in a **private placement** rather than a public offering. In this case, the firm (using an investment banker) sells shares directly to a small group of institutional or wealthy investors. Private placements can be far cheaper than public offerings. This is because Rule 144A of the SEC allows corporations to make these placements without preparing the extensive and costly registration statements required of a public offering. On the other hand, because private placements are not made available to the general public, they generally will be less suited for very large offerings. Moreover, private placements do not trade in secondary markets like stock exchanges. This greatly reduces their liquidity and presumably reduces the prices that investors will pay for the issue.

Initial Public Offerings

Investment bankers manage the issuance of new securities to the public. Once the SEC has commented on the registration statement and a preliminary prospectus has been distributed to interested investors, the investment bankers organize *road shows* in which they travel around the country to publicize the imminent offering. These road shows serve two purposes. First, they generate interest among potential investors and provide information about the offering. Second, they provide information to the issuing firm and its underwriters about the price at which they will be able to market the securities. Large investors communicate their interest in purchasing shares of the IPO to the underwriters; these indications of interest are called a *book* and the process of polling potential investors is called *bookbuilding*. These indications of interest provide valuable information to the issuing firm because institutional investors often will have useful insights about both the market demand for the security as well as the prospects of the firm and its competitors. It is common for investment bankers to revise both their initial estimates of the offering price of a security and the number of shares offered based on feedback from the investing community.

Why do investors truthfully reveal their interest in an offering to the investment banker? Might they be better off expressing little interest, in the hope that this will drive down the offering price? Truth is the better policy in this case because truth telling is rewarded. Shares of IPOs are allocated across investors in part based on the strength of each investor's expressed interest in the offering. If a firm wishes to get a large allocation when it is optimistic about the security, it needs to reveal its optimism. In turn, the underwriter needs to offer the security at a bargain price to these investors to induce them to participate in book-building and share their information. Thus, IPOs commonly are underpriced compared to the price at which they could be marketed. Such underpricing is reflected in price jumps that occur on the date when the shares are first traded in public security markets. The most dramatic case of underpricing occurred in December 1999 when shares in VA Linux were sold in an IPO at $30 a share and closed on the first day of trading at $239.25, a 698% 1-day return.[1]

---

[1] It is worth noting, however, that by December 2000, shares in VA Linux (now renamed VA Software) were selling for less than $9 a share, and by 2002, for less than $1. This example is extreme, but consistent with the generally disappointing long-term investment performance of IPOs.

While the explicit costs of an IPO tend to be around 7% of the funds raised, such underpricing should be viewed as another cost of the issue. For example, if VA Linux had sold its shares for the $239 that investors obviously were willing to pay for them, its IPO would have raised 8 times as much as it actually did. The money "left on the table" in this case far exceeded the explicit cost of the stock issue. This degree of underpricing is far more dramatic than is common, but underpricing seems to be a universal phenomenon.

Figure 3.2 presents average first-day returns on IPOs of stocks across the world. The results consistently indicate that IPOs are marketed to investors at attractive prices. Underpricing of IPOs makes them appealing to all investors, yet institutional investors are allocated the bulk of a typical new issue. Some view this as unfair discrimination against small investors. However, our analysis suggests that the apparent discounts on IPOs may be in part payments for a valuable service, specifically, the information contributed by the institutional investors. The right to allocate shares in this way may contribute to efficiency by promoting the collection and dissemination of such information.[2]

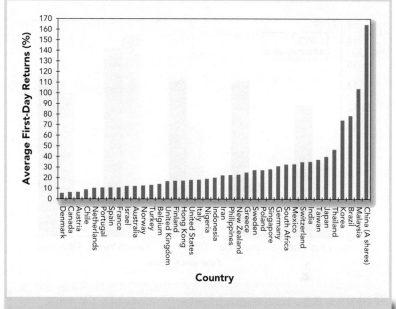

FIGURE 3.2 Average initial returns for IPOs in various countries

Source: Provided by Professor J. Ritter of the University of Florida, 2005; **bear.cba.ufl. edu/ritter**. This is an updated version of the information contained in T. Loughran, J. Ritter, and K. Rydqvist, "Initial Public Offerings," *Pacific-Basin Finance Journal* 2 (1994), pp. 165–199. Copyright 1994 with permission from Elsevier Science. Updated August 2007.

Both views of IPO allocations probably contain some truth. IPO allocations to institutions do serve a valid economic purpose as an information-gathering tool. Nevertheless, the system can be—and has been—abused. Part of the Wall Street scandals of 2000–2002 centered on the allocation of shares in IPOs. In a practice known as "spinning," some investment bankers used IPO allocations to corporate insiders to curry favors, in effect as implicit kickback schemes. These underwriters would award generous IPO allocations to executives of particular firms in return for the firm's future investment banking business.

Pricing of IPOs is not trivial and not all IPOs turn out to be underpriced. Some do poorly after issue. The 2006 IPO of Vonage was a notable disappointment. The stock lost about 30% of its value in its first 7 days of trading. Other IPOs cannot even be fully sold to the market. Underwriters left with unmarketable securities are forced to sell them at a loss on the secondary market. Therefore, the investment banker bears price risk for an underwritten issue.

---

[2]An elaboration of this point and a more complete discussion of the bookbuilding process is provided in Lawrence Benveniste and William Wilhelm, "Going by the Book," *Journal of Applied Corporate Finance* 9 (Spring 1997).

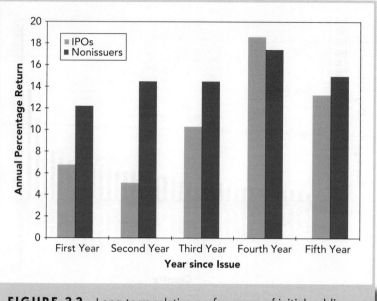

FIGURE 3.3   Long-term relative performance of initial public offerings

Source: Professor Jay R. Ritter's Web site, University of Florida, May 2005, **bear.cba.ufl. edu/ritter/ipodata.htm.**

Interestingly, despite their dramatic initial investment performance, IPOs have been poor long-term investments. Figure 3.3 compares the stock price performance of IPOs with shares of other firms of the same size for each of the 5 years after issue of the IPO. The year-by-year underperformance of the IPOs is dramatic, suggesting that, on average, the investing public may be too optimistic about the prospects of these firms. Such long-lived systematic errors on the part of investors would be surprising. An interesting study by Brav, Geczy, and Gompers,[3] however, suggests that apparent IPO underperformance may be illusory. When they carefully match firms based on size and ratios of book values to market values, they find that IPO returns are actually similar to those of comparison firms.

3.2   HOW SECURITIES ARE TRADED

Financial markets develop to meet the needs of particular traders. Consider what would happen if organized markets did not exist. Any household wishing to invest in some type of financial asset would have to find others wishing to sell. Soon, venues where interested traders could meet would become popular. Eventually, financial markets would emerge from these meeting places. Thus, a pub in old London called Lloyd's launched the maritime insurance industry. A Manhattan curb on Wall Street became synonymous with the financial world.

Types of Markets

We can differentiate four types of markets: direct search markets, brokered markets, dealer markets, and auction markets.

Direct Search Markets   A *direct search market* is the least organized market. Buyers and sellers must seek each other out directly. An example of a transaction in such a market is the sale of a used refrigerator where the seller advertises for buyers in a local newspaper. Such markets are characterized by sporadic participation and low-priced and nonstandard goods. It does not pay most people or firms to seek profits by specializing in such an environment.

[3]Alon Brav, Christopher Geczy, and Paul A. Gompers, "Is the Abnormal Return Following Equity Issuances Anomalous?" *Journal of Financial Economics* 56 (2000), pp. 209–49.

Brokered Markets The next level of organization is a *brokered market*. In markets where trading in a good is active, brokers find it profitable to offer search services to buyers and sellers. A good example is the real estate market, where economies of scale in searches for available homes and for prospective buyers make it worthwhile for participants to pay brokers to conduct the searches. Brokers in particular markets develop specialized knowledge on valuing assets traded in that market.

An important brokered investment market is the *primary market,* where new issues of securities are offered to the public. In the primary market, investment bankers who market a firm's securities to the public act as brokers; they seek investors to purchase securities directly from the issuing corporation.

Another brokered market is that for large block transactions, in which very large blocks of stock are bought or sold. These blocks are so large (technically more than 10,000 shares but usually much larger) that brokers or "block houses" often are engaged to search directly for other large traders, rather than bring the trade directly to the markets where relatively smaller investors trade.

Dealer Markets When trading activity in a particular type of asset increases, **dealer markets** arise. Dealers specialize in various assets, purchase these assets for their own accounts, and later sell them for a profit from their inventory. The spreads between dealers' buy (or "bid") prices and sell (or "ask") prices are a source of profit. Dealer markets save traders on search costs because market participants can easily look up the prices at which they can buy from or sell to dealers. A fair amount of market activity is required before dealing in a market is an attractive source of income. The over-the-counter (OTC) securities market is one example of a dealer market.

Auction Markets The most integrated market is an **auction market,** in which all traders converge at one place (either physically or "electronically") to buy or sell an asset. The New York Stock Exchange (NYSE) is an example of an auction market. An advantage of auction markets over dealer markets is that one need not search across dealers to find the best price for a good. If all participants converge, they can arrive at mutually agreeable prices and save the bid–ask spread.

Continuous auction markets (as opposed to periodic auctions, such as in the art world) require very heavy and frequent trading to cover the expense of maintaining the market. For this reason, the NYSE and other exchanges set up listing requirements, which limit the stocks traded on the exchange to those of firms in which sufficient trading interest is likely to exist.

The organized stock exchanges are also secondary markets. They are organized for investors to trade existing securities among themselves.

CONCEPT CHECK 2

Many assets trade in more than one type of market. What types of markets do the following trade in?

a. Used cars
b. Paintings
c. Rare coins

Types of Orders

Before comparing alternative trading practices and competing security markets, it is helpful to begin with an overview of the types of trades an investor might wish to have executed in these markets. Broadly speaking, there are two types of orders: market orders and orders contingent on price.

Market Orders Market orders are buy or sell orders that are to be executed immediately at current market prices. For example, our investor might call her broker and ask for the market price of IBM. The broker might report back that the best **bid price** is $90 and the best **ask price** is $90.05, meaning that the investor would need to pay $90.05 to purchase a share, and could receive $90 a share if she wished to sell some of her own holdings of IBM. The **bid–ask spread** in this case is $.05. So an order to buy 100 shares "at market" would result in purchase at $90.05, and an order to "sell at market" would be executed at $90.

This simple scenario is subject to a few potential complications. First, the posted price quotes actually represent commitments to trade up to a specified number of shares. If the market order is for more than this number of shares, the order may be filled at multiple prices. For example, if the asked price is good for orders up to 1,000 shares, and the investor wishes to purchase 1,500 shares, it may be necessary to pay a slightly higher price for the last 500 shares. Second, another trader may beat our investor to the quote, meaning that her order would then be executed at a worse price. Finally, the best price quote may change before her order arrives, again causing execution at a price different from the one at the moment of the order.

Price-Contingent Orders Investors also may place orders specifying prices at which they are willing to buy or sell a security. A limit buy order may instruct the broker to buy some number of shares if and when IBM may be obtained *at or below* a stipulated price. Conversely, a limit sell instructs the broker to sell if and when the stock price rises *above* a specified limit. A collection of **limit orders** waiting to be executed is called a *limit order book*.

Figure 3.4 is a portion of the limit order book for shares in Intel taken from the Archipelago exchange (one of several electronic exchanges; more on these shortly) on one day in 2007. Notice that the best orders are at the top of the list: the offers to buy at the highest price and to sell at the lowest price. The buy and sell orders at the top of the list—$20.77 and $20.78—are called the *inside quotes;* they are the highest buy and lowest sell orders. For Intel, the inside spread is only 1 cent. Note, however, that order sizes at the inside quotes are often fairly small. Therefore, investors interested in larger trades face an *effective* spread greater than the nominal one because they cannot execute their entire trades at the inside price quotes.

Until 2001, when U.S. markets adopted

INTC Intel Corp

NYSE Arca. [INTC] [Go>>]

	Bid				Ask		
ID	Price	Size	Time	ID	Price	Size	Time
ARCA	20.77	23100	14:08:23	ARCA	20.78	27200	14:08:23
ARCA	20.76	35725	14:08:22	ARCA	20.79	31800	14:08:23
ARCA	20.75	37391	14:08:21	ARCA	20.80	32000	14:08:22
ARCA	20.74	24275	14:08:23	ARCA	20.81	30500	14:08:22
ARCA	20.73	20524	14:08:23	ARCA	20.82	17090	14:08:21
ARCA	20.72	6890	14:08:21	ARCA	20.83	19650	14:08:01

FIGURE 3.4 The limit order book for Intel on the Archipelago market, January 19, 2007

Source: New York Stock Exchange Euronext Web site, **www.nyse.com.**

decimal pricing, the minimum possible spread was "one tick," which on the New York Stock Exchange was $\$\frac{1}{8}$ until 1997 and $\$\frac{1}{16}$ thereafter. With decimal pricing, the spread can be far lower. The average quoted bid–ask spread on the NYSE is less than 5 cents.

Stop orders are similar to limit orders in that the trade is not to be executed unless the stock hits a price limit. For *stop-loss orders,* the stock is to be *sold* if its price falls *below* a stipulated level. As the name suggests, the order lets the stock be sold to stop further losses from accumulating. Similarly, *stop-buy orders* specify that a stock should be bought when its price rises above a limit. These trades often accompany *short sales* (sales of securities you don't own but have borrowed from your broker) and are used to limit potential losses from the short position. Short sales are discussed in greater detail later in this chapter. Figure 3.5 organizes these types of trades in a convenient matrix.

	Condition	
	Price below the Limit	**Price above the Limit**
Action — Buy	Limit-Buy Order	Stop-Buy Order
Action — Sell	Stop-Loss Order	Limit-Sell Order

FIGURE 3.5 Price-contingent orders

CONCEPT CHECK 3

What type of trading order might you give to your broker in each of the following circumstances?

a. You want to buy shares of Intel to diversify your portfolio. You believe the share price is approximately at the "fair" value, and you want the trade done quickly and cheaply.

b. You want to buy shares of Intel, but believe that the current stock price is too high given the firm's prospects. If the shares could be obtained at a price 5% lower than the current value, you would like to purchase shares for your portfolio.

c. You plan to purchase a condominium sometime in the next month or so and will sell your shares of Intel to provide the funds for your down payment. While you believe that the Intel share price is going to rise over the next few weeks, if you are wrong and the share price drops suddenly, you will not be able to afford the purchase. Therefore, you want to hold on to the shares for as long as possible, but still protect yourself against the risk of a big loss.

Trading Mechanisms

Broadly speaking, there are three trading systems employed in the United States: over-the-counter dealer markets, electronic communication networks, and formal exchanges. The best-known markets such as NASDAQ or the New York Stock Exchange actually use a variety of trading procedures, so before delving into specific markets, it is useful to understand the basic operation of each type of trading system.

Dealer Markets   Roughly 35,000 securities trade on the **over-the-counter** or **OTC market.** Thousands of brokers register with the SEC as security dealers. Dealers quote prices at which they are willing to buy or sell securities. A broker then executes a trade by contacting a dealer listing an attractive quote.

Before 1971, all OTC quotations were recorded manually and published daily on so-called pink sheets. In 1971, the National Association of Securities Dealers Automatic Quotations System, or NASDAQ, was developed to link brokers and dealers in a computer network where price quotes could be displayed and revised. Dealers could use the network to display the bid price at which they were willing to purchase a security and the ask price at which they were willing to sell. The difference in these prices, the bid–ask spread, was the source of the dealer's profit. Brokers representing clients could examine quotes over the computer network, contact the dealer with the best quote, and execute a trade.

As originally organized, NASDAQ was more of a price-quotation system than a trading system. While brokers could survey bid and ask prices across the network of dealers in the search for the best trading opportunity, actual trades required direct negotiation (often over the phone) between the investor's broker and the dealer in the security. However, as we will see shortly, NASDAQ has effectively evolved into an electronic market. While dealers still post bid and ask prices over the network, the bulk of trades are executed electronically, without need of direct negotiation.

Electronic Communication Networks (ECNs)   Electronic communication networks allow participants to post market and limit orders over computer networks. The limit-order book is available to all participants. An example of such an order book from Archipelago, one of the leading ECNs, appeared in Figure 3.4. Orders that can be "crossed," that is, matched against another order, are done so automatically without requiring the intervention of a broker. For example, an order to buy a share at a price of $50 or lower will be immediately executed if there is an outstanding asked price of $50. Therefore, ECNs are true trading systems, not merely price-quotation systems.

ECNs offer several attractions. Direct crossing of trades without using a broker-dealer system eliminates the bid–ask spread that otherwise would be incurred. Instead, trades are automatically crossed at a modest cost, typically less than a penny per share. ECNs are attractive as well because of the speed with which a trade can be executed. Finally, these systems offer investors considerable anonymity in their trades.

Specialist Markets   In formal exchanges such as the New York Stock Exchange, trading in each security is managed by a **specialist** assigned responsibility for that security. Brokers who wish to buy or sell shares on behalf of their clients must direct the trade to the specialist's post on the floor of the exchange.

Each security is assigned to one specialist, but each specialist firm—currently there are fewer than 10 on the NYSE—makes a market in many securities. This task may require the specialist to act as either a broker or a dealer. The specialist's role as a broker is simply to execute the orders of other brokers. Specialists also may buy or sell shares of stock for their own portfolios. When no other trader can be found to take the other side of a trade, specialists will do so even if it means they must buy for or sell from their own accounts. Specialist firms earn income both from commissions for managing orders (as implicit brokers) and from the spreads at which they buy and sell securities (as implicit dealers).

Part of the specialist's job as a broker is simply clerical. The specialist maintains a limit-order book of all outstanding unexecuted limit orders entered by brokers on behalf of clients. When limit orders can be executed at market prices, the specialist executes, or "crosses," the trade.

The specialist is required to use the highest outstanding offered purchase price and the lowest outstanding offered selling price when matching trades. Therefore, the specialist system results in an auction market, meaning all buy and all sell orders come to one location, and the best orders "win" the trades. In this role, the specialist acts merely as a facilitator.

The more interesting function of the specialist is to maintain a "fair and orderly market" by acting as a dealer in the stock. In return for the exclusive right to make the market in a specific stock on the exchange, the specialist is required by the exchange to maintain an orderly market by buying and selling shares from inventory. Specialists maintain their own portfolios of stock and quoted bid and ask prices at which they are obligated to meet at least a limited amount of market orders.

Ordinarily, in an active market, specialists can match buy and sell orders without using their own accounts. That is, the specialist's own inventory of securities need not be the primary means of order execution. Sometimes, however, the specialist's bid and ask prices are better than those offered by any other market participant. Therefore, at any point, the effective ask price in the market is the lower of either the specialist's ask price or the lowest of the unfilled limit-sell orders. Similarly, the effective bid price is the highest of the unfilled limit-buy orders or the specialist's bid. These procedures ensure that the specialist provides liquidity to the market. In practice, specialists participate in approximately one-quarter of the transactions on the NYSE.

Specialists strive to maintain a narrow bid–ask spread for at least two reasons. First, one source of the specialist's income is frequent trading at the bid and ask prices, with the spread as a trading profit. A too-large spread would make the specialist's quotes uncompetitive with the limit orders placed by other traders. If the specialist's bid and asked quotes are consistently worse than those of public traders, the specialist will not participate in any trades and will lose the ability to profit from the bid–ask spread.

An equally important reason for narrow specialist spreads is that specialists are obligated to provide *price continuity* to the market. To illustrate price continuity, suppose the highest limit-buy order for a stock is $30, while the lowest limit-sell order is $32. When a market buy order comes in, it is matched to the best limit sell at $32. A market sell order would be matched to the best limit buy at $30. As market buys and sells come to the floor randomly, the stock price would fluctuate between $30 and $32. The exchange authorities would consider this excessive volatility, and the specialist would be expected to step in with bid and/or ask prices between these values to reduce the bid–ask spread to an acceptable level, typically below $.05 for large firms. When a firm is newly listed on an exchange, specialist firms vigorously compete to be awarded the rights to maintain the market in those shares. Since specialists are evaluated in part on their past performance in maintaining price continuity, they have considerable incentive to maintain tight spreads.

3.3   U.S. SECURITIES MARKETS

We have briefly sketched the three major trading mechanisms used in the United States: over-the-counter dealer markets, exchange trading managed by specialists, and direct trading among brokers or investors over electronic networks. Originally, NASDAQ was primarily a dealer market and the NYSE was primarily a specialist market. As we will see, however, these markets have evolved in response to new information technology and both have dramatically increased their commitment to automated electronic trading.

NASDAQ

While any security can be traded in the over-the-counter network of security brokers and dealers, not all securities were included in the original National Association of Security Dealers Automated Quotations System. That system, now called the **NASDAQ Stock Market,** lists about 3,200 firms and offers three listing options. The NASDAQ Global Select Market lists over 1,000 of the largest, most actively traded firms, the NASDAQ Global Market is for the next tier of firms, and the NASDAQ Capital Market is the third tier of listed firms. Some of the requirements for initial listing are presented in Table 3.1. For even smaller firms that may not be eligible for listing or that wish to avoid disclosure requirements associated with listing on regulated markets, Pink Sheets LLC offers real-time stock quotes on **www.pinksheets.com,** as well as Pink Link, an electronic messaging and trade negotiation service.

TABLE 3.1

Partial requirements for initial listing on NASDAQ markets

	NASDAQ Global Market	NASDAQ Capital Market
Shareholders' equity	$15 million	$5 million
Shares in public hands	1.1 million	1 million
Market value of publicly traded shares	$8 million	$5 million
Minimum price of stock	$5	$4
Pretax income	$1 million	$750,000
Shareholders	400	300

Source: The NASDAQ Stock Market, **www.nasdaq.com.** December 2006, The NASDAQ Stock Market, Inc. Reprinted with permission.

Because the NASDAQ system does not use a specialist, trades do not require a centralized trading floor as do exchange-listed stocks. Dealers can be located anywhere they can communicate effectively with other buyers and sellers.

NASDAQ has three levels of subscribers. The highest, level 3 subscribers, are for firms dealing, or "making markets," in securities. These market makers maintain inventories of a security and constantly stand ready to buy or sell these shares from or to the public at the quoted bid and ask prices. They earn profits from the spread between the bid and ask prices. Level 3 subscribers may enter the bid and ask prices at which they are willing to buy or sell stocks into the computer network and may update these quotes as desired.

Level 2 subscribers receive all bid and ask quotes, but they cannot enter their own quotes. These subscribers tend to be brokerage firms that execute trades for clients but do not actively deal in the stocks on their own account. Brokers buying or selling shares trade with the market maker (a level 3 subscriber) displaying the best price quote.

Level 1 subscribers receive only the *inside quotes* (i.e., the highest bid and lowest ask prices on each stock). Level 1 subscribers tend to be investors who are not actively buying and selling securities but want information on current prices.

As noted, NASDAQ was originally more a price-quotation system than a trading system. But that has changed. Investors on NASDAQ today (through their brokers) typically access bids and offers electronically without human interaction. NASDAQ has steadily developed ever-more-sophisticated electronic trading platforms, which today handle the great majority of its trades. The latest version, called the NASDAQ Market Center, was introduced in 2004 and consolidates all of NASDAQ's previous electronic markets into one integrated system.

Market Center is NASDAQ's competitive response to the growing popularity of ECNs, which have captured a large share of order flow. By enabling automatic trade execution, Market Center allows NASDAQ to function much like an ECN. In addition, NASDAQ purchased the BRUT ECN and merged with Instinet, which runs the INET ECN, to capture a greater share of the electronic trading market. Nevertheless, larger orders may still be negotiated among brokers and dealers, so NASDAQ retains some features of a pure dealer market.

The New York Stock Exchange

The New York Stock Exchange is by far the largest **stock exchange** in the United States. Shares of about 2,800 firms trade there, with a combined market capitalization in early 2008 of around $15 trillion. Daily trading on the NYSE averaged 2.1 billion shares in 2007, with a dollar value of approximately $87 billion.

An investor who wishes to trade shares on the NYSE places an order with a brokerage firm, which either sends the order to the floor of the exchange via computer network or contacts its broker on the floor of the exchange to "work" the order. Smaller orders are almost always sent electronically for automatic execution, while larger orders that may require negotiation or judgment are more likely sent to a floor broker. A floor broker sent a trade order takes the order to the specialist's post. At the post is a monitor called the Display Book that presents current offers from interested traders to buy or sell given numbers of shares at various prices. The specialist can cross the trade with that of another broker if that is feasible or match the trade using its own inventory of shares. Brokers might also seek out traders willing to take the other side of a trade at a price better than those currently appearing in the Display Book. If they can do so, they will bring the agreed-upon trade to the specialist for final execution.

Brokers must purchase the right to trade on the floor of the NYSE. Originally, the NYSE was organized as a not-for-profit company owned by its members or "seat holders." For example, in 2005 there were 1,366 seat-holding members of the NYSE. Each seat entitled its owner to place a broker on the floor of the exchange, where he or she could execute trades. Member firms could charge investors for executing trades on their behalf, which made a seat a valuable asset. The commissions that members might earn by trading on behalf of clients determined the market value of the seats, which were bought and sold like any other asset. Seat prices fluctuated widely, ranging from as low as $4,000 (in 1878) to as high as $4 million (in 2005).

More recently, however, many exchanges have decided to switch from a mutual form of organization, in which seat holders are joint owners, to publicly traded corporations owned by shareholders. In 2006, the NYSE merged with the Archipelago Exchange to form a publicly held company called the NYSE Group. (In 2007, the NYSE Group merged with Euronext to form NYSE Euronext.) As a publicly traded corporation, its share price rather than the price of a seat on the exchange is the best indicator of its financial health. Each seat on the exchange has been replaced by an annual license permitting traders to conduct business on the exchange floor.

The move toward public listing of exchanges is widespread. Other exchanges that have recently gone public include the Chicago Mercantile Exchange (derivatives trading, 2002), the International Securities Exchange (options, 2005), and the Chicago Board of Trade (derivatives, 2005), which has since merged with the CME. The Chicago Board Options Exchange reportedly also is considering going public.

Table 3.2 gives some of the initial listing requirements for the NYSE. These requirements ensure that a firm is of significant trading interest before the NYSE will allocate facilities for it to be traded on the floor of the exchange. If a listed company suffers a decline and fails to meet the criteria in Table 3.2, it may be delisted.

Regional exchanges and the Amex also sponsor trading of some firms that are listed on the NYSE. This arrangement enables local brokerage firms to trade in shares of large firms without obtaining a floor license on the NYSE.

About 75% of the share volume transacted in NYSE-listed securities actually is executed on the NYSE. The NYSE's market share measured by trades rather than share volume is considerably lower, as smaller retail orders are far more likely to be executed off the exchange. Nevertheless, the NYSE remains the venue of choice for large trades.

		TABLE 3.2
Minimum annual pretax income in previous 2 years	$ 2,000,000	
Revenue	$ 75,000,000	**Some initial listing**
Market value of publicly held stock	$100,000,000	**requirements for the**
Shares publicly held	1,100,000	**NYSE**
Number of holders of 100 shares or more	2,200	

Source: New York Stock Exchange, **www.nyse.com** January 2007.

TABLE 3.3

Block transactions on the New York Stock Exchange

Year	Shares (millions)	% Reported Volume	Average Number of Block Transactions per Day
1965	48	3.1%	9
1970	451	15.4	68
1975	779	16.6	136
1980	3,311	29.2	528
1985	14,222	51.7	2,139
1990	19,682	49.6	3,333
1995	49,737	57.0	7,793
2000	135,772	51.7	21,941
2005	112,027	27.7	17,445
2006	97,576	21.3	14,360
2007	57,079	10.7	7,332

Source: Data from the New York Stock Exchange Euronext Web site, **www.nyse.com.**

Block Sales   Institutional investors frequently trade blocks of tens of thousands of shares of stock. Table 3.3 shows that **block transactions** of over 10,000 shares account for a good deal of all trading on the NYSE. The larger block transactions are often too large for specialists to handle, as they do not wish to hold such large blocks of stock in their inventory. For example, one large block transaction in 2006 was for $972 million worth of shares in Direct TV.

"Block houses" have evolved to aid in the placement of larger block trades. Block houses are brokerage firms that specialize in matching block buyers and sellers. Once a buyer and a seller have been matched, the block is sent to the exchange floor where specialists execute the trade. If a buyer cannot be found, the block house might purchase all or part of a block sale for its own account. The block house then can resell the shares to the public.

You can observe in Table 3.3 that the volume of block trading has declined dramatically in the last decade. This reflects changing trading practices since the advent of electronic markets. Large trades are now much more likely to be split up into multiple small trades and executed electronically. The lack of depth on the electronic exchanges reinforces this pattern: because the inside quote on these exchanges is valid only for small trades, it generally is preferable to buy or sell a large stock position in a series of smaller transactions.

SuperDot and Electronic Trading on the NYSE   SuperDot is an electronic order-routing system that enables NYSE member firms to send market and limit orders directly to the specialist over computer lines. In 2006, it processed about 13 million trades per day, which were executed in a matter of seconds. The vast majority of all orders are submitted electronically through SuperDot, but these tend to be smaller orders, and account for about 70% of NYSE trading volume.

SuperDot is especially useful to program traders. A **program trade** is a coordinated purchase or sale of an entire portfolio of stocks. Many trading strategies (such as index arbitrage, a topic we will study in Chapter 23) require that an entire portfolio of stocks be purchased or sold simultaneously in a coordinated program. SuperDot is the tool that enables many trading orders to be sent out at once and executed almost simultaneously.

The NYSE has recently stepped up its commitment to electronic trading, instituting a fully automated trade-execution system called DirectPlus or Direct+. It matches orders against the inside bid or ask price with execution times of less than one-half second. In 2006, Direct+ handled about 17% of NYSE trade volume, largely because the system would accept only smaller trades (up to 1,099 shares). However, the NYSE is in the process of eliminating size and other limitations on Direct+ orders, so the fraction of shares cleared electronically is quickly rising. In stocks for which the size limitation was eliminated in the latter part of 2006, electronic trades rose to 80% of share volume within 4 months.

Settlement   Since June 1995, an order executed on the exchange must be settled within 3 working days. This requirement is often called T + 3, for trade date plus 3 days. The purchaser must deliver the cash, and the seller must deliver the stock to the broker, who in turn delivers it to the buyer's broker. Frequently, a firm's clients keep their securities in *street name,* which means the broker holds the shares registered in the firm's own name on behalf of the client. This convention can speed security transfer. T + 3 settlement has made such arrangements more important: It can be quite difficult for a seller of a security to complete delivery to the purchaser within the 3-day period if the stock is kept in a safe deposit box.

Settlement is simplified further by the existence of a clearinghouse. The trades of all exchange members are recorded each day, with members' transactions netted out, so that each member need transfer or receive only the net number of shares sold or bought that day. An exchange member then settles with the clearinghouse instead of individually with every firm with which it made trades.

Electronic Communication Networks

ECNs are private computer networks that directly link buyers with sellers. As an order is received, the system determines whether there is a matching order, and if so, the trade is executed immediately. Brokers that have an affiliation with an ECN have computer access and can enter orders in the limit-order book. Moreover, these brokers may make their terminals (or Internet access) available directly to individual traders who then can enter their own orders into the system.

ECNs have been highly successful and have captured more than half of the trading volume in NASDAQ-listed stocks. They must be certified by the SEC and registered with the National Association of Security Dealers to participate in the NASDAQ market. The two biggest ECNs by far are INET, formed by a merger of Island and Instinet, and Archipelago.

As noted, the NYSE and Archipelago have merged into a new publicly traded company called the NYSE Group (which then merged with Euronext). In principle, the merged firm can fill simple orders quickly without human interaction through ArcaEx (the Archipelago Exchange) and large complex orders using human traders on the floor of the NYSE. At the same time, NASDAQ purchased the other leading ECN, Instinet, which operates INET. Thus, the securities markets appear to be consolidating and it seems that each market will, at least for a time, offer multiple trading platforms.

The National Market System

The Securities Act Amendments of 1975 directed the Securities and Exchange Commission to implement a national competitive securities market. Such a market would entail centralized reporting of transactions as well as a centralized quotation system, with the aim of enhanced competition among market makers.

In 1975, Consolidated Tape began reporting trades on the NYSE, Amex, and major regional exchanges, as well as trades of NASDAQ-listed stocks. In 1977, the Consolidated Quotations Service began providing online bid and ask quotes for NYSE securities also traded on various other exchanges. In 1978, the Intermarket Trading System (ITS) was implemented. ITS currently links nine exchanges by computer: NYSE, Amex, Boston, National (formerly Cincinnati), Pacific, Philadelphia, Chicago, NASDAQ, and the Chicago Board Options Exchange. The system allows brokers and market makers to display and view quotes for all markets and to execute cross-market trades when the Consolidated Quotation System shows better prices in other markets.

However, the ITS has been only a limited success. Orders need to be directed to markets with the best prices by participants who might find it inconvenient or unprofitable to do so. However, the growth of automated electronic trading has made market integration more feasible. The SEC reaffirmed its so-called trade-through rule in 2005. Its Regulation NMS requires that investors' orders be filled at the best price that can be executed immediately, even if that price is available in a different market.

The trade-through rule is meant to improve speed of execution and enhance integration of competing stock markets. Linking these markets electronically through a unified book displaying all limit orders would be a logical extension of the ITS, enabling trade execution across markets. But this degree of integration has not yet been realized. Regulation NMS requires only that the inside quotes of each market be publicly shared. Because the inside or best quote is typically available only for a specified number of shares, there is still no guarantee that an investor will receive the best available prices for an entire trade, especially for larger trades.

Bond Trading

The New York Stock Exchange also operates a bond exchange where U.S. government, corporate, municipal, and foreign bonds may be traded. The centerpiece of the NYSE bond market is the Automated Bond System (ABS), which is an automated trading system that allows trading firms to obtain market information, to enter and execute trades over a computer network, and to receive immediate confirmations of trade execution.

However, the vast majority of bond trading occurs in the OTC market among bond dealers, even for bonds that are actually listed on the NYSE. This market is a network of bond dealers such as Merrill Lynch, Salomon Smith Barney (a division of Citigroup), or Goldman, Sachs that is linked by a computer quotation system. However, because these dealers do not carry extensive inventories of the wide range of bonds that have been issued to the public, they cannot necessarily offer to sell bonds from their inventory to clients or even buy bonds for their own inventory. They may instead work to locate an investor who wishes to take the opposite side of a trade. In practice, however, the corporate bond market often is quite "thin," in that there may be few investors interested in trading a specific bond at any particular time. As a result, the bond market is subject to a type of liquidity risk, for it can be difficult to sell one's holdings quickly if the need arises.

In 2006, the NYSE obtained regulatory approval to expand its bond trading system to include the debt issues of any NYSE-listed firm. In the past, each bond needed to be registered before listing; such a requirement was too onerous to justify listing most bonds. With the change, the NYSE now lists about 6,000 bond issues, an enormous increase from the roughly 1,000 bonds listed in 2006. In conjunction with these new listings, the NYSE has expanded its electronic bond-trading platform, which is now called NYSE Bonds. If the new trading system is successful, it will provide an alternative to the over-the-counter dealer market in bonds and improve the transparency of bond pricing for the public.

3.4   MARKET STRUCTURE IN OTHER COUNTRIES

The structure of security markets varies considerably from one country to another. A full cross-country comparison is far beyond the scope of this text. Therefore, we will instead briefly review three of the biggest non-U.S. stock markets: the London, Euronext, and Tokyo exchanges. Figure 3.6 shows the market capitalization of firms trading in the major world stock markets.

London

The London Stock Exchange uses an electronic trading system dubbed SETS (Stock Exchange Electronic Trading Service) for trading in large, liquid securities. This is an electronic clearing system similar to ECNs in which buy and sell orders are submitted via computer networks and any buy and sell orders that can be crossed are executed automatically. However, less-liquid shares are traded in a more traditional dealer market called the SEAQ (Stock Exchange Automated Quotations) system, where market makers enter bid and ask prices at which they are willing to transact.

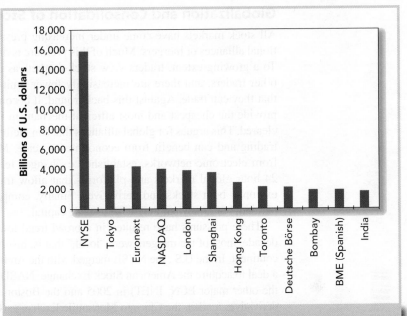

FIGURE 3.6 Market capitalization of major world stock exchanges, 2007
Source: World Federation of Exchanges.

Euronext

Euronext was formed in 2000 by a merger of the Paris, Amsterdam, and Brussels exchanges and itself merged with the NYSE Group in 2007. Euronext, like most European exchanges, uses an electronic trading system. Its system, called NSC (for Nouveau Système de Cotation, or New Quotation System), has fully automated order routing and execution. In fact, investors can enter their orders directly without contacting their brokers. An order submitted to the system is executed immediately if it can be crossed against an order in the public limit-order book; if it cannot be executed, it is entered into the limit-order book.

Euronext has established cross-trading agreements with several other European exchanges such as Helsinki or Luxembourg. In 2001, it also purchased LIFFE, the London International Financial Futures and Options Exchange.

Tokyo

The Tokyo Stock Exchange (TSE) is among the largest in the world, measured either by trading volume or the market capitalization of its roughly 2,400 listed firms. It exemplifies many of the general trends that we have seen affecting stock markets throughout the world. In 1999, it closed its trading floor and switched to all-electronic trading. It switched from a membership form of organization to a corporate form in 2001.

The TSE maintains three "sections." The First section is for large companies, the Second is for midsized firms, and the "Mothers" section is for emerging and high-growth stocks. About three-quarters of all listed firms trade on the First section, and about 200 trade in the Mothers section.

The two major stock market indexes for the TSE are the Nikkei 225 index, which is a price-weighted average of 225 top-tier Japanese firms, and the TOPIX index, which is a value-weighted index of the First section companies.

Globalization and Consolidation of Stock Markets

All stock markets have come under increasing pressure in recent years to make international alliances or mergers. Much of this pressure is due to the impact of electronic trading. To a growing extent, traders view stock markets as computer networks that link them to other traders, and there are increasingly fewer limits on the securities around the world that they can trade. Against this background, it becomes more important for exchanges to provide the cheapest and most efficient mechanism by which trades can be executed and cleared. This argues for global alliances that can facilitate the nuts and bolts of cross-border trading and can benefit from economies of scale. Moreover, in the face of competition from electronic networks, established exchanges feel that they eventually need to offer 24-hour global markets and platforms that allow trading of different security types, for example, both stocks and derivatives. Finally, companies want to be able to go beyond national borders when they wish to raise capital.

These pressures have resulted in a broad trend toward market consolidation. In the last decade, most of the mergers were "local," that is, involving exchanges operating in the same continent. In the U.S., the NYSE merged with the Archipelago ECN, and in 2008 announced a deal to acquire the American Stock Exchange. NASDAQ acquired Instinet (which operated the other major ECN, INET) in 2005 and the Boston Stock Exchange in 2007, and, in the derivatives market, the Chicago Mercantile Exchange (CME) acquired the Chicago Board of Trade. In 2008, the CME entered into merger talks with the New York Mercantile Exchange. In Europe, Euronext was formed by the merger of the Paris, Brussels, Lisbon, and Amsterdam exchanges and shortly thereafter purchased Liffe, the derivatives exchange based in London. Now a new wave of intercontinental mergers seems to be brewing. The NYSE Group and Euronext merged in 2007. The NYSE has purchased 5% of India's National Stock Exchange and has entered a cooperation agreement with the Tokyo Stock Exchange. In March 2006, NASDAQ made an offer to acquire the London Stock Exchange, but the LSE rejected that proposal. However, NASDAQ appears finally to have established a foothold in Europe in 2007, when it joined forces with Börse Dubai to acquired the Swedish exchange OMX. In the derivatives market, Deutsche Börse agreed to buy International Securities Exchange Holdings.

3.5 TRADING COSTS

Part of the cost of trading a security is obvious and explicit. Your broker must be paid a commission. Individuals may choose from two kinds of brokers: full-service or discount brokers. Full-service brokers who provide a variety of services often are referred to as account executives or financial consultants.

Besides carrying out the basic services of executing orders, holding securities for safe-keeping, extending margin loans, and facilitating short sales, brokers routinely provide information and advice relating to investment alternatives.

Full-service brokers usually depend on a research staff that prepares analyses and forecasts of general economic as well as industry and company conditions and often makes specific buy or sell recommendations. Some customers take the ultimate leap of faith and allow a full-service broker to make buy and sell decisions for them by establishing a *discretionary account*. In this account, the broker can buy and sell prespecified securities whenever deemed fit. (The broker cannot withdraw any funds, though.) This action requires an unusual degree of trust on the part of the customer, for an unscrupulous broker can "churn" an account, that is, trade securities excessively with the sole purpose of generating commissions.

Discount brokers, on the other hand, provide "no-frills" services. They buy and sell securities, hold them for safekeeping, offer margin loans, facilitate short sales, and that is all. The only information they provide about the securities they handle is price quotations. Discount brokerage services have become increasingly available in recent years. Many banks, thrift institutions, and mutual fund management companies now offer such services to the investing public as part of a general trend toward the creation of one-stop "financial supermarkets." Stock trading fees have fallen steadily over the last decade, and discount brokerage firms such as Schwab, E*Trade, or Ameritrade now offer commissions below $15 or even less than $10 for preferred customers.

In addition to the explicit part of trading costs—the broker's commission—there is an implicit part—the dealer's bid–ask spread. Sometimes the broker is also a dealer in the security being traded and charges no commission but instead collects the fee entirely in the form of the bid–ask spread. Another implicit cost of trading that some observers would distinguish is the price concession an investor may be forced to make for trading in any quantity that exceeds the quantity the dealer is willing to trade at the posted bid or asked price.

An ongoing controversy between the NYSE and its competitors is the extent to which better execution on the NYSE offsets the generally lower explicit costs of trading in other markets. Execution refers to the size of the effective bid–ask spread and the possibility of price improvement in a market. The NYSE believes that many investors focus too intently on the costs they can see, despite the fact that quality of execution can be a far more important determinant of total costs. Many NYSE trades are executed at a price inside the quoted spread. This can happen because floor brokers at the specialist's post can bid above or sell below the specialist's quote. In this way, two public orders can cross without incurring the specialist's spread.

To illustrate, suppose IBM is trading at $83.03 bid, $83.07 asked. A broker who has received a market buy order can meet a broker with a market sell order, and agree to a price of $83.05. By meeting in the middle of the quoted spread, both buyer and seller obtain "price improvement," that is, transaction prices better than the best quoted prices. Such "meetings" of brokers are more than accidental. Because all trading takes place at the specialist's post, floor brokers know where to look for counterparties to a trade.

3.6   BUYING ON MARGIN

When purchasing securities, investors have easy access to a source of debt financing called *broker's call loans*. The act of taking advantage of broker's call loans is called *buying on margin*.

Purchasing stocks on margin means the investor borrows part of the purchase price of the stock from a broker. The **margin** in the account is the portion of the purchase price contributed by the investor; the remainder is borrowed from the broker. The brokers in turn borrow money from banks at the call money rate to finance these purchases; they then charge their clients that rate (defined in Chapter 2), plus a service charge for the loan. All securities purchased on margin must be maintained with the brokerage firm in street name, for the securities are collateral for the loan.

The Board of Governors of the Federal Reserve System limits the extent to which stock purchases can be financed using margin loans. The current initial margin requirement is 50%, meaning that at least 50% of the purchase price must be paid for in cash, with the rest borrowed.

EXAMPLE 3.1   Margin

The percentage margin is defined as the ratio of the net worth, or the "equity value," of the account to the market value of the securities. To demonstrate, suppose an investor initially pays $6,000 toward the purchase of $10,000 worth of stock (100 shares at $100 per share), borrowing the remaining $4,000 from a broker. The initial balance sheet looks like this:

Assets		Liabilities and Owners' Equity	
Value of stock	$10,000	Loan from broker	$4,000
		Equity	$6,000

The initial percentage margin is

$$\text{Margin} = \frac{\text{Equity in account}}{\text{Value of stock}} = \frac{\$6,000}{\$10,000} = .60, \text{ or } 60\%$$

If the price declines to $70 per share, the account balance becomes:

Assets		Liabilities and Owners' Equity	
Value of stock	$7,000	Loan from broker	$4,000
		Equity	$3,000

The assets in the account fall by the full decrease in the stock value, as does the equity. The percentage margin is now

$$\text{Margin} = \frac{\text{Equity in account}}{\text{Value of stock}} = \frac{\$3,000}{\$7,000} = .43, \text{ or } 43\%$$

If the stock value in Example 3.1 were to fall below $4,000, owners' equity would become negative, meaning the value of the stock is no longer sufficient collateral to cover the loan from the broker. To guard against this possibility, the broker sets a *maintenance margin.* If the percentage margin falls below the maintenance level, the broker will issue a *margin call,* which requires the investor to add new cash or securities to the margin account. If the investor does not act, the broker may sell securities from the account to pay off enough of the loan to restore the percentage margin to an acceptable level.

EXAMPLE 3.2   Maintenance Margin

Suppose the maintenance margin is 30%. How far could the stock price fall before the investor would get a margin call?

Let P be the price of the stock. The value of the investor's 100 shares is then $100P$, and the equity in the account is $100P - \$4,000$. The percentage margin is $(100P - \$4,000)/100P$. The price at which the percentage margin equals the maintenance margin of .3 is found by solving the equation

$$\frac{100P - 4,000}{100P} = .3$$

which implies that $P = \$57.14$. If the price of the stock were to fall below $57.14 per share, the investor would get a margin call.

The Online Learning Center (**www.mhhe.com/bkm**) contains the Excel spreadsheet model below, which makes it easy to analyze the impacts of different margin levels and the volatility of stock prices. It also allows you to compare return on investment for a margin trade with a trade using no borrowed funds.

	A	B	C	D	E	F	G	H
1								
2			Action or Formula	Ending	Return on		Ending	Return with
3			for Column B	St Price	Investment		St Price	No Margin
4	Initial Equity Investment	$10,000.00	Enter data		−41.60%			−18.80%
5	Amount Borrowed	$10,000.00	(B4/B10)−B4	$20.00	−121.60%		$20.00	−58.80%
6	Initial Stock Price	$50.00	Enter data	25.00	−101.60%		25.00	−48.80%
7	Shares Purchased	400	(B4/B10)/B6	30.00	−81.60%		30.00	−38.80%
8	Ending Stock Price	$40.00	Enter data	35.00	−61.60%		35.00	−28.80%
9	Cash Dividends During Hold Per.	$0.60	Enter data	40.00	−41.60%		40.00	−18.80%
10	Initial Margin Percentage	50.00%	Enter data	45.00	−21.60%		45.00	−8.80%
11	Maintenance Margin Percentage	30.00%	Enter data	50.00	−1.60%		50.00	1.20%
12				55.00	18.40%		55.00	11.20%
13	Rate on Margin Loan	8.00%	Enter data	60.00	38.40%		60.00	21.20%
14	Holding Period in Months	6	Enter data	65.00	58.40%		65.00	31.20%
15				70.00	78.40%		70.00	41.20%
16	Return on Investment			75.00	98.40%		75.00	51.20%
17	Capital Gain on Stock	−$4,000.00	B7*(B8−B6)	80.00	118.40%		80.00	61.20%
18	Dividends	$240.00	B7*B9					
19	Interest on Margin Loan	$400.00	B5*(B14/12)*B13					
20	Net Income	−$4,160.00	B17+B18−B19				LEGEND:	
21	Initial Investment	$10,000.00	B4				Enter data	
22	Return on Investment	−41.60%	B20/B21				Value calculated	

Why do investors buy securities on margin? They do so when they wish to invest an amount greater than their own money allows. Thus, they can achieve greater upside potential, but they also expose themselves to greater downside risk.

CONCEPT CHECK 4

Suppose the maintenance margin in Example 3.2 is 40%. How far can the stock price fall before the investor gets a margin call?

To see how, let's suppose an investor is bullish on IBM stock, which is selling for $100 per share. An investor with $10,000 to invest expects IBM to go up in price by 30% during the next year. Ignoring any dividends, the expected rate of return would be 30% if the investor invested $10,000 to buy 100 shares.

But now assume the investor borrows another $10,000 from the broker and invests it in IBM, too. The total investment in IBM would be $20,000 (for 200 shares). Assuming an interest rate on the margin loan of 9% per year, what will the investor's rate of return be now (again ignoring dividends) if IBM stock goes up 30% by year's end?

The 200 shares will be worth $26,000. Paying off $10,900 of principal and interest on the margin loan leaves $15,100 (i.e., $26,000 − $10,900). The rate of return in this case will be

$$\frac{\$15,100 - \$10,000}{\$10,000} = 51\%$$

The investor has parlayed a 30% rise in the stock's price into a 51% rate of return on the $10,000 investment.

Doing so, however, magnifies the downside risk. Suppose that, instead of going up by 30%, the price of IBM stock goes down by 30% to $70 per share. In that case, the 200 shares

TABLE 3.4

Illustration of buying stock on margin

Change in Stock Price	End-of-Year Value of Shares	Repayment of Principal and Interest*	Investor's Rate of Return
30% increase	$26,000	$10,900	51%
No change	20,000	10,900	−9
30% decrease	14,000	10,900	−69

*Assuming the investor buys $20,000 worth of stock, borrowing $10,000 of the purchase price at an interest rate of 9% per year.

will be worth $14,000, and the investor is left with $3,100 after paying off the $10,900 of principal and interest on the loan. The result is a disastrous return of

$$\frac{\$3,100 - \$10,000}{\$10,000} = -69\%$$

Table 3.4 summarizes the possible results of these hypothetical transactions. If there is no change in IBM's stock price, the investor loses 9%, the cost of the loan.

CONCEPT CHECK 5

Suppose that in this margin example, the investor borrows only $5,000 at the same interest rate of 9% per year. What will the rate of return be if the price of IBM goes up by 30%? If it goes down by 30%? If it remains unchanged?

3.7 SHORT SALES

Normally, an investor would first buy a stock and later sell it. With a short sale, the order is reversed. First, you sell and then you buy the shares. In both cases, you begin and end with no shares.

A **short sale** allows investors to profit from a decline in a security's price. An investor borrows a share of stock from a broker and sells it. Later, the short-seller must purchase a share of the same stock in order to replace the share that was borrowed. This is called *covering the short position*. Table 3.5 compares stock purchases to short sales.

The short-seller anticipates the stock price will fall, so that the share can be purchased later at a lower price than it initially sold for; if so, the short-seller will reap a profit. Short-sellers must not only replace the shares but also pay the lender of the security any dividends paid during the short sale.

In practice, the shares loaned out for a short sale are typically provided by the short-seller's brokerage firm, which holds a wide variety of securities of its other investors in street name (i.e., the broker holds the shares registered in its own name on behalf of the client). The owner of the shares need not know that the shares have been lent to the short-seller. If the owner wishes to sell the shares, the brokerage firm will simply borrow shares from another investor. Therefore, the short sale may have an indefinite term. However, if the brokerage firm cannot locate new shares to replace the ones sold, the short-seller will need to repay the loan immediately by purchasing shares in the market and turning them over to the brokerage house to close out the loan.

eXcel APPLICATIONS: short sale

The Online Learning Center (**www.mhhe.com/bkm**) contains this Excel spreadsheet model, built using the text example for Dot Bomb. The model allows you to analyze the effects of returns, margin calls, and different levels of initial and maintenance margins. The model also includes a sensitivity analysis for ending stock price and returnt on investment.

	A	B	C	D	E
1					
2			Action or Formula	Ending	Return on
3			for Column B	St Price	Investment
4	Initial Investment	$50,000.00	Enter data		60.00%
5	Initial Stock Price	$100.00	Enter data	$170.00	–140.00%
6	Number of Shares Sold Short	1,000	(B4/B9)/B5	160.00	–120.00%
7	Ending Stock Price	$70.00	Enter data	150.00	–100.00%
8	Cash Dividends Per Share	$0.00	Enter data	140.00	–80.00%
9	Initial Margin Percentage	50.00%	Enter data	130.00	–60.00%
10	Maintenance Margin Percentage	30.00%	Enter data	120.00	–40.00%
11				110.00	–20.00%
12	Return on Short Sale			100.00	0.00%
13	Capital Gain on Stock	$30,000.00	B6*(B5–B7)	90.00	20.00%
14	Dividends Paid	$0.00	B8*B6	80.00	40.00%
15	Net Income	$30,000.00	B13–B14	70.00	60.00%
16	Initial Investment	$50,000.00	B4	60.00	80.00%
17	Return on Investment	60.00%	B15/B16	50.00	100.00%
18				40.00	120.00%
19	Margin Positions			30.00	140.00%
20	Margin Based on Ending Price	114.29%	(B4+(B5*B6)–B14–(B6*B7))/(B6*B7)	20.00	160.00%
21				10.00	180.00%
22	Price for Margin Call	$115.38	(B4+(B5*B6)–B14)/(B6*(1+B10))		
23				LEGEND:	
24				Enter data	
25				Value calculated	

Finally, exchange rules require that proceeds from a short sale must be kept on account with the broker. The short-seller cannot invest these funds to generate income, although large or institutional investors typically will receive some income from the proceeds of a short sale being held with the broker. Short-sellers also are required to post margin (cash or collateral) with the broker to cover losses should the stock price rise during the short sale.

Purchase of Stock		
Time	Action	Cash Flow*
0	Buy share	− Initial price
1	Receive dividend, sell share	Ending price + Dividend
Profit = (Ending price + Dividend) − Initial price		

Short Sale of Stock		
Time	Action	Cash Flow*
0	Borrow share; sell it	+ Initial price
1	Repay dividend and buy share to replace the share originally borrowed	− (Ending price + Dividend)
Profit = Initial price − (Ending price + Dividend)		

*A negative cash flow implies a cash *outflow*.

TABLE 3.5

Cash flows from purchasing versus short-selling shares of stock

EXAMPLE 3.3   Short Sales

To illustrate the mechanics of short-selling, suppose you are bearish (pessimistic) on Dot Bomb stock, and its market price is $100 per share. You tell your broker to sell short 1,000 shares. The broker borrows 1,000 shares either from another customer's account or from another broker.

The $100,000 cash proceeds from the short sale are credited to your account. Suppose the broker has a 50% margin requirement on short sales. This means you must have other cash or securities in your account worth at least $50,000 that can serve as margin on the short sale. Let's say that you have $50,000 in Treasury bills. Your account with the broker after the short sale will then be:

Assets		Liabilities and Owners' Equity	
Cash	$100,000	Short position in Dot Bomb stock (1,000 shares owed)	$100,000
T-bills	50,000	Equity	50,000

Your initial percentage margin is the ratio of the equity in the account, $50,000, to the current value of the shares you have borrowed and eventually must return, $100,000:

$$\text{Percentage margin} = \frac{\text{Equity}}{\text{Value of stock owed}} = \frac{\$50,000}{\$100,000} = .50$$

Suppose you are right and Dot Bomb falls to $70 per share. You can now close out your position at a profit. To cover the short sale, you buy 1,000 shares to replace the ones you borrowed. Because the shares now sell for $70, the purchase costs only $70,000.[4] Because your account was credited for $100,000 when the shares were borrowed and sold, your profit is $30,000: The profit equals the decline in the share price times the number of shares sold short.

Like investors who purchase stock on margin, a short-seller must be concerned about margin calls. If the stock price rises, the margin in the account will fall; if margin falls to the maintenance level, the short-seller will receive a margin call.

EXAMPLE 3.4   Margin Calls on Short Positions

Suppose the broker has a maintenance margin of 30% on short sales. This means the equity in your account must be at least 30% of the value of your short position at all times. How much can the price of Dot Bomb stock rise before you get a margin call?

Let P be the price of Dot Bomb stock. Then the value of the shares you must pay back is $1,000P$ and the equity in your account is $\$150,000 - 1,000P$. Your short position

---

[4]Notice that when buying on margin, you borrow a given amount of dollars from your broker, so the amount of the loan is independent of the share price. In contrast, when short-selling you borrow a given number of *shares*, which must be returned. Therefore, when the price of the shares changes, the value of the loan also changes.

margin ratio is equity/value of stock = $(150,000 - 1,000P)/1,000P$. The critical value of P is thus

$$\frac{\text{Equity}}{\text{Value of shares owed}} = \frac{150,000 - 1,000P}{1,000P} = .3$$

which implies that $P = \$115.38$ per share. If Dot Bomb stock should *rise* above $\$115.38$ per share, you will get a margin call, and you will either have to put up additional cash or cover your short position by buying shares to replace the ones borrowed.

CONCEPT CHECK **6**	*a.* Construct the balance sheet if Dot Bomb in Example 3.4 goes up to $110. *b.* If the short position maintenance margin in the Dot Bomb example is 40%, how far can the stock price rise before the investor gets a margin call?

You can see now why stop-buy orders often accompany short sales. Imagine that you short-sell Dot Bomb when it is selling at $100 per share. If the share price falls, you will profit from the short sale. On the other hand, if the share price rises, let's say to $130, you will lose $30 per share. But suppose that when you initiate the short sale, you also enter a stop-buy order at $120. The stop-buy will be executed if the share price surpasses $120, thereby limiting your losses to $20 per share. (If the stock price drops, the stop-buy will never be executed.) The stop-buy order thus provides protection to the short-seller if the share price moves up.

3.8   REGULATION OF SECURITIES MARKETS

Trading in securities markets in the United States is regulated by a myriad of laws. The major governing legislation includes the Securities Act of 1933 and the Securities Exchange Act of 1934. The 1933 Act requires full disclosure of relevant information relating to the issue of new securities. This is the act that requires registration of new securities and issuance of a prospectus that details the financial prospects of the firm. SEC approval of a prospectus or financial report is not an endorsement of the security as a good investment. The SEC cares only that the relevant facts are disclosed; investors must make their own evaluation of the security's value.

The 1934 Act established the Securities and Exchange Commission to administer the provisions of the 1933 Act. It also extended the disclosure principle of the 1933 Act by requiring periodic disclosure of relevant financial information by firms with already-issued securities on secondary exchanges.

The 1934 Act also empowers the SEC to register and regulate securities exchanges, OTC trading, brokers, and dealers. While the SEC is the administrative agency responsible for broad oversight of the securities markets, it shares responsibility with other regulatory agencies. The Commodity Futures Trading Commission (CFTC) regulates trading in futures markets, while the Federal Reserve has broad responsibility for the health of the U.S. financial system. In this role, the Fed sets margin requirements on stocks and stock options and regulates bank lending to security market participants.

The Securities Investor Protection Act of 1970 established the Securities Investor Protection Corporation (SIPC) to protect investors from losses if their brokerage firms fail.

Just as the Federal Deposit Insurance Corporation provides depositors with federal protection against bank failure, the SIPC ensures that investors will receive securities held for their account in street name by a failed brokerage firm up to a limit of $500,000 per customer. The SIPC is financed by levying an "insurance premium" on its participating, or member, brokerage firms.

In addition to federal regulations, security trading is subject to state laws, known generally as *blue sky laws* because they are intended to give investors a clearer view of investment prospects. State laws to outlaw fraud in security sales existed before the Securities Act of 1933. Varying state laws were somewhat unified when many states adopted portions of the Uniform Securities Act, which was enacted in 1956.

Self-Regulation

Although the SEC is charged with oversight of the securities markets and participating firms, in practice it delegates much of its work to the exchanges themselves. The stock markets are therefore largely self-regulating organizations. The National Association of Securities Dealers (NASD) oversees participants in the NASDAQ stock market, and the NYSE has its own regulatory arm. NYSE Regulation, Inc., was created during the merger between the NYSE and Archipelago and is now a subsidiary of NYSE Euronext. It is charged with monitoring and regulating the activities of NYSE member firms and listed companies, and enforcing compliance with both NYSE rules and federal securities laws. At the end of 2006, the NYSE and NASD agreed to merge portions of their regulatory arms into one agency to reduce the costs of overlapping and redundant regulation. The plan is to consolidate routine examinations, rule-making, enforcement, and arbitration into one "self-regulatory organization," or SRO.

In addition to exchange regulation, there is also self-regulation among the community of investment professionals. For example, the CFA Institute has developed standards of professional conduct that govern the behavior of members with the Chartered Financial Analysts designation, commonly referred to as CFAs. The nearby box presents a brief outline of those principles.

Regulatory Responses to Recent Scandals

The scandals of 2000–2002 centered largely on three broad practices: allocations of shares in initial public offerings, tainted securities research and recommendations put out to the public, and, probably most important, misleading financial statements and accounting practices. The regulatory response to these issues is still evolving, but some initiatives have been put in place. Many of these are contained in the Sarbanes-Oxley Act passed by Congress in 2002. Among the key reforms are:

- Creation of a Public Company Accounting Oversight Board to oversee the auditing of public companies.

- Rules requiring independent financial experts to serve on audit committees of a firm's board of directors.

- CEOs and CFOs must now personally certify that their firms' financial reports "fairly represent, in all material respects, the operations and financial condition of the company," and are subject to personal penalties if those reports turn out to be misleading. Following the letter of GAAP rules may still be necessary, but it is no longer sufficient accounting practice.

- Auditors may no longer provide several other services to their clients. This is intended to prevent potential profits on consulting work from influencing the quality of their audit.

EXCERPTS FROM CFA INSTITUTE STANDARDS OF PROFESSIONAL CONDUCT

I. Professionalism

- Knowledge of law. Members must understand, have knowledge of, and comply with all applicable laws, rules, and regulations including the Code of Ethics and Standards of Professional Conduct.
- Independence and objectivity. Members shall maintain independence and objectivity in their professional activities.
- Misrepresentation. Members must not knowingly misrepresent investment analysis, recommendations, or other professional activities.

II. Integrity of Capital Markets

- Non-public information. Members must not exploit material non-public information.
- Market manipulation. Members shall not attempt to distort prices or trading volume with the intent to mislead market participants.

III. Duties to Clients

- Loyalty, prudence, and care. Members must place their clients' interests before their own and act with reasonable care on their behalf.
- Fair dealing. Members shall deal fairly and objectively with clients when making investment recommendations or taking actions.
- Suitability. Members shall make a reasonable inquiry into a client's financial situation, investment experience, and investment objectives prior to making appropriate investment recommendations.
- Performance presentation. Members shall attempt to ensure that investment performance is presented fairly, accurately, and completely.
- Confidentiality. Members must keep information about clients confidential unless the client permits disclosure.

IV. Duties to Employers

- Loyalty. Members must act for the benefit of their employer.
- Compensation. Members must not accept compensation from sources that would create a conflict of interest with their employer's interests without written consent from all involved parties.
- Supervisors. Members must make reasonable efforts to detect and prevent violation of applicable laws and regulations by anyone subject to their supervision.

V. Investment Analysis and Recommendations

- Diligence. Members must exercise diligence and have reasonable basis for investment analysis, recommendations, or actions.
- Communication. Members must distinguish fact from opinion in their presentation of analysis and disclose general principles of investment processes used in analysis.

VI. Conflicts of Interest

- Disclosure of conflicts. Members must disclose all matters that reasonably could be expected to impair their objectivity or interfere with their other duties.
- Priority of transactions. Transactions for clients and employers must have priority over transactions for the benefit of a member.

VII. Responsibilities as Member of CFA Institute

- Conduct. Members must not engage in conduct that compromises the reputation or integrity of the CFA Institute or CFA designation.

- The Board of Directors must be composed of independent directors and hold regular meetings of directors in which company management is not present (and therefore cannot impede or influence the discussion).

More recently, there has been a fair amount of push-back on Sarbanes-Oxley. Many observers believe that the compliance costs associated with the law are too onerous, especially for smaller firms, and that heavy-handed regulatory oversight is giving foreign locales an undue advantage over the United States when firms decide where to list their

THE RULES OF THE GAME

Financial innovation has proceeded at a head-spinning rate in recent years. Hedge funds have ballooned to account for more than $1.3 trillion in assets worldwide. They also bear some responsibility for the growing volatility of global financial markets and pose difficult questions for regulators. Complex new products that are created in one financial center involve assets in another and are sold to investors in a third, so who is supposed to keep an eye on them?

It is up to regulators to sort out the balance between control and adaptability, but the complexities of rapid trading, particularly across multiple borders and asset classes, are stretching the capacity of even the most sophisticated regulators. There is talk of "regulatory arbitrage", meaning that financial firms look for the most favorable environments to operate in.

Current American financial regulation—divided among many agencies at both federal and state levels—strikes many firms as complex and confusing. The Securities and Exchange Commission (SEC), which regulates share trading, banks and other parts of the financial markets, takes a "rules-based" approach, spelling out in detail what can and cannot be done. The Commodities Futures Trading Commission (CFTC), which monitors the futures markets, is generally more risk-based and less legalistic than the SEC—more like Britain's Financial Services Authority (FSA).

The debate over regulation is noisiest in America. There are worries in financial circles that markets there may be losing some of their business to financial centers abroad. The Sarbanes-Oxley act, passed five years ago, which imposed far tougher controls on public companies, is also often blamed for making America a less attractive place for doing business. Many in the financial community have called for America to combine its jumble of financial regulators under a single umbrella, as Britain has done with the FSA, but views on what exactly should be done are far from unanimous.

Britain's financial system, which has served as a model for regulators from Hong Kong to Dubai, is based on broad principles and "risk-based" regulation. Stocks, futures products, banking, insurance and over-the-counter products (private transactions between parties) are grouped under a single regulator, the FSA.

Yet there is an added layer of regulatory complication in Europe as the European Commission in Brussels pushes for a single regional market in financial services. From November 2007, European financial-services providers will be subject to the Markets in Financial Instruments Directive (MiFID), designed to increase competition and improve transparency across a broad swathe of financial services.

Because of the increasingly global nature of capital markets, these regulations are being tested in new ways. The growing volume of cross-border exchange deals, for instance, has forced regulators to work much more closely together. "Just as the United States can't go it alone, neither can any other country," says Christopher Cox, chairman of America's SEC.

Source: The *Economist*, September 13, 2007.

securities. Moreover, the efficacy of single-country regulation is being tested in the face of increasing globalization and the ease with which funds can move across national borders. The nearby box considers some of these issues.

The SEC's Regulation FD (for Fair Disclosure), introduced in 2000, prohibits firms from divulging material information to one outside group (e.g., stock analysts) before making it available to the entire market. In addition, to settle charges concerning their publication of biased stock research as a quid pro quo for IPO allocations and investment banking contracts, major investment banks agreed in late 2002 to fence off stock research from the investment banking side of the firm.

Circuit Breakers

The market collapse of October 19, 1987, prompted several suggestions for regulatory change. Among these was a call for "circuit breakers" to slow or stop trading during periods of extreme volatility. Some of the current circuit breakers still being used entail trading halts. If the Dow Jones Industrial Average falls by 10%, trading will be halted for 1 hour if the drop occurs before 2:00 p.m. (Eastern Standard Time), for ½ hour if the drop occurs between 2:00 and 2:30, but not at all if the drop occurs after 2:30. If the Dow falls by 20%, trading will be halted for 2 hours if the drop occurs before 1:00 p.m., for 1 hour if the drop occurs between 1:00 and 2:00, and for the rest of the day if the drop occurs after 2:00. A 30% drop in the Dow would close the market for the rest of the day, regardless of the time.

The idea behind circuit breakers is that a temporary halt in trading during periods of very high volatility can help mitigate informational problems that might contribute to excessive price swings. For example, even if a trader is unaware of any specific adverse economic news, if he sees the market plummeting, he will suspect that there might be a good reason for the price drop and will become unwilling to buy shares. In fact, he might decide to sell shares to avoid losses. Thus, feedback from price swings to trading behavior can exacerbate market movements. Circuit breakers give participants a chance to assess market fundamentals while prices are temporarily frozen. In this way, they have a chance to decide whether price movements are warranted while the market is closed.

Of course, circuit breakers have no bearing on trading in non-U.S. markets. It is quite possible that they simply have induced those who engage in program trading to move their operations into foreign exchanges.

Insider Trading

Regulations also prohibit insider trading. It is illegal for anyone to transact in securities to profit from **inside information,** that is, private information held by officers, directors, or major stockholders that has not yet been divulged to the public. But the definition of insiders can be ambiguous. While it is obvious that the chief financial officer of a firm is an insider, it is less clear whether the firm's biggest supplier can be considered an insider. Yet a supplier may deduce the firm's near-term prospects from significant changes in orders. This gives the supplier a unique form of private information, yet the supplier is not technically an insider. These ambiguities plague security analysts, whose job is to uncover as much information as possible concerning the firm's expected prospects. The distinction between legal private information and illegal inside information can be fuzzy.

The SEC requires officers, directors, and major stockholders to report all transactions in their firm's stock. A compendium of insider trades is published monthly in the SEC's *Official Summary of Securities Transactions and Holdings*. The idea is to inform the public of any implicit vote of confidence or no confidence made by insiders.

Insiders *do* exploit their knowledge. Three forms of evidence support this conclusion. First, there have been well-publicized convictions of principals in insider trading schemes.

Second, there is considerable evidence of "leakage" of useful information to some traders before any public announcement of that information. For example, share prices of firms announcing dividend increases (which the market interprets as good news concerning the firm's prospects) commonly increase in value a few days *before* the public announcement of the increase. Clearly, some investors are acting on the good news before it is released to the public. Share prices still rise substantially on the day of the public release of good news, however, indicating that insiders, or their associates, have not fully bid up the price of the stock to the level commensurate with the news.

A third form of evidence on insider trading has to do with returns earned on trades by insiders. Researchers have examined the SEC's summary of insider trading to measure the performance of insiders. In one of the best known of these studies, Jaffee[5] examined the abnormal return of stocks over the months following purchases or sales by insiders. For months in which insider purchasers of a stock exceeded insider sellers of the stock by three or more, the stock had an abnormal return in the following 8 months of about 5%. Moreover, when insider sellers exceeded insider buyers, the stock tended to perform poorly.

SUMMARY

1. Firms issue securities to raise the capital necessary to finance their investments. Investment bankers market these securities to the public on the primary market. Investment bankers generally act as underwriters who purchase the securities from the firm and resell them to the public at a markup. Before the securities may be sold to the public, the firm must publish an SEC-accepted prospectus that provides information on the firm's prospects.

2. Already-issued securities are traded on the secondary market, that is, on organized stock exchanges; the over-the-counter market; and for large trades, through direct negotiation. Only license holders of exchanges may trade on the exchange. Brokerage firms holding licenses to trade on the exchange sell their services to individuals, charging commissions for executing trades on their behalf.

3. Trading may take place in dealer markets, via electronic communication networks, or in specialist markets. In dealer markets, security dealers post bid and ask prices at which they are willing to trade. Brokers for individuals execute trades at the best available prices. In electronic markets, the existing book of limit orders provides the terms at which trades can be executed. Mutually agreeable offers to buy or sell securities are automatically crossed by the computer system operating the market. In specialist markets, the specialist acts to maintain an orderly market with price continuity. Specialists maintain a limit-order book, but also sell from or buy for their own inventories of stock. Thus, liquidity in specialist markets comes from both the limit-order book and the specialist's inventory.

4. NASDAQ was traditionally a dealer market in which a network of dealers negotiated directly over sales of securities. The NYSE was traditionally a specialist market. In recent years, as ECNs have commanded a greater share of trading activity, both exchanges have increased their commitment to electronic and automated trading. Most trades on NASDAQ today are electronic, and the NYSE has increased its electronic capabilities through an expansion of Direct + as well as its mergers with Archipelago and Euronext.

5. Trading costs include explicit commissions as well as the bid–ask spread. An ongoing controversy among markets concerns overall trading costs including the effect of spreads. The NYSE argues that it is often the cheapest trading venue when quality of execution (including the possibility of price improvement) is recognized.

6. Buying on margin means borrowing money from a broker to buy more securities than can be purchased with one's own money alone. By buying securities on a margin, an investor magnifies both the upside potential and the downside risk. If the equity in a margin account falls below the required maintenance level, the investor will get a margin call from the broker.

7. Short-selling is the practice of selling securities that the seller does not own. The short-seller borrows the securities sold through a broker and may be required to cover the short position at any time on demand. The cash proceeds of a short sale are kept in escrow by the broker, and the

[5]Jeffrey E. Jaffee, "Special Information and Insider Trading," *Journal of Business* 47 (July 1974).

broker usually requires that the short-seller deposit additional cash or securities to serve as margin (collateral) for the short sale.

8. Securities trading is regulated by the Securities and Exchange Commission, by other government agencies, and through self-regulation of the exchanges. Many of the important regulations have to do with full disclosure of relevant information concerning the securities in question. Insider trading rules also prohibit traders from attempting to profit from inside information.

Related Web sites for this chapter are available at www.mhhe.com/bkm

---

KEY TERMS

primary market	ask price	NASDAQ
secondary market	bid–ask spread	stock exchanges
initial public offerings (IPOs)	limit order	block transactions
underwriters	stop orders	program trade
prospectus	over-the-counter (OTC)	margin
private placement	market	short sale
dealer markets	electronic communication	inside information
auction market	networks (ECNs)	
bid price	specialist	

PROBLEM SETS

Quiz

1. Call one full-service broker and one discount broker and find out the transaction costs of implementing the following strategies:
   a. Buying 100 shares of IBM now and selling them 6 months from now.
   b. Investing an equivalent amount in 6-month at-the-money call options on IBM stock now and selling them 6 months from now.

2. What purpose does the SuperDot system serve on the New York Stock Exchange?

3. Who sets the bid and asked price for a stock traded over the counter? Would you expect the spread to be higher on actively or inactively traded stocks?

Problems

4. Suppose you short sell 100 shares of IBM, now selling at $120 per share.
   a. What is your maximum possible loss?
   b. What happens to the maximum loss if you simultaneously place a stop-buy order at $128?

5. Dée Trader opens a brokerage account and purchases 300 shares of Internet Dreams at $40 per share. She borrows $4,000 from her broker to help pay for the purchase. The interest rate on the loan is 8%.
   a. What is the margin in Dée's account when she first purchases the stock?
   b. If the share price falls to $30 per share by the end of the year, what is the remaining margin in her account? If the maintenance margin requirement is 30%, will she receive a margin call?
   c. What is the rate of return on her investment?

6. Old Economy Traders opened an account to short sell 1,000 shares of Internet Dreams from the previous problem. The initial margin requirement was 50%. (The margin account pays no interest.) A year later, the price of Internet Dreams has risen from $40 to $50, and the stock has paid a dividend of $2 per share.
   a. What is the remaining margin in the account?
   b. If the maintenance margin requirement is 30%, will Old Economy receive a margin call?
   c. What is the rate of return on the investment?

7. Do you think it is possible to replace market-making specialists with a fully automated, computerized trade-matching system?

8. Consider the following limit-order book of a specialist. The last trade in the stock occurred at a price of $50.

Limit Buy Orders		Limit Sell Orders	
Price	Shares	Price	Shares
$49.75	500	$50.25	100
49.50	800	51.50	100
49.25	500	54.75	300
49.00	200	58.25	100
48.50	600		

  a. If a market buy order for 100 shares comes in, at what price will it be filled?
  b. At what price would the next market buy order be filled?
  c. If you were the specialist, would you want to increase or decrease your inventory of this stock?

9. You are bullish on Telecom stock. The current market price is $50 per share, and you have $5,000 of your own to invest. You borrow an additional $5,000 from your broker at an interest rate of 8% per year and invest $10,000 in the stock.

  a. What will be your rate of return if the price of Telecom stock goes up by 10% during the next year? (Ignore the expected dividend.)
  b. How far does the price of Telecom stock have to fall for you to get a margin call if the maintenance margin is 30%? Assume the price fall happens immediately.

10. You are bearish on Telecom and decide to sell short 100 shares at the current market price of $50 per share.

  a. How much in cash or securities must you put into your brokerage account if the broker's initial margin requirement is 50% of the value of the short position?
  b. How high can the price of the stock go before you get a margin call if the maintenance margin is 30% of the value of the short position?

11. Suppose that Intel currently is selling at $40 per share. You buy 500 shares using $15,000 of your own money, borrowing the remainder of the purchase price from your broker. The rate on the margin loan is 8%.

  a. What is the percentage increase in the net worth of your brokerage account if the price of Intel *immediately* changes to: (i) $44; (ii) $40; (iii) $36? What is the relationship between your percentage return and the percentage change in the price of Intel?
  b. If the maintenance margin is 25%, how low can Intel's price fall before you get a margin call?
  c. How would your answer to (b) change if you had financed the initial purchase with only $10,000 of your own money?
  d. What is the rate of return on your margined position (assuming again that you invest $15,000 of your own money) if Intel is selling *after 1 year* at: (i) $44; (ii) $40; (iii) $36? What is the relationship between your percentage return and the percentage change in the price of Intel? Assume that Intel pays no dividends.
  e. Continue to assume that a year has passed. How low can Intel's price fall before you get a margin call?

12. Suppose that you sell short 500 shares of Intel, currently selling for $40 per share, and give your broker $15,000 to establish your margin account.
  a. If you earn no interest on the funds in your margin account, what will be your rate of return after 1 year if Intel stock is selling at: (i) $44; (ii) $40; (iii) $36? Assume that Intel pays no dividends.
  b. If the maintenance margin is 25%, how high can Intel's price rise before you get a margin call?

c. Redo parts (*a*) and (*b*), but now assume that Intel also has paid a year-end dividend of $1 per share. The prices in part (*a*) should be interpreted as ex-dividend, that is, prices after the dividend has been paid.

13. Here is some price information on Marriott:

	Bid	Asked
Marriott	37.95	38.05

You have placed a stop-loss order to sell at $38. What are you telling your broker? Given market prices, will your order be executed?

14. Here is some price information on Fincorp stock. Suppose first that Fincorp trades in a dealert market.

	Bid	Asked
	55.25	55.50

a. Suppose you have submitted an order to your broker to buy at market. At what price will your trade be executed?
b. Suppose you have submitted an order to sell at market. At what price will your trade be executed?
c. Suppose you have submitted a limit order to sell at $55.62. What will happen?
d. Suppose you have submitted a limit order to buy at $55.37. What will happen?

15. Now reconsider Problem 14 assuming that Fincorp sells in an exchange market like the NYSE.

a. Is there any chance for price improvement in the market orders considered in parts (*a*) and (*b*)?
b. Is there any chance of an immediate trade at $55.37 for the limit-buy order in part (*d*)?

16. You've borrowed $20,000 on margin to buy shares in Disney, which is now selling at $40 per share. Your account starts at the initial margin requirement of 50%. The maintenance margin is 35%. Two days later, the stock price falls to $35 per share.

a. Will you receive a margin call?
b. How low can the price of Disney shares fall before you receive a margin call?

17. On January 1, you sold short one round lot (that is, 100 shares) of Zenith stock at $14 per share. On March 1, a dividend of $2 per share was paid. On April 1, you covered the short sale by buying the stock at a price of $9 per share. You paid 50 cents per share in commissions for each transaction. What is the value of your account on April 1?

---

1. FBN, Inc., has just sold 100,000 shares in an initial public offering. The underwriter's explicit fees were $70,000. The offering price for the shares was $50, but immediately upon issue, the share price jumped to $53.

a. What is your best guess as to the total cost to FBN of the equity issue?
b. Is the entire cost of the underwriting a source of profit to the underwriters?

2. If you place a stop-loss order to sell 100 shares of stock at $55 when the current price is $62, how much will you receive for each share if the price drops to $50?

a. $50.
b. $55.
c. $54.87.
d. Cannot tell from the information given.

Visit us at www.mhhe.com/bkm

3. Specialists on the New York Stock Exchange do all of the following *except:*

   a. Act as dealers for their own accounts.
   b. Execute limit orders.
   c. Help provide liquidity to the marketplace.
   d. Act as odd-lot dealers.

E-Investments

Stock Market Listing Standards

Each exchange sets different criteria that must be satisfied for a stock to be listed there. The NYSE refers to their requirements as "Listing Standards." NASDAQ refers to the requirements as "Listing Qualifications." Listing requirements for these markets can be found at **www.nyse.com** and **www.nasdaq.com.** Find the listing requirements for firms with securities traded on each exchange. The NYSE also provides "continued listing standards." What are those requirements? Using the security search engine on either the NYSE or NASDAQ, search for stocks that do not meet the continued listing standards of the NYSE. Which variables would lead to the stock being delisted from the NYSE? What do you think is the likelihood that this stock will continue to be listed on the NYSE?

**STANDARD
&POOR'S**

1. Go to **www.mhhe.com/edumarketinsight.** Select the Company tab and enter ticker symbol IQW. Click on the Compustat Reports section and find the link for the company's profile. Where is the company's headquarters located? On what exchange does the company's stock primarily trade?

2. Now link to the Corporate Actions section of the Compustat Reports. Briefly summarize what you find out about the company's history with regard to its name and its ticker symbol.

3. Link to the Financial Highlights section of the Compustat Reports. What firm is the primary auditor of Quebecor's financial statements? Is the auditor's opinion qualified in any way?

4. In the S&P Stock Reports section, link to the company's Stock Report. Scroll down to the Business Summary section of the report. What are some of the magazines that Quebecor prints? For which companies does it print advertising inserts or circulars? What catalogs does it print? What firm(s) does Quebecor use as its Transfer Agent and Registrar? (*Hint:* If you have difficulty finding this, use the search tool on the Adobe menu that looks like a pair of field glasses. You can enter the word "transfer" and it will find the Transfer Agent.)

SOLUTIONS TO CONCEPT CHECKS

1. Limited time shelf registration was introduced because of its favorable trade-off of saving issue cost against mandated disclosure. Allowing unlimited shelf registration would circumvent "blue sky" laws that ensure proper disclosure as the financial circumstances of the firm change over time.

2. *a.* Used cars trade in dealer markets (used-car lots or auto dealerships) and in direct search markets when individuals advertise in local newspapers.

   b. Paintings trade in broker markets when clients commission brokers to buy or sell art for them, in dealer markets at art galleries, and in auction markets.

   c. Rare coins trade mostly in dealer markets in coin shops, but they also trade in auctions and in direct search markets when individuals advertise they want to buy or sell coins.

3. *a.* You should give your broker a market order. It will be executed immediately and is the cheapest type of order in terms of brokerage fees.

   b. You should give your broker a limit-buy order, which will be executed only if the shares can be obtained at a price about 5% below the current price.

   c. You should give your broker a stop-loss order, which will be executed if the share price starts falling. The limit or stop price should be close to the current price to avoid the possibility of large losses.

4. Solving

$$\frac{100P - \$4,000}{100P} = .4$$

yields $P = \$66.67$ per share.

5. The investor will purchase 150 shares, with a rate of return as follows:

Year-End Change in Price	Year-End Value of Shares	Repayment of Principal and Interest	Investor's Rate of Return
30%	$19,500	$5,450	40.5%
No change	15,000	5,450	− 4.5
−30%	10,500	5,450	−49.5

6. *a.* Once Dot Bomb stock goes up to $110, your balance sheet will be:

Assets		Liabilities and Owner's Equity	
Cash	$100,000	Short position in Dot Bomb	$110,000
T-bills	50,000	Equity	40,000

   b. Solving

$$\frac{\$150,000 - 1,000P}{1,000P} = .4$$

yields $P = \$107.14$ per share.

CHAPTER FOUR

MUTUAL FUNDS AND OTHER INVESTMENT COMPANIES

THE PREVIOUS CHAPTER introduced you to the mechanics of trading securities and the structure of the markets in which securities trade. Commonly, however, individual investors do not trade securities directly for their own accounts. Instead, they direct their funds to investment companies that purchase securities on their behalf. The most important of these financial intermediaries are open-end investment companies, more commonly known as mutual funds, to which we devote most of this chapter. We also touch briefly on other types of investment companies such as unit investment trusts, hedge funds, and closed-end funds. We begin the chapter by describing and comparing the various types of investment companies available to investors. We then examine the functions of mutual funds, their investment styles and policies, and the costs of investing in these funds. Next we take a first look at the investment performance of these funds. We consider the impact of expenses and turnover on net performance and examine the extent to which performance is consistent from one period to the next. In other words, will the mutual funds that were the best *past* performers be the best *future* performers? Finally, we discuss sources of information on mutual funds, and we consider in detail the information provided in the most comprehensive guide, Morningstar's *Mutual Fund Sourcebook*.

4.1   INVESTMENT COMPANIES

Investment companies are financial intermediaries that collect funds from individual investors and invest those funds in a potentially wide range of securities or other assets. Pooling of assets is the key idea behind investment companies. Each investor has a claim to the portfolio established by the investment company in proportion to the amount invested. These companies thus provide a mechanism for small investors to "team up" to obtain the benefits of large-scale investing.

Investment companies perform several important functions for their investors:

1. *Record keeping and administration.* Investment companies issue periodic status reports, keeping track of capital gains distributions, dividends, investments, and redemptions, and they may reinvest dividend and interest income for shareholders.

2. *Diversification and divisibility.* By pooling their money, investment companies enable investors to hold fractional shares of many different securities. They can act as large investors even if any individual shareholder cannot.

3. *Professional management.* Many, but not all, investment companies have full-time staffs of security analysts and portfolio managers who attempt to achieve superior investment results for their investors.

4. *Lower transaction costs.* Because they trade large blocks of securities, investment companies can achieve substantial savings on brokerage fees and commissions.

While all investment companies pool assets of individual investors, they also need to divide claims to those assets among those investors. Investors buy shares in investment companies, and ownership is proportional to the number of shares purchased. The value of each share is called the **net asset value,** or **NAV.** Net asset value equals assets minus liabilities expressed on a per-share basis:

$$\text{Net asset value} = \frac{\text{Market value of assets minus liabilities}}{\text{Shares outstanding}}$$

EXAMPLE 4.1   Net Asset Value

Consider a mutual fund that manages a portfolio of securities worth $120 million. Suppose the fund owes $4 million to its investment advisers and owes another $1 million for rent, wages due, and miscellaneous expenses. The fund has 5 million shares outstanding.

$$\text{Net asset value} = \frac{\$120 \text{ million} - \$5 \text{ million}}{5 \text{ million shares}} = \$23 \text{ per share}$$

CONCEPT CHECK 1	Consider these data from the December 31, 2006, balance sheet of Fidelity's Contrafund. What was the net asset value of the fund?
	Assets: $69,265.99 million
	Liabilities: $ 689.72 million
	Shares: 1,051.69 million

4.2   TYPES OF INVESTMENT COMPANIES

In the United States, investment companies are classified by the Investment Company Act of 1940 as either unit investment trusts or managed investment companies. The portfolios of unit investment trusts are essentially fixed and thus are called "unmanaged." In contrast, managed companies are so named because securities in their investment portfolios continually are bought and sold: The portfolios are managed. Managed companies are further classified as either closed-end or open-end. Open-end companies are what we commonly call mutual funds.

Unit Investment Trusts

Unit investment trusts are pools of money invested in a portfolio that is fixed for the life of the fund. To form a unit investment trust, a sponsor, typically a brokerage firm, buys a portfolio of securities that are deposited into a trust. It then sells to the public shares, or "units," in the trust, called *redeemable trust certificates*. All income and payments of principal from the portfolio are paid out by the fund's trustees (a bank or trust company) to the shareholders.

There is little active management of a unit investment trust because once established, the portfolio composition is fixed; hence these trusts are referred to as *unmanaged*. Trusts tend to invest in relatively uniform types of assets; for example, one trust may invest in municipal bonds, another in corporate bonds. The uniformity of the portfolio is consistent with the lack of active management. The trusts provide investors a vehicle to purchase a pool of one particular type of asset that can be included in an overall portfolio as desired.

Sponsors of unit investment trusts earn their profit by selling shares in the trust at a premium to the cost of acquiring the underlying assets. For example, a trust that has purchased $5 million of assets may sell 5,000 shares to the public at a price of $1,030 per share, which (assuming the trust has no liabilities) represents a 3% premium over the net asset value of the securities held by the trust. The 3% premium is the trustee's fee for establishing the trust.

Investors who wish to liquidate their holdings of a unit investment trust may sell the shares back to the trustee for net asset value. The trustees can either sell enough securities from the asset portfolio to obtain the cash necessary to pay the investor, or they may instead sell the shares to a new investor (again at a slight premium to net asset value). Unit investment trusts have steadily lost market share to mutual funds in recent years. Assets in such trusts declined from $105 billion in 1990 to only $50 billion in early 2007.

Managed Investment Companies

There are two types of managed companies: closed-end and open-end. In both cases, the fund's board of directors, which is elected by shareholders, hires a management company to manage the portfolio for an annual fee that typically ranges from .2% to 1.5% of assets. In many cases the management company is the firm that organized the fund. For example, Fidelity Management and Research Corporation sponsors many Fidelity mutual funds and is responsible for managing the portfolios. It assesses a management fee on each Fidelity fund. In other cases, a mutual fund will hire an outside portfolio manager. For example, Vanguard has hired Wellington Management as the investment adviser for its Wellington Fund. Most management companies have contracts to manage several funds.

Open-end funds stand ready to redeem or issue shares at their net asset value (although both purchases and redemptions may involve sales charges). When investors in open-end funds wish to "cash out" their shares, they sell them back to the fund at NAV. In contrast, **closed-end funds** do not redeem or issue shares. Investors in closed-end funds who wish to cash out must sell their shares to other investors. Shares of closed-end funds are traded on organized exchanges and can be purchased through brokers just like other common stock; their prices, therefore, can differ from NAV.

Figure 4.1 is a listing of closed-end funds. The first column gives the name and ticker symbol of the fund. The next two columns give the fund's most recent net asset value and closing share price. The premium or discount in the next column is the percentage difference between price and NAV: (Price – NAV)/NAV. Notice that there are more funds selling at discounts to NAV (indicated by negative differences) than premiums. Finally, the 52-week return based on the percentage change in share price plus dividend income is presented in the last column.

The common divergence of price from net asset value, often by wide margins, is a puzzle that has yet to be fully explained. To see why this is a puzzle, consider a closed-end fund that is selling at a discount from net asset value. If the fund were to sell all the assets in the portfolio, it would realize proceeds equal to net asset value. The difference between the market price of the fund and the fund's NAV would represent the per-share increase in the wealth of the fund's investors. Moreover, several studies[1] have shown that on average, fund premiums or discounts tend to dissipate over time, so funds selling at a discount receive a boost to their rate of return as the discount shrinks. Pontiff[2] estimates that a fund selling at a 20% discount would have an expected 12-month return more than 6% greater than funds selling at net asset value.

Interestingly, while many closed-end funds sell at a discount from net asset value, the prices of these funds when originally issued are often above NAV. This is a further puzzle, as it is hard to explain why investors would purchase these newly issued funds at a premium to NAV when the shares tend to fall to a discount shortly after issue.

In contrast to closed-end funds, the price of open-end funds cannot fall below NAV, because these funds stand ready to redeem shares at NAV. The offering price will exceed NAV, however, if the fund carries a **load.** A load is, in effect, a sales charge, which is paid to the seller. Load funds are sold by securities brokers and directly by mutual fund groups.

Unlike closed-end funds, open-end mutual funds do not trade on organized exchanges. Instead, investors simply buy shares from and liquidate through the investment company at net asset value. Thus the number of outstanding shares of these funds changes daily. In early 2007, about $300 billion of assets were held in closed-end funds.

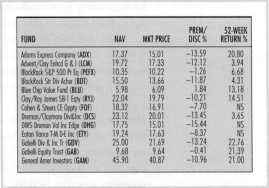

FUND	NAV	MKT PRICE	PREM/ DISC %	52-WEEK RETURN %
Adams Express Company (ADX)	17.37	15.01	−13.59	20.80
Advent/Clay Enhcd G & I (LCM)	19.72	17.33	−12.12	3.94
BlackRock S&P 500 Pr Eq (PEFX)	10.35	10.22	−1.26	6.68
BlackRock Str Div Achvr (BDT)	15.50	13.66	−11.87	4.31
Blue Chip Value Fund (BLU)	5.98	6.09	1.84	13.18
Clay/Ray James SB-1 Eqty (RYJ)	22.04	19.79	−10.21	14.51
Cohen & Steers CE Oppty (FOF)	18.32	16.91	−7.70	NS
Dreman/Claymore Div&Inc (DCS)	23.12	20.01	−13.45	3.65
DWS Dreman Val Inc Edge (DHG)	17.75	15.01	−15.44	NS
Eaton Vance T-M D-E Inc (ETY)	19.24	17.63	−8.37	NS
Gabelli Div & Inc Tr (GDV)	25.00	21.69	−13.24	22.76
Gabelli Equity Trust (GAB)	9.68	9.64	−0.41	21.39
General Amer Investors (GAM)	45.90	40.87	−10.96	21.00

FIGURE 4.1   Closed-end mutual funds

Source: Data compiled from *The Wall Street Journal* Online, September 28, 2007.

Other Investment Organizations

There are intermediaries not formally organized or regulated as investment companies that nevertheless serve functions similar to investment companies. Three of the more important are commingled funds, real estate investment trusts, and hedge funds.

Commingled Funds   Commingled funds are partnerships of investors that pool their funds. The management firm that organizes the partnership, for example, a bank or insurance company, manages the funds for a fee. Typical partners in a commingled fund might be trust or retirement accounts with portfolios much larger than those of most individual investors, but still too small to warrant managing on a separate basis.

Commingled funds are similar in form to open-end mutual funds. Instead of shares, though, the fund offers *units,* which are bought and sold at net asset value. A bank or insurance company may offer an array of different commingled funds, for example, a money market fund, a bond fund, and a common stock fund.

Real Estate Investment Trusts (REITs)   A REIT is similar to a closed-end fund. REITs invest in real estate or loans secured by real estate. Besides issuing shares, they raise capital

[1]See, for example, Rex Thompson, "The Information Content of Discounts and Premiums on Closed-End Fund Shares," *Journal of Financial Economics* 6 (1978), pp.151–86.

[2]Jeffrey Pontiff, "Costly Arbitrage: Evidence from Closed-End Funds," *Quarterly Journal of Economics* 111 (November 1996), pp. 1135–51.

by borrowing from banks and issuing bonds or mortgages. Most of them are highly leveraged, with a typical debt ratio of 70%.

There are two principal kinds of REITs. *Equity trusts* invest in real estate directly, whereas *mortgage trusts* invest primarily in mortgage and construction loans. REITs generally are established by banks, insurance companies, or mortgage companies, which then serve as investment managers to earn a fee.

Hedge Funds   Like mutual funds, **hedge funds** are vehicles that allow private investors to pool assets to be invested by a fund manager. Unlike mutual funds, however, hedge funds are commonly structured as private partnerships and thus subject to only minimal SEC regulation. They typically are open only to wealthy or institutional investors. Many require investors to agree to initial "lock-ups," that is, periods as long as several years in which investments cannot be withdrawn. Lock-ups allow hedge funds to invest in illiquid assets without worrying about meeting demands for redemption of funds. Moreover, because hedge funds are only lightly regulated, their managers can pursue investment strategies involving, for example, heavy use of derivatives, short sales, and leverage; such strategies typically are not open to mutual fund managers.

Hedge funds by design are empowered to invest in a wide range of investments, with various funds focusing on derivatives, distressed firms, currency speculation, convertible bonds, emerging markets, merger arbitrage, and so on. Other funds may jump from one asset class to another as perceived investment opportunities shift.

Hedge funds have enjoyed great growth in the last several years, with assets under management ballooning from about $50 billion in 1990 to around $1.4 trillion in 2007. Because of their recent prominence, we devote all of Chapter 26 to these funds.

4.3   MUTUAL FUNDS

Mutual funds are the common name for open-end investment companies. This is the dominant investment company today, accounting for more than 90% of investment company assets. Assets under management in the U.S. mutual fund industry were over $10 trillion in 2007, and approximately another $9 trillion was held in non-U.S. funds.

Investment Policies

Each mutual fund has a specified investment policy, which is described in the fund's prospectus. For example, money market mutual funds hold the short-term, low-risk instruments of the money market (see Chapter 2 for a review of these securities), while bond funds hold fixed-income securities. Some funds have even more narrowly defined mandates. For example, some bond funds will hold primarily Treasury bonds, others primarily mortgage-backed securities.

Management companies manage a family, or "complex," of mutual funds. They organize an entire collection of funds and then collect a management fee for operating them. By managing a collection of funds under one umbrella, these companies make it easy for investors to allocate assets across market sectors and to switch assets across funds while still benefiting from centralized record keeping. Some of the most well-known management companies are Fidelity, Vanguard, Putnam, and Dreyfus. Each offers an array of open-end mutual funds with different investment policies. In early 2007, there were more than 8,000 mutual funds in the U.S., which were offered by fewer than 500 fund complexes.

Some of the more important fund types, classified by investment policy, are discussed next.

Money Market Funds   These funds invest in money market securities such as commercial paper, repurchase agreements, or certificates of deposit. The average maturity of these assets tends to be a bit more than 1 month. Money market funds usually offer check-writing features, and net asset value is fixed at $1 per share, so that there are no tax implications such as capital gains or losses associated with redemption of shares.

Equity Funds   Equity funds invest primarily in stock, although they may, at the portfolio manager's discretion, also hold fixed-income or other types of securities. Funds commonly will hold between 4% and 5% of total assets in money market securities to provide liquidity necessary to meet potential redemption of shares.

It is traditional to classify stock funds according to their emphasis on capital appreciation versus current income. Thus, *income funds* tend to hold shares of firms with consistently high dividend yields. *Growth funds* are willing to forgo current income, focusing instead on prospects for capital gains. While the classification of these funds is couched in terms of income versus capital gains, it is worth noting that in practice the more relevant distinction concerns the level of risk these funds assume. Growth stocks, and therefore growth funds, are typically riskier and respond far more dramatically to changes in economic conditions than do income funds.

Sector Funds   Some equity funds, called *sector* funds, concentrate on a particular industry. For example, Fidelity markets dozens of "select funds," each of which invests in a specific industry such as biotechnology, utilities, precious metals, or telecommunications. Other funds specialize in securities of particular countries.

Bond Funds   As the name suggests, these funds specialize in the fixed-income sector. Within that sector, however, there is considerable room for specialization. For example, various funds will concentrate on corporate bonds, Treasury bonds, mortgage-backed securities, or municipal (tax-free) bonds. Indeed, some of the municipal bond funds will invest only in bonds of a particular state (or even city!) to satisfy the investment desires of residents of that state who wish to avoid local as well as federal taxes on the interest paid on the bonds. Many funds will also specialize by the maturity of the securities, ranging from short-term to intermediate to long-term, or by the credit risk of the issuer, ranging from very safe to high-yield or "junk" bonds.

International Funds   Many funds have international focus. *Global funds* invest in securities worldwide, including the United States. In contrast, *international funds* invest in securities of firms located outside the United States. *Regional funds* concentrate on a particular part of the world, and *emerging market funds* invest in companies of developing nations.

Balanced Funds   Some funds are designed to be candidates for an individual's entire investment portfolio. These balanced funds hold both equities and fixed-income securities in relatively stable proportions. *Life-cycle funds* are balanced funds in which the asset mix can range from aggressive (primarily marketed to younger investors) to conservative (directed at older investors). Static allocation life-cycle funds maintain a stable mix across stocks and bonds, while *targeted-maturity funds* gradually become more conservative as the investor ages.

Asset Allocation and Flexible Funds   These funds are similar to balanced funds in that they hold both stocks and bonds. However, asset allocation funds may dramatically vary the proportions allocated to each market in accord with the portfolio manager's forecast of the relative performance of each sector. Hence these funds are engaged in market timing and are not designed to be low-risk investment vehicles.

Index Funds   An index fund tries to match the performance of a broad market index. The fund buys shares in securities included in a particular index in proportion to each security's representation in that index. For example, the Vanguard 500 Index Fund is a mutual fund that replicates the composition of the Standard & Poor's 500 stock price index. Because the S&P 500 is a value-weighted index, the fund buys shares in each S&P 500 company in proportion to the market value of that company's outstanding equity. Investment in an index fund is a low-cost way for small investors to pursue a passive investment strategy— that is, to invest without engaging in security analysis. Of course, index funds can be tied to nonequity indexes as well. For example, Vanguard offers a bond index fund and a real estate index fund.

Table 4.1 breaks down the number of mutual funds by investment orientation. Often a fund name describes its investment policy. For example, Vanguard's GNMA fund invests in mortgage-backed securities, the Municipal Intermediate fund invests in intermediate-term municipal bonds, and the High-Yield Corporate bond fund invests in large part in speculative grade, or "junk," bonds with high yields. However, names of common stock funds frequently reflect little or nothing about their investment policies. Examples are Vanguard's Windsor and Wellington funds.

TABLE 4.1 U.S. mutual funds by investment classification		Assets ($ billion)	% of Total Assets	Number of Funds
	Equity funds			
	Capital appreciation focus	$ 2,701.0	25.9%	3,070
	World/international	1,314.1	12.6	915
	Total return	1,896.5	18.2	785
	Total equity funds	$ 5,911.6	56.8%	4,770
	Bond funds			
	Corporate	$ 272.2	2.6%	289
	High yield	156.2	1.5	207
	World	59.4	0.6	113
	Government	193.0	1.9	309
	Strategic income	448.6	4.3	364
	Single-state municipal	154.9	1.5	481
	National municipal	210.0	2.0	230
	Total bond funds	$ 1,494.4	14.4%	1,993
	Hybrid (bond/stock) funds	$ 653.1	6.3%	508
	Money market funds			
	Taxable	$ 1,988.1	19.1%	576
	Tax-exempt	366.4	3.5	273
	Total money market funds	$ 2,354.5	22.6%	849
	Total	$10,413.6	100.0%	8,120

Note: Column sums subject to rounding error.
Source: Investment Company Institute, 2007 *Mutual Fund Fact Book*.

How Funds Are Sold

Most mutual funds have an underwriter that has exclusive rights to distribute shares to investors. Mutual funds are generally marketed to the public either directly by the fund underwriter or indirectly through brokers acting on behalf of the underwriter. Direct-marketed funds are sold through the mail, various offices of the fund, over the phone, or, more so, over the Internet. Investors contact the fund directly to purchase shares.

About half of fund sales today are distributed through a sales force. Brokers or financial advisers receive a commission for selling shares to investors. (Ultimately, the commission is paid by the investor. More on this shortly.) In some cases, funds use a "captive" sales force that sells only shares in funds of the mutual fund group they represent.

Investors who rely on their broker's advice to select their mutual funds should be aware that brokers may have a conflict of interest with regard to fund selection. This arises from a practice called *revenue sharing,* in which fund companies pay the brokerage firm for preferential treatment when making investment recommendations.

Revenue sharing poses potential conflicts of interest if it induces brokers to recommend mutual funds based on criteria other than the best interests of their clients. In addition, the mutual fund may be violating its obligation to its existing investors if it uses fund assets to pay brokers for favored status in new sales. SEC rules require brokerage firms to explicitly reveal any compensation or other incentives they receive to sell a particular fund, both at the time of sale and in the trade confirmation.

Many funds also are sold through "financial supermarkets" that sell shares in funds of many complexes. Instead of charging customers a sales commission, the broker splits management fees with the mutual fund company. Another advantage is unified record keeping for all funds purchased from the supermarket, even if the funds are offered by different complexes. On the other hand, many contend that these supermarkets result in higher expense ratios because mutual funds pass along the costs of participating in these programs in the form of higher management fees.

4.4   COSTS OF INVESTING IN MUTUAL FUNDS

Fee Structure

An individual investor choosing a mutual fund should consider not only the fund's stated investment policy and past performance but also its management fees and other expenses. Comparative data on virtually all important aspects of mutual funds are available in the annual reports prepared by CDA Wiesenberger Investment Companies Services or in Morningstar's *Mutual Fund Sourcebook,* which can be found in many academic and public libraries. You should be aware of four general classes of fees.

Operating Expenses   Operating expenses are the costs incurred by the mutual fund in operating the portfolio, including administrative expenses and advisory fees paid to the investment manager. These expenses, usually expressed as a percentage of total assets under management, may range from 0.2% to 2%. Shareholders do not receive an explicit bill for these operating expenses; however, the expenses periodically are deducted from the assets of the fund. Shareholders pay for these expenses through the reduced value of the portfolio.

In addition to operating expenses, many funds assess fees to pay for marketing and distribution costs. These charges are used primarily to pay the brokers or financial advisers who sell the funds to the public. Investors can avoid these expenses by buying shares directly from the fund sponsor, but many investors are willing to incur these distribution fees in return for the advice they may receive from their broker.

Front-End Load   A front-end load is a commission or sales charge paid when you purchase the shares. These charges, which are used primarily to pay the brokers who sell the funds, may not exceed 8.5%, but in practice they are rarely higher than 6%. *Low-load funds* have loads that range up to 3% of invested funds. *No-load funds* have no front-end sales charges. Loads effectively reduce the amount of money invested. For example, each $1,000 paid for a fund with a 6% load results in a sales charge of $60 and fund investment of only $940. You need cumulative returns of 6.4% of your net investment (60/940 = .064) just to break even.

Back-End Load   A back-end load is a redemption, or "exit," fee incurred when you sell your shares. Typically, funds that impose back-end loads start them at 5% or 6% and reduce them by 1 percentage point for every year the funds are left invested. Thus an exit fee that starts at 6% would fall to 4% by the start of your third year. These charges are known more formally as "contingent deferred sales charges."

12b-1 Charges   The Securities and Exchange Commission allows the managers of so-called 12b-1 funds to use fund assets to pay for distribution costs such as advertising, promotional literature including annual reports and prospectuses, and, most important, commissions paid to brokers who sell the fund to investors. These **12b-1 fees** are named after the SEC rule that permits use of these plans. Funds may use 12b-1 charges instead of, or in addition to, front-end loads to generate the fees with which to pay brokers. As with operating expenses, investors are not explicitly billed for 12b-1 charges. Instead, the fees are deducted from the assets of the fund. Therefore, 12b-1 fees (if any) must be added to operating expenses to obtain the true annual expense ratio of the fund. The SEC requires that all funds include in the prospectus a consolidated expense table that summarizes all relevant fees. The 12b-1 fees are limited to 1% of a fund's average net assets per year.[3]

Many funds offer "classes" that represent ownership in the same portfolio of securities, but with different combinations of fees. For example Class A shares might have front-end loads while Class B shares rely on 12b-1 fees.

EXAMPLE 4.2   Fees for Various Classes (Dreyfus Founders Core Equity Fund)

Here are fees for different classes of the Dreyfus Founders Core Equity Fund in 2007. Notice the trade-off between the front-end loads versus 12b-1 charges.

	Class A	Class B	Class C	Class T
Front-end load	0–5.75%[a]	0	0	0–4.50%[a]
Back-end load	0	0–4%[b]	0–1%[b]	0
12b-1 fees[c]	.25%	1.0%	1.0%	.50%
Expense ratio	1.16%	1.35%	1.17%	1.27%

[a]Depending on size of investment.
[b]Depending on years until holdings are sold.
[c]Including service fee.

---

[3]The maximum 12b-1 charge for the sale of the fund is .75%. However, an additional service fee of .25% of the fund's assets also is allowed for personal service and/or maintenance of shareholder accounts.

Each investor must choose the best combination of fees. Obviously, pure no-load no-fee funds distributed directly by the mutual fund group are the cheapest alternative, and these will often make most sense for knowledgeable investors. However, as we have noted, many investors are willing to pay for financial advice, and the commissions paid to advisers who sell these funds are the most common form of payment. Alternatively, investors may choose to hire a fee-only financial manager who charges directly for services and does not accept commissions. These advisers can help investors select portfolios of low- or no-load funds (as well as provide other financial advice). Independent financial planners have become increasingly important distribution channels for funds in recent years.

If you do buy a fund through a broker, the choice between paying a load and paying 12b-1 fees will depend primarily on your expected time horizon. Loads are paid only once for each purchase, whereas 12b-1 fees are paid annually. Thus, if you plan to hold your fund for a long time, a one-time load may be preferable to recurring 12b-1 charges.

Fees and Mutual Fund Returns

The rate of return on an investment in a mutual fund is measured as the increase or decrease in net asset value plus income distributions such as dividends or distributions of capital gains expressed as a fraction of net asset value at the beginning of the investment period. If we denote the net asset value at the start and end of the period as NAV_0 and NAV_1, respectively, then

$$\text{Rate of return} = \frac{NAV_1 - NAV_0 + \text{Income and capital gain distributions}}{NAV_0}$$

For example, if a fund has an initial NAV of $20 at the start of the month, makes income distributions of $.15 and capital gain distributions of $.05, and ends the month with NAV of $20.10, the monthly rate of return is computed as

$$\text{Rate of return} = \frac{\$20.10 - \$20.00 + \$.15 + \$.05}{\$20.00} = .015, \text{ or } 1.5\%$$

Notice that this measure of the rate of return ignores any commissions such as front-end loads paid to purchase the fund.

On the other hand, the rate of return is affected by the fund's expenses and 12b-1 fees. This is because such charges are periodically deducted from the portfolio, which reduces net asset value. Thus the rate of return on the fund equals the gross return on the underlying portfolio minus the total expense ratio.

EXAMPLE 4.3   Fees and Net Returns

To see how expenses can affect rate of return, consider a fund with $100 million in assets at the start of the year and with 10 million shares outstanding. The fund invests in a portfolio of stocks that provides no income but increases in value by 10%. The expense ratio, including 12b-1 fees, is 1%. What is the rate of return for an investor in the fund?

The initial NAV equals $100 million/10 million shares = $10 per share. In the absence of expenses, fund assets would grow to $110 million and NAV would grow to $11 per share, for a 10% rate of return. However, the expense ratio of the fund is 1%. Therefore, $1 million will be deducted from the fund to pay these fees, leaving the portfolio worth only $109 million, and NAV equal to $10.90. The rate of return on the fund is only 9%, which equals the gross return on the underlying portfolio minus the total expense ratio.

TABLE 4.2

Impact of costs on investment performance

	Cumulative Proceeds (All Dividends Reinvested)		
	Fund A	Fund B	Fund C
Initial investment*	$10,000	$10,000	$ 9,200
5 years	17,234	16,474	15,502
10 years	29,699	27,141	26,123
15 years	51,183	44,713	44,018
20 years	88,206	73,662	74,173

*After front-end load, if any.
Notes:
1. Fund A is no-load with .5% expense ratio.
2. Fund B is no-load with 1.5% expense ratio.
3. Fund C has an 8% load on purchases and a 1% expense ratio.
4. Gross return on all funds is 12% per year before expenses.

Fees can have a big effect on performance. Table 4.2 considers an investor who starts with $10,000 and can choose among three funds that all earn an annual 12% return on investment before fees but have different fee structures. The table shows the cumulative amount in each fund after several investment horizons. Fund A has total operating expenses of .5%, no load, and no 12b-1 charges. This might represent a low-cost producer like Vanguard. Fund B has no load but has 1% in management expenses and .5% in 12b-1 fees. This level of charges is fairly typical of actively managed equity funds. Finally, Fund C has 1% in management expenses, no 12b-1 charges, but assesses an 8% front-end load on purchases.

Note the substantial return advantage of low-cost Fund A. Moreover, that differential is greater for longer investment horizons.

CONCEPT CHECK 2

The Equity Fund sells Class A shares with a front-end load of 4% and Class B shares with 12b-1 fees of .5% annually as well as back-end load fees that start at 5% and fall by 1% for each full year the investor holds the portfolio (until the fifth year). Assume the rate of return on the fund portfolio net of operating expenses is 10% annually. What will be the value of a $10,000 investment in Class A and Class B shares if the shares are sold after (a) 1 year, (b) 4 years, (c) 10 years? Which fee structure provides higher net proceeds at the end of the investment horizon?

Although expenses can have a big impact on net investment performance, it is sometimes difficult for the investor in a mutual fund to measure true expenses accurately. This is because of the common practice of paying for some expenses in **soft dollars.** A portfolio manager earns soft-dollar credits with a brokerage firm by directing the fund's trades to that broker. Based on those credits, the broker will pay for some of the mutual fund's expenses, such as databases, computer hardware, or stock-quotation systems. The soft-dollar arrangement means that the stockbroker effectively returns part of the trading commission to the fund. Purchases made with soft dollars are not included in the fund's expenses, so funds with extensive soft dollar arrangements may report artificially low expense ratios to the public. However, the fund may have paid its broker needlessly high commissions to obtain its soft-dollar "rebate." The impact of the higher trading commission shows up in net investment performance rather than the reported expense ratio.

Late Trading and Market Timing

Mutual funds calculate net asset value (NAV) at the end of each trading day. All buy or sell orders arriving during the day are executed at that NAV following the market close at 4:00 p.m. New York time. Allowing some favored investors to buy shares in the fund below NAV or redeem their shares for more than NAV would obviously benefit those investors, but at the expense of the remaining shareholders. Yet, that is precisely what many mutual funds did until these practices were exposed in 2003.

Late trading refers to the practice of accepting buy or sell orders after the market closes and NAV is determined. Suppose that based on market closing prices at 4:00, a fund's NAV equals $100, but at 4:30, some positive economic news is announced. While NAV already has been fixed, it is clear that the fair market value of each share now exceeds $100. If they are able to submit a late order, investors can buy shares at the now-stale NAV and redeem them the next day after prices and NAV have adjusted to reflect the news. Late traders therefore can buy shares in the fund at a price below what NAV would be if it reflected up-to-date information. This transfers value from the other shareholders to the privileged traders and shows up as a reduction in the rate of return of the mutual fund.

Market timing also exploits stale prices. Consider the hypothetical "Pacific Basin Mutual Fund," which specializes in Japanese stocks. Because of time-zone differences, the Japanese market closes several hours before trading ends in New York. NAV is set based on the closing price of the Japanese shares. If the U.S. market jumps significantly while the Japanese market is closed, however, it is likely that Japanese prices will rise when the market opens in Japan the next day. A market timer will buy the Pacific Basin fund in the U.S. today at its now-stale NAV, planning to redeem those shares the next day for a likely profit. While such activity often is characterized as rapid in-and-out trading, the more salient issue is that the market timer is allowed to transact at a stale price.

While late trading clearly violates securities laws, market timing does not. However, many funds that claimed to prohibit or discourage such trading actually allowed it, at least for some customers. Why did they engage in practices that reduced the rate of return to most shareholders? The answer is the management fee. Market timers and late traders in essence paid for their access to such practices by investing large amounts in the funds on which the fund manager charged its management fee. Of course, the traders possibly earned far more than those fees through their trading activity, but those costs were borne by the other shareholders, not the fund sponsor.

By mid-2004, mutual fund sponsors had paid more than $1.65 billion in penalties to settle allegations of improper trading. In addition, new rules have been implemented and others proposed to eliminate these illicit practices. These include:

- *4:00 p.m. hard cutoff.* Strict policies that a trade order must arrive at the mutual fund (not merely an intermediary such as a broker) by 4:00 to be executed. Orders arriving after 4:00 are deferred until the close of the next trading day.

- *Fair-value pricing.* When computing fund NAV, prices of securities in closed markets are adjusted to reflect the likely impact of big price changes in open markets.

- *Redemption fees.* A redemption fee of 2% or more to be charged on mutual fund shares sold within 1 week of purchase. These fees would be paid not to the management company, but directly into the fund to compensate other investors for potential losses due to the rapid trading.

4.5   TAXATION OF MUTUAL FUND INCOME

Investment returns of mutual funds are granted "pass-through status" under the U.S. tax code, meaning that taxes are paid only by the investor in the mutual fund, not by the fund itself. The income is treated as passed through to the investor as long as the fund meets several requirements, most notably that virtually all income is distributed to shareholders. A fund's short-term capital gains, long-term capital gains, and dividends are passed through to investors as though the investor earned the income directly.

The pass-through of investment income has one important disadvantage for individual investors. If you manage your own portfolio, you decide when to realize capital gains and losses on any security; therefore, you can time those realizations to efficiently manage your tax liabilities. When you invest through a mutual fund, however, the timing of the sale of securities from the portfolio is out of your control, which reduces your ability to engage in tax management.[4] Of course, if the mutual fund is held in a tax-deferred retirement account such as an IRA or 401(k) account, these tax management issues are irrelevant.

A fund with a high portfolio turnover rate can be particularly "tax inefficient." **Turnover** is the ratio of the trading activity of a portfolio to the assets of the portfolio. It measures the fraction of the portfolio that is "replaced" each year. For example, a $100 million portfolio with $50 million in sales of some securities with purchases of other securities would have a turnover rate of 50%. High turnover means that capital gains or losses are being realized constantly, and therefore that the investor cannot time the realizations to manage his or her overall tax obligation.

Turnover rates in equity funds in the last decade have typically been around 60% when weighted by assets under management. By contrast, a low-turnover fund such as an index fund may have turnover as low as 2%, which is both tax-efficient and economical with respect to trading costs.

**CONCEPT
CHECK
3**

An investor's portfolio currently is worth $1 million. During the year, the investor sells 1,000 shares of Microsoft at a price of $80 per share and 2,000 shares of Ford at a price of $40 per share. The proceeds are used to buy 1,600 shares of IBM at $100 per share.

a. What was the portfolio turnover rate?

b. If the shares in Microsoft originally were purchased for $70 each and those in Ford were purchased for $35, and the investor's tax rate on capital gains income is 20%, how much extra will the investor owe on this year's taxes as a result of these transactions?

4.6   EXCHANGE–TRADED FUNDS

Exchange-traded funds (ETFs), first introduced in 1993, are offshoots of mutual funds that allow investors to trade index portfolios just as they do shares of stock. The first ETF was the "spider," a nickname for SPDR, or Standard & Poor's Depository Receipt, which

---

[4]An interesting problem that an investor needs to be aware of derives from the fact that capital gains and dividends on mutual funds are typically paid out to shareholders once or twice a year. This means that an investor who has just purchased shares in a mutual fund can receive a capital gain distribution (and be taxed on that distribution)on transactions that occurred long before he or she purchased shares in the fund. This is particularly a concern late in the year when such distributions typically are made.

is a unit investment trust holding a portfolio matching the S&P 500 index. Unlike mutual funds, which can be bought or sold only at the end of the day when NAV is calculated, investors can trade spiders throughout the day, just like any other share of stock. Spiders gave rise to many similar products such as "diamonds" (based on the Dow Jones Industrial Average, ticker DIA), "Cubes" (based on the NASDAQ 100 index, ticker QQQQ), and "WEBS" (World Equity Benchmark Shares, which are shares in portfolios of foreign stock market indexes). By 2007, about $425 billion were invested in over 300 ETFs. Table 4.3, panel A, presents some of the major sponsors of ETFs; panel B gives a flavor of the types of funds offered.

ETFs offer several advantages over conventional mutual funds. First, as we just noted, a mutual fund's net asset value is quoted—and therefore, investors can buy or sell their shares in the fund—only once a day. In contrast, ETFs trade continuously. Moreover, like other shares, but unlike mutual funds, ETFs can be sold short or purchased on margin.

ETFs also offer a potential tax advantage over mutual funds. When large numbers of mutual fund investors redeem their shares, the fund must sell securities to meet the redemptions. This can trigger capital gains taxes, which are passed through to and must be paid by the remaining shareholders. In contrast, when small investors wish to redeem their position in an ETF, they simply sell their shares to other traders, with no need for the fund to sell

A. ETF Sponsors	
Sponsor	**Product Name**
Barclays Global Investors	i-Shares
Merrill Lynch	HOLDRS (Holding Company Depository Receipts: "Holders")
StateStreet/Merrill Lynch	Select Sector SPDRs (S&P Depository Receipts: "Spiders")
Vanguard	VIPER (Vanguard Index Participation Equity Receipts: "Vipers")

B. Sample of ETF Products		
Name	**Ticker**	**Index Tracked**
Broad U.S. indexes		
Spiders	SPY	S&P 500
Diamonds	DIA	Dow Jones Industrials
Cubes	QQQQ	NASDAQ 100
iShares Russell 2000	IWM	Russell 2000
Total Stock Market VIPERS	VTI	Wilshire 5000
Industry indexes		
Energy Select Spider	XLE	S&P 500 energy companies
iShares Energy Sector	IYE	Dow Jones energy companies
Financial Sector Spider	XLF	S&P 500 financial companies
iShares Financial Sector	IYF	Dow Jones financial companies
International indexes		
WEBS United Kingdom	EWU	MCSI U.K. Index
WEBS France	EWQ	MCSI France Index
WEBS Japan	EWJ	MCSI Japan Index

TABLE 4.3

ETF sponsors and products

any of the underlying portfolio. Large investors can exchange their ETF shares for shares in the underlying portfolio; this form of redemption also avoids a tax event.

ETFs are also cheaper than mutual funds. Investors who buy ETFs do so through brokers rather than buying directly from the fund. Therefore, the fund saves the cost of marketing itself directly to small investors. This reduction in expenses translates into lower management fees.

There are some disadvantages to ETFs, however. Because they trade as securities, there is the possibility that their prices can depart by small amounts from net asset value before arbitrage activity restores equality. Even small discrepancies can easily swamp the cost advantage of ETFs over mutual funds. Second, while mutual funds can be bought at no expense from no-load funds, ETFs must be purchased from brokers for a fee.

4.7   MUTUAL FUND INVESTMENT PERFORMANCE: A FIRST LOOK

We noted earlier that one of the benefits of mutual funds for the individual investor is the ability to delegate management of the portfolio to investment professionals. The investor retains control over the broad features of the overall portfolio through the asset allocation decision: Each individual chooses the percentages of the portfolio to invest in bond funds versus equity funds versus money market funds, and so forth, but can leave the specific security selection decisions within each investment class to the managers of each fund. Shareholders hope that these portfolio managers can achieve better investment performance than they could obtain on their own.

What is the investment record of the mutual fund industry? This seemingly straightforward question is deceptively difficult to answer because we need a standard against which to evaluate performance. For example, we clearly would not want to compare the investment performance of an equity fund to the rate of return available in the money market. The vast differences in the risk of these two markets dictate that year-by-year as well as average performance will differ considerably. We would expect to find that equity funds outperform money market funds (on average) as compensation to investors for the extra risk incurred in equity markets. How then can we determine whether mutual fund portfolio managers are performing up to par *given* the level of risk they incur? In other words, what is the proper benchmark against which investment performance ought to be evaluated?

Measuring portfolio risk properly and using such measures to choose an appropriate benchmark is an extremely difficult task. We devote all of Parts Two and Three of the text to issues surrounding the proper measurement of portfolio risk and the trade-off between risk and return. In this chapter, therefore, we will satisfy ourselves with a first look at the question of fund performance by using only very simple performance benchmarks and ignoring the more subtle issues of risk differences across funds. However, we will return to this topic in Chapter 11, where we take a closer look at mutual fund performance after adjusting for differences in the exposure of portfolios to various sources of risk.

Here we use as a benchmark for the performance of equity fund managers the rate of return on the Wilshire 5000 index. Recall from Chapter 2 that this is a value-weighted index of more than 5,400 stocks that trade on the NYSE, NASDAQ, and Amex stock markets. It is the most inclusive index of the performance of U.S. equities. The performance of the Wilshire 5000 is a useful benchmark with which to evaluate professional managers because it corresponds to a simple passive investment strategy: Buy all the shares in the index in proportion to their outstanding market value. Moreover, this is a feasible strategy for even small investors, because the Vanguard Group offers an index fund (its Total Stock Market Portfolio) designed to replicate the performance of the Wilshire 5000 index. Using the Wilshire 5000 index as a benchmark, we may pose the problem of evaluating the performance of mutual fund portfolio managers this way: How does the typical performance of actively managed equity mutual funds compare to the performance of a passively managed portfolio that simply replicates the composition of a broad index of the stock market?

Casual comparisons of the performance of the Wilshire 5000 index versus that of professionally managed mutual funds reveal disappointing results for active managers. Figure 4.2 shows that the average return on diversified equity funds was below the return on the Wilshire index in 21 of the 37 years from 1971 to 2007. The average annual return on the index was 12.8%, which was 1% greater than that of the average mutual fund.[5]

This result may seem surprising. After all, it would not seem unreasonable to expect that professional money managers should be able to outperform a very simple rule such as "hold an indexed portfolio." As it turns out, however, there may be good reasons to expect such a result. We explore them in detail in Chapter 11, where we discuss the efficient market hypothesis.

Of course, one might argue that there are good managers and bad managers, and that good managers can, in fact, consistently outperform the index. To test this notion, we examine whether managers with good performance in one year are likely to repeat that performance in a following year. Is superior performance in any particular year due to luck, and therefore random, or due to skill, and therefore consistent from year to year?

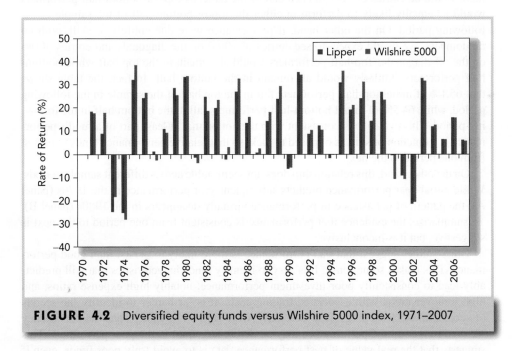

FIGURE 4.2 Diversified equity funds versus Wilshire 5000 index, 1971–2007

[5]Of course, actual funds incur trading costs while indexes do not, so a fair comparison between the returns on actively managed funds versus those on a passive index would first reduce the return on the Wilshire 5000 by an estimate of such costs. Vanguard's Total Stock Market Index portfolio, which tracks the Wilshire 5000, charges an expense ratio of .19%, and, because it engages in little trading, incurs low trading costs. Therefore, it would be reasonable to reduce the returns on the index by about .30%. This reduction would not erase the difference in average performance.

TABLE 4.4

Consistency
of investment results

Initial Period Performance	Successive Period Performance	
	Top Half	Bottom Half
A. Malkiel study, 1970s		
Top half	65.1%	34.9%
Bottom half	35.5	64.5
B. Malkiel study, 1980s		
Top half	51.7	48.3
Bottom half	47.5	52.5

Source: Burton G. Malkiel, "Returns from Investing in Equity Mutual Funds 1971–1991," *Journal of Finance* 50 (June 1995), pp. 549–72. Reprinted by permission of the publisher, Blackwell Publishing, Inc.

To answer this question, we can examine the performance of a large sample of equity mutual fund portfolios, divide the funds into two groups based on total investment return, and ask: "Do funds with investment returns in the top half of the sample in one period continue to perform well in a subsequent period?"

Table 4.4 presents such an analysis from a study by Malkiel.[6] The table shows the fraction of "winners" (i.e., top-half performers) in each year that turn out to be winners or losers in the following year. If performance were purely random from one period to the next, there would be entries of 50% in each cell of the table, as top- or bottom-half performers would be equally likely to perform in either the top or bottom half of the sample in the following period. On the other hand, if performance were due entirely to skill, with no randomness, we would expect to see entries of 100% on the diagonals and entries of 0% on the off-diagonals: Top-half performers would all remain in the top half while bottom-half performers similarly would all remain in the bottom half. In fact, the table shows that 65.1% of initial top-half performers fall in the top half of the sample in the following period, while 64.5% of initial bottom-half performers fall in the bottom half in the following period. This evidence is consistent with the notion that at least part of a fund's performance is a function of skill as opposed to luck, so that relative performance tends to persist from one period to the next.[7]

On the other hand, this relationship does not seem stable across different sample periods. While initial-year performance predicts subsequent-year performance in the 1970s (panel A), the pattern of persistence in performance virtually disappears in the 1980s (panel B). To summarize, the evidence that performance is consistent from one period to the next is suggestive, but it is inconclusive.

Other studies suggest that bad performance is more likely to persist than good performance. This makes some sense: It is easy to identify fund characteristics that will predictably lead to consistently poor investment performance, notably high expense ratios, and high turnover ratios with associated trading costs. It is far harder to identify the secrets of successful stock picking. (If it were easy, we would all be rich!) Thus the consistency we do observe in fund performance may be due in large part to the poor performers. This suggests that the real value of past performance data is to avoid truly poor funds, even if identifying the future top performers is still a daunting task.

[6]Burton G. Malkiel, "Returns from Investing in Equity Mutual Funds 1971–1991," *Journal of Finance* 50 (June 1995), pp. 549–72.

[7]Another possibility is that performance consistency is due to variation in fee structure across funds. We return to this possibility in Chapter 11.

CONCEPT CHECK 4	Suppose you observe the investment performance of 400 portfolio managers and rank them by investment returns during the year. Twenty percent of all managers are truly skilled, and therefore always fall in the top half, but the others fall in the top half purely because of good luck. What fraction of this year's top-half managers would you expect to be top-half performers next year?

4.8   INFORMATION ON MUTUAL FUNDS

The first place to find information on a mutual fund is in its prospectus. The Securities and Exchange Commission requires that the prospectus describe the fund's investment objectives and policies in a concise "Statement of Investment Objectives" as well as in lengthy discussions of investment policies and risks. The fund's investment adviser and its portfolio manager are also described. The prospectus also presents the costs associated with purchasing shares in the fund in a fee table. Sales charges such as front-end and back-end loads as well as annual operating expenses such as management fees and 12b-1 fees are detailed in the fee table.

Funds provide information about themselves in two other sources. The Statement of Additional Information or SAI, also known as Part B of the prospectus, includes a list of the securities in the portfolio at the end of the fiscal year, audited financial statements, a list of the directors and officers of the fund—as well as their personal investments in the fund, and data on brokerage commissions paid by the fund. However, unlike the fund prospectus, investors do not receive the SAI unless they specifically request it; one industry joke is that SAI stands for "something always ignored." The fund's annual report also includes portfolio composition and financial statements, as well as a discussion of the factors that influenced fund performance over the last reporting period.

With more than 8,000 mutual funds to choose from, it can be difficult to find and select the fund that is best suited for a particular need. Several publications now offer "encyclopedias" of mutual fund information to help in the search process. Two prominent sources are Wiesenberger's *Investment Companies* and Morningstar's *Mutual Fund Sourcebook.* Morningstar's Web site, **www.morningstar.com,** is another excellent source of information, as is Yahoo!'s site, **finance.yahoo.com/funds.** The Investment Company Institute (**www.ici.org**), the national association of mutual funds, closed-end funds, and unit investment trusts, publishes an annual *Directory of Mutual Funds* that includes information on fees as well as phone numbers to contact funds. To illustrate the range of information available about funds, we consider Morningstar's report on Fidelity's Magellan Fund, reproduced in Figure 4.3.

Some of Morningstar's analysis is qualitative. The top box on the left-hand side of the page of the report reproduced in the figure provides a short description of fund strategy, in particular the types of securities in which the fund manager tends to invest. The bottom box on the left ("Morningstar's Take") is a more detailed discussion of the fund's income strategy. The short statement of the fund's investment policy is in the top right-hand corner: Magellan is a "large growth" fund, meaning that it tends to invest in large firms, with an emphasis on growth over value stocks.

The table on the left in the figure labeled "Performance" reports on the fund's quarterly returns over the last few years and then over longer periods up to 15 years. Comparisons of returns to relevant indexes, in this case, the S&P 500 and the Russell 1000 indexes, are provided to serve as benchmarks in evaluating the performance of the fund. The values under

Data through June 30, 2007. Reprinted by permission of Morningstar.

Fidelity Magellan

	Ticker	Load	NAV	Yield	Total Assets	Mstar Category
	FMAGX	Closed	$93.80	0.3%	$44,373 mil	Large Growth

Governance and Management

Stewardship Grade: B

Portfolio Manager(s)

Before taking over this fund on Oct. 31, 2005, Harry Lange ran Fidelity Capital Appreciation for nearly 10 years and Fidelity Advisor Small Cap for nearly seven years. Lange joined Fidelity as an analyst in 1987, served as a research director in Japan, and managed the firm's technology offerings before moving on to run diversified funds. As manager of one of Fidelity's flagships, Lange is backed by scores of the firm's analysts. He also collaborates with other growth-oriented Fidelity managers, such as Will Danoff and Fergus Shiel.

Strategy

Harry Lange favors fast-growing companies that are benefiting from larger trends. He is valuation conscious, however, and typically likes to lighten his positions in companies that are trading richly and buy in when they're slumping. Lange invests heavily in traditional growth sectors, such as tech hardware, but he won't let sector weightings deviate from those of the S&P 500 as much as he did at his previous charge. He holds between 250 and 300 names here and will go overseas for opportunities. Fidelity does not hedge foreign currency exposure.

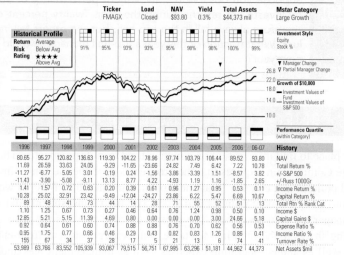

Historical Profile
Return Average
Risk   Below Avg
Rating ★★★★ Above Avg

	1996	1997	1998	1999	2000	2001	2002	2003	2004	2005	2006	06-07	History
	80.65	95.27	120.82	136.63	119.30	104.22	78.96	97.74	103.79	106.44	89.52	93.80	NAV
	11.69	26.59	33.63	24.05	-9.29	-11.65	-23.66	24.82	7.49	6.42	7.22	10.78	Total Return %
	-11.27	-6.77	5.05	3.01	-0.19	0.24	-1.56	-3.86	-3.39	1.51	-8.57	3.82	+/-S&P 500
	-11.43	-3.90	-5.08	-9.11	13.13	8.77	4.22	-4.93	1.19	1.16	-1.85	2.65	+/-Russ 1000Gr
	1.41	1.57	0.72	0.63	0.20	0.39	0.61	0.96	1.27	0.95	0.53	0.11	Income Return %
	10.28	24.02	32.91	23.42	-9.49	-12.04	-24.27	23.86	6.22	5.47	6.69	10.67	Capital Return %
	89	48	41	73	44	14	28	71	55	52	51	13	Total Rtn % Rank Cat
	1.10	1.25	0.67	0.73	0.27	0.46	0.64	0.76	1.24	0.98	0.50	0.10	Income $
	12.85	5.21	5.15	11.39	4.69	0.80	0.00	0.00	0.00	3.30	24.66	5.18	Capital Gains $
	0.92	0.64	0.61	0.60	0.74	0.88	0.88	0.76	0.70	0.62	0.56	0.53	Expense Ratio %
	0.95	1.75	0.77	0.66	0.46	0.29	0.43	0.82	0.83	1.26	0.86	0.41	Income Ratio %
	155	67	34	37	28	17	5	21	13	6	74	41	Turnover Rate %
	53,989	63,766	83,552	105,939	93,067	79,515	56,751	67,995	63,296	51,181	44,962	44,373	Net Assets $mil

Investment Style
Equity
Stock %

91% 95% 93% 93% 95% 98% 96% 100% 99%

▼ Manager Change
▽ Partial Manager Change

Growth of $10,000
— Investment Values of Fund
— Investment Values of S&P 500

Performance Quartile (within Category)

Performance 06-30-07

	1st Qtr	2nd Qtr	3rd Qtr	4th Qtr	Total
2003	-2.87	14.25	1.48	10.85	24.82
2004	1.42	0.77	-2.77	8.17	7.49
2005	-2.69	1.51	3.55	4.04	6.42
2006	5.98	-3.99	0.32	5.04	7.22
2007	2.01	8.60	—	—	—

Trailing	Total Return%	+/- S&P 500	+/- Russ 1000Gr	%Rank Cat	Growth of $10,000
3 Mo	8.60	2.32	1.74	15	10,860
6 Mo	10.78	3.82	2.65	13	11,078
1 Yr	16.74	-3.85	-2.30	54	11,674
3 Yr Avg	9.96	-1.72	1.26	35	13,295
5 Yr Avg	8.81	-1.90	-0.47	47	15,253
10 Yr Avg	6.51	-0.62	2.12	33	18,789
15 Yr Avg	10.31	-0.88	1.28	34	43,574

Tax Analysis	Tax-Adj Rtn%	%Rank Cat	Tax-Cost Rat	%Rank Cat
3 Yr (estimated)	8.00	55	1.78	87
5 Yr (estimated)	7.51	61	1.19	89
10 Yr (estimated)	5.26	34	1.17	57

Potential Capital Gain Exposure: 31% of assets

Morningstar's Take by Dan Lefkovitz 04-04-07

Fidelity Magellan is revving its engines.

If and when a growth-stock rally materializes, this long-closed fund will be ready. During 2006, manager Harry Lange added to stakes in fast-growing tech stocks, such as Corning and Seagate Technology, which join Nokia and Google in Magellan's top five. As of year-end 2006, the portfolio had twice as much exposure to the hardware and software sectors than the benchmark S&P 500 Index. Lange thinks such stocks are cheap, given their growth potential.

Technology has been one of the market's least favorite sectors since Lange took the helm here on Oct. 31, 2005, which is why growth funds, such as this one, have struggled relative to the S&P 500. But technology is Lange's specialty. He compiled a terrific 9.5-year record on Fidelity Capital Appreciation, in large part by loading up on tech when it was down and selling after runups. During Lange's brief tenure here, the fund has beaten its new peers in the large-growth category.

We moved the fund from large blend to large growth because Lange gave the once-stodgy portfolio a racy makeover. Gone are the blue chips that made the fund look and act like the S&P 500. Lange's growth bias can also be seen in the energy and financials sectors, where he prefers fast growers, such as coal concern Peabody Energy and investment bank Merrill Lynch, to oil majors and big banks. Lange focuses more on Japan (where he sees big-time growth potential) than his predecessor did, and he's able to pay more attention to mid-caps and smaller large caps. He has more flexibility, thanks to an asset base that, while still huge, is less than half its 1999 level.

Lange's more-aggressive approach has indeed ratcheted up volatility. Magellan lost more than its peer group and benchmark when the market pulled back in May and June 2006 and in late February and early March 2007. But the fund has the same potential on the upside. We think it would be a mistake to sell now.

Rating and Risk

Time Period	Load-Adj Return %	Morningstar Rtn vs Cat	Morningstar Risk vs Cat	Morningstar Risk-Adj Rating
1 Yr	16.74			
3 Yr	9.96	Avg	-Avg	★★★★
5 Yr	8.81	Avg	Avg	★★★
10 Yr	6.51	Avg	-Avg	★★★★
Incept	18.38			

Other Measures	Standard Index S&P 500	Best Fit Index Russ MG
Alpha	-1.9	-1.3
Beta	1.05	0.71
R-Squared	79	87

Standard Deviation	8.72
Mean	9.96
Sharpe Ratio	0.69

Portfolio Analysis 03-31-07

Share change since 12-06 Total Stocks:252	Sector	PE	Tot Ret%	% Assets
Nokia Corporation ADR	Hardware	19.9	41.41	4.92
Corning Inc.	Hardware	21.3	36.56	3.97
Google, Inc.	Business	47.0	13.66	2.88
⊕ Seagate Technology	Hardware	36.9	-17.16	2.57
⊖ American International G	Financial	12.2	-1.81	2.54
⊕ ASML Holding NV	Hardware	16.1	11.45	1.86
⊖ Peabody Energy Corporati	Energy	23.3	20.04	1.78
⊖ Canadian Natural Resourc	Energy	15.1	24.97	1.66
⊖ Schlumberger, Ltd.	Energy	25.1	35.15	1.64
⊖ Allergan, Inc.	Health	42.7	-3.56	1.64
⊕ Staples, Inc.	Consumer	17.4	-10.13	1.50
Burlington Northern Sant	Business	17.1	16.05	1.31
⊕ Johnson & Johnson	Health	17.5	-6.12	1.31
Merrill Lynch & Company,	Financial	8.9	-9.55	1.20
⊕ Gilead Sciences, Inc.	Health	-33.9	19.51	1.20
AT&T, Inc.	Telecom	21.1	18.36	1.19
⊕ Canon	Goods	—	—	1.19
China Life Insurance	Financial	—	—	1.13
Honeywell International,	Ind Mtrls	21.1	25.59	1.05
State Street Corporation	Financial	20.4	2.08	1.04

Current Investment Style

Value Blnd Growth

Market Cap	%
Giant	35.2
Large	41.4
Mid	20.7
Small	2.5
Micro	0.3

Avg $mil: 24,194

Value Measures		Rel Category
Price/Earnings	18.38	0.97
Price/Book	2.70	0.82
Price/Sales	1.64	0.87
Price/Cash Flow	9.67	0.79
Dividend Yield %	0.98	0.93

Growth Measures	%	Rel Category
Long-Term Erngs	14.61	1.02
Book Value	13.80	1.08
Sales	11.54	0.91
Cash Flow	12.33	0.83
Historical Erngs	25.83	1.08

Profitability	%	Rel Category
Return on Equity	18.52	0.92
Return on Assets	10.37	0.96
Net Margin	13.05	0.94

Sector Weightings

	% of Stocks	Rel S&P 500	3 Year High Low
⟳ Info	31.08	1.52	
Software	3.93	1.08	6 4
Hardware	22.14	2.29	22 11
Media	1.36	0.40	9 1
Telecom	3.65	0.97	4 1
⟲ Service	47.04	1.06	
Health	11.84	1.01	16 11
Consumer	9.14	1.18	11 7
Business	10.60	2.57	11 2
Financial	15.46	0.74	20 15
Mfg	21.90	0.62	
Goods	3.94	0.47	6 4
Ind Mtrls	10.01	0.79	12 7
Energy	7.65	0.72	12 8
Utilities	0.30	0.09	1 0

Composition

● Cash	1.1
● Stocks	98.9
● Bonds	0.0
● Other	0.0
Foreign (% of Stock)	23.5

Address:	82 Devonshire St Boston MA 02109 800-544-9797	Minimum Purchase:	Closed	Add: —	IRA: —
		Min Auto Inv Plan:	Closed	Add: —	
		Sales Fees:	No-load		
Web Address:	www.fidelity.com	Management Fee:	0.50%		
Inception:	05-02-63	Actual Fees:	Mgt:0.35%	Dist: —	
Advisor:	Fidelity Mgmt & Research (FMR)	Expense Projections:	3Yr:$173	5Yr:$302	10Yr:$677
Subadvisor:	Fidelity Intl Invest Advisors (uk) Ltd	Income Distrib:	Semi-Annually		
NTF Plans:	Fidelity Retail-NTF, CommonWealth NTF				

 Mutual Funds

---

FIGURE 4.3 Morningstar report

MUTUAL-FUND RATINGS COME UNDER FIRE

Two methods for rating mutual funds, including the widely used Morningstar system, have come under fire.

A new study concludes that mutual funds given high ratings by Morningstar and Value Line—both used by investors to choose among funds—don't necessarily perform better than those with middling ratings.

"Mutual-fund ratings services can't really predict winners," says the study's author, finance professor Matthew R. Morey of New York's Pace University.

To test ratings' predictive abilities, Prof. Morey sifted the fund market for diversified stock funds that had at least three years of history at the end of 1994. He then tracked the performance of these funds over the next six years to see how funds with high ratings from Morningstar and Value Line compared with those with lower ratings.

Prof. Morey found that, from 1995 through 2000, lower-rated funds kept slumping to some extent. But highly rated funds, which draw heavy promotion and sales, didn't tend to perform any better than funds with middle-of-the-pack ratings.

So, how should investors use fund ratings? Cautiously.

The best approach is to research how a rating is derived and, if you're comfortable with its criteria, only use it as a first cut to winnow the vast field of options. A ratings screen will leave you with a more manageable pack of funds to study closely and shoe-horn into a well-diversified portfolio.

Source: Abridged from Ian McDonald, "Mutual-Fund Ratings Come under Fire," *The Wall Street Journal*, January 15, 2003.

---

these columns give the performance of the fund relative to the index. The returns reported for the fund are calculated net of expenses, 12b-1 fees, and any other fees automatically deducted from fund assets, but they do not account for any sales charges such as front-end loads or back-end charges. Next appear the percentile ranks of the fund compared to all other funds with the same investment objective (see column headed by %Rank Cat). A rank of 1 means the fund is a top performer. A rank of 80 would mean that it was beaten by 80% of funds in the comparison group. Finally, growth of $10,000 invested in the fund over various periods ranging from the past 3 months to the past 15 years is given in the last column.

More data on the performance of the fund are provided in the graph near the top of the figure. The line graph compares the growth of $10,000 invested in the fund and the S&P 500 over the last 10 years. Below the graph are boxes for each year that depict the relative performance of the fund for that year. The shaded area on the box shows the quartile in which the fund's performance falls relative to other funds with the same objective. If the shaded band is at the top of the box, the firm was a top quartile performer in that period, and so on. The table below the bar charts presents historical data on characteristics of the fund such as return data and expense ratios.

The table on the right entitled Portfolio Analysis presents the 20 largest holdings of the portfolio, showing the price–earnings ratio and year-to-date return of each of those securities. Investors can thus get a quick look at the manager's biggest bets.

Below the portfolio analysis table is a box labeled Current Investment Style. In this box, Morningstar evaluates style along two dimensions: One dimension is the size of the firms held in the portfolio as measured by the market value of outstanding equity; the other dimension is a value/growth measure. Morningstar defines *value stocks* as those with low ratios of market price per share to various measures of value. It puts stocks on a growth-value continuum based on the ratios of stock price to the firm's earnings, book value, sales, cash flow, and dividends. Value stocks are those with a low price relative to these measures of value. In contrast, *growth stocks* have high ratios, suggesting that investors in these firms must believe that the firm will experience rapid growth to justify the prices at which the stocks sell. The shaded box for Magellan shows that the portfolio tends to hold larger firms (top row) and growth stocks (right column). A year-by-year history of Magellan's investment style is presented in the sequence of such boxes at the top of Figure 4.3.

The center of the figure, labeled Rating and Risk, is one of the more complicated but interesting facets of Morningstar's analysis. The column labeled Load-Adj Return rates a fund's return compared to other funds with the same investment policy. Returns for periods ranging from 1 to 10 years are calculated with all loads and back-end fees applicable to that investment period subtracted from total income. The return is then compared to the average return for the comparison group of funds to obtain the Morningstar Return vs. Category. Similarly, risk measures compared to category are computed and reported in the next column.

The last column presents Morningstar's risk-adjusted rating, ranging from one to five stars. The rating is based on the fund's return score minus risk score compared to other funds with similar investment styles. To allow funds to be compared to other funds with similar investment styles, Morningstar recently increased the number of categories; there are now 48 separate stock and bond fund categories. Of course, we are accustomed to the disclaimer that "past performance is not a reliable measure of future results," and this is true as well of the coveted Morningstar 5-star rating. The nearby box discusses the predictive value of the Morningstar ranking. Consistent with both the conventional disclaimer and Table 4.4, past results have little predictive power for future performance.

The tax analysis box shown on the left in Figure 4.3 provides some evidence on the tax efficiency of the fund. The after-tax return, given in the first column, is computed based on the dividends paid to the portfolio as well as realized capital gains, assuming the investor is in the maximum federal tax bracket at the time of the distribution. State and local taxes are ignored. The tax efficiency of the fund is measured by the "Tax-Cost Ratio," which is an estimate of the impact of taxes on the investor's after-tax return. Morningstar ranks each fund compared to its category for both tax-adjusted return and tax-cost ratio.

The bottom of the page in Figure 4.3 provides information on the expenses and loads associated with investments in the fund, as well as information on the fund's investment adviser. Thus, Morningstar provides a considerable amount of the information you would need to decide among several competing funds.

SUMMARY

1. Unit investment trusts, closed-end management companies, and open-end management companies are all classified and regulated as investment companies. Unit investment trusts are essentially unmanaged in the sense that the portfolio, once established, is fixed. Managed investment companies, in contrast, may change the composition of the portfolio as deemed fit by the portfolio manager. Closed-end funds are traded like other securities; they do not redeem shares for their investors. Open-end funds will redeem shares for net asset value at the request of the investor.

2. Net asset value equals the market value of assets held by a fund minus the liabilities of the fund divided by the shares outstanding.

3. Mutual funds free the individual from many of the administrative burdens of owning individual securities and offer professional management of the portfolio. They also offer advantages that are available only to large-scale investors, such as discounted trading costs. On the other hand, funds are assessed management fees and incur other expenses, which reduce the investor's rate of return. Funds also eliminate some of the individual's control over the timing of capital gains realizations.

4. Mutual funds are often categorized by investment policy. Major policy groups include money market funds; equity funds, which are further grouped according to emphasis on income versus growth; fixed-income funds; balanced and income funds; asset allocation funds; index funds; and specialized sector funds.

5. Costs of investing in mutual funds include front-end loads, which are sales charges; back-end loads, which are redemption fees or, more formally, contingent-deferred sales charges; fund operating expenses; and 12b-1 charges, which are recurring fees used to pay for the expenses of marketing the fund to the public.

6. Income earned on mutual fund portfolios is not taxed at the level of the fund. Instead, as long as the fund meets certain requirements for pass-through status, the income is treated as being earned by the investors in the fund.

7. The average rate of return of the average equity mutual fund in the last 35 years has been below that of a passive index fund holding a portfolio to replicate a broad-based index like the S&P 500 or Wilshire 5000. Some of the reasons for this disappointing record are the costs incurred by actively managed funds, such as the expense of conducting the research to guide stock-picking activities, and trading costs due to higher portfolio turnover. The record on the consistency of fund performance is mixed. In some sample periods, the better-performing funds continue to perform well in the following periods; in other sample periods they do not.

Related Web sites for this chapter are available at www.mhhe.com/bkm

KEY TERMS

investment company	closed-end fund	soft dollars
net asset value (NAV)	load	turnover
unit investment trust	hedge fund	exchange-traded funds
open-end fund	12b-1 fees	

PROBLEM SETS

Quiz

1. Would you expect a typical open-end fixed-income mutual fund to have higher or lower operating expenses than a fixed-income unit investment trust? Why?

2. What are some comparative advantages of investing in the following:
   a. Unit investment trusts.
   b. Open-end mutual funds.
   c. Individual stocks and bonds that you choose for yourself.

3. Open-end equity mutual funds find it necessary to keep a significant percentage of total investments, typically around 5% of the portfolio, in very liquid money market assets. Closed-end funds do not have to maintain such a position in "cash equivalent" securities. What difference between open-end and closed-end funds might account for their differing policies?

4. Balanced funds, life-cycle funds, and asset allocation funds all invest in both the stock and bond markets. What are the differences among these types of funds?

Problems

5. An open-end fund has a net asset value of $10.70 per share. It is sold with a front-end load of 6%. What is the offering price?

6. If the offering price of an open-end fund is $12.30 per share and the fund is sold with a front-end load of 5%, what is its net asset value?

7. The composition of the Fingroup Fund portfolio is as follows:

Stock	Shares	Price
A	200,000	$35
B	300,000	40
C	400,000	20
D	600,000	25

The fund has not borrowed any funds, but its accrued management fee with the portfolio manager currently totals $30,000. There are 4 million shares outstanding. What is the net asset value of the fund?

8. Reconsider the Fingroup Fund in the previous problem. If during the year the portfolio manager sells all of the holdings of stock D and replaces it with 200,000 shares of stock E at $50 per share and 200,000 shares of stock F at $25 per share, what is the portfolio turnover rate?

9. The Closed Fund is a closed-end investment company with a portfolio currently worth $200 million. It has liabilities of $3 million and 5 million shares outstanding.

   a. What is the NAV of the fund?
   b. If the fund sells for $36 per share, what is its premium or discount as a percent of net asset value?

10. Corporate Fund started the year with a net asset value of $12.50. By year-end, its NAV equaled $12.10. The fund paid year-end distributions of income and capital gains of $1.50. What was the (pretax) rate of return to an investor in the fund?

11. A closed-end fund starts the year with a net asset value of $12.00. By year-end, NAV equals $12.10. At the beginning of the year, the fund was selling at a 2% premium to NAV. By the end of the year, the fund is selling at a 7% discount to NAV. The fund paid year-end distributions of income and capital gains of $1.50.

   a. What is the rate of return to an investor in the fund during the year?
   b. What would have been the rate of return to an investor who held the same securities as the fund manager during the year?

12. a. Impressive Fund had excellent investment performance last year, with portfolio returns that placed it in the top 10% of all funds with the same investment policy. Do you expect it to be a top performer next year? Why or why not?
    b. Suppose instead that the fund was among the poorest performers in its comparison group. Would you be more or less likely to believe its relative performance will persist into the following year? Why?

13. Consider a mutual fund with $200 million in assets at the start of the year and with 10 million shares outstanding. The fund invests in a portfolio of stocks that provides dividend income at the end of the year of $2 million. The stocks included in the fund's portfolio increase in price by 8%, but no securities are sold, and there are no capital gains distributions. The fund charges 12b-1 fees of 1%, which are deducted from portfolio assets at year-end. What is net asset value at the start and end of the year? What is the rate of return for an investor in the fund?

14. The New Fund had average daily assets of $2.2 billion last year. The fund sold $400 million worth of stock and purchased $500 million during the year. What was its turnover ratio?

15. If New Fund's expense ratio (see Problem 14) was 1.1% and the management fee was .7%, what were the total fees paid to the fund's investment managers during the year? What were other administrative expenses?

16. You purchased 1,000 shares of the New Fund at a price of $20 per share at the beginning of the year. You paid a front-end load of 4%. The securities in which the fund invests increase in value by 12% during the year. The fund's expense ratio is 1.2%. What is your rate of return on the fund if you sell your shares at the end of the year?

17. The Investments Fund sells Class A shares with a front-end load of 6% and Class B shares with 12b-1 fees of .5% annually as well as back-end load fees that start at 5% and fall by 1% for each full year the investor holds the portfolio (until the fifth year). Assume the portfolio rate of return net of operating expenses is 10% annually. If you plan to sell the fund after 4 years, are Class A or Class B shares the better choice for you? What if you plan to sell after 15 years?

18. You are considering an investment in a mutual fund with a 4% load and expense ratio of .5%. You can invest instead in a bank CD paying 6% interest.

   a. If you plan to invest for 2 years, what annual rate of return must the fund portfolio earn for you to be better off in the fund than in the CD? Assume annual compounding of returns.

b. How does your answer change if you plan to invest for 6 years? Why does your answer change?

c. Now suppose that instead of a front-end load the fund assesses a 12b-1 fee of .75% per year. What annual rate of return must the fund portfolio earn for you to be better off in the fund than in the CD? Does your answer in this case depend on your time horizon?

19. Suppose that every time a fund manager trades stock, transaction costs such as commissions and bid–asked spreads amount to .4% of the value of the trade. If the portfolio turnover rate is 50%, by how much is the total return of the portfolio reduced by trading costs?

20. You expect a tax-free municipal bond portfolio to provide a rate of return of 4%. Management fees of the fund are .6%. What fraction of portfolio income is given up to fees? If the management fees for an equity fund also are .6%, but you expect a portfolio return of 12%, what fraction of portfolio income is given up to fees? Why might management fees be a bigger factor in your investment decision for bond funds than for stock funds? Can your conclusion help explain why unmanaged unit investment trusts tend to focus on the fixed-income market?

21. Suppose you observe the investment performance of 350 portfolio managers for 5 years and rank them by investment returns during each year. After 5 years, you find that 11 of the funds have investment returns that place the fund in the top half of the sample in each and every year of your sample. Such consistency of performance indicates to you that these must be the funds whose managers are in fact skilled, and you invest your money in these funds. Is your conclusion warranted?

Challenge Problem

1. Go to **www.mhhe.com/edumarketinsight.** Select the *Industry* tab and click on the arrow in the GICS box. Scroll down in the list until you find Hypermarkets & Super Centers. Click on the Go! Icon.

   In the Compustat Reports section of the left side menu, click on the Constituents link. Select one of the firms listed and click on its name. On the screen that comes up, follow the link for Financial Highlights. What is the market capitalization for this firm? What is the 5-year growth rate of sales? Based on this information, for which type of mutual fund objective(s) would this stock be a good fit?

   Go back to the list of the Hypermarkets & Super Centers constituents and choose another company. Locate the same data for the second company and indicate which type of mutual fund would be likely to hold this stock.

   STANDARD &POOR'S

2. Go to the **www.mhhe.com/edumarketinsight** home page and repeat the process for two firms in the biotechnology industry. How do the results compare with those of firms in the Hypermarkets & Super Centers sector?

E-Investments

Choosing a Mutual Fund

Go to the **finance.yahoo.com.** Click on Mutual Funds under the Investing tab. Look for the Mutual Fund Screener. Use the drop-down boxes to select the criteria for mutual funds that are of interest to you. How many funds are shown in your results? If there are no funds or only a few funds that meet your criteria, try loosening your standards. If there are too many funds, try stricter standards. You can click on any column heading in the results list to sort by that criterion.

SOLUTIONS TO CONCEPT CHECKS

1. $\text{NAV} = \dfrac{\$69{,}265.99 - \$689.72}{1{,}051.69} = \$65.21$

2. The net investment in the Class A shares after the 4% commission is $9,600. If the fund earns a 10% return, the investment will grow after n years to $\$9{,}600 \times (1.10)^n$. The Class B shares have no front-end load. However, the net return to the investor after 12b-1 fees will be only 9.5%. In addition, there is a back-end load that reduces the sales proceeds by a percentage equal to (5 – years until sale) until the fifth year, when the back-end load expires.

Horizon	Class A Shares $\$9{,}600 \times (1.10)^n$	Class B Shares $\$10{,}000 \times (1.095)^n \times (1 - \text{percentage exit fee})$
1 year	$10,560	$\$10{,}000 \times (1.095) \times (1 - .04) = \$10{,}512$
4 years	$14,055	$\$10{,}000 \times (1.095)^4 \times (1 - .01) = \$14{,}233$
10 years	$24,900	$\$10{,}000 \times (1.095)^{10} \quad\quad = \$24{,}782$

For a very short horizon such as 1 year, the Class A shares are the better choice. The front-end and back-end loads are equal, but the Class A shares don't have to pay the 12b-1 fees. For moderate horizons such as 4 years, the Class B shares dominate because the front-end load of the Class A shares is more costly than the 12b-1 fees and the now-smaller exit fee. For long horizons of 10 years or more, Class A again dominates. In this case, the one-time front-end load is less expensive than the continuing 12b-1 fees.

3. *a.* Turnover = $160,000 in trades per $1 million of portfolio value = 16%.

   b. Realized capital gains are $10 × 1,000 = $10,000 on Microsoft and $5 × 2,000 = $10,000 on Ford. The tax owed on the capital gains is therefore .20 × $20,000 = $4,000.

4. Twenty percent of the managers are skilled, which accounts for .2 × 400 = 80 of those managers who appear in the top half. There are 120 slots left in the top half, and 320 other managers, so the probability of an unskilled manager "lucking into" the top half in any year is 120/320, or .375. Therefore, of the 120 lucky managers in the first year, we would expect .375 × 120 = 45 to repeat as top-half performers next year. Thus, we should expect a total of 80 + 45 = 125, or 62.5%, of the better initial performers to repeat their top-half performance.

LEARNING ABOUT RETURN AND RISK FROM THE HISTORICAL RECORD

CASUAL OBSERVATION AND formal research both suggest that investment risk is as important to investors as expected return. While we have theories about the relationship between risk and expected return that would prevail in rational capital markets, there is no theory about the levels of risk we should find in the marketplace. We can at best estimate the level of risk likely to confront investors by analyzing historical experience.

This situation is to be expected because prices of investment assets fluctuate in response to news about the fortunes of corporations, as well as to macroeconomic developments that affect interest rates. There is no theory about the frequency and importance of such events; hence we cannot determine a "natural" level of risk.

Compounding this difficulty is the fact that neither expected returns nor risk are directly observable. We observe only *realized* rates of return after the fact. Hence, to make forecasts about future expected returns and risk, we first must learn how to "forecast" their *past* values, that is, the expected returns and risk that investors actually anticipated, from historical data. (There is an old saying that forecasting the future is even more difficult than forecasting the past.) In this chapter, we present the essential tools for estimating expected returns and risk from the historical record and consider the implications of this record for future investments.

We begin by discussing interest rates and investments in safe assets and examine the history of risk-free investments in the U.S over the last 80 years. Moving to risky assets, we begin with scenario analysis of risky investments and the data inputs necessary to conduct it. With this in mind, we develop statistical tools needed to make inferences from historical time series of portfolio returns. We present a global view of the history of returns over 100 years from stocks and bonds in various countries and analyze the historical record of five broad asset-class portfolios. We end the chapter with discussions of implications of the historical record for future investments and a variety of risk measures commonly used in the industry.

5.1　DETERMINANTS OF THE LEVEL OF INTEREST RATES

Interest rates and forecasts of their future values are among the most important inputs into an investment decision. For example, suppose you have $10,000 in a savings account. The bank pays you a variable interest rate tied to some short-term reference rate such as the 30-day Treasury bill rate. You have the option of moving some or all of your money into a longer-term certificate of deposit that offers a fixed rate over the term of the deposit.

Your decision depends critically on your outlook for interest rates. If you think rates will fall, you will want to lock in the current higher rates by investing in a relatively long-term CD. If you expect rates to rise, you will want to postpone committing any funds to long-term CDs.

Forecasting interest rates is one of the most notoriously difficult parts of applied macro-economics. Nonetheless, we do have a good understanding of the fundamental factors that determine the level of interest rates:

1. The supply of funds from savers, primarily households.
2. The demand for funds from businesses to be used to finance investments in plant, equipment, and inventories (real assets or capital formation).
3. The government's net supply of or demand for funds as modified by actions of the Federal Reserve Bank.

Before we elaborate on these forces and resultant interest rates, we need to distinguish real from nominal interest rates.

Real and Nominal Rates of Interest

An interest rate is a promised rate of return denominated in some unit of account (dollars, yen, euros, or even purchasing power units) over some time period (a month, a year, 20 years, or longer). Thus, when we say the interest rate is 5%, we must specify both the unit of account and the time period.

Assuming there is no default risk, we can refer to the promised rate of interest as a risk-free rate for that particular unit of account and time period. But if an interest rate is risk-free for one unit of account and time period, it will not be risk-free for other units or periods. For example, interest rates that are absolutely safe in dollar terms will be risky when evaluated in terms of purchasing power because of inflation uncertainty.

To illustrate, consider a 1-year dollar (nominal) risk-free interest rate. Suppose exactly 1 year ago you deposited $1,000 in a 1-year time deposit guaranteeing a rate of interest of 10%. You are about to collect $1,100 in cash. What is the real return on your investment? That depends on what money can buy these days, relative to what you *could* buy a year ago. The consumer price index (CPI) measures purchasing power by averaging the prices of goods and services in the consumption basket of an average urban family of four.

Suppose the rate of inflation (the percent change in the CPI, denoted by i) for the last year amounted to $i = 6\%$. This tells you that the purchasing power of money is reduced by 6% a year. The value of each dollar depreciates by 6% a year in terms of the goods it can buy. Therefore, part of your interest earnings are offset by the reduction in the purchasing power of the dollars you will receive at the end of the year. With a 10% interest rate, after you net out the 6% reduction in the purchasing power of money, you are left with a net increase in purchasing power of about 4%. Thus we need to distinguish between a **nominal interest rate**—the growth rate of your money—and a **real interest rate**—the growth rate of your purchasing power. If we call R the nominal rate, r the real rate, and i the inflation rate, then we conclude

$$r \approx R - i \qquad (5.1)$$

In words, the real rate of interest is the nominal rate reduced by the loss of purchasing power resulting from inflation. If inflation turns out higher than 6%, your *realized* real return will be lower than 4%; if inflation is lower, your real rate will be higher.

In fact, the exact relationship between the real and nominal interest rate is given by

$$1 + r = \frac{1 + R}{1 + i} \qquad (5.2)$$

This is because the growth factor of your purchasing power, $1 + r$, equals the growth factor of your money, $1 + R$, divided by the new price level, that is, $1 + i$ times its value in the previous period. The exact relationship can be rearranged to

$$r = \frac{R - i}{1 + i} \qquad (5.3)$$

which shows that the approximation rule overstates the real rate by the factor $1 + i$.

EXAMPLE 5.1   Approximating the Real Rate

If the nominal interest rate on a 1-year CD is 8%, and you expect inflation to be 5% over the coming year, then using the approximation formula, you expect the real rate of interest to be $r = 8\% - 5\% = 3\%$. Using the exact formula, the real rate is $r = \dfrac{.08 - .05}{1 + .05} = .0286$, or 2.86%. Therefore, the approximation rule overstates the expected real rate by only .14% (14 basis points). The approximation rule is more exact for small inflation rates and is perfectly exact for continuously compounded rates. We discuss further details in the next section.

Before the decision to invest, you should realize that conventional certificates of deposit offer a guaranteed *nominal* rate of interest. Thus you can only infer the expected real rate on these investments by subtracting your expectation of the rate of inflation.

It is always possible to calculate the real rate after the fact. The inflation rate is published by the Bureau of Labor Statistics (BLS). The future real rate, however, is unknown, and one has to rely on expectations. In other words, because future inflation is risky, the real rate of return is risky even when the nominal rate is risk-free.

The Equilibrium Real Rate of Interest

Three basic factors—supply, demand, and government actions—determine the *real* interest rate. The nominal interest rate, which is the rate we actually observe, is the real rate plus the expected rate of inflation. So a fourth factor affecting the interest rate is the expected rate of inflation.

Although there are many different interest rates economywide (as many as there are types of securities), these rates tend to move together, so economists frequently talk as if there were a single representative rate. We can use this abstraction to gain some insights into the real rate of interest if we consider the supply and demand curves for funds.

Figure 5.1 shows a downward-sloping demand curve and an upward-sloping supply curve. On the horizontal axis, we measure the quantity of funds, and on the vertical axis, we measure the real rate of interest.

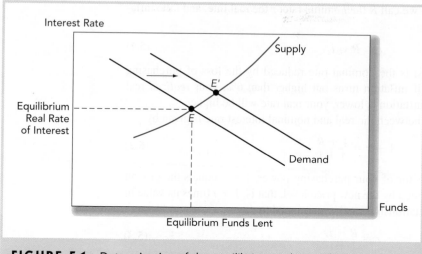

Interest Rate

Supply

E'

Equilibrium
Real Rate
of Interest

E

Demand

Funds

Equilibrium Funds Lent

FIGURE 5.1   Determination of the equilibrium real rate of interest

The supply curve slopes up from left to right because the higher the real interest rate, the greater the supply of household savings. The assumption is that at higher real interest rates households will choose to postpone some current consumption and set aside or invest more of their disposable income for future use.[1]

The demand curve slopes down from left to right because the lower the real interest rate, the more businesses will want to invest in physical capital. Assuming that businesses rank projects by the expected real return on invested capital, firms will undertake more projects the lower the real interest rate on the funds needed to finance those projects.

Equilibrium is at the point of intersection of the supply and demand curves, point E in Figure 5.1.

The government and the central bank (the Federal Reserve) can shift these supply and demand curves either to the right or to the left through fiscal and monetary policies. For example, consider an increase in the government's budget deficit. This increases the government's borrowing demand and shifts the demand curve to the right, which causes the equilibrium real interest rate to rise to point E'. That is, a forecast that indicates higher than previously expected government borrowing increases expected future interest rates. The Fed can offset such a rise through an expansionary monetary policy, which will shift the supply curve to the right.

Thus, although the fundamental determinants of the real interest rate are the propensity of households to save and the expected productivity (or we could say profitability) of investment in physical capital, the real rate can be affected as well by government fiscal and monetary policies.

The Equilibrium Nominal Rate of Interest

We've seen that the real rate of return on an asset is approximately equal to the nominal rate minus the inflation rate. Because investors should be concerned with their real returns—the increase in their purchasing power—we would expect that as the inflation rate increases, investors will demand higher nominal rates of return on their investments. This higher rate is necessary to maintain the expected real return offered by an investment.

Irving Fisher (1930) argued that the nominal rate ought to increase one-for-one with increases in the expected inflation rate. If we use the notation $E(i)$ to denote the current

---

[1]There is considerable disagreement among experts on the extent to which household saving does increase in response to an increase in the real interest rate.

expectation of the inflation rate that will prevail over the coming period, then we can state the so-called Fisher equation formally as

$$R = r + E(i) \qquad (5.4)$$

The equation implies that if real rates are reasonably stable, then increases in nominal rates ought to predict higher inflation rates. This relationship has been debated and empirically investigated. The results are mixed; although the data do not strongly support this relationship, nominal interest rates seem to predict inflation as well as alternative methods, in part because we are unable to forecast inflation well with any method.

One reason it is difficult to determine the empirical validity of the Fisher hypothesis that changes in nominal rates predict changes in future inflation rates is that the real rate also changes unpredictably over time. Nominal interest rates can be viewed as the sum of the required real rate on nominally risk-free assets, plus a "noisy" forecast of inflation.

In Part Four we discuss the relationship between short- and long-term interest rates. Longer rates incorporate forecasts for long-term inflation. For this reason alone, interest rates on bonds of different maturity may diverge. In addition, we will see that prices of longer-term bonds are more volatile than those of short-term bonds. This implies that expected returns on longer-term bonds may include a risk premium, so that the expected real rate offered by bonds of varying maturity also may vary.

CONCEPT CHECK 1	a. Suppose the real interest rate is 3% per year and the expected inflation rate is 8%. What is the nominal interest rate?
	b. Suppose the expected inflation rate rises to 10%, but the real rate is unchanged. What happens to the nominal interest rate?

Taxes and the Real Rate of Interest

Tax liabilities are based on *nominal* income and the tax rate determined by the investor's tax bracket. Congress recognized the resultant "bracket creep" (when nominal income grows due to inflation and pushes taxpayers into higher brackets) and mandated index-linked tax brackets in the Tax Reform Act of 1986.

Index-linked tax brackets do not provide relief from the effect of inflation on the taxation of savings, however. Given a tax rate (t) and a nominal interest rate (R), the after-tax interest rate is $R(1 - t)$. The real after-tax rate is approximately the after-tax nominal rate minus the inflation rate:

$$R(1 - t) - i = (r + i)(1 - t) - i = r(1 - t) - it \qquad (5.5)$$

Thus the after-tax real rate of return falls as the inflation rate rises. Investors suffer an inflation penalty equal to the tax rate times the inflation rate. If, for example, you are in a 30% tax bracket and your investments yield 12%, while inflation runs at the rate of 8%, then your before-tax real rate is approximately 4%, and you *should,* in an inflation-protected tax system, net after taxes a real return of 4%(1 − .3) = 2.8%. But the tax code does not recognize that the first 8% of your return is no more than compensation for inflation—not real income—and hence your after-tax return is reduced by 8% × .3 = 2.4%, so that your after-tax real interest rate, at .4%, is almost wiped out.

Compounding Period	T	EAR = [1 + r_f(T)]^{1/T} − 1 = .058		APR = r_f(T)*(1/T) = .058	
		$r_f(T)$	APR = [(1 + EAR)^T − 1]/T	$r_f(T)$	EAR = (1 + APR*T)^{(1/T)} −1
1 year	1.0000	.0580	.05800	.0580	.05800
6 months	0.5000	.0286	.05718	.0290	.05884
1 quarter	0.2500	.0142	.05678	.0145	.05927
1 month	0.0833	.0047	.05651	.0048	.05957
1 week	0.0192	.0011	.05641	.0011	.05968
1 day	0.0027	.0002	.05638	.0002	.05971
Continuous		$r_{cc} = \ln(1 + EAR) = .05638$		EAR = exp (r_{cc}) − 1 = .05971	

TABLE 5.1

Annual percentage rate (APR) and effective annual rates (EAR). In the first set of columns, we hold the equivalent annual rate (EAR) fixed at 5.8%, and find APR for each holding period. In the second set of columns, we hold APR fixed and solve for EAR.

eXcel
Please visit us at
www.mhhe.com/bkm

two rates diverge as the compounding frequency continues to grow? Put differently, what is the limit of $[1 + T \times APR]^{1/T}$, as T gets ever smaller? As T approaches zero, we effectively approach *continuous compounding (CC)*, and the relation of EAR to the annual percentage rate, denoted by r_{cc} for the continuously compounded case, is given by the exponential function

$$1 + EAR = \exp(r_{cc}) = e^{r_{cc}} \tag{5.9}$$

where e is approximately 2.71828.

To find r_{cc} from the effective annual rate, we solve Equation 5.9 for r_{cc} as follows:

$$\ln(1 + EAR) = r_{cc}$$

where ln (•) is the natural logarithm function, the inverse of exp (•). Both the exponential and logarithmic functions are available in Excel, and are called LN() and EXP(), respectively.

EXAMPLE 5.5   Continuously Compounded Rates

The continuously compounded annual percentage rate, r_{cc}, that provides an EAR of 5.8% is 5.638% (see Table 5.1). This is virtually the same as the APR for daily compounding. But for less frequent compounding, for example, semiannually, the APR necessary to provide the same EAR is noticeably higher, 5.718%. With less frequent compounding, a higher APR is necessary to provide an equivalent effective return.

While continuous compounding may at first seem to be a mathematical nuisance, working with such rates in many cases can actually simplify calculations of expected return and risk. For example, given a continuously compounded rate, the total return for any period T, $r_{cc}(T)$, is simply $\exp(T \times r_{cc})$.[4] In other words, the total return scales up in direct

---

[4]This follows from Equation 5.9. If $1 + EAR = e^{r_{cc}}$, then $(1 + EAR)^T = e^{r_{cc}T}$.

proportion to the time period, T. This is far simpler than working with the exponents that arise using discrete period compounding. As another example, look again at Equation 5.1. There, the relationship between the real rate, r, the nominal rate R, and the inflation rate i, $r \approx R - i$, was only an approximation, as demonstrated by Equation 5.3. But if we express all rates as continuously compounded, then Equation 5.1 is exact,[5] that is, $r_{cc}(\text{real}) = r_{cc}(\text{nominal}) - i_{cc}$.

CONCEPT CHECK **2**	A bank offers you two alternative interest schedules for a savings account of $100,000 locked in for 3 years: (a) a monthly rate of 1%; (b) an annually, continuously compounded rate (r_{cc}) of 12%. Which alternative should you choose?

5.3 BILLS AND INFLATION, 1926–2005

In this chapter we will often work with a history that begins in 1926, and it is fair to ask why. The reason is simply that January 1, 1926, is the starting date of the most widely available accurate return database.

Table 5.2 summarizes the history of short-term interest rates in the U.S., the inflation rate, and the resultant real rate. You can find the entire post-1926 history of the annual rates of these series on the text's Web site, **www.mhhe.com/bkm** (link to the student material for Chapter 5). The annual rates on T-bills are computed from rolling over twelve 1-month bills during each year. The real rate is computed from the annual T-bill rate and the percent change in the CPI according to Equation 5.2.

Table 5.2 shows the averages, standard deviations, and the first-order serial correlations for the full 80-year history (1926–2005) as well as for various subperiods. The first-order serial correlation measures the relationship between the interest rate in one year with the rate in the preceding year. If this correlation is positive, then a high rate tends to be followed by another high rate, whereas if it is negative, a high rate tends to be followed by a low rate.

The discussion of equilibrium real rates of interest in Section 5.1 suggests that we should start with the series of real rates. The average real rate for the full 80-year period, .72%, is quite different from the average over the 40-year period 1966–2005, which is 1.25%. We see that the real rate has been steadily rising, reaching a level of 2.28% for the generation of 1981–2005. The standard deviation of the real rate over the whole period, 3.97%, was driven by much higher variability in the early years. The real rate was far more stable in the period of 1981–2005, with a standard deviation of only 2.35%.

We can attribute a good part of these trends to policies of the Federal Reserve Board. Since the early 1980s, the Fed has adopted a policy of maintaining a low rate of inflation and a stable real rate. Some believe that the higher level of real rates in recent years may also be attributable to increased productivity of capital, particularly investments in information technology when applied to a better educated labor force.

---

[5] $1 + r(\text{real}) = \dfrac{1 + r(\text{nominal})}{1 + \text{inflation}}$

$\Rightarrow \ln[1 + r(\text{real})] = \ln\left(\dfrac{1 + r(\text{nominal})}{1 + \text{inflation}}\right) = \ln[1 + r(\text{nominal})] - \ln(1 + \text{inflation})$

$\Rightarrow r_{cc}(\text{real}) = r_{cc}(\text{nominal}) - i_{cc}$

between 1966 and 2005. These rates may not seem impressive, but are sufficient to reduce the terminal value of $1 invested in 1966 from a nominal value of $10.08 in 2005 to a real (constant purchasing power) value of only $1.63.

5.4   RISK AND RISK PREMIUMS

Holding-Period Returns

You are considering investing in a stock-index fund. The fund currently sells for $100 per share. With an investment horizon of 1 year, the realized rate of return on your investment will depend on (a) the price per share at year's end and (b) the cash dividends you will collect over the year.

Suppose the price per share at year's end is $110 and cash dividends over the year amount to $4. The realized return, called the *holding-period return,* HPR (in this case, the holding period is 1 year), is defined as

$$HPR = \frac{\text{Ending price of a share} - \text{Beginning price} + \text{Cash dividend}}{\text{Beginning price}} \tag{5.10}$$

In our case we have

$$HPR = \frac{\$110 - \$100 + \$4}{\$100} = .14, \text{ or } 14\%$$

This definition of the HPR assumes the dividend is paid at the end of the holding period. To the extent that dividends are received earlier, the HPR ignores reinvestment income between the receipt of the payment and the end of the holding period. The percent return from dividends is called the **dividend yield,** and so the dividend yield plus the capital gains yield equals the HPR.

Expected Return and Standard Deviation

There is considerable uncertainty about the price of a share plus dividend income 1 year from now, however, so you cannot be sure about your eventual HPR. We can quantify our beliefs about the state of the economy and the stock market in terms of three possible scenarios with probabilities as presented in columns A through E of Spreadsheet 5.1.

How can we evaluate this probability distribution? Throughout this book we will characterize probability distributions of rates of return in terms of their expected or mean return, $E(r)$, and their standard deviation, σ. The expected rate of return is a probability-weighted average of the rates of return in each scenario. Calling $p(s)$ the probability of each scenario and $r(s)$ the HPR in each scenario, where scenarios are labeled or "indexed" by s, we may write the expected return as

$$E(r) = \sum_s p(s)r(s) \tag{5.11}$$

Applying this formula to the data in Spreadsheet 5.1, we find that the expected rate of return on the index fund is

$$E(r) = (0.30 \times 34\%) + (.5 \times 14\%) + [0.20 \times (-16\%)] = 14\%$$

Spreadsheet 5.1 shows that this sum can be evaluated easily in Excel, using the SUM-PRODUCT function, which first calculates the products of a series of number pairs, and

	A	B	C	D	E	F	G	H
1								
2								
3	Rates of return expressed as decimals							
4	Purchase Price =		$100		T-bill Rate =	0.06		
5								
6						Squared		Squared
7	State of the		Year-end	Cash		Deviations	Excess	Deviations
8	Economy	Probability	Price	Dividends	HPR	from Mean	Returns	from Mean
9	Boom	0.3	129.50	4.50	0.34	0.040	0.28	0.040
10	Normal growth	0.5	110.00	4.00	0.14	0.000	0.08	0.000
11	Recession	0.2	80.50	3.50	−0.16	0.090	−0.22	0.090
12	Expected value (mean)		SUMPRODUCT(B9:B11, E9:E11) =		0.14			
13	Standard deviation of HPR			SUMPRODUCT(B9:B11, F9:F11)^.5 =		0.1732		
14	Risk premium			SUMPRODUCT(B9:B11, G9:G11) =			0.08	
15	Standard deviation of excess return				SUMPRODUCT(B9:B11, H9:H11)^0.5 = 0.1732			

SPREADSHEET 5.1

eXcel

Please visit us at
www.mhhe.com/bkm

Distribution of HPR on the stock-index fund

then sums the products. Here, the number pair is the probability of each scenario and the rate of return.

The standard deviation of the rate of return (σ) is a measure of risk. It is defined as the square root of the variance, which in turn is the expected value of the squared deviations from the expected return. The higher the volatility in outcomes, the higher will be the average value of these squared deviations. Therefore, variance and standard deviation measure the uncertainty of outcomes. Symbolically,

$$\sigma^2 = \sum_s p(s) \, [r(s) - E(r)]^2 \tag{5.12}$$

Therefore, in our example

$$\sigma^2 = 0.3(34 - 14)^2 + .5(14 - 14)^2 + 0.2(-16 - 14)^2 = 300,$$

and

$$\sigma = \sqrt{300} = 17.32\%$$

Clearly, what would trouble potential investors in the index fund is the downside risk of a −16% rate of return, not the upside potential of a 34% rate of return. The standard deviation of the rate of return does not distinguish between these two; it treats both simply as deviations from the mean. As long as the probability distribution is more or less symmetric about the mean, σ is an adequate measure of risk. In the special case where we can assume that the probability distribution is normal—represented by the well-known bell-shaped curve—$E(r)$ and σ are perfectly adequate to characterize the distribution.

Excess Returns and Risk Premiums

How much, if anything, should you invest in the index fund? First, you must ask how much of an expected reward is offered for the risk involved in investing money in stocks.

We measure the reward as the difference between the *expected* HPR on the index stock fund and the **risk-free rate,** that is, the rate you can earn by leaving money in risk-free assets such as T-bills, money market funds, or the bank. We call this difference the **risk premium** on common stocks. If the risk-free rate in the example is 6% per year, and the expected index fund return is 14%, then the risk premium on stocks is 8% per year. The difference in any particular period between the *actual* rate of return on a risky asset and the risk-free rate is called **excess return.** Therefore, the risk premium is the expected value of the excess return, and the standard deviation of the excess return is an appropriate measure of its risk. (See Spreadsheet 5.1 for these calculations.)

The degree to which investors are willing to commit funds to stocks depends on **risk aversion.** Financial analysts generally assume investors are risk averse in the sense that, if the risk premium were zero, people would not be willing to invest any money in stocks. In theory, then, there must always be a positive risk premium on stocks in order to induce risk-averse investors to hold the existing supply of stocks instead of placing all their money in risk-free assets.

Although this sample scenario analysis illustrates the concepts behind the quantification of risk and return, you may still wonder how to get a more realistic estimate of $E(r)$ and σ for common stocks and other types of securities. Here, history has insights to offer. Analysis of the historical record of portfolio returns, however, makes use of a variety of important statistical tools and concepts, and so we first turn to a preparatory discussion.

CONCEPT CHECK 3

You invest $27,000 in a corporate bond selling for $900 per $1,000 par value. Over the coming year, the bond will pay interest of $75 per $1,000 of par value. The price of the bond at year's end will depend on the level of interest rates that will prevail at that time. You construct the following scenario analysis:

Interest Rates	Probability	Year-End Bond Price
High	.2	$850
Unchanged	.5	915
Low	.3	985

Your alternative investment is a T-bill that yields a sure rate of return of 5%. Calculate the HPR for each scenario, the expected rate of return, and the risk premium on your investment. What is the expected end-of-year dollar value of your investment?

5.5 TIME SERIES ANALYSIS OF PAST RATES OF RETURN

Time Series versus Scenario Analysis

In a forward-looking scenario analysis we determine a set of relevant scenarios and associated investment outcomes (rates of return), assign probabilities to each, and conclude by computing the risk premium (the reward) and standard deviation (the risk) of the proposed investment. In contrast, asset and portfolio return histories come in the form of time series of past realized returns that do not explicitly provide investors' original assessments of the probabilities of those observed returns; we observe only dates and associated HPRs. We must infer from this limited data the probability distributions from which these returns might have been drawn or, at least, some of its characteristics such as expected return and standard deviation.

Expected Returns and the Arithmetic Average

When we use historical data, we treat each observation as an equally likely "scenario." So if there are n observations, we substitute equal probabilities of magnitude $1/n$ for each $p(s)$

in Equation 5.11. The expected return, $E(r)$, is then estimated by the arithmetic average of the sample rates of return:

$$E(r) = \sum_{s=1}^{n} p(s)r(s) = \frac{1}{n}\sum_{s=1}^{n} r(s) \tag{5.13}$$

$$= \text{arithmetic average of rates of return}$$

EXAMPLE 5.6 Arithmetic Average and Expected Return

Spreadsheet 5.2 presents a (short) time series of annual holding-period returns for the S&P 500 index over the period 2001–2005. We treat each HPR of the $n = 5$ observations in the time series as an equally likely annual outcome during the sample years and assign it an equal probability of 1/5, or .2. Column B in Spreadsheet 5.2 therefore uses .2 as probabilities, and Column C shows the annual HPRs. Applying Equation 5.13 (using Excel's SUMPRODUCT function) to the time series in Spreadsheet 5.2 demonstrates that adding up the products of probability times HPR amounts to taking the arithmetic average of the HPRs (compare cells C10 and C11).

Example 5.6 illustrates the logic for the wide use of the arithmetic average in investments. If the time series of historical returns fairly represents the true underlying probability distribution, then the arithmetic average return from a historical period provides a good forecast of the investment's expected HPR.

The Geometric (Time-Weighted) Average Return

We saw that the arithmetic average provides an unbiased estimate of the *expected* rate of return. But what does the time series tell us about the *actual* performance of the portfolio over the full sample period? Column F in Spreadsheet 5.2 shows the wealth index from investing $1 in an S&P 500 index fund at the beginning of 2001. The value of the wealth index at the end of 2005, $1.0275, is the terminal value of the $1 investment, which implies a *5-year* holding-period return (HPR) of 2.75%.

	A	B	C	D	E	F
1						
2						
3		Implicitly Assumed		Squared	Gross HPR =	Wealth
4	Period	Probability = 1/5	HPR (decimal)	Deviation	1 + HPR	Index*
5	2001	.2	−0.1189	0.0196	0.8811	0.8811
6	2002	.2	−0.2210	0.0586	0.7790	0.6864
7	2003	.2	0.2869	0.0707	1.2869	0.8833
8	2004	.2	0.1088	0.0077	1.1088	0.9794
9	2005	.2	0.0491	0.0008	1.0491	1.0275
10	Arithmetic average	AVERAGE(C5:C9) =	0.0210			
11	Expected HPR	SUMPRODUCT(B5:B9, C5:C9) =	0.0210			
12		Standard deviation	SUMPRODUCT(B5:B9, D5:D9)^.5 =	0.1774		Check:
13			STDEV(C5:C9) =	0.1983		1.0054^5=
14			Geometric average return	GEOMEAN(E5:E9) − 1 =	0.0054	1.0275
15	*The value of $1 invested at the beginning of the sample period (1/1/2001).					

SPREADSHEET 5.2

eXcel

Please visit us at
www.mhhe.com/bkm

Time series of HPR for the S&P 500

An intuitive measure of performance over the sample period is the (fixed) annual HPR that would compound over the period to the same terminal value as obtained from the sequence of actual returns in the time series. Denote this rate by g, so that

$$\text{Terminal value} = (1 + r_1) \times (1 + r_2) \times \cdots \times (1 + r_5) = 1.0275$$
$$(1 + g)^n = \text{Terminal value} = 1.0275 \quad \text{(cell F9 in Spreadsheet 5.2)} \qquad \textbf{(5.14)}$$
$$g = \text{Terminal value}^{1/n} - 1 = 1.0275^{1/5} - 1 = .0054 = .54\% \quad \text{(cell E14)}$$

where $1 + g$ is the geometric average of the gross returns $(1 + r)$ from the time series (which can be computed with Excel's GEOMEAN function) and g is the annual HPR that would replicate the final value of our investment.

Practitioners of investments also call g the *time-weighted* (as opposed to dollar-weighted) average return, to emphasize that each past return receives an equal weight in the process of averaging. This distinction is important because investment managers often experience significant changes in funds under management as investors purchase or redeem shares. Rates of return obtained during periods when the fund is large produce larger dollar profits than rates obtained when the fund is small. We discuss this distinction further in the chapter on performance evaluation.

EXAMPLE 5.7   Geometric versus Arithmetic Average

The geometric average in Example 5.6 (.54%) is substantially less than the arithmetic average (2.10%). This discrepancy sometimes is a source of confusion. It arises from the asymmetric effect of positive and negative rates of returns on the terminal value of the portfolio.

Observe the returns in years 2002 ($-.2210$) and 2003 (.2869). The arithmetic average return over the 2 years is $(-.2210 + .2869)/2 = .03295$ (3.295%). However, if you had invested \$100 at the beginning of 2002, you would have only \$77.90 at the end of the year. In order to simply break even, you would then have needed to earn \$21.10 in 2003, which would amount to a whopping return of 27.09% (21.10/77.90). Why is such a high rate necessary to break even, rather than the 22.10% you lost in 2002? Because your base for 2003 was much smaller than \$100; the lower base means that it takes a greater subsequent percentage gain to just break even. Even a rate as high as the 28.69% realized in 2003 yields a portfolio value in 2003 of \$77.90 $\times$ 1.2869 = \$100.25, barely greater than \$100. This implies a 2-year annually compounded rate (the geometric average) of only .12%, significantly less than the arithmetic average of 3.295%.

The larger the swings in rates of return, the greater the discrepancy between the arithmetic and geometric averages, that is, between the compound rate earned over the sample period and the average of the annual returns. If returns come from a normal distribution, the difference exactly equals half the variance of the distribution, that is,

$$\text{Geometric average} = \text{Arithmetic average} - \tfrac{1}{2}\sigma^2 \qquad \textbf{(5.15)}$$

(A warning: to use Equation 5.15, you must express returns as decimals, not percentages.)

Variance and Standard Deviation

When thinking about risk, we are interested in the likelihood of deviations from the *expected* return. In practice, we usually cannot directly observe expectations, so we estimate the variance by averaging squared deviations from our *estimate* of the expected return, the arithmetic average, $\bar{r}$. Adapting Equation 5.12 for historic data, we again use equal probabilities for each observation, and use the sample average in place of the unobservable $E(r)$.

$$\text{Variance} = \text{expected value of squared deviations}$$

$$\sigma^2 = \sum p(s) \, [r(s) - E(r)]^2$$

Using historical data with n observations, we *estimate* variance as

$$\sigma^2 = \frac{1}{n} \sum_{s=1}^{n} [r(s) - \bar{r}]^2 \tag{5.16}$$

EXAMPLE 5.8   Variance and Standard Deviation

Take another look at Spreadsheet 5.2. Column D shows the square deviations from the arithmetic average, and cell D12 gives the standard deviation as the square root of the sum of products of the (equal) probabilities times the squared deviations (.1774).

The variance estimate from Equation 5.16 is downward biased, however. The reason is that we have taken deviations from the sample arithmetic average, $\bar{r}$, instead of the unknown, true expected value, $E(r)$, and so have introduced a bit of estimation error. This is sometimes called a *degrees of freedom* bias. We can eliminate the bias by multiplying the arithmetic average of squared deviations by the factor $n/(n-1)$. The variance and standard deviation then become

$$\sigma^2 = \left(\frac{n}{n-1} \right) \times \frac{1}{n} \sum_{j=1}^{n} [r(s) - \bar{r}]^2 = \frac{1}{n-1} \sum_{j=1}^{n} [r(s) - \bar{r}]^2$$

$$\sigma = \sqrt{\frac{1}{n-1} \sum_{j=1}^{n} [r(s) - \bar{r}]^2} \tag{5.17}$$

Cell D13 shows that the unbiased estimate of the standard deviation is .1983, which is a bit higher than the .1774 value obtained in cell D12.

The Reward-to-Volatility (Sharpe) Ratio

Finally, it is worth noting that investors presumably are interested in the expected *excess* return they can earn over the T-bill rate by replacing T-bills with a risky portfolio as well as the risk they would thereby incur. While the T-bill rate is not fixed each period, we still know with certainty what rate we will earn if we purchase a bill and hold it to maturity. Other investments typically entail accepting some risk in return for the prospect of earning more than the safe T-bill rate. Investors price risky assets so that the risk premium will be commensurate with the risk of that expected *excess* return, and hence it's best to measure risk by the standard deviation of excess, not total, returns.

The importance of the trade-off between reward (the risk premium) and risk (as measured by standard deviation or SD) suggests that we measure the attraction of an investment portfolio by the ratio of its risk premium to the SD of its excess returns.

$$\text{Sharpe ratio (for portfolios)} = \frac{\text{Risk premium}}{\text{SD of excess return}} \tag{5.18}$$

This reward-to-volatility measure (first proposed by William Sharpe and hence called the *Sharpe ratio*) is widely used to evaluate the performance of investment managers.

EXAMPLE 5.9   Sharpe Ratio

Take another look at Spreadsheet 5.1. The scenario analysis for the proposed investment in the stock-index fund resulted in a risk premium of 8%, and standard deviation of excess returns of 17.32%. This implies a Sharpe ratio of .46, a value that is pretty much in line with past performance of stock-index funds. We elaborate on this important measure in future chapters and show that while it is an adequate measure of the risk–return trade-off for diversified portfolios (the subject of this chapter), it is inadequate when applied to individual assets such as shares of stock that may be held as part of larger diversified portfolios.

CONCEPT CHECK

4

Using the annual returns for years 2003–2005 in Spreadsheet 5.2,

a. Compute the arithmetic average return.

b. Compute the geometric average return.

c. Compute the standard deviation of returns.

d. Compute the Sharpe ratio assuming the risk-free rate was 6% per year.

5.6   THE NORMAL DISTRIBUTION

The bell-shaped **normal distribution** appears naturally in many applications. For example, heights and weights of the population are well described by the normal distribution. In fact, many variables that are the end result of multiple random influences will exhibit a normal distribution. By the same logic, if return expectations implicit in asset prices are rational, actual rates of return realized should be normally distributed around these expectations.

To see why the normal curve is "normal," consider a newspaper stand that turns a profit of $100 on a good day and breaks even on a bad day, with equal probabilities of .5. Thus, the mean daily profit is $50 dollars. We can build a tree that compiles all the possible outcomes at the end of any period. Here is an **event tree** showing outcomes after 2 days:

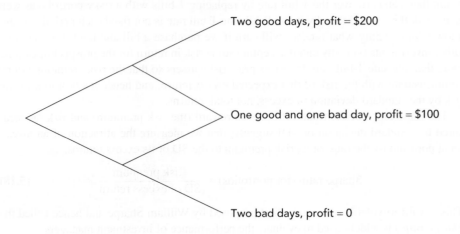

Two good days, profit = $200

One good and one bad day, profit = $100

Two bad days, profit = $0

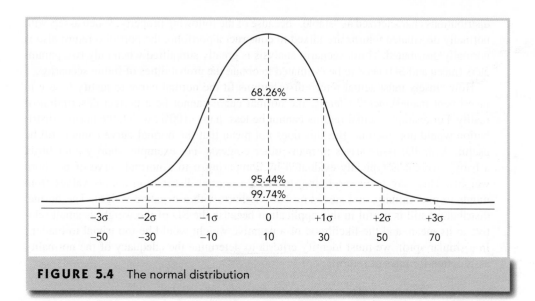

FIGURE 5.4 The normal distribution

Notice that 2 days can produce three different outcomes and, in general, *n* days can produce *n* + 1 possible outcomes. The most likely 2-day outcome is "one good and one bad day," which can happen in two ways (first a good day, or first a bad day). The probability of this outcome is .5. Less likely are the two extreme outcomes (both good days or both bad days) with probability .25 each.

What is the distribution of profits at the end of many business days? For example, after 200 days, there are 201 possible outcomes and, again, the midrange outcomes are the more likely because there are more sequences that lead to them. For example, while there is only one sequence that results in 200 consecutive bad days, there are an enormous number of sequences that result in 100 good days and 100 bad days. The probability distribution will eventually take on the appearance of the bell-shaped normal distribution, with midrange outcomes most likely, and extreme outcomes least likely.[6]

Figure 5.4 is a graph of the normal curve with mean of 10% and standard deviation of 20%. The graph shows the theoretical probability of rates of return within various ranges given these parameters. A smaller SD means that possible outcomes cluster more tightly around the mean, while a higher SD implies more diffuse distributions. The likelihood of realizing any particular outcome when sampling from a normal distribution is fully determined by the number of standard deviations that separate that outcome from the mean. Put differently, the normal distribution is completely characterized by two parameters, the mean and SD.

Investment management is far more tractable when rates of return can be well approximated by the normal distribution. First, the normal distribution is symmetric, that is, the probability of any positive deviation above the mean is equal to that of a negative deviation of the same magnitude. Absent symmetry, measuring risk as the standard deviation of returns is inadequate. Second, the normal distribution belongs to a special family of

---

[6]As a historical footnote, early descriptions of the normal distribution in the eighteenth century were based on the outcomes of a "binomial tree" like the one we have drawn for the newspaper stand, extended out to many periods. This representation is used in practice to price many option contracts, as we will see in Chapter 21. For a nice demonstration of how the binomial distribution quickly approximates the normal, go to **www.jcu.edu/math/isep/ Quincunx/Quincunx.html.**

distributions characterized as "stable," because of the following property: When assets with normally distributed returns are mixed to construct a portfolio, the portfolio return also is normally distributed. Third, scenario analysis is greatly simplified when only two parameters (mean and SD) need to be estimated to obtain the probabilities of future scenarios.

How closely must actual return distributions fit the normal curve to justify its use in investment management? Clearly, the normal curve cannot be a perfect description of reality. For example, actual returns cannot be less than -100%, which the normal distribution would not rule out. But this does not mean that the normal curve cannot still be useful. A similar issue arises in many other contexts. For example, shortly after birth, a baby's weight is typically evaluated by comparing it to a normal curve of newborn weights. This may seem surprising, because a normal distribution admits values from minus to plus infinity, and surely no baby is born with a negative weight. The normal distribution still is useful in this application because the SD of the weight is small relative to its mean, and the likelihood of a negative weight would be too trivial to matter.[7] In a similar spirit, we must identify criteria to determine the adequacy of the normality assumption for rates of return.

EXAMPLE 5.10   Normal Distribution Function in Excel

Suppose the monthly rate of return on the S&P 500 is approximately normally distributed with a mean of 1% and standard deviation of 6%. What is the probability that the return on the index in any month will be negative? We can use Excel's built-in functions to quickly answer this question. The probability of observing an outcome less than some cutoff according to the normal distribution function is given as NORMDIST(cutoff, mean, standard deviation, TRUE). In this case, we want to know the probability of an outcome below zero, when the mean is 1% and the standard deviation is 6%, so we compute NORMDIST(0, 1, 6, TRUE) = .4338. We could also use Excel's built-in *standard* normal function and ask for the probability of an outcome 1/6 of a standard deviation below the mean. This would be the same: NORMSDIST($-1/6$) = .4338.

CONCEPT CHECK **5**	What is the probability that the return on the index in Example 5.10 will be below -15%?

5.7 DEVIATIONS FROM NORMALITY

To assess the adequacy of the assumption of normality we focus on deviations from normality that would invalidate the use of standard deviation as an adequate measure of risk. Our first criterion is symmetry. A measure of asymmetry called **skew** uses the ratio of the

---

[7]In fact, the standard deviation is 511 grams while the mean is 3,958 grams. A negative weight would therefore be 7.74 standard deviations below the mean, and according to the normal distribution would have probability of only 4.97×10^{-15}. The issue of negative birth weight clearly isn't a *practical* concern.

average *cubed* deviations from the mean, called the third moment, to the cubed standard deviation to measure any asymmetry or "skewness" of a distribution.

$$\text{Skew} = \frac{E[r(s) - E(r)]^3}{\sigma^3} \quad (5.19)$$

Cubing deviations maintains their sign (for example, the cube of a negative number is negative). Thus, if the distribution is "skewed to the right," as is the dark curve in Figure 5.5A, the extreme positive values, when cubed, will dominate the third moment, resulting in a positive measure of skew. If the distribution is "skewed to the left," the cubed extreme negative values will dominate, and the skew will be negative.

When the distribution is positively skewed (the skew is greater than zero), the standard deviation overestimates risk, because extreme positive deviations from expectation (which are not a source of concern to the investor) nevertheless increase the estimate of volatility. Conversely, and more importantly, when the distribution is negatively skewed, the SD will underestimate risk.

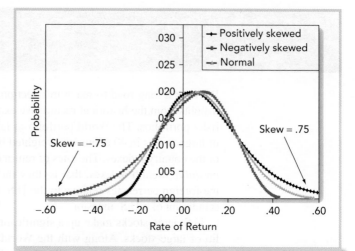

FIGURE 5.5A Normal and skewed distributions (mean = 6%, SD = 17%)

Another potentially important deviation from normality concerns the likelihood of extreme values on either side of the mean at the expense of a smaller fraction of moderate deviations. Graphically speaking, when the tails of a distribution are "fat," there is more probability mass in the tails of the distribution than predicted by the normal distribution, at the expense of "slender shoulders," that is, less probability mass near the center of the distribution. Figure 5.5B superimposes a "fat-tailed" distribution on a normal with the same mean and SD. Although symmetry is still preserved, the SD will underestimate the likelihood of extreme events: large losses as well as large gains.

Kurtosis is a measure of the degree of fat tails. In this case, we use the expectation of deviations from the mean raised to the *fourth* power and standardize by dividing by the fourth power of the SD, that is,

$$\text{Kurtosis} = \frac{E[r(s) - E(r)]^4}{\sigma^4} - 3 \quad (5.20)$$

We subtract 3 from the ratio in Equation 5.20, because the ratio for a normal distribution would be 3. Thus, the kurtosis of a normal distribution is defined as zero, and any kurtosis above zero is a sign of fatter tails than would be observed in a normal distribution. The kurtosis of the distribution in Figure 5.5B, which has visible fat tails, is .36.

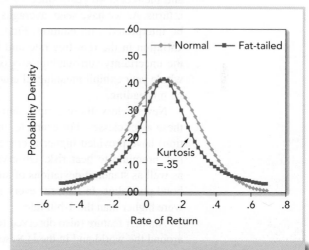

FIGURE 5.5B Normal and fat-tailed distributions (mean = .1, SD = .2)

| CONCEPT CHECK 6 | Estimate the skew and kurtosis of the five rates in Spreadsheet 5.2. |

We took a long road to reach this section, but now we are in a position to derive useful insights from the historical record. We examine the time series of five broadly diversified risky portfolios. The World portfolio of large stocks includes the market-index portfolios of large stocks in 40 countries, weighted by the market capitalization (total market value) of the country indexes. The rates of return on this (and the World bond) portfolio are based on *dollar* wealth indexes, that is, they include gains/losses from changes in the value of the foreign currencies relative to the U.S. dollar. Thus, the picture we present is from the standpoint of a U.S. investor.

U.S. large stocks make up a significant part, approximately 40%, of the World portfolio of large stocks. Along with the World large equities, we show results for a portfolio of large U.S. stocks, specifically, the S&P 500 index. The riskier portfolio composed of smaller U.S. stocks shows up next. Finally, we present statistics for two long-term bond portfolios. "World bonds" averages the return on long-term government bond indexes of 16 countries, weighted by the GDP of these countries. Here, too, U.S. Treasury bonds make up a significant, although somewhat smaller, fraction of the portfolio returns.

Average Returns and Standard Deviations

Table 5.3 compiles the average rates of return and their standard deviations over generational periods of 25 years, as well as summaries for the overall period of 80 years and the recent 40 years since 1966. Figure 5.6 presents frequency distributions of those returns. As we have seen, averages and standard deviations of raw annual returns should be interpreted with caution. First, standard deviations of total returns are affected by variation in the risk-free rate and thus do not measure the true source of risk, namely, the uncertainty surrounding *excess* returns. Second, annual rates that compound over a whole year exhibit meaningful amounts of skewness, and estimates of kurtosis also may be misleading.

Nevertheless, these simple statistics still reveal much about the nature of returns for these asset classes. For example, the asset classes with higher volatility (standard deviation) have provided higher average returns, supporting the idea that investors demand a risk premium to bear risk. Observe, for example, the consistently larger average return as well as standard deviations of small compared with large stocks, or stock compared to bond portfolios. In fact, for every generation, the average returns on the stock portfolios were higher than the T-bill rate.

Another feature (also observed for T-bill and inflation rates) is that the nature of returns around the world and in the U.S. seems to have changed since the 1960s. Standard deviations of stock portfolios have fallen, particularly for small stocks, but have remained about the same for bonds.

Other Statistics of the Risky Portfolios

Table 5.4 summarizes the essential statistics of the annual *excess* returns of the five risky portfolios. The statistics from which we can make inferences about the nature of the return distributions—skew, kurtosis, and serial correlation—are computed from the excess continuously compounded rates, that is, the difference between the continuously compounded rates on the risky portfolios and the continuously compounded T-bill rate.

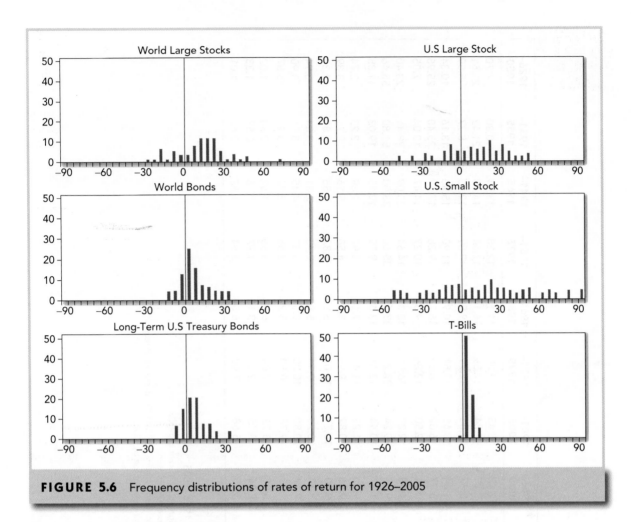

FIGURE 5.6 Frequency distributions of rates of return for 1926–2005

Sharpe Ratios

The reward-to-volatility (Sharpe) ratios of the five risky portfolios are of the same order of magnitude. The Sharpe ratios of the more recent 40 years, 1966–2005, are somewhat lower and generally more uniform across portfolios, in the range of .30 to .34. Notice, however, that the portfolio of U.S. long-term T-bonds has a significantly lower Sharpe measure (.21) than the other four, possibly for a good reason. Although the year-to-year rate of return on these bonds will vary, these bonds may serve as "the" risk-free choice for investors with long-term horizons. Consider a pension fund that must provide a known future cash flow to pay beneficiaries. The only risk-free vehicle to accomplish this objective would be to invest in a portfolio of U.S. T-bonds providing cash flows that match the pension fund's obligations. Hence, investors with a long horizon may not demand a risk premium commensurate with the risk as measured by the standard deviation of short-term returns.

Serial Correlation

In well-functioning capital markets, we would expect excess returns from successive years to be uncorrelated, that is, the serial correlation of excess returns should be nearly zero. Suppose, for example, that the serial correlation of the annual rate of return on a stock

TABLE 5.3

History of rates of return of asset classes for generations, 1926–2005

Portfolio	Statistic	1926–2005	1966–2005	1981–2005	1971–1995	1961–1985	1951–1975	1941–1965	1931–1955	1926–1950
World large stocks	Arithmetic avg.	11.46	12.12	13.45	14.20	11.17	12.28	13.01	10.80	7.70
	SD	18.57	17.72	17.84	17.59	16.10	17.64	14.18	21.42	21.61
	Geometric avg.	9.85	10.67	12.03	12.79	9.99	10.89	12.15	8.77	5.59
U.S. large stocks	Arithmetic avg.	12.15	11.64	13.65	13.51	10.92	11.90	15.70	13.16	10.34
	SD	20.26	16.97	16.02	16.62	16.74	19.28	17.17	25.40	25.98
	Geometric avg.	10.17	10.31	12.50	12.26	9.63	10.27	14.47	10.04	7.05
U.S. small stocks	Arithmetic avg.	17.95	14.98	12.27	16.01	18.37	14.64	23.09	28.41	23.40
	SD	38.71	29.58	20.24	27.21	33.65	35.68	33.00	51.80	55.46
	Geometric avg.	12.01	11.27	10.44	12.61	13.62	9.59	19.15	19.03	11.85
World bonds	Arithmetic avg.	6.14	9.40	11.22	11.48	7.10	3.92	1.69	2.23	2.74
	SD	9.09	9.56	10.89	9.96	8.39	4.58	5.16	8.76	8.89
	Geometric avg.	5.77	9.00	10.71	11.07	6.80	3.82	1.56	1.88	2.38
Long-term U.S. treasury bonds	Arithmetic avg.	5.68	8.17	10.28	9.94	5.52	2.75	2.31	3.34	3.94
	SD	8.09	9.97	10.80	10.20	8.59	6.37	4.45	3.96	3.90
	Geometric avg.	5.38	7.73	9.78	9.50	5.20	2.56	2.22	3.27	3.87
U.S. T-bills	Arithmetic avg.	3.75	5.98	5.73	7.04	6.55	3.66	1.62	0.63	1.02
	SD	3.15	2.84	3.15	2.87	3.15	1.97	1.16	0.57	1.33
	Geometric avg.	3.70	5.95	5.68	7.00	6.50	3.64	1.62	0.62	1.01

Sources: World portfolio: Datastream (16 countries index returns weighted by market capitalization).
U.S. stock returns for 1926–1995: Center for Research in Security Prices (CRSP).
U.S. stock returns since 1996: Returns on appropriate index portfolios: Large stocks, S&P 500; Small stocks, Russell 2000.
World bonds: Elroy Dimson, Paul Marsh, and Mike Staunton (16 countries weighted by GDP).
Long-term Government bonds: Lehman Bros. LT Treasury index.
T-bills: Salomon Smith Barney 3-month U.S. T-bill index.

TABLE 5.4

History of excess rates of return of asset classes for generations, 1926–2005

* Skew, kurtosis, and serial correlation are estimated from continuously compounded excess rates of return.

Portfolio	Statistic	1926–2005	1966–2005	1981–2005	1971–1995	1961–1985	1951–1975	1941–1965	1931–1955	1926–1950
World large stocks	Average excess return	7.71	6.14	7.73	7.16	4.63	8.62	11.39	10.18	6.68
	SD of excess return	18.90	18.21	18.33	18.33	16.67	18.87	14.30	21.38	21.66
	Sharpe ratio	0.41	0.34	0.42	0.39	0.28	0.46	0.80	0.48	0.31
	Skew	−0.61	−0.62	−0.53	−0.93	−0.78	−0.65	−0.12	−0.70	−0.57
	Kurtosis	0.98	−0.38	−0.57	0.48	0.32	0.38	0.55	3.05	1.88
	Serial correlation	0.14	0.05	0.13	−0.01	−0.16	0.03	0.04	0.03	0.23
U.S. large stocks	Average excess return	8.39	5.66	7.92	6.47	4.38	8.24	14.08	12.54	9.32
	SD of excess return	20.54	17.10	16.12	16.97	17.22	20.47	17.43	25.39	26.01
	Sharpe ratio	0.41	0.33	0.49	0.38	0.25	0.40	0.81	0.49	0.36
	Skew	−0.80	−0.70	−0.65	−1.00	−0.79	−0.39	−0.14	−1.15	−0.91
	Kurtosis	1.03	−0.20	−0.46	0.91	−0.02	0.03	−0.67	1.62	0.62
	Serial correlation	0.08	0.02	0.07	−0.15	−0.18	−0.08	−0.20	−0.05	0.16
U.S. small stocks	Average excess return	14.20	9.00	6.54	8.97	11.82	10.98	21.47	27.78	22.38
	SD of excess return	39.31	29.89	20.70	27.50	34.06	36.38	33.40	51.92	55.86
	Sharpe ratio	0.36	0.30	0.32	0.33	0.35	0.30	0.64	0.54	0.40
	Skew	−0.22	−0.30	−0.42	−0.86	−0.41	−0.07	0.45	−0.28	−0.31
	Kurtosis	0.86	0.20	−0.20	0.41	−0.03	−0.26	−0.84	0.75	−0.17
	Serial correlation	0.16	0.07	−0.26	0.12	0.12	0.01	0.11	0.05	0.26
World bonds	Average excess return	2.39	3.42	5.49	4.44	0.55	0.26	0.07	1.61	1.72
	SD of excess return	8.97	10.36	11.58	11.20	9.02	4.71	4.92	8.78	8.81
	Sharpe ratio	0.27	0.33	0.47	0.40	0.06	0.05	0.01	0.18	0.20
	Skew	0.48	0.23	−0.06	0.02	0.36	0.14	−1.13	0.69	0.65
	Kurtosis	0.70	−0.42	−0.63	−0.36	1.29	0.09	2.26	2.50	2.39
	Serial correlation	0.13	0.11	−0.14	0.16	0.07	0.16	0.13	0.19	0.16
Long-term U.S. Treasury bonds	Average excess return	1.93	2.18	4.55	2.90	−1.02	−0.91	0.69	2.72	2.92
	SD of excess return	7.91	10.18	11.01	10.70	8.44	6.36	4.60	4.21	4.19
	Sharpe ratio	0.24	0.21	0.41	0.27	−0.12	−0.14	0.15	0.64	0.70
	Skew	0.23	0.23	−0.04	0.45	0.87	0.17	0.08	−0.21	−0.38
	Kurtosis	0.28	−0.57	−0.78	−0.49	1.60	−0.01	−0.51	−0.20	0.09
	Serial correlation	−0.07	−0.05	−0.31	0.01	0.23	0.02	−0.19	−0.14	−0.25

Sources: World portfolio: Datastream (16 countries index returns weighted by market capitalization).
U.S. stock returns for 1926–1995: Center for Research in Security Prices (CRSP).
U.S. stock returns since 1996: Returns on appropriate index portfolios: Large stocks, S&P 500; Small stocks, Russell 2000.
World bonds: Elroy Dimson, Paul Marsh, and Mike Staunton (16 countries weighted by GDP).
Long-term Government bonds: Lehman Bros. LT Treasury index.
T-bills: Salomon Smith Barney 3-month U.S. T-bill index.

index were negative and that the index fell last year. Investors therefore could predict that stock prices are more likely than usual to rise in the coming year. But armed with this insight, they would *immediately* buy shares and bid up stock prices, thereby eliminating the prospect of an above-normal return in the coming year. We elaborate on this mechanism in the chapter on market efficiency.

Such a consideration does not apply to the T-bill rate, whose return is known in advance. The positive serial correlation of T-bill rates (.83 for the last 40 years) indicates that the short-term rate follows periods in which it predictably tends to rise or fall. However, this predictability in the baseline risk-free rate is not a source of abnormal profits (i.e., excessive profits relative to risk borne). This is a reason why the serial correlation of the *total* return on risky assets will be "contaminated" by that of the risk-free rate, and why we instead prefer to measure serial correlation from excess rates. Indeed, we find that the serial correlation is practically zero for four of the five portfolios. The serial correlation for World bond portfolio returns is somewhat high, but the fact that it was negative for the most recent years 1981–2005 suggests it is not economically significant.

Skewness and Kurtosis

Skewness and kurtosis are computed from the continuously compounded rate. Therefore, if the true underlying distribution of continuously compounded returns is normal, both should be zero. In fact, the skews of the large stock portfolios are significantly negative, −.62 for the World and −.70 to −.80 for the U.S. This negative skew may result from "lumpiness" of bad news (compared with good news) that produces occasional but large negative "jumps" in prices. It appears that the much larger standard deviation of the small stock portfolio reduces the relative impact of such negative jumps, and so the negative skew of the distribution is less pronounced (in the range of −.22 to −.30). Returns on the World and U.S. government bond portfolios are slightly positively skewed.

Negative skews imply that the standard deviation underestimates the actual level of risk. Take another look at Figure 5.5A; it shows two distributions with identical annual means (6%) and standard deviations (17%), similar to those of the excess returns of U.S. large stocks. But the skews of −.75 and .75 suggest a significant difference in risk, as is evident from the magnitude of possible losses. The probability of an annual loss greater than 40% is significantly higher for the negatively skewed distribution than for the normal distribution with the same mean and standard deviation.

Concern expressed in the literature about the presence of fat tails in stock return distributions does not manifest itself in this history. It appears that observed fat tails are largely due to older history. The most recent 40 years show no kurtosis for the large stock index, and only a small value for small stocks.

Estimates of Historical Risk Premiums

The striking observation here, again, is that the average excess return was positive for every generation over the entire 80-year history. In fact, research shows that this pattern characterizes periods as short as decades. Average excess returns of large stocks are somewhat lower in the more recent 40-year history and, overall, suggest a risk premium of 6–8%. Average excess returns for small U.S. stocks, as well as their standard deviation, were much lower over the recent 40-year history than over the full 80-year period.

An often-overlooked fact about the precision of estimates of expected returns and standard deviation needs to be clarified. Suppose we observe the time series of a stock price over 10 years. We compute the 10-year HPR from the price at the beginning, $P(0)$, and at the end of the 10 years, $P(10)$, by $r(10) = P(10)/P(1) - 1$. We can then annualize the 10-year return. Notice from this calculation that we obtain the average return *solely* from the start and ending prices. Prices from more frequent observations *during* the 10-year period would change neither the final value of the stock nor, therefore, our estimate of its expected return. The only way to increase the precision of this estimate of the expected annual return would be to obtain a sample longer than 10 years. But as we dig deeper into the past to obtain a longer sample, we have to ask whether the return distribution of more-distant history is representative of more-recent periods. This is precisely the dilemma we face when we observe a large difference between 80-year and 40-year historical averages.

Interestingly, this limitation does *not* apply to estimates of variance and standard deviation. Increasing the number of observations by slicing a 10-year sample into progressively shorter intervals does increase the accuracy of the estimate of the standard deviation of annual returns, even if the overall sample period remains 10 years. This is because we learn about volatility by observing fluctuations of returns within the sample period. (In contrast, intra-period fluctuations do not teach us about the general trend of stock prices, which is the basis of the estimate of expected return.) For this reason, estimates of risk (standard deviation) can be made more reliable than estimates of expected returns by sampling more frequently.[8]

Our estimate of risk may also sharpen our estimates of expected return. For example, when we observe that broadly diversified portfolios show similar Sharpe ratios, we have more confidence in the estimates of their expected returns from historical averages. Similarly, when we observe that the average return of small stocks fell in tandem with their standard deviation (the latter was 39% from 1926 to 2005 but only 29% between 1966 and 2005), we have more confidence that the more recent averages better estimate expected returns for the near future.

A Global View of the Historical Record

As financial markets around the world grow and become more transparent, U.S. investors look to improve diversification by investing internationally. Foreign investors that traditionally used U.S. financial markets as a safe haven to supplement home-country investments also seek international diversification to reduce risk. The question arises as to how historical U.S. experience compares with that of stock markets around the world.

Figure 5.7 shows a century-long history (1900–2000) of average nominal and real returns in stock markets of 16 developed countries. We find the United States in fourth place in terms of average real returns, behind Sweden, Australia, and South Africa. Figure 5.8 shows the standard deviations of real stock and bond returns for these same countries. We find the United States tied with four other countries for third place in terms of lowest standard deviation of real stock returns. So the United States has done well, but not abnormally so, compared with these countries.

One interesting feature of these figures is that the countries with the worst results, measured by the ratio of average real returns to standard deviation, are Italy, Belgium, Germany, and Japan—the countries most devastated by World War II. The top-performing countries are Australia, Canada, and the United States, the countries least devastated by the wars of the twentieth century. Another, perhaps more telling feature, is the insignificant difference between the real returns in the different countries. The difference between the highest average real rate (Sweden, at 7.6%) from the average return across the 16 countries (5.1%) is 2.5%. Similarly, the difference between the average and the lowest country return (Belgium, at 2.5%) is 2.6%. Using the average standard deviation of 23%, the *t*-statistic for a difference of 2.6% with 100 observations is

$$t\text{- Statistic} = \frac{\text{Difference in mean}}{\text{Standard deviation}/\sqrt{n}} = \frac{2.6}{23/\sqrt{100}} = 1.3$$

---

[8]The 10-year average return $r(10)$ is a geometric average. We know from Equation 5.15 that the arithmetic average is greater by $\frac{1}{2}\sigma^2$. Any improved accuracy in estimating σ^2 will still leave us with the original imprecision in the geometric average return.

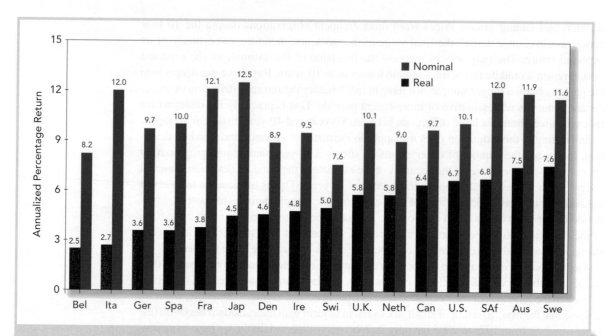

FIGURE 5.7 Nominal and real equity returns around the world, 1900–2000

Source: Elroy Dimson, Paul Marsh, and Mike Staunton, *Triumph of the Optimists: 101 Years of Global Investment Returns* (Princeton University Press, 2002), p. 50. Reprinted by permission of the Princeton University Press.

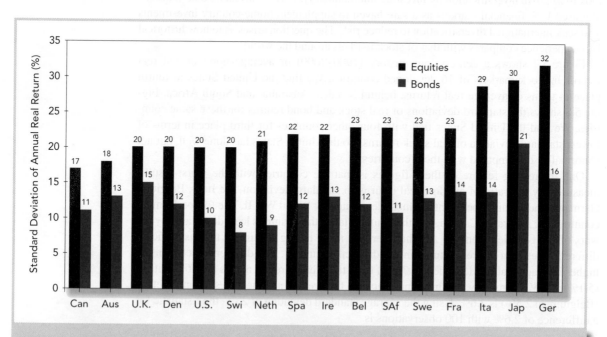

FIGURE 5.8 Standard deviations of real equity and bond returns around the world, 1900–2000

Source: Elroy Dimson, Paul Marsh, and Mike Staunton, *Triumph of the Optimists: 101 Years of Global Investment Returns* (Princeton University Press, 2002), p. 61. Reprinted by permission of the Princeton University Press.

which is far below conventional levels of statistical significance. We conclude that the U.S. experience cannot be dismissed as an outlier case. Hence, using the U.S. stock market as a yardstick for return characteristics may be reasonable.

These days, practitioners and scholars are debating whether the historical U.S. average risk-premium of large stocks over T-bills of 8.39% (Table 5.4) is a reasonable forecast for the long term. This debate centers around two questions: First, do economic factors that prevailed over that historic period (1926–2005) adequately represent those that may prevail over the forecasting horizon? Second, is the arithmetic average from the available history a good yardstick for long-term forecasts?

5.9   LONG–TERM INVESTMENTS*

Consider an investor saving $1 today toward retirement in 25 years, or 300 months. Investing the dollar in a risky stock portfolio (reinvesting dividends until retirement) with an expected rate of return of 1% per month, this retirement "fund" is expected to grow almost 20-fold to a terminal value of $(1 + .01)^{300} = \$19.79$ (providing total growth of 1,879%). Compare this impressive result to an investment in a 25-year Treasury bond with a risk-free EAR of 6% (.407% per month) that yields a retirement fund of $1.06^{25} = \$4.29$. We see that a monthly risk premium of just .593% produces a retirement fund that is more than four times that of the risk-free alternative. Such is the power of compound interest. Why, then, would anyone invest in Treasuries? Obviously, this is an issue of trading excess return for risk. What is the nature of this return-to-risk trade-off? The risk of an investment that compounds at fluctuating rates over the long run is widely misunderstood, and it is important to figure it out.

We can construct the probability distribution of the stock-fund terminal value from a binomial tree just as we did earlier for the newspaper stand, except that instead of *adding* monthly profits, the portfolio value *compounds* monthly by a rate drawn from a given distribution. For example, suppose we can approximate the portfolio monthly distribution as follows: Each month the rate of return is either 5.54% or –3.54%, with equal probabilities of .5. This configuration generates an expected return of 1% per month. The portfolio risk is measured as the monthly standard deviation: $\sqrt{.5 \times (5.54 - 1)^2 + .5 \times (-3.54 - 1)^2} = 4.54\%$. After 2 months, the event tree looks like this:

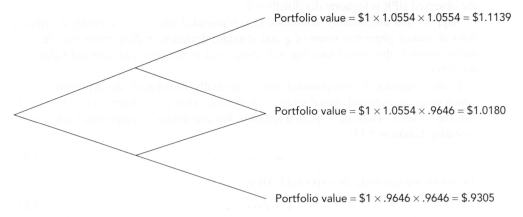

Portfolio value = $1 × 1.0554 × 1.0554 = $1.1139

Portfolio value = $1 × 1.0554 × .9646 = $1.0180

Portfolio value = $1 × .9646 × .9646 = $.9305

---

*The material in this and the next subsection addresses important and ongoing debates about risk and return, but is more challenging. It may be skipped in shorter courses without impairing the ability to understand later chapters.

Despite the low probability that a portfolio insurance policy would have to pay up (only 3.8% for the 25-year policy), the magnitude and timing[9] of possible losses would make such long-term insurance surprisingly costly. For example, standard option-pricing models suggest that the value of insurance against shortfall risk over a 10-year horizon would cost nearly 20% of the initial value of the portfolio. And contrary to any intuition that a longer horizon reduces shortfall risk, the value of portfolio insurance increases dramatically with the maturity of the contract. For example, a 25-year policy would be about 50% more costly, or about 30% of the initial portfolio value.

The Sharpe Ratio Revisited

The Sharpe ratio (the reward-to-volatility ratio) divides average excess return by its standard deviation. You should be aware, however, that the Sharpe ratio has a time dimension, in that the Sharpe ratio for any given portfolio will vary systematically with the assumed investment holding period.

We have seen that as the holding period grows longer, the average continuously compounded return grows proportionally to the investment horizon (this is approximately true as well for short-term effective rates). The standard deviation, however, grows at a slower pace, the square root of time. Therefore, the Sharpe ratio *grows* with the length of the holding period at the rate of the square root of time. Hence, when comparing Sharpe ratios from a series of monthly rates to those from a series of annual rates, we must first multiply the monthly Sharpe ratio by the square root of 12.

EXAMPLE 5.12   Sharpe Ratios

For the long-term risky portfolio (with a monthly expected return of 1% and standard deviation of 5%), given a risk-free rate of .5%, the Sharpe ratio is $(1 - .5)/5 = .10$. The expected annual return would be 12% and annual standard deviation would be $5\% \times \sqrt{12} = 16.6\%$ so the Sharpe ratio using annual returns would be $(12 - 6)/16.6 = .36$, similar to values we find in the historical record of well-diversified portfolios.

Simulation of Long-Term Future Rates of Return

The frequency distributions in Figure 5.6 provide only rough descriptions of the nature of the return distributions and are even harder to interpret for long-term investments. A good way to use history to learn about the distribution of long-term future returns is to simulate these future returns from the available sample. A popular method to accomplish this task is called *bootstrapping*.

Bootstrapping is a procedure that avoids any assumptions about the return distribution, except that all rates of return in the sample history are equally likely. For example, we could simulate a 25-year sample of possible future returns by sampling (with replacement) 25 randomly selected returns from our available 80-year history. We compound those 25 returns to obtain one possible 25-year holding-period return. This procedure is repeated thousands of times to generate a probability distribution of long-term total returns that is anchored in the historical frequency distribution.

---

[9]By "timing," we mean that a decline in stock prices is associated with a bad economy when extra income would be most important to an investor. The fact that the insurance policy would pay off in these scenarios contributes to its market value.

The cardinal decision when embarking on a bootstrapping exercise is the choice of how far into the past we should go to draw observations for "future" return sequences. We will use our entire 80-year sample so that we are more likely to include low probability events of extreme value.

One important objective of this exercise is to assess the potential effect of deviations from the normality assumption on the probability distribution of a long-term investment in U.S. stocks. For this purpose, we simulate a 25-year distribution of annual returns for large and small stocks and contrast these samples to similar samples drawn from normal distributions that (due to compounding) result in lognormally distributed long-term total returns. Results are shown in Figure 5.10. Panel A shows the frequency distributions of the paired samples of large U.S. stocks, constructed by sampling both from actual returns and from the normal distribution. Panel B shows the same frequency distributions for small U.S. stocks. The boxes inside Figure 5.10 show the statistics of the distributions.

We first review the results for large stocks in panel A. Viewing the frequency distributions, we see that the difference between the simulated history and the normal draw is small but distinct. Despite the very small differences between the averages of 1-year and

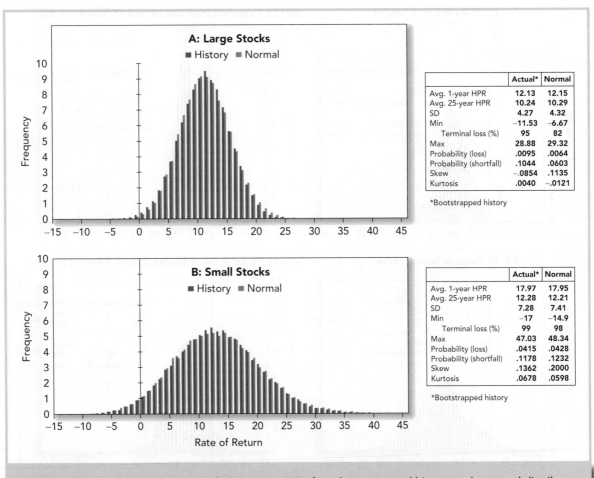

	Actual*	Normal
Avg. 1-year HPR	12.13	12.15
Avg. 25-year HPR	10.24	10.29
SD	4.27	4.32
Min	−11.53	−6.67
Terminal loss (%)	95	82
Max	28.88	29.32
Probability (loss)	.0095	.0064
Probability (shortfall)	.1044	.0603
Skew	−.0854	.1135
Kurtosis	.0040	−.0121

*Bootstrapped history

	Actual*	Normal
Avg. 1-year HPR	17.97	17.95
Avg. 25-year HPR	12.28	12.21
SD	7.28	7.41
Min	−17	−14.9
Terminal loss (%)	99	98
Max	47.03	48.34
Probability (loss)	.0415	.0428
Probability (shortfall)	.1178	.1232
Skew	.1362	.2000
Kurtosis	.0678	.0598

*Bootstrapped history

FIGURE 5.10 Annually compounded, 25-year HPRs from bootstrapped history and a normal distribution (50,000 observations)

25-year annual returns, as well as between the standard deviations, the small differences in skewness and kurtosis combine to produce significant differences in the probabilities of shortfalls and losses, as well as in the potential terminal loss. For small stocks, shown in panel B, the smaller differences in skewness and kurtosis lead to almost identical figures for the probability and magnitude of losses.

What about risk for investors with other long-term horizons? Figure 5.11 compares 25-year to 10-year investments in large and small stocks. For an appropriate comparison, we must account for the fact that the 10-year investment will be supplemented with a 15-year investment in T-bills. To accomplish this comparison, we bootstrap 15-year samples from the 80-year history of T-bill rates and augment each sample with 10 annual rates drawn from the history of the risky investment. Panels A1 and A2 in Figure 5.11 show the comparison for large stocks. The frequency distributions reveal a substantial difference in the risks of the terminal portfolio. This difference is clearly manifested in the portfolio performance statistics. The same picture arises in panels B1 and B2 for small stocks.

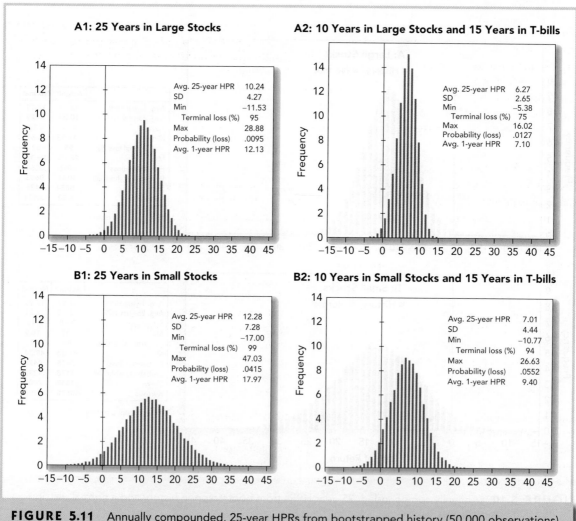

FIGURE 5.11   Annually compounded, 25-year HPRs from bootstrapped history (50,000 observations)

Figure 5.12 shows the trajectories of the wealth indexes of possible outcomes of a 25-year investment in large stocks, compared with the wealth index of the average outcome of a T-bill portfolio. The outcomes of the stock portfolio in Figure 5.12 range from the worst, through the bottom 1% and 5% of terminal value, and up to the mean and median terminal values. The bottom 5% still results in a significant shortfall relative to the T-bill portfolio. In sum, the analysis clearly demonstrates that the notion that investments in stocks become less risky in the long run must be rejected.

Yet many practitioners hold on to the view that investment risk is less pertinent to long-term investors. A typical demonstration shown in the nearby box relies on

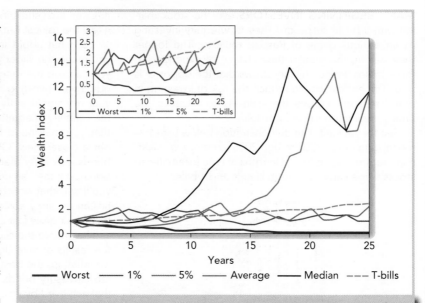

FIGURE 5.12   Wealth indexes of selected outcomes of large stock portfolios and the average T-bill portfolio. Inset: Focus on worst, 1%, and 5% outcomes versus bills.

the fact that the standard deviation (or range of likely outcomes) of *annualized* returns is lower for longer-term horizons. But the demonstration is silent on the range of *total* returns.

Forecasts for the Long Haul

We use arithmetic averages to forecast future rates of return because they are unbiased estimates of expected rates over equivalent holding periods. But the arithmetic average of short-term returns can be misleading when used to forecast long-term cumulative returns. This is because sampling errors in the estimate of expected return will have asymmetric impact when compounded over long periods. Positive sampling variation will compound to greater upward errors than negative variation.

Jacquier, Kane, and Marcus[10] show that an unbiased forecast of total return over long horizons requires compounding at a weighted average of the arithmetic and geometric historical averages. The proper weight applied to the geometric average equals the ratio of the length of the forecast horizon to the length of the estimation period. For example, if we wish to forecast the cumulative return for a 25-year horizon from a 80-year history, an unbiased estimate would be to compound at a rate of

$$\text{Geometric average} \times \frac{25}{80} + \text{Arithmetic average} \times \frac{(80 - 25)}{80}$$

This correction would take about .6% off the historical arithmetic average risk premium on large stocks and about 2% off the arithmetic average of small stocks. A forecast for the next 80 years would require compounding at only the geometric average, and for longer horizons at an even lower number. The forecast horizons that are relevant for current middle-aged investors would depend on their life expectancies.

---

[10]Eric Jacquier, Alex Kane, and Alan J. Marcus, "Geometric or Arithmetic Means: A Reconsideration," *Financial Analysts Journal,* November/December 2003.

TIME VS. RISK

MANY BEGINNING INVESTORS eye the stock market with a bit of suspicion. They view equity investing as an anxious game of Russian roulette: The longer they stay in, the greater their chance of experiencing more losses. In fact, history shows that the opposite is true. The easiest way to reduce the risk of investing in equities—and improve the gain—is to increase the time you hang on to your portfolio.

See for yourself. The demonstration below uses historical data from 1950 through 2005 to compare investment returns over different lengths of time for small-cap stocks, large caps, long-term bonds and T-bills.

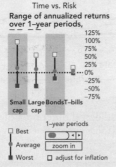

Time vs. Risk
Range of annualized returns over 1-year periods,

Small cap   Large cap   Bonds   T-bills

1-year periods

Best
Average
Worst

zoom in
adjust for inflation

Source: CRSP, Federal Reserve

The graph starts out showing results for investments held over one-year periods. There's no doubt about

it: Over such short intervals, small-cap stocks are definitely the riskiest bet.

But what about investing for more than a year? If you move the slider at the bottom right of the graph, you can see the range of returns for longer time periods. Even investing for two years instead of one cuts your risk significantly. As the length of time increases, the volatility of equities decreases sharply—so much so that you may need to click the "zoom in" button to get a closer view. Over 10-year periods, government bonds look safer than large-cap equities on the downside. Click the "adjust for inflation" box, however, and you'll see that bond "safety" can be illusory. Inflation has an uncanny ability to erode the value of securities that don't grow fast enough.

Now move the slider all the way to the right to see the results of investing for 20-year intervals. Adjusting for inflation, the best 20-year gain a portfolio of long-term Treasury bonds could muster is much lower than that achieved by small- and large-cap stocks. And contrary to popular belief, over their worst 20-year period, long-term bonds actually *lost* money when adjusted for inflation. Meanwhile, small-cap investors still had gains over a 20-year-period, even when stocks were at their worst.

Source: Abridged from **www.smartmoney.com/university/Investing101/RiskvsReward/index.cfm?story=timevsrisk,** accessed October 15, 2007.

5.10 MEASUREMENT OF RISK WITH NON-NORMAL DISTRIBUTIONS

The realization that rates of return on stock portfolios are not quite normally distributed, and that as a result, standard deviations may not adequately measure risk, has preoccupied practitioners for quite some time. As we have seen, this concern is indeed well placed. Three methods to augment the measurement of risk are common in the industry: Value at Risk (VaR), Conditional Tail Expectations (CTE), and Lower Partial Standard Deviation (LPSD). We show these statistics for the bootstrapped distributions, contrasted with those for the normal distribution in Table 5.5.

Value at Risk (VaR)

Professional investors extensively use a risk measure that highlights the potential loss from extreme negative returns, called **value at risk,** denoted by **VaR** (to distinguish it from VAR or Var, commonly used to denote variance). The VaR is another name for the *quantile* of a distribution. The quantile (q) of a distribution is the value below which lie q% of the values. Thus the median of the distribution is the 50% quantile. Practitioners commonly use the 5% quantile as the VaR of the distribution. It tells us that, with a probability of 5%, we

| | Large U.S. Stocks | | Small U.S. Stocks | | TABLE 5.5 |
	History	Normal	History	Normal	Risk measures for non-normal distributions
Value at Risk					
VaR 1%	0.02%	0.18%	−0.63%	−0.64%	
VaR 5%	1.16	1.27	0.17	0.13	
VaR 10%	2.17	2.26	1.13	1.04	
VaR 50%	10.58	10.29	16.41	15.99	
Conditional Tail Expectation					
CTE 1%	−0.28%	−0.14%	−0.77%	−0.76%	
CTE 5%	0.46	0.62	−0.33	−0.35	
CTE 10%	1.07	1.20	0.16	0.12	
CTE 50%	5.07	4.99	5.80	5.49	
Lower Partial Standard Deviation					
LPSD of 25-year HPR	4.34%	4.23%	7.09%	7.14%	
LPSD of 1-year HPR	21.71	21.16	35.45	35.72	
Average 1-year HPR	12.13	12.15	17.97	17.95	

can expect a loss equal to or greater than the VaR. For a normal distribution, which is completely described by its mean and standard deviation, the 5% VaR always lies 1.65 standard deviations below the mean, and thus, while it may be a convenient benchmark, it adds no information about risk. But if the distribution is not adequately described by the normal, the VaR does give useful information about the magnitude of loss we can expect in a "bad" (e.g., 5% quantile) scenario.

The first four lines in Table 5.5 show the VaR from the bootstrapped distributions and the paired normal samples. The VaR values provide important input for investments in large stocks. The commonly used 5% VaR for large stocks is a 25-year annual holding-period return of 1.16%, compared with 1.27% for the paired normal distribution. The distribution of the portfolio of small stocks is more reasonably approximated by the normal, as is evident in the similarity of the VaR values.

Conditional Tail Expectation (CTE)

The 5% **conditional tail expectation (CTE)** provides the answer to the question, "Assuming the terminal value of the portfolio falls in the bottom 5% of possible outcomes, what is its expected value?" This value for large stocks is a 25-year holding-period return of .46%. Notice the difference from the 5% VaR (1.16%). The 5% VaR is in fact the outcome at the upper boundary of these worst-case outcomes. This is of course the highest holding-period return among the 5% worst-case scenarios, and by construction is higher than the CTE. CTE improves on VaR, as it is more like an expected value that accounts for the entire tail of the distribution, in particular worst-case scenarios, and thus provides a fuller sense of potential losses from low-probability events.

Lower Partial Standard Deviation (LPSD)

An appropriate measure of risk for non-normal distributions is the standard deviation computed solely from values below the expected return. This is a measure of "downside risk" and is called the **lower partial standard deviation (LPSD).** Some practitioners even go as far as using the LPSD in place of the regular standard deviation to compute the Sharpe

8. Derive the probability distribution of the 1-year HPR on a 30-year U.S. Treasury bond with an 8% coupon if it is currently selling at par and the probability distribution of its yield to maturity a year from now is as follows:

State of the Economy	Probability	YTM
Boom	.20	11.0%
Normal growth	.50	8.0
Recession	.30	7.0

For simplicity, assume the entire 8% coupon is paid at the end of the year rather than every 6 months.

9. What is the standard deviation of a random variable q with the following probability distribution:

Value of q	Probability
0	.25
1	.25
2	.50

10. The continuously compounded annual return on a stock is normally distributed with a mean of 20% and standard deviation of 30%. With 95.44% confidence, we should expect its actual return in any particular year to be between which pair of values? *Hint:* look again at Figure 5.4.

  a. −40.0% and 80.0%
  b. −30.0% and 80.0%
  c. −20.6% and 60.6%
  d. −10.4% and 50.4%

11. Using historical risk premiums over the 1926–1995 period as your guide, what would be your estimate of the expected annual HPR on the S&P 500 stock portfolio if the current risk-free interest rate is 6%?

12. You can find annual holding-period returns for several asset classes at our Web site (**www. mhhe.com/bkm**); look for links to Chapter 5. Compute the means, standard deviations, skewness, and kurtosis of the annual HPR of large stocks and long-term Treasury bonds using only the 30 years of data between 1976 and 2005. How do these statistics compare with those computed from the data for the period 1926–1941? Which do you think are the most relevant statistics to use for projecting into the future?

13. During a period of severe inflation, a bond offered a nominal HPR of 80% per year. The inflation rate was 70% per year.

  a. What was the real HPR on the bond over the year?
  b. Compare this real HPR to the approximation $r \approx R - i$.

14. Suppose that the inflation rate is expected to be 3% in the near future. Using the historical data provided in this chapter, what would be your predictions for:

  a. The T-bill rate?
  b. The expected rate of return on large stocks?
  c. The risk premium on the stock market?

15. An economy is making a rapid recovery from steep recession, and businesses foresee a need for large amounts of capital investment. Why would this development affect real interest rates?

Challenge Problems 16 and 17 are more difficult. You may need to review the definitions of call and put options in Chapter 2.

16. You are faced with the probability distribution of the HPR on the stock market index fund given in Spreadsheet 5.1 of the text. Suppose the price of a put option on a share of the index fund with exercise price of $110 and time to expiration of 1 year is $12.

  a. What is the probability distribution of the HPR on the put option?
  b. What is the probability distribution of the HPR on a portfolio consisting of one share of the index fund and a put option?

c. In what sense does buying the put option constitute a purchase of insurance in this case?

17. Take as given the conditions described in the previous problem, and suppose the risk-free interest rate is 6% per year. You are contemplating investing $107.55 in a 1-year CD and simultaneously buying a call option on the stock market index fund with an exercise price of $110 and expiration of 1 year. What is the probability distribution of your dollar return at the end of the year?

1. Given $100,000 to invest, what is the expected risk premium in dollars of investing in equities versus risk-free T-bills (U.S. Treasury bills) based on the following table?

Action	Probability	Expected Return
Invest in equities	.6	$ 50,000
	.4	–$ 30,000
Invest in risk-free T-bill	1.0	$ 5,000

2. Based on the scenarios below, what is the expected return for a portfolio with the following return profile?

	Market Condition		
	Bear	Normal	Bull
Probability	.2	.3	.5
Rate of return	–25%	10%	24%

Use the following scenario analysis for Stocks X and Y to answer CFA Problems 3 through 6 (round to the nearest percent).

	Bear Market	Normal Market	Bull Market
Probability	0.2	0.5	0.3
Stock X	–20%	18%	50%
Stock Y	–15%	20%	10%

3. What are the expected rates of return for Stocks X and Y?

4. What are the standard deviations of returns on Stocks X and Y?

5. Assume that of your $10,000 portfolio, you invest $9,000 in Stock X and $1,000 in Stock Y. What is the expected return on your portfolio?

6. Probabilities for three states of the economy and probabilities for the returns on a particular stock in each state are shown in the table below.

State of Economy	Probability of Economic State	Stock Performance	Probability of Stock Performance in Given Economic State
Good	.3	Good	.6
		Neutral	.3
		Poor	.1
Neutral	.5	Good	.4
		Neutral	.3
		Poor	.3
Poor	.2	Good	.2
		Neutral	.3
		Poor	.5

RISK AVERSION AND CAPITAL ALLOCATION TO RISKY ASSETS

THE PROCESS OF constructing an investor portfolio can be viewed as a sequence of two steps: (1) selecting the composition of one's portfolio of risky assets such as stocks and long-term bonds, and (2) deciding how much to invest in that risky portfolio versus in a safe asset such as short-term Treasury bills. Obviously, an investor cannot decide how to allocate investment funds between the risk-free asset and that risky portfolio without knowing its expected return and degree of risk, so a fundamental part of the asset allocation problem is to characterize the risk–return trade-off for this portfolio.

While the task of constructing an optimal risky portfolio is technically complex, it can be delegated to a professional because it largely entails well-defined optimization techniques. In contrast, the decision of how much to invest in that portfolio depends on an investor's *personal* preferences about risk versus expected return, and therefore it cannot easily be delegated. As we will see in the chapter on behavioral finance, many investors stumble over this cardinal step. We therefore begin our journey into

portfolio theory by establishing a framework to explore this fundamental decision, namely, capital allocation between the risk-free and the risky portfolio.

We begin by introducing two themes in portfolio theory that are centered on risk. The first is the tenet that investors will avoid risk unless they can anticipate a reward for engaging in risky investments. The second theme allows us to quantify investors' personal trade-offs between portfolio risk and expected return. To do this we introduce a personal *utility function,* which allows each investor to assign welfare or "utility" scores to alternative portfolios based on expected return and risk and choose the portfolio with the highest score. We elaborate on the historical and empirical basis for the utility model in the appendix to this chapter.

Armed with the utility model, we can resolve the investment decision that is most consequential to investors, that is, how much of their wealth to put at risk for the greater expected return that can thus be achieved. We assume that the construction of the risky portfolio from the universe of available risky assets has already taken place and defer the discussion of how to construct that risky portfolio to the next chapter. At this point the investor can assess the expected return and risk of the overall portfolio. Using the expected return and risk parameters in the utility model yields the optimal allocation of capital between the risky portfolio and risk-free asset.

6.1 RISK AND RISK AVERSION

In Chapter 5 we introduced the concepts of the holding-period return (HPR) and the excess return over the risk-free rate. We also discussed estimation of the **risk premium** (the *expected* excess return) and the standard deviation of the rate of return, which we use as the measure of portfolio risk. We demonstrated these concepts with a scenario analysis of a specific risky portfolio (Spreadsheet 5.1). To emphasize that bearing risk typically must be accompanied by a reward in the form of a risk premium, we first distinguish between speculation and gambling.

Risk, Speculation, and Gambling

One definition of *speculation* is "the assumption of considerable investment risk to obtain commensurate gain." Although this definition is fine linguistically, it is useless without first specifying what is meant by "considerable risk" and "commensurate gain."

By "considerable risk" we mean that the risk is sufficient to affect the decision. An individual might reject an investment that has a positive risk premium because the potential gain is insufficient to make up for the risk involved. By "commensurate gain" we mean a positive risk premium, that is, an expected profit greater than the risk-free alternative.

To gamble is "to bet or wager on an uncertain outcome." If you compare this definition to that of speculation, you will see that the central difference is the lack of "commensurate gain." Economically speaking, a gamble is the assumption of risk for no purpose but enjoyment of the risk itself, whereas speculation is undertaken *in spite* of the risk involved because one perceives a favorable risk–return trade-off. To turn a gamble into a speculative prospect requires an adequate risk premium to compensate risk-averse investors for the risks they bear. Hence, *risk aversion and speculation are not inconsistent.* Notice that a risky investment with a risk premium of zero, sometimes called a **fair game,** amounts to a gamble. A risk-averse investor will reject it.

In some cases a gamble may appear to the participants as speculation. Suppose two investors disagree sharply about the future exchange rate of the U.S. dollar against the British pound. They may choose to bet on the outcome. Suppose that Paul will pay Mary $100 if the value of £1 exceeds $1.90 one year from now, whereas Mary will pay Paul if the pound is worth less than $1.90. There are only two relevant outcomes: (1) the pound will exceed $1.90, or (2) it will fall below $1.90. If both Paul and Mary agree on the probabilities of the two possible outcomes, and if neither party anticipates a loss, it must be that they assign $p = .5$ to each outcome. In that case the expected profit to both is zero and each has entered one side of a gambling prospect.

What is more likely, however, is that the bet results from differences in the probabilities that Paul and Mary assign to the outcome. Mary assigns it $p > .5$, whereas Paul's assessment is $p < .5$. They perceive, subjectively, two different prospects. Economists call this case of differing beliefs "heterogeneous expectations." In such cases investors on each side of a financial position see themselves as speculating rather than gambling.

Both Paul and Mary should be asking, Why is the other willing to invest in the side of a risky prospect that I believe offers a negative expected profit? The ideal way to resolve heterogeneous beliefs is for Paul and Mary to "merge their information," that is, for each party to verify that he or she possesses all relevant information and processes the information properly. Of course, the acquisition of information and the extensive communication that is required to eliminate all heterogeneity in expectations is costly, and thus up to a point heterogeneous expectations cannot be taken as irrational. If, however, Paul and Mary enter such contracts frequently, they would recognize the information problem in one of two ways: Either they will realize that they are creating gambles when each wins half of the bets, or the consistent loser will admit that he or she has been betting on the basis of inferior forecasts.

CONCEPT CHECK 1	Assume that dollar-denominated T-bills in the United States and pound-denominated bills in the United Kingdom offer equal yields to maturity. Both are short-term assets, and both are free of default risk. Neither offers investors a risk premium. However, a U.S. investor who holds U.K. bills is subject to exchange rate risk, because the pounds earned on the U.K. bills eventually will be exchanged for dollars at the future exchange rate. Is the U.S. investor engaging in speculation or gambling?

Risk Aversion and Utility Values

The history of rates of return on various asset classes presented in Chapter 5, as well as numerous elaborate empirical studies, leave no doubt that risky assets command a risk premium in the marketplace. This implies that most investors are risk averse.

Investors who are **risk averse** reject investment portfolios that are fair games or worse. Risk-averse investors are willing to consider only risk-free or speculative prospects with positive risk premiums. Loosely speaking, a risk-averse investor "penalizes" the expected rate of return of a risky portfolio by a certain percentage (or penalizes the expected profit by a dollar amount) to account for the risk involved. The greater the risk, the larger the penalty. One might wonder why we assume risk aversion as fundamental. We believe that most investors would accept this view from simple introspection, but we discuss the question more fully in the Appendix of this chapter.

To illustrate the issues we confront when choosing among portfolios with varying degrees of risk, consider a specific example. Suppose the risk-free rate is 5% and that an investor considers three alternative risky portfolios with risk premiums, expected returns, and standard deviations as given in Table 6.1. The risk premiums and degrees of risk (standard deviation, SD) of the portfolios in the table are chosen to represent the properties of low-risk bonds (L), high-risk bonds (M), and large stocks (H). Accordingly, these portfolios offer progressively higher risk premiums to compensate for greater risk. How might investors choose among them?

TABLE 6.1	Portfolio	Risk Premium	Expected Return	Risk (SD)
Available risky portfolios (Risk-free rate = 5%)	L (low risk)	2%	7%	5%
	M (medium risk)	4	9	10
	H (high risk)	8	13	20

Intuitively, one would rank each portfolio as more attractive when its expected return is higher, and lower when its risk is higher. But when risk increases along with return, the most attractive portfolio is not obvious. How can investors quantify the rate at which they are willing to trade off return against risk?

We will assume that each investor can assign a welfare, or **utility,** score to competing investment portfolios based on the expected return and risk of those portfolios. Higher utility values are assigned to portfolios with more attractive risk-return profiles. Portfolios receive higher utility scores for higher expected returns and lower scores for higher volatility. Many particular "scoring" systems are legitimate. One reasonable function that has been employed by both financial theorists and the CFA Institute assigns a portfolio with expected return $E(r)$ and variance of returns σ^2 the following utility score:

$$U = E(r) - \tfrac{1}{2}A\sigma^2 \tag{6.1}$$

where U is the utility value and A is an index of the investor's risk aversion. The factor of $\tfrac{1}{2}$ is just a scaling convention. To use Equation 6.1, rates of return must be expressed as decimals rather than percentages.

Equation 6.1 is consistent with the notion that utility is enhanced by high expected returns and diminished by high risk. Notice that risk-free portfolios receive a utility score equal to their (known) rate of return, because they receive no penalty for risk. The extent to which the variance of risky portfolios lowers utility depends on A, the investor's degree of risk aversion. More risk-averse investors (who have the larger values of A) penalize risky investments more severely. Investors choosing among competing investment portfolios will select the one providing the highest utility level. The nearby box discusses some techniques that financial advisers use to gauge the risk aversion of their clients.

EXAMPLE 6.1   Evaluating Investments by Using Utility Scores

Consider three investors with different degrees of risk aversion: $A_1 = 2$, $A_2 = 3.5$, and $A_3 = 5$, all of whom are evaluating the three portfolios in Table 6.1. Because the risk-free rate is assumed to be 5%, Equation 6.1 implies that all three investors would assign a utility score of .05 to the risk-free alternative. Table 6.2 presents the utility scores that would be assigned by each investor to each portfolio. The portfolio with the highest utility score for each investor appears in bold. Notice that the high-risk portfolio, H, would be chosen only by the investor with the lowest degree of risk aversion, $A_1 = 2$, while the low-risk portfolio, L, would be passed over even by the most risk-averse of our three investors. All three portfolios beat the risk-free alternative for the investors with levels of risk aversion given in the table.

Investor Risk Aversion (A)	Utility Score of Portfolio L $[E(r) = .07; \sigma = .05]$	Utility Score of Portfolio M $[E(r) = .09; \sigma = .10]$	Utility Score of Portfolio H $[E(r) = .13; \sigma = .20]$
2.0	$.07 - \tfrac{1}{2} \times 2 \times .05^2 = .0675$	$.09 - \tfrac{1}{2} \times 2 \times .1^2 = .0800$	$\mathbf{.13 - \tfrac{1}{2} \times 2 \times .2^2 = .09}$
3.5	$.07 - \tfrac{1}{2} \times 3.5 \times .05^2 = .0656$	$\mathbf{.09 - \tfrac{1}{2} \times 3.5 \times .1^2 = .0725}$	$.13 - \tfrac{1}{2} \times 3.5 \times .2^2 = .06$
5.0	$.07 - \tfrac{1}{2} \times 5 \times .05^2 = .0638$	$\mathbf{.09 - \tfrac{1}{2} \times 5 \times .1^2 = .0650}$	$.13 - \tfrac{1}{2} \times 5 \times .2^2 = .03$

TABLE 6.2

Utility scores of alternative portfolios for investors with varying degrees of risk aversion

We can interpret the utility score of *risky* portfolios as a **certainty equivalent rate** of return. The certainty equivalent rate is the rate that risk-free investments would need to offer to provide the same utility score as the risky portfolio. In other words, it is the rate that, if earned with certainty, would provide a utility score equivalent to that of the portfolio in question. The certainty equivalent rate of return is a natural way to compare the utility values of competing portfolios.

Now we can say that a portfolio is desirable only if its certainty equivalent return exceeds that of the risk-free alternative. A sufficiently risk-averse investor may assign any risky portfolio, even one with a positive risk premium, a certainty equivalent rate of return that is below the risk-free rate, which will cause the investor to reject the risky portfolio. At the same time, a less risk-averse investor may assign the same portfolio a certainty equivalent rate that exceeds the risk-free rate and thus will prefer the portfolio to the risk-free alternative. If the risk premium is zero or negative to begin with, any downward adjustment to utility only makes the portfolio look worse. Its certainty equivalent rate will be below that of the risk-free alternative for all risk-averse investors.

CONCEPT CHECK 2	A portfolio has an expected rate of return of 20% and standard deviation of 30%. T-bills offer a safe rate of return of 7%. Would an investor with risk-aversion parameter $A = 4$ prefer to invest in T-bills or the risky portfolio? What if $A = 2$?

In contrast to risk-averse investors, **risk-neutral** investors (with $A = 0$) judge risky prospects solely by their expected rates of return. The level of risk is irrelevant to the risk-neutral investor, meaning that there is no penalty for risk. For this investor a portfolio's certainty equivalent rate is simply its expected rate of return.

A **risk lover** (for whom $A < 0$) is willing to engage in fair games and gambles; this investor adjusts the expected return *upward* to take into account the "fun" of confronting the prospect's risk. Risk lovers will always take a fair game because their upward adjustment of utility for risk gives the fair game a certainty equivalent that exceeds the alternative of the risk-free investment.

We can depict the individual's trade-off between risk and return by plotting the characteristics of potential investment portfolios that the individual would view as equally attractive on a graph with axes measuring the expected value and standard deviation of portfolio returns. Figure 6.1 plots the characteristics of one portfolio denoted P.

Portfolio *P*, which has expected return $E(r_P)$ and standard deviation σ_P is preferred by risk-averse investors to any portfolio in quadrant IV because it has an expected return equal to or greater than any portfolio in that quadrant

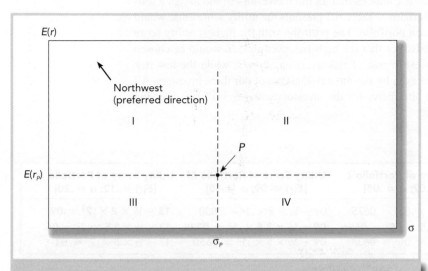

FIGURE 6.1   The trade-off between risk and return of a potential investment portfolio, *P*

and a standard deviation equal to or smaller than any portfolio in that quadrant. Conversely, any portfolio in quadrant I is preferable to portfolio P because its expected return is equal to or greater than P's and its standard deviation is equal to or smaller than P's.

This is the mean-standard deviation, or equivalently, **mean-variance (M-V) criterion.** It can be stated as follows: portfolio A dominates B if

$$E(r_A) \geq E(r_B)$$

and

$$\sigma_A \leq \sigma_B$$

and at least one inequality is strict (rules out the equality).

In the expected return–standard deviation plane in Figure 6.1, the preferred direction is northwest, because in this direction we simultaneously increase the expected return *and* decrease the variance of the rate of return. This means that any portfolio that lies northwest of P is superior to it.

What can be said about portfolios in quadrants II and III? Their desirability, compared with P, depends on the exact nature of the investor's risk aversion. Suppose an investor identifies all portfolios that are equally attractive as portfolio P. Starting at P, an increase in standard deviation lowers utility; it must be compensated for by an increase in expected return. Thus point Q in Figure 6.2 is equally desirable to this investor as P. Investors will be equally attracted to portfolios with high risk and high expected returns compared with other portfolios with lower risk but lower expected returns. These equally preferred portfolios will lie in the mean–standard deviation plane on a curve called the **indifference curve** that connects all portfolio points with the same utility value (Figure 6.2).

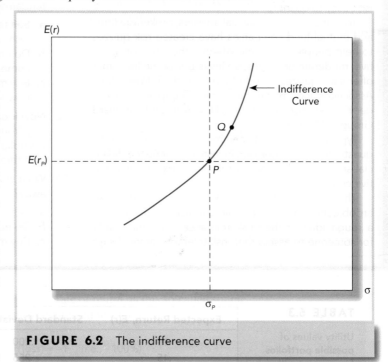

FIGURE 6.2   The indifference curve

To determine some of the points that appear on the indifference curve, examine the utility values of several possible portfolios for an investor with $A = 4$, presented in Table 6.3. Note that each portfolio offers identical utility, because the portfolios with higher expected return also have higher risk (standard deviation).

Estimating Risk Aversion

How might we go about estimating the levels of risk aversion we might expect to observe in practice? One way is to observe individuals' decisions when confronted with risk. For example, we can observe how much people are willing to pay to avoid risk, such as when they buy insurance against large losses. Consider

> **CONCEPT CHECK 3**
>
> a. How will the indifference curve of a less risk-averse investor compare to the indifference curve drawn in Figure 6.2?
> b. Draw both indifference curves passing through point P.

What about variance and standard deviation of the investor's position? The deviations from expectation, $r - E(r)$, for each outcome are

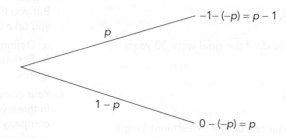

$$-1 - (-p) = p - 1$$
$$p$$
$$1 - p$$
$$0 - (-p) = p$$

The variance of the rate of return equals the expectation of the squared deviation:

$$\sigma^2(r) = p \times (p - 1)^2 + (1 - p) \times p^2 = p(1 - p) \tag{6.3}$$

To calculate the utility score of this simple prospect we use the risk-aversion coefficient, A, the expected return, $E(r)$ (from Equation 6.2), and the variance, $\sigma^2(r)$ (from Equation 6.3) in Equation 6.1 and obtain

$$U = E(r) - \tfrac{1}{2}A\sigma^2(r)$$
$$= -p - \tfrac{1}{2}Ap(1 - p) \tag{6.4}$$

Now we can relate the risk-aversion parameter to the amount that an individual would be willing to pay for insurance against the potential loss. Suppose an insurance company offers to cover any loss over the year for a fee of v dollars per dollar of insured property. The individual who pays $\$v$ per dollar of real estate value to the insurance company will face no risk—the insurance company will reimburse any losses, so the real estate will be worth its original value at year-end. Taking out such a policy amounts to a sure negative rate of return of $-v$, with a utility score: $U = -v$.

How much will our investor pay for the policy, that is, what is the maximum value of v he or she will be willing to pay? To find this value, we equate the utility score of the uninsured property (given in Equation 6.4) to that of the insured property (which is $-v$):

$$U = -p - \tfrac{1}{2}A\, p(1 - p) = -v \tag{6.5}$$

We can solve Equation 6.5 for the policy cost at which the investor would be indifferent between purchasing insurance or going uninsured. This is the maximum amount that he or she will be willing pay for the insurance policy:

$$v = p[1 + \tfrac{1}{2}A(1 - p)] \tag{6.6}$$

Remember that the expected loss on the property is p. Therefore, the term in the square brackets in Equation 6.6 tells us the *multiple* of the expected loss, p, the investor is willing to pay for the policy. Obviously, a risk-neutral investor, with $A = 0$, will be willing to pay no more than the expected loss, $v = p$. With $A = 1$, the term in square brackets is almost 1.5 (because p is small), so v will be close to $1.5p$. In other words, the investor is willing to pay almost 50% more than the expected loss for the policy. For each additional increment to the degree of risk aversion ($A = 2, 3$, and so on), the investor is willing to add (almost) another 50% of the expected loss to the insurance premium.

TABLE 6.4

Investor's willingness to pay for catastrophe insurance

Investor Risk Aversion, A	Expected Rate of Loss, $p = .0001$	Expected Rate of Loss, $p = .01$
	Maximum Premium, v, as a Multiple of Expected Loss, p	Maximum Premium, v, as a Multiple of Expected Loss, p
0	1.0000	1.0000
1	1.5000	1.4950
2	1.9999	1.9900
3	2.4999	2.4850
4	2.9998	2.9800
5	3.4998	3.4750

Table 6.4 shows how many multiples of the expected loss the investor is willing to pay for insurance for two values of the probability of disaster, p, as a function of the degree of risk aversion. Based on individuals' actual willingness to pay for insurance against catastrophic loss as in this example, economists estimate that investors seem to exhibit degrees of risk aversion in the range of 2 to 4, that is, would be likely to be willing to pay as much as two to three times the expected loss but not much more.

By the way, this analysis also tells you something about the merits of competitive insurance markets. Insurance companies that are able to share their risk with many co-insurers will be willing to offer coverage for premiums that are only slightly higher than the expected loss, even though each investor may *value* the coverage at several multiples of the expected loss. The large savings that investors thus derive from competitive insurance markets are analogous to the consumer surplus derived from competition in other markets.

More support for the hypothesis that A is somewhere in the range of 2 to 4 can be obtained from estimates of the expected rate of return and risk on a broad stock-index portfolio. We will present this argument shortly after we describe how investors might determine their optimal allocation of wealth to risky assets.

6.2   CAPITAL ALLOCATION ACROSS RISKY AND RISK–FREE PORTFOLIOS

History shows us that long-term bonds have been riskier investments than investments in Treasury bills and that stock investments have been riskier still. On the other hand, the riskier investments have offered higher average returns. Investors, of course, do not make all-or-nothing choices from these investment classes. They can and do construct their portfolios using securities from all asset classes. Some of the portfolio may be in risk-free Treasury bills, some in high-risk stocks.

The most straightforward way to control the risk of the portfolio is through the fraction of the portfolio invested in Treasury bills and other safe money market securities versus risky assets. This capital allocation decision is an example of an asset allocation choice—a choice among broad investment classes, rather than among the specific securities within each asset class. Most investment professionals consider asset allocation the most important part of portfolio construction. Consider this statement by John Bogle, made when he was chairman of the Vanguard Group of Investment Companies:

> The most fundamental decision of investing is the allocation of your assets: How much should you own in stock? How much should you own in bonds? How much should you own in cash reserves? . . . That decision [has been shown to account] for an astonishing 94% of the differences in total returns achieved by institutionally managed pension funds. . . . There is no reason to believe that the same relationship does not also hold true for individual investors.[1]

Therefore, we start our discussion of the risk–return trade-off available to investors by examining the most basic asset allocation choice: the choice of how much of the portfolio to place in risk-free money market securities versus other risky asset classes.

We will denote the investor's portfolio of risky assets as P and the risk-free asset as F. We will assume for the sake of illustration that the risky component of the investor's overall portfolio comprises two mutual funds, one invested in stocks and the other invested in long-term bonds. For now, we take the composition of the risky portfolio as given and focus only on the allocation between it and risk-free securities. In the next chapter, we turn to asset allocation and security selection across risky assets.

When we shift wealth from the risky portfolio to the risk-free asset, we do not change the relative proportions of the various risky assets within the risky portfolio. Rather, we reduce the relative weight of the risky portfolio as a whole in favor of risk-free assets.

For example, assume that the total market value of an initial portfolio is $300,000, of which $90,000 is invested in the Ready Asset money market fund, a risk-free asset for practical purposes. The remaining $210,000 is invested in risky securities—$113,400 in equities ($E$) and $96,600 in long-term bonds (B). The equities and long bond holdings comprise "the" risky portfolio, 54% in E and 46% in B:

$$E: \quad w_E = \frac{113,400}{210,000} = .54$$

$$B: \quad w_B = \frac{96,600}{210,000} = .46$$

The weight of the risky portfolio, P, in the **complete portfolio,** including risk-free *and* risky investments, is denoted by y:

$$y = \frac{210,000}{300,000} = .7 \text{ (risky assets)}$$

$$1 - y = \frac{90,000}{300,000} = .3 \text{ (risky-free assets)}$$

The weights of each asset class in the complete portfolio are as follows:

$$E: \quad \frac{\$113,400}{\$300,000} = .378$$

$$B: \quad \frac{\$96,600}{\$300,000} = .322$$

$$\text{Risky portfolio} = E + B = .700$$

The risky portfolio makes up 70% of the complete portfolio.

[1]John C. Bogle, *Bogle on Mutual Funds* (Burr Ridge, IL: Irwin Professional Publishing, 1994), p. 235.

EXAMPLE 6.2   The Risky Portfolio

Suppose that the owner of this portfolio wishes to decrease risk by reducing the allocation to the risky portfolio from $y = .7$ to $y = .56$. The risky portfolio would then total only .56 $\times$ \$300,000 = \$168,000, requiring the sale of \$42,000 of the original \$210,000 of risky holdings, with the proceeds used to purchase more shares in Ready Asset (the money market fund). Total holdings in the risk-free asset will increase to \$300,000 $\times$ $(1 - .56)$ = \$132,000, the original holdings plus the new contribution to the money market fund:

$$\$90,000 + \$42,000 = \$132,000$$

The key point, however, is that we leave the proportions of each asset in the risky portfolio unchanged. Because the weights of E and B in the risky portfolio are .54 and .46, respectively, we sell .54 $\times$ \$42,000 = \$22,680 of E and .46 $\times$ \$42,000 = \$19,320 of B. After the sale, the proportions of each asset in the risky portfolio are in fact unchanged:

$$E: \quad w_E = \frac{113,400 - 22,680}{210,000 - 42,000} = .54$$

$$B: \quad w_B = \frac{96,600 - 19,320}{210,000 - 42,000} = .46$$

Rather than thinking of our risky holdings as E and B separately, we may view our holdings as if they were in a single fund that holds equities and bonds in fixed proportions. In this sense we may treat the risky fund as a single risky asset, that asset being a particular bundle of securities. As we shift in and out of safe assets, we simply alter our holdings of that bundle of securities commensurately.

Given this simplification, we can now turn to the desirability of reducing risk by changing the risky/risk-free asset mix, that is, reducing risk by decreasing the proportion y. As long as we do not alter the weights of each security within the risky portfolio, the probability distribution of the rate of return on the risky portfolio remains unchanged by the asset reallocation. What will change is the probability distribution of the rate of return on the *complete* portfolio that consists of the risky asset and the risk-free asset.

CONCEPT CHECK 4	What will be the dollar value of your position in equities (*E*), and its proportion in your overall portfolio, if you decide to hold 50% of your investment budget in Ready Asset?

6.3   THE RISK–FREE ASSET

By virtue of its power to tax and control the money supply, only the government can issue default-free bonds. Even the default-free guarantee by itself is not sufficient to make the bonds risk-free in real terms. The only risk-free asset in real terms would be a perfectly price-indexed bond. Moreover, a default-free perfectly indexed bond offers a guaranteed real rate to an investor only if the maturity of the bond is identical to the investor's desired holding period. Even indexed bonds are subject to interest rate risk, because real

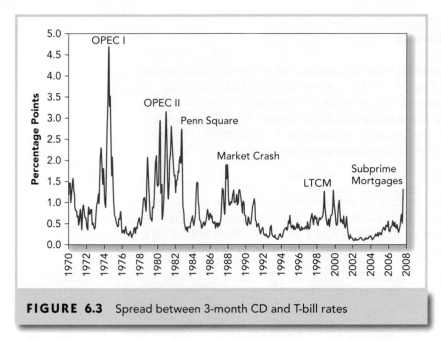

FIGURE 6.3 Spread between 3-month CD and T-bill rates

interest rates change unpredictably through time. When future real rates are uncertain, so is the future price of indexed bonds.

Nevertheless, it is common practice to view Treasury bills as "the" **risk-free asset.** Their short-term nature makes their values insensitive to interest rate fluctuations. Indeed, an investor can lock in a short-term nominal return by buying a bill and holding it to maturity. Moreover, inflation uncertainty over the course of a few weeks, or even months, is negligible compared with the uncertainty of stock market returns.

In practice, most investors use a broader range of money market instruments as a risk-free asset. All the money market instruments are virtually free of interest rate risk because of their short maturities and are fairly safe in terms of default or credit risk.

Most money market funds hold, for the most part, three types of securities—Treasury bills, bank certificates of deposit (CDs), and commercial paper (CP)—differing slightly in their default risk. The yields to maturity on CDs and CP for identical maturity, for example, are always somewhat higher than those of T-bills. The recent history of this yield spread for 90-day CDs is shown in Figure 6.3.

Money market funds have changed their relative holdings of these securities over time but, by and large, T-bills make up only about 15% of their portfolios. Nevertheless, the risk of such blue-chip short-term investments as CDs and CP is minuscule compared with that of most other assets such as long-term corporate bonds, common stocks, or real estate. Hence we treat money market funds as the most easily accessible risk-free asset for most investors.

6.4 PORTFOLIOS OF ONE RISKY ASSET AND A RISK–FREE ASSET

In this section we examine the risk–return combinations available to investors. This is the "technical" part of asset allocation; it deals only with the opportunities available to investors given the features of the broad asset markets in which they can invest. In the next section we address the "personal" part of the problem—the specific individual's choice of the best risk–return combination from the set of feasible combinations.

Suppose the investor has already decided on the composition of the risky portfolio. Now the concern is with the proportion of the investment budget, y, to be allocated to the risky portfolio, P. The remaining proportion, $1 - y$, is to be invested in the risk-free asset, F.

Denote the risky rate of return of P by r_P, its expected rate of return by $E(r_P)$, and its standard deviation by σ_P. The rate of return on the risk-free asset is denoted as r_f. In the numerical example we assume that $E(r_P) = 15\%$, $\sigma_P = 22\%$, and that the risk-free rate is $r_f = 7\%$. Thus the risk premium on the risky asset is $E(r_P) - r_f = 8\%$.

With a proportion, y, in the risky portfolio, and $1 - y$ in the risk-free asset, the rate of return on the *complete* portfolio, denoted C, is r_C where

$$r_C = yr_P + (1 - y)r_f \tag{6.7}$$

Taking the expectation of this portfolio's rate of return,

$$E(r_C) = yE(r_P) + (1 - y)r_f$$
$$= r_f + y[E(r_P) - r_f] = 7 + y(15 - 7) \tag{6.8}$$

This result is easily interpreted. The base rate of return for any portfolio is the risk-free rate. In addition, the portfolio is *expected* to earn a risk premium that depends on the risk premium of the risky portfolio, $E(r_P) - r_f$, and the investor's position in that risky asset, y. Investors are assumed to be risk averse and thus unwilling to take on a risky position without a positive risk premium.

When we combine a risky asset and a risk-free asset in a portfolio, the standard deviation of the resulting complete portfolio is the standard deviation of the risky asset multiplied by the weight of the risky asset in that portfolio.[2] Because the standard deviation of the risky portfolio is $\sigma_P = 22\%$,

$$\sigma_C = y\sigma_P = 22y \tag{6.9}$$

which makes sense because the standard deviation of the portfolio is proportional to both the standard deviation of the risky asset and the proportion invested in it. In sum, the rate of return of the complete portfolio will have expected value $E(r_C) = r_f + y[E(r_P) - r_f] = 7 + 8y$ and standard deviation $\sigma_C = 22y$.

The next step is to plot the portfolio characteristics (given the choice for y) in the expected return–standard deviation plane. This is done in Figure 6.4. The risk-free asset, F, appears on the vertical axis because its standard deviation is zero. The risky asset, P, is plotted with a standard deviation, $\sigma_P = 22\%$, and expected return of 15%. If an investor chooses to invest solely in the risky asset, then $y = 1.0$, and the complete portfolio is P. If the chosen position is $y = 0$, then $1 - y = 1.0$, and the complete portfolio is the risk-free portfolio F.

What about the more interesting midrange portfolios where y lies between 0 and 1? These portfolios will graph on the straight line connecting points F and P. The slope of that line is $[E(r_P) - r_f]/\sigma_P$ (or rise/run), in this case, 8/22.

The conclusion is straightforward. Increasing the fraction of the overall portfolio invested in the risky asset increases expected return according to Equation 6.8 at a rate of 8%. It also increases portfolio standard deviation according to Equation 6.9 at the rate of 22%. The extra return per extra risk is thus 8/22 = .36.

To derive the exact equation for the straight line between F and P, we rearrange Equation 6.9 to find that $y = \sigma_C/\sigma_P$, and we substitute for y in Equation 6.8 to describe the expected return–standard deviation trade-off:

$$E(r_C) = r_f + y[E(r_P) - r_f]$$
$$= r_f + \frac{\sigma_C}{\sigma_P}[E(r_P) - r_f] = 7 + \frac{8}{22}\sigma_C \tag{6.10}$$

---

[2]This is an application of a basic rule from statistics: If you multiply a random variable by a constant, the standard deviation is multiplied by the same constant. In our application, the random variable is the rate of return on the risky asset, and the constant is the fraction of that asset in the complete portfolio. We will elaborate on the rules for portfolio return and risk in the following chapter.

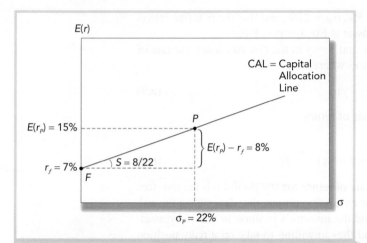

FIGURE 6.4 The investment opportunity set with a risky asset and a risk-free asset in the expected return–standard deviation plane

Thus the expected return of the complete portfolio as a function of its standard deviation is a straight line, with intercept r_f and slope

$$S = \frac{E(r_P) - r_f}{\sigma_P} = \frac{8}{22} \qquad \textbf{(6.11)}$$

Figure 6.4 graphs the *investment opportunity set,* which is the set of feasible expected return and standard deviation pairs of all portfolios resulting from different values of y. The graph is a straight line originating at r_f and going through the point labeled P.

This straight line is called the **capital allocation line** (CAL). It depicts all the risk–return combinations available to investors. The slope of the CAL, denoted S, equals the increase in the expected return of the complete portfolio per unit of additional standard deviation—in other words, incremental return per incremental risk. For this reason, the slope is called the **reward-to-volatility ratio.** It also is called the Sharpe ratio (see Chapter 5).

A portfolio equally divided between the risky asset and the risk-free asset, that is, where $y = .5$, will have an expected rate of return of $E(r_C) = 7 + .5 \times 8 = 11\%$, implying a risk premium of 4%, and a standard deviation of $\sigma_C = .5 \times 22 = 11\%$. It will plot on the line FP midway between F and P. The reward-to-volatility ratio is $S = 4/11 = .36$, precisely the same as that of portfolio P.

What about points on the CAL to the right of portfolio P? If investors can borrow at the (risk-free) rate of $r_f = 7\%$, they can construct portfolios that may be plotted on the CAL to the right of P.

EXAMPLE 6.3 Leverage

Suppose the investment budget is $300,000 and our investor borrows an additional $120,000, investing the total available funds in the risky asset. This is a *leveraged* position in the risky asset; it is financed in part by borrowing. In that case

$$y = \frac{420,000}{300,000} = 1.4$$

and $1 - y = 1 - 1.4 = -.4$, reflecting a short (borrowing) position in the risk-free asset. Rather than lending at a 7% interest rate, the investor borrows at 7%. The distribution of the portfolio rate of return still exhibits the same reward-to-volatility ratio:

$$E(r_C) = 7\% + (1.4 \times 8\%) = 18.2\%$$

$$\sigma_C = 1.4 \times 22\% = 30.8\%$$

$$S = \frac{E(r_C) - r_f}{\sigma_C} = \frac{18.2 - 7}{30.8} = .36$$

As one might expect, the leveraged portfolio has a higher standard deviation than does an unleveraged position in the risky asset.

Of course, nongovernment investors cannot borrow at the risk-free rate. The risk of a borrower's default causes lenders to demand higher interest rates on loans. Therefore, the nongovernment investor's borrowing cost will exceed the lending rate of $r_f = 7\%$. Suppose the borrowing rate is $r_f^B = 9\%$. Then in the borrowing range, the reward-to-volatility ratio, the slope of the CAL, will be $[E(r_P) - r_f^B]/\sigma_P = 6/22 = .27$. The CAL will therefore be "kinked" at point P, as shown in Figure 6.5. To the left of P the investor is lending at 7%, and the slope of the CAL is .36. To the right of P, where $y > 1$, the investor is borrowing at 9% to finance extra investments in the risky asset, and the slope is .27.

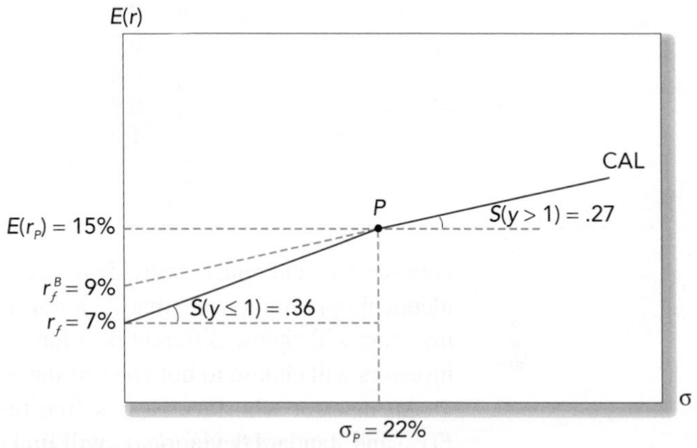

In practice, borrowing to invest in the risky portfolio is easy and straightforward if you have a margin account with a broker. All you have to do is tell your broker that you want to buy "on margin." Margin purchases may not exceed 50% of the purchase value. Therefore, if your net worth in the account is $300,000, the broker is allowed to lend you up to $300,000 to purchase additional stock.[3] You would then have $600,000 on the asset side of your account and $300,000 on the liability side, resulting in $y = 2.0$.

FIGURE 6.5   The opportunity set with differential borrowing and lending rates

CONCEPT CHECK 6	Suppose that there is an upward shift in the expected rate of return on the risky asset, from 15% to 17%. If all other parameters remain unchanged, what will be the slope of the CAL for $y \le 1$ and $y > 1$?

6.5   RISK TOLERANCE AND ASSET ALLOCATION

We have shown how to develop the CAL, the graph of all feasible risk–return combinations available from different asset allocation choices. The investor confronting the CAL now must choose one optimal portfolio, C, from the set of feasible choices. This choice entails a trade-off

[3]Margin purchases require the investor to maintain the securities in a margin account with the broker. If the value of the securities declines below a "maintenance margin," a "margin call" is sent out, requiring a deposit to bring the net worth of the account up to the appropriate level. If the margin call is not met, regulations mandate that some or all of the securities be sold by the broker and the proceeds used to reestablish the required margin. See Chapter 3, Section 3.6, for further discussion. As we will see in Chapter 22, futures contracts also offer leverage. If the risky portfolio is an index fund on which a contract trades, the implicit rate on the loan will be close to the T-bill rate.

TABLE 6.5

Utility levels for various positions in risky assets (y) for an investor with risk aversion A = 4

(1) y	(2) E(r_C)	(3) σ_C	(4) U = E(r) − ½Aσ^2
0	.070	0	.0700
0.1	.078	.022	.0770
0.2	.086	.044	.0821
0.3	.094	.066	.0853
0.4	.102	.088	.0865
0.5	.110	.110	.0858
0.6	.118	.132	.0832
0.7	.126	.154	.0786
0.8	.134	.176	.0720
0.9	.142	.198	.0636
1.0	.150	.220	.0532

between risk and return. Individual investor differences in risk aversion imply that, given an identical opportunity set (that is, a risk-free rate and a reward-to-volatility ratio), different investors will choose different positions in the risky asset. In particular, the more risk-averse investors will choose to hold less of the risky asset and more of the risk-free asset.

An investor who faces a risk-free rate, r_f, and a risky portfolio with expected return $E(r_P)$ and standard deviation σ_P will find that, for any choice of y, the expected return of the complete portfolio is given by Equation 6.8:

$$E(r_C) = r_f + y[E(r_P) − r_f]$$

From Equation 6.9, the variance of the overall portfolio is

$$\sigma_C^2 = y^2\sigma_P^2$$

Investors attempt to maximize utility by choosing the best allocation to the risky asset, y. The utility function is given by Equation 6.1 as $U = E(r) − \frac{1}{2}A\sigma^2$. As the allocation to the risky asset increases (higher y), expected return increases, but so does volatility, so utility can increase or decrease. To illustrate, Table 6.5 shows utility levels corresponding to different values of y. Initially, utility increases as y increases, but eventually it declines.

Figure 6.6 is a plot of the utility function from Table 6.5. The graph shows that utility is highest at $y = .41$. When y is less than .41, investors are willing to assume more risk to increase expected return. But at higher levels of y, risk is higher,

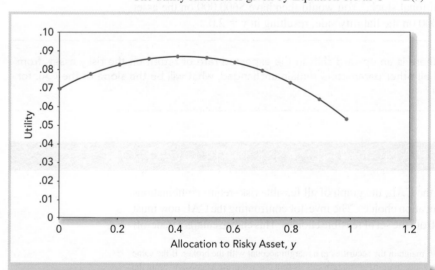

FIGURE 6.6 Utility as a function of allocation to the risky asset, y

and additional allocations to the risky asset are undesirable—beyond this point, further increases in risk dominate the increase in expected return and reduce utility.

To solve the utility maximization problem more generally, we write the problem as follows:

$$\text{Max}_{y} \; U = E(r_C) - \tfrac{1}{2}A\sigma_C^2 = r_f + y[E(r_P) - r_f] - \tfrac{1}{2}Ay^2\sigma_P^2$$

Students of calculus will remember that the maximization problem is solved by setting the derivative of this expression to zero. Doing so and solving for y yields the optimal position for risk-averse investors in the risky asset, y^*, as follows:[4]

$$y^* = \frac{E(r_P) - r_f}{A\sigma_P^2} \tag{6.12}$$

This solution shows that the optimal position in the risky asset is, as one would expect, *inversely* proportional to the level of risk aversion and the level of risk (as measured by the variance) and directly proportional to the risk premium offered by the risky asset.

EXAMPLE 6.4   *Capital Allocation*

Using our numerical example [$r_f = 7\%$, $E(r_P) = 15\%$, and $\sigma_P = 22\%$], and expressing all returns as decimals, the optimal solution for an investor with a coefficient of risk aversion $A = 4$ is

$$y^* = \frac{.15 - .07}{4 \times .22^2} = .41$$

In other words, this particular investor will invest 41% of the investment budget in the risky asset and 59% in the risk-free asset. As we saw in Figure 6.6, this is the value of y at which utility is maximized.

With 41% invested in the risky portfolio, the expected return and standard deviation of the complete portfolio are

$$E(r_C) = 7 + [.41 \times (15 - 7)] = 10.28\%$$
$$\sigma_C = .41 \times 22 = 9.02\%$$

The risk premium of the complete portfolio is $E(r_C) - r_f = 3.28\%$, which is obtained by taking on a portfolio with a standard deviation of 9.02%. Notice that $3.28/9.02 = .36$, which is the reward-to-volatility (Sharpe) ratio assumed for this example.

A graphical way of presenting this decision problem is to use indifference curve analysis. To illustrate how to build an indifference curve, consider an investor with risk aversion $A = 4$ who currently holds all her wealth in a risk-free portfolio yielding $r_f = 5\%$. Because the variance of such a portfolio is zero, Equation 6.1 tells us that its utility value is $U = .05$. Now we find the expected return the investor would require to maintain the *same* level of utility when holding a risky portfolio, say, with $\sigma = 1\%$. We use Equation 6.1 to find how much $E(r)$ must increase to compensate for the higher value of σ:

$$U = E(r) - \tfrac{1}{2} \times A \times \sigma^2$$
$$.05 = E(r) - \tfrac{1}{2} \times 4 \times .01^2$$

---

[4]The derivative with respect to y equals $E(r_P) - r_f - yA\sigma_P^2$. Setting this expression equal to zero and solving for y yields Equation 6.12.

TABLE 6.6

Spreadsheet calculations of indifference curves (Entries in columns 2–4 are expected returns necessary to provide specified utility value.)

	A = 2		A = 4	
σ	U = .05	U = .09	U = .05	U = .09
0	.0500	.0900	.050	.090
.05	.0525	.0925	.055	.095
.10	.0600	.1000	.070	.110
.15	.0725	.1125	.095	.135
.20	.0900	.1300	.130	.170
.25	.1125	.1525	.175	.215
.30	.1400	.1800	.230	.270
.35	.1725	.2125	.295	.335
.40	.2100	.2500	.370	.410
.45	.2525	.2925	.455	.495
.50	.3000	.3400	.550	.590

This implies that the necessary expected return increases to

$$\text{Required } E(r) = .05 + \tfrac{1}{2} \times A \times \sigma^2$$
$$= .05 + \tfrac{1}{2} \times 4 \times .01^2 = .0502 \qquad \textbf{(6.13)}$$

We can repeat this calculation for many other levels of σ, each time finding the value of $E(r)$ necessary to maintain $U = .05$. This process will yield all combinations of expected return and volatility with utility level of .05; plotting these combinations gives us the indifference curve.

We can readily generate an investor's indifference curves using a spreadsheet. Table 6.6 contains risk–return combinations with utility values of .05 and .09 for two investors, one with $A = 2$ and the other with $A = 4$. For example, column (2) uses Equation 6.13 to calculate the expected return that must be paired with the standard deviation in column (1) for an investor with $A = 2$ to derive a utility value of $U = .05$. Column (3) repeats the calculations for a higher utility value, $U = .09$. The plot of these expected return–standard deviation combinations appears in Figure 6.7 as the two curves labeled $A = 2$. Notice that the intercepts of the indifference curves are at .05 and .09, exactly the level of utility corresponding to the two curves.

Given the choice, any investor would prefer a portfolio on the higher indifference curve, the one with a higher certainty equivalent (utility). Portfolios on higher indifference curves offer a higher expected return for any given level of risk. For

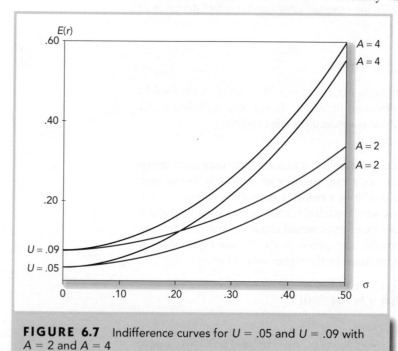

FIGURE 6.7 Indifference curves for $U = .05$ and $U = .09$ with $A = 2$ and $A = 4$

example, both indifference curves for $A = 2$ have the same shape, but for any level of volatility, a portfolio on the curve with utility of .09 offers an expected return 4% greater than the corresponding portfolio on the lower curve, for which $U = .05$.

Columns (4) and (5) of Table 6.6 repeat this analysis for a more risk-averse investor, with $A = 4$. The resulting pair of indifference curves in Figure 6.7 demonstrates that more risk-averse investors have steeper indifference curves than less risk-averse investors. Steeper curves mean that investors require a greater increase in expected return to compensate for an increase in portfolio risk.

Higher indifference curves correspond to higher levels of utility. The investor thus attempts to find the complete portfolio on the highest possible indifference

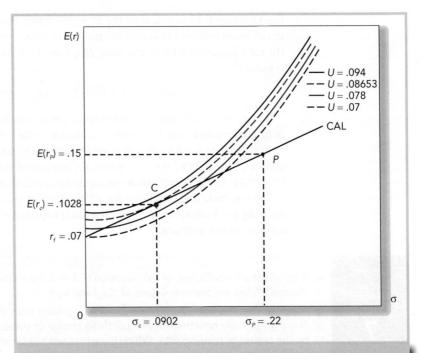

FIGURE 6.8 Finding the optimal complete portfolio by using indifference curves

curve. When we superimpose plots of indifference curves on the investment opportunity set represented by the capital allocation line as in Figure 6.8, we can identify the *highest possible* indifference curve that still touches the CAL. That indifference curve is tangent to the CAL, and the tangency point corresponds to the standard deviation and expected return of the optimal complete portfolio.

To illustrate, Table 6.7 provides calculations for four indifference curves (with utility levels of .07, .078, .08653, and .094) for an investor with $A = 4$. Columns (2)–(5)

σ	$U = .07$	$U = .078$	$U = .08653$	$U = .094$	CAL
0	.0700	.0780	.0865	.0940	.0700
.02	.0708	.0788	.0873	.0948	.0773
.04	.0732	.0812	.0897	.0972	.0845
.06	.0772	.0852	.0937	.1012	.0918
.08	.0828	.0908	.0993	.1068	.0991
.0902	.0863	.0943	.1028	.1103	.1028
.10	.0900	.0980	.1065	.1140	.1064
.12	.0988	.1068	.1153	.1228	.1136
.14	.1092	.1172	.1257	.1332	.1209
.18	.1348	.1428	.1513	.1588	.1355
.22	.1668	.1748	.1833	.1908	.1500
.26	.2052	.2132	.2217	.2292	.1645
.30	.2500	.2580	.2665	.2740	.1791

TABLE 6.7

Expected returns on four indifference curves and the CAL. Investor's risk aversion is $A = 4$.

use Equation 6.13 to calculate the expected return that must be paired with the standard deviation in column (1) to provide the utility value corresponding to each curve. Column (6) uses Equation 6.10 to calculate $E(r_C)$ on the CAL for the standard deviation σ_C in column (1):

$$E(r_C) = r_f + [E(r_P) - r_f]\frac{\sigma_C}{\sigma_P} = 7 + [15 - 7]\frac{\sigma_C}{22}$$

Figure 6.8 graphs the four indifference curves and the CAL. The graph reveals that the indifference curve with $U = .08653$ is tangent to the CAL; the tangency point corresponds to the complete portfolio that maximizes utility. The tangency point occurs at $\sigma_C = 9.02\%$ and $E(r_C) = 10.28\%$, the risk–return parameters of the optimal complete portfolio with $y^* = 0.41$. These values match our algebraic solution using Equation 6.12.

We conclude that the choice for y^*, the fraction of overall investment funds to place in the risky portfolio versus the safer but lower expected-return risk-free asset, is in large part a matter of risk aversion.

CONCEPT CHECK 7

a. If an investor's coefficient of risk aversion is $A = 3$, how does the optimal asset mix change? What are the new values of $E(r_C)$ and σ_C?

b. Suppose that the borrowing rate, $r_f^B = 9\%$ is greater than the lending rate, $r_f = 7\%$. Show graphically how the optimal portfolio choice of some investors will be affected by the higher borrowing rate. Which investors will *not* be affected by the borrowing rate?

6.6   PASSIVE STRATEGIES: THE CAPITAL MARKET LINE

The CAL is derived with the risk-free and "the" risky portfolio, P. Determination of the assets to include in risky portfolio P may result from a passive or an active strategy. A **passive strategy** describes a portfolio decision that avoids *any* direct or indirect security analysis.[5] At first blush, a passive strategy would appear to be naive. As will become apparent, however, forces of supply and demand in large capital markets may make such a strategy a reasonable choice for many investors.

In Chapter 5, we presented a compilation of the history of rates of return on different asset classes. The data are available at Professor Kenneth French's Web site, **mba.tuck. dartmouth.edu/pages/faculty/ken.french/data_library.html.** We can use these data to examine various passive strategies.

A natural candidate for a passively held risky asset would be a well-diversified portfolio of common stocks. Because a passive strategy requires that we devote no resources to acquiring information on any individual stock or group of stocks, we must follow a "neutral" diversification strategy. One way is to select a diversified portfolio of stocks that mirrors the value of the corporate sector of the U.S. economy. This results in a portfolio in which, for example, the proportion invested in Microsoft stock will be the ratio of Microsoft's total market value to the market value of all listed stocks.

---

[5] By "indirect security analysis" we mean the delegation of that responsibility to an intermediary such as a professional money manager.

	Average Annual Returns		S&P 500 Portfolio			Probability of Observing This Subperiod Estimate*
Period	S&P 500 Portfolio	1-Month T-bills	Risk Premium	Standard Deviation	Sharpe Ratio (Reward-to-Volatility)	
1926–2005	12.15	3.75	8.39	20.54	.41	
1986–2005	13.16	4.56	8.60	16.24	.53	.63
1966–1985	10.12	7.41	2.72	17.83	.15	.30
1946–1965	14.97	1.97	13.00	17.65	.74	.20
1926–1945	10.33	1.07	9.26	27.95	.33	.73

TABLE 6.8

Average annual return on large stocks and 1-month T-bills; standard deviation, and reward-to-volatility ratio of large stocks over time

*The probability that the estimate of 1926–2005 is true and we observe the reported (or an even more different) value for the subperiod.

The most popular value-weighted index of U.S. stocks is the Standard & Poor's Composite Index of 500 large capitalization U.S. corporations (the S&P 500). Table 6.8 summarizes the performance of the S&P 500 portfolio over the 80-year period 1926–2005, as well as for the four 20-year subperiods. Table 6.8 shows the average return for the portfolio, the return on rolling over 1-month T-bills for the same period, as well as the resultant average excess return and its standard deviation. The reward-to-volatility (Sharpe) ratio was .41 for the overall period, 1926–2005. In other words, stock market investors enjoyed a .41% average excess return relative to the T-bill rate for every 1% of standard deviation. The large standard deviation of the excess return (20.54%) is one reason we observe a wide range of average excess returns and reward-to-volatility ratios across subperiods (varying from .15 for 1966–1985 to .74 for 1946–1965). Using the statistical distribution of the difference between the Sharpe ratios of two portfolios, we can estimate the probability of observing a deviation of the Sharpe measure for a particular subperiod from that of the overall period, assuming the latter is the true value. The last column of Table 6.8 shows that the probabilities of finding such widely different Sharpe ratios over the subperiods are actually quite substantial.

We call the capital allocation line provided by 1-month T-bills and a broad index of common stocks the **capital market line** (CML). A passive strategy generates an investment opportunity set that is represented by the CML.

How reasonable is it for an investor to pursue a passive strategy? Of course, we cannot answer such a question without comparing the strategy to the costs and benefits accruing to an active portfolio strategy. Some thoughts are relevant at this point, however.

First, the alternative active strategy is not free. Whether you choose to invest the time and cost to acquire the information needed to generate an optimal active portfolio of risky assets, or whether you delegate the task to a professional who will charge a fee, constitution of an active portfolio is more expensive than a passive one. The passive portfolio requires only small commissions on purchases of T-bills (or zero commissions if you purchase bills directly from the government) and management fees to either an exchange-traded fund or a mutual fund company that operates a market index fund. Vanguard, for example, operates the Index 500 Portfolio that mimics the S&P 500 index fund. It purchases shares of the

SUMMARY

1. Speculation is the undertaking of a risky investment for its risk premium. The risk premium has to be large enough to compensate a risk-averse investor for the risk of the investment.

2. A fair game is a risky prospect that has a zero risk premium. It will not be undertaken by a risk-averse investor.

3. Investors' preferences toward the expected return and volatility of a portfolio may be expressed by a utility function that is higher for higher expected returns and lower for higher portfolio variances. More risk-averse investors will apply greater penalties for risk. We can describe these preferences graphically using indifference curves.

4. The desirability of a risky portfolio to a risk-averse investor may be summarized by the certainty equivalent value of the portfolio. The certainty equivalent rate of return is a value that, if it is received with certainty, would yield the same utility as the risky portfolio.

5. Shifting funds from the risky portfolio to the risk-free asset is the simplest way to reduce risk. Other methods involve diversification of the risky portfolio and hedging. We take up these methods in later chapters.

6. T-bills provide a perfectly risk-free asset in nominal terms only. Nevertheless, the standard deviation of real rates on short-term T-bills is small compared to that of other assets such as long-term bonds and common stocks, so for the purpose of our analysis we consider T-bills as the risk-free asset. Money market funds hold, in addition to T-bills, short-term relatively safe obligations such as CP and CDs. These entail some default risk, but again, the additional risk is small relative to most other risky assets. For convenience, we often refer to money market funds as risk-free assets.

7. An investor's risky portfolio (the risky asset) can be characterized by its reward-to-volatility ratio, $S = [E(r_P) - r_f]/\sigma_P$. This ratio is also the slope of the CAL, the line that, when graphed, goes from the risk-free asset through the risky asset. All combinations of the risky asset and the risk-free asset lie on this line. Other things equal, an investor would prefer a steeper-sloping CAL, because that means higher expected return for any level of risk. If the borrowing rate is greater than the lending rate, the CAL will be "kinked" at the point of the risky asset.

8. The investor's degree of risk aversion is characterized by the slope of his or her indifference curve. Indifference curves show, at any level of expected return and risk, the required risk premium for taking on one additional percentage point of standard deviation. More risk-averse investors have steeper indifference curves; that is, they require a greater risk premium for taking on more risk.

9. The optimal position, y^*, in the risky asset, is proportional to the risk premium and inversely proportional to the variance and degree of risk aversion:

$$y^* = \frac{E(r_P) - r_f}{A\sigma_P^2}$$

Graphically, this portfolio represents the point at which the indifference curve is tangent to the CAL.

10. A passive investment strategy disregards security analysis, targeting instead the risk-free asset and a broad portfolio of risky assets such as the S&P 500 stock portfolio. If in 2005 investors took the mean historical return and standard deviation of the S&P 500 as proxies for its expected return and standard deviation, then the values of outstanding assets would imply a degree of risk aversion of about $A = 2.7$ for the average investor. This is in line with other studies, which estimate typical risk aversion in the range of 2.0 through 4.0.

risk premium	risk neutral	risk-free asset
fair game	risk lover	capital allocation line
risk averse	mean-variance (M-V) criterion	reward-to-volatility ratio
utility	indifference curve	passive strategy
certainty equivalent rate	complete portfolio	capital market line

PROBLEM SETS

Quiz

1. Which of the following choices best completes the following statement? Explain. An investor with a higher degree of risk aversion, compared to one with a lower degree, will prefer investment portfolios

   a. with higher risk premiums.
   b. that are riskier (with higher standard deviations).
   c. with lower Sharpe ratios.
   d. with higher Sharpe ratios.
   e. None of the above is true.

2. Which of the following statements are true? Explain.

   a. A lower allocation to the risky portfolio reduces the Sharpe (reward-to-volatility) ratio.
   b. The higher the borrowing rate, the lower the Sharpe ratios of levered portfolios.
   c. With a fixed risk-free rate, doubling the expected return and standard deviation of the risky portfolio will double the Sharpe ratio.
   d. Holding constant the risk premium of the risky portfolio, a higher risk-free rate will increase the Sharpe ratio of investments with a positive allocation to the risky asset.

3. What do you think would happen to the expected return on stocks if investors perceived higher volatility in the equity market? Relate your answer to Equation 6.12.

Problems

4. Consider a risky portfolio. The end-of-year cash flow derived from the portfolio will be either $70,000 or $200,000 with equal probabilities of .5. The alternative risk-free investment in T-bills pays 6% per year.

   a. If you require a risk premium of 8%, how much will you be willing to pay for the portfolio?
   b. Suppose that the portfolio can be purchased for the amount you found in (*a*). What will be the expected rate of return on the portfolio?
   c. Now suppose that you require a risk premium of 12%. What is the price that you will be willing to pay?
   d. Comparing your answers to (*a*) and (*c*), what do you conclude about the relationship between the required risk premium on a portfolio and the price at which the portfolio will sell?

5. Consider a portfolio that offers an expected rate of return of 12% and a standard deviation of 18%. T-bills offer a risk-free 7% rate of return. What is the maximum level of risk aversion for which the risky portfolio is still preferred to bills?

6. Draw the indifference curve in the expected return–standard deviation plane corresponding to a utility level of .05 for an investor with a risk aversion coefficient of 3. (*Hint:* Choose several possible standard deviations, ranging from .05 to .25, and find the expected rates of return providing a utility level of .05. Then plot the expected return–standard deviation points so derived.)

7. Now draw the indifference curve corresponding to a utility level of .04 for an investor with risk aversion coefficient $A = 4$. Comparing your answers to Problems 6 and 7, what do you conclude?

8. Draw an indifference curve for a risk-neutral investor providing utility level .05.

9. What must be true about the sign of the risk aversion coefficient, A, for a risk lover? Draw the indifference curve for a utility level of .05 for a risk lover.

For Problems 10 through 12: Consider historical data showing that the average annual rate of return on the S&P 500 portfolio over the past 80 years has averaged roughly 8.5% more than the Treasury bill return and that the S&P 500 standard deviation has been about 20% per year. Assume these values are representative of investors' expectations for future performance and that the current T-bill rate is 5%.

10. Calculate the expected return and variance of portfolios invested in T-bills and the S&P 500 index with weights as follows:

W_{bills}	W_{index}
0	1.0
0.2	0.8
0.4	0.6
0.6	0.4
0.8	0.2
1.0	0

11. Calculate the utility levels of each portfolio of Problem 10 for an investor with $A = 3$. What do you conclude?

12. Repeat Problem 11 for an investor with $A = 5$. What do you conclude?

Use these inputs for Problems 13 through 22: You manage a risky portfolio with expected rate of return of 18% and standard deviation of 28%. The T-bill rate is 8%.

13. Your client chooses to invest 70% of a portfolio in your fund and 30% in a T-bill money market fund. What is the expected value and standard deviation of the rate of return on his portfolio?

14. Suppose that your risky portfolio includes the following investments in the given proportions:

Stock A	25%
Stock B	32%
Stock C	43%

What are the investment proportions of your client's overall portfolio, including the position in T-bills?

15. What is the reward-to-volatility ratio (S) of your risky portfolio? Your client's?

16. Draw the CAL of your portfolio on an expected return–standard deviation diagram. What is the slope of the CAL? Show the position of your client on your fund's CAL.

17. Suppose that your client decides to invest in your portfolio a proportion y of the total investment budget so that the overall portfolio will have an expected rate of return of 16%.

    a. What is the proportion y?
    b. What are your client's investment proportions in your three stocks and the T-bill fund?
    c. What is the standard deviation of the rate of return on your client's portfolio?

18. Suppose that your client prefers to invest in your fund a proportion y that maximizes the expected return on the complete portfolio subject to the constraint that the complete portfolio's standard deviation will not exceed 18%.

    a. What is the investment proportion, y?
    b. What is the expected rate of return on the complete portfolio?

19. Your client's degree of risk aversion is $A = 3.5$.

    a. What proportion, y, of the total investment should be invested in your fund?

b. What is the expected value and standard deviation of the rate of return on your client's optimized portfolio?

20. Look at the data in Table 6.8 on the average risk premium of the S&P 500 over T-bills, and the standard deviation of that risk premium. Suppose that the S&P 500 is your risky portfolio.

    a. If your risk-aversion coefficient is $A = 4$ and you believe that the entire 1926–2005 period is representative of future expected performance, what fraction of your portfolio should be allocated to T-bills and what fraction to equity?
    b. What if you believe that the 1986–2005 period is representative?
    c. What do you conclude upon comparing your answers to (*a*) and (*b*)?

21. Consider the following information about a risky portfolio that you manage, and a risk-free asset: $E(r_P) = 11\%$, $\sigma_P = 15\%$, $r_f = 5\%$.

    a. Your client wants to invest a proportion of her total investment budget in your risky fund to provide an expected rate of return on her overall or complete portfolio equal to 8%. What proportion should she invest in the risky portfolio, *P*, and what proportion in the risk-free asset?
    b. What will be the standard deviation of the rate of return on her portfolio?
    c. Another client wants the highest return possible subject to the constraint that you limit his standard deviation to be no more than 12%. Which client is more risk averse?

For Problems 22 through 25: Suppose that the borrowing rate that your client faces is 9%. Assume that the S&P 500 index has an expected return of 13% and standard deviation of 25%, that $r_f = 5\%$, and that your fund has the parameters given in Problem 21.

22. Draw a diagram of your client's CML, accounting for the higher borrowing rate. Superimpose on it two sets of indifference curves, one for a client who will choose to borrow, and one who will invest in both the index fund and a money market fund.

23. What is the range of risk aversion for which a client will neither borrow nor lend, that is, for which $y = 1$?

24. Solve Problems 22 and 23 for a client who uses your fund rather than an index fund.

25. What is the largest percentage fee that a client who currently is lending ($y < 1$) will be willing to pay to invest in your fund? What about a client who is borrowing ($y > 1$)?

For Challenge Problems 26 and 27: You estimate that a passive portfolio, that is, one invested in a risky portfolio that mimics the S&P 500 stock index, yields an expected rate of return of 13% with a standard deviation of 25%. You manage an active portfolio with expected return 18% and standard deviation 28%. The risk-free rate is 8%.

Challenge Problems

26. Draw the CML and your funds' CAL on an expected return–standard deviation diagram.

    a. What is the slope of the CML?
    b. Characterize in one short paragraph the advantage of your fund over the passive fund.

27. Your client ponders whether to switch the 70% that is invested in your fund to the passive portfolio.

    a. Explain to your client the disadvantage of the switch.
    b. Show him the maximum fee you could charge (as a percentage of the investment in your fund, deducted at the end of the year) that would leave him at least as well off investing in your fund as in the passive one. (*Hint:* The fee will lower the slope of his CAL by reducing the expected return net of the fee.)

28. Consider again the client in Problem 19 with $A = 3.5$.

    a. If he chose to invest in the passive portfolio, what proportion, *y*, would he select?
    b. Is the fee (percentage of the investment in your fund, deducted at the end of the year) that you can charge to make the client indifferent between your fund and the passive strategy affected by his capital allocation decision (i.e., his choice of *y*)?

Use the following data in answering CFA Problems 1–3:

Utility Formula Data

Investment	Expected Return, $E(r)$	Standard Deviation, σ
1	.12	.30
2	.15	.50
3	.21	.16
4	.24	.21

$U = E(r) - \frac{1}{2}A\sigma^2$, where $A = 4$

1. Based on the utility formula above, which investment would you select if you were risk averse with $A = 4$?

2. Based on the utility formula above, which investment would you select if you were risk neutral?

3. The variable (A) in the utility formula represents the:

   a. investor's return requirement.
   b. investor's aversion to risk.
   c. certainty equivalent rate of the portfolio.
   d. preference for one unit of return per four units of risk.

Use the following graph to answer CFA Problems 4 and 5.

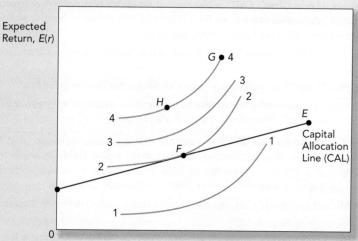

4. Which indifference curve represents the greatest level of utility that can be achieved by the investor?

5. Which point designates the optimal portfolio of risky assets?

6. Given $100,000 to invest, what is the expected risk premium in dollars of investing in equities versus risk-free T-bills based on the following table?

Action	Probability	Expected Return
Invest in	.6	$50,000
equities	.4	−$30,000
Invest in risk-free		
T-bills	1.0	$ 5,000

7. The change from a straight to a kinked capital allocation line is a result of the:

    a. Reward-to-volatility ratio increasing.
    b. Borrowing rate exceeding the lending rate.
    c. Investor's risk tolerance decreasing.
    d. Increase in the portfolio proportion of the risk-free asset.

8. You manage an equity fund with an expected risk premium of 10% and an expected standard deviation of 14%. The rate on Treasury bills is 6%. Your client chooses to invest $60,000 of her portfolio in your equity fund and $40,000 in a T-bill money market fund. What is the expected return and standard deviation of return on your client's portfolio?

9. What is the reward-to-volatility ratio for the *equity fund* in CFA Problem 8?

---

1. Go to **www.mhhe.com/edumarketinsight** (Have you remembered to bookmark this page?) and link to *Company,* then *Population.* Select a company of interest to you and link to the *Stock Reports* page. Observe the menu of company information reports on the left. Link to the *Recent News* and review the most recent *Business Wire* articles. What recent event or information release had an apparent impact upon your company's stock price? (You can find a history of stock prices under *Excel Analytics.*)

2. Go to **www.mhhe.com/edumarketinsight** and link to *Industry.* From the pull-down menu, link to an industry that is of interest to you. From the menu on the left side, select the *S&P 500* report under *Industry GICS Sub-Industry Financial Highlights.* How many companies from this industry are in the S&P 500? What percentage of the Main Industry Group does this Industry Group represent in the S&P 500? Look at the ratios provided for the industry and their comparisons to the *GICS Sub-Industry Benchmarks.* How did the industry perform relative to S&P 500 companies during the last year?

E-Investments

Risk Aversion

There is a difference between an investor's *willingness* to take risk and his or her *ability* to take risk. Take the quizzes offered at the Web sites below and compare the results. If they are significantly different, which one would you use to determine an investment strategy?

http://mutualfunds.about.com/library/personalitytests/blrisktolerance.htm

http://mutualfunds.about.com/library/personalitytests/blriskcapacity.htm

---

SOLUTIONS TO CONCEPT CHECKS

1. The investor is taking on exchange rate risk by investing in a pound-denominated asset. If the exchange rate moves in the investor's favor, the investor will benefit and will earn more from the U.K. bill than the U.S. bill. For example, if both the U.S. and U.K. interest rates are 5%, and the current exchange rate is $2 per pound, a $2 investment today can buy 1 pound, which can be invested in England at a certain rate of 5%, for a year-end value of 1.05 pounds. If the year-end exchange rate is $2.10 per pound, the 1.05 pounds can be exchanged for $1.05 \times \$2.10 = \$2.205$ for a rate of return in dollars of $1 + r = \$2.205/\$2 = 1.1025$, or $r = 10.25\%$, more than is

available from U.S. bills. Therefore, if the investor expects favorable exchange rate movements, the U.K. bill is a speculative investment. Otherwise, it is a gamble.

2. For the $A = 4$ investor the utility of the risky portfolio is

$$U = .20 - (\tfrac{1}{2} \times 4 \times .3^2) = .02$$

while the utility of bills is

$$U = .07 - (\tfrac{1}{2} \times 4 \times 0) = .07$$

The investor will prefer bills to the risky portfolio. (Of course, a mixture of bills and the portfolio might be even better, but that is not a choice here.)

Even for the $A = 2$ investor, the utility of the risky portfolio is

$$U = .20 - (\tfrac{1}{2} \times 2 \times .3^2) = .11$$

while the utility of bills is again .07. The less risk-averse investor prefers the risky portfolio.

3. The less risk-averse investor has a shallower indifference curve. An increase in risk requires less increase in expected return to restore utility to the original level.

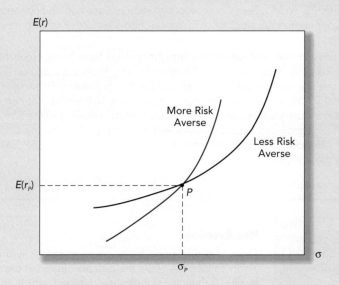

4. Holding 50% of your invested capital in Ready Assets means that your investment proportion in the risky portfolio is reduced from 70% to 50%.

Your risky portfolio is constructed to invest 54% in E and 46% in B. Thus the proportion of E in your overall portfolio is $.5 \times 54\% = 27\%$, and the dollar value of your position in E is $\$300,000 \times .27 = \$81,000$.

5. In the expected return–standard deviation plane all portfolios that are constructed from the same risky and risk-free funds (with various proportions) lie on a line from the risk-free rate through the risky fund. The slope of the CAL (capital allocation line) is the same everywhere; hence the reward-to-volatility ratio is the same for all of these portfolios. Formally, if you invest a proportion, y, in a risky fund with expected return $E(r_P)$ and standard deviation σ_P, and the remainder, $1 - y$, in a risk-free asset with a sure rate r_f, then the portfolio's expected return and standard deviation are

$$E(r_C) = r_f + y[E(r_P) - r_f]$$
$$\sigma_C = y\sigma_P$$

and therefore the reward-to-volatility ratio of this portfolio is

$$S_C = \frac{E(r_C) - r_f}{\sigma_C} = \frac{y[E(r_P) - r_f]}{y\sigma_P} = \frac{E(r_P) - r_f}{\sigma_P}$$

which is independent of the proportion y.

6. The lending and borrowing rates are unchanged at $r_f = 7\%$, $r_f^B = 9\%$. The standard deviation of the risky portfolio is still 22%, but its expected rate of return shifts from 15% to 17%.

The slope of the two-part CAL is

$$\frac{E(r_P) - r_f}{\sigma_P} \quad \text{for the lending range}$$

$$\frac{E(r_P) - r_f^B}{\sigma_P} \quad \text{for the borrowing range}$$

Thus in both cases the slope increases: from 8/22 to 10/22 for the lending range, and from 6/22 to 8/22 for the borrowing range.

7. *a.* The parameters are $r_f = .07$, $E(r_P) = .15$, $\sigma_P = .22$. An investor with a degree of risk aversion A will choose a proportion y in the risky portfolio of

$$y = \frac{E(r_P) - r_f}{A\sigma_P^2}$$

With the assumed parameters and with $A = 3$ we find that

$$y = \frac{.15 - .07}{3 \times .0484} = .55$$

When the degree of risk aversion decreases from the original value of 4 to the new value of 3, investment in the risky portfolio increases from 41% to 55%. Accordingly, the expected return and standard deviation of the optimal portfolio increase:

$$E(r_C) = .07 + (.55 \times .08) = .114 \text{ (before: .1028)}$$
$$\sigma_C = .55 \times .22 = .121 \text{ (before: .0902)}$$

b. All investors whose degree of risk aversion is such that they would hold the risky portfolio in a proportion equal to 100% or less ($y < 1.00$) are lending rather than borrowing, and so are unaffected by the borrowing rate. The least risk-averse of these investors hold 100% in the risky portfolio ($y = 1$). We can solve for the degree of risk aversion of these "cut off" investors from the parameters of the investment opportunities:

$$y = 1 = \frac{E(r_P) - r_f}{A\sigma_P^2} = \frac{.08}{.0484\,A}$$

which implies

$$A = \frac{.08}{.0484} = 1.65$$

Any investor who is more risk tolerant (that is, $A < 1.65$) would borrow if the borrowing rate were 7%. For borrowers,

$$y = \frac{E(r_P) - r_f^B}{A\sigma_P^2}$$

Suppose, for example, an investor has an A of 1.1. When $r_f = r_f^B = 7\%$, this investor chooses to invest in the risky portfolio:

$$y = \frac{.08}{1.1 \times .0484} = 1.50$$

which means that the investor will borrow an amount equal to 50% of her own investment capital. Raise the borrowing rate, in this case to $r_f^B = 9\%$, and the investor will invest less in the risky asset. In that case:

$$y = \frac{.06}{1.1 \times .0484} = 1.13$$

and "only" 13% of her investment capital will be borrowed. Graphically, the line from r_f to the risky portfolio shows the CAL for lenders. The dashed part *would* be relevant if the borrowing rate equaled the lending rate. When the borrowing rate exceeds the lending rate, the CAL is kinked at the point corresponding to the risky portfolio.

The following figure shows indifference curves of two investors. The steeper indifference curve portrays the more risk-averse investor, who chooses portfolio C_0, which involves lending. This investor's choice is unaffected by the borrowing rate. The more risk-tolerant investor is portrayed by the shallower-sloped indifference curves. If the lending rate equaled the borrowing rate, this investor would choose portfolio C_1 on the dashed part of the CAL. When the borrowing rate goes up, this investor chooses portfolio C_2 (in the borrowing range of the kinked CAL), which involves less borrowing than before. This investor is hurt by the increase in the borrowing rate.

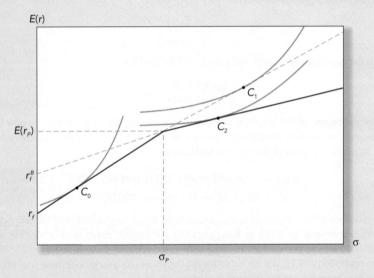

8. If all the investment parameters remain unchanged, the only reason for an investor to decrease the investment proportion in the risky asset is an increase in the degree of risk aversion. If you think that this is unlikely, then you have to reconsider your faith in your assumptions. Perhaps the S&P 500 is not a good proxy for the optimal risky portfolio. Perhaps investors expect a higher real rate on T-bills.

APPENDIX A: Risk Aversion, Expected Utility, and the St. Petersburg Paradox

We digress in this appendix to examine the rationale behind our contention that investors are risk averse. Recognition of risk aversion as central in investment decisions goes back at least to 1738. Daniel Bernoulli, one of a famous Swiss family of distinguished mathematicians, spent the years 1725 through 1733 in St. Petersburg, where he analyzed the following coin-toss game. To enter the game one pays an entry fee. Thereafter, a coin is tossed until the *first* head appears. The number of tails, denoted by n, that appears until the first head is tossed is used to compute the payoff, R, to the participant, as

$$R(n) = 2^n$$

The probability of no tails before the first head ($n = 0$) is 1/2 and the corresponding payoff is $2^0 = \$1$. The probability of one tail and then heads ($n = 1$) is $1/2 \times 1/2$ with payoff $2^1 = \$2$, the probability of two tails and then heads ($n = 2$) is $1/2 \times 1/2 \times 1/2$ and so forth.

The following table illustrates the probabilities and payoffs for various outcomes:

Tails	Probability	Payoff = $ $R(n)$	Probability × Payoff
0	1/2	$1	$1/2
1	1/4	$2	$1/2
2	1/8	$4	$1/2
3	1/16	$8	$1/2
$\vdots$	$\vdots$	$\vdots$	$\vdots$
n	$(1/2)^{n+1}$	$\$2^n$	$1/2

The expected payoff is therefore

$$E(R) = \sum_{n=0}^{\infty} \Pr(n)R(n) = \text{½} + \text{½} + \cdots = \infty$$

The evaluation of this game is called the "St. Petersburg Paradox." Although the expected payoff is infinite, participants obviously will be willing to purchase tickets to play the game only at a finite, and possibly quite modest, entry fee.

Bernoulli resolved the paradox by noting that investors do not assign the same value per dollar to all payoffs. Specifically, the greater their wealth, the less their "appreciation" for each extra dollar. We can make this insight mathematically precise by assigning a welfare or utility value to any level of investor wealth. Our utility function should increase as wealth is higher, but each extra dollar of wealth should increase utility by progressively smaller amounts.[8] (Modern economists would say that investors exhibit "decreasing marginal utility" from an additional payoff dollar.) One particular function that assigns a subjective value to the investor from a payoff of R, which has a smaller value per dollar the greater the payoff, is the function $\ln(R)$ where ln is the natural logarithm function. If this function measures utility values of wealth, the subjective utility value of the game is indeed finite, equal to .693.[9] The certain wealth level necessary to yield this utility value is $2.00, because $\ln(2.00) = .693$. Hence the certainty equivalent value of the risky payoff is $2.00, which is the maximum amount that this investor will pay to play the game.

Von Neumann and Morgenstern adapted this approach to investment theory in a complete axiomatic system in 1946. Avoiding unnecessary technical detail, we restrict ourselves here to an intuitive exposition of the rationale for risk aversion.

---

[8]This utility is similar in spirit to the one that assigns a satisfaction level to portfolios with given risk and return attributes. However, the utility function here refers not to investors' satisfaction with alternative portfolio choices but only to the subjective welfare they derive from different levels of wealth.

[9]If we substitute the "utility" value, $\ln(R)$, for the dollar payoff, R, to obtain an expected utility value of the game (rather than expected dollar value), we have, calling $V(R)$ the expected utility,

$$V(R) = \sum_{n=0}^{\infty} \Pr(n) \ln[R(n)] = \sum_{n=0}^{\infty} (1/2)^{n+1} \ln(2^n) = .693$$

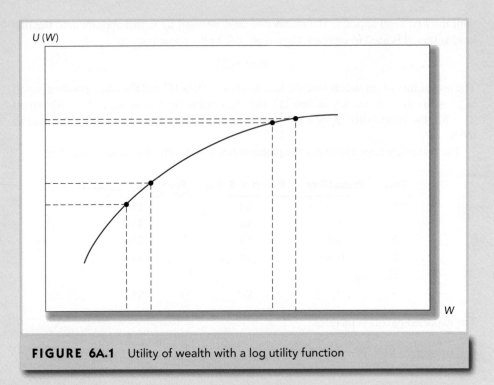

FIGURE 6A.1   Utility of wealth with a log utility function

Imagine two individuals who are identical twins, except that one of them is less fortunate than the other. Peter has only $1,000 to his name while Paul has a net worth of $200,000. How many hours of work would each twin be willing to offer to earn one extra dollar? It is likely that Peter (the poor twin) has more essential uses for the extra money than does Paul. Therefore, Peter will offer more hours. In other words, Peter derives a greater personal welfare or assigns a greater "utility" value to the 1,001st dollar than Paul does to the 200,001st. Figure 6A.1 depicts graphically the relationship between the wealth and the utility value of wealth that is consistent with this notion of decreasing marginal utility.

Individuals have different rates of decrease in their marginal utility of wealth. What is constant is the *principle* that the per-dollar increment to utility decreases with wealth. Functions that exhibit the property of decreasing per-unit value as the number of units grows are called concave. A simple example is the log function, familiar from high school mathematics. Of course, a log function will not fit all investors, but it is consistent with the risk aversion that we assume for all investors.

Now consider the following simple prospect:

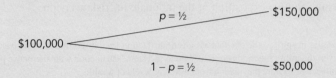

This is a fair game in that the expected profit is zero. Suppose, however, that the curve in Figure 6A.1 represents the investor's utility value of wealth, assuming a log utility function. Figure 6A.2 shows this curve with numerical values marked.

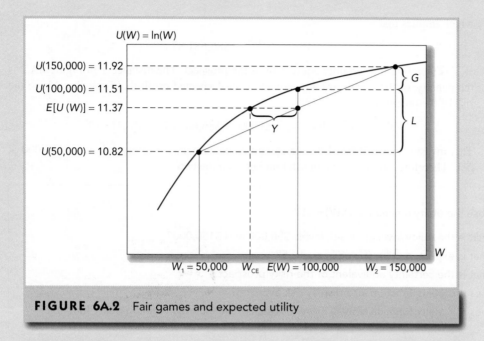

FIGURE 6A.2   Fair games and expected utility

Figure 6A.2 shows that the loss in utility from losing $50,000 exceeds the gain from winning $50,000. Consider the gain first. With probability $p = .5$, wealth goes from $100,000 to $150,000. Using the log utility function, utility goes from $\ln(100,000) = 11.51$ to $\ln(150,000) = 11.92$, the distance G on the graph. This gain is $G = 11.92 - 11.51 = .41$. In expected utility terms, then, the gain is $pG = .5 \times .41 = .21$.

Now consider the possibility of coming up on the short end of the prospect. In that case, wealth goes from $100,000 to $50,000. The loss in utility, the distance L on the graph, is $L = \ln(100,000) - \ln(50,000) = 11.51 - 10.82 = .69$. Thus the loss in expected utility terms is $(1 - p)L = .5 \times .69 = .35$, which exceeds the gain in expected utility from the possibility of winning the game.

We compute the expected utility from the risky prospect:

$$E[U(W)] = pU(W_1) + (1 - p)U(W_2)$$
$$= \tfrac{1}{2}\ln(50,000) + \tfrac{1}{2}\ln(150,000) = 11.37$$

If the prospect is rejected, the utility value of the (sure) $100,000 is $\ln(100,000) = 11.51$, greater than that of the fair game (11.37). Hence the risk-averse investor will reject the fair game.

Using a specific investor utility function (such as the log utility function) allows us to compute the certainty equivalent value of the risky prospect to a given investor. This is the amount that, if received with certainty, she would consider equally attractive as the risky prospect.

If log utility describes the investor's preferences toward wealth outcomes, then Figure 6A.2 can also tell us what is, for her, the dollar value of the prospect. We ask, What sure level of wealth has a utility value of 11.37 (which equals the expected utility from the prospect)? A horizontal line drawn at the level 11.37 intersects the utility curve at the level of wealth W_{CE}. This means that

$$\ln(W_{CE}) = 11.37$$

which implies that

$$W_{CE} = e^{11.37} = \$86,681.87$$

W_{CE} is therefore the certainty equivalent of the prospect. The distance Y in Figure 6A.2 is the penalty, or the downward adjustment, to the expected profit that is attributable to the risk of the prospect.

$$Y = E(W) - W_{CE} = \$100,000 - \$86,681.87 = \$13,318.13$$

This investor views $86,681.87 for certain as being equal in utility value as $100,000 at risk. Therefore, she would be indifferent between the two.

CONCEPT CHECK

A.1

Suppose the utility function is $U(W) = \sqrt{W}$.

a. What is the utility level at wealth levels $50,000 and $150,000?

b. What is expected utility if p still equals .5?

c. What is the certainty equivalent of the risky prospect?

d. Does this utility function also display risk aversion?

e. Does this utility function display more or less risk aversion than the log utility function?

APPENDIX B: Utility Functions and Equilibrium Prices of Insurance Contracts

The utility function of an individual investor allows us to measure the subjective value the individual would place on a dollar at various levels of wealth. Essentially, a dollar in bad times (when wealth is low) is more valuable than a dollar in good times (when wealth is high).

Suppose that all investors hold the risky S&P 500 portfolio. Then, if the portfolio value falls in a worse-than-expected economy, all investors will, albeit to different degrees, experience a "low wealth" scenario. Therefore, the equilibrium value of a dollar in the low-wealth economy would be higher than the value of a dollar when the portfolio performs better than expected. This observation helps explain the apparently high cost of portfolio insurance that we encountered when considering long-term investments in the previous chapter. It also helps explain why an investment in a stock portfolio (and hence in individual stocks) has a risk premium that appears to be so high and results in probability of shortfall that is so low. Despite the low probability of shortfall risk, stocks still do not dominate the lower-return risk-free bond, because if an investment shortfall should transpire, it will coincide with states in which the value of dollar returns is high.

Does revealed behavior of investors demonstrate risk aversion? Looking at prices and past rates of return in financial markets, we can answer with a resounding yes. With remarkable consistency, riskier bonds are sold at lower prices than are safer ones with otherwise similar characteristics. Riskier stocks also have provided higher average rates of return over long periods of time than less risky assets such as T-bills. For example, over the 1926 to 2005 period, the average rate of return on the S&P 500 portfolio exceeded the T-bill return by more than 8% per year.

It is abundantly clear from financial data that the average, or representative, investor exhibits substantial risk aversion. For readers who recognize that financial assets are priced to compensate for risk by providing a risk premium and at the same time feel the urge for some gambling, we have a constructive recommendation: Direct your gambling impulse to investment in financial markets. As Von Neumann once said, "The stock market is a casino with the odds in your favor." A small risk-seeking investment may provide all the excitement you want with a positive expected return to boot!

1. Suppose that your wealth is $250,000. You buy a $200,000 house and invest the remainder in a risk-free asset paying an annual interest rate of 6%. There is a probability of .001 that your house will burn to the ground and its value will be reduced to zero. With a log utility of end-of-year wealth, how much would you be willing to pay for insurance (at the beginning of the year)? (Assume that if the house does not burn down, its end-of-year value still will be $200,000.)

2. If the cost of insuring your house is $1 per $1,000 of value, what will be the certainty equivalent of your end-of-year wealth if you insure your house at:

   a. ½ its value.
   b. Its full value.
   c. 1½ times its value.

PROBLEMS: APPENDIX

SOLUTIONS TO CONCEPT CHECKS

A.1. *a.* $U(W) = \sqrt{W}$

$$U(50,000) = \sqrt{50,000} = 223.61$$

$$U(150,000) = 387.30$$

b. $E(U) = (.5 \times 223.61) + (.5 \times 387.30) = 305.45$

c. We must find W_{CE} that has utility level 305.45. Therefore

$$\sqrt{W_{CE}} = 305.45$$

$$W_{CE} = 305.45^2 = \$93,301$$

d. Yes. The certainty equivalent of the risky venture is less than the expected outcome of $100,000.

e. The certainty equivalent of the risky venture to this investor is greater than it was for the log utility investor considered in the text. Hence this utility function displays less risk aversion.

OPTIMAL RISKY PORTFOLIOS

THE INVESTMENT DECISION can be viewed as a top-down process: (i) *Capital allocation* between the risky portfolio and risk-free assets, (ii) *asset allocation* across broad asset classes (e.g., U.S. stocks, international stocks, and long-term bonds), and (iii) *security selection* of individual assets within each asset class.

Capital allocation, as we saw in Chapter 6, determines the investor's exposure to risk. The optimal capital allocation is determined by risk aversion as well as expectations for the risk–return trade-off of the optimal risky portfolio. In principle, asset allocation and security selection are technically identical; both aim at identifying that optimal risky portfolio, namely, the combination of risky assets that provides the best risk–return trade-off. In practice, however, asset allocation and security selection are typically separated into two steps, in which the broad outlines of the portfolio are established first (asset allocation), while details concerning specific securities are filled in later (security selection). After we show how the optimal risky portfolio may be constructed, we will consider the cost and benefits of pursuing this two-step approach.

We first motivate the discussion by illustrating the potential gains from simple diversification into many assets. We then proceed to examine the process of *efficient* diversification from the ground up, starting with an investment menu of only two risky assets, then adding the risk-free asset, and finally, incorporating the entire universe of available risky securities. We learn how diversification can reduce risk without affecting expected returns. This accomplished, we re-examine the hierarchy of capital allocation, asset allocation, and security selection. Finally, we offer insight into the power of diversification by drawing an analogy between it and the workings of the insurance industry.

The portfolios we discuss in this and the following chapters are of a short-term horizon—even if the overall investment horizon is long, portfolio composition can be rebalanced or updated almost continuously. For these short horizons, the skewness that characterizes long-term compounded returns is absent. Therefore, the assumption of normality is sufficiently accurate to describe holding-period returns, and we will be concerned only with portfolio means and variances.

In Appendix A, we demonstrate how construction of the optimal risky portfolio can easily be accomplished with Excel. Appendix B provides a review of portfolio statistics with emphasis on the intuition behind covariance and correlation measures. Even if you have had a good quantitative methods course, it may well be worth skimming.

7.1 DIVERSIFICATION AND PORTFOLIO RISK

Suppose your portfolio is composed of only one stock, say, Dell Computer Corporation. What would be the sources of risk to this "portfolio"? You might think of two broad sources of uncertainty. First, there is the risk that comes from conditions in the general economy, such as the business cycle, inflation, interest rates, and exchange rates. None of these macroeconomic factors can be predicted with certainty, and all affect the rate of return on Dell stock. In addition to these macroeconomic factors there are firm-specific influences, such as Dell's success in research and development, and personnel changes. These factors affect Dell without noticeably affecting other firms in the economy.

Now consider a naive **diversification** strategy, in which you include additional securities in your portfolio. For example, place half your funds in ExxonMobil and half in Dell. What should happen to portfolio risk? To the extent that the firm-specific influences on the two stocks differ, diversification should reduce portfolio risk. For example, when oil prices fall, hurting ExxonMobil, computer prices might rise, helping Dell. The two effects are offsetting and stabilize portfolio return.

But why end diversification at only two stocks? If we diversify into many more securities, we continue to spread out our exposure to firm-specific factors, and portfolio volatility should continue to fall. Ultimately, however, even with a large number of stocks we cannot avoid risk altogether, because virtually all securities are affected by the common macroeconomic factors. For example, if all stocks are affected by the business cycle, we cannot avoid exposure to business cycle risk no matter how many stocks we hold.

When all risk is firm-specific, as in Figure 7.1, panel A, diversification can reduce risk to arbitrarily low levels. The reason is that with all risk sources independent, the exposure to any particular source of risk is reduced to a negligible level. The reduction of risk to very low levels in the case of independent risk sources is sometimes called the **insurance principle,** because of the notion that an insurance company depends on the risk reduction achieved through diversification when it writes many policies insuring against many independent sources of risk, each policy being a small part of the company's overall portfolio. (See Section 7.5 for a discussion of the insurance principle.)

When common sources of risk affect all firms, however, even extensive diversification cannot eliminate risk. In Figure 7.1, panel B, portfolio standard deviation falls as the number of securities increases, but it cannot be reduced to zero. The risk that remains even after extensive diversification is called **market risk,** risk that is attributable to marketwide risk sources. Such risk is also called **systematic risk,** or **nondiversifiable risk.** In contrast, the risk that *can* be eliminated by diversification is called **unique risk, firm-specific risk, nonsystematic risk,** or **diversifiable risk.**

This analysis is borne out by empirical studies. Figure 7.2 shows the effect of portfolio diversification, using data on NYSE stocks.[1] The figure shows the average standard

[1]Meir Statman, "How Many Stocks Make a Diversified Portfolio?" *Journal of Financial and Quantitative Analysis* 22 (September 1987).

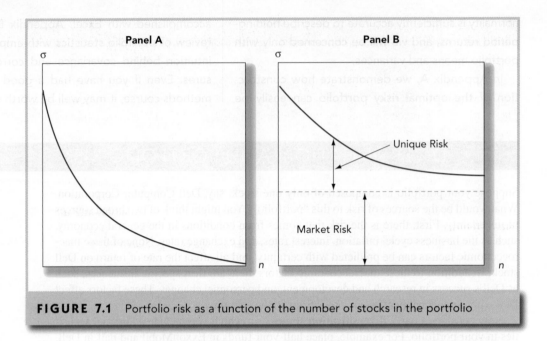

FIGURE 7.1   Portfolio risk as a function of the number of stocks in the portfolio

deviation of equally weighted portfolios constructed by selecting stocks at random as a function of the number of stocks in the portfolio. On average, portfolio risk does fall with diversification, but the power of diversification to reduce risk is limited by systematic or common sources of risk.

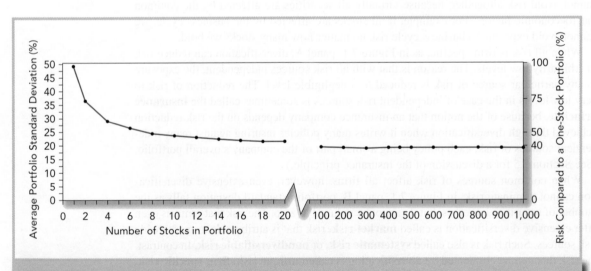

FIGURE 7.2   Portfolio diversification. The average standard deviation of returns of portfolios composed of only one stock was 49.2%. The average portfolio risk fell rapidly as the number of stocks included in the portfolio increased. In the limit, portfolio risk could be reduced to only 19.2%.

Source: From Meir Statman, "How Many Stocks Make a Diversified Portfolio? *Journal of Financial and Quantitative Analysis* 22 (September 1987). Reprinted by permission.

7.2 PORTFOLIOS OF TWO RISKY ASSETS

In the last section we considered naive diversification using equally weighted portfolios of several securities. It is time now to study *efficient* diversification, whereby we construct risky portfolios to provide the lowest possible risk for any given level of expected return. The nearby box provides an introduction to the relationship between diversification and portfolio construction.

Portfolios of two risky assets are relatively easy to analyze, and they illustrate the principles and considerations that apply to portfolios of many assets. It makes sense to think about a two-asset portfolio as an asset allocation decision, and so we consider two mutual funds, a bond portfolio specializing in long-term debt securities, denoted D, and a stock fund that specializes in equity securities, E. Table 7.1 lists the parameters describing the rate-of-return distribution of these funds.

A proportion denoted by w_D is invested in the bond fund, and the remainder, $1 - w_D$, denoted w_E, is invested in the stock fund. The rate of return on this portfolio, r_p, will be[2]

$$r_p = w_D r_D + w_E r_E \tag{7.1}$$

where r_D is the rate of return on the debt fund and r_E is the rate of return on the equity fund.

The expected return on the portfolio is a weighted average of expected returns on the component securities with portfolio proportions as weights:

$$E(r_p) = w_D E(r_D) + w_E E(r_E) \tag{7.2}$$

The variance of the two-asset portfolio is

$$\sigma_p^2 = w_D^2 \sigma_D^2 + w_E^2 \sigma_E^2 + 2w_D w_E \text{Cov}(r_D, r_E) \tag{7.3}$$

Our first observation is that the variance of the portfolio, unlike the expected return, is *not* a weighted average of the individual asset variances. To understand the formula for the portfolio variance more clearly, recall that the covariance of a variable with itself is the variance of that variable; that is

$$\text{Cov}(r_D, r_D) = \sum_{\text{scenarios}} \text{Pr(scenario)}[r_D - E(r_D)][r_D - E(r_D)]$$

$$= \sum_{\text{scenarios}} \text{Pr(scenario)}[r_D - E(r_D)]^2 \tag{7.4}$$

$$= \sigma_D^2$$

Therefore, another way to write the variance of the portfolio is

$$\sigma_p^2 = w_D w_D \text{Cov}(r_D, r_D) + w_E w_E \text{Cov}(r_E, r_E) + 2w_D w_E \text{Cov}(r_D, r_E) \tag{7.5}$$

	Debt	Equity	TABLE 7.1
Expected return, $E(r)$	8%	13%	Descriptive statistics for two mutual funds
Standard deviation, σ	12%	20%	
Covariance, $\text{Cov}(r_D, r_E)$		72	
Correlation coefficient, ρ_{DE}		.30	

[2]See Appendix B of this chapter for a review of portfolio statistics.

INTRODUCTION TO DIVERSIFICATION

Diversification is a familiar term to most investors. In the most general sense, it can be summed up with this phrase: "Don't put all of your eggs in one basket." While that sentiment certainly captures the essence of the issue, it provides little guidance on the practical implications of the role diversification plays in an investor's portfolio and offers no insight into how a diversified portfolio is actually created.

WHAT IS DIVERSIFICATION?

Taking a closer look at the concept of diversification, the idea is to create a portfolio that includes multiple investments in order to reduce risk. Consider, for example, an investment that consists of only the stock issued by a single company. If that company's stock suffers a serious downturn, your portfolio will sustain the full brunt of the decline. By splitting your investment between the stocks of two different companies, you reduce the potential risk to your portfolio.

Another way to reduce the risk in your portfolio is to include bonds and cash. Because cash is generally used as a short-term reserve, most investors develop an asset allocation strategy for their portfolios based primarily on the use of stocks and bonds. It is never a bad idea to keep a portion of your invested assets in cash, or short-term money-market securities. Cash can be used in case of an emergency, and short-term money-market securities can be liquidated instantly in the event your usual cash requirements spike and you need to sell investments to make payments.

Regardless of whether you are aggressive or conservative, the use of asset allocation to reduce risk through the selection of a balance of stocks and bonds for your portfolio is a more detailed description of how a diversified portfolio is created than the simplistic eggs in one basket concept. The specific balance of stocks and bonds in a given portfolio is designed to create a specific risk-reward ratio that offers the opportunity to achieve a certain rate of return on your investment in exchange for your willingness to accept a certain amount of risk.

WHAT ARE MY OPTIONS?

If you are a person of limited means or you simply prefer uncomplicated investment scenarios, you could choose a single balanced mutual fund and invest all of your assets in the fund. For most investors, this strategy is far too simplistic. Furthermore, while investing in a single mutual fund provides diversification among the basic asset classes of stocks, bonds and cash, the opportunities for diversification go far beyond these basic categories. A host of alternative investments provide the opportunity for further diversification. Real estate investment trusts, hedge funds, art and other investments provide the opportunity to invest in vehicles that do not necessarily move in tandem with the traditional financial markets.

CONCLUSION

Regardless of your means or method, keep in mind that there is no generic diversification model that will meet the needs of every investor. Your personal time horizon, risk tolerance, investment goals, financial means and level of investment experience will play a large role in dictating your investment mix.

Source: Adapted from Jim McWhinney, *Introduction to Diversification*, December 16, 2005, **www.investopedia.com/articles/basics/05/diversification.asp**, retrieved April 25, 2006.

In words, the variance of the portfolio is a weighted sum of covariances, and each weight is the product of the portfolio proportions of the pair of assets in the covariance term.

Table 7.2 shows how portfolio variance can be calculated from a spreadsheet. Panel A of the table shows the *bordered* covariance matrix of the returns of the two mutual funds. The bordered matrix is the covariance matrix with the portfolio weights for each fund placed on the borders, that is, along the first row and column. To find portfolio variance, multiply each element in the covariance matrix by the pair of portfolio weights in its row and column borders. Add up the resultant terms, and you have the formula for portfolio variance given in Equation 7.5.

We perform these calculations in panel B, which is the *border-multiplied* covariance matrix: Each covariance has been multiplied by the weights from the row and the column in the borders. The bottom line of panel B confirms that the sum of all the terms in this matrix (which we obtain by adding up the column sums) is indeed the portfolio variance in Equation 7.5.

This procedure works because the covariance matrix is symmetric around the diagonal, that is, $\text{Cov}(r_D, r_E) = \text{Cov}(r_E, r_D)$. Thus each covariance term appears twice.

A. Bordered Covariance Matrix			TABLE 7.2
Portfolio Weights	w_D	w_E	Computation of portfolio variance from the covariance matrix
w_D	$Cov(r_D, r_D)$	$Cov(r_D, r_E)$	
w_E	$Cov(r_E, r_D)$	$Cov(r_E, r_E)$	
B. Border-multiplied Covariance Matrix			
Portfolio Weights	w_D	w_E	
w_D	$w_D w_D Cov(r_D, r_D)$	$w_D w_E Cov(r_D, r_E)$	
w_E	$w_E w_D Cov(r_E, r_D)$	$w_E w_E Cov(r_E, r_E)$	
$w_D + w_E = 1$	$w_D w_D Cov(r_D, r_D) + w_E w_D Cov(r_E, r_D)$	$w_D w_E Cov(r_D, r_E) + w_E w_E Cov(r_E, r_E)$	
Portfolio variance	$w_D w_D Cov(r_D, r_D) + w_E w_D Cov(r_E, r_D) + w_D w_E Cov(r_D, r_E) + w_E w_E Cov(r_E, r_E)$		

This technique for computing the variance from the border-multiplied covariance matrix is general; it applies to any number of assets and is easily implemented on a spreadsheet. Concept Check 1 asks you to try the rule for a three-asset portfolio. Use this problem to verify that you are comfortable with this concept.

CONCEPT CHECK 1

a. First confirm for yourself that our simple rule for computing the variance of a two-asset portfolio from the bordered covariance matrix is consistent with Equation 7.3.

b. Now consider a portfolio of three funds, X, Y, Z, with weights w_X, w_Y, and w_Z. Show that the portfolio variance is

$$w_X^2 \sigma_X^2 + w_Y^2 \sigma_Y^2 + w_Z^2 \sigma_Z^2 + 2w_X w_Y Cov(r_X, r_Y) + 2w_X w_Z Cov(r_X, r_Z) + 2w_Y w_Z Cov(r_Y, r_Z)$$

Equation 7.3 reveals that variance is reduced if the covariance term is negative. It is important to recognize that even if the covariance term is positive, the portfolio standard deviation *still* is less than the weighted average of the individual security standard deviations, unless the two securities are perfectly positively correlated.

To see this, notice that the covariance can be computed from the correlation coefficient, ρ_{DE}, as

$$Cov(r_D, r_E) = \rho_{DE}\sigma_D\sigma_E \qquad (7.6)$$

Therefore,

$$\sigma_p^2 = w_D^2 \sigma_D^2 + w_E^2 \sigma_E^2 + 2w_D w_E \sigma_D \sigma_E \rho_{DE} \qquad (7.7)$$

Other things equal, portfolio variance is higher when ρ_{DE} is higher. In the case of perfect positive correlation, $\rho_{DE} = 1$, the right-hand side of Equation 7.7 is a perfect square and simplifies to

$$\sigma_p^2 = (w_D \sigma_D + w_E \sigma_E)^2 \qquad (7.8)$$

or

$$\sigma_p = w_D \sigma_D + w_E \sigma_E \qquad (7.9)$$

Therefore, the standard deviation of the portfolio with perfect positive correlation is just the weighted average of the component standard deviations. In all other cases, the correlation coefficient is less than 1, making the portfolio standard deviation *less* than the weighted average of the component standard deviations.

A hedge asset has *negative* correlation with the other assets in the portfolio. Equation 7.7 shows that such assets will be particularly effective in reducing total risk. Moreover, Equation 7.2 shows that expected return is unaffected by correlation between returns. Therefore, other things equal, we will always prefer to add to our portfolios assets with low or, even better, negative correlation with our existing position.

Because the portfolio's expected return is the weighted average of its component expected returns, whereas its standard deviation is less than the weighted average of the component standard deviations, *portfolios of less than perfectly correlated assets always offer better risk–return opportunities than the individual component securities on their own.* The lower the correlation between the assets, the greater the gain in efficiency.

How low can portfolio standard deviation be? The lowest possible value of the correlation coefficient is -1, representing perfect negative correlation. In this case, Equation 7.7 simplifies to

$$\sigma_p^2 = (w_D\sigma_D - w_E\sigma_E)^2 \qquad (7.10)$$

and the portfolio standard deviation is

$$\sigma_p = \text{Absolute value } (w_D\sigma_D - w_E\sigma_E) \qquad (7.11)$$

When $\rho = -1$, a perfectly hedged position can be obtained by choosing the portfolio proportions to solve

$$w_D\sigma_D - w_E\sigma_E = 0$$

The solution to this equation is

$$w_D = \frac{\sigma_E}{\sigma_D + \sigma_E}$$

$$w_E = \frac{\sigma_D}{\sigma_D + \sigma_E} = 1 - w_D \qquad (7.12)$$

These weights drive the standard deviation of the portfolio to zero.

EXAMPLE 7.1 Portfolio Risk and Return

Let us apply this analysis to the data of the bond and stock funds as presented in Table 7.1. Using these data, the formulas for the expected return, variance, and standard deviation of the portfolio as a function of the portfolio weights are

$$E(r_p) = 8w_D + 13w_E$$

$$\sigma_p^2 = 12^2 w_D^2 + 20^2 w_E^2 + 2 \times 12 \times 20 \times .3 \times w_D w_E$$

$$= 144w_D^2 + 400w_E^2 + 144w_D w_E$$

$$\sigma_p = \sqrt{\sigma_p^2}$$

We can experiment with different portfolio proportions to observe the effect on portfolio expected return and variance. Suppose we change the proportion invested in bonds. The effect on expected return is tabulated in Table 7.3 and plotted in Figure 7.3. When the proportion invested in debt varies from zero to 1 (so that the proportion in equity varies from

			Portfolio Standard Deviation for Given Correlation				TABLE 7.3
w_D	w_E	$E(r_P)$	$\rho = -1$	$\rho = 0$	$\rho = .30$	$\rho = 1$	Expected return and standard deviation with various correlation coefficients
0.00	1.00	13.00	20.00	20.00	20.00	20.00	
0.10	0.90	12.50	16.80	18.04	18.40	19.20	
0.20	0.80	12.00	13.60	16.18	16.88	18.40	
0.30	0.70	11.50	10.40	14.46	15.47	17.60	
0.40	0.60	11.00	7.20	12.92	14.20	16.80	
0.50	0.50	10.50	4.00	11.66	13.11	16.00	
0.60	0.40	10.00	0.80	10.76	12.26	15.20	
0.70	0.30	9.50	2.40	10.32	11.70	14.40	
0.80	0.20	9.00	5.60	10.40	11.45	13.60	
0.90	0.10	8.50	8.80	10.98	11.56	12.80	
1.00	0.00	8.00	12.00	12.00	12.00	12.00	

			Minimum Variance Portfolio				
burnd w_D			0.6250	0.7353	0.8200	—	
stock w_E			0.3750	0.2647	0.1800	—	
Expected return $E(r_P)$			9.8750	9.3235	8.9000	—	
SD σ_P			0.0000	10.2899	11.4473	—	

1 to zero), the portfolio expected return goes from 13% (the stock fund's expected return) to 8% (the expected return on bonds).

What happens when $w_D > 1$ and $w_E < 0$? In this case portfolio strategy would be to sell the equity fund short and invest the proceeds of the short sale in the debt fund. This will decrease

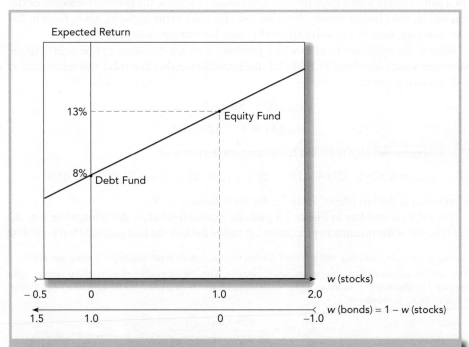

FIGURE 7.3 Portfolio expected return as a function of investment proportions

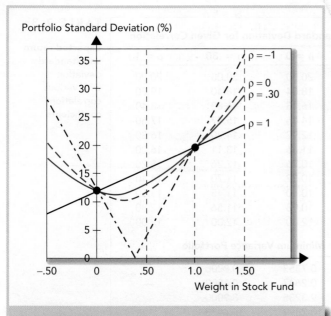

FIGURE 7.4 Portfolio standard deviation as a function of investment proportions

the expected return of the portfolio. For example, when $w_D = 2$ and $w_E = -1$, expected portfolio return falls to $2 \times 8 + (-1) \times 13 = 3\%$. At this point the value of the bond fund in the portfolio is twice the net worth of the account. This extreme position is financed in part by short-selling stocks equal in value to the portfolio's net worth.

The reverse happens when $w_D < 0$ and $w_E > 1$. This strategy calls for selling the bond fund short and using the proceeds to finance additional purchases of the equity fund.

Of course, varying investment proportions also has an effect on portfolio standard deviation. Table 7.3 presents portfolio standard deviations for different portfolio weights calculated from Equation 7.7 using the assumed value of the correlation coefficient, .30, as well as other values of ρ. Figure 7.4 shows the relationship between standard deviation and portfolio weights. Look first at the solid curve for $\rho_{DE} = .30$. The graph shows that as the portfolio weight in the equity fund increases from zero to 1, portfolio standard deviation first falls with the initial diversification from bonds into stocks, but then rises again as the portfolio becomes heavily concentrated in stocks, and again is undiversified. This pattern will generally hold as long as the correlation coefficient between the funds is not too high.[3] For a pair of assets with a large positive correlation of returns, the portfolio standard deviation will increase monotonically from the low-risk asset to the high-risk asset. Even in this case, however, there is a positive (if small) value from diversification.

What is the minimum level to which portfolio standard deviation can be held? For the parameter values stipulated in Table 7.1, the portfolio weights that solve this minimization problem turn out to be[4]

$$w_{\text{Min}}(D) = .82$$
$$w_{\text{Min}}(E) = 1 - .82 = .18$$

This minimum-variance portfolio has a standard deviation of

$$\sigma_{\text{Min}} = [(.82^2 \times 12^2) + (.18^2 \times 20^2) + (2 \times .82 \times .18 \times 72)]^{1/2} = 11.45\%$$

as indicated in the last line of Table 7.3 for the column $\rho = .30$.

The solid colored line in Figure 7.4 plots the portfolio standard deviation when $\rho = .30$ as a function of the investment proportions. It passes through the two undiversified portfolios

---

[3]As long as $\rho < \sigma_D/\sigma_E$, volatility will initially fall when we start with all bonds and begin to move into stocks.

[4]This solution uses the minimization techniques of calculus. Write out the expression for portfolio variance from Equation 7.3, substitute $1 - w_D$ for w_E, differentiate the result with respect to w_D, set the derivative equal to zero, and solve for w_D to obtain

$$w_{\text{Min}}(D) = \frac{\sigma_E^2 - \text{Cov}(r_D, r_E)}{\sigma_D^2 + \sigma_E^2 - 2\text{Cov}(r_D, r_E)}$$

Alternatively, with a spreadsheet program such as Excel, you can obtain an accurate solution by using the Solver to minimize the variance. See Appendix A for an example of a portfolio optimization spreadsheet.

of $w_D = 1$ and $w_E = 1$. Note that the **minimum-variance portfolio** has a standard deviation *smaller than that of either of the individual component assets*. This illustrates the effect of diversification.

The other three lines in Figure 7.4 show how portfolio risk varies for other values of the correlation coefficient, holding the variances of each asset constant. These lines plot the values in the other three columns of Table 7.3.

The solid dark line connecting the undiversified portfolios of all bonds or all stocks, $w_D = 1$ or $w_E = 1$, shows portfolio standard deviation with perfect positive correlation, $\rho = 1$. In this case there is no advantage from diversification, and the portfolio standard deviation is the simple weighted average of the component asset standard deviations.

The dashed colored curve depicts portfolio risk for the case of uncorrelated assets, $\rho = 0$. With lower correlation between the two assets, diversification is more effective and portfolio risk is lower (at least when both assets are held in positive amounts). The minimum portfolio standard deviation when $\rho = 0$ is 10.29% (see Table 7.3), *again lower than the standard deviation of either asset.*

Finally, the triangular broken line illustrates the perfect hedge potential when the two assets are perfectly negatively correlated ($\rho = -1$). In this case the solution for the minimum-variance portfolio is, by Equation 7.12,

$$w_{\text{Min}}(D; \rho = -1) = \frac{\sigma_E}{\sigma_D + \sigma_E} = \frac{20}{12 + 20} = .625$$

$$w_{\text{Min}}(E; \rho = -1) = 1 - .625 = .375$$

and the portfolio variance (and standard deviation) is zero.

We can combine Figures 7.3 and 7.4 to demonstrate the relationship between portfolio risk (standard deviation) and expected return—given the parameters of the available assets. This is done in Figure 7.5. For any pair of investment proportions, w_D, w_E, we read the expected return from Figure 7.3 and the standard deviation from Figure 7.4. The resulting pairs of expected return and standard deviation are tabulated in Table 7.3 and plotted in Figure 7.5.

The solid colored curve in Figure 7.5 shows the **portfolio opportunity set** for $\rho = .30$. We call it the portfolio opportunity set because it shows all combinations of portfolio expected return and standard deviation that can be constructed from the two available assets. The other lines show the portfolio opportunity set for other values of the correlation coefficient. The solid black line connecting the two funds shows that there is no benefit from diversification when the correlation between the two is perfectly positive ($\rho = 1$). The opportunity set is not "pushed" to the northwest. The dashed colored line demonstrates the greater benefit from diversification when the correlation coefficient is lower than .30.

Finally, for $\rho = -1$, the portfolio opportunity set is linear, but now it offers a perfect hedging opportunity and the maximum advantage from diversification.

To summarize, although the expected return of any portfolio is simply the weighted average of the

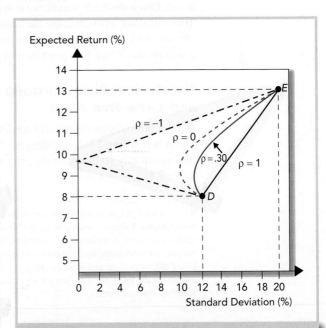

FIGURE 7.5 Portfolio expected return as a function of standard deviation

asset expected returns, this is not true of the standard deviation. Potential benefits from diversification arise when correlation is less than perfectly positive. The lower the correlation, the greater the potential benefit from diversification. In the extreme case of perfect negative correlation, we have a perfect hedging opportunity and can construct a zero-variance portfolio.

Suppose now an investor wishes to select the optimal portfolio from the opportunity set. The best portfolio will depend on risk aversion. Portfolios to the northeast in Figure 7.5 provide higher rates of return but impose greater risk. The best trade-off among these choices is a matter of personal preference. Investors with greater risk aversion will prefer portfolios to the southwest, with lower expected return but lower risk.[5]

CONCEPT CHECK 2	Compute and draw the portfolio opportunity set for the debt and equity funds when the correlation coefficient between them is $\rho = .25$.

7.3 ASSET ALLOCATION WITH STOCKS, BONDS, AND BILLS

In the previous chapter we examined the capital allocation decision, the choice of how much of the portfolio to leave in risk-free money market securities versus in a risky portfolio. Now we have taken a further step, specifying that the risky portfolio comprises a stock and a bond fund. We still need to show how investors can decide on the proportion of their risky portfolios to allocate to the stock versus the bond market. This is an asset allocation decision. As the nearby box emphasizes, most investment professionals recognize that "the really critical decision is how to divvy up your money among stocks, bonds and supersafe investments such as Treasury bills."

In the last section, we derived the properties of portfolios formed by mixing two risky assets. Given this background, we now reintroduce the choice of the third, risk-free, portfolio. This will allow us to complete the basic problem of asset allocation across the three key asset classes: stocks, bonds, and risk-free money market securities. Once you understand this case, it will be easy to see how portfolios of many risky securities might best be constructed.

The Optimal Risky Portfolio with Two Risky Assets and a Risk-Free Asset

What if our risky assets are still confined to the bond and stock funds, but now we can also invest in risk-free T-bills yielding 5%? We start with a graphical solution. Figure 7.6 shows the opportunity set based on the properties of the bond and stock funds, using the data from Table 7.1.

---

[5]Given a level of risk aversion, one can determine the portfolio that provides the highest level of utility. Recall from Chapter 6 that we were able to describe the utility provided by a portfolio as a function of its expected return, $E(r_p)$, and its variance, σ_p^2, according to the relationship $U = E(r_p) - 0.5A\sigma_p^2$. The portfolio mean and variance are determined by the portfolio weights in the two funds, w_E and w_D, according to Equations 7.2 and 7.3. Using those equations and some calculus, we find the optimal investment proportions in the two funds. A warning: to use the following equation (or any equation involving the risk aversion parameter, A), you must express returns in decimal form.

$$w_D = \frac{E(r_D) - E(r_E) + A(\sigma_E^2 - \sigma_D\sigma_E\rho_{DE})}{A(\sigma_D^2 + \sigma_E^2 - 2\sigma_D\sigma_E\rho_{DE})}$$

$$w_E = 1 - w_D$$

Here, too, Excel's Solver or similar software can be used to maximize utility subject to the constraints of Equations 7.2 and 7.3, plus the portfolio constraint that $w_D + w_E = 1$ (i.e., that portfolio weights sum to 1).

RECIPE FOR SUCCESSFUL INVESTING: FIRST, MIX ASSETS WELL

First things first.

If you want dazzling investment results, don't start your day foraging for hot stocks and stellar mutual funds. Instead, say investment advisers, the really critical decision is how to divvy up your money among stocks, bonds, and supersafe investments such as Treasury bills.

In Wall Street lingo, this mix of investments is called your asset allocation. "The asset-allocation choice is the first and most important decision," says William Droms, a finance professor at Georgetown University. "How much you have in [the stock market] really drives your results."

"You cannot get [stock market] returns from a bond portfolio, no matter how good your security selection is or how good the bond managers you use," says William John Mikus, a managing director of Financial Design, a Los Angeles investment adviser.

For proof, Mr. Mikus cites studies such as the 1991 analysis done by Gary Brinson, Brian Singer and Gilbert Beebower. That study, which looked at the 10-year results for 82 large pension plans, found that a plan's asset-allocation policy explained 91.5% of the return earned.

DESIGNING A PORTFOLIO

Because your asset mix is so important, some mutual fund companies now offer free services to help investors design their portfolios.

Gerald Perritt, editor of the *Mutual Fund Letter*, a Chicago newsletter, says you should vary your mix of assets depending on how long you plan to invest. The further away your investment horizon, the more you should have in stocks. The closer you get, the more you should lean toward bonds and money-market instruments, such as Treasury bills. Bonds and money-market instruments may generate lower returns than stocks. But for those who need money in the near future, conservative investments make more sense, because there's less chance of suffering a devastating short-term loss.

SUMMARIZING YOUR ASSETS

"One of the most important things people can do is summarize all their assets on one piece of paper and figure out their asset allocation," says Mr. Pond.

Once you've settled on a mix of stocks and bonds, you should seek to maintain the target percentages, says Mr. Pond. To do that, he advises figuring out your asset allocation once every six months. Because of a stock-market plunge, you could find that stocks are now a far smaller part of your portfolio than you envisaged. At such a time, you should put more into stocks and lighten up on bonds.

When devising portfolios, some investment advisers consider gold and real estate in addition to the usual trio of stocks, bonds and money-market instruments. Gold and real estate give "you a hedge against hyper-inflation," says Mr. Droms. "But real estate is better than gold, because you'll get better long-run returns."

Source: Jonathan Clements, "Recipe for Successful Investing: First, Mix Assets Well," *The Wall Street Journal*, October 6, 1993. Reprinted by permission of *The Wall Street Journal*, © 1993 Dow Jones & Company, Inc. All rights reserved worldwide.

Two possible capital allocation lines (CALs) are drawn from the risk-free rate ($r_f = 5\%$) to two feasible portfolios. The first possible CAL is drawn through the minimum-variance portfolio A, which is invested 82% in bonds and 18% in stocks (Table 7.3, bottom panel, last column). Portfolio A's expected return is 8.90%, and its standard deviation is 11.45%. With a T-bill rate of 5%, the **reward-to-volatility (Sharpe) ratio,** which is the slope of the CAL combining T-bills and the minimum-variance portfolio, is

Treynor ratio =

$$\frac{Portfolio\ Return - risk\ free}{\beta\ (portfolio\ beta)}$$

$$S_A = \frac{E(r_A) - r_f}{\sigma_A} = \frac{8.9 - 5}{11.45} = .34$$

Now consider the CAL that uses portfolio B instead of A. Portfolio B invests 70% in bonds and 30% in stocks. Its expected return is 9.5% (a risk premium of 4.5%), and its standard deviation is 11.70%. Thus the reward-to-volatility ratio on the CAL that is supported by portfolio B is

$$S_B = \frac{9.5 - 5}{11.7} = .38$$

which is higher than the reward-to-volatility ratio of the CAL that we obtained using the minimum-variance portfolio and T-bills. Hence, portfolio B dominates A.

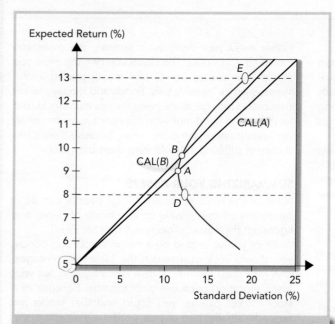

FIGURE 7.6 The opportunity set of the debt and equity funds and two feasible CALs

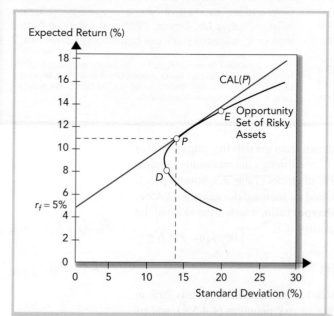

FIGURE 7.7 The opportunity set of the debt and equity funds with the optimal CAL and the optimal risky portfolio

But why stop at portfolio B? We can continue to ratchet the CAL upward until it ultimately reaches the point of tangency with the investment opportunity set. This must yield the CAL with the highest feasible reward-to-volatility ratio. Therefore, the tangency portfolio, labeled P in Figure 7.7, is the optimal risky portfolio to mix with T-bills. We can read the expected return and standard deviation of portfolio P from the graph in Figure 7.7:

$$E(r_P) = 11\%$$
$$\sigma_P = 14.2\%$$

In practice, when we try to construct optimal risky portfolios from more than two risky assets, we need to rely on a spreadsheet or another computer program. The spreadsheet we present in Appendix A can be used to construct efficient portfolios of many assets. To start, however, we will demonstrate the solution of the portfolio construction problem with only two risky assets (in our example, long-term debt and equity) and a risk-free asset. In this simpler two-asset case, we can derive an explicit formula for the weights of each asset in the optimal portfolio. This will make it easy to illustrate some of the general issues pertaining to portfolio optimization.

The objective is to find the weights w_D and w_E that result in the highest slope of the CAL (i.e., the weights that result in the risky portfolio with the highest reward-to-volatility ratio). Therefore, the objective is to maximize the slope of the CAL for any possible portfolio, p. Thus our *objective function* is the slope (equivalently, the Sharpe ratio) S_p:

$$S_p = \frac{E(r_p) - r_f}{\sigma_p}$$

For the portfolio with two risky assets, the expected return and standard deviation of portfolio p are

$$E(r_p) = w_D E(r_D) + w_E E(r_E)$$
$$= 8w_D + 13w_E$$
$$\sigma_p = [w_D^2 \sigma_D^2 + w_E^2 \sigma_E^2 + 2w_D w_E \text{Cov}(r_D, r_E)]^{1/2}$$
$$= [144w_D^2 + 400w_E^2 + (2 \times 72 w_D w_E)]^{1/2}$$

When we maximize the objective function, S_p, we have to satisfy the constraint that the portfolio weights sum to 1.0 (100%), that is, $w_D + w_E = 1$. Therefore, we solve an optimization problem formally written as

$$\text{Max}_{w_i} \; S_p = \frac{E(r_p) - r_f}{\sigma_p}$$

subject to $\Sigma w_i = 1$. This is a nonlinear problem that can be solved using standard tools of calculus.

In the case of two risky assets, the solution for the weights of the **optimal risky portfolio, P,** is given by Equation 7.13. Notice that the solution employs *excess* rates of return (denoted R) rather than total returns (denoted r).[6]

$$w_D = \frac{E(R_D)\sigma_E^2 - E(R_E)\text{Cov}(R_D, R_E)}{E(R_D)\sigma_E^2 + E(R_E)\sigma_D^2 - [E(R_D) + E(R_E)]\text{Cov}(R_D, R_E)}$$

$$w_E = 1 - w_D$$

(7.13)

EXAMPLE 7.2 Optimal Risky Portfolio

Using our data, the solution for the optimal risky portfolio is

$$w_D = \frac{(8-5)400 - (13-5)72}{(8-5)400 + (13-5)144 - (8-5+13-5)72} = .40$$

$$w_E = 1 - .40 = .60$$

The expected return and standard deviation of this optimal risky portfolio are

$$E(r_P) = (.4 \times 8) + (.6 \times 13) = 11\%$$

$$\sigma_P = [(.4^2 \times 144) + (.6^2 \times 400) + (2 \times .4 \times .6 \times 72)]^{1/2} = 14.2\%$$

The CAL of this optimal portfolio has a slope of

$$S_P = \frac{11-5}{14.2} = .42$$

which is the reward-to-volatility (Sharpe) ratio of portfolio P. Notice that this slope exceeds the slope of any of the other feasible portfolios that we have considered, as it must if it is to be the slope of the best feasible CAL.

In Chapter 6 we found the optimal *complete* portfolio given an optimal *risky* portfolio and the CAL generated by a combination of this portfolio and T-bills. Now that we have constructed the optimal risky portfolio, P, we can use the individual investor's degree of risk aversion, A, to calculate the optimal proportion of the complete portfolio to invest in the risky component.

[6]The solution procedure for two risky assets is as follows. Substitute for $E(r_P)$ from Equation 7.2 and for σ_P from Equation 7.7. Substitute $1 - w_D$ for w_E. Differentiate the resulting expression for S_p with respect to w_D, set the derivative equal to zero, and solve for w_D.

EXAMPLE 7.3   Optimal Complete Portfolio

An investor with a coefficient of risk aversion $A = 4$ would take a position in portfolio P of[7]

$$y = \frac{E(r_P) - r_f}{A\sigma_P^2} = \frac{.11 - .05}{4 \times .142^2} = .7439 \qquad \textbf{(7.14)}$$

Thus the investor will invest 74.39% of his or her wealth in portfolio P and 25.61% in T-bills. Portfolio P consists of 40% in bonds, so the fraction of wealth in bonds will be $y w_D = .4 \times .7439 = .2976$, or 29.76%. Similarly, the investment in stocks will be $y w_E = .6 \times .7439 = .4463$, or 44.63%. The graphical solution of this asset allocation problem is presented in Figures 7.8 and 7.9.

Once we have reached this point, generalizing to the case of many risky assets is straightforward. Before we move on, let us briefly summarize the steps we followed to arrive at the complete portfolio.

1. Specify the return characteristics of all securities (expected returns, variances, covariances).
2. Establish the risky portfolio:
   a. Calculate the optimal risky portfolio, P (Equation 7.13).
   b. Calculate the properties of portfolio P using the weights determined in step (*a*) and Equations 7.2 and 7.3.

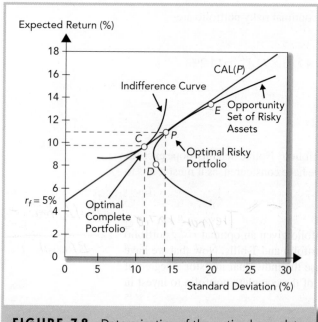

FIGURE 7.8   Determination of the optimal complete portfolio

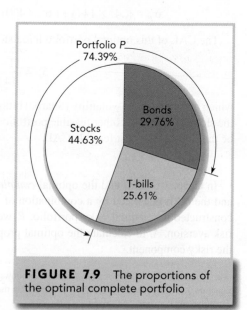

FIGURE 7.9   The proportions of the optimal complete portfolio

[7]Notice that we express returns as decimals in Equation 7.14. This is necessary when using the risk aversion parameter, A, to solve for capital allocation.

3. Allocate funds between the risky portfolio and the risk-free asset:

   a. Calculate the fraction of the complete portfolio allocated to portfolio P (the risky portfolio) and to T-bills (the risk-free asset) (Equation 7.14).

   b. Calculate the share of the complete portfolio invested in each asset and in T-bills.

Recall that our two risky assets, the bond and stock mutual funds, are already diversified portfolios. The diversification *within* each of these portfolios must be credited for a good deal of the risk reduction compared to undiversified single securities. For example, the standard deviation of the rate of return on an average stock is about 50% (see Figure 7.2). In contrast, the standard deviation of our stock-index fund is only 20%, about equal to the historical standard deviation of the S&P 500 portfolio. This is evidence of the importance of diversification within the asset class. Optimizing the asset allocation between bonds and stocks contributed incrementally to the improvement in the reward-to-volatility ratio of the complete portfolio. The CAL with stocks, bonds, and bills (Figure 7.7) shows that the standard deviation of the complete portfolio can be further reduced to 18% while maintaining the same expected return of 13% as the stock portfolio.

CONCEPT CHECK

3

The universe of available securities includes two risky stock funds, A and B, and T-bills. The data for the universe are as follows:

	Expected Return	Standard Deviation
A	10%	20%
B	30	60
T-bills	5	0

The correlation coefficient between funds A and B is −.2.

a. Draw the opportunity set of funds A and B.

b. Find the optimal risky portfolio, P, and its expected return and standard deviation.

c. Find the slope of the CAL supported by T-bills and portfolio P.

d. How much will an investor with A = 5 invest in funds A and B and in T-bills?

7.4 THE MARKOWITZ PORTFOLIO SELECTION MODEL

Security Selection

We can generalize the portfolio construction problem to the case of many risky securities and a risk-free asset. As in the two risky assets example, the problem has three parts. First, we identify the risk–return combinations available from the set of risky assets. Next, we identify the optimal portfolio of risky assets by finding the portfolio weights that result in the steepest CAL. Finally, we choose an appropriate complete portfolio by mixing the risk-free asset with the optimal risky portfolio. Before describing the process in detail, let us first present an overview.

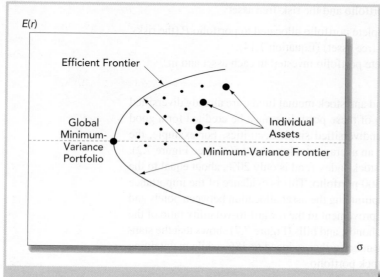

FIGURE 7.10   The minimum-variance frontier of risky assets

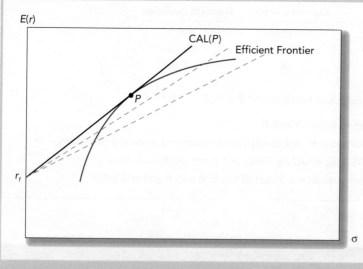

FIGURE 7.11   The efficient frontier of risky assets with the optimal CAL

The first step is to determine the risk–return opportunities available to the investor. These are summarized by the **minimum-variance frontier** of risky assets. This frontier is a graph of the lowest possible variance that can be attained for a given portfolio expected return. Given the input data for expected returns, variances, and covariances, we can calculate the minimum-variance portfolio for any targeted expected return. The plot of these expected return–standard deviation pairs is presented in Figure 7.10.

Notice that all the individual assets lie to the right inside the frontier, at least when we allow short sales in the construction of risky portfolios.[8] This tells us that risky portfolios comprising only a single asset are inefficient. Diversifying investments leads to portfolios with higher expected returns and lower standard deviations.

All the portfolios that lie on the minimum-variance frontier from the global minimum-variance portfolio and upward provide the best risk–return combinations and thus are candidates for the optimal portfolio. The part of the frontier that lies above the global minimum-variance portfolio, therefore, is called the **efficient frontier of risky assets.** For any portfolio on the lower portion of the minimum-variance frontier, there is a portfolio with the same standard deviation and a greater expected return positioned directly above it. Hence the bottom part of the minimum-variance frontier is inefficient.

The second part of the optimization plan involves the risk-free asset. As before, we search for the capital allocation line with the highest reward-to-volatility ratio (that is, the steepest slope) as shown in Figure 7.11.

[8]When short sales are prohibited, single securities may lie on the frontier. For example, the security with the highest expected return must lie on the frontier, as that security represents the *only* way that one can obtain a return that high, and so it must also be the minimum-variance way to obtain that return. When short sales are feasible, however, portfolios can be constructed that offer the same expected return and lower variance. These portfolios typically will have short positions in low-expected-return securities.

The accompanying spreadsheet can be used to measure the return and risk of a portfolio of two risky assets. The model calculates the return and risk for varying weights of each security along with the optimal risky and minimum-variance portfolio. Graphs are automatically generated for various model inputs. The model allows you to specify a target rate of return and solves for optimal combinations using the risk-free asset and the optimal risky portfolio. The spreadsheet is constructed with the two-security return data from Table 7.1. This spreadsheet is available at **www.mhhe.com/bkm.**

	A	B	C	D	E	F
1	Asset Allocation Analysis: Risk and Return					
2		Expected	Standard	Correlation		
3		Return	Deviation	Coefficient	Covariance	
4	Security 1	0.08	0.12	0.3	0.0072	
5	Security 2	0.13	0.2			
6	T-Bill	0.05	0			
7						
8	Weight	Weight		Expected	Standard	Reward to
9	Security 1	Security 2		Return	Deviation	Volatility
10	1	0		0.08000	0.12000	0.25000
11	0.9	0.1		0.08500	0.11559	0.30281
12	0.8	0.2		0.09000	0.11454	0.34922
13	0.7	0.3		0.09500	0.11696	0.38474
14	0.6	0.4		0.10000	0.12264	0.40771

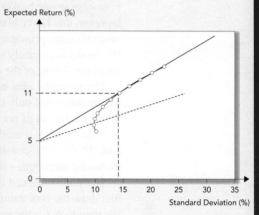

The CAL that is supported by the optimal portfolio, P, is tangent to the efficient frontier. This CAL dominates all alternative feasible lines (the broken lines that are drawn through the frontier). Portfolio P, therefore, is the optimal risky portfolio.

Finally, in the last part of the problem the individual investor chooses the appropriate mix between the optimal risky portfolio P and T-bills, exactly as in Figure 7.8.

Now let us consider each part of the portfolio construction problem in more detail. In the first part of the problem, risk–return analysis, the portfolio manager needs as inputs a set of estimates for the expected returns of each security and a set of estimates for the covariance matrix. (In Part Five on security analysis we will examine the security valuation techniques and methods of financial analysis that analysts use. For now, we will assume that analysts already have spent the time and resources to prepare the inputs.)

The portfolio manager is now armed with the n estimates of $E(r_i)$ and the $n \times n$ estimates of the covariance matrix in which the n diagonal elements are estimates of the variances, σ_i^2, and the $n^2 - n = n(n - 1)$ off-diagonal elements are the estimates of the covariances between each pair of asset returns. (You can verify this from Table 7.2 for the case $n = 2$.) We know that each covariance appears twice in this table, so actually we have $n(n - 1)/2$ different covariance estimates. If our portfolio management unit covers 50 securities, our security analysts need to deliver 50 estimates of expected returns, 50 estimates of variances, and $50 \times 49/2 = 1,225$ different estimates of covariances. This is a daunting task! (We show later how the number of required estimates can be reduced substantially.)

Once these estimates are compiled, the expected return and variance of any risky portfolio with weights in each security, w_i, can be calculated from the bordered covariance matrix or, equivalently, from the following formulas:

$$E(r_p) = \sum_{i=1}^{n} w_i E(r_i) \qquad (7.15)$$

$$\sigma_p^2 = \sum_{i=1}^{n} \sum_{j=1}^{n} w_i w_j \text{Cov}(r_i, r_j) \qquad (7.16)$$

An extended worked example showing you how to do this using a spreadsheet is presented in Appendix A of this chapter.

We mentioned earlier that the idea of diversification is age-old. The phrase "don't put all your eggs in one basket" existed long before modern finance theory. It was not until 1952, however, that Harry Markowitz published a formal model of portfolio selection embodying diversification principles, thereby paving the way for his 1990 Nobel Prize in Economics.[9] His model is precisely step one of portfolio management: the identification of the efficient set of portfolios, or the *efficient frontier of risky assets*.

The principal idea behind the frontier set of risky portfolios is that, for any risk level, we are interested only in that portfolio with the highest expected return. Alternatively, the frontier is the set of portfolios that minimizes the variance for any target expected return.

Indeed, the two methods of computing the efficient set of risky portfolios are equivalent. To see this, consider the graphical representation of these procedures. Figure 7.12 shows the minimum-variance frontier.

The points marked by squares are the result of a variance-minimization program. We first draw the constraints, that is, horizontal lines at the level of required expected returns. We then look for the portfolio with the lowest standard deviation that plots on each horizontal line—we look for the portfolio that will plot farthest to the left (smallest standard deviation) on that line. When we repeat this for many levels of required expected returns, the shape of the minimum-variance frontier emerges. We then discard the bottom (dashed) half of the frontier, because it is inefficient.

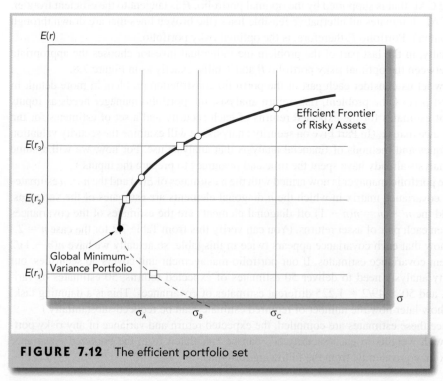

FIGURE 7.12   The efficient portfolio set

[9]Harry Markowitz, "Portfolio Selection," *Journal of Finance,* March 1952.

In the alternative approach, we draw a vertical line that represents the standard deviation constraint. We then consider all portfolios that plot on this line (have the same standard deviation) and choose the one with the highest expected return, that is, the portfolio that plots highest on this vertical line. Repeating this procedure for many vertical lines (levels of standard deviation) gives us the points marked by circles that trace the upper portion of the minimum-variance frontier, the efficient frontier.

When this step is completed, we have a list of efficient portfolios, because the solution to the optimization program includes the portfolio proportions, w_i, the expected return, $E(r_p)$, and the standard deviation, σ_p.

Let us restate what our portfolio manager has done so far. The estimates generated by the security analysts were transformed into a set of expected rates of return and a covariance matrix. This group of estimates we shall call the **input list.** This input list is then fed into the optimization program.

Before we proceed to the second step of choosing the optimal risky portfolio from the frontier set, let us consider a practical point. Some clients may be subject to additional constraints. For example, many institutions are prohibited from taking short positions in any asset. For these clients the portfolio manager will add to the optimization program constraints that rule out negative (short) positions in the search for efficient portfolios. In this special case it is possible that single assets may be, in and of themselves, efficient risky portfolios. For example, the asset with the highest expected return will be a frontier portfolio because, without the opportunity of short sales, the only way to obtain that rate of return is to hold the asset as one's entire risky portfolio.

Short-sale restrictions are by no means the only such constraints. For example, some clients may want to ensure a minimal level of expected dividend yield from the optimal portfolio. In this case the input list will be expanded to include a set of expected dividend yields $d_1, \ldots, d_n$ and the optimization program will include an additional constraint that ensures that the expected dividend yield of the portfolio will equal or exceed the desired level, d.

Portfolio managers can tailor the efficient set to conform to any desire of the client. Of course, any constraint carries a price tag in the sense that an efficient frontier constructed subject to extra constraints will offer a reward-to-volatility ratio inferior to that of a less constrained one. The client should be made aware of this cost and should carefully consider constraints that are not mandated by law.

Another type of constraint is aimed at ruling out investments in industries or countries considered ethically or politically undesirable. This is referred to as *socially responsible investing,* which entails a cost in the form of a lower reward-to-volatility on the resultant constrained, optimal portfolio. This cost can be justifiably viewed as a contribution to the underlying cause.

Capital Allocation and the Separation Property

Now that we have the efficient frontier, we proceed to step two and introduce the risk-free asset. Figure 7.13 shows the efficient frontier plus three CALs representing various portfolios from the efficient set. As before, we ratchet up the CAL by selecting different portfolios until we reach portfolio P, which is the tangency point of a line from F to the efficient frontier. Portfolio P maximizes the reward-to-volatility ratio, the slope of the line from F to portfolios on the efficient frontier. At this point our portfolio manager is done. Portfolio P is the optimal risky portfolio for the manager's clients. This is a good time to ponder our results and their implementation.

A spreadsheet model featuring optimal risky portfolios is available on the Online Learning Center at **www.mhhe.com/bkm.** It contains a template that is similar to the template developed in this section. The model can be used to find optimal mixes of securities for targeted levels of returns for both restricted and unrestricted portfolios. Graphs of the efficient frontier are generated for each set of inputs. The example available at our Web site applies the model to portfolios constructed from equity indexes (called WEBS securities) of several countries.

	A	B	C	D	E	F
1	**Efficient Frontier for World Equity Benchmark Securities (WEBS)**					
2						
3		Mean	Standard			
4	**WEBS**	Return	Deviation	Country		
5	EWD	15.5393	26.4868	Sweden		
6	EWH	6.3852	41.1475	Hong Kong		
7	EWI	26.5999	26.0514	Italy		
8	EWJ	1.4133	26.0709	Japan		
9	EWL	18.0745	21.6916	Switzerland		
10	EWP	18.6347	25.0779	Spain		
11	EWW	16.2243	38.7686	Mexico		
12	S&P 500	17.2306	17.1944			

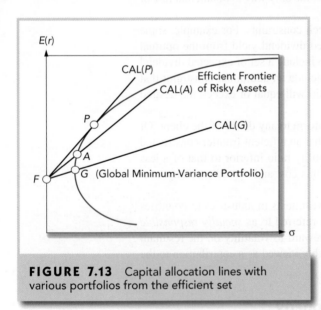

FIGURE 7.13 Capital allocation lines with various portfolios from the efficient set

The most striking conclusion is that a portfolio manager will offer the same risky portfolio, P, to all clients regardless of their degree of risk aversion.[10] The degree of risk aversion of the client comes into play only in the selection of the desired point along the CAL. Thus the only difference between clients' choices is that the more risk-averse client will invest more in the risk-free asset and less in the optimal risky portfolio than will a less risk-averse client. However, both will use portfolio P as their optimal risky investment vehicle.

This result is called a **separation property;** it tells us that the portfolio choice problem may be separated into two independent tasks.[11] The first task, determination of the optimal risky portfolio, is purely technical. Given the manager's input list, the best risky portfolio is the same for all clients, regardless of risk aversion. The second task, however, allocation of the complete portfolio to T-bills versus the risky portfolio, depends on personal preference. Here the client is the decision maker.

The crucial point is that the optimal portfolio P that the manager offers is the same for all clients. Put another way, investors with varying degrees of risk aversion would be satisfied with a universe of only two mutual funds: a money market fund for risk-free investments and a mutual fund that hold the optimal risky portfolio, P, on the tangency point of the CAL and the efficient frontier. This result makes professional management more

[10]Clients who impose special restrictions (constraints) on the manager, such as dividend yield, will obtain another optimal portfolio. Any constraint that is added to an optimization problem leads, in general, to a different and inferior optimum compared to an unconstrained program.

[11]The separation property was first noted by Nobel laureate James Tobin, "Liquidity Preference as Behavior toward Risk," *Review of Economic Statistics* 25 (February 1958), pp. 65–86.

efficient and hence less costly. One management firm can serve any number of clients with relatively small incremental administrative costs.

In practice, however, different managers will estimate different input lists, thus deriving different efficient frontiers, and offer different "optimal" portfolios to their clients. The source of the disparity lies in the security analysis. It is worth mentioning here that the universal rule of GIGO (garbage in–garbage out) also applies to security analysis. If the quality of the security analysis is poor, a passive portfolio such as a market index fund will result in a better CAL than an active portfolio that uses low-quality security analysis to tilt portfolio weights toward seemingly favorable (mispriced) securities.

One particular input list that would lead to a worthless estimate of the efficient frontier is based on recent security average returns. If sample average returns over recent years are used as proxies for the true expected return on the security, the noise in those estimates will make the resultant efficient frontier virtually useless for portfolio construction.

Consider a stock with an annual standard deviation of 50%. Even if one were to use a 10-year average to estimate its expected return (and 10 years is almost ancient history in the life of a corporation), the standard deviation of that estimate would still be $50 / \sqrt{10} = 15.8\%$. The chances that this average represents expected returns for the coming year are negligible.[12] In Chapter 25, we see an example demonstrating that efficient frontiers constructed from past data may be wildly optimistic in terms of the *apparent* opportunities they offer to improve Sharpe ratios.

As we have seen, optimal risky portfolios for different clients also may vary because of portfolio constraints such as dividend-yield requirements, tax considerations, or other client preferences. Nevertheless, this analysis suggests that a limited number of portfolios may be sufficient to serve the demands of a wide range of investors. This is the theoretical basis of the mutual fund industry.

The (computerized) optimization technique is the easiest part of the portfolio construction problem. The real arena of competition among portfolio managers is in sophisticated security analysis. This analysis, as well as its proper interpretation, is part of the art of portfolio construction.[13]

CONCEPT CHECK

4

Suppose that two portfolio managers who work for competing investment management houses each employ a group of security analysts to prepare the input list for the Markowitz algorithm. When all is completed, it turns out that the efficient frontier obtained by portfolio manager A seems to dominate that of manager B. By dominate, we mean that A's optimal risky portfolio lies northwest of B's. Hence, given a choice, investors will all prefer the risky portfolio that lies on the CAL of A.

a. What should be made of this outcome?

b. Should it be attributed to better security analysis by A's analysts?

c. Could it be that A's computer program is superior?

d. If you were advising clients (and had an advance glimpse at the efficient frontiers of various managers), would you tell them to periodically switch their money to the manager with the most northwesterly portfolio?

---

[12]Moreover, you cannot avoid this problem by observing the rate of return on the stock more frequently. In Chapter 5 we showed that the accuracy of the sample average as an estimate of expected return depends on the length of the sample period, and is not improved by sampling more frequently within a given sample period.

[13]You can find a nice discussion of some practical issues in implementing efficient diversification in a white paper prepared by Wealthcare Capital Management at this address: **www.financeware.com/ruminations/WP_EfficiencyDeficiency.pdf.** A copy of the report is also available at the Online Learning Center for this text, **www.mhhe.com/bkm.**

The Power of Diversification

Section 7.1 introduced the concept of diversification and the limits to the benefits of diversification resulting from systematic risk. Given the tools we have developed, we can reconsider this intuition more rigorously and at the same time sharpen our insight regarding the power of diversification.

Recall from Equation 7.16, restated here, that the general formula for the variance of a portfolio is

$$\sigma_p^2 = \sum_{i=1}^{n} \sum_{j=1}^{n} w_i w_j \text{Cov}(r_i, r_j) \tag{7.16}$$

Consider now the naive diversification strategy in which an *equally weighted* portfolio is constructed, meaning that $w_i = 1/n$ for each security. In this case Equation 7.16 may be rewritten as follows, where we break out the terms for which $i = j$ into a separate sum, noting that $\text{Cov}(r_i, r_i) = \sigma_i^2$:

$$\sigma_p^2 = \frac{1}{n} \sum_{i=1}^{n} \frac{1}{n} \sigma_i^2 + \sum_{\substack{j=1 \\ j \neq i}}^{n} \sum_{i=1}^{n} \frac{1}{n^2} \text{Cov}(r_i, r_j) \tag{7.17}$$

Note that there are n variance terms and $n(n - 1)$ covariance terms in Equation 7.17.

If we define the average variance and average covariance of the securities as

$$\overline{\sigma}^2 = \frac{1}{n} \sum_{i=1}^{n} \sigma_i^2 \tag{7.18}$$

$$\overline{\text{Cov}} = \frac{1}{n(n-1)} \sum_{\substack{j=1 \\ j \neq i}}^{n} \sum_{i=1}^{n} \text{Cov}(r_i, r_j) \tag{7.19}$$

we can express portfolio variance as

$$\sigma_p^2 = \frac{1}{n} \overline{\sigma}^2 + \frac{n-1}{n} \overline{\text{Cov}} \tag{7.20}$$

Now examine the effect of diversification. When the average covariance among security returns is zero, as it is when all risk is firm-specific, portfolio variance can be driven to zero. We see this from Equation 7.20. The second term on the right-hand side will be zero in this scenario, while the first term approaches zero as n becomes larger. Hence when security returns are uncorrelated, the power of diversification to reduce portfolio risk is unlimited.

However, the more important case is the one in which economy-wide risk factors impart positive correlation among stock returns. In this case, as the portfolio becomes more highly diversified (n increases) portfolio variance remains positive. Although firm-specific risk, represented by the first term in Equation 7.20, is still diversified away, the second term simply approaches $\overline{\text{Cov}}$ as n becomes greater. [Note that $(n - 1)/n = 1 - 1/n$, which approaches 1 for large n.] Thus the irreducible risk of a diversified portfolio depends on the covariance of the returns of the component securities, which in turn is a function of the importance of systematic factors in the economy.

To see further the fundamental relationship between systematic risk and security correlations, suppose for simplicity that all securities have a common standard deviation, σ, and all security pairs have a common correlation coefficient, ρ. Then the covariance between all pairs of securities is $\rho\sigma^2$, and Equation 7.20 becomes

$$\sigma_p^2 = \frac{1}{n}\sigma^2 + \frac{n-1}{n}\rho\sigma^2 \tag{7.21}$$

The effect of correlation is now explicit. When $\rho = 0$, we again obtain the insurance principle, where portfolio variance approaches zero as n becomes greater. For $\rho > 0$, however, portfolio variance remains positive. In fact, for $\rho = 1$, portfolio variance equals σ^2 regardless of n, demonstrating that diversification is of no benefit: In the case of perfect correlation, all risk is systematic. More generally, as n becomes greater, Equation 7.21 shows that systematic risk becomes $\rho\sigma^2$.

Table 7.4 presents portfolio standard deviation as we include ever-greater numbers of securities in the portfolio for two cases, $\rho = 0$ and $\rho = .40$. The table takes σ to be 50%. As one would expect, portfolio risk is greater when $\rho = .40$. More surprising, perhaps, is that portfolio risk diminishes far less rapidly as n increases in the positive correlation case. The correlation among security returns limits the power of diversification.

Note that for a 100-security portfolio, the standard deviation is 5% in the uncorrelated case—still significant compared to the potential of zero standard deviation. For $\rho = .40$, the standard deviation is high, 31.86%, yet it is very close to undiversifiable systematic risk in the infinite-sized security universe, $\sqrt{\rho\sigma^2} = \sqrt{.4 \times 50^2} = 31.62\%$. At this point, further diversification is of little value.

Perhaps the most important insight from the exercise is this: When we hold diversified portfolios, the contribution to portfolio risk of a particular security will depend on the *covariance* of that security's return with those of other securities, and *not* on the security's variance. As we shall see in Chapter 9, this implies that fair risk premiums also should depend on covariances rather than total variability of returns.

CONCEPT CHECK 5	Suppose that the universe of available risky securities consists of a large number of stocks, identically distributed with $E(r) = 15\%$, σ = 60%, and a common correlation coefficient of $\rho = .5$. *a.* What are the expected return and standard deviation of an equally weighted risky portfolio of 25 stocks? *b.* What is the smallest number of stocks necessary to generate an efficient portfolio with a standard deviation equal to or smaller than 43%? *c.* What is the systematic risk in this security universe? *d.* If T-bills are available and yield 10%, what is the slope of the CAL?

Asset Allocation and Security Selection

As we have seen, the theories of security selection and asset allocation are identical. Both activities call for the construction of an efficient frontier, and the choice of a particular portfolio from along that frontier. The determination of the optimal combination of securities proceeds in the same manner as the analysis of the optimal combination of asset classes. Why, then, do we (and the investment community) distinguish between asset allocation and security selection?

Three factors are at work. First, as a result of greater need and ability to save (for college educations, recreation, longer life in retirement, health care needs, etc.), the demand

TABLE 7.4

Risk reduction of equally weighted portfolios in correlated and uncorrelated universes

Universe Size n	Portfolio Weights $w = 1/n$ (%)	$\rho = 0$		$\rho = .4$	
		Standard Deviation (%)	Reduction in σ	Standard Deviation (%)	Reduction in σ
1	100	50.00	14.64	50.00	8.17
2	50	35.36		41.83	
5	20	22.36	1.95	36.06	0.70
6	16.67	20.41		35.36	
10	10	15.81	0.73	33.91	0.20
11	9.09	15.08		33.71	
20	5	11.18	0.27	32.79	0.06
21	4.76	10.91		32.73	
100	1	5.00	0.02	31.86	0.00
101	0.99	4.98		31.86	

for sophisticated investment management has increased enormously. Second, the widening spectrum of financial markets and financial instruments has put sophisticated investment beyond the capacity of many amateur investors. Finally, there are strong economies of scale in investment analysis. The end result is that the size of a competitive investment company has grown with the industry, and efficiency in organization has become an important issue.

A large investment company is likely to invest both in domestic and international markets and in a broad set of asset classes, each of which requires specialized expertise. Hence the management of each asset-class portfolio needs to be decentralized, and it becomes impossible to simultaneously optimize the entire organization's risky portfolio in one stage, although this would be prescribed as optimal on *theoretical* grounds.

The practice is therefore to optimize the security selection of each asset-class portfolio independently. At the same time, top management continually updates the asset allocation of the organization, adjusting the investment budget allotted to each asset-class portfolio.

7.5 RISK POOLING, RISK SHARING, AND RISK IN THE LONG RUN

Consider an insurance company that offers a 1-year policy on a residential property valued at $100,000. Suppose the following event tree gives the probability distribution of year-end payouts on the policy:

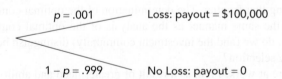

$p = .001$ — Loss: payout = $100,000

$1 - p = .999$ — No Loss: payout = 0

Assume for simplicity that the insurance company sets aside $100,000 to cover its potential payout on the policy. The funds may be invested in T-bills for the coverage year, earning the risk-free rate of 5%. Of course, the *expected* payout on the policy is far smaller; it equals $p \times$ potential payout $= .001 \times 100,000 = \$100$. The insurer may charge an up-front premium of \$120. The \$120 yields (with 5% interest) \$126 by year-end. Therefore, the insurer's expected profit on the policy is \$126 − \$100 = \$26, which makes for a risk premium of 2.6 basis points (.026%) on the \$100,000 set aside to cover potential losses. Relative to what appears a paltry expected profit of \$26, the standard deviation is enormous, \$3,160.70 (try checking this); this implies a standard deviation of return of $\sigma = 3.16\%$ of the \$100,000 investment, compared to a risk premium of only 0.26%.

By now you may be thinking about diversification and the insurance principle. Because the company will cover many such properties, each of which has independent risk, perhaps the large one-policy risk (relative to the risk premium) can be brought down to a "satisfactory" level. Before we proceed, however, we pause for a digression on why this discussion is relevant to understanding portfolio risk. It is because the analogy between the insurance principle and portfolio diversification is essential to understanding risk in the long run.

Risk Pooling and the Insurance Principle

Suppose the insurance company sells 10,000 of these uncorrelated policies. In the context of portfolio diversification, one might think that 10,000 uncorrelated assets would diversify away practically all risk. The expected rate of return on each of the 10,000 identical, independent policies is .026%, and this is the rate of return of the collection of policies as well. To find the standard deviation of the rate of return we use Equation 7.20. Because the covariance between any two policies is zero and σ is the same for each policy, the variance and standard deviation of the rate of return on the 10,000-policy portfolio are

$$\sigma_P^2 = \frac{1}{n}\sigma^2$$

$$\sigma_P = \frac{\sigma}{\sqrt{n}} = \frac{3.16\%}{\sqrt{10,000}} = .0316\%$$

(7.22)

Now the standard deviation is of the same order as the risk premium, and in fact could be further decreased by selling even more policies. This is the insurance principle.

It seems that as the firm sells more policies, its risk continues to fall. The standard deviation of the rate of return on equity capital falls relative to the expected return, and the probability of loss with it. Sooner or later, it appears, the firm will earn a risk-free risk premium. Sound too good to be true? It is.

This line of reasoning might remind you of the familiar argument that investing in stocks for the long run reduces risk. In both cases, scaling up the bet (either by adding more policies or extending the investment to longer periods) appears to reduce risk. And, in fact, the flaw in this argument is the same as the one that we encountered when we looked at the claim that stock investments become less risky in the long run. We saw then that the probability of loss is an inadequate measure of risk, as it does not account for the magnitude of the possible loss. In the insurance application, the maximum possible loss is $10,000 \times \$100,000 = \$1$ billion, and hence a comparison with a one-policy "portfolio" (with a maximum loss of \$100,000) cannot be made on the basis of means and standard deviations of rates of return.

This claim may be surprising. After all, the profits from many policies are normally distributed,[14] so the distribution is symmetric and the standard deviation should be an

---

[14]This argument for normality is similar to that of the newsstand example in Chapter 5. With many policies, the most likely outcomes for total payout are near the expected value. Deviations in either direction are less likely, and the probability distribution of payouts approaches the familiar bell-shaped curve.

appropriate measure of risk. Accordingly, it would seem that the steady decline of the portfolio standard deviation faithfully reflects risk reduction.

The problem with the argument is that increasing the size of the bundle of policies does not make for diversification! Diversifying a portfolio means dividing *a fixed investment budget* across more assets. If an investment of $100,000 in Microsoft is to be diversified, the same $100,000 must be divided between shares of Microsoft and shares of Wal-Mart and other firms. In contrast, an investor who currently has $100,000 invested in Microsoft does *not* reduce total risk by adding another $100,000 investment in Wal-Mart.

An investment of $200,000 divided equally between Microsoft and Wal-Mart, cannot be compared to an investment of $100,000 in Microsoft alone using *rate of return* statistics. This is because the scales of the investments are different. Put differently, if we wish to compare these two investments, the distribution of the rate of return is not reliable. We must compare the distribution of *dollar profits* from the two investments.[15]

When we combine n uncorrelated insurance policies, each with an expected profit of $\$\pi$, both expected total profit *and* standard deviation (SD) grow in direct proportion to n. This is so because

$$E(n\pi) = nE(\pi)$$
$$\text{Var}(n\pi) = n^2\text{Var}(\pi) = n^2 \sigma^2$$
$$\text{SD}(n\pi) = n\sigma$$

The ratio of mean to standard deviation does not change when n increases. The risk–return trade-off therefore does not improve with the assumption of additional policies. Ironically, the economics of the insurance industry has little to do with what is commonly called the insurance principle. Before we turn to the principle that does drive the industry, let's first turn back to see what this example suggests about risk in the long run.

Consider the investor with a $100,000 portfolio. Keeping the $100,000 in the risky portfolio for a second year does not diversify the risk associated with the first year investment. Keeping $100,000 in a risky investment for an additional year is analogous to the insurance company selling an additional $100,000 policy. Average rates of return cannot be used to meaningfully compare a 2-year investment in the risky portfolio with a 1-year investment in the same risky portfolio. Instead, we must compare the distribution of *terminal values* (or 2-year HPRs) of alternative *2-year* investments: 2 years in the risky portfolio versus 1 year in the risky portfolio *and* 1 year in a risk-free investment.

Risk Sharing

If risk *pooling* (the sale of additional independent policies) does not explain the insurance industry, then what does? The answer is risk *sharing,* the distribution of a fixed amount of risk among many investors.

The birth of the insurance industry is believed to have taken place in Edward Lloyd's coffee house in the late 1600s. The economic model underlying Lloyd's underwriters today is quite similar to insurance underwriting when the firm was founded. Suppose a U.S. corporation desires to insure the launch of a satellite valued at $100 million. It can contact one of Lloyd's independent underwriters. That underwriter will contact other underwriters who each will take a piece of the action—each will choose to insure a *fraction* of the project risk. When the lead underwriter successfully puts together a consortium that is

---

[15]Think back to your corporate finance class and you will see the analogy to ranking mutually exclusive projects of different magnitude. The rate of return, or IRR of two investments, can incorrectly rank the projects because it ignores size; only the net present value criterion can be relied on to correctly rank competing projects. This is so because NPV accounts for the dollar magnitude of the investment and subsequent cash flows.

willing to cover 100% of the risk, a proposal is made to the launch company. Notice that each underwriter has a *fixed amount* of equity capital. The underwriter diversifies its risk by allocating its investment budget across many projects that are not perfectly correlated, which is why one underwriter will decline to underwrite too large a fraction of any single project. In other words, the underwriters engage in risk sharing. They limit their exposure to any single source of risk by sharing that risk with other underwriters. Each one diversifies a largely fixed portfolio across many projects, and the risk of each project is shared with many other underwriters. This is the proper use of risk pooling: pooling many sources of risk in a portfolio of *given* size.[16]

Let's return to the property insurance. Suppose an insurance entrepreneur can market every year 10,000 policies of the type we discussed (each with $100,000 of coverage), for $1 billion of total coverage. With such prowess, this entrepreneur can go public and sell shares in the enterprise. Let's say 10,000 investors purchase one share of the billion-dollar company and share equally in the risk premium. If a particular policy pays off, each investor is at risk for only $100,000/10,000 = $10. There is minimal risk from any single policy.

Moreover, even if the insurance company has not pooled many policies, individual investors can still limit their risk by diversifying their own holdings. Shareholders of corporations do not look for the corporation to reduce their portfolio risk. Rather, they diversify their investment portfolios by divvying them up across stocks of many companies.

Keeping with the assumption that all policies are truly independent, it actually makes no difference how many separate insurance companies cover a given number of policies currently outstanding in an insurance market. Suppose that instead of the billion-dollar company, shares of two $500-million insurance companies trade, each with a "portfolio" of 5,000 policies. The distribution of the aggregate profit of the two companies is identical to that of the billion-dollar company. Therefore, buying one share in the large company provides the same diversification value as buying one share in each of the two smaller firms.

The bottom line is that portfolio risk management is about the allocation of a fixed investment budget to assets that are not perfectly correlated. In this environment, rate of return statistics, that is, expected returns, variances, and covariances, are sufficient to optimize the investment portfolio. Choices among alternative investments of a different magnitude require that we abandon rates of return in favor of dollar profits. This applies as well to investments for the long run.

[16]Underwriters that, through successful marketing and efficient administration, can underwrite profitable risks beyond the capacity of their own equity capital may turn to reinsurance companies to cover a fraction of the risk of a large venture. Competition in the reinsurance market keeps rates low and allows the underwriter to keep a good share of the profits of the reinsured risks. This is how insurers can leverage their equity capital.

SUMMARY

1. The expected return of a portfolio is the weighted average of the component security expected returns with the investment proportions as weights.

2. The variance of a portfolio is the weighted sum of the elements of the covariance matrix with the product of the investment proportions as weights. Thus the variance of each asset is weighted by the square of its investment proportion. The covariance of each pair of assets appears twice in the covariance matrix; thus the portfolio variance includes twice each covariance weighted by the product of the investment proportions in each of the two assets.

3. Even if the covariances are positive, the portfolio standard deviation is less than the weighted average of the component standard deviations, as long as the assets are not perfectly positively correlated. Thus portfolio diversification is of value as long as assets are less than perfectly correlated.

4. The greater an asset's covariance with the other assets in the portfolio, the more it contributes to portfolio variance. An asset that is perfectly negatively correlated with a portfolio can serve as a perfect hedge. The perfect hedge asset can reduce the portfolio variance to zero.

5. The efficient frontier is the graphical representation of a set of portfolios that maximize expected return for each level of portfolio risk. Rational investors will choose a portfolio on the efficient frontier.

6. A portfolio manager identifies the efficient frontier by first establishing estimates for asset expected returns and the covariance matrix. This input list is then fed into an optimization program that reports as outputs the investment proportions, expected returns, and standard deviations of the portfolios on the efficient frontier.

7. In general, portfolio managers will arrive at different efficient portfolios because of differences in methods and quality of security analysis. Managers compete on the quality of their security analysis relative to their management fees.

8. If a risk-free asset is available and input lists are identical, all investors will choose the same portfolio on the efficient frontier of risky assets: the portfolio tangent to the CAL. All investors with identical input lists will hold an identical risky portfolio, differing only in how much each allocates to this optimal portfolio and to the risk-free asset. This result is characterized as the separation principle of portfolio construction.

9. Diversification is based on the allocation of a *fixed* portfolio across several assets, limiting the exposure to any one source of risk. Adding additional risky assets to a portfolio, thereby increasing the total amounts invested, does not reduce dollar risk, even if it makes the rate of return more predictable. This is because that uncertainty is applied to a larger investment base. Nor does investing over longer horizons reduce risk. Increasing the investment horizon is analogous to investing in more assets. It increases total risk. Analogously, the key to the insurance industry is risk sharing—the spreading of risk across many investors, each of whom takes on only a small exposure to any given source of risk. Risk pooling—the assumption of ever-more sources of risk—may increase rate of return predictability, but not the predictability of total dollar returns.

Related Web sites for this chapter are available at **www.mhhe.com/bkm**

KEY TERMS

diversification	firm-specific risk	optimal risky portfolio
insurance principle	nonsystematic risk	minimum-variance frontier
market risk	diversifiable risk	efficient frontier of risky assets
systematic risk	minimum-variance portfolio	input list
nondiversifiable risk	portfolio opportunity set	separation property
unique risk	reward-to-volatility ratio	

PROBLEM SETS

Quiz

1. Which of the following factors reflect *pure* market risk for a given corporation?
    a. Increased short-term interest rates.
    b. Fire in the corporate warehouse.
    c. Increased insurance costs.
    d. Death of the CEO.
    e. Increased labor costs.

2. When adding real estate to an asset allocation program that currently includes only stocks, bonds, and cash, which of the properties of real estate returns affect portfolio *risk?* Explain.
    a. Standard deviation.
    b. Expected return.
    c. Correlation with returns of the other asset classes.

3. Which of the following statements about the minimum variance portfolio of all risky securities are valid? (Assume short sales are allowed.) Explain.
    a. Its variance must be lower than those of all other securities or portfolios.
    b. Its expected return can be lower than the risk-free rate.

 c. It may be the optimal risky portfolio.
 d. It must include all individual securities.

The following data apply to Problems 4 through 10: A pension fund manager is considering three mutual funds. The first is a stock fund, the second is a long-term government and corporate bond fund, and the third is a T-bill money market fund that yields a rate of 8%. The probability distribution of the risky funds is as follows:

	Expected Return	Standard Deviation
Stock fund (S)	20%	30%
Bond fund (B)	12	15

The correlation between the fund returns is .10.

4. What are the investment proportions in the minimum-variance portfolio of the two risky funds, and what is the expected value and standard deviation of its rate of return?

5. Tabulate and draw the investment opportunity set of the two risky funds. Use investment proportions for the stock fund of zero to 100% in increments of 20%.

6. Draw a tangent from the risk-free rate to the opportunity set. What does your graph show for the expected return and standard deviation of the optimal portfolio?

7. Solve numerically for the proportions of each asset and for the expected return and standard deviation of the optimal risky portfolio.

8. What is the reward-to-volatility ratio of the best feasible CAL?

9. You require that your portfolio yield an expected return of 14%, and that it be efficient, on the best feasible CAL.
 a. What is the standard deviation of your portfolio?
 b. What is the proportion invested in the T-bill fund and each of the two risky funds?

10. If you were to use only the two risky funds, and still require an expected return of 14%, what would be the investment proportions of your portfolio? Compare its standard deviation to that of the optimized portfolio in Problem 9. What do you conclude?

11. Stocks offer an expected rate of return of 18%, with a standard deviation of 22%. Gold offers an expected return of 10% with a standard deviation of 30%.

 a. In light of the apparent inferiority of gold with respect to both mean return and volatility, would anyone hold gold? If so, demonstrate graphically why one would do so.

 b. Given the data above, reanswer (a) with the additional assumption that the correlation coefficient between gold and stocks equals 1. Draw a graph illustrating why one would or would not hold gold in one's portfolio. Could this set of assumptions for expected returns, standard deviations, and correlation represent an equilibrium for the security market?

12. Suppose that there are many stocks in the security market and that the characteristics of Stocks A and B are given as follows:

Stock	Expected Return	Standard Deviation
A	10%	5%
B	15	10
	Correlation = −1	

Suppose that it is possible to borrow at the risk-free rate, r_f. What must be the value of the risk-free rate? (*Hint:* Think about constructing a risk-free portfolio from stocks A and B.)

13. Assume that expected returns and standard deviations for all securities (including the risk-free rate for borrowing and lending) are known. In this case all investors will have the same optimal risky portfolio. (True or false?)

14. The standard deviation of the portfolio is always equal to the weighted average of the standard deviations of the assets in the portfolio. (True or false?)

15. Suppose you have a project that has a .7 chance of doubling your investment in a year and a .3 chance of halving your investment in a year. What is the standard deviation of the rate of return on this investment?

16. Suppose that you have $1 million and the following two opportunities from which to construct a portfolio:
    a. Risk-free asset earning 12% per year.
    b. Risky asset with expected return of 30% per year and standard deviation of 40%.

    If you construct a portfolio with a standard deviation of 30%, what is its expected rate of return?

The following data are for Problems 17 through 19: The correlation coefficients between pairs of stocks are as follows: Corr(A,B) = .85; Corr(A,C) = .60; Corr(A,D) = .45. Each stock has an expected return of 8% and a standard deviation of 20%.

17. If your entire portfolio is now composed of stock A and you can add some of only one stock to your portfolio, would you choose (explain your choice):
    a. B.
    b. C.
    c. D.
    d. Need more data.

18. Would the answer to Problem 17 change for more risk-averse or risk-tolerant investors? Explain.

19. Suppose that in addition to investing in one more stock you can invest in T-bills as well. Would you change your answers to Problems 17 and 18 if the T-bill rate is 8%?

Challenge Problems

The following table of compound annual returns by decade applies to Challenge Problems 20 and 21.

	1920s*	1930s	1940s	1950s	1960s	1970s	1980s	1990s
Small-company stocks	−3.72%	7.28%	20.63%	19.01%	13.72%	8.75%	12.46%	13.84%
Large-company stocks	18.36	−1.25	9.11	19.41	7.84	5.90	17.60	18.20
Long-term government	3.98	4.60	3.59	0.25	1.14	6.63	11.50	8.60
Intermediate-term government	3.77	3.91	1.70	1.11	3.41	6.11	12.01	7.74
Treasury bills	3.56	0.30	0.37	1.87	3.89	6.29	9.00	5.02
Inflation	−1.00	−2.04	5.36	2.22	2.52	7.36	5.10	2.93

*Based on the period 1926–1929.

20. Input the data from the table into a spreadsheet. Compute the serial correlation in decade returns for each asset class and for inflation. Also find the correlation between the returns of various asset classes. What do the data indicate?

21. Convert the asset returns by decade presented in the table into real rates. Repeat the analysis of Challenge Problem 20 for the real rates of return.

CFA® PROBLEMS

The following data apply to CFA Problems 1 through 3: Hennessy & Associates manages a $30 million equity portfolio for the multimanager Wilstead Pension Fund. Jason Jones, financial vice president of Wilstead, noted that Hennessy had rather consistently achieved the best record among the Wilstead's six equity managers. Performance of the Hennessy portfolio had been clearly superior to that of the S&P 500 in 4 of the past 5 years. In the one less-favorable year, the shortfall was trivial.

Hennessy is a "bottom-up" manager. The firm largely avoids any attempt to "time the market." It also focuses on selection of individual stocks, rather than the weighting of favored industries.

There is no apparent conformity of style among the six equity managers. The five managers, other than Hennessy, manage portfolios aggregating $250 million made up of more than 150 individual issues.

Jones is convinced that Hennessy is able to apply superior skill to stock selection, but the favorable returns are limited by the high degree of diversification in the portfolio. Over the years, the portfolio generally held 40–50 stocks, with about 2%–3% of total funds committed to each issue. The reason Hennessy seemed to do well most years was that the firm was able to identify each year 10 or 12 issues that registered particularly large gains.

Based on this overview, Jones outlined the following plan to the Wilstead pension committee:

Let's tell Hennessy to limit the portfolio to no more than 20 stocks. Hennessy will double the commitments to the stocks that it really favors, and eliminate the remainder. Except for this one new restriction, Hennessy should be free to manage the portfolio exactly as before.

All the members of the pension committee generally supported Jones's proposal because all agreed that Hennessy had seemed to demonstrate superior skill in selecting stocks. Yet the proposal was a considerable departure from previous practice, and several committee members raised questions. Respond to each of the following questions.

1. *a.* Will the limitation to 20 stocks likely increase or decrease the risk of the portfolio? Explain.
   b. Is there any way Hennessy could reduce the number of issues from 40 to 20 without significantly affecting risk? Explain.

2. One committee member was particularly enthusiastic concerning Jones's proposal. He suggested that Hennessy's performance might benefit further from reduction in the number of issues to 10. If the reduction to 20 could be expected to be advantageous, explain why reduction to 10 might be less likely to be advantageous. (Assume that Wilstead will evaluate the Hennessy portfolio independently of the other portfolios in the fund.)

3. Another committee member suggested that, rather than evaluate each managed portfolio independently of other portfolios, it might be better to consider the effects of a change in the Hennessy portfolio on the total fund. Explain how this broader point of view could affect the committee decision to limit the holdings in the Hennessy portfolio to either 10 or 20 issues.

4. Which one of the following portfolios cannot lie on the efficient frontier as described by Markowitz?

	Portfolio	Expected Return (%)	Standard Deviation (%)
a.	W	15	36
b.	X	12	15
c.	Z	5	7
d.	Y	9	21

5. Which statement about portfolio diversification is correct?
   a. Proper diversification can reduce or eliminate systematic risk.
   b. Diversification reduces the portfolio's expected return because it reduces a portfolio's total risk.
   c. As more securities are added to a portfolio, total risk typically would be expected to fall at a decreasing rate.
   d. The risk-reducing benefits of diversification do not occur meaningfully until at least 30 individual securities are included in the portfolio.

6. The measure of risk for a security held in a diversified portfolio is:
   a. Specific risk.
   b. Standard deviation of returns.
   c. Reinvestment risk.
   d. Covariance.

7. Portfolio theory as described by Markowitz is most concerned with:
   a. The elimination of systematic risk.
   b. The effect of diversification on portfolio risk.

  c. The identification of unsystematic risk.

  d. Active portfolio management to enhance return.

8. Assume that a risk-averse investor owning stock in Miller Corporation decides to add the stock of either Mac or Green Corporation to her portfolio. All three stocks offer the same expected return and total variability. The covariance of return between Miller and Mac is $-.05$ and between Miller and Green is $+.05$. Portfolio risk is expected to:

  a. Decline more when the investor buys Mac.

  b. Decline more when the investor buys Green.

  c. Increase when either Mac or Green is bought.

  d. Decline or increase, depending on other factors.

9. Stocks *A*, *B*, and *C* have the same expected return and standard deviation. The following table shows the correlations between the returns on these stocks.

	Stock A	Stock B	Stock C
Stock A	+1.0		
Stock B	+0.9	+1.0	
Stock C	+0.1	−0.4	+1.0

Given these correlations, the portfolio constructed from these stocks having the lowest risk is a portfolio:

  a. Equally invested in stocks *A* and *B*.

  b. Equally invested in stocks *A* and *C*.

  c. Equally invested in stocks *B* and *C*.

  d. Totally invested in stock *C*.

10. Statistics for three stocks, *A*, *B*, and *C*, are shown in the following tables.

Standard Deviations of Returns

Stock:	A	B	C
Standard deviation (%):	40	20	40

Correlations of Returns

Stock	A	B	C
A	1.00	0.90	0.50
B		1.00	0.10
C			1.00

Based *only* on the information provided in the tables, and given a choice between a portfolio made up of equal amounts of stocks *A* and *B or* a portfolio made up of equal amounts of stocks *B* and *C*, which portfolio would you recommend? Justify your choice.

11. George Stephenson's current portfolio of $2 million is invested as follows:

Summary of Stephenson's Current Portfolio

	Value	Percent of Total	Expected Annual Return	Annual Standard Deviation
Short-term bonds	$ 200,000	10%	4.6%	1.6%
Domestic large-cap equities	600,000	30%	12.4%	19.5%
Domestic small-cap equities	1,200,000	60%	16.0%	29.9%
Total portfolio	$2,000,000	100%	13.8%	23.1%

Stephenson soon expects to receive an additional $2 million and plans to invest the entire amount in an index fund that best complements the current portfolio. Stephanie Coppa, CFA, is evaluating the four index funds shown in the following table for their ability to produce a portfolio that will meet two criteria relative to the current portfolio: (1) maintain or enhance expected return and (2) maintain or reduce volatility.

Each fund is invested in an asset class that is not substantially represented in the current portfolio.

Index Fund Characteristics

Index Fund	Expected Annual Return	Expected Annual Standard Deviation	Correlation of Returns with Current Portfolio
Fund A	15%	25%	+0.80
Fund B	11	22	+0.60
Fund C	16	25	+0.90
Fund D	14	22	+0.65

State which fund Coppa should recommend to Stephenson. Justify your choice by describing how your chosen fund *best* meets both of Stephenson's criteria. No calculations are required.

12. Abigail Grace has a $900,000 fully diversified portfolio. She subsequently inherits ABC Company common stock worth $100,000. Her financial adviser provided her with the following forecast information:

Risk and Return Characteristics

	Expected Monthly Returns	Standard Deviation of Monthly Returns
Original Portfolio	0.67%	2.37%
ABC Company	1.25	2.95

The correlation coefficient of ABC stock returns with the original portfolio returns is .40.

a. The inheritance changes Grace's overall portfolio and she is deciding whether to keep the ABC stock. Assuming Grace keeps the ABC stock, calculate the:

   i. Expected return of her new portfolio which includes the ABC stock.
   ii. Covariance of ABC stock returns with the original portfolio returns.
   iii. Standard deviation of her new portfolio which includes the ABC stock.

b. If Grace sells the ABC stock, she will invest the proceeds in risk-free government securities yielding .42% monthly. Assuming Grace sells the ABC stock and replaces it with the government securities, calculate the

   i. Expected return of her new portfolio, which includes the government securities.
   ii. Covariance of the government security returns with the original portfolio returns.
   iii. Standard deviation of her new portfolio, which includes the government securities.

c. Determine whether the systematic risk of her new portfolio, which includes the government securities, will be higher or lower than that of her original portfolio.

d. Based on conversations with her husband, Grace is considering selling the $100,000 of ABC stock and acquiring $100,000 of XYZ Company common stock instead. XYZ stock has the same expected return and standard deviation as ABC stock. Her husband comments, "It doesn't matter whether you keep all of the ABC stock or replace it with $100,000 of XYZ stock." State whether her husband's comment is correct or incorrect. Justify your response.

e. In a recent discussion with her financial adviser, Grace commented, "If I just don't lose money in my portfolio, I will be satisfied." She went on to say, "I am more afraid of losing money than I am concerned about achieving high returns."

   i. Describe *one* weakness of using standard deviation of returns as a risk measure for Grace.
   ii. Identify an alternate risk measure that is more appropriate under the circumstances.

Visit us at www.mhhe.com/bkm

13. Dudley Trudy, CFA, recently met with one of his clients. Trudy typically invests in a master list of 30 equities drawn from several industries. As the meeting concluded, the client made the following statement: "I trust your stock-picking ability and believe that you should invest my funds in your five best ideas. Why invest in 30 companies when you obviously have stronger opinions on a few of them?" Trudy plans to respond to his client within the context of Modern Portfolio Theory.

   a. Contrast the concepts of systematic risk and firm-specific risk, and give an example of *each* type of risk.

   b. Critique the client's suggestion. Discuss how both systematic and firm-specific risk change as the number of securities in a portfolio is increased.

E-Investments

Diversification

Go to the **www.investopedia.com/articles/basics/03/050203.asp** Web site to learn more about diversification, the factors that influence investors' risk preferences, and the types of investments that fit into each of the risk categories. Then check out **www.investopedia.com/articles/pf/05/061505.asp** for asset allocation guidelines for various types of portfolios from conservative to very aggressive. What do you conclude about your own risk preferences and the best portfolio type for you? What would you expect to happen to your attitude toward risk as you get older? How might your portfolio composition change?

SOLUTIONS TO CONCEPT CHECKS

1. *a.* The first term will be $w_D \times w_D \times \sigma_D^2$, because this is the element in the top corner of the matrix (σ_D^2) times the term on the column border (w_D) times the term on the row border (w_D). Applying this rule to each term of the covariance matrix results in the sum $w_D^2\sigma_D^2 + w_D w_E \text{Cov}(r_E, r_D) + w_E w_D \text{Cov}(r_D, r_E) + w_E^2\sigma_E^2$, which is the same as Equation 7.3, because $\text{Cov}(r_E, r_D) = \text{Cov}(r_D, r_E)$.

   b. The bordered covariance matrix is

	w_X	w_Y	w_Z
w_X	σ_X^2	$\text{Cov}(r_X, r_Y)$	$\text{Cov}(r_X, r_Z)$
w_Y	$\text{Cov}(r_Y, r_X)$	σ_Y^2	$\text{Cov}(r_Y, r_Z)$
w_Z	$\text{Cov}(r_Z, r_X)$	$\text{Cov}(r_Z, r_Y)$	σ_Z^2

   There are nine terms in the covariance matrix. Portfolio variance is calculated from these nine terms:

$$\sigma_P^2 = w_X^2\sigma_X^2 + w_Y^2\sigma_Y^2 + w_Z^2\sigma_Z^2$$
$$+ w_X w_Y \text{Cov}(r_X, r_Y) + w_Y w_X \text{Cov}(r_Y, r_X)$$
$$+ w_X w_Z \text{Cov}(r_X, r_Z) + w_Z w_X \text{Cov}(r_Z, r_X)$$
$$+ w_Y w_Z \text{Cov}(r_Y, r_Z) + w_Z w_Y \text{Cov}(r_Z, r_Y)$$
$$= w_X^2\sigma_X^2 + w_Y^2\sigma_Y^2 + w_Z^2\sigma_Z^2$$
$$+ 2w_X w_Y \text{Cov}(r_X, r_Y) + 2w_X w_Z \text{Cov}(r_X, r_Z) + 2w_Y w_Z \text{Cov}(r_Y, r_Z)$$

2. The parameters of the opportunity set are $E(r_D) = 8\%$, $E(r_E) = 13\%$, $\sigma_D = 12\%$, $\sigma_E = 20\%$, and $\rho(D,E) = .25$. From the standard deviations and the correlation coefficient we generate the covariance matrix:

Fund	D	E
D	144	60
E	60	400

The *global minimum-variance* portfolio is constructed so that

$$w_D = \frac{\sigma_E^2 - \text{Cov}(r_D, r_E)}{\sigma_D^2 + \sigma_E^2 - 2\,\text{Cov}(r_D, r_E)}$$

$$= \frac{400 - 60}{(144 + 400) - (2 \times 60)} = .8019$$

$$w_E = 1 - w_D = .1981$$

Its expected return and standard deviation are

$$E(r_P) = (.8019 \times 8) + (.1981 \times 13) = 8.99\%$$
$$\sigma_P = [w_D^2 \sigma_D^2 + w_E^2 \sigma_E^2 + 2w_D w_E \text{Cov}(r_D, r_E)]^{1/2}$$
$$= [(.8019^2 \times 144) + (.1981^2 \times 400) + (2 \times .8019 \times .1981 \times 60)]^{1/2}$$
$$= 11.29\%$$

For the other points we simply increase w_D from .10 to .90 in increments of .10; accordingly, w_E ranges from .90 to .10 in the same increments. We substitute these portfolio proportions in the formulas for expected return and standard deviation. Note that when $w_E = 1.0$, the portfolio parameters equal those of the stock fund; when $w_D = 1$, the portfolio parameters equal those of the debt fund.

We then generate the following table:

w_E	w_D	E(r)	σ
0.0	1.0	8.0	12.00
0.1	0.9	8.5	11.46
0.2	0.8	9.0	11.29
0.3	0.7	9.5	11.48
0.4	0.6	10.0	12.03
0.5	0.5	10.5	12.88
0.6	0.4	11.0	13.99
0.7	0.3	11.5	15.30
0.8	0.2	12.0	16.76
0.9	0.1	12.5	18.34
1.0	0.0	13.0	20.00
0.1981	0.8019	8.99	11.29 minimum variance portfolio

You can now draw your graph.

3. *a.* The computations of the opportunity set of the stock and risky bond funds are like those of Question 2 and will not be shown here. You should perform these computations, however, in order to give a graphical solution to part *a*. Note that the covariance between the funds is

$$\text{Cov}(r_A, r_B) = \rho(A, B) \times \sigma_A \times \sigma_B$$
$$= -.2 \times 20 \times 60 = -240$$

b. The proportions in the optimal risky portfolio are given by

$$w_A = \frac{(10-5)60^2 - (30-5)(-240)}{(10-5)60^2 + (30-5)20^2 - 30(-240)}$$

$$= .6818$$

$$w_B = 1 - w_A = .3182$$

The expected return and standard deviation of the optimal risky portfolio are

$$E(r_P) = (.6818 \times 10) + (.3182 \times 30) = 16.36\%$$

$$\sigma_P = \{(.6818^2 \times 20^2) + (.3182^2 \times 60^2) + [2 \times .6818 \times .3182(-240)]\}^{1/2}$$

$$= 21.13\%$$

Note that in this case the standard deviation of the optimal risky portfolio is smaller than the standard deviation of stock A. Note also that portfolio P is not the global minimum-variance portfolio. The proportions of the latter are given by

$$w_A = \frac{60^2 - (-240)}{60^2 + 20^2 - 2(-240)} = .8571$$

$$w_B = 1 - w_A = .1429$$

With these proportions, the standard deviation of the minimum-variance portfolio is

$$\sigma(\min) = \{(.8571^2 \times 20^2) + (.1429^2 \times 60^2) + [2 \times .8571 \times .1429 \times (-240)]\}^{1/2}$$

$$= 17.57\%$$

which is less than that of the optimal risky portfolio.

c. The CAL is the line from the risk-free rate through the optimal risky portfolio. This line represents all efficient portfolios that combine T-bills with the optimal risky portfolio. The slope of the CAL is

$$S = \frac{E(r_P) - r_f}{\sigma_P} = \frac{16.36 - 5}{21.13} = .5376$$

d. Given a degree of risk aversion, A, an investor will choose a proportion, y, in the optimal risky portfolio of (remember to express returns as decimals when using A):

$$y = \frac{E(r_P) - r_f}{A\sigma_P^2} = \frac{.1636 - .05}{5 \times .2113^2} = .5089$$

This means that the optimal risky portfolio, with the given data, is attractive enough for an investor with A = 5 to invest 50.89% of his or her wealth in it. Because stock A makes up 68.18% of the risky portfolio and stock B makes up 31.82%, the investment proportions for this investor are

Stock A:	.5089 × 68.18 =	34.70%
Stock B:	.5089 × 31.82 =	16.19%
Total		50.89%

4. Efficient frontiers derived by portfolio managers depend on forecasts of the rates of return on various securities and estimates of risk, that is, the covariance matrix. The forecasts themselves do not control outcomes. Thus preferring managers with rosier forecasts (northwesterly frontiers) is tantamount to rewarding the bearers of good news and punishing the bearers of bad news. What we should do is reward bearers of *accurate* news. Thus if you get a glimpse of the frontiers (forecasts) of portfolio managers on a regular basis, what you want to do is develop the track record of their forecasting accuracy and steer your advisees toward the more accurate forecaster. Their portfolio choices will, in the long run, outperform the field.

5. The parameters are $E(r) = 15$, $\sigma = 60$, and the correlation between any pair of stocks is $\rho = .5$.

a. The portfolio expected return is invariant to the size of the portfolio because all stocks have identical expected returns. The standard deviation of a portfolio with $n = 25$ stocks is

$$\sigma_P = [\sigma^2/n + \rho \times \sigma^2(n-1)/n]^{1/2}$$
$$= [60^2/25 + .5 \times 60^2 \times 24/25]^{1/2} = 43.27\%$$

b. Because the stocks are identical, efficient portfolios are equally weighted. To obtain a standard deviation of 43%, we need to solve for n:

$$43^2 = \frac{60^2}{n} + .5 \times \frac{60^2(n-1)}{n}$$
$$1,849n = 3,600 + 1,800n - 1,800$$
$$n = \frac{1,800}{49} = 36.73$$

Thus we need 37 stocks and will come in with volatility slightly under the target.

c. As n gets very large, the variance of an efficient (equally weighted) portfolio diminishes, leaving only the variance that comes from the covariances among stocks, that is

$$\sigma_P = \sqrt{\rho \times \sigma^2} = \sqrt{.5 \times 60^2} = 42.43\%$$

Note that with 25 stocks we came within .84% of the systematic risk, that is, the nonsystematic risk of a portfolio of 25 stocks is only .84%. With 37 stocks the standard deviation is 43%, of which nonsystematic risk is .57%.

d. If the risk-free is 10%, then the risk premium on any size portfolio is $15 - 10 = 5\%$. The standard deviation of a well-diversified portfolio is (practically) 42.43%; hence the slope of the CAL is

$$S = 5/42.43 = .1178$$

APPENDIX A: A Spreadsheet Model for Efficient Diversification

Several software packages can be used to generate the efficient frontier. We will demonstrate the method using Microsoft Excel. Excel is far from the best program for this purpose and is limited in the number of assets it can handle, but working through a simple portfolio optimizer in Excel can illustrate concretely the nature of the calculations used in more sophisticated "black-box" programs. You will find that even in Excel, the computation of the efficient frontier is fairly easy.

We apply the Markowitz portfolio optimization program to a practical problem of international diversification. We take the perspective of a portfolio manager serving U.S. clients, who wishes to construct for the next year an optimal risky portfolio of large stocks in the U.S and six developed capital markets (Japan, Germany, U.K., France, Canada, and Australia). First we describe the input list: forecasts of risk premiums and the covariance matrix. Next, we describe Excel's Solver, and finally we show the solution to the manager's problem.

The Covariance Matrix

To capture recent risk parameters the manager compiles an array of 60 recent monthly (annualized) rates of return, as well as the monthly T-bill rates for the same period.

The standard deviations of excess returns are shown in Table 7A.1 (column C). They range from 14.93% (U.K. large stocks) to 22.7% (Germany). For perspective on how these parameters can change over time, standard deviations for the period 1991–2000 are also shown (column B). In addition, we present the correlation coefficient between large stocks in the six foreign markets with U.S. large stocks for the same two periods. Here we see that correlations are higher in the more recent period, consistent with the process of globalization.

The covariance matrix shown in Table 7A.2 was estimated from the array of 60 returns of the seven countries using the COVARIANCE function from the dialog box of *Data Analysis* in Excel's Tools menu. Due to a quirk in the Excel software, the covariance matrix is not corrected for degrees-of-freedom bias; hence, each of the elements in the matrix was multiplied by 60/59 to eliminate downward bias.

Expected Returns

While estimation of the risk parameters (the covariance matrix) from excess returns is a simple technical matter, estimating the risk premium (the expected excess return) is a daunting task. As we discussed in Chapter 5, estimating expected returns using historical data is unreliable. Consider, for example, the negative average excess returns on U.S. large stocks over the period 2001–2005 (cell G6) and, more generally, the big differences in average returns between the 1991–2000 and 2001–2005 periods, as demonstrated in columns F and G.

In this example, we simply present the manager's forecasts of future returns as shown in column H. In Chapter 8 we will establish a framework that makes the forecasting process more explicit.

The Bordered Covariance Matrix and Portfolio Variance

The covariance matrix in Table 7A.2 is bordered by the portfolio weights, as explained in Section 7.2 and Table 7.2. The values in cells A18–A24, to the left of the covariance matrix, will be selected by the optimization program. For now, we arbitrarily input 1.0 for the U.S. and zero for the others. Cells A16–I16, above the covariance matrix, must be set equal to the column of weights on the left, so that they will change in tandem as the column weights are changed by Excel's Solver. Cell A25 sums the column weights and is used to force the optimization program to set the sum of portfolio weights to 1.0.

Cells C25–I25, below the covariance matrix, are used to compute the portfolio variance for any set of weights that appears in the borders. Each cell accumulates the contribution to portfolio variance from the column above it. It uses the function SUMPRODUCT to accomplish this task. For example, row 33 shows the formula used to derive the value that appears in cell C25.

Finally, the short column A26–A28 below the bordered covariance matrix presents portfolio statistics computed from the bordered covariance matrix. First is the portfolio risk premium in cell A26, with formula shown in row 35, which multiplies the column of portfolio weights by the column of forecasts (H6–H12) from Table 7A.1. Next is the portfolio standard deviation in cell A27. The variance is given by the sum of cells C25–I25 below the bordered covariance matrix. Cell A27 takes the square root of this sum to produce the standard deviation. The last statistic is the portfolio Sharpe ratio, cell A28, which is the slope of the CAL (capital allocation line) that runs through the portfolio constructed using the column weights (the value in cell A28 equals cell A26 divided by cell A27). The optimal risky portfolio is the one that maximizes the Sharpe ratio.

Using the Excel Solver

Excel's Solver is a user-friendly, but quite powerful, optimizer. It has three parts: (1) an objective function, (2) decision variables, and (3) constraints. Figure 7A.1 shows three pictures of the Solver. For the current discussion we refer to picture A.

eXcel

Please visit us at
www.mhhe.com/bkm

7A.1 Country Index Statistics and Forecasts of Excess Returns

	A	B	C	D	E	F	G	H
	Country	Standard Deviation		Correlation with the U.S.		Average Excess Return		Forecast
		1991–2000	2001–2005	1991–2000	2001–2005	1991–2000	2001–2005	2006
6	US	0.1295	0.1495	1	1	0.1108	−0.0148	0.0600
7	UK	0.1466	0.1493	0.64	0.83	0.0536	0.0094	0.0530
8	France	0.1741	0.2008	0.54	0.83	0.0837	0.0247	0.0700
9	Germany	0.1538	0.2270	0.53	0.85	0.0473	0.0209	0.0800
10	Australia	0.1808	0.1617	0.52	0.81	0.0468	0.1225	0.0580
11	Japan	0.2432	0.1878	0.41	0.43	−0.0177	0.0398	0.0450
12	Canada	0.1687	0.1727	0.72	0.79	0.0727	0.1009	0.0590

7A.2 The Bordered Covariance Matrix

	A	B	C	D	E	F	G	H	I
	Portfolio Weights →		1.0000	0.0000	0.0000	0.0000	0.0000	0.0000	0.0000
17			US	UK	France	Germany	Australia	Japan	Canada
18	1.0000	US	0.0224	0.0184	0.0250	0.0288	0.0195	0.0121	0.0205
19	0.0000	UK	0.0184	0.0223	0.0275	0.0299	0.0204	0.0124	0.0206
20	0.0000	France	0.0250	0.0275	0.0403	0.0438	0.0259	0.0177	0.0273
21	0.0000	Germany	0.0288	0.0299	0.0438	0.0515	0.0301	0.0183	0.0305
22	0.0000	Australia	0.0195	0.0204	0.0259	0.0301	0.0261	0.0147	0.0234
23	0.0000	Japan	0.0121	0.0124	0.0177	0.0183	0.0147	0.0353	0.0158
24	0.0000	Canada	0.0205	0.0206	0.0273	0.0305	0.0234	0.0158	0.0298
25	1.0000		0.0224	0.0000	0.0000	0.0000	0.0000	0.0000	0.0000
26	0.0600	Mean							
27	0.1495	SD							
28	0.4013	Slope							

30	Cell A18 - A24	A18 is set arbitrarily to 1 while A19 to A24 are set to 0
31	Formula in cell C16	=A18 ... Formula in cell I16 = A24
32	Formula in cell A25	=SUM(A18:A24)
33	Formula in cell C25	=C16*SUMPRODUCT($A$18:$A$24,C18:C24)
34	Formula in cell D25-I25	Copied from C25 (note the absolute addresses)
35	Formula in cell A26	=SUMPRODUCT($A$18:$A$24,H6:H12)
36	Formula in cell A27	=SUM(C25:I25)^0.5
37	Formula in cell A28	=A26/A27

7A.3 The Efficient Frontier

	A	B	C	D	E	F	G	H	I	J	K	L
41	Cell to store constraint on risk premium				0.0400							
43			Min Var					Optimum				
44	Mean		0.0383	0.0400	0.0450	0.0500	0.0550	0.0564	0.0575	0.0600	0.0700	0.0800
45	SD	0.1	0.1132	0.1135	0.1168	0.1238	0.1340	0.1374	0.1401	0.1466	0.1771	0.2119
46	Slope		0.3386	0.3525	0.3853	0.4037	0.4104	0.4107	0.4106	0.4092	0.3953	0.3774
47	US		0.6112	0.6195	0.6446	0.6696	0.6947	0.7018	0.7073	0.7198	0.7699	0.8201
48	UK		0.8778	0.8083	0.5992	0.3900	0.1809	0.1214	0.0758	−0.0283	−0.4465	−0.8648
49	France		−0.2140	−0.2029	−0.1693	−0.1357	−0.1021	−0.0926	−0.0852	−0.0685	−0.0014	0.0658
50	Germany		−0.5097	−0.4610	−0.3144	−0.1679	−0.0213	0.0205	0.0524	0.1253	0.4185	0.7117
51	Australia		0.0695	0.0748	0.0907	0.1067	0.1226	0.1271	0.1306	0.1385	0.1704	0.2023
52	Japan		0.2055	0.1987	0.1781	0.1575	0.1369	0.1311	0.1266	0.1164	0.0752	0.0341
53	Canada		−0.0402	−0.0374	−0.0288	−0.0203	−0.0118	−0.0093	−0.0075	−0.0032	0.0139	0.0309
54	CAL*	0.0411	0.0465	0.0466	0.0480	0.0509	0.0550	0.0564	0.0575	0.0602	0.0727	0.0871
55	*Risk premium on CAL = SD × slope of optimal risky portfolio											

TABLE 7A.1, 7A.2, 7A.3

Spreadsheet model for international diversification

Visit us at www.mhhe.com/bkm

The top panel of the Solver lets you choose a target cell for the "objective function," that is, the variable you are trying to optimize. In picture A, the target cell is A27, the portfolio standard deviation. Below the target cell, you can choose whether your objective is to maximize, minimize, or set your objective function equal to a value that you specify. Here we choose to minimize the portfolio standard deviation.

The next panel contains the decision variables. These are cells that the Solver can change in order to optimize the objective function in the target cell. Here, we input cells A18–A24, the portfolio weights that we select to minimize portfolio volatility.

The bottom panel of the Solver can include any number of constraints. One constraint that must always appear in portfolio optimization is the "feasibility constraint," namely, that portfolio weights sum to 1.0. When we bring up the constraint dialogue box, we specify that cell A25 (the sum of weights) be set equal to 1.0.

Finding the Minimum Variance Portfolio

It is helpful to begin by identifying the global minimum variance portfolio (G). This provides the starting point of the efficient part of the frontier. Once we input the target cell, the decision variable cells, and the feasibility constraint, as in picture A, we can select "solve" and the Solver returns portfolio G. We copy the portfolio statistics and weights to our output Table 7A.3. Column C in Table 7A.3 shows that the lowest standard deviation (SD) that can be achieved with our input list is 11.32%. Notice that the SD of portfolio G is considerably lower than even the lowest SD of the individual indexes. From the risk premium of portfolio G (3.83%) we begin building the efficient frontier with ever-larger risk premiums.

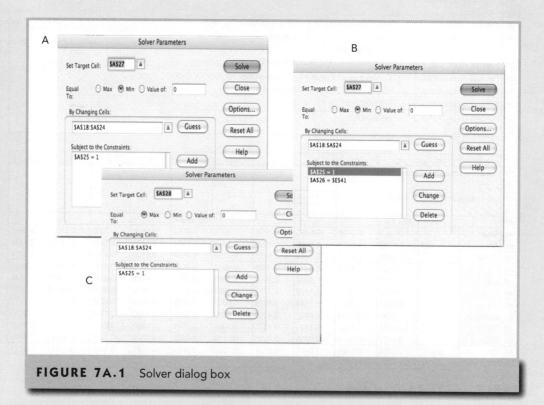

FIGURE 7A.1   Solver dialog box

Charting the Efficient Frontier of Risky Portfolios

We determine the desired risk premiums (points on the efficient frontier) that we wish to use to construct the graph of the efficient frontier. It is good practice to choose more points in the neighborhood of portfolio *G* because the frontier has the greatest curvature in that region. It is sufficient to choose for the highest point the highest risk premium from the input list (here, 8% for Germany). You can produce the entire efficient frontier in minutes following this procedure.

1. Input to the Solver a constraint that says: Cell A26 (the portfolio risk premium) must equal the value in cell E41. The Solver at this point is shown in picture B of Figure 7A.1. Cell E41 will be used to change the required risk premium and thus generate different points along the frontier.

2. For each additional point on the frontier, you input a different desired risk premium into cell E41, and ask the Solver to solve again.

3. Every time the Solver gives you a solution to the request in (2), copy the results into Table 7A.3, which tabulates the collection of points along the efficient frontier. For the next step, change cell E41 and repeat from step 2.

Finding the Optimal Risky Portfolio on the Efficient Frontier

Now that we have an efficient frontier, we look for the portfolio with the highest Sharpe ratio (i.e., reward-to-volatility ratio). This is the efficient frontier portfolio that is tangent to the CAL. To find it, we just need to make two changes to the Solver. First, change the target cell from cell A27 to cell A28, the Sharpe ratio of the portfolio, and request that the value in this cell be maximized. Next, eliminate the constraint on the risk premium that may be left over from the last time you used the Solver. At this point the Solver looks like picture C in Figure 7A.1.

The Solver now yields the optimal risky portfolio. Copy the statistics for the optimal portfolio and its weights to your Table 7A.3. In order to get a clean graph, place the column of the optimal portfolio in Table 7A.3 so that the risk premiums of all portfolios in the table are steadily increasing from the risk premium of portfolio *G* (3.83%) all the way up to 8%.

The efficient frontier is graphed using the data in cells C45–I45 (the horizontal or *x*-axis is portfolio standard deviation) and C44–I44 (the vertical or *y*-axis is portfolio risk premium). The resulting graph appears in Figure 7A.2.

The Optimal CAL

It is instructive to superimpose on the graph of the efficient frontier in Figure 7A.2 the CAL that identifies the optimal risky portfolio. This CAL has a slope equal to the Sharpe ratio of the optimal risky portfolio. Therefore, we add at the bottom of Table 7A.3 a row with entries obtained by multiplying the SD of each column's portfolio by the Sharpe ratio of the optimal risky portfolio from cell H46. This results in the risk premium for each portfolio along the CAL efficient frontier. We now add a series to the graph with the standard deviations in B45–I45 as the *x*-axis and cells B54–I54 as the *y*-axis. You can see this CAL in Figure 7A.2.

The Optimal Risky Portfolio and the Short-Sales Constraint

With the input list used by the portfolio manager, the optimal risky portfolio calls for significant short positions in the stocks of France and Canada (see column H of Table 7A.3). In many cases the portfolio manager is prohibited from taking short positions. If so, we need to amend the program to preclude short sales.

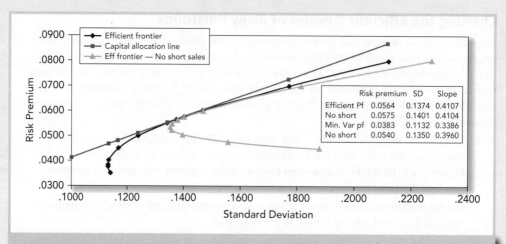

FIGURE 7A.2   Efficient frontier and CAL for country stock indexes

To accomplish this task, we repeat the exercise, but with one change. We add to the Solver the following constraint: Each element in the column of portfolio weights, A18–A24, must be greater than or equal to zero. You should try to produce the short-sale constrained efficient frontier in your own spreadsheet. The graph of the constrained frontier is also shown in Figure 7A.2.

APPENDIX B: Review of Portfolio Statistics

We base this review of scenario analysis on a two-asset portfolio. We denote the assets D and E (which you may think of as debt and equity), but the risk and return parameters we use in this appendix are not necessarily consistent with those used in Section 7.2.

Expected Returns

We use "expected value" and "mean" interchangeably. For an analysis with n scenarios, where the rate of return in scenario i is $r(i)$ with probability $p(i)$, the expected return is

$$E(r) = \sum_{i=1}^{n} p(i)r(i) \tag{7B.1}$$

If you were to increase the rate of return assumed for each scenario by some amount Δ, then the mean return will increase by Δ. If you multiply the rate in each scenario by a factor w, the new mean will be multiplied by that factor:

$$\sum_{i=1}^{n} p(i) \times [r(i) + \Delta] = \sum_{i=1}^{n} p(i) \times r(i) + \Delta \sum_{i=1}^{n} p(i) = E(r) + \Delta \tag{7B.2}$$

$$\sum_{i=1}^{n} p(i) \times [wr(i)] = w \sum_{i=1}^{n} p(i) \times r(i) = wE(r)$$

	A	B	C	D	E	F	G
1							
2			Scenario rates of return				
3	Scenario	Probability	$r_D(i)$	$r_D(i) + 0.03$	$0.4 * r_D(i)$		
4	1	0.14	−0.10	−0.07	−0.040		
5	2	0.36	0.00	0.03	0.000		
6	3	0.30	0.10	0.13	0.040		
7	4	0.20	0.32	0.35	0.128		
8		Mean	0.080	0.110	0.032		
9		Cell C8	=SUMPRODUCT($B$4:$B$7,C4:C7)				
10							
11							
12							

TABLE 7B.1

Scenario analysis for bonds

EXAMPLE 7B.1   Expected Rates of Return

Column C of Table 7B.1 shows scenario rates of return for debt, D. In column D we add 3% to each scenario return and in column E we multiply each rate by .4. The table shows how we compute the expected return for columns C, D, and E. It is evident that the mean increases by 3% (from .08 to .11) in column D and is multiplied by .4 (from .08 to 0.032) in column E.

Now let's construct a portfolio that invests a fraction of the investment budget, $w(D)$, in bonds and the fraction $w(E)$ in stocks. The portfolio's rate of return in each scenario and its expected return are given by

$$r_P(i) = w_D r_D(i) + w_E r_E(i) \tag{7B.3}$$

$$E(r_P) = \sum p(i)[w_D r_D(i) + w_E r_E(i)] = \sum p(i) w_D r_D(i) + \sum p(i) w_E r_E(i)$$
$$= w_D E(r_D) + w_E E(r_E)$$

The rate of return on the portfolio in each scenario is the weighted average of the component rates. The weights are the fractions invested in these assets, that is, the portfolio weights. The expected return on the portfolio is the weighted average of the asset means.

EXAMPLE 7B.2   Portfolio Rate of Return

Table 7B.2 lays out rates of return for both stocks and bonds. Using assumed weights of .4 for debt and .6 for equity, the portfolio return in each scenario appears in column L. Cell L8 shows the portfolio expected return as .1040, obtained using the SUMPRODUCT function, which multiplies each scenario return (column L) by the scenario probability (column I) and sums the results.

	H	I	J	K	L
1					
2			Scenario rates of return		Portfolio return
3	Scenario	Probability	$r_D(i)$	$r_E(i)$	$0.4*r_D(i)+0.6*r_E(i)$
4	1	0.14	−0.10	−0.35	−0.2500
5	2	0.36	0.00	0.20	0.1200
6	3	0.30	0.10	0.45	0.3100
7	4	0.20	0.32	−0.19	0.0140
8		Mean	0.08	0.12	0.1040
9		Cell L4	=0.4*J4+0.6*K4		
10		Cell L8	=SUMPRODUCT($I$4:$I$7,L4:L7)		
11					
12					

TABLE 7B.2

Scenario analysis for bonds and stocks

Variance and Standard Deviation

The variance and standard deviation of the rate of return on an asset from a scenario analysis are given by[17]

$$\sigma^2(r) = \sum_{i=1}^{n} p(i)[r(i) - E(r)]^2 \qquad (7B.4)$$

$$\sigma(r) = \sqrt{\sigma^2(r)}$$

Notice that the unit of variance is percent squared. In contrast, standard deviation, the square root of variance, has the same dimension as the original returns, and therefore is easier to interpret as a measure of return variability.

When you add a fixed incremental return, Δ, to each scenario return, you increase the mean return by that same increment. Therefore, the deviation of the realized return in each scenario from the mean return is unaffected, and both variance and SD are unchanged. In contrast, when you multiply the return in each scenario by a factor w, the variance is multiplied by the square of that factor (and the SD is multiplied by w):

$$\text{Var}(wr) = \sum_{i=1}^{n} p(i) \times [wr(i) - E(wr)]^2 = w^2 \sum_{i=1}^{n} p(i)[r(i) - E(r)]^2 = w^2\sigma^2 \qquad (7B.5)$$

$$\text{SD}(wr) = \sqrt{w^2\sigma^2} = w\sigma(r)$$

Excel does not have a direct function to compute variance and standard deviation for a scenario analysis. Its STDEV and VAR functions are designed for time series. We need to calculate the probability-weighted squared deviations directly. To avoid having

---

[17]Variance (here, of an asset rate of return) is not the only possible choice to quantify variability. An alternative would be to use the *absolute* deviation from the mean instead of the *squared* deviation. Thus, the mean absolute deviation (MAD) is sometimes used as a measure of variability. The variance is the preferred measure for several reasons. First, it is mathematically more difficult to work with absolute deviations. Second, squaring deviations gives more weight to larger deviations. In investments, giving more weight to large deviations (hence, losses) is compatible with risk aversion. Third, when returns are normally distributed, the variance is one of the two parameters that fully characterize the distribution.

	A	B	C	D	E	F	G
13							
14				Scenario rates of return			
15	Scenario	Probability	$r_D(i)$	$r_D(i) + 0.03$	$0.4 \cdot r_D(i)$		
16	1	0.14	–0.10	–0.07	–0.040		
17	2	0.36	0.00	0.03	0.000		
18	3	0.30	0.10	0.13	0.040		
19	4	0.20	0.32	0.35	0.128		
20		Mean	0.0800	0.1100	0.0240		
21		Variance	0.0185	0.0185	0.0034		
22		SD	0.1359	0.1359	0.0584		
23	Cell C21	=SUMPRODUCT($B$16:$B$19,C16:C19,C16:C19)–C20^2					
24	Cell C22	=C21^0.5					

TABLE 7B.3

Scenario analysis for bonds

to first compute columns of squared deviations from the mean, however, we can simplify our problem by expressing the variance as a difference between two easily computable terms:

$$\sigma^2(r) = E[r - E(r)]^2 = E\{r^2 + [E(r)]^2 - 2rE(r)\}$$
$$= E(r^2) + [E(r)]^2 - 2E(r)E(r)$$
$$= E(r^2) - [E(r)]^2 = \sum_{i=1}^{n} p(i)r(i)^2 - \left[\sum_{i=1}^{n} p(i)r(i) \right]^2 \quad \text{(7B.6)}$$

EXAMPLE 7B.3 Calculating the Variance of a Risky Asset in Excel

You can compute the first expression, $E(r^2)$, in Equation 7B.6 using Excel's SUMPRODUCT function. For example, in Table 7B.3, $E(r^2)$ is first calculated in cell C21 by using SUMPRODUCT to multiply the scenario probability times the asset return times the asset return again. Then $[E(r)]^2$ is subtracted (notice the subtraction of C20^2 in cell C21), to arrive at variance.

The variance of a *portfolio* return is not as simple to compute as the mean. The portfolio variance is *not* the weighted average of the asset variances. The deviation of the portfolio rate of return in any scenario from its mean return is

$$r_P - E(r_P) = w_D r_D(i) + w_E r_E(i) - [w_D E(r_D) + w_E E(r_E)]$$
$$= w_D[r_D(i) - E(r_D)] + w_E[r_E(i) - E(r_E)] \quad \text{(7B.7)}$$
$$= w_D d(i) + w_E e(i)$$

where the lowercase variables denote deviations from the mean:

$$d(i) = r_D(i) - E(r_D)$$
$$e(i) = r_E(i) - E(r_E)$$

We express the variance of the portfolio return in terms of these deviations from the mean in Equation 7B.7:

$$\sigma_P^2 = \sum_{i=1}^{n} p(i)[r_P - E(r_P)]^2 = \sum_{i=1}^{n} p(i)[w_D d(i) + w_E e(i)]^2$$

$$= \sum_{i=1}^{n} p(i)[w_D^2 d(i)^2 + w_E^2 e(i)^2 + 2w_D w_E d(i)e(i)]$$

$$= w_D^2 \sum_{i=1}^{n} p(i)d(i)^2 + w_E^2 \sum_{i=1}^{n} p(i)e(i)^2 + 2w_D w_E \sum_{i=1}^{n} p(i)d(i)e(i) \tag{7B.8}$$

$$= w_D^2 \sigma_D^2 + w_E^2 \sigma_E^2 + 2w_D w_E \sum_{i=1}^{n} p(i)d(i)e(i)$$

The last line in Equation 7B.8 tells us that the variance of a portfolio is the weighted sum of portfolio variances (notice that the weights are the squares of the portfolio weights), plus an additional term that, as we will soon see, makes all the difference.

Notice also that $d(i) \times e(i)$ is the product of the deviations of the scenario returns of the two assets from their respective means. The probability-weighted average of this product is its expected value, which is called *covariance* and is denoted $\text{Cov}(r_D, r_E)$. The covariance between the two assets can have a big impact on the variance of a portfolio.

Covariance

The covariance between two variables equals

$$\text{Cov}(r_D, r_E) = E(d \times e) = E\{[r_D - E(r_D)][r_E - E(r_E)]\} \tag{7B.9}$$

$$= E(r_D r_E) - E(r_D)E(r_E)$$

The covariance is an elegant way to quantify the covariation of two variables. This is easiest seen through a numerical example.

Imagine a three-scenario analysis of stocks and bonds as given in Table 7B.4. In scenario 1, bonds go down (negative deviation) while stocks go up (positive deviation). In scenario 3, bonds are up, but stocks are down. When the rates move in opposite directions, as in this case, the product of the deviations is negative; conversely, if the rates moved in the same direction, the sign of the product would be positive. The magnitude of the product shows the extent of the opposite or common movement in that scenario. The probability-weighted average of these products therefore summarizes the *average* tendency for the variables to co-vary across scenarios. In the last line of the spreadsheet, we see that the covariance is -80 (cell H6).

Suppose our scenario analysis had envisioned stocks generally moving in the same direction as bonds. To be concrete, let's switch the forecast rates on stocks in the first and

	A	B	C	D	E	F	G	H
1		Rates of Return			Deviation from Mean			Product of
2	Probability	Bonds	Stocks		Bonds	Stocks		Deviations
3	0.25	−2	30		−8	20		−160
4	0.50	6	10		0	0		0
5	0.25	14	−10		8	−20		−160
6	Mean:	6	10		0	0		−80

TABLE 7B.4

Three-scenario analysis for stocks and bonds

third scenarios, that is, let the stock return be -10% in the first scenario and 30% in the third. In this case, the absolute value of both products of these scenarios remains the same, but the signs are positive, and thus the covariance is positive, at $+80$, reflecting the tendency for both asset returns to vary in tandem. If the levels of the scenario returns change, the intensity of the covariation also may change, as reflected by the magnitude of the product of deviations. The change in the magnitude of the covariance quantifies the change in both direction and intensity of the covariation.

If there is no comovement at all, because positive and negative products are equally likely, the covariance is zero. Also, if one of the assets is risk-free, its covariance with any risky asset is zero, because its deviations from its mean are identically zero.

The computation of covariance using Excel can be made easy by using the last line in Equation 7B.9. The first term, $E(r_D \times r_E)$, can be computed in one stroke using Excel's SUMPRODUCT function. Specifically, in Table 7B.4, SUMPRODUCT(A3:A5, B3:B5, C3:C5) multiplies the probability times the return on debt times the return on equity in each scenario and then sums those three products.

Notice that adding Δ to each rate would not change the covariance because deviations from the mean would remain unchanged. But if you *multiply* either of the variables by a fixed factor, the covariance will increase by that factor. Multiplying both variables results in a covariance multiplied by the products of the factors because

$$\text{Cov}(w_D r_D, w_E r_E) = E\{[w_D r_D - w_D E(r_D)][w_E r_E - w_E E(r_E)]\}$$
$$= w_D w_E \text{Cov}(r_D, r_E) \qquad \text{(7B.10)}$$

The covariance in Equation 7B.10 is actually the term that we add (twice) in the last line of the equation for portfolio variance, Equation 7B.8. So we find that portfolio variance is the weighted sum (not average) of the individual asset variances, *plus* twice their covariance weighted by the two portfolio weights ($w_D \times w_E$).

Like variance, the dimension (unit) of covariance is percent squared. But here we cannot get to a more easily interpreted dimension by taking the square root, because the average product of deviations can be negative, as it was in Table 7B.4. The solution in this case is to scale the covariance by the standard deviations of the two variables, producing the *correlation coefficient*.

Correlation Coefficient

Dividing the covariance by the product of the standard deviations of the variables will generate a pure number called *correlation*. We define correlation as follows:

$$\text{Corr}(r_D, r_E) = \frac{\text{Cov}(r_D, r_E)}{\sigma_D \sigma_E} \qquad \text{(7B.11)}$$

The correlation coefficient must fall within the range $[-1, 1]$. This can be explained as follows. What two variables should have the highest degree comovement? Logic says a variable with itself, so let's check it out.

$$\text{Cov}(r_D, r_D) = E\{[r_D - E(r_D)] \times [r_D - E(r_D)]\}$$
$$= E[r_D - E(r_D)]^2 = \sigma_D^2$$
$$\text{Corr}(r_D, r_D) = \frac{\text{Cov}(r_D, r_D)}{\sigma_D \sigma_D} = \frac{\sigma_D^2}{\sigma_D^2} = 1 \qquad \text{(7B.12)}$$

Similarly, the lowest (most negative) value of the correlation coefficient is -1. (Check this for yourself by finding the correlation of a variable with its own negative.)

Visit us at www.mhhe.com/bkm

An important property of the correlation coefficient is that it is unaffected by both addition and multiplication. Suppose we start with a return on debt, r_D, multiply it by a constant, w_D, and then add a fixed amount Δ. The correlation with equity is unaffected:

$$\text{Corr}(\Delta + w_D r_D, r_E) = \frac{\text{Cov}(\Delta + w_D r_D, r_E)}{\sqrt{\text{Var}(\Delta + w_D r_D)} \times \sigma_E} \qquad \text{(7B.13)}$$

$$= \frac{w_D \text{Cov}(r_D, r_E)}{\sqrt{w_D^2 \sigma_D^2} \times \sigma_E} = \frac{w_D \text{Cov}(r_D, r_E)}{w_D \sigma_D \times \sigma_E}$$

$$= \text{Corr}(r_D, r_E)$$

Because the correlation coefficient gives more intuition about the relationship between rates of return, we sometimes express the covariance in terms of the correlation coefficient. Rearranging Equation 7B.11, we can write covariance as

$$\text{Cov}(r_D, r_E) = \sigma_D \sigma_E \text{Corr}(r_D, r_E) \qquad \text{(7B.14)}$$

EXAMPLE 7B.4   Calculating Covariance and Correlation

Table 7B.5 shows the covariance and correlation between stocks and bonds using the same scenario analysis as in the other examples in this appendix. Covariance is calculated using Equation 7B.9. The SUMPRODUCT function used in cell J22 gives us $E(r_D \times r_E)$, from which we subtract $E(r_D) \times E(r_E)$ (i.e., we subtract J20 × K20). Then we calculate correlation in cell J23 by dividing covariance by the product of the asset standard deviations.

Portfolio Variance

We have seen in Equation 7B.8, with the help of Equation 7B.10, that the variance of a two-asset portfolio is the sum of the individual variances multiplied by the square of the portfolio weights, plus twice the covariance between the rates, multiplied by the product of the portfolio weights:

$$\sigma_P^2 = w_D^2 \sigma_D^2 + w_E^2 \sigma_E^2 + 2w_D w_E \text{Cov}(r_D, r_E)$$
$$= w_D^2 \sigma_D^2 + w_E^2 \sigma_E^2 + 2w_D w_E \sigma_D \sigma_E \text{Corr}(r_D, r_E) \qquad \text{(7B.15)}$$

	H	I	J	K	L	M
13						
14			Scenario rates of return			
15	Scenario	Probability	$r_D(i)$	$r_E(i)$		
16	1	0.14	−0.10	−0.35		
17	2	0.36	0.00	0.20		
18	3	0.30	0.10	0.45		
19	4	0.20	0.32	−0.19		
20		Mean	0.08	0.12		
21		SD	0.1359	0.2918		
22		Covariance	−0.0034			
23		Correlation	−0.0847			
24	Cell J22	=SUMPRODUCT(I16:I19,J16:J19,K16:K19)–J20*K20				
25	Cell J23	=J22/(J21*K21)				

TABLE 7B.5

Scenario analysis for bonds and stocks

	A	B	C	D	E	F	G
25							
26							
27							
28			Scenario rates of return		Portfolio return		
29	Scenario	Probability	$r_D(i)$	$r_E(i)$	$0.4*r_D(i)+0.6r_E(i)$		
30	1	0.14	−0.10	−0.35	−0.25		
31	2	0.36	0.00	0.20	0.12		
32	3	0.30	0.10	0.45	0.31		
33	4	0.20	0.32	−0.19	0.014		
34		Mean	0.08	0.12	0.1040		
35		SD	0.1359	0.2918	0.1788		
36		Covariance	−0.0034		SD:	0.1788	
37		Correlation	−0.0847				
38	Cell E35	=SUMPRODUCT(B30:B33,E30:E33,E30:E33)−E34^2)^0.5					
39	Cell E36	=(0.4*C35)^2+(0.6*D35)^2+2*0.4*0.6*C36)^0.5					

e**X**cel

Please visit us at
www.mhhe.com/bkm

TABLE 7B.6

Scenario analysis for bonds and stocks

EXAMPLE 7B.5　Calculating Portfolio Variance

We calculate portfolio variance in Table 7B.6. Notice there that we calculate the portfolio standard deviation in two ways: once from the scenario portfolio returns (cell E35) and again (in cell E36) using the first line of Equation 7B.15. The two approaches yield the same result. You should try to repeat the second calculation using the correlation coefficient from the second line in Equation 7B.15 instead of covariance in the formula for portfolio variance.

Suppose that one of the assets, say, *E,* is replaced with a money market instrument, that is, a risk-free asset. The variance of *E* is then zero, as is the covariance with *D*. In that case, as seen from Equation 7B.15, the portfolio standard deviation is just $w_D \sigma_D$. In other words, when we mix a risky portfolio with the risk-free asset, portfolio standard deviation equals the risky asset's standard deviation times the weight invested in that asset. This result was used extensively in Chapter 6.

Visit us at www.mhhe.com/bkm

INDEX MODELS

THE MARKOWITZ PROCEDURE introduced in the preceding chapter suffers from two drawbacks. First, the model requires a huge number of estimates to fill the covariance matrix. Second, the model does not provide any guideline to the forecasting of the security risk premiums that are essential to construct the efficient frontier of risky assets. Because past returns are unreliable guides to expected future returns, this drawback can be telling.

In this chapter we introduce index models that simplify estimation of the covariance matrix and greatly enhance the analysis of security risk premiums. By allowing us to explicitly decompose risk into systematic and firm-specific components, these models also shed considerable light on both the power and limits of diversification. Further, they allow us to measure these components of risk for particular securities and portfolios.

We begin the chapter by describing a single-factor security market and show how it can justify a single-index model of security returns. Once its properties are analyzed, we proceed to an extensive example of estimation of the single-index model. We review the statistical properties of these estimates and show how they relate to the practical issues facing portfolio managers.

Despite the simplification they offer, index models remain true to the concepts of the efficient frontier and portfolio optimization. Empirically, index models are as valid as the assumption of normality of the rates of return on available securities. To the extent that short-term returns are well approximated by normal distributions, index models can be used to select optimal portfolios nearly as accurately as the Markowitz algorithm. Finally, we examine optimal risky portfolios constructed using the index model. While the principles are the same as those employed in the previous chapter, the properties of the portfolio are easier to derive and interpret in this context. We illustrate how to use the index model by constructing an optimal risky portfolio using a small sample of firms. This portfolio is compared to the corresponding portfolio constructed from the Markowitz model. We conclude with a discussion of several practical issues that arise when implementing the index model.

8.1   A SINGLE–FACTOR SECURITY MARKET

The Input List of the Markowitz Model

The success of a portfolio selection rule depends on the quality of the input list, that is, the estimates of expected security returns and the covariance matrix. In the long run, efficient portfolios will beat portfolios with less reliable input lists and consequently inferior reward-to-risk trade-offs.

Suppose your security analysts can thoroughly analyze 50 stocks. This means that your input list will include the following:

$$n = \quad 50 \quad \text{estimates of expected returns}$$
$$n = \quad 50 \quad \text{estimates of variances}$$
$$\underline{(n^2 - n)/2 = 1{,}225} \quad \text{estimates of covariances}$$
$$1{,}325 \quad \text{total estimates}$$

This is a formidable task, particularly in light of the fact that a 50-security portfolio is relatively small. Doubling n to 100 will nearly quadruple the number of estimates to 5,150. If $n = 3{,}000$, roughly the number of NYSE stocks, we need more than 4.5 *million* estimates.

Another difficulty in applying the Markowitz model to portfolio optimization is that errors in the assessment or estimation of correlation coefficients can lead to nonsensical results. This can happen because some sets of correlation coefficients are mutually inconsistent, as the following example demonstrates:[1]

Asset	Standard Deviation (%)	Correlation Matrix		
		A	**B**	**C**
A	20	1.00	0.90	0.90
B	20	0.90	1.00	0.00
C	20	0.90	0.00	1.00

Suppose that you construct a portfolio with weights: -1.00; 1.00; 1.00, for assets A; B; C, respectively, and calculate the portfolio variance. You will find that the portfolio variance appears to be negative (-200). This of course is not possible because portfolio variances cannot be negative: we conclude that the inputs in the estimated correlation matrix must be mutually inconsistent. Of course, *true* correlation coefficients are always consistent.[2] But we do not know these true correlations and can only estimate them with some imprecision. Unfortunately, it is difficult to determine at a quick glance whether a correlation matrix is inconsistent, providing another motivation to seek a model that is easier to implement.

Introducing a model that simplifies the way we describe the sources of security risk allows us to use a smaller, consistent set of estimates of risk parameters and risk premiums. The simplification emerges because positive covariances among security returns arise from common economic forces that affect the fortunes of most firms. Some examples of common economic factors are business cycles, interest rates, and the cost of natural resources. The unexpected changes in these variables cause, simultaneously, unexpected changes

---

[1]We are grateful to Andrew Kaplin and Ravi Jagannathan, Kellogg Graduate School of Management, Northwestern University, for this example.

[2]The mathematical term for a correlation matrix that cannot generate negative portfolio variance is "positive definite."

in the rates of return on the entire stock market. By decomposing uncertainty into these system-wide versus firm-specific sources, we vastly simplify the problem of estimating covariance and correlation.

Normality of Returns and Systematic Risk

We can always decompose the rate of return on any security, i, into the sum of its expected plus unanticipated components:

$$r_i = E(r_i) + e_i \tag{8.1}$$

where the unexpected return, e_i, has a mean of zero and a standard deviation of σ_i that measures the uncertainty about the security return.

When security returns can be well approximated by normal distributions that are correlated across securities, we say that they are *joint normally distributed*. This assumption alone implies that, at any time, security returns are driven by one or more common variables. When more than one variable drives normally distributed security returns, these returns are said to have a *multivariate normal distribution*. We begin with the simpler case where only one variable drives the joint normally distributed returns, resulting in a single-factor security market. Extension to the multivariate case is straightforward and is discussed in later chapters.

Suppose the common factor, m, that drives innovations in security returns is some macroeconomic variable that affects all firms. Then we can decompose the sources of uncertainty into uncertainty about the economy as a whole, which is captured by m, and uncertainty about the firm in particular, which is captured by e_i. In this case, we amend Equation 8.1 to accommodate two sources of variation in return:

$$r_i = E(r_i) + m + e_i \tag{8.2}$$

The macroeconomic factor, m, measures unanticipated macro surprises. As such, it has a mean of zero (over time, surprises will average out to zero), with standard deviation of σ_m. In contrast, e_i measures only the firm-specific surprise. Notice that m has no subscript because the same common factor affects all securities. Most important is the fact that m and e_i are uncorrelated, that is, because e_i is firm-specific, it is independent of shocks to the common factor that affect the entire economy. The variance of r_i thus arises from two uncorrelated sources, systematic and firm specific. Therefore,

$$\sigma_i^2 = \sigma_m^2 + \sigma^2(e_i) \tag{8.3}$$

The common factor, m, generates correlation across securities, because all securities will respond to the same macroeconomic news, while the firm-specific surprises, captured by e_i, are assumed to be uncorrelated across firms. Because m is also uncorrelated with any of the firm-specific surprises, the covariance between any two securities i and j is

$$\text{Cov}(r_i, r_j) = \text{Cov}(m + e_i, m + e_j) = \sigma_m^2 \tag{8.4}$$

Finally, we recognize that some securities will be more sensitive than others to macroeconomic shocks. For example, auto firms might respond more dramatically to changes in general economic conditions than pharmaceutical firms. We can capture this refinement by assigning each firm a sensitivity coefficient to macro conditions. Therefore, if we denote the sensitivity coefficient for firm i by the Greek letter beta, β_i, we modify Equation 8.2 to obtain the **single-factor model**:

$$r_i = E(r_i) + \beta_i m + e_i \tag{8.5}$$

Equation 8.5 tells us the systematic risk of security i is determined by its beta coefficient. "Cyclical" firms have greater sensitivity to the market and therefore higher systematic risk. The systematic risk of security i is $\beta_i^2\sigma_m^2$, and its total risk is

$$\sigma_i^2 = \beta_i^2\sigma_m^2 + \sigma^2(e_i) \tag{8.6}$$

The covariance between any pair of securities also is determined by their betas:

$$\text{Cov}(r_i, r_j) = \text{Cov}(\beta_i m + e_i, \beta_j m + e_j) = \beta_i\beta_j\sigma_m^2 \tag{8.7}$$

In terms of systematic risk and market exposure, this equation tells us that firms are close substitutes. Equivalent beta securities give equivalent market positions.

Up to this point we have used only statistical implications from the joint normality of security returns. Normality of security returns alone guarantees that portfolio returns are also normal (from the "stability" of the normal distribution discussed in Chapter 5) and that there is a linear relationship between security returns and the common factor. This greatly simplifies portfolio analysis. Statistical analysis, however, does not identify the common factor, nor does it specify how that factor might operate over a longer investment period. However, it seems plausible (and can be empirically verified) that the variance of the common factor usually changes relatively slowly through time, as do the variances of individual securities and the covariances among them. We seek a variable that can proxy for this common factor. To be useful, this variable must be observable, so we can estimate its volatility as well as the sensitivity of individual securities returns to variation in its value.

8.2   THE SINGLE-INDEX MODEL

A reasonable approach to making the single-factor model operational is to assert that the rate of return on a broad index of securities such as the S&P 500 is a valid proxy for the common macroeconomic factor. This approach leads to an equation similar to the single-factor model, which is called a **single-index model** because it uses the market index to proxy for the common factor.

The Regression Equation of the Single-Index Model

Because the S&P 500 is a portfolio of stocks whose prices and rates of return can be observed, we have a considerable amount of past data with which to estimate systematic risk. We denote the market index by M, with excess return of $R_M = r_M - r_f$, and standard deviation of σ_M. Because the index model is linear, we can estimate the sensitivity (or beta) coefficient of a security on the index using a single-variable linear regression. We regress the excess return of a security, $R_i = r_i - r_f$, on the excess return of the index, R_M. To estimate the regression, we collect a historical sample of paired observations, $R_i(t)$ and $R_M(t)$, where t denotes the date of each pair of observations (e.g., the excess returns on the stock and the index in a particular month).[3] The **regression equation** is

$$R_i(t) = \alpha_i + \beta_i R_M(t) + e_i(t) \tag{8.8}$$

The intercept of this equation (denoted by the Greek letter alpha, or α) is the security's expected excess return *when the market excess return is zero*. The slope coefficient, β_i, is

---

[3]Practitioners often use a "modified" index model that is similar to Equation 8.8 but that uses total rather than excess returns. This practice is most common when daily data are used. In this case the rate of return on bills is on the order of only about .01% per day, so total and excess returns are almost indistinguishable.

the security beta. Beta is the security's sensitivity to the index: it is the amount by which the security return tends to increase or decrease for every 1% increase or decrease in the return on the index. e_i is the zero-mean, firm-specific surprise in the security return in time t, also called the **residual.**

The Expected Return–Beta Relationship

Because $E(e_i) = 0$, if we take the expected value of $E(R_i)$ in Equation 8.8, we obtain the expected return–beta relationship of the single-index model:

$$E(R_i) = \alpha_i + \beta_i E(R_M) \tag{8.9}$$

The second term in Equation 8.9 tells us that part of a security's risk premium is due to the risk premium of the index. The market risk premium is multiplied by the relative sensitivity, or beta, of the individual security. We call this the *systematic* risk premium because it derives from the risk premium that characterizes the entire market, which proxies for the condition of the full economy or economic system.

The remainder of the risk premium is given by the first term in the equation, α. Alpha is a *nonmarket* premium. For example, α may be large if you think a security is underpriced and therefore offers an attractive expected return. Later on, we will see that when security prices are in equilibrium, such attractive opportunities ought to be competed away, in which case α will be driven to zero. But for now, let's assume that each security analyst comes up with his or her own estimates of alpha. If managers believe that they can do a superior job of security analysis, then they will be confident in their ability to find stocks with nonzero values of alpha.

We will see shortly that the index model decomposition of an individual security's risk premium to market and nonmarket components greatly clarifies and simplifies the operation of macroeconomic and security analysis within an investment company.

Risk and Covariance in the Single-Index Model

Remember that one of the problems with the Markowitz model is the overwhelming number of parameter estimates required to implement it. Now we will see that the index model simplification vastly reduces the number of parameters that must be estimated. Equation 8.8 yields the systematic and firm-specific components of the overall risk of each security, and the covariance between any pair of securities. Both variances and covariances are determined by the security betas and the properties of the market index:

Total risk = Systematic risk + Firm-specific risk

$$\sigma_i^2 = \beta_i^2 \sigma_M^2 + \sigma^2(e_i)$$

Covariance = Product of betas × Market index risk

$$\text{Cov}(r_i, r_j) = \beta_i \beta_j \sigma_M^2 \tag{8.10}$$

Correlation = Product of correlations with the market index

$$\text{Corr}(r_i, r_j) = \frac{\beta_i \beta_j \sigma_M^2}{\sigma_i \sigma_j} = \frac{\beta_i \sigma_M^2 \beta_j \sigma_M^2}{\sigma_i \sigma_M \sigma_j \sigma_M} = \text{Corr}(r_i, r_M) \times \text{Corr}(r_j, r_M)$$

Equations 8.9 and 8.10 imply that the set of parameter estimates needed for the single-index model consists of only α, β, and $\sigma(e)$ for the individual securities, plus the risk premium and variance of the market index.

<table>
<tr><td rowspan="3" style="background:black;color:white">CONCEPT CHECK

1</td><td colspan="2">The data below describe a three-stock financial market that satisfies the single-index model.</td></tr>
</table>

	Stock	Capitalization	Beta	Mean Excess Return	Standard Deviation
	A	$3,000	1.0	10%	40%
	B	$1,940	0.2	2	30
	C	$1,360	1.7	17	50

The standard deviation of the market index portfolio is 25%.

a. What is the mean excess return of the index portfolio?

b. What is the covariance between stock A and stock B?

c. What is the covariance between stock B and the index?

d. Break down the variance of stock B into its systematic and firm-specific components.

The Set of Estimates Needed for the Single-Index Model

We summarize the results for the single-index model in the table below.

	Symbol
1. The stock's expected return if the market is neutral, that is, if the market's excess return, $r_M - r_f$, is zero	α_i
2. The component of return due to movements in the overall market; β_i is the security's responsiveness to market movements	$\beta_i(r_M - r_f)$
3. The unexpected component of return due to unexpected events that are relevant only to this security (firm specific)	e_i
4. The variance attributable to the uncertainty of the common macroeconomic factor	$\beta_i^2 \sigma_M^2$
5. The variance attributable to firm-specific uncertainty	$\sigma^2(e_i)$

These calculations show that if we have:

- n estimates of the extra-market expected excess returns, α_i
- n estimates of the sensitivity coefficients, β_i
- n estimates of the firm-specific variances, $\sigma^2(e_i)$
- 1 estimate for the market risk premium, $E(R_M)$
- 1 estimate for the variance of the (common) macroeconomic factor, σ_M^2

then these $(3n + 2)$ estimates will enable us to prepare the entire input list for this single-index security universe. Thus for a 50-security portfolio we will need 152 estimates rather than 1,325; for the entire New York Stock Exchange, about 3,000 securities, we will need 9,002 estimates rather than approximately 4.5 million!

It is easy to see why the index model is such a useful abstraction. For large universes of securities, the number of estimates required for the Markowitz procedure using the index model is only a small fraction of what otherwise would be needed.

Another advantage is less obvious but equally important. The index model abstraction is crucial for specialization of effort in security analysis. If a covariance term had to be calculated directly for each security pair, then security analysts could not specialize by industry. For example, if one group were to specialize in the computer industry and another in the auto industry, who would have the common background to estimate the covariance *between* IBM and GM? Neither group would have the deep understanding of other industries necessary to make an informed judgment of co-movements among industries. In contrast, the index model suggests a simple way to compute covariances. Covariances among securities are due to the influence of the single common factor, represented by the market index return, and can be easily estimated using the regression Equation 8.8 on (p. 247).

The simplification derived from the index model assumption is, however, not without cost. The "cost" of the model lies in the restrictions it places on the structure of asset return uncertainty. The classification of uncertainty into a simple dichotomy—macro versus micro risk—oversimplifies sources of real-world uncertainty and misses some important sources of dependence in stock returns. For example, this dichotomy rules out industry events, events that may affect many firms within an industry without substantially affecting the broad macroeconomy.

This last point is potentially important. Imagine that the single-index model is perfectly accurate, except that the residuals of two stocks, say, British Petroleum (BP) and Royal Dutch Shell, are correlated. The index model will ignore this correlation (it will assume it is zero), while the Markowitz algorithm (which accounts for the full covariance between every pair of stocks) will automatically take the residual correlation into account when minimizing portfolio variance. If the universe of securities from which we must construct the optimal portfolio is small, the two models will yield substantively different optimal portfolios. The portfolio of the Markowitz algorithm will place a smaller weight on both BP and Shell (because their mutual covariance reduces their diversification value), resulting in a portfolio with lower variance. Conversely, when correlation among residuals is negative, the index model will ignore the potential diversification value of these securities. The resulting "optimal" portfolio will place too little weight on these securities, resulting in an unnecessarily high variance.

The optimal portfolio derived from the single-index model therefore can be significantly inferior to that of the full-covariance (Markowitz) model when stocks with correlated residuals have large alpha values and account for a large fraction of the portfolio. If many pairs of the covered stocks exhibit residual correlation, it is possible that a *multi-index* model, which includes additional factors to capture those extra sources of cross-security correlation, would be better suited for portfolio analysis and construction. We will demonstrate the effect of correlated residuals in the spreadsheet example in this chapter, and discuss multi-index models in later chapters.

CONCEPT CHECK 2

Suppose that the index model for the excess returns of stocks A and B is estimated with the following results:

$$R_A = 1.0\% + .9R_M + e_A$$

$$R_B = -2.0\% + 1.1R_M + e_B$$

$$\sigma_M = 20\%$$

$$\sigma(e_A) = 30\%$$

$$\sigma(e_B) = 10\%$$

Find the standard deviation of each stock and the covariance between them.

The Index Model and Diversification

The index model, first suggested by Sharpe,[4] also offers insight into portfolio diversification. Suppose that we choose an equally weighted portfolio of *n* securities. The excess rate of return on each security is given by

$$R_i = \alpha_i + \beta_i R_M + e_i$$

[4]William F. Sharpe, "A Simplified Model of Portfolio Analysis," *Management Science,* January 1963.

Similarly, we can write the excess return on the portfolio of stocks as

$$R_P = \alpha_P + \beta_P R_M + e_P \tag{8.11}$$

We now show that, as the number of stocks included in this portfolio increases, the part of the portfolio risk attributable to nonmarket factors becomes ever smaller. This part of the risk is diversified away. In contrast, market risk remains, regardless of the number of firms combined into the portfolio.

To understand these results, note that the excess rate of return on this equally weighted portfolio, for which each portfolio weight $w_i = 1/n$, is

$$
\begin{aligned}
R_P &= \sum_{i=1}^{n} w_i R_i = \frac{1}{n} \sum_{i=1}^{n} R_i = \frac{1}{n} \sum_{i=1}^{n} (\alpha_i + \beta_i R_M + e_i) \\
&= \frac{1}{n} \sum_{i=1}^{n} \alpha_i + \left(\frac{1}{n} \sum_{i=1}^{n} \beta_i \right) R_M + \frac{1}{n} \sum_{i=1}^{n} e_i
\end{aligned}
\tag{8.12}
$$

Comparing Equations 8.11 and 8.12, we see that the portfolio has a sensitivity to the market given by

$$\beta_P = \frac{1}{n} \sum_{i=1}^{n} \beta_i \tag{8.13}$$

which is the average of the individual β_is. It has a nonmarket return component of

$$\alpha_P = \frac{1}{n} \sum_{i=1}^{n} \alpha_i \tag{8.14}$$

which is the average of the individual alphas, plus the zero mean variable

$$e_P = \frac{1}{n} \sum_{i=1}^{n} e_i \tag{8.15}$$

which is the average of the firm-specific components. Hence the portfolio's variance is

$$\sigma_P^2 = \beta_P^2 \sigma_M^2 + \sigma^2(e_P) \tag{8.16}$$

The systematic risk component of the portfolio variance, which we defined as the component that depends on marketwide movements, is $\beta_P^2 \sigma_M^2$ and depends on the sensitivity coefficients of the individual securities. This part of the risk depends on portfolio beta and σ_M^2 and will persist regardless of the extent of portfolio diversification. No matter how many stocks are held, their common exposure to the market will be reflected in portfolio systematic risk.[5]

In contrast, the nonsystematic component of the portfolio variance is $\sigma^2(e_P)$ and is attributable to firm-specific components, e_i. Because these e_is are independent, and all have zero expected value, the law of averages can be applied to conclude that as more and more stocks are added to the portfolio, the firm-specific components tend to cancel out, resulting in ever-smaller nonmarket risk. Such risk is thus termed *diversifiable*. To see this more rigorously, examine the formula for the variance of the equally weighted "portfolio" of firm-specific components. Because the e_is are uncorrelated,

$$\sigma^2(e_P) = \sum_{i=1}^{n} \left(\frac{1}{n} \right)^2 \sigma^2(e_i) = \frac{1}{n} \overline{\sigma}^2(e) \tag{8.17}$$

where $\overline{\sigma}^2(e)$ is the average of the firm-specific variances. Because this average is independent of n, when n gets large, $\sigma^2(e_P)$ becomes negligible.

---

[5]Of course, one can construct a portfolio with zero systematic risk by mixing negative β and positive β assets. The point of our discussion is that the vast majority of securities have a positive β, implying that well-diversified portfolios with small holdings in large numbers of assets will indeed have positive systematic risk.

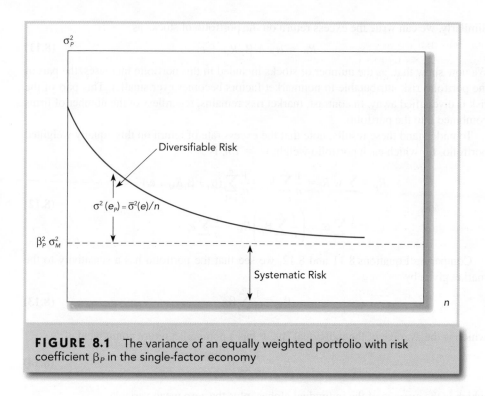

FIGURE 8.1   The variance of an equally weighted portfolio with risk coefficient β_P in the single-factor economy

To summarize, as diversification increases, the total variance of a portfolio approaches the systematic variance, defined as the variance of the market factor multiplied by the square of the portfolio sensitivity coefficient, β_P^2. This is shown in Figure 8.1.

Figure 8.1 shows that as more and more securities are combined into a portfolio, the portfolio variance decreases because of the diversification of firm-specific risk. However, the power of diversification is limited. Even for very large n, part of the risk remains because of the exposure of virtually all assets to the common, or market, factor. Therefore, this systematic risk is said to be nondiversifiable.

CONCEPT CHECK 3	Reconsider the two stocks in Concept Check 2. Suppose we form an equally weighted portfolio of A and B. What will be the nonsystematic standard deviation of that portfolio?

This analysis is borne out by empirical evidence. We saw the effect of portfolio diversification on portfolio standard deviations in Figure 7.2. These empirical results are similar to the theoretical graph presented here in Figure 8.1.

8.3   ESTIMATING THE SINGLE–INDEX MODEL

Armed with the theoretical underpinnings of the single-index model, we now provide an extended example that begins with estimation of the regression equation (8.8) and continues through to the estimation of the full covariance matrix of security returns.

To keep the presentation manageable, we focus on only six large U.S. corporations: Hewlett-Packard and Dell from the information technology (IT) sector of the S&P 500, Target and Wal-Mart from the retailing sector, and British Petroleum and Royal Dutch Shell from the energy sector.

We work with monthly observations of rates of return for the six stocks, the S&P 500 portfolio, and T-bills over the period April 2001 to March 2006 (60 observations). As a first step, the excess returns on the seven risky assets are computed. We start with a detailed look at the preparation of the input list for Hewlett-Packard (HP), and then proceed to display the entire input list. Later in the chapter, we will show how these estimates can be used to construct the optimal risky portfolio.

The Security Characteristic Line for Hewlett-Packard

The index model regression Equation 8.8 (on p. 247), restated for Hewlett-Packard (HP) is

$$R_{HP}(t) = \alpha_{HP} + \beta_{HP} R_{S\&P\,500}(t) + e_{HP}(t)$$

The equation describes the (linear) dependence of HP's excess return on changes in the state of the economy as represented by the excess returns of the S&P 500 index portfolio. The regression estimates describe a straight line with intercept α_{HP} and slope β_{HP}, which we call the **security characteristic line** (SCL) for HP.

Figure 8.2 shows a graph of the excess returns on HP and the S&P 500 portfolio over the 60-month period from April 2001 to March 2006. The graph shows that HP returns generally follow those of the index, but with much larger swings. Indeed, the annualized standard deviation of the excess return on the S&P 500 portfolio over the period was 13.58%, while that of HP was 38.17%. The swings in HP's excess returns suggest a greater-than-average sensitivity to the index, that is, a beta greater than 1.0.

The relationship between the returns of HP and the S&P 500 is made clearer by the **scatter diagram** in Figure 8.3, where the regression line is drawn through the scatter. The vertical distance of each point from the regression line is the value of HP's residual, $e_{HP}(t)$, corresponding to that particular date. The rates in Figures 8.2 and 8.3 are not annualized, and the scatter diagram shows monthly swings of over ±30% for HP, but returns in the range of −11% to 8.5% for the S&P 500. The regression analysis output obtained by using Excel is shown in Table 8.1.

The Explanatory Power of the SCL for HP

Considering the top panel of Table 8.1 first, we see that the correlation of HP with the S&P 500 is quite high (.7238), telling us that HP tracks changes in the returns of the S&P 500 fairly closely. The R-square (.5239) tells us that variation in the S&P 500 excess returns explains about 52% of the variation in the HP series. The adjusted R-square (which is slightly smaller) corrects for an upward bias in R-square that arises because we use the fitted values of two parameters,[6] the slope (beta) and intercept (alpha), rather than their true, but unobservable,

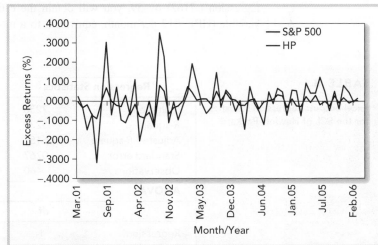

FIGURE 8.2 Excess returns on HP and S&P 500 for April 2001 to March 2006

[6]In general, the adjusted R-square (R_A^2) is derived from the unadjusted by $R_A^2 = 1 - (1 - R^2)\dfrac{n-1}{n-k-1}$, where k is the number of independent variables (here, $k = 1$). An additional degree of freedom is lost to the estimate of the intercept.

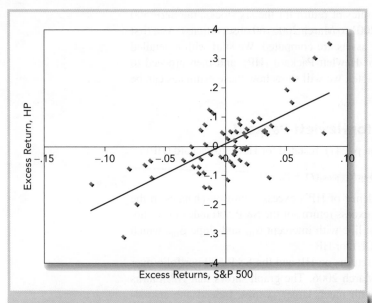

FIGURE 8.3 Scatter diagram of HP, the S&P 500, and the security characteristic line (SCL) for HP

values. With 60 observations, this bias is small. The standard error of the regression is the standard deviation of the residual, which we discuss in more detail shortly. This is a measure of the slippage in the average relationship between the stock and the index due to the impact of firm-specific factors, and is based on *in-sample* data. A more severe test is to look at returns from periods after the one covered by the regression sample and test the power of the independent variable (the S&P 500) to predict the dependent variable (the return on HP). Correlation between regression forecasts and realizations of *out-of-sample* data is almost always considerably lower than in-sample correlation.

Analysis of Variance

The next panel of Table 8.1 shows the analysis of variance (ANOVA) for the SCL. The sum of squares (SS) of the regression (.3752) is the portion of the variance of the dependent variable (HP's return) that is explained by the independent variable (the S&P 500 return); it is equal to $\beta_{HP}^2 \sigma_{S\&P\,500}^2$. The MS column for the residual (.0059) shows the variance of the *unexplained* portion of HP's return, that is, the portion of return that is independent of the market index. The square root of this value is the standard error (SE) of the regression (.0767) reported in the first panel. If you divide the total SS of the regression (.7162) by 59, you will obtain the estimate of the variance of the dependent variable (HP), .012 per month, equivalent to a monthly standard deviation of 11%. When

TABLE 8.1

Excel output: Regression statistics for the SCL of Hewlett-Packard

Regression Statistics				
Multiple *R*	.7238			
R-square	.5239			
Adjusted *R*-square	.5157			
Standard error	.0767			
Observations	60			

ANOVA				
	df	SS	MS	
Regression	1	.3752	.3752	
Residual	58	.3410	.0059	
Total	59	.7162		

	Coefficients	Standard Error	t-Stat	p-Value
Intercept	0.0086	.0099	0.8719	.3868
S&P 500	2.0348	.2547	7.9888	.0000

annualized,[7] we obtain an annualized standard deviation of 38.17%, as reported earlier. Notice that the R-square (the ratio of explained to total variance) equals the explained (regression) SS divided by the total SS.[8]

The Estimate of Alpha

Moving to the bottom panel, the intercept (.0086 = .86% per month) is the estimate of HP's alpha for the sample period. Although this is an economically large value (10.32% on an annual basis), it is statistically insignificant. This can be seen from the three statistics next to the estimated coefficient. The first is the standard error of the estimate (0.0099).[9] This is a measure of the imprecision of the estimate. If the standard error is large, the range of likely estimation error is correspondingly large.

The t-statistic reported in the bottom panel is the ratio of the regression parameter to its standard error. This statistic equals the number of standard errors by which our estimate exceeds zero, and therefore can be used to assess the likelihood that the true but unobserved value might actually equal zero rather than the estimate derived from the data.[10] The intuition is that if the true value were zero, we would be unlikely to observe estimated values far away (i.e., many standard errors) from zero. So large t-statistics imply low probabilities that the true value is zero.

In the case of alpha, we are interested in the average value of HP's return net of the impact of market movements. Suppose we define the nonmarket component of HP's return as its actual return minus the return attributable to market movements during any period. Call this HP's firm-specific return, which we abbreviate as R_{fs}.

$$R_{\text{firm-specific}} = R_{fs} = R_{\text{HP}} - \beta_{\text{HP}} R_{\text{S\&P500}}$$

If R_{fs} were normally distributed with a mean of zero, the ratio of its estimate to its standard error would have a t-distribution. From a table of the t-distribution (or using Excel's TINV function) we can find the probability that the true alpha is actually zero or even lower given the positive estimate of its value and the standard error of the estimate. This is called the *level of significance* or, as in Table 8.1, the probability or *p-value*. The conventional cut-off for statistical significance is a probability of less than 5%, which requires a t-statistic of about 2.0. The regression output shows the t-statistic for HP's alpha to

---

[7]When annualizing monthly data, average return and variance are multiplied by 12. However, because variance is multiplied by 12, standard deviation is multiplied by $\sqrt{12}$.

[8]
$$R\text{-Square} = \frac{\beta_{\text{HP}}^2 \sigma_{\text{S\&P500}}^2}{\beta_{\text{HP}}^2 \sigma_{\text{S\&P500}}^2 + \sigma^2(e_{\text{HP}})} = \frac{.3752}{.7162} = .5239$$

Equivalently, R-square equals 1 minus the fraction of variance that is *not* explained by market returns, i.e., 1 minus the ratio of firm-specific risk to total risk. For HP, this is

$$1 - \frac{\sigma^2(e_{\text{HP}})}{\beta_{\text{HP}}^2 \sigma_{\text{S\&P500}}^2 + \sigma^2(e_{\text{HP}})} = 1 - \frac{.3410}{.7162} = .5239$$

[9]We can relate the standard error of the alpha estimate to the standard error of the residuals as follows:

$$\text{SE}(\alpha_{\text{HP}}) = \sigma(e_{\text{HP}}) \sqrt{\frac{1}{n} + \frac{(\text{AvgS\&P500})^2}{\text{Var(S\&P500)} \times (n-1)}}$$

[10]The t-statistic is based on the assumption that returns are normally distributed. In general, if we standardize the estimate of a normally distributed variable by computing its difference from a hypothesized value and dividing by the standard error of the estimate (to express the difference as a number of standard errors), the resulting variable will have a t-distribution. With a large number of observations, the bell-shaped t-distribution approaches the normal distribution.

be .8719, indicating that the estimate is not significantly different from zero. That is, we cannot reject the hypothesis that the true value of alpha equals zero with an acceptable level of confidence. The *p*-value for the alpha estimate (.3868) indicates that if the true alpha were zero, the probability of obtaining an estimate as high as .0086 (given the large standard error of .0099) would be .3868, which is not so unlikely. We conclude that the sample average of R_{fs} is too low to reject the hypothesis that the true value of alpha is zero.

But even if the alpha value were both economically *and* statistically significant *within the sample,* we still would not use that alpha as a forecast for a future period. Overwhelming empirical evidence shows that 5-year alpha values do not persist over time, that is, there seems to be virtually no correlation between estimates from one sample period to the next. In other words, while the alpha estimated from the regression tells us the average return on the security when the market was flat during that estimation period, it does *not* forecast what the firm's performance will be in future periods. This is why security analysis is so hard. The past does not readily foretell the future. We elaborate on this issue in Chapter 11 on market efficiency.

The Estimate of Beta

The regression output in Table 8.1 shows the beta estimate for HP to be 2.0348, more than twice that of the S&P 500. Such high market sensitivity is not unusual for technology stocks. The standard error (SE) of the estimate is .2547.[11]

The value of beta and its SE produce a large *t*-statistic (7.9888), and a *p*-value of practically zero. We can confidently reject the hypothesis that HP's true beta is zero. A more interesting *t*-statistic might test a null hypothesis that HP's beta is greater than the market-wide average beta of 1. This *t*-statistic would measure how many standard errors separate the estimated beta from a hypothesized value of 1. Here too, the difference is easily large enough to achieve statistical significance:

$$\frac{\text{Estimated value} - \text{Hypothesized value}}{\text{Standard error}} = \frac{2.03 - 1}{.2547} = 4.00$$

However, we should bear in mind that even here, precision is not what we might like it to be. For example, if we wanted to construct a confidence interval that includes the true but unobserved value of beta with 95% probability, we would take the estimated value as the center of the interval and then add and subtract about two standard errors. This produces a range between 1.43 and 2.53, which is quite wide.

Firm-Specific Risk

The monthly standard deviation of HP's residual is 7.67%, or 26.6% annually. This is quite large, on top of HP's high-level systematic risk. The standard deviation of systematic risk is $\beta \times \sigma(\text{S\&P } 500) = 2.03 \times 13.58 = 27.57\%$. Notice that HP's firm-specific risk is as large as its systematic risk, a common result for individual stocks.

Correlation and Covariance Matrix

Figure 8.4 graphs the excess returns of the pairs of securities from each of the three sectors with the S&P 500 index on the same scale. We see that the IT sector is the most variable, followed by the retail sector, and then the energy sector, which has the lowest volatility.

Panel 1 in Spreadsheet 8.1 shows the estimates of the risk parameters of the S&P 500 portfolio and the six analyzed securities. You can see from the high residual standard deviations (column E) how important diversification is. These securities have tremendous

---

[11] $\text{SE}(\beta) = \dfrac{\sigma(e_{\text{HP}})}{\sigma_{\text{HP}}\sqrt{n-1}}$

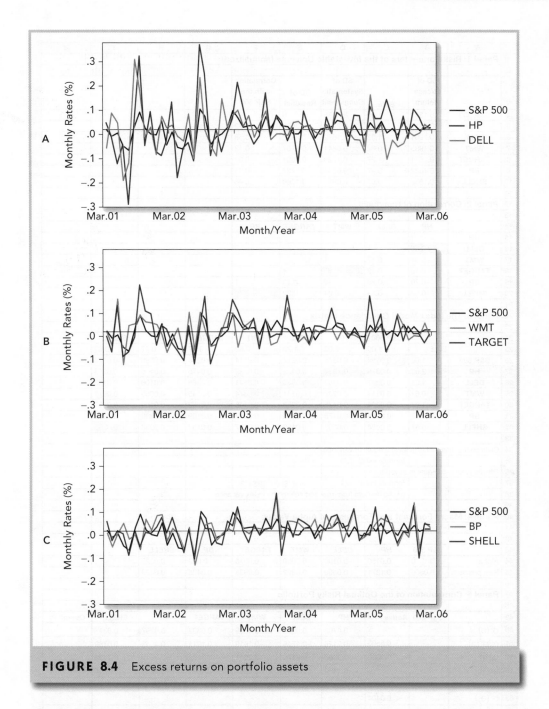

FIGURE 8.4 Excess returns on portfolio assets

firm-specific risk. Portfolios concentrated in these (or other) securities would have unnecessarily high volatility and inferior Sharpe ratios.

Panel 2 shows the correlation matrix of the residuals from the regressions of excess returns on the S&P 500. The shaded cells show correlations of same-sector stocks, which are as high as .7 for the two oil stocks (BP and Shell). This is in contrast to the assumption of the index model that all residuals are uncorrelated. Of course, these correlations are, to a great extent, high by design, because we selected pairs of firms from the same industry. Cross-industry correlations are typically far smaller, and the empirical estimates

	A	B	C	D	E	F	G	H	I	J
1	Panel 1: Risk Parameters of the Investable Universe (annualized)									
2										
3		SD of Excess Return	Beta	SD of Systematic Component	SD of Residual	Correlation with the S&P 500				
4	S&P 500	0.1358	1.00	0.1358	0	1				
5	HP	0.3817	2.03	0.2762	0.2656	0.72				
6	DELL	0.2901	1.23	0.1672	0.2392	0.58				
7	WMT	0.1935	0.62	0.0841	0.1757	0.43				
8	TARGET	0.2611	1.27	0.1720	0.1981	0.66				
9	BP	0.1822	0.47	0.0634	0.1722	0.35				
10	SHELL	0.1988	0.67	0.0914	0.1780	0.46				
11										
12	Panel 2: Correlation of Residuals									
13										
14		HP	DELL	WMT	TARGET	BP				
15	HP	1								
16	DELL	0.08	1							
17	WMT	−0.34	0.17	1						
18	TARGET	−0.10	0.12	0.50	1					
19	BP	−0.20	−0.28	−0.19	−0.13	1				
20	SHELL	−0.06	−0.19	−0.24	−0.22	0.70				
21										
22	Panel 3: The Index Model Covariance Matrix									
23										
24			S&P 500	HP	DELL	WMT	TARGET	BP	SHELL	
25		Beta	1.00	2.03	1.23	0.62	1.27	0.47	0.67	
26	S&P 500	1.00	0.0184	0.0375	0.0227	0.0114	0.0234	0.0086	0.0124	
27	HP	2.03	0.0375	0.1457	0.0462	0.0232	0.0475	0.0175	0.0253	
28	DELL	1.23	0.0227	0.0462	0.0842	0.0141	0.0288	0.0106	0.0153	
29	WMT	0.62	0.0114	0.0232	0.0141	0.0374	0.0145	0.0053	0.0077	
30	TARGET	1.27	0.0234	0.0475	0.0288	0.0145	0.0682	0.0109	0.0157	
31	BP	0.47	0.0086	0.0175	0.0106	0.0053	0.0109	0.0332	0.0058	
32	SHELL	0.67	0.0124	0.0253	0.0153	0.0077	0.0157	0.0058	0.0395	
33										
34	Cells on the diagonal (shadowed) equal to variance									
35			formula in cell C26	= B4^2						
36	Off-diagonal cells equal to covariance									
37			formula in cell C27	= C$25*$B27*$B$4^2						
38			multiplies beta from row and column by index variance							
39										
40	Panel 4: Macro Forecast and Forecasts of Alpha Values									
41										
42										
43		S&P 500	HP	DELL	WMT	TARGET	BP	SHELL		
44	Alpha	0	0.0150	−0.0100	−0.0050	0.0075	0.012	0.0025		
45	Risk premium	0.0600	0.1371	0.0639	0.0322	0.0835	0.0400	0.0429		
46										
47	Panel 5: Computation of the Optimal Risky Portfolio									
48										
49		S&P 500	Active Pf A	HP	DELL	WMT	TARGET	BP	SHELL	Overall Pf
50	$\sigma^2(e)$			0.0705	0.0572	0.0309	0.0392	0.0297	0.0317	
51	$\alpha/\sigma^2(e)$		0.5505	0.2126	−0.1748	−0.1619	0.1911	0.4045	0.0789	
52	$w^0(i)$		1.0000	0.3863	−0.3176	−0.2941	0.3472	0.7349	0.1433	
53	$[w^0(i)]^2$			0.1492	0.1009	0.0865	0.1205	0.5400	0.0205	
54	α_A		0.0222							
55	$\sigma^2(e_A)$		0.0404							
56	w_A^0		0.1691							
57	w^*(Risky portf)	0.8282	0.1718							
58	Beta	1	1.0922	2.0348	1.2315	0.6199	1.2672	0.4670	0.6736	1.0158
59	Risk premium	0.06	0.0878	0.1371	0.0639	0.0322	0.0835	0.0400	0.0429	0.0648
60	SD	0.1358	0.2497							0.1422
61	Sharpe ratio	0.44	0.35							0.46

SPREADSHEET 8.1

eXcel

Please visit us at
www.mhhe.com/bkm

Implementing the index model

of correlations of residuals for industry indexes (rather than individual stocks in the same industry) would be far more in accord with the model. In fact, a few of the stocks in this sample actually seem to have negatively correlated residuals. Of course, correlation also is subject to statistical sampling error, and this may be a fluke.

Panel 3 produces covariances derived from Equation 8.10 of the single-index model. Variances of the S&P 500 index and the individual covered stocks appear on the diagonal. The variance estimates for the individual stocks equal $\beta_i^2 \sigma_M^2 + \sigma^2(e_i)$. The off-diagonal terms are covariance values and equal $\beta_i \beta_j \sigma_M^2$.

8.4 PORTFOLIO CONSTRUCTION AND THE SINGLE–INDEX MODEL

In this section, we look at the implications of the index model for portfolio construction.[12] We will see that the model offers several advantages, not only in terms of parameter estimation, but also for the analytic simplification and organizational decentralization that it makes possible.

Alpha and Security Analysis

Perhaps the most important advantage of the single-index model is the framework it provides for macroeconomic and security analysis in the preparation of the input list that is so critical to the efficiency of the optimal portfolio. The Markowitz model requires estimates of risk premiums for each security. The estimate of expected return depends on both macroeconomic and individual-firm forecasts. But if many different analysts perform security analysis for a large organization such as a mutual fund company, a likely result is inconsistency in the macroeconomic forecasts that partly underlie expectations of returns across securities. Moreover, the underlying assumptions for market-index risk and return often are not explicit in the analysis of individual securities.

The single-index model creates a framework that separates these two quite different sources of return variation and makes it easier to ensure consistency across analysts. We can lay down a hierarchy of the preparation of the input list using the framework of the single-index model.

1. Macroeconomic analysis is used to estimate the risk premium and risk of the market index.
2. Statistical analysis is used to estimate the beta coefficients of all securities and their residual variances, $\sigma^2(e_i)$.
3. The portfolio manager uses the estimates for the market-index risk premium and the beta coefficient of a security to establish the expected return of that security *absent* any contribution from security analysis. The market-driven expected return is conditional on information common to all securities, not on information gleaned from security analysis of particular firms. This market-driven expected return can be used as a benchmark.
4. Security-specific expected return forecasts (specifically, security alphas) are derived from various security-valuation models (such as those discussed in Part Five). Thus, the alpha value distills the incremental risk premium attributable to private information developed from security analysis.

---

[12] The use of the index model to construct optimal risky portfolios was originally developed in Jack Treynor and Fischer Black, "How to Use Security Analysis to Improve Portfolio Selection," *Journal of Business,* January 1973.

In the context of Equation 8.9, the risk premium on a security not subject to security analysis would be $\beta_i E(R_M)$. In other words, the risk premium would derive solely from the security's tendency to follow the market index. Any expected return beyond this benchmark risk premium (the security alpha) would be due to some nonmarket factor that would be uncovered through security analysis.

The end result of security analysis is the list of alpha values. Statistical methods of estimating beta coefficients are widely known and standardized; hence, we would not expect this portion of the input list to differ greatly across portfolio managers. In contrast, macro and security analysis are far less of an exact science and therefore provide an arena for distinguished performance. Using the index model to disentangle the premiums due to market and nonmarket factors, a portfolio manager can be confident that macro analysts compiling estimates of the market-index risk premium and security analysts compiling alpha values are using consistent estimates for the overall market.

In the context of portfolio construction, alpha is more than just one of the components of expected return. It is the key variable that tells us whether a security is a good or a bad buy. Consider an individual stock for which we have a beta estimate from statistical considerations and an alpha value from security analysis. We easily can find many other securities with identical betas and therefore identical systematic components of their risk premiums. Therefore, what really makes a security attractive or unattractive to a portfolio manager is its alpha value. In fact, we've suggested that a security with a positive alpha is providing a premium over and above the premium it derives from its tendency to track the market index. This security is a bargain and therefore should be overweighted in the overall portfolio compared to the passive alternative of using the market-index portfolio as the risky vehicle. Conversely, a negative-alpha security is overpriced and, other things equal, its portfolio weight should be reduced. In more extreme cases, the desired portfolio weight might even be negative, that is, a short position (if permitted) would be desirable.

The Index Portfolio as an Investment Asset

The process of charting the efficient frontier using the single-index model can be pursued much like the procedure we used in Chapter 7, where we used the Markowitz model to find the optimal risky portfolio. Here, however, we can benefit from the simplification the index model offers for deriving the input list. Moreover, portfolio optimization highlights another advantage of the single-index model, namely, a simple and intuitively revealing representation of the optimal risky portfolio. Before we get into the mechanics of optimization in this setting, however, we start by considering the role of the index portfolio in the optimal portfolio.

Suppose the prospectus of an investment company limits the universe of investable assets to only stocks included in the S&P 500 portfolio. In this case, the S&P 500 index captures the impact of the economy on the large stocks the firm may include in its portfolio. Suppose that the resources of the company allow coverage of only a relatively small subset of this so-called *investable universe*. If these analyzed firms are the only ones allowed in the portfolio, the portfolio manager may well be worried about limited diversification.

A simple way to avoid inadequate diversification is to include the S&P 500 portfolio as one of the assets of the portfolio. Examination of Equations 8.8 and 8.9 reveals that if we treat the S&P 500 portfolio as the market index, it will have a beta of 1.0 (its sensitivity to itself), no firm-specific risk, and an alpha of zero—there is no nonmarket component in its expected return. Equation 8.10 shows that the covariance of any security, i, with the index is $\beta_i \sigma_M^2$. To distinguish the S&P 500 from the n securities covered by the firm, we will designate it the $(n + 1)$th asset. We can think of the S&P 500 as a *passive portfolio* that the manager would select in the absence of security analysis. It gives broad market exposure without the need for expensive security analysis. However, if the manager is willing to engage in such research, she may devise an *active portfolio* that can be mixed with the index to provide an even better risk–return trade-off.

The Single-Index-Model Input List

If the portfolio manager plans to compile a portfolio from a list of *n* actively researched firms and a passive market index portfolio, the input list will include the following estimates:

1. Risk premium on the S&P 500 portfolio.
2. Estimate of the standard deviation of the S&P 500 portfolio.
3. *n* sets of estimates of (a) beta coefficients, (b) stock residual variances, and (c) alpha values. (The alpha values for each security, together with the risk premium of the S&P 500 and the beta of each security, will allow for determination of the expected return on each security.)

The Optimal Risky Portfolio of the Single-Index Model

The single-index model allows us to solve for the optimal risky portfolio directly and to gain insight into the nature of the solution. First we confirm that we easily can set up the optimization process to chart the efficient frontier in this framework along the lines of the Markowitz model.

With the estimates of the beta and alpha coefficients, plus the risk premium of the index portfolio, we can generate the $n + 1$ expected returns using Equation 8.9. With the estimates of the beta coefficients and residual variances, together with the variance of the index portfolio, we can construct the covariance matrix using Equation 8.10. Given a column of risk premiums and the covariance matrix, we can conduct the optimization program described in Chapter 7.

We can take the description of how diversification works in the single-index framework of Section 8.2 a step further. We showed earlier that the alpha, beta, and residual variance of an equally weighted portfolio are the simple averages of those parameters across component securities. Moreover, this result is not limited to equally weighted portfolios. It applies to any portfolio, where we need only replace "simple average" with "weighted average," using the portfolio weights. Specifically,

$$\alpha_P = \sum_{i=1}^{n+1} w_i \alpha_i \qquad \text{for the index } \alpha_{n+1} = \alpha_M = 0$$

$$\beta_P = \sum_{i=1}^{n+1} w_i \beta_i \qquad \text{for the index } \beta_{n+1} = \beta_M = 1 \qquad \textbf{(8.18)}$$

$$\sigma^2(e_P) = \sum_{i=1}^{n+1} w_i^2 \sigma^2(e_i) \quad \text{for the index } \sigma^2(e_{n+1}) = \sigma^2(e_M) = 0$$

The objective is to maximize the Sharpe ratio of the portfolio by using portfolio weights, $w_1, \ldots, w_{n+1}$. With this set of weights, the expected return, standard deviation, and Sharpe ratio of the portfolio are

$$E(R_P) = \alpha_P + E(R_M)\beta_P = \sum_{i=1}^{n+1} w_i \alpha_i + E(R_M) \sum_{i=1}^{n+1} w_i \beta_i$$

$$\sigma_P = [\beta_P^2 \sigma_M^2 + \sigma^2(e_P)]^{1/2} = \left[\sigma_M^2 \left(\sum_{i=1}^{n+1} w_i \beta_i \right)^2 + \sum_{i=1}^{n+1} w_i^2 \sigma^2(e_i) \right]^{1/2} \qquad \textbf{(8.19)}$$

$$S_P = \frac{E(R_P)}{\sigma_P}$$

At this point, as in the standard Markowitz procedure, we could use Excel's optimization program to maximize the Sharpe ratio subject to the adding-up constraint that the portfolio weights sum to 1. However, this is not necessary because the optimal portfolio can be derived explicitly using the index model. Moreover, the solution for the optimal portfolio provides considerable insight into the efficient use of security analysis in portfolio construction. It is instructive to outline the logical thread of the solution. We will not show every algebraic step, but will instead present the major results and interpretation of the procedure.

Before delving into the results, let us first explain the basic trade-off the model reveals. If we were interested only in diversification, we would just hold the market index. Security analysis gives us the chance to uncover securities with a nonzero alpha and to take a differential position in those securities. The cost of that differential position is a departure from efficient diversification, in other words, the assumption of unnecessary firm-specific risk. The model shows us that the optimal risky portfolio trades off the search for alpha against the departure from efficient diversification.

The optimal risky portfolio turns out to be a combination of two component portfolios: (1) an *active portfolio,* denoted by *A,* comprised of the *n* analyzed securities (we call this the *active* portfolio because it follows from active security analysis), and (2) the market-index portfolio, the $(n + 1)$th asset we include to aid in diversification, which we call the *passive portfolio* and denote by *M.*

Assume first that the active portfolio has a beta of 1. In that case, the optimal weight in the active portfolio would be proportional to the ratio $\alpha_A/\sigma^2(e_A)$. This ratio balances the contribution of the active portfolio (its alpha) against its contribution to the portfolio variance (residual variance). The analogous ratio for the index portfolio is $E(R_M) / \sigma_M^2$, and hence the initial position in the active portfolio (i.e., if its beta were 1) is

$$w_A^0 = \frac{\dfrac{\alpha_A}{\sigma_A^2}}{\dfrac{E(R_M)}{\sigma_M^2}} \tag{8.20}$$

Next, we amend this position to account for the actual beta of the active portfolio. For any level of σ_A^2, the correlation between the active and passive portfolios is greater when the beta of the active portfolio is higher. This implies less diversification benefit from the passive portfolio and a lower position in it. Correspondingly, the position in the active portfolio increases. The precise modification for the position in the active portfolio is:[13]

$$w_A^* = \frac{w_A^0}{1 + (1 - \beta_A)w_A^0} \tag{8.21}$$

Notice that when $\beta_A = 1$, $w_A^* = w_A^0$.

The Information Ratio

Equations 8.20 and 8.21 yield the optimal position in the active portfolio once we know its alpha, beta, and residual variance. With w_A^* in the active portfolio and $1 - w_A^*$ invested in the index portfolio, we can compute the expected return, standard deviation, and Sharpe ratio of the optimal risky portfolio. The Sharpe ratio of an optimally constructed risky

[13]With a little algebraic manipulation, beta can be shown to equal the product of correlation between the index and the active portfolio and the ratio of SD(index)/SD(active portfolio). If $\beta_A > 1$, then correlation is higher than envisioned in Equation 8.20, so the diversification value of the index is lower. This requires the modification in Equation 8.21.

portfolio will exceed that of the index portfolio (the passive strategy). The exact relationship is

$$S_P^2 = S_M^2 + \left[\frac{\alpha_A}{\sigma(e_A)} \right]^2 \qquad (8.22)$$

Equation 8.22 shows us that the contribution of the active portfolio (when held in its optimal weight, w_A^*) to the Sharpe ratio of the overall risky portfolio is determined by the ratio of its alpha to its residual standard deviation. This important ratio is called the **information ratio.** This ratio measures the extra return we can obtain from security analysis compared to the firm-specific risk we incur when we over- or underweight securities relative to the passive market index. Equation 8.22 therefore implies that to maximize the overall Sharpe ratio, we must maximize the information ratio of the active portfolio.

It turns out that the information ratio of the active portfolio will be maximized if we invest in each security in proportion to its ratio of $\alpha_i/\sigma^2(e_i)$. Scaling this ratio so that the total position in the active portfolio adds up to w_A^*, the weight in each security is

$$w_i^* = w_A^* \frac{\dfrac{\alpha_i}{\sigma^2(e_i)}}{\displaystyle\sum_{i=1}^{n} \dfrac{\alpha_i}{\sigma^2(e_i)}} \qquad (8.23)$$

With this set of weights, we find that the contribution of each security to the information ratio of the active portfolio depends on its *own* information ratio, that is,

$$\left[\frac{\alpha_A}{\sigma(e_A)} \right]^2 = \sum_{i=1}^{n} \left[\frac{\alpha_i}{\sigma(e_i)} \right]^2 \qquad (8.24)$$

The model thus reveals the central role of the information ratio in efficiently taking advantage of security analysis. The positive contribution of a security to the portfolio is made by its addition to the nonmarket risk premium (its alpha). Its negative impact is to increase the portfolio variance through its firm-specific risk (residual variance).

In contrast to alpha, notice that the market (systematic) component of the risk premium, $\beta_i E(R_M)$, is offset by the security's nondiversifiable (market) risk, $\beta_i^2 \sigma_M^2$, and both are driven by the same beta. This trade-off is not unique to any security, as any security with the same beta makes the same balanced contribution to both risk and return. Put differently, the beta of a security is neither vice nor virtue. It is a property that simultaneously affects the risk *and* risk premium of a security. Hence we are concerned only with the aggregate beta of the active portfolio, rather than the beta of each individual security.

We see from Equation 8.23 that if a security's alpha is negative, the security will assume a short position in the optimal risky portfolio. If short positions are prohibited, a negative-alpha security would simply be taken out of the optimization program and assigned a portfolio weight of zero. As the number of securities with nonzero alpha values (or the number with positive alphas if short positions are prohibited) increases, the active portfolio will itself be better diversified and its weight in the overall risky portfolio will increase at the expense of the passive index portfolio.

Finally, we note that the index portfolio is an efficient portfolio only if all alpha values are zero. This makes intuitive sense. Unless security analysis reveals that a security has a nonzero alpha, including it in the active portfolio would make the portfolio less attractive. In addition to the security's systematic risk, which is compensated for by the market risk premium (through beta), the security would add its firm-specific risk to portfolio variance.

With a zero alpha, however, the latter is not compensated by an addition to the nonmarket risk premium. Hence, if all securities have zero alphas, the optimal weight in the active portfolio will be zero, and the weight in the index portfolio will be 1. However, when security analysis uncovers securities with nonmarket risk premiums (nonzero alphas), the index portfolio is no longer efficient.

Summary of Optimization Procedure

To summarize, once security analysis is complete, and the index-model estimates of security and market index parameters are established, the optimal risky portfolio can be formed using these steps:

1. Compute the initial position of each security in the active portfolio as $w_i^0 = \alpha_i / \sigma^2(e_i)$.

2. Scale those initial positions to force portfolio weights to sum to 1 by dividing by their sum, that is, $w_i = \dfrac{w_i^0}{\sum\limits_{i=1}^{n} w_i^0}$.

3. Compute the alpha of the active portfolio: $\alpha_A = \sum_{i=1}^{n} w_i \alpha_i$.

4. Compute the residual variance of the active portfolio: $\sigma^2(e_A) = \sum_{i=1}^{n} w_i^2 \sigma^2(e_i)$.

5. Compute the initial position in the active portfolio: $w_A^0 = \left[\dfrac{\alpha_A / \sigma^2(e_A)}{E(R_M) / \sigma_M^2} \right]$.

6. Compute the beta of the active portfolio: $\beta_A = \sum_{i=1}^{n} w_i \beta_i$.

7. Adjust the initial position in the active portfolio: $w_A^* = \dfrac{w_A^0}{1 + (1 - \beta_A)w_A^0}$.

8. Note: the optimal risky portfolio now has weights: $w_M^* = 1 - w_A^*$; $w_i^* = w_A^* w_i$.

9. Calculate the risk premium of the optimal risky portfolio from the risk premium of the index portfolio and the alpha of the active portfolio: $E(R_P) = (w_M^* + w_A^* \beta_A)E(R_M) + w_A^* \alpha_A$. Notice that the beta of the risky portfolio is $w_M^* + w_A^* \beta_A$ because the beta of the index portfolio is 1.

10. Compute the variance of the optimal risky portfolio from the variance of the index portfolio and the residual variance of the active portfolio: $\sigma_P^2 = (w_M^* + w_A^* \beta_A)^2 \sigma_M^2 + [w_A^* \sigma(e_A)]^2$.

An Example

We can illustrate the implementation of the index model by constructing an optimal portfolio from the S&P 500 index and the six stocks for which we analyzed risk parameters in Section 8.3.

This example entails only six analyzed stocks, but by virtue of selecting three *pairs* of firms from the same industry, it is designed to produce relatively high residual correlations. This should put the index model to a severe test, as the model ignores the correlation between residuals when producing estimates for the covariance matrix. Therefore, comparison of results from the index model with the full-blown covariance (Markowitz) model should be instructive.

Risk Premium Forecasts   Panel 4 of Spreadsheet 8.1 contains estimates of alpha and the risk premium for each stock. These alphas ordinarily would be the most important production of the investment company in a real-life procedure. Statistics plays a small role here; in this arena, macro/security analysis is king. In this example, we simply use illustrative values to demonstrate the portfolio construction process and possible results. You may wonder why we have chosen such small, forecast alpha values. The reason is that even when security analysis uncovers a large apparent mispricing, that is, large alpha values, these forecasts must be substantially trimmed to account for the fact that such forecasts are subject to large estimation error. We discuss the important procedure of adjusting actual forecasts in Chapter 27.

The Optimal Risky Portfolio   Panel 5 of Spreadsheet 8.1 displays calculations for the optimal risky portfolio. They follow the summary procedure of Section 8.4 (you should try to replicate these calculations in your own spreadsheet). In this example we allow short sales. Notice that the weight of each security in the active portfolio (see row 52) has the same sign as the alpha value. Allowing short sales, the positions in the active portfolio are quite large (e.g., the position in BP is .7349); this is an aggressive portfolio. As a result, the alpha of the active portfolio (2.22%) is larger than that of any of the individual alpha forecasts. However, this aggressive stance also results in a large residual variance (.0404, which corresponds to a residual standard deviation of 20%). Therefore, the position in the active portfolio is scaled down (see Equation 8.20) and ends up quite modest (.1718; cell C57), reinforcing the notion that diversification considerations are paramount in the optimal risky portfolio.

The optimal risky portfolio has a risk premium of 6.48%, standard deviation of 14.22%, and a Sharpe ratio of .46 (cells J58–J61). By comparison, the Sharpe ratio of the index portfolio is .06/.1358 = .44 (cell B61), which is quite close to that of the optimal risky portfolio. The small improvement is a result of the modest alpha forecasts that we used. In Chapter 11 on market efficiency and Chapter 24 on performance evaluation we demonstrate that such results are common in the mutual fund industry. Of course, some portfolio managers can and do produce portfolios with better performance.

The interesting question here is the extent to which the index model produces results that are inferior to that of the full-covariance (Markowitz) model. Figure 8.5 shows the efficient frontiers from the two models with the example data. We find that the difference is infact negligible. Table 8.2 compares the compositions and expected performance of the global minimum variance (G) and the optimal risky portfolios derived from the two models. The significant difference between the two portfolios is limited to the minimum-variance portfolios that are driven only by considerations of variance. As we move up the efficient frontier, the required expected returns obviate the impact of the differences in covariance and the portfolios become similar in performance.

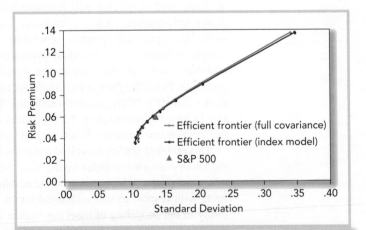

FIGURE 8.5   Efficient frontiers with the index model and full-covariance matrix

TABLE 8.2

Comparison of portfolios from the single-index and full-covariance models

	Global Minimum Variance Portfolio		Optimal Portfolio	
	Full-Covariance Model	**Index Model**	**Full-Covariance Model**	**Index Model**
Mean	.0371	.0354	.0677	.0649
SD	.1089	.1052	.1471	.1423
Sharpe ratio	.3409	.3370	.4605	.4558
Portfolio Weights				
S&P 500	.88	.83	.75	.83
HP	−.11	−.17	.10	.07
DELL	−.01	−.05	−.04	−.06
WMT	.23	.14	−.03	−.05
TARGET	−.18	−.08	.10	.06
BP	.22	.20	.25	.13
SHELL	−.02	.12	−.12	.03

8.5   PRACTICAL ASPECTS OF PORTFOLIO MANAGEMENT WITH THE INDEX MODEL

The tone of our discussions in this chapter indicates that the index model is the preferred one for practical portfolio management. Switching from the Markowitz to an index model is an important decision and hence the first question is whether the index model is really inferior to the Markowitz full-covariance model.

Is the Index Model Inferior to the Full-Covariance Model?

This question is partly related to a more general question of the value of parsimonious models. As an analogy, consider the question of adding additional explanatory variables in a regression equation. We know that adding explanatory variables will in most cases increase R-square, and in no case will R-square fall. But this does not necessarily imply a better regression equation.[14] A better criterion is contribution to the predictive power of the regression. The appropriate question is whether inclusion of a variable that contributes to in-sample explanatory power is likely to contribute to out-of-sample forecast precision. Adding variables, even ones that may appear significant, sometimes can be hazardous to forecast precision. Put differently, a parsimonious model that is stingy about inclusion of independent variables is often superior. Predicting the value of the dependent variable depends on two factors, the precision of the coefficient estimates and the precision of the forecasts of the independent variables. When we add variables, we introduce errors on both counts.

This problem applies as well to replacing the single-index with the full-blown Markowitz model, or even a multi-index model of security returns. To add another index, we need both a forecast of the risk premium of the additional index portfolio and estimates of security betas with respect to that additional factor. The Markowitz model allows far more flexibility in our modeling of asset covariance structure compared to the single-index model. But that advantage may be illusory if we can't estimate those covariances with any degree

---

[14]In fact, the adjusted R-square may fall if the additional variable does not contribute enough explanatory power to compensate for the extra degree of freedom it uses.

of confidence. Using the full-covariance matrix invokes estimation risk of thousands of terms. Even if the full Markowitz model would be better *in principle*, it is very possible that cumulative effect of so many estimation errors will result in a portfolio that is actually inferior to that derived from the single-index model.

Against the potential superiority of the full-covariance model, we have the clear practical advantage of the single-index framework. Its aid in decentralizing macro and security analysis is another decisive advantage.

The Industry Version of the Index Model

Not surprisingly, the index model has attracted the attention of practitioners. To the extent that it is approximately valid, it provides a convenient benchmark for security analysis.

A portfolio manager who has no special information about a security nor insight that is unavailable to the general public will take the security's alpha value as zero, and, according to Equation 8.9, will forecast a risk premium for the security equal to $\beta_i R_M$. If we restate this forecast in terms of total returns, one would expect

$$E(r_{\text{HP}}) = r_f + \beta_{\text{HP}}[E(r_M) - r_f] \tag{8.25}$$

A portfolio manager who has a forecast for the market index, $E(r_M)$, and observes the risk-free T-bill rate, r_f, can use the model to determine the benchmark expected return for any stock. The beta coefficient, the market risk, σ_M^2, and the firm-specific risk, $\sigma^2(e)$, can be estimated from historical SCLs, that is, from regressions of security excess returns on market index excess returns.

There are many sources for such regression results. One widely used source is Research Computer Services Department of Merrill Lynch, which publishes a monthly *Security Risk Evaluation* book, commonly called the "beta book." The Web sites for this chapter at the Online Learning Center (**www.mhhe.com/bkm**) also provide security betas.

Security Risk Evaluation uses the S&P 500 as the proxy for the market portfolio. It relies on the 60 most recent monthly observations to calculate regression parameters. Merrill Lynch and most services[15] use total returns, rather than excess returns (deviations from T-bill rates), in the regressions. In this way they estimate a variant of our index model, which is

$$r = a + br_M + e^* \tag{8.26}$$

instead of

$$r - r_f = \alpha + \beta(r_M - r_f) + e \tag{8.27}$$

To see the effect of this departure, we can rewrite Equation 8.27 as

$$r = r_f + \alpha + \beta r_M - \beta r_f + e = \alpha + r_f(1 - \beta) + \beta r_M + e \tag{8.28}$$

Comparing Equations 8.26 and 8.28, you can see that if r_f is constant over the sample period, both equations have the same independent variable, r_M, and residual, e. Therefore, the slope coefficient will be the same in the two regressions.[16]

However, the intercept that Merrill Lynch calls alpha is really an estimate of $\alpha + r_f(1 - \beta)$. The apparent justification for this procedure is that, on a monthly basis, $r_f(1 - \beta)$ is small and is apt to be swamped by the volatility of actual stock returns. But it is worth noting that for $\beta \neq 1$, the regression intercept in Equation 8.26 will not equal the index model alpha as it does when excess returns are used as in Equation 8.27.

---

[15] Value Line is another common source of security betas. Value Line uses weekly rather than monthly data and uses the New York Stock Exchange index instead of the S&P 500 as the market proxy.

[16] Actually, r_f does vary over time and so should not be grouped casually with the constant term in the regression. However, variations in r_f are tiny compared with the swings in the market return. The actual volatility in the T-bill rate has only a small impact on the estimated value of β.

Another way the Merrill Lynch procedure departs from the index model is in its use of percentage changes in price instead of total rates of return. This means that the index model variant of Merrill Lynch ignores the dividend component of stock returns.

Table 8.3 illustrates a page from the beta book which includes estimates for Hewlett-Packard. The third column, Close Price, shows the stock price at the end of the sample period. The next two columns show the beta and alpha coefficients. Remember that Merrill Lynch's alpha is actually an estimate of $\alpha + r_f(1 - \beta)$.

Much of the output that Merrill Lynch reports is similar to the Excel output (Table 8.1) that we discussed when estimating the index model for Hewlett-Packard. The R-square statistic is the ratio of systematic variance to total variance, the fraction of total volatility attributable to market movements. Merrill Lynch actually reports adjusted R-squares (see footnote 6), which accounts for the instances of negative values. For most firms, R-square is substantially below .5, indicating that stocks have far more firm-specific than systematic risk. This highlights the practical importance of diversification.

The *Resid Std Dev-n* column is the standard deviation of the monthly regression residuals, also sometimes called the standard error of the regression. Like Excel, Merrill Lynch also reports the standard errors of the alpha and beta estimates so we can evaluate the precision of the estimates. Notice that the estimates of beta are far more precise than those of alpha.

The next-to-last column is called Adjusted Beta. The motivation for adjusting beta estimates is that, on average, the beta coefficients of stocks seem to move toward 1 over time. One explanation for this phenomenon is intuitive. A business enterprise usually is established to produce a specific product or service, and a new firm may be more unconventional than an older one in many ways, from technology to management style. As it grows, however, a firm often diversifies, first expanding to similar products and later to more diverse operations. As the firm becomes more conventional, it starts to resemble the rest of the economy even more. Thus its beta coefficient will tend to change in the direction of 1.

Another explanation for this phenomenon is statistical. We know that the average beta over all securities is 1. Thus, before estimating the beta of a security, our best forecast of the beta would be that it is 1. When we estimate this beta coefficient over a particular sample period, we sustain some unknown sampling error of the estimated beta. The greater the difference between our beta estimate and 1, the greater is the chance that we incurred a large estimation error and that beta in a subsequent sample period will be closer to 1.

The sample estimate of the beta coefficient is the best guess for that sample period. Given that beta has a tendency to evolve toward 1, however, a forecast of the future beta coefficient should adjust the sample estimate in that direction.

Merrill Lynch adjusts beta estimates in a simple way.[17] It takes the sample estimate of beta and averages it with 1, using weights of two-thirds and one-third:

$$\text{Adjusted beta} = \tfrac{2}{3} \text{ sample beta} + \tfrac{1}{3} (1) \tag{8.29}$$

CONCEPT CHECK 4	What was HP's index-model alpha per month during the period covered by the Merrill Lynch regression if during this period the average monthly rate of return on T-bills was .4%?

Always remember that these alpha estimates are ex post (after the fact) measures. They do not mean that anyone could have forecast these alpha values ex ante (before the fact). In fact, the name of the game in security analysis is to forecast alpha values

[17]A more sophisticated method is described in Oldrich A. Vasicek, "A Note on Using Cross-Sectional Information in Bayesian Estimation of Security Betas," *Journal of Finance* 28 (1973), pp. 1233–39.

Ticker Symbol	Security Nam		2004/12 Close Price	Beta	Alpha	R-Sqr	Resid Std Dev-n	Std Error		Adjusted Beta	Number of Observ
								Beta	Alpha		
HTBK	HERITAGE COMM CORP		19.020	0.23	0.72	0.01	6.86	0.19	0.89	0.49	60
HPC	HERCULES INC		14.850	0.78	−0.09	0.07	12.13	0.34	1.57	0.85	60
HFWA	HERITAGE FINL CORP WASH		22.120	0.09	1.69	−0.01	4.27	0.12	0.55	0.40	60
HRLY	HERLEY INDS INC		20.340	−0.04	1.66	−0.02	10.37	0.29	1.34	0.31	60
HT	HERSHA HOSPITALITY TR	PRIORITY A SHS	11.450	0.46	1.67	0.12	5.62	0.16	0.73	0.64	60
HSY	HERSHEY FOODS CORP		55.540	−0.21	1.66	0.00	7.72	0.21	1.00	0.20	60
HSKA	HESKA CORP		1.169	1.87	3.88	0.06	31.26	0.86	4.04	1.58	60
HPQ	HEWLETT PACKARD CO		20.970	1.76	−0.45	0.40	10.05	0.28	1.30	1.50	60
HXL	HEXCEL CORP NEW		14.500	0.85	4.08	0.02	21.63	0.60	2.80	0.90	60
HIFN	HI/FN INC		9.220	2.33	0.88	0.21	20.55	0.57	2.66	1.88	60
HIBB	HIBBETT SPORTING GOODS		26.610	1.03	4.05	0.11	13.03	0.36	1.68	1.02	60
HIB	HIBERNIA CORP	CLASS A	29.510	0.59	2.08	0.14	6.53	0.18	0.84	0.73	60
HICK A	HICKOK INC	CLASS A	7.500	0.29	2.35	−0.01	19.21	0.53	2.48	0.53	60
HTCO	HICKORY TECH CORP		10.690	0.13	−0.02	−0.01	10.74	0.30	1.39	0.42	60
HSVL Y	HIGHVELD STL & VANADIUM ADR		8.200	0.34	2.64	0.00	14.42	0.40	1.86	0.56	60
HIW	HIGHWOODS PROPERTIES IN		27.700	0.10	0.45	−0.01	5.70	0.16	0.74	0.40	60

TABLE 8.3

Merrill Lynch, Pierce, Fenner & Smith, Inc.: Market sensitivity statistics*

*Based on S&P 500 index using straight regression.

EXAMPLE 8.1   Adjusted Beta

For the 60 months used in Table 8.3, HP's beta was estimated at 1.76. Therefore, its adjusted beta is $\frac{2}{3} \times 1.76 + \frac{1}{3} = 1.51$, taking it a third of the way toward 1.

In the absence of special information concerning HP, if our forecast for the market index is 11% and T-bills pay 5%, we learn from the Merrill Lynch beta book that the forecast for the rate of return on HP stock is

$$E(r_{\text{HP}}) = r_f + \text{adjusted beta} \times [E(r_M) - r_f]$$
$$= 5 + 1.51(11 - 5) = 14.06\%$$

The sample period regression alpha is $-.45\%$. Because HP's beta is greater than 1, we know that this means that the index-model alpha estimate is somewhat larger. As in Equation 8.28, we have to subtract $(1 - \beta)r_f$ from the regression alpha to obtain the index model alpha. In any event, the standard error of the alpha estimate is 1.30%. The estimate of alpha is far less than twice its standard error. Consequently, we cannot reject the hypothesis that the true alpha is zero.

ahead of time. A well-constructed portfolio that includes long positions in future positive-alpha stocks and short positions in future negative-alpha stocks will outperform the market index. The key term here is "well constructed," meaning that the portfolio has to balance concentration on high-alpha stocks with the need for risk-reducing diversification as discussed earlier in the chapter.

Note that HP's RESID STD DEV-N is 10.05% per month and its R^2 is .40. This tells us that $\sigma_{\text{HP}}^2(e) = 10.05^2 = 101.0$ and, because $R^2 = 1 - \sigma^2(e)/\sigma^2$, we can solve for the estimate of HP's total standard deviation by rearranging as follows:

$$\sigma_{\text{HP}} = \left[\frac{\sigma_{\text{HP}}^2(e)}{1 - R^2}\right]^{1/2} = \left(\frac{101}{.60}\right)^{1/2} = 12.97\% \text{ per month}$$

This is HP's monthly standard deviation for the sample period. Therefore, the annualized standard deviation for that period was $12.97\sqrt{12} = 44.93\%$.

Finally, the last column shows the number of observations, which is 60 months, unless the stock is newly listed and fewer observations are available.

Predicting Betas

Merrill Lynch's adjusted betas are a simple way to recognize that betas estimated from past data may not be the best estimates of future betas: Betas seem to drift toward 1 over time. This suggests that we might want a forecasting model for beta.

One simple approach would be to collect data on beta in different periods and then estimate a regression equation:

$$\text{Current beta} = a + b \text{ (Past beta)} \tag{8.30}$$

Given estimates of a and b, we would then forecast future betas using the rule

$$\text{Forecast beta} = a + b \text{ (Current beta)} \tag{8.31}$$

There is no reason, however, to limit ourselves to such simple forecasting rules. Why not also investigate the predictive power of other financial variables in forecasting beta? For example, if we believe that firm size and debt ratios are two determinants of beta, we might specify an expanded version of Equation 8.30 and estimate

$$\text{Current beta} = a + b_1(\text{Past beta}) + b_2(\text{Firm size}) + b_3(\text{Debt ratio})$$

Now we would use estimates of a and b_1 through b_3 to forecast future betas.

Such an approach was followed by Rosenberg and Guy[18] who found the following variables to help predict betas:

1. Variance of earnings.
2. Variance of cash flow.
3. Growth in earnings per share.
4. Market capitalization (firm size).
5. Dividend yield.
6. Debt-to-asset ratio.

Rosenberg and Guy also found that even after controlling for a firm's financial characteristics, industry group helps to predict beta. For example, they found that the beta values of gold mining companies are on average .827 lower than would be predicted based on financial characteristics alone. This should not be surprising; the −.827 "adjustment factor" for the gold industry reflects the fact that gold values are inversely related to market returns.

Table 8.4 presents beta estimates and adjustment factors for a subset of firms in the Rosenberg and Guy study.

CONCEPT CHECK 5

Compare the first five and last four industries in Table 8.4. What characteristic seems to determine whether the adjustment factor is positive or negative?

Index Models and Tracking Portfolios

Suppose a portfolio manager believes she has identified an underpriced portfolio. Her security analysis team estimates the index model equation for this portfolio (using the S&P 500 index) in excess return form and obtains the following estimates:

$$R_P = .04 + 1.4R_{S\&P500} + e_P \tag{8.32}$$

Therefore, P has an alpha value of 4% and a beta of 1.4. The manager is confident in the quality of her security analysis but is wary about the performance of the broad market in the

Industry	Beta	Adjustment Factor
Agriculture	0.99	−.140
Drugs and medicine	1.14	−.099
Telephone	0.75	−.288
Energy utilities	0.60	−.237
Gold	0.36	−.827
Construction	1.27	.062
Air transport	1.80	.348
Trucking	1.31	.098
Consumer durables	1.44	.132

TABLE 8.4

Industry betas and adjustment factors

[18]Barr Rosenberg and J. Guy, "Prediction of Beta from Investment Fundamentals, Parts 1 and 2," *Financial Analysts Journal,* May–June and July–August 1976.

18. Recalculate Problem 17 for a portfolio manager who is not allowed to short sell securities.

    a. What is the cost of the restriction in terms of Sharpe's measure?

    b. What is the utility loss to the investor ($A = 2.8$) given his new complete portfolio?

19. Suppose that based on the analyst's past record, you estimate that the relationship between forecast and actual alpha is:

$$\text{Actual abnormal return} = .3 \times \text{Forecast of alpha}$$

Use the alphas from Problem 17. How much is expected performance affected by recognizing the imprecision of alpha forecasts?

Challenge Problem

20. Suppose that the alpha forecasts in row 44 of Spreadsheet 8.1 are doubled. All the other data remain the same. Recalculate the optimal risky portfolio. Before you do any calculations, however, use the Summary of Optimization Procedure to estimate a back-of-the-envelope calculation of the information ratio and Sharpe ratio of the newly optimized portfolio. Then recalculate the entire spreadsheet example and verify your back-of-the-envelope calculation.

---

1. When the annualized monthly percentage rates of return for a stock market index were regressed against the returns for ABC and XYZ stocks over a 5-year period ending in 2008, using an ordinary least squares regression, the following results were obtained:

Statistic	ABC	XYZ
Alpha	−3.20%	7.3%
Beta	0.60	0.97
R^2	0.35	0.17
Residual standard deviation	13.02%	21.45%

Explain what these regression results tell the analyst about risk–return relationships for each stock over the sample period. Comment on their implications for future risk–return relationships, assuming both stocks were included in a diversified common stock portfolio, especially in view of the following additional data obtained from two brokerage houses, which are based on 2 years of weekly data ending in December 2008.

Brokerage House	Beta of ABC	Beta of XYZ
A	.62	1.45
B	.71	1.25

2. Assume the correlation coefficient between Baker Fund and the S&P 500 Stock Index is .70. What percentage of Baker Fund's total risk is specific (i.e., nonsystematic)?

3. The correlation between the Charlottesville International Fund and the EAFE Market Index is 1.0. The expected return on the EAFE Index is 11%, the expected return on Charlottesville International Fund is 9%, and the risk-free return in EAFE countries is 3%. Based on this analysis, what is the implied beta of Charlottesville International?

4. The concept of *beta* is most closely associated with:

    a. Correlation coefficients.

    b. Mean-variance analysis.

    c. Nonsystematic risk.

    d. Systematic risk.

5. Beta and standard deviation differ as risk measures in that beta measures:

    a. Only unsystematic risk, while standard deviation measures total risk.

    b. Only systematic risk, while standard deviation measures total risk.

c. Both systematic and unsystematic risk, while standard deviation measures only unsystematic risk.

d. Both systematic and unsystematic risk, while standard deviation measures only systematic risk.

Go to **www.mhhe.com/edumarketinsight** and click on the *Company* link. Enter the ticker symbol for the stock of your choice and click on the *Go* button. In the *Excel Analytics* section go to the *Market Data* section and get the *Monthly Adjusted Prices* data for the past 4 years. The page will also show monthly returns for your stock and for the S&P 500. Copy the data into an *Excel* worksheet and then do a regression to generate the characteristic line for the stock. (Use the menus for *Tools, Data Analysis, Regression*, input the X range and the Y range, select *New Worksheet Ply* under *Output Options*, and click on *OK*.) Based on the regression results, what is the beta coefficient for your stock?

Next use *Excel* to plot an X-Y Scatter graph of the stock's returns versus the S&P 500's returns. Once the graph is constructed, select one of the data points and right click on it. Choose the *Add Trendline* option and select the *Linear* type. On the *Options* tab, select *Display Equation on Chart.* How does the equation compare with your regression results?

Go back to the main page for your stock's information and select *S&P Stock Reports* from the menu. Choose *Stock Report* from the submenu and when the stock report opens, find the beta coefficient for the firm. How does this beta compare to your results? What are possible reasons for any differences?

STANDARD
&POOR'S

E-Investments

Beta Estimates

Go to **http://finance.yahoo.com** and click on *Stocks* link under the *Investing* tab. Look for the *Stock Screener* link under *Research Tools*. The *Java Yahoo! Finance Screener* lets you create your own screens. In the *Click to Add Criteria* box, find *Trading and Volume* on the menu and choose *Beta.* In the *Conditions* box, choose < = and in the *Values* box, enter *1.* Hit the *Enter* key and then request the top 200 matches in the *Return Top_Matches* box. Click on the *Run Screen* button.

Select the *View Table* tab and sort the results to show the lowest betas at the top of the list by clicking on the *Beta* column header. Which firms have the lowest betas? In which industries do they operate?

Select the *View Histogram* tab and when the histogram appears, look at the bottom of the screen to see the *Show Histogram for* box. Use the menu that comes up when you click on the down arrow to select *beta.* What pattern(s), if any, do you see in the distributions of betas for firms that have betas less than 1?

SOLUTIONS TO CONCEPT CHECKS

1. *a.* Total market capitalization is $3{,}000 + 1{,}940 + 1{,}360 = 6{,}300$. Therefore, the mean excess return of the index portfolio is

$$\frac{3{,}000}{6{,}300} \times 10 + \frac{1{,}940}{6{,}300} \times 2 + \frac{1{,}360}{6{,}300} \times 17 = 9.05\% = .0905$$

b. The covariance between stocks A and B equals

$$\text{Cov}(R_A, R_B) = \beta_A\beta_B\sigma_M^2 = 1 \times .2 \times .25^2 = .0125$$

c. The covariance between stock B and the index portfolio equals

$$\text{Cov}(R_B, R_M) = \beta_B\sigma_M^2 = .2 \times .25^2 = .0125$$

d. The total variance of B equals

$$\sigma_B^2 = \text{Var}(\beta_B R_M + e_B) = \beta_B^2\sigma_M^2 + \sigma^2(e_B)$$

Systematic risk equals $\beta_B^2\sigma_M^2 = .2^2 \times .25^2 = .0025$.

Thus the firm-specific variance of B equals

$$\sigma^2(e_B) = \sigma_B^2 - \beta_B^2\sigma_M^2 = .30^2 - .2^2 \times .25^2 = .0875$$

2. The variance of each stock is $\beta^2\sigma_M^2 + \sigma^2(e)$.

For stock A, we obtain

$$\sigma_A^2 = .9^2(20)^2 + 30^2 = 1,224$$
$$\sigma_A = 35\%$$

For stock B,

$$\sigma_B^2 = 1.1^2(20)^2 + 10^2 = 584$$
$$\sigma_B = 24\%$$

The covariance is

$$\beta_A\beta_B\sigma_M^2 = .9 \times 1.1 \times 20^2 = 396$$

3. $\sigma^2(e_P) = (\frac{1}{2})^2[\sigma^2(e_A) + \sigma^2(e_B)]$
   $= \frac{1}{4}(.30^2 + .10^2)$
   $= .0250$

Therefore $\sigma(e_P) = .158 = 15.8\%$

4. Merrill Lynch's alpha is related to the index-model alpha by

$$\alpha_{\text{Merrill}} = \alpha_{\text{index model}} + (1 - \beta)r_f$$

For HP, $\alpha_{\text{Merrill}} = -.45\%$, $\beta = 1.76$, and we are told that r_f was .4%. Thus

$$\alpha_{\text{index model}} = -.45\% - (1 - 1.76).4\% = -.146\%.$$

HP's return was somewhat disappointing even after correcting Merrill Lynch's alpha. It under-performed its "benchmark" return by an average of .146% per month.

5. The industries with positive adjustment factors are most sensitive to the economy. Their betas would be expected to be higher because the business risk of the firms is higher. In contrast, the industries with negative adjustment factors are in business fields with a lower sensitivity to the economy. Therefore, for any given financial profile, their betas are lower.

CHAPTER NINE

THE CAPITAL ASSET PRICING MODEL

THE CAPITAL ASSET pricing model, almost always referred to as the CAPM, is a centerpiece of modern financial economics. The model gives us a precise prediction of the relationship that we should observe between the risk of an asset and its expected return. This relationship serves two vital functions. First, it provides a benchmark rate of return for evaluating possible investments. For example, if we are analyzing securities, we might be interested in whether the expected return we forecast for a stock is more or less than its "fair" return given its risk. Second, the model helps us to make an educated guess as to the expected return on assets that have not yet been traded in the marketplace. For example, how do we price an initial public offering of stock? How will a major new investment project affect the return investors require on a company's stock? Although the CAPM does not fully withstand empirical tests, it is widely used because of the insight it offers and because its accuracy is deemed acceptable for important applications.

9.1 THE CAPITAL ASSET PRICING MODEL

The capital asset pricing model is a set of predictions concerning equilibrium expected returns on risky assets. Harry Markowitz laid down the foundation of modern portfolio management in 1952. The CAPM was developed 12 years later in articles by William Sharpe,[1] John Lintner,[2] and Jan Mossin.[3] The time for this gestation indicates that the leap from Markowitz's portfolio selection model to the CAPM is not trivial.

We will approach the CAPM by posing the question "what if," where the "if" part refers to a simplified world. Positing an admittedly unrealistic world allows a relatively easy leap to the "then" part. Once we accomplish this, we can add complexity to the hypothesized

[1]William Sharpe, "Capital Asset Prices: A Theory of Market Equilibrium," *Journal of Finance,* September 1964.

[2]John Lintner, "The Valuation of Risk Assets and the Selection of Risky Investments in Stock Portfolios and Capital Budgets," *Review of Economics and Statistics,* February 1965.

[3]Jan Mossin, "Equilibrium in a Capital Asset Market," *Econometrica,* October 1966.

environment one step at a time and see how the conclusions must be amended. This process allows us to derive a reasonably realistic and comprehensible model.

We summarize the simplifying assumptions that lead to the basic version of the CAPM in the following list. The thrust of these assumptions is that we try to ensure that individuals are as alike as possible, with the notable exceptions of initial wealth and risk aversion. We will see that conformity of investor behavior vastly simplifies our analysis.

1. There are many investors, each with an endowment (wealth) that is small compared to the total endowment of all investors. Investors are price-takers, in that they act as though security prices are unaffected by their own trades. This is the usual perfect competition assumption of microeconomics.

2. All investors plan for one identical holding period. This behavior is myopic (short-sighted) in that it ignores everything that might happen after the end of the single-period horizon. Myopic behavior is, in general, suboptimal.

3. Investments are limited to a universe of publicly traded financial assets, such as stocks and bonds, and to risk-free borrowing or lending arrangements. This assumption rules out investment in nontraded assets such as education (human capital), private enterprises, and governmentally funded assets such as town halls and international airports. It is assumed also that investors may borrow or lend any amount at a fixed, risk-free rate.

4. Investors pay no taxes on returns and no transaction costs (commissions and service charges) on trades in securities. In reality, of course, we know that investors are in different tax brackets and that this may govern the type of assets in which they invest. For example, tax implications may differ depending on whether the income is from interest, dividends, or capital gains. Furthermore, actual trading is costly, and commissions and fees depend on the size of the trade and the good standing of the individual investor.

5. All investors are rational mean-variance optimizers, meaning that they all use the Markowitz portfolio selection model.

6. All investors analyze securities in the same way and share the same economic view of the world. The result is identical estimates of the probability distribution of future cash flows from investing in the available securities; that is, for any set of security prices, they all derive the same input list to feed into the Markowitz model. Given a set of security prices and the risk-free interest rate, all investors use the same expected returns and covariance matrix of security returns to generate the efficient frontier and the unique optimal risky portfolio. This assumption is often referred to as **homogeneous expectations** or beliefs.

These assumptions represent the "if" of our "what if" analysis. Obviously, they ignore many real-world complexities. With these assumptions, however, we can gain some powerful insights into the nature of equilibrium in security markets.

We can summarize the equilibrium that will prevail in this hypothetical world of securities and investors briefly. The rest of the chapter explains and elaborates on these implications.

1. All investors will choose to hold a portfolio of risky assets in proportions that duplicate representation of the assets in the **market portfolio** (*M*), which includes all traded assets. For simplicity, we generally refer to all risky assets as *stocks*. The proportion of each stock in the market portfolio equals the market value of the stock

(price per share multiplied by the number of shares outstanding) divided by the total market value of all stocks.

2. Not only will the market portfolio be on the efficient frontier, but it also will be the tangency portfolio to the optimal capital allocation line (CAL) derived by each and every investor. As a result, the *capital market line* (CML), the line from the risk-free rate through the market portfolio, *M*, is also the best attainable capital allocation line. All investors hold *M* as their optimal risky portfolio, differing only in the amount invested in it versus in the risk-free asset.

3. The risk premium on the market portfolio will be proportional to its risk and the degree of risk aversion of the representative investor. Mathematically,

$$E(r_M) - r_f = \overline{A}\sigma_M^2$$

where σ_M^2 is the variance of the market portfolio and $\overline{A}$ is the average degree of risk aversion across investors. Note that because *M* is the optimal portfolio, which is efficiently diversified across all stocks, σ_M^2 is the systematic risk of this universe.

4. The risk premium on *individual* assets will be proportional to the risk premium on the market portfolio, *M*, and the *beta coefficient* of the security relative to the market portfolio. Beta measures the extent to which returns on the stock and the market move together. Formally, beta is defined as

$$\beta_i = \frac{\text{Cov}(r_i, r_M)}{\sigma_M^2}$$

and the risk premium on individual securities is

$$E(r_i) - r_f = \frac{\text{Cov}(r_i, r_M)}{\sigma_M^2}[E(r_M) - r_f] = \beta_i[E(r_M) - r_f]$$

Why Do All Investors Hold the Market Portfolio?

What is the market portfolio? When we sum over, or aggregate, the portfolios of all individual investors, lending and borrowing will cancel out (because each lender has a corresponding borrower), and the value of the aggregate risky portfolio will equal the entire wealth of the economy. This is the market portfolio, *M*. The proportion of each stock in this portfolio equals the market value of the stock (price per share times number of shares outstanding) divided by the sum of the market values of all stocks.[4] The CAPM implies that as individuals attempt to optimize their personal portfolios, they each arrive at the same portfolio, with weights on each asset equal to those of the market portfolio.

Given the assumptions of the previous section, it is easy to see that all investors will desire to hold identical risky portfolios. If all investors use identical Markowitz analysis (Assumption 5) applied to the same universe of securities (Assumption 3) for the same time horizon (Assumption 2) and use the same input list (Assumption 6), they all must arrive at the same composition of the optimal risky portfolio, the portfolio on the efficient frontier identified by the tangency line from T-bills to that frontier, as in Figure 9.1. This

[4]As noted previously, we use the term "stock" for convenience; the market portfolio properly includes all assets in the economy.

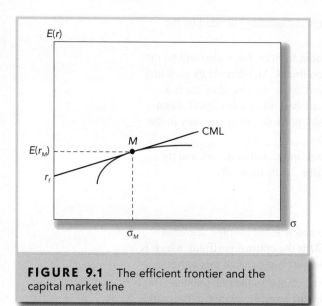

FIGURE 9.1   The efficient frontier and the capital market line

implies that if the weight of GE stock, for example, in each common risky portfolio is 1%, then GE also will comprise 1% of the market portfolio. The same principle applies to the proportion of any stock in each investor's risky portfolio. As a result, the optimal risky portfolio of all investors is simply a share of the market portfolio in Figure 9.1.

Now suppose that the optimal portfolio of our investors does not include the stock of some company, such as Delta Airlines. When all investors avoid Delta stock, the demand is zero, and Delta's price takes a free fall. As Delta stock gets progressively cheaper, it becomes ever more attractive and other stocks look relatively less attractive. Ultimately, Delta reaches a price where it is attractive enough to include in the optimal stock portfolio.

Such a price adjustment process guarantees that all stocks will be included in the optimal portfolio. It shows that *all* assets have to be included in the market portfolio. The only issue is the price at which investors will be willing to include a stock in their optimal risky portfolio.

This may seem a roundabout way to derive a simple result: If all investors hold an identical risky portfolio, this portfolio has to be *M,* the market portfolio. Our intention, however, is to demonstrate a connection between this result and its underpinnings, the equilibrating process that is fundamental to security market operation.

The Passive Strategy Is Efficient

In Chapter 6 we defined the CML (capital market line) as the CAL (capital allocation line) that is constructed from a money market account (or T-bills) and the market portfolio. Perhaps now you can fully appreciate why the CML is an interesting CAL. In the simple world of the CAPM, *M* is the optimal tangency portfolio on the efficient frontier, as shown in Figure 9.1.

In this scenario, the market portfolio held by all investors is based on the common input list, thereby incorporating all relevant information about the universe of securities. This means that investors can skip the trouble of doing security analysis and obtain an efficient portfolio simply by holding the market portfolio. (Of course, if everyone were to follow this strategy, no one would perform security analysis and this result would no longer hold. We discuss this issue in greater depth in Chapter 11 on market efficiency.)

Thus the passive strategy of investing in a market index portfolio is efficient. For this reason, we sometimes call this result a **mutual fund theorem.** The mutual fund theorem is another incarnation of the separation property discussed in Chapter 7. Assuming that all investors choose to hold a market index mutual fund, we can separate portfolio selection into two components—a technical problem, creation of mutual funds by professional managers—and a personal problem that depends on an investor's risk aversion, allocation of the *complete* portfolio between the mutual fund and risk-free assets.

In reality, different investment managers do create risky portfolios that differ from the market index. We attribute this in part to the use of different input lists in the formation of the optimal risky portfolio. Nevertheless, the practical significance of the mutual fund theorem is that a passive investor may view the market index as a reasonable first approximation to an efficient risky portfolio.

THE PARABLE OF THE MONEY MANAGERS

Some years ago, in a land called Indicia, revolution led to the overthrow of a socialist regime and the restoration of a system of private property. Former government enterprises were reformed as corporations, which then issued stocks and bonds. These securities were given to a central agency, which offered them for sale to individuals, pension funds, and the like (all armed with newly printed money).

Almost immediately a group of money managers came forth to assist these investors. Recalling the words of a venerated elder, uttered before the previous revolution ("Invest in Corporate Indicia"), they invited clients to give them money, with which they would buy a cross-section of all the newly issued securities. Investors considered this a reasonable idea, and soon everyone held a piece of Corporate Indicia.

Before long the money managers became bored because there was little for them to do. Soon they fell into the habit of gathering at a beachfront casino where they passed the time playing roulette, craps, and similar games, for low stakes, with their own money.

After a while, the owner of the casino suggested a new idea. He would furnish an impressive set of rooms which would be designated the Money Managers' Club. There the members could place bets with one another about the fortunes of various corporations, industries, the level of the Gross National Product, foreign trade, etc. To make the betting more exciting, the casino owner suggested that the managers use their clients' money for this purpose.

The offer was immediately accepted, and soon the money managers were betting eagerly with one another. At the end of each week, some found that they had won money for their clients, while others found

that they had lost. But the losses always exceeded the gains, for a certain amount was deducted from each bet to cover the costs of the elegant surroundings in which the gambling took place.

Before long a group of professors from Indicia U. suggested that investors were not well served by the activities being conducted at the Money Managers' Club. "Why pay people to gamble with your money? Why not just hold your own piece of Corporate Indicia?" they said.

This argument seemed sensible to some of the investors, and they raised the issue with their money managers. A few capitulated, announcing that they would henceforth stay away from the casino and use their clients' money only to buy proportionate shares of all the stocks and bonds issued by corporations.

The converts, who became known as managers of Indicia funds, were initially shunned by those who continued to frequent the Money Managers' Club, but in time, grudging acceptance replaced outright hostility. The wave of puritan reform some had predicted failed to materialize, and gambling remained legal. Many managers continued to make their daily pilgrimage to the casino. But they exercised more restraint than before, placed smaller bets, and generally behaved in a manner consonant with their responsibilities. Even the members of the Lawyers' Club found it difficult to object to the small amount of gambling that still went on.

And everyone but the casino owner lived happily ever after.

Source: William F. Sharpe, "The Parable of the Money Managers," *The Financial Analysts' Journal* 32 (July/August 1976), p. 4. Copyright 1976, CFA Institute. Reproduced from *The Financial Analysts' Journal* with permission from the CFA Institute. All rights reserved.

The nearby box contains a parable illustrating the argument for indexing. If the passive strategy is efficient, then attempts to beat it simply generate trading and research costs with no offsetting benefit, and ultimately inferior results.

CONCEPT CHECK 1	If there are only a few investors who perform security analysis, and all others hold the market portfolio, *M*, would the CML still be the efficient CAL for investors who do not engage in security analysis? Why or why not?

The Risk Premium of the Market Portfolio

In Chapter 6 we discussed how individual investors go about deciding how much to invest in the risky portfolio. Returning now to the decision of how much to invest in portfolio *M* versus in the risk-free asset, what can we deduce about the equilibrium risk premium of portfolio *M?*

We asserted earlier that the equilibrium risk premium on the market portfolio, $E(r_M) - r_f$, will be proportional to the average degree of risk aversion of the investor population and the risk of the market portfolio, σ_M^2. Now we can explain this result.

Recall that each individual investor chooses a proportion y, allocated to the optimal portfolio M, such that

$$y = \frac{E(r_M) - r_f}{A\sigma_M^2} \tag{9.1}$$

In the simplified CAPM economy, risk-free investments involve borrowing and lending among investors. Any borrowing position must be offset by the lending position of the creditor. This means that net borrowing and lending across all investors must be zero, and in consequence, substituting the representative investor's risk aversion, $\overline{A}$, for A, the average position in the risky portfolio is 100%, or $\overline{y} = 1$. Setting $y = 1$ in Equation 9.1 and rearranging, we find that the risk premium on the market portfolio is related to its variance by the average degree of risk aversion:

$$E(r_M) - r_f = \overline{A}\sigma_M^2 \tag{9.2}$$

CONCEPT CHECK **2**	Data from the last eight decades (see Table 5.3) for the S&P 500 index yield the following statistics: average excess return, 8.4%; standard deviation, 20.3%. a. To the extent that these averages approximated investor expectations for the period, what must have been the average coefficient of risk aversion? b. If the coefficient of risk aversion were actually 3.5, what risk premium would have been consistent with the market's historical standard deviation?

Expected Returns on Individual Securities

The CAPM is built on the insight that the appropriate risk premium on an asset will be determined by its contribution to the risk of investors' overall portfolios. Portfolio risk is what matters to investors and is what governs the risk premiums they demand.

Remember that all investors use the same input list, that is, the same estimates of expected returns, variances, and covariances. We saw in Chapter 7 that these covariances can be arranged in a covariance matrix, so that the entry in the fifth row and third column, for example, would be the covariance between the rates of return on the fifth and third securities. Each diagonal entry of the matrix is the covariance of one security's return with itself, which is simply the variance of that security.

Suppose, for example, that we want to gauge the portfolio risk of GE stock. We measure the contribution to the risk of the overall portfolio from holding GE stock by its covariance with the market portfolio. To see why this is so, let us look again at the way the variance of the market portfolio is calculated. To calculate the variance of the market portfolio, we use the bordered covariance matrix with the market portfolio weights, as discussed in Chapter 7. We highlight GE in this depiction of the n stocks in the market portfolio.

Portfolio Weights	w_1	w_2	. . .	w_{GE}	. . .	w_n
w_1	$Cov(r_1, r_1)$	$Cov(r_1, r_2)$	. . .	$Cov(r_1, r_{GE})$	. . .	$Cov(r_1, r_n)$
w_2	$Cov(r_2, r_1)$	$Cov(r_2, r_2)$	. . .	$Cov(r_2, r_{GE})$	. . .	$Cov(r_2, r_n)$
$\vdots$	$\vdots$	$\vdots$		$\vdots$		$\vdots$
w_{GE}	$Cov(r_{GE}, r_1)$	$Cov(r_{GE}, r_2)$	. . .	$Cov(r_{GE}, r_{GE})$	. . .	$Cov(r_{GE}, r_n)$
$\vdots$	$\vdots$	$\vdots$		$\vdots$		$\vdots$
w_n	$Cov(r_n, r_1)$	$Cov(r_n, r_2)$	. . .	$Cov(r_n, r_{GE})$	. . .	$Cov(r_n, r_n)$

Recall that we calculate the variance of the portfolio by summing over all the elements of the covariance matrix, first multiplying each element by the portfolio weights from the row and the column. The contribution of one stock to portfolio variance therefore can be expressed as the sum of all the covariance terms in the column corresponding to the stock, where each covariance is first multiplied by both the stock's weight from its row and the weight from its column.[5]

For example, the contribution of GE's stock to the variance of the market portfolio is

$$w_{GE}[w_1 Cov(r_1, r_{GE}) + w_2 Cov(r_2, r_{GE}) + \ldots + w_{GE} Cov(r_{GE}, r_{GE}) + \ldots$$
$$+ w_n Cov(r_n, r_{GE})] \quad \textbf{(9.3)}$$

Equation 9.3 provides a clue about the respective roles of variance and covariance in determining asset risk. When there are many stocks in the economy, there will be many more covariance terms than variance terms. Consequently, the covariance of a particular stock with all other stocks will dominate that stock's contribution to total portfolio risk. Notice that the sum inside the square brackets in Equation 9.3 is the covariance of GE with the market portfolio. In other words, we can best measure the stock's contribution to the risk of the market portfolio by its covariance with that portfolio:

$$GE\text{'s contribution to variance} = w_{GE} Cov(r_{GE}, r_M)$$

This should not surprise us. For example, if the covariance between GE and the rest of the market is negative, then GE makes a "negative contribution" to portfolio risk: By providing returns that move inversely with the rest of the market, GE stabilizes the return on the overall portfolio. If the covariance is positive, GE makes a positive contribution to overall portfolio risk because its returns reinforce swings in the rest of the portfolio.

To demonstrate this more rigorously, note that the rate of return on the market portfolio may be written as

$$r_M = \sum_{k=1}^{n} w_k r_k$$

---

[5]An alternative approach would be to measure GE's contribution to market variance as the sum of the elements in the row *and* the column corresponding to GE. In this case, GE's contribution would be twice the sum in Equation 9.3. The approach that we take in the text allocates contributions to portfolio risk among securities in a convenient manner in that the sum of the contributions of each stock equals the total portfolio variance, whereas the alternative measure of contribution would sum to twice the portfolio variance. This results from a type of double-counting, because adding both the rows and the columns for each stock would result in each entry in the matrix being added twice.

Therefore, the covariance of the return on GE with the market portfolio is

$$\text{Cov}(r_{GE}, r_M) = \text{Cov}\left(r_{GE}, \sum_{k=1}^{n} w_k r_k\right) = \sum_{k=1}^{n} w_k \text{Cov}(r_k, r_{GE}) \tag{9.4}$$

Notice that the last term of Equation 9.4 is precisely the same as the term in brackets in Equation 9.3. Therefore, Equation 9.3, which is the contribution of GE to the variance of the market portfolio, may be simplified to $w_{GE} \text{Cov}(r_{GE}, r_M)$. We also observe that the contribution of our holding of GE to the risk premium of the market portfolio is $w_{GE}[E(r_{GE}) - r_f]$.

Therefore, the reward-to-risk ratio for investments in GE can be expressed as

$$\frac{\text{GE's contribution to risk premium}}{\text{GE's contribution to variance}} = \frac{w_{GE}[E(r_{GE}) - r_f]}{w_{GE}\text{Cov}(r_{GE}, r_M)} = \frac{E(r_{GE}) - r_f}{\text{Cov}(r_{GE}, r_M)}$$

The market portfolio is the tangency (efficient mean-variance) portfolio. The reward-to-risk ratio for investment in the market portfolio is

$$\frac{\text{Market risk premium}}{\text{Market variance}} = \frac{E(r_M) - r_f}{\sigma_M^2} \tag{9.5}$$

The ratio in Equation 9.5 is often called the **market price of risk**[6] because it quantifies the extra return that investors demand to bear portfolio risk. Notice that for *components* of the efficient portfolio, such as shares of GE, we measure risk as the *contribution* to portfolio variance (which depends on its *covariance* with the market). In contrast, for the efficient portfolio itself, its variance is the appropriate measure of risk.

A basic principle of equilibrium is that all investments should offer the same reward-to-risk ratio. If the ratio were better for one investment than another, investors would rearrange their portfolios, tilting toward the alternative with the better trade-off and shying away from the other. Such activity would impart pressure on security prices until the ratios were equalized. Therefore we conclude that the reward-to-risk ratios of GE and the market portfolio should be equal:

$$\frac{E(r_{GE}) - r_f}{\text{Cov}(r_{GE}, r_M)} = \frac{E(r_M) - r_f}{\sigma_M^2} \tag{9.6}$$

To determine the fair risk premium of GE stock, we rearrange Equation 9.6 slightly to obtain

$$E(r_{GE}) - r_f = \frac{\text{Cov}(r_{GE}, r_M)}{\sigma_M^2}[E(r_M) - r_f] \tag{9.7}$$

---

[6]We open ourselves to ambiguity in using this term, because the market portfolio's reward-to-volatility ratio

$$\frac{E(r_M) - r_f}{\sigma_M}$$

sometimes is referred to as the market price of risk. Note that because the appropriate risk measure of GE is its covariance with the market portfolio (its contribution to the variance of the market portfolio), this risk is measured in percent squared. Accordingly, the price of this risk, $[E(r_M) - r_f]/\sigma^2$, is defined as the percentage expected return per percent square of variance.

The ratio $\text{Cov}(r_{\text{GE}}, r_M)/\sigma_M^2$ measures the contribution of GE stock to the variance of the market portfolio as a fraction of the total variance of the market portfolio. The ratio is called **beta** and is denoted by β. Using this measure, we can restate Equation 9.7 as

$$E(r_{\text{GE}}) = r_f + \beta_{\text{GE}}[E(r_M) - r_f] \tag{9.8}$$

This **expected return–beta relationship** is the most familiar expression of the CAPM to practitioners. We will have a lot more to say about the expected return–beta relationship shortly.

We see now why the assumptions that made individuals act similarly are so useful. If everyone holds an identical risky portfolio, then everyone will find that the beta of each asset with the market portfolio equals the asset's beta with his or her own risky portfolio. Hence everyone will agree on the appropriate risk premium for each asset.

Does the fact that few real-life investors actually hold the market portfolio imply that the CAPM is of no practical importance? Not necessarily. Recall from Chapter 7 that reasonably well-diversified portfolios shed firm-specific risk and are left with mostly systematic or market risk. Even if one does not hold the precise market portfolio, a well-diversified portfolio will be so very highly correlated with the market that a stock's beta relative to the market will still be a useful risk measure.

In fact, several authors have shown that modified versions of the CAPM will hold true even if we consider differences among individuals leading them to hold different portfolios. For example, Brennan[7] examined the impact of differences in investors' personal tax rates on market equilibrium, and Mayers[8] looked at the impact of nontraded assets such as human capital (earning power). Both found that although the market portfolio is no longer each investor's optimal risky portfolio, the expected return–beta relationship should still hold in a somewhat modified form.

If the expected return–beta relationship holds for any individual asset, it must hold for any combination of assets. Suppose that some portfolio P has weight w_k for stock k, where k takes on values $1, \ldots, n$. Writing out the CAPM Equation 9.8 for each stock, and multiplying each equation by the weight of the stock in the portfolio, we obtain these equations, one for each stock:

$$
\begin{aligned}
w_1 E(r_1) &= w_1 r_f + w_1 \beta_1 [E(r_M) - r_f] \\
+ w_2 E(r_2) &= w_2 r_f + w_2 \beta_2 [E(r_M) - r_f] \\
+ \quad \cdots &= \cdots \\
\underline{+ w_n E(r_n)} &= \underline{w_n r_f + w_n \beta_n [E(r_M) - r_f]} \\
E(r_P) &= r_f + \beta_P [E(r_M) - r_f]
\end{aligned}
$$

Summing each column shows that the CAPM holds for the overall portfolio because $E(r_P) = \sum_k w_k E(r_k)$ is the expected return on the portfolio, and $\beta_P = \sum_k w_k \beta_k$ is the portfolio beta. Incidentally, this result has to be true for the market portfolio itself,

$$E(r_M) = r_f + \beta_M [E(r_M) - r_f]$$

---

[7]Michael J. Brennan, "Taxes, Market Valuation, and Corporate Finance Policy," *National Tax Journal,* December 1973.

[8]David Mayers, "Nonmarketable Assets and Capital Market Equilibrium under Uncertainty," in *Studies in the Theory of Capital Markets,* ed. M. C. Jensen (New York: Praeger, 1972). We will look at this model more closely later in the chapter.

Indeed, this is a tautology because $\beta_M = 1$, as we can verify by noting that

$$\beta_M = \frac{\text{Cov}(r_M, r_M)}{\sigma_M^2} = \frac{\sigma_M^2}{\sigma_M^2}$$

This also establishes 1 as the weighted-average value of beta across all assets. If the market beta is 1, and the market is a portfolio of all assets in the economy, the weighted-average beta of all assets must be 1. Hence betas greater than 1 are considered aggressive in that investment in high-beta stocks entails above-average sensitivity to market swings. Betas below 1 can be described as defensive.

A word of caution: We are all accustomed to hearing that well-managed firms will provide high rates of return. We agree this is true if one measures the *firm's* return on investments in plant and equipment. The CAPM, however, predicts returns on investments in the *securities* of the firm.

Let us say that everyone knows a firm is well run. Its stock price will therefore be bid up, and consequently returns to stockholders who buy at those high prices will not be excessive. Security prices, in other words, already reflect public information about a firm's prospects; therefore only the risk of the company (as measured by beta in the context of the CAPM) should affect expected returns. In an efficient market investors receive high expected returns only if they are willing to bear risk.

Of course, investors do not directly observe or determine expected returns on securities. Rather, they observe security prices and bid those prices up or down. Expected rates of return are determined by the prices investors must pay compared to the cash flows those investments might garner.

CONCEPT CHECK 3	Suppose that the risk premium on the market portfolio is estimated at 8% with a standard deviation of 22%. What is the risk premium on a portfolio invested 25% in GM and 75% in Ford, if they have betas of 1.10 and 1.25, respectively?

The Security Market Line

We can view the expected return–beta relationship as a reward–risk equation. The beta of a security is the appropriate measure of its risk because beta is proportional to the risk that the security contributes to the optimal risky portfolio.

Risk-averse investors measure the risk of the optimal risky portfolio by its variance. In this world we would expect the reward, or the risk premium on individual assets, to depend on the *contribution* of the individual asset to the risk of the portfolio. The beta of a stock measures its contribution to the variance of the market portfolio. Hence we expect, for any asset or portfolio, the required risk premium to be a function of beta. The CAPM confirms this intuition, stating further that the security's risk premium is directly proportional to both the beta and the risk premium of the market portfolio; that is, the risk premium equals $\beta[E(r_M) - r_f]$.

The expected return–beta relationship can be portrayed graphically as the **security market line (SML)** in Figure 9.2. Because the market's beta is 1, the slope is the risk premium of the market portfolio. At the point on the horizontal axis where $\beta = 1$, we can read off the vertical axis the expected return on the market portfolio.

It is useful to compare the security market line to the capital market line. The CML graphs the risk premiums of *efficient* portfolios (i.e., portfolios composed of the market and the risk-free asset) as a function of portfolio standard deviation. This is appropriate because standard deviation is a valid measure of risk for efficiently diversified portfolios that are candidates for an investor's overall portfolio. The SML, in contrast, graphs *individual asset* risk premiums as a function of asset risk. The relevant measure of risk for individual assets held as parts of well-diversified portfolios is not the asset's standard deviation or variance; it is, instead, the contribution of the asset to the portfolio variance, which we measure by the asset's beta. The SML is valid for both efficient portfolios and individual assets.

The security market line provides a benchmark for the evaluation of investment performance. Given the risk of an investment, as measured by its beta, the SML provides the required rate of return necessary to compensate investors for both risk as well as the time value of money.

Because the security market line is the graphic representation of the expected return–beta relationship, "fairly priced" assets plot exactly on the SML; that is, their expected returns are commensurate with their risk. Given the assumptions we made at the start of this section, all securities must lie on the SML in market equilibrium. Nevertheless, we see here how the CAPM may be of use in the money-management industry. Suppose that the SML relation is used as a benchmark to assess the fair expected return on a risky asset. Then security analysis is performed to calculate the return actually expected. (Notice that we depart here from the simple CAPM world in that some investors now apply their own unique analysis to derive an "input list" that may differ from their competitors'.) If a stock is perceived to be a good buy, or underpriced, it will provide an expected return in excess of the fair return stipulated by the SML. Underpriced stocks therefore plot above the SML: Given their betas, their expected returns are greater than dictated by the CAPM. Overpriced stocks plot below the SML.

The difference between the fair and actually expected rates of return on a stock is called the stock's **alpha,** denoted by α. For example, if the market return is expected to be 14%, a stock has a beta of 1.2, and the T-bill rate is 6%, the SML would predict an expected return on the stock of $6 + 1.2(14 - 6) = 15.6\%$. If one believed the stock would provide an expected return of 17%, the implied alpha would be 1.4% (see Figure 9.3).

One might say that security analysis (which we treat in Part Five) is about uncovering securities with nonzero alphas. This analysis suggests that the starting point of

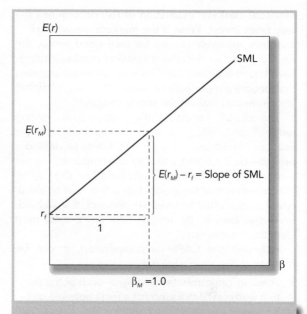

FIGURE 9.2   The security market line

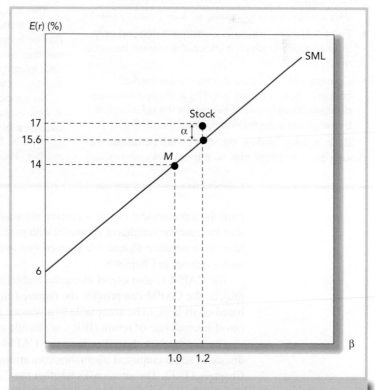

FIGURE 9.3   The SML and a positive-alpha stock

TALES FROM THE FAR SIDE

Financial markets' evaluation of risk determines the way firms invest. What if the markets are wrong?

Investors are rarely praised for their good sense. But for the past two decades a growing number of firms have based their decisions on a model which assumes that people are perfectly rational. If they are irrational, are businesses making the wrong choices?

The model, known as the "capital-asset pricing model," or CAPM, has come to dominate modern finance. Almost any manager who wants to defend a project—be it a brand, a factory or a corporate merger—must justify his decision partly based on the CAPM. The reason is that the model tells a firm how to calculate the return that its investors demand. If shareholders are to benefit, the returns from any project must clear this "hurdle rate."

Although the CAPM is complicated, it can be reduced to five simple ideas:

- Investors can eliminate some risks—such as the risk that workers will strike, or that a firm's boss will quit—by diversifying across many regions and sectors.

- Some risks, such as that of a global recession, cannot be eliminated through diversification. So even a basket of all of the stocks in a stock market will still be risky.

- People must be rewarded for investing in such a risky basket by earning returns above those that they can get on safer assets, such as Treasury bills.

- The rewards on a specific investment depend only on the extent to which it affects the market basket's risk.

- Conveniently, that contribution to the market basket's risk can be captured by a single measure—dubbed "beta"—which expresses the relationship between the investment's risk and the market's.

Beta is what makes the CAPM so powerful. Although an investment may face many risks, diversified

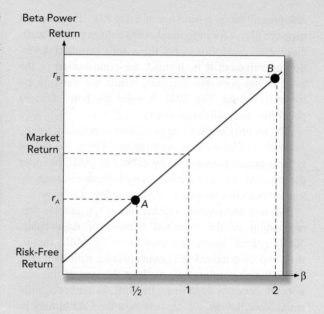

investors should care only about those that are related to the market basket. Beta not only tells managers how to measure those risks, but it also allows them to translate them directly into a hurdle rate. If the future profits from a project will not exceed that rate, it is not worth shareholders' money.

The diagram shows how the CAPM works. Safe investments, such as Treasury bills, have a beta of zero. Riskier investments should earn a premium over the risk-free rate which increases with beta. Those whose risks roughly match the market's have a beta of one, by definition, and should earn the market return.

So suppose that a firm is considering two projects, A and B. Project A has a beta of ½: when the market rises or falls by 10%, its returns tend to rise or fall by 5%. So its risk premium is only half that of the market. Project B's risk premium is twice that of the

portfolio management can be a passive market-index portfolio. The portfolio manager will then increase the weights of securities with positive alphas and decrease the weights of securities with negative alphas. We showed one strategy for adjusting the portfolio weights in such a manner in Chapter 8.

The CAPM is also useful in capital budgeting decisions. For a firm considering a new project, the CAPM can provide the *required rate of return* that the project needs to yield, based on its beta, to be acceptable to investors. Managers can use the CAPM to obtain this cutoff internal rate of return (IRR), or "hurdle rate" for the project.

The nearby box describes how the CAPM can be used in capital budgeting. It also discusses some empirical anomalies concerning the model, which we address in detail in Chapters 11–13. The article asks whether the CAPM is useful for capital budgeting in light of these shortcomings; it concludes that even given the anomalies cited, the model still can be useful to managers who wish to increase the fundamental value of their firms.

market, so it must earn a higher return to justify the expenditure.

NEVER KNOWINGLY UNDERPRICED

But there is one small problem with the CAPM: Financial economists have found that beta is not much use for explaining rates of return on firms' shares. Worse, there appears to be another measure which explains these returns quite well.

That measure is the ratio of a firm's book value (the value of its assets at the time they entered the balance sheet) to its market value. Several studies have found that, on average, companies that have high book-to-market ratios tend to earn excess returns over long periods, even after adjusting for the risks that are associated with beta.

The discovery of this book-to-market effect has sparked a fierce debate among financial economists. All of them agree that some risks ought to carry greater rewards. But they are now deeply divided over how risk should be measured. Some argue that since investors are rational, the book-to-market effect must be capturing an extra risk factor. They conclude, therefore, that managers should incorporate the book-to-market effect into their hurdle rates. They have labeled this alternative hurdle rate the "new estimator of expected return," or NEER.

Other financial economists, however, dispute this approach. Since there is no obvious extra risk associated with a high book-to-market ratio, they say, investors must be mistaken. Put simply, they are underpricing high book-to-market stocks, causing them to earn abnormally high returns. If managers of such firms try to exceed those inflated hurdle rates, they will forgo many profitable investments. With economists now at odds, what is a conscientious manager to do?

Jeremy Stein, an economist at the Massachusetts Institute of Technology's business school, offers a paradoxical answer.* If investors are rational, then beta cannot be the only measure of risk, so managers should stop using it. Conversely, if investors are irrational, then beta is still the right measure in many cases. Mr. Stein argues that if beta captures an asset's fundamental risk—that is, its contribution to the market basket's risk—then it will often make sense for managers to pay attention to it, even if investors are somehow failing to.

Often, but not always. At the heart of Mr. Stein's argument lies a crucial distinction—that between (a) boosting a firm's long-term value and (b) trying to raise its share price. If investors are rational, these are the same thing: any decision that raises long-term value will instantly increase the share price as well. But if investors are making predictable mistakes, a manager must choose.

For instance, if he wants to increase today's share price—perhaps because he wants to sell his shares, or to fend off a takeover attempt—he must usually stick with the NEER approach, accommodating investors' misperceptions. But if he is interested in long-term value, he should usually continue to use beta. Showing a flair for marketing, Mr. Stein labels this far-sighted alternative to NEER the "fundamental asset risk"—or FAR—approach.

Mr. Stein's conclusions will no doubt irritate many company bosses, who are fond of denouncing their investors' myopia. They have resented the way in which CAPM—with its assumption of investor infallibility—has come to play an important role in boardroom decision-making. But it now appears that if they are right, and their investors are wrong, then those same far-sighted managers ought to be the CAPM's biggest fans.

*Jeremy Stein, "Rational Capital Budgeting in an Irrational World," *The Journal of Business*, October 1996.

EXAMPLE 9.1   Using the CAPM

Yet another use of the CAPM is in utility rate-making cases.[9] In this case the issue is the rate of return that a regulated utility should be allowed to earn on its investment in plant and equipment. Suppose that the equityholders have invested $100 million in the firm and that the beta of the equity is .6. If the T-bill rate is 6% and the market risk premium is 8%, then the fair profits to the firm would be assessed as $6 + .6 \times 8 = 10.8\%$ of the $100 million investment, or $10.8 million. The firm would be allowed to set prices at a level expected to generate these profits.

---

[9]This application is fast disappearing, as many states are in the process of deregulating their public utilities and allowing a far greater degree of free market pricing. Nevertheless, a considerable amount of rate setting still takes place.

CONCEPT CHECK

4 and 5

Stock XYZ has an expected return of 12% and risk of $\beta = 1$. Stock ABC has expected return of 13% and $\beta = 1.5$. The market's expected return is 11%, and $r_f = 5\%$.

a. According to the CAPM, which stock is a better buy?

b. What is the alpha of each stock? Plot the SML and each stock's risk–return point on one graph. Show the alphas graphically.

The risk-free rate is 8% and the expected return on the market portfolio is 16%. A firm considers a project that is expected to have a beta of 1.3.

a. What is the required rate of return on the project?

b. If the expected IRR of the project is 19%, should it be accepted?

9.2   THE CAPM AND THE INDEX MODEL

Actual Returns versus Expected Returns

The CAPM is an elegant model. The question is whether it has real-world value—whether its implications are borne out by experience. Chapter 13 provides a range of empirical evidence on this point, but for now we focus briefly on a more basic issue: Is the CAPM testable even in principle?

For starters, one central prediction of the CAPM is that the market portfolio is a mean-variance efficient portfolio. Consider that the CAPM treats all traded risky assets. To test the efficiency of the CAPM market portfolio, we would need to construct a value-weighted portfolio of a huge size and test its efficiency. So far, this task has not been feasible. An even more difficult problem, however, is that the CAPM implies relationships among *expected* returns, whereas all we can observe are actual or realized holding-period returns, and these need not equal prior expectations. Even supposing we could construct a portfolio to represent the CAPM market portfolio satisfactorily, how would we test its mean-variance efficiency? We would have to show that the reward-to-volatility ratio of the market portfolio is higher than that of any other portfolio. However, this reward-to-volatility ratio is set in terms of expectations, and we have no way to observe these expectations directly.

The problem of measuring expectations haunts us as well when we try to establish the validity of the second central set of CAPM predictions, the expected return–beta relationship. This relationship is also defined in terms of expected returns $E(r_i)$ and $E(r_M)$:

$$E(r_i) = r_f + \beta_i[E(r_M) - r_f] \tag{9.9}$$

The upshot is that, as elegant and insightful as the CAPM is, we must make additional assumptions to make it implementable and testable.

The Index Model and Realized Returns

We have said that the CAPM is a statement about ex ante or expected returns, whereas in practice all anyone can observe directly are ex post or realized returns. To make the leap from expected to realized returns, we can employ the index model, which we will use in excess return form as

$$R_i = \alpha_i + \beta_i R_M + e_i \qquad (9.10)$$

We saw in Chapter 8 how to apply standard regression analysis to estimate Equation 9.10 using observable realized returns over some sample period. Let us now see how this framework for statistically decomposing actual stock returns meshes with the CAPM.

We start by deriving the covariance between the returns on stock i and the market index. By definition, the firm-specific or nonsystematic component is independent of the market wide or systematic component, that is, $\text{Cov}(R_M, e_i) = 0$. From this relationship, it follows that the covariance of the excess rate of return on security i with that of the market index is

$$\begin{aligned} \text{Cov}(R_i, R_M) &= \text{Cov}(\beta_i R_M + e_i, R_M) \\ &= \beta_i \text{Cov}(R_M, R_M) + \text{Cov}(e_i, R_M) \\ &= \beta_i \sigma_M^2 \end{aligned}$$

Note that we can drop α_i from the covariance terms because α_i is a constant and thus has zero covariance with all variables.

Because $\text{Cov}(R_i, R_M) = \beta_i \sigma_M^2$, the sensitivity coefficient, β_i, in Equation 9.10, which is the slope of the regression line representing the index model, equals

$$\beta_i = \frac{\text{Cov}(R_i, R_M)}{\sigma_M^2}$$

The index model beta coefficient turns out to be the same beta as that of the CAPM expected return–beta relationship, except that we replace the (theoretical) market portfolio of the CAPM with the well-specified and observable market index.

The Index Model and the Expected Return–Beta Relationship

Recall that the CAPM expected return–beta relationship is, for any asset i and the (theoretical) market portfolio,

$$E(r_i) - r_f = \beta_i [E(r_M) - r_f]$$

where $\beta_i = \text{Cov}(R_i, R_M)/\sigma_M^2$. This is a statement about the mean or expected excess returns of assets relative to the mean excess return of the (theoretical) market portfolio.

If the index M in Equation 9.10 represents the true market portfolio, we can take the expectation of each side of the equation to show that the index model specification is

$$E(r_i) - r_f = \alpha_i + \beta_i [E(r_M) - r_f]$$

A comparison of the index model relationship to the CAPM expected return–beta relationship (Equation 9.9) shows that the CAPM predicts that α_i should be zero for all assets. The alpha of a stock is its expected return in excess of (or below) the fair expected return as predicted by the CAPM. If the stock is fairly priced, its alpha must be zero.

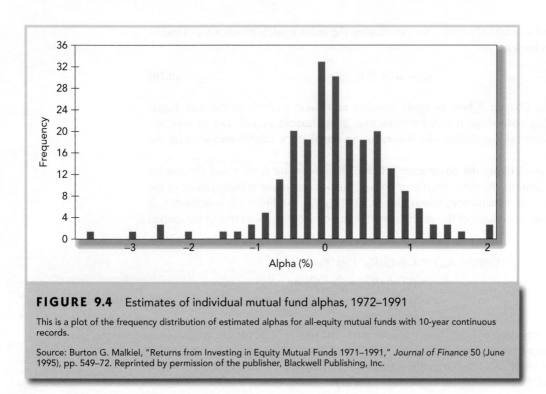

FIGURE 9.4   Estimates of individual mutual fund alphas, 1972–1991

This is a plot of the frequency distribution of estimated alphas for all-equity mutual funds with 10-year continuous records.

Source: Burton G. Malkiel, "Returns from Investing in Equity Mutual Funds 1971–1991," *Journal of Finance* 50 (June 1995), pp. 549–72. Reprinted by permission of the publisher, Blackwell Publishing, Inc.

We emphasize again that this is a statement about *expected* returns on a security. After the fact, of course, some securities will do better or worse than expected and will have returns higher or lower than predicted by the CAPM; that is, they will exhibit positive or negative alphas over a sample period. But this superior or inferior performance could not have been forecast in advance.

Therefore, if we estimate the index model for several firms, using Equation 9.10 as a regression equation, we should find that the ex post or realized alphas (the regression intercepts) for the firms in our sample center around zero. If the initial expectation for alpha were zero, as many firms would be expected to have a positive as a negative alpha for some sample period. The CAPM states that the *expected* value of alpha is zero for all securities, whereas the index model representation of the CAPM holds that the *realized* value of alpha should average out to zero for a sample of historical observed returns. Just as important, the sample alphas should be unpredictable, that is, independent from one sample period to the next.

Indirect evidence on the efficiency of the market portfolio can be found in a study by Burton Malkiel,[10] who estimates alpha values for a large sample of equity mutual funds. The results, which appear in Figure 9.4, show that the distribution of alphas is roughly bell shaped, with a mean that is slightly negative but statistically indistinguishable from zero. On average, it does not appear that mutual funds outperform the market index (the S&P 500) on a risk-adjusted basis.[11]

[10]Burton G. Malkiel, "Returns from Investing in Equity Mutual Funds 1971–1991," *Journal of Finance* 50 (June 1995), pp. 549–72.

[11]Notice that the study included all mutual funds with at least 10 years of continuous data. This suggests the average alpha from this sample would be upward biased because funds that failed after less than 10 years were ignored and omitted from the left tail of the distribution. This *survivorship bias* makes the finding that the average fund underperformed the index even more telling. We discuss survivorship bias further in Chapter 11.

This result is quite meaningful. While we might expect realized alpha values of individual securities to center around zero, professionally managed mutual funds might be expected to demonstrate average positive alphas. Funds with superior performance (and we do expect this set to be non-empty) should tilt the sample average to a positive value. The small impact of superior funds on this distribution suggests the difficulty in beating the passive strategy that the CAPM deems to be optimal.

There is yet another applicable variation on the intuition of the index model, the **market model.** Formally, the market model states that the return "surprise" of any security is proportional to the return surprise of the market, plus a firm-specific surprise:

$$r_i - E(r_i) = \beta_i[r_M - E(r_M)] + e_i$$

This equation divides returns into firm-specific and systematic components somewhat differently from the index model. If the CAPM is valid, however, you can confirm that, substituting for $E(r_i)$ from Equation 9.9, the market model equation becomes identical to the index model. For this reason the terms "index model" and "market model" often are used interchangeably.

CONCEPT CHECK 6	Can you sort out the nuances of the following maze of models? *a.* CAPM *c.* Single-index model *b.* Single-factor model *d.* Market model

9.3   IS THE CAPM PRACTICAL?

To discuss the role of the CAPM in real-life investments we have to answer two questions. First, even if we all agreed that the CAPM were the best available theoretical model to explain rates of return on risky assets, how would this affect practical investment policy? Second, how can we determine whether the CAPM is in fact the best available model to explain rates of return on risky assets?

Notice the wording of the first question. We don't pose it as: "Suppose the CAPM perfectly explains the rates of return on risky assets. . . ." All models, whether in economics or science, are based on simplifications that enable us to come to grips with a complicated reality, which means that perfection is an unreasonable and unusable standard. In our context, we must clarify what "perfectly explains" would mean. From the previous section we know that if the CAPM were valid, a single-index model in which the index includes all traded securities (i.e., all risky securities in the investable universe as in Assumption 3) also would be valid. In this case, "perfectly explains" would mean that all alpha values in security risk premiums would be identically zero.

The notion that all alpha values can be identically zero is feasible in principle, but such a configuration cannot be expected to emerge in real markets. This was demonstrated by Grossman and Stiglitz, who showed that such an equilibrium may be one that the real economy can approach, but not necessarily reach.[12] Their basic idea is that the

[12]Sanford J. Grossman and Joseph E. Stiglitz, "On the Impossibility of Informationally Efficient Markets," *American Economic Review* 70 (June 1981).

actions of security analysts are the forces that drive security prices to "proper" levels at which alpha is zero. But if all alphas were identically zero, there would be no incentive to engage in such security analysis. Instead, the market equilibrium will be characterized by prices hovering "near" their proper values, at which alphas are almost zero, but with enough slippage (and therefore reward for superior insight) to induce analysts to continue their efforts.

A more reasonable standard, that the CAPM is the "best available model to explain rates of return on risky assets," means that in the absence of security analysis, one should take security alphas as zero. A security is mispriced if and only if its alpha is nonzero—underpriced if alpha is positive and overpriced if alpha is negative—and positive or negative alphas are revealed only by superior security analysis. Absent the investment of significant resources in such analysis, an investor would obtain the best investment portfolio on the assumption that all alpha values are zero. This definition of the superiority of the CAPM over any other model also determines its role in real-life investments.

Under the assumption that the CAPM is the best available model, investors willing to expend resources to construct a superior portfolio must (1) identify a practical index to work with and (2) deploy macro analysis to obtain good forecasts for the index and security analysis to identify mispriced securities. This procedure was described in Chapter 8 and is further elaborated on in Part Five (Security Analysis) and Part Seven (Applied Portfolio Management).

We will examine several tests of the CAPM in Chapter 13. But it is important to explain the results of these tests and their implications.

Is the CAPM Testable?

Let us consider for a moment what testability means. A model consists of (i) a set of assumptions, (ii) logical/mathematical development of the model through manipulation of those assumptions, and (iii) a set of predictions. Assuming the logical/mathematical manipulations are free of errors, we can test a model in two ways, *normative* and *positive*. Normative tests examine the assumptions of the model, while positive tests examine the predictions.

If a model's assumptions are valid, and the development is error-free, then the predictions of the model must be true. In this case, testing the assumptions is synonymous with testing the model. But few, if any, models can pass the normative test. In most cases, as with the CAPM, the assumptions are admittedly invalid—we recognize that we have simplified reality, and therefore to this extent are relying on "untrue" assumptions. The motivation for invoking unrealistic assumptions is clear; we simply cannot solve a model that is perfectly consistent with the full complexity of real-life markets. As we've noted, the need to use simplifying assumptions is not peculiar to economics—it characterizes all of science.

Assumptions are chosen first and foremost to render the model solvable. But we prefer assumptions to which the model is "robust." A model is robust with respect to an assumption if its predictions are not highly sensitive to violation of the assumption. If we use only assumptions to which the model is robust, the model's predictions will be reasonably accurate despite its shortcomings. The upshot of all this is that tests of models are almost always positive—we judge a model on the success of its empirical predictions. This standard brings statistics into any science and requires us to take a stand on what are acceptable levels of significance and power.[13] Because the nonrealism of the assumptions precludes a normative test, the positive test is really a test of the robustness of the model to its assumptions.

The CAPM implications are embedded in two predictions: (1) the market portfolio is efficient, and (2) the security market line (the expected return–beta relationship) accurately describes the risk–return trade-off, that is, alpha values are zero. In fact, the second implication can be derived from the first, and therefore both stand or fall together in a test that the market portfolio is mean-variance efficient. The central problem in testing this prediction is that the hypothesized market portfolio is unobservable. The "market portfolio" includes *all* risky assets that can be held by investors. This is far more extensive than an equity index. It would include bonds, real estate, foreign assets, privately held businesses, and human capital. These assets are often traded thinly or (for example, in the case of human capital) not traded at all. It is difficult to test the efficiency of an observable portfolio, let alone an unobservable one. These problems alone make adequate testing of the model infeasible.[14] Moreover, even small departures from efficiency in the market portfolio can lead to large departures from the expected return–beta relationship of the SML, which would negate the practical usefulness of the model.

The CAPM Fails Empirical Tests

Because the market portfolio cannot be observed, tests of the CAPM revolve around the expected return–beta relationship. The tests use proxies such as the S&P 500 index to stand in for the true market portfolio. These tests therefore appeal to robustness of the assumption that the market proxy is sufficiently close to the true, unobservable market portfolio. The CAPM fails these tests, that is, the data reject the hypothesis that alpha values are uniformly zero at acceptable levels of significance. For example, we find that, on average, low-beta securities have positive alphas and high-beta securities have negative alphas.

It is possible that this is a result of a failure of our data, the validity of the market proxy, or statistical method. If so, we would conclude the following: There is no better model out there, but we measure beta and alpha values with unsatisfactory precision. This situation

---

[13] To illustrate the meanings of significance and power, consider a test of the efficacy of a new drug. The agency testing the drug may make two possible errors. The drug may be useless (or even harmful), but the agency may conclude that it is useful. This is called a "Type I" error. The *significance level* of a test is the probability of a Type I error. Typical practice is to fix the level of significance at some low level, for example, 5%. In the case of drug testing, for example, the first goal is to avoid introducing ineffective or harmful treatments. The other possible error is that the drug is actually useful, but the testing procedure concludes it is not. This mistake, called "Type II" error, would lead us to discard a useful treatment. The *power* of the test is the probability of avoiding Type II error (i.e., one minus the probability of making such an error), that is, the probability of accepting the drug if it is indeed useful. We want tests that, at a given level of significance, have the most power, so we will admit effective drugs with high probability. In social sciences in particular, available tests often have low power, in which case they are susceptible to Type II error and will reject a correct model (a "useful drug") with high frequency. "The drug is useful" is analogous in the CAPM to alphas being zero. When the test data reject the hypothesis that observed alphas are zero at the desired level of significance, the CAPM fails. However, if the test has low power, the probability that we accept the model when true is not all that high.

[14] The best-known discussion of the difficulty in testing the CAPM is now called "Roll's critique." See Richard Roll, "A Critique of the Asset Pricing Theory's Tests: Part I: On Past and Potential Testability of the Theory," *Journal of Financial Economics* 4 (1977). The issue is developed further in Richard Roll and Stephen A. Ross, "On the Cross-Sectional Relation between Expected Return and Betas," *Journal of Finance* 50 (1995); and Schmuel Kandel and Robert F. Stambaugh, "Portfolio Inefficiency and the Cross-Section of Expected Returns," *Journal of Finance* 50 (1995).

would call for improved technique. But if the rejection of the model is not an artifact of statistical problems, then we must search for extensions to the CAPM, or substitute models. We will consider several extensions of the model later in the chapter.

The Economy and the Validity of the CAPM

For better or worse, some industries are regulated, with rate commissions either setting or approving prices. Imagine a commission pondering a rate case for a regulated utility. The rate commission must decide whether the rates charged by the company are sufficient to grant shareholders a fair rate of return on their investments. The normative framework of the typical rate hearing is that shareholders, who have made an investment in the firm, are entitled to earn a "fair" rate of return on their equity investment. The firm is therefore allowed to charge prices that are expected to generate a profit consistent with that fair rate of return.

The question of fairness of the rate of return to the company shareholders cannot be divorced from the level of risk of these returns. The CAPM provides the commission a clear criterion: If the rates under current regulation are too low, then the rate of return to equity investors would be less than commensurate with risk, and alpha would be negative. As we pointed out in Example 9.1, the commissioner's problem may now be organized around arguments about estimates of risk and the security market line.

Similar applications arise in many legal settings. For example, contracts with payoffs that are contingent on a fair rate of return can be based on the index rate of return and the beta of appropriate assets. Many disputes involving damages require that a stream of losses be discounted to a present value. The proper discount rate depends on risk, and disputes about fair compensation to litigants can be (and often are) set on the basis of the SML, using past data that differentiate systematic from firm-specific risk.

It may be surprising to find that the CAPM is an accepted norm in the U.S. and many other developed countries, despite its empirical shortcomings. We can offer a twofold explanation. First, the logic of the decomposition to systematic and firm-specific risk is compelling. Absent a better model to assess nonmarket components of risk premiums, we must use the best method available. As improved methods of generating equilibrium security returns become empirically validated, they gradually will be incorporated into institutional decision making. Such improvements may come either from extensions of the CAPM and its companion, arbitrage pricing theory (discussed in the next chapter), or from a yet-undiscovered new model.

Second, there is impressive, albeit less-formal, evidence that the central conclusion of the CAPM—the efficiency of the market portfolio—may not be all that far from being valid. Thousands of mutual funds within hundreds of investment companies compete for investor money. These mutual funds employ professional analysts and portfolio managers and expend considerable resources to construct superior portfolios. But the number of funds that consistently outperform a simple strategy of investing in passive market index portfolios is extremely small, suggesting that the single-index model with ex ante zero alpha values may be a reasonable working approximation for most investors.

The Investments Industry and the Validity of the CAPM

More than other practitioners, investment firms must take a stand on the validity of the CAPM. If they judge the CAPM invalid, they must turn to a substitute framework to guide them in constructing optimal portfolios.

For example, the CAPM provides discount rates that help security analysts assess the intrinsic value of a firm. If an analyst believes that some actual prices differ from intrinsic values, then those securities have nonzero alphas, and there is an opportunity to construct an active portfolio with a superior risk–return profile. But if the discount rate used to assess intrinsic value is incorrect because of a failure in the CAPM, the estimate of alpha will be biased, and both the Markowitz model of Chapter 7 and the index model of Chapter 8 will actually lead to inferior portfolios. When constructing their presumed optimal risky portfolios, practitioners must be satisfied that the passive index they use for that purpose is satisfactory and that the ratios of alpha to residual variance are appropriate measures of investment attractiveness. This would not be the case if the CAPM is invalid. Yet it appears many practitioners do use index models (albeit often with additional indexes) when assessing security prices. The curriculum of the CFA Institute also suggests a widespread acceptance of the CAPM, at least as a starting point for thinking about the risk–return relationship. An explanation similar to the one we offered in the previous subsection is equally valid here.

The central conclusion from our discussion so far is that, explicitly or implicitly, practitioners do use a CAPM. If they use a single-index model and derive optimal portfolios from ratios of alpha forecasts to residual variance, they behave as if the CAPM is valid.[15] If they use a multi-index model, then they use one of the extensions of the CAPM (discussed later in this chapter) or arbitrage pricing theory (discussed in the next chapter). Thus, theory and evidence on the CAPM should be of interest to all sophisticated practitioners.

9.4 ECONOMETRICS AND THE EXPECTED RETURN–BETA RELATIONSHIP

When assessing the empirical success of the CAPM, we must also consider our econometric technique. If our tests are poorly designed, we may mistakenly reject the model. Similarly, some empirical tests implicitly introduce additional assumptions that are not part of the CAPM, for example, that various parameters of the model such as beta or residual variance are constant over time. If these extraneous additional assumptions are too restrictive, we also may mistakenly reject the model.

To begin, notice that all the coefficients of a regression equation are estimated simultaneously, and these estimates are not independent. In particular, the estimate of the intercept (alpha) of a single- (independent) variable regression depends on the estimate of the slope coefficient. Hence, if the beta estimate is inefficient and/or biased, so will be the estimate of the intercept. Unfortunately, statistical bias is easily introduced.

An example of this hazard was pointed out in an early paper by Miller and Scholes,[16] who demonstrated how econometric problems could lead one to reject the CAPM even if it were perfectly valid. They considered a checklist of difficulties encountered in testing the model and showed how these problems potentially could bias conclusions. To prove the point, they simulated rates of return that were *constructed* to satisfy the predictions of the CAPM and used these rates to "test" the model with standard statistical techniques of the day. The result of these tests was a rejection of the model that looks surprisingly similar to what we find in tests of returns from actual data—this despite the fact that the "data" were constructed to satisfy the CAPM. Miller and Scholes thus demonstrated that econometric technique alone could be responsible for the rejection of the model in actual tests.

---

[15]We need to be a bit careful here. On its face, the CAPM asserts that alpha values will equal zero in security market equilibrium. But as we argued earlier, consistent with the vast amount of security analysis that actually takes place, a better way to interpret the CAPM is that equilibrium really means that alphas should be taken to be zero in the absence of security analysis. With private information or superior insight one presumably would be able to identify stocks that are mispriced by the market and thus offer nonzero alphas.

[16]Merton H. Miller and Myron Scholes, "Rates of Return in Relations to Risk: A Re-examination of Some Recent Findings," in *Studies in the Theory of Capital Markets,* Michael C. Jensen, ed. (New York: Praeger, 1972).

There are several potential problems with the estimation of beta coefficients. First, when residuals are correlated (as is common for firms in the same industry), standard beta estimates are not efficient. A simple approach to this problem would be to use statistical techniques designed for these complications. For example, we might replace OLS (ordinary least squares) regressions with GLS (generalized least squares) regressions, which account for correlation across residuals. Moreover, both coefficients, alpha and beta, as well as residual variance, are likely time varying. There is nothing in the CAPM that precludes such time variation, but standard regression techniques rule it out and thus may lead to false rejection of the model. There are now well-known techniques to account for time-varying parameters. In fact, Robert Engle won the Nobel Prize for his pioneering work on econometric techniques to deal with time-varying volatility, and a good portion of the applications of these new techniques have been in finance.[17] Moreover, betas may vary not purely randomly over time, but in response to changing economic conditions. A "conditional" CAPM allows risk and return to change with a set of "conditioning variables."[18]

As importantly, Campbell and Vuolteenaho[19] find that the beta of a security can be decomposed into two components, one of which measures sensitivity to changes in corporate profitability and another which measures sensitivity to changes in the market's discount rates. These are found to be quite different in many cases. Improved econometric techniques such as those proposed in this short survey may help resolve part of the empirical failure of the simple CAPM.

9.5   EXTENSIONS OF THE CAPM

The CAPM uses a number of simplifying assumptions. We can gain greater predictive accuracy at the expense of greater complexity by relaxing some of those assumptions. In this section, we will consider a few of the more important attempts to extend the model. This discussion is not meant to be exhaustive. Rather, it introduces a few extensions of the basic model to provide insight into the various attempts to improve empirical content.

The Zero-Beta Model

Efficient frontier portfolios have a number of interesting characteristics, independently derived by Merton and Roll.[20] Three of these are

1. Any portfolio that is a combination of two frontier portfolios is itself on the efficient frontier.

---

[17]Engle's work gave rise to the widespread use of so-called ARCH models. ARCH stands for autoregressive conditional heteroskedasticity, which is a fancy way of saying that volatility changes over time, and that recent levels of volatility can be used to form optimal estimates of future volatility.

[18]There is now a large literature on conditional models of security market equilibrium. Much of it derives from Ravi Jagannathan and Zhenyu Wang, "The Conditional CAPM and the Cross-Section of Expected Returns," *Journal of Finance* 51 (March 1996), vol pp. 3–53.

[19]John Campbell and Tuomo Vuolteenaho, "Bad Beta, Good Beta," *American Economic Review* 94 (December 2004), pp. 1249–75.

[20]Robert C. Merton, "An Analytic Derivation of the Efficient Portfolio Frontier," *Journal of Financial and Quantitative Analysis*, 1972. Roll, see footnote 14.

2. The expected return of any asset can be expressed as an exact linear function of the expected return on any two efficient-frontier portfolios P and Q according to the following equation:

$$E(r_i) - E(r_Q) = [E(r_P) - E(r_Q)]\frac{\text{Cov}(r_i, r_P) - \text{Cov}(r_P, r_Q)}{\sigma_P^2 - \text{Cov}(r_P, r_Q)} \qquad (9.11)$$

3. Every portfolio on the efficient frontier, except for the global minimum-variance portfolio, has a "companion" portfolio on the bottom (inefficient) half of the frontier with which it is uncorrelated. Because it is uncorrelated, the companion portfolio is referred to as the **zero-beta portfolio** of the efficient portfolio. If we choose the market portfolio M and its zero-beta companion portfolio Z, then Equation 9.11 simplifies to the CAPM-like equation

$$E(r_i) - E(r_Z) = [E(R_M) - E(R_Z)]\frac{\text{Cov}(r_i, r_M)}{\sigma_M^2} = \beta_i[E(r_M) - E(r_Z)] \qquad (9.12)$$

Equation 9.12 resembles the SML of the CAPM, except that the risk-free rate is replaced with the expected return on the zero-beta companion of the market index portfolio.

Fischer Black used these properties to show that Equation 9.12 is the CAPM equation that results when investors face restrictions on borrowing and/or investment in the risk-free asset.[21] In this case, at least some investors will choose portfolios on the efficient frontier that are not necessarily the market index portfolio. Because average returns on the zero-beta portfolio are greater than observed T-bill rates, the zero-beta model can explain why average estimates of alpha values are positive for low-beta securities and negative for high-beta securities, contrary to the prediction of the CAPM. Despite this, the model is not sufficient to rescue the CAPM from empirical rejection.

Labor Income and Nontraded Assets

An important departure from realism is the CAPM assumption that all risky assets are traded. Two important asset classes that are *not* traded are human capital and privately held businesses. The discounted value of future labor income exceeds the total market value of traded assets. The market value of privately held corporations and businesses is of the same order of magnitude. Human capital and private enterprises are different types of assets with possibly different implications for equilibrium returns on traded securities.

Privately held business may be the lesser of the two sources of departures from the CAPM. Nontraded firms can be incorporated or sold at will, save for liquidity considerations that we discuss in the next section. Owners of private business also can borrow against their value, further diminishing the material difference between ownership of private and public business. Suppose that privately held business have similar risk characteristics as those of traded assets. In this case, individuals can partially offset the diversification problems posed by their nontraded entrepreneurial assets by reducing their portfolio demand for securities of similar, traded assets. Thus, the CAPM expected return–beta equation may not be greatly disrupted by the presence of entrepreneurial income.

To the extent that risk characteristics of private enterprises differ from those of traded securities, a portfolio of traded assets that best hedges the risk of typical private business

---

[21]Fischer Black, "Capital Market Equilibrium with Restricted Borrowing," *Journal of Business,* July 1972.

would enjoy excess demand from the population of private business owners. The price of assets in this portfolio will be bid up relative to the CAPM considerations, and the expected returns on these securities will be lower in relation to their systematic risk. Conversely, securities highly correlated with such risk will have high equilibrium risk premiums and may appear to exhibit positive alphas relative to the conventional SML. In fact, Heaton and Lucas show that adding proprietary income to a standard asset-pricing model improves its predictive performance.[22]

The size of labor income and its special nature is of greater concern for the validity of the CAPM. The possible effect of labor income on equilibrium returns can be appreciated from its important effect on personal portfolio choice. Despite the fact that an individual can borrow against labor income (via a home mortgage) and reduce some of the uncertainty about future labor income via life insurance, human capital is less "portable" across time and may be more difficult to hedge using traded securities than nontraded business. This may induce pressure on security prices and result in departures from the CAPM expected return–beta equation. For one example, surely an individual seeking diversification should avoid investing in his employer's stock and limit investments in the same industry. Thus, the demand for stocks of labor-intensive firms may be reduced, and these stocks may require a higher expected return than predicted by the CAPM.

Mayers[23] derives the equilibrium expected return–beta equation for an economy in which individuals are endowed with labor income of varying size relative to their nonlabor capital. The resultant SML equation is

$$E(R_i) = E(R_M) \frac{\text{Cov}(R_i, R_M) + \dfrac{P_H}{P_M}\text{Cov}(R_i, R_H)}{\sigma_M^2 + \dfrac{P_H}{P_M}\text{Cov}(R_M, R_H)} \tag{9.13}$$

where

P_H = value of aggregate human capital,

P_M = market value of traded assets (market portfolio),

R_H = excess rate of return on aggregate human capital.

The CAPM measure of systematic risk, beta, is replaced in the extended model by an adjusted beta that also accounts for covariance with the portfolio of aggregate human capital. Notice that the ratio of human capital to market value of all traded assets, P_H/P_M, may well be greater than 1, and hence the effect of the covariance of a security with labor income, $\text{Cov}(R_i, R_H)$, relative to the average, $\text{Cov}(R_M, R_H)$, is likely to be economically significant. When $\text{Cov}(R_i, R_H)$ is positive, the adjusted beta is greater when the CAPM beta is smaller than 1, and vice versa. Because we expect $\text{Cov}(R_i, R_H)$ to be positive for the average security, the risk premium in this model will be greater, on average, than predicted by the CAPM for securities with beta less than 1, and smaller for securities with beta greater than 1. The model thus predicts a security market line that is less steep than that of the standard CAPM. This may help explain the average negative alpha of high-beta securities and positive alpha of low-beta securities that lead to the statistical failure of the CAPM equation. In Chapter 13 on empirical evidence we present additional results along these lines.

[22]John Heaton and Deborah Lucas, "Portfolio Choice and Asset Prices: The Importance of Entrepreneurial Risk, *Journal of Finance* 55 (June 2000). This paper offers evidence of the effect of entrepreneurial risk on both portfolio choice and the risk–return relationship.

[23]See footnote 8.

A Multiperiod Model and Hedge Portfolios

Robert C. Merton revolutionized financial economics by using continuous-time models to extend many of our models of asset pricing.[24] While his (Nobel Prize–winning) contributions to option-pricing theory and financial engineering (along with those of Fischer Black and Myron Scholes) may have had greater impact on the investment industry, his solo contribution to portfolio theory was equally important for our understanding of the risk–return relationship.

In his basic model, Merton relaxes the "single-period" myopic assumptions about investors. He envisions individuals who optimize a lifetime consumption/investment plan, and who continually adapt consumption/investment decisions to current wealth and planned retirement age. When uncertainty about portfolio returns is the only source of risk and investment opportunities remain unchanged through time, that is, there is no change in the probability distribution of the return on the market portfolio or individual securities, Merton's so-called intertemporal capital asset pricing model (ICAPM) predicts the same expected return–beta relationship as the single-period equation.[25]

But the situation changes when we include additional sources of risk. These extra risks are of two general kinds. One concerns changes in the parameters describing investment opportunities, such as future risk-free rates, expected returns, or the risk of the market portfolio. For example, suppose that the real interest rate may change over time. If it falls in some future period, one's level of wealth will now support a lower stream of real consumption. Future spending plans, for example, for retirement spending, may be put in jeopardy. To the extent that returns on some securities are correlated with changes in the risk-free rate, a portfolio can be formed to hedge such risk, and investors will bid up the price (and bid down the expected return) of those hedge assets. Investors will sacrifice some expected return if they can find assets whose returns will be higher when other parameters (in this case, the risk-free rate) change adversely.

The other additional source of risk concerns the prices of the consumption goods that can be purchased with any amount of wealth. Consider as an example inflation risk. In addition to the expected level and volatility of their nominal wealth, investors must be concerned about the cost of living—what those dollars can buy. Therefore, inflation risk is an important extramarket source of risk, and investors may be willing to sacrifice some expected return to purchase securities whose returns will be higher when the cost of living changes adversely. If so, hedging demands for securities that help to protect against inflation risk would affect portfolio choice and thus expected return. One can push this conclusion even further, arguing that empirically significant hedging demands may arise for important subsectors of consumer expenditures; for example, investors may bid up share prices of energy companies that will hedge energy price uncertainty. These sorts of effects may characterize any assets that hedge important extramarket sources of risk.

More generally, suppose we can identify K sources of extramarket risk and find K associated hedge portfolios. Then, Merton's ICAPM expected return–beta equation would generalize the SML to a multi-index version:

$$E(R_i) = \beta_{iM}E(R_M) + \sum_{k=1}^{K}\beta_{ik}E(R_k) \qquad (9.14)$$

where β_{iM} is the familiar security beta on the market-index portfolio, and β_{ik} is the beta on the kth hedge portfolio.

[24]Merton's classic works are collected in *Continuous-Time Finance* (Oxford, U.K.: Basil Blackwell, 1992).

[25]Eugene F. Fama also made this point in "Multiperiod Consumption-Investment Decisions," *American Economic Review* 60 (1970).

Other multifactor models using additional factors that do not arise from extramarket sources of risk have been developed and lead to SMLs of a form identical to that of the ICAPM. These models also may be considered extensions of the CAPM in the broad sense. We examine these models in the next chapter.

A Consumption-Based CAPM

The logic of the CAPM together with the hedging demands noted in the previous subsection suggests that it might be useful to center the model directly on consumption. Such models were first proposed by Mark Rubinstein, Robert Lucas, and Douglas Breeden.[26]

In a lifetime consumption plan, the investor must in each period balance the allocation of current wealth between today's consumption and the savings and investment that will support future consumption. When optimized, the utility value from an additional dollar of consumption today must be equal to the utility value of the expected future consumption that can be financed by that additional dollar of wealth.[27] Future wealth will grow from labor income, as well as returns on that dollar when invested in the optimal complete portfolio.

Suppose risky assets are available and you wish to increase expected consumption growth by allocating some of your savings to a risky portfolio. How would we measure the risk of these assets? As a general rule, investors will value additional income more highly during difficult economic times (when consumption opportunities are scarce) than in affluent times (when consumption is already abundant). An asset will therefore be viewed as riskier in terms of consumption if it has positive covariance with consumption growth—in other words, if its payoff is higher when consumption is already high and lower when consumption is relatively restricted. Therefore, equilibrium risk premiums will be greater for assets that exhibit higher covariance with consumption growth. Developing this insight, we can write the risk premium on an asset as a function of its "consumption risk" as follows:

$$E(R_i) = \beta_{iC}\text{RP}_C \tag{9.15}$$

where portfolio C may be interpreted as a *consumption-tracking portfolio* (also called a *consumption-mimicking portfolio*), that is, the portfolio with the highest correlation with consumption growth; β_{iC} is the slope coefficient in the regression of asset i's excess returns, R_i, on those of the consumption-tracking portfolio; and, finally, RP_C is the risk premium associated with consumption uncertainty, which is measured by the expected excess return on the consumption-tracking portfolio:

$$\text{RP}_C = E(R_C) = E(r_C) - r_f \tag{9.16}$$

Notice how similar this conclusion is to the conventional CAPM. The consumption-tracking portfolio in the CCAPM plays the role of the market portfolio in the conventional CAPM. This is in accord with its focus on the risk of *consumption* opportunities rather than the risk and return of the *dollar* value of the portfolio. The excess return on the

[26]Mark Rubinstein, "The Valuation of Uncertain Income Streams and the Pricing of Options," *Bell Journal of Economics and Management Science* 7 (1976), pp. 407–25; Robert Lucas, "Asset Prices in an Exchange Economy," *Econometrica* 46 (1978), pp. 1429–45; Douglas Breeden, "An Intertemporal Asset Pricing Model with Stochastic Consumption and Investment Opportunities," *Journal of Financial Economics* 7 (1979), pp. 265–96.

[27]Wealth at each point in time equals the market value of assets in the balance sheet plus the present value of future labor income. These models of consumption and investment decisions are often made tractable by assuming investors exhibit constant relative risk aversion, or CRRA. CRRA implies that an individual invests a constant proportion of wealth in the optimal risky portfolio regardless of the level of wealth. You might recall that our prescription for optimal capital allocation in Chapter 6 also called for an optimal investment proportion in the risky portfolio regardless of the level of wealth. The utility function we employed there also exhibited CRRA.

consumption-tracking portfolio plays the role of the excess return on the market portfolio, M. Both approaches result in linear, single-factor models that differ mainly in the identity of the factor they use.

In contrast to the CAPM, the beta of the market portfolio on the market factor of the CCAPM is not necessarily 1. It is perfectly plausible and empirically evident that this beta is substantially greater than 1. This means that in the linear relationship between the market index risk premium and that of the consumption portfolio,

$$E(R_M) = \alpha_M + \beta_{MC}E(R_C) + \varepsilon_M \qquad (9.17)$$

where α_M and ε_M allow for empirical deviation from the exact model in Equation 9.15, and β_{MC} is not necessarily equal to 1.

Because the CCAPM is so similar to the CAPM, one might wonder about its usefulness. Indeed, just as the CAPM is empirically flawed because not all assets are traded, so is the CCAPM. The attractiveness of this model is in that it compactly incorporates consumption hedging and possible changes in investment opportunities, that is, in the parameters of the return distributions in a single-factor framework. There is a price to pay for this compactness, however. Consumption growth figures are published infrequently (monthly at the most) compared with financial assets, and are measured with significant error. Nevertheless, recent empirical research[28] indicates that this model is more successful in explaining realized returns than the CAPM, which is a reason why students of investments should be familiar with it. We return to this issue, as well as empirical evidence concerning the CCAPM, in Chapter 13.

9.6   LIQUIDITY AND THE CAPM

Standard models of asset pricing (such as the CAPM) assume frictionless markets, meaning that securities can be traded costlessly. But these models actually have little to say about trading activity. For example, in the equilibrium of the CAPM, all investors share all available information and demand identical portfolios of risky assets. The awkward implication of this result is that there is no reason for trade. If all investors hold identical portfolios of risky assets, then when new (unexpected) information arrives, prices will change commensurately, but each investor will continue to hold a piece of the market portfolio, which requires no exchange of assets. How do we square this implication with the observation that on a typical day, more than 3 billion shares change hands on the New York Stock Exchange alone? One obvious answer is heterogeneous expectations, that is, beliefs not shared by the entire market. Such private information will give rise to trading as investors attempt to profit by rearranging portfolios in accordance with their now-heterogeneous demands. In reality, trading (and trading costs) will be of great importance to investors.

The **liquidity** of an asset is the ease and speed with which it can be sold at fair market value. Part of liquidity is the cost of engaging in a transaction, particularly the bid–ask spread. Another part is price impact—the adverse movement in price one would encounter when attempting to execute a larger trade. Yet another component is immediacy—the ability to sell the asset quickly without reverting to fire-sale prices. Conversely, **illiquidity** can be measured in part by the discount from fair market value a seller must accept if the asset is to be sold quickly. A perfectly liquid asset is one that would entail no illiquidity discount.

---

[28]Ravi Jagannathan and Yong Wang, "Lazy Investors, Discretionary Consumption, and the Cross-Section of Stock Returns," *Journal of Finance* 62 (August 2007), pp. 1633–61.

STOCK INVESTORS PAY HIGH PRICE FOR LIQUIDITY

Given a choice between liquid and illiquid stocks, most investors, to the extent they think of it at all, opt for issues they know are easy to get in and out of.

But for long-term investors who don't trade often—which includes most individuals—that may be unnecessarily expensive. Recent studies of the performance of listed stocks show that, on average, less-liquid issues generate substantially higher returns—as much as several percentage points a year at the extremes.

ILLIQUIDITY PAYOFF

Among the academic studies that have attempted to quantify this illiquidity payoff is a recent work by two finance professors, Yakov Amihud of New York University and Tel Aviv University, and Haim Mendelson of the University of Rochester. Their study looks at New York Stock Exchange issues over the 1961–1980 period and defines liquidity in terms of bid–asked spreads as a percentage of overall share price.

Market makers use spreads in quoting stocks to define the difference between the price they'll bid to take stock off an investor's hands and the price they'll offer to sell stock to any willing buyer. The bid price is always somewhat lower because of the risk to the broker of tying up precious capital to hold stock in inventory until it can be resold.

If a stock is relatively illiquid, which means there's not a ready flow of orders from customers clamoring to buy it, there's more of a chance the broker will lose money on the trade. To hedge this risk, market makers demand an even bigger discount to service potential sellers, and the spread will widen further.

The study by Profs. Amihud and Mendelson shows that liquidity spreads—measured as a percentage discount from the stock's total price—ranged from less than 0.1%, for widely held International Business Machines

Corp., to as much as 4% to 5%. The widest-spread group was dominated by smaller, low-priced stocks.

The study found that, overall, the least-liquid stocks averaged an 8.5 percent-a-year higher return than the most-liquid stocks over the 20-year period. On average, a one percentage point increase in the spread was associated with a 2.5% higher annual return for New York Stock Exchange stocks. The relationship held after results were adjusted for size and other risk factors.

An extension of the study of Big Board stocks done at *The Wall Street Journal*'s request produced similar findings. It shows that for the 1980–85 period, a one percentage-point-wider spread was associated with an extra average annual gain of 2.4%. Meanwhile, the least-liquid stocks outperformed the most-liquid stocks by almost six percentage points a year.

COST OF TRADING

Since the cost of the spread is incurred each time the stock is traded, illiquid stocks can quickly become prohibitively expensive for investors who trade frequently. On the other hand, long-term investors needn't worry so much about spreads, since they can amortize them over a longer period.

In terms of investment strategy, this suggests "that the small investor should tailor the types of stocks he or she buys to his expected holding period," Prof. Mendelson says. If the investor expects to sell within three months, he says, it's better to pay up for the liquidity and get the lowest spread. If the investor plans to hold the stock for a year or more, it makes sense to aim at stocks with spreads of 3% or more to capture the extra return.

Source: Barbara Donnelly, *The Wall Street Journal*, April 28, 1987, p. 37. Reprinted by permission of *The Wall Street Journal*. © 1987 Dow Jones & Company, Inc. All Rights Reserved Worldwide.

Liquidity (or the lack of it) has long been recognized as an important characteristic that affects asset values. For example, in legal cases, courts have routinely applied very steep discounts to the values of businesses that cannot be publicly traded. But liquidity has not always been appreciated as an important factor in security markets, presumably due to the relatively small trading cost per transaction compared with the large costs of trading assets such as real estate. The breakthrough came in the work of Amihud and Mendelson[29] (see the nearby box) and today, liquidity is increasingly viewed as an important determinant of prices and expected returns. We supply only a brief synopsis of this important topic here and provide empirical evidence in Chapter 13.

[29] Yakov Amihud and Haim Mendelson, "Asset Pricing and the Bid–Ask Spread," *Journal of Financial Economics* 17(1986). A summary of the ensuing large body of literature on liquidity can be found in Yakov Amihud, Haim Mendelson, and Lasse Heje Pedersen, "Liquidity and Asset Prices," *Foundations and Trends in Finance* 1, no. 4 (2005).

Early models of liquidity focused on the inventory management problem faced by security dealers. Dealers in over-the-counter markets post prices at which they are willing to buy a security (the bid price) or sell it (the ask price). The willingness of security dealers to add to their inventory or sell shares from their inventory makes them crucial contributors to overall market liquidity. The fee they earn for supplying this liquidity is the bid–ask spread. Part of the bid–ask spread may be viewed as compensation for bearing the price risk involved in holding an inventory of securities and allowing their inventory levels to absorb the fluctuations in overall security demand. Assuming the fair price of the stock is the average of the bid and ask prices, an investor pays half the spread upon purchase and another half upon sale of the stock. A dealer on the other side of the transaction earns these spreads. The spread is one important component of liquidity—it is the cost of transacting in a security.

The advent of electronic trading has steadily diminished the role of dealers, but traders still must contend with a bid–ask spread. For example, in electronic markets, the limit-order book contains the "inside spread," that is, the difference between the highest price at which some investor will purchase any shares and the lowest price at which another investor is willing to sell. The effective bid–ask spread will also depend on the size of the desired transaction. Larger purchases will require a trader to move deeper into the limit-order book and accept less-attractive prices. While inside spreads on electronic markets often appear extremely low, effective spreads can be much larger, because the limit orders are good for only small numbers of shares.

Even without the inventory problems faced by traditional securities dealers, the importance of the spread persists. There is greater emphasis today on the component of the spread that is due to asymmetric information. By asymmetric information, we mean the potential for one trader to have private information about the value of the security that is not known to the trading partner. To see why such an asymmetry can affect the market, think about the problems facing someone buying a used car. The seller knows more about the car than the buyer, so the buyer naturally wonders if the seller is trying to get rid of the car because it is a "lemon." At the least, buyers worried about overpaying will shave the prices they are willing to pay for a car of uncertain quality. In extreme cases of asymmetric information, trading may cease altogether.[30] Similarly, traders who post offers to buy or sell at limit prices need to be worried about being picked off by better-informed traders who hit their limit prices only when they are out of line with the intrinsic value of the firm.

Broadly speaking, we may envision investors trading securities for two reasons. Some trades are driven by "noninformational" motives, for example, selling assets to raise cash for a big purchase, or even just for portfolio rebalancing. These sorts of trades, which are not motivated by private information that bears on the value of the traded security, are called *noise trades*. Security dealers will earn a profit from the bid–ask spread when transacting with noise traders (also called *liquidity traders* because their trades may derive from needs for liquidity, i.e., cash).

Other transactions are motivated by private information known only to the seller or buyer. These transactions are generated when traders believe they have come across information that a security is mispriced, and try to profit from that analysis. If an information trader identifies an advantageous opportunity, it must be disadvantageous to the other party in the transaction. If private information indicates a stock is overpriced, and the trader decides to sell it, a dealer who has posted a bid price or another trader who has posted a

---

[30]The problem of informational asymmetry in markets was introduced by the 2001 Nobel Laureate George A. Akerlof and has since become known as the *lemons problem*. A good introduction to Akerlof's contributions can be found in George A. Akerlof, *An Economic Theorist's Book of Tales* (Cambridge, U.K.: Cambridge University Press, 1984).

limit-buy order and ends up on the other side of the transaction will purchase the stock at what will later be revealed to have been an inflated price. Conversely, when private information results in a decision to buy, the price at which the security is traded will eventually be recognized as less than fair value.

Information traders impose a cost on both dealers and other investors who post limit orders. Although on average dealers make money from the bid–ask spread when transacting with liquidity traders, they will absorb losses from information traders. Similarly, any trader posting a limit order is at risk from information traders. The response is to increase limit-ask prices and decrease limit-bid orders—in other words, the spread must widen. The greater the relative importance of information traders, the greater the required spread to compensate for the potential losses from trading with them. In the end, therefore, liquidity traders absorb most of the cost of the information trades because the bid–ask spread that they must pay on their "innocent" trades widens when informational asymmetry is more severe.

The discount in a security price that results from illiquidity can be surprisingly large, far larger than the bid–ask spread. Consider a security with a bid–ask spread of 1%. Suppose it will change hands once a year for the next 3 years and then will be held forever by the third buyer. For the last trade, the investor will pay for the security 99.5% or .995 of its fair price; the price is reduced by half the spread that will be incurred when the stock is sold. The second buyer, knowing the security will be sold a year later for .995 of fair value, and having to absorb half the spread upon purchase, will be willing to pay $.995 - .005/1.05 = .9902$ (i.e., 99.02% of fair value), if the cost of trading is discounted at a rate of 5%. Finally, the current buyer, knowing the loss next year, when the stock will be sold for .9902 of fair value (a discount of .0098), will pay for the security only $.995 - .0098/1.05 = .9857$. Thus the discount has ballooned from .5% to 1.43%. In other words, the present values of all three future trading costs (spreads) are discounted into the current price.[31] To extend this logic, if the security will be traded once a year forever, its current illiquidity cost will equal immediate cost plus the present value of a perpetuity of .5%. At an annual discount rate of 5%, this sum equals $.005 + .005/.05 = .105$, or 10.5%! Obviously, liquidity is of potentially large value and should not be ignored in deriving the equilibrium value of securities.

Consider three stocks with equal bid–ask spreads of 1%. The first trades once a year, the second once every 2 years, and the third every 3 years. We have already calculated the price discount due to illiquidity as the present value of illiquidity costs for the first as 10.5%. The discount for the second security is .5% plus the present value of a biannual perpetuity of .5%, which at a discount rate of 5% amounts to $.5 + .5/(1.05^2 - 1) = 5.38\%$. Similarly, the cost for the security that trades only every 3 years is 3.67%. From this pattern of discounts—10.5%, 5.38%, and 3.67%—it seems that for any *given* spread, the price discount will increase almost in proportion to the frequency of trading. It also would appear that the discount should be proportional to the bid–ask spread. However, trading frequency may well vary inversely with the spread, and this will impede the response of the price discount to the spread.

An investor who plans to hold a security for a given period will calculate the impact of illiquidity costs on expected rate of return; liquidity costs will be amortized over the anticipated holding period. Investors who trade less frequently therefore will be less affected by high trading costs. The reduction in the rate of return due to trading costs is lower the longer the security is held. Hence in equilibrium, investors with long holding periods will,

---

[31] We will see another instance of such capitalization of trading costs in Chapter 13, where one explanation for large discounts on closed-end funds is the substantial present value of a *stream* of apparently small per-period expenses.

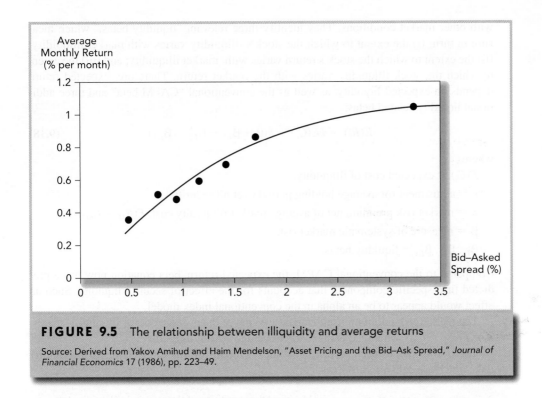

FIGURE 9.5   The relationship between illiquidity and average returns

Source: Derived from Yakov Amihud and Haim Mendelson, "Asset Pricing and the Bid–Ask Spread," *Journal of Financial Economics* 17 (1986), pp. 223–49.

on average, hold more of the illiquid securities, while short-horizon investors will more strongly prefer liquid securities. This "clientele effect" mitigates the effect of the bid–ask spread for illiquid securities. The end result is that the liquidity premium should increase with the bid–ask spread at a decreasing rate. Figure 9.5 confirms this prediction.

So far, we have shown that the expected level of liquidity can affect prices, and therefore expected rates of return. What about unanticipated changes in liquidity? Investors may also demand compensation for *liquidity risk.* The bid–ask spread of a security is not constant through time, nor is the ability to sell a security at a fair price with little notice. Both depend on overall conditions in security markets. If asset liquidity fails at times when it is most desired, then investors will require an additional price discount beyond that required for the expected cost of illiquidity.[32] In other words, there may be a *systematic* component to liquidity risk that affects the equilibrium rate of return and hence the expected return–beta relationship.

As a concrete example of such a model, Acharya and Pedersen[33] consider the impacts of both the level and the risk of liquidity on security pricing. They include three components to liquidity risk—each captures the extent to which liquidity varies systematically

[32] A good example of systematic effects in liquidity risk surrounds the demise of Long-Term Capital Management in the summer of 1998. Despite extensive analysis that indicated its portfolio was highly diversified, many of its assets went bad at the same time when Russia defaulted on its debt. The problem was that despite the fact that short and long positions were expected to balance price changes based on normal market fluctuations, a massive decline in the market liquidity and prices of some assets was not offset by increased prices of more liquid assets. As a supplier of liquidity to others, LTCM was a large holder of less-liquid securities and a liquidity shock of this magnitude was at that time an unimaginable event. While its portfolio may have been diversified in terms of exposure to traditional business condition shocks, it was undiversified in terms of exposure to liquidity shocks.

[33] V. V. Acharya and L. H. Pedersen, "Asset Pricing with Liquidity Risk," *Journal of Financial Economics* 77 (2005).

with other market conditions. They identify three relevant "liquidity betas," which measure in turn: (i) the extent to which the stock's illiquidity varies with market illiquidity; (ii) the extent to which the stock's return varies with market illiquidity; and (iii) the extent to which the stock illiquidity varies with the market return. Therefore, expected return depends on expected liquidity, as well as the conventional "CAPM beta" and three additional liquidity-related betas:

$$E(R_i) = kE(C_i) + \lambda(\beta + \beta_{L1} - \beta_{L2} - \beta_{L3}) \tag{9.18}$$

where

$E(C_i)$ = expected cost of illiquidity,

k = adjustment for average holding period over all securities,

λ = market risk premium net of average market illiquidity cost, $E(R_M - C_M)$,

β = measure of systematic market risk,

$\beta_{L1}, \beta_{L2}, \beta_{L3}$ = liquidity betas.

Compared to the conventional CAPM, the expected return–beta equation now has a predicted firm-specific component that accounts for the effect of security liquidity. Such an effect would appear to be an alpha in the conventional index model.

The market risk premium itself is measured net of the average cost of illiquidity, that is, $\lambda = E(R_M - C_M)$, where C_M is the market-average cost of illiquidity.

The overall risk of each security now must account for the three elements of liquidity risk, which are defined as follows:[34]

$$\beta_{L1} = \frac{\text{Cov}(C_i, C_M)}{\text{Var}(R_M - C_M)}$$

Measures the sensitivity of the security's illiquidity to market illiquidity. Investors want additional compensation for holding a security that becomes illiquid when general liquidity is low.[34]

$$\beta_{L2} = \frac{\text{Cov}(R_i, C_M)}{\text{Var}(R_M - C_M)}$$

Measures the sensitivity of the stock's return to market illiquidity. This coefficient appears with a negative sign in Equation 9.18 because investors are willing to accept a lower average return on stocks that will provide higher returns when market illiquidity is greater.

$$\beta_{L3} = \frac{\text{Cov}(C_i, R_M)}{\text{Var}(R_M - C_M)}$$

Measures the sensitivity of security illiquidity to the market rate of return. This sensitivity also appears with a negative sign, because investors will be willing to accept a lower average return on securities that can be sold more easily (have low illiquidity costs) when the market declines.

A good number of variations on this model can be found in the current (and rapidly growing) literature on liquidity.[35] What is common to all liquidity variants is that they improve on the explanatory power of the CAPM equation and hence there is no doubt that, sooner or later, practitioner optimization models and, more important, security analysis will incorporate the empirical content of these models.

---

[34]Several papers have shown that there is important covariance across asset illiquidity. See for example, T. Chordia, R. Roll, and A. Subramanyam, "Commonality in Liquidity," *Journal of Financial Economics* 56 (2000), pp. 3–28 or J. Hasbrouck and D. H. Seppi "Common Factors in Prices, Order Flows and Liquidity," *Journal of Financial Economics* 59 (2001), pp. 383–411.

[35] Another influential study of liquidity risk and asset pricing is L. Pastor and R. Stambaugh, "Liquidity Risk and Expected Stock Returns," *Journal of Political Economy* 111 (2003), pp. 642–85.

1. The CAPM assumes that investors are single-period planners who agree on a common input list from security analysis and seek mean-variance optimal portfolios.

2. The CAPM assumes that security markets are ideal in the sense that:

   a. They are large, and investors are price-takers.

   b. There are no taxes or transaction costs.

   c. All risky assets are publicly traded.

   d. Investors can borrow and lend any amount at a fixed risk-free rate.

3. With these assumptions, all investors hold identical risky portfolios. The CAPM holds that in equilibrium the market portfolio is the unique mean-variance efficient tangency portfolio. Thus a passive strategy is efficient.

4. The CAPM market portfolio is a value-weighted portfolio. Each security is held in a proportion equal to its market value divided by the total market value of all securities.

5. If the market portfolio is efficient and the average investor neither borrows nor lends, then the risk premium on the market portfolio is proportional to its variance, σ_M^2, and to the average coefficient of risk aversion across investors, A:

$$E(r_M) - r_f = \overline{A}\sigma_M^2$$

6. The CAPM implies that the risk premium on any individual asset or portfolio is the product of the risk premium on the market portfolio and the beta coefficient:

$$E(r_i) - r_f = \beta_i[E(r_M) - r_f]$$

where the beta coefficient is the covariance of the asset with the market portfolio as a fraction of the variance of the market portfolio

$$\beta_i = \frac{\text{Cov}(r_i, r_M)}{\sigma_M^2}$$

7. When risk-free investments are restricted but all other CAPM assumptions hold, then the simple version of the CAPM is replaced by its zero-beta version. Accordingly, the risk-free rate in the expected return–beta relationship is replaced by the zero-beta portfolio's expected rate of return:

$$E(r_i) = E[r_{Z(M)}] + \beta_i E[r_M - r_{Z(M)}]$$

8. The simple version of the CAPM assumes that investors are myopic. When investors are assumed to be concerned with lifetime consumption and bequest plans, but investors' tastes and security return distributions are stable over time, the market portfolio remains efficient and the simple version of the expected return–beta relationship holds. But if those distributions change unpredictably, or if investors seek to hedge nonmarket sources of risk to their consumption, the simple CAPM will give way to a multifactor version in which the security's exposure to these nonmarket sources of risk command risk premiums.

9. The consumption-based capital asset pricing model (CCAPM) is a single-factor model in which the market portfolio excess return is replaced by that of a consumption-tracking portfolio. By appealing directly to consumption, the model naturally incorporates consumption-hedging considerations and changing investment opportunities within a single-factor framework.

10. The Security Market Line of the CAPM must be modified to account for labor income and other significant nontraded assets.

11. Liquidity costs and liquidity risk can be incorporated into the CAPM relationship. Investors demand compensation for both expected costs of illiquidity as well as the risk surrounding those costs.

Related Web sites for this chapter are available at **www.mhhe.com/bkm**

Visit us at www.mhhe.com/bkm

KEY TERMS

homogeneous expectations	expected return–beta	market model
market portfolio	relationship	zero-beta portfolio
mutual fund theorem	security market line (SML)	liquidity
market price of risk	alpha	illiquidity
beta		

PROBLEM SETS

Quiz

1. What must be the beta of a portfolio with $E(r_P) = 18\%$, if $r_f = 6\%$ and $E(r_M) = 14\%$?

2. The market price of a security is $50. Its expected rate of return is 14%. The risk-free rate is 6% and the market risk premium is 8.5%. What will be the market price of the security if its correlation coefficient with the market portfolio doubles (and all other variables remain unchanged)? Assume that the stock is expected to pay a constant dividend in perpetuity.

3. Are the following true or false? Explain.

   a. Stocks with a beta of zero offer an expected rate of return of zero.
   b. The CAPM implies that investors require a higher return to hold highly volatile securities.
   c. You can construct a portfolio with beta of .75 by investing .75 of the investment budget in T-bills and the remainder in the market portfolio.

Problems

4. You are a consultant to a large manufacturing corporation that is considering a project with the following net after-tax cash flows (in millions of dollars):

Years from Now	After-Tax Cash Flow
0	−40
1–10	15

The project's beta is 1.8. Assuming that $r_f = 8\%$ and $E(r_M) = 16\%$, what is the net present value of the project? What is the highest possible beta estimate for the project before its NPV becomes negative?

5. Consider the following table, which gives a security analyst's expected return on two stocks for two particular market returns:

Market Return	Aggressive Stock	Defensive Stock
5%	−2%	6%
25	38	12

   a. What are the betas of the two stocks?
   b. What is the expected rate of return on each stock if the market return is equally likely to be 5% or 25%?
   c. If the T-bill rate is 6% and the market return is equally likely to be 5% or 25%, draw the SML for this economy.
   d. Plot the two securities on the SML graph. What are the alphas of each?
   e. What hurdle rate should be used by the management of the aggressive firm for a project with the risk characteristics of the defensive firm's stock?

For Problems 6 to 12: If the simple CAPM is valid, which of the following situations are possible? Explain. Consider each situation independently.

6.

Portfolio	Expected Return	Beta
A	20	1.4
B	25	1.2

7.

Portfolio	Expected Return	Standard Deviation
A	30	35
B	40	25

8.

Portfolio	Expected Return	Standard Deviation
Risk-free	10	0
Market	18	24
A	16	12

9.

Portfolio	Expected Return	Standard Deviation
Risk-free	10	0
Market	18	24
A	20	22

10.

Portfolio	Expected Return	Beta
Risk-free	10	0
Market	18	1.0
A	16	1.5

11.

Portfolio	Expected Return	Beta
Risk-free	10	0
Market	18	1.0
A	16	0.9

12.

Portfolio	Expected Return	Standard Deviation
Risk-free	10	0
Market	18	24
A	16	22

For Problems 13 to 15 assume that the risk-free rate of interest is 6% and the expected rate of return on the market is 16%.

13. A share of stock sells for $50 today. It will pay a dividend of $6 per share at the end of the year. Its beta is 1.2. What do investors expect the stock to sell for at the end of the year?

14. I am buying a firm with an expected perpetual cash flow of $1,000 but am unsure of its risk. If I think the beta of the firm is .5, when in fact the beta is really 1, how much *more* will I offer for the firm than it is truly worth?

15. A stock has an expected rate of return of 4%. What is its beta?

16. Two investment advisers are comparing performance. One averaged a 19% rate of return and the other a 16% rate of return. However, the beta of the first investor was 1.5, whereas that of the second was 1.

   a. Can you tell which investor was a better selector of individual stocks (aside from the issue of general movements in the market)?

   b. If the T-bill rate were 6% and the market return during the period were 14%, which investor would be the superior stock selector?

   c. What if the T-bill rate were 3% and the market return were 15%?

17. Suppose the rate of return on short-term government securities (perceived to be risk-free) is about 5%. Suppose also that the expected rate of return required by the market for a portfolio with a beta of 1 is 12%. According to the capital asset pricing model:

   a. What is the expected rate of return on the market portfolio?
   b. What would be the expected rate of return on a stock with $\beta = 0$?
   c. Suppose you consider buying a share of stock at $40. The stock is expected to pay $3 dividends next year and you expect it to sell then for $41. The stock risk has been evaluated at $\beta = -.5$. Is the stock overpriced or underpriced?

18. Suppose that borrowing is restricted so that the zero-beta version of the CAPM holds. The expected return on the market portfolio is 17%, and on the zero-beta portfolio it is 8%. What is the expected return on a portfolio with a beta of .6?

19. a. A mutual fund with beta of .8 has an expected rate of return of 14%. If $r_f = 5\%$, and you expect the rate of return on the market portfolio to be 15%, should you invest in this fund? What is the fund's alpha?
   b. What passive portfolio comprised of a market-index portfolio and a money market account would have the same beta as the fund? Show that the difference between the expected rate of return on this passive portfolio and that of the fund equals the alpha from part (*a*).

**Challenge
Problem**

20. Outline how you would incorporate the following into the CCAPM:

   a. Liquidity
   b. Nontraded assets (Do you have to worry about labor income?)

1. a. John Wilson is a portfolio manager at Austin & Associates. For all of his clients, Wilson manages portfolios that lie on the Markowitz efficient frontier. Wilson asks Mary Regan, CFA, a managing director at Austin, to review the portfolios of two of his clients, the Eagle Manufacturing Company and the Rainbow Life Insurance Co. The expected returns of the two portfolios are substantially different. Regan determines that the Rainbow portfolio is virtually identical to the market portfolio and concludes that the Rainbow portfolio must be superior to the Eagle portfolio. Do you agree or disagree with Regan's conclusion that the Rainbow portfolio is superior to the Eagle portfolio? Justify your response with reference to the capital market line.

   b. Wilson remarks that the Rainbow portfolio has a higher expected return because it has greater nonsystematic risk than Eagle's portfolio. Define nonsystematic risk and explain why you agree or disagree with Wilson's remark.

2. Wilson is now evaluating the expected performance of two common stocks, Furhman Labs Inc. and Garten Testing Inc. He has gathered the following information:

   • The risk-free rate is 5%.
   • The expected return on the market portfolio is 11.5%.
   • The beta of Furhman stock is 1.5.
   • The beta of Garten stock is .8.

   Based on his own analysis, Wilson's forecasts of the returns on the two stocks are 13.25% for Furhman stock and 11.25% for Garten stock. Calculate the required rate of return for Furhman Labs stock and for Garten Testing stock. Indicate whether each stock is undervalued, fairly valued, or overvalued.

3. The security market line depicts:

   a. A security's expected return as a function of its systematic risk.
   b. The market portfolio as the optimal portfolio of risky securities.

   c. The relationship between a security's return and the return on an index.

   d. The complete portfolio as a combination of the market portfolio and the risk-free asset.

4. Within the context of the capital asset pricing model (CAPM), assume:

   • Expected return on the market = 15%.

   • Risk-free rate = 8%.

   • Expected rate of return on XYZ security = 17%.

   • Beta of XYZ security = 1.25.

   Which one of the following is correct?

   a. XYZ is overpriced.

   b. XYZ is fairly priced.

   c. XYZ's alpha is −.25%.

   d. XYZ's alpha is .25%.

5. What is the expected return of a zero-beta security?

   a. Market rate of return.

   b. Zero rate of return.

   c. Negative rate of return.

   d. Risk-free rate of return.

6. Capital asset pricing theory asserts that portfolio returns are best explained by:

   a. Economic factors.

   b. Specific risk.

   c. Systematic risk.

   d. Diversification.

7. According to CAPM, the expected rate of return of a portfolio with a beta of 1.0 and an alpha of 0 is:

   a. Between r_M and r_f.

   b. The risk-free rate, r_f.

   c. $\beta (r_M - r_f)$.

   d. The expected return on the market, r_M.

The following table shows risk and return measures for two portfolios.

Portfolio	Average Annual Rate of Return	Standard Deviation	Beta
R	11%	10%	0.5
S&P 500	14%	12%	1.0

8. When plotting portfolio *R* on the preceding table relative to the SML, portfolio *R* lies:

   a. On the SML.

   b. Below the SML.

   c. Above the SML.

   d. Insufficient data given.

9. When plotting portfolio *R* relative to the capital market line, portfolio *R* lies:

   a. On the CML.

   b. Below the CML.

   c. Above the CML.

   d. Insufficient data given.

10. Briefly explain whether investors should expect a higher return from holding portfolio *A* versus portfolio *B* under capital asset pricing theory (CAPM). Assume that both portfolios are fully diversified.

	Portfolio A	Portfolio B
Systematic risk (beta)	1.0	1.0
Specific risk for each individual security	High	Low

11. Joan McKay is a portfolio manager for a bank trust department. McKay meets with two clients, Kevin Murray and Lisa York, to review their investment objectives. Each client expresses an interest in changing his or her individual investment objectives. Both clients currently hold well-diversified portfolios of risky assets.

   a. Murray wants to increase the expected return of his portfolio. State what action McKay should take to achieve Murray's objective. Justify your response in the context of the CML.

   b. York wants to reduce the risk exposure of her portfolio but does not want to engage in borrowing or lending activities to do so. State what action McKay should take to achieve York's objective. Justify your response in the context of the SML.

12. Karen Kay, a portfolio manager at Collins Asset Management, is using the capital asset pricing model for making recommendations to her clients. Her research department has developed the information shown in the following exhibit.

Forecast Returns, Standard Deviations, and Betas

	Forecast Return	Standard Deviation	Beta
Stock X	14.0%	36%	0.8
Stock Y	17.0	25	1.5
Market index	14.0	15	1.0
Risk-free rate	5.0		

   a. Calculate expected return and alpha for each stock.
   b. Identify and justify which stock would be more appropriate for an investor who wants to

   i. add this stock to a well-diversified equity portfolio.
   ii. hold this stock as a single-stock portfolio.

STANDARD &POOR'S

Go to **www.mhhe.com/edumarketinsight** and link to *Company*, then *Population*. Select a company of interest to you and link to the Company Research page. Look for the *Excel Analytics section*, and choose *Valuation Data*, then review the *Profitability* report. Find the row that shows the historical betas for your firm. Is beta stable from year to year? Go back to the *Company Research* page and look at the latest available *S&P Stock Report* for your firm. What beta does the report indicate for your firm? Why might this be different from the one in the *Profitability Report*? Based on current risk-free rates (available at **finance.yahoo.com**), and the historical risk premiums discussed in Chapter 5, estimate the expected rate of return on your company's stock by using the CAPM.

Visit us at www.mhhe.com/bkm

E-Investments

Beta and Security Returns

Fidelity provides data on the risk and return of its funds at **www.fidelity.com**. Click on the *Research* link, then choose *Mutual Funds* from the submenu. In the *Fund Evaluator* section, choose *Advanced Search*. Scroll down until you find the *Risk/ Volatility Measures* section and indicate that you want to screen for funds with betas less than or equal to .50. Click *Search Funds* to see the results. Click on the link that says *View All Matching Fidelity Funds*. Select five funds from the resulting list and click *Compare*. Rank the five funds according to their betas and then according to their standard deviations. Do both lists rank the funds in the same order? How would you explain any difference in the rankings? Note the 1-Year return for one of the funds (use the load-adjusted return if it is available). Repeat the exercise to compare five funds that have betas greater than or equal to 1.50.

SOLUTIONS TO CONCEPT CHECKS

1. We can characterize the entire population by two representative investors. One is the "uninformed" investor, who does not engage in security analysis and holds the market portfolio, whereas the other optimizes using the Markowitz algorithm with input from security analysis. The uninformed investor does not know what input the informed investor uses to make portfolio purchases. The uninformed investor knows, however, that if the other investor is informed, the market portfolio proportions will be optimal. Therefore, to depart from these proportions would constitute an uninformed bet, which will, on average, reduce the efficiency of diversification with no compensating improvement in expected returns.

2. *a.* Substituting the historical mean and standard deviation in Equation 9.2 yields a coefficient of risk aversion of

$$\overline{A} = \frac{E(r_M) - r_f}{\sigma_M^2} = \frac{.084}{.203^2} = 2.04$$

   b. This relationship also tells us that for the historical standard deviation and a coefficient of risk aversion of 3.5 the risk premium would be

$$E(r_M) - r_f = \overline{A}\sigma_M^2 = 3.5 \times .203^2 = .144 = 14.4\%$$

3. For these investment proportions, w_{Ford}, w_{GM}, the portfolio β is

$$\beta_P = w_{Ford}\beta_{Ford} + w_{GM}\beta_{GM}$$
$$= (.75 \times 1.25) + (.25 \times 1.10) = 1.2125$$

As the market risk premium, $E(r_M) - r_f$, is 8%, the portfolio risk premium will be

$$E(r_P) - r_f = \beta_P[E(r_M) - r_f]$$
$$= 1.2125 \times 8 = 9.7\%$$

4. The alpha of a stock is its expected return in excess of that required by the CAPM.

$$\alpha = E(r) - \{r_f + \beta[E(r_M) - r_f]\}$$
$$\alpha_{XYZ} = 12 - [5 + 1.0(11 - 5)] = 1\%$$
$$\alpha_{ABC} = 13 - [5 + 1.5(11 - 5)] = -1\%$$

ABC plots below the SML, while *XYZ* plots above.

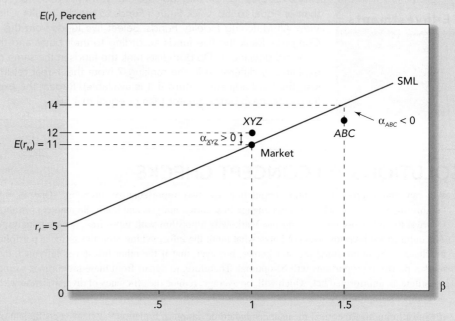

5. The project-specific required return is determined by the project beta coupled with the market risk premium and the risk-free rate. The CAPM tells us that an acceptable expected rate of return for the project is

$$r_f + \beta[E(r_M) - r_f] = 8 + 1.3(16 - 8) = 18.4\%$$

which becomes the project's hurdle rate. If the IRR of the project is 19%, then it is desirable. Any project with an IRR equal to or less than 18.4% should be rejected.

6. The CAPM is a model that relates expected rates of return to risk. It results in the expected return–beta relationship, where the expected risk premium on any asset is proportional to the expected risk premium on the market portfolio with beta as the proportionality constant. As such the model is impractical for two reasons: (i) expectations are unobservable, and (ii) the theoretical market portfolio includes every risky asset and is in practice unobservable. The next three models incorporate additional assumptions to overcome these problems.

   The single-factor model assumes that one economic factor, denoted *F*, exerts the only common influence on security returns. Beyond it, security returns are driven by independent, firm-specific factors. Thus for any security, *i*,

$$r_i = E(r_i) + \beta_i F + e_i$$

The single-index model assumes that in the single-factor model, the factor *F* can be replaced by a broad-based index of securities that can proxy for the CAPM's theoretical market portfolio. The index model can be stated as $R_i = \alpha_i + \beta_i R_M + e_i$.

   At this point it should be said that many interchange the meaning of the index and market models. The concept of the market model is that rate of return *surprises* on a stock are proportional to corresponding surprises on the market index portfolio, again with proportionality constant β.

10

ARBITRAGE PRICING THEORY AND MULTIFACTOR MODELS OF RISK AND RETURN

THE EXPLOITATION OF security mispricing in such a way that risk-free profits can be earned is called arbitrage. It involves the simultaneous purchase and sale of equivalent securities in order to profit from discrepancies in their prices. Perhaps the most basic principle of capital market theory is that equilibrium market prices are rational in that they rule out arbitrage opportunities. If actual security prices allow for arbitrage, the result will be strong pressure to restore equilibrium. Therefore, security markets ought to satisfy a "no-arbitrage condition." In this chapter, we show how such no-arbitrage conditions together with the factor model introduced in Chapter 8 allow us to generalize the security market line of the CAPM to gain richer insight into the risk–return relationship.

We begin by showing how the decomposition of risk into market versus firm-specific influences that we introduced in earlier chapters can be extended to deal with the multifaceted nature of systematic risk. Multifactor models of security returns can be used to measure and manage exposure to each of many economy-wide factors such as business-cycle risk, interest or inflation rate risk, energy price risk, and so on. These models also lead us to a multifactor version of the security market line in which risk premiums derive from exposure to multiple risk sources, each with their own risk premium.

We show how factor models combined with a no-arbitrage condition lead to a simple relationship between expected return and risk. This approach to the risk–return trade-off is called Arbitrage Pricing Theory, or APT. We derive the APT, and show why it implies a multifactor security market line. We ask next what factors are likely to be the most important sources of risk. These will be the factors generating substantial hedging demands that brought us to the multifactor CAPM introduced in Chapter 9. Both the APT and the CAPM therefore lead to multiple-risk versions of the security market line, thereby enriching the insights we can derive about the risk–return relationship.

10.1   MULTIFACTOR MODELS: AN OVERVIEW

The index model introduced in Chapter 8 gave us a way of decomposing stock variability into market or systematic risk, due largely to macroeconomic events, versus firm-specific or idiosyncratic effects that can be diversified in large portfolios. In the index model, the return on the market portfolio summarized the broad impact of macro factors. Sometimes, however, rather than using a market proxy, it is more useful to focus directly on the ultimate sources of risk. This can be useful in risk assessment when measuring one's exposures to particular sources of uncertainty. Factor models are tools that allow us to describe and quantify the different factors that affect the rate of return on a security during any time period.

Factor Models of Security Returns

To illustrate, we will start by examining a single-factor model like the one introduced in Chapter 8. As noted there, uncertainty in asset returns has two sources: a common or macroeconomic factor, and firm-specific events. The common factor is constructed to have zero expected value, because we use it to measure *new* information concerning the macro-economy which, by definition, has zero expected value.

If we call F the deviation of the common factor from its expected value, β_i the sensitivity of firm i to that factor, and e_i the firm-specific disturbance, the factor model states that the actual return on firm i will equal its initially expected return plus a (zero expected value) random amount attributable to unanticipated economywide events, plus another (zero expected value) random amount attributable to firm-specific events.

Formally, the **single-factor model** is described by Equation 10.1:

$$r_i = E(r_i) + \beta_i F + e_i \tag{10.1}$$

where $E(r_i)$ is the expected return on stock i. Notice that if the macro factor has a value of 0 in any particular period (i.e., no macro surprises), the return on the security will equal its previously expected value, $E(r_i)$, plus the effect of firm-specific events only. The nonsystematic components of returns, the e_is, are assumed to be uncorrelated among themselves and uncorrelated with the factor F.

EXAMPLE 10.1   Factor Models

To make the factor model more concrete, consider an example. Suppose that the macro factor, F, is taken to be news about the state of the business cycle, measured by the unexpected percentage change in gross domestic product (GDP), and that the consensus is that GDP will increase by 4% this year. Suppose also that a stock's β value is 1.2. If GDP increases by only 3%, then the value of F would be -1%, representing a 1% disappointment in actual growth versus expected growth. Given the stock's beta value, this disappointment would translate into a return on the stock that is 1.2% lower than previously expected. This macro surprise, together with the firm-specific disturbance, e_i, determine the total departure of the stock's return from its originally expected value.

CONCEPT CHECK

1

Suppose you currently expect the stock in Example 10.1 to earn a 10% rate of return. Then some macroeconomic news suggests that GDP growth will come in at 5% instead of 4%. How will you revise your estimate of the stock's expected rate of return?

The factor model's decomposition of returns into systematic and firm-specific components is compelling, but confining systematic risk to a single factor is not. Indeed, when we motivated the index model in Chapter 8, we noted that the systematic or macro factor summarized by the market return arises from a number of sources, for example, uncertainty about the business cycle, interest rates, inflation, and so on. The market return reflects both macro factors as well as the average sensitivity of firms to those factors. When we estimate a single-index regression, therefore, we implicitly impose an (incorrect) assumption that each stock has the same relative sensitivity to each risk factor. If stocks actually differ in their betas relative to the various macroeconomic factors, then lumping all systematic sources of risk into one variable such as the return on the market index will ignore the nuances that better explain individual-stock returns.

It stands to reason that a more explicit representation of systematic risk, allowing for the possibility that different stocks exhibit different sensitivities to its various components, would constitute a useful refinement of the single-factor model. It is easy to see that models that allow for several factors—**multifactor models**—can provide better descriptions of security returns.

Apart from their use in building models of equilibrium security pricing, multifactor models are useful in risk management applications. These models give us a simple way to measure our exposure to various macroeconomic risks, and construct portfolios to hedge those risks.

Let's start with a two-factor model. Suppose the two most important macroeconomic sources of risk are uncertainties surrounding the state of the business cycle, news of which we will again measure by unanticipated growth in GDP and changes in interest rates. We will denote by IR any unexpected change in interest rates. The return on any stock will respond both to sources of macro risk as well as to its own firm-specific influences. We therefore can write a two-factor model describing the rate of return on stock i in some time period as follows:

$$r_i = E(r_i) + \beta_{iGDP}GDP + \beta_{iIR}IR + e_i \qquad \textbf{(10.2)}$$

The two macro factors on the right-hand side of the equation comprise the systematic factors in the economy. As in the single-factor model, both of these macro factors have zero expectation: they represent changes in these variables that have not already been anticipated. The coefficients of each factor in Equation 10.2 measure the sensitivity of share returns to that factor. For this reason the coefficients are sometimes called **factor sensitivities, factor loadings,** or, equivalently, **factor betas.** An increase in interest rates is bad news for most firms, so we would expect interest rate betas generally to be negative. As before, e_i reflects firm-specific influences.

To illustrate the advantages of multifactor models, consider two firms, one a regulated electric-power utility in a mostly residential area, the other an airline. Because residential demand for electricity is not very sensitive to the business cycle, the utility has a low beta on GDP. But the utility's stock price may have a relatively high sensitivity to interest rates. Because the cash flow generated by the utility is relatively stable, its present value behaves much like that of a bond, varying inversely with interest rates. Conversely, the performance of the airline is very sensitive to economic activity but is less sensitive to interest rates. It will have a high GDP beta and a lower interest rate beta. Suppose that on a particular day, there is a piece of news suggesting that the economy will expand. GDP is expected to increase, but so are interest rates. Is the "macro news" on this day good or bad? For the utility, this is bad news: its dominant sensitivity is to rates. But for the airline, which responds more to GDP, this is good news. Clearly a one-factor or single-index model cannot capture such differential responses to varying sources of macroeconomic uncertainty.

EXAMPLE 10.2 Risk Assessment Using Multifactor Models

Suppose we estimate the two-factor model in Equation 10.2 for Northeast Airlines and find the following result:

$$r = .133 + 1.2(\text{GDP}) - .3(\text{IR}) + e$$

This tells us that based on currently available information, the expected rate of return for Northeast is 13.3%, but that for every percentage point increase in GDP beyond current expectations, the return on Northeast shares increases on average by 1.2%, while for every unanticipated percentage point that interest rates increases, Northeast's shares fall on average by .3%.

Factor betas can provide a framework for a hedging strategy. The idea for an investor who wishes to hedge a source of risk is to establish an opposite factor exposure to offset that particular source of risk. Often, futures contracts can be used to hedge particular factor exposures. We explore this application in Chapter 22.

A Multifactor Security Market Line

As it stands, the multifactor model is no more than a *description* of the factors that affect security returns. There is no "theory" in the equation. The obvious question left unanswered by a factor model like Equation 10.2 is where $E(r)$ comes from, in other words, what determines a security's expected rate of return. This is where we need a theoretical model of equilibrium security returns.

In previous chapters we developed one example of such a model: the security market line (SML) of the capital asset pricing model (CAPM). The CAPM asserts that securities will be priced to give investors an expected return comprised of two components: the risk-free rate, which is compensation for the time value of money, and a risk premium, determined by multiplying a benchmark risk premium (i.e., the risk premium offered by the market portfolio) times the relative measure of risk, beta:

$$E(r) = r_f + \beta[E(r_M) - r_f] \tag{10.3}$$

If we denote the risk premium of the market portfolio by RP_M, then a useful way to rewrite Equation 10.3 is as follows:

$$E(r) = r_f + \beta\text{RP}_M \tag{10.4}$$

We pointed out in Chapter 8 that you can think of beta as measuring the exposure of a stock or portfolio to marketwide or macroeconomic risk factors. Therefore, one interpretation of the SML is that investors are rewarded with a higher expected return for their exposure to macro risk, based on both the sensitivity to that risk (beta) as well as the compensation for bearing each unit of that source of risk (i.e., the risk premium, RP_M), but are *not* rewarded for exposure to firm-specific uncertainty (the residual term e_i in Equation 10.1).

How might this single-factor view of the world generalize once we recognize the presence of multiple sources of systematic risk? We will work out the details of the argument in the next section, but before getting lost in the trees, we will start with the lay of the forest, motivating intuitively the results that are to come. Perhaps not surprisingly, a multifactor index model gives rise to a multifactor security market line in which the risk premium is determined by the exposure to *each* systematic risk factor, and by a risk premium associated with each of those factors.

For example, in a two-factor economy in which risk exposures can be measured by Equation 10.2, we would conclude that the expected rate of return on a security would be the sum of:

1. The risk-free rate of return.
2. The sensitivity to GDP risk (i.e., the GDP beta) times the risk premium for bearing GDP risk.
3. The sensitivity to interest rate risk (i.e., the interest rate beta) times the risk premium for bearing interest rate risk.

This assertion is expressed as follows in Equation 10.5. In that equation, β_{GDP} denotes the sensitivity of the security return to unexpected changes in GDP growth, and RP_{GDP} is the risk premium associated with "one unit" of GDP exposure, that is, the exposure corresponding to a GDP beta of 1.0. Here then is a two-factor security market line.

$$E(r) = r_f + \beta_{GDP}RP_{GDP} + \beta_{IR}RP_{IR} \tag{10.5}$$

If you look back at Equation 10.4, you will see that Equation 10.5 is a generalization of the simple security market line. In the single-factor SML, the benchmark risk premium is given by the market portfolio, $RP_M = E(r_M) - r_f$, but once we generalize to multiple risk sources, each with its own risk premium, we see that the insights are highly similar.

However, one difference between a single and multiple factor economy is that a factor risk premium can be negative. For example, a security with a positive interest rate beta performs better when rates increase, and thus would hedge the value of a portfolio against interest rate risk. Investors might well accept a lower rate of return, that is, a negative risk premium, as the cost of this hedging attribute. In contrast, a more typical security that does worse when rates increase (a negative IR beta) adds to interest rate exposure, and therefore has a higher required rate of return. Equation 10.5 shows that the contribution of interest rate risk to required return for such a security would then be positive, the product of a negative-factor beta times a negative-factor risk premium.[1]

We still need to specify how to estimate the risk premium for each factor. Analogously to the simple CAPM, the risk premium associated with each factor can be thought of as the risk premium of a portfolio that has a beta of 1.0 on that particular factor and a beta of zero on all other factors. In other words, it is the risk premium one might expect to earn by taking a "pure play" on that factor. We will return to this below, but for now, let's just take the factor risk premiums as given and see how a multifactor SML might be used.

---

[1]A warning: predicting the sign of a risk premium can be tricky. For example, taken in isolation, an unanticipated drop in interest rates could signal a decline in GDP. On this basis, the interest rate factor would proxy for general economic activity and presumably carry a positive risk premium. However, because unexpected changes in GDP are also included in Equation 10.2, the interest rate beta measures sensitivity to interest rates controlling for surprises in GDP. Therefore, we expect the IR factor to have a negative risk premium. Nevertheless, it is possible that an unanticipated decline in interest rates may signal a fall in GDP in *future* periods, not captured by the contemporaneous GDP factor. In that case, a positive risk premium still would be possible.

EXAMPLE 10.3   A Multifactor SML

Think about our regression estimates for Northeast Airlines in Example 10.2. Northeast has a GDP beta of 1.2 and an interest rate beta of $-.3$. Suppose the risk premium for one unit of exposure to GDP risk is 6%, while the risk premium for one unit of exposure to interest rate risk is -7%. Then the overall risk premium on the Northeast portfolio should equal the sum of the risk premiums required as compensation for each source of systematic risk.

The risk premium attributable to GDP risk should be the stock's exposure to that risk multiplied by the risk premium of the first factor portfolio, 6%. Therefore, the portion of the firm's risk premium that is compensation for its exposure to the first factor is $1.2 \times 6\% = 7.2\%$. Similarly, the risk premium attributable to interest rate risk is $-.3 \times (-7\%) = 2.1\%$. The total risk premium should be $7.2 + 2.1 = 9.3\%$. Therefore, if the risk-free rate is 4%, the total return on Northeast Airlines should be

4.0%	Risk-free rate
+ 7.2	+ Risk premium for exposure to GDP risk
+ 2.1	+ Risk premium for exposure to interest rate risk
13.3%	Total expected return

More concisely, using Equation 10.5,

$$E(r) = 4\% + 1.2 \times 6\% + (-.3) \times (-7\%) = 13.3\%$$

The multifactor model clearly gives us a much richer way to think about risk exposures and compensation for those exposures than the single-index model or CAPM. Let us now fill in some of the gaps in the argument and more carefully explore the link between multifactor models of security returns and multifactor security market lines.

CONCEPT CHECK 2	Suppose the factor risk premiums in Example 10.3 were $RP_{GDP} = 4\%$ and $RP_{IR} = -2\%$. What would be the new value for the equilibrium expected rate of return on Northeast Airlines?

10.2   ARBITRAGE PRICING THEORY

Stephen Ross developed the **arbitrage pricing theory** (APT) in 1976.[2] Like the CAPM, the APT predicts a security market line linking expected returns to risk, but the path it takes to the SML is quite different. Ross's APT relies on three key propositions: (i) security returns can be described by a factor model; (ii) there are sufficient securities to diversify away idiosyncratic risk; and (iii) well-functioning security markets do not allow for the persistence of arbitrage opportunities. We begin with a simple version of Ross's model, which assumes that only one systematic factor affects security returns. However, the usual discussion of the APT is concerned with the multifactor case, so we treat this more general case as well.

[2]Stephen A. Ross, "Return, Risk and Arbitrage," in I. Friend and J. Bicksler, eds., *Risk and Return in Finance* (Cambridge, MA: Ballinger, 1976).

Arbitrage, Risk Arbitrage, and Equilibrium

An **arbitrage** opportunity arises when an investor can earn riskless profits without making a net investment. A trivial example of an arbitrage opportunity would arise if shares of a stock sold for different prices on two different exchanges. For example, suppose IBM sold for $95 on the NYSE but only $93 on NASDAQ. Then you could buy the shares on NASDAQ and simultaneously sell them on the NYSE, clearing a riskless profit of $2 per share without tying up any of your own capital. The **Law of One Price** states that if two assets are equivalent in all economically relevant respects, then they should have the same market price. The Law of One Price is enforced by arbitrageurs: if they observe a violation of the law, they will engage in *arbitrage activity*—simultaneously buying the asset where it is cheap and selling where it is expensive. In the process, they will bid up the price where it is low and force it down where it is high until the arbitrage opportunity is eliminated.

The idea that market prices will move to rule out arbitrage opportunities is perhaps the most fundamental concept in capital market theory. Violation of this restriction would indicate the grossest form of market irrationality.

The critical property of a risk-free arbitrage portfolio is that any investor, regardless of risk aversion or wealth, will want to take an infinite position in it. Because those large positions will quickly force prices up or down until the opportunity vanishes, security prices should satisfy a "no-arbitrage condition," that is, a condition that rules out the existence of arbitrage opportunities.

There is an important difference between arbitrage and risk–return dominance arguments in support of equilibrium price relationships. A dominance argument holds that when an equilibrium price relationship is violated, many investors will make limited portfolio changes, depending on their degree of risk aversion. Aggregation of these limited portfolio changes is required to create a large volume of buying and selling, which in turn restores equilibrium prices. By contrast, when arbitrage opportunities exist, each investor wants to take as large a position as possible; hence it will not take many investors to bring about the price pressures necessary to restore equilibrium. Therefore, implications for prices derived from no-arbitrage arguments are stronger than implications derived from a risk–return dominance argument.

The CAPM is an example of a dominance argument, implying that all investors hold mean-variance efficient portfolios. If a security is mispriced, then investors will tilt their portfolios toward the underpriced and away from the overpriced securities. Pressure on equilibrium prices results from many investors shifting their portfolios, each by a relatively small dollar amount. The assumption that a large number of investors are mean-variance sensitive is critical. In contrast, the implication of a no-arbitrage condition is that a few investors who identify an arbitrage opportunity will mobilize large dollar amounts and quickly restore equilibrium.

Practitioners often use the terms "arbitrage" and "arbitrageurs" more loosely than our strict definition. "Arbitrageur" often refers to a professional searching for mispriced securities in specific areas such as merger-target stocks, rather than to one who seeks strict (risk-free) arbitrage opportunities. Such activity is sometimes called **risk arbitrage** to distinguish it from pure arbitrage.

To leap ahead, in Part Four we will discuss "derivative" securities such as futures and options, whose market values are determined by prices of other securities. For example, the value of a call option on a stock is determined by the price of the stock. For such securities, strict arbitrage is a practical possibility, and the condition of no-arbitrage leads to exact pricing. In the case of stocks and other "primitive" securities whose values are not determined strictly by another asset or bundle of assets, no-arbitrage conditions must be obtained by appealing to diversification arguments.

Well-Diversified Portfolios

Now we look at the risk of a portfolio of stocks. We first show that if a portfolio is well diversified, its firm-specific or nonfactor risk becomes negligible, so that only factor (or systematic) risk remains. If we construct an n-stock portfolio with weights w_i, $\Sigma w_i = 1$, then the rate of return on this portfolio is as follows:

$$r_P = E(r_P) + \beta_P F + e_P \tag{10.6}$$

where

$$\beta_P = \Sigma w_i \beta_i; \quad E(r_P) = \Sigma w_i E(r_i)$$

are the weighted averages of the β_i and expected returns of the n securities. The portfolio nonsystematic component (which is uncorrelated with F) is $e_P = \Sigma w_i e_i$ which similarly is a weighted average of the e_i of the n securities.

We can divide the variance of this portfolio into systematic and nonsystematic sources, as we saw in Chapter 8. The portfolio variance is

$$\sigma_P^2 = \beta_P^2 \sigma_F^2 + \sigma^2(e_P)$$

where σ_F^2 is the variance of the factor F and $\sigma^2(e_P)$ is the nonsystematic risk of the portfolio, which is given by

$$\sigma^2(e_P) = \text{Variance}(\Sigma w_i e_i) = \Sigma w_i^2 \sigma^2(e_i)$$

Note that in deriving the nonsystematic variance of the portfolio, we depend on the fact that the firm-specific e_is are uncorrelated and hence that the variance of the "portfolio" of nonsystematic e_is is the weighted sum of the individual nonsystematic variances with the *square* of the investment proportions as weights.

If the portfolio were equally weighted, $w_i = 1/n$, then the nonsystematic variance would be

$$\sigma^2(e_P) = \text{Variance}(\Sigma w_i e_i) = \sum \left(\frac{1}{n}\right)^2 \sigma^2(e_i) = \frac{1}{n} \sum \frac{\sigma^2(e_i)}{n} = \frac{1}{n} \bar{\sigma}^2(e_i)$$

where the last term is the average value across securities of nonsystematic variance. In words, the nonsystematic variance of the portfolio equals the average nonsystematic variance divided by n. Therefore, when the portfolio gets large in the sense that n is large, its nonsystematic variance approaches zero. This is the effect of diversification.

We conclude that for the equally weighted portfolio, the nonsystematic variance approaches zero as n becomes ever larger. This property is true of portfolios other than the equally weighted one. *Any* portfolio for which each w_i becomes consistently smaller as n gets large (more precisely, for which each w_i^2 approaches zero as n increases) will satisfy the condition that the portfolio nonsystematic risk will approach zero. In fact, this property motivates us to define a **well-diversified portfolio** as one that is diversified over a large enough number of securities, with each weight, w_i, small enough that for practical purposes the nonsystematic variance, $\sigma^2(e_P)$, is negligible.

Because the expected value of e_P for any well-diversified portfolio is zero, and its variance also is effectively zero, we can conclude that any realized value of e_P will be virtually zero. Rewriting Equation 10.1, we conclude that for a well-diversified portfolio, for all practical purposes

$$r_P = E(r_P) + \beta_P F$$

Large (mostly institutional) investors can hold portfolios of hundreds and even thousands of securities; thus the concept of well-diversified portfolios clearly is operational in contemporary financial markets.

a. A portfolio is invested in a very large number of shares (n is large). The standard deviation of the residual return of any of these stocks is not so large as to overwhelm the rest of the portfolio. (More precisely, $\text{Var}(e_i)$ is of lower order than $n\text{Var}(r_M)$ for all firms.) However, one-half of the portfolio is invested in stock 1, and the rest of the portfolio is equally divided among the other $n - 1$ shares. Is this portfolio well diversified?

b. Another portfolio also is invested in the same n shares, where n is very large. Instead of equally weighting with portfolio weights of $1/n$ in each stock, the weights in half the securities are $1.5/n$ while the weights in the other shares are $.5/n$. Is this portfolio well diversified?

Betas and Expected Returns

Because nonfactor risk can be diversified away, only factor risk should command a risk premium in market equilibrium. Nonsystematic risk across firms cancels out in well-diversified portfolios; one would not expect investors to be rewarded for bearing risk that can be eliminated through diversification. Instead, only the systematic risk of a portfolio of securities should be related to its expected returns.

The solid line in Figure 10.1A plots the return of a well-diversified portfolio A with $\beta_A = 1$ for various realizations of the systematic factor. The expected return of portfolio A is 10%; this is where the solid line crosses the vertical axis. At this point the systematic factor is zero, implying no macro surprises. If the macro factor is positive, the portfolio's return exceeds its expected value; if it is negative, the portfolio's return falls short of its mean. The return on the portfolio is therefore

$$E(r_A) + \beta_A F = 10\% + 1.0 \times F$$

Compare Figure 10.1A with Figure 10.1B, which is a similar graph for a single stock (S) with $\beta_s = 1$. The undiversified stock is subject to nonsystematic risk, which is seen in a scatter of points around the line. The well-diversified portfolio's return, in contrast, is determined completely by the systematic factor.

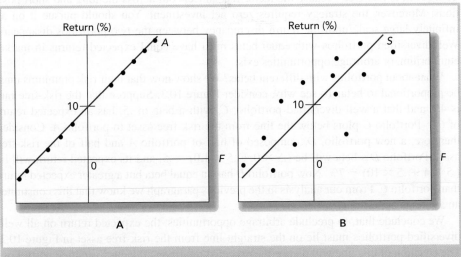

FIGURE 10.1   Returns as a function of the systematic factor.
Panel A, well-diversified portfolio A. **Panel B,** single stock (S).

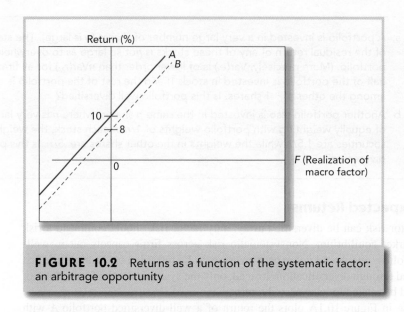

FIGURE 10.2   Returns as a function of the systematic factor: an arbitrage opportunity

Now consider Figure 10.2, where the dashed line plots the return on another well-diversified portfolio, portfolio *B,* with an expected return of 8% and β_B also equal to 1. Could portfolios *A* and *B* coexist with the return pattern depicted? Clearly not: No matter what the systematic factor turns out to be, portfolio *A* outperforms portfolio *B,* leading to an arbitrage opportunity.

If you sell short $1 million of *B* and buy $1 million of *A,* a zero net investment strategy, your riskless payoff would be $20,000, as follows:

$$\begin{array}{ll} (.10 + 1.0 \times F) \times \$1 \text{ million} & \text{from long position in } A \\ \underline{-(.08 + 1.0 \times F) \times \$1 \text{ million}} & \text{from short position in } B \\ .02 \times \$1 \text{ million} = \$20{,}000 & \text{net proceeds} \end{array}$$

Your profit is risk-free because the factor risk cancels out across the long and short positions. Moreover, the strategy requires zero net investment. You should pursue it on an infinitely large scale until the return discrepancy between the two portfolios disappears. Well-diversified portfolios with equal betas must have equal expected returns in market equilibrium, or arbitrage opportunities exist.

What about portfolios with different betas? We show now that their risk premiums must be proportional to beta. To see why, consider Figure 10.3. Suppose that the risk-free rate is 4% and that a well-diversified portfolio, *C,* with a beta of .5, has an expected return of 6%. Portfolio *C* plots below the line from the risk-free asset to portfolio *A.* Consider, therefore, a new portfolio, *D,* composed of half of portfolio *A* and half of the risk-free asset. Portfolio *D*'s beta will be $(.5 \times 0 + .5 \times 1.0) = .5$, and its expected return will be $(.5 \times 4 + .5 \times 10) = 7\%$. Now portfolio *D* has an equal beta but a greater expected return than portfolio *C.* From our analysis in the previous paragraph we know that this constitutes an arbitrage opportunity.

We conclude that, to preclude arbitrage opportunities, the expected return on all well-diversified portfolios must lie on the straight line from the risk-free asset in Figure 10.3. The equation of this line will dictate the expected return on all well-diversified portfolios.

Notice in Figure 10.3 that risk premiums are indeed proportional to portfolio betas. The risk premium is depicted by the vertical arrow, which measures the distance between the

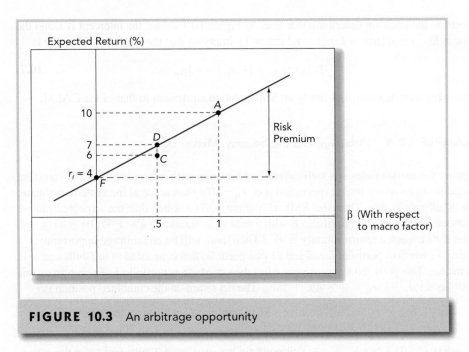

FIGURE 10.3 An arbitrage opportunity

risk-free rate and the expected return on the portfolio. The risk premium is zero for $\beta = 0$ and rises in direct proportion to β.

The One-Factor Security Market Line

Now consider the market index portfolio, *M*, as a well-diversified portfolio, and let us measure the systematic factor as the unexpected return on that portfolio. Because the index portfolio must be on the line in Figure 10.4 and the beta of the index portfolio is 1, we can

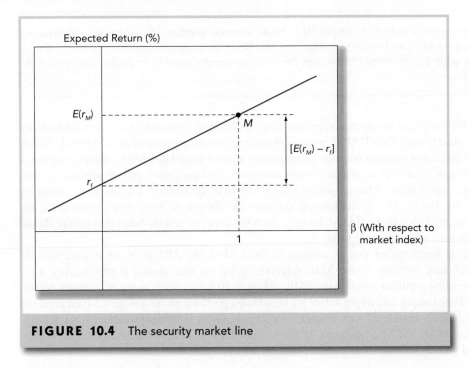

FIGURE 10.4 The security market line

determine the equation describing that line. As Figure 10.4 shows, the intercept is r_f and the slope is $E(r_M) - r_f$ [rise $= E(r_M) - r_f$; run $= 1$], implying that the equation of the line is

$$E(r_P) = r_f + [E(r_M) - r_f]\beta_P \qquad (10.7)$$

Hence, Figures 10.3 and 10.4 imply an SML relation equivalent to that of the CAPM.

EXAMPLE 10.4   Arbitrage and the Security Market Line

Suppose the market index is a well-diversified portfolio with expected return 10% and that deviations of its return from expectation (i.e., $r_M - 10\%$) can serve as the systematic factor. The T-bill rate is 4%. Then the SML (Equation 10.7) implies that the expected rate of return on well-diversified portfolio E with a beta of $\frac{2}{3}$ should be $4\% + \frac{2}{3}(10 - 4) = 8\%$. What if its expected return actually is 9%? Then there will be an arbitrage opportunity.

Buy $1 worth of portfolio E and sell $1 of a portfolio that is invested $\frac{1}{3}$ in T-bills and $\frac{2}{3}$ in the market. This portfolio by construction has the same beta as portfolio E. The return on this portfolio is $\frac{1}{3}r_f + \frac{2}{3}r_M = \frac{1}{3} \times 4\% + \frac{2}{3}r_M$. The net return on the combined position is:

$1 \times [.09 + \frac{2}{3}(r_M - .10)]$	Invest $1 in portfolio E, with expected return 9% and beta of $\frac{2}{3}$ on surprise in market return.
$-\$1(\frac{1}{3} \times .04 + \frac{2}{3}r_M)$	Sell portfolio invested $\frac{1}{3}$ in T-bills and $\frac{2}{3}$ in the market index.
$1 \times .01$	Total

The profit per dollar invested is risk-free and precisely equal to the deviation of the expected return on portfolio E from the SML.

CONCEPT CHECK 4

Continue to use the data in Example 10.4. Now consider portfolio G, which is well diversified with a beta of $\frac{1}{3}$ and expected return of 5%. Does an arbitrage opportunity exist? If so, what is the arbitrage strategy? Show that the strategy results in risk-free profits with zero net investment.

We have used the no-arbitrage condition to obtain an expected return–beta relationship identical to that of the CAPM, without the restrictive assumptions of the CAPM. As noted, this derivation depends on three assumptions: a factor model describing security returns, a sufficient number of securities to form well-diversified portfolios, and the absence of arbitrage opportunities. This last restriction gives rise to the name of the approach: Arbitrage Pricing Theory. Our demonstration suggests that despite its restrictive assumptions, the main conclusion of the CAPM, namely, the SML expected return–beta relationship, should be at least approximately valid.

It is worth noting that in contrast to the CAPM, the APT does not require that the benchmark portfolio in the SML relationship be the true market portfolio. Any well-diversified portfolio lying on the SML of Figure 10.4 may serve as the benchmark portfolio. For example, one might define the benchmark portfolio as the well-diversified portfolio most highly correlated with whatever systematic factor is thought to affect stock returns. Accordingly, the APT has more flexibility than does the CAPM because problems associated with an unobservable market portfolio are not a concern.

In addition, the APT provides further justification for use of the index model in the practical implementation of the SML relationship. Even if the index portfolio is not a precise proxy for the true market portfolio, which is a cause of considerable concern in the context of the CAPM, we now know that if the index portfolio is sufficiently well diversified, the SML relationship should still hold true according to the APT.

So far we have demonstrated the APT relationship for well-diversified portfolios only. The CAPM expected return–beta relationship applies to single assets, as well as to portfolios. In the next section we generalize the APT result one step further.

10.3 INDIVIDUAL ASSETS AND THE APT

We have demonstrated that if arbitrage opportunities are to be ruled out, each well-diversified portfolio's expected excess return must be proportional to its beta. The question is whether this relationship tells us anything about the expected returns on the component stocks. The answer is that if this relationship is to be satisfied by all well-diversified portfolios, it must be satisfied by *almost* all individual securities, although a full proof of this proposition is somewhat difficult. We can illustrate the argument less formally.

Suppose that the expected return–beta relationship is violated for all single assets. Now create a pair of well-diversified portfolios from these assets. What are the chances that in spite of the fact that for any pair of assets the relationship does *not* hold, the relationship *will* hold for both well-diversified portfolios? The chances are small, but it is possible that the relationships among the single securities are violated in offsetting ways so that somehow it holds for the pair of well-diversified portfolios.

Now construct yet a third well-diversified portfolio. What are the chances that the violations of the relationships for single securities are such that the third portfolio also will fulfill the no-arbitrage expected return–beta relationship? Obviously, the chances are smaller still, but the relationship is possible. Continue with a fourth well-diversified portfolio, and so on. If the no-arbitrage expected return–beta relationship has to hold for infinitely many different, well-diversified portfolios, it must be virtually certain that the relationship holds for all but a small number of individual securities.

We use the term *virtually certain* advisedly because we must distinguish this conclusion from the statement that all securities surely fulfill this relationship. The reason we cannot make the latter statement has to do with a property of well-diversified portfolios.

Recall that to qualify as well diversified, a portfolio must have very small positions in all securities. If, for example, only one security violates the expected return–beta relationship, then the effect of this violation on a well-diversified portfolio will be too small to be of importance for any practical purpose, and meaningful arbitrage opportunities will not arise. But if many securities violate the expected return–beta relationship, the relationship will no longer hold for well-diversified portfolios, and arbitrage opportunities will be available. Consequently, we conclude that imposing the no-arbitrage condition on a single-factor security market implies maintenance of the expected return–beta relationship for all well-diversified portfolios and for all but possibly a *small* number of individual securities.

The APT and the CAPM

The APT serves many of the same functions as the CAPM. It gives us a benchmark for rates of return that can be used in capital budgeting, security valuation, or investment performance evaluation. Moreover, the APT highlights the crucial distinction between nondiversifiable risk (factor risk) that requires a reward in the form of a risk premium and diversifiable risk that does not.

The APT is an extremely appealing model. It depends on the assumption that a rational equilibrium in capital markets precludes arbitrage opportunities. A violation of the APT's pricing relationships will cause extremely strong pressure to restore them even if only a limited number of investors become aware of the disequilibrium. Furthermore, the APT yields an expected return–beta relationship using a well-diversified portfolio that practically can be constructed from a large number of securities.

In contrast, the CAPM is derived assuming an inherently unobservable "market" portfolio. The CAPM argument rests on mean-variance efficiency; that is, if any security violates the expected return–beta relationship, then many investors (each relatively small) will tilt their portfolios so that their combined overall pressure on prices will restore an equilibrium that satisfies the relationship.

In spite of these apparent advantages, the APT does not fully dominate the CAPM. The CAPM provides an unequivocal statement on the expected return–beta relationship for all securities, whereas the APT implies that this relationship holds for all but perhaps a small number of securities. Because it focuses on the no-arbitrage condition, without the further assumptions of the market or index model, the APT cannot rule out a violation of the expected return–beta relationship for any particular asset. For this, we need the CAPM assumptions and its dominance arguments.

10.4 A MULTIFACTOR APT

We have assumed so far that there is only one systematic factor affecting stock returns. This simplifying assumption is in fact too simplistic. We've noted that it is easy to think of several factors driven by the business cycle that might affect stock returns: interest rate fluctuations, inflation rates, oil prices, and so on. Presumably, exposure to any of these factors will affect a stock's risk and hence its expected return. We can derive a multifactor version of the APT to accommodate these multiple sources of risk.

Suppose that we generalize the factor model expressed in Equation 10.1 to a two-factor model:

$$r_i = E(r_i) + \beta_{i1}F_1 + \beta_{i2}F_2 + e_i \tag{10.8}$$

In Example 10.2, factor 1 was the departure of GDP growth from expectations, and factor 2 was the unanticipated change in interest rates. Each factor has zero expected value because each measures the *surprise* in the systematic variable rather than the level of the variable. Similarly, the firm-specific component of unexpected return, e_i, also has zero expected value. Extending such a two-factor model to any number of factors is straightforward.

Establishing a multifactor APT is similar to the one-factor case. But first we must introduce the concept of a **factor portfolio,** which is a well-diversified portfolio constructed to have a beta of 1 on one of the factors and a beta of zero on any other factor. We can think of a factor portfolio as a *tracking portfolio.* That is, the returns on such a portfolio track the evolution of particular sources of macroeconomic risk, but are uncorrelated with other sources of risk. It is possible to form such factor portfolios because we have a large number of securities to choose from, and a relatively small number of factors. Factor portfolios will serve as the benchmark portfolios for a multifactor security market line.

EXAMPLE 10.5 Multifactor SML

Suppose that the two factor portfolios, portfolios 1 and 2, have expected returns $E(r_1) = 10\%$ and $E(r_2) = 12\%$. Suppose further that the risk-free rate is 4%. The risk premium on the first factor portfolio is $10\% - 4\% = 6\%$, whereas that on the second factor portfolio is $12\% - 4\% = 8\%$.

Now consider a well-diversified portfolio, portfolio A, with beta on the first factor, $\beta_{A1} = .5$, and beta on the second factor, $\beta_{A2} = .75$. The multifactor APT states that the overall risk premium on this portfolio must equal the sum of the risk premiums required as compensation for each source of systematic risk. The risk premium attributable to risk factor 1 should be the portfolio's exposure to factor 1, β_{A1}, multiplied by the risk premium earned on the first factor portfolio, $E(r_1) - r_f$. Therefore, the portion of portfolio A's risk premium that is compensation for its exposure to the first factor is $\beta_{A1}[E(r_1) - r_f] = .5(10\% - 4\%) = 3\%$, whereas the risk premium attributable to risk factor 2 is $\beta_{A2}[E(r_2) - r_f] = .75(12\% - 4\%) = 6\%$. The total risk premium on the portfolio should be $3 + 6 = 9\%$ and the total return on the portfolio should be $4\% + 9\% = 13\%$.

To generalize the argument in Example 10.5, note that the factor exposures of any portfolio, P, are given by its betas, β_{P1} and β_{P2}. A competing portfolio, Q, can be formed by investing in factor portfolios with the following weights: β_{P1} in the first factor portfolio, β_{P2} in the second factor portfolio, and $1 - \beta_{P1} - \beta_{P2}$ in T-bills. By construction, portfolio Q will have betas equal to those of portfolio P and expected return of

$$E(r_Q) = \beta_{P1}E(r_1) + \beta_{P2}E(r_2) + (1 - \beta_{P1} - \beta_{P2})r_f$$
$$= r_f + \beta_{P1}[E(r_1) - r_f] + \beta_{P2}[E(r_2) - r_f] \tag{10.9}$$

Using the numbers in Example 10.5:

$$E(r_Q) = 4 + .5 \times (10 - 4) + .75 \times (12 - 4) = 13\%$$

EXAMPLE 10.6 Mispricing and Arbitrage

Suppose that the expected return on portfolio A from Example 10.5 were 12% rather than 13%. This return would give rise to an arbitrage opportunity. Form a portfolio from the factor portfolios with the same betas as portfolio A. This requires weights of .5 on the first factor portfolio, .75 on the second factor portfolio, and $-.25$ on the risk-free asset. This portfolio has exactly the same factor betas as portfolio A: It has a beta of .5 on the first factor because of its .5 weight on the first factor portfolio, and a beta of .75 on the second factor. (The weight of $-.25$ on risk-free T-bills does not affect the sensitivity to either factor.)

Now invest $1 in portfolio Q and sell (short) $1 in portfolio A. Your net investment is zero, but your expected dollar profit is positive and equal to

$$\$1 \times E(r_Q) - \$1 \times E(r_A) = \$1 \times .13 - \$1 \times .12 = \$.01$$

Moreover, your net position is riskless. Your exposure to each risk factor cancels out because you are long $1 in portfolio Q and short $1 in portfolio A, and both of these well-diversified portfolios have exactly the same factor betas. Thus, if portfolio A's expected return differs from that of portfolio Q's, you can earn positive risk-free profits on a zero net investment position. This is an arbitrage opportunity.

Because portfolio Q has precisely the same exposures as portfolio A to the two sources of risk, their expected returns also ought to be equal. So portfolio A also ought to have an expected return of 13%. If it does not, then there will be an arbitrage opportunity.[3]

We conclude that any well-diversified portfolio with betas β_{P1} and β_{P2} must have the return given in Equation 10.9 if arbitrage opportunities are to be precluded. If you compare Equations 10.3 and 10.9, you will see that Equation 10.9 is simply a generalization of the one-factor SML.

Finally, the extension of the multifactor SML of Equation 10.9 to individual assets is precisely the same as for the one-factor APT. Equation 10.9 cannot be satisfied by every well-diversified portfolio unless it is satisfied by virtually every security taken individually. Equation 10.9 thus represents the multifactor SML for an economy with multiple sources of risk.

We pointed out earlier that one application of the CAPM is to provide "fair" rates of return for regulated utilities. The multifactor APT can be used to the same ends. The nearby box summarizes a study in which the APT was applied to find the cost of capital for regulated electric companies. Notice that empirical estimates for interest rate and inflation risk premiums in the box are negative, as we argued was reasonable in our discussion of Example 10.2.

| CONCEPT CHECK 5 | Using the factor portfolios of Example 10.5, find the equilibrium rate of return on a portfolio with $\beta_1 = .2$ and $\beta_2 = 1.4$. |

10.5 WHERE SHOULD WE LOOK FOR FACTORS?

One shortcoming of the multifactor APT is that it gives no guidance concerning the determination of the relevant risk factors or their risk premiums. Two principles guide us when we specify a reasonable list of factors. First, we want to limit ourselves to systematic factors with considerable ability to explain security returns. If our model calls for many explanatory variables, it does little to simplify our description of security returns. Second, we wish to choose factors that seem likely to be important risk factors, that is, factors that concern investors sufficiently that they will demand meaningful risk premiums to bear exposure to those sources of risk.

One example of the multifactor approach is the work of Chen, Roll, and Ross[4] who chose the following set of factors based on the ability of these factors to paint a broad picture of the macroeconomy. Their set is obviously but one of many possible sets that might be considered.

IP = % change in industrial production

EI = % change in expected inflation

UI = % change in unanticipated inflation

CG = excess return of long-term corporate bonds over long-term government bonds

GB = excess return of long-term government bonds over T-bills

---

[3]The risk premium on portfolio A is 9% (more than the historical risk premium of the S&P 500) despite the fact that its betas, which are both below 1, might *seem* defensive. This highlights another distinction between multifactor and single-factor models. Whereas a beta greater than 1 in a single-factor market is aggressive, we cannot say in advance what would be aggressive or defensive in a multifactor economy where risk premiums depend on the sum of the contributions of several factors.

[4]N. Chen, R. Roll, and S. Ross, "Economic Forces and the Stock Market," *Journal of Business* 59 (1986), pp. 383–403.

USING THE APT TO FIND COST OF CAPITAL

Elton, Gruber, and Mei* use the APT to derive the cost of capital for electric utilities. They assume that the relevant risk factors are unanticipated developments in the term structure of interest rates, the level of interest rates, inflation rates, the business cycle (measured by GDP), foreign exchange rates, and a summary measure they devise to measure other macro factors.

Their first step is to estimate the risk premium associated with exposure to each risk source. They accomplish this in a two-step strategy (which we will describe in considerable detail in Chapter 13):

1. *Estimate "factor loadings" (i.e., betas) of a large sample of firms.* Regress returns of 100 randomly selected stocks against the systematic risk factors. They use a time-series regression for each stock (e.g., 60 months of data), therefore estimating 100 regressions, one for each stock.

2. *Estimate the reward earned per unit of exposure to each risk factor.* For each month, regress the return of each stock against the five betas estimated. The coefficient on each beta is the extra average return earned as beta increases, i.e., it is an estimate of the risk premium for that risk factor from that month's data. These estimates are of course subject to sampling error. Therefore, average the risk premium estimates across the 12 months in each year. The *average* response of return to risk is less subject to sampling error.

The risk premiums are in the second column of the table at the top of the next column.

Notice that some risk premiums are negative. The interpretation of this result is that risk premium should be positive for risk factors you don't want exposure to, but *negative* for factors you *do* want exposure to. For example, you should desire securities that have higher returns when inflation increases and be willing to accept lower expected returns on such securities; this shows up as a negative risk premium.

Factor	Factor Risk Premium	Factor Betas for Niagra Mohawk
Term structure	.425	1.0615
Interest rates	−.051	−2.4167
Exchange rates	−.049	1.3235
Business cycle	.041	.1292
Inflation	−.069	−.5220
Other macro factors	.530	.3046

Therefore, the expected return on any security should be related to its factor betas as follows:

$$r_f + .425\,\beta_{\text{term struc}} - .051\,\beta_{\text{int rate}}$$
$$-.049\,\beta_{\text{ex rate}} + .041\,\beta_{\text{bus cycle}} - .069\,\beta_{\text{inflation}} + .530\,\beta_{\text{other}}$$

Finally, to obtain the cost of capital for a particular firm, the authors estimate the firm's betas against each source of risk, multiply each factor beta by the "cost of factor risk" from the table above, sum over all risk sources to obtain the total risk premium, and add the risk-free rate.

For example, the beta estimates for Niagra Mohawk appear in the last column of the table above. Therefore, its cost of capital is

$$\text{Cost of capital} = r_f + .425 \times 1.0615 - .051(-2.4167)$$
$$- .049(1.3235) + .041(.1292)$$
$$- .069(-.5220) + .530(.3046)$$
$$= r_f + .72$$

In other words, the monthly cost of capital for Niagra Mohawk is .72% above the monthly risk-free rate. Its annualized risk premium is therefore .72% × 12 = 8.64%.

*Edwin J. Elton, Martin J. Gruber, and Jianping Mei, "Cost of Capital Using Arbitrage Pricing Theory: A Case Study of Nine New York Utilities," *Financial Markets, Institutions, and Instruments* 3 (August 1994), pp. 46–68.

This list gives rise to the following five-factor model of security returns during holding period *t* as a function of the change in the set of macroeconomic indicators:

$$r_{it} = \alpha_i + \beta_{i\text{IP}}\text{IP}_t + \beta_{i\text{EI}}\text{EI}_t + \beta_{i\text{UI}}\text{UI}_t + \beta_{i\text{CG}}\text{CG}_t + \beta_{i\text{GB}}\text{GB}_t + e_{it} \qquad \textbf{(10.10)}$$

Equation 10.10 is a multidimensional security characteristic line (SCL), with five factors. As before, to estimate the betas of a given stock we can use regression analysis. Here, however, because there is more than one factor, we estimate a *multiple* regression of the returns of the stock in each period on the five macroeconomic factors. The residual variance of the regression estimates the firm-specific risk. We discuss the results of this model in Chapter 13, which focuses on empirical evidence on security pricing.

The Fama-French (FF) Three-Factor Model

An alternative approach to specifying macroeconomic factors as candidates for relevant sources of systematic risk uses firm characteristics that seem on empirical grounds to proxy for exposure to systematic risk. The factors chosen are variables that on past evidence seem to predict average returns well and therefore may be capturing risk premiums. One example of this approach is the Fama and French three-factor model, which has come to dominate empirical research and industry applications:[5]

$$r_{it} = \alpha_i + \beta_{iM}R_{Mt} + \beta_{iSMB}\text{SMB}_t + \beta_{iHML}\text{HML}_t + e_{it} \tag{10.11}$$

where

SMB = Small Minus Big, i.e., the return of a portfolio of small stocks in excess of the return on a portfolio of large stocks.

HML = High Minus Low, i.e., the return of a portfolio of stocks with a high book-to-market ratio in excess of the return on a portfolio of stocks with a low book-to-market ratio.

Note that in this model the market index does play a role and is expected to capture systematic risk originating from macroeconomic factors.

These two firm-characteristic variables are chosen because of long-standing observations that corporate capitalization (firm size) and book-to-market ratio predict deviations of average stock returns from levels consistent with the CAPM. Fama and French justify this model on empirical grounds: While SMB and HML are not themselves obvious candidates for relevant risk factors, the hope is that these variables proxy for yet-unknown more-fundamental variables. For example, Fama and French point out that firms with high ratios of book-to-market value are more likely to be in financial distress and that small stocks may be more sensitive to changes in business conditions. Thus, these variables may capture sensitivity to risk factors in the macroeconomy. More evidence on the Fama-French model appears in Chapter 13.

The problem with empirical approaches such as the Fama-French model, which use proxies for extramarket sources of risk, is that none of the factors in the proposed models can be clearly identified as hedging a significant source of uncertainty. Black[6] points out that when researchers scan and rescan the database of security returns in search of explanatory factors (an activity often called data-snooping), they may eventually uncover past "patterns" that are due purely to chance. Black observes that return premiums to factors such as firm size have proven to be inconsistent since first discovered. However, Fama and French have shown that size and book-to-market ratios have predicted average returns in various time periods and in markets all over the world, thus mitigating potential effects of data-snooping.

The firm-characteristic basis of the Fama-French factors raises the question of whether they reflect an APT model or an approximation to a multi-index ICAPM based on extramarket hedging demands. This is an important distinction for the debate over the proper interpretation of the model, because the validity of FF-style models may constitute either a deviation from rational equilibrium (as there is no rational reason to prefer one or another of these firm characteristics per se), or that firm characteristics identified as empirically associated with average returns are correlated with other (yet unknown) risk factors.

The issue is still unresolved and is discussed in Chapter 13.

---

[5]Eugene F. Fama and Kenneth R. French, "Multifactor Explanations of Asset Pricing Anomalies," *The Journal of Finance* 51 (1996), pp. 55–84.

[6]Fischer Black, "Beta and Return," *Journal of Portfolio Management* 20 (1993), pp. 8–18.

10.6 THE MULTIFACTOR CAPM AND THE APT

It is important to distinguish the multifactor APT from the multi-index CAPM. In the latter, the factors are derived from a multiperiod consideration of a stream of consumption as well as randomly evolving investment opportunities pertaining to the distributions of rates of return. Hence, the hedge index portfolios must be derived from considerations of the utility of consumption, nontraded assets, and changes in investment opportunities.

A multi-index CAPM therefore will inherit its risk factors from sources of risk that a broad group of investors deem important enough to hedge. If hedging demands are common to many investors, the prices of securities with desirable hedging characteristics will be bid up and their expected return reduced. This process requires a multifactor model to explain expected returns, where each factor arises from a particular hedging motive. Risk sources that are "priced" in market equilibrium (that is, are sufficiently important to result in detectable risk premiums) presumably will be systematic sources of uncertainty that affect investors broadly.

In contrast, the APT is largely silent on where to look for priced sources of risk. This lack of guidance is problematic, but by the same token, it accommodates a less structured search for relevant risk factors. These may reflect the concerns of a broader set of investors, including institutions such as endowment or pension funds that may be concerned about exposures to risks that would not be obvious from an examination of individual consumption/investment decisions.

CONCEPT CHECK 6	Consider the following regression results for stock X. $$r_X = 2\% + 1.2 \text{ (percentage change in oil prices)}$$ a. If I live in Louisiana, where the local economy is heavily dependent on oil industry profits, does stock X represent a useful asset to hedge my overall economic well-being? b. What if I live in Massachusetts, where most individuals and firms are energy *consumers*? c. If energy consumers are far more numerous than energy producers, will high oil-beta stocks have higher or lower expected rates of return in market equilibrium than low oil-beta stocks?

SUMMARY

1. Multifactor models seek to improve the explanatory power of single-factor models by explicitly accounting for the various systematic components of security risk. These models use indicators intended to capture a wide range of macroeconomic risk factors.

2. Once we allow for multiple risk factors, we conclude that the security market line also ought to be multidimensional, with exposure to each risk factor contributing to the total risk premium of the security.

3. A (risk-free) arbitrage opportunity arises when two or more security prices enable investors to construct a zero net investment portfolio that will yield a sure profit. The presence of arbitrage opportunities will generate a large volume of trades that puts pressure on security prices. This pressure will continue until prices reach levels that preclude such arbitrage.

4. When securities are priced so that there are no risk-free arbitrage opportunities, we say that they satisfy the no-arbitrage condition. Price relationships that satisfy the no-arbitrage condition are important because we expect them to hold in real-world markets.

Visit us at www.mhhe.com/bkm

a. How could you construct an arbitrage portfolio? (*Hint:* Consider combinations of portfolios A and B, and compare the resultant portfolio to C.)

b. Some researchers have examined the relationship between average returns on diversified portfolios and the β and β^2 of those portfolios. What should they have discovered about the effect of β^2 on portfolio return?

10. Consider the following multifactor (APT) model of security returns for a particular stock.

Factor	Factor Beta	Factor Risk Premium
Inflation	1.2	6%
Industrial production	0.5	8
Oil prices	0.3	3

a. If T-bills currently offer a 6% yield, find the expected rate of return on this stock if the market views the stock as fairly priced.

b. Suppose that the market expected the values for the three macro factors given in column 1 below, but that the actual values turn out as given in column 2. Calculate the revised expectations for the rate of return on the stock once the "surprises" become known.

Factor	Expected Rate of Change	Actual Rate of Change
Inflation	5%	4%
Industrial production	3	6
Oil prices	2	0

11. Suppose that the market can be described by the following three sources of systematic risk with associated risk premiums.

Factor	Risk Premium
Industrial production (I)	6%
Interest rates (R)	2
Consumer confidence (C)	4

The return on a particular stock is generated according to the following equation:

$$r = 15\% + 1.0I + .5R + .75C + e$$

Find the equilibrium rate of return on this stock using the APT. The T-bill rate is 6%. Is the stock over- or underpriced? Explain.

12. As a finance intern at Pork Products, Jennifer Wainwright's assignment is to come up with fresh insights concerning the firm's cost of capital. She decides that this would be a good opportunity to try out the new material on the APT that she learned last semester. She decides that three promising factors would be (i) the return on a broad-based index such as the S&P 500; (ii) the level of interest rates, as represented by the yield to maturity on 10-year Treasury bonds; and (iii) the price of hogs, which are particularly important to her firm. Her plan is to find the beta of Pork Products against each of these factors by using a multiple regression and to estimate the risk premium associated with each exposure factor. Comment on Jennifer's choice of factors. Which are most promising with respect to the likely impact on her firm's cost of capital? Can you suggest improvements to her specification?

Challenge Problems

13. Assume a universe of n (large) securities for which the largest residual variance is of an order not larger than $n\sigma_M^2$. Construct as many different weighting schemes as you can that generate well-diversified portfolios.

14. Derive a more general (than the numerical example in the chapter) demonstration of the APT security market line:

a. For a single-factor market.

b. For a multifactor market.

15. Small firms will have relatively high loadings (high betas) on the SMB (small minus big) factor.

    a. Explain why.

    b. Now suppose two unrelated small firms merge. Each will be operated as an independent unit of the merged company. Would you expect the stock market behavior of the merged firm to differ from that of a portfolio of the two previously independent firms? How does the merger affect market capitalization? What is the prediction of the Fama-French model for the risk premium on the combined firm? Do we see here a flaw in the FF model?

---

1. Jeffrey Bruner, CFA, uses the capital asset pricing model (CAPM) to help identify mispriced securities. A consultant suggests Bruner use arbitrage pricing theory (APT) instead. In comparing CAPM and APT, the consultant made the following arguments:

   a. Both the CAPM and APT require a mean-variance efficient market portfolio.

   b. Neither the CAPM nor APT assumes normally distributed security returns.

   c. The CAPM assumes that one specific factor explains security returns but APT does not.

   State whether each of the consultant's arguments is correct or incorrect. Indicate, for each incorrect argument, why the argument is incorrect.

2. Assume that both X and Y are well-diversified portfolios and the risk-free rate is 8%.

Portfolio	Expected Return	Beta
X	16%	1.00
Y	12	0.25

   In this situation you would conclude that portfolios X and Y:

   a. Are in equilibrium.

   b. Offer an arbitrage opportunity.

   c. Are both underpriced.

   d. Are both fairly priced.

3. A zero-investment portfolio with a positive alpha could arise if:

   a. The expected return of the portfolio equals zero.

   b. The capital market line is tangent to the opportunity set.

   c. The Law of One Price remains unviolated.

   d. A risk-free arbitrage opportunity exists.

4. According to the theory of arbitrage:

   a. High-beta stocks are consistently overpriced.

   b. Low-beta stocks are consistently overpriced.

   c. Positive alpha investment opportunities will quickly disappear.

   d. Rational investors will pursue arbitrage consistent with their risk tolerance.

5. The arbitrage pricing theory (APT) differs from the single-factor capital asset pricing model (CAPM) because the APT:

   a. Places more emphasis on market risk.

   b. Minimizes the importance of diversification.

   c. Recognizes multiple unsystematic risk factors.

   d. Recognizes multiple systematic risk factors.

6. An investor takes as large a position as possible when an equilibrium price relationship is violated. This is an example of:

   a. A dominance argument.

   b. The mean-variance efficient frontier.

   c. Arbitrage activity.

   d. The capital asset pricing model.

7. The feature of arbitrage pricing theory (APT) that offers the greatest potential advantage over the *simple* CAPM is the:
   a. Identification of anticipated changes in production, inflation, and term structure of interest rates as key factors explaining the risk–return relationship.
   b. Superior measurement of the risk-free rate of return over historical time periods.
   c. Variability of coefficients of sensitivity to the APT factors for a given asset over time.
   d. Use of several factors instead of a single market index to explain the risk–return relationship.

8. In contrast to the capital asset pricing model, arbitrage pricing theory:
   a. Requires that markets be in equilibrium.
   b. Uses risk premiums based on micro variables.
   c. Specifies the number and identifies specific factors that determine expected returns.
   d. Does not require the restrictive assumptions concerning the market portfolio.

STANDARD &POOR'S

Go to **www.mhhe.com/edumarketinsight** and link to *Industry*. From the pull-down menu link to the *Air Freight and Logistics* industry and click on *Go!*. Review the latest *S&P Industry Survey*. What are the current major risk factors that affect this industry? Which of these factors would you expect to be priced, that is, to command a significant risk premium? Now find the latest *S&P Industry Survey* for the *Biotechnology* sector. What risk factors does this industry face? Which of these factors are likely to affect the firm in the long term and which are likely to change over time?

E-Investments

Unanticipated Inflation

One of the factors in the APT model specified by Chen, Roll, and Ross is the percent change in unanticipated inflation. Who gains and who loses when inflation change? Go to **http://hussmanfunds.com/rsi/infsurprises.htm** to see a graph Inflation Surprise Index and Economists' Inflation Forecasts.

SOLUTIONS TO CONCEPT CHECKS

1. The GDP beta is 1.2 and GDP growth is 1% better than previously expected. So you will increase your forecast for the stock return by $1.2 \times 1\% = 1.2\%$. The revised forecast is for an 11.2% return.

2. With these lower risk premiums, the expected return on the stock will be lower:

$$E(r) = 4\% + 1.2 \times 4\% + (-.3) \times (-2\%) = 9.4\%$$

3. a. This portfolio is not well diversified. The weight on the first security does not decline as n increases. Regardless of how much diversification there is in the rest of the portfolio, you will not shed the firm-specific risk of this security.

   b. This portfolio is well diversified. Even though some stocks have three times the weight as other stocks ($1.5/n$ versus $.5/n$), the weight on all stocks approaches zero as n increases. The impact of any individual stock's firm-specific risk will approach zero as n becomes ever larger.

4. The SML says that the expected return on the portfolio should be $4\% + (\frac{1}{3})(10 - 4) = 6\%$. The return actually expected is only 5%, implying that the stock is overpriced and that there is an arbitrage opportunity. Buy $1 of a portfolio that is $\frac{2}{3}$ invested in T-bills and $\frac{1}{3}$ in the market. The return on this portfolio is $\frac{2}{3} r_f + \frac{1}{3} r_M = \frac{2}{3} \times 4\% + \frac{1}{3} r_M$. Sell $1 of portfolio G. The net return on the combined position is:

$\$1 \times [\frac{2}{3} \times .04 + \frac{1}{3} r_M]$	Buy portfolio invested $\frac{2}{3}$ in T-bills and $\frac{1}{3}$ in the market index.
$-\$1 \times [.05 + \frac{1}{3}(r_M - .10)]$	Sell \$1 in portfolio G, with expected return of 5% and beta of $\frac{1}{3}$ on surprise in market return.
$\$1 \times .01$	Total

The profit per dollar invested is risk-free and precisely equal to the deviation of expected return from the SML.

5. The equilibrium return is $E(r) = r_f + \beta_{P1} [E(r_1) - r_f] + \beta_{P2} [E(r_2) - r_f]$. Using the data in Example 10.5:

$$E(r) = 4 + .2 \times (10 - 4) + 1.4 \times (12 - 4) = 16.4\%$$

6. *a.* For Louisiana residents, the stock is not a hedge. When their economy does poorly (low energy prices), the stock also does poorly, thereby aggravating their problems.

   b. For Massachusetts residents, the stock is a hedge. When energy prices increase, the stock will provide greater wealth with which to purchase energy.

   c. If energy consumers (who are willing to bid up the price of the stock for its hedge value) dominate the economy, then high oil-beta stocks will have lower expected rates of return than would be predicted by the simple CAPM.

THE EFFICIENT MARKET HYPOTHESIS

ONE OF THE early applications of computers in economics in the 1950s was to analyze economic time series. Business cycle theorists felt that tracing the evolution of several economic variables over time would clarify and predict the progress of the economy through boom and bust periods. A natural candidate for analysis was the behavior of stock market prices over time. Assuming that stock prices reflect the prospects of the firm, recurrent patterns of peaks and troughs in economic performance ought to show up in those prices.

Maurice Kendall examined this proposition in 1953.[1] He found to his great surprise that he could identify no predictable patterns in stock prices. Prices seemed to evolve randomly. They were as likely to go up as they were to go down on any particular day, regardless of past performance. The data provided no way to predict price movements.

At first blush, Kendall's results were disturbing to some financial economists. They seemed to imply that the stock market is dominated by erratic market psychology, or "animal spirits"—that it follows no logical rules. In short, the results appeared to confirm the irrationality of the market. On further reflection, however, economists came to reverse their interpretation of Kendall's study.

It soon became apparent that random price movements indicated a well-functioning or efficient market, not an irrational one. In this chapter we explore the reasoning behind what may seem a surprising conclusion. We show how competition among analysts leads naturally to market efficiency, and we examine the implications of the efficient market hypothesis for investment policy. We also consider empirical evidence that supports and contradicts the notion of market efficiency.

[1]Maurice Kendall, "The Analysis of Economic Time Series, Part I: Prices," *Journal of the Royal Statistical Society* 96 (1953).

11.1   RANDOM WALKS AND THE EFFICIENT MARKET HYPOTHESIS

Suppose Kendall had discovered that stock prices are predictable. What a gold mine this would have been. If they could use Kendall's equations to predict stock prices, investors would reap unending profits simply by purchasing stocks that the computer model implied were about to increase in price and by selling those stocks about to fall in price.

A moment's reflection should be enough to convince yourself that this situation could not persist for long. For example, suppose that the model predicts with great confidence that XYZ stock price, currently at $100 per share, will rise dramatically in 3 days to $110. What would all investors with access to the model's prediction do today? Obviously, they would place a great wave of immediate buy orders to cash in on the prospective increase in stock price. No one holding XYZ, however, would be willing to sell. The net effect would be an *immediate* jump in the stock price to $110. The forecast of a future price increase will lead instead to an immediate price increase. In other words, the stock price will immediately reflect the "good news" implicit in the model's forecast.

This simple example illustrates why Kendall's attempt to find recurrent patterns in stock price movements was likely to fail. A forecast about favorable *future* performance leads instead to favorable *current* performance, as market participants all try to get in on the action before the price jump.

More generally, one might say that any information that could be used to predict stock performance should already be reflected in stock prices. As soon as there is any information indicating that a stock is underpriced and therefore offers a profit opportunity, investors flock to buy the stock and immediately bid up its price to a fair level, where only ordinary rates of return can be expected. These "ordinary rates" are simply rates of return commensurate with the risk of the stock.

However, if prices are bid immediately to fair levels, given all available information, it must be that they increase or decrease only in response to new information. New information, by definition, must be unpredictable; if it could be predicted, then the prediction would be part of today's information. Thus stock prices that change in response to new (unpredictable) information also must move unpredictably.

This is the essence of the argument that stock prices should follow a **random walk,** that is, that price changes should be random and unpredictable.[2] Far from a proof of market irrationality, randomly evolving stock prices would be the necessary consequence of intelligent investors competing to discover relevant information on which to buy or sell stocks before the rest of the market becomes aware of that information.

Don't confuse randomness in price *changes* with irrationality in the *level* of prices. If prices are determined rationally, then only new information will cause them to change. Therefore, a random walk would be the natural result of prices that always reflect all current knowledge. Indeed, if stock price movements were predictable, that would be damning evidence of stock market inefficiency, because the ability to predict prices

---

[2]Actually, we are being a little loose with terminology here. Strictly speaking, we should characterize stock prices as following a submartingale, meaning that the expected change in the price can be positive, presumably as compensation for the time value of money and systematic risk. Moreover, the expected return may change over time as risk factors change. A random walk is more restrictive in that it constrains successive stock returns to be independent *and* identically distributed. Nevertheless, the term "random walk" is commonly used in the looser sense that price changes are essentially unpredictable. We will follow this convention.

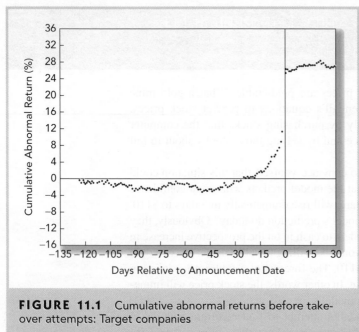

FIGURE 11.1 Cumulative abnormal returns before take-over attempts: Target companies

Source: Arthur Keown and John Pinkerton, "Merger Announcements and Insider Trading Activity," *Journal of Finance* 36 (September 1981). Reprinted by permission of the publisher, Blackwell Publishing, Inc.

would indicate that all available information was not already reflected in stock prices. Therefore, the notion that stocks already reflect all available information is referred to as the **efficient market hypothesis** (EMH).[3]

Figure 11.1 illustrates the response of stock prices to new information in an efficient market. The graph plots the price response of a sample of 194 firms that were targets of takeover attempts. In most take-overs, the acquiring firm pays a substantial premium over current market prices. Therefore, announcement of a takeover attempt should cause the stock price to jump. The figure shows that stock prices jump dramatically on the day the news becomes public. However, there is no further drift in prices *after* the announcement date, suggesting that prices reflect the new information, including the likely magnitude of the takeover premium, by the end of the trading day.

Even more dramatic evidence of rapid response to new information may be found in intraday prices. For example, Patell and Wolfson show that most of the stock price response to corporate dividend or earnings announcements occurs within 10 minutes of the announcement.[4] A nice illustration of such rapid adjustment is provided in a study by Busse and Green, who track minute-by-minute stock prices of firms that are featured on CNBC's "Morning" or "Midday Call" segments.[5] Minute 0 in Figure 11.2 is the time at which the stock is mentioned on the midday show. The top line is the average price movement of stocks that receive positive reports, while the bottom line reports returns on stocks with negative reports. Notice that the top line levels off, indicating that the market has fully digested the news, within 5 minutes of the report. The bottom line levels off within about 12 minutes.

Competition as the Source of Efficiency

Why should we expect stock prices to reflect "all available information"? After all, if you are willing to spend time and money on gathering information, it might seem reasonable that you could turn up something that has been overlooked by the rest of the investment community. When information is costly to uncover and analyze, one would expect investment analysis calling for such expenditures to result in an increased expected return.

---

[3]Market efficiency should not be confused with the idea of efficient portfolios introduced in Chapter 7. An informationally efficient *market* is one in which information is rapidly disseminated and reflected in prices. An efficient *portfolio* is one with the highest expected return for a given level of risk.

[4]J. M. Patell and M. A. Wolfson, "The Intraday Speed of Adjustment of Stock Prices to Earnings and Dividend Announcements," *Journal of Financial Economics* 13 (June 1984), pp. 223–52.

[5]J. A. Busse and T. C. Green, "Market Efficiency in Real Time," *Journal of Financial Economics* 65 (2002), pp. 415–37. You can find a nice intraday movie version of this figure at **www.bus.emory.edu/cgreen/cnbc.html**.

This point has been stressed by Grossman and Stiglitz.[6] They argued that investors will have an incentive to spend time and resources to analyze and uncover new information only if such activity is likely to generate higher investment returns. Thus, in market equilibrium, efficient information-gathering activity should be fruitful. Moreover, it would not be surprising to find that the degree of efficiency differs across various markets. For example, emerging markets that are less intensively analyzed than U.S. markets and in which accounting disclosure requirements are less rigorous may be less efficient than U.S. markets. Small stocks that receive relatively little coverage by Wall Street analysts may be less efficiently priced than large ones. Therefore, while we would not go so far as to say that you absolutely cannot come up with new information, it makes sense to consider and respect your competition.

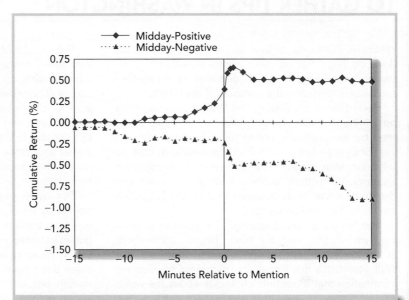

FIGURE 11.2   Stock price reaction to CNBC reports. The figure shows the reaction of stock prices to on-air stock reports during the "Midday Call" segment on CNBC. The chart plots cumulative returns beginning 15 minutes before the stock report.

Source: Reprinted from J. A. Busse and T. C. Green, "Market Efficiency in Real Time," *Journal of Financial Economics* 65 (2002), p. 422. Copyright 2002 with permission from Elsevier Science.

EXAMPLE 11.1   Rewards for Incremental Performance

Consider an investment management fund currently managing a $5 billion portfolio. Suppose that the fund manager can devise a research program that could increase the portfolio rate of return by one-tenth of 1% per year, a seemingly modest amount. This program would increase the dollar return to the portfolio by $5 billion × .001, or $5 million. Therefore, the fund would be willing to spend up to $5 million per year on research to increase stock returns by a mere tenth of 1% per year. With such large rewards for such small increases in investment performance, it should not be surprising that professional portfolio managers are willing to spend large sums on industry analysts, computer support, and research effort, and therefore that price changes are, generally speaking, difficult to predict.

With so many well-backed analysts willing to spend considerable resources on research, easy pickings in the market are rare. Moreover, the incremental rates of return on research activity may be so small that only managers of the largest portfolios will find them worth pursuing.

Although it may not literally be true that "all" relevant information will be uncovered, it is virtually certain that there are many investigators hot on the trail of most leads that seem likely to improve investment performance. Competition among these many well-backed,

[6]Sanford J. Grossman and Joseph E. Stiglitz, "On the Impossibility of Informationally Efficient Markets," *American Economic Review* 70 (June 1980).

HEDGE FUNDS HIRE LOBBYISTS TO GATHER TIPS IN WASHINGTON

WASHINGTON—As federal authorities try to crack down on illegal trading using secrets leaked from companies, some hedge-fund managers are tapping another source of information: the corridors of the Capitol.

Hedge funds are finding that Washington can be a gold mine of market-moving information, easily gathered by the politically connected. The funds are hiring lobbyists—not to influence government, but to tell them what it's going to do. Several lobbying firms are ramping up their "political-intelligence" units and charging hedge funds between $5,000 and $20,000 a month for tips and predictions.

The Securities and Exchange Commission is looking into whether laws are being broken somewhere in the transfer of information between Congress and Wall Street. It's not illegal for lawmakers to disclose information that is not publicly known about the workings of Congress, even if it could affect stock prices. It breaks congressional ethics rules only if they or their aides profit directly. But one question the SEC is trying to resolve is whether the passing of market-sensitive information by lobbyists to investors could violate insider-trading law.

The use of lobbyists as tipsters also is drawing attention from Congress. Democrats are considering requiring lobbyists to disclose their political-intelligence clients. Right now, lobbyists only have to disclose their work for clients seeking to influence government, while hedge funds and other clients seeking market-beating tips can stay in the shadows. Increasingly, lobbyists acting as advocates for a company on an issue may also have a client looking to trade on information about the same issue.

Employees of publicly traded companies are tightly bound by insider-trading laws, which also ban investors from trading public securities using material, nonpublic information that has been passed on improperly. But in most cases, members of Congress and their aides don't have a duty under the law to keep information private. They routinely exchange information about politics and policy with lobbyists—often not realizing that mere morsels are being sold to hedge funds who trade on the tidbits.

Source: Brody Mullins and Kara Scannell, *The Wall Street Journal*, December 8, 2006, p. A1. © 2006. All rights reserved worldwide.

highly paid, aggressive analysts ensures that, as a general rule, stock prices ought to reflect available information regarding their proper levels.

A concrete illustration of this point appears in the above box, which reports on hedge funds paying lobbying firms up to $20,000 per *month* for tips on upcoming legislation that may affect the prospects of particular firms. These "investments in information" can easily pay for themselves when applied to very large portfolios. The article also notes that both Congress and the SEC are uneasy about the ethics and legalities of such arrangements.

Versions of the Efficient Market Hypothesis

It is common to distinguish among three versions of the EMH: the weak, semistrong, and strong forms of the hypothesis. These versions differ by their notions of what is meant by the term "all available information."

The **weak-form** hypothesis asserts that stock prices already reflect all information that can be derived by examining market trading data such as the history of past prices, trading volume, or short interest. This version of the hypothesis implies that trend analysis is fruitless. Past stock price data are publicly available and virtually costless to obtain. The weak-form hypothesis holds that if such data ever conveyed reliable signals about future performance, all investors already would have learned to exploit the signals. Ultimately, the signals lose their value as they become widely known because a buy signal, for instance, would result in an immediate price increase.

The **semistrong-form** hypothesis states that all publicly available information regarding the prospects of a firm must be reflected already in the stock price. Such information includes, in addition to past prices, fundamental data on the firm's product line, quality of management, balance sheet composition, patents held, earning forecasts, and accounting practices. Again, if investors have access to such information from publicly available sources, one would expect it to be reflected in stock prices.

Finally, the **strong-form** version of the efficient market hypothesis states that stock prices reflect all information relevant to the firm, even including information available only to company insiders. This version of the hypothesis is quite extreme. Few would argue with the proposition that corporate officers have access to pertinent information long enough before public release to enable them to profit from trading on that information. Indeed, much of the activity of the Securities and Exchange Commission is directed toward preventing insiders from profiting by exploiting their privileged situation. Rule 10b-5 of the Security Exchange Act of 1934 sets limits on trading by corporate officers, directors, and substantial owners, requiring them to report trades to the SEC. These insiders, their relatives, and any associates who trade on information supplied by insiders are considered in violation of the law.

Defining insider trading is not always easy, however. After all, stock analysts are in the business of uncovering information not already widely known to market participants. As we saw in Chapter 3, the distinction between private and inside information is sometimes murky.

CONCEPT CHECK **1**	*a.* Suppose you observed that high-level managers make superior returns on investments in their company's stock. Would this be a violation of weak-form market efficiency? Would it be a violation of strong-form market efficiency? *b.* If the weak form of the efficient market hypothesis is valid, must the strong form also hold? Conversely, does strong-form efficiency imply weak-form efficiency?

11.2   IMPLICATIONS OF THE EMH

Technical Analysis

Technical analysis is essentially the search for recurrent and predictable patterns in stock prices. Although technicians recognize the value of information regarding future economic prospects of the firm, they believe that such information is not necessary for a successful trading strategy. This is because whatever the fundamental reason for a change in stock price, if the stock price responds slowly enough, the analyst will be able to identify a trend that can be exploited during the adjustment period. The key to successful technical analysis is a sluggish response of stock prices to fundamental supply-and-demand factors. This prerequisite, of course, is diametrically opposed to the notion of an efficient market.

Technical analysts are sometimes called *chartists* because they study records or charts of past stock prices, hoping to find patterns they can exploit to make a profit. As an example of technical analysis, consider the *relative strength* approach. The chartist compares stock performance over a recent period to performance of the market or other stocks in the same industry. A simple version of relative strength takes the ratio of the stock price to a market indicator such as the S&P 500 index. If the ratio increases over time, the stock is said to exhibit relative strength because its price performance is better than that of the broad market. Such strength presumably may continue for a long enough period of time to offer profit opportunities.

One of the most commonly heard components of technical analysis is the notion of **resistance levels** or **support levels.** These values are said to be price levels above which it is difficult for stock prices to rise, or below which it is unlikely for them to fall, and they are believed to be levels determined by market psychology.

EXAMPLE 11.2   Resistance Levels

Consider stock XYZ, which traded for several months at a price of $72, and then declined to $65. If the stock eventually begins to increase in price, $72 is considered a resistance level (according to this theory) because investors who bought originally at $72 will be eager to sell their shares as soon as they can break even on their investment. Therefore, at prices near $72 a wave of selling pressure would exist. Such activity imparts a type of "memory" to the market that allows past price history to influence current stock prospects.

The efficient market hypothesis implies that technical analysis is without merit. The past history of prices and trading volume is publicly available at minimal cost. Therefore, any information that was ever available from analyzing past prices has already been reflected in stock prices. As investors compete to exploit their common knowledge of a stock's price history, they necessarily drive stock prices to levels where expected rates of return are exactly commensurate with risk. At those levels one cannot expect abnormal returns.

As an example of how this process works, consider what would happen if the market believed that a level of $72 truly were a resistance level for stock XYZ in Example 11.2. No one would be willing to purchase the stock at a price of $71.50, because it would have almost no room to increase in price, but ample room to fall. However, if no one would buy it at $71.50, then $71.50 would become a resistance level. But then, using a similar analysis, no one would buy it at $71, or $70, and so on. The notion of a resistance level is a logical conundrum. Its simple resolution is the recognition that if the stock is ever to sell at $71.50, investors *must* believe that the price can as easily increase as fall. The fact that investors are willing to purchase (or even hold) the stock at $71.50 is evidence of their belief that they can earn a fair expected rate of return at that price.

> **CONCEPT CHECK 2**
>
> If everyone in the market believes in resistance levels, why do these beliefs not become self-fulfilling prophecies?

An interesting question is whether a technical rule that seems to work will continue to work in the future once it becomes widely recognized. A clever analyst may occasionally uncover a profitable trading rule, but the real test of efficient markets is whether the rule itself becomes reflected in stock prices once its value is discovered. Once a useful technical rule (or price pattern) is discovered, it ought to be invalidated when the mass of traders attempts to exploit it. In this sense, price patterns ought to be *self-destructing.*

Thus the market dynamic is one of a continual search for profitable trading rules, followed by destruction by overuse of those rules found to be successful, followed by more search for yet-undiscovered rules.

Fundamental Analysis

Fundamental analysis uses earnings and dividend prospects of the firm, expectations of future interest rates, and risk evaluation of the firm to determine proper stock prices. Ultimately, it represents an attempt to determine the present discounted value of all the payments a stockholder will receive from each share of stock. If that value exceeds the stock price, the fundamental analyst would recommend purchasing the stock.

Fundamental analysts usually start with a study of past earnings and an examination of company balance sheets. They supplement this analysis with further detailed economic analysis, ordinarily including an evaluation of the quality of the firm's management, the firm's standing within its industry, and the prospects for the industry as a whole. The hope is to attain insight into future performance of the firm that is not yet recognized by the rest of the market. Chapters 17 through 19 provide a detailed discussion of the types of analyses that underlie fundamental analysis.

Once again, the efficient market hypothesis predicts that *most* fundamental analysis also is doomed to failure. If the analyst relies on publicly available earnings and industry information, his or her evaluation of the firm's prospects is not likely to be significantly more accurate than those of rival analysts. There are many well-informed, well-financed firms conducting such market research, and in the face of such competition it will be difficult to uncover data not also available to other analysts. Only analysts with a unique insight will be rewarded.

Fundamental analysis is much more difficult than merely identifying well-run firms with good prospects. Discovery of good firms does an investor no good in and of itself if the rest of the market also knows those firms are good. If the knowledge is already public, the investor will be forced to pay a high price for those firms and will not realize a superior rate of return.

The trick is not to identify firms that are good, but to find firms that are *better* than everyone else's estimate. Similarly, poorly run firms can be great bargains if they are not quite as bad as their stock prices suggest.

This is why fundamental analysis is difficult. It is not enough to do a good analysis of a firm; you can make money only if your analysis is better than that of your competitors because the market price will already reflect all commonly available information.

Active versus Passive Portfolio Management

By now it is apparent that casual efforts to pick stocks are not likely to pay off. Competition among investors ensures that any easily implemented stock evaluation technique will be used widely enough so that any insights derived will be reflected in stock prices. Only serious analysis and uncommon techniques are likely to generate the *differential* insight necessary to yield trading profits.

Moreover, these techniques are economically feasible only for managers of large portfolios. If you have only $100,000 to invest, even a 1% per year improvement in performance generates only $1,000 per year, hardly enough to justify herculean efforts. The billion-dollar manager, however, reaps extra income of $10 million annually from the same 1% increment.

If small investors are not in a favored position to conduct active portfolio management, what are their choices? The small investor probably is better off investing in mutual funds. By pooling resources in this way, small investors can gain from economies of scale.

More difficult decisions remain, though. Can investors be sure that even large mutual funds have the ability or resources to uncover mispriced stocks? Furthermore, will any mispricing be sufficiently large to repay the costs entailed in active portfolio management?

Proponents of the efficient market hypothesis believe that active management is largely wasted effort and unlikely to justify the expenses incurred. Therefore, they advocate a **passive investment strategy** that makes no attempt to outsmart the market. A passive strategy aims only at establishing a well-diversified portfolio of securities without attempting to find under- or overvalued stocks. Passive management is usually characterized by a buy-and-hold strategy. Because the efficient market theory indicates that stock prices are at fair levels, given all available information, it makes no sense to buy and sell securities frequently, which generates large brokerage fees without increasing expected performance.

One common strategy for passive management is to create an **index fund,** which is a fund designed to replicate the performance of a broad-based index of stocks. For example, Vanguard's Index 500 Portfolio holds stocks in direct proportion to their weight in the Standard & Poor's 500 stock price index. The performance of the Index 500 fund therefore replicates the performance of the S&P 500. Investors in this fund obtain broad diversification with relatively low management fees. The fees can be kept to a minimum because Vanguard does not need to pay analysts to assess stock prospects and does not incur transaction costs from high portfolio turnover. Indeed, while the typical annual charge for an actively managed equity fund is more than 1% of assets, Vanguard charges a bit less than .2% for the Index 500 Portfolio. Today, Vanguard's Index 500 Portfolio is among the largest equity mutual funds with over $125 billion of assets in mid-2007, and about 10% of equity funds are indexed.

Indexing need not be limited to the S&P 500, however. For example, some of the funds offered by the Vanguard Group track the Wilshire 5000 index, the Salomon Brothers Broad Investment Grade Bond Index, the MSCI index of small-capitalization U.S. companies, the European equity market, and the Pacific Basin equity market. Several other mutual fund complexes have introduced indexed portfolios, but Vanguard dominates the retail market for indexed products.

Exchange-traded funds, or ETFs, are a close (and usually lower-expense) alternative to indexed mutual funds. As noted in Chapter 4, these are shares in diversified portfolios that can be bought or sold just like shares of individual stock. ETFs matching several broad stock market indexes such as the S&P 500 or Wilshire 5000 indexes and dozens of international and industry stock indexes are available to investors who want to hold a diversified sector of a market without attempting active security selection.

CONCEPT CHECK 3	What would happen to market efficiency if *all* investors attempted to follow a passive strategy?

A hybrid strategy also is fairly common, where the fund maintains a *passive core,* which is an indexed position, and augments that position with one or more actively managed portfolios.

The Role of Portfolio Management in an Efficient Market

If the market is efficient, why not pick stocks by throwing darts at *The Wall Street Journal* instead of trying rationally to choose a stock portfolio? This is a tempting conclusion to draw from the notion that security prices are fairly set, but it is far too facile. There is a role for rational portfolio management, even in perfectly efficient markets.

You have learned that a basic principle in portfolio selection is diversification. Even if all stocks are priced fairly, each still poses firm-specific risk that can be eliminated through diversification. Therefore, rational security selection, even in an efficient market, calls for the selection of a well-diversified portfolio providing the systematic risk level that the investor wants.

Rational investment policy also requires that tax considerations be reflected in security choice. High-tax-bracket investors generally will not want the same securities that low-bracket investors find favorable. At an obvious level, high-bracket investors find it advantageous to buy tax-exempt municipal bonds despite their relatively low pretax yields, whereas those same bonds are unattractive to low-tax-bracket or tax-exempt investors. At a more subtle level, high-bracket investors might want to tilt their portfolios in the direction of capital gains as opposed to interest income, because capital gains are taxed less heavily and because the option to defer the realization of capital gains income is more valuable the higher the current tax bracket. Hence these investors may prefer stocks that yield low dividends yet offer greater expected capital gain income. They also will be more attracted to investment opportunities for which returns are sensitive to tax benefits, such as real estate ventures.

A third argument for rational portfolio management relates to the particular risk profile of the investor. For example, a General Motors executive whose annual bonus depends on GM's profits generally should not invest additional amounts in auto stocks. To the extent that his or her compensation already depends on GM's well-being, the executive is already overinvested in GM and should not exacerbate the lack of diversification.

Investors of varying ages also might warrant different portfolio policies with regard to risk bearing. For example, older investors who are essentially living off savings might choose to avoid long-term bonds whose market values fluctuate dramatically with changes in interest rates (discussed in Part Four). Because these investors are living off accumulated savings, they require conservation of principal. In contrast, younger investors might be more inclined toward long-term inflation-indexed bonds. The steady flow of real income over long periods of time that is locked in with these bonds can be more important than preservation of principal to those with long life expectancies.

In conclusion, there is a role for portfolio management even in an efficient market. Investors' optimal positions will vary according to factors such as age, tax bracket, risk aversion, and employment. The role of the portfolio manager in an efficient market is to tailor the portfolio to these needs, rather than to beat the market.

Resource Allocation

We've focused so far on the investment implications of the efficient market hypothesis. Deviations from efficiency may offer profit opportunities to better-informed traders at the expense of less-informed traders.

However, deviations from informational efficiency would also result in a large cost that will be borne by all citizens, namely, inefficient resource allocation. Recall that in a capitalist economy, investments in *real* assets such as plant, equipment, and know-how are guided in large part by the prices of financial assets. For example, if the values of biotech assets as reflected in the stock market prices of biotech firms exceed the cost of acquiring those assets, the managers of such firms have a strong signal that further investments in the firm will be regarded by the market as a positive net present value venture. In this manner, capital market prices guide resource allocation. Security mispricing thus could entail severe social costs by fostering inappropriate investments on the real side of the economy.

Corporations with overpriced securities will be able to obtain capital too cheaply, and corporations with undervalued securities might forgo investment opportunities because the cost of raising capital will be too high. Therefore, inefficient capital markets would diminish one of the most potent benefits of a market economy.

11.3   EVENT STUDIES

The notion of informationally efficient markets leads to a powerful research methodology. If security prices reflect all currently available information, then price changes must reflect new information. Therefore, it seems that one should be able to measure the importance of an event of interest by examining price changes during the period in which the event occurs.

An **event study** describes a technique of empirical financial research that enables an observer to assess the impact of a particular event on a firm's stock price. A stock market analyst might want to study the impact of dividend changes on stock prices, for example. An event study would quantify the relationship between dividend changes and stock returns.

Analyzing the impact of any particular event is more difficult than it might at first appear. On any day, stock prices respond to a wide range of economic news such as updated forecasts for GDP, inflation rates, interest rates, or corporate profitability. Isolating the part of a stock price movement that is attributable to a specific event is not a trivial exercise.

The general approach starts with a proxy for what the stock's return would have been in the absence of the event. The **abnormal return** due to the event is estimated as the difference between the stock's actual return and this benchmark. Several methodologies for estimating the benchmark return are used in practice. For example, a very simple approach measures the stock's abnormal return as its return minus that of a broad market index. An obvious refinement is to compare the stock's return to those of other stocks matched according to criteria such as firm size, beta, recent performance, or ratio of price to book value per share. Another approach estimates normal returns using an asset pricing model such as the CAPM or one of its multifactor generalizations such as the Fama-French three-factor model.

Many researchers have used a "market model" to estimate abnormal returns. This approach is based on the index models we introduced in Chapter 9. Recall that a single-index model holds that stock returns are determined by a market factor and a firm-specific factor. The stock return, r_t, during a given period t, would be expressed mathematically as

$$r_t = a + br_{Mt} + e_t \qquad (11.1)$$

where r_{Mt} is the market's rate of return during the period and e_t is the part of a security's return resulting from firm-specific events. The parameter b measures sensitivity to the market return, and a is the average rate of return the stock would realize in a period with a zero market return.[7] Equation 11.1 therefore provides a decomposition of r_t into market and firm-specific factors. The firm-specific or abnormal return may be interpreted as the unexpected return that results from the event.

Determination of the abnormal return in a given period requires that we obtain an estimate of the term e_t. Therefore, we rewrite Equation 11.1:

$$e_t = r_t - (a + br_{Mt}) \qquad (11.2)$$

Equation 11.2 has a simple interpretation: The residual, e_t, that is, the component presumably due to the event in question, is the stock's return over and above what one would predict based on broad market movements in that period, given the stock's sensitivity to the market.

The market model is a highly flexible tool, because it can be generalized to include richer models of benchmark returns, for example, by including industry as well as broad market returns on the right-hand side of Equation 11.1, or returns on indexes constructed to match characteristic such as firm size. However, one must be careful that regression parameters in Equation 11.1 (the intercept a and slope b) are estimated properly. In particular, they must be estimated using data sufficiently separated in time from the event in question that they are not affected by event-period abnormal stock performance. In part

---

[7]We know from Chapter 9 that the CAPM implies that the intercept a in Equation 11.1 should equal $r_f(1 - \beta)$. Nevertheless, it is customary to estimate the intercept in this equation empirically rather than imposing the CAPM value. One justification for this practice is that empirically fitted security market lines seem flatter than predicted by the CAPM (see Chapter 13), which would make the intercept implied by the CAPM too small.

because of this vulnerability of the market model, returns on characteristic-matched port-folios have become more widely used benchmarks in recent years.

EXAMPLE 11.3   Abnormal Returns

Suppose that the analyst has estimated that $a = .05\%$ and $b = .8$. On a day that the market goes up by 1%, you would predict from Equation 11.1 that the stock should rise by an expected value of $.05\% + .8 \times 1\% = .85\%$. If the stock actually rises by 2%, the analyst would infer that firm-specific news that day caused an additional stock return of $2\% - .85\% = 1.15\%$. This is the abnormal return for the day.

We measure the impact of an event by estimating the abnormal return on a stock (or group of stocks) at the moment the information about the event becomes known to the market. For example, in a study of the impact of merger attempts on the stock prices of target firms, the announcement date is the date on which the public is informed that a merger is to be attempted. The abnormal returns of each firm surrounding the announcement date are computed, and the statistical significance and magnitude of the typical abnormal return are assessed to determine the impact of the newly released information.

One concern that complicates event studies arises from *leakage* of information. Leakage occurs when information regarding a relevant event is released to a small group of investors before official public release. In this case the stock price might start to increase (in the case of a "good news" announcement) days or weeks before the official announcement date. Any abnormal return on the announcement date is then a poor indicator of the total impact of the information release. A better indicator would be the **cumulative abnormal return,** which is simply the sum of all abnormal returns over the time period of interest. The cumulative abnormal return thus captures the total firm-specific stock movement for an entire period when the market might be responding to new information.

Figure 11.1 (earlier in the chapter) presents the results from a fairly typical event study. The authors of this study were interested in leakage of information before merger announcements and constructed a sample of 194 firms that were targets of takeover attempts. In most takeovers, stockholders of the acquired firms sell their shares to the acquirer at substantial premiums over market value. Announcement of a takeover attempt is good news for shareholders of the target firm and therefore should cause stock prices to jump.

Figure 11.1 confirms the good-news nature of the announcements. On the announcement day, called day 0, the average cumulative abnormal return (CAR) for the sample of takeover candidates increases substantially, indicating a large and positive abnormal return on the announcement date. Notice that immediately after the announcement date the CAR no longer increases or decreases significantly. This is in accord with the efficient market hypothesis. Once the new information became public, the stock prices jumped almost immediately in response to the good news. With prices once again fairly set, reflecting the effect of the new information, further abnormal returns on any particular day are equally likely to be positive or negative. In fact, for a sample of many firms, the average abnormal return should be extremely close to zero, and thus the CAR will show neither upward nor downward drift. This is precisely the pattern shown in Figure 11.1.

The pattern of returns for the days preceding the public announcement date yields some interesting evidence about efficient markets and information leakage. If insider trading rules were perfectly obeyed and perfectly enforced, stock prices should show no abnormal returns on days before the public release of relevant news, because no special firm-specific information would be available to the market before public announcement. Instead, we should observe a clean jump in the stock price only on the announcement day. In fact, Figure 11.1 shows that the prices of the takeover targets clearly start an upward drift 30 days before the public announcement. There are two possible interpretations of this pattern. One is that information is leaking to some market participants who then purchase the stocks before the public announcement. At least some abuse of insider trading rules is occurring.

Another interpretation is that in the days before a takeover attempt the public becomes suspicious of the attempt as it observes someone buying large blocks of stock. As acquisition intentions become more evident, the probability of an attempted merger is gradually revised upward so that we see a gradual increase in CARs. Although this interpretation is certainly possible, evidence of leakage appears almost universally in event studies, even in cases where the public's access to information is not gradual.

Actually, the SEC itself can take some comfort from patterns such as that in Figure 11.1. If insider trading rules were widely and flagrantly violated, we would expect to see abnormal returns earlier than they appear in these results. For example, in the case of mergers, the CAR would turn positive as soon as acquiring firms decided on their takeover targets, because insiders would start trading immediately. By the time of the public announcement, the insiders would have bid up the stock prices of target firms to levels reflecting the merger attempt, and the abnormal returns on the actual public announcement date would be close to zero. The dramatic increase in the CAR that we see on the announcement date indicates that a good deal of these announcements are indeed news to the market and that stock prices did not already reflect complete knowledge about the takeovers. It would appear, therefore, that SEC enforcement does have a substantial effect on restricting insider trading, even if some amount of it still persists.

Event study methodology has become a widely accepted tool to measure the economic impact of a wide range of events. For example, the SEC regularly uses event studies to measure illicit gains captured by traders who may have violated insider trading or other securities laws.[8] Event studies are also used in fraud cases, where the courts must assess damages caused by a fraudulent activity.

EXAMPLE 11.4   Using Abnormal Returns to Infer Damages

Suppose the stock of a company with market value of $100 million falls by 4% on the day that news of an accounting scandal surfaces. The rest of the market, however, generally did well that day. The market indexes were up sharply, and based on the usual relationship between the stock and the market, one would have expected a 2% gain on the stock. We would conclude that the impact of the scandal was a 6% drop in value, the difference between the 2% gain that we would have expected and the 4% drop actually observed. One might then infer that the damages sustained from the scandal were $6 million, because the value of the firm (after adjusting for general market movements) fell by 6% of $100 million when investors became aware of the news and reassessed the value of the stock.

| CONCEPT CHECK **4** | Suppose that we see negative abnormal returns (declining CARs) after an announcement date. Is this a violation of efficient markets? |

---

[8]For a review of SEC applications of this technique, see Mark Mitchell and Jeffry Netter, "The Role of Financial Economics in Securities Fraud Cases: Applications at the Securities and Exchange Commission," *The Business Lawyer* 49 (February 1994), pp. 545–90.

11.4   ARE MARKETS EFFICIENT?

The Issues

Not surprisingly, the efficient market hypothesis does not exactly arouse enthusiasm in the community of professional portfolio managers. It implies that a great deal of the activity of portfolio managers—the search for undervalued securities—is at best wasted effort, and quite probably harmful to clients because it costs money and leads to imperfectly diversified portfolios. Consequently, the EMH has never been widely accepted on Wall Street, and debate continues today on the degree to which security analysis can improve investment performance. Before discussing empirical tests of the hypothesis, we want to note three factors that together imply that the debate probably never will be settled: the *magnitude issue,* the *selection bias issue,* and the *lucky event issue.*

The Magnitude Issue   We noted that an investment manager overseeing a $5 billion portfolio who can improve performance by only 0.1% per year will increase investment earnings by .001 × $5 billion = $5 million annually. This manager clearly would be worth her salary! Yet can we, as observers, statistically measure her contribution? Probably not: A 0.1% contribution would be swamped by the yearly volatility of the market. Remember, the annual standard deviation of the well-diversified S&P 500 index has been around 20%. Against these fluctuations a small increase in performance would be hard to detect.

All might agree that stock prices are very close to fair values and that only managers of large portfolios can earn enough trading profits to make the exploitation of minor mispricing worth the effort. According to this view, the actions of intelligent investment managers are the driving force behind the constant evolution of market prices to fair levels. Rather than ask the qualitative question, Are markets efficient? we ought instead to ask a more quantitative question: How efficient are markets?

The Selection Bias Issue   Suppose that you discover an investment scheme that could really make money. You have two choices: either publish your technique in *The Wall Street Journal* to win fleeting fame, or keep your technique secret and use it to earn millions of dollars. Most investors would choose the latter option, which presents us with a conundrum. Only investors who find that an investment scheme cannot generate abnormal returns will be willing to report their findings to the whole world. Hence opponents of the efficient markets view of the world always can use evidence that various techniques do not provide investment rewards as proof that the techniques that do work simply are not being reported to the public. This is a problem in *selection bias;* the outcomes we are able to observe have been preselected in favor of failed attempts. Therefore, we cannot fairly evaluate the true ability of portfolio managers to generate winning stock market strategies.

The Lucky Event Issue   In virtually any month it seems we read an article about some investor or investment company with a fantastic investment performance over the recent past. Surely the superior records of such investors disprove the efficient market hypothesis.

Yet this conclusion is far from obvious. As an analogy to the investment game, consider a contest to flip the most number of heads out of 50 trials using a fair coin. The expected outcome for any person is, of course, 50% heads and 50% tails. If 10,000 people, however, compete in this contest, it would not be surprising if at least one or two contestants flipped

HOW TO GUARANTEE A SUCCESSFUL MARKET NEWSLETTER

Suppose you want to make your fortune publishing a market newsletter. You need first to convince potential subscribers that you have talent worth paying for. But what if you have no talent? The solution is simple: start eight newsletters.

In year 1, let four of your newsletters predict an up-market and four a down-market. In year 2, let half of the originally optimistic group of newsletters continue to predict an up-market and the other half a down-market. Do the same for the originally pessimistic group. Continue in this manner to obtain the pattern of predictions in the table that follows (U = prediction of an up-market, D = prediction of a down-market).

After 3 years, no matter what has happened to the market, one of the newsletters would have had a perfect prediction record. This is because after 3 years there are $2^3 = 8$ outcomes for the market, and we have covered all eight possibilities with the eight newsletters. Now, we simply slough off the seven unsuccessful newsletters, and market the eighth newsletter based on its perfect track record. If we want to establish a newsletter with a perfect track record over a 4-year

period, we need $2^4 = 16$ newsletters. A 5-year period requires 32 newsletters, and so on.

After the fact, the one newsletter that was always right will attract attention for your uncanny foresight and investors will rush to pay large fees for its advice. Your fortune is made, and you have never even researched the market!

WARNING: This scheme is illegal! The point, however, is that with hundreds of market newsletters, you can find one that has stumbled onto an apparently remarkable string of successful predictions without any real degree of skill. After the fact, someone's prediction history can seem to imply great forecasting skill. This person is the one we will read about in The Wall Street Journal; the others will be forgotten.

Newsletter Predictions								
Year	1	2	3	4	5	6	7	8
1	U	U	U	U	D	D	D	D
2	U	U	D	D	U	U	D	D
3	U	D	U	D	U	D	U	D

more than 75% heads. In fact, elementary statistics tells us that the expected number of contestants flipping 75% or more heads would be two. It would be silly, though, to crown these people the "head-flipping champions of the world." Obviously, they are simply the contestants who happened to get lucky on the day of the event. (See the above box.)

The analogy to efficient markets is clear. Under the hypothesis that any stock is fairly priced given all available information, any bet on a stock is simply a coin toss. There is equal likelihood of winning or losing the bet. However, if many investors using a variety of schemes make fair bets, statistically speaking, some of those investors will be lucky and win a great majority of the bets. For every big winner, there may be many big losers, but we never hear of these managers. The winners, though, turn up in The Wall Street Journal as the latest stock market gurus; then they can make a fortune publishing market newsletters.

Our point is that after the fact there will have been at least one successful investment scheme. A doubter will call the results luck, the successful investor will call it skill. The proper test would be to see whether the successful investors can repeat their performance in another period, yet this approach is rarely taken.

With these caveats in mind, we turn now to some of the empirical tests of the efficient market hypothesis.

CONCEPT CHECK 5

Legg Mason's Value Trust, managed by Bill Miller, outperformed the S&P 500 in each of the 15 years ending in 2005. Is Miller's performance sufficient to dissuade you from a belief in efficient markets? If not, would any performance record be sufficient to dissuade you?

Weak-Form Tests: Patterns in Stock Returns

Returns over Short Horizons   Early tests of efficient markets were tests of the weak form. Could speculators find trends in past prices that would enable them to earn abnormal profits? This is essentially a test of the efficacy of technical analysis.

One way of discerning trends in stock prices is by measuring the *serial correlation* of stock market returns. Serial correlation refers to the tendency for stock returns to be related to past returns. Positive serial correlation means that positive returns tend to follow positive returns (a momentum type of property). Negative serial correlation means that positive returns tend to be followed by negative returns (a reversal or "correction" property). Both Conrad and Kaul[9] and Lo and MacKinlay[10] examine weekly returns of NYSE stocks and find positive serial correlation over short horizons. However, the correlation coefficients of weekly returns tend to be fairly small, at least for large stocks for which price data are the most reliably up-to-date. Thus, while these studies demonstrate weak price trends over short periods,[11] the evidence does not clearly suggest the existence of trading opportunities.

While broad market indexes demonstrate only weak serial correlation, there appears to be stronger momentum in performance across market sectors exhibiting the best and worst recent returns. In an investigation of intermediate-horizon stock price behavior (using 3- to 12-month holding periods), Jegadeesh and Titman[12] found a **momentum effect** in which good or bad recent performance of particular stocks continues over time. They conclude that while the performance of individual stocks is highly unpredictable, *portfolios* of the best-performing stocks in the recent past appear to outperform other stocks with enough reliability to offer profit opportunities. Thus, it appears that there is evidence of short- to intermediate-horizon price momentum in both the aggregate market and cross-sectionally (i.e., across particular stocks).

Returns over Long Horizons   Although studies of short- to intermediate-horizon returns have detected momentum in stock market prices, tests[13] of long-horizon returns (i.e., returns over multiyear periods) have found suggestions of pronounced *negative* long-term serial correlation in the performance of the aggregate market. The latter result has given rise to a "fads hypothesis," which asserts that the stock market might overreact to relevant news. Such overreaction leads to positive serial correlation (momentum) over short time horizons. Subsequent correction of the overreaction leads to poor performance following good performance and vice versa. The corrections mean that a run of positive returns eventually will tend to be followed by negative returns, leading to

[9]Jennifer Conrad and Gautam Kaul, "Time-Variation in Expected Returns," *Journal of Business* 61 (October 1988), pp. 409–25.

[10]Andrew W. Lo and A. Craig MacKinlay, "Stock Market Prices Do Not Follow Random Walks: Evidence from a Simple Specification Test," *Review of Financial Studies* 1 (1988), pp. 41–66.

[11]On the other hand, there is evidence that share prices of individual securities (as opposed to broad market indexes) are more prone to reversals than continuations at very short horizons. See, for example, B. Lehmann, "Fads, Martingales and Market Efficiency," *Quarterly Journal of Economics* 105 (February 1990), pp. 1–28; and N. Jegadeesh, "Evidence of Predictable Behavior of Security Returns," *Journal of Finance* 45 (September 1990), pp. 881–98. However, as Lehmann notes, this is probably best interpreted as due to liquidity problems after big movements in stock prices as market makers adjust their positions in the stock.

[12]Narasimhan Jegadeesh and Sheridan Titman, "Returns to Buying Winners and Selling Losers: Implications for Stock Market Efficiency," *Journal of Finance* 48 (March 1993), pp. 65–91.

[13]Eugene F. Fama and Kenneth R. French, "Permanent and Temporary Components of Stock Prices," *Journal of Political Economy* 96 (April 1988), pp. 24–73; James Poterba and Lawrence Summers, "Mean Reversion in Stock Prices: Evidence and Implications," *Journal of Financial Economics* 22 (October 1988), pp. 27–59.

negative serial correlation over longer horizons. These episodes of apparent overshooting followed by correction give the stock market the appearance of fluctuating around its fair value.

These long-horizon results are dramatic, but the studies offer far from conclusive evidence regarding efficient markets. First, the study results need not be interpreted as evidence for stock market fads. An alternative interpretation of these results holds that they indicate only that the market risk premium varies over time. For example, when the risk premium and the required return on the market rises, stock prices will fall. When the market then rises (on average) at this higher rate of return, the data convey the impression of a stock price recovery. The apparent overshooting and correction are in fact no more than a rational response of market prices to changes in discount rates.

In addition to studies suggestive of overreaction in overall stock market returns over long horizons, many other studies suggest that over long horizons, extreme performance in particular securities also tends to reverse itself: The stocks that have performed best in the recent past seem to underperform the rest of the market in following periods, while the worst past performers tend to offer above-average future performance. DeBondt and Thaler[14] and Chopra, Lakonishok, and Ritter[15] find strong tendencies for poorly performing stocks in one period to experience sizable reversals over the subsequent period, while the best-performing stocks in a given period tend to follow with poor performance in the following period.

For example, the DeBondt and Thaler study found that if one were to rank the performance of stocks over a 5-year period and then group stocks into portfolios based on investment performance, the base-period "loser" portfolio (defined as the 35 stocks with the worst investment performance) outperformed the "winner" portfolio (the top 35 stocks) by an average of 25% (cumulative return) in the following 3-year period. This **reversal effect,** in which losers rebound and winners fade back, suggests that the stock market overreacts to relevant news. After the overreaction is recognized, extreme investment performance is reversed. This phenomenon would imply that a *contrarian* investment strategy—investing in recent losers and avoiding recent winners—should be profitable. Moreover, these returns seem pronounced enough to be exploited profitably.

Thus it appears that there may be short-run momentum but long-run reversal patterns in price behavior both for the market as a whole and across sectors of the market. One interpretation of this pattern is that short-run overreaction (which causes momentum in prices) may lead to long-term reversals (when the market recognizes its past error).

Predictors of Broad Market Returns

Several studies have documented the ability of easily observed variables to predict market returns. For example, Fama and French[16] showed that the return on the aggregate stock market tends to be higher when the dividend/price ratio, the dividend yield, is high. Campbell and Shiller[17] found that the earnings yield can predict market returns. Keim and

---

[14]Werner F. M. DeBondt and Richard Thaler, "Does the Stock Market Overreact?" *Journal of Finance* 40 (1985), pp. 793–805.

[15]Navin Chopra, Josef Lakonishok, and Jay R. Ritter, "Measuring Abnormal Performance: Do Stocks Overreact?" *Journal of Financial Economics* 31 (1992), pp. 235–68.

[16]Eugene F. Fama and Kenneth R. French, "Dividend Yields and Expected Stock Returns," *Journal of Financial Economics* 22 (October 1988), pp. 3–25.

[17]John Y. Campbell and Robert Shiller, "Stock Prices, Earnings and Expected Dividends," *Journal of Finance* 43 (July 1988), pp. 661–76.

Stambaugh[18] showed that bond market data such as the spread between yields on high- and low-grade corporate bonds also help predict broad market returns.

Again, the interpretation of these results is difficult. On the one hand, they may imply that stock returns can be predicted, in violation of the efficient market hypothesis. More probably, however, these variables are proxying for variation in the market risk premium. For example, given a level of dividends or earnings, stock prices will be lower and dividend and earnings yields will be higher when the risk premium (and therefore the expected market return) is higher. Thus a high dividend or earnings yield will be associated with higher market returns. This does not indicate a violation of market efficiency. The predictability of market returns is due to predictability in the risk premium, not in risk-adjusted abnormal returns.

Fama and French[19] showed that the yield spread between high- and low-grade bonds has greater predictive power for returns on low-grade bonds than for returns on high-grade bonds, and greater predictive power for stock returns than for bond returns, suggesting that the predictability in returns is in fact a risk premium rather than evidence of market inefficiency. Similarly, the fact that the dividend yield on stocks helps to predict bond market returns suggests that the yield captures a risk premium common to both markets rather than mispricing in the equity market.

Semistrong Tests: Market Anomalies

Fundamental analysis uses a much wider range of information to create portfolios than does technical analysis. Investigations of the efficacy of fundamental analysis ask whether publicly available information beyond the trading history of a security can be used to improve investment performance, and therefore are tests of semistrong-form market efficiency. Surprisingly, several easily accessible statistics, for example a stock's price–earnings ratio or its market capitalization, seem to predict abnormal risk-adjusted returns. Findings such as these, which we will review in the following pages, are difficult to reconcile with the efficient market hypothesis, and therefore are often referred to as efficient market **anomalies.**

A difficulty in interpreting these tests is that we usually need to adjust for portfolio risk before evaluating the success of an investment strategy. Many tests, for example, have used the CAPM to adjust for risk. However, we know that even if beta is a relevant descriptor of stock risk, the empirically measured quantitative trade-off between risk as measured by beta and expected return differs from the predictions of the CAPM. (We review this evidence in Chapter 13.) If we use the CAPM to adjust portfolio returns for risk, inappropriate adjustments may lead to the conclusion that various portfolio strategies can generate superior returns, when in fact it simply is the risk adjustment procedure that has failed.

Another way to put this is to note that tests of risk-adjusted returns are *joint tests* of the efficient market hypothesis *and* the risk adjustment procedure. If it appears that a portfolio strategy can generate superior returns, we must then choose between rejecting the EMH and rejecting the risk adjustment technique. Usually, the risk adjustment technique is based on more-questionable assumptions than is the EMH; by opting to reject the procedure, we are left with no conclusion about market efficiency.

[18]Donald B. Keim and Robert F. Stambaugh, "Predicting Returns in the Stock and Bond Markets," *Journal of Financial Economics* 17 (1986), pp. 357–90.

[19]Eugene F. Fama and Kenneth R. French, "Business Conditions and Expected Returns on Stocks and Bonds," *Journal of Financial Economics* 25 (November 1989), pp. 3–22.

An example of this issue is the discovery by Basu[20] that portfolios of low price–earnings (P/E) ratio stocks have provided higher returns than high P/E portfolios. The **P/E effect** holds up even if returns are adjusted for portfolio beta. Is this a confirmation that the market systematically misprices stocks according to P/E ratio? This would be an extremely surprising and, to us, disturbing conclusion, because analysis of P/E ratios is such a simple procedure. Although it may be possible to earn superior returns by using hard work and much insight, it hardly seems plausible that such a simplistic technique is enough to generate abnormal returns.

Another interpretation of these results is that returns are not properly adjusted for risk. If two firms have the same expected earnings, the riskier stock will sell at a lower price and lower P/E ratio. Because of its higher risk, the low P/E stock also will have higher expected returns. Therefore, unless the CAPM beta fully adjusts for risk, P/E will act as a useful additional descriptor of risk, and will be associated with abnormal returns if the CAPM is used to establish benchmark performance.

The Small-Firm-in-January Effect   The so-called size or **small-firm effect,** originally documented by Banz,[21] is illustrated in Figure 11.3. It shows the historical performance of portfolios formed by dividing the NYSE stocks into 10 portfolios each year according to firm size (i.e., the total value of outstanding equity). Average annual returns between 1926 and 2006 are consistently higher on the small-firm portfolios. The difference in average

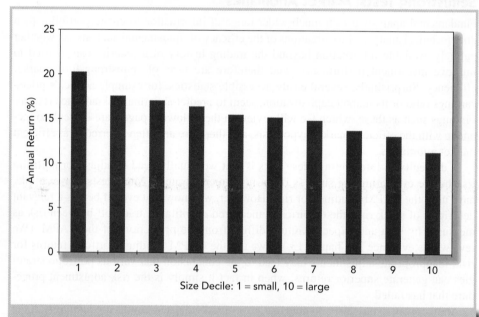

FIGURE 11.3   Average annual return for 10 size-based portfolios, 1926–2006

Source: Authors' calculations, using data obtained from Professor Ken French's data library at **http://mba. tuck.dartmouth.edu/pages/faculty/ken.french/data_library.html.**

[20]Sanjoy Basu, "The Investment Performance of Common Stocks in Relation to Their Price-Earnings Ratios: A Test of the Efficient Market Hypothesis," *Journal of Finance* 32 (June 1977), pp. 663–82; and "The Relationship between Earnings Yield, Market Value, and Return for NYSE Common Stocks: Further Evidence," *Journal of Financial Economics* 12 (June 1983).

[21]Rolf Banz, "The Relationship between Return and Market Value of Common Stocks," *Journal of Financial Economics* 9 (March 1981).

annual return between portfolio 10 (with the largest firms) and portfolio 1 (with the smallest firms) is 8.86%. Of course, the smaller-firm portfolios tend to be riskier. But even when returns are adjusted for risk using the CAPM, there is still a consistent premium for the smaller-sized portfolios.

Imagine earning a premium of this size on a billion-dollar portfolio. Yet it is remarkable that following a simple (even simplistic) rule such as "invest in low-capitalization stocks" should enable an investor to earn excess returns. After all, any investor can measure firm size at little cost. One would not expect such minimal effort to yield such large rewards.

Later studies (Keim,[22] Reinganum,[23] and Blume and Stambaugh[24]) showed that the small-firm effect occurs virtually entirely in January, in fact, in the first 2 weeks of January. The size effect is in fact a "small-firm-in-January" effect.

The Neglected-Firm Effect and Liquidity Effects   Arbel and Strebel[25] gave another interpretation of the small-firm-in-January effect. Because small firms tend to be neglected by large institutional traders, information about smaller firms is less available. This information deficiency makes smaller firms riskier investments that command higher returns. "Brand-name" firms, after all, are subject to considerable monitoring from institutional investors, which promises high-quality information, and presumably investors do not purchase "generic" stocks without the prospect of greater returns.

As evidence for the **neglected-firm effect,** Arbel[26] divided firms into highly researched, moderately researched, and neglected groups based on the number of institutions holding the stock. The January effect was in fact largest for the neglected firms. An article by Merton[27] shows that neglected firms might be expected to earn higher equilibrium returns as compensation for the risk associated with limited information. In this sense the neglected firm premium is not strictly a market inefficiency, but is a type of risk premium.

Work by Amihud and Mendelson[28] on the effect of liquidity on stock returns might be related to both the small-firm and neglected-firm effects. As we noted in Chapter 9, investors will demand a rate-of-return premium to invest in less-liquid stocks that entail higher trading costs. In accord with this hypothesis, Amihud and Mendelson showed that these stocks show a strong tendency to exhibit abnormally high risk-adjusted rates of return. Because small and less-analyzed stocks as a rule are less liquid, the liquidity effect might be a partial explanation of their abnormal returns. However, this theory does not explain why the abnormal returns of small firms should be concentrated in January. In any case, exploiting these effects can be more difficult than it would appear. The high trading costs on small stocks can easily wipe out any apparent abnormal profit opportunity.

[22]Donald B. Keim, "Size Related Anomalies and Stock Return Seasonality: Further Empirical Evidence," *Journal of Financial Economics* 12 (June 1983).

[23]Marc R. Reinganum, "The Anomalous Stock Market Behavior of Small Firms in January: Empirical Tests for Tax-Loss Effects," *Journal of Financial Economics* 12 (June 1983).

[24]Marshall E. Blume and Robert F. Stambaugh, "Biases in Computed Returns: An Application to the Size Effect," *Journal of Financial Economics,* 1983.

[25]Avner Arbel and Paul J. Strebel, "Pay Attention to Neglected Firms," *Journal of Portfolio Management,* Winter 1983.

[26]Avner Arbel, "Generic Stocks: An Old Product in a New Package," *Journal of Portfolio Management,* Summer 1985.

[27]Robert C. Merton, "A Simple Model of Capital Market Equilibrium with Incomplete Information," *Journal of Finance* 42 (1987), pp. 483–510.

[28]Yakov Amihud and Haim Mendelson, "Asset Pricing and the Bid–Ask Spread," *Journal of Financial Economics* 17 (December 1986), pp. 223–50; and "Liquidity, Asset Prices, and Financial Policy," *Financial Analysts Journal* 47 (November/December 1991), pp. 56–66.

Book-to-Market Ratios Fama and French[29] showed that a powerful predictor of returns across securities is the ratio of the book value of the firm's equity to the market value of equity. Fama and French stratified firms into 10 groups according to book-to-market ratios and examined the average monthly rate of return of each of the 10 groups. Figure 11.4 is an updated version of their results. The decile with the highest book-to-market ratio had an average annual return of 16.84%, while the lowest-ratio decile averaged only 11.12%. The dramatic dependence of returns on book-to-market ratio is independent of beta, suggesting either that high book-to-market ratio firms are relatively underpriced, or that the book-to-market ratio is serving as a proxy for a risk factor that affects equilibrium expected returns.

In fact, Fama and French found that after controlling for the size and **book-to-market effects,** beta seemed to have no power to explain average security returns.[30] This finding is an important challenge to the notion of rational markets, because it seems to imply that a factor that should affect returns—systematic risk—seems not to matter, while a factor that should not matter—the book-to-market ratio—seems capable of predicting future returns. We will return to the interpretation of this anomaly.

Post–Earnings-Announcement Price Drift A fundamental principle of efficient markets is that any new information ought to be reflected in stock prices very rapidly. When good news is made public, for example, the stock price should jump immediately. A puzzling anomaly, therefore, is the apparently sluggish response of stock prices to firms' earnings announcements, as uncovered by Ball and Brown.[31] Their results were later confirmed and extended in many other papers.[32]

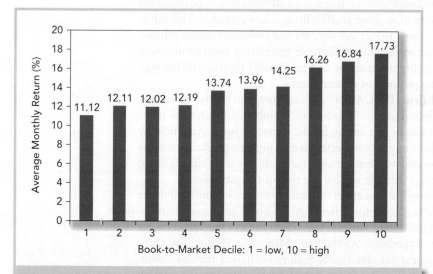

FIGURE 11.4 Average return as a function of book-to-market ratio, 1926–2006

Source: Authors' calculations, using data obtained from Professor Ken French's data library at http://mba.tuck.dartmouth.edu/pages/faculty/ken.french/data_library.html.

[29]Eugene F. Fama and Kenneth R. French, "The Cross Section of Expected Stock Returns," *Journal of Finance* 47 (1992), pp. 427–65

[30]However, a study by S. P. Kothari, Jay Shanken, and Richard G. Sloan, "Another Look at the Cross-Section of Expected Stock Returns," *Journal of Finance* 50 (March 1995), pp. 185–224, finds that when betas are estimated using annual rather than monthly returns, securities with high beta values do in fact have higher average returns. Moreover, the authors find a book-to-market effect that is attenuated compared to the results in Fama and French and furthermore is inconsistent across different samples of securities. They conclude that the empirical case for the importance of the book-to-market ratio may be somewhat weaker than the Fama and French study would suggest.

[31]R. Ball and P. Brown, "An Empirical Evaluation of Accounting Income Numbers," *Journal of Accounting Research* 9 (1968), pp. 159–78.

[32]There is a voluminous literature on this phenomenon, often referred to as post–earnings-announcement price drift. For more recent papers that focus on why such drift may be observed, see V. Bernard and J. Thomas, "Evidence That Stock Prices Do Not Fully Reflect the Implications of Current Earnings for Future Earnings," *Journal of Accounting and Economics* 13 (1990), pp. 305–40, or R. H. Battalio and R. Mendenhall, "Earnings Expectation, Investor Trade Size, and Anomalous Returns Around Earnings Announcements," *Journal of Financial Economics* 77 (2005). pp. 289–319.

The "news content" of an earnings announcement can be evaluated by comparing the announcement of actual earnings to the value previously expected by market participants. The difference is the "earnings surprise." (Market expectations of earnings can be roughly measured by averaging the published earnings forecasts of Wall Street analysts or by applying trend analysis to past earnings.) Rendleman, Jones, and Latané[33] provide an influential study of sluggish price response to earnings announcements. They calculate earnings surprises for a large sample of firms, rank the magnitude of the surprise, divide firms into 10 deciles based on the size of the surprise, and calculate abnormal returns for each decile. Figure 11.5 plots cumulative abnormal returns by decile.

Their results are dramatic. The correlation between ranking by earnings surprise and abnormal returns across deciles is as predicted. There is a large abnormal return (a jump in cumulative abnormal return) on the earnings announcement day (time 0). The abnormal return is positive for positive-surprise firms and negative for negative-surprise firms.

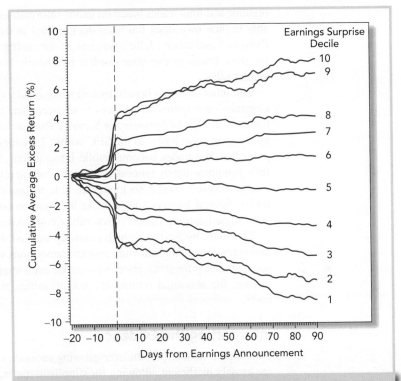

FIGURE 11.5   Cumulative abnormal returns in response to earnings announcements

Source: Reprinted from R.J. Rendleman Jr., C. P. Jones, and H. A. Latané, "Empirical Anomalies Based on Unexpected Earnings and the Importance of Risk Adjustments," *Journal of Financial Economics* 10 (1982), pp. 269–287. Copyright 1982 with permission from Elsevier Science.

The more remarkable, and interesting, result of the study concerns stock price movement *after* the announcement date. The cumulative abnormal returns of positive-surprise stocks continue to rise—in other words, exhibit momentum—even after the earnings information becomes public, while the negative-surprise firms continue to suffer negative abnormal returns. The market appears to adjust to the earnings information only gradually, resulting in a sustained period of abnormal returns.

Evidently, one could have earned abnormal profits simply by waiting for earnings announcements and purchasing a stock portfolio of positive-earnings-surprise companies. These are precisely the types of predictable continuing trends that ought to be impossible in an efficient market.

Strong-Form Tests: Inside Information

It would not be surprising if insiders were able to make superior profits trading in their firm's stock. In other words, we do not expect markets to be strong-form efficient; we

[33]Richard J. Rendleman Jr., Charles P. Jones, and Henry A. Latané, "Empirical Anomalies Based on Unexpected Earnings and the Importance of Risk Adjustments," *Journal of Financial Economics* 10 (November 1982), pp. 269–87.

regulate and limit trades based on inside information. The ability of insiders to trade profitably in their own stock has been documented in studies by Jaffe,[34] Seyhun,[35] Givoly and Palmon,[36] and others. Jaffe's was one of the earlier studies that documented the tendency for stock prices to rise after insiders intensively bought shares and to fall after intensive insider sales.

Can other investors benefit by following insiders' trades? The Securities and Exchange Commission requires all insiders to register their trading activity and it publishes these trades in an *Official Summary of Security Transactions and Holdings.* Since 2002, insiders must report large trades to the SEC within 2 business days. Once the *Official Summary* is published, the trades become public information. At that point, if markets are efficient, fully and immediately processing the information released in the *Official Summary* of trading, an investor should no longer be able to profit from following the pattern of those trades. Several Internet sites contain information on insider trading. See the Web sites at our Online Learning Center (**www.mhhe.com/bkm**) for some suggestions.

The study by Seyhun, which carefully tracked the public release dates of the *Official Summary,* found that following insider transactions would be to no avail. Although there is some tendency for stock prices to increase even after the *Official Summary* reports insider buying, the abnormal returns are not of sufficient magnitude to overcome transaction costs.

Interpreting the Evidence

How should we interpret the ever-growing anomalies literature? Does it imply that markets are grossly inefficient, allowing for simplistic trading rules to offer large profit opportunities? Or are there other, more-subtle interpretations?

Risk Premiums or Inefficiencies?   The price-earnings, small-firm, market-to-book, momentum, and long-term reversal effects are currently among the most puzzling phenomena in empirical finance. There are several interpretations of these effects. First note that to some extent, some of these phenomena may be related. The feature that small firms, low-market-to-book firms, and recent "losers" seem to have in common is a stock price that has fallen considerably in recent months or years. Indeed, a firm can become a small firm or a low-market-to-book firm by suffering a sharp drop in price. These groups therefore may contain a relatively high proportion of distressed firms that have suffered recent difficulties.

Fama and French[37] argue that these effects can be explained as manifestations of risk premiums. Using their three-factor model, introduced in the previous chapter, they show that stocks with higher "betas" (also known as factor loadings) on size or market-to-book factors have higher average returns; they interpret these returns as evidence of a risk premium associated with the factor. This model does a much better job than the one-factor CAPM in explaining security returns. While size or book-to-market ratios per se are obviously not risk factors, they perhaps might act as proxies for more fundamental determinants of risk. Fama and French argue that these patterns of returns may therefore be consistent with

[34]Jeffrey F. Jaffe, "Special Information and Insider Trading," *Journal of Business* 47 (July 1974).

[35]H. Nejat Seyhun, "Insiders' Profits, Costs of Trading and Market Efficiency," *Journal of Financial Economics* 16 (1986).

[36]Dan Givoly and Dan Palmon, "Insider Trading and Exploitation of Inside Information: Some Empirical Evidence," *Journal of Business* 58 (1985).

[37]Eugene F. Fama and Kenneth R. French, "Common Risk Factors in the Returns on Stocks and Bonds," *Journal of Financial Economics* 33 (1993), pp. 3–56.

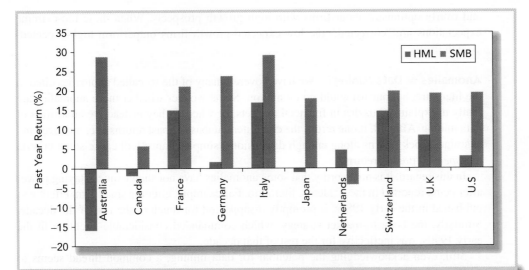

FIGURE 11.6 Return to style portfolio as a predictor of GDP growth. Average difference in the return on the style portfolio in years before good GDP growth versus in years with bad GDP growth. Positive value means the style portfolio does better in years prior to good macroeconomic performance. HML = high minus low portfolio, sorted on ratio of book-to-market value. SMB = small minus big portfolio, sorted on firm size.

Source: Reprinted from J. Liew and M. Vassalou, "Can Book-to-Market, Size, and Momentum Be Risk Factors That Predict Economic Growth?" *Journal of Financial Economics* 57 (2000), pp. 221–45. Copyright 2000 with permission from Elsevier Science.

an efficient market in which expected returns are consistent with risk. In this regard, it is worth noting that returns to "style factors," for example, the return on portfolios constructed based on the ratio of book-to-market value (specifically, the Fama-French high minus low book-to-market portfolio) or firm size (the return on the small-minus big-firm portfolio) do indeed seem to predict business cycles in many countries. Figure 11.6 shows that returns on these portfolios tend to have positive returns in years prior to rapid growth in gross domestic product. We examine the Fama-French paper in more detail in Chapter 13.

The opposite interpretation is offered by Lakonishok, Shleifer, and Vishney,[38] who argue that these phenomena are evidence of inefficient markets, more specifically, of systematic errors in the forecasts of stock analysts. They believe that analysts extrapolate past performance too far into the future, and therefore overprice firms with recent good performance and underprice firms with recent poor performance. Ultimately, when market participants recognize their errors, prices reverse. This explanation is consistent with the reversal effect and also, to a degree, is consistent with the small-firm and book-to-market effects because firms with sharp price drops may tend to be small or have high book-to-market ratios.

If Lakonishok, Shleifer, and Vishney are correct, we ought to find that analysts systematically err when forecasting returns of recent "winner" versus "loser" firms. A study by La Porta[39] is consistent with this pattern. He finds that equity of firms for which analysts predict low growth rates of earnings actually perform better than those with high expected earnings growth. Analysts seem overly pessimistic about firms with low growth prospects

[38]Josef Lakonishok, Andrei Shleifer, and Robert W. Vishney, "Contrarian Investment, Extrapolation, and Risk," *Journal of Finance* 50 (1995), pp. 541–78.

[39]Raphael La Porta, "Expectations and the Cross Section of Stock Returns," *Journal of Finance* 51 (December 1996), pp. 1715–42.

and overly optimistic about firms with high growth prospects. When these too-extreme expectations are "corrected," the low-expected-growth firms outperform high-expected-growth firms.

Anomalies or Data Mining?   We have covered many of the so-called anomalies cited in the literature, but our list could go on and on. Some wonder whether these anomalies are really unexplained puzzles in financial markets, or whether they instead are an artifact of data mining. After all, if one reruns the computer database of past returns over and over and examines stock returns along enough dimensions, simple chance will cause some criteria to *appear* to predict returns.

In this regard, it is noteworthy that some anomalies have not shown much staying power after being reported in the academic literature. For example, after the small-firm effect was published in the early 1980s, it promptly disappeared for much of the rest of the decade. Similarly, the book-to-market strategy, which commanded considerable attention in the early 1990s, was ineffective for the rest of that decade.

Still, even acknowledging the potential for data mining, a common thread seems to run through many of the anomalies we have considered, lending support to the notion that there is a real puzzle to explain. Value stocks—defined by low P/E ratio, high book-to-market ratio, or depressed prices relative to historic levels—seem to have provided higher average returns than "glamour" or growth stocks.

One way to address the problem of data mining is to find a data set that has not already been researched and see whether the relationship in question shows up in the new data. Such studies have revealed size, momentum, and book-to-market effects in other security markets around the world. While these phenomena may be a manifestation of a systematic risk premium, the precise nature of that risk is not fully understood.

The "Noisy Market Hypothesis" and Fundamental Indexing

The efficient market hypothesis argues in favor of capitalization-weighted indexed portfolios that provide broad diversification with minimal trading costs. But several researchers and practitioners have forcefully argued that such "cap-weighted" indexing is necessarily inferior to a strategy they call fundamental indexing.[40] The rational for their argument goes by the name "noisy market hypothesis."

The hypothesis begins with the observation that market prices may well contain pricing errors or "noise" relative to the intrinsic or "true" value of a firm. Even if prices are correct on average, at any time some stocks will be overvalued and others undervalued. Overpriced stocks have inflated market values relative to intrinsic value, while the market values of underpriced stocks are too low. Because indexed portfolios invest in proportion to market capitalization, portfolio weights will track these pricing errors, with greater amounts invested in overpriced stocks (which have poor expected returns) and lesser amounts invested in underpriced stocks (which have high expected returns). The conclusion is that a capitalization-weighted strategy is destined to overweight precisely the firms with the worst return prospects. In contrast, a fundamental index that invests in proportion to intrinsic value would avoid the detrimental association between portfolio weights and the market's pricing errors, and would therefore outperform a capitalization-weighted index.

However, while this conclusion is correct, it begs the crucial question. How can we find the intrinsic values necessary to form a fundamental index? The necessary inputs are in fact the holy grail of all active managers: true stock values or, equivalently, market pricing errors. Clearly, *given* the errors in market prices, we could outperform passive

---

[40]See, for example, Robert Arnott, "Orthodoxy Overwrought," *Institutional Investor,* December 18, 2006.

cap-weighted portfolios by tilting toward undervalued stocks and away from overpriced ones. This is hardly a surprise. The problem is finding a guide to these pricing errors. Unfortunately, market capitalization by itself tells us *nothing* about potential mispricing (indeed, this is the starting assumption of the noisy market hypothesis), and therefore, gives us no guidance as to how to tilt our portfolio.[41]

Advocates of fundamental indexing propose that portfolio weights determined by indicators of intrinsic value such as dividends or earnings be used to construct an alternative to a cap-weighted index. These rules would result in allocations that are skewed (compared to cap weighting) toward firms with high value indicators. But notice that these indicators are precisely the tools used in the value-investing strategies that we discussed earlier in this section (e.g., dividend yield or price–earnings ratios). There may be good reasons to pursue value investing, chiefly the evidence reviewed earlier that value stocks have typically outperformed growth stocks over long periods in many countries. But we've also noted that there may be other, risk-premium-based, explanations for that performance. Regardless of your interpretation of the value premium, you should recognize that fundamental indexing is at heart nothing more than a value tilt, a point emphasized by Asness.[42] It is therefore, despite its name, *not* indexing, but rather a form of active investing, and it is hardly a radical new approach to either indexation or investment policy.

11.5   MUTUAL FUND AND ANALYST PERFORMANCE

We have documented some of the apparent chinks in the armor of efficient market proponents. For investors, the issue of market efficiency boils down to whether skilled investors can make consistent abnormal trading profits. The best test is to look at the performance of market professionals to see if they can generate performance superior to that of a passive index fund that buys and holds the market. We will look at two facets of professional performance: that of stock market analysts who recommend investment positions and that of mutual fund managers who actually manage portfolios.

Stock Market Analysts

Stock market analysts historically have worked for brokerage firms, which presents an immediate problem in interpreting the value of their advice: analysts have tended to be overwhelmingly positive in their assessment of the prospects of firms.[43] For example, on a scale of 1 (strong buy) to 5 (strong sell), the average recommendation for 5,628 covered firms in 1996 was 2.04.[44] As a result, we cannot take positive recommendations (e.g., to buy) at face value. Instead, we must look at either the relative strength of analyst

---

[41]For a more rigorous demonstration of this point and an insightful discussion of fundamental indexing, see André Perold, "Fundamentally Flawed Indexing," *Financial Analysts Journal,* November/December 2007, vol. 63, pp. 31–37.

[42]Cliff Asness, "The Value of Fundamental Indexing," *Institutional Investor,* October 16, 2006, pp. 94–99.

[43]This problem may be less severe in the future; one recent reform intended to mitigate the conflict of interest in having brokerage firms that sell stocks also provide investment advice is to separate analyst coverage from the other activities of the firm.

[44]B. Barber, R. Lehavy, M. McNichols, and B. Trueman, "Can Investors Profit from the Prophets? Security Analyst Recommendations and Stock Returns," *Journal of Finance* 56 (April 2001), pp. 531–63.

recommendations compared to those for other firms, or at the change in consensus recommendations.

Womack[45] focuses on changes in analysts' recommendations and finds that positive changes are associated with increased stock prices of about 5%, and negative changes result in average price decreases of 11%. One might wonder whether these price changes reflect the market's recognition of analysts' superior information or insight about firms or, instead, simply result from new buy or sell pressure brought on by the recommendations themselves. Womack argues that price impact seems to be permanent, and therefore consistent with the hypothesis that analysts do in fact reveal new information. Jegadeesh, Kim, Krische, and Lee[46] also find that changes in consensus recommendations are associated with price changes, but that the *level* of consensus recommendations is an inconsistent predictor of future stock performance.

Barber, Lehavy, McNichols, and Trueman[47] focus on the level of consensus recommendations and show that firms with the most-favorable recommendations outperform those with the least-favorable recommendations. While their results seem impressive, the authors note that portfolio strategies based on analyst consensus recommendations would result in extremely heavy trading activity with associated costs that probably would wipe out the potential profits from the strategy.

In sum, the literature suggests some value added by analysts, but ambiguity remains. Are superior returns following analyst upgrades due to revelation of new information or due to changes in investor demand in response to the changed outlook? Also, are these results exploitable by investors who necessarily incur trading costs?

Mutual Fund Managers

As we pointed out in Chapter 4, casual evidence does not support the claim that professionally managed portfolios can consistently beat the market. Figure 4.2 in that chapter demonstrated that between 1972 and 2007 the returns of a passive portfolio indexed to the Wilshire 5000 typically would have been better than those of the average equity fund. On the other hand, there was some (admittedly inconsistent) evidence of persistence in performance, meaning that the better managers in one period tended to be better managers in following periods. Such a pattern would suggest that the better managers can with some consistency outperform their competitors, and it would be inconsistent with the notion that market prices already reflect all relevant information.

The analyses cited in Chapter 4 were based on total returns; they did not properly adjust returns for exposure to systematic risk factors. In this section we revisit the question of mutual fund performance, paying more attention to the benchmark against which performance ought to be evaluated.

As a first pass, we might examine the risk-adjusted returns (i.e., the alpha, or return in excess of required return based on beta and the market index return in each period) of a large sample of mutual funds. But the market index may not be an adequate benchmark against which to evaluate mutual fund returns. Because mutual funds tend to maintain considerable holdings in equity of small firms, whereas the capitalization-weighted index is dominated by large firms, mutual funds as a whole will tend to outperform the index when small firms outperform large ones and underperform when small firms fare worse. Thus a

[45]K. L. Womack, "Do Brokerage Analysts' Recommendations Have Investment Value?" *Journal of Finance* 51 (March 1996), pp. 137–67.

[46]N. Jegadeesh, J. Kim, S. D. Krische, and C. M. Lee, "Analyzing the Analysts: When Do Recommendations Add Value?" *Journal of Finance* 59 (June 2004), pp. 1083–124.

[47]Barber et al., op. cit.

better benchmark for the performance of funds would be an index that separately incorporates the stock market performance of smaller firms.

The importance of the benchmark can be illustrated by examining the returns on small stocks in various subperiods.[48] In the 20-year period between 1945 and 1964, a small-stock index underperformed the S&P 500 by about 4% per year (i.e., the alpha of the small-stock index after adjusting for systematic risk was −4%). In the following 20-year period between 1965 and 1984, small stocks outperformed the S&P index by 10%. Thus if one were to examine mutual fund returns in the earlier period, they would tend to look poor, not necessarily because fund managers were poor stock pickers, but simply because mutual funds as a group tended to hold more small stocks than were represented in the S&P 500. In the later period, funds would look better on a risk-adjusted basis relative to the S&P 500 because small stocks performed better. The "style choice," that is, the exposure to small stocks (which is an asset allocation decision) would dominate the evaluation of performance even though it has little to do with managers' stock-picking ability.[49]

Elton, Gruber, Das, and Hlavka attempted to control for the impact of non–S&P assets on mutual fund performance. They used a multifactor version of the index model of security returns and calculated fund alphas by using regressions that include as explanatory variables the excess returns of three benchmark portfolios rather than just one proxy for the market index. Their three factors are the excess return on the S&P 500 index, the excess return on an equity index of non–S&P low capitalization (i.e., small) firms, and the excess return on a bond market index. Some of their results are presented in Table 11.1, which shows that average alphas are negative for each type of equity fund, although generally not of statistically significant magnitude. They concluded that after controlling for the relative performance of these three asset classes—large stocks, small stocks, and bonds—mutual fund managers as

Type of Fund (Wiesenberger Classification)	Number of Funds	Alpha (%)	t-Statistic for Alpha
Equity funds			
Maximum capital gain	12	−4.59	−1.87
Growth	33	−1.55	−1.23
Growth and income	40	−0.68	−1.65
Balanced funds	31	−1.27	−2.73

TABLE 11.1

Performance of mutual funds based on three-index model

Note: The three-index model calculates the alpha of each fund as the intercept of the following regression:

$$r - r_f = \alpha + \beta_M(r_M - r_f) + \beta_S(r_S - r_f) + \beta_D(r_D - r_f) + e$$

where r is the return on the fund, r_f is the risk-free rate, r_M is the return on the S&P 500 index, r_s is the return on a non–S&P small-stock index, r_D is the return on a bond index, e is the fund's residual return, and the betas measure the sensitivity of fund returns to the various indexes.
Source: E. J. Elton, M. J. Gruber, S. Das, and M. Hlavka, "Efficiency with Costly Information: A Reinterpretation of Evidence from Managed Portfolios," *Review of Financial Studies* 6 (1993), pp. 1–22.

[48]This illustration and the statistics cited are based on E. J. Elton, M. J. Gruber, S. Das, and M. Hlavka, "Efficiency with Costly Information: A Reinterpretation of Evidence from Managed Portfolios," *Review of Financial Studies* 6 (1993), pp. 1–22, which is discussed shortly.

[49]Remember that the asset allocation decision is usually in the hands of the individual investor. Investors allocate their investment portfolios to funds in asset classes they desire to hold, and they can reasonably expect only that mutual fund portfolio managers will choose stocks advantageously *within* those asset classes.

a group do not demonstrate an ability to beat passive index strategies that would simply mix index funds from among these asset classes. They also found that mutual fund performance is worse for firms that have higher expense ratios and higher turnover ratios. Thus it appears that funds with higher fees do not increase gross returns by enough to justify those fees.

The conventional performance benchmark today is a four-factor model, which employs the three Fama-French factors (the return on the market index, and returns to portfolios based on size and book-to-market ratio) augmented by a momentum factor (a portfolio constructed based on prior-year stock return). Alphas constructed using an expanded index model using these four factors control for a wide range of mutual fund style choices that may affect average returns, for example, an inclination to growth versus value or small versus large capitalization stocks. Figure 11.7 shows a frequency distribution of four-factor alphas for U.S. domestic equity funds.[50] The results show that the distribution of alpha is roughly bell shaped, with a slightly negative mean. On average, it does not appear that these funds outperform their style-adjusted benchmarks.

Carhart[51] reexamines the issue of consistency in mutual fund performance—sometimes called the "hot hands" phenomenon—using the same 4-factor model. He finds that after controlling for these factors, there is some small persistence in relative performance across managers. However, much of that persistence seems due to expenses and transactions costs rather than gross investment returns. This last point is important; while there can be no consistently superior performers in a fully efficient market, there *can* be consistently inferior performers. Repeated weak performance would not be due to an ability to pick bad stocks consistently (that would be impossible in an efficient market!) but could result from a consistently high expense ratio, high portfolio turnover, or higher-than-average transaction costs per trade. In this regard, it is interesting that in another study documenting apparent

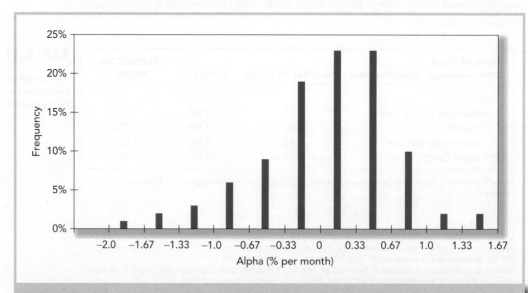

FIGURE 11.7 Mutual fund alphas computed using a 4-factor model of expected return, 1993–2007. (The best and worst 2.5% of observations are excluded from this distribution.)

Source: Professor Richard Evans, University of Virginia, Darden School of Business.

[50]We are grateful to Professor Richard Evans for these data.

[51]Mark M. Carhart, "On Persistence in Mutual Fund Performance," *Journal of Finance* 52 (1997), pp. 57–82.

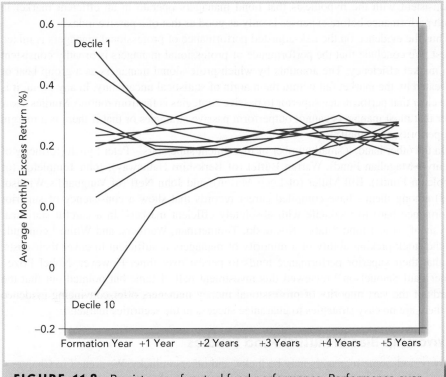

FIGURE 11.8   Persistence of mutual fund performance. Performance over time of mutual fund groups ranked by initial year performance

Source: Mark M. Carhart, "On Persistence in Mutual Fund Performance," *Journal of Finance* 52 (March 1997), pp. 57–82. Reprinted by permission of the publisher, Blackwell Publishing, Inc.

consistency across managers, Hendricks, Patel, and Zeckhauser[52] also found the strongest consistency among the weakest performers.

Even allowing for expenses and turnover, some amount of performance persistence seems to be due to differences in investment strategy. Carhart found, however, that the evidence of persistence is concentrated at the two extremes. Figure 11.8 from Carhart's study documents performance persistence. Equity funds are ranked into one of 10 groups by performance in the formation year, and the performance of each group in the following years is plotted. It is clear that except for the best-performing top-decile group and the worst-performing 10th decile group, performance in future periods is almost independent of earlier-year returns. Carhart's results suggest that there may be a small group of exceptional managers who can with some consistency outperform a passive strategy, but that for the majority of managers over- or underperformance in any period is largely a matter of chance.

In contrast to the extensive studies of equity fund managers, there have been few studies of the performance of bond fund managers. Blake, Elton, and Gruber[53] examined the performance of fixed-income mutual funds. They found that, on average, bond funds underperform passive fixed-income indexes by an amount roughly equal to expenses, and that there is no evidence that past performance can predict future performance. Their evidence

[52]Darryll Hendricks, Jayendu Patel, and Richard Zeckhauser, "Hot Hands in Mutual Funds: Short-Run Persistence of Relative Performance, 1974–1988," *Journal of Finance* 43 (March 1993), pp. 93–130.

[53]Christopher R. Blake, Edwin J. Elton, and Martin J. Gruber, "The Performance of Bond Mutual Funds," *Journal of Business* 66 (July 1993), pp. 371–404.

is consistent with the hypothesis that bond managers operate in an efficient market in which performance before expenses is only as good as that of a passive index.

Thus the evidence on the risk-adjusted performance of professional managers is mixed at best. We conclude that the performance of professional managers is broadly consistent with market efficiency. The amounts by which professional managers as a group beat or are beaten by the market fall within the margin of statistical uncertainty. In any event, it is quite clear that performance superior to passive strategies is far from routine. Studies show either that most managers cannot outperform passive strategies or that if there is a margin of superiority, it is small.

On the other hand, a small number of investment superstars—Peter Lynch (formerly of Fidelity's Magellan Fund), Warren Buffet (of Berkshire Hathaway), John Templeton (of Templeton Funds), Bill Miller (of Legg Mason), and John Neff (of Vanguard's Windsor Fund) among them—have compiled career records that show a consistency of superior performance hard to reconcile with absolutely efficient markets. In a careful statistical analysis of mutual fund "stars," Kosowski, Timmerman, Wermers, and White[54] conclude that the stock-picking ability of a minority of managers is sufficient to cover their costs, and that their superior performance tends to persist over time. However, Nobel Prize–winner Paul Samuelson[55] reviewed this investment hall of fame but pointed out that the records of the vast majority of professional money managers offer convincing evidence that there are no easy strategies to guarantee success in the securities markets.

Survivorship Bias in Mutual Fund Studies

In any period, some managers may be lucky, and others unlucky. We argued in Chapter 4 that a good way to separate skill from luck is to see whether the managers who perform well in one period tend to be above-average performers in subsequent periods. If they are, we should be more willing to ascribe their success to skill. Unfortunately, studies of mutual fund performance can be affected by *survivorship bias,* the tendency for less successful funds to go out of business over time, thus leaving the sample. This can give rise to the appearance of persistence in performance, even if there is none in reality.

Define a "winner" fund as one in the top half of the distribution of returns in a given period and a "loser" fund as one in the bottom half of the sample. If performance is due solely to chance, the probability of being a winner or loser in the next period is the same regardless of first-period performance. A 2×2 tabulation of performance in two consecutive periods would look like this:

	Second Period	
First Period	**Winners**	**Losers**
Winners	.25	.25
Losers	.25	.25

For example, the first period winners (50% of the sample) are equally likely to be winners or losers in the second period, so 25% of total outcomes fall in each cell in the first row.

But what happens if losing funds or managers are removed from the sample because they are shut down by their management companies? This can lead to the appearance of

[54]R. Kosowski, A. Timmerman, R. Wermers, and H. White. "Can Mutual Fund 'Stars' Really Pick Stocks? New Evidence from a Bootstrap Analysis," *Journal of Finance* 61 (December 2006), pp. 2551–95.

[55]Paul Samuelson, "The Judgment of Economic Science on Rational Portfolio Management," *Journal of Portfolio Management* 16 (Fall 1989), pp. 4–12.

	Second-Period Winners	Second-Period Losers
A. No cut-off (*n* = 600)		
First-period winners	150.09	149.51
First-period losers	149.51	150.09
B. 5% cut-off (*n* = 494)		
First-period winners	127.49	119.51
First-period losers	119.51	127.49
C. 10% cut-off (*n* = 398)		
First-period winners	106.58	92.42
First-period losers	92.42	106.58

TABLE 11.2

Two-way table of managers classified by risk-adjusted returns over successive intervals

Source: S. J. Brown, W. Goetzmann, and S. A. Ross, "Survivorship Bias in Performance Studies," *Review of Financial Studies* 5 (1992).

performance persistence. Brown, Goetzmann, Ibbotson, and Ross[56] use a sample of mutual fund returns to simulate the potential import of survivorship bias. They simulate annual returns over a 4-year period for 600 managers drawing from distributions constructed to mimic historical equity and fund returns in the United States, compute performance over two 2-year periods, and construct 2 × 2 tables of winner/loser performance like the one above. Their results appear in Table 11.2. If all 600 managers remain in the simulated sample, the results look much like the ones above (see panel A). But if the bottom 5% of first-period performers are removed from the sample each year (5% cut-off, panel B), the diagonal terms are larger than the off-diagonal terms: winners seem more likely to remain winners, and losers to remain losers. If a higher fraction of poor performers are removed from the sample (panel C), there is even greater appearance of performance persistence.

The appearance of persistence in the simulation is due to survivorship bias. Average alphas are constructed to be zero for all groups. These results serve as a warning that data sets used to assess performance of professional managers must be free of survivorship bias. Unfortunately, many are not.

So, Are Markets Efficient?

There is a telling joke about two economists walking down the street. They spot a $20 bill on the sidewalk. One starts to pick it up, but the other one says, "Don't bother; if the bill were real someone would have picked it up already."

The lesson is clear. An overly doctrinaire belief in efficient markets can paralyze the investor and make it appear that no research effort can be justified. This extreme view is probably unwarranted. There are enough anomalies in the empirical evidence to justify the search for underpriced securities that clearly goes on.

The bulk of the evidence, however, suggests that any supposedly superior investment strategy should be taken with many grains of salt. The market is competitive *enough* that only differentially superior information or insight will earn money; the easy pickings have been picked. In the end it is likely that the margin of superiority that any professional manager can add is so slight that the statistician will not easily be able to detect it.

We conclude that markets are very efficient, but that rewards to the especially diligent, intelligent, or creative may in fact be waiting.

[56]S. J. Brown, W. Goetzmann, R. G. Ibbotson, and S. A. Ross, "Survivorship Bias in Performance Studies," *Review of Financial Studies* 5 (1992).

SUMMARY

1. Statistical research has shown that to a close approximation stock prices seem to follow a random walk with no discernible predictable patterns that investors can exploit. Such findings are now taken to be evidence of market efficiency, that is, evidence that market prices reflect all currently available information. Only new information will move stock prices, and this information is equally likely to be good news or bad news.

2. Market participants distinguish among three forms of the efficient market hypothesis. The weak form asserts that all information to be derived from past trading data already is reflected in stock prices. The semistrong form claims that all publicly available information is already reflected. The strong form, which generally is acknowledged to be extreme, asserts that all information, including insider information, is reflected in prices.

3. Technical analysis focuses on stock price patterns and on proxies for buy or sell pressure in the market. Fundamental analysis focuses on the determinants of the underlying value of the firm, such as current profitability and growth prospects. Because both types of analysis are based on public information, neither should generate excess profits if markets are operating efficiently.

4. Proponents of the efficient market hypothesis often advocate passive as opposed to active investment strategies. The policy of passive investors is to buy and hold a broad-based market index. They expend resources neither on market research nor on frequent purchase and sale of stocks. Passive strategies may be tailored to meet individual investor requirements.

5. Event studies are used to evaluate the economic impact of events of interest, using abnormal stock returns. Such studies usually show that there is some leakage of inside information to some market participants before the public announcement date. Therefore, insiders do seem to be able to exploit their access to information to at least a limited extent.

6. Empirical studies of technical analysis do not generally support the hypothesis that such analysis can generate superior trading profits. One notable exception to this conclusion is the apparent success of momentum-based strategies over intermediate-term horizons.

7. Several anomalies regarding fundamental analysis have been uncovered. These include the P/E effect, the small-firm-in-January effect, the neglected-firm effect, post–earnings-announcement price drift, and the book-to-market effect. Whether these anomalies represent market inefficiency or poorly understood risk premiums is still a matter of debate.

8. The noisy markets hypothesis holds that random errors in market valuations will make capitalization-weighted indexing strategies inefficient since they will overweight overvalued securities and underweight undervalued securities. Fundamental indexing is advocated as means to construct indexes free of such biases. But without a means to identify mispriced securities, fundamental indexing in practice amounts to little more than a portfolio strategy tilted toward value stocks.

9. By and large, the performance record of professionally managed funds lends little credence to claims that most professionals can consistently beat the market.

Related Web sites for this chapter are available at **www.mhhe.com/bkm**

KEY TERMS

random walk	support levels	momentum effect
efficient market hypothesis	fundamental analysis	reversal effect
weak-form EMH	passive investment strategy	anomalies
semistrong-form EMH	index fund	P/E effect
strong-form EMH	event study	small-firm effect
technical analysis	abnormal return	neglected-firm effect
resistance levels	cumulative abnormal return	book-to-market effect

9. *a.* Briefly explain the concept of the efficient market hypothesis (EMH) and each of its three forms—weak, semistrong, and strong—and briefly discuss the degree to which existing empirical evidence supports each of the three forms of the EMH.

   b. Briefly discuss the implications of the efficient market hypothesis for investment policy as it applies to:

   i. Technical analysis in the form of charting.
   ii. Fundamental analysis.

   c. Briefly explain the roles or responsibilities of portfolio managers in an efficient market environment.

10. Growth and value can be defined in several ways. "Growth" usually conveys the idea of a portfolio emphasizing or including only issues believed to possess above-average future rates of per-share earnings growth. Low current yield, high price-to-book ratios, and high price-to-earnings ratios are typical characteristics of such portfolios. "Value" usually conveys the idea of portfolios emphasizing or including only issues currently showing low price-to-book ratios, low price-to-earnings ratios, above-average levels of dividend yield, and market prices believed to be below the issues' intrinsic values.

    a. Identify and provide reasons why, over an extended period of time, value-stock investing might outperform growth-stock investing.

    b. Explain why the outcome suggested in (*a*) should not be possible in a market widely regarded as being highly efficient.

---

1. Collect the following data for a sample of firms from Market Insight (**www.mhhe.com/edumarketinsight**):

   a. Price/Book ratio.
   b. Price/EPS from operations ratio.
   c. Market capitalization (size).
   d. Price/Cash Flow ratio.
   e. Another criterion that interests you.

   You can find this information by choosing a company, then clicking on the *Financial Hlts.* link in the *Compustat Reports* section. Rank the firms based on each of the criteria separately and divide the firms into five groups based on their ranking for each criterion. Calculate the average rate of return for each group of firms.

   Do you confirm or reject any of the anomalies cited in this chapter? Can you uncover a new anomaly? Note: For your test to be valid, you must form your portfolios based on criteria observed at the *beginning* of the period when you form the stock groups. Why?

2. Use the price history from Market Insight (**www.mhhe.com/edumarketinsight**) to calculate the beta of each of the firms in the previous question. Use this beta, the T-bill rate, and the return on the S&P 500 to calculate the risk-adjusted abnormal return of each stock group. Does any anomaly uncovered in the previous question persist after controlling for risk?

3. Now form stock groups that use two criteria simultaneously. For example, form a portfolio of stocks that are both in the lowest quintile of price–earnings ratios and in the lowest quintile of market-to-book ratio. Does selecting stocks based on more than one characteristic improve your ability to devise portfolios with abnormal returns? Repeat the analysis by forming groups that meet three criteria simultaneously. Does this yield any further improvement in abnormal returns?

STANDARD &POOR'S

E-Investments

Earnings Surprises

Several Web sites list information on earnings surprises. Much of the information supplied is from Zacks.com. Each day the largest positive and negative surprises are listed. Go to **www.zacks.com/research/earnings/today_eps.php** and identify the top positive and the top negative earnings surprises for the day. The table will list the time and date of the announcement. Do you notice any difference between the times of day positive announcements tend to be made versus negative announcements?

Identify the tickers for the top three positive surprises. Once you have identified the top surprises, go to **finance.yahoo.com.** Enter the ticker symbols and obtain quotes for these securities. Examine the 5-day charts for each of the companies. Is the information incorporated into price quickly? Is there any evidence of prior knowledge or anticipation of the disclosure in advance of the trading?

Choose one of the stocks listed and click on its symbol to follow the link for more information. Click on the link for Interactive Chart that appears under the graph. You can move the cursor over various parts of the graph to investigate what happened to the price and trading volume of the stock on each trading day. Do you notice any patterns?

SOLUTIONS TO CONCEPT CHECKS

1. *a.* A high-level manager might well have private information about the firm. Her ability to trade profitably on that information is not surprising. This ability does not violate weak-form efficiency: The abnormal profits are not derived from an analysis of past price and trading data. If they were, this would indicate that there is valuable information that can be gleaned from such analysis. But this ability does violate strong-form efficiency. Apparently, there is some private information that is not already reflected in stock prices.

    b. The information sets that pertain to the weak, semistrong, and strong form of the EMH can be described by the following illustration:

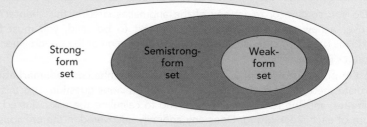

The weak-form information set includes only the history of prices and volumes. The semistrong-form set includes the weak form set *plus* all publicly available information. In turn, the strong-form set includes the semistrong set *plus* insiders' information. It is illegal to act on this incremental information (insiders' private information). The direction of *valid* implication is

Strong-form EMH $\Rightarrow$ Semistrong-form EMH $\Rightarrow$ Weak-form EMH

The reverse direction implication is *not* valid. For example, stock prices may reflect all past price data (weak-form efficiency) but may not reflect relevant fundamental data (semistrong-form inefficiency).

2. The point made in the preceding discussion is that the very fact that we observe stock prices near so-called resistance levels belies the assumption that the price can be a resistance level. If a stock is observed to sell *at any price,* then investors must believe that a fair rate of return can be earned if the stock is purchased at that price. It is logically impossible for a stock to have a resistance level *and* offer a fair rate of return at prices just below the resistance level. If we accept that prices are appropriate, we must reject any presumption concerning resistance levels.

3. If *everyone* follows a passive strategy, sooner or later prices will fail to reflect new information. At this point there are profit opportunities for active investors who uncover mispriced securities. As they buy and sell these assets, prices again will be driven to fair levels.

4. Predictably declining CARs do violate the EMH. If one can predict such a phenomenon, a profit opportunity emerges: Sell (or short sell) the affected stocks on an event date just before their prices are predicted to fall.

5. The answer depends on your prior beliefs about market efficiency. Miller's record has been incredibly strong. On the other hand, with so many funds in existence, it is less surprising that *some* fund would appear to be consistently superior after the fact. Exceptional past performance of a small number of managers is possible by chance even in an efficient market. A better test is provided in "continuation studies." Are better performers in one period more likely to repeat that performance in later periods?

BEHAVIORAL FINANCE
AND TECHNICAL ANALYSIS

THE EFFICIENT MARKET hypothesis makes two important predictions. First, it implies that security prices properly reflect whatever information is available to investors. A second implication follows immediately: active traders will find it difficult to outperform passive strategies such as holding market indexes. To do so would require differential insight; this in a highly competitive market is very hard to come by.

Unfortunately, it is hard to devise measures of the "true" or intrinsic value of a security, and correspondingly difficult to test directly whether prices match those values. Therefore, most tests of market efficiency have focused on the performance of active trading strategies. These tests have been of two kinds. The anomalies literature has examined strategies that apparently *would* have provided superior risk-adjusted returns (e.g., investing in stocks with momentum or in value rather than glamour stocks). Other tests have looked at the results of *actual* investments by asking whether professional managers have been able to beat the market.

Neither class of tests has proven fully conclusive. The anomalies literature suggests that several strategies would have provided superior returns. But there are questions as to whether some of these apparent anomalies reflect risk premiums not captured by simple models of risk and return, or even if they merely reflect data mining. Moreover, the apparent inability of the typical money manager to turn these anomalies into superior returns on actual portfolios casts additional doubt on their "reality."

A relatively new school of thought dubbed *behavioral finance* argues that the sprawling literature on trading strategies has missed a larger and more important point by overlooking the first implication of efficient markets—the correctness of security prices. This may be the more important implication, because market economies rely on prices to allocate resources efficiently. The behavioral school argues that even if security prices are wrong, it still can be difficult to exploit them and, therefore, that the failure to uncover obviously successful trading rules or traders cannot be taken as proof of market efficiency.

Whereas conventional theories presume that investors are rational, behavioral finance starts with the assumption that they might not be. We will examine some of the information-processing and behavioral irrationalities uncovered by psychologists in other contexts and show how these tendencies applied to financial markets might result in some of the anomalies discussed in the previous chapter. We then examine the limitations of strategies designed to take advantage of behaviorally induced mispricing. If the limits to such arbitrage activity are severe, mispricing can survive even if some rational investors attempt to exploit it. We turn next to technical analysis and show how behavioral models give some support to techniques that clearly would be useless in efficient markets. We close the chapter with a brief survey of some of these technical strategies.

12.1 THE BEHAVIORAL CRITIQUE

The premise of **behavioral finance** is that conventional financial theory ignores how real people make decisions and that people make a difference.[1] A growing number of economists have come to interpret the anomalies literature as consistent with several "irrationalities" that seem to characterize individuals making complicated decisions. These irrationalities fall into two broad categories: first, that investors do not always process information correctly and therefore infer incorrect probability distributions about future rates of return; and second, that even given a probability distribution of returns, they often make inconsistent or systematically suboptimal decisions.

Of course, the existence of irrational investors would not by itself be sufficient to render capital markets inefficient. If such irrationalities did affect prices, then sharp-eyed arbitrageurs taking advantage of profit opportunities might be expected to push prices back to their proper values. Thus, the second leg of the behavioral critique is that in practice the actions of such arbitrageurs are limited and therefore insufficient to force prices to match intrinsic value.

This leg of the argument is important. Virtually everyone agrees that if prices are right (i.e., price = intrinsic value), then there are no easy profit opportunities. But the reverse is not necessarily true. If behaviorists are correct about limits to arbitrage activity, then the absence of profit opportunities does not necessarily imply that markets are efficient. We've noted that most tests of the efficient market hypothesis have focused on the existence of profit opportunities, often as reflected in the performance of money managers. But their failure to systematically outperform passive investment strategies need not imply that markets are in fact efficient.

We will start our summary of the behavioral critique with the first leg of the argument, surveying a sample of the informational processing errors uncovered by psychologists in other areas. We next examine a few of the behavioral irrationalities that seem to characterize decision makers. Finally, we look at limits to arbitrage activity, and conclude with a tentative assessment of the import of the behavioral debate.

Information Processing

Errors in information processing can lead investors to misestimate the true probabilities of possible events or associated rates of return. Several such biases have been uncovered. Here are four of the more important ones.

---

[1]The discussion in this section is largely based on Nicholas Barberis and Richard Thaler, "A Survey of Behavioral Finance," in the *Handbook of the Economics of Finance*, eds. G. M. Constantinides, M. Harris, and R. Stulz (Amsterdam: Elsevier, 2003).

Forecasting Errors   A series of experiments by Kahneman and Tversky[2] indicate that people give too much weight to recent experience compared to prior beliefs when making forecasts (sometimes dubbed a *memory bias*) and tend to make forecasts that are too extreme given the uncertainty inherent in their information. DeBondt and Thaler[3] argue that the P/E effect can be explained by earnings expectations that are too extreme. In this view, when forecasts of a firm's future earnings are high, perhaps due to favorable recent performance, they tend to be *too* high relative to the objective prospects of the firm. This results in a high initial P/E (due to the excessive optimism built into the stock price) and poor subsequent performance when investors recognize their error. Thus, high P/E firms tend to be poor investments.

Overconfidence   People tend to overestimate the precision of their beliefs or forecasts, and they tend to overestimate their abilities. In one famous survey, 90% of drivers in Sweden ranked themselves as better-than-average drivers. Such overconfidence may be responsible for the prevalence of active versus passive investment management—itself an anomaly to adherents of the efficient market hypothesis. Despite the growing popularity of indexing, only about 10% of the equity in the mutual fund industry is held in indexed accounts. The dominance of active management in the face of the typical underperformance of such strategies (consider the disappointing performance of actively managed mutual funds reviewed in Chapter 4 as well as in the previous chapter) is consistent with a tendency to overestimate ability.

An interesting example of overconfidence in financial markets is provided by Barber and Odean,[4] who compare trading activity and average returns in brokerage accounts of men and women. They find that men (in particular single men) trade far more actively than women, consistent with the greater overconfidence among men well documented in the psychology literature. They also find that trading activity is highly predictive of poor investment performance. The top 20% of accounts ranked by portfolio turnover had average returns 7 percentage points lower than the 20% of the accounts with the lowest turnover rates. As they conclude, "trading [and by implication, overconfidence] is hazardous to your wealth."

Conservatism   A **conservatism** bias means that investors are too slow (too conservative) in updating their beliefs in response to new evidence. This means that they might initially underreact to news about a firm, so that prices will fully reflect new information only gradually. Such a bias would give rise to momentum in stock market returns.

Sample Size Neglect and Representativeness   The notion of **representativeness** holds that people commonly do not take into account the size of a sample, apparently reasoning that a small sample is just as representative of a population as a large one. They may therefore infer a pattern too quickly based on a small sample and extrapolate apparent trends too far into the future. It is easy to see how such a pattern would be consistent with overreaction and correction anomalies. A short-lived run of good earnings reports or high stock returns would lead such investors to revise their assessments of likely future

---

[2]D. Kahneman and A. Tversky, "On the Psychology of Prediction," *Psychology Review* 80 (1973), pp. 237–51 and "Subjective Probability: A Judgment of Representativeness," *Cognitive Psychology* 3 (1972), pp. 430–54.

[3]W.F.M. De Bondt and R. H. Thaler, "Do Security Analysts Overreact?" *American Economic Review* 80 (1990), pp. 52–57.

[4]Brad Barber and Terrance Odean, "Boys Will Be Boys: Gender, Overconfidence, and Common Stock Investment," *Quarterly Journal of Economics* 16 (2001), pp. 262–92, and "Trading Is Hazardous to Your Wealth: The Common Stock Investment Performance of Individual Investors," *Journal of Finance* 55 (2000), pp. 773–806.

performance, and thus generate buying pressure that exaggerates the price run-up. Eventually, the gap between price and intrinsic value becomes glaring and the market corrects its initial error. Interestingly, stocks with the best recent performance suffer reversals precisely in the few days surrounding earnings announcements, suggesting that the correction occurs just as investors learn that their initial beliefs were too extreme.[5]

CONCEPT CHECK 1	We saw in the last chapter that stocks seem to exhibit a pattern of short- to middle-term momentum, along with long-term reversals. How might this pattern arise from an interplay between the conservatism and representativeness biases?

Behavioral Biases

Even if information processing were perfect, many studies conclude that individuals would tend to make less-than-fully-rational decisions using that information. These behavioral biases largely affect how investors frame questions of risk versus return, and therefore make risk–return trade-offs.

Framing   Decisions seem to be affected by how choices are **framed.** For example, an individual may reject a bet when it is posed in terms of the risk surrounding possible gains but may accept that same bet when described in terms of the risk surrounding potential losses. In other words, individuals may act risk averse in terms of gains but risk seeking in terms of losses. But in many cases, the choice of how to frame a risky venture—as involving gains or losses—can be arbitrary.

EXAMPLE 12.1   Framing

Consider a coin toss with a payoff of $50 for tails. Now consider a gift of $50 that is bundled with a bet that imposes a loss of $50 if that coin toss comes up heads. In both cases, you end up with zero for heads and $50 for tails. But the former description frames the coin toss as posing a risky gain while the latter frames the coin toss in terms of risky losses. The difference in framing can lead to different attitudes toward the bet.

Mental Accounting   **Mental accounting** is a specific form of framing in which people segregate certain decisions. For example, an investor may take a lot of risk with one investment account, but establish a very conservative position with another account that is dedicated to her child's education. Rationally, it might be better to view both accounts as part of the investor's overall portfolio with the risk–return profiles of each integrated into a unified framework. Statman[6] argues that mental accounting is consistent with some investors' irrational preference for stocks with high cash dividends (they feel free to spend dividend income, but would not "dip into capital" by selling a few shares of another stock with the same total rate of return) and with a tendency to ride losing stock positions for too long (because "behavioral investors" are reluctant to realize losses). In fact, investors

---

[5]N. Chopra, J. Lakonishok, and J. Ritter, "Measuring Abnormal Performance: Do Stocks Overreact?" *Journal of Financial Economics* 31 (1992), pp. 235–68.

[6]Meir Statman, "Behavioral Finance," *Contemporary Finance Digest* 1 (Winter 1997), pp. 5–22.

are more likely to sell stocks with gains than those with losses, precisely contrary to a tax-minimization strategy.[7]

Mental accounting effects also can help explain momentum in stock prices. The *house money effect* refers to gamblers' greater willingness to accept new bets if they currently are ahead. They think of (i.e., frame) the bet as being made with their "winnings account," that is, with the casino's and not with their own money, and thus are more willing to accept risk. Analogously, after a stock market run-up, individuals may view investments as largely funded out of a "capital gains account," become more tolerant of risk, discount future cash flows at a lower rate, and thus further push up prices.

Regret Avoidance Psychologists have found that individuals who make decisions that turn out badly have more regret (blame themselves more) when that decision was more unconventional. For example, buying a blue-chip portfolio that turns down is not as painful as experiencing the same losses on an unknown start-up firm. Any losses on the blue-chip stocks can be more easily attributed to bad luck rather than bad decision making and cause less regret. De Bondt and Thaler[8] argue that such **regret avoidance** is consistent with both the size and book-to-market effect. Higher book-to-market firms tend to have depressed stock prices. These firms are "out of favor" and more likely to be in a financially precarious position. Similarly, smaller less well known firms are also less conventional investments. Such firms require more "courage" on the part of the investor, which increases the required rate of return. Mental accounting can add to this effect. If investors focus on the gains or losses of individual stocks, rather than on broad portfolios, they can become more risk averse concerning stocks with recent poor performance, discount their cash flows at a higher rate, and thereby create a value-stock risk premium.

CONCEPT CHECK 2

How might the P/E effect (discussed in the previous chapter) also be explained as a consequence of regret avoidance?

Prospect Theory Prospect theory modifies the analytic description of rational risk-averse investors found in standard financial theory.[9] Figure 12.1, panel A, illustrates the conventional description of a risk-averse investor. Higher wealth provides higher satisfaction or "utility," but at a diminishing rate (the curve flattens as the individual becomes wealthier). This gives rise to risk aversion: A gain of $1,000 increases utility by less than a loss of $1,000 reduces it; therefore, investors will reject risky prospects that don't offer a risk premium.

Figure 12.1, panel B, shows a competing description of preferences characterized by "loss aversion." Utility depends not on the *level* of wealth as in panel A, but on *changes* in wealth from current levels. Moreover, to the left of zero (zero denotes no change from current wealth), the curve is convex rather than concave. This has several implications. Whereas many conventional utility functions imply that investors may become less risk averse as wealth increases, the function in panel B always re-centers on current wealth, thereby ruling out such decreases in risk aversion and possibly helping to explain high

---

[7]H. Shefrin and M. Statman, "The Disposition to Sell Winners Too Early and Ride Losers Too Long: Theory and Evidence," *Journal of Finance* 40 (July 1985), pp. 777–90; and T. Odean, "Are Investors Reluctant to Realize Their Losses?" *Journal of Finance* 53 (1998), pp. 1775–98.

[8]W.F.M. De Bondt and R. H. Thaler, "Further Evidence on Investor Overreaction and Stock Market Seasonality," *Journal of Finance* 42 (1987), pp. 557–81.

[9]Prospect theory originated with a highly influential paper about decision making under uncertainty by D. Kahneman and A. Tversky, "Prospect Theory: An Analysis of Decision under Risk," *Econometrica* 47 (1979), pp. 263–91.

average historical equity risk premiums. Moreover, the convex curvature to the left of the origin in panel B will induce investors to be risk seeking rather than risk averse when it comes to losses. Consistent with loss aversion, traders in the T-bond futures contract have been observed to assume significantly greater risk in afternoon sessions following morning sessions in which they have lost money.[10]

These are only a sample of many behavioral biases uncovered in the literature. Many have implications for investor behavior. The nearby box offers some good examples.

Limits to Arbitrage

Behavioral biases would not matter for stock pricing if rational arbitrageurs could fully exploit the mistakes of behavioral investors. Trades of profit-seeking investors would correct any misalignment of prices. However, behavioral advocates argue that in practice, several factors limit the ability to profit from mispricing.[11]

Fundamental Risk   Suppose that a share of IBM is underpriced. Buying it may present a profit opportunity, but it is hardly risk-free, because the presumed market underpricing can get worse. While price eventually should converge to intrinsic value, this may not happen until after the trader's investment horizon. For example, the investor may be a mutual fund manager who may lose clients (not to mention a job!) if short-term performance is poor, or a trader who

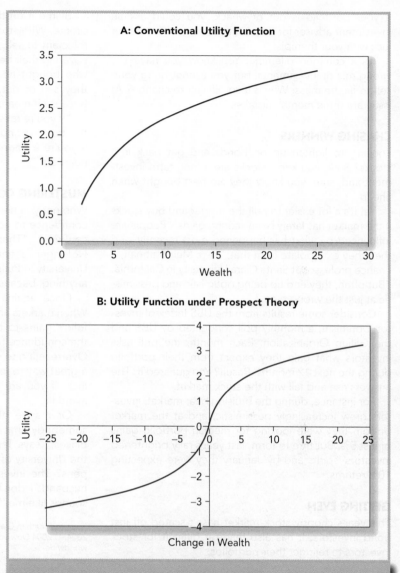

FIGURE 12.1   Prospect theory. *Panel A:* A conventional utility function is defined in terms of wealth and is concave, resulting in risk aversion. *Panel B:* Under loss aversion, the utility function is defined in terms of losses relative to current wealth. It is also convex to the left of the origin, giving rise to risk-seeking behavior in terms of losses.

[10]J. D. Coval and T. Shumway, "Do Behavioral Biases Affect Prices?" *Journal of Finance* 60 (February 2005), pp. 1–34.

[11]Some of the more influential references on limits to arbitrage are J. B. DeLong, A. Schleifer, L. Summers, and R. Waldmann, "Noise Trader Risk in Financial Markets," *Journal of Political Economy* 98 (August 1990), pp. 704–38; and A. Schleifer and R. Vishny, "The Limits of Arbitrage," *Journal of Finance* 52 (March 1997), pp. 35–55.

WHY IT'S SO TOUGH TO FIX YOUR PORTFOLIO

If your portfolio is out of whack, you could ask an investment adviser for help. But you might have better luck with your therapist.

It's a common dilemma: You know you have the wrong mix of investments, but you cannot bring yourself to fix the mess. Why is it so difficult to change? At issue are three mental mistakes.

CHASING WINNERS

Looking to lighten up on bonds and get back into stocks? Sure, you know stocks are a long-term investment and, sure, you know they are best bought when cheap.

Yet it's a lot easier to pull the trigger and buy stocks if the market has lately been scoring gains. "People are influenced by what has happened most recently, and then they extrapolate from that," says Meir Statman, a finance professor at Santa Clara University in California. "But often, they end up being optimistic and pessimistic at just the wrong time."

Consider some results from the UBS Index of Investor Optimism, a monthly poll conducted by UBS and the Gallup Organization. Each month, the poll asks investors what gain they expect from their portfolio during the next 12 months. Result? You guessed it: The answers rise and fall with the stock market.

For instance, during the bruising bear market, investors grew increasingly pessimistic, and at the market bottom they were looking for median portfolio gains of just 5%. But true to form, last year's rally brightened investors' spirits and by January they were expecting 10% returns.

GETTING EVEN

This year's choppy stock market hasn't scared off just bond investors. It has also made it difficult for stock investors to rejigger their portfolios.

Blame it on the old "get even, then get out" syndrome. With stocks treading water, many investors are reluctant to sell, because they are a long way from recovering their bear-market losses. To be sure, investors who bought near the peak are underwater, whether they sell or not. But selling losers is still agonizing, because it means admitting you made a mistake.

"If you're rational and you have a loss, you sell, take the tax loss and move on," Prof. Statman says. "But if you're a normal person, selling at a loss tears your heart out."

MUSTERING COURAGE

Whether you need to buy stocks or buy bonds, it takes confidence to act. And right now, investors just aren't confident. "There's this status-quo bias," says John Nofsinger, a finance professor at Washington State University in Pullman, Washington. "We're afraid to do anything, because we're afraid we'll regret it."

Once again, it's driven by recent market action When markets are flying high, folks attribute their portfolio's gains to their own brilliance. That gives them the confidence to trade more and to take greater risks Overreacting to short-term market results is, of course, a great way to lose a truckload of money. But with any luck, if you are aware of this pitfall, maybe you will avoid it.

Or maybe [this is] too optimistic. "You can tell somebody that investors have all these behavioral biases," says Terrance Odean, a finance professor at the University of California at Berkeley. "So what happens? The investor thinks, 'Oh, that sounds like my husband. I don't think many investors say, 'Oh, that sounds like me.'"

Source: Jonathan Clements, *The Wall Street Journal Online*, June 23, 2004. © 2004 Dow Jones & Company, Inc. All rights reserved worldwide.

---

may run through her capital if the market turns against her, even temporarily. The **fundamental risk** incurred in exploiting the apparent profit opportunity presumably will limit the activity of the traders.

EXAMPLE 12.2 Fundamental Risk

In much of 2007, the NASDAQ index fluctuated at a level around 2,600. From that perspective, the value the index had reached 5 years earlier, around 5,000, seemed obviously crazy. Surely some investors living through the Internet "bubble" of the late 1990s must have identified the index as grossly overvalued, suggesting a good selling opportunity. But

---

this hardly would have been a riskless arbitrage opportunity. Consider that NASDAQ may also have been overvalued in 1999 when it first crossed above 3,500 (35% higher than its value in 2007). An investor in 1999 who believed (as it turns out, quite correctly) that NASDAQ was overvalued at 3,500 and decided to sell it short would have suffered enormous losses as the index increased by another 1,500 points before finally peaking at 5,000. While the investor might have derived considerable satisfaction at eventually being proven right about the overpricing, by entering a year before the market "corrected," he might also have gone broke.

Implementation Costs Exploiting overpricing can be particularly difficult. Short selling a security entails costs; short-sellers may have to return the borrowed security on little notice, rendering the horizon of the short sale uncertain; other investors such as many pension or mutual fund managers face strict limits on their discretion to short securities. This can limit the ability of arbitrage activity to force prices to fair value.

Model Risk One always has to worry that an apparent profit opportunity is more apparent than real. Perhaps you are using a faulty model to value the security, and the price actually is right. Mispricing may make a position a good bet, but it is still a risky one, which limits the extent to which it will be pursued.

Limits to Arbitrage and the Law of One Price

While one can debate the implications of much of the anomalies literature, surely the Law of One Price (positing that effectively identical assets should have identical prices) should be satisfied in rational markets. Yet there are several instances where the law seems to have been violated. These instances are good case studies of the limits to arbitrage.

"Siamese Twin" Companies[12] In 1907, Royal Dutch Petroleum and Shell Transport merged their operations into one firm. The two original companies, which continued to trade separately, agreed to split all profits from the joint company on a 60/40 basis. Shareholders of Royal Dutch receive 60% of the cash flow, and those of Shell receive 40%. One would therefore expect that Royal Dutch should sell for exactly 60/40 = 1.5 times the price of Shell. But this is not the case. Figure 12.2 shows that the relative value of the two firms has departed considerably from this "parity" ratio for extended periods of time.

Doesn't this mispricing give rise to an arbitrage opportunity? If Royal Dutch sells for more than 1.5 times Shell, why not buy relatively underpriced Shell and short sell overpriced Royal? This seems like a reasonable strategy, but if you had followed it in February 1993 when Royal sold for about 10% more than its parity value, Figure 12.2 shows that you would have lost a lot of money as the premium widened to about 17% before finally reversing after 1999. As in Example 12.2, this opportunity posed fundamental risk.

Equity Carve-outs Several equity carve-outs also have violated the Law of One Price.[13] To illustrate, consider the case of 3Com, which in 1999 decided to spin off its Palm division. It first sold 5% of its stake in Palm in an IPO, announcing that it would distribute the

[12]This discussion is based on K. A. Froot and E. M. Dabora, "How Are Stock Prices Affected by the Location of Trade?" *Journal of Financial Economics* 53 (1999), pp. 189–216.

[13]O. A. Lamont and R. H. Thaler, "Can the Market Add and Subtract? Mispricing in Tech Carve-outs," *Journal of Political Economy* 111 (2003), pp. 227–68.

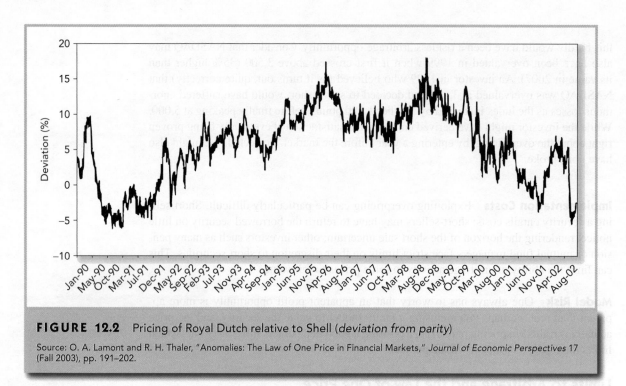

FIGURE 12.2   Pricing of Royal Dutch relative to Shell (*deviation from parity*)

Source: O. A. Lamont and R. H. Thaler, "Anomalies: The Law of One Price in Financial Markets," *Journal of Economic Perspectives* 17 (Fall 2003), pp. 191–202.

remaining 95% of its Palm shares to 3Com shareholders 6 months later in a spinoff. Each 3Com shareholder would receive 1.5 shares of Palm in the spinoff.

Once Palm shares began trading, but prior to the spinoff, the share price of 3Com should have been *at least* 1.5 times that of Palm. After all, each share of 3Com entitled its owner to 1.5 shares of Palm *plus* an ownership stake in a profitable company. Instead, Palm shares at the IPO actually sold for *more* than the 3Com shares. The *stub value* of 3Com (i.e., the value of each 3Com share net of the value of the claim to Palm represented by that share) could be computed as the price of 3Com minus 1.5 times the price of Palm. This calculation, however, implies that 3Com's stub value was negative, despite the fact that it was a profitable company with cash assets alone of about $10 per share.

Again, an arbitrage strategy seems obvious. Why not buy 3Com and sell Palm? The limit to arbitrage in this case was the inability of investors to sell Palm short. Virtually all available shares in Palm were already borrowed and sold short, and the negative stub values persisted for more than 2 months.

Closed-End Funds   We noted in Chapter 4 that closed-end funds often sell for substantial discounts or premiums from net asset value. This is "nearly" a violation of the Law of One Price, because one would expect the value of the fund to equal the value of the shares it holds. We say nearly because, in practice, there are a few wedges between the value of the closed-end fund and its underlying assets. One is expenses. The fund incurs expenses that ultimately are paid for by investors, and these will reduce share price. On the other hand, if managers can invest fund assets to generate positive risk-adjusted returns, share price might exceed net asset value.

Lee, Shleifer, and Thaler[14] argue that the patterns of discounts and premiums on closed-end funds are driven by changes in investor sentiment. They note that discounts on various

---

[14]C. M. Lee, A. Shleifer, and R. H. Thaler, "Investor Sentiment and the Closed-End Fund Puzzle," *Journal of Finance* 46 (March 1991), pp. 75–109.

funds move together and are correlated with the return on small stocks, suggesting that all are affected by common variation in sentiment. One might consider buying funds selling at a discount from net asset value and selling those trading at a premium, but discounts and premiums can widen, subjecting this strategy too to fundamental risk. Pontiff[15] demonstrates that deviations of price from net asset value in closed-end funds tend to be higher in funds that are more difficult to arbitrage, for example, those with more idiosyncratic volatility.

Closed-end fund discounts are a good example of so-called anomalies that also may have rational explanations. Ross demonstrates that they can be reconciled with rational investors even if expenses or fund abnormal returns are modest.[16] He shows that if a fund has a dividend yield of δ, an alpha (risk-adjusted abnormal return) of α, and expense ratio of ε, then using the constant-growth dividend discount model (see Chapter 18), the premium of the fund over its net asset value will be

$$\frac{\text{Price} - \text{NAV}}{\text{NAV}} = \frac{\alpha - \varepsilon}{\delta + \varepsilon - \alpha}$$

If the fund manager's performance more than compensates for expenses (i.e., if $\alpha > \varepsilon$), the fund will sell at a premium to NAV; otherwise it will sell at a discount. For example, suppose $\alpha = .015$, the expense ratio is $\varepsilon = .0125$, and the dividend yield is $\delta = .02$. Then the premium will be .14, or 14%. But if the market turns sour on the manager and revises its estimate of α downward to .005, that premium quickly turns into a discount of 43%.

This analysis might explain why closed-end funds often are issued to the public at a premium; if investors do not expect α to exceed ε, they won't purchase shares in the fund. But the fact that most premiums eventually turn into discounts indicates how difficult it is for management to fulfill these expectations.[17]

CONCEPT CHECK 3

Fundamental risk may be limited by a "deadline" that forces a convergence between price and intrinsic value. What do you think would happen to a closed-end fund's discount if the fund announced that it plans to liquidate in 6 months, at which time it will distribute NAV to its shareholders?

Bubbles and Behavioral Economics

In Example 12.2 above, we pointed out that the stock market run-up of the late 1990s, and even more spectacularly, the run-up of the technology-heavy NASDAQ market, seems in retrospect to have been an obvious bubble. In a 6-year period beginning in 1995, the NASDAQ index increased by a factor of more than 6. Former Fed Chairman Alan Greenspan famously characterized the dot-com boom as an example of "irrational exuberance," and his assessment turned out to be correct: by October 2002, the index fell to less than one-fourth the peak value it had reached only 2½ years earlier. This episode seems to be

---

[15]Jeffrey Pontiff, "Costly Arbitrage: Evidence from Closed-End Funds," *Quarterly Journal of Economics* 111 (November 1996), pp. 1135–51.

[16]S. A. Ross, "Neoclassical Finance, Alternative Finance and the Closed End Fund Puzzle," *European Financial Management* 8 (2002), pp. 129–37, **http://ssrn.com/abstract=313444.**

[17]We might ask why this logic of discounts and premiums does not apply to open-end mutual funds because they incur similar expense ratios. Because investors in these funds can redeem shares for NAV, the shares cannot sell at a discount to NAV. Expenses in open-end funds reduce returns in each period rather than being capitalized into price and inducing a discount.

a case in point for advocates of the behavioral school, exemplifying a market moved by irrational investor sentiment. Moreover, in accord with behavioral patterns, as the dot-com boom developed, it seemed to feed on itself, with investors increasingly confident of their investment prowess (overconfidence bias) and apparently willing to extrapolate short-term patterns into the distant future (representativeness bias).

On the other hand, bubbles are a lot easier to identify as such once they are over. While they are going on, it is not as clear that prices are irrationally exuberant and, indeed, many financial commentators at the time justified the boom as consistent with glowing forecasts for the "new economy." A simple example shows how hard it can be to tie down the fair value of stock investments.[18]

EXAMPLE 12.3   A Stock Market Bubble?

In 2000, the dividends paid by the firms included in the S&P 500 totaled $154.6 million. If the discount rate for the index was 9.2% and the expected dividend growth rate was 8%, the value of these shares according to the constant-growth dividend discount model (see Chapter 18 for more on this model) would be

$$\text{Value} = \frac{\text{Dividend}}{\text{Discount rate} - \text{Growth rate}} = \frac{\$154.6}{.092 - .08} = \$12,883 \text{ million}$$

This was quite close to the actual total value of those firms at the time. But the estimate is highly sensitive to the input values, and even a small reassessment of their prospects would result in a big revision of price. Suppose the expected dividend growth rate fell to 7.4%. This would reduce the value of the index to

$$\text{Value} = \frac{\text{Dividend}}{\text{Discount rate} - \text{Growth rate}} = \frac{\$154.6}{.092 - .074} = \$8,589 \text{ million}$$

which was about the value to which the S&P 500 firms had fallen by October 2002. In light of this example, the run-up and crash of the 1990s seems easier to reconcile with rational behavior.

Still, other evidence seems to tag the dot-com boom as at least partially irrational. Consider, for example, the results of a study documenting that firms adding ".com" to the end of their names during this period enjoyed a meaningful stock price increase.[19] That doesn't sound like rational valuation to us.

Evaluating the Behavioral Critique

As investors, we are concerned with the existence of profit opportunities. The behavioral explanations of efficient market anomalies do not give guidance as to how to exploit any irrationality. For investors, the question is still whether there is money to be made from mispricing, and the behavioral literature is largely silent on this point.

However, as we have emphasized above, one of the important implications of the efficient market hypothesis is that security prices serve as reliable guides to the allocation of

---

[18]The following example is taken from R. A. Brealey, S. C. Myers, and F. Allen, *Principles of Corporate Finance,* 8th ed. (Burr Ridge, IL: McGraw-Hill Irwin, 2006).

[19]P. R. Rau, O. Dimitrov, and M. Cooper, "A Rose.com by Any Other Name," *Journal of Finance* 56 (2001), pp. 2371–88.

real capital. If prices are distorted, then capital markets will give misleading signals (and incentives) as to where the economy may best allocate resources. In this crucial dimension, the behavioral critique of the efficient market hypothesis is certainly important irrespective of any implication for investment strategies.

There is considerable debate among financial economists concerning the strength of the behavioral critique. Many believe that the behavioral approach is too unstructured, in effect allowing virtually any anomaly to be explained by some combination of irrationalities chosen from a laundry list of behavioral biases. While it is easy to "reverse engineer" a behavioral explanation for any particular anomaly, these critics would like to see a consistent or unified behavioral theory that can explain a *range* of behavioral anomalies.

More fundamentally, others are not convinced that the anomalies literature as a whole is a convincing indictment of the efficient market hypothesis. Fama[20] notes that the anomalies are inconsistent in terms of their support for one type of irrationality versus another. For example, some papers document long-term corrections (consistent with overreaction) while others document long-term continuations of abnormal returns (consistent with underreaction). Moreover, the statistical significance of many of these results is less than meets the eye. Even small errors in choosing a benchmark against which to compare returns can cumulate to large apparent abnormalities in long-term returns.

Behavioral finance is still relatively new, however. Its critique of full rationality in investor decision making is well taken, but the extent to which limited rationality affects asset pricing is controversial. Whether or not investor irrationality affects asset prices, however, behavioral finance already makes important points about portfolio management. Investors who are aware of the potential pitfalls in information processing and decision making that seem to characterize their peers should be better able to avoid such errors. Ironically, the insights of behavioral finance may lead to some of the same policy conclusions embraced by efficient market advocates. For example, an easy way to avoid some of the behavioral minefields is to pursue passive, largely indexed, portfolio strategies. It seems that only rare individuals can consistently beat passive strategies; this conclusion may hold true whether your fellow investors are behavioral or rational.

12.2   TECHNICAL ANALYSIS AND BEHAVIORAL FINANCE

Technical analysis attempts to exploit recurring and predictable patterns in stock prices to generate superior investment performance. Technicians do not deny the value of fundamental information, but believe that prices only gradually close in on intrinsic value. As fundamentals shift, astute traders can exploit the adjustment to a new equilibrium.

For example, one of the best-documented behavioral tendencies is the *disposition effect,* which refers to the tendency of investors to hold on to losing investments. Behavioral investors seem reluctant to realize losses. This disposition effect can lead to momentum in stock prices even if fundamental values follow a random walk.[21] The fact that the demand of "disposition investors" for a company's shares depends on the price history of those shares means that prices close in on fundamental values only over time, consistent with the central motivation of technical analysis.

Behavioral biases may also be consistent with technical analysts' use of volume data. An important behavioral trait noted above is overconfidence, a systematic tendency to

[20]E. F. Fama, "Market Efficiency, Long-Term Returns, and Behavioral Finance," *Journal of Financial Economics* 49 (September 1998), pp. 283–306.

[21]Mark Grinblatt and Bing Han, "Prospect Theory, Mental Accounting, and Momentum," *Journal of Financial Economics* 78 (November 2005), pp. 311–39.

TECHNICAL FAILURE

PRACTICAL traders, who believe themselves to be quite exempt from any intellectual influences, are usually slaves of some defunct mathematician. That is what Keynes might have said had he considered the faith placed by some investors in the work of Leonardo of Pisa, a 12th and 13th century number-cruncher.

Better known as Fibonacci, Leonardo produced the sequence formed by adding consecutive components of a series—1, 1, 2, 3, 5, 8 and so on. Numbers in this series crop up frequently in nature and the relationship between components tends towards 1.618, a figure known as the golden ratio in architecture and design.

If it works for plants (and appears in "The Da Vinci Code"), why shouldn't it work for financial markets? Some traders believe that markets will change trend when they reach, say, 61.8% of the previous high, or are 61.8% above their low.

Believers in Fibonacci numbers are part of a school known as technical analysis, or chartism, which believes the future movement of asset prices can be divined from past data. But there is bad news for the numerologists. A new study* by Professor Roy Batchelor and Richard Ramyar of the Cass Business School, finds no evidence that Fibonacci numbers work in American stockmarkets.

This research may well fall on stony ground. Experience suggests that chartists defend their territory with an almost religious zeal. But their arguments are often anecdotal: "If technical analysis doesn't work, how come so-and-so is a multi-millionaire?" This "survivorship bias" ignores the many traders whose losses from using charts drive them out of the market. Furthermore, the recommendations of technical analysts can be so hedged about with qualifications that they can validate almost any market outcome.

If the efficient market theory is correct, technical analysis should not work at all; the prevailing market price should reflect all information, including past price movements. However, academic fashion has moved in favor of behavioral finance, which suggests that investors may not be completely rational and that their psychological biases could cause prices to deviate from their "correct" level. Technical analysts also make the perfectly fair argument that those who analyze markets on the basis of fundamentals (such as economic statistics or corporate profits) are no more successful.

All that talk of long waves is distinctly mystical and seems to take the deterministic view of history that human activity is subject to some pre-ordained pattern. Chartists fall prey to their own behavioral flaw, finding "confirmation" of patterns everywhere, as if they were reading clouds in their coffee futures.

Besides, technical analysis tends to increase trading activity, creating extra costs. Hedge funds may be able to rise above these costs; small investors will not. As illusionists often proclaim, don't try this at home.

*"No Magic in the Dow—Debunking Fibonacci's Code," working paper, Cass Business School, September 2006.

Source: *The Economist*, September 21, 2006.

---

overestimate one's abilities. As traders become overconfident, they may trade more, inducing an association between trading volume and market returns.[22] Technical analysis thus uses volume data as well as price history to direct trading strategy.

Finally, technicians believe that market fundamentals can be perturbed by irrational or behavioral factors, sometimes labeled sentiment variables. More or less random price fluctuations will accompany any underlying price trend, creating opportunities to exploit corrections as these fluctuations dissipate. The nearby box explores the link between technical analysis and behavioral finance.

Trends and Corrections

Much of technical analysis seeks to uncover trends in market prices. This is in effect a search for momentum. Momentum can be absolute, in which case one searches for upward price trends, or relative, in which case the analyst looks to invest in one sector over another (or even take on a long-short position in the two sectors). Relative strength statistics (see the previous chapter) are designed to uncover these potential opportunities.

[22]S. Gervais and T. Odean, "Learning to Be Overconfident," *Review of Financial Studies* 14 (2001), pp. 1–27.

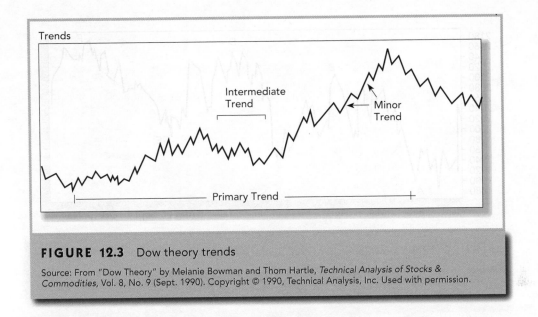

FIGURE 12.3   Dow theory trends

Source: From "Dow Theory" by Melanie Bowman and Thom Hartle, *Technical Analysis of Stocks & Commodities*, Vol. 8, No. 9 (Sept. 1990). Copyright © 1990, Technical Analysis, Inc. Used with permission.

Dow Theory   The grandfather of trend analysis is the **Dow theory,** named after its creator Charles Dow (who established *The Wall Street Journal*). Many of today's more technically sophisticated methods are essentially variants of Dow's approach.

The Dow theory posits three forces simultaneously affecting stock prices:

1. The *primary trend* is the long-term movement of prices, lasting from several months to several years.
2. *Secondary* or *intermediate trends* are caused by short-term deviations of prices from the underlying trend line. These deviations are eliminated via *corrections* when prices revert back to trend values.
3. *Tertiary* or *minor trends* are daily fluctuations of little importance.

Figure 12.3 represents these three components of stock price movements. In this figure, the primary trend is upward, but intermediate trends result in short-lived market declines lasting a few weeks. The intraday minor trends have no long-run impact on price.

Figure 12.4 depicts the course of the DJIA during 1988. The primary trend is upward, as evidenced by the fact that each market peak is higher than the previous peak (point *F* versus *D* versus *B*). Similarly, each low is higher than the previous low (*E* versus *C* versus *A*). This pattern of upward-moving "tops" and "bottoms" is one of the key ways to identify the underlying primary trend. Notice in Figure 12.4 that, despite the upward primary trend, intermediate trends still can lead to short periods of declining prices (points *B* through *C*, or *D* through *E*).

In evaluating the Dow theory, don't forget the lessons of the efficient market hypothesis. The Dow theory is based on a notion of predictably recurring price patterns. Yet the EMH holds that if any pattern is exploitable, many investors would attempt to profit from such predictability, which would ultimately move stock prices and cause the trading strategy to selfdestruct. While Figure 12.3 certainly appears to describe a classic upward primary trend, we have to wonder whether we can see that trend only *after* the fact. Recognizing patterns as they emerge is far more difficult.

Recent variations on the Dow theory are the Elliott wave theory and the theory of Kondratieff waves. Like the Dow theory, the idea behind Elliott waves is that stock prices

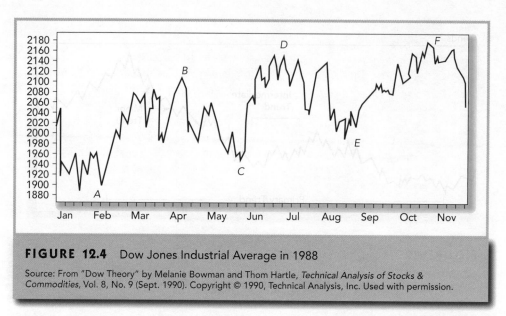

FIGURE 12.4 Dow Jones Industrial Average in 1988

Source: From "Dow Theory" by Melanie Bowman and Thom Hartle, *Technical Analysis of Stocks & Commodities*, Vol. 8, No. 9 (Sept. 1990). Copyright © 1990, Technical Analysis, Inc. Used with permission.

can be described by a set of wave patterns. Long-term and short-term wave cycles are superimposed and result in a complicated pattern of price movements, but by interpreting the cycles, one can, according to the theory, predict broad movements. Similarly, Kondratieff waves are named after a Russian economist who asserted that the macroeconomy (and therefore the stock market) moves in broad waves lasting between 48 and 60 years. The Kondratieff waves are therefore analogous to Dow's primary trend, although they are of far longer duration. Kondratieff's assertion is hard to evaluate empirically, however, because cycles that last about 50 years provide only two independent data points per century, which is hardly enough data to test the predictive power of the theory.

Moving Averages   The moving average of a stock index is the average level of the index over a given interval of time. For example, a 52-week moving average tracks the average index value over the most recent 52 weeks. Each week, the moving average is recomputed by dropping the oldest observation and adding the latest. Figure 12.5 is a moving

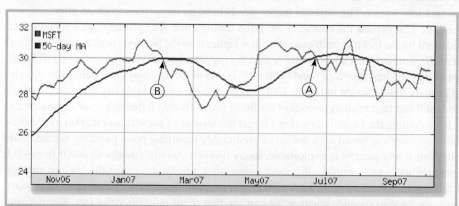

FIGURE 12.5   Moving average for Microsoft

Source: Yahoo! Finance, October 4, 2007 (**finance.yahoo.com**). Reproduced with permission of Yahoo! Inc. © 2007 by Yahoo! Inc. Yahoo! and the Yahoo! logo are trademarks of Yahoo! Inc.

average chart for Microsoft. Notice that the moving average plot (the colored curve) is a "smoothed" version of the original data series (dark curve).

After a period in which prices have generally been falling, the moving average will be above the current price (because the moving average "averages in" the older and higher prices). When prices have been rising, the moving average will be below the current price.

When the market price breaks through the moving average line from below, as at point A in Figure 12.5, it is taken as a bullish signal because it signifies a shift from a falling trend (with prices below the moving average) to a rising trend (with prices above the moving average). Conversely, when prices fall below the moving average, as at point B, it's considered time to sell.

There is some variation in the length of the moving average considered most predictive of market movements. Two popular measures are 200-day and 53-week moving averages.

EXAMPLE 12.4   Moving Averages

Consider the following price data. Each observation represents the closing level of the Dow Jones Industrial Average (DJIA) on the last trading day of the week. The 5-week moving average for each week is the average of the DJIA over the previous 5 weeks. For example, the first entry, for week 5, is the average of the index value between weeks 1 and 5: 13,290, 13,380, 13,399, 13,379, and 13,450. The next entry is the average of the index values between weeks 2 and 6, and so on.

Week	DJIA	5-Week Moving Average	Week	DJIA	5-Week Moving Average
1	13,290		11	13,590	13,555
2	13,380		12	13,652	13,586
3	13,399		13	13,625	13,598
4	13,379		14	13,657	13,624
5	13,450	13,380	15	13,699	13,645
6	13,513	13,424	16	13,647	13,656
7	13,500	13,448	17	13,610	13,648
8	13,565	13,481	18	13,595	13,642
9	13,524	13,510	19	13,499	13,610
10	13,597	13,540	20	13,466	13,563

Figure 12.6 plots the level of the index and the 5-week moving average. Notice that while the index itself moves up and down rather abruptly, the moving average is a relatively smooth series, because the impact of each week's price movement is averaged with that of the previous weeks. Week 16 is a bearish point according to the moving average rule. The price series crosses from above the moving average to below it, signifying the beginning of a downward trend in stock prices.

Breadth   The **breadth** of the market is a measure of the extent to which movement in a market index is reflected widely in the price movements of all the stocks in the

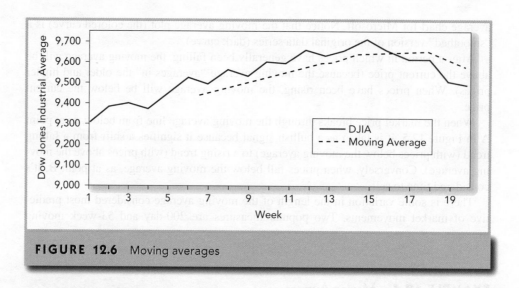

FIGURE 12.6   Moving averages

Trading Diary: Volume, Advancers, Decliners

	NYSE	% chg from 65-day avg	Nasdaq	% chg from 65-day avg	AMEX	% chg from 65-day avg
Issues traded	3,412	**-0.1**	3,086	**-1.9**	1,254	**-1.1**
Advances	1,233	**-25.2**	1,137	**-21.5**	479	**-19.1**
Declines	2,068	**23.3**	1,807	**15.0**	684	**16.5**
Unchanged	111	**24.1**	142	**13.3**	91	**3.1**
New highs	85	**-18.9**	114	**47.2**	47	**9.6**
New lows	24	**-85.5**	35	**-68.7**	15	**-68.8**
Adv. volume*	467,560,150	**-41.4**	685,769,070	**-34.6**	10,816,500	**-41.9**
Decl. volume*	766,901,460	**-7.6**	1,143,477,485	**13.4**	19,158,379	**2.2**
Total volume*	1,246,345,660	**-24.2**	1,857,988,473	**-11.1**	33,068,379	**-15.3**
Closing tick	-169	...	-264	...	-64	...
Closing Arms (TRIN)*	0.98	...	1.05	...	1.24	...
Block trades*	p4,457	...	p8,629	...	p421	...

FIGURE 12.7   Market Diary

Source: The Wall Street Journal, October 4, 2007. Reprinted by permission of Dow Jones & Company, Inc. via Copyright Clearance Center, Inc. © 2007 Dow Jones & Company, Inc. All Rights Reserved Worldwide.

market. The most common measure of breadth is the spread between the number of stocks that advance and decline in price. If advances outnumber declines by a wide margin, then the market is viewed as being stronger because the rally is widespread. These breadth numbers are reported in *The Wall Street Journal* (see Figure 12.7).

Some analysts cumulate breadth data each day as in Table 12.1. The cumulative breadth for each day is obtained by adding that day's net advances (or declines) to the previous day's total. The direction of the cumulated series is then used to discern broad market trends. Analysts might use a moving average of cumulative breadth to gauge broad trends.

Sentiment Indicators

Trin Statistic   Market volume is sometimes used to measure the strength of a market rise or fall. Increased investor participation in a market advance or retreat is viewed as a measure of the significance of the movement. Technicians consider market advances to be a more favorable omen of continued price increases when they are associated with increased trading volume. Similarly, market reversals are considered more bearish when associated with higher volume. The **trin statistic** is defined as

$$\text{Trin} = \frac{\text{Volume declining/Number declining}}{\text{Volume advancing/Number advancing}}$$

Trading Day	Computers, Inc.	Industry Index	Trading Day	Computers, Inc.	Industry Index
1	19.63	50.0	21	19.63	54.1
2	20	50.1	22	21.50	54.0
3	20.50	50.5	23	22	53.9
4	22	50.4	24	23.13	53.7
5	21.13	51.0	25	24	54.8
6	22	50.7	26	25.25	54.5
7	21.88	50.5	27	26.25	54.6
8	22.50	51.1	28	27	54.1
9	23.13	51.5	29	27.50	54.2
10	23.88	51.7	30	28	54.8
11	24.50	51.4	31	28.50	54.2
12	23.25	51.7	32	28	54.8
13	22.13	52.2	33	27.50	54.9
14	22	52.0	34	29	55.2
15	20.63	53.1	35	29.25	55.7
16	20.25	53.5	36	29.50	56.1
17	19.75	53.9	37	30	56.7
18	18.75	53.6	38	28.50	56.7
19	17.50	52.9	39	27.75	56.5
20	19	53.4	40	28	56.1

TABLE 12A

Computers, Inc., stock price history

Day	Advances	Declines	Day	Advances	Declines
1	906	704	6	970	702
2	653	986	7	1002	609
3	721	789	8	903	722
4	503	968	9	850	748
5	497	1095	10	766	766

TABLE 12B

Market advances and declines

13. Table 12B contains data on market advances and declines. Calculate cumulative breadth and decide whether this technical signal is bullish or bearish.

14. If the trading volume in advancing shares on day 1 in the previous problem was 330 million shares, while the volume in declining issues was 240 million shares, what was the trin statistic for that day? Was trin bullish or bearish?

15. Given the following data, is the confidence index rising or falling? What might explain the pattern of yield changes?

	This Year	Last Year
Yield on top-rated corporate bonds	8%	8.5%
Yield on intermediate-grade corporate bonds	10.5	10

16. Go to **www.mhhe.com/bkm** and link to the material for Chapter 12, where you will find 5 years of weekly returns for the S&P 500.

    a. Set up a spreadsheet to calculate the 26-week moving average of the index. Set the value of the index at the beginning of the sample period equal to 100. The index value in each week is then updated by multiplying the previous week's level by (1 + rate of return over previous week).

    b. Identify every instance in which the index crosses through its moving average from below. In how many of the weeks following a cross-through does the index increase? Decrease?

    c. Identify every instance in which the index crosses through its moving average from above. In how many of the weeks following a cross-through does the index increase? Decrease?

    d. How well does the moving average rule perform in identifying buy or sell opportunities?

17. Go to **www.mhhe.com/bkm** and link to the material for Chapter 12, where you will find 5 years of weekly returns for the S&P 500 and Fidelity's Select Banking Fund (ticker FSRBX).

    a. Set up a spreadsheet to calculate the relative strength of the banking sector compared to the broad market. Hint: as in the previous problem, set the initial value of the sector index and the S&P 500 index equal to 100, and use each week's rate of return to update the level of each index.

    b. Identify every instance in which the relative strength ratio increases by at least 5% from its value 5 weeks earlier. In how many of the weeks following a substantial increase in relative strength does the banking sector outperform the S&P 500? In how many of those weeks does the banking sector underperform the S&P 500?

    c. Identify every instance in which the relative strength ratio decreases by at least 5% from its value 5 weeks earlier. In how many of the weeks following a substantial decrease in relative strength does the banking sector underperform the S&P 500? In how many of those weeks does the banking sector outperform the S&P 500?

    d. How well does the relative strength rule perform in identifying buy or sell opportunities?

Challenge Problem

18. One seeming violation of the Law of One Price is the pervasive discrepancy of closed-end fund prices from their net asset values. Would you expect to observe greater discrepancies on diversified or less-diversified funds? Why?

1. Don Sampson begins a meeting with his financial adviser by outlining his investment philosophy as shown below:

Statement Number	Statement
1	Investments should offer strong return potential but with very limited risk. I prefer to be conservative and to minimize losses, even if I miss out on substantial growth opportunities.
2	All nongovernmental investments should be in industry-leading and financially strong companies.
3	Income needs should be met entirely through interest income and cash dividends. All equity securities held should pay cash dividends.
4	Investment decisions should be based primarily on consensus forecasts of general economic conditions and company-specific growth.
5	If an investment falls below the purchase price, that security should be retained until it returns to its original cost. Conversely, I prefer to take quick profits on successful investments.
6	I will direct the purchase of investments, including derivative securities, periodically. These aggressive investments result from personal research and may not prove consistent with my investment policy. I have not kept records on the performance of similar past investments, but I have had some "big winners."

They showed that the estimated values of γ_0 and γ_1 will be biased by a term proportional to the relative efficiency of the market proxy. If the market index used in the regression is fully efficient, the test will be well specified. But the second-pass regression will provide a poor test of the CAPM if the proxy for the market portfolio is not efficient. Thus, while GLS regressions may not give totally arbitrary results, as Roll and Ross demonstrate may occur using standard OLS regressions, we still cannot test the model in a meaningful way without a reasonably efficient market proxy. Unfortunately, it is difficult to tell how efficient our market index is relative to the theoretical true market portfolio, so we cannot tell how good our tests are.

Measurement Error in Beta

Roll's critique tells us that CAPM tests are handicapped from the outset. But suppose that we could get past Roll's problem by obtaining data on the returns of the true market portfolio. We still would have to deal with the statistical problems caused by measurement error in the estimates of beta from the first-stage regressions.

It is well known in statistics that if the right-hand-side variable of a regression equation is measured with error (in our case, beta is measured with error and is the right-hand-side variable in the second-pass regression), then the slope coefficient of the regression equation will be biased downward and the intercept biased upward. This is consistent with the findings cited above, which found that the estimate of γ_0 was higher than predicted by the CAPM and that the estimate of γ_1 was lower than predicted.

Indeed, a well-controlled simulation test by Miller and Scholes[6] confirms these arguments. In this test a random-number generator simulated rates of return with covariances similar to observed ones. The average returns were made to agree exactly with the CAPM expected return–beta relationship. Miller and Scholes then used these randomly generated rates of return in the tests we have described as if they were observed from a sample of stock returns. The results of this "simulated" test were virtually identical to those reached using real data, despite the fact that the simulated returns were *constructed* to obey the SML, that is, the true γ coefficients were $\gamma_0 = 0$, $\gamma_1 = \overline{r_M - r_f}$, and $\gamma_2 = 0$.

This postmortem of the early test gets us back to square one. We can explain away the disappointing test results, but we have no positive results to support the CAPM-APT implications.

The next wave of tests was designed to overcome the measurement error problem that led to biased estimates of the SML. The innovation in these tests, pioneered by Black, Jensen, and Scholes,[7] was to use portfolios rather than individual securities. Combining securities into portfolios diversifies away most of the firm-specific part of returns, thereby enhancing the precision of the estimates of beta and the expected rate of return of the portfolio of securities. This mitigates the statistical problems that arise from measurement error in the beta estimates.

Obviously, however, combining stocks into portfolios reduces the number of observations left for the second-pass regression. For example, suppose that we group our sample of 100 stocks into five portfolios of 20 stocks each. If the assumption of a single-factor market is reasonably accurate, then the residuals of the 20 stocks in each portfolio will be practically uncorrelated and, hence, the variance of the portfolio residual will be about one-twentieth the residual variance of the average stock. Thus the portfolio beta in the

---

[6]Miller and Scholes, "Rate of Return in Relation to Risk: A Reexamination of Some Recent Findings," in *Studies in the Theory of Capital Markets,* ed. Michael C. Jensen (New York: Praeger, 1972).

[7]Fischer Black, Michael C. Jensen, and Myron Scholes, "The Capital Asset Pricing Model: Some Empirical Tests," in *Studies in the Theory of Capital Markets,* ed. Michael C. Jensen (New York: Praeger, 1972).

first-pass regression will be estimated with far better accuracy. However, now consider the second-pass regression. With individual securities, we had 100 observations to estimate the second-pass coefficients. With portfolios of 20 stocks each, we are left with only five observations for the second-pass regression.

To get the best of this trade-off, we need to construct portfolios with the largest possible dispersion of beta coefficients. Other things being equal, a sample yields more accurate regression estimates the more widely spaced are the observations of the independent variables. Consider the first-pass regressions where we estimate the SCL, that is, the relationship between the excess return on each stock and the market's excess return. If we have a sample with a great dispersion of market returns, we have a greater chance of accurately estimating the effect of a change in the market return on the return of the stock. In our case, however, we have no control over the range of the market returns. But we can control the range of the independent variable of the second-pass regression, the portfolio betas. Rather than allocate 20 stocks to each portfolio randomly, we can rank portfolios by betas. Portfolio 1 will include the 20 highest-beta stocks and portfolio 5 the 20 lowest-beta stocks. In that case a set of portfolios with small nonsystematic components, e_P, and widely spaced betas will yield reasonably powerful tests of the SML.

Fama and MacBeth[8] used this methodology to verify that the observed relationship between average excess returns and beta is indeed linear and that nonsystematic risk does not explain average excess returns. Using 20 portfolios constructed according to the Black, Jensen, and Scholes methodology, Fama and MacBeth expanded the estimation of the SML equation to include the square of the beta coefficient (to test for linearity of the relationship between returns and betas) and the estimated standard deviation of the residual (to test for the explanatory power of nonsystematic risk). For a sequence of many subperiods, they estimated for each subperiod the equation

$$r_i = \gamma_0 + \gamma_1\beta_i + \gamma_2\beta_i^2 + \gamma_3\sigma(e_i) \tag{13.5}$$

The term γ_2 measures potential nonlinearity of return, and γ_3 measures the explanatory power of nonsystematic risk, $\sigma(e_i)$. According to the CAPM, both γ_2 and γ_3 should have coefficients of zero in the second-pass regression.

Fama and MacBeth estimated Equation 13.5 for every month of the period January 1935 through June 1968. The results are summarized in Table 13.1, which shows average coefficients and t-statistics for the overall period as well as for three subperiods. Fama

TABLE 13.1 Summary of Fama and MacBeth (1973) study (all rates in basis points per month)	**Period**	**1935/6–1968**	**1935–1945**	**1946–1955**	**1956/6–1968**
	Av. r_f	13	2	9	26
	Av. $\gamma_0 - r_f$	8	10	8	5
	Av. $t(\gamma_0 - r_f)$	0.20	0.11	0.20	0.10
	Av. $r_M - r_f$	130	195	103	95
	Av. γ_1	114	118	209	34
	Av. $t(\gamma_1)$	1.85	0.94	2.39	0.34
	Av. γ_2	−26	−9	−76	0
	Av. $t(\gamma_2)$	−0.86	−0.14	−2.16	0
	Av. γ_3	516	817	−378	960
	Av. $t(\gamma_3)$	1.11	0.94	−0.67	1.11
	Av. R-SQR	0.31	0.31	0.32	0.29

[8]Eugene Fama and James MacBeth, "Risk, Return, and Equilibrium: Empirical Tests," *Journal of Political Economy* 81 (March 1973).

and MacBeth observed that the coefficients on residual standard deviation (nonsystematic risk), denoted by γ_3, fluctuate greatly from month to month and were insignificant, consistent with the hypothesis that nonsystematic risk is not rewarded by higher average returns. Likewise, the coefficients on the square of beta, denoted by γ_2, were insignificant, consistent with the hypothesis that the expected return–beta relationship is linear.

With respect to the expected return–beta relationship, however, the picture is mixed. The estimated SML is too flat, consistent with previous studies, as can be seen from the fact that $\gamma_0 - r_f$ is positive, and that γ_1 is, on average, less than $r_M - r_f$. On the positive side, the difference does not appear to be significant, so that the CAPM is not clearly rejected.

> **CONCEPT CHECK 3**
>
> According to the CAPM and the data in Table 13.1, what are the predicted values of γ_0, γ_1, γ_2, and γ_3 in the Fama-MacBeth regressions for the period 1946–1955?

In conclusion, these tests of the CAPM provide mixed evidence on the validity of the theory. We can summarize the results as follows:

1. The insights that are supported by the single-factor CAPM and APT are as follows:

   a. Expected rates of return are linear and increase with beta, the measure of systematic risk.

   b. Expected rates of return are not affected by nonsystematic risk.

2. The single-variable expected return–beta relationship predicted by either the risk-free rate or the zero-beta version of the CAPM is not fully consistent with empirical observation.

Thus, although the CAPM seems *qualitatively* correct in that β matters and $\sigma(e_i)$ does not, empirical tests do not validate its *quantitative* predictions.

> **CONCEPT CHECK 4**
>
> What would you conclude if you performed the Fama and MacBeth tests and found that the coefficients on β^2 and $\sigma(e)$ were positive?

The EMH and the CAPM

Roll's critique also provides a positive avenue to view the empirical content of the CAPM and APT. Recall, as Roll pointed out, that the CAPM and the expected return–beta relationship follow directly from the efficiency of the market portfolio. This means that if we can establish that the market portfolio is efficient, we would have no need to further test the expected return–beta relationship.

As demonstrated in Chapter 11 on the efficient market hypothesis, proxies for the market portfolio such as the S&P 500 and the NYSE index have proven hard to beat by professional investors. This is perhaps the strongest evidence for the empirical content of the CAPM and APT.

Accounting for Human Capital and Cyclical Variations in Asset Betas

We are reminded of two important deficiencies of the tests of the single-index models:

1. Only a fraction of the value of assets in the United States is traded in capital markets; perhaps the most important nontraded asset is human capital.

2. There is ample evidence that asset betas are cyclical and that accounting for this cyclicality may improve the predictive power of the CAPM.

One of the CAPM assumptions is that all assets are traded and accessible to all investors. Mayers[9] proposed a version of the CAPM that accounts for a violation of this assumption; this requires an additional term in the expected return–beta relationship.

An important nontraded asset that may partly account for the deficiency of standard market proxies such as the S&P 500 is human capital. The value of future wages and compensation for expert services is a significant component of the wealth of investors who expect years of productive careers prior to retirement. Moreover, it is reasonable to expect that changes in human capital are far less than perfectly correlated with asset returns, and hence they diversify the risk of investor portfolios.

Jagannathan and Wang[10] used a proxy for changes in the value of human capital based on the rate of change in aggregate labor income. In addition to the standard security betas estimated using the value-weighted stock market index, which we denote β^{vw}, Jagannathan and Wang also estimated the betas of assets with respect to labor income growth, which we denote β^{labor}. Finally, they considered the possibility that business cycles affect asset betas, an issue that has been examined in a number of other studies.[11] They used the difference between the yields on low- and high-grade corporate bonds as a proxy for the state of the business cycle and estimate asset betas relative to this business cycle variable; we denote this beta as β^{prem}. With the estimates of these three betas for several stock portfolios, Jagannathan and Wang estimated a second-pass regression which includes firm size (market value of equity, denoted ME):

$$E(R_i) = c_0 + c_{size}\log(\text{ME}) + c_{vw}\beta^{vw} + c_{prem}\beta^{prem} + c_{labor}\beta^{labor} \qquad (13.6)$$

Equation 13.6 shows that Jagannathan and Wang chose an indirect way to add a cyclical component to the expected return–beta relationship, as the default premium can be very different from the expected return on the market index. As mentioned in Chapter 9 (The CAPM), multifactor models fall into two classes: models that are motivated by hedging considerations (such as the ICAPM) and models that are motivated by APT considerations, for which multiple systematic factors drive asset returns. Both these models are the topic of the next section. Equation 13.6 combines the labor factor that would be a natural ICAPM factor with two other factors (size and the default premium) that might be justified on APT grounds. Absent the APT factors, this version of the model would really be a two-factor ICAPM that replaces the single-index CAPM with an adjusted beta as in Equation 9.13 of Chapter 9. This is the reason we present the results here.

Jagannathan and Wang test their model with 100 portfolios that are designed to spread securities on the basis of size and beta. Stocks are sorted to 10 size portfolios, and the stocks within each size decile are further sorted by beta into 10 subportfolios, resulting in 100 portfolios in total. Table 13.2 shows a subset of the various versions of the second-pass estimates. The first two rows in the table show the coefficients and t-statistics of a test of the CAPM along the lines of the Fama and MacBeth tests introduced in the previous section. The result is a sound rejection of the model, as the coefficient on beta is negative, albeit not significant.

The next two rows show that the model is not helped by the addition of the size factor. The dramatic increase in R-square (from 1.35% to 57%) shows that size explains variations in average returns quite well while beta does not. Substituting the default premium and labor

[9]David Mayers, "Nonmarketable Assets and Capital Market Equilibrium under Uncertainty," in *Studies in the Theory of Capital Markets,* ed. Michael C. Jensen (New York: Praeger, 1972), pp. 223–48.

[10]Ravi Jagannathan and Zhenyu Wang, "The Conditional CAPM and the Cross-Section of Expected Returns," *Journal of Finance* 51 (March 1996), pp. 3–54.

[11]For example, Campbell Harvey, "Time-Varying Conditional Covariances in Tests of Asset Pricing Models," *Journal of Financial Economics* 24 (October 1989), pp. 289–317; Wayne Ferson and Campbell Harvey, "The Variation of Economic Risk Premiums," *Journal of Political Economy* 99 (April 1991), pp. 385–415; and Wayne Ferson and Robert Korajczyk, "Do Arbitrage Pricing Models Explain the Predictability of Stock Returns?" *Journal of Business* 68 (July 1995), pp. 309–49.

Coefficient	c_0	c_{vw}	c_{prem}	c_{labor}	c_{size}	R^2
A. The Static CAPM without Human Capital						
Estimate	1.24	−0.10				1.35
t-value	5.16	−0.28				
Estimate	2.08	−0.32			−0.11	57.56
t-value	5.77	−0.94			−2.30	
B. The Conditional CAPM with Human Capital						
Estimate	1.24	−0.40	0.34	0.22		55.21
t-value	4.10	−0.88	1.73	2.31		
Estimate	1.70	−0.40	0.20	0.10	−0.07	64.73
t-value	4.14	−1.06	2.72	2.09	−1.30	

TABLE 13.2

Evaluation of various CAPM specifications

This table gives the estimates for the cross-sectional regression model

$$E(R_{it}) = c_0 + c_{size}\log(ME_i) + c_{vw}\beta_i^{vw} + c_{prem}\beta_i^{prem} + c_{labor}\beta_i^{labor}$$

with either a subset or all of the variables. Here, R_{it} is the return on portfolio i ($i = 1, 2, \ldots, 100$) in month t (July 1963–December 1990), R_t^{vw} is the return on the value-weighted index of stocks, R_{t-1}^{prem} is the yield spread between low- and high-grade corporate bonds, and R_t^{labor} is the growth rate in per capita labor income. The β_i^{vw} is the slope coefficient in the OLS regression of R_{it} on a constant and R_t^{vw}. The other betas are estimated in a similar way. The portfolio size, log (ME_i), is calculated as the equally weighted average of the logarithm of the market value (in millions of dollars) of the stocks in portfolio i. The regression models are estimated by using the Fama-MacBeth procedure. The "corrected t-values" take sampling errors in the estimated betas into account. All R^2s are reported as percentages.

income for size results in a similar increase in explanatory power (R-square of 55%), but the CAPM expected return–beta relationship is not redeemed. The default premium is significant, while labor income is borderline significant. When we add size as well, in the last two rows, we find it is no longer significant and only marginally increases explanatory power.

Despite the clear rejection of the CAPM, we do learn two important facts from Table 13.2. First, conventional first-pass estimates of security betas are greatly deficient. They clearly do not fully capture the cyclicality of stock returns and thus do not accurately measure the systematic risk of stocks. This actually can be interpreted as good news for the CAPM in that it may be possible to replace the simple beta with better estimates of systematic risk and transfer the explanatory power of instrumental variables such as size and the default premium to the index rate of return. Second, and more relevant to the work of Jagannathan and Wang, is the conclusion that human capital will be important in any version of the CAPM that better explains the systematic risk of securities.

Accounting for Nontraded Business

Heaton and Lucas[12] estimate the importance of proprietary business in portfolio choice. We expect that private-business owners will reduce demand for traded securities that are positively correlated with their specific entrepreneurial income. If this effect is sufficiently important, aggregate demand for traded securities will be determined in part by the covariance with aggregate noncorporate business income. The risk premium on securities with high covariance with noncorporate business income will be commensurately higher.

The extensive empirical work of Heaton and Lucas produces many interesting observations, and we show but a few. Table 13.3 shows portfolio shares relative to total assets by

---

[12]John Heaton and Debora Lucas, "Portfolio Choice and Asset Prices: The Importance of Entrepreneurial Risk," *Journal of Finance* 55, no. 3 (June 2000), pp. 1163–98.

TABLE 13.3

Portfolio shares relative to total assets by age and net worth

Assets	Net Worth					
	$10 K to $100 K		$100 K to $1 M		>$1 M	
	<65	≥65	<65	≥65	<65	≥65
Stocks	0.040/0.012 (0.083)	0.085/0.023 (0.164)	0.068/0.037 (0.086)	0.132/0.101 (0.113)	0.135/0.063 (0.172)	0.257/0.177 (0.226)
Bonds	0.009/0.000 (0.032)	0.064/0.008 (0.181)	0.026/0.003 (0.055)	0.076/0.011 (0.120)	0.061/0.015 (0.107)	0.174/0.100 (0.202)
Cash	0.021/0.007 (0.038)	0.075/0.038 (0.076)	0.039/0.016 (0.064)	0.153/0.090 (0.169)	0.052/0.027 (0.088)	0.106/0.061 (0.106)
Business	0.002/0.000 (0.014)	0.000/0.000 (0.000)	0.046/0.000 (0.109)	0.010/0.000 (0.050)	0.181/0.046 (0.241)	0.098/0.000 (0.200)
Pension	0.009/0.000 (0.028)	0.004/0.000 (0.017)	0.026/0.001 (0.051)	0.001/0.000 (0.007)	0.061/0.006 (0.111)	0.001/0.000 (0.011)
Real estate	0.125/0.104 (0.136)	0.261/0.217 (0.269)	0.228/0.169 (0.174)	0.290/0.273 (0.170)	0.268/0.213 (0.268)	0.257/0.244 (0.194)
Cap. labor*	0.662/0.793 (0.308)	0.018/0.000 (0.052)	0.482/0.575 (0.290)	0.020/0.000 (0.065)	0.211/0.173 (0.200)	0.005/0.000 (0.019)
Cap. SS + pension*	0.131/0.047 (0.178)	0.494/0.542 (0.269)	0.085/0.045 (0.109)	0.318/0.295 (0.190)	0.030/0.018 (0.047)	0.101/0.067 (0.103)
Debt/assets	0.076/0.064 (0.084)	0.052/0.009 (0.073)	0.065/0.051 (0.071)	0.013/0.000 (0.032)	0.038/0.025 (0.048)	0.014/0.000 (0.035)
Total assets (billion $)	3,706	111	8,655	1,768	5,703	1,828
Imputed no. of households	5,685,551	551,333	8,277,319	3,321,638	1,415,286	567,332

*Capitalized values of income (from either labor, Social Security, or pensions) is the estimated present value of that income source.

Note: Data are reported as mean/median (standard deviation).

Source: John Heaton and Debora Lucas, "Portfolio Choice and Asset Prices: The Importance of Entrepreneurial Risk," *Journal of Finance* 55, no. 3 (June 2000), pp. 1163–98. Reprinted by permission of the publisher, Blackwell Publishing, Inc.

age and net worth for households with net worth over $10,000 and at least $500 of stock holdings in 1995. The number of households in this category totaled 19.8 million, about 15% of the population. Of these, about 10% had net worth over $1 million. In general, the large standard deviations and differences between average and median values indicate the distributions are highly positively skewed.

Consistent with theory, Heaton and Lucas find that households with higher investments in private business do in fact reduce the fraction of total wealth invested in equity. Table 13.4 presents excerpts from their regression analysis, in which allocation of the overall portfolio to stocks is the dependent variable. The share of private business in total wealth (labeled "relative business") receives negative and statistically significant coefficients in these regressions. Notice also the negative and significant coefficient on risk-attitude based on a self-reported degree of risk aversion.

Finally, Heaton and Lucas extend Jagannathan and Wang's equation to include the rate of change in proprietary-business wealth. They find that this variable also is significant and improves the explanatory power of the regression. Here, too, the market rate of return does not help explain the rate of return on individual securities and, hence, this implication of the CAPM still must be rejected.

TABLE 13.4

Determinants of stockholdings

	Share of Stock in Assets		
	Stock Relative to Liquid Assets	**Stock Relative to Financial Assets**	**Stock Relative to Total Assets**
Intercept	0.71	0.53	0.24
	(14.8)	(21.28)	(10.54)
Total income $\times 10^{-10}$	−1.80	−.416	−1.72
	(−0.435)	(−0.19)	(−0.85)
Net worth $\times 10^{-10}$	2.75	5.04	7.37
	(0.895)	(3.156)	(5.02)
Relative business	−0.14	−0.50	−0.32
	(−4.34)	(−29.31)	(−20.62)
Age of respondent	-7.94×10^{-4}	-6.99×10^{-5}	2.44×10^{-3}
	(−1.26)	(−0.21)	(−4.23)
Risk attitude	−0.05	−0.02	−0.02
	(−4.74)	(−3.82)	(−4.23)
Relative mortgage	0.05	0.43	0.30
	(1.31)	(20.90)	(16.19)
Relative pension	0.07	−0.41	−0.31
	(1.10)	(−11.67)	(−9.60)
Relative real estate	−0.04	−0.44	−0.31
	(−1.41)	(−27.00)	(−20.37)
Adjusted R-square	0.03	0.48	0.40

Note: *t*-statistics in parentheses.
Source: John Heaton and Debora Lucas, "Portfolio Choice and Asset Prices: The Importance of Entrepreneurial Risk," *Journal of Finance* 55, no. 3 (June 2000), pp. 1163–98. Reprinted by permission of the publisher, Blackwell Publishing, Inc.

13.2   TESTS OF MULTIFACTOR CAPM AND APT

The multifactor CAPM and APT are elegant theories of how exposure to systematic risk factors should influence expected returns, but they provide little guidance concerning which factors (sources of risk) ought to result in risk premiums. A test of this hypothesis would require three stages:

1. Specification of risk factors.
2. Identification of portfolios that hedge these fundamental risk factors.
3. Test of the explanatory power and risk premiums of the hedge portfolios.

A Macro Factor Model

Chen, Roll, and Ross[13] identify several possible variables that might proxy for systematic factors:

IP = Growth rate in industrial production.

EI = Changes in expected inflation measured by changes in short-term (T-bill) interest rates.

UI = Unexpected inflation defined as the difference between actual and expected inflation.

CG = Unexpected changes in risk premiums measured by the difference between the returns on corporate Baa-rated bonds and long-term government bonds.

GB = Unexpected changes in the term premium measured by the difference between the returns on long- and short-term government bonds.

With the identification of these potential economic factors, Chen, Roll, and Ross skipped the procedure of identifying factor portfolios (the portfolios that have the highest correlation with the factors). Instead, by using the factors themselves, they implicitly assumed that factor portfolios exist that can proxy for the factors. They use these factors in a test similar to that of Fama and MacBeth.

A critical part of the methodology is the grouping of stocks into portfolios. Recall that in the single-factor tests, portfolios were constructed to span a wide range of betas to enhance the power of the test. In a multifactor framework the efficient criterion for grouping is less obvious. Chen, Roll, and Ross chose to group the sample stocks into 20 portfolios by size (market value of outstanding equity), a variable that is known to be associated with average stock returns.

They first used 5 years of monthly data to estimate the factor betas of the 20 portfolios in a first-pass regression. This is accomplished by estimating the following regressions for each portfolio:

$$r = a + \beta_M r_M + \beta_{IP}\text{IP} + \beta_{EI}\text{EI} + \beta_{UI}\text{UI} + \beta_{CG}\text{CG} + \beta_{GB}\text{GB} + e \qquad \textbf{(13.7a)}$$

where M stands for the stock market index. Chen, Roll, and Ross used as the market index both the value-weighted NYSE index (VWNY) and the equally weighted NYSE index (EWNY).

---

[13]Nai-Fu Chen, Richard Roll, and Stephen Ross, "Economic Forces and the Stock Market," *Journal of Business* 59 (1986).

A	EWNY	IP	EI	UI	CG	GB	Constant
	5.021	14.009	−0.128	−0.848	0.130	−5.017	6.409
	(1.218)	(3.774)	(−1.666)	(−2.541)	(2.855)	(−1.576)	(1.848)
B	**VWNY**	**IP**	**EI**	**UI**	**CG**	**GB**	**Constant**
	−2.403	11.756	−0.123	−0.795	8.274	−5.905	10.713
	(−0.633)	(3.054)	(−1.600)	(−2.376)	(2.972)	(−1.879)	(2.755)

TABLE 13.5

Economic variables and pricing (percent per month × 10), multivariate approach

VWNY = Return on the value-weighted NYSE index; EWNY = Return on the equally weighted NYSE index; IP = Monthly growth rate in industrial production; EI = Change in expected inflation; UI = Unanticipated inflation; CG = Unanticipated change in the risk premium (Baa and under return − long-term government bond return); GB = Unanticipated change in the term structure (long-term government bond return − Treasury-bill rate); Note that t-statistics are in parentheses.
Source: Modified from Nai-Fu Chen, Richard Roll, and Stephen Ross, "Economic Forces and the Stock Market," *Journal of Business* 59 (1986). Reprinted by permission of the publisher, The University of Chicago Press.

Using the 20 sets of first-pass estimates of factor betas as the independent variables, they now estimated the second-pass regression (with 20 observations, one for each portfolio):

$$r = \gamma_0 + \gamma_M\beta_M + \gamma_{IP}\beta_{IP} + \gamma_{EI}\beta_{EI} + \gamma_{UI}\beta_{UI} + \gamma_{CG}\beta_{CG} + \gamma_{GB}\beta_{GB} + e \quad \textbf{(13.7b)}$$

where the gammas become estimates of the risk premiums on the factors.

Chen, Roll, and Ross ran this second-pass regression for every month of their sample period, reestimating the first-pass factor betas once every 12 months. The estimated risk premiums (the values for the parameters, γ) were averaged over all the second-pass regressions.

Note in Table 13.5, that the two market indexes EWNY and VWNY are not statistically significant (their t-statistics of 1.218 and −.633 are less than 2). Note also that the VWNY factor has the "wrong" sign in that it seems to imply a negative market-risk premium. Industrial production (IP), the risk premium on corporate bonds (CG), and unanticipated inflation (UI) are the factors that appear to have significant explanatory power.

13.3   THE FAMA–FRENCH THREE–FACTOR MODEL

The multifactor model that occupies center stage these days is the three-factor model introduced by Fama and French. The systematic factors in the Fama-French model are firm size and book-to-market ratio as well as the market index.[14] These additional factors are empirically motivated by the observations, documented in Chapter 11, that historical-average returns on stocks of small firms and on stocks with high ratios of book equity to market equity (B/M) are higher than predicted by the security market line of the CAPM. These observations suggest that size or the book-to-market ratio may be proxies for exposures to sources of systematic risk not captured by the CAPM beta and thus result in the return premiums we see associated with these factors.

How can we make the Fama-French model operational? Fama and French propose measuring the size factor in each period as the differential return on small firms versus large

[14]A four-factor model that also accounts for recent stock returns (a *momentum factor*) is also widely used.

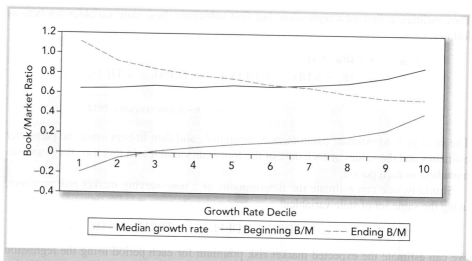

FIGURE 13.3 The book-to-market ratio reflects past growth, but not future growth prospects. B/M tends to fall with income growth experienced at the *end* of a 5-year period, but actually increases slightly with future income growth rates.

Source: L.K.C. Chan, J. Karceski, and J. Lakonishok, "The Level and Persistence of Growth Rates," *Journal of Finance* 58 (April 2003), pp. 643–84. Reprinted by permission of the publisher, Blackwell Publishing, Inc.

Figure 13.3, from a study by Chan, Karceski, and Lakonishok,[20] makes the case for overreaction. Firms are sorted into deciles based on income growth in the past 5 years. By construction, the growth rates uniformly increase from the first through the tenth decile. The book-to-market ratio for each decile at the *end* of the 5-year period (the dashed line) tracks recent growth very well. B/M falls steadily with growth over past 5 years. This is evidence that *past* growth is extrapolated and then impounded in price. High past growth leads to higher prices and lower B/M ratios.

But B/M at the *beginning* of a 5-year period shows little or even a positive association with subsequent growth (the solid colored line) implying that market capitalization today is *inversely* related to growth prospects. In other words, the firms with lower B/M (glamour firms) experience no better or even worse average future income growth than other firms. The implication is that the market ignores evidence that past growth cannot be extrapolated far into the future. Book-to-market may reflect past growth better than future growth, consistent with extrapolation error.

More direct evidence supporting extrapolation error is provided by La Porta, Lakonishok, Shleifer, and Vishny,[21] who examine stock price performance when actual earnings are released to the public. Firms are classified as growth versus value stocks, and the stock price performance at earnings announcements for 4 years following the classification date is then examined. Figure 13.4 demonstrates that growth stocks underperform value stocks surrounding these announcements. We conclude that when news of actual

---

[20]L.K.C. Chan, J. Karceski, and J. Lakonishok, "The Level and Persistence of Growth Rates," *Journal of Finance* 58 (April 2003), pp. 643–84.

[21]R. La Porta, J. Lakonishok, A. Shleifer, and R.W. Vishny, "Good News for Value Stocks," *Journal of Finance* 51 (1997), pp. 1715–42.

earnings is released to the public, the market is relatively disappointed in stocks it has been pricing as growth firms.

In the end, we would have to characterize the debate as unsettled. The Fama-French model and its extensions (e.g., a four-factor model with a momentum effect added to the FF factors) is clearly a highly useful tool for comparing performance against a well-defined set of benchmarks. Whether the return premiums to those factors reflect fully rational risk premiums, market irrationality, or some of both still is a matter of considerable controversy.

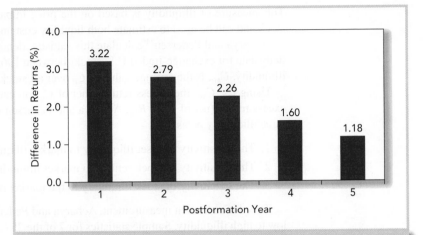

FIGURE 13.4 Value minus glamour returns surrounding earnings announcements, 1971–1992. Announcement effects are measured for each of 4 years following classification as a value versus a growth firm.

Source: R. La Porta, J. Lakonishok, A. Shleifer, and R.W. Vishny, "Good News for Value Stocks," *Journal of Finance* 51 (1997), pp. 1715–42. Reprinted by permission of the publisher, Blackwell Publishing, Inc.

13.4 LIQUIDITY AND ASSET PRICING

In Chapter 9 we saw that an important extension of the CAPM incorporates considerations of asset liquidity. Unfortunately, measuring liquidity is far from trivial. We know that the effect of liquidity on an asset's expected return is composed of two factors:

1. Transaction costs that are dominated by the bid–ask spread that dealers set to compensate for losses incurred when trading with informed traders.[22]

2. Liquidity *risk* resulting from covariance between *changes* in asset liquidity cost with both *changes* in market-index liquidity cost and with market-index rates of return.

Both of these factors are unobservable and their effect on equilibrium rates of return is difficult to estimate.

Observed (inside) bid–ask spreads apply only to small trades and therefore may be highly unreliable indicators of trading costs for larger transactions; therefore, most studies of liquidity instead use a proxy variable that can distinguish liquidity costs across firms and then calibrate the distribution of such costs to average observed spreads. One widely used measure of **illiquidity cost** was proposed by Amihud:[23]

$$ILLIQ = \text{Monthly average of daily} \left[\frac{\text{Absolute value (Stock return)}}{\text{Dollar volume}} \right]$$

[22]In nondealer markets, the spread may be the difference between bid and ask prices in the limit-order book. In markets where traders transact directly, bid–ask spreads are unobserved. Yet observed transaction prices and resultant rates of return will reflect the cost of the implicit bid–ask spread as uninformed buyers reduce bid prices and sellers increase offer prices to compensate for expected losses to informed traders.

[23]Yakov Amihud, "Illiquidity and Stock Returns: Cross-section and Time-Series Effects," *Journal of Financial Markets* 5 (2002), pp. 31–56.

This measure of illiquidity is based on the price impact per dollar of transactions in the stock and can be used to estimate both liquidity cost and liquidity risk.

Acharya and Pedersen[24] calculate this statistic, denoted C_{it} for stock i in month t, using daily data for exchange-traded U.S. stocks between 1963 and 1999. The market measure of illiquidity, C_{Mt}, is the average value of C_{it} over all stocks in month t.

Using C_{it}, C_{Mt}, the excess returns (net of C_{it}) on each stock, R_{it}, as well as the market excess return (net of C_{Mt}), R_{Mt}, Acharya and Pedersen calculate the market beta (β_M) and three illiquidity betas:

1. The sensitivity of asset illiquidity to market illiquidity: β_{L1}
2. The sensitivity of stock returns to market illiquidity: β_{L2}
3. The sensitivity of stock illiquidity to the market return: β_{L3}

To reduce errors in measurement, Acharya and Pedersen form 25 portfolios sorted from low to high illiquidity. Sample statistics for 7 of the 25 (equally weighted) portfolios appear in Table 13.7. The variables in the first three rows show that liquidity is correlated with all three Fama-French factors, suggesting that some of the predictive power of the FF factors for average returns may in fact be liquidity related. Average excess return increases with portfolio illiquidity, although part of that increase is attributable to the higher systematic risk associated with higher illiquidity.[25]

Liquidity cost (the effective bid–ask spread) increases dramatically with illiquidity, ultimately becoming quite large (8.83% per month). This reflects the cost of investing in each portfolio for 1 month and then selling it, something which hardly any investor will do. But even after adjustment for the more typical holding periods, as reflected by monthly turnover, the row "Average Illiquidity Cost" in Table 13.7 shows that this cost is economically significant for illiquid portfolios, on the order of 2.5% per year (.21% per month), and this value still does not account for the effect of liquidity risk on the portfolio risk premium. Notice also from Table 13.7 that portfolio turnover falls with liquidity; as noted in Chapter 9, this reflects the fact that illiquid assets will be unattractive to investors with short time horizons. Finally, the liquidity betas are small relative to the market beta and highly collinear (note the high correlations in panel B), but may still significantly improve the explanatory power of a CAPM augmented with liquidity considerations. This can be determined by comparing the explanatory power of the standard CAPM specification with an augmented model that includes liquidity betas.

We show results for three of the specifications estimated by Acharya and Pedersen in Table 13.8. The first pair of rows provides surprising support for the single-factor CAPM: the intercept is not significantly different from zero, and the statistically significant slope of 1.4% is actually higher than the market monthly average excess return. However, the adjusted R-square of the equation estimate, 0.322, is low.

The next pair of rows presents results for a liquidity-adjusted CAPM. In model 1, β^{NET} is the sum of the usual market beta plus the three liquidity betas: $\beta^{NET} = \beta_M + \beta_{L1} + \beta_{L2} + \beta_{L3}$.

---

[24]Viral V. Acharya and Lasse Heje Pedersen, "Asset Pricing with Liquidity Risk," *Journal of Financial Economics* 77 (2005), pp. 375–410.

[25]A drawback of using these portfolios to test risk-return relationships is the narrow range of market betas that result when portfolios are sorted by liquidity. This reduces the power of the tests to measure the impact of beta on average return.

Panel A: Summary statistics

Liquidity Portfolio	Most Liquid 1	5	9	13	17	21	Least Liquid 25
Market beta	0.551	0.747	0.819	0.853	0.879	0.927	0.845
Capitalization ($billion)	12.50	1.20	0.48	0.24	0.13	0.06	0.02
B/M ratio	0.53	0.71	0.73	0.77	0.88	0.99	1.15
Avg. excess return (% per month)	0.48	0.60	0.71	0.77	0.80	1.13	1.10
Turnover (% per month)	3.25	4.17	3.82	3.47	2.96	2.97	2.60
Illiquidity cost* = $E(C_P)$(%)	0.25	0.27	0.32	0.43	0.71	1.61	8.83
Average illiquidity cost** (%/month)	0.01	0.01	0.01	0.01	0.02	0.04	0.21
β_{L1} ($\times$100)	0.00	0.00	0.01	0.01	0.04	0.09	0.42
β_{L2} ($\times$100)	−0.80	−1.24	−1.37	−1.47	−1.59	−1.69	−1.69
β_{L3} ($\times$100)	0.00	−0.07	−0.18	−0.40	−0.98	−2.10	−4.52
β^{NET}*** ($\times$100)	55.90	75.98	83.49	87.17	90.50	96.61	91.17

Panel B: Correlation matrix of liquidity portfolio betas

	β_M	β_{L1}	β_{L2}	β_{L3}
β_M	1	0.441	−0.972	−0.628
β_{L1}		1	−0.573	−0.941
β_{L2}			1	0.726
β_{L3}				1

TABLE 13.7

Properties of liquidity portfolios

* Illiquidity cost if the portfolio is held for only 1 month = effective bid–ask spread.
** Average illiquidity cost (for the average investor) = 0.5 $\times$ effective bid–ask spread $\times$ turnover $\times$ [1 + 1/(1 + discount rate)$^{1/turnover}$]. The monthly discount rate used here is 0.6%.
*** $\beta^{NET} = \beta_M + \beta_{L1} + \beta_{L2} + \beta_{L3}$.
Source: Viral V. Acharya and Lasse Heje Pedersen, "Asset Pricing with Liquidity Risk," *Journal of Financial Economics* 77 (2005), pp. 375–410.

Combining the market beta with the three liquidity betas in this manner amounts to assuming that risk premiums for all sources of systematic risk are equal. This is a reasonable assumption if the risk premiums on the various betas are roughly comparable. The estimated coefficients show a statistically insignificant intercept and a slope coefficient of .996% per month, which is closer to the risk premium of the market portfolio during this

Explanatory Variable	Model(1)	Model(2)	Model(3)
Constant	−0.530	−0.299	−0.053
	(−1.082)	(−0.737)	(−0.060)
$E(C_P)$		0.062	0.117
		(−3.878)	(−0.837)
β_M	1.374		1.207
	−2.085		(−0.343)
β^{NET}		0.996	
		(−4.848)	
β_{L1}			−346.55
			(−0.769)
β_{L2}			33.043
			−0.186
β_{L3}			−17.36
			(−0.981)
R-square	0.350	0.846	0.913
Adjusted R-square	0.322	0.832	0.890

TABLE 13.8

Estimates of the CAPM with and without liquidity factors

Model specifications

(1) Single-factor CAPM, $\quad E(R_P) = \lambda_M * \beta_M$

(2) Liquidity-adjusted CAPM, $E(R_P) = k * E(C_P) + \lambda_M * \beta_M + \lambda^{NET} * \beta^{NET}$

(3) Liquidity-adjusted CAPM, $E(R_P) = E(C_P) + \lambda_M * \beta_M + \lambda_{L1} * \beta_{L1} + \lambda_{L2} * \beta_{L2} + \lambda_{L3} * \beta_{L3}$

Notes: t-statistics appear in parentheses below regression coefficients. λ is the risk premium for each source of risk from a second-pass regression.

Source: Viral V. Acharya and Lasse Heje Pedersen, "Asset Pricing with Liquidity Risk," *Journal of Financial Economics* 77 (2005), pp. 375–410.

period. More impressive is the increase in explanatory power, reflected in the adjusted R-square of 0.832. Thus, despite the fact that the liquidity adjustments to the market beta are relatively small, accounting for portfolio liquidity materially improves the fit of the model.

The coefficient on the level of liquidity premium, 0.062, reflects the fact that Acharya and Pedersen measure illiquidity cost assuming a holding period of 1 month. The actual amortized monthly cost to particular investors would depend on their holding periods. The average holding period is the inverse of the monthly turnover; for the most illiquid portfolio, with a monthly turnover of 2.6%, the holding period is 38 months. In comparison, the holding period of the fifth most liquid portfolio, with monthly turnover of 4.15%, corresponds to 24 months. Regardless of the precise impact on investor returns, Acharya and Pedersen's work establishes the important point that liquidity is a priced factor that significantly affects asset returns.

Finally, the last pair of rows presents estimates of the model allowing for each individual liquidity beta to have its own return premium. Unfortunately, the high correlation among the various liquidity betas prevents accurate estimation of their individual premiums. However, the higher adjusted R-square, 0.89, further highlights the attraction of incorporating liquidity into the CAPM.

13.5   TIME–VARYING VOLATILITY

We may associate the variance of the rate of return on the stock with the rate of arrival of new information because new information may lead investors to revise their assessment of intrinsic value. As a casual survey of the media would indicate, the rate of revision in predictions of business cycles, industry ascents or descents, and the fortunes of individual enterprises fluctuate regularly; in other words, the rate of arrival of new information is time varying. Consequently, we should expect the variances of the rates of return on stocks (as well as the covariances among them) to be time varying.

In an exploratory study of the volatility of NYSE stocks over more than 150 years (using monthly returns over 1835–1987), Pagan and Schwert[26] computed estimates of the variance of monthly returns. Their results, depicted in Figure 13.5, show just how important it may be to consider time variation in stock variance. The centrality of the risk–return trade-off suggests that once we make sufficient progress in the modeling, estimation, and prediction of the time variation in return variances and covariances, we should expect a significant refinement in our understanding of expected returns as well.

When we consider a time-varying return distribution, we must refer to the *conditional* mean, variance, and covariance, that is, the mean, variance, or covariance conditional on currently available information. The "conditions" that vary over time are the values of variables that determine the level of these parameters. In contrast, the usual estimate of return variance, the average of squared deviations over the sample period, provides an *unconditional* estimate, because it treats the variance as constant over time.

In 1982 Robert F. Engle published a study[27] of U.K. inflation rates that measured their time-varying volatility. His model, named ARCH (autoregressive conditional heteroskedasticity), is based on the idea that a natural way to update a variance forecast is to average it with the most recent squared "surprise" (i.e., the squared deviation of the rate of return from its mean).

Today, the most widely used model to estimate the conditional (hence time-varying) variance of stocks and stock-index returns is the *generalized* autoregressive conditional heteroskedasticity (GARCH) model, also pioneered by Robert F. Engle.[28] (The generalized ARCH model allows greater flexibility in the specification of how volatility evolves over time.)

The GARCH model uses rate-of-return history as the information set used to form our estimates of variance. The model posits that the forecast of market volatility evolves relatively smoothly each period in response to new

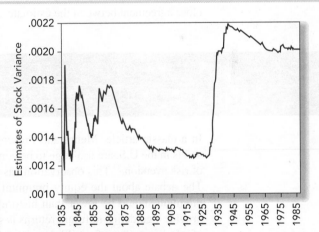

FIGURE 13.5   Estimates of the monthly stock return variance, 1835–1987

Source: Reprinted from *Journal of Econometrics* 45 (1990), Adrian R. Pagan and G. William Schwert, "Alternative Models for Conditional Stock Volatility," pp. 267–290. Copyright 1990, with permission from Elsevier Science.

[26]Adrian Pagan and G. William Schwert, "Alternative Models for Conditional Stock Volatility," *Journal of Econometrics* 45 (1990), pp. 267–90.

[27]Robert F. Engle, "Autoregressive Conditional Heteroskedasticity with Estimates of the Variance of U.K. Inflation," *Econometrica* 50 (1982), pp. 987–1008.

[28]Ibid.

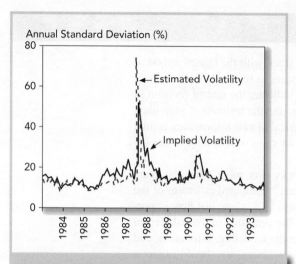

FIGURE 13.6 Implied versus estimated volatility. Implied volatility is derived from options on the S&P 100 index. Estimated volatility is derived from an ARCH model.

observations on market returns. The updated estimate of market-return variance in each period depends on both the previous estimate and the most recent squared residual return on the market. The squared residual is an unbiased estimate of variance, so this technique essentially mixes in a statistically efficient manner the previous volatility estimate with an unbiased estimate based on the new observation of market return. The updating formula is

$$\sigma_t^2 = a_0 + a_1 \epsilon_{t-1}^2 + a_2 \sigma_{t-1}^2 \qquad (13.10)$$

As noted, Equation 13.10 asserts that the updated forecast of variance is a function of the most recent variance forecast σ_{t-1}^2, and the most recent squared prediction error in market return, ϵ_{t-1}^2. The parameters a_0, a_1, and a_2 are estimated from past data.

Evidence on the relationship between mean and variance has been mixed. Whitelaw[29] found that average returns and volatility are negatively related, but Kane, Marcus, and Noh[30] found a positive relationship.

ARCH-type models clearly capture much of the variation in stock market volatility. Figure 13.6 compares volatility estimates from an ARCH model to volatility estimates derived from prices on market-index options, called *implied volatility*.[31] The variation in volatility, as well as the close agreement between the estimates, is evident.

13.6 CONSUMPTION–BASED ASSET PRICING AND THE EQUITY PREMIUM PUZZLE

In a classic article, Mehra and Prescott observed that historical excess returns on risky assets in the U.S. are too large to be consistent with economic theory and reasonable levels of risk aversion.[32] This observation has come to be known as the "equity premium puzzle." The debate about the equity premium puzzle suggests that forecasts of the market risk premium should be lower than historical averages. The question of whether past returns provide a guideline to future returns is sufficiently important to justify stretching the scope of our discussions of equilibrium in capital markets.

Consumption Growth and Market Rates of Return

As discussed in Chapter 9, the ICAPM is derived from a lifetime consumption/investment plan of a representative consumer/investor. Each individual's plan is set to maximize a

[29]Robert F. Whitelaw, "Time Variation and Covariations in the Expectation and Volatility of Stock Returns," *Journal of Finance* 49 (1994), pp. 515–42.

[30]Alex Kane, Alan J. Marcus, and Jaesun Noh, "The P/E Multiple and Market Volatility," *Financial Analysts Journal* 52 (July–August 1996), pp. 16–24.

[31]We will show you how such estimates can be derived from option prices in Chapter 21.

[32]Jarnish Mehra and Edward Prescott, "The Equity Premium: A Puzzle," *Journal of Monetary Economics*, March 1985.

utility function of lifetime consumption, and consumption/investment in each period is based on age and current wealth, as well as the risk-free rate and the market portfolio's risk and risk premium.

The consumption model implies that what matters to investors is not their wealth per se, but their lifetime flow of consumption. There can be slippage between wealth and consumption due to variation in factors such as the risk-free rate, the market portfolio risk premium, or prices of major consumption items. Therefore, a better measure of consumer well-being than wealth is the consumption flow that such wealth can support.

Given this framework, the generalization of the basic CAPM is that instead of measuring security risk based on the covariance of returns with the market return (a measure that focuses only on wealth), we are better off using the covariance of returns with aggregate consumption. Hence, we would expect the risk premium of the market index to be related to that covariance as follows:

$$E(r_M) - r_f = A\mathrm{Cov}(r_M, r_C) \tag{13.11}$$

where A depends on the average coefficient of risk aversion and r_C is the rate of return on a consumption-tracking portfolio constructed to have the highest possible correlation with growth in aggregate consumption.[33]

The first wave of attempts to estimate consumption-based asset pricing models used consumption data directly rather than returns on consumption-tracking portfolios. By and large, these tests found the CCAPM no better than the conventional CAPM in explaining risk premiums. Part of the difficulty originated from the fact that consumption data are collected far less frequently (monthly at best) than rate of return data and with substantial error. This prevented researchers from taking advantage of the more frequent and accurate observation of rates of return on financial assets.

Recent research improves the quality of estimation in several ways. First, rather than using consumption growth directly, it uses consumption-tracking portfolios. The available (infrequent) data on aggregate consumption is used only to construct the consumption-tracking portfolio. The frequent and accurate data on the return on these portfolios may then be used to test the asset pricing model. (On the other hand, any inaccuracy in the construction of the consumption-mimicking portfolios will muddy the relationship between asset returns and consumption risk.)

Second, investors seem to adjust consumption levels most substantially in the fourth quarter of a calendar year. Using data from other quarters may obscure the reaction of annual consumption to annual portfolio returns.

Finally, the standard CCAPM focuses on a representative consumer/investor, thereby ignoring information about heterogeneous investors with different levels of wealth and consumption habits. To improve the model's power to explain returns, some newer studies allow for several classes of investors with differences in wealth and consumption behavior. They also may separate expenditures on consumer nondurables versus durable goods.

For example, a recent study by Jagannathan and Wang focuses on year-over-year fourth-quarter consumption and employs a consumption-mimicking portfolio.[34] Table 13.9,

---

[33]This equation is analogous to the equation for the risk premium in the conventional CAPM, i.e., that $E(r_M) - r_f = A\mathrm{Cov}(r_M, r_M) = A\mathrm{Var}(r_M)$. In the one-factor version of Merton's ICAPM, this equation for the market risk premium also would be valid. In the multifactor version of the ICAPM, however, the market is no longer mean-variance efficient, so the risk premium of the market index will not be proportional to its variance. The APT also implies a linear relationship between risk premium and covariance with relevant factors, but it is silent about the slope of the relationship because it avoids assumptions about utility.

[34]Ravi Jagannathan and Yong Wang, "Lazy Investors, Discretionary Consumption, and the Cross-Section of Stock Returns," *Journal of Finance* 62 (August 2006), pp. 1623–61.

TABLE 13.9

Annual consumption growth,* 1954–2003 (%)

	Q1-Q1	Q2-Q2	Q3-Q3	Q4-Q4	Annual–Annual	Dec–Dec
Mean	2.38	2.38	2.41	2.44	2.40	2.49
SD	1.38	1.31	1.29	1.38	1.21	1.43
Min	−0.36	−0.27	−0.49	−0.78	−0.07	−0.79
Max	5.72	5.40	4.83	5.70	4.52	5.17

*Consumption is measured by real per capita consumption expenditure on nondurables and services.

Notes: Q1-Q1 annual consumption growth is calculated using Quarter 1 consumption data. Q2-Q2, Q3-Q3, and Q4-Q4 annual consumption growth are calculated in a similar way. Annual–Annual consumption growth is calculated using annual consumption data. Dec–Dec consumption growth is calculated from December consumption data.

Source: Ravi Jagannathan and Yong Wang, "Lazy Investors, Discretionary Consumption, and the Cross-Section of Stock Returns," *Journal of Finance* 62 (August 2006), pp. 1623–61.

excerpted from their study, shows the difference in consumption growth between 1954 and 2003 computed in different ways. On the surface, these values appear similar. Nevertheless, Jagannathan and Wang find that annual consumption growth measured by comparing fourth-quarter data in successive years is substantially better than the other intervals in explaining portfolio returns. This finding echoes the results on liquidity, where we saw that even small liquidity betas seemed to materially improve the success of the model in explaining returns. Here again, small differences in data seem telling.

Table 13.10 shows that the Fama-French factors are in fact associated with consumption betas as well as excess returns. The top panel contains familiar results: moving across each row, we see that higher book-to-market ratios are associated with higher average returns. Similarly, moving down each column, we see that larger size generally implies lower average returns. The novel results are in the lower panel: a high book-to-market ratio is associated with higher consumption beta, and larger firm size is associated with lower consumption beta. The suggestion is that the explanatory power of the Fama-French

TABLE 13.10

Annual excess returns and consumption betas

Size	Book-to-Market		
	Low	Medium	High
Average annual excess returns* (%)			
Small	6.19	12.24	17.19
Medium	6.93	10.43	13.94
Big	7.08	8.52	9.5
Consumption beta*			
Small	3.46	4.26	5.94
Medium	2.88	4.35	5.71
Big	3.39	2.83	4.41

*Average annual excess returns on the 25 Fama-French portfolios from 1954 to 2003 Consumption betas estimated by the time series regression

$$R_{i,t} = \alpha_i + \beta_{i,c}g_{ct} + \epsilon_{i,t},$$

where $R_{i,t}$ is the excess return over the risk-free rate, and g_{ct} is annual consumption growth calculated using fourth-quarter consumption data.

Source: Ravi Jagannathan and Yong Wang, "Lazy Investors, Discretionary Consumption, and the Cross-Section of Stock Returns," *Journal of Finance* 62 (August 2006), pp. 1623–61.

factors for average returns may in fact reflect the differing consumption risk of those portfolios. Figure 13.7 shows that the average returns of the 25 Fama-French portfolios are strongly associated with their consumption betas. Other tests reported by Jagannathan and Wang show that the CCAPM explains returns even better than the Fama-French three-factor model, which in turn is superior to the single-factor CAPM.

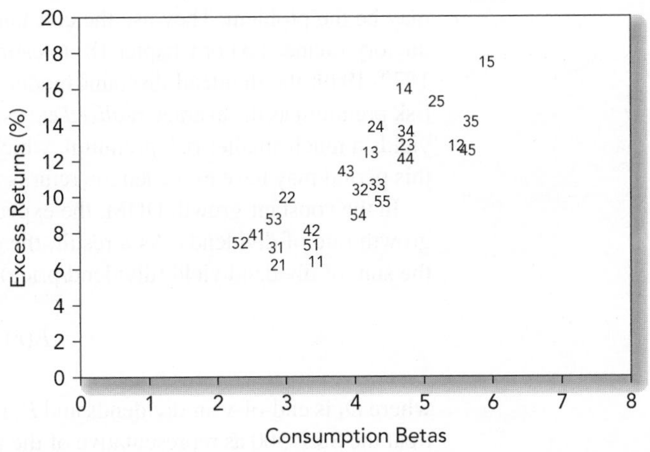

The equity premium puzzle refers to the fact that using reasonable estimates of A, the covariance of consumption growth with the market-index return, $Cov(r_M, r_C)$, is far too low to justify observed historical-average excess returns on the market-index portfolio, which may be viewed as an estimate of the left-hand side of Equation 13.11.[35] Thus, the risk premium puzzle says in effect that historical excess returns are too high and/or our usual estimates of risk aversion are too low.

The equity premium puzzle can be interpreted in several ways. One approach focuses on observed historical returns, and asks whether Equation 13.11 fails empirical tests only because those historical returns were actually not representative of investors' expectations at the time. A second, conflicting, interpretation is that the puzzle is real, and is yet another nail in the coffin of the CAPM. The next two subsections pursue these lines of inquiry. A third approach suggests that extensions of the CAPM may resolve the puzzle. In contrast, a fourth interpretation from the field of behavioral finance pins the puzzle on irrational behavior.

FIGURE 13.7   Cross-section of stock returns: Fama-French 25 portfolios, 1954–2003

Annual excess returns and consumption betas. This figure plots the average annual excess returns on the 25 Fama-French portfolios and their consumption betas. Each two-digit number represents one portfolio. The first digit refers to the size quintile (1 = smallest, 5 = largest), and the second digit refers to the book-to-market quintile (1 = lowest, 5 = highest).

Expected versus Realized Returns

Fama and French[36] offer another interpretation of the equity premium puzzle. Using stock index returns from 1872 to 1999, they report the average risk-free rate, average return on equity (represented by the S&P 500 index), and resultant risk premium for the overall period and subperiods:

Period	Risk-Free Rate	S&P 500 Return	Equity Premium
1872–1999	4.87	10.97	6.10
1872–1949	4.05	8.67	4.62
1950–1999	6.15	14.56	8.41

The big increase in the average excess return on equity after 1949 suggests that the equity premium puzzle is largely a creature of modern times.

[35]Notice that the conventional CAPM does not pose such problems. In the CAPM, $E(r_M) - r_f = A\text{Var}(r_M)$. A risk premium of .085 (8.5%) and a standard deviation of .20 (20%, or variance of .04) imply a coefficient of risk aversion of .085/.04 = 2.125, which is quite plausible.

[36]Eugene Fama and Kenneth French, "The Equity Premium," *Journal of Finance* 57, no. 2 (2002).

Fama and French suspect that estimating the risk premium from average realized returns may be the problem. They use the constant-growth dividend-discount model (see an introductory finance text or Chapter 18) to estimate expected returns and find that for the period 1872–1949, the dividend discount model (DDM) yields similar estimates of the *expected* risk premium as the average *realized* excess return. But for the period 1950–1999, the DDM yields a much smaller risk premium, which suggests that the high average excess return in this period may have exceeded the returns investors actually expected to earn at the time.

In the constant-growth DDM, the expected capital gains rate on the stock will equal the growth rate of dividends. As a result, the expected total return on the firm's stock will be the sum of dividend yield (dividend/price) plus the expected dividend growth rate, g:

$$E(r) = \frac{D_1}{P_0} + g \qquad (13.12)$$

where D_1 is end-of-year dividends and P_0 is the current price of the stock. Fama and French treat the S&P 500 as representative of the average firm, and use Equation 13.12 to produce estimates of $E(r)$.

For any sample period, $t = 1, \ldots, T$, Fama and French estimate expected return from the arithmetic average of the dividend yield (D_t/P_{t-1}) plus the dividend growth rate $(g_t = D_t/D_{t-1} - 1)$. In contrast, the *realized* return is the dividend yield plus the rate of capital gains $(P_t/P_{t-1} - 1)$. Because the dividend yield is common to both estimates, the difference between the expected and realized return equals the difference between the dividend growth and capital gains rates. While dividend growth and capital gains were similar in the earlier period, capital gains significantly exceeded the dividend growth rate in modern times. Hence, Fama and French conclude that the equity premium puzzle may be due at least in part to unanticipated capital gains in the latter period.

Fama and French argue that dividend growth rates produce more reliable estimates of the capital gains investors actually expected to earn than the average of their realized capital gains. They point to three reasons:

1. Average realized returns over 1950–1999 exceeded the internal rate of return on corporate investments. If those average returns were representative of expectations, we would have to conclude that firms were willingly engaging in negative-NPV investments.

2. The statistical precision of estimates from the DDM are far higher than those using average historical returns. The standard error of the estimates of the risk premium from realized returns greatly exceed the standard error from the dividend discount model (see the following table).

3. The reward-to-volatility (Sharpe) ratio derived from the DDM is far more stable than that derived from realized returns. If risk aversion remains the same over time, we would expect the Sharpe ratio to be stable.

The evidence for the second and third points is shown in the following table, where estimates from the dividend model (DDM) and from realized returns (Realized) are shown side by side.

	Mean Return		Standard Error		t-Statistic		Sharpe Ratio	
Period	DDM	Realized	DDM	Realized	DDM	Realized	DDM	Realized
1872–1999	4.03	6.10	1.14	1.65	3.52	3.70	0.22	0.34
1872–1949	4.35	4.62	1.76	2.20	2.47	2.10	0.23	0.24
1950–1999	3.54	8.41	1.03	2.45	3.42	3.43	0.21	0.51

Fama and French's study provides a simple explanation for the equity premium puzzle, namely, that observed rates of return in the recent half-century were unexpectedly high. It also implies that forecasts of future excess returns will be lower than past averages. (Coincidentally, their study was published in 1999, and so far appears prophetic in light of low subsequent average returns since then.)

Work by Goetzmann and Ibbotson[37] lends support to Fama and French's argument. Goetzmann and Ibbotson combine research that extends data on rates of return on stocks and long-term corporate bonds back to 1792. Summary statistics for these values between 1792 and 1925 are as follows:

	Arithmetic Average	Geometric Average	Standard Deviation
NYSE total return	7.93%	6.99%	14.64%
U.S. bond yields	4.17%	4.16%	4.17%

These statistics suggest a risk premium that is much lower than the historical average for 1926–2005 (much less 1950–1999), which is the period that produces the equity premium puzzle.[38] Thus, the period for which Fama and French claim realized rates were unexpected is actually relatively short in historical perspective.

Survivorship Bias

The equity premium puzzle emerged from long-term averages of U.S. stock returns. There are reasons to suspect that these estimates of the risk premium are subject to survivorship bias, as the United States has arguably been the most successful capitalist system in the world, an outcome that probably would not have been anticipated several decades ago. Jurion and Goetzmann[39] assembled a database of capital appreciation indexes for the stock markets of 39 countries over the period 1921–1996. Figure 13.8 shows that U.S. equities had the highest real return of all countries, at 4.3% annually, versus a median of .8% for other countries. Moreover, unlike the United States, many other countries have had equity markets that actually closed, either permanently or for extended periods of time.

The implication of these results is that using average U.S. data may impart a form of survivorship bias to our estimate of expected returns, because unlike many other countries, the United States has never been a victim of

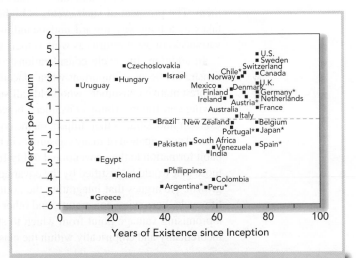

FIGURE 13.8   Real returns on global stock markets. The figure displays average real returns for 39 markets over the period 1921 to 1996. Markets are sorted by years of existence. The graph shows that markets with long histories typically have higher returns. An asterisk indicates that the market suffered a long-term break.

[37]William N. Goetzmann and Roger G. Ibbotson, "History and the Equity Risk Premium," working paper, Yale University, October 18, 2005.

[38]The short-term risk-free rate is a lot more difficult to assess because short-term bonds in this period were quite risky and average rates exceeded the yields on long-term corporate bonds.

[39]Philippe Jurion and William N. Goetzmann, "Global Stock Markets in the Twentieth Century," *Journal of Finance* 54, no. 3 (June 1999).

such extreme problems. Estimating risk premiums from the experience of the most successful country and ignoring the evidence from stock markets that did not survive for the full sample period will impart an upward bias in estimates of expected returns. The high realized equity premium obtained for the United States may not be indicative of required returns.

As an analogy, think of the effect of survivorship bias in the mutual fund industry. We know that some companies regularly close down their worst-performing mutual funds. If performance studies include only mutual funds for which returns are available during an entire sample period, the average returns of the funds that make it into the sample will be reflective of the performance of long-term survivors only. With the failed funds excluded from the sample, the average measured performance of mutual fund managers will be better than one could reasonably expect from the full sample of managers. Think back to the box in Chapter 11, "How to Guarantee a Successful Market Newsletter." If one starts many newsletters with a range of forecasts, and continues only the newsletters that turned out to have successful advice, then it will *appear* from the sample of survivors that the average newsletter had forecasting skill.

Extensions to the CAPM May Resolve the Equity Premium Puzzle

Constantinides[40] argues that the standard CAPM can be extended to account for observed excess returns by relaxing some of its assumptions, in particular, by recognizing that consumers face uninsurable and idiosyncratic income shocks, for example, the loss of employment. The prospect of such events is higher in economic downturns and this observation takes us a long way toward understanding both the unconditional moments (means and variances) of asset returns as well as their variation along the business cycle.

In addition, life-cycle considerations are important and often overlooked. Borrowing constraints become important when placed in the context of the life cycle. The imaginary "representative consumer" who holds all stock and bond market wealth does not face borrowing constraints. Young consumers, however, do face meaningful borrowing constraints. Constantinides traces their impact on the equity premium, the demand for bonds, and on the limited participation of many consumers in the capital markets. Finally, he shows that adding habit formation to the conventional utility function helps explain higher risk premiums than those that would be justified by the covariance of stock returns with aggregate consumption growth. He argues that integrating the notions of habit formation, incomplete markets, the life cycle, borrowing constraints, and other sources of limited stock market participation is a promising vantage point from which to study the prices of assets and their returns, both theoretically and empirically within the class of rational asset-pricing models.

Behavioral Explanations of the Equity Premium Puzzle

Barberis and Huang[41] explain the puzzle as an outcome of irrational investor behavior. The key elements of their approach are loss aversion and narrow framing, two well-known features of decision making under risk in experimental settings. Narrow framing is the idea that investors evaluate every risk they face in isolation. Thus, investors will ignore low correlation of the risk of a stock portfolio with other components of wealth, and therefore

[40]George M. Constantinides, "Understanding the Equity Risk Premium Puzzle," in *Handbooks in Finance: Handbook of the Equity Risk Premium,* ed. Rajnish Mehra (Amsterdam: Elsevier, 2008), pp. 331–59.

[41]Nicholas Barberis and Ming Huang, "The Loss Aversion/Narrow Framing Approach to the Equity Premium Puzzle," in *Handbooks in Finance: Handbook of the Equity Risk Premium* ed. Rajnish Mehra (Amsterdam: Elsevier, 2008), pp. 199–229.

require a higher risk premium than rational models would predict. Combined with loss aversion, investor behavior will generate large risk premiums despite the fact that traditionally measured risk aversion is plausibly low. (See Chapter 12 for more discussion of such behavioral biases.)

Models that incorporate these effects can generate a large equilibrium equity risk premium and a low and stable risk-free rate, even when consumption growth is smooth and only weakly correlated with the stock market. Moreover, they can do so for parameter values that correspond to plausible predictions about attitudes to independent monetary gambles. The analysis for the equity premium also has implications for a closely related portfolio puzzle, the stock market participation puzzle. They suggest some possible directions for future research.

The approach of Barberis and Huang, when accounting for heterogeneity of preferences, can explain why a segment of the population that predictably would participate in the stock market despite frictions and other rational explanations, still avoids it. Narrow framing also explains the disconnect between consumption growth and market rates of return. The assessment of stock market return in isolation ignores the limited impact on consumption via smoothing and other hedges. Loss aversion that exaggerates disutility of losses relative to a reference point magnifies this effect. The development of empirical literature on the tenets of these theories may determine the validity and implications of the equity premium puzzle.

SUMMARY

1. Although the single-factor expected return–beta relationship has not been confirmed by scientific standards, its use is already commonplace in economic life.

2. Early tests of the single-factor CAPM rejected the SML, finding that nonsystematic risk did explain average security returns.

3. Later tests controlling for the measurement error in beta found that nonsystematic risk does not explain portfolio returns but also that the estimated SML is too flat compared with what the CAPM would predict.

4. Roll's critique implied that the usual CAPM test is a test only of the mean-variance efficiency of a prespecified market *proxy* and therefore that tests of the linearity of the expected return–beta relationship do not bear on the validity of the model.

5. Tests of the mean-variance efficiency of professionally managed portfolios against the benchmark of a prespecified market index conform with Roll's critique in that they provide evidence on the efficiency of the prespecific market index.

6. Empirical evidence suggests that most professionally managed portfolios are outperformed by market indexes, which lends weight to acceptance of the efficiency of those indexes and hence the CAPM.

7. Work with economic factors suggests that factors such as unanticipated inflation do play a role in the expected return–beta relationship of security returns.

8. Tests of the single-index model that account for human capital and cyclical variations in asset betas are far more consistent with the single-index CAPM and APT. These tests suggest that macroeconomic variables are not necessary to explain expected returns. Moreover, anomalies such as effects of size and book-to-market ratios disappear once these variables are accounted for.

9. Volatility of stock returns is constantly changing. Empirical evidence on stock returns must account for this phenomenon. Contemporary researchers use the variations of the ARCH algorithm to estimate the level of volatility and its effect on mean returns.

10. The equity premium puzzle originates from the observation that equity returns exceeded the risk-free rate to an extent that is inconsistent with reasonable levels of risk aversion—at least when average rates of return are taken to represent expectations. Fama and French show that the puzzle emerges primarily from excess returns over the last 50 years. Alternative estimates of expected returns using the dividend growth model instead of average returns suggest that excess returns on stocks were high because of unexpected large capital gains. The study suggests that future excess returns will be lower than realized in recent decades.

11. Early research on consumption-based capital asset pricing models was disappointing, but more recent work is far more encouraging. In some studies, consumption betas explain average portfolio returns as well as the Fama-French three-factor model. These results support Fama and French's conjecture that their factors proxy for more fundamental sources of risk.

KEY TERMS

first-pass regression   benchmark error   illiquidity cost
second-pass regression

PROBLEM SETS

Quiz

1. Suppose you find, as research indicates, that in the cross-section regression of the CCAPM, the coefficients of factor loadings on the Fama-French model are significant predictors of average return factors (in addition to consumption beta). How would you explain this phenomenon?

2. Search the Internet for a recent graph of market volatility. What does this history suggest about the history of consumption growth?

Problems

The following annual excess rates of return were obtained for nine individual stocks and a market index:

	Market	Stock Excess Returns (%)								
Year	Index	A	B	C	D	E	F	G	H	I
1	29.65	33.88	−25.20	36.48	42.89	−39.89	39.67	74.57	40.22	90.19
2	−11.91	−49.87	24.70	−25.11	−54.39	44.92	−54.33	−79.76	−71.58	−26.64
3	14.73	65.14	−25.04	18.91	−39.86	−3.91	−5.69	26.73	14.49	18.14
4	27.68	14.46	−38.64	−23.31	−0.72	−3.21	92.39	−3.82	13.74	0.09
5	5.18	15.67	61.93	63.95	−32.82	44.26	−42.96	101.67	24.24	8.98
6	25.97	−32.17	44.94	−19.56	69.42	90.43	76.72	1.72	77.22	72.38
7	10.64	−31.55	−74.65	50.18	74.52	15.38	21.95	−43.95	−13.40	28.95
8	1.02	−23.79	47.02	−42.28	28.61	−17.64	28.83	98.01	28.12	39.41
9	18.82	−4.59	28.69	−0.54	2.32	42.36	18.93	−2.45	37.65	94.67
10	23.92	−8.03	48.61	23.65	26.26	−3.65	23.31	15.36	80.59	52.51
11	−41.61	78.22	−85.02	−0.79	−68.70	−85.71	−45.64	2.27	−72.47	−80.26
12	−6.64	4.75	42.95	−48.60	26.27	13.24	−34.34	−54.47	−1.50	−24.46

3. Perform the first-pass regressions and tabulate the summary statistics.

4. Specify the hypotheses for a test of the second-pass regression for the SML.

5. Perform the second-pass SML regression by regressing the average excess return of each portfolio on its beta.

6. Summarize your test results and compare them to the results reported in the text.

7. Group the nine stocks into three portfolios, maximizing the dispersion of the betas of the three resultant portfolios. Repeat the test and explain any changes in the results.

8. Explain Roll's critique as it applies to the tests performed in Problems 3 to 7.

9. Plot the capital market line (CML), the nine stocks, and the three portfolios on a graph of average returns versus standard deviation. Compare the mean-variance efficiency of the three portfolios and the market index. Does the comparison support the CAPM?

Suppose that, in addition to the market factor that has been considered in Problems 3 to 9, a second factor is considered. The values of this factor for years 1 to 12 were as follows:

Year	% Change in Factor Value	Year	% Change in Factor Value
1	−9.84	7	−3.52
2	6.46	8	8.43
3	16.12	9	8.23
4	−16.51	10	7.06
5	17.82	11	−15.74
6	−13.31	12	2.03

10. Perform the first-pass regressions as did Chen, Roll, and Ross and tabulate the relevant summary statistics. (*Hint:* Use a multiple regression as in a standard spreadsheet package. Estimate the betas of the 12 stocks on the two factors.)

11. Specify the hypothesis for a test of a second-pass regression for the two-factor SML.

12. Do the data suggest a two-factor economy?

13. Can you identify a factor portfolio for the second factor?

14. Suppose you own your own business, which now makes up about half your net worth. Based on what you have learned in this chapter, how would you structure your portfolio of financial assets?

Challenge Problem

---

1. Identify and briefly discuss three criticisms of beta as used in the capital asset pricing model.

2. Richard Roll, in an article on using the capital asset pricing model (CAPM) to evaluate portfolio performance, indicated that it may not be possible to evaluate portfolio management ability if there is an error in the benchmark used.

   a. In evaluating portfolio performance, describe the general procedure, with emphasis on the benchmark employed.
   b. Explain what Roll meant by the benchmark error and identify the specific problem with this benchmark.
   c. Draw a graph that shows how a portfolio that has been judged as superior relative to a "measured" security market line (SML) can be inferior relative to the "true" SML.
   d. Assume that you are informed that a given portfolio manager has been evaluated as superior when compared to the Dow Jones Industrial Average, the S&P 500, and the NYSE Composite Index. Explain whether this consensus would make you feel more comfortable regarding the portfolio manager's true ability.
   e. Although conceding the possible problem with benchmark errors as set forth by Roll, some contend this does not mean the CAPM is incorrect, but only that there is a measurement problem when implementing the theory. Others contend that because of benchmark errors the whole technique should be scrapped. Take and defend one of these positions.

3. Bart Campbell, CFA, is a portfolio manager who has recently met with a prospective client, Jane Black. After conducting a survey market line (SML) performance analysis using the Dow Jones Industrial Average as her market proxy, Black claims that her portfolio has experienced superior performance. Campbell uses the capital asset pricing model as an investment performance measure and finds that Black's portfolio plots below the SML. Campbell concludes that Black's apparent superior performance is a function of an incorrectly specified market proxy, not superior investment management. Justify Campbell's conclusion by addressing the likely effects of an incorrectly specified market proxy on both beta and the slope of the SML.

STANDARD
&POOR'S

First obtain monthly returns for a sample of 10 firms and the S&P 500 from the Market Insight database at **www.mhhe.com/edumarketinsight.** Then obtain the corresponding returns on the HML (high minus low book value) and SMB (small minus big) portfolios from Ken French's Web site at **mba.tuck.dartmouth.edu/pages/faculty/ken.french/data_library. html.** Finally, obtain monthly interest rates from the Fed's Web site at **www.federalreserve. gov/releases/h15/data.htm.** Evaluate the alphas of each firm over the last 3 years as the intercept in a first-pass regression using excess returns in a single-index model. Then evaluate the alphas using a first-pass Fama-French three-factor multiple regression. Under which model is alpha more variable across firms? What do you conclude?

E-Investments

Mutual Funds and the Index Model

Go to **www.morningstar.com** and select the *Funds* tab. When the *Mutual Funds* page opens, scroll down to the *Find a Fund* (Fund Screener) section. Get a list of the funds that satisfy specifications of your choosing. Choose three of the listed funds, with the constraint that the funds have different investment styles (e.g., small cap, global, precious metals, emerging markets).

For each fund, click on its name to get a *Snapshot Report,* then click on the link for *Risk Measures* on the left menu. Identity each fund's beta, alpha, and R-squared coefficients. Compare both the Standard Index and the Best Fit Index. Given the risk levels of the funds, which of them outperformed the market? Which fund had the highest level of risk-adjusted performance?

SOLUTIONS TO CONCEPT CHECKS

1. The SCL is estimated for each stock; hence we need to estimate 100 equations. Our sample consists of 60 monthly rates of return for each of the 100 stocks and for the market index. Thus each regression is estimated with 60 observations. Equation 13.1 in the text shows that when stated in excess return form, the SCL should pass through the origin, that is, have a zero intercept.

2. When the SML has a positive intercept and its slope is less than the mean excess return on the market portfolio, it is flatter than predicted by the CAPM. Low-beta stocks therefore have yielded returns that, on average, were higher than they should have been on the basis of their beta. Conversely, high-beta stocks were found to have yielded, on average, lower returns than they should have on the basis of their betas. The positive coefficient on γ_2 implies that stocks with higher values of firm-specific risk had on average higher returns. This pattern, of course, violates the predictions of the CAPM.

3. According to Equation 13.5, γ_0 is the average return earned on a stock with zero beta and zero firm-specific risk. According to the CAPM, this should be the risk-free rate, which for the 1946–1955 period was 9 basis points, or .09% per month (see Table 13.1). According to the CAPM, γ_1 should equal the average market risk premium, which for the 1946–1955 period was 103 basis points, or 1.03% per month. Finally, the CAPM predicts that γ_3, the coefficient on firm-specific risk, should be zero.

4. A positive coefficient on beta-squared would indicate that the relationship between risk and return is nonlinear. High-beta securities would provide expected returns more than proportional to risk. A positive coefficient on $\sigma(e)$ would indicate that firm-specific risk affects expected return, a direct contradiction of the CAPM and APT.

CHAPTER FOURTEEN

BOND PRICES AND YIELDS

IN THE PREVIOUS chapters on risk and return relationships, we have treated securities at a high level of abstraction. We assumed implicitly that a prior, detailed analysis of each security already had been performed, and that its risk and return features had been assessed.

We turn now to specific analyses of particular security markets. We examine valuation principles, determinants of risk and return, and portfolio strategies commonly used within and across the various markets.

We begin by analyzing **debt securities.** A debt security is a claim on a specified periodic stream of income. Debt securities are often called *fixed-income securities* because they promise either a fixed stream of income or a stream of income that is determined according to a specified formula. These securities have the advantage of being relatively easy to understand because the payment formulas are specified in advance. Risk considerations are minimal as long as the issuer

of the security is sufficiently creditworthy. That makes these securities a convenient starting point for our analysis of the universe of potential investment vehicles.

The bond is the basic debt security, and this chapter starts with an overview of the universe of bond markets, including Treasury, corporate, and international bonds. We turn next to bond pricing, showing how bond prices are set in accordance with market interest rates and why bond prices change with those rates. Given this background, we can compare the myriad measures of bond returns such as yield to maturity, yield to call, holding-period return, or realized compound rate of return. We show how bond prices evolve over time, discuss certain tax rules that apply to debt securities, and show how to calculate after-tax returns. Finally, we consider the impact of default or credit risk on bond pricing and look at the determinants of credit risk and the default premium built into bond yields.

14.1   BOND CHARACTERISTICS

A **bond** is a security that is issued in connection with a borrowing arrangement. The borrower issues (i.e., sells) a bond to the lender for some amount of cash; the bond is the "IOU" of the borrower. The arrangement obligates the issuer to make specified payments to the bondholder on specified dates. A typical coupon bond obligates the issuer to make semiannual payments of interest to the bondholder for the life of the bond. These are called *coupon payments* because in precomputer days, most bonds had coupons that investors would clip off and present to claim the interest payment. When the bond matures, the issuer repays the debt by paying the bondholder the bond's **par value** (equivalently, its **face value**). The **coupon rate** of the bond serves to determine the interest payment: The annual payment is the coupon rate times the bond's par value. The coupon rate, maturity date, and par value of the bond are part of the **bond indenture,** which is the contract between the issuer and the bondholder.

To illustrate, a bond with par value of $1,000 and coupon rate of 8% might be sold to a buyer for $1,000. The bondholder is then entitled to a payment of 8% of $1,000, or $80 per year, for the stated life of the bond, say, 30 years. The $80 payment typically comes in two semiannual installments of $40 each. At the end of the 30-year life of the bond, the issuer also pays the $1,000 par value to the bondholder.

Bonds usually are issued with coupon rates set just high enough to induce investors to pay par value to buy the bond. Sometimes, however, **zero-coupon bonds** are issued that make no coupon payments. In this case, investors receive par value at the maturity date but receive no interest payments until then: The bond has a coupon rate of zero. These bonds are issued at prices considerably below par value, and the investor's return comes solely from the difference between issue price and the payment of par value at maturity. We will return to these bonds later.

Treasury Bonds and Notes

Figure 14.1 is an excerpt from the listing of Treasury issues. Treasury note maturities range up to 10 years, while Treasury bonds with maturities ranging from 10 to 30 years appear in the figure. Most bonds and notes are issued in denominations of $1,000 or more, but the minimum denomination was reduced to $100 in 2008. Both make semiannual coupon payments.

The highlighted bond in Figure 14.1 matures in January 2011. The *n* after 2011 denotes that this is a Treasury note, not a bond. Its coupon rate is 4.25%. Par value typically is $1,000; thus the bond pays interest of $42.50 per year in two semiannual payments of $21.25. Payments are made in January and July of each year. The bid and asked prices[1] are quoted in points plus fractions of $\frac{1}{32}$ of a point (the numbers after the colons are the fractions of a point). Although bonds usually are sold in denominations of $1,000, the prices are quoted as a percentage of par value. Therefore, the bid price of the bond is $98:07 = 98\frac{7}{32} = 98.219\%$ of par value, or $982.19, whereas the asked price is $99\frac{8}{32}\%$ of par, or $982.50.

The last column, labeled "Ask Yld," is the yield to maturity on the bond based on the asked price. The yield to maturity is a measure of the average rate of return to an investor who purchases the bond for the asked price and holds it until its maturity date. We will have much to say about yield to maturity below.[2]

---

[1]Recall that the bid price is the price at which you can sell the bond to a dealer. The asked price, which is slightly higher, is the price at which you can buy the bond from a dealer.

[2]Notice that some of the bonds in Figure 14.1 have the letter *i* after the maturity year and that these bonds have lower reported yields to maturity. These are inflation-indexed bonds, and their yields should be interpreted as after-inflation, or real returns. We discuss these bonds in detail later in the chapter.

U.S. Government Bonds and Notes

Representative Over-the-Counter quotation based on transactions of $1 million or more.
Treasury bond, note and bill quotes are from midafternoon. Colons in bond and note bid-and-asked quotes represent 32nds; 101:01 means 101 1/32. Net change in 32nds. n-Treasury Note. i-inflation-indexed issue. Treasury bill quotes in hundredths, quoted in terms of a rate of discount. Days to maturity calculated from settlement date. All yields are to maturity and based on the asked quote. For bonds callable prior to maturity, yields are computed to the earliest call date for issues quoted above par and to the maturity date for issues quoted below par.
*-When issued. Daily change expressed in basis points.

RATE	MATURITY MO/YR	BID	ASKED	CHG	ASK YLD
5.250	Feb 29	104:14	104:15	+9	4.92
3.875	Apr 29i	124:17	124:18	+16	2.44
6.125	Aug 29	116:12	116:13	+9	4.91
6.250	May 30	118:19	118:20	+10	4.90
5.375	Feb 31	106:20	106:21	+8	4.90
3.375	Apr 32i	119:09	119:10	+16	2.35
4.500	Feb 36	94:19	94:20	+9	4.84

RATE	MATURITY MO/YR	BID	ASKED	CHG	ASK YLD	RATE	MATURITY MO/YR	BID	ASKED	CHG	ASK YLD
3.125	Jan 07n	99:29	99:30	....	4.83	2.375	Apr 11i	99:11	99:12	+2	2.53
2.250	Feb 07n	99:24	99:25	....	4.88	4.875	Apr 11n	100:16	100:17	+3	4.73
6.250	Feb 07n	100:02	100:03	....	4.88	4.875	May 11n	100:17	100:18	+3	4.73
3.375	Feb 07n	99:25	99:26	....	4.97	5.125	Jun 11n	101:17	101:18	+4	4.73
3.750	Mar 07n	99:23	99:24	+1	4.97	4.875	Jul 11n	100:18	100:19	+4	4.73
3.625	Apr 07n	99:18	99:19	....	4.99	4.625	Dec 11n	99:15	99:16	+4	4.74
5.750	Aug 10n	103:09	103:10	+2	4.73	3.375	Jan 12i	104:01	104:02	+3	2.50
4.125	Aug 10n	98:00	98:01	+3	4.73	4.875	Feb 12n	100:24	100:25	+4	4.70
3.875	Sep 10n	97:03	97:04	+3	4.73	3.000	Jul 12i	102:17	102:18	+2	2.49
4.250	Oct 10n	98:10	98:11	+3	4.73	4.375	Aug 12n	98:13	98:14	+4	4.69
4.500	Nov 10n	99:05	99:06	+3	4.73	4.000	Nov 12n	96:13	96:14	+4	4.71
4.375	Dec 10n	98:22	98:23	+3	4.74	10.375	Nov 12	104:11	104:12	+2	4.87
4.250	Jan 11n	98:07	98:08	+3	4.74	3.375	Feb 13n	95:17	95:18	+4	4.72
3.500	Jan 11i	103:26	103:27	+3	2.48	3.625	May 13n	94:02	94:03	+5	4.71
5.000	Feb 11n	101:03	101:04	+3	4.69	1.375	Jul 13i	96:09	96:10	+4	2.49
4.500	Feb 11n	99:04	99:05	+3	4.73	4.250	Aug 13n	97:10	97:11	+6	4.72
4.750	Mar 11n	100:01	100:02	+3	4.73	5.250	Nov 28	104:12	104:13	+8	4.92

Treasury Bills

MATURITY	DAYS TO MAT	BID	ASKED	CHG	ASK YLD
Mar 22 07	64	4.96	4.95	+0.02	5.06
Mar 29 07	71	4.96	4.95	+0.01	5.07
Apr 05 07	78	4.96	4.95	+0.01	5.07
Apr 12 07	85	4.96	4.95	....	5.08
Apr 19 07	92	4.98	4.97	+0.02	5.10
Apr 26 07	99	4.96	4.95	....	5.09
May 03 07	106	4.96	4.95	+0.01	5.09
May 10 07	113	4.96	4.95	....	5.10
May 17 07	120	4.97	4.96	+0.01	5.11
May 24 07	127	4.97	4.96	+0.01	5.12
May 31 07	134	4.95	4.94	+0.01	5.10
Jun 07 07	141	4.94	4.93	+0.01	5.10
Jun 14 07	148	4.94	4.93	....	5.10
Jun 21 07	155	4.94	4.93	....	5.11
Jun 28 07	162	4.94	4.93	....	5.11
Jul 05 07	169	4.95	4.94	....	5.13
Jul 12 07	176	4.95	4.94	....	5.13

FIGURE 14.1   Listing of Treasury issues

Source: *The Wall Street Journal Online*, January 16, 2007. Reprinted by permission of Dow Jones & Company, Inc. via Copyright Clearance Center, Inc. © 2007 Dow Jones & Company. All Rights Reserved Worldwide.

Accrued Interest and Quoted Bond Prices   The bond prices that you see quoted in the financial pages are not actually the prices that investors pay for the bond. This is because the quoted price does not include the interest that accrues between coupon payment dates.

If a bond is purchased between coupon payments, the buyer must pay the seller for accrued interest, the prorated share of the upcoming semiannual coupon. For example, if 30 days have passed since the last coupon payment, and there are 182 days in the semiannual coupon period, the seller is entitled to a payment of accrued interest of 30/182 of the semiannual coupon. The sale, or *invoice,* price of the bond would equal the stated price plus the accrued interest.

In general, the formula for the amount of accrued interest between two dates is

$$\text{Accrued interest} = \frac{\text{Annual coupon payment}}{2} \times \frac{\text{Days since last coupon payment}}{\text{Days separating coupon payments}}$$

EXAMPLE 14.1   Accrued Interest

Suppose that the coupon rate is 8%. Then the annual coupon is $80 and the semiannual coupon payment is $40. Because 30 days have passed since the last coupon payment, the accrued interest on the bond is $40 × (30/182) = $6.59. If the quoted price of the bond is $990, then the invoice price will be $990 + $6.59 = $996.59.

The practice of quoting bond prices net of accrued interest explains why the price of a maturing bond is listed at $1,000 rather than $1,000 plus one coupon payment. A purchaser of an 8% coupon bond 1 day before the bond's maturity would receive $1,040 (par value plus semiannual interest) on the following day and so should be willing to pay a total price of $1,040 for the bond. The bond price is quoted net of accrued interest in the financial pages and thus appears as $1,000.[3]

Corporate Bonds

Like the government, corporations borrow money by issuing bonds. Figure 14.2 is a sample of corporate bond listings for a few actively traded corporate bonds. Although some bonds trade on a formal exchange operated by the New York Stock Exchange, most bonds are traded over-the-counter in a network of bond dealers linked by a computer quotation system. (See Chapter 3 for a comparison of exchange versus OTC trading.) In practice, the bond market can be quite "thin," in that there are few investors interested in trading a particular issue at any particular time.

The bond listings in Figure 14.2 include the coupon, maturity, price, and yield to maturity of each bond. The "rating" column is the estimation of bond safety given by the three major bond-rating agencies—Moody's, Standard & Poor's, and Fitch. Bonds with gradations of A ratings are safer than those with B ratings or below. Notice that as a general rule, safer bonds with higher ratings promise lower yields to maturity than other bonds with similar maturities. We will return to this topic toward the end of the chapter.

Call Provisions on Corporate Bonds   Although the Treasury no longer issues callable bonds, some corporate bonds are issued with call provisions allowing the issuer to repurchase the bond at a specified *call price* before the maturity date. For example, if a company issues a bond with a high coupon rate when market interest rates are high, and interest rates later fall, the firm might like to retire the high-coupon debt and issue new bonds at a lower coupon rate to reduce interest payments. This is called *refunding*. Callable bonds typically come with a period of call protection, an initial time during which the bonds are not callable. Such bonds are referred to as *deferred* callable bonds.

ISSUER NAME	SYMBOL	COUPON	MATURITY	RATING MOODY'S/S&P/ FITCH	HIGH	LOW	LAST	CHANGE	YIELD %
Gatx	GMT.IK	8.875%	Jun 2009	Baa1/BBB/BBB−	107.545	107.538	107.545	−0.100	5.433
Marshall & Ilsley	MI.YL	3.800%	Feb 2008	Aa3/A+/A+	98.514	98.470	98.514	0.064	5.263
Capital One	COF.HK	7.686%	Aug 2036	Baa2/BBB−/BBB−	113.895	113.390	113.733	0.257	6.621
Entergy Gulf States	ETR.KC	6.180%	Mar 2035	Baa3/BBB+/BBB	99.950	94.616	99.469	0.219	6.220
AOL Time Warner	AOL.HG	6.875%	May 2012	Baa2/BBB+/BBB	107.205	105.402	106.565	0.720	5.427
Household Intl	HI.HJG	8.875%	Feb 2008	Aa3/AA−/AA−	100.504	100.504	100.504	−0.109	5.348
SBC Comm	SBC.IF	5.875%	Feb 2012	A2/A/A	102.116	102.001	102.001	−0.156	5.415
American General Finance	AIG.GOU	5.750%	Sep 2016	A1/A+/A+	101.229	101.135	101.135	−0.530	5.595

FIGURE 14.2   Listing of corporate bonds

Source: *The Wall Street Journal Online*, January 12, 2007. Reprinted by permission of Dow Jones & Company, Inc. via Copyright Clearance Center, Inc. © 2007 Dow Jones & Company, Inc. All Rights Reserved Worldwide.

[3]In contrast to bonds, stocks do not trade at flat prices with adjustments for "accrued dividends." Whoever owns the stock when it goes "ex-dividend" receives the entire dividend payment, and the stock price reflects the value of the upcoming dividend. The price therefore typically falls by about the amount of the dividend on the "ex-day." There is no need to differentiate between reported and invoice prices for stocks.

The option to call the bond is valuable to the firm, allowing it to buy back the bonds and refinance at lower interest rates when market rates fall. Of course, the firm's benefit is the bondholder's burden. Holders of called bonds must forfeit their bonds for the call price, thereby giving up the attractive coupon rate on their original investment. To compensate investors for this risk, callable bonds are issued with higher coupons and promised yields to maturity than noncallable bonds.

| CONCEPT CHECK 1 | Suppose that Verizon issues two bonds with identical coupon rates and maturity dates. One bond is callable, however, whereas the other is not. Which bond will sell at a higher price? |

Convertible Bonds   **Convertible bonds** give bondholders an option to exchange each bond for a specified number of shares of common stock of the firm. The *conversion ratio* is the number of shares for which each bond may be exchanged. Suppose a convertible bond is issued at par value of $1,000 and is convertible into 40 shares of a firm's stock. The current stock price is $20 per share, so the option to convert is not profitable now. Should the stock price later rise to $30, however, each bond may be converted profitably into $1,200 worth of stock. The *market conversion value* is the current value of the shares for which the bonds may be exchanged. At the $20 stock price, for example, the bond's conversion value is $800. The *conversion premium* is the excess of the bond value over its conversion value. If the bond were selling currently for $950, its premium would be $150.

Convertible bondholders benefit from price appreciation of the company's stock. Again, this benefit comes at a price: Convertible bonds offer lower coupon rates and stated or promised yields to maturity than do nonconvertible bonds. However, the actual return on the convertible bond may exceed the stated yield to maturity if the option to convert becomes profitable.

We discuss convertible and callable bonds further in Chapter 20.

Puttable Bonds   While the callable bond gives the issuer the option to extend or retire the bond at the call date, the *extendable* or **put bond** gives this option to the bondholder. If the bond's coupon rate exceeds current market yields, for instance, the bondholder will choose to extend the bond's life. If the bond's coupon rate is too low, it will be optimal not to extend; the bondholder instead reclaims principal, which can be invested at current yields.

Floating-Rate Bonds   **Floating-rate bonds** make interest payments that are tied to some measure of current market rates. For example, the rate might be adjusted annually to the current T-bill rate plus 2%. If the 1-year T-bill rate at the adjustment date is 4%, the bond's coupon rate over the next year would then be 6%. This arrangement means that the bond always pays approximately current market rates.

The major risk involved in floaters has to do with changes in the firm's financial strength. The yield spread is fixed over the life of the security, which may be many years. If the financial health of the firm deteriorates, then investors will demand a greater yield premium than is offered by the security. In this case, the price of the bond will fall. Although the coupon rate on floaters adjusts to changes in the general level of market interest rates, it does not adjust to changes in the financial condition of the firm.

Preferred Stock

Although preferred stock strictly speaking is considered to be equity, it often is included in the fixed-income universe. This is because, like bonds, preferred stock promises to pay a specified stream of dividends. However, unlike bonds, the failure to pay the promised dividend does not result in corporate bankruptcy. Instead, the dividends owed simply cumulate, and the common stockholders may not receive any dividends until the preferred stockholders have been paid in full. In the event of bankruptcy, preferred stockholders' claims to the firm's assets have lower priority than those of bondholders, but higher priority than those of common stockholders.

Preferred stock commonly pays a fixed dividend. Therefore, it is in effect a perpetuity, providing a level cash flow indefinitely. In the last two decades, however, adjustable or floating-rate preferred stock has become popular, in some years accounting for about half of new issues. Floating-rate preferred stock is much like floating-rate bonds. The dividend rate is linked to a measure of current market interest rates and is adjusted at regular intervals.

Unlike interest payments on bonds, dividends on preferred stock are not considered tax-deductible expenses to the firm. This reduces their attractiveness as a source of capital to issuing firms. On the other hand, there is an offsetting tax advantage to preferred stock. When one corporation buys the preferred stock of another corporation, it pays taxes on only 30% of the dividends received. For example, if the firm's tax bracket is 35%, and it receives $10,000 in preferred dividend payments, it will pay taxes on only $3,000 of that income: Total taxes owed on the income will be $.35 \times \$3,000 = \$1,050$. The firm's effective tax rate on preferred dividends is therefore only $.30 \times 35\% = 10.5\%$. Given this tax rule, it is not surprising that most preferred stock is held by corporations.

Preferred stock rarely gives its holders full voting privileges in the firm. However, if the preferred dividend is skipped, the preferred stockholders may then be provided some voting power.

Other Issuers

There are, of course, several issuers of bonds in addition to the Treasury and private corporations. For example, state and local governments issue municipal bonds. The outstanding feature of these is that interest payments are tax-free. We examined municipal bonds and the value of the tax exemption in Chapter 2.

Government agencies such as the Federal Home Loan Bank Board, the Farm Credit agencies, and the mortgage pass-through agencies Ginnie Mae, Fannie Mae, and Freddie Mac also issue considerable amounts of bonds. These too were reviewed in Chapter 2.

International Bonds

International bonds are commonly divided into two categories, *foreign bonds* and *Eurobonds*. Foreign bonds are issued by a borrower from a country other than the one in which the bond is sold. The bond is denominated in the currency of the country in which it is marketed. For example, if a German firm sells a dollar-denominated bond in the United States, the bond is considered a foreign bond. These bonds are given colorful names based on the countries in which they are marketed. For example, foreign bonds sold in the United States are called *Yankee bonds*. Like other bonds sold in the United States, they are registered with the Securities and Exchange Commission. Yen-denominated bonds sold in Japan by non-Japanese issuers are called *Samurai bonds*. British pound-denominated foreign bonds sold in the United Kingdom are called *bulldog bonds*.

In contrast to foreign bonds, Eurobonds are bonds issued in the currency of one country but sold in other national markets. For example, the Eurodollar market refers to dollar-denominated bonds sold outside the United States (not just in Europe), although London is the largest market for Eurodollar bonds. Because the Eurodollar market falls outside U.S. jurisdiction, these bonds are not regulated by U.S. federal agencies. Similarly, Euroyen bonds are yen-denominated bonds selling outside Japan, Eurosterling bonds are pound denominated Eurobonds selling outside the United Kingdom, and so on.

Innovation in the Bond Market

Issuers constantly develop innovative bonds with unusual features; these issues illustrate that bond design can be extremely flexible. Here are examples of some novel bonds. They should give you a sense of the potential variety in security design.

Inverse Floaters These are similar to the floating-rate bonds we described earlier, except that the coupon rate on these bonds *falls* when the general level of interest rates rises. Investors in these bonds suffer doubly when rates rise. Not only does the present value of each dollar of cash flow from the bond fall as the discount rate rises, but the level of those cash flows falls as well. Of course, investors in these bonds benefit doubly when rates fall.

Asset-Backed Bonds Walt Disney has issued bonds with coupon rates tied to the financial performance of several of its films. Similarly, "David Bowie bonds" have been issued with payments that will be tied to royalties on some of his albums. These are examples of asset-backed securities. The income from a specified group of assets is used to service the debt. More conventional asset-backed securities are mortgage-backed securities or securities backed by auto or credit card loans, as we discussed in Chapter 2.

Catastrophe Bonds Oriental Land Company, which manages Tokyo Disneyland, issued a bond in 1999 with a final payment that depended on whether there had been an earthquake near the park. The Swiss insurance firm Winterthur has issued a bond whose payments will be cut if a severe hailstorm in Switzerland results in extensive payouts on Winterthur policies. These bonds are a way to transfer "catastrophe risk" from the firm to the capital markets. Investors in these bonds receive compensation for taking on the risk in the form of higher coupon rates. But in the event of a catastrophe, the bondholders will give up all or part of their investments. "Disaster" can be defined by total insured losses or by criteria such as wind speed in a hurricane or Richter level in an earthquake. Issuance of catastrophe bonds has surged in recent years, rising from about $1 billion in 2000 to $9 billion in 2006, as insurers have sought ways to spread their risks across a wider spectrum of the capital market.

Indexed Bonds Indexed bonds make payments that are tied to a general price index or the price of a particular commodity. For example, Mexico has issued 20-year bonds with payments that depend on the price of oil. Some bonds are indexed to the general price level. The United States Treasury started issuing such inflation-indexed bonds in January 1997. They are called Treasury Inflation Protected Securities (TIPS). By tying the par value of the bond to the general level of prices, coupon payments as well as the final repayment of par value on these bonds increase in direct proportion to the Consumer Price Index. Therefore, the interest rate on these bonds is a risk-free real rate.

To illustrate how TIPS work, consider a newly issued bond with a 3-year maturity, par value of $1,000, and a coupon rate of 4%. For simplicity, we will assume the bond makes annual coupon payments. Assume that inflation turns out to be 2%, 3%, and 1% in the next 3 years. Table 14.1 shows how the bond cash flows will be calculated. The first payment comes at the end of the first year, at $t = 1$. Because inflation over the year was 2%, the par value of the bond increases from $1,000 to $1,020; because the coupon rate is 4%, the coupon payment is 4% of this amount, or $40.80. Notice that par value increases by the

TABLE 14.1

Principal and interest payments for a Treasury Inflation Protected Security

Time	Inflation in Year Just Ended	Par Value	Coupon Payment	+	Principal Repayment	=	Total Payment
0		$1,000.00					
1	2%	1,020.00	$40.80		$ 0		$ 40.80
2	3	1,050.60	42.02		0		42.02
3	1	1,061.11	42.44		1,061.11		1,103.55

inflation rate, and because the coupon payments are 4% of par, they too increase in proportion to the general price level. Therefore, the cash flows paid by the bond are fixed in *real* terms. When the bond matures, the investor receives a final coupon payment of $42.44 plus the (price-level-indexed) repayment of principal, $1,061.11.[4]

The *nominal* rate of return on the bond in the first year is

$$\text{Nominal return} = \frac{\text{Interest} + \text{Price Appreciation}}{\text{Initial Price}} = \frac{40.80 + 20}{1000} = 6.08\%$$

The real rate of return is precisely the 4% real yield on the bond:

$$\text{Real return} = \frac{1 + \text{Nominal return}}{1 + \text{Inflation}} - 1 = \frac{1.0608}{1.02} - 1 = .04, \text{ or } 4\%$$

One can show in a similar manner (see Problem 16 in the end-of-chapter problems) that the rate of return in each of the 3 years is 4% as long as the real yield on the bond remains constant. If real yields do change, then there will be capital gains or losses on the bond. In early 2008, the real yield on long-term TIPS bonds was about 1.75%.

14.2   BOND PRICING

Because a bond's coupon and principal repayments all occur months or years in the future, the price an investor would be willing to pay for a claim to those payments depends on the value of dollars to be received in the future compared to dollars in hand today. This "present value" calculation depends in turn on market interest rates. As we saw in Chapter 5, the nominal risk-free interest rate equals the sum of (1) a real risk-free rate of return and (2) a premium above the real rate to compensate for expected inflation. In addition, because most bonds are not riskless, the discount rate will embody an additional premium that reflects bond-specific characteristics such as default risk, liquidity, tax attributes, call risk, and so on.

We simplify for now by assuming there is one interest rate that is appropriate for discounting cash flows of any maturity, but we can relax this assumption easily. In practice, there may be different discount rates for cash flows accruing in different periods. For the time being, however, we ignore this refinement.

To value a security, we discount its expected cash flows by the appropriate discount rate. The cash flows from a bond consist of coupon payments until the maturity date plus the final payment of par value. Therefore,

Bond value = Present value of coupons + Present value of par value

[4]By the way, total nominal income (i.e., coupon plus that year's increase in principal) is treated as taxable income in each year.

If we call the maturity date T and call the interest rate r, the bond value can be written as

$$\text{Bond value} = \sum_{t=1}^{T} \frac{\text{Coupon}}{(1+r)^t} + \frac{\text{Par value}}{(1+r)^T} \tag{14.1}$$

The summation sign in Equation 14.1 directs us to add the present value of each coupon payment; each coupon is discounted based on the time until it will be paid. The first term on the right-hand side of Equation 14.1 is the present value of an annuity. The second term is the present value of a single amount, the final payment of the bond's par value.

You may recall from an introductory finance class that the present value of a $1 annuity that lasts for T periods when the interest rate equals r is $\dfrac{1}{r}\left[1 - \dfrac{1}{(1+r)^T}\right]$. We call this expression the T-period *annuity factor* for an interest rate of r.[5] Similarly, we call $\dfrac{1}{(1+r)^T}$ the *PV factor*, that is, the present value of a single payment of $1 to be received in T periods. Therefore, we can write the price of the bond as

$$\text{Price} = \text{Coupon} \times \frac{1}{r}\left[1 - \frac{1}{(1+r)^T}\right] + \text{Par value} \times \frac{1}{(1+r)^T} \tag{14.2}$$

$$= \text{Coupon} \times \text{Annuity factor}(r, T) + \text{Par value} \times \text{PV factor}(r, T)$$

EXAMPLE 14.2 Bond Pricing

We discussed earlier an 8% coupon, 30-year maturity bond with par value of $1,000 paying 60 semiannual coupon payments of $40 each. Suppose that the interest rate is 8% annually, or $r = 4\%$ per 6-month period. Then the value of the bond can be written as

$$\text{Price} = \sum_{t=1}^{60} \frac{\$40}{(1.04)^t} + \frac{\$1,000}{(1.04)^{60}} \tag{14.3}$$

$$= \$40 \times \text{Annuity factor}(4\%, 60) + \$1,000 \times \text{PV factor}(4\%, 60)$$

It is easy to confirm that the present value of the bond's 60 semiannual coupon payments of $40 each is $904.94 and that the $1,000 final payment of par value has a present value of $95.06, for a total bond value of $1,000. You can either calculate the value directly from Equation 14.2, perform these calculations on any financial calculator,[6] use a spreadsheet program (see the Excel Applications box), or use a set of present value tables.

---

[5]Here is a quick derivation of the formula for the present value of an annuity. An annuity lasting T periods can be viewed as equivalent to a perpetuity whose first payment comes at the end of the current period *less* another perpetuity whose first payment comes at the end of the $(T+1)$st period. The immediate perpetuity net of the delayed perpetuity provides exactly T payments. We know that the value of a $1 per period perpetuity is $1/r. Therefore, the present value of the delayed perpetuity is $1/r discounted for T additional periods, or $\dfrac{1}{r} \times \dfrac{1}{(1+r)^T}$. The present value of the annuity is the present value of the first perpetuity minus the present value of the delayed perpetuity, or $\dfrac{1}{r}\left[1 - \dfrac{1}{(1+r)^T}\right]$.

[6]On your financial calculator, you would enter the following inputs: n (number of periods) = 60; FV (face or future value) = 1000; PMT (payment each period) = 40; i (per period interest rate) = 4%; then you would compute the price of the bond (COMP PV or CPT PV). You should find that the price is $1,000. Actually, most calculators will display the result as *negative* $1,000. This is because most (but not all) calculators treat the initial purchase price of the bond as a cash *outflow*. We will discuss calculators and spreadsheets more fully in a few pages.

In this example, the coupon rate equals the market interest rate, and the bond price equals par value. If the interest rate were not equal to the bond's coupon rate, the bond would not sell at par value. For example, if the interest rate were to rise to 10% (5% per 6 months), the bond's price would fall by $189.29 to $810.71, as follows:

$$\$40 \times \text{Annuity factor}(5\%,\ 60) + \$1,000 \times \text{PV factor}(5\%,\ 60)$$
$$= \$757.17 + \$53.54 = \$810.71$$

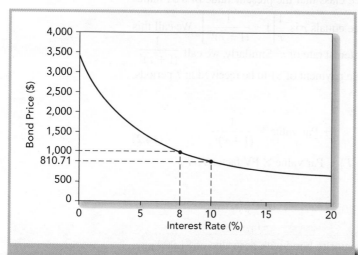

FIGURE 14.3 The inverse relationship between bond prices and yields. Price of an 8% coupon bond with 30-year maturity making semiannual payments

At a higher interest rate, the present value of the payments to be received by the bondholder is lower. Therefore, the bond price will fall as market interest rates rise. This illustrates a crucial general rule in bond valuation. When interest rates rise, bond prices must fall because the present value of the bond's payments is obtained by discounting at a higher interest rate.

Figure 14.3 shows the price of the 30-year, 8% coupon bond for a range of interest rates, including 8%, at which the bond sells at par, and 10%, at which it sells for $810.71. The negative slope illustrates the inverse relationship between prices and yields. Note also from the figure (and from Table 14.2) that the shape of the curve implies that an increase in the interest rate results in a price decline that is smaller than the price gain resulting from a decrease of equal magnitude in the interest rate. This property of bond prices is called *convexity* because of the convex shape of the bond price curve. This curvature reflects the fact that progressive increases in the interest rate result in progressively smaller reductions in the bond price.[7] Therefore, the price curve becomes flatter at higher interest rates. We return to the issue of convexity in Chapter 16.

CONCEPT CHECK 2	Calculate the price of the 30-year, 8% coupon bond for a market interest rate of 3% per half-year. Compare the capital gains for the interest rate decline to the losses incurred when the rate increases to 5%.

Corporate bonds typically are issued at par value. This means that the underwriters of the bond issue (the firms that market the bonds to the public for the issuing corporation) must choose a coupon rate that very closely approximates market yields. In a primary issue of bonds, the underwriters attempt to sell the newly issued bonds directly to their customers. If the coupon rate is inadequate, investors will not pay par value for the bonds.

After the bonds are issued, bondholders may buy or sell bonds in secondary markets, such as the one operated by the New York Stock Exchange or the over-the-counter market,

---

[7]The progressively smaller impact of interest increases results from the fact that at higher rates the bond is worth less. Therefore, an additional increase in rates operates on a smaller initial base, resulting in a smaller price reduction.

Time to Maturity	Bond Price at Given Market Interest Rate					TABLE 14.2
	4%	6%	8%	10%	12%	Bond prices at different interest rates (8% coupon bond, coupons paid semiannually)
1 year	1,038.83	1,029.13	1,000.00	981.41	963.33	
10 years	1,327.03	1,148.77	1,000.00	875.35	770.60	
20 years	1,547.11	1,231.15	1,000.00	828.41	699.07	
30 years	1,695.22	1,276.76	1,000.00	810.71	676.77	

where most bonds trade. In these secondary markets, bond prices move in accordance with market forces. The bond prices fluctuate inversely with the market interest rate.

The inverse relationship between price and yield is a central feature of fixed-income securities. Interest rate fluctuations represent the main source of risk in the fixed-income market, and we devote considerable attention in Chapter 16 to assessing the sensitivity of bond prices to market yields. For now, however, it is sufficient to highlight one key factor that determines that sensitivity, namely, the maturity of the bond.

A general rule in evaluating bond price risk is that, keeping all other factors the same, the longer the maturity of the bond, the greater the sensitivity of price to fluctuations in the interest rate. For example, consider Table 14.2, which presents the price of an 8% coupon bond at different market yields and times to maturity. For any departure of the interest rate from 8% (the rate at which the bond sells at par value), the change in the bond price is greater for longer times to maturity.

This makes sense. If you buy the bond at par with an 8% coupon rate, and market rates subsequently rise, then you suffer a loss: You have tied up your money earning 8% when alternative investments offer higher returns. This is reflected in a capital loss on the bond—a fall in its market price. The longer the period for which your money is tied up, the greater the loss, and correspondingly the greater the drop in the bond price. In Table 14.2, the row for 1-year maturity bonds shows little price sensitivity—that is, with only 1 year's earnings at stake, changes in interest rates are not too threatening. But for 30-year maturity bonds, interest rate swings have a large impact on bond prices. The force of discounting is greatest for the longest-term bonds.

This is why short-term Treasury securities such as T-bills are considered to be the safest. They are free not only of default risk but also largely of price risk attributable to interest rate volatility.

Bond Pricing between Coupon Dates

Equation 14.2 for bond prices assumes that the next coupon payment is in precisely one payment period, either a year for an annual payment bond or 6 months for a semiannual payment bond. But you probably want to be able to price bonds all 365 days of the year, not just on the one or two dates each year that it makes a coupon payment!

In principle, the fact that the bond is between coupon dates does not affect the pricing problem. The procedure is always the same: compute the present value of each remaining payment and sum up. But if you are between coupon dates, there will be fractional periods remaining until each payment, and this does complicate the arithmetic computations.

Fortunately, bond pricing functions are included in most spreadsheet programs such as Excel. The spreadsheet allows you to enter today's date as well as the maturity date of the bond, and so can provide prices for bonds at any date. The nearby box shows you how.

As we pointed out earlier, bond prices are typically quoted net of accrued interest. These prices, which appear in the financial press, are called *flat prices*. The actual *invoice price* that a buyer pays for the bond includes accrued interest. Thus,

$$\text{Invoice price} = \text{Flat price} + \text{Accrued interest}$$

When a bond pays its coupon, flat price equals invoice price, because at that moment accrued interest reverts to zero. However, this will be the exceptional case, not the rule.

Excel pricing functions provide the flat price of the bond. To find the invoice price, we need to add accrued interest. Fortunately, Excel also provides functions that count the days since the last coupon payment date and thus can be used to compute accrued interest. The nearby box also illustrates how to use these functions. The box provides examples using bonds that have just paid a coupon and so have zero accrued interest, as well as a bond that is between coupon dates.

14.3 BOND YIELDS

We have noted that the current yield of a bond measures only the cash income provided by the bond as a percentage of bond price and ignores any prospective capital gains or losses. We would like a measure of rate of return that accounts for both current income and the price increase or decrease over the bond's life. The yield to maturity is the standard measure of the total rate of return. However, it is far from perfect, and we will explore several variations of this measure.

Yield to Maturity

In practice, an investor considering the purchase of a bond is not quoted a promised rate of return. Instead, the investor must use the bond price, maturity date, and coupon payments to infer the return offered by the bond over its life. The **yield to maturity** (YTM) is defined as the interest rate that makes the present value of a bond's payments equal to its price. This interest rate is often interpreted as a measure of the average rate of return that will be earned on a bond if it is bought now and held until maturity. To calculate the yield to maturity, we solve the bond price equation for the interest rate given the bond's price.

EXAMPLE 14.3 Yield to Maturity

Suppose an 8% coupon, 30-year bond is selling at $1,276.76. What average rate of return would be earned by an investor purchasing the bond at this price? We find the interest rate at which the present value of the remaining 60 semiannual payments equals the bond price. This is the rate consistent with the observed price of the bond. Therefore, we solve for r in the following equation:

$$\$1,276.76 = \sum_{t=1}^{60} \frac{\$40}{(1+r)^t} + \frac{\$1,000}{(1+r)^{60}}$$

or, equivalently,

$$1,276.76 = 40 \times \text{Annuity factor}(r, 60) + 1,000 \times \text{PV factor}(r, 60)$$

These equations have only one unknown variable, the interest rate, r. You can use a financial calculator or spreadsheet to confirm that the solution is $r = .03$, or 3%, per half-year.[8] This is considered the bond's yield to maturity.

The financial press reports yields on an annualized basis, and annualizes the bond's semi-annual yield using simple interest techniques, resulting in an annual percentage rate, or APR. Yields annualized using simple interest are also called "bond equivalent yields." Therefore, the semiannual yield would be doubled and reported in the newspaper as a bond equivalent yield of 6%. The *effective* annual yield of the bond, however, accounts for compound interest. If one earns 3% interest every 6 months, then after 1 year, each dollar invested grows with interest to $1 \times (1.03)^2 = \$1.0609$, and the effective annual interest rate on the bond is 6.09%.

Excel also provides a function for yield to maturity that is especially useful in between coupon dates. It is

= YIELD(settlement date, maturity date, annual coupon rate, bond price, redemption
    value as percent of par value, number of coupon payments per year)

The bond price used in the function should be the reported flat price, without accrued interest. For example, to find the yield to maturity of the bond in Example 14.3, we would use column B of Spreadsheet 14.1. If the coupons were paid only annually, we would change the entry for payments per year to 1 (see cell D8), and the yield would fall slightly to 5.99%.

The bond's yield to maturity is the internal rate of return on an investment in the bond. The yield to maturity can be interpreted as the compound rate of return over the life of the bond under the assumption that all bond coupons can be reinvested at that yield.[9] Yield to maturity is widely accepted as a proxy for average return.

	A	B	C	D	E
1		**Semiannual coupons**		**Annual coupons**	
2					
3	Settlement date	1/1/2000		1/1/2000	
4	Maturity date	1/1/2030		1/1/2030	
5	Annual coupon rate	0.08		0.08	
6	Bond price (flat)	127.676		127.676	
7	Redemption value (% of face value)	100		100	
8	Coupon payments per year	2		1	
9					
10	**Yield to maturity (decimal)**	0.0600		0.0599	
11					
12		The formula entered here is: =YIELD(B3,B4,B5,B6,B7,B8)			

SPREADSHEET 14.1

Finding yield to maturity in Excel

eXcel

Please visit us at

www.mhhe.com/bkm

---

[8]On your financial calculator, you would enter the following inputs: $n = 60$ periods; PV $= -1,276.76$; FV $= 1000$; PMT $= 40$; then you would compute the interest rate (COMP i or CPT i). Notice that we enter the present value, or PV, of the bond as *minus* $1,276.76. Again, this is because most calculators treat the initial purchase price of the bond as a cash outflow. Spreadsheet 14.1 shows how to find yield to maturity using Excel. Without a financial calculator or spreadsheet, you still could solve the equation, but you would need to use a trial-and-error approach.

[9]If the reinvestment rate does not equal the bond's yield to maturity, the compound rate of return will differ from YTM. This is demonstrated in Examples 14.5 and 14.6.

Example 14.5 highlights the problem with conventional yield to maturity when reinvestment rates can change over time. Conventional yield to maturity will not equal realized compound return. However, in an economy with future interest rate uncertainty, the rates at which interim coupons will be reinvested are not yet known. Therefore, although realized compound return can be computed *after* the investment period ends, it cannot be computed in advance without a forecast of future reinvestment rates. This reduces much of the attraction of the realized return measure.

Forecasting the realized compound yield over various holding periods or investment horizons is called **horizon analysis.** The forecast of total return depends on your forecasts of *both* the price of the bond when you sell it at the end of your horizon *and* the rate at which you are able to reinvest coupon income. The sales price depends in turn on the yield to maturity at the horizon date. With a longer investment horizon, however, reinvested coupons will be a larger component of your final proceeds.

EXAMPLE 14.6   Horizon Analysis

Suppose you buy a 30-year, 7.5% (annual payment) coupon bond for $980 (when its yield to maturity is 7.67%) and plan to hold it for 20 years. Your forecast is that the bond's yield to maturity will be 8% when it is sold and that the reinvestment rate on the coupons will be 6%. At the end of your investment horizon, the bond will have 10 years remaining until expiration, so the forecast sales price (using a yield to maturity of 8%) will be $966.45. The 20 coupon payments will grow with compound interest to $2,758.92. (This is the future value of a 20-year $75 annuity with an interest rate of 6%.)

Based on these forecasts, your $980 investment will grow in 20 years to $966.45 + $2,758.92 = $3,725.37. This corresponds to an annualized compound return of 6.90%:

$$V_0(1 + r)^{20} = V_{20}$$
$$\$980(1 + r)^{20} = \$3,725.37$$
$$r = .0690 = 6.90\%$$

Examples 14.5 and 14.6 demonstrate that as interest rates change, bond investors are actually subject to two sources of offsetting risk. On the one hand, when rates rise, bond prices fall, which reduces the value of the portfolio. On the other hand, reinvested coupon income will compound more rapidly at those higher rates. This **reinvestment rate risk** will offset the impact of price risk. In Chapter 16, we will explore this trade-off in more detail and will discover that by carefully tailoring their bond portfolios, investors can precisely balance these two effects for any given investment horizon.

14.4   BOND PRICES OVER TIME

As we noted earlier, a bond will sell at par value when its coupon rate equals the market interest rate. In these circumstances, the investor receives fair compensation for the time value of money in the form of the recurring coupon payments. No further capital gain is necessary to provide fair compensation.

When the coupon rate is lower than the market interest rate, the coupon payments alone will not provide investors as high a return as they could earn elsewhere in the market. To receive a fair return on such an investment, investors also need to earn price appreciation on their bonds. The bonds, therefore, would have to sell below par value to provide a "built-in" capital gain on the investment.

EXAMPLE 14.7 Fair Holding-Period Return

To illustrate built-in capital gains or losses, suppose a bond was issued several years ago when the interest rate was 7%. The bond's annual coupon rate was thus set at 7%. (We will suppose for simplicity that the bond pays its coupon annually.) Now, with 3 years left in the bond's life, the interest rate is 8% per year. The bond's market price is the present value of the remaining annual coupons plus payment of par value. That present value is[10]

$$\$70 \times \text{Annuity factor}(8\%,\ 3) + \$1,000 \times \text{PV factor}(8\%,\ 3) = \$974.23$$

which is less than par value.

In another year, after the next coupon is paid, the bond would sell at

$$\$70 \times \text{Annuity factor}(8\%,\ 2) + \$1,000 \times \text{PV factor}(8\%,\ 2) = \$982.17$$

thereby yielding a capital gain over the year of $7.94. If an investor had purchased the bond at $974.23, the total return over the year would equal the coupon payment plus capital gain, or $70 + $7.94 = $77.94. This represents a rate of return of $77.94/$974.23, or 8%, exactly the current rate of return available elsewhere in the market.

When bond prices are set according to the present value formula, any discount from par value provides an anticipated capital gain that will augment a below-market coupon rate just sufficiently to provide a fair total rate of return. Conversely, if the

CONCEPT CHECK 6

At what price will the bond in Example 14.7 sell in yet another year, when only 1 year remains until maturity? What is the rate of return to an investor who purchases the bond at $982.17 and sells it 1 year hence?

coupon rate exceeds the market interest rate, the interest income by itself is greater than that available elsewhere in the market. Investors will bid up the price of these bonds above their par values. As the bonds approach maturity, they will fall in value because fewer of these above-market coupon payments remain. The resulting capital losses offset the large coupon payments so that the bondholder again receives only a fair rate of return.

Problem 12 at the end of the chapter asks you to work through the case of the high-coupon bond. Figure 14.6 traces out the price paths of high- and low-coupon bonds (net of accrued interest) as time to maturity approaches, at least for the case in which the market interest rate is constant. The low-coupon bond enjoys capital gains, whereas the high-coupon bond suffers capital losses.[11]

We use these examples to show that each bond offers investors the same total rate of return. Although the capital gain versus income components differ, the price of each bond is set to provide competitive rates, as we should expect in well-functioning capital markets. Security returns all should be comparable on an after-tax risk-adjusted basis. It they are not, investors will try to sell low-return securities, thereby driving down their prices until the total return at the now-lower price is competitive with other securities. Prices should

---

[10]Using a calculator, enter $n = 3$, $i = 8$, PMT = 70, FV = 1,000, and compute PV.

[11]If interest rates are volatile, the price path will be "jumpy," vibrating around the price path in Figure 14.6 and reflecting capital gains or losses as interest rates fluctuate. Ultimately, however, the price must reach par value at the maturity date, so the price of the premium bond will fall over time while that of the discount bond will rise.

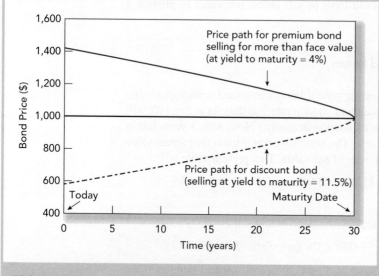

FIGURE 14.6 Prices over time of 30-year maturity, 6.5% coupon bonds. Bond price approaches par value as maturity approaches.

continue to adjust until all securities are fairly priced in that expected returns are comparable, given appropriate risk and tax adjustments.

Yield to Maturity versus Holding-Period Return

In Example 14.7, the holding-period return and the yield to maturity were equal. The bond yield started and ended the year at 8%, and the bond's holding-period return also equaled 8%. This turns out to be a general result. When the yield to maturity is unchanged over the period, the rate of return on the bond will equal that yield. As we noted, this should not be surprising: The bond must offer a rate of return competitive with those available on other securities.

However, when yields fluctuate, so will a bond's rate of return. Unanticipated changes in market rates will result in unanticipated changes in bond returns and, after the fact, a bond's holding-period return can be better or worse than the yield at which it initially sells. An increase in the bond's yield acts to reduce its price, which means that the holding-period return will be less than the initial yield. Conversely, a decline in yield will result in a holding-period return greater than the initial yield.

EXAMPLE 14.8   Yield to Maturity versus Holding-Period Return

Consider a 30-year bond paying an annual coupon of $80 and selling at par value of $1,000. The bond's initial yield to maturity is 8%. If the yield remains at 8% over the year, the bond price will remain at par, so the holding-period return also will be 8%. But if the yield falls below 8%, the bond price will increase. Suppose the yield falls and the price increases to $1,050. Then the holding-period return is greater than 8%:

$$\text{Holding-period return} = \frac{\$80 + (\$1,050 - \$1,000)}{\$1,000} = .13, \text{ or } 13\%$$

CONCEPT CHECK 7

Show that if yield to maturity increases, then holding-period return is *less* than initial yield. For example, suppose in Example 14.8 that by the end of the first year, the bond's yield to maturity is 8.5%. Find the 1-year holding-period return and compare it to the bond's initial 8% yield to maturity.

Here is another way to think about the difference between yield to maturity and holding-period return. Yield to maturity depends only on the bond's coupon, *current* price, and par value at maturity. All of these values are observable today, so yield to maturity can be easily calculated. Yield to maturity can be interpreted as a measure of the *average* rate of return if the investment in the bond is held until the bond matures. In contrast, holding-period return is the rate of return over a particular investment period and depends on the market price of the bond at the end of that holding period; of course this price is *not* known today. Because bond prices over the holding period will respond to unanticipated changes in interest rates, holding-period return can at most be forecast.

Zero-Coupon Bonds and Treasury Strips

Original-issue discount bonds are less common than coupon bonds issued at par. These are bonds that are issued intentionally with low coupon rates that cause the bond to sell at a discount from par value. An extreme example of this type of bond is the *zero-coupon bond,* which carries no coupons and provides all its return in the form of price appreciation. Zeros provide only one cash flow to their owners, on the maturity date of the bond.

U.S. Treasury bills are examples of short-term zero-coupon instruments. If the bill has face value of $10,000, the Treasury issues or sells it for some amount less than $10,000, agreeing to repay $10,000 at maturity. All of the investor's return comes in the form of price appreciation.

Longer-term zero-coupon bonds are commonly created from coupon-bearing notes and bonds with the help of the U.S. Treasury. A bond dealer who purchases a Treasury coupon bond may ask the Treasury to break down the cash flows to be paid by the bond into a series of independent securities, where each security is a claim to one of the payments of the original bond. For example, a 10-year coupon bond would be "stripped" of its 20 semiannual coupons, and each coupon payment would be treated as a stand-alone zero-coupon bond. The maturities of these bonds would thus range from 6 months to 10 years. The final payment of principal would be treated as another stand-alone zero-coupon security. Each of the payments is now treated as an independent security and is assigned its own CUSIP number (by the Committee on Uniform Securities Identification Procedures), the security identifier that allows for electronic trading over the Fedwire system, a network that connects all Federal Reserve banks and their branches. The payments are still considered obligations of the U.S. Treasury. The Treasury program under which coupon stripping is performed is called STRIPS (Separate Trading of Registered Interest and Principal of Securities), and these zero-coupon securities are called Treasury *strips.*

What should happen to prices of zeros as time passes? On their maturity dates, zeros must sell for par value. Before maturity, however, they should sell at discounts from par, because of the time value of money. As time passes, price should approach par value. In fact, if the interest rate is constant, a zero's price will increase at exactly the rate of interest.

To illustrate this property, consider a zero with 30 years until maturity, and suppose the market interest rate is 10% per year. The price of the bond today will be $1,000/(1.10)^{30} = \$57.31$. Next year, with only 29 years until maturity, if the yield is still 10%, the price will be $1,000/(1.10)^{29} = \$63.04$, a 10% increase over its previous-year value. Because the par value of the bond is now discounted for 1 year fewer, its price has increased by the 1-year discount factor.

Figure 14.7 presents the price path of a 30-year zero-coupon bond until its maturity date for an

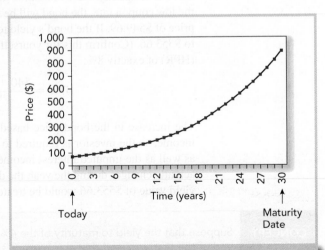

FIGURE 14.7 The price of a 30-year zero-coupon bond over time at a yield to maturity of 10%. Price equals $1,000/(1.10)^T$, where T is time until maturity.

annual market interest rate of 10%. The bond prices rise exponentially, not linearly, until its maturity.

After-Tax Returns

The tax authorities recognize that the "built-in" price appreciation on original-issue discount (OID) bonds such as zero-coupon bonds represents an implicit interest payment to the holder of the security. The IRS, therefore, calculates a price appreciation schedule to impute taxable interest income for the built-in appreciation during a tax year, even if the asset is not sold or does not mature until a future year. Any additional gains or losses that arise from changes in market interest rates are treated as capital gains or losses if the OID bond is sold during the tax year.

EXAMPLE 14.9   Taxation of Original-Issue Discount Bonds

If the interest rate originally is 10%, the 30-year zero would be issued at a price of $1,000/(1.10)^{30} = 57.31. The following year, the IRS calculates what the bond price would be if the yield were still 10%. This is $1,000/(1.10)^{29} = 63.04. Therefore, the IRS imputes interest income of $63.04 - $57.31 = 5.73. This amount is subject to tax. Notice that the *imputed* interest income is based on a "constant yield method" that ignores any changes in market interest rates.

If interest rates actually fall, let's say to 9.9%, the bond price will be $1,000/(1.099)^{29} = 64.72. If the bond is sold, then the difference between $64.72 and $63.04 is treated as capital gains income and taxed at the capital gains tax rate. If the bond is not sold, then the price difference is an unrealized capital gain and does not result in taxes in that year. In either case, the investor must pay taxes on the $5.73 of imputed interest at the rate on ordinary income.

The procedure illustrated in Example 14.9 applies as well to the taxation of other original-issue discount bonds, even if they are not zero-coupon bonds. Consider, as an example, a 30-year maturity bond that is issued with a coupon rate of 4% and a yield to maturity of 8%. For simplicity, we will assume that the bond pays coupons once annually. Because of the low coupon rate, the bond will be issued at a price far below par value, specifically at a price of $549.69. If the bond's yield to maturity is still 8%, then its price in 1 year will rise to $553.66. (Confirm this for yourself.) This would provide a pretax holding-period return (HPR) of exactly 8%:

$$\text{HPR} = \frac{\$40 + (\$553.66 - \$549.69)}{\$549.69} = .08$$

The increase in the bond price based on a constant yield, however, is treated as interest income, so the investor is required to pay taxes on both the explicit coupon income, $40, as well as the imputed interest income of $553.66 - $549.69 = 3.97. If the bond's yield actually changes during the year, the difference between the bond's price and the constant-yield value of $553.66 would be treated as capital gains income if the bond is sold.

CONCEPT CHECK 8

Suppose that the yield to maturity of the 4% coupon, 30-year maturity bond falls to 7% by the end of the first year and that the investor sells the bond after the first year. If the investor's federal plus state tax rate on interest income is 38% and the combined tax rate on capital gains is 20%, what is the investor's after-tax rate of return?

14.5 DEFAULT RISK AND BOND PRICING

Although bonds generally *promise* a fixed flow of income, that income stream is not risk-less unless the investor can be sure the issuer will not default on the obligation. While U.S. government bonds may be treated as free of default risk, this is not true of corporate bonds. Therefore, the actual payments on these bonds are uncertain, for they depend to some degree on the ultimate financial status of the firm.

Bond default risk, usually called **credit risk,** is measured by Moody's Investor Services, Standard & Poor's Corporation, and Fitch Investors Service, all of which provide financial information on firms as well as quality ratings of large corporate and municipal bond issues. International sovereign bonds, which also entail default risk, especially in emerging markets, also are commonly rated for default risk. Each rating firm assigns letter grades to the bonds of corporations and municipalities to reflect their assessment of the safety of the bond issue. The top rating is AAA or Aaa, a designation awarded to only about a dozen firms. Moody's modifies each rating class with a 1, 2, or 3 suffix (e.g., Aaa1, Aaa2, Aaa3) to provide a finer gradation of ratings. The other agencies use a + or − modification.

Those rated BBB or above (S&P, Fitch) or Baa and above (Moody's) are considered **investment-grade bonds,** whereas lower-rated bonds are classified as **speculative-grade** or **junk bonds.** Defaults on low-grade issues are not uncommon. For example, almost half of the bonds that were rated CCC by Standard & Poor's at issue have defaulted within 10 years. Highly rated bonds rarely default, but even these bonds are not free of credit risk. For example, in May 2001 WorldCom sold $11.8 billion of bonds with an investment-grade rating. Only a year later, the firm filed for bankruptcy and its bondholders lost more than 80% of their investment. Certain regulated institutional investors such as insurance companies have not always been allowed to invest in speculative-grade bonds.

Figure 14.8 provides the definitions of each bond rating classification.

Junk Bonds

Junk bonds, also known as *high-yield bonds,* are nothing more than speculative-grade (low-rated or unrated) bonds. Before 1977, almost all junk bonds were "fallen angels," that is, bonds issued by firms that originally had investment-grade ratings but that had since been downgraded. In 1977, however, firms began to issue "original-issue junk."

Much of the credit for this innovation is given to Drexel Burnham Lambert, and especially its trader Michael Milken. Drexel had long enjoyed a niche as a junk bond trader and had established a network of potential investors in junk bonds. Firms not able to muster an investment-grade rating were happy to have Drexel (and other investment bankers) market their bonds directly to the public, as this opened up a new source of financing. Junk issues were a lower-cost financing alternative than borrowing from banks.

High-yield bonds gained considerable notoriety in the 1980s when they were used as financing vehicles in leveraged buyouts and hostile takeover attempts. Shortly thereafter, however, the junk bond market suffered. The legal difficulties of Drexel and Michael Milken in connection with Wall Street's insider trading scandals of the late 1980s tainted the junk bond market.

At the height of Drexel's difficulties, the high-yield bond market nearly dried up. Since then, the market has rebounded dramatically. However, it is worth noting that the average credit quality of high-yield debt issued today is higher than the average quality in the boom years of the 1980s.

Bond Ratings					
	Very High Quality	**High Quality**	**Speculative**		**Very Poor**
Standard & Poor's	AAA AA	A BBB	BB B		CCC D
Moody's	Aaa Aa	A Baa	Ba B		Caa C

At times both Moody's and Standard & Poor's have used adjustments to these ratings: S&P uses plus and minus signs: A + is the strongest A rating and A − the weakest. Moody's uses a 1, 2, or 3 designation, with 1 indicating the strongest.

Moody's	S&P	
Aaa	AAA	Debt rated Aaa and AAA has the highest rating. Capacity to pay interest and principal is extremely strong.
Aa	AA	Debt rated Aa and AA has a very strong capacity to pay interest and repay principal. Together with the highest rating, this group comprises the high-grade bond class.
A	A	Debt rated A has a strong capacity to pay interest and repay principal, although it is somewhat more susceptible to the adverse effects of changes in circumstances and economic conditions than debt in higher-rated categories.
Baa	BBB	Debt rated Baa and BBB is regarded as having an adequate capacity to pay interest and repay principal. Whereas it normally exhibits adequate protection parameters, adverse economic conditions or changing circumstances are more likely to lead to a weakened capacity to pay interest and repay principal for debt in this category than in higher-rated categories. These bonds are medium-grade obligations.
Ba B Caa Ca	BB B CCC CC	Debt rated in these categories is regarded, on balance, as predominantly speculative with respect to capacity to pay interest and repay principal in accordance with the terms of the obligation. BB and Ba indicate the lowest degree of speculation, and CC and Ca the highest degree of speculation. Although such debt will likely have some quality and protective characteristics, these are outweighed by large uncertainties or major risk exposures to adverse conditions. Some issues may be in default.
C	C	This rating is reserved for income bonds on which no interest is being paid.
D	D	Debt rated D is in default, and payment of interest and/or repayment of principal is in arrears.

FIGURE 14.8   Definitions of each bond rating class

Source: Stephen A. Ross and Randolph W. Westerfield, *Corporate Finance*, Copyright 1988 (St. Louis: Times Mirror/ Mosby College Publishing, reproduced with permission from the McGarw-Hill Companies, Inc.). Data from various editions of *Standard & Poor's Bond Guide* and *Moody's Bond Guide*.

Determinants of Bond Safety

Bond rating agencies base their quality ratings largely on an analysis of the level and trend of some of the issuer's financial ratios. The key ratios used to evaluate safety are

1. *Coverage ratios*—Ratios of company earnings to fixed costs. For example, the *times-interest-earned ratio* is the ratio of earnings before interest payments and taxes to interest obligations. The *fixed-charge coverage ratio* includes lease payments and

sinking fund payments with interest obligations to arrive at the ratio of earnings to all fixed cash obligations (sinking funds are described below). Low or falling coverage ratios signal possible cash flow difficulties.

2. *Leverage ratio—Debt-to-equity ratio.* A too-high leverage ratio indicates excessive indebtedness, signaling the possibility the firm will be unable to earn enough to satisfy the obligations on its bonds.

3. *Liquidity ratios*—The two most common liquidity ratios are the *current ratio* (current assets/current liabilities) and the *quick ratio* (current assets excluding inventories/current liabilities). These ratios measure the firm's ability to pay bills coming due with its most liquid assets.

4. *Profitability ratios*—Measures of rates of return on assets or equity. Profitability ratios are indicators of a firm's overall financial health. The *return on assets* (earnings before interest and taxes divided by total assets) or *return on equity* (net income/equity) are the most popular of these measures. Firms with higher returns on assets or equity should be better able to raise money in security markets because they offer prospects for better returns on the firm's investments.

5. *Cash flow-to-debt ratio*—This is the ratio of total cash flow to outstanding debt.

Standard & Poor's periodically computes median values of selected ratios for firms in several rating classes, which we present in Table 14.3. Of course, ratios must be evaluated in the context of industry standards, and analysts differ in the weights they place on particular ratios. Nevertheless, Table 14.3 demonstrates the tendency of ratios to improve along with the firm's rating class. And default rates vary dramatically with bond rating. Historically, only about 1% of bonds originally rated AA or better at issuance had defaulted after 15 years. That ratio is around 7.5% for BBB-rated bonds, and 40% for B-rated bonds. Credit risk clearly varies dramatically across rating classes.

Many studies have tested whether financial ratios can in fact be used to predict default risk. One of the best-known series of tests was conducted by Edward Altman, who used discriminant analysis to predict bankruptcy. With this technique a firm is assigned a score based on its financial characteristics. If its score exceeds a cut-off value, the firm is deemed

	3-year (2002 to 2004) medians						
	AAA	AA	A	BBB	BB	B	CCC
EBIT interest coverage multiple	23.8	19.5	8.0	4.7	2.5	1.2	0.4
EBITDA interest coverage multiple	25.5	24.6	10.2	6.5	3.5	1.9	0.9
Funds from operations/total debt (%)	203.3	79.9	48.0	35.9	22.4	11.5	5.0
Free operating cash flow/total debt (%)	127.6	44.5	25.0	17.3	8.3	2.8	(2.1)
Total debt/EBITDA multiple	0.4	0.9	1.6	2.2	3.5	5.3	7.9
Return on capital (%)	27.6	27.0	17.5	13.4	11.3	8.7	3.2
Total debt/total debt + equity (%)	12.4	28.3	37.5	42.5	53.7	75.9	113.5

TABLE 14.3

Financial ratios by rating class, long-term debt

Note: EBITDA is earnings before interest, taxes, depreciation, and amortization
Source: *Corporate Rating Criteria*, Standard & Poor's, 2006.

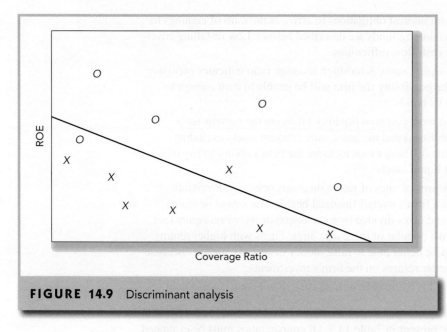

FIGURE 14.9 Discriminant analysis

creditworthy. A score below the cut-off value indicates significant bankruptcy risk in the near future.

To illustrate the technique, suppose that we were to collect data on the return on equity (ROE) and coverage ratios of a sample of firms, and then keep records of any corporate bankruptcies. In Figure 14.9 we plot the ROE and coverage ratios for each firm using X for firms that eventually went bankrupt and O for those that remained solvent. Clearly, the X and O firms show different patterns of data, with the solvent firms typically showing higher values for the two ratios.

The discriminant analysis determines the equation of the line that best separates the X and O observations. Suppose that the equation of the line is $.75 = .9 \times \text{ROE} + .4 \times \text{Coverage}$. Then, based on its own financial ratios, each firm is assigned a "Z-score" equal to $.9 \times \text{ROE} + .4 \times \text{Coverage}$. If its Z-score exceeds .75, the firm plots above the line and is considered a safe bet; Z-scores below .75 foretell financial difficulty.

Altman[12] found the following equation to best separate failing and nonfailing firms:

$$Z = 3.3 \frac{\text{EBIT}}{\text{Total assets}} + 99.9 \frac{\text{Sales}}{\text{Assets}} + .6 \frac{\text{Market value of equity}}{\text{Book value of debt}}$$
$$+ 1.4 \frac{\text{Retained earnings}}{\text{Total assets}} + 1.2 \frac{\text{Working capital}}{\text{Total assets}}$$

where EBIT = earnings before interest and taxes.

CONCEPT CHECK 9

Suppose we add a new variable equal to current liabilities/current assets to Altman's equation. Would you expect this variable to receive a positive or negative coefficient?

Bond Indentures

A bond is issued with an *indenture,* which is the contract between the issuer and the bondholder. Part of the indenture is a set of restrictions that protect the rights of the bondholders. Such restrictions include provisions relating to collateral, sinking funds, dividend policy, and further borrowing. The issuing firm agrees to these *protective covenants* in order to market its bonds to investors concerned about the safety of the bond issue.

Sinking Funds Bonds call for the payment of par value at the end of the bond's life. This payment constitutes a large cash commitment for the issuer. To help ensure the commitment

---

[12]Edward I. Altman, "Financial Ratios, Discriminant Analysis, and the Prediction of Corporate Bankruptcy," *Journal of Finance* 23 (September 1968).

does not create a cash flow crisis, the firm agrees to establish a **sinking fund** to spread the payment burden over several years. The fund may operate in one of two ways:

1. The firm may repurchase a fraction of the outstanding bonds in the open market each year.
2. The firm may purchase a fraction of the outstanding bonds at a special call price associated with the sinking fund provision. The firm has an option to purchase the bonds at either the market price or the sinking fund price, whichever is lower. To allocate the burden of the sinking fund call fairly among bondholders, the bonds chosen for the call are selected at random based on serial number.[13]

The sinking fund call differs from a conventional bond call in two important ways. First, the firm can repurchase only a limited fraction of the bond issue at the sinking fund call price. At best, some indentures allow firms to use a *doubling option,* which allows repurchase of double the required number of bonds at the sinking fund call price. Second, while callable bonds generally have call prices above par value, the sinking fund call price usually is set at the bond's par value.

Although sinking funds ostensibly protect bondholders by making principal repayment more likely, they can hurt the investor. The firm will choose to buy back discount bonds (selling below par) at market price, while exercising its option to buy back premium bonds (selling above par) at par. Therefore, if interest rates fall and bond prices rise, firms will benefit from the sinking fund provision that enables them to repurchase their bonds at below-market prices. In these circumstances, the firm's gain is the bondholder's loss.

One bond issue that does not require a sinking fund is a *serial bond* issue. In a serial bond issue, the firm sells bonds with staggered maturity dates. As bonds mature sequentially, the principal repayment burden for the firm is spread over time, just as it is with a sinking fund. One advantage of serial bonds over sinking fund issues is that there is no uncertainty introduced by the possibility that a particular bond will be called for the sinking fund. The disadvantage of serial bonds, however, is that bonds of different maturity dates are not interchangeable, which reduces the liquidity of the issue.

Subordination of Further Debt   One of the factors determining bond safety is total outstanding debt of the issuer. If you bought a bond today, you would be understandably distressed to see the firm tripling its outstanding debt tomorrow. Your bond would be of lower credit quality than it appeared when you bought it. To prevent firms from harming bondholders in this manner, **subordination clauses** restrict the amount of additional borrowing. Additional debt might be required to be subordinated in priority to existing debt; that is, in the event of bankruptcy, *subordinated* or *junior* debtholders will not be paid unless and until the prior senior debt is fully paid off. For this reason, subordination is sometimes called a "me-first rule," meaning the senior (earlier) bondholders are to be paid first in the event of bankruptcy.

Dividend Restrictions   Covenants also limit the dividends firms may pay. These limitations protect the bondholders because they force the firm to retain assets rather than paying them out to stockholders. A typical restriction disallows payments of dividends

---

[13]Although it is less common, the sinking fund provision also may call for periodic payments to a trustee, with the payments invested so that the accumulated sum can be used for retirement of the entire issue at maturity.

if cumulative dividends paid since the firm's inception exceed cumulative retained earnings plus proceeds from sales of stock.

Collateral Some bonds are issued with specific collateral behind them. **Collateral** can take several forms, but it represents a particular asset of the firm that the bondholders receive if the firm defaults on the bond. If the collateral is property, the bond is called a *mortgage bond.* If the collateral takes the form of other securities held by the firm, the bond is a *collateral trust bond.* In the case of equipment, the bond is known as an *equipment obligation bond.* This last form of collateral is used most commonly by firms such as railroads, where the equipment is fairly standard and can be easily sold to another firm should the firm default and the bondholders acquire the collateral.

Because of the specific collateral that backs them, collateralized bonds generally are considered the safest variety of corporate bonds. General **debenture** bonds by contrast do not provide for specific collateral; they are *unsecured* bonds. The bondholder relies solely on the general earning power of the firm for the bond's safety. If the firm defaults, debenture owners become general creditors of the firm. Because they are safer, collateralized bonds generally offer lower yields than general debentures.

& Mobil Corp. debenture 8s, due 2032:
Rating — Aa2

AUTH—$250,000,000.
OUTSTG—Dec. 31, 1993, $250,000,000.
DATED—Oct. 30, 1991.
INTEREST—F&A 12.
TRUSTEE—Chemical Bank.
DENOMINATION—Fully registered, $1,000 and integral multiplies thereof. Transferable and exchangeable without service charge.
CALLABLE—As a whole or in part, at any time, on or after Aug. 12, 2002, at the option of Co. on at least 30 but not more than the 60 days' notice to each Aug. 11 as follows:

2003..........105.007	2004..........104.756	2005..........104.506
2006..........104.256	2007..........104.005	2008..........103.755
2009..........103.505	2010..........103.254	2011..........103.004
2012..........102.754	2013..........102.503	2014..........102.253
2015..........102.003	2016..........101.752	2017..........101.502
2018..........101.252	2019..........101.001	2020..........100.751
2021..........100.501	2022..........100.250	

and thereafter at 100 plus accrued interest.
SECURITY—Not secured. Ranks equally with all other unsecured and unsubordinated indebtedness of Co. Co. nor any Affiliate will not incur any indebtedness; provided that Co. will not create as security for any indebtedness for borrowed money, any mortgage, pledge, security interest or lien on any stock or indebtedness is directly owned by Co. without effectively providing that the debt securities shall be secured equally and ratably with such indebtedness. so long as such indebtedness shall be so secured.
INDENTURE MODIFICATION—Indenture may be modified, except as provided with, consent of 66 2/3% of debs. outstg.
RIGHTS ON DEFAULT—Trustee, or 25% of debs. outstg., may declare principal due and payable (30 days' grace for payment of interest).

LISTED—On New York Stock Exchange.
PURPOSE—Proceeds used for general corporate purposes.
OFFERED—($250,000,000) at 99.51 plus accrued interest (proceeds to Co., 99.11) on Aug. 5, 1992 thru Merrill Lynch & Co., Donaldson, Lufkin & Jenerette Securities Corp., PaineWebber Inc., Prudential Securities Inc., Smith Barney, Harris Upham & Co. Inc. and associates.

FIGURE 14.10 Callable bond issued by Mobil

Source: *Mergent's Industrial Manual,* Mergent's Investor Services, 1994. Reprinted with permission. All rights reserved.

Figure 14.10 shows the terms of a bond issued by Mobil as described in *Moody's Industrial Manual.* The bond is registered and listed on the NYSE. It was issued in 1991 but was not callable until 2002. Although the call price started at 105.007% of par value, it falls gradually until it reaches par after 2020. Most of the terms of the bond are typical and illustrate many of the indenture provisions we have mentioned. However, in recent years there has been a marked trend away from the use of call provisions.

Yield to Maturity and Default Risk

Because corporate bonds are subject to default risk, we must distinguish between the bond's promised yield to maturity and its expected yield. The promised or stated yield will be realized only if the firm meets the obligations of the bond issue. Therefore, the stated yield is the *maximum possible* yield to maturity of the bond. The expected yield to maturity must take into account the possibility of a default.

For example, in November 2001, as Enron approached bankruptcy, its 6.4% coupon bonds due in 2006 were selling at about 20% of par value, resulting in a yield to maturity of about 57%. Investors did not really expect these bonds to provide a 57% rate of return. They recognized that bondholders were very unlikely to receive all the payments promised in the bond contract and that the yield based on *expected* cash flows was far less than the yield based on *promised* cash flows.

EXAMPLE 14.10 Expected vs. Promised Yield to Maturity

Suppose a firm issued a 9% coupon bond 20 years ago. The bond now has 10 years left until its maturity date but the firm is having financial difficulties. Investors believe that the firm will be able to make good on the remaining interest payments, but that at the maturity date, the firm will be forced into bankruptcy, and bondholders will receive only 70% of par value. The bond is selling at $750.

Yield to maturity (YTM) would then be calculated using the following inputs:

	Expected YTM	**Stated YTM**
Coupon payment	$45	$45
Number of semiannual periods	20 periods	20 periods
Final payment	$700	$1,000
Price	$750	$750

The yield to maturity based on promised payments is 13.7%. Based on the expected payment of $700 at maturity, however, the yield to maturity would be only 11.6%. The stated yield to maturity is greater than the yield investors actually expect to receive.

Example 14.10 suggests that when a bond becomes more subject to default risk, its price will fall, and therefore its promised yield to maturity will rise. Similarly, the default premium, the spread between the stated yield to maturity and that on otherwise-comparable Treasury bonds, will rise. However, its expected yield to maturity, which ultimately is tied to the systematic risk of the bond, will be far less affected. Let's continue Example 14.10.

EXAMPLE 14.11 Default Risk and the Default Premium

Suppose that the condition of the firm in Example 14.10 deteriorates further, and investors now believe that the bond will pay off only 55% of face value at maturity. Investors now demand an expected yield to maturity of 12% (i.e., 6% semiannually), which is 0.4% higher than in Example 14.10. But the price of the bond will fall from $750 to $688 [$n = 20$; $i = 6$; FV = 550; PMT = $45]. At this price, the stated yield to maturity based on promised cash flows is 15.2%. While the expected yield to maturity has increased by 0.4%, the drop in price has caused the promised yield to maturity to rise by 1.5%.

To compensate for the possibility of default, corporate bonds must offer a **default premium.** The default premium is the difference between the promised yield on a corporate bond and the yield of an otherwise-identical government bond that is riskless in terms of default. If the firm remains solvent and actually pays the investor all of the promised cash flows, the investor will realize a

CONCEPT CHECK 10

What is the expected yield to maturity if the firm is in even worse condition? Investors expect a final payment of only $500, and the bond price has fallen to $650.

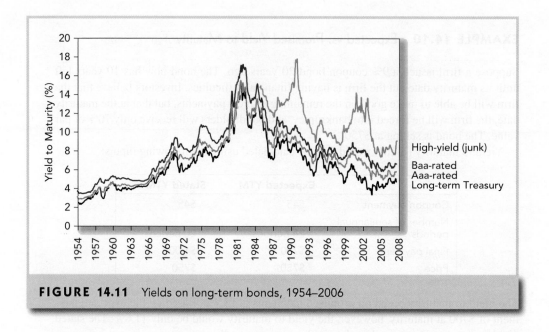

FIGURE 14.11 Yields on long-term bonds, 1954–2006

higher yield to maturity than would be realized from the government bond. If, however, the firm goes bankrupt, the corporate bond is likely to provide a lower return than the government bond. The corporate bond has the potential for both better and worse performance than the default-free Treasury bond. In other words, it is riskier.

The pattern of default premiums offered on risky bonds is sometimes called the *risk structure of interest rates*. The greater the default risk, the higher the default premium. Figure 14.11 shows yield to maturity of bonds of different risk classes since 1954 and yields on junk bonds since 1986. You can see here clear evidence of credit-risk premiums on promised yields.

One particular manner in which yield spreads seem to vary over time is related to the business cycle. Yield spreads tend to be wider when the economy is in a recession. Apparently, investors perceive a higher probability of bankruptcy when the economy is faltering, even holding bond rating constant. They require a commensurately higher default premium. This is sometimes termed a *flight to quality,* meaning that investors move their funds into safer bonds unless they can obtain larger premiums on lower-rated securities.

Credit Risk and Collateralized Debt Obligations

Collateralized debt obligations, or **CDO**s, emerged in the last decade as a major mechanism to reallocate credit risk in the fixed-income markets. To create a CDO, a financial institution, commonly a bank, first establishes a legally distinct entity to buy and later resell a portfolio of bonds or other loans. A common vehicle for this purpose is the so-called Structured Investment Vehicle (SIV).[14] The SIV raises funds, often by issuing short-term commercial paper, and uses the proceeds to buy corporate bonds or other

[14]The legal separation of the bank from the SIV allows the ownership of the loans to be conducted off the bank's balance sheet, and thus avoids capital requirements the bank would otherwise encounter.

		Senior-Subordinated Tranche Structure	Typical Terms
		Senior tranche	70–90% of notional principal, coupon similar to Aa-Aaa rated bonds
		Mezzanine 1	5–15% of principal, investment-grade rating
Bank	Structured Investment Vehicle, SIV		
		Mezzanine 2	5–15% of principal, higher-quality junk rating
		Equity/first loss/ residual tranche	<2%, unrated, coupon rate with 20% credit spread

FIGURE 14.12 Collateralized debt obligations

forms of debt such as mortgage loans or credit card debt. These loans are first pooled together and then split into a series of classes known as *tranches*. (*Tranche* is the French word for "slice.")

Each tranche is given a different level of seniority in terms of its claims on the underlying loan pool, and each can be sold as a stand-alone security. As the loans in the underlying pool make their interest payments, the proceeds are distributed to pay interest to each tranche in order of seniority. This priority structure implies that each tranche has a different exposure to credit risk.

Figure 14.12 illustrates a typical setup. The senior tranche is on top. Its investors may account for perhaps 80% of the principal of the entire pool. But it has first claim on *all* the debt service, and therefore bears little credit exposure. For example, using our numbers, even if 20% of the debt pool defaults, the senior tranche can be paid in full. Once the highest seniority tranche is paid off, the next-lower class (e.g., the mezzanine 1 tranche in Figure 14.12) receives the proceeds from the pool of loans until its claims also are satisfied.

Of course, shielding senior tranches from default risk means that the risk is concentrated on the lower tranches. The bottom tranche—called alternatively the equity, first-loss, or residual tranche—has last call on payments from the pool of loans, or, put differently, is at the head of the line in terms of absorbing default or delinquency risk. Using junior tranches to insulate senior tranches from credit risk in this manner, one can create Aaa-rated bonds even from a junk-bond portfolio. And, in fact, while Aaa-rated bonds are extremely few and far between, Aaa-rated CDO tranches are common.

Not surprisingly, investors in tranches with the greatest exposure to credit risk demand the highest coupon rates. Therefore, while the lower mezzanine and equity tranches bear the most risk, they will provide the highest returns if credit experience turns out favorably. Ideally, investors with greater expertise in evaluating credit risk are the natural investors in these securities. Often, the originating bank holds the residual tranche. This arrangement makes sense, because it provides incentives to the originator to perform careful credit analysis of the bonds included in the structure. The bank

CREDIT AND BLAME

The rating agencies Standard & Poor's (S&P), Moody's, and Fitch have earned huge sums in the past ten years offering opinions on the creditworthiness of an alphabet soup of mortgage-related securities created by over-eager banks. But did the fat fees lead to a drop in standards?

The agencies feel aggrieved at the criticism. So far, defaults have hit only three of the mortgage tranches it has rated. Of more complex products, collateralized-debt obligations (CDOs) downgrades have affected just 1% of securities by value.

The agencies are neither the only, nor indeed the main, culprits for the subprime crisis. The American mortgage industry was rotten from top to bottom, from buyers lying about their incomes to qualify for loans, through brokers accepting buyers with poor credit histories, to investors who bought bonds in the secondary market without conducting enough research.

Nevertheless, the agencies' business is built upon a rather shaky foundation. Rules devised by regulators, such as America's Securities Exchange Commission (SEC) and bank watchdogs, have made ratings a formal part of the financial system. The agencies have thus been handed a lucrative oligopoly. Moreover, they have a conflict of interest, since they are paid by the issuers whose securities they rate.

It is very hard to see how this combination can be justified. If the agencies' views are given a regulatory imprimatur, they should be subject to legal challenge. Alternatively, if they are simply independent expressions of opinion, then either investors, not issuers, should pay them, or they should be divorced from the regulatory system.

Joshua Rosner of Graham Fisher, an investment firm, thinks that the agencies should both be more transparent and improve their monitoring. Following bonds once they trade in the secondary market is much less lucrative for the agencies, he argues, and they devote far fewer resources to it. Although the agencies' models make it clear what rating they will give a bond on issue, it is less clear what will cause them to downgrade it later on.

Another response would be to make the agencies legally liable for their views. But the potential damage claim for making a duff rating would be so large that agencies might either be driven out of business or made excessively cautious by the threat of legal action.

The agencies could be asked to earn their fees from someone other than the issuers. But who? It is hard to believe that investors would pay: By hook or by crook, ratings would become public knowledge. The problem of free-riders means that there would not be enough research.

therefore retains significant interest in the management of the relationship with the borrowers.

Mortgage-backed CDOs were an investment disaster in 2007. These were CDOs formed by pooling not corporate debt, but subprime mortgage loans made to individuals whose credit standing did not allow them to qualify for conventional mortgages. When home prices stalled in 2007 and interest rates on these typically adjustable-rate loans reset to market levels, mortgage delinquencies and home foreclosures soared, and investors in these securities lost billions of dollars. Even some highly rated tranches suffered extreme losses as default rates turned out to be far higher than anticipated. The SIVs, which had financed their purchase of these loans by issuing short-term asset-backed commercial paper, came under extreme pressure as investors were unwilling to roll over the paper into new issues once they reassessed the credit risk of the loan pools backing their investments.

Not surprisingly, the rating agencies that had certified these tranches as investment-grade came under considerable fire. Questions were raised concerning conflicts of interest: Because the rating agencies are paid by bond issuers, the agencies were accused of responding to pressure to ease their standards. See the above box for more on the ensuing controversy.

1. Fixed-income securities are distinguished by their promise to pay a fixed or specified stream of income to their holders. The coupon bond is a typical fixed-income security.

2. Treasury notes and bonds have original maturities greater than 1 year. They are issued at or near par value, with their prices quoted net of accrued interest.

3. Callable bonds should offer higher promised yields to maturity to compensate investors for the fact that they will not realize full capital gains should the interest rate fall and the bonds be called away from them at the stipulated call price. Bonds often are issued with a period of call protection. In addition, discount bonds selling significantly below their call price offer implicit call protection.

4. Put bonds give the bondholder rather than the issuer the option to terminate or extend the life of the bond.

5. Convertible bonds may be exchanged, at the bondholder's discretion, for a specified number of shares of stock. Convertible bondholders "pay" for this option by accepting a lower coupon rate on the security.

6. Floating-rate bonds pay a coupon rate at a fixed premium over a reference short-term interest rate. Risk is limited because the rate is tied to current market conditions.

7. The yield to maturity is the single interest rate that equates the present value of a security's cash flows to its price. Bond prices and yields are inversely related. For premium bonds, the coupon rate is greater than the current yield, which is greater than the yield to maturity. The order of these inequalities is reversed for discount bonds.

8. The yield to maturity is often interpreted as an estimate of the average rate of return to an investor who purchases a bond and holds it until maturity. This interpretation is subject to error, however. Related measures are yield to call, realized compound yield, and expected (versus promised) yield to maturity.

9. Prices of zero-coupon bonds rise exponentially over time, providing a rate of appreciation equal to the interest rate. The IRS treats this built-in price appreciation as imputed taxable interest income to the investor.

10. When bonds are subject to potential default, the stated yield to maturity is the maximum possible yield to maturity that can be realized by the bondholder. In the event of default, however, that promised yield will not be realized. To compensate bond investors for default risk, bonds must offer default premiums, that is, promised yields in excess of those offered by default-free government securities. If the firm remains healthy, its bonds will provide higher returns than government bonds. Otherwise the returns may be lower.

11. Bond safety is often measured using financial ratio analysis. Bond indentures are another safeguard to protect the claims of bondholders. Common indentures specify sinking fund requirements, collateralization of the loan, dividend restrictions, and subordination of future debt.

12. Collateralized debt obligations are used to reallocate the credit risk of a pool of loans. The pool is sliced into tranches, with each tranche assigned a different level of seniority in terms of its claims on the cash flows from the underlying loans. High seniority tranches are usually quite safe, with credit risk concentrated on the lower level tranches. Each tranche can be sold as a stand-alone security.

SUMMARY

Related web sites for this chapter are available at www.mhhe.com/bkm

KEY TERMS

debt securities	floating-rate bonds	investment-grade bonds
bond	yield to maturity	speculative-grade or junk
par value	current yield	bonds
face value	premium bonds	sinking fund
coupon rate	discount bonds	subordination clauses
bond indenture	realized compound return	collateral
zero-coupon bonds	horizon analysis	debenture
convertible bonds	reinvestment rate risk	default premium
put bond	credit risk	collateralized debt obligations

PROBLEM SETS

Quiz

Problems

1. Two bonds have identical times to maturity and coupon rates. One is callable at 105, the other at 110. Which should have the higher yield to maturity? Why?

2. The stated yield to maturity and realized compound yield to maturity of a (default-free) zero-coupon bond will always be equal. Why?

3. Why do bond prices go down when interest rates go up? Don't lenders like high interest rates?

4. Which security has a higher *effective* annual interest rate?

   a. A 3-month T-bill selling at $97,645 with par value $100,000.
   b. A coupon bond selling at par and paying a 10% coupon semiannually.

5. Treasury bonds paying an 8% coupon rate with *semiannual* payments currently sell at par value. What coupon rate would they have to pay in order to sell at par if they paid their coupons *annually?* (Hint: what is the effective annual yield on the bond?)

6. Consider a bond with a 10% coupon and with yield to maturity = 8%. If the bond's yield to maturity remains constant, then in 1 year, will the bond price be higher, lower, or unchanged? Why?

7. Consider an 8% coupon bond selling for $953.10 with 3 years until maturity making *annual* coupon payments. The interest rates in the next 3 years will be, with certainty, $r_1 = 8\%$, $r_2 = 10\%$, and $r_3 = 12\%$. Calculate the yield to maturity and realized compound yield of the bond.

8. Assume you have a 1-year investment horizon and are trying to choose among three bonds. All have the same degree of default risk and mature in 10 years. The first is a zero-coupon bond that pays $1,000 at maturity. The second has an 8% coupon rate and pays the $80 coupon once per year. The third has a 10% coupon rate and pays the $100 coupon once per year.

   a. If all three bonds are now priced to yield 8% to maturity, what are their prices?
   b. If you expect their yields to maturity to be 8% at the beginning of next year, what will their prices be then? What is your before-tax holding-period return on each bond? If your tax bracket is 30% on ordinary income and 20% on capital gains income, what will your after-tax rate of return be on each?
   c. Recalculate your answer to (b) under the assumption that you expect the yields to maturity on each bond to be 7% at the beginning of next year.

9. A 20-year maturity bond with par value of $1,000 makes semiannual coupon payments at a coupon rate of 8%. Find the bond equivalent and effective annual yield to maturity of the bond if the bond price is:

   a. $950.
   b. $1,000.
   c. $1,050.

10. Repeat Problem 9 using the same data, but assuming that the bond makes its coupon payments annually. Why are the yields you compute lower in this case?

11. Fill in the table below for the following zero-coupon bonds, all of which have par values of $1,000.

Price	Maturity (years)	Bond-Equivalent Yield to Maturity
$400	20	—
$500	20	—
$500	10	—
—	10	10%
—	10	8%
$400	—	8%

12. Consider a bond paying a coupon rate of 10% per year semiannually when the market interest rate is only 4% per half-year. The bond has 3 years until maturity.

    a. Find the bond's price today and 6 months from now after the next coupon is paid.
    b. What is the total (6-month) rate of return on the bond?

13. A bond with a coupon rate of 7% makes semiannual coupon payments on January 15 and July 15 of each year. *The Wall Street Journal* reports the asked price for the bond on January 30 at 100:02. What is the invoice price of the bond? The coupon period has 182 days.

14. A bond has a current yield of 9% and a yield to maturity of 10%. Is the bond selling above or below par value? Explain.

15. Is the coupon rate of the bond in Problem 14 more or less than 9%?

16. Return to Table 14.1 and calculate both the real and nominal rates of return on the TIPS bond in the second and third years.

17. A newly issued 20-year maturity, zero-coupon bond is issued with a yield to maturity of 8% and face value $1,000. Find the imputed interest income in the first, second, and last year of the bond's life.

18. A newly issued 10-year maturity, 4% coupon bond making *annual* coupon payments is sold to the public at a price of $800. What will be an investor's taxable income from the bond over the coming year? The bond will not be sold at the end of the year. The bond is treated as an original-issue discount bond.

19. A 30-year maturity, 8% coupon bond paying coupons semiannually is callable in 5 years at a call price of $1,100. The bond currently sells at a yield to maturity of 7% (3.5% per half-year).

    a. What is the yield to call?
    b. What is the yield to call if the call price is only $1,050?
    c. What is the yield to call if the call price is $1,100, but the bond can be called in 2 years instead of 5 years?

20. A 10-year bond of a firm in severe financial distress has a coupon rate of 14% and sells for $900. The firm is currently renegotiating the debt, and it appears that the lenders will allow the firm to reduce coupon payments on the bond to one-half the originally contracted amount. The firm can handle these lower payments. What is the stated and expected yield to maturity of the bonds? The bond makes its coupon payments annually.

21. A 2-year bond with par value $1,000 making annual coupon payments of $100 is priced at $1,000. What is the yield to maturity of the bond? What will be the realized compound yield to maturity if the 1-year interest rate next year turns out to be (*a*) 8%, (*b*) 10%, (*c*) 12%?

22. Suppose that today's date is April 15. A bond with a 10% coupon paid semiannually every January 15 and July 15 is listed in *The Wall Street Journal* as selling at an asked price of 101:04. If you buy the bond from a dealer today, what price will you pay for it?

23. Assume that two firms issue bonds with the following characteristics. Both bonds are issued at par.

	ABC Bonds	XYZ Bonds
Issue size	$1.2 billion	$150 million
Maturity	10 years*	20 years
Coupon	9%	10%
Collateral	First mortgage	General debenture
Callable	Not callable	In 10 years
Call price	None	110
Sinking fund	None	Starting in 5 years

*Bond is extendible at the discretion of the bondholder for an additional 10 years.

Ignoring credit quality, identify four features of these issues that might account for the lower coupon on the ABC debt. Explain.

24. A large corporation issued both fixed and floating-rate notes 5 years ago, with terms given in the following table:

	9% Coupon Notes	Floating-Rate Note
Issue size	$250 million	$280 million
Original maturity	20 years	10 years
Current price (% of par)	93	98
Current coupon	9%	8%
Coupon adjusts	Fixed coupon	Every year
Coupon reset rule	—	1-year T-bill rate + 2%
Callable	10 years after issue	10 years after issue
Call price	106	102.50
Sinking fund	None	None
Yield to maturity	9.9%	—
Price range since issued	$85–$112	$97–$102

a. Why is the price range greater for the 9% coupon bond than the floating-rate note?
b. What factors could explain why the floating-rate note is not always sold at par value?
c. Why is the call price for the floating-rate note not of great importance to investors?
d. Is the probability of call for the fixed-rate note high or low?
e. If the firm were to issue a fixed-rate note with a 15-year maturity, what coupon rate would it need to offer to issue the bond at par value?
f. Why is an entry for yield to maturity for the floating-rate note not appropriate?

25. Masters Corp. issues two bonds with 20-year maturities. Both bonds are callable at $1,050. The first bond is issued at a deep discount with a coupon rate of 4% and a price of $580 to yield 8.4%. The second bond is issued at par value with a coupon rate of 8¾%.

a. What is the yield to maturity of the par bond? Why is it higher than the yield of the discount bond?
b. If you expect rates to fall substantially in the next 2 years, which bond would you prefer to hold?
c. In what sense does the discount bond offer "implicit call protection"?

Challenge Problem

26. A newly issued bond pays its coupons once annually. Its coupon rate is 5%, its maturity is 20 years, and its yield to maturity is 8%.

a. Find the holding-period return for a 1-year investment period if the bond is selling at a yield to maturity of 7% by the end of the year.
b. If you sell the bond after 1 year, what taxes will you owe if the tax rate on interest income is 40% and the tax rate on capital gains income is 30%? The bond is subject to original-issue discount tax treatment.
c. What is the after-tax holding-period return on the bond?
d. Find the realized compound yield *before taxes* for a 2-year holding period, assuming that (1) you sell the bond after 2 years, (2) the bond yield is 7% at the end of the second year, and (3) the coupon can be reinvested for 1 year at a 3% interest rate.
e. Use the tax rates in (*b*) above to compute the *after-tax* 2-year realized compound yield. Remember to take account of OID tax rules.

CFA® PROBLEMS

1. Leaf Products may issue a 10-year maturity fixed-income security, which might include a sinking fund provision and either refunding or call protection.

a. Describe a sinking fund provision.
b. Explain the impact of a sinking fund provision on:
  i. The expected average life of the proposed security.
  ii. Total principal and interest payments over the life of the proposed security.
c. From the investor's point of view, explain the rationale for demanding a sinking fund provision.

2. Bonds of Zello Corporation with a par value of $1,000 sell for $960, mature in 5 years, and have a 7% annual coupon rate paid semiannually.

   a. Calculate the:

      i. Current yield.
      ii. Yield to maturity (to the nearest whole percent, i.e., 3%, 4%, 5%, etc.).
      iii. Realized compound yield for an investor with a 3-year holding period and a reinvestment rate of 6% over the period. At the end of 3 years the 7% coupon bonds with 2 years remaining will sell to yield 7%.

   b. Cite one major shortcoming for each of the following fixed-income yield measures:

      i. Current yield.
      ii. Yield to maturity.
      iii. Realized compound yield.

3. On May 30, 2008, Janice Kerr is considering one of the newly issued 10-year AAA corporate bonds shown in the following exhibit.

Description	Coupon	Price	Callable	Call Price
Sentinal, due May 30, 2018	6.00%	100	Noncallable	NA
Colina, due May 30, 2018	6.20%	100	Currently callable	102

   a. Suppose that market interest rates decline by 100 basis points (i.e., 1%). Contrast the effect of this decline on the price of each bond.
   b. Should Kerr prefer the Colina over the Sentinal bond when rates are expected to rise or to fall?
   c. What would be the effect, if any, of an increase in the *volatility* of interest rates on the prices of each bond?

4. A convertible bond has the following features:

Coupon	5.25%
Maturity	June 15, 2027
Market price of bond	$77.50
Market price of underlying common stock	$28.00
Annual dividend	$1.20
Conversion ratio	20.83 shares

   Calculate the conversion premium for this bond.

5. a. Explain the impact on the offering yield of adding a call feature to a proposed bond issue.
   b. Explain the impact on the bond's expected life of adding a call feature to a proposed bond issue.
   c. Describe one advantage and one disadvantage of including callable bonds in a portfolio.

6. a. An investment in a coupon bond will provide the investor with a return equal to the bond's yield to maturity at the time of purchase if:

      i. The bond is not called for redemption at a price that exceeds its par value.
      ii. All sinking fund payments are made in a prompt and timely fashion over the life of the issue.
      iii. The reinvestment rate is the same as the bond's yield to maturity and the bond is held until maturity.
      iv. All of the above.

   b. A bond with a call feature:

      i. Is attractive because the immediate receipt of principal plus premium produces a high return.
      ii. Is more apt to be called when interest rates are high because the interest savings will be greater.

iii. Will usually have a higher yield to maturity than a similar noncallable bond.

iv. None of the above.

c. In which *one* of the following cases is the bond selling at a discount?

  i. Coupon rate is greater than current yield, which is greater than yield to maturity.

  ii. Coupon rate, current yield, and yield to maturity are all the same.

  iii. Coupon rate is less than current yield, which is less than yield to maturity.

  iv. Coupon rate is less than current yield, which is greater than yield to maturity.

d. Consider a 5-year bond with a 10% coupon that has a present yield to maturity of 8%. If interest rates remain constant, 1 year from now the price of this bond will be:

  i. Higher

  ii. Lower

  iii. The same

  iv. Par

STANDARD &POOR'S

Use the *Financial Highlights* section of Market Insight (**www.mhhe.com/edumarketinsight**) to obtain Standard & Poor's Issuer Credit Ratings of at least ten firms in the database. Try to choose a sample with a wide range of ratings. Next use Market Insight's Annual Ratio Report (in the *Excel Analytics* section) to obtain for each firm the financial ratios shown in Table 14.3. What is the relationship between the firms' credit ratings and their ratios? Can you tell from your sample firms which of these ratios are the more important determinants of credit rating?

E-Investments

Credit Spreads

At **www.bondsonline.com** review the *Industrial Spreads* for various ratings (click the links on the left-side menus to follow the links to *Today's Markets, Corporate Bond Spreads*). These are spreads above U.S. Treasuries of comparable maturities. What factors tend to explain the yield differences? How might these yield spreads differ during an economic boom versus a recession?

From the home page, select *Today's Markets* from the left-side menu and then select the link for *Composite Bond Yields*. How do the Yield Curves for Treasury, Agency, Corporate, and Municipal bonds compare to each other?

SOLUTIONS TO CONCEPT CHECKS

1. The callable bond will sell at the *lower* price. Investors will not be willing to pay as much if they know that the firm retains a valuable option to reclaim the bond for the call price if interest rates fall.

2. At a semiannual interest rate of 3%, the bond is worth $40 × Annuity factor (3%, 60) + $1,000 × PV factor(3%, 60) = $1,276.76, which results in a capital gain of $276.76. This exceeds the capital loss of $189.29 ($1,000 − $810.71) when the semiannual interest rate increased to 5%.

3. Yield to maturity exceeds current yield, which exceeds coupon rate. Take as an example the 8% coupon bond with a yield to maturity of 10% per year (5% per half year). Its price is $810.71, and therefore its current yield is 80/810.71 = .0987, or 9.87%, which is higher than the coupon rate but lower than the yield to maturity.

4. The bond with the 6% coupon rate currently sells for 30 × Annuity factor (3.5%, 20) + 1,000 × PV factor(3.5%, 20) = $928.94. If the interest rate immediately drops to 6% (3% per half-year), the bond price will rise to $1,000, for a capital gain of $71.06, or 7.65%. The 8% coupon bond currently sells for $1,071.06. If the interest rate falls to 6%, the present value of the *scheduled* payments increases to $1,148.77. However, the bond will be called at $1,100, for a capital gain of only $28.94, or 2.70%.

5. The current price of the bond can be derived from its yield to maturity. Using your calculator, set: $n = 40$ (semiannual periods); payment = $45 per period; future value = $1,000; interest rate = 4% per semiannual period. Calculate present value as $1,098.96. Now we can calculate yield to call. The time to call is 5 years, or 10 semiannual periods. The price at which the bond will be called is $1,050. To find yield to call, we set: $n = 10$ (semiannual periods); payment = $45 per period; future value = $1,050; present value = $1,098.96. Calculate yield to call as 3.72%.

6. Price = $70 × Annuity factor(8%, 1) + $1,000 × PV factor(8%, 1) = $990.74

$$\text{Rate of return to investor} = \frac{\$70 + (\$990.74 - \$982.17)}{\$982.17} = .080 = 8\%$$

7. By year-end, remaining maturity is 29 years. If the yield to maturity were still 8%, the bond would still sell at par and the holding-period return would be 8%. At a higher yield, price and return will be lower. Suppose, for example, that the yield to maturity rises to 8.5%. With annual payments of $80 and a face value of $1,000, the price of the bond will be $946.70 [$n = 29$; $i = 8.5\%$; PMT = $80; FV = $1,000]. The bond initially sold at $1,000 when issued at the start of the year. The holding-period return is

$$\text{HPR} = \frac{80 + (946.70 - 1,000)}{1,000} = .0267 = 2.67\%$$

which is less than the initial yield to maturity of 8%.

8. At the lower yield, the bond price will be $631.67 [$n = 29$, $i = 7\%$, FV = $1,000, PMT = $40]. Therefore, total after-tax income is

Coupon	$40 × (1 − .38)	= $24.80
Imputed interest	($553.66 − $549.69) × (1 − .38) =	2.46
Capital gains	($631.67 − $553.66) × (1 − .20) =	62.41
Total income after taxes		$89.67
Rate of return = 89.67/549.69 = .163 = 16.3%.		

9. It should receive a negative coefficient. A high ratio of liabilities to assets is a poor omen for a firm that should lower its credit rating.

10. The coupon payment is $45. There are 20 semiannual periods. The final payment is assumed to be $500. The present value of expected cash flows is $650. The expected yield to maturity is 6.317% semiannual or annualized, 12.63%, bond equivalent yield.

THE TERM STRUCTURE OF INTEREST RATES

IN CHAPTER 14 we assumed for the sake of simplicity that the same constant interest rate is used to discount cash flows of any maturity. In the real world this is rarely the case. We have seen, for example, that in early 2007 short-term bonds and notes carried yields to maturity of about 4.7% while the longest-term bonds offered yields of about 5%. At the time when these bond prices were quoted, anyway, the longer-term securities had higher yields. This, in fact, is a typical pattern, but as we shall see below, the relationship between time to maturity and yield to maturity can vary dramatically from one period to another. In this chapter we explore the pattern of interest rates for different-term assets. We attempt to identify the factors that account for that pattern and determine what information may be derived from an analysis of the so-called **term structure of interest rates,** the structure of interest rates for discounting cash flows of different maturities.

We demonstrate how the prices of Treasury bonds may be derived from prices and yields of stripped zero-coupon Treasury securities. We also examine the extent to which the term structure reveals market-consensus forecasts of future interest rates and how the presence of interest rate risk may affect those inferences. Finally, we show how traders can use the term structure to compute forward rates that represent interest rates on "forward" or deferred loans, and consider the relationship between forward rates and future interest rates.

15.1   THE YIELD CURVE

Figure 14.1 demonstrated that bonds of different maturities typically sell at different yields to maturity. When these bond prices and yields were compiled, long-term bonds sold at slightly higher yields than short-term bonds. Practitioners commonly summarize the relationship between yield and maturity graphically in a **yield curve,** which is a plot of yield to maturity as a function of time to maturity. The yield curve is one of the key concerns of fixed-income investors. We will see in this chapter that the yield curve is central to bond valuation and, as well, allows investors to gauge their expectations for future interest rates

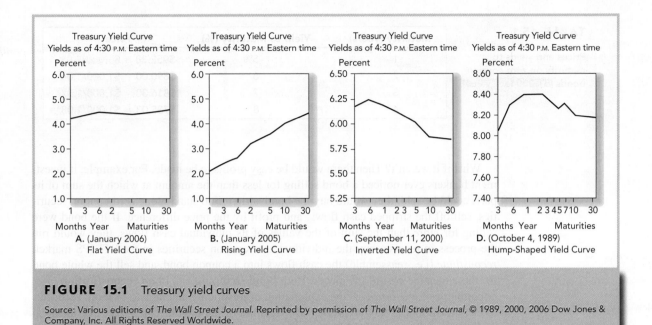

FIGURE 15.1 Treasury yield curves

Source: Various editions of *The Wall Street Journal*. Reprinted by permission of *The Wall Street Journal*, © 1989, 2000, 2006 Dow Jones & Company, Inc. All Rights Reserved Worldwide.

against those of the market. Such a comparison is often the starting point in the formulation of a fixed-income portfolio strategy.

In late 2007, the yield curve was nearly flat, with long-term bonds offering yields only slightly higher than those of short-term bonds. But the relationship between yield and maturity can vary widely. Figure 15.1 illustrates yield curves of several different shapes. Panel A is the almost-flat curve of early 2006. Panel B is a more typical upward-sloping curve from a year earlier. Panel C is a downward-sloping or "inverted" curve, and panel D is humped-shaped, first rising and then falling.

Bond Pricing

If yields on different-maturity bonds are not all equal, how should we value coupon bonds that make payments at many different times? For example, suppose that yields on zero-coupon Treasury bonds of different maturities are as given in Table 15.1. The table tells us that zero-coupon bonds with 1-year maturity sell at a yield to maturity of $y_1 = 5\%$, 2-year zeros sell at yields of $y_2 = 6\%$, and 3-year zeros sell at yields of $y_3 = 7\%$. Which of these rates should we use to discount bond cash flows? The answer: all of them. The trick is to consider each bond cash flow—either coupon or principal payment—as at least potentially sold off separately as a stand-alone zero-coupon bond.

Recall the Treasury STRIPS program we introduced in the last chapter (Section 14.4). Stripped Treasuries are zero-coupon bonds created by selling each coupon or principal payment from a whole Treasury bond as a separate cash flow. For example, a 1-year maturity T-bond paying semiannual coupons can be split into a 6-month maturity zero (by selling the first coupon payment as a stand-alone security) and a 12-month zero (corresponding to payment of final coupon and principal). Treasury stripping suggests exactly how to value a coupon bond. If each cash flow can be (and in practice often is) sold off as a separate security, then the value of the whole bond should be the same as the value of its cash flows bought piece by piece in the STRIPS market.

TABLE 15.1

Prices and yields to maturity on zero-coupon bonds ($1,000 face value)

Maturity (years)	Yield to Maturity (%)	Price
1	5%	$952.38 = \$1,000/1.05$
2	6	$890.00 = \$1,000/1.06^2$
3	7	$816.30 = \$1,000/1.07^3$
4	8	$735.03 = \$1,000/1.08^4$

What if it weren't? Then there would be easy profits to be made. For example, if investment bankers ever noticed a bond selling for less than the amount at which the sum of its parts could be sold, they would buy the bond, strip it into stand-alone zero-coupon securities, sell off the stripped cash flows, and profit by the price difference. If the bond were selling for *more* than the sum of the values of its individual cash flows, they would run the process in reverse: buy the individual zero-coupon securities in the STRIPS market, *reconstitute* (i.e., reassemble) the cash flows into a coupon bond, and sell the whole bond for more than the cost of the pieces. Both **bond stripping** and **bond reconstitution** offer opportunities for *arbitrage*—the exploitation of mispricing among two or more securities to clear a riskless economic profit. Any violation of the Law of One Price, that identical cash flow bundles must sell for identical prices, gives rise to arbitrage opportunities.

Now, we know how to value each stripped cash flow. We simply look up its appropriate discount rate in *The Wall Street Journal.* Because each coupon payment matures at a different time, we discount by using the yield appropriate to its particular maturity—this is the yield on a Treasury strip maturing at the time of that cash flow. We can illustrate with an example.

EXAMPLE 15.1   Valuing Coupon Bonds

Suppose the yields on stripped Treasuries are as given in Table 15.1, and we wish to value a 10% coupon bond with a maturity of 3 years. For simplicity, assume the bond makes its payments annually. Then the first cash flow, the $100 coupon paid at the end of the first year, is discounted at 5%; the second cash flow, the $100 coupon at the end of the second year, is discounted at 6%; and the final cash flow consisting of the final coupon plus par value, or $1,100, is discounted at 7%. The value of the coupon bond is therefore

$$\frac{100}{1.05} + \frac{100}{1.06^2} + \frac{1100}{1.07^3} = 95.238 + 89.000 + 897.928 = \$1,082.17$$

Calculate the yield to maturity of the coupon bond in Example 15.1, and you may be surprised. Its yield to maturity is 6.88%; so while its maturity matches that of the 3-year zero in Table 15.1, its yield is a bit lower.[1] This reflects the fact that the 3-year coupon bond may usefully be thought of as a *portfolio* of three implicit zero-coupon bonds, one corresponding to each cash flow. The yield on the coupon bond is then an amalgam of the yields on each of the three components of the "portfolio." Think about what this means: If their coupon rates differ, bonds of the same maturity generally will not have the same yield to maturity.

What then do we mean by "the" yield curve? In fact, in practice, traders refer to several yield curves. The **pure yield curve** refers to the curve for stripped, or zero-coupon,

[1] Remember that the yield to maturity of a coupon bond is the *single* interest rate at which the present value of cash flows equals market price. To calculate the yield to maturity on this bond on your calculator or spreadsheet, set $n = 3$; price $= 1,082.17$; future value $= 1,000$; payment $= 100$. Then compute the interest rate.

Treasuries. In contrast, the **on-the-run yield curve** refers to the plot of yield as a function of maturity for recently issued coupon bonds selling at or near par value. As we've just seen, there may be significant differences in these two curves. The yield curves published in the financial press, for example, in Figure 15.1, are typically on-the-run curves. On-the-run Treasuries have the greatest liquidity, so traders have keen interest in their yield curve.

CONCEPT CHECK 1	Calculate the price and yield to maturity of a 3-year bond with a coupon rate of 4% making annual coupon payments. Does its yield match that of either the 3-year zero or the 10% coupon bond considered in Example 15.1? Why is the yield spread between the 4% bond and the zero smaller than the yield spread between the 10% bond and the zero?

15.2 THE YIELD CURVE AND FUTURE INTEREST RATES

We've told you what the yield curve is, but we haven't yet had much to say about where it comes from. For example, why is the curve sometimes upward-sloping and other times downward-sloping? How do expectations for the evolution of interest rates affect the shape of today's yield curve?

These questions do not have simple answers, so we will begin with an admittedly idealized framework, and then extend the discussion to more realistic settings. To start, consider a world with no uncertainty, specifically, one in which all investors already know the path of future interest rates.

The Yield Curve under Certainty

If interest rates are certain, what should we make of the fact that the yield on the 2-year zero coupon bond in Table 15.1 is greater than that on the 1-year zero? It can't be that one bond is expected to provide a higher rate of return than the other. This would not be possible in a certain world—with no risk, all bonds (in fact, all securities!) must offer identical returns, or investors will bid up the price of the high-return bond until its rate of return is no longer superior to that of other bonds.

Instead, the upward-sloping yield curve is evidence that short-term rates are going to be higher next year than they are now. To see why, consider two 2-year bond strategies. The first strategy entails buying the 2-year zero offering a 2-year yield to maturity of $y_2 = 6\%$, and holding it until maturity. The zero with face value $1,000 is purchased today for $\$1,000/1.06^2 = \$890$ and matures in 2 years to $1,000. The total 2-year growth factor for the investment is therefore $\$1,000/\$890 = 1.06^2 = 1.1236$.

Now consider an alternative 2-year strategy. Invest the same $890 in a 1-year zero-coupon bond with a yield to maturity of 5%. When that bond matures, reinvest the proceeds in another 1-year bond. Figure 15.2 illustrates these two strategies. The interest rate that 1-year bonds will offer next year is denoted as r_2.

Remember, both strategies must provide equal returns—neither entails any risk. Therefore, the proceeds after 2 years to either strategy must be equal:

$$\text{Buy and hold 2-year zero} = \text{Roll over 1-year bonds}$$
$$\$890 \times 1.06^2 = \$890 \times 1.05 \times (1 + r_2)$$

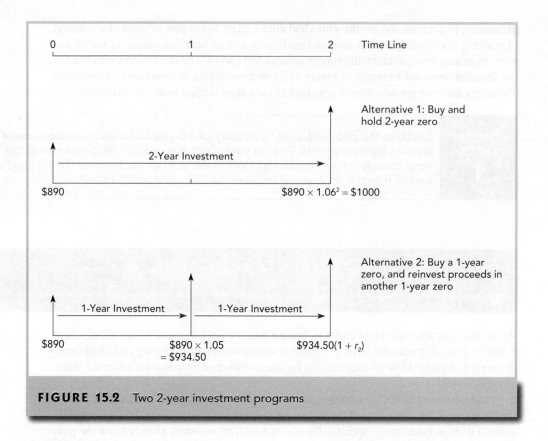

FIGURE 15.2   Two 2-year investment programs

We find next year's interest rate by solving $1 + r_2 = 1.06^2/1.05 = 1.0701$, or $r_2 = 7.01\%$. So while the 1-year bond offers a lower yield to maturity than the 2-year bond (5% versus 6%), we see that it has a compensating advantage: it allows you to roll over your funds into another short-term bond next year when rates will be higher. Next year's interest rate is higher than today's by just enough to make rolling over 1-year bonds equally attractive as investing in the 2-year bond.

To distinguish between yields on long-term bonds versus short-term rates that will be available in the future, practitioners use the following terminology. They call the yield to maturity on zero-coupon bonds the **spot rate,** meaning the rate that prevails *today* for a time period corresponding to the zero's maturity. In contrast, the **short rate** for a given time interval (e.g., 1 year) refers to the interest rate for that interval available at different points in time. In our example, the short rate today is 5%, and the short rate next year will be 7.01%.

Not surprisingly, the 2-year spot rate is an average of today's short rate and next year's short rate. But because of compounding, that average is a geometric one.[2] We see this by again equating the total return on the two competing 2-year strategies:

$$(1 + y_2)^2 = (1 + r_1) \times (1 + r_2)$$
$$1 + y_2 = [(1 + r_1) \times (1 + r_2)]^{1/2}$$

(15.1)

---

[2] In an arithmetic average, we add n numbers and divide by n. In a geometric average, we multiply n numbers and take the nth root.

Equation 15.1 begins to tell us why the yield curve might take on different shapes at different times. When next year's short rate, r_2, is greater than this year's short rate, r_1, the average of the two rates is higher than today's rate, so $y_2 > r_1$ and the yield curve slopes upward. If next year's short rate were less than r_1, the yield curve would slope downward. Thus, at least in part, the yield curve reflects the market's assessments of coming interest rates. The following example uses a similar analysis to find the short rate that will prevail in year 3.

EXAMPLE 15.2 Finding a Future Short Rate

Now we compare two 3-year strategies. One is to buy a 3-year zero, with a yield to maturity from Table 15.1 of 7%, and hold it until maturity. The other is to buy a 2-year zero yielding 6%, and roll the proceeds into a 1-year bond in year 3, at the short rate r_3. The growth factor for the invested funds under each policy will be:

$$\text{Buy and hold 3-year zero} = \text{Buy 2-year zero; roll proceeds into 1-year bond}$$
$$(1 + y_3)^3 = (1 + y_2)^2 \times (1 + r_3)$$
$$1.07^3 = 1.06^2 \times (1 + r_3)$$

which implies that $r_3 = 1.07^3/1.06^2 - 1 = .09025 = 9.025\%$. Again, notice that the yield on the 3-year bond reflects a geometric average of the discount factors for the next 3 years:

$$1 + y_3 = [(1 + r_1) \times (1 + r_2) \times (1 + r_3)]^{1/3}$$
$$1.07 = [1.05 \times 1.0701 \times 1.09025]^{1/3}$$

We conclude that the yield or spot rate on a long-term bond reflects the path of short rates anticipated by the market over the life of the bond.

Figure 15.3 summarizes the results of our analysis and emphasizes the difference between short rates and spot rates. The top line presents the short rates for each year. The lower lines present spot rates—or, equivalently, yields to maturity on zero-coupon bonds for different holding periods—extending from the present to each relevant maturity date.

CONCEPT CHECK 2	Use Table 15.1 to find the short rate that will prevail in the fourth year. Confirm that the yield on the 4-year zero is a geometric average of the short rates in the next 4 years.

Holding-Period Returns

We've argued that the multiyear cumulative returns on all of our competing bonds ought to be equal. What about holding-period returns over shorter periods such as a year? You might think that bonds selling at higher yields to maturity will offer higher 1-year returns, but this is not the case. In fact, once you stop to think about it, it's clear that this *cannot* be true. In a world of certainty, all bonds must offer identical returns, or investors will flock to the higher-return securities, bidding up their prices, and reducing their returns. We can illustrate by using the bonds in Table 15.1.

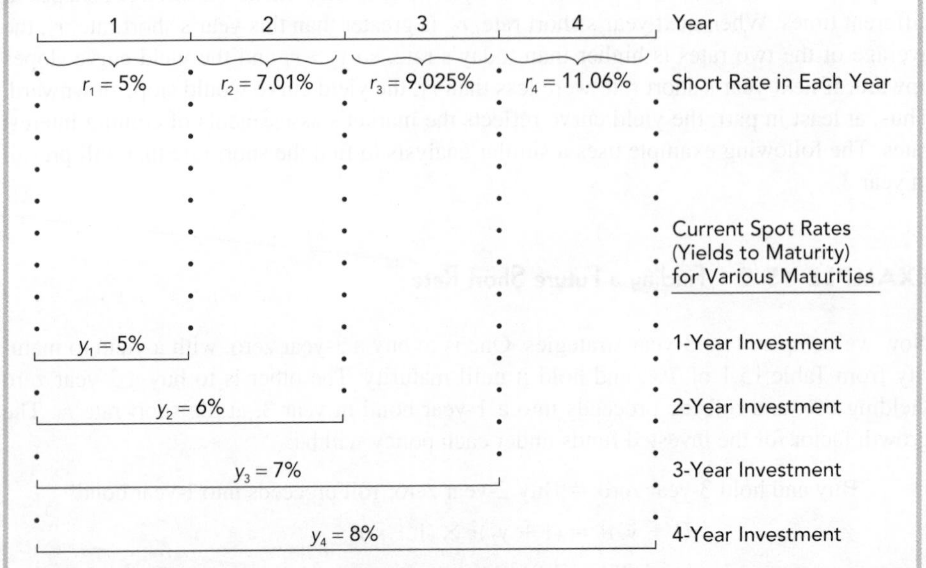

FIGURE 15.3 Short rates versus spot rates

EXAMPLE 15.3 Holding-Period Returns on Zero-Coupon Bonds

The 1-year bond in Table 15.1 can be bought today for $1,000/1.05 = $952.38 and will mature to its par value in 1 year. It pays no coupons, so total investment income is just its price appreciation, and its rate of return is ($1,000 − $952.38)/$952.38 = .05. The 2-year bond can be bought for $1,000/1.06² = $890.00. Next year, the bond will have a remaining maturity of 1 year and the 1-year interest rate will be 7.01%. Therefore, its price next year will be $1,000/1.0701 = $934.49, and its 1-year holding-period rate of return will be ($934.49 − $890.00)/$890.00 = .05, for an identical 5% rate of return.

CONCEPT CHECK 3

Show that the rate of return on the 3-year zero in Table 15.1 also will be 5%. Hint: next year, the bond will have a maturity of 2 years. Use the short rates derived in Figure 15.3 to compute the 2-year spot rate that will prevail a year from now.

Forward Rates

The following equation generalizes our approach to inferring a future short rate from the yield curve of zero-coupon bonds. It equates the total return on two n-year investment strategies: buying and holding an n-year zero-coupon bond versus buying an $(n − 1)$-year zero and rolling over the proceeds into a 1-year bond.

$$(1 + y_n)^n = (1 + y_{n-1})^{n-1} \times (1 + r_n) \tag{15.2}$$

where n denotes the period in question, and y_n is the yield to maturity of a zero-coupon bond with an n-period maturity. Given the observed yield curve, we can solve Equation 15.2 for the short rate in the last period:

$$(1 + r_n) = \frac{(1 + y_n)^n}{(1 + y_{n-1})^{n-1}} \tag{15.3}$$

Equation 15.3 has a simple interpretation. The numerator on the right-hand side is the total growth factor of an investment in an n-year zero held until maturity. Similarly, the denominator is the growth factor of an investment in an $(n-1)$-year zero. Because the former investment lasts for one more year than the latter, the difference in these growth factors must be the rate of return available in year n when the $(n-1)$-year zero can be rolled over into a 1-year investment.

Of course, when future interest rates are uncertain, as they are in reality, there is no meaning to inferring "the" future short rate. No one knows today what the future interest rate will be. At best, we can speculate as to its expected value and associated uncertainty. Nevertheless, it still is common to use Equation 15.3 to investigate the implications of the yield curve for future interest rates. Recognizing that future interest rates are uncertain, we call the interest rate that we infer in this matter the **forward interest rate** rather than the *future short rate,* because it need not be the interest rate that actually will prevail at the future date.

If the forward rate for period n is denoted f_n, we then define f_n by the equation

$$(1 + f_n) = \frac{(1 + y_n)^n}{(1 + y_{n-1})^{n-1}} \tag{15.4}$$

Equivalently, we may rewrite Equation 15.4 as

$$(1 + y_n)^n = (1 + y_{n-1})^{n-1}(1 + f_n) \tag{15.5}$$

In this formulation, the forward rate is *defined* as the "break-even" interest rate that equates the return on an n-period zero-coupon bond to that of an $(n-1)$-period zero-coupon bond rolled over into a 1-year bond in year n. The actual total returns on the two n-year strategies will be equal if the short interest rate in year n turns out to equal f_n.

EXAMPLE 15.4 Forward Rates

Suppose a bond trader uses the data presented in Table 15.1. The forward rate for year 4 would be computed as

$$1 + f_4 = \frac{(1 + y_4)^4}{(1 + y_3)^3} = \frac{1.08^4}{1.07^3} = 1.1106$$

Therefore, the forward rate is $f_4 = .1106$, or 11.06%.

We emphasize again that the interest rate that actually will prevail in the future need not equal the forward rate, which is calculated from today's data. Indeed, it is not even necessarily the case that the forward rate equals the expected value of the future short interest rate. This is an issue that we address in the next section. For now, however, we note that forward rates equal future short rates in the *special case* of interest rate certainty.

 CONCEPT CHECK 4 You've been exposed to many "rates" in the last few pages. Explain the differences between spot rates, short rates, and forward rates.

The spreadsheet below (available at **www.mhhe.com/bkm**) can be used to estimate prices and yields of coupon bonds and to calculate the forward rates for both single-year and multiyear periods. Spot yields are derived for the yield curve of bonds that are selling at their par value, also referred to as the current coupon or "on-the-run" bond yield curve.

The spot rates for each maturity date are used to calculate the present value of each period's cash flow. The sum of these cash flows is the price of the bond. Given its price, the bond's yield to maturity can then be computed. If you were to err and use the yield to maturity of the on-the-run bond to discount each of the bond's coupon payments, you could find a significantly different price. That difference is calculated in the worksheet.

	A	B	C	D	E	F	G	H
56		**Forward Rate Calculations**						
57								
58		**Spot Rate**	**1-yr for.**	**2-yr for.**	**3-yr for.**	**4-yr for.**	**5-yr for.**	**6-yr for.**
59	**Period**							
60	1	8.0000%	7.9792%	7.6770%	7.2723%	6.9709%	6.8849%	6.7441%
61	2	7.9896%	7.3757%	6.9205%	6.6369%	6.6131%	6.4988%	6.5520%
62	3	7.7846%	6.4673%	6.2695%	6.3600%	6.2807%	6.3880%	6.1505%
63	4	7.4537%	6.0720%	6.3065%	6.2186%	6.3682%	6.0872%	6.0442%
64	5	7.1760%	6.5414%	6.2920%	6.4671%	6.0910%	6.0387%	5.8579%
65	6	7.0699%	6.0432%	6.4299%	5.9413%	5.9134%	5.7217%	5.6224%
66	7	6.9227%	6.8181%	5.8904%	5.8701%	5.6414%	5.5384%	5.3969%
67	8	6.9096%	4.9707%	5.3993%	5.2521%	5.2209%	5.1149%	5.1988%

15.3   INTEREST RATE UNCERTAINTY AND FORWARD RATES

Let us turn now to the more difficult analysis of the term structure when future interest rates are uncertain. We have argued so far that, in a certain world, different investment strategies with common terminal dates must provide equal rates of return. For example, two consecutive 1-year investments in zeros would need to offer the same total return as an equal-sized investment in a 2-year zero. Therefore, under certainty,

$$(1 + r_1)(1 + r_2) = (1 + y_2)^2 \qquad \text{(15.6)}$$

What can we say when r_2 is not known today?

For example, suppose that today's rate is $r_1 = 5\%$ and that the *expected* short rate for the following year is $E(r_2) = 6\%$. If investors cared only about the expected value of the interest rate, then the yield to maturity on a 2-year zero would be determined by using the expected short rate in Equation 15.6:

$$(1 + y_2)^2 = (1 + r_1) \times [1 + E(r_2)] = 1.05 \times 1.06$$

The price of a 2-year zero would be $\$1,000/(1 + y_2)^2 = \$1,000/(1.05 \times 1.06) = \$898.47$.

But now consider a short-term investor who wishes to invest only for 1 year. She can purchase the 1-year zero for $\$1,000/1.05 = \$952.38$, and lock in a riskless 5% return because she knows that at the end of the year, the bond will be worth its maturity value of $\$1,000$. She also can purchase the 2-year zero. Its *expected* rate of return also is 5%: Next year, the bond will have 1 year to maturity, and we expect that the 1-year interest rate will be 6%, implying a price of $\$943.40$ and a holding-period return of 5%.

But the rate of return on the 2-year bond is risky. If next year's interest rate turns out to be above expectations, that is, greater than 6%, the bond price will be below $943.40; conversely if r_2 turns out to be less than 6%, the bond price will exceed $943.40. Why should this short-term investor buy the *risky* 2-year bond when its expected return is 5%, no better than that of the *risk-free* 1-year bond? Clearly, she would not hold the 2-year bond unless it offered a higher expected rate of return. This requires that the 2-year bond sell at a price lower than the $898.47 value we derived when we ignored risk.

EXAMPLE 15.5   Bond Prices and Forward Rates with Interest Rate Risk

Suppose that most investors have short-term horizons and therefore are willing to hold the 2-year bond only if its price falls to $881.83. At this price, the expected holding-period return on the 2-year bond is 7% (because 943.40/881.83 = 1.07). The risk premium of the 2-year bond, therefore, is 2%; it offers an expected rate of return of 7% versus the 5% risk-free return on the 1-year bond. At this risk premium, investors are willing to bear the price risk associated with interest rate uncertainty.

When bond prices reflect a risk premium, however, the forward rate, f_2, no longer equals the expected short rate, $E(r_2)$. Although we have assumed that $E(r_2) = 6\%$, it is easy to confirm that $f_2 = 8\%$. The yield to maturity on the 2-year zeros selling at $881.83 is 6.49%, and

$$1 + f_2 = \frac{(1 + y_2)^2}{1 + y_1} = \frac{1.0649^2}{1.05} = 1.08$$

The result in Example 15.5—that the forward rate exceeds the expected short rate—should not surprise us. We defined the forward rate as the interest rate that would need to prevail in the second year to make the long- and short-term investments equally attractive, *ignoring risk*. When we account for risk, it is clear that short-term investors will shy away from the long-term bond unless it offers an expected return greater than that of the 1-year bond. Another way of putting this is to say that investors will require a risk premium to hold the longer-term bond. The risk-averse investor would be willing to hold the long-term bond only if the expected value of the short rate is less than the break-even value, f_2, because the lower the expectation of r_2, the greater the anticipated return on the long-term bond.

Therefore, if most individuals are short-term investors, bonds must have prices that make f_2 greater than $E(r_2)$. The forward rate will embody a premium compared with the expected future short-interest rate. This **liquidity premium** compensates short-term investors for the uncertainty about the price at which they will be able to sell their long-term bonds at the end of the year.[3]

Perhaps surprisingly, we also can imagine scenarios in which long-term bonds can be perceived by investors to be *safer* than short-term bonds. To see how, we now consider a "long-term" investor, who wishes to invest for a full 2-year period. Suppose that the investor can purchase a $1,000 par value 2-year zero-coupon bond for $890 and lock in a guaranteed yield to maturity of $y_2 = 6\%$.

> **CONCEPT CHECK**
> **5**
>
> Suppose that the required liquidity premium for the short-term investor is 1%. What must $E(r_2)$ be if f_2 is 7%?

---

[3]*Liquidity* refers to the ability to sell an asset easily at a predictable price. Because long-term bonds have greater price risk, they are considered less liquid in this context and thus must offer a premium.

implying that $1 + y_2 = 1.055$. Similarly, if f_3 also equals 6%, then the yield on 3-year bonds would be determined by

$$(1 + y_3)^3 = (1 + r_1)(1 + f_2)(1 + f_3)$$
$$= 1.05 \times 1.06 \times 1.06 = 1.17978$$

implying that $1 + y_3 = 1.0567$. The plot of the yield curve in this situation would be given as in Figure 15.4, panel A. Such an upward-sloping yield curve is commonly observed in practice.

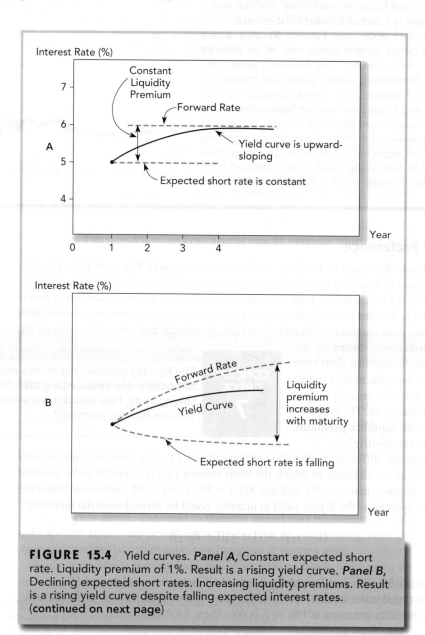

FIGURE 15.4 Yield curves. *Panel A,* Constant expected short rate. Liquidity premium of 1%. Result is a rising yield curve. *Panel B,* Declining expected short rates. Increasing liquidity premiums. Result is a rising yield curve despite falling expected interest rates. **(continued on next page)**

If interest rates are expected to change over time, then the liquidity premium may be overlaid on the path of expected spot rates to determine the forward interest rate. Then the yield to maturity for each date will be an average of the single-period forward rates. Several such possibilities for increasing and declining interest rates appear in Figure 15.4, panels B to D.

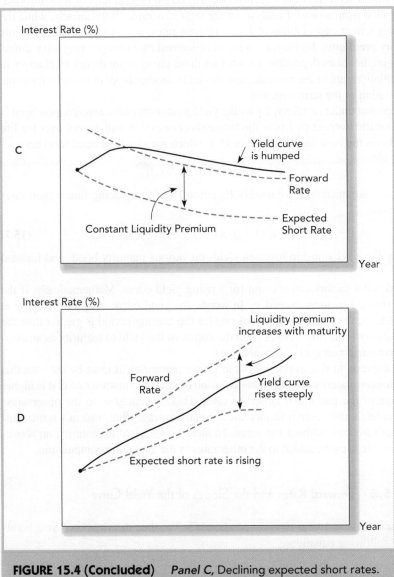

FIGURE 15.4 (Concluded) *Panel C*, Declining expected short rates. Constant liquidity premiums. Result is a hump-shaped yield curve. *Panel D*, Increasing expected short rates. Increasing liquidity premiums. Result is a sharply rising yield curve.

15.5   INTERPRETING THE TERM STRUCTURE

If the yield curve reflects expectations of future short rates, then it offers a potentially powerful tool for fixed-income investors. If we can use the term structure to infer the expectations of other investors in the economy, we can use those expectations as benchmarks for our own analysis. For example, if we are relatively more optimistic than other investors that interest rates will fall, we will be more willing to extend our portfolios into longer-term bonds. Therefore, in this section, we will take a careful look at what information can be gleaned from a careful analysis of the term structure. Unfortunately, while the yield curve does reflect expectations of future interest rates, it also reflects other factors such as liquidity premiums. Moreover, forecasts of interest rate changes may have different investment implications depending on whether those changes are driven by changes in the expected inflation rate or the real rate, and this adds another layer of complexity to the proper interpretation of the term structure.

We have seen that under certainty, 1 plus the yield to maturity on a zero-coupon bond is simply the geometric average of 1 plus the future short rates that will prevail over the life of the bond. This is the meaning of Equation 15.1, which we give in general form here:

$$1 + y_n = [(1 + r_1)(1 + r_2) \cdots (1 + r_n)]^{1/n}$$

When future rates are uncertain, we modify Equation 15.1 by replacing future short rates with forward rates:

$$1 + y_n = [(1 + r_1)(1 + f_2)(1 + f_3) \cdots (1 + f_n)]^{1/n} \tag{15.7}$$

Thus there is a direct relationship between yields on various maturity bonds and forward interest rates.

First, we ask what factors can account for a rising yield curve. Mathematically, if the yield curve is rising, f_{n+1} must exceed y_n. In words, the yield curve is upward-sloping at any maturity date, n, for which the forward rate for the coming period is greater than the yield at that maturity. This rule follows from the notion of the yield to maturity as an average (albeit a geometric average) of forward rates.

If the yield curve is to rise as one moves to longer maturities, it must be the case that extension to a longer maturity results in the inclusion of a "new" forward rate that is higher than the average of the previously observed rates. This is analogous to the observation that if a new student's test score is to increase the class average, that student's score must exceed the class's average without her score. To increase the yield to maturity, an above-average forward rate must be added to the other rates in the averaging computation.

EXAMPLE 15.6   Forward Rates and the Slopes of the Yield Curve

If the yield to maturity on 3-year zero-coupon bonds is 7%, then the yield on 4-year bonds will satisfy the following equation:

$$(1 + y_4)^4 = (1.07)^3(1 + f_4)$$

If $f_4 = .07$, then y_4 also will equal .07. (Confirm this!) If f_4 is greater than 7%, y_4 will exceed 7%, and the yield curve will slope upward. For example, if $f_4 = .08$, then $(1 + y_4)^4 = (1.07)^3(1.08) = 1.3230$, and $y_4 = .0725$.

Given that an upward-sloping yield curve is always associated with a forward rate higher than the spot, or current, yield to maturity, we ask next what can account for that higher forward rate. Unfortunately, there always are two possible

answers to this question. Recall that the forward rate can be related to the expected future short rate according to this equation:

$$f_n = E(r_n) + \text{Liquidity premium} \qquad (15.8)$$

where the liquidity premium might be necessary to induce investors to hold bonds of maturities that do not correspond to their preferred investment horizons.

By the way, the liquidity premium need not be positive, although that is the position generally taken by advocates of the liquidity premium hypothesis. We showed previously that if most investors have long-term horizons, the liquidity premium in principle could be negative.

In any case, Equation 15.8 shows that there are two reasons that the forward rate could be high. Either investors expect rising interest rates, meaning that $E(r_n)$ is high, or they require a large premium for holding longer-term bonds. Although it is tempting to infer from a rising yield curve that investors believe that interest rates will eventually increase, this is not a valid inference. Indeed, panel A in Figure 15.4 provides a simple counter-example to this line of reasoning. There, the short rate is expected to stay at 5% forever. Yet there is a constant 1% liquidity premium so that all forward rates are 6%. The result is that the yield curve continually rises, starting at a level of 5% for 1-year bonds, but eventually approaching 6% for long-term bonds as more and more forward rates at 6% are averaged into the yields to maturity.

Therefore, although it is true that expectations of increases in future interest rates can result in a rising yield curve, the converse is not true: A rising yield curve does not in and of itself imply expectations of higher future interest rates. This is the heart of the difficulty in drawing conclusions from the yield curve. The effects of possible liquidity premiums confound any simple attempt to extract expectations from the term structure. But estimating the market's expectations is a crucial task, because only by comparing your own expectations to those reflected in market prices can you determine whether you are relatively bullish or bearish on interest rates.

One very rough approach to deriving expected future spot rates is to assume that liquidity premiums are constant. An estimate of that premium can be subtracted from the forward rate to obtain the market's expected interest rate. For example, again making use of the example plotted in panel A of Figure 15.4, the researcher would estimate from historical data that a typical liquidity premium in this economy is 1%. After calculating the forward rate from the yield curve to be 6%, the expectation of the future spot rate would be determined to be 5%.

This approach has little to recommend it for two reasons. First, it is next to impossible to obtain precise estimates of a liquidity premium. The general approach to doing so would be to compare forward rates and eventually realized future short rates and to calculate the average difference between the two. However, the deviations between the two values can be quite large and unpredictable because of unanticipated economic events that affect the realized short rate. The data are too noisy to calculate a reliable estimate of the expected premium. Second, there is no reason to believe that the liquidity premium should be constant.

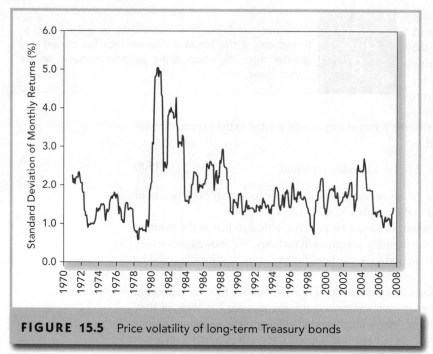

FIGURE 15.5   Price volatility of long-term Treasury bonds

Figure 15.5 shows the rate of return variability of prices of long-term Treasury bonds since 1971. Interest rate risk fluctuated dramatically during the period. So we might expect risk premiums on various maturity bonds to fluctuate, and empirical evidence suggests that liquidity premiums do in fact fluctuate over time.

Still, very steep yield curves are interpreted by many market professionals as warning signs of impending rate increases. In fact, the yield curve is a good predictor of the business cycle as a whole, because long-term rates tend to rise in anticipation of an expansion in economic activity. When the curve is steep, there is a far lower probability of a recession in the next year than when it is inverted or falling. For this reason, the yield curve is a component of the index of leading economic indicators.

The usually observed upward slope of the yield curve, especially for short maturities, is the empirical basis for the liquidity premium doctrine that long-term bonds offer a positive liquidity premium. In the face of this empirical regularity, perhaps it is valid to interpret a downward-sloping yield curve as evidence that interest rates are expected to decline. If **term premiums,** the spread between yields on long- and short-term bonds, generally are positive, then a downward-sloping yield curve might signal anticipated declines in rates, possibly associated with an impending recession.

Figure 15.6 presents a history of yields on 90-day Treasury bills and 10-year Treasury bonds. Yields on the longer-term bonds *generally* exceed those on the bills, meaning that the yield curve generally slopes upward. Moreover, the exceptions to this rule do seem to precede episodes of falling short rates, which, if anticipated, would induce a downward-sloping yield curve. For example, the figure shows that 1980–81 were years in which 90-day yields exceeded long-term yields. These years preceded both a drastic drop in the general level of rates and a steep recession.

Why might interest rates fall? There are two factors to consider: the real rate and the inflation premium. Recall that the nominal interest rate is composed of the real rate plus a factor to compensate for the effect of inflation:

$$1 + \text{Nominal rate} = (1 + \text{Real rate})(1 + \text{Inflation rate})$$

or, approximately,

$$\text{Nominal rate} \approx \text{Real rate} + \text{Inflation rate}$$

Therefore, an expected change in interest rates can be due to changes in either expected real rates or expected inflation rates. Usually, it is important to distinguish between these

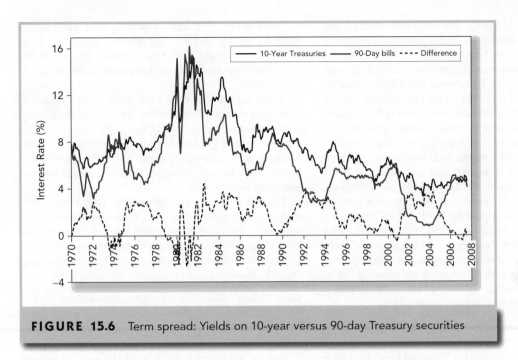

FIGURE 15.6 Term spread: Yields on 10-year versus 90-day Treasury securities

two possibilities because the economic environments associated with them may vary substantially. High real rates may indicate a rapidly expanding economy, high government budget deficits, and tight monetary policy. Although high inflation rates can arise out of a rapidly expanding economy, inflation also may be caused by rapid expansion of the money supply or supply-side shocks to the economy such as interruptions in oil supplies. These factors have very different implications for investments. Even if we conclude from an analysis of the yield curve that rates will fall, we need to analyze the macroeconomic factors that might cause such a decline.

For example, the nearby box notes that inversion of the yield curve in early 2007 was interpreted by many observers as a signal that a recession might be imminent. However, optimists at the time argued that even if the inversion presaged lower nominal interest rates, those lower rates might reflect declines in long-term inflation rates rather than declines in real interest rates due to a recession. Again, the term structure reflects several factors, including real rates, inflation premiums, and risk premiums. Backing out an exact message from the yield curve is always a delicate business.

15.6 FORWARD RATES AS FORWARD CONTRACTS

We have seen that forward rates may be derived from the yield curve, using Equation 15.5. In general, forward rates will not equal the eventually realized short rate, or even today's expectation of what that short rate will be. But there is still an important sense in which the forward rate is a market interest rate. Suppose that you wanted to arrange *now* to make a loan at some future date. You would agree today on the interest rate that will be charged, but the loan would not commence until some time in the future. How would the interest rate on

GRADING BONDS ON INVERTED CURVE

The bond market is having relationship issues that are getting harder to ignore. Normally, yields on long-term government bonds are higher than yields on short-term ones. Investors demand a bigger return for the risk that comes with holding an investment that takes longer to repay. The relationship has been upside-down since July, however, with yields on short-term U.S. Treasury bills exceeding those on long-term Treasury notes.

This unusual state of affairs—known as an inverted yield curve—has some economists wondering whether the bond market is signaling that the economy itself could turn upside down. Yield inversions, many analysts say, are harbingers of hard times. When bond investors see a recession coming, they tend to buy long-term Treasury securities for two reasons. First, they are safer than stocks. Second, they are appealing when inflation is low, and recessions tend to beat down inflation. The buying that comes with recession fears drives down a long-term bond's yield, sometimes below the prevailing yield on short-term Treasury securities.

The market, in effect, is betting that the Federal Reserve, which dictates short-term rates, will have to cut its overnight fund rate to boost the economy, and investors are pushing long-term rates down in anticipation.

Some economists doubt the yield curve's effectiveness as a recession-forecasting tool. They think long-term rates are exceptionally low right now for other reasons, including lower long-term expectations about inflation and growing demand for U.S. government bonds from foreign investors needing somewhere to park their money.

But those who think highly of the yield curve's predictive power have history on their side. Seven times between 1965 and 2005, yields on the 10-year note have dropped below those on the three-month Treasury bill for an extended span. In six of those instances, the U.S. economy went into recession soon after.

Source: Michael Hudson, "Grading Bonds on Inverted Curve," *The Wall Street Journal Online*, January 8, 2007, P. C1.

---

such a "forward loan" be determined? Perhaps not surprisingly, it would be the forward rate of interest for the period of the loan. Let's use an example to see how this might work.

EXAMPLE 15.7 Forward Interest Rate Contract

Suppose the price of 1-year maturity zero-coupon bonds with face value $1,000 is 952.38 and the price of 2-year zeros with $1,000 face value is $890. The yield to maturity on the 1-year bond is therefore 5%, while that on the 2-year bond is 6%. The forward rate for the second year is thus

$$f_2 = \frac{(1 + y_2)^2}{(1 + y_1)} - 1 = \frac{1.06^2}{1.05} - 1 = .0701, \text{ or } 7.01\%$$

Now consider the strategy laid out in the following table. In the first column we present data for this example, and in the last column we generalize. We denote by $B_0(T)$ today's price of a zero maturing at time T.

	Initial Cash Flow	In General
Buy a 1-year zero-coupon bond	−952.38	$-B_0(1)$
Sell 1.0701 2-year zeros	+890 × 1.0701 = 952.38	$+B_0(2) \times (1 + f_2)$
	0	0

The initial cash flow (at time 0) is zero. You pay $952.38, or in general $B_0(1)$, for a zero maturing in 1 year, and you receive $890, or in general $B_0(2)$, for each zero you sell maturing in 2 years. By selling 1.0701 of these bonds, you set your initial cash flow to zero.[4]

---

[4]Of course, in reality one cannot sell a fraction of a bond, but you can think of this part of the transaction as follows. If you sold one of these bonds, you would effectively be borrowing $890 for a 2-year period. Selling 1.0701 of these bonds simply means that you are borrowing $890 × 1.0701 = $952.38.

At time 1, the 1-year bond matures and you receive $1,000. At time 2, the 2-year maturity zero-coupon bonds that you sold mature, and you have to pay $1.0701 \times \$1,000 = \$1,070.10$. Your cash flow stream is shown in Figure 15.7, panel A. Notice that you have created a "synthetic" forward loan: You effectively *will* borrow $1,000 a year from now, and repay $1,070.10 a year later. The rate on this forward loan is therefore 7.01%, precisely equal to the forward rate for the second year.

In general, to construct the synthetic forward loan, you sell $(1 + f_2)$ 2-year zeros for every 1-year zero that you buy. This makes your initial cash flow zero because the prices of the 1- and 2-year zeros differ by the factor $(1 + f_2)$; notice that

$$B_0(1) = \frac{\$1,000}{(1 + y_1)} \quad \text{while} \quad B_0(2) = \frac{\$1,000}{(1 + y_2)^2} = \frac{\$1,000}{(1 + y_1)(1 + f_2)}$$

Therefore, when you sell $(1 + f_2)$ 2-year zeros you generate just enough cash to buy one 1-year zero. Both zeros mature to a face value of $1,000, so the difference between the cash inflow at time 1 and the cash outflow at time 2 is the same factor, $1 + f_2$, as illustrated in Figure 15.7, panel B. As a result, f_2 is the rate on the forward loan.

Obviously, you can construct a synthetic forward loan for periods beyond the second year, and you can construct such loans for multiple periods. Challenge Problems 14 and 15 at the end of the chapter lead you through some of these variants.

CONCEPT CHECK 9	Suppose that the price of 3-year zero-coupon bonds is $816.30. What is the forward rate for the third year? How would you construct a synthetic 1-year forward loan that commences at $t = 2$ and matures at $t = 3$?

A. Forward Rate = 7.01%

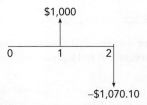

B. For a General Forward Rate. The short rates in the two periods are r_1 (which is observable today) and r_2 (which is not). The rate that can be locked in for a one-period-ahead loan is f_2.

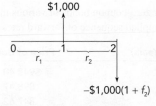

FIGURE 15.7 Engineering a synthetic forward loan

SUMMARY

1. The term structure of interest rates refers to the interest rates for various terms to maturity embodied in the prices of default-free zero-coupon bonds.

2. In a world of certainty all investments must provide equal total returns for any investment period. Short-term holding-period returns on all bonds would be equal in a risk-free economy, and all equal to the rate available on short-term bonds. Similarly, total returns from rolling over short-term bonds over longer periods would equal the total return available from long-maturity bonds.

3. The forward rate of interest is the break-even future interest rate that would equate the total return from a rollover strategy to that of a longer-term zero-coupon bond. It is defined by the equation

$$(1 + y_n)^n (1 + f_{n+1}) = (1 + y_{n+1})^{n+1}$$

where n is a given number of periods from today. This equation can be used to show that yields to maturity and forward rates are related by the equation

$$(1 + y_n)^n = (1 + r_1)(1 + f_2)(1 + f_3) \cdots (1 + f_n)$$

4. A common version of the expectations hypothesis holds that forward interest rates are unbiased estimates of expected future interest rates. However, there are good reasons to believe that forward rates differ from expected short rates because of a risk premium known as a *liquidity premium*. A positive liquidity premium can cause the yield curve to slope upward even if no increase in short rates is anticipated.

5. The existence of liquidity premiums makes it extremely difficult to infer expected future interest rates from the yield curve. Such an inference would be made easier if we could assume the liquidity premium remained reasonably stable over time. However, both empirical and theoretical considerations cast doubt on the constancy of that premium.

6. Forward rates are market interest rates in the important sense that commitments to forward (i.e., deferred) borrowing or lending arrangements can be made at these rates.

KEY TERMS

term structure of interest rates	on-the-run yield curve	expectations hypothesis
yield curve	spot rate	liquidity preference theory
bond stripping	short rate	liquidity premium
bond reconstitution	forward interest rate	term premiums
pure yield curve	liquidity premium	

PROBLEM SETS

Quiz

1. What is the relationship between forward rates and the market's expectation of future short rates? Explain in the context of both the expectations and liquidity preference theories of the term structure of interest rates.

2. Under the expectations hypothesis, if the yield curve is upward- sloping, the market must expect an increase in short-term interest rates. True/false/uncertain? Why?

3. Under the liquidity preference theory, if inflation is expected to be falling over the next few years, long-term interest rates will be higher than short-term rates. True/false/uncertain? Why?

Problems

4. The following is a list of prices for zero-coupon bonds of various maturities. Calculate the yields to maturity of each bond and the implied sequence of forward rates.

Maturity (Years)	Price of Bond
1	$943.40
2	898.47
3	847.62
4	792.16

5. Assuming that the expectations hypothesis is valid, compute the expected price path of the 4-year bond in Problem 4 as time passes. What is the rate of return of the bond in each year? Show that the expected return equals the forward rate for each year.

6. The term structure for zero-coupon bonds is currently:

Maturity (Years)	YTM (%)
1	4%
2	5
3	6

Next year at this time, *you* expect it to be:

Maturity (Years)	YTM (%)
1	5%
2	6
3	7

a. What do *you* expect the rate of return to be over the coming year on a 3-year zero-coupon bond?

b. Under the expectations theory, what yields to maturity does *the market* expect to observe on 1- and 2-year zeros over the coming year? Is the market's expectation of the return on the 3-year bond greater or less than yours?

7. The yield to maturity on 1-year zero-coupon bonds is currently 7%; the YTM on 2-year zeros is 8%. The Treasury plans to issue a 2-year maturity *coupon* bond, paying coupons once per year with a coupon rate of 9%. The face value of the bond is $100.

a. At what price will the bond sell?

b. What will the yield to maturity on the bond be?

c. If the expectations theory of the yield curve is correct, what is the market expectation of the price that the bond will sell for next year?

d. Recalculate your answer to (c) if you believe in the liquidity preference theory and you believe that the liquidity premium is 1%.

8. Below is a list of prices for zero-coupon bonds of various maturities.

Maturity	Price of $1,000 Par Bond (Zero-Coupon)
1 year	943.40
2	873.52
3	816.37

a. An 8.5% coupon $1,000 par bond pays an annual coupon and will mature in 3 years. What should the yield to maturity on the bond be?

b. If at the end of the first year the yield curve flattens out at 8%, what will be the 1-year holding-period return on the coupon bond?

9. Prices of zero-coupon bonds reveal the following pattern of forward rates:

Year	Forward Rate
1	5%
2	7
3	8

In addition to the zero-coupon bond, investors also may purchase a 3-year bond making annual payments of $60 with par value $1,000.

a. What is the price of the coupon bond?

b. What is the yield to maturity of the coupon bond?

Bond Characteristics

	Bond A	Bond B
Coupons	Annual	Annual
Maturity	3 years	3 years
Coupon rate	10%	6%
Yield to maturity	10.65%	10.75%
Price	98.40	88.34

Spot Interest Rates

Term (Years)	Spot Rates (Zero-Coupon)
1	5%
2	8
3	11

6. Sandra Kapple is a fixed-income portfolio manager who works with large institutional clients. Kapple is meeting with Maria VanHusen, consultant to the Star Hospital Pension Plan, to discuss management of the fund's approximately $100 million Treasury bond portfolio. The current U.S. Treasury yield curve is given in the following exhibit. VanHusen states, "Given the large differential between 2-and 10-year yields, the portfolio would be expected to experience a higher return over a 10-year horizon by buying 10-year Treasuries, rather than buying 2-year Treasuries and reinvesting the proceeds into 2-year T-bonds at each maturity date."

Maturity	Yield	Maturity	Yield
1 year	2.00%	6 years	4.15%
2	2.90	7	4.30
3	3.50	8	4.45
4	3.80	9	4.60
5	4.00	10	4.70

a. Indicate whether VanHusen's conclusion is correct, based on the pure expectations hypothesis.
b. VanHusen discusses with Kapple alternative theories of the term structure of interest rates and gives her the following information about the U.S. Treasury market:

Maturity (years)	2	3	4	5	6	7	8	9	10
Liquidity premium (%)	.55	.55	.65	.75	.90	1.10	1.20	1.50	1.60

Use this additional information and the liquidity preference theory to determine what the slope of the yield curve implies about the direction of future expected short-term interest rates.

7. A portfolio manager at Superior Trust Company is structuring a fixed-income portfolio to meet the objectives of a client. The portfolio manager compares coupon U.S. Treasuries with zero-coupon stripped U.S. Treasuries and observes a significant yield advantage for the stripped bonds:

Term	Coupon U.S. Treasuries	Zero-Coupon Stripped U.S. Treasuries
3 years	5.50%	5.80%
7	6.75	7.25
10	7.25	7.60
30	7.75	8.20

Briefly discuss why zero-coupon stripped U.S. Treasuries could yield more than coupon U.S. Treasuries with the same final maturity.

8. The shape of the U.S. Treasury yield curve appears to reflect two expected Federal Reserve reductions in the Federal Funds rate. The current short-term interest rate is 5%. The first reduction of approximately 50 basis points (bp) is expected 6 months from now and the second reduction of approximately 50 bp is expected 1 year from now. The current U.S. Treasury term premiums are 10 bp per year for each of the next 3 years (out through the 3-year benchmark).

However, the market also believes that the Federal Reserve reductions will be reversed in a single 100 bp increase in the Federal Funds rate 2½ years from now. You expect liquidity premiums to remain 10 bp per year for each of the next 3 years (out through the 3-year benchmark).

Describe or draw the shape of the Treasury yield curve out through the 3-year benchmark. Which term structure theory supports the shape of the U.S. Treasury yield curve you've described?

9. U.S. Treasuries represent a significant holding in many pension portfolios. You decide to analyze the yield curve for U.S. Treasury notes.

 a. Using the data in the table below, calculate the 5-year spot and forward rates assuming annual compounding. Show your calculations.

U.S. Treasury Note Yield Curve Data

Years to Maturity	Par Coupon Yield to Maturity	Calculated Spot Rates	Calculated Forward Rates
1	5.00	5.00	5.00
2	5.20	5.21	5.42
3	6.00	6.05	7.75
4	7.00	7.16	10.56
5	7.00	?	?

 b. Define and describe each of the following three concepts:

   i. Short rate
   ii. Spot rate
   iii. Forward rate

   Explain how these concepts are related.

 c. You are considering the purchase of a zero-coupon U.S. Treasury note with 4 years to maturity. Based on the above yield-curve analysis, calculate both the expected yield to maturity and the price for the security. Show your calculations.

10. The spot rates of interest for five U.S. Treasury Securities are shown in the following exhibit. Assume all securities pay interest annually.

Spot Rates of Interest

Term to Maturity	Spot Rate of Interest
1 year	13.00%
2	12.00
3	11.00
4	10.00
5	9.00

 a. Compute the 2-year implied forward rate for a deferred loan beginning in 3 years.
 b. Compute the price of a 5-year annual-pay Treasury security with a coupon rate of 9% by using the information in the exhibit.

E-Investments

The Yield Curve

Go to **www.smartmoney.com**. Access the *Living Yield Curve* (look for the *Economy and Bonds* tab), a moving picture of the yield curve. Is the yield curve usually upward- or downward-sloping? What about today's yield curve? How much does the slope of the curve vary? Which varies more: short-term or long-term rates? Can you explain why this might be the case?

SOLUTIONS TO CONCEPT CHECKS

1. The price of the 3-year bond paying a $40 coupon is

$$\frac{40}{1.05} + \frac{40}{1.06^2} + \frac{1040}{1.07^3} = 38.095 + 35.600 + 848.950 = \$922.65$$

At this price, the yield to maturity is 6.945% [$n = 3$; PV $= (-)922.65$; FV $= 1,000$; PMT $= 40$]. This bond's yield to maturity is closer to that of the 3-year zero-coupon bond than is the yield to maturity of the 10% coupon bond in Example 15.1. This makes sense: this bond's coupon rate is lower than that of the bond in Example 15.1. A greater fraction of its value is tied up in the final payment in the third year, and so it is not surprising that its yield is closer to that of a pure 3-year zero-coupon security.

2. We compare two investment strategies in a manner similar to Example 15.2:

Buy and hold 4-year zero = Buy 3-year zero; roll proceeds into 1-year bond

$$(1 + y_4)^4 = (1 + y_3)^3 \times (1 + r_4)$$
$$1.08^4 = 1.07^3 \times (1 + r_4)$$

which implies that $r_4 = 1.08^4/1.07^3 - 1 = .11056 = 11.056\%$. Now we confirm that the yield on the 4-year zero is a geometric average of the discount factors for the next 3 years:

$$1 + y_4 = [(1 + r_1) \times (1 + r_2) \times (1 + r_3) \times (1 + r_4)]^{1/4}$$
$$1.08 = [1.05 \times 1.0701 \times 1.09025 \times 1.11056]^{1/4}$$

3. The 3-year bond can be bought today for $1,000/1.07^3 = \$816.30$. Next year, it will have a remaining maturity of 2 years. The short rate in year 2 will be 7.01% and the short rate in year 3 will be 9.025%. Therefore, the bond's yield to maturity next year will be related to these short rates according to

$$(1 + y_2)^2 = 1.0701 \times 1.09025 = 1.1667$$

and its price next year will be $1,000/(1 + y_2)^2 = \$1,000/1.1667 = \$857.12$. The 1-year holding-period rate of return is therefore ($857.12 - $816.30)/$816.30 = .05, or 5%.

4. The *n*-period *spot* rate is the yield to maturity on a zero-coupon bond with a maturity of *n* periods. The *short* rate for period *n* is the *one-period* interest rate that will prevail in period *n*. Finally, the *forward* rate for period *n* is the short rate that would satisfy a "break-even condition" equating the total returns on two *n*-period investment strategies. The first strategy is an investment in an *n*-period zero-coupon bond; the second is an investment in an $n - 1$ period zero-coupon bond "rolled over" into an investment in a one-period zero. Spot rates and forward rates are observable today, but because interest rates evolve with uncertainty, future short rates are not. *In the special case* in which there is no uncertainty in future interest rates, the forward rate calculated from the yield curve would equal the short rate that will prevail in that period.

5. 7% − 1% = 6%.

6. The risk premium will be zero.

7. If issuers prefer to issue long-term bonds, they will be willing to accept higher expected interest costs on long bonds over short bonds. This willingness combines with investors' demands for higher rates on long-term bonds to reinforce the tendency toward a positive liquidity premium.

8. In general, from Equation 15.5, $(1 + y_n)^n = (1 + y_{n-1})^{n-1} \times (1 + f_n)$. In this case, $(1 + y_4)^4 = (1.07)^3 \times (1 + f_4)$. If $f_4 = .07$, then $(1 + y_4)^4 = (1.07)^4$ and $y_4 = .07$. If f_4 is greater than .07, then y_4 also will be greater, and conversely if f_4 is less than .07, then y_4 will be as well.

9. The 3-year yield to matuwrity is $\left(\dfrac{1,000}{816.30} \right)^{1/3} - 1 = .07 = 7.0\%$

   The forward rate for the third year is therefore

   $$f_3 = \frac{(1 + y_3)^3}{(1 + y_2)^2} - 1 = \frac{1.07^3}{1.06^2} - 1 = .0903 = 9.03\%$$

   (Alternatively, note that the ratio of the price of the 2-year zero to the price of the 3-year zero is $1 + f_3 = 1.0903$.) To construct the synthetic loan, buy one 2-year maturity zero, and sell 1.0903 3-year maturity zeros. Your initial cash flow is zero, your cash flow at time 2 is $+\$1,000$, and your cash flow at time 3 is $-\$1,090.30$, which corresponds to the cash flows on a 1-year forward loan commencing at time 2 with an interest rate of 9.03%.

CHAPTER SIXTEEN

MANAGING BOND PORTFOLIOS

IN THIS CHAPTER we turn to various strategies that bond portfolio managers can pursue, making a distinction between passive and active strategies. A *passive investment strategy* takes market prices of securities as set fairly. Rather than attempting to beat the market by exploiting superior information or insight, passive managers act to maintain an appropriate risk–return balance given market opportunities. One special case of passive management is an immunization strategy that attempts to insulate or immunize the portfolio from interest rate risk. In contrast, an *active investment strategy* attempts to achieve returns greater than those commensurate with the risk borne. In the context of bond management this style of management can take two forms. Active managers use either interest rate forecasts to predict movements in the entire bond market or some form of intramarket analysis to identify particular sectors of the market or particular bonds that are relatively mispriced.

Because interest rate risk is crucial to formulating both active and passive strategies, we begin our discussion with an analysis of the sensitivity of bond prices to interest rate fluctuations. This sensitivity is measured by the duration of the bond, and we devote considerable attention to what determines bond duration. We discuss several passive investment strategies, and show how duration-matching techniques can be used to immunize the holding-period return of a portfolio from interest rate risk. After examining the broad range of applications of the duration measure, we consider refinements in the way that interest rate sensitivity is measured, focusing on the concept of bond convexity. Duration is important in formulating active investment strategies as well, and we conclude the chapter with a discussion of active fixed-income strategies. These include policies based on interest rate forecasting as well as intramarket analysis that seeks to identify relatively attractive sectors or securities within the fixed-income market.

16.1 INTEREST RATE RISK

We have seen already that an inverse relationship exists between bond prices and yields, and we know that interest rates can fluctuate substantially. As interest rates rise and fall, bondholders experience capital losses and gains. These gains or losses make fixed-income investments risky, even if the coupon and principal payments are guaranteed, as in the case of Treasury obligations.

Why do bond prices respond to interest rate fluctuations? Remember that in a competitive market all securities must offer investors fair expected rates of return. If a bond is issued with an 8% coupon when competitive yields are 8%, then it will sell at par value. If the market rate rises to 9%, however, who would purchase an 8% coupon bond at par value? The bond price must fall until its expected return increases to the competitive level of 9%. Conversely, if the market rate falls to 7%, the 8% coupon on the bond is attractive compared to yields on alternative investments. In response, investors eager for that return would bid the bond price above its par value until the total rate of return falls to the market rate.

Interest Rate Sensitivity

The sensitivity of bond prices to changes in market interest rates is obviously of great concern to investors. To gain some insight into the determinants of interest rate risk, turn to Figure 16.1, which presents the percentage change in price corresponding to changes in yield to maturity for four bonds that differ according to coupon rate, initial yield to maturity, and time to maturity. All four bonds illustrate that bond prices decrease when yields rise, and that the price curve is convex, meaning that decreases in yields have bigger

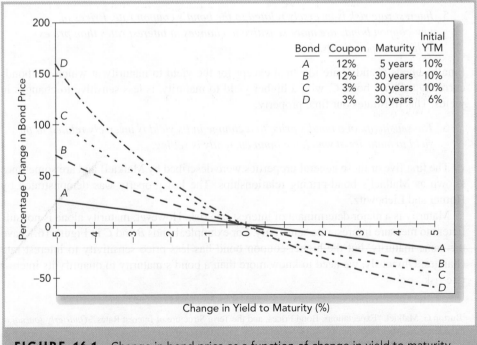

Bond	Coupon	Maturity	Initial YTM
A	12%	5 years	10%
B	12%	30 years	10%
C	3%	30 years	10%
D	3%	30 years	6%

FIGURE 16.1 Change in bond price as a function of change in yield to maturity

impacts on price than increases in yields of equal magnitude. We summarize these observations in the following two propositions:

1. *Bond prices and yields are inversely related: as yields increase, bond prices fall; as yields fall, bond prices rise.*
2. *An increase in a bond's yield to maturity results in a smaller price change than a decrease in yield of equal magnitude.*

Now compare the interest rate sensitivity of bonds *A* and *B*, which are identical except for maturity. Figure 16.1 shows that bond *B*, which has a longer maturity than bond *A*, exhibits greater sensitivity to interest rate changes. This illustrates another general property:

3. *Prices of long-term bonds tend to be more sensitive to interest rate changes than prices of short-term bonds.*

This is not surprising. If rates increase, for example, the bond is less valuable as its cash flows are discounted at a now-higher rate. The impact of the higher discount rate will be greater as that rate is applied to more-distant cash flows.

Notice that while bond *B* has six times the maturity of bond *A*, it has less than six times the interest rate sensitivity. Although interest rate sensitivity seems to increase with maturity, it does so less than proportionally as bond maturity increases. Therefore, our fourth property is that:

4. *The sensitivity of bond prices to changes in yields increases at a decreasing rate as maturity increases. In other words, interest rate risk is less than proportional to bond maturity.*

Bonds *B* and *C*, which are alike in all respects except for coupon rate, illustrate another point. The lower-coupon bond exhibits greater sensitivity to changes in interest rates. This turns out to be a general property of bond prices:

5. *Interest rate risk is inversely related to the bond's coupon rate. Prices of low-coupon bonds are more sensitive to changes in interest rates than prices of high-coupon bonds.*

Finally, bonds *C* and *D* are identical except for the yield to maturity at which the bonds currently sell. Yet bond *C*, with a higher yield to maturity, is less sensitive to changes in yields. This illustrates our final property:

6. *The sensitivity of a bond's price to a change in its yield is inversely related to the yield to maturity at which the bond currently is selling.*

The first five of these general properties were described by Malkiel[1] and are sometimes known as Malkiel's bond-pricing relationships. The last property was demonstrated by Homer and Liebowitz.[2]

Maturity is a major determinant of interest rate risk. However, maturity alone is not sufficient to measure interest rate sensitivity. For example, bonds *B* and *C* in Figure 16.1 have the same maturity, but the higher-coupon bond has less price sensitivity to interest rate changes. Obviously, we need to know more than a bond's maturity to quantify its interest rate risk.

---

[1]Burton G. Malkiel, "Expectations, Bond Prices, and the Term Structure of Interest Rates," *Quarterly Journal of Economics* 76 (May 1962), pp. 197–218.

[2]Sidney Homer and Martin L. Liebowitz, *Inside the Yield Book: New Tools for Bond Market Strategy* (Englewood Cliffs, NJ: Prentice Hall, 1972).

Yield to Maturity (APR)	T = 1 Year	T = 10 Years	T = 20 Years	TABLE 16.1
8%	1,000.00	1,000.00	1,000.00	Prices of 8% coupon bond
9%	990.64	934.96	907.99	(coupons paid semiannually)
Fall in price (%)*	0.94%	6.50%	9.20%	

*Equals value of bond at a 9% yield to maturity divided by value of bond at (the original) 8% yield, minus 1.

To see why bond characteristics such as coupon rate or yield to maturity affect interest rate sensitivity, let's start with a simple numerical example. Table 16.1 gives bond prices for 8% semiannual coupon bonds at different yields to maturity and times to maturity, T. [The interest rates are expressed as annual percentage rates (APRs), meaning that the true 6-month yield is doubled to obtain the stated annual yield.] The shortest-term bond falls in value by less than 1% when the interest rate increases from 8% to 9%. The 10-year bond falls by 6.5%, and the 20-year bond by over 9%.

Let us now look at a similar computation using a zero-coupon bond rather than the 8% coupon bond. The results are shown in Table 16.2. Notice that for each maturity, the price of the zero-coupon bond falls by a greater proportional amount than the price of the 8% coupon bond. Because we know that long-term bonds are more sensitive to interest rate movements than are short-term bonds, this observation suggests that in some sense a zero-coupon bond represents a longer-term bond than an equal-time-to-maturity coupon bond.

In fact, this insight about the effective maturity of a bond is a useful one that we can make mathematically precise. To start, note that the times to maturity of the two bonds in this example are not perfect measures of the long- or short-term nature of the bonds. The 20-year 8% bond makes many coupon payments, most of which come years before the bond's maturity date. Each of these payments may be considered to have its own "maturity date." In the previous chapter, we pointed out that it can be useful to view a coupon bond as a "portfolio" of coupon payments. The effective maturity of the bond is therefore some sort of average of the maturities of *all* the cash flows paid out by the bond. The zero-coupon bond, by contrast, makes only one payment at maturity. Its time to maturity is, therefore, a well-defined concept.

Higher-coupon-rate bonds have a higher fraction of value tied to coupons rather than final payment of par value, and so the "portfolio of coupons" is more heavily weighted toward the earlier, short-maturity payments, which gives it lower "effective maturity." This explains Malkiel's fifth rule, that price sensitivity falls with coupon rate.

Similar logic explains our sixth rule, that price sensitivity falls with yield to maturity. A higher yield reduces the present value of all of the bond's payments, but more so for more-distant payments. Therefore, at a higher yield, a higher fraction of the bond's value is due to its earlier payments, which have lower effective maturity and interest rate sensitivity. The overall sensitivity of the bond price to changes in yields is thus lower.

Yield to Maturity (APR)	T = 1 Year	T = 10 Years	T = 20 Years	TABLE 16.2
8%	924.56	456.39	208.29	Prices of zero-coupon bond
9%	915.73	414.64	171.93	(semiannual compounding)
Fall in price (%)*	0.96%	9.15%	17.46%	

*Equals value of bond at a 9% yield to maturity divided by value of bond at (the original) 8% yield, minus 1.

Duration

To deal with the ambiguity of the "maturity" of a bond making many payments, we need a measure of the average maturity of the bond's promised cash flows to serve as a useful summary statistic of the effective maturity of the bond. We would like also to use the measure as a guide to the sensitivity of a bond to interest rate changes, because we have noted that price sensitivity tends to increase with time to maturity.

Frederick Macaulay[3] termed the effective maturity concept the duration of the bond. **Macaulay's duration** equals the weighted average of the times to each coupon or principal payment made by the bond. The weight associated with each payment time clearly should be related to the "importance" of that payment to the value of the bond. In fact, the weight applied to each payment time is the proportion of the total value of the bond accounted for by that payment, that is, the present value of the payment divided by the bond price.

We define the weight, w_t, associated with the cash flow made at time t (denoted CF_t) as:

$$w_t = \frac{CF_t / (1 + y)^t}{\text{Bond price}}$$

where y is the bond's yield to maturity. The numerator on the right-hand side of this equation is the present value of the cash flow occurring at time t while the denominator is the value of all the payments forthcoming from the bond. These weights sum to 1.0 because the sum of the cash flows discounted at the yield to maturity equals the bond price.

Using these values to calculate the weighted average of the times until the receipt of each of the bond's payments, we obtain Macaulay's duration formula:

$$D = \sum_{t=1}^{T} t \times w_t \tag{16.1}$$

As an example of the application of Equation 16.1, we derive in Spreadsheet 16.1 the durations of an 8% coupon and zero-coupon bond, each with 2 years to maturity. We

	A	B	C	D	E	F	G
1			Time until				Column (C)
2			Payment		PV of CF (Discount rate =		times
3		Period	(Years)	Cash Flow	5% per period)	Weight*	Column (F)
4	**A.** 8% coupon bond	1	0.5	40	38.095	0.0395	0.0197
5		2	1.0	40	36.281	0.0376	0.0376
6		3	1.5	40	34.554	0.0358	0.0537
7		4	2.0	1040	855.611	0.8871	1.7741
8	Sum:				964.540	1.0000	1.8852
9							
10	**B.** Zero-coupon	1	0.5	0	0.000	0.0000	0.0000
11		2	1.0	0	0.000	0.0000	0.0000
12		3	1.5	0	0.000	0.0000	0.0000
13		4	2.0	1000	822.702	1.0000	2.0000
14	Sum:				822.702	1.0000	2.0000
15							
16	Semiannual int rate:	0.05					
17							
18	*Weight = Present value of each payment (column E) divided by the bond price.						

SPREADSHEET 16.1   Calculating the duration of two bonds   **eXcel**

Please visit us at
www.mhhe.com/bkm

Column sums subject to rounding error.

[3]Frederick Macaulay, *Some Theoretical Problems Suggested by the Movements of Interest Rates, Bond Yields, and Stock Prices in the United States since 1856* (New York: National Bureau of Economic Research, 1938).

	A	B	C	D	E	F	G
1			Time until		PV of CF		Column (C)
2			Payment		(Discount rate =		times
3		Period	(Years)	Cash Flow	5% per period)	Weight	Column (F)
4	A. 8% coupon bond	1	0.5	40	=D4/(1+$B$16)^B4	=E4/E$8	=F4*C4
5		2	1	40	=D5/(1+$B$16)^B5	=E5/E$8	=F5*C5
6		3	1.5	40	=D6/(1+$B$16)^B6	=E6/E$8	=F6*C6
7		4	2	1040	=D7/(1+$B$16)^B7	=E7/E$8	=F7*C7
8	Sum:				=SUM(E4:E7)	=SUM(F4:F7)	=SUM(G4:G7)
9							
10	B. Zero-coupon	1	0.5	0	=D10/(1+$B$16)^B10	=E10/E$14	=F10*C10
11		2	1	0	=D11/(1+$B$16)^B11	=E11/E$14	=F11*C11
12		3	1.5	0	=D12/(1+$B$16)^B12	=E12/E$14	=F12*C12
13		4	2	1000	=D13/(1+$B$16)^B13	=E13/E$14	=F13*C13
14	Sum:				=SUM(E10:E13)	=SUM(F10:F13)	=SUM(G10:G13)
15							
16	Semiannual int rate:	0.05					

SPREADSHEET 16.2

Spreadsheet formulas for calculating duration

eXcel

Please visit us at
www.mhhe.com/bkm

assume that the yield to maturity on each bond is 10%, or 5% per half-year. The present value of each payment is discounted at 5% per period for the number of (semiannual) periods shown in column B. The weight associated with each payment time (column F) is the present value of the payment for that period (column E) divided by the bond price (the sum of the present values in column E).

The numbers in column G are the products of time to payment and payment weight. Each of these products corresponds to one of the terms in Equation 16.1. According to that equation, we can calculate the duration of each bond by adding the numbers in column G.

The duration of the zero-coupon bond is exactly equal to its time to maturity, 2 years. This makes sense, because with only one payment, the average time until payment must be the bond's maturity. In contrast, the 2-year coupon bond has a shorter duration of 1.8852 years.

Spreadsheet 16.2 shows the spreadsheet formulas used to produce the entries in Spreadsheet 16.1. The inputs in the spreadsheet—specifying the cash flows the bond will pay—are given in columns B–D. In column E we calculate the present value of each cash flow using the assumed yield to maturity, in column F we calculate the weights for Equation 16.1, and in column G we compute the product of time to payment and payment weight. Each of these terms corresponds to one of the values that is summed in Equation 16.1. The sums computed in cells G8 and G14 are therefore the durations of each bond. Using the spreadsheet, you can easily answer several "what if" questions such as the one in Concept Check 1.

Duration is a key concept in fixed-income portfolio management for at least three reasons. First, as we have noted, it is a simple summary statistic of the effective average maturity of the portfolio. Second, it turns out

> **CONCEPT CHECK 1**
>
> Suppose the interest rate decreases to 9% as an annual percentage rate. What will happen to the prices and durations of the two bonds in Spreadsheet 16.1?

to be an essential tool in immunizing portfolios from interest rate risk. We explore this application in Section 16.3. Third, duration is a measure of the interest rate sensitivity of a portfolio, which we explore here.

duration

We have seen that long-term bonds are more sensitive to interest rate movements than are short-term bonds. The duration measure enables us to quantify this relationship. Specifically, it can be shown that when interest rates change, the proportional change in a bond's price can be related to the change in its yield to maturity, y, according to the rule

$$\frac{\Delta P}{P} = -D \times \left[\frac{\Delta(1 + y)}{1 + y} \right] \tag{16.2}$$

The proportional price change equals the proportional change in 1 plus the bond's yield times the bond's duration.

Practitioners commonly use Equation 16.2 in a slightly different form. They define **modified duration** as $D^* = D/(1 + y)$, note that $\Delta(1 + y) = \Delta y$, and rewrite Equation 16.2 as

$$\frac{\Delta P}{P} = -D^* \Delta y \tag{16.3}$$

interest rate

The percentage change in bond price is just the product of modified duration and the change in the bond's yield to maturity. Because the percentage change in the bond price is proportional to modified duration, modified duration is a natural measure of the bond's exposure to changes in interest rates. Actually, as we will see below, Equation 16.2, or equivalently 16.3, is only approximately valid for large changes in the bond's yield. The approximation becomes exact as one considers smaller, or localized, changes in yields.[4]

EXAMPLE 16.1   Duration

Consider the 2-year maturity, 8% coupon bond in Spreadsheet 16.1 making semiannual coupon payments and selling at a price of $964.540, for a yield to maturity of 10%. The duration of this bond is 1.8852 years. For comparison, we will also consider a zero-coupon bond with maturity *and* duration of 1.8852 years. As we found in Spreadsheet 16.1, because the coupon bond makes payments semiannually, it is best to treat one "period" as a half-year. So the duration of each bond is $1.8852 \times 2 = 3.7704$ (semiannual) periods, with a per period interest rate of 5%. The modified duration of each bond is therefore $3.7704/1.05 = 3.591$ periods.

Suppose the semiannual interest rate increases from 5% to 5.01%. According to Equation 16.3, the bond prices should fall by

$$\Delta P/P = -D^* \Delta y = -3.591 \times .01\% = -.03591\%$$

Now compute the price change of each bond directly. The coupon bond, which initially sells at $964.540, falls to $964.1942 when its yield increases to 5.01%, which is a

---

[4]Students of calculus will recognize that modified duration is proportional to the derivative of the bond's price with respect to changes in the bond's yield. For small changes in yield, Equation 16.3 can be restated as

$$D^* = -\frac{1}{P}\frac{dP}{dy}$$

As such, it gives a measure of the slope of the bond price curve only in the neighborhood of the current price. In fact, Equation 16.3′ can be derived by differentiating the following bond pricing equation with respect to y:

$$P = \sum_{t=1}^{T} \frac{CF_t}{(1 + y)^t}$$

where CF_t is the cash flow paid to the bondholder at date t; CF_t represents either a coupon payment before maturity or final coupon plus par value at the maturity date.

percentage decline of .0359%. The zero-coupon bond initially sells for $\$1,000/1.05^{3.7704} = 831.9704$. At the higher yield, it sells for $\$1,000/1.0501^{3.7704} = 831.6717$. This price also falls by .0359%.

We conclude that bonds with equal durations do in fact have equal interest rate sensitivity and that (at least for small changes in yields) the percentage price change is the modified duration times the change in yield.

CONCEPT CHECK 2	*a.* In Concept Check 1, you calculated the price and duration of a 2-year maturity, 8% coupon bond making semiannual coupon payments when the market interest rate is 9%. Now suppose the interest rate increases to 9.05%. Calculate the new value of the bond and the percentage change in the bond's price.
	b. Calculate the percentage change in the bond's price predicted by the duration formula in Equation 16.2 or 16.3. Compare this value to your answer for (*a*).

What Determines Duration?

Malkiel's bond price relations, which we laid out in the previous section, characterize the determinants of interest rate sensitivity. Duration allows us to quantify that sensitivity, which greatly enhances our ability to formulate investment strategies. For example, if we wish to speculate on interest rates, duration tells us how strong a bet we are making. Conversely, if we wish to remain "neutral" on rates, and simply match the interest rate sensitivity of a chosen bond-market index, duration allows us to measure that sensitivity and mimic it in our own portfolio. For these reasons, it is crucial to understand the determinants of duration. Therefore, in this section, we present several "rules" that summarize most of the important properties of duration. These rules are also illustrated in Figure 16.2, where durations of bonds of various coupon rates, yields to maturity, and times to maturity are plotted.

We have already established:

Rule 1 for Duration   The duration of a zero-coupon bond equals its time to maturity.

We have also seen that a coupon bond has a lower duration than a zero with equal maturity because coupons early in the bond's life lower the bond's weighted average time until payments. This illustrates another general property:

Rule 2 for Duration   Holding maturity constant, a bond's duration is lower when the coupon rate is higher.

This property corresponds to Malkiel's fifth relationship and is attributable to the impact of early coupon payments on the weighted-average maturity of a bond's payments. The higher these coupons, the higher the weights on the early payments and the lower is the weighted average maturity of the payments. In other words, a higher fraction of the total value of the bond is tied up in the (earlier) coupon payments whose values are relatively insensitive to yields rather than the (later and more yield-sensitive) repayment of par value. Compare the plots in Figure 16.2 of the durations of the 3% coupon and 15% coupon bonds, each with identical yields of 15%. The plot of the duration of the 15% coupon bond lies below the corresponding plot for the 3% coupon bond.

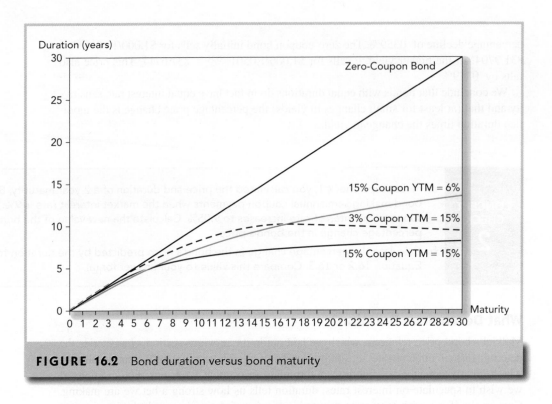

FIGURE 16.2   Bond duration versus bond maturity

Rule 3 for Duration   Holding the coupon rate constant, a bond's duration generally increases with its time to maturity. Duration always increases with maturity for bonds selling at par or at a premium to par.

This property of duration corresponds to Malkiel's third relationship, and it is fairly intuitive. What is surprising is that duration need not always increase with time to maturity. It turns out that for some deep-discount bonds (such as the 3% coupon bond in Figure 16.2), duration may fall with increases in maturity. However, for virtually all traded bonds it is safe to assume that duration increases with maturity.

Notice in Figure 16.2 that for the zero-coupon bond, maturity and duration are equal. However, for coupon bonds, duration increases by less than a year with a year's increase in maturity. The slope of the duration graph is less than 1.0.

Although long-maturity bonds generally will be high-duration bonds, duration is a better measure of the long-term nature of the bond because it also accounts for coupon payments. Time to maturity is an adequate statistic only when the bond pays no coupons; then, maturity and duration are equal.

Notice also in Figure 16.2 that the two 15% coupon bonds have different durations when they sell at different yields to maturity. The lower-yield bond has longer duration. This makes sense, because at lower yields the more distant payments made by the bond have relatively greater present values and account for a greater share of the bond's total value. Thus in the weighted-average calculation of duration the distant payments receive greater weights, which results in a higher duration measure. This establishes rule 4:

Rule 4 for Duration   Holding other factors constant, the duration of a coupon bond is higher when the bond's yield to maturity is lower.

As we noted above, the intuition for this property is that while a higher yield reduces the present value of all of the bond's payments, it reduces the value of more-distant payments by a greater proportional amount. Therefore, at higher yields a higher fraction of the total value of the bond lies in its earlier payments, thereby reducing effective maturity. Rule 4, which is the sixth bond-pricing relationship above, applies to coupon bonds. For zeros, of course, duration equals time to maturity, regardless of the yield to maturity.

Finally, we present a formula for the duration of a perpetuity. This rule is derived from and consistent with the formula for duration given in Equation 16.1 but may be easier to use for infinitely lived bonds.

Rule 5 for Duration   The duration of a level perpetuity is

$$\text{Duration of perpetuity} = \frac{1+y}{y} \qquad (16.4)$$

For example, at a 10% yield, the duration of a perpetuity that pays $100 once a year forever is 1.10/.10 = 11 years, but at an 8% yield it is 1.08/.08 = 13.5 years.

Equation 16.4 makes it obvious that maturity and duration can differ substantially. The maturity of the perpetuity is infinite, whereas the duration of the instrument at a 10%

CONCEPT CHECK **3**

Show that the duration of the perpetuity increases as the interest rate decreases in accordance with rule 4.

yield is only 11 years. The present-value-weighted cash flows early on in the life of the perpetuity dominate the computation of duration.

Notice from Figure 16.2 that as their maturities become ever longer, the durations of the two coupon bonds with yields of 15% both converge to the duration of the perpetuity with the same yield, 7.67 years.

The equations for the durations of coupon bonds are somewhat tedious and spreadsheets like Spreadsheet 16.1 are cumbersome to modify for different maturities and coupon rates. Moreover, they assume that the bond is at the beginning of a coupon payment period. Fortunately, spreadsheet programs such as Excel come with generalizations of these equations that can accommodate bonds between coupon payment dates. Spreadsheet 16.3 illustrates how to use Excel to compute duration. The spreadsheet uses many of the same conventions as the bond-pricing spreadsheets described in Chapter 14.

	A	B	C
1	**Inputs**		Formula in column B
2	Settlement date	1/1/2000	=DATE(2000,1,1)
3	Maturity date	1/1/2002	=DATE(2002,1,1)
4	Coupon rate	0.08	0.08
5	Yield to maturity	0.10	0.10
6	Coupons per year	2	2
7			
8	**Outputs**		
9	Macaulay duration	1.8852	=DURATION(B2,B3,B4,B5,B6)
10	Modified duration	1.7955	=MDURATION(B2,B3,B4,B5,B6)

SPREADSHEET 16.3

Using Excel functions to compute duration

e**X**cel

Please visit us at
www.mhhe.com/bkm

TABLE 16.3

Bond durations (yield to maturity = 8% APR; semiannual coupons)

Years to Maturity	Coupon Rates (per Year)			
	6%	8%	10%	12%
1	0.985	0.981	0.976	0.972
5	4.361	4.218	4.095	3.990
10	7.454	7.067	6.772	6.541
20	10.922	10.292	9.870	9.568
Infinite (perpetuity)	13.000	13.000	13.000	13.000

The settlement date (i.e., today's date) and maturity date are entered in cells B2 and B3 using Excel's date function, DATE(year, month, day). The coupon and maturity rates are entered as decimals in cells B4 and B5, and the payment periods per year are entered in cell B6. Macaulay and modified duration appear in cells B9 and B10. The spreadsheet confirms that the duration of the bond we looked at in Spreadsheet 16.1 is indeed 1.8852 years. For this 2-year maturity bond, we don't have a specific settlement date. We arbitrarily set the settlement date to January 1, 2000, and use a maturity date precisely 2 years later.

CONCEPT CHECK 4

Use Spreadsheet 16.3 to test some of the rules for duration presented a few pages ago. What happens to duration when you change the coupon rate of the bond? The yield to maturity? The maturity? What happens to duration if the bond pays its coupons annually rather than semiannually? Why intuitively is duration shorter with semiannual coupons?

Durations can vary widely among traded bonds. Table 16.3 presents durations computed from Spreadsheet 16.3 for several bonds all assumed to pay semiannual coupons and to yield 4% per half-year. Notice that duration decreases as coupon rates increase, and duration generally increases with time to maturity. According to Table 16.3 and Equation 16.2, if the interest rate were to increase from 8% to 8.1%, the 6% coupon 20-year bond would fall in value by about 1.05% (10.922 × .1%/1.04), whereas the 10% coupon 1-year bond would fall by only .976 × .1%/1.04 = .094%.[5] Notice also from Table 16.3 that duration is independent of coupon rate only for perpetuities.

16.2   CONVEXITY

As a measure of interest rate sensitivity, duration clearly is a key tool in fixed-income portfolio management. Yet the duration rule for the impact of interest rates on bond prices is only an approximation. Equation 16.2, or its equivalent, 16.3, which we repeat here, states that the percentage change in the value of a bond approximately equals the product of modified duration times the change in the bond's yield:

$$\frac{\Delta P}{P} = -D^* \Delta y$$

This equation asserts that the percentage price change is directly proportional to the change in the bond's yield. If this were *exactly* so, however, a graph of the percentage

[5]Notice that because the bonds pay their coupons semiannually, we calculate modified duration using the semiannual yield to maturity, 4%, in the denominator.

change in bond price as a function of the change in its yield would plot as a straight line, with slope equal to $-D^*$. Yet Figure 16.1 makes it clear that the relationship between bond prices and yields is *not* linear. The duration rule is a good approximation for small changes in bond yield, but it is less accurate for larger changes.

Figure 16.3 illustrates this point. Like Figure 16.1, the figure presents the percentage change in bond price in response to a change in the bond's yield to maturity. The curved line is the percentage price change for a 30-year maturity, 8% annual payment coupon bond, selling at an initial yield to maturity of 8%.

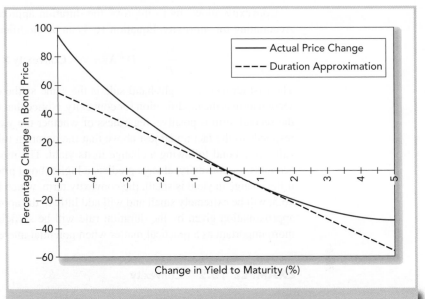

FIGURE 16.3 Bond price convexity: 30-year maturity, 8% coupon bond; initial yield to maturity = 8%

The straight line is the percentage price change predicted by the duration rule. The slope of the straight line is the modified duration of the bond at its initial yield to maturity. The modified duration of the bond at this yield is 11.26 years, so the straight line is a plot of $-D^*\Delta y = -11.26 \times \Delta y$. Notice that the two plots are tangent at the initial yield. Thus for small changes in the bond's yield to maturity, the duration rule is quite accurate. However, for larger changes in yield, there is progressively more "daylight" between the two plots, demonstrating that the duration rule becomes progressively less accurate.

Notice from Figure 16.3 that the duration approximation (the straight line) always understates the value of the bond; it underestimates the increase in bond price when the yield falls, and it overestimates the decline in price when the yield rises. This is due to the curvature of the true price-yield relationship. Curves with shapes such as that of the price-yield relationship are said to be *convex,* and the curvature of the price-yield curve is called the **convexity** of the bond.

We can quantify convexity as the rate of change of the slope of the price-yield curve, expressed as a fraction of the bond price.[6] As a practical rule, you can view bonds with higher convexity as exhibiting higher curvature in the price-yield relationship. The convexity of noncallable bonds such as that in Figure 16.3 is positive: The slope increases (i.e., becomes less negative) at higher yields.

[6]We pointed out in footnote 4 that Equation 16.2 for modified duration can be written as $dP/P = -D^*dy$. Thus $D^* = -1/P \times dP/dy$ is the slope of the price-yield curve expressed as a fraction of the bond price. Similarly, the convexity of a bond equals the *second* derivative (the rate of change of the slope) of the price-yield curve divided by bond price: Convexity $= 1/P \times d^2P/dy^2$. The formula for the convexity of a bond with a maturity of T years making annual coupon payments is

$$\text{Convexity} = \frac{1}{P \times (1 + y)^2} \sum_{t=1}^{T} \left[\frac{\text{CF}_t}{(1 + y)^t} (t^2 + t) \right]$$

where CF_t is the cash flow paid to the bondholder at date t; CF_t represents either a coupon payment before maturity or final coupon plus par value at the maturity date.

Convexity allows us to improve the duration approximation for bond price changes. Accounting for convexity, Equation 16.3 can be modified as follows:[7]

$$\frac{\Delta P}{P} = -D^* \Delta y + \tfrac{1}{2} \times \text{Convexity} \times (\Delta y)^2 \qquad (16.5)$$

The first term on the right-hand side is the same as the duration rule, Equation 16.3. The second term is the modification for convexity. Notice that for a bond with positive convexity, the second term is positive, regardless of whether the yield rises or falls. This insight corresponds to the fact noted just above that the duration rule always underestimates the new value of a bond following a change in its yield. The more accurate Equation 16.5, which accounts for convexity, always predicts a higher bond price than Equation 16.2. Of course, if the change in yield is small, the convexity term, which is multiplied by $(\Delta y)^2$ in Equation 16.5, will be extremely small and will add little to the approximation. In this case, the linear approximation given by the duration rule will be sufficiently accurate. Thus convexity is more important as a practical matter when potential interest rate changes are large.

EXAMPLE 16.2 Convexity

The bond in Figure 16.3 has a 30-year maturity, an 8% coupon, and sells at an initial yield to maturity of 8%. Because the coupon rate equals yield to maturity, the bond sells at par value, or $1,000. The modified duration of the bond at its initial yield is 11.26 years, and its convexity is 212.4, which can be verified using the formula in footnote 6. (You can find a spreadsheet to calculate the convexity of a 30-year bond at the Online Learning Center at **www.mhhe. com/bkm**.) If the bond's yield increases from 8% to 10%, the bond price will fall to $811.46, a decline of 18.85%. The duration rule, Equation 16.2, would predict a price decline of

$$\frac{\Delta P}{P} = -D^* \Delta y = -11.26 \times .02 = -.2252, \text{ or } -22.52\%$$

which is considerably more than the bond price actually falls. The duration-with-convexity rule, Equation 16.4, is considerably more accurate:

$$\frac{\Delta P}{P} = -D^* \Delta y + \tfrac{1}{2} \times \text{Convexity} \times (\Delta y)^2$$

$$= -11.26 \times .02 + \tfrac{1}{2} \times 212.4 \times (.02)^2 = -.1827, \text{ or } -18.27\%$$

which is far closer to the exact change in bond price. (Notice that when we use Equation 16.5, we express interest rates as decimals rather than percentages. The change in rates from 8% to 10% is represented as $\Delta y = .02$.)

Notice that if the change in yield were smaller, say, .1%, convexity would matter less. The price of the bond actually would fall to $988.85, a decline of 1.115%. Without accounting for convexity, we would predict a price decline of

$$\frac{\Delta P}{P} = -D^* \Delta y = -11.26 \times .001 = -.01126, \text{ or } -1.126\%$$

Accounting for convexity, we get almost the precisely correct answer:

$$\frac{\Delta P}{P} = -11.26 \times .001 + \tfrac{1}{2} \times 212.4 \times (.001)^2 = -.01115, \text{ or } -1.115\%$$

Nevertheless, the duration rule is quite accurate in this case, even without accounting for convexity.

---

[7]To use the convexity rule, you must express interest rates as decimals rather than percentages.

Why Do Investors Like Convexity?

Convexity is generally considered a desirable trait. Bonds with greater curvature gain more in price when yields fall than they lose when yields rise. For example, in Figure 16.4 bonds A and B have the same duration at the initial yield. The plots of their proportional price changes as a function of interest rate changes are tangent, meaning that their sensitivities to changes in yields at that point are equal. However, bond A is more convex than bond B. It enjoys greater price increases and smaller price decreases when interest rates fluctuate by larger amounts. If

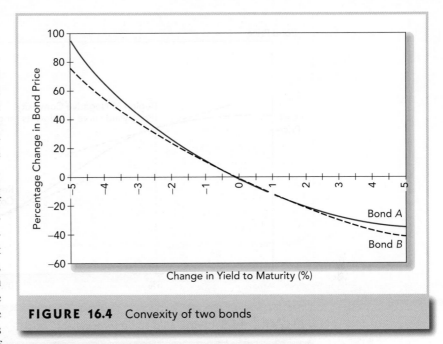

FIGURE 16.4   Convexity of two bonds

interest rates are volatile, this is an attractive asymmetry that increases the expected return on the bond, because bond A will benefit more from rate decreases and suffer less from rate increases. Of course, if convexity is desirable, it will not be available for free: investors will have to pay higher prices and accept lower yields to maturity on bonds with greater convexity.

Duration and Convexity of Callable Bonds

Look at Figure 16.5, which depicts the price-yield curve for a callable bond. When interest rates are high, the curve is convex, as it would be for a straight bond. For example, at an interest rate of 10%, the price-yield curve lies above its tangency line. But as rates fall, there is a ceiling on the possible price: The bond cannot be worth more than its call price. So as rates fall, we sometimes say that the bond is subject to price compression—its value is "compressed" to the call price. In this region, for example at an interest rate of 5%, the price-yield curve lies *below* its tangency line, and the curve is said to have *negative convexity.*[8]

Notice that in the region of negative convexity, the price-yield curve exhibits an *unattractive* asymmetry. Interest rate increases result in a larger price decline than the price gain corresponding to an interest rate decrease of equal magnitude. The asymmetry arises from the fact that the bond issuer has retained an option to call back the bond. If rates rise, the bondholder loses, as would be the case for a straight bond. But if rates fall, rather than reaping a large capital gain, the investor may have the bond called back from her. The bondholder is thus in a "heads I lose, tails I don't win" position. Of course, she was compensated for this unattractive situation when she purchased the bond. Callable bonds sell at lower initial prices (higher initial yields) than otherwise comparable straight bonds.

The effect of negative convexity is highlighted in Equation 16.5. When convexity is negative, the second term on the right-hand side is necessarily negative, meaning that bond

---

[8]If you've taken a calculus course, you will recognize that the curve is *concave* in this region. However, rather than saying that these bonds exhibit concavity, bond traders prefer the terminology "negative convexity."

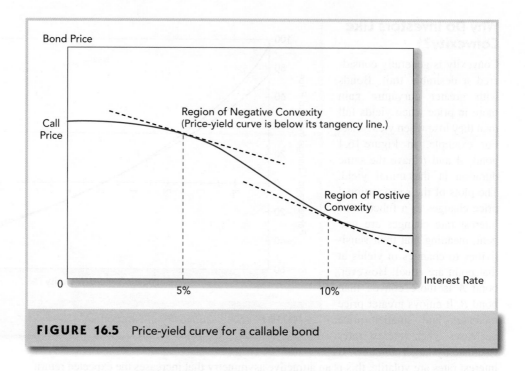

FIGURE 16.5 Price-yield curve for a callable bond

price performance will be worse than would be predicted by the duration approximation. However, callable bonds or, more generally, bonds with "embedded options," are difficult to analyze in terms of Macaulay's duration. This is because in the presence of such options, the future cash flows provided by the bonds are no longer known. If the bond may be called, for example, its cash flow stream may be terminated and its principal repaid earlier than was initially anticipated. Because cash flows are random, we can hardly take a weighted average of times until each future cash flow, as would be necessary to compute Macaulay's duration.

The convention on Wall Street is to compute the **effective duration** of bonds with embedded options. Effective duration cannot be computed with a simple formula such as 16.1 that requires known cash flows. Instead, more complex bond valuation approaches that account for the embedded options are used, and effective duration is *defined* as the proportional change in the bond price per unit change in market interest rates:

$$\text{Effective duration} = -\frac{\Delta P/P}{\Delta r} \qquad (16.6)$$

This equation *seems* merely like a slight manipulation of the modified duration formula 16.3. However, there are important differences. First, note that we do not compute effective duration relative to a change in the bond's own yield to maturity. (The denominator is Δr, not Δy.) This is because for bonds with embedded options, which may be called early, the yield to maturity is often not a relevant statistic. Instead, we calculate price change relative to a shift in the level of the term structure of interest rates. Second, the effective duration formula relies on a pricing methodology that accounts for embedded options. This means that the effective duration will be a function of variables that would not matter to conventional duration, for example, the volatility of interest rates. In contrast, modified or Macaulay duration can be computed directly from the promised bond cash flows and yield to maturity.

EXAMPLE 16.3 Effective Duration

Suppose that a callable bond with a call price of $1,050 is selling today for $980. If the yield curve shifts up by .5%, the bond price will fall to $930. If it shifts down by .5%, the bond price will rise to $1,010. To compute effective duration, we compute:

$$\Delta r = \text{Assumed increase in rates} - \text{Assumed decrease in rates}$$
$$= .5\% - (-.5\%) = 1\% = .01$$
$$\Delta P = \text{Price at .5\% increase in rates} - \text{Price at .5\% decrease in rates}$$
$$= \$930 - \$1,010 = -\$80$$

Then the effective duration of the bond is

$$\text{Effective duration} = -\frac{\Delta P/P}{\Delta r} = -\frac{-\$80 / \$980}{.01} = 8.16 \text{ years}$$

In other words, the bond price changes by 8.16% for a 1 percentage point swing in rates around current values.

CONCEPT CHECK 5 What are the differences between Macaulay duration, modified duration, and effective duration?

Duration and Convexity of Mortgage-Backed Securities

In practice, the biggest market for which call provisions are important is the market for mortgage-backed securities. In recent years, firms have been less apt to issue bonds with call provisions, and the number of outstanding callable corporate bonds has steadily declined. In contrast, the mortgage-backed market has enjoyed rapid growth over the last two decades. In 2007, the size of the mortgage-backed securities market ($3.8 trillion) was considerably larger than the *entire* corporate bond market ($3.1 trillion).

Lenders that originate mortgage loans commonly sell those loans to federal agencies such as the Federal National Mortgage Association (FNMA, or Fannie Mae) or the Federal Home Loan Mortgage Corporation (FHLMC, or Freddie Mac). The original borrowers (the homeowners) continue to make their monthly payments to their lenders, but the lenders pass these payments along to the agency that has purchased the loan. In turn, the agencies may combine many mortgages into a pool called a mortgage-backed security, and then sell that security in the fixed-income market. These securities are called *pass-throughs* because the cash flows from the borrowers are first passed through to the agency (Fannie Mae or Freddie Mac) and then passed through again to the ultimate purchaser of the mortgage-backed security. Fannie and Freddie together hold the lion's share of the market for so-called conforming loans that satisfy size limitations and underwriting standards, but there is also a very large market among private firms such as Citigroup for nonconforming mortgages. These are either "jumbo" loans that are too large to meet guidelines for agency securitization or subprime loans that do not meet agency standards for the creditworthiness of the borrower.

As an example, suppose that ten 30-year mortgages, each with principal value of $100,000, are grouped together into a million-dollar pool. If the mortgage rate is 8%, then the monthly payment on each loan would be $733.76. (The interest component of the first payment is $.08 \times 1/12 \times \$100{,}000 = \$666.67$; the remaining $67.09 is "amortization," or scheduled repayment of principal. In later periods, with a lower principal balance, less of the monthly payments goes to interest and more to amortization.) The owner of the mortgage-backed security would receive $7,337.60, the total payment from the 10 mortgages in the pool.[9]

But now recall that the homeowner has the right to prepay the loan at any time. For example, if mortgage rates go down, the homeowner may very well decide to take a new loan at a lower rate, using the proceeds to pay off the original loan. The right to prepay the loan is, of course, precisely analogous to the right to refund a callable bond. The call price for the mortgage is simply the remaining principal balance on the loan. Therefore, the mortgage-backed security is best viewed as a portfolio of *callable* amortizing loans.

Mortgage-backs are subject to the same negative convexity as other callable bonds. When rates fall and homeowners prepay their mortgages, the repayment of principal is passed through to the investors. Rather than enjoying capital gains on their investment, they simply receive the outstanding principal balance on the loan. Therefore, the value of the mortgage-backed security as a function of interest rates, presented in Figure 16.6, looks much like the plot for a callable bond.

There are some differences between the mortgage-backs and callable corporate bonds, however. For example, you will commonly find mortgage-backs selling for more than their principal balance. This is because homeowners do not refinance their loans as soon as interest rates drop. Some homeowners do not want to incur the costs or hassles of refinancing unless the benefit is great enough, others may decide not to refinance if they are planning to move shortly, and others may simply be unsophisticated in making the refinancing decision. Therefore, while the mortgage-backed security exhibits negative convexity at low rates, its implicit call price (the principal balance on the loan) is not a firm ceiling on its value.

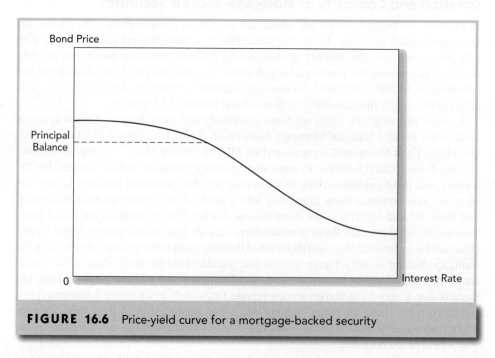

FIGURE 16.6   Price-yield curve for a mortgage-backed security

---

[9]Actually, the financial institution that continues to service the loan and the pass-through agency that guarantees the loan each retain a portion of the monthly payment as a charge for their services. Thus, the monthly payment received by the investor is a bit less than the amount paid by the borrower.

Mortgage-backed securities are among the most successful examples of financial engineering, the repackaging of cash flows from one security (in this case, the original mortgage) into new securities (the mortgage pass-through security). They have become the model for many other asset-backed securities and illustrate other important aspects of this market. For example, *credit enhancement* is a common feature of the asset-backed market. In the mortgage market, the credit risk of the underlying borrower is enhanced by the guarantee of Freddie or Fannie that any mortgage default will be treated from the point of view of the investor as if the mortgage had been prepaid. Rather than resulting in a loss of principal, the loan is in effect treated as if it has been paid off, with the principal balance passed through to the investor. But remember that while the securities are thereby guaranteed in terms of payment of interest and principal, their rates of return are not guaranteed. They still are subject to the interest rate risk that is the topic of this chapter.

Simple mortgage-backs have also given rise to a rich set of mortgage-backed derivatives that can be used to help investors manage interest rate risk. For example, a CMO (collateralized mortgage obligation) further redirects the cash flow stream of the mortgage-backed security to several classes of derivative securities called "tranches." These tranches may be designed to allocate interest rate risk to investors most willing to bear that risk.[10]

The following table is an example of a very simple CMO structure. The underlying mortgage pool is divided into three tranches, each with a different effective maturity and therefore interest rate risk exposure. Suppose the original pool has $10 million of 15-year-maturity mortgages, each with an interest rate of 10.5%, and is subdivided into three tranches as follows:

Tranche A = $4 million principal	"Short-pay" tranche
Tranche B = $3 million principal	"Intermediate-pay" tranche
Tranche C = $3 million principal	"Long-pay" tranche

Suppose further that in each year, 8% of outstanding loans in the pool prepay. Then total cash flows in each year to the whole mortgage pool are given in panel A of Figure 16.7. Total payments shrink by 8% each year, as that percentage of the loans in the original pool is paid off. The light portions of each bar represent interest payments, while the dark colored portions are principal payments, comprising both loan amortization and prepayments.

In each period, each tranche receives the interest owed it based on the promised coupon rate and outstanding principal balance. But initially, *all* principal payments, both prepayments and amortization, go to tranche A (Figure 16.7, panel B). Notice from panels C and D that tranches B and C receive only interest payments until tranche A is retired. Once tranche A is fully paid off, all principal payments go to tranche B. Finally, when B is retired, all principal payments go to C. This makes tranche A a "short-pay" class, with the lowest effective duration, while tranche C is the longest-pay tranche. This is therefore a relatively simple way to allocate interest rate risk among tranches.

Many variations on the theme are possible and employed in practice. Different tranches may receive different coupon rates. Some tranches may be given preferential treatment in terms of uncertainty over mortgage prepayment speeds. Complex formulas may be used to dictate the cash flows allocated to each tranche. In essence, the mortgage pool is treated as a source of cash flows that can be reallocated to different investors in accordance with the tastes of different investors.

---

[10]In Chapter 14, we examined how collateralized debt obligations or CDOs used tranche structures to reallocate *credit risk* among different classes. There is at most minimal credit risk in agency-guaranteed mortgage-backed securities; in the CMO market, tranche structure is used to allocate *interest rate risk* across classes.

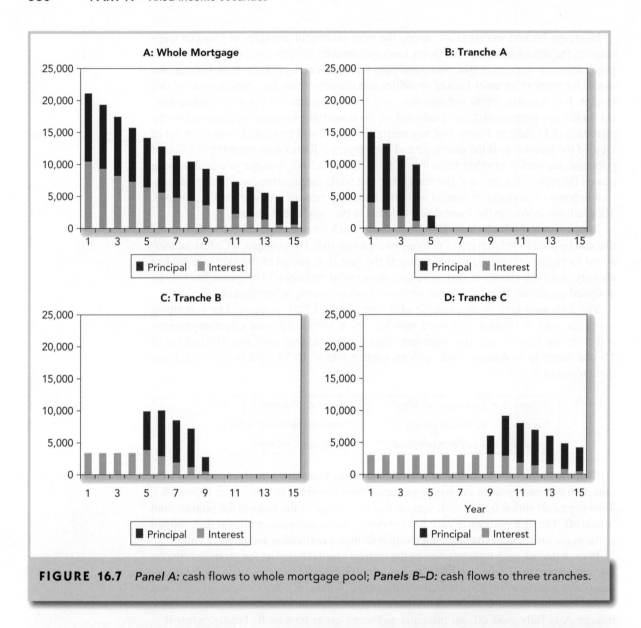

FIGURE 16.7 *Panel A:* cash flows to whole mortgage pool; *Panels B–D:* cash flows to three tranches.

16.3 PASSIVE BOND MANAGEMENT

Passive managers take bond prices as fairly set and seek to control only the risk of their fixed-income portfolio. Two broad classes of passive management are pursued in the fixed-income market. The first is an indexing strategy that attempts to replicate the performance of a given bond index. The second broad class of passive strategies is known as immunization techniques; they are used widely by financial institutions such as insurance companies and pension funds, and are designed to shield the overall financial status of the institution from exposure to interest rate fluctuations.

Although indexing and immunization strategies are alike in that they accept market prices as correctly set, they are very different in terms of risk exposure. A bond-index portfolio will have the same risk–reward profile as the bond market index to which it is tied. In contrast, immunization strategies seek to establish a virtually zero-risk profile, in which interest rate movements have no impact on the value of the firm. We discuss both types of strategies in this section.

Bond-Index Funds

In principle, bond market indexing is similar to stock market indexing. The idea is to create a portfolio that mirrors the composition of an index that measures the broad market. In the U.S. equity market, for example, the S&P 500 is the most commonly used index for stock-index funds, and these funds simply buy shares of each firm in the S&P 500 in proportion to the market value of outstanding equity. A similar strategy is used for bond-index funds, but as we shall see shortly, several modifications are required because of difficulties unique to the bond market and its indexes.

Three major indexes of the broad bond market are the Lehman Aggregate Bond Index, the Salomon Smith Barney Broad Investment Grade (BIG) Index, and the Merrill Lynch U.S. Broad Market Index. All are market-value-weighted indexes of total returns. All three include government, corporate, mortgage-backed, and Yankee bonds in their universes. (Yankee bonds are dollar-denominated, SEC-registered bonds of foreign issuers sold in the United States.) All three indexes include only bonds with maturities greater than 1 year. As time passes, and the maturity of a bond falls below 1 year, the bond is dropped from the index.

The first problem that arises in the formation of an indexed bond portfolio arises from the fact that these indexes include more than 5,000 securities, making it quite difficult to purchase each security in the index in proportion to its market value. Moreover, many bonds are very thinly traded, meaning that identifying their owners and purchasing the securities at a fair market price can be difficult.

Bond-index funds also face more difficult rebalancing problems than do stock-index funds. Bonds are continually dropped from the index as their maturities fall below 1 year. Moreover, as new bonds are issued, they are added to the index. Therefore, in contrast to equity indexes, the securities used to compute bond indexes constantly change. As they do, the manager must update or rebalance the portfolio to ensure a close match between the composition of the portfolio and the bonds included in the index. The fact that bonds generate considerable interest income that must be reinvested further complicates the job of the index fund manager.

In practice, it is deemed infeasible to precisely replicate the broad bond indexes. Instead, a stratified sampling or *cellular* approach is often pursued. Figure 16.8 illustrates the idea behind the cellular approach. First, the bond market is stratified into several subclasses. Figure 16.8 shows a simple two-way breakdown by maturity and issuer; in practice, however, criteria such as the bond's coupon rate or the credit risk of the issuer also would be used to form cells. Bonds falling within each cell are then considered reasonably homogeneous. Next, the percentages of the entire universe (i.e., the bonds included in the index that is to be matched) falling within each cell are computed and reported, as we have done for a few cells in Figure 16.8. Finally, the portfolio manager establishes a bond portfolio with representation for each cell that matches the representation of that cell in the bond universe. In this way, the characteristics of the portfolio in terms of maturity, coupon rate, credit risk, industrial representation, and so on, will match the characteristics of the index, and the performance of the portfolio likewise should match the index.

Immunization

In contrast to indexing strategies, many institutions try to insulate their portfolios from interest rate risk altogether. Generally, there are two ways of viewing this risk, depending

Sector / Term to Maturity	Treasury	Agency	Mortgage-backed	Industrial	Finance	Utility	Yankee
<1 year	12.1%						
1–3 years	5.4%						
3–5 years			4.1%				
5–7 years							
7–10 years		0.1%					
10–15 years							
15–30 years			9.2%			3.4%	
30+ years							

FIGURE 16.8 Stratification of bonds into cells

on the circumstances of the particular investor. Some institutions, such as banks, are concerned with protecting the current net worth or net market value of the firm against interest rate fluctuations. Other investors, such as pension funds, may face an obligation to make payments after a given number of years. These investors are more concerned with protecting the future values of their portfolios.

What is common to the bank and the pension fund, however, is interest rate risk. The net worth of the firm or the ability to meet future obligations fluctuates with interest rates. These institutions presumably might be interested in methods to control that risk. **Immunization** techniques refer to strategies used by such investors to shield their overall financial status from exposure to interest rate fluctuations.

Many banks and thrift institutions have a natural mismatch between asset and liability maturity structures. Bank liabilities are primarily the deposits owed to customers, most of which are very short-term in nature and, consequently, of low duration. Bank assets by contrast are composed largely of outstanding commercial and consumer loans or mortgages. These assets are of longer duration than are deposits, and their values are correspondingly more sensitive to interest rate fluctuations. In periods when interest rates increase unexpectedly, banks can suffer serious decreases in net worth—their assets fall in value by more than their liabilities.

Similarly, a pension fund may have a mismatch between the interest rate sensitivity of the assets held in the fund and the present value of its liabilities—the promise to make payments to retirees. The nearby box illustrates the dangers that pension funds face when they neglect the interest rate exposure of *both* assets and liabilities. The article points out that when interest rates change, the present value of the fund's liabilities change. For example, in some recent years pension funds lost ground despite the fact that they enjoyed excellent investment returns. As interest rates fell, the value of their liabilities grew even faster than the value of their assets. The lesson is that funds should match the interest rate exposure of assets and liabilities so that the value of assets will track the value of liabilities whether rates rise or fall. In other words, the financial manager might want to *immunize* the fund against interest rate volatility.

PENSION FUNDS LOST GROUND DESPITE BROAD MARKET GAINS

With the S&P 500 providing a rate of return in excess of 25%, 2003 was a banner year for the stock market. Not surprisingly, this performance showed up in the balance sheets of U.S. pension funds: assets in these funds rose by more than $100 billion. Despite this boost, pension funds actually *lost* ground in 2003, with the gap between assets and liabilities growing by about $45 billion.

How could this happen? Blame the decline in interest rates during the year that were in large part the force behind the stock market gains. As rates fell during the year, the present value of pension obligations to retirees rose even faster than the value of the assets backing those promises. It turns out that the value of pension liabilities is more sensitive to interest rate changes than the value of the typical assets held in those funds. So even though falling rates tend to pump up asset returns, they pump up liabilities even more so. In other words, the duration of fund investments tends to be shorter than the duration of its obligations. This duration mismatch makes funds vulnerable to interest rate declines.

Why don't funds better match asset and liability durations? One reason is that fund managers are often evaluated based on their performance relative to standard bond market indexes. Those indexes tend to have far shorter durations than pension fund liabilities. So to some extent, managers may be keeping their eyes on the wrong ball, one with the wrong interest rate sensitivity.

Pension funds are not alone in this concern. Any institution with a future fixed obligation might consider immunization a reasonable risk management policy. Insurance companies, for example, also pursue immunization strategies. Indeed, the notion of immunization was introduced by F. M. Redington,[11] an actuary for a life insurance company. The idea behind immunization is that duration-matched assets and liabilities let the asset portfolio meet the firm's obligations despite interest rate movements.

Consider, for example, an insurance company that issues a guaranteed investment contract, or GIC, for $10,000. (Essentially, GICs are zero-coupon bonds issued by the insurance company to its customers. They are popular products for individuals' retirement-savings accounts.) If the GIC has a 5-year maturity and a guaranteed interest rate of 8%, the insurance company is obligated to pay $10,000 \times (1.08)^5 = $14,693.28 in 5 years.

Suppose that the insurance company chooses to fund its obligation with $10,000 of 8% *annual* coupon bonds, selling at par value, with 6 years to maturity. As long as the market interest rate stays at 8%, the company has fully funded the obligation, as the present value of the obligation exactly equals the value of the bonds.

Table 16.4A shows that if interest rates remain at 8%, the accumulated funds from the bond will grow to exactly the $14,693.28 obligation. Over the 5-year period, year-end coupon income of $800 is reinvested at the prevailing 8% market interest rate. At the end of the period, the bonds can be sold for $10,000; they still will sell at par value because the coupon rate still equals the market interest rate. Total income after 5 years from reinvested coupons and the sale of the bond is precisely $14,693.28.

If interest rates change, however, two offsetting influences will affect the ability of the fund to grow to the targeted value of $14,693.28. If interest rates rise, the fund will suffer a capital loss, impairing its ability to satisfy the obligation. The bonds will be worth less in 5 years than if interest rates had remained at 8%. However, at a higher interest rate, reinvested coupons will grow at a faster rate, offsetting the capital loss. In other words, fixed-income investors face two offsetting types of interest rate risk: *price risk* and *reinvestment rate risk*. Increases in interest rates cause capital losses but at the same time increase the rate at which reinvested income will grow. If the portfolio duration is chosen appropriately,

[11]F. M. Redington, "Review of the Principle of Life-Office Valuations," *Journal of the Institute of Actuaries* 78 (1952).

these two effects will cancel out exactly. When the portfolio duration is set equal to the investor's horizon date, the accumulated value of the investment fund at the horizon date will be unaffected by interest rate fluctuations. *For a horizon equal to the portfolio's duration, price risk and reinvestment risk exactly cancel out.*

In the example we are discussing, the duration of the 6-year maturity bonds used to fund the GIC is 5 years. Because the fully funded plan has equal duration for its assets and liabilities, the insurance company should be immunized against interest rate fluctuations. To confirm that this is the case, let us now investigate whether the bond can generate enough income to pay off the obligation 5 years from now regardless of interest rate movements.

Tables 16.4B and C consider two possible interest rate scenarios: Rates either fall to 7%, or increase to 9%. In both cases, the annual coupon payments from the bond are reinvested at the new interest rate, which is assumed to change before the first coupon payment, and the bond is sold in year 5 to help satisfy the obligation of the GIC.

Table 16.4B shows that if interest rates fall to 7%, the total funds will accumulate to $14,694.05, providing a small surplus of $.77. If rates increase to 9% as in Table 16.4C, the fund accumulates to $14,696.02, providing a small surplus of $2.74.

Payment Number	Years Remaining until Obligation	Accumulated Value of Invested Payment		
A. Rates remain at 8%				
1	4	$800 \times (1.08)^4$	=	1,088.39
2	3	$800 \times (1.08)^3$	=	1,007.77
3	2	$800 \times (1.08)^2$	=	933.12
4	1	$800 \times (1.08)^1$	=	864.00
5	0	$800 \times (1.08)^0$	=	800.00
Sale of bond	0	10,800/1.08	=	10,000.00
				14,693.28
B. Rates fall to 7%				
1	4	$800 \times (1.07)^4$	=	1,048.64
2	3	$800 \times (1.07)^3$	=	980.03
3	2	$800 \times (1.07)^2$	=	915.92
4	1	$800 \times (1.07)^1$	=	856.00
5	0	$800 \times (1.07)^0$	=	800.00
Sale of bond	0	10,800/1.07	=	10,093.46
				14,694.05
C. Rates increase to 9%				
1	4	$800 \times (1.09)^4$	=	1,129.27
2	3	$800 \times (1.09)^3$	=	1,036.02
3	2	$800 \times (1.09)^2$	=	950.48
4	1	$800 \times (1.09)^1$	=	872.00
5	0	$800 \times (1.09)^0$	=	800.00
Sale of bond	0	10,800/1.09	=	9,908.26
				14,696.02

TABLE 16.4

Terminal value of a bond portfolio after 5 years (all proceeds reinvested)

Note: The sale price of the bond portfolio equals the portfolio's final payment ($10,800) divided by $1 + r$, because the time to maturity of the bonds will be 1 year at the time of sale.

Several points are worth highlighting. First, duration matching balances the difference between the accumulated value of the coupon payments (reinvestment rate risk) and the sale value of the bond (price risk). That is, when interest rates fall, the coupons grow less than in the base case, but the gain on the sale of the bond offsets this. When interest rates rise, the re-sale value of the bond falls, but the coupons more than make up for this loss because they are reinvested at the higher rate. Figure 16.9 illustrates this case. The solid curve traces out the accumulated value of the bonds if interest rates remain at 8%. The dashed curve shows that value if interest rates happen to increase. The initial impact is a capital loss, but this loss eventually is offset by the now-faster growth rate of reinvested funds. At the 5-year horizon date, equal to the bond's duration, the two effects just cancel, leaving the company able to satisfy its obligation with the accumulated proceeds from the bond.

We can also analyze immunization in terms of present as opposed to future values. Table 16.5A shows the initial balance sheet for the insurance company's GIC account. Both assets and the obligation have market values of $10,000, so that the plan is just fully funded. Tables 16.5B and C show that whether the interest rate increases or decreases, the value of the bonds funding the GIC and the present value of the company's obligation change by virtually identical amounts. Regardless of the interest rate change, the plan remains fully funded, with the surplus in Table 16.5B and C just about zero. The duration-matching strategy has ensured that both assets and liabilities react equally to interest rate fluctuations.

Figure 16.10 is a graph of the present values of the bond and the single-payment obligation as a function of the interest rate. At the current rate of 8%, the values are equal, and the obligation is fully funded by the bond. Moreover, the two present value curves are tangent at $y = 8\%$. As interest rates change, the change in value of both the asset and the obligation is equal, so the obligation remains fully funded. For greater changes in the interest rate, however, the present value curves diverge. This reflects the fact that the fund actually shows a small surplus in Table 16.4 at market interest rates other than 8%.

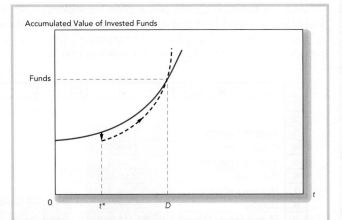

Accumulated Value of Invested Funds

FIGURE 16.9 Growth of invested funds. The solid colored curve represents the growth of portfolio value at the original interest rate. If interest rates increase at time t^*, the portfolio value initially falls but increases thereafter at the faster rate represented by the broken curve. At time D (duration) the curves cross.

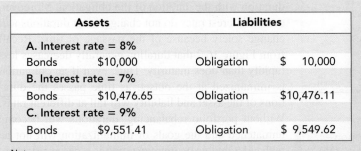

Assets		Liabilities	
A. Interest rate = 8%			
Bonds	$10,000	Obligation	$ 10,000
B. Interest rate = 7%			
Bonds	$10,476.65	Obligation	$10,476.11
C. Interest rate = 9%			
Bonds	$9,551.41	Obligation	$ 9,549.62

TABLE 16.5

Market value balance sheet

Notes:

Value of bonds = 800 × Annuity factor(r, 6) + 10,000 × PV factor(r, 6)

$$\text{Value of obligation} = \frac{14{,}693.28}{(1 + r)^5} = 14{,}693.28 \times \text{PV factor}(r, 5)$$

The Online Learning Center (**www.mhhe.com/bkm**) contains a spreadsheet that is useful in understanding the concept of holding-period immunization. The spreadsheet calculates duration and holding-period returns on bonds of any maturity. The spreadsheet shows how price risk and reinvestment risk offset if a bond is sold at its duration.

	A	B	C	D	E	F	G	H
1								
2								
3	Yield to maturity	11.580%						
4	Coupon rate	14.000%						
5	Years to maturity	7.0						
6	Par value	$1,000.00						
7	Holding period	5.0						
8	Duration	5.000251		5.000251				
9	Market price	$1,111.929		$1,111.929				
10								
11	If YTM increases 200 basis points:			2.00%		If YTM increases 200 basis points:		
12	Yield to maturity	13.580%				Yield to maturity	12.580%	
13	Future value of coupons	$917.739		$917.739		Future value of coupons	$899.705	
14	Sale of bond	$1,006.954		1,006.954		Sale of bond	$1,023.817	
15	Accumulated value	$1,924.693				Accumulated value	$1,923.522	
16	Internal rate of return	11.5981%				Internal rate of return	11.5845%	
17								

If the obligation was immunized, why is there any surplus in the fund? The answer is convexity. Figure 16.10 shows that the coupon bond has greater convexity than the obligation it funds. Hence, when rates move substantially, the bond value exceeds the present value of the obligation by a noticeable amount. Another way to think about it is that although the duration of the bond is indeed equal to 5 years at a yield to maturity of 8%, it rises to 5.02 years when its yield falls to 7% and drops to 4.97 years at $y = 9\%$; that is, the bond and the obligation were not duration-matched *across* the interest rate shift.

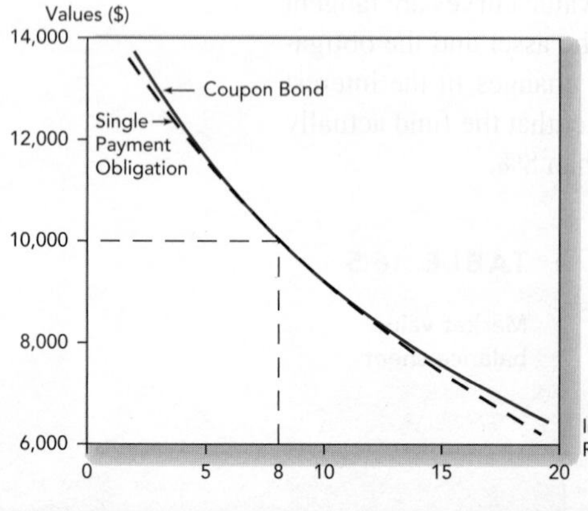

This example highlights the importance of **rebalancing** immunized portfolios. As interest rates and asset durations change, a manager must rebalance the portfolio of fixed-income assets continually to realign its duration with the duration of the obligation. Moreover, even if interest rates do not change, asset durations *will* change solely because of the passage of time. Recall from Figure 16.2 that duration generally decreases less rapidly than does maturity. Thus, even if an obligation is immunized at the outset, as time passes the durations of the asset and liability will fall at different rates. Without portfolio rebalancing, durations will become unmatched and the goals of immunization will not be realized. Obviously, immunization is a passive strategy only in the sense that it does not involve attempts to identify undervalued securities. Immunization managers still actively update and monitor their positions.

FIGURE 16.10 Immunization. The coupon bond fully funds the obligation at an interest rate of 8%. Moreover, the present value curves are tangent at 8%, so the obligation will remain fully funded even if rates change by a small amount.

EXAMPLE 16.4   Constructing an Immunized Portfolio

An insurance company must make a payment of $19,487 in 7 years. The market interest rate is 10%, so the present value of the obligation is $10,000. The company's portfolio manager wishes to fund the obligation using 3-year zero-coupon bonds and perpetuities paying annual coupons. (We focus on zeros and perpetuities to keep the algebra simple.) How can the manager immunize the obligation?

Immunization requires that the duration of the portfolio of assets equal the duration of the liability. We can proceed in four steps:

1. *Calculate the duration of the liability.* In this case, the liability duration is simple to compute. It is a single-payment obligation with duration of 7 years.

2. *Calculate the duration of the asset portfolio.* The portfolio duration is the weighted average of duration of each component asset, with weights proportional to the funds placed in each asset. The duration of the zero-coupon bond is simply its maturity, 3 years. The duration of the perpetuity is $1.10/.10 = 11$ years. Therefore, if the fraction of the portfolio invested in the zero is called w, and the fraction invested in the perpetuity is $(1 - w)$, the portfolio duration will be

$$\text{Asset duration} = w \times 3 \text{ years} + (1 - w) \times 11 \text{ years}$$

3. *Find the asset mix that sets the duration of assets equal to the 7-year duration of liabilities.* This requires us to solve for w in the following equation:

$$w \times 3 \text{ years} + (1 - w) \times 11 \text{ years} = 7 \text{ years}$$

   This implies that $w = \frac{1}{2}$. The manager should invest half the portfolio in the zero and half in the perpetuity. This will result in an asset duration of 7 years.

4. *Fully fund the obligation.* Because the obligation has a present value of $10,000, and the fund will be invested equally in the zero and the perpetuity, the manager must purchase $5,000 of the zero-coupon bond and $5,000 of the perpetuity. (Note that the *face value* of the zero will be $5,000 \times (1.10)^3 = \$6,655$.)

Even if a position is immunized, however, the portfolio manager still cannot rest. This is because of the need for rebalancing in response to changes in interest rates. Moreover, even if rates do not change, the passage of time also will affect duration and require rebalancing. Let us continue Example 16.4 and see how the portfolio manager can maintain an immunized position.

EXAMPLE 16.5   Rebalancing

Suppose that 1 year has passed, and the interest rate remains at 10%. The portfolio manager of Example 16.4 needs to reexamine her position. Is the position still fully funded? Is it still immunized? If not, what actions are required?

First, examine funding. The present value of the obligation will have grown to $11,000, as it is 1 year closer to maturity. The manager's funds also have grown to $11,000: The zero-coupon bonds have increased in value from $5,000 to $5,500 with the passage of time, while the perpetuity has paid its annual $500 coupons and remains worth $5,000. Therefore, the obligation is still fully funded.

The portfolio weights must be changed, however. The zero-coupon bond now will have a duration of 2 years, while the perpetuity duration remains at 11 years. The obligation is now due in 6 years. The weights must now satisfy the equation

$$w \times 2 + (1 - w) \times 11 = 6$$

which implies that $w = \frac{5}{9}$ To rebalance the portfolio and maintain the duration match, the manager now must invest a total of $\$11,000 \times \frac{5}{9} = \$6,111.11$ in the zero-coupon bond. This requires that the entire $500 coupon payment be invested in the zero, with an additional $111.11 of the perpetuity sold and invested in the zero-coupon bond.

Of course, rebalancing of the portfolio entails transaction costs as assets are bought or sold, so one cannot rebalance continuously. In practice, an appropriate compromise must be established between the desire for perfect immunization, which requires continual rebalancing, and the need to control trading costs, which dictates less frequent rebalancing.

> **CONCEPT CHECK 6**
>
> Look again at Example 16.5. What would be the immunizing weights in the second year if the interest rate had fallen to 8%?

Cash Flow Matching and Dedication

The problems associated with immunization seem to have a simple solution. Why not simply buy a zero-coupon bond that provides a payment in an amount exactly sufficient to cover the projected cash outlay? If we follow the principle of **cash flow matching** we automatically immunize the portfolio from interest rate movement because the cash flow from the bond and the obligation exactly offset each other.

Cash flow matching on a multiperiod basis is referred to as a **dedication strategy.** In this case, the manager selects either zero-coupon or coupon bonds that provide total cash flows in each period that match a series of obligations. The advantage of dedication is that it is a once-and-for-all approach to eliminating interest rate risk. Once the cash flows are matched, there is no need for rebalancing. The dedicated portfolio provides the cash necessary to pay the firm's liabilities regardless of the eventual path of interest rates.

Cash flow matching is not more widely pursued probably because of the constraints that it imposes on bond selection. Immunization or dedication strategies are appealing to firms that do not wish to bet on general movements in interest rates, but these firms may want to immunize using bonds that they perceive are undervalued. Cash flow matching, however, places so many more constraints on the bond selection process that it can be impossible to pursue a dedication strategy using only "underpriced" bonds. Firms looking for underpriced bonds give up exact and easy dedication for the possibility of achieving superior returns from the bond portfolio.

Sometimes, cash flow matching is simply not possible. To cash flow match for a pension fund that is obligated to pay out a perpetual flow of income to current and future retirees, the pension fund would need to purchase fixed-income securities with maturities ranging up to hundreds of years. Such securities do not exist, making exact dedication infeasible.

> **CONCEPT CHECK 7**
>
> How would an increase in trading costs affect the attractiveness of dedication versus immunization?

Other Problems with Conventional Immunization

If you look back at the definition of duration in Equation 16.1, you note that it uses the bond's yield to maturity to calculate the weight applied to the time until each coupon payment. Given this definition and limitations on the proper use of yield to maturity, it is perhaps not surprising that this notion of duration is strictly valid only for a flat yield curve for which all payments are discounted at a common interest rate.

If the yield curve is not flat, then the definition of duration must be modified and $CF_t/(1 + y)^t$ replaced with the present value of CF_t, where the present value of each cash flow is calculated by discounting with the appropriate spot interest rate from the zero-coupon yield curve corresponding to the date of the *particular* cash flow, instead of by discounting with the *bond's* yield to maturity. Moreover, even with this modification, duration matching will immunize portfolios only for parallel shifts in the yield curve. Clearly, this sort of restriction is unrealistic. As a result, much work has been devoted to generalizing the notion of duration. Multifactor duration models have been developed to allow for tilts and other distortions in the shape of the yield curve, in addition to shifts in its level. However, it does not appear that the added complexity of such models pays off in terms of substantially greater effectiveness.[12]

Finally, immunization can be an inappropriate goal in an inflationary environment. Immunization is essentially a nominal notion and makes sense only for nominal liabilities. It makes no sense to immunize a projected obligation that will grow with the price level using nominal assets such as bonds. For example, if your child will attend college in 15 years and if the annual cost of tuition is expected to be $40,000 at that time, immunizing your portfolio at a locked-in terminal value of $40,000 is not necessarily a risk-reducing strategy. The tuition obligation will vary with the realized inflation rate, whereas the asset portfolio's final value will not. In the end, the tuition obligation will not necessarily be matched by the value of the portfolio.

16.4   ACTIVE BOND MANAGEMENT

Sources of Potential Profit

Broadly speaking, there are two sources of potential value in active bond management. The first is interest rate forecasting, which tries to anticipate movements across the entire spectrum of the fixed-income market. If interest rate declines are anticipated, managers will increase portfolio duration (and vice versa). The second source of potential profit is identification of relative mispricing within the fixed-income market. An analyst, for example, might believe that the default premium on one particular bond is unnecessarily large and therefore that the bond is underpriced.

These techniques will generate abnormal returns only if the analyst's information or insight is superior to that of the market. You cannot profit from knowledge that rates are about to fall if prices already reflect this information. You know this from our discussion of market efficiency. Valuable information is differential information. In this context it is worth noting that interest rate forecasters have a notoriously poor track record. If you consider this record, you will approach attempts to time the bond market with caution.

---

[12]G. O. Bierwag, G. C. Kaufman, and A. Toevs, eds., *Innovations in Bond Portfolio Management: Duration Analysis and Immunization* (Greenwich, CT: JAI Press, 1983).

Homer and Liebowitz (see footnote 2) coined a popular taxonomy of active bond portfolio strategies. They characterize portfolio rebalancing activities as one of four types of *bond swaps.* In the first two swaps the investor typically believes that the yield relationship between bonds or sectors is only temporarily out of alignment. When the aberration is eliminated, gains can be realized on the underpriced bond. The period of realignment is called the *workout period.*

1. The **substitution swap** is an exchange of one bond for a nearly identical substitute. The substituted bonds should be of essentially equal coupon, maturity, quality, call features, sinking fund provisions, and so on. This swap would be motivated by a belief that the market has temporarily mispriced the two bonds, and that the discrepancy between the prices of the bonds represents a profit opportunity.

   An example of a substitution swap would be a sale of a 20-year maturity, 8% coupon Toyota bond that is priced to provide a yield to maturity of 8.05%, coupled with a purchase of an 8% coupon Honda bond with the same time to maturity that yields 8.15%. If the bonds have about the same credit rating, there is no apparent reason for the Honda bonds to provide a higher yield. Therefore, the higher yield actually available in the market makes the Honda bond seem relatively attractive. Of course, the equality of credit risk is an important condition. If the Honda bond is in fact riskier, then its higher yield does not represent a bargain.

2. The **intermarket spread swap** is pursued when an investor believes that the yield spread between two sectors of the bond market is temporarily out of line. For example, if the current spread between corporate and government bonds is considered too wide and is expected to narrow, the investor will shift from government bonds into corporate bonds. If the yield spread does in fact narrow, corporates will outperform governments. For example, if the yield spread between 10-year Treasury bonds and 10-year Baa-rated corporate bonds is now 3%, and the historical spread has been only 2%, an investor might consider selling holdings of Treasury bonds and replacing them with corporates. If the yield spread eventually narrows, the Baa-rated corporate bonds will outperform the Treasuries.

   Of course, the investor must consider carefully whether there is a good reason that the yield spread seems out of alignment. For example, the default premium on corporate bonds might have increased because the market is expecting a severe recession. In this case, the wider spread would not represent attractive pricing of corporates relative to Treasuries, but would simply be an adjustment for a perceived increase in credit risk.

3. The **rate anticipation swap** is pegged to interest rate forecasting. In this case if investors believe that rates will fall, they will swap into bonds of longer duration. Conversely, when rates are expected to rise, they will swap into shorter duration bonds. For example, the investor might sell a 5-year maturity Treasury bond, replacing it with a 25-year maturity Treasury bond. The new bond has the same lack of credit risk as the old one, but has longer duration.

4. The **pure yield pickup swap** is pursued not in response to perceived mispricing, but as a means of increasing return by holding higher-yield bonds. When the yield curve is upward-sloping, the yield pickup swap entails moving into longer-term bonds. This must be viewed as an attempt to earn an expected term premium in higher-yield bonds. The investor is willing to bear the interest rate risk that this strategy entails. The investor who swaps the shorter-term bond for the longer one will earn a higher rate of return as long as the yield curve does not shift up

during the holding period. Of course if it does, the longer-duration bond will suffer a greater capital loss.

We can add a fifth swap, called a **tax swap,** to this list. This simply refers to a swap to exploit some tax advantage. For example, an investor may swap from one bond that has decreased in price to another if realization of capital losses is advantageous for tax purposes.

Horizon Analysis

One form of interest rate forecasting, which we encountered in Chapter 14, is called **horizon analysis.** The analyst using this approach selects a particular holding period and predicts the yield curve at the end of that period. Given a bond's time to maturity at the end of the holding period, its yield can be read from the predicted yield curve and its end-of-period price calculated. Then the analyst adds the coupon income and prospective capital gain of the bond to obtain the total return on the bond over the holding period.

EXAMPLE 16.6   Horizon Analysis

A 20-year maturity bond with a 10% coupon rate (paid annually) currently sells at a yield to maturity of 9%. A portfolio manager with a 2-year horizon needs to forecast the total return on the bond over the coming 2 years. In 2 years, the bond will have an 18-year maturity. The analyst forecasts that 2 years from now, 18-year bonds will sell at yields to maturity of 8%, and that coupon payments can be reinvested in short-term securities over the coming 2 years at a rate of 7%.

To calculate the 2-year return on the bond, the analyst would perform the following calculations:

1. Current price = $100 × Annuity factor(9%, 20 years)
    $\qquad\qquad + \$1,000 \times$ PV factor(9%, 20 years)
    $\qquad = \$1,091.29$

2. Forecast price = $100 × Annuity factor(8%, 18 years)
    $\qquad\qquad + \$1,000 \times$ PV factor(8%, 18 years)
    $\qquad = \$1,187.44$

3. The future value of reinvested coupons will be ($100 × 1.07) + $100 = $207

4. The 2-year return is $\dfrac{\$207 + (\$1,187.44 - \$1,091.29)}{\$1,091.29} = 0.278$, or 27.8%

The annualized rate of return over the 2-year period would then be $(1.278)^{1/2} - 1 = 0.13$, or 13%.

CONCEPT CHECK 8

What will be the rate of return in Example 16.6 if the manager forecasts that in 2 years the yield on 18-year bonds will be 10%, and that the reinvestment rate for coupons will be 8%?

Contingent Immunization

Contingent immunization is a mixed passive-active strategy suggested by Liebowitz and Weinberger.[13] To illustrate, suppose that interest rates currently are 10% and that a manager's portfolio is worth $10 million right now. At current rates the manager could lock in, via conventional immunization techniques, a future portfolio value of $12.1 million after 2 years. Now suppose that the manager wishes to pursue active management but is willing to risk losses only to the extent that the terminal value of the portfolio would not drop lower than $11 million. Because only $9.09 million (i.e., the present value of $11 million, or $11 million/$1.10^2$) is required to achieve this minimum acceptable terminal value, and the portfolio currently is worth $10 million, the manager can afford to risk some losses at the outset and might start off with an active strategy rather than immediately immunizing.

The key is to calculate the funds required to lock in via immunization a future value of $11 million at current rates. If T denotes the time left until the horizon date, and r is the market interest rate at any particular time, then the value of the fund necessary to guarantee an ability to reach the minimum acceptable terminal value is $11 million/$(1 + r)^T$, because this size portfolio, if immunized, will grow risk-free to $11 million by the horizon date. This value becomes the trigger point: If and when the actual portfolio value dips to the trigger point, active management will cease. *Contingent* upon reaching the trigger, an immunization strategy is initiated instead, guaranteeing that the minimal acceptable performance can be realized.

> **CONCEPT CHECK 9**
>
> What would be the trigger point with a 3-year horizon, an interest rate of 12%, and a minimum acceptable terminal value of $10 million?

Figure 16.11 illustrates two possible outcomes in a contingent immunization strategy. In Figure 16.11A, the portfolio falls in value and hits the trigger at time t^*. At that point, immunization is pursued and the portfolio rises smoothly to the $11 million terminal value. In Figure 16.11B, the portfolio does well, never reaches the trigger point, and is worth more than $11 million at the horizon date.

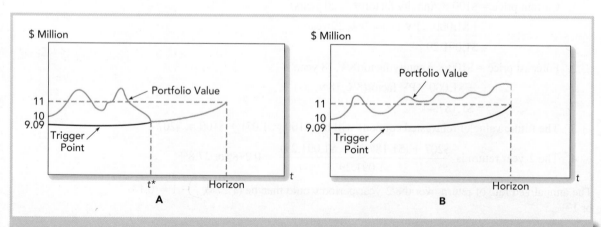

FIGURE 16.11   Contingent immunization.
Panel A: The portfolio is immunized when its value falls to the trigger point at time t^*. *Panel B:* The portfolio value remains above the trigger point and can be managed actively for the whole period.

[13]Martin L. Liebowitz and Alfred Weinberger, "Contingent Immunization—Part I: Risk Control Procedures," *Financial Analysts Journal* 38 (November–December 1982).

1. Even default-free bonds such as Treasury issues are subject to interest rate risk. Longer-term bonds generally are more sensitive to interest rate shifts than are short-term bonds. A measure of the average life of a bond is Macaulay's duration, defined as the weighted average of the times until each payment made by the security, with weights proportional to the present value of the payment.

2. Duration is a direct measure of the sensitivity of a bond's price to a change in its yield. The proportional change in a bond's price equals the negative of duration multiplied by the proportional change in $1 + y$.

3. Convexity refers to the curvature of a bond's price-yield relationship. Accounting for convexity can substantially improve on the accuracy of the duration approximation for bond price sensitivity to changes in yields.

4. Immunization strategies are characteristic of passive fixed-income portfolio management. Such strategies attempt to render the individual or firm immune from movements in interest rates. This may take the form of immunizing net worth or, instead, immunizing the future accumulated value of a fixed-income portfolio.

5. Immunization of a fully funded plan is accomplished by matching the durations of assets and liabilities. To maintain an immunized position as time passes and interest rates change, the portfolio must be periodically rebalanced. Classic immunization also depends on parallel shifts in a flat yield curve. Given that this assumption is unrealistic, immunization generally will be less than complete. To mitigate the problem, multifactor duration models can be used to allow for variation in the shape of the yield curve.

6. A more direct form of immunization is dedication, or cash flow matching. If a portfolio is perfectly matched in cash flow with projected liabilities, rebalancing will be unnecessary.

7. Active bond management consists of interest rate forecasting techniques and intermarket spread analysis. One popular taxonomy classifies active strategies as substitution swaps, intermarket spread swaps, rate anticipation swaps, or pure yield pickup swaps.

8. Horizon analysis is a type of interest rate forecasting. In this procedure the analyst forecasts the position of the yield curve at the end of some holding period, and from that yield curve predicts corresponding bond prices. Bonds then can be ranked according to expected total returns (coupon plus capital gain) over the holding period.

Related Web sites for this chapter are available at www.mhhe.com/bkm

Visit us at www.mhhe.com/bkm

KEY TERMS

Macaulay's duration	rebalancing	rate anticipation swap
modified duration	cash flow matching	pure yield pickup swap
convexity	dedication strategy	tax swap
effective duration	substitution swap	horizon analysis
immunization	intermarket spread swap	contingent immunization

PROBLEM SETS

Quiz

Problems

1. Prices of long-term bonds are more volatile than prices of short-term bonds. However, yields to maturity of short-term bonds fluctuate more than yields of long-term bonds. How do you reconcile these two empirical observations?

2. How can a perpetuity, which has an infinite maturity, have a duration as short as 10 or 20 years?

3. A 9-year bond has a yield of 10% and a duration of 7.194 years. If the market yield changes by 50 basis points, what is the percentage change in the bond's price?

4. Find the duration of a 6% coupon bond making *annual* coupon payments if it has 3 years until maturity and has a yield to maturity of 6%. What is the duration if the yield to maturity is 10%?

5. Find the duration of the bond in Problem 4 if the coupons are paid semiannually.

6. Rank the durations or effective durations of the following pairs of bonds:

   a. Bond *A* is an 8% coupon bond, with a 20-year time to maturity selling at par value. Bond *B* is an 8% coupon bond, with a 20-year maturity time selling below par value.

   b. Bond *A* is a 20-year noncallable coupon bond with a coupon rate of 8%, selling at par. Bond *B* is a 20-year callable bond with a coupon rate of 9%, also selling at par.

7. An insurance company must make payments to a customer of $10 million in 1 year and $4 million in 5 years. The yield curve is flat at 10%.

   a. If it wants to fully fund and immunize its obligation to this customer with a *single* issue of a zero-coupon bond, what maturity bond must it purchase?

   b. What must be the face value and market value of that zero-coupon bond?

8. Long-term Treasury bonds currently are selling at yields to maturity of nearly 8%. You expect interest rates to fall. The rest of the market thinks that they will remain unchanged over the coming year. In each question, choose the bond that will provide the higher holding-period return over the next year if you are correct. Briefly explain your answer.

   a. i. A Baa-rated bond with coupon rate 8% and time to maturity 20 years.
      ii. An Aaa-rated bond with coupon rate of 8% and time to maturity 20 years.

   b. i. An A-rated bond with coupon rate 4% and maturity 20 years, callable at 105.
      ii. An A-rated bond with coupon rate 8% and maturity 20 years, callable at 105.

   c. i. A 6% coupon noncallable T-bond with maturity 20 years and YTM = 8%.
      ii. A 9% coupon noncallable T-bond with maturity 20 years and YTM = 8%.

9. Currently, the term structure is as follows: 1-year bonds yield 7%, 2-year bonds yield 8%, 3-year bonds and longer-maturity bonds all yield 9%. An investor is choosing between 1-, 2-, and 3-year maturity bonds all paying annual coupons of 8%, once a year. Which bond should you buy if you strongly believe that at year-end the yield curve will be flat at 9%?

10. You will be paying $10,000 a year in tuition expenses at the end of the next 2 years. Bonds currently yield 8%.

    a. What is the present value and duration of your obligation?

    b. What maturity zero-coupon bond would immunize your obligation?

    c. Suppose you buy a zero-coupon bond with value and duration equal to your obligation. Now suppose that rates immediately increase to 9%. What happens to your net position, that is, to the difference between the value of the bond and that of your tuition obligation? What if rates fall to 7%?

11. Pension funds pay lifetime annuities to recipients. If a firm will remain in business indefinitely, the pension obligation will resemble a perpetuity. Suppose, therefore, that you are managing a pension fund with obligations to make perpetual payments of $2 million per year to beneficiaries. The yield to maturity on all bonds is 16%.

    a. If the duration of 5-year maturity bonds with coupon rates of 12% (paid annually) is 4 years and the duration of 20-year maturity bonds with coupon rates of 6% (paid annually) is 11 years, how much of each of these coupon bonds (in market value) will you want to hold to both fully fund and immunize your obligation?

    b. What will be the par value of your holdings in the 20-year coupon bond?

12. You are managing a portfolio of $1 million. Your target duration is 10 years, and you can choose from two bonds: a zero-coupon bond with maturity of 5 years, and a perpetuity, each currently yielding 5%.

    a. How much of each bond will you hold in your portfolio?

    b. How will these fractions change *next year* if target duration is now 9 years?

13. My pension plan will pay me $10,000 once a year for a 10-year period. The first payment will come in exactly 5 years. The pension fund wants to immunize its position.

    a. What is the duration of its obligation to me? The current interest rate is 10% per year.

    b. If the plan uses 5-year and 20-year zero-coupon bonds to construct the immunized position, how much money ought to be placed in each bond? What will be the *face value* of the holdings in each zero?

14. A 30-year maturity bond making annual coupon payments with a coupon rate of 12% has duration of 11.54 years and convexity of 192.4. The bond currently sells at a yield to maturity of 8%. Use a financial calculator or spreadsheet to find the price of the bond if its yield to maturity falls to 7% or rises to 9%. What prices for the bond at these new yields would be predicted by the duration rule and the duration-with-convexity rule? What is the percentage error for each rule? What do you conclude about the accuracy of the two rules?

15. A fixed-income portfolio manager is unwilling to realize a rate of return of less than 3% annually over a 5-year investment period on a portfolio currently valued at $1 million. Three years later, the interest rate is 8%. What is the trigger point of the portfolio at this time, that is, how low can the value of the portfolio fall before the manager will be forced to immunize to be assured of achieving the minimum acceptable return?

16. A 30-year maturity bond has a 7% coupon rate, paid annually. It sells today for $867.42. A 20-year maturity bond has 6.5% coupon rate, also paid annually. It sells today for $879.50. A bond market analyst forecasts that in 5 years, 25-year maturity bonds will sell at yields to maturity of 8% and 15-year maturity bonds will sell at yields of 7.5%. Because the yield curve is upward sloping, the analyst believes that coupons will be invested in short-term securities at a rate of 6%. Which bond offers the higher expected rate of return over the 5-year period?

17. *a.* Use a spreadsheet to calculate the durations of the two bonds in Spreadsheet 16.1 if the annual interest rate increases to 12%. Why does the duration of the coupon bond fall while that of the zero remains unchanged? (*Hint:* examine what happens to the weights computed in column F.)
    b. Use the same spreadsheet to calculate the duration of the coupon bond if the coupon were 12% instead of 8% and the semiannual interest rate is again 5%. Explain why duration is lower than in Spreadsheet 16.1. (Again, start by looking at column F.)

18. *a.* Footnote 6 presents the formula for the convexity of a bond. Build a spreadsheet to calculate the convexity of a 5-year, 8% coupon bond making annual payments at the initial yield to maturity of 10%.
    b. What is the convexity of a 5-year zero-coupon bond?

19. A 12.75-year maturity zero-coupon bond selling at a yield to maturity of 8% (effective annual yield) has convexity of 150.3 and modified duration of 11.81 years. A 30-year maturity 6% coupon bond making annual coupon payments also selling at a yield to maturity of 8% has nearly identical duration—11.79 years—but considerably higher convexity of 231.2.

    a. Suppose the yield to maturity on both bonds increases to 9%. What will be the actual percentage capital loss on each bond? What percentage capital loss would be predicted by the duration-with-convexity rule?
    b. Repeat part (*a*), but this time assume the yield to maturity decreases to 7%.
    c. Compare the performance of the two bonds in the two scenarios, one involving an increase in rates, the other a decrease. Based on the comparative investment performance, explain the attraction of convexity.
    d. In view of your answer to (*c*), do you think it would be possible for two bonds with equal duration but different convexity to be priced initially at the same yield to maturity if the yields on both bonds always increased or decreased by equal amounts, as in this example? Would anyone be willing to buy the bond with lower convexity under these circumstances?

20. A newly issued bond has a maturity of 10 years and pays a 7% coupon rate (with coupon payments coming once annually). The bond sells at par value.

    a. What are the convexity and the duration of the bond? Use the formula for convexity in footnote 6.
    b. Find the actual price of the bond assuming that its yield to maturity immediately increases from 7% to 8% (with maturity still 10 years).
    c. What price would be predicted by the duration rule (Equation 16.3)? What is the percentage error of that rule?
    d. What price would be predicted by the duration-with-convexity rule (Equation 16.5)? What is the percentage error of that rule?

Challenge Problems

1. *a.* Explain the impact on the offering yield of adding a call feature to a proposed bond issue.

   b. Explain the impact on *both* effective bond duration and convexity of adding a call feature to a proposed bond issue.

2. *a.* A 6% coupon bond paying interest annually has a modified duration of 10 years, sells for $800, and is priced at a yield to maturity of 8%. If the YTM increases to 9%, what is the predicted change in price using the duration concept?

   b. A 6% coupon bond with semiannual coupons has a convexity (in years) of 120, sells for 80% of par, and is priced at a yield to maturity of 8%. If the YTM increases to 9.5%, what is the predicted contribution to the percentage change in price due to convexity?

   c. A bond with annual coupon payments has a coupon rate of 8%, yield to maturity of 10%, and Macaulay duration of 9 years. What is the bond's modified duration?

   d. When interest rates decline, the duration of a 30-year bond selling at a premium:

       i. Increases.
       ii. Decreases.
       iii. Remains the same.
       iv. Increases at first, then declines.

   e. If a bond manager swaps a bond for one that is identical in terms of coupon rate, maturity, and credit quality but offers a higher yield to maturity, the swap is:

       i. A substitution swap.
       ii. An interest rate anticipation swap.
       iii. A tax swap.
       iv. An intermarket spread swap.

   f. Which bond has the longest duration?

       i. 8-year maturity, 6% coupon.
       ii. 8-year maturity, 11% coupon.
       iii. 15-year maturity, 6% coupon.
       iv. 15-year maturity, 11% coupon.

3. A newly issued bond has the following characteristics:

Coupon	Yield to Maturity	Maturity	Macaulay Duration
8%	8%	15 years	10 years

   a. Calculate modified duration using the information above.

   b. Explain why modified duration is a better measure than maturity when calculating the bond's sensitivity to changes in interest rates.

   c. Identify the direction of change in modified duration if:

       i. The coupon of the bond were 4%, not 8%.
       ii. The maturity of the bond were 7 years, not 15 years.

   d. Define convexity and explain how modified duration and convexity are used to approximate the bond's percentage change in price, given a change in interest rates.

4. Bonds of Zello Corporation with a par value of $1,000 sell for $960, mature in 5 years, and have a 7% annual coupon rate paid semiannually.

   a. Calculate each of the following yields:

       i. Current yield.
       ii. Yield to maturity (to the nearest whole percent, i.e., 3%, 4%, 5%, etc.).
       iii. Horizon yield (also called total compound return) for an investor with a 3-year holding period and a reinvestment rate of 6% over the period. At the end of 3 years the 7% coupon bonds with 2 years remaining will sell to yield 7%.

   b. Cite a major shortcoming for each of the following fixed-income yield measures:

       i. Current yield.
       ii. Yield to maturity.
       iii. Horizon yield (also called total compound return).

5. Sandra Kapple presents Maria VanHusen with a description, given in the following table, of the bond portfolio held by the Star Hospital Pension Plan. All securities in the bond portfolio are noncallable U.S. Treasury securities.

Par Value (U.S. $)	Treasury Security	Market Value (U.S. $)	Current Price	Price If Yields Change		Effective Duration
				Up 100 Basis Points	Down 100 Basis Points	
48,000,000	2.375% due 2006	48,667,680	101.391	99.245	103.595	2.15
50,000,000	4.75% due 2031	50,000,000	100.000	86.372	116.887	—
98,000,000	Total Bond Portfolio	98,667,680	—	—	—	—

a. Calculate the effective duration of each of the following:

  i. The 4.75% Treasury security due 2031.

  ii. The total bond portfolio.

b. VanHusen remarks to Kapple, "If you changed the maturity structure of the bond portfolio to result in a portfolio duration of 5.25, the price sensitivity of that portfolio would be identical to the price sensitivity of a single, noncallable Treasury security that has a duration of 5.25." In what circumstance would VanHusen's remark be correct?

6. One common goal among fixed-income portfolio managers is to earn high incremental returns on corporate bonds versus government bonds of comparable durations. The approach of some corporate-bond portfolio managers is to find and purchase those corporate bonds having the largest initial spreads over comparable-duration government bonds. John Ames, HFS's fixed-income manager, believes that a more rigorous approach is required if incremental returns are to be maximized.

The following table presents data relating to one set of corporate/government spread relationships present in the market at a given date:

Bond Rating	Initial Spread over Governments	Expected Horizon Spread	Initial Duration	Expected Duration 1 Year from Now
Aaa	31 b.p.	31 b.p.	4 years	3.1 years
Aa	40 b.p.	50 b.p.	4 years	3.1 years

Note: 1 b.p. means 1 basis point, or .01%.

a. Recommend purchase of either Aaa or Aa bonds for a 1-year investment horizon given a goal of maximizing incremental returns.

b. Ames chooses not to rely *solely* on initial spread relationships. His analytical framework considers a full range of other key variables likely to impact realized incremental returns, including call provisions and potential changes in interest rates. Describe variables, in addition to those identified above, that Ames should include in his analysis and explain how each of these could cause realized incremental returns to differ from those indicated by initial spread relationships.

7. Patrick Wall is considering the purchase of one of the two bonds described in the following table. Wall realizes his decision will depend primarily on effective duration, and he believes that interest rates will decline by 50 basis points at all maturities over the next 6 months.

Characteristic	CIC	PTR
Market price	101.75	101.75
Maturity date	June 1, 2019	June 1, 2019
Call date	Noncallable	June 1, 2014
Annual coupon	6.25%	7.35%
Interest payment	Semiannual	Semiannual
Effective duration	7.35	5.40
Yield to maturity	6.02%	7.10%
Credit rating	A	A

a. Calculate the percentage price change forecasted by effective duration for both the CIC and PTR bonds if interest rates decline by 50 basis points over the next 6 months.

b. Calculate the 6-month horizon return (in percent) for each bond, if the actual CIC bond price equals 105.55 and the actual PTR bond price equals 104.15 at the end of 6 months. Assume you purchased the bonds to settle on June 1, 2009.

c. Wall is surprised by the fact that although interest rates fell by 50 basis points, the actual price change for the CIC bond was greater than the price change forecasted by effective duration, whereas the actual price change for the PTR bond was less than the price change forecasted by effective duration. Explain why the actual price change would be greater for the CIC bond and the actual price change would be less for the PTR bond.

8. You are the manager for the bond portfolio of a pension fund. The policies of the fund allow for the use of active strategies in managing the bond portfolio.

It appears that the economic cycle is beginning to mature, inflation is expected to accelerate, and in an effort to contain the economic expansion, central bank policy is moving toward constraint. For each of the situations below, state which one of the two bonds you would prefer. Briefly justify your answer in each case.

a. Government of Canada (Canadian pay) 6% due in 2012 and priced at 98.75 to yield 6.50% to maturity.

or

Government of Canada (Canadian pay) 6% due in 2022 and priced at 91.75 to yield 7.19% to maturity.

b. Texas Power and Light Co. 6½ due in 2016, rated AAA, and priced at 90 to yield 7.02% to maturity.

or

Arizona Public Service Co. 5.45 due in 2016, rated A–, and priced at 85 to yield 8.05% to maturity.

c. Commonwealth Edison 2¾ due in 2012, rated Baa, and priced at 81 to yield 9.2% to maturity.

or

Commonwealth Edison 12⅜ due in 2012, rated Baa, and priced at 114.40 to yield 9.2% to maturity.

d. Shell Oil Co. 7½ sinking fund debentures due in 2020, rated AAA (sinking fund begins September 2007 at par), and priced at 78 to yield 9.91% to maturity.

or

Warner-Lambert 7⅞ sinking fund debentures due in 2020, rated AAA (sinking fund begins April 2014 at par), and priced at 84 to yield 9.31% to maturity.

e. Bank of Montreal (Canadian pay) 5% certificates of deposit due in 2010, rated AAA, and priced at 100 to yield 5% to maturity.

or

Bank of Montreal (Canadian pay) floating-rate note due in 2014, rated AAA. Coupon currently set at 5.1% and priced at 100 (coupon adjusted semiannually to .5% above the 3-month Government of Canada Treasury bill rate).

9. A member of a firm's investment committee is very interested in learning about the management of fixed-income portfolios. He would like to know how fixed-income managers position portfolios to capitalize on their expectations concerning three factors which influence interest rates:

a. Changes in the level of interest rates.

b. Changes in yield spreads across/between sectors.

c. Changes in yield spreads as to a particular instrument.

Formulate and describe a fixed-income portfolio management strategy for each of these factors that could be used to exploit a portfolio manager's expectations about that factor. (*Note:* Three strategies are required, one for each of the listed factors.)

10. Carol Harrod is the investment officer for a $100 million U.S. pension fund. The fixed-income portion of the portfolio is actively managed, and a substantial portion of the fund's large capitalization U.S. equity portfolio is indexed and managed by Webb Street Advisors.

    Harrod has been impressed with the investment results of Webb Street's equity index strategy and is considering asking Webb Street to index a portion of the actively managed fixed-income portfolio.

    a. Describe advantages and disadvantages of bond indexing relative to active bond management.

    b. Webb Street manages indexed bond portfolios. Discuss how an indexed bond portfolio is constructed under stratified sampling (cellular) methods.

    c. Describe the main source of tracking error for the cellular method.

11. Janet Meer is a fixed-income portfolio manager. Noting that the current shape of the yield curve is flat, she considers the purchase of a newly issued, 7% coupon, 10-year maturity, option-free corporate bond priced at par. The bond has the following features:

	Change in Yields	
	Up 10 Basis Points	Down 10 Basis Points
Price	99.29	100.71
Convexity measure	35.00	
Convexity adjustment	0.0035	

    a. Calculate the modified duration of the bond.

    b. Meer is also considering the purchase of a newly issued, 7.25% coupon, 12-year maturity option-free corporate bond. She wants to evaluate this second bond's price sensitivity to an instantaneous, downward parallel shift in the yield curve of 200 basis points. Based on the following data, what will be its price change in this yield-curve scenario?

Original issue price	Par value, to yield 7.25%
Modified duration (at original price)	7.90
Convexity measure	41.55
Convexity adjustment (yield change of 200 basis points)	1.66

    c. Meer asks her assistant to analyze several callable bonds, given the expected downward parallel shift in the yield curve. Meer's assistant argues that if interest rates fall enough, convexity for a callable bond will become negative. Is the assistant's argument correct?

12. Noah Kramer, a fixed-income portfolio manager based in the country of Sevista, is considering the purchase of a Sevista government bond. Kramer decides to evaluate two strategies for implementing his investment in Sevista bonds. Table 16A gives the details of the two strategies, and Table 16B contains the assumptions that apply to both strategies.

Strategy	5-Year Maturity (Modified Duration = 4.83)	15-Year Maturity (Modified Duration = 14.35)	25-Year Maturity (Modified Duration = 23.81)
I	$5 million	0	$5 million
II	0	$10 million	0

TABLE 16A

Investment strategies (amounts are market value invested)

Market value of bonds	$10 million
Bond maturities	5 and 25 years or 15 years
Bond coupon rates	0.00% (zero coupon)
Target modified duration	15 years

TABLE 16B

Investment strategy assumptions

TABLE 16C

Instantaneous interest rate shift immediately after investment

Maturity	Interest Rate Change
5 year	Down 75 basis points (bps)
15 year	Up 25 bps
25 year	Up 50 bps

Before choosing one of the two bond-investment strategies, Kramer wants to analyze how the market value of the bonds will change if an instantaneous interest rate shift occurs immediately after his investment. The details of the interest rate shift are shown in Table 16C. Calculate, for the instantaneous interest rate shift shown in Table 16C, the percent change in the market value of the bonds that will occur under each strategy.

13. As part of your analysis of debt issued by Monticello Corporation, you are asked to evaluate two of its bond issues, shown in the following table.

	Bond A (Callable)	Bond B (Noncallable)
Maturity	2020	2020
Coupon	11.50%	7.25%
Current price	125.75	100.00
Yield to maturity	7.70%	7.25%
Modified duration to maturity	6.20	6.80
Call date	2014	—
Call price	105	—
Yield to call	5.10%	—
Modified duration to call	3.10	—

a. Using the duration and yield information in the table above, compare the price and yield behavior of the two bonds under each of the following two scenarios:
   i. Strong economic recovery with rising inflation expectations.
   ii. Economic recession with reduced inflation expectations.

b. Using the information in the table, calculate the projected price change for bond B if its yield to maturity falls by 75 basis points.

c. Describe the shortcoming of analyzing bond A strictly to call or to maturity.

1. Go to the **www.mhhe.com/edumarketinsight** Web site. Click on the *Company* tab and enter the stock ticker symbol "T" for AT&T. In the *S&P Stock Reports* section, review the most recent *Industry Outlook* report for the telecom industry. How is AT&T faring relative to other members of its Peer Group?

2. Review the variety of AT&T bonds outstanding by looking at the latest EDGAR 10K report for AT&T. (Bonds are listed in the first few pages.)

3. Then go to **www.finra.org/marketdata** and search for AT&T bonds. (Choose *Search* and enter the ticker symbol "T"; select BONDS to find all outstanding AT&T bonds. Choose "Sort by" *Issuer Name* so the AT&T bonds will be grouped together.) What are the current ratings and yields to maturity for the AT&T debt securities? What factors explain the yield levels? For what type of investor or bond portfolio would AT&T bonds be most interesting?

E-Investments	**Duration and Convexity Calculators**
	Go to **www.investinginbonds.com/story.asp?id=207.** Choose the link for the general-purpose bond calculator. The calculator provides yield to maturity, modified duration, and bond convexity as the bond's price changes. Experiment by trying different inputs. What happens to duration and convexity as coupon increases? As maturity increases? As price increases (holding coupon fixed)?

SOLUTIONS TO CONCEPT CHECKS

1. Use Spreadsheet 16.1 with a semiannual discount rate of 4.5%.

	Period	Time until Payment (Years)	Cash Flow	PV of CF (Discount rate = 4.5% per period)	Weight	Weight × Time
A. 8% coupon bond	1	0.5	40	38.278	0.0390	0.0195
	2	1.0	40	36.629	0.0373	0.0373
	3	1.5	40	35.052	0.0357	0.0535
	4	2.0	1040	872.104	0.8880	1.7761
Sum:				982.062	1.0000	1.8864
B. Zero-coupon	1	0.5	0	0.000	0.0000	0.0000
	2	1.0	0	0.000	0.0000	0.0000
	3	1.5	0	0.000	0.0000	0.0000
	4	2.0	1000	838.561	1.0000	2.0000
Sum:				838.561	1.0000	2.0000

The duration of the 8% coupon bond increases to 1.8864 years. Price increases to $982.062. The duration of the zero-coupon bond is unchanged at 2 years, although its price also increases (to $838.561) when the interest rate falls.

2. *a.* If the interest rate increases from 9% to 9.05%, the bond price falls from $982.062 to $981.177. The percentage change in price is −0.0901%.

   b. Using the initial semiannual rate of 4.5%, duration is 1.8864 years (see Concept Check 1), so the duration formula would predict a price change of

$$-\frac{1.8864}{1.045} \times .0005 = -.000903 = -.0903\%$$

   which is almost the same answer that we obtained from direct computation in part (*a*).

3. The duration of a level perpetuity is $(1 + y)/y$ or $1 + 1/y$, which clearly falls as y increases. Tabulating duration as a function of y we get

y	D
.01	101 years
.02	51
.05	21
.10	11
.20	6
.25	5
.40	3.5

Visit us at www.mhhe.com/bkm

4. In accord with the duration rules presented in the chapter, you should find that duration is shorter when the coupon rate or yield to maturity is higher. Duration increases with maturity for most bonds. Duration is shorter when coupons are paid semiannually rather than annually because on average, payments come earlier. Instead of waiting until year-end to receive the annual coupon, investors receive half the coupon midyear.

5. Macaulay's duration is defined as the weighted average of the time until receipt of each bond payment. Modified duration is defined as Macaulay's duration divided by $1 + y$ (where y is yield per payment period, e.g., a semiannual yield if the bond pays semiannual coupons). One can demonstrate that for a straight bond, modified duration equals the percentage change in bond price per change in yield. Effective duration captures this last property of modified duration. It is *defined* as percentage change in bond price per change in market interest rates. Effective duration for a bond with embedded options requires a valuation method that allows for such options in computing price changes. Effective duration cannot be related to a weighted average of times until payments, because those payments are themselves uncertain.

6. The perpetuity's duration now would be $1.08/.08 = 13.5$. We need to solve the following equation for w:

$$w \times 2 + (1 - w) \times 13.5 = 6$$

Therefore $w = .6522$.

7. Dedication would be more attractive. Cash flow matching eliminates the need for rebalancing and thus saves transaction costs.

8. Current price $= \$1,091.29$

   Forecasted price $= \$100 \times$ Annuity factor (10%, 18 years) $+ \$1,000 \times$ PV factor(10%, 18 years)
   $= \$1,000$

   The future value of reinvested coupons will be $(\$100 \times 1.08) + \$100 = \$208$

   The 2-year return is $\dfrac{\$208 + (\$1,000 - \$1,091.29)}{\$1,091.29} = 0.107$, or 10.7%

   The annualized rate of return over the 2-year period would then be $(1.107)^{1/2} - 1 = .052$, or 5.2%.

9. The trigger point is 10 million$/(1.12)^3 = \$7.118$ million.

CHAPTER SEVENTEEN

MACROECONOMIC AND INDUSTRY ANALYSIS

TO DETERMINE A proper price for a firm's stock, the security analyst must forecast the dividend and earnings that can be expected from the firm. This is the heart of **fundamental analysis**—that is, the analysis of the determinants of value such as earnings prospects. Ultimately, the business success of the firm determines the dividends it can pay to shareholders and the price it will command in the stock market. Because the prospects of the firm are tied to those of the broader economy, however, fundamental analysis must consider the business environment in which the firm operates. For some firms, macroeconomic and industry circumstances might have a greater influence on profits than the firm's relative performance within its industry. In other words, investors need to keep the big economic picture in mind.

Therefore, in analyzing a firm's prospects it often makes sense to start with the broad economic environment, examining the state of the aggregate economy and even the international economy. From there, one considers the implications of the outside environment on the industry in which the firm operates. Finally, the firm's position within the industry is examined.

This chapter treats the broad-based aspects of fundamental analysis—macroeconomic and industry analysis. The two chapters following cover firm-specific analysis. We begin with a discussion of international factors relevant to firm performance, and move on to an overview of the significance of the key variables usually used to summarize the state of the macroeconomy. We then discuss government macroeconomic policy. We conclude the analysis of the macroenvironment with a discussion of business cycles. Finally, we move to industry analysis, treating issues concerning the sensitivity of the firm to the business cycle, the typical life cycle of an industry, and strategic issues that affect industry performance.

A top-down analysis of a firm's prospects must start with the global economy. The international economy might affect a firm's export prospects, the price competition it faces from competitors, or the profits it makes on investments abroad. Nevertheless, despite the fact that the economies of most countries are linked in a global macroeconomy, there is considerable variation in the economic performance across countries at any time. Consider, for example, Table 17.1, which presents data on several so-called emerging economies. The table documents striking variation in growth rates of economic output in 2007. For example, while the Chinese economy grew by 11.5%, Mexican output grew by only 2.8%. Similarly, there was considerable variation in stock market returns in these countries in 2007, ranging from 2.7% in Colombia (in dollar terms) to a 133.8% gain in China.

These data illustrate that the national economic environment can be a crucial determinant of industry performance. It is far harder for businesses to succeed in a contracting economy than in an expanding one. This observation highlights the role of a big-picture macroeconomic analysis as a fundamental part of the investment process.

In addition, the global environment presents political risks of far greater magnitude than are typically encountered in U.S.-based investments. In the last decade, we have seen several instances where political developments had major impacts on economic prospects. For example, the biggest international economic story in late 1997 and 1998 was the turmoil in several Asian economies, notably Thailand, Indonesia, and South Korea. The close interplay between politics and economics was also highlighted by these episodes, as both currency and stock values swung with enormous volatility in response to developments concerning the prospects for aid from the International Monetary Fund. In August 1998, the shockwaves following Russia's devaluation of the ruble and its default on some of its

TABLE 17.1			**Stock Market Return**	
Economic Performance in Selected Emerging Markets		**Growth in Real GDP**	**Local Currency**	**$ Terms**
	Argentina	7.7	7.2	4.1
	Brazil	4.7	42.1	68.0
	China	11.5	125.1	133.8
	Colombia	6.6	(8.9)	2.7
	Hong Kong	6.2	46.8	47.2
	India	8.0	35.8	51.9
	Indonesia	6.3	46.3	44.7
	Mexico	2.8	23.7	23.9
	Russia	7.2	6.2	12.3
	Singapore	7.0	28.6	34.8
	South Africa	4.8	24.7	29.0
	South Korea	4.9	38.3	40.1
	Taiwan	4.3	22.2	22.1
	Turkey	5.2	48.1	73.8
	Venezuela	6.5	(28.8)	10.8

Source: *The Economist*, October 18, 2007. © 2007 The Economist Newspaper Group, Inc. Reprinted with permission. Further reproduction is prohibited. www.economist.com. All rights reserved.

debt created havoc in world security markets, ultimately requiring a rescue of the giant hedge fund Long Term Capital Management to avoid further major disruptions. Currently, the aftermath of the war in Iraq and the security of energy supplies are weighing heavily on stock markets around the world.

Other political issues that are less sensational but still extremely important to economic growth and investment returns include issues of protectionism and trade policy, the free flow of capital, and the status of a nation's workforce.

One obvious factor that affects the international competitiveness of a country's industries is the exchange rate between that country's currency and other currencies. The **exchange rate** is the rate at which domestic currency can be converted into foreign currency. For example, in mid-2007, it took about 118 Japanese yen to purchase 1 U.S. dollar. We would say that the exchange rate is ¥118 per dollar or, equivalently, $.0085 per yen.

As exchange rates fluctuate, the dollar value of goods priced in foreign currency similarly fluctuates. For example, in 1980, the dollar–yen exchange rate was about $.0045 per yen. Because the exchange rate in 2007 was $.0085 per yen, a U.S. citizen would need almost twice as many dollars in 2007 to buy a product selling for ¥10,000 as would have been required in 1980. If the Japanese producer were to maintain a fixed yen price for its product, the price expressed in U.S. dollars would nearly double. This would make Japanese products more expensive to U.S. consumers, however, and result in lost sales. Obviously, appreciation of the yen creates a problem for Japanese producers that must compete with U.S. producers.

In this vein, see the nearby box, which discusses how the depreciation of the dollar in 2007 was expected to benefit Walt Disney. The firm anticipated an increase in foreign visitors (taking advantage of a relatively cheap dollar) to its parks as well as domestic visitors who would stay in the U.S. because overseas travel became more expensive to them.

Figure 17.1 shows the change in the purchasing power of the U.S. dollar relative to the purchasing power of the currencies of several major industrial countries in the period between 1999 and 2006. The ratio of purchasing powers is called the "real," or inflation adjusted,

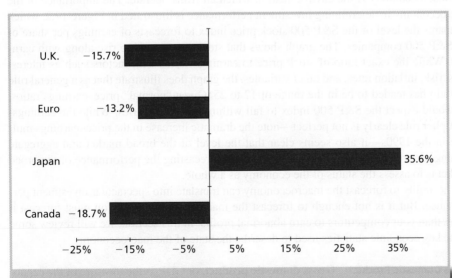

FIGURE 17.1 Change in real exchange rate: U.S. dollar versus major currencies, 1999–2006

Source: Computed from data in the *Economic Report of the President,* 2007.

WEAK DOLLAR COULD HELP FILL MICKEY'S WALLET

The weak dollar has been benefiting businesses with operations overseas—but it could also lend a hand to a struggling domestic industry: tourism. One beneficiary could be Walt Disney.

The U.S. tourism industry was seriously set back after Sept. 11, 2001. Last year was the first time money spent by foreign travelers in the U.S. reached pre-2001 levels, according to the Commerce Department.

Even more is likely to be spent this year. A weak dollar makes it more expensive for U.S. citizens to travel overseas, leading more to choose the beaches of Florida over the boulevards of Paris. Conversely, foreign visitors whose home currencies now fetch more dollars find it cheaper to visit the U.S.

The dollar's impact on Disney may be most apparent in its parks and resorts operations. But even Disney's movie business may benefit from the slumping greenback. Thanks in part to recent depreciation, the dollar value of overseas sales for the third "Pirates of the Caribbean" have hit $640 million, already outstripping the total overseas sales of $637 million of its predecessor, according to Worldwide Boxoffice.

Source: Scott Patterson, "Weak Dollar could Help Fill Mickey's Wallet," *The Wall Street Journal*, August 1, 2007, p. C1.

exchange rate. The change in the real exchange rate measures how much more or less expensive foreign goods have become to U.S. citizens, accounting for both exchange rate fluctuations and inflation differentials across countries. A positive value in Figure 17.1 means that the dollar has gained purchasing power relative to another currency; a negative number indicates a depreciating dollar. For example, the figure shows that goods priced in terms of the Canadian dollar have become far more expensive to U.S. consumers but that goods priced in Japanese yen have become cheaper. Conversely, goods priced in U.S. dollars have become more affordable to Canadian consumers, but more expensive to Japanese consumers.

17.2 THE DOMESTIC MACROECONOMY

The macroeconomy is the environment in which all firms operate. The importance of the macroeconomy in determining investment performance is illustrated in Figure 17.2, which compares the level of the S&P 500 stock price index to forecasts of earnings per share of the S&P 500 companies. The graph shows that stock prices tend to rise along with earnings. While the exact ratio of stock price to earnings varies with factors such as interest rates, risk, inflation rates, and other variables, the graph does illustrate that as a general rule the ratio has tended to be in the range of 12 to 25. Given "normal" price–earnings ratios, we would expect the S&P 500 index to fall within these boundaries. While the earnings-multiplier rule clearly is not perfect—note the dramatic increase in the price–earnings multiple in the 1990s—it also seems clear that the level of the broad market and aggregate earnings do trend together. Thus the first step in forecasting the performance of the broad market is to assess the status of the economy as a whole.

The ability to forecast the macroeconomy can translate into spectacular investment performance. But it is not enough to forecast the macroeconomy well. You must forecast it *better* than your competitors to earn abnormal profits. In this section, we will review some of the key economic statistics used to describe the state of the macroeconomy.

Gross Domestic Product   **Gross domestic product,** or GDP, is the measure of the economy's total production of goods and services. Rapidly growing GDP indicates an expanding economy with ample opportunity for a firm to increase sales. Another popular measure of the economy's output is *industrial production*. This statistic provides a measure of economic activity more narrowly focused on the manufacturing side of the economy.

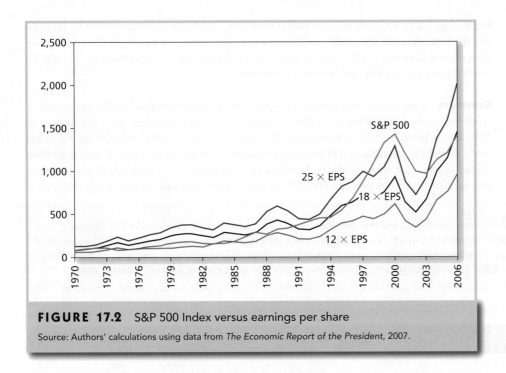

FIGURE 17.2   S&P 500 Index versus earnings per share

Source: Authors' calculations using data from *The Economic Report of the President*, 2007.

Employment   The **unemployment rate** is the percentage of the total labor force (i.e., those who are either working or actively seeking employment) yet to find work. The unemployment rate measures the extent to which the economy is operating at full capacity. The unemployment rate is a factor related to workers only, but further insight into the strength of the economy can be gleaned from the unemployment rate for other factors of production. Analysts also look at the factory *capacity utilization rate,* which is the ratio of actual output from factories to potential output.

Inflation   The rate at which the general level of prices rise is called **inflation.** High rates of inflation often are associated with "overheated" economies, that is, economies where the demand for goods and services is outstripping productive capacity, which leads to upward pressure on prices. Most governments walk a fine line in their economic policies. They hope to stimulate their economies enough to maintain nearly full employment, but not so much as to bring on inflationary pressures. The perceived trade-off between inflation and unemployment is at the heart of many macroeconomic policy disputes. There is considerable room for disagreement as to the relative costs of these policies as well as the economy's relative vulnerability to these pressures at any particular time.

Interest Rates   High interest rates reduce the present value of future cash flows, thereby reducing the attractiveness of investment opportunities. For this reason, real interest rates are key determinants of business investment expenditures. Demand for housing and high-priced consumer durables such as automobiles, which are commonly financed, also is highly sensitive to interest rates because interest rates affect interest payments. (In Chapter 5, Section 5.1, we examined the determinants of interest rates.)

Budget Deficit   The **budget deficit** of the federal government is the difference between government spending and revenues. Any budgetary shortfall must be offset by government borrowing. Large amounts of government borrowing can force up interest rates by increasing the total demand for credit in the economy. Economists generally believe excessive government borrowing will "crowd out" private borrowing and investing by forcing up interest rates and choking off business investment.

Sentiment   Consumers' and producers' optimism or pessimism concerning the economy is an important determinant of economic performance. If consumers have confidence in their future income levels, for example, they will be more willing to spend on big-ticket items. Similarly, businesses will increase production and inventory levels if they anticipate higher demand for their products. In this way, beliefs influence how much consumption and investment will be pursued and affect the aggregate demand for goods and services.

CONCEPT CHECK 1	Consider an economy where the dominant industry is automobile production for domestic consumption as well as export. Now suppose the auto market is hurt by an increase in the length of time people use their cars before replacing them. Describe the probable effects of this change on (a) GDP, (b) unemployment, (c) the government budget deficit, and (d) interest rates.

17.3   DEMAND AND SUPPLY SHOCKS

A useful way to organize your analysis of the factors that might influence the macroeconomy is to classify any impact as a supply or demand shock. A **demand shock** is an event that affects the demand for goods and services in the economy. Examples of positive demand shocks are reductions in tax rates, increases in the money supply, increases in government spending, or increases in foreign export demand. A **supply shock** is an event that influences production capacity and costs. Examples of supply shocks are changes in the price of imported oil; freezes, floods, or droughts that might destroy large quantities of agricultural crops; changes in the educational level of an economy's workforce; or changes in the wage rates at which the labor force is willing to work.

Demand shocks are usually characterized by aggregate output moving in the same direction as interest rates and inflation. For example, a big increase in government spending will tend to stimulate the economy and increase GDP. It also might increase interest rates by increasing the demand for borrowed funds by the government as well as by businesses that might desire to borrow to finance new ventures. Finally, it could increase the inflation rate if the demand for goods and services is raised to a level at or beyond the total productive capacity of the economy.

Supply shocks are usually characterized by aggregate output moving in the opposite direction of inflation and interest rates. For example, a big increase in the price of imported oil will be inflationary because costs of production will rise, which eventually will lead to increases in prices of finished goods. The increase in inflation rates over the near term can lead to higher nominal interest rates. Against this background, aggregate output will be falling. With raw materials more expensive, the productive capacity of the economy is reduced, as is the ability of individuals to purchase goods at now-higher prices. GDP, therefore, tends to fall.

How can we relate this framework to investment analysis? You want to identify the industries that will be most helped or hurt in any macroeconomic scenario you envision. For example, if you forecast a tightening of the money supply, you might want to avoid industries such as automobile producers that might be hurt by the likely increase in interest rates. We caution you again that these forecasts are no easy task. Macroeconomic predictions are notoriously unreliable. And again, you must be aware that in all likelihood your forecast will be made using only publicly available information. Any investment advantage you have will be a result only of better analysis—not better information.

17.4 FEDERAL GOVERNMENT POLICY

As the previous section would suggest, the government has two broad classes of macroeconomic tools—those that affect the demand for goods and services and those that affect the supply. For much of postwar history, demand-side policy was of primary interest. The focus was on government spending, tax levels, and monetary policy. Since the 1980s, however, increasing attention has been focused on supply-side economics. Broadly interpreted, supply-side concerns have to do with enhancing the productive capacity of the economy, rather than increasing the demand for the goods and services the economy can produce. In practice, supply-side economists have focused on the appropriateness of the incentives to work, innovate, and take risks that result from our system of taxation. However, issues such as national policies on education, infrastructure (such as communication and transportation systems), and research and development also are properly regarded as part of supply-side macroeconomic policy.

Fiscal Policy

Fiscal policy refers to the government's spending and tax actions and is part of "demand-side management." Fiscal policy is probably the most direct way either to stimulate or to slow the economy. Decreases in government spending directly deflate the demand for goods and services. Similarly, increases in tax rates immediately siphon income from consumers and result in fairly rapid decreases in consumption.

Ironically, although fiscal policy has the most immediate impact on the economy, the formulation and implementation of such policy is usually painfully slow and involved. This is because fiscal policy requires enormous amounts of compromise between the executive and legislative branches. Tax and spending policy must be initiated and voted on by Congress, which requires considerable political negotiations, and any legislation passed must be signed by the president, requiring more negotiation. Thus, although the impact of fiscal policy is relatively immediate, its formulation is so cumbersome that fiscal policy cannot in practice be used to fine-tune the economy.

Moreover, much of government spending, such as that for Medicare or Social Security, is nondiscretionary, meaning that it is determined by formula rather than policy and cannot be changed in response to economic conditions. This places even more rigidity into the formulation of fiscal policy.

A common way to summarize the net impact of government fiscal policy is to look at the government's budget deficit or surplus, which is simply the difference between revenues and expenditures. A large deficit means the government is spending considerably more than it is taking in by way of taxes. The net effect is to increase the demand for goods (via spending) by more than it reduces the demand for goods (via taxes), thereby stimulating the economy.

Monetary Policy

Monetary policy refers to the manipulation of the money supply to affect the macroeconomy and is the other main leg of demand-side policy. Monetary policy works largely through its impact on interest rates. Increases in the money supply lower short-term interest rates, ultimately encouraging investment and consumption demand. Over longer periods, however, most economists believe a higher money supply leads only to a higher price level and does not have a permanent effect on economic activity. Thus the monetary authorities face a difficult balancing act. Expansionary monetary policy probably will lower interest rates and thereby stimulate investment and some consumption demand in the short run, but these circumstances ultimately will lead only to higher prices. The stimulation/inflation trade-off is implicit in all debate over proper monetary policy.

Fiscal policy is cumbersome to implement but has a fairly direct impact on the economy, whereas monetary policy is easily formulated and implemented but has a less immediate impact. Monetary policy is determined by the Board of Governors of the Federal Reserve System. Board members are appointed by the president for 14-year terms and are reasonably insulated from political pressure. The board is small enough, and often sufficiently dominated by its chairperson, that policy can be formulated and modulated relatively easily.

Implementation of monetary policy also is quite direct. The most widely used tool is the open market operation, in which the Fed buys or sells bonds for its own account. When the Fed buys securities, it simply "writes a check," thereby increasing the money supply. (Unlike us, the Fed can pay for the securities without drawing down funds at a bank account.) Conversely, when the Fed sells a security, the money paid for it leaves the money supply. Open market operations occur daily, allowing the Fed to fine-tune its monetary policy.

Other tools at the Fed's disposal are the discount rate, which is the interest rate it charges banks on short-term loans, and the reserve requirement, which is the fraction of deposits that banks must hold as cash on hand or as deposits with the Fed. Reductions in the discount rate signal a more expansionary monetary policy. Lowering reserve requirements allows banks to make more loans with each dollar of deposits and stimulates the economy by increasing the effective money supply.

While the discount rate is under the direct control of the Fed, it is changed relatively infrequently. The *federal funds rate* is by far the better guide to Federal Reserve policy. The federal funds rate is the interest rate at which banks make short-term, usually overnight, loans to each other. These loans occur because some banks need to borrow funds to meet reserve requirements, while other banks have excess funds. Unlike the discount rate, the fed funds rate is a market rate, meaning that it is determined by supply and demand rather than being set administratively. Nevertheless, the Federal Reserve Board targets the fed funds rate, expanding or contracting the money supply through open market operations as it nudges the fed funds rate to its targeted value. This is the benchmark short-term U.S. interest rate, and as such has considerable influence on other interest rates in the United States and the rest of the world.

Monetary policy affects the economy in a more roundabout way than fiscal policy. Whereas fiscal policy directly stimulates or dampens the economy, monetary policy works largely through its impact on interest rates. Increases in the money supply lower interest rates, which stimulates investment demand. As the quantity of money in the economy increases, investors will find that their portfolios of assets include too much money. They will rebalance their portfolios by buying securities such as bonds, forcing bond prices up and interest rates down. In the longer run, individuals may increase their holdings of stocks as well and ultimately buy real assets, which stimulates consumption demand directly. The ultimate effect of monetary policy on investment and consumption demand, however, is less immediate than that of fiscal policy.

CONCEPT CHECK 2	Suppose the government wants to stimulate the economy without increasing interest rates. What combination of fiscal and monetary policy might accomplish this goal?

Supply-Side Policies

Fiscal and monetary policy are demand-oriented tools that affect the economy by stimulating the total demand for goods and services. The implicit belief is that the economy will not by itself arrive at a full employment equilibrium and that macroeconomic policy can push the economy toward this goal. In contrast, supply-side policies treat the issue of the productive capacity of the economy. The goal is to create an environment in which workers and owners of capital have the maximum incentive and ability to produce and develop goods.

Supply-side economists also pay considerable attention to tax policy. Whereas demand-siders look at the effect of taxes on consumption demand, supply-siders focus on incentives and marginal tax rates. They argue that lowering tax rates will elicit more investment and improve incentives to work, thereby enhancing economic growth. Some go so far as to claim that reductions in tax rates can lead to increases in tax revenues because the lower tax rates will cause the economy and the revenue tax base to grow by more than the tax rate is reduced.

CONCEPT CHECK 3	Large tax cuts in 2001 were followed by relatively rapid growth in GDP. How would demand-side and supply-side economists differ in their interpretations of this phenomenon?

17.5 BUSINESS CYCLES

We've looked at the tools the government uses to fine-tune the economy, attempting to maintain low unemployment and low inflation. Despite these efforts, economies repeatedly seem to pass through good and bad times. One determinant of the broad asset allocation decision of many analysts is a forecast of whether the macroeconomy is improving or deteriorating. A forecast that differs from the market consensus can have a major impact on investment strategy.

The Business Cycle

The economy recurrently experiences periods of expansion and contraction, although the length and depth of those cycles can be irregular. This recurring pattern of recession and recovery is called the **business cycle.** Figure 17.3 presents graphs of several measures of production and output. The production series all show clear variation around a generally rising trend. The bottom graph of capacity utilization also evidences a clear cyclical (although irregular) pattern.

The transition points across cycles are called peaks and troughs, indicated by the left and right edges of the shaded regions in Figure 17.3. A **peak** is the transition from the end of an expansion to the start of a contraction. A **trough** occurs at the bottom of a recession just as the economy enters a recovery. The shaded areas in Figure 17.3 therefore all represent periods of recession.

As the economy passes through different stages of the business cycle, the relative performance of different industry groups might be expected to vary. For example, at a trough, just before the economy begins to recover from a recession, one would expect that **cyclical industries,** those with above-average sensitivity to the state of the economy, would tend to outperform other industries. Examples of cyclical industries are producers of durable goods such as automobiles. Because purchases of these goods can be deferred during a recession, sales are particularly sensitive to macroeconomic conditions. Other cyclical

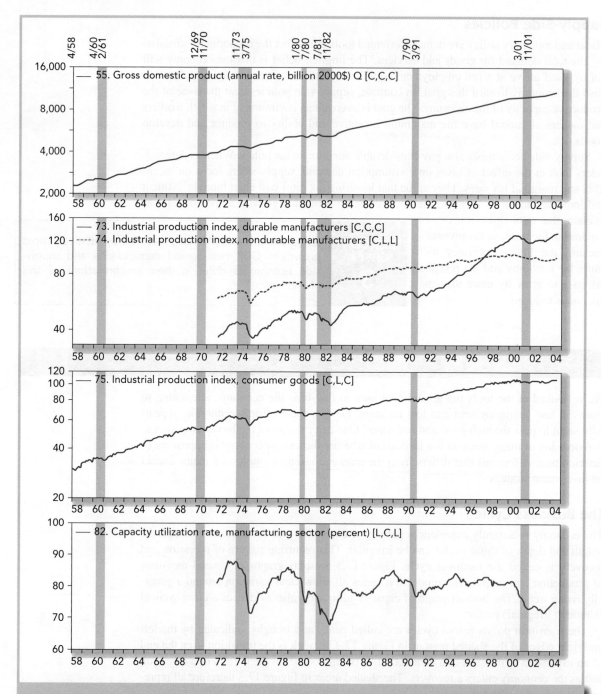

FIGURE 17.3   Cyclical indicators

Source: The Conference Board, *Business Cycle Indicators*, August 2004.

industries are producers of capital goods, that is, goods used by other firms to produce their own products. When demand is slack, few companies will be expanding and purchasing capital goods. Therefore, the capital goods industry bears the brunt of a slowdown but does well in an expansion.

In contrast to cyclical firms, **defensive industries** have little sensitivity to the business cycle. These are industries that produce goods for which sales and profits are least sensitive to the state of the economy. Defensive industries include food producers and processors, pharmaceutical firms, and public utilities. These industries will outperform others when the economy enters a recession.

The cyclical/defensive classification corresponds well to the notion of systematic or market risk introduced in our discussion of portfolio theory. When perceptions about the health of the economy become more optimistic, for example, the prices of most stocks will increase as forecasts of profitability rise. Because the cyclical firms are most sensitive to such developments, their stock prices will rise the most. Thus firms in cyclical industries will tend to have high-beta stocks. In general, then, stocks of cyclical firms will show the best results when economic news is positive but the worst results when that news is bad. Conversely, defensive firms will have low betas and performance that is relatively unaffected by overall market conditions.

If your assessments of the state of the business cycle were reliably more accurate than those of other investors, you would simply choose cyclical industries when you are relatively more optimistic about the economy and defensive firms when you are relatively more pessimistic. Unfortunately, it is not so easy to determine when the economy is passing through a peak or a trough. It if were, choosing between cyclical and defensive industries would be easy. As we know from our discussion of efficient markets, however, attractive investment choices will rarely be obvious. It usually is not apparent that a recession or expansion has started or ended until several months after the fact. With hindsight, the transitions from expansion to recession and back might be apparent, but it is often quite difficult to say whether the economy is heating up or slowing down at any moment.

Economic Indicators

Given the cyclical nature of the business cycle, it is not surprising that to some extent the cycle can be predicted. A set of cyclical indicators computed by the Conference Board helps forecast, measure, and interpret short-term fluctuations in economic activity. **Leading economic indicators** are those economic series that tend to rise or fall in advance of the rest of the economy. *Coincident* and *lagging indicators,* as their names suggest, move in tandem with or somewhat after the broad economy.

Ten series are grouped into a widely followed composite index of leading economic indicators. Similarly, four coincident and seven lagging indicators form separate indexes. The composition of these indexes appears in Table 17.2.

Figure 17.4 graphs these three series. The numbers on the top of the chart indicate the date of each turning point (in year:month format) between expansions and contractions. The chart shows that the index of leading indicators consistently turns before the rest of the economy, but its lead time is somewhat erratic. Moreover, the lead time for peaks is consistently longer than that for troughs.

The stock market price index is a leading indicator. This is as it should be, as stock prices are forward-looking predictors of future profitability. Unfortunately, this makes the series of leading indicators much less useful for investment policy—by the time the series predicts an upturn, the market has already made its move. Although the business cycle may

TABLE 17.2

Indexes of economic indicators

A. Leading indicators
1. Average weekly hours of production workers (manufacturing)
2. Initial claims for unemployment insurance
3. Manufacturers' new orders (consumer goods and materials industries)
4. Fraction of companies reporting slower deliveries diffusion index
5. New orders for nondefense capital goods
6. New private housing units authorized by local building permits
7. Yield curve slope: 10-year Treasury minus federal funds rate
8. Stock prices, 500 common stocks
9. Money supply (M2) growth rate
10. Index of consumer expectations
B. Coincident indicators
1. Employees on nonagricultural payrolls
2. Personal income less transfer payments
3. Industrial production
4. Manufacturing and trade sales
C. Lagging indicators
1. Average duration of unemployment
2. Ratio of trade inventories to sales
3. Change in index of labor cost per unit of output
4. Average prime rate charged by banks
5. Commercial and industrial loans outstanding
6. Ratio of consumer installment credit outstanding to personal income
7. Change in consumer price index for services

Source: The Conference Board, *Business Cycle Indicators,* February 2007.

be somewhat predictable, the stock market may not be. This is just one more manifestation of the efficient markets hypothesis.

The money supply is another leading indicator. This makes sense in light of our earlier discussion concerning the lags surrounding the effects of monetary policy on the economy. An expansionary monetary policy can be observed fairly quickly, but it might not affect the economy for several months. Therefore, today's monetary policy might well predict future economic activity.

Other leading indicators focus directly on decisions made today that will affect production in the near future. For example, manufacturers' new orders for goods, contracts and orders for plant and equipment, and housing starts all signal a coming expansion in the economy.

A wide range of economic indicators is released to the public on a regular "economic calendar." Table 17.3 is an "economic calendar," listing the public announcement dates and sources for about 20 statistics of interest. These announcements are reported in the financial press, for example, *The Wall Street Journal,* as they are released. They also are available at many sites on the Web, for example, at the Yahoo! Finance Web site. Figure 17.5 (on p. 567) is an excerpt from the Economic Calendar page at Yahoo! The page gives a list of the announcements released the week of October 16. Notice that recent forecasts of each variable are provided along with the actual value of each statistic. This is useful, because

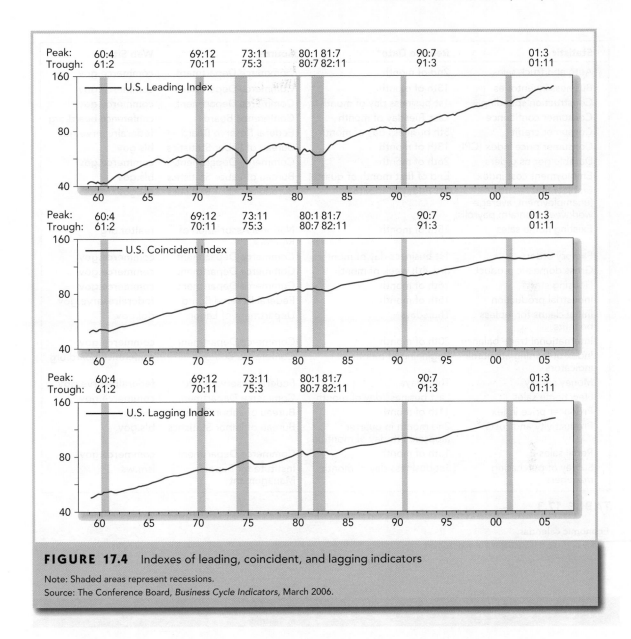

FIGURE 17.4   Indexes of leading, coincident, and lagging indicators

Note: Shaded areas represent recessions.

Source: The Conference Board, *Business Cycle Indicators*, March 2006.

in an efficient market, security prices already will reflect market expectations. The *new* information in the announcement will determine the market response.

Other Indicators

You can find lots of important information about the state of the economy from sources other than the official components of the economic calendar or the components of business cycle indicators. Table 17.4 (on p. 567), which is derived from some suggestions in *Inc.* magazine,[1] contains a few.

---

[1]Gene Sperling, "The Insider's Guide to Economic Forecasting," *Inc.,* August 2003, p. 96.

Statistic	Release Date*	Source	Web Site
Auto and truck sales	2nd of month	Commerce Department	commerce.gov
Business inventories	15th of month	Commerce Department	commerce.gov
Construction spending	1st business day of month	Commerce Department	commerce.gov
Consumer confidence	Last Tuesday of month	Conference Board	conference-board.org
Consumer credit	5th business day of month	Federal Reserve Board	federalreserve.gov
Consumer price index (CPI)	13th of month	Bureau of Labor Statistics	bls.gov
Durable goods orders	26th of month	Commerce Department	commerce.gov
Employment cost index	End of first month of quarter	Bureau of Labor Statistics	bls.gov
Employment record (unemployment, average workweek, nonfarm payrolls)	1st Friday of month	Bureau of Labor Statistics	bls.gov
Existing home sales	25th of month	National Association of Realtors	realtor.org
Factory orders	1st business day of month	Commerce Department	commerce.gov
Gross domestic product	3rd–4th week of month	Commerce Department	commerce.gov
Housing starts	16th of month	Commerce Department	commerce.gov
Industrial production	15th of month	Federal Reserve Board	federalreserve.gov
Initial claims for jobless benefits	Thursdays	Department of Labor	dol.gov
International trade balance	20th of month	Commerce Department	commerce.gov
Index of leading economic indicators	Beginning of month	Conference Board	conference-board.org
Money supply	Thursdays	Federal Reserve Board	federalreserve.gov
New home sales	Last business day of month	Commerce Department	commerce.gov
Producer price index	11th of month	Bureau of Labor Statistics	bls.gov
Productivity and costs	2nd month in quarter (approx. 7th day of month)	Bureau of Labor Statistics	bls.gov
Retail sales	13th of month	Commerce Department	commerce.gov
Survey of purchasing managers	1st business day of month	Institute for Supply Management	ism.ws

TABLE 17.3

Economic calendar

*Many of these release dates are approximate.

17.6 INDUSTRY ANALYSIS

Industry analysis is important for the same reason that macroeconomic analysis is. Just as it is difficult for an industry to perform well when the macroeconomy is ailing, it is unusual for a firm in a troubled industry to perform well. Similarly, just as we have seen that economic performance can vary widely across countries, performance also can vary widely across industries. Figure 17.6 (see p. 568) illustrates the dispersion of industry performance. It shows return on equity based on 2007 profitability for several major industry groups. ROE ranged from 8.5% for airlines to 35.0% for the cigarette industry.

Given the wide variation in profitability, it is not surprising that industry groups exhibit considerable dispersion in their stock market performance. Figure 17.7 (see p. 569) presents the stock market performance of several industry-specific iShares during 2007. The spread in performance is remarkable, ranging from a 35.7% return in the oil equipment

Economic Calendar   Week of October 15, 2007

Last Week

Date	Time (ET)	Statistic	For	Actual	Briefing Forecast	Market Expects	Prior
Oct 16	9:15 AM	Industrial Production	Sep	0.1%	0.1%	0.1%	0.0%
Oct 16	9:15 AM	Capacity Utilization	Sep	82.1%	82.2%	82.1%	82.2%
Oct 17	8:30 AM	CPI	Sep	0.3%	0.2%	0.2%	−0.1%
Oct 17	8:30 AM	Housing Starts	Sep	1191K	1300K	1285K	1327K
Oct 17	8:30 AM	Building Permits	Sep	1226K	1310K	1300K	1326K

FIGURE 17.5   Economic calendar at Yahoo!

Source: Yahoo! Finance, **biz.yahoo.com.** Reproduced by permission of Yahoo! Inc. © 2007 by Yahoo! Inc. Yahoo! and the Yahoo! logo are trademarks of Yahoo! Inc.

industry to a 51.9% loss in home construction. Recall that iShares are exchange-traded funds (see Chapter 4) that trade like stocks and thus allow even small investors to take a position in each traded industry. So this range of performance was very much available to virtually all investors in 2007. Alternatively, one can invest in mutual funds with

		TABLE 17.4
CEO polls www.businessroundtable.org	The business roundtable surveys CEOs about planned capital spending, a good measure of their optimism about the economy.	Useful economic indicators
Temp jobs (search for "Temporary Help Services") www.bls.gov	A useful leading indicator. Businesses often hire temporary workers as the economy first picks up, until it is clear that an upturn is going to be sustained. This series is available at the Bureau of Labor Statistics Web site.	
Wal-Mart sales www.walmartstores.com	Wal-Mart sales are a good indicator of the retail sector. It publishes its same-store sales weekly.	
Commercial and industrial loans www.federalreserve.gov	These loans are used by small and medium-sized firms. Information is published weekly by the Federal Reserve.	
Semiconductors www.semi.org	The book-to-bill ratio (i.e., new sales versus actual shipments) indicates whether demand in the technology sector is increasing (ratio > 1) or falling. This ratio is published by Semiconductor Equipment and Materials International.	
Commercial structures http://bea.doc.gov	Investment in structures is an indicator of businesses' forecasts of demand for their products in the near future. This series is compiled by the Bureau of Economic Analysis as part of its GDP series.	

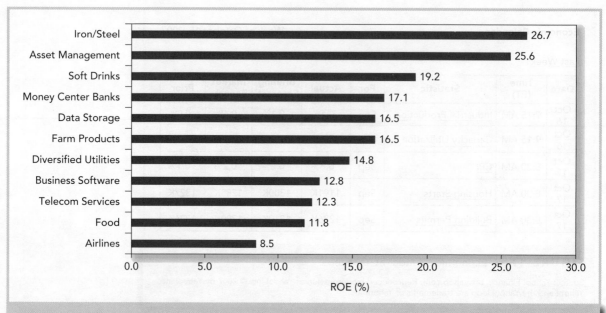

FIGURE 17.6 Return on equity, 2007

Source: Yahoo! Finance, November 5, 2007. **finance.yahoo.com.** Reproduced with permission of Yahoo! Inc. © 2007 by Yahoo! Inc. Yahoo! and the Yahoo! logo are trademarks of Yahoo! Inc.

an industry focus. For example, Fidelity offers about 40 Select Funds, each of which is invested in a particular industry.

Defining an Industry

Although we know what we mean by an "industry," it can be difficult in practice to decide where to draw the line between one industry and another. Consider, for example, one of the industries depicted in Figure 17.6, money center banks. Industry ROE in 2007 was 17.1%. But there is substantial variation within this group by size, focus, and region, and one might well be justified in further dividing these banks into distinct subindustries. Their differences may result in considerable dispersion in financial performance. Figure 17.8 shows ROE for a sample of the banks included in this industry, confirming that 2007 performance did indeed vary widely: from 11.7% for Sun Trust to 24.9% for TCF Financial.

A useful way to define industry groups in practice is given by the North American Industry Classification System, or **NAICS codes.**[2] These are codes assigned to group firms for statistical analysis. The first two digits of the NAICS codes denote very broad industry classifications. For example, Table 17.5 shows that the codes for all construction firms start with 23. The next digits define the industry grouping more narrowly. For example, codes starting with 236 denote *building* construction, 2361 denotes *residential* construction, and

---

[2]These codes are used for firms operating inside the NAFTA (North American Free Trade Agreement) region, which includes the U.S., Mexico, and Canada. NAICS codes have replaced the Standard Industry Classification or SIC codes previously used in the U.S.

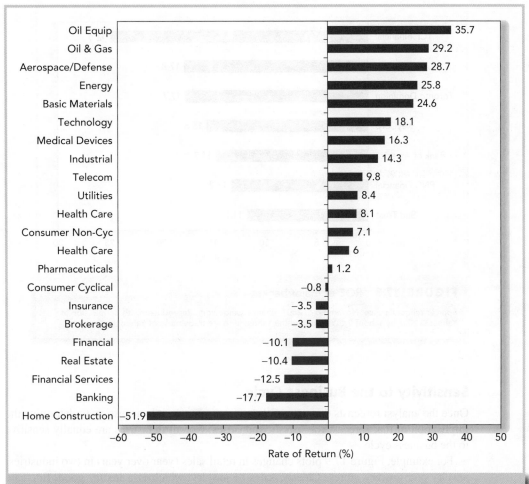

FIGURE 17.7   Industry stock price performance as measured by rate of return on Dow Jones Sector iShares, January–October 2007

236115 denotes *single-family* construction. Firms with the same four-digit NAICS codes are commonly taken to be in the same industry.

NAICS industry classifications are not perfect. For example, both J.C. Penney and Neiman Marcus might be classified as "Department Stores." Yet the former is a high-volume "value" store, whereas the latter is a high-margin elite retailer. Are they really in the same industry? Still, these classifications are a tremendous aid in conducting industry analysis because they provide a means of focusing on very broad or fairly narrowly defined groups of firms.

Several other industry classifications are provided by other analysts; for example, Standard & Poor's reports on the performance of about 100 industry groups. S&P computes stock price indexes for each group, which is useful in assessing past investment performance. The *Value Line Investment Survey* reports on the conditions and prospects of about 1,700 firms, grouped into about 90 industries. Value Line's analysts prepare forecasts of the performance of industry groups as well as of each firm.

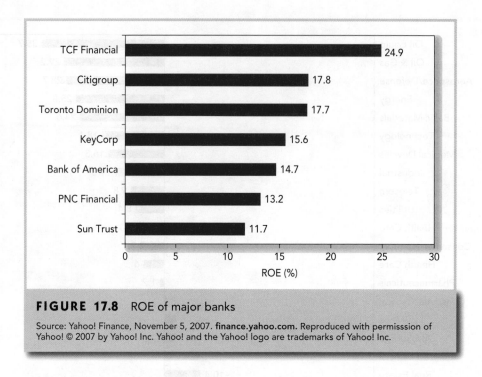

FIGURE 17.8 ROE of major banks

Source: Yahoo! Finance, November 5, 2007. **finance.yahoo.com.** Reproduced with permisssion of Yahoo! © 2007 by Yahoo! Inc. Yahoo! and the Yahoo! logo are trademarks of Yahoo! Inc.

Sensitivity to the Business Cycle

Once the analyst forecasts the state of the macroeconomy, it is necessary to determine the implication of that forecast for specific industries. Not all industries are equally sensitive to the business cycle.

For example, Figure 17.9 plots changes in retail sales (year over year) in two industries: jewelry and grocery stores. Clearly, sales of jewelry, which is a luxury good, fluctuate more widely than those of groceries. The downturn in jewelry sales in 2001 when the economy was in a recession is notable. In contrast, sales growth in the grocery industry

TABLE 17.5

Examples of NAICS industry codes

NAICS Code	NAICS Title
23	Construction
236	Construction of Buildings
2361	Residential Building Construction
23611	Residential Building Construction
236115	New Single-Family Housing Construction
236116	New Multifamily Housing Construction
236117	New Housing Operative Builders
236118	Residential Remodelers
2362	Nonresidential Building Construction
23621	Industrial Building Construction
236210	Industrial Building Construction
23622	Commercial and Institutional Building Construction
236220	Commercial and Institutional Building Construction

is relatively stable, with no years in which sales decline. These patterns reflect that fact that jewelry is a discretionary good, whereas most grocery products are staples for which demand will not fall significantly even in hard times.

Three factors will determine the sensitivity of a firm's earnings to the business cycle. First is the sensitivity of sales. Necessities will show little sensitivity to business conditions. Examples of industries in this group are food, drugs, and medical services. Other industries with low sensitivity are those for which income is not a crucial determinant of demand. Tobacco products are an example of this type of industry. Another industry in this group is movies, because consumers

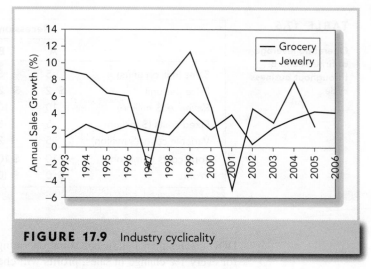

FIGURE 17.9 Industry cyclicality

tend to substitute movies for more expensive sources of entertainment when income levels are low. In contrast, firms in industries such as machine tools, steel, autos, and transportation are highly sensitive to the state of the economy.

The second factor determining business cycle sensitivity is operating leverage, which refers to the division between fixed and variable costs. (Fixed costs are those the firm incurs regardless of its production levels. Variable costs are those that rise or fall as the firm produces more or less product.) Firms with greater amounts of variable as opposed to fixed costs will be less sensitive to business conditions. This is because in economic downturns, these firms can reduce costs as output falls in response to falling sales. Profits for firms with high fixed costs will swing more widely with sales because costs do not move to offset revenue variability. Firms with high fixed costs are said to have high operating leverage, because small swings in business conditions can have large impacts on profitability.

EXAMPLE 17.1 Operating Leverage

Consider two firms operating in the same industry with identical revenues in all phases of the business cycle: recession, normal, and expansion. Firm A has short-term leases on most of its equipment and can reduce its lease expenditures when production slackens. It has fixed costs of $5 million and variable costs of $1 per unit of output. Firm B has long-term leases on most of its equipment and must make lease payments regardless of economic conditions. Its fixed costs are higher, $8 million, but its variable costs are only $.50 per unit. Table 17.6 shows that Firm A will do better in recessions than Firm B, but not as well in expansions. A's costs move in conjunction with its revenues to help performance in downturns and impede performance in upturns.

We can quantify operating leverage by measuring how sensitive profits are to changes in sales. The **degree of operating leverage,** or DOL, is defined as

$$DOL = \frac{\text{Percentage change in profits}}{\text{Percentage change in sales}}$$

TABLE 17.6

Operating leverage
of firms A and B
throughout business
cycle

	Recession		Normal		Expansion	
	A	**B**	**A**	**B**	**A**	**B**
Sales (million units)	5	5	6	6	7	7
Price per unit	$ 2	$ 2	$ 2	$ 2	$ 2	$ 2
Revenue ($ million)	10	10	12	12	14	14
Fixed costs ($ million)	5	8	5	8	5	8
Variable costs ($ million)	5	2.5	6	3	7	3.5
Total costs ($ million)	$10	$ 10.5	$11	$11	$12	$11.5
Profits	$ 0	$ (0.5)	$ 1	$ 1	$ 2	$ 2.5

DOL greater than 1 indicates some operating leverage. For example, if DOL = 2, then for every 1% change in sales, profits will change by 2% in the same direction, either up or down.

We have seen that the degree of operating leverage increases with a firm's exposure to fixed costs. In fact, one can show that DOL depends on fixed costs in the following manner:[3]

$$DOL = 1 + \frac{\text{Fixed costs}}{\text{Profits}}$$

EXAMPLE 17.2   Degree of Operating Leverage

Return to the two firms illustrated in Table 17.6 and compare profits and sales in the "normal" scenario for the economy with those in a recession. Profits of Firm A fall by 100% (from $1 million to zero) when sales fall by 16.7% (from $6 million to $5 million):

$$DOL(\text{Firm A}) = \frac{\text{Percentage change in profits}}{\text{Percentage change in sales}} = \frac{-100\%}{-16.7\%} = 6$$

We can confirm the relationship between DOL and fixed costs as follows:

$$DOL(\text{Firm A}) = 1 + \frac{\text{Fixed costs}}{\text{Profits}} = 1 + \frac{\$5 \text{ million}}{\$1 \text{ million}} = 6$$

Firm B has higher fixed costs, and its operating leverage is higher. Again, compare data for a normal scenario to a recession. Profits for Firm B fall by 150%, from $1 million to –$.5 million. Operating leverage for Firm B is therefore

$$DOL(\text{Firm B}) = \frac{\text{Percentage change in profits}}{\text{Percentage change in sales}} = \frac{-150\%}{-16.7\%} = 9$$

which reflects its higher level of fixed costs:

$$DOL(\text{Firm B}) = 1 + \frac{\text{Fixed costs}}{\text{Profits}} = 1 + \frac{\$8 \text{ million}}{\$1 \text{ million}} = 9$$

[3]Operating leverage and DOL are treated in more detail in most corporate finance texts.

The third factor influencing business cycle sensitivity is financial leverage, which is the use of borrowing. Interest payments on debt must be paid regardless of sales. They are fixed costs that also increase the sensitivity of profits to business conditions. (We will have more to say about financial leverage in Chapter 19.)

Investors should not always prefer industries with lower sensitivity to the business cycle. Firms in sensitive industries will have high-beta stocks and are riskier. But while they swing lower in downturns, they also swing higher in upturns. As always, the issue you need to address is whether the expected return on the investment is fair compensation for the risks borne.

CONCEPT CHECK 4	What will be profits in the three scenarios for Firm C with fixed costs of $2 million and variable costs of $1.50 per unit? What are your conclusions regarding operating leverage and business risk?

Sector Rotation

One way that many analysts think about the relationship between industry analysis and the business cycle is the notion of **sector rotation.** The idea is to shift the portfolio more heavily into industry or sector groups that are expected to outperform based on one's assessment of the state of the business cycle.

Figure 17.10 is a stylized depiction of the business cycle. Near the peak of the business cycle, the economy might be overheated with high inflation and interest rates, and price pressures on basic commodities. This might be a good time to invest in firms engaged in natural resource extraction and processing such as minerals or petroleum.

Following a peak, when the economy enters a contraction or recession, one would expect defensive industries that are less sensitive to economic conditions, for example, pharmaceuticals, food, and other necessities, to be the best performers. At the height of the contraction, financial firms will be hurt by shrinking loan volume and higher default rates. Toward the end of the recession, however, contractions induce lower inflation and interest rates, which favor financial firms.

At the trough of a recession, the economy is poised for recovery and subsequent expansion. Firms might thus be spending on purchases of new equipment to meet anticipated increases in demand. This, then, would be a good time to invest in capital goods industries, such as equipment, transportation, or construction.

Finally, in an expansion, the economy is growing rapidly. Cyclical industries such as consumer durables and luxury items will be most profitable in this stage of the cycle. Banks might also do well in expansions, since loan volume will be high and default exposure low when the economy is growing rapidly.

Figure 17.11 illustrates sector rotation. When investors are relatively pessimistic

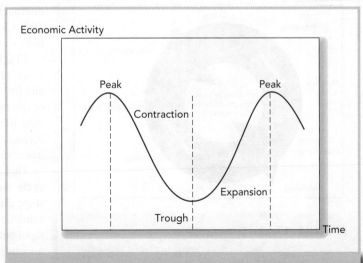

FIGURE 17.10 A stylized depiction of the business cycle.

about the economy, they will shift into noncyclical industries such as consumer staples or health care. When anticipating an expansion, they will prefer more cyclical industries such as materials and technology.

Let us emphasize again that sector rotation, like any other form of market timing, will be successful only if one anticipates the next stage of the business cycle better than other investors. The business cycle depicted in Figure 17.10 is highly stylized. In real life, it is never as clear how long each phase of the cycle will last, nor how extreme it will be. These forecasts are where analysts need to earn their keep.

CONCEPT CHECK 5

In which phase of the business cycle would you expect the following industries to enjoy their best performance?

a. Newspapers

b. Machine tools

c. Beverages

d. Timber

Industry Life Cycles

Examine the biotechnology industry and you will find many firms with high rates of investment, high rates of return on investment, and low dividend payout rates. Do the same for the public utility industry and you will find lower rates of return, lower investment rates, and higher dividend payout rates. Why should this be?

The biotech industry is still new. Recently, available technologies have created opportunities for highly profitable investment of resources. New products are protected by patents, and profit margins are high. With such lucrative investment opportunities, firms find it advantageous to put all profits back into the firm. The companies grow rapidly on average.

Eventually, however, growth must slow. The high profit rates will induce new firms to enter the industry. Increasing competition will hold down prices and profit margins. New technologies become proven and more predictable, risk levels fall, and entry becomes even easier. As internal investment opportunities become less attractive, a lower fraction of profits is reinvested in the firm. Cash dividends increase.

Ultimately, in a mature industry, we observe "cash cows," firms with stable dividends and cash flows and little risk. Growth rates might be similar to that of the overall economy. Industries in early states of their life cycles offer high-risk/high-potential-return investments. Mature industries offer lower-risk, lower-return profiles.

This analysis suggests that a typical **industry life cycle** might be described by four stages: a start-up stage, characterized by extremely rapid growth; a consolidation stage, characterized by growth that is less rapid but still faster than that of the general economy; a maturity stage, characterized by growth no faster than the general economy; and a stage of relative decline, in which the industry grows less rapidly than

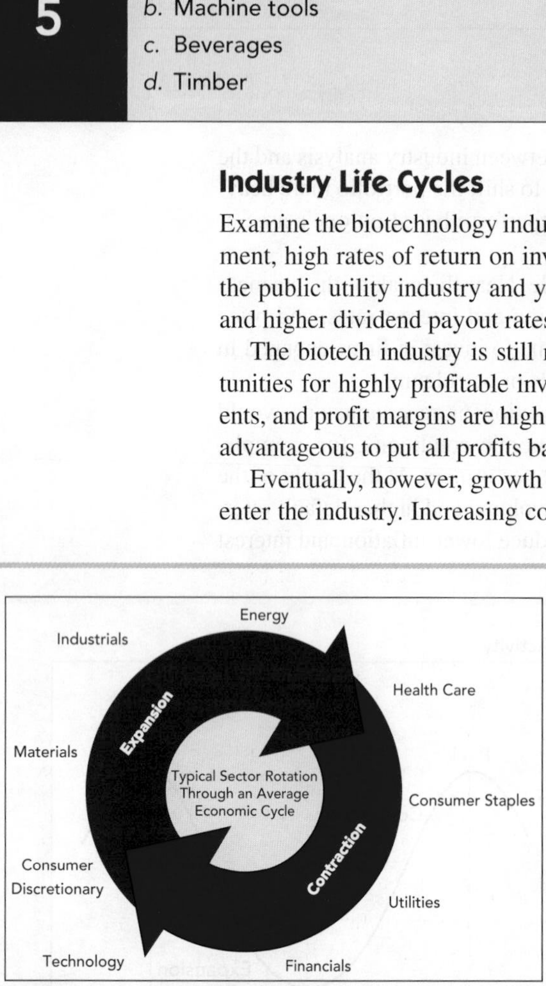

FIGURE 17.11   Sector rotation

Source: Sam Stovall, *BusinessWeek Online,* "A Cyclical Take on Performance." Reprinted with special permission from the July 8, 2004, issue of *BusinessWeek.* © 2004 McGraw-Hill Companies, Inc.

the rest of the economy, or actually shrinks. This industry life cycle is illustrated in Figure 17.12. Let us turn to an elaboration of each of these stages.

Start-Up Stage   The early stages of an industry are often characterized by a new technology or product such as VCRs or personal computers in the 1980s, cell phones in the 1990s, or flat-screen televisions more recently. At this stage, it is difficult to predict which firms will emerge as industry leaders. Some firms will turn out to be wildly successful, and others will fail altogether. Therefore, there is considerable risk in selecting one particular firm within the industry. For example, in the flat-screen television industry, there is still a battle among competing technologies, such as LCD versus plasma screens, and it is still difficult to predict which firms or technologies ultimately will dominate the market.

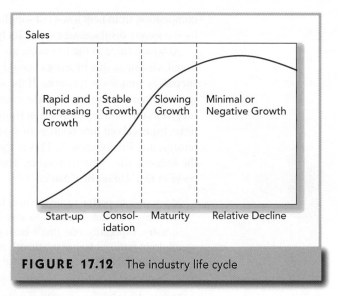

FIGURE 17.12   The industry life cycle

At the industry level, however, sales and earnings will grow at an extremely rapid rate, because the new product has not yet saturated its market. For example, in 1980 very few households had VCRs. The potential market for the product therefore was the entire set of television-watching households. In contrast to this situation, consider the market for a mature product like refrigerators. Almost all households in the United States already have refrigerators, so the market for this good is primarily comprised of households replacing old refrigerators. Obviously, the growth rate in this market in the next decade will be far lower than that for flat-screen TVs.

Consolidation Stage   After a product becomes established, industry leaders begin to emerge. The survivors from the start-up stage are more stable, and market share is easier to predict. Therefore, the performance of the surviving firms will more closely track the performance of the overall industry. The industry still grows faster than the rest of the economy as the product penetrates the marketplace and becomes more commonly used.

Maturity Stage   At this point, the product has reached its full potential for use by consumers. Further growth might merely track growth in the general economy. The product has become far more standardized, and producers are forced to compete to a greater extent on the basis of price. This leads to narrower profit margins and further pressure on profits. Firms at this stage sometimes are characterized as cash cows, having reasonably stable cash flow but offering little opportunity for profitable expansion. The cash flow is best "milked from" rather than reinvested in the company.

We pointed to VCRs as a start-up industry in the 1980s. By the mid-1990s it was a mature industry, with high market penetration, considerable price competition, low profit margins, and slowing sales. By the late 1990s, VCR sales were giving way to DVD players, which were in their own start-up phase. By today, one would have to judge DVD players as already having entered a maturity stage, with standardization, price competition, and considerable market penetration.

Relative Decline   In this stage, the industry might grow at less than the rate of the overall economy, or it might even shrink. This could be due to obsolescence of the product, competition from new low-cost suppliers, or competition from new products, as illustrated by the steady displacement of VCRs by DVD players.

At which stage in the life cycle are investments in an industry most attractive? Conventional wisdom is that investors should seek firms in high-growth industries. This recipe for success is simplistic, however. If the security prices already reflect the likelihood for high growth, then it is too late to make money from that knowledge. Moreover, high growth and fat profits encourage competition from other producers. The exploitation of profit opportunities brings about new sources of supply that eventually reduce prices, profits, investment returns, and finally growth. This is the dynamic behind the progression from one stage of the industry life cycle to another. The famous portfolio manager Peter Lynch makes this point in *One Up on Wall Street*:

> Many people prefer to invest in a high-growth industry, where there's a lot of sound and fury. Not me. I prefer to invest in a low-growth industry. . . . In a low-growth industry, especially one that's boring and upsets people [such as funeral homes or the oil-drum retrieval business], there's no problem with competition. You don't have to protect your flanks from potential rivals . . . and this gives you the leeway to continue to grow. [p. 131]

In fact, Lynch uses an industry classification system in a very similar spirit to the life-cycle approach we have described. He places firms in the following six groups:

Slow Growers Large and aging companies that will grow only slightly faster than the broad economy. These firms have matured from their earlier fast-growth phase. They usually have steady cash flow and pay a generous dividend, indicating that the firm is generating more cash than can be profitably reinvested in the firm.

Stalwarts Large, well-known firms like Coca-Cola, Hershey's, or Colgate-Palmolive. They grow faster than the slow growers, but are not in the very rapid growth start-up stage. They also tend to be in noncyclical industries that are relatively unaffected by recessions.

Fast Growers Small and aggressive new firms with annual growth rates in the neighborhood of 20% to 25%. Company growth can be due to broad industry growth or to an increase in market share in a more mature industry.

Cyclicals These are firms with sales and profits that regularly expand and contract along with the business cycle. Examples are auto companies, steel companies, or the construction industry.

Turnarounds These are firms that are in bankruptcy or soon might be. If they can recover from what might appear to be imminent disaster, they can offer tremendous investment returns. A good example of this type of firm would be Chrysler in 1982, when it required a government guarantee on its debt to avoid bankruptcy. The stock price rose fifteenfold in the next 5 years.

Asset Plays These are firms that have valuable assets not currently reflected in the stock price. For example, a company may own or be located on valuable real estate that is worth as much as or more than the company's business enterprises. Sometimes the hidden asset can be tax-loss carryforwards. Other times the assets may be intangible. For example, a cable company might have a valuable list of cable subscribers. These assets do not immediately generate cash flow, and so may be more easily overlooked by other analysts attempting to value the firm.

Industry Structure and Performance

The maturation of an industry involves regular changes in the firm's competitive environment. As a final topic, we examine the relationship among industry structure, competitive strategy, and profitability. Michael Porter[4] has highlighted these five determinants of competition: threat of entry from new competitors, rivalry between existing competitors, price pressure from substitute products, bargaining power of buyers, and bargaining power of suppliers.

Threat of Entry   New entrants to an industry put pressure on price and profits. Even if a firm has not yet entered an industry, the potential for it to do so places pressure on prices, because high prices and profit margins will encourage entry by new competitors. Therefore, barriers to entry can be a key determinant of industry profitability. Barriers can take many forms. For example, existing firms may already have secure distribution channels for their products based on long-standing relationships with customers or suppliers that would be costly for a new entrant to duplicate. Brand loyalty also makes it difficult for new entrants to penetrate a market and gives firms more pricing discretion. Proprietary knowledge or patent protection also may give firms advantages in serving a market. Finally, an existing firm's experience in a market may give it cost advantages due to the learning that takes place over time.

Rivalry between Existing Competitors   When there are several competitors in an industry, there will generally be more price competition and lower profit margins as competitors seek to expand their share of the market. Slow industry growth contributes to this competition, because expansion must come at the expense of a rival's market share. High fixed costs also create pressure to reduce prices, because fixed costs put greater pressure on firms to operate near full capacity. Industries producing relatively homogeneous goods are also subject to considerable price pressure, because firms cannot compete on the basis of product differentiation.

Pressure from Substitute Products   Substitute products means that the industry faces competition from firms in related industries. For example, sugar producers compete with corn syrup producers. Wool producers compete with synthetic fiber producers. The availability of substitutes limits the prices that can be charged to customers.

Bargaining Power of Buyers   If a buyer purchases a large fraction of an industry's output, it will have considerable bargaining power and can demand price concessions. For example, auto producers can put pressure on suppliers of auto parts. This reduces the profitability of the auto parts industry.

Bargaining Power of Suppliers   If a supplier of a key input has monopolistic control over the product, it can demand higher prices for the good and squeeze profits out of the industry. One special case of this issue pertains to organized labor as a supplier of a key input to the production process. Labor unions engage in collective bargaining to increase the wages paid to workers. When the labor market is highly unionized, a significant share of the potential profits in the industry can be captured by the workforce.

The key factor determining the bargaining power of suppliers is the availability of substitute products. If substitutes are available, the supplier has little clout and cannot extract higher prices.

---

[4]Michael Porter, *Competitive Advantage: Creating and Sustaining Superior Performance* (New York: Free Press, 1985).

SUMMARY

1. Macroeconomic policy aims to maintain the economy near full employment without aggravating inflationary pressures. The proper trade-off between these two goals is a source of ongoing debate.

2. The traditional tools of macropolicy are government spending and tax collection, which comprise fiscal policy, and manipulation of the money supply via monetary policy. Expansionary fiscal policy can stimulate the economy and increase GDP but tends to increase interest rates. Expansionary monetary policy works by lowering interest rates.

3. The business cycle is the economy's recurring pattern of expansions and recessions. Leading economic indicators can be used to anticipate the evolution of the business cycle because their values tend to change before those of other key economic variables.

4. Industries differ in their sensitivity to the business cycle. More sensitive industries tend to be those producing high-priced durable goods for which the consumer has considerable discretion as to the timing of purchase. Examples are jewelry, automobiles, or consumer durables. Other sensitive industries are those that produce capital equipment for other firms. Operating leverage and financial leverage increase sensitivity to the business cycle.

KEY TERMS

fundamental analysis	supply shock	defensive industries
exchange rate	fiscal policy	leading economic indicators
gross domestic product	monetary policy	NAICS codes
unemployment rate	business cycle	degree of operating leverage
inflation	peak	sector rotation
budget deficit	trough	industry life cycle
demand shock	cyclical industries	

PROBLEM SETS

Quiz

1. What monetary and fiscal policies might be prescribed for an economy in a deep recession?

2. If you believe the U.S. dollar will depreciate more dramatically than do other investors, what will be your stance on investments in U.S. auto producers?

3. Choose an industry and identify the factors that will determine its performance in the next 3 years. What is your forecast for performance in that time period?

4. What are the differences between bottom-up and top-down approaches to security valuation? What are the advantages of a top-down approach?

5. What characteristics will give firms greater sensitivity to business cycles?

Problems

6. Unlike other investors, you believe the Fed is going to loosen monetary policy. What would be your recommendations about investments in the following industries?

    a. Gold mining
    b. Construction

7. According to supply-side economists, what will be the long-run impact on prices of a reduction in income tax rates?

8. Consider two firms producing DVD recorders. One uses a highly automated robotics process, whereas the other uses workers on an assembly line and pays overtime when there is heavy production demand.

    a. Which firm will have higher profits in a recession? In a boom?
    b. Which firm's stock will have a higher beta?

9. Here are four industries and four forecasts for the macroeconomy. Match the industry to the scenario in which it is likely to be the best performer.

Industry	Economic Forecast
a. Housing construction	(i) *Deep recession:* falling inflation, interest rates, and GDP
b. Health care	(ii) *Superheated economy:* rapidly rising GDP, increasing inflation and interest rates
c. Gold mining	
d. Steel production	(iii) *Healthy expansion:* rising GDP, mild inflation, low unemployment
	(iv) *Stagflation:* falling GDP, high inflation

10. In which stage of the industry life cycle would you place the following industries?

(*Note:* There is considerable room for disagreement concerning the "correct" answers to this question.)

   a. Oil well equipment.
   b. Computer hardware.
   c. Computer software.
   d. Genetic engineering.
   e. Railroads.

11. For each pair of firms, choose the one that you think would be more sensitive to the business cycle.

   a. General Autos or General Pharmaceuticals.
   b. Friendly Airlines or Happy Cinemas.

12. Why do you think the index of consumer expectations is a useful leading indicator of the macroeconomy? (See Table 17.2.)

13. Why do you think the change in the index of labor cost per unit of output is a useful lagging indicator of the macroeconomy? (See Table 17.2.)

14. General Weedkillers dominates the chemical weed control market with its patented product Weed-ex. The patent is about to expire, however. What are your forecasts for changes in the industry? Specifically, what will happen to industry prices, sales, the profit prospects of General Weedkillers, and the profit prospects of its competitors? What stage of the industry life cycle do you think is relevant for the analysis of this market?

15. Your business plan for your proposed start-up firm envisions first-year revenues of $120,000, fixed costs of $30,000, and variable costs equal to one-third of revenue.

   a. What are expected profits based on these expectations?
   b. What is the degree of operating leverage based on the estimate of fixed costs and expected profits?
   c. If sales are 10% below expectation, what will be the decrease in profits?
   d. Show that the percentage decrease in profits equals DOL times the 10% drop in sales.
   e. Based on the DOL, what is the largest percentage shortfall in sales relative to original expectations that the firm can sustain before profits turn negative? What are break-even sales at this point?
   f. Confirm that your answer to (*e*) is correct by calculating profits at the break-even level of sales.

1. Briefly discuss what actions the U.S. Federal Reserve would likely take in pursuing an *expansionary* monetary policy using each of the following three monetary tools:

   a. Reserve requirements.
   b. Open market operations.
   c. Discount rate.

CFA®
PROBLEMS

2. An unanticipated expansionary monetary policy has been implemented. Indicate the impact of this policy on each of the following four variables:

   a. Inflation rate.
   b. Real output and employment.
   c. Real interest rate.
   d. Nominal interest rate.

3. Universal Auto is a large multinational corporation headquartered in the United States. For segment reporting purposes, the company is engaged in two businesses: production of motor vehicles and information processing services.

   The motor vehicle business is by far the larger of Universal's two segments. It consists mainly of domestic U.S. passenger car production, but it also includes small truck manufacturing operations in the United States and passenger car production in other countries. This segment of Universal has had weak operating results for the past several years, including a large loss in 2007. Although the company does not reveal the operating results of its domestic passenger car segments, that part of Universal's business is generally believed to be primarily responsible for the weak performance of its motor vehicle segment.

   Idata, the information processing services segment of Universal, was started by Universal about 15 years ago. This business has shown strong, steady growth that has been entirely internal; no acquisitions have been made.

   An excerpt from a research report on Universal prepared by Paul Adams, a CFA candidate, states: "Based on our assumption that Universal will be able to increase prices significantly on U.S. passenger cars in 2009, we project a multibillion dollar profit improvement."

   a. Discuss the concept of an industrial life cycle by describing each of its four phases.
   b. Identify where each of Universal's two primary businesses—passenger cars and information processing—is in such a cycle.
   c. Discuss how product pricing should differ between Universal's two businesses, based on the location of each in the industrial life cycle.

4. Adams's research report (see the preceding problem) continued as follows: "With a business recovery already under way, the expected profit surge should lead to a much higher price for Universal Auto stock. We strongly recommend purchase."

   a. Discuss the business cycle approach to investment timing. (Your answer should describe actions to be taken on both stocks and bonds at different points over a typical business cycle.)
   b. Assuming Adams's assertion is correct (that a business recovery is already under way), evaluate the timeliness of his recommendation to purchase Universal Auto, a cyclical stock, based on the business cycle approach to investment timing.

5. Janet Ludlow is preparing a report on U.S.-based manufacturers in the electric toothbrush industry and has gathered the information shown in Tables 17A and 17B. Ludlow's report concludes that the electric toothbrush industry is in the maturity (i.e., late) phase of its industry life cycle.

   a. Select and justify three factors from Table 17A that *support* Ludlow's conclusion.
   b. Select and justify three factors from Table 17B that *refute* Ludlow's conclusion.

6. As a securities analyst you have been asked to review a valuation of a closely held business, Wigwam Autoparts Heaven, Inc. (WAH), prepared by the Red Rocks Group (RRG). You are to give an opinion on the valuation and to support your opinion by analyzing each part of the valuation. WAH's sole business is automotive parts retailing. The RRG valuation includes a section called "Analysis of the Retail Autoparts Industry," based completely on the data in Table 17C and the following additional information:

   - WAH and its principal competitors each operated more than 150 stores at year-end 2006.
   - The average number of stores operated per company engaged in the retail autoparts industry is 5.3.
   - The major customer base for autoparts sold in retail stores consists of young owners of old vehicles. These owners do their own automotive maintenance out of economic necessity.

	2001	2002	2003	2004	2005	2006
Return on equity						
Electric toothbrush industry index	12.5%	12.0%	15.4%	19.6%	21.6%	21.6%
Market index	10.2	12.4	14.6	19.9	20.4	21.2
Average P/E						
Electric toothbrush industry index	28.5×	23.2×	19.6×	18.7×	18.5×	16.2×
Market index	10.2	12.4	14.6	19.9	18.1	19.1
Dividend payout ratio						
Electric toothbrush industry index	8.8%	8.0%	12.1%	12.1%	14.3%	17.1%
Market index	39.2	40.1	38.6	43.7	41.8	39.1
Average dividend yield						
Electric toothbrush industry index	0.3%	0.3%	0.6%	0.7%	0.8%	1.0%
Market index	3.8	3.2	2.6	2.2	2.3	2.1

TABLE 17A

Ratios for electric toothbrush industry index and broad stock market index

a. One of RRG's conclusions is that the retail autoparts industry as a whole is in the maturity stage of the industry life cycle. Discuss three relevant items of data from Table 17C that support this conclusion.
b. Another RRG conclusion is that WAH and its principal competitors are in the consolidation stage of their life cycle.
   i. Cite three relevant items of data from Table 17C that support this conclusion.
   ii. Explain how WAH and its principal competitors can be in a consolidation stage while their industry as a whole is in the maturity stage.

7. Dynamic Communication dominates a segment of the consumer electronics industry. A small competitor in that segment is Wade Goods & Co. Wade has just introduced a new product, the Carrycom, which will replace the existing Wade product line and could significantly affect the industry segment. Mike Brandreth is preparing an industry research update that focuses on Wade, including an analysis that makes extensive use of the five competitive forces identified by Michael Porter. Wade's president, Toby White, makes the following statements:

· "Wade has an exclusive 3-year production license for Carrycom technology from the patent owners of the new technology. This will provide us a window of opportunity to

- **Industry Sales Growth**—Industry sales have grown at 15–20% per year in recent years and are expected to grow at 10–15% per year over the next 3 years.
- **Non-U.S. Markets**—Some U.S. manufacturers are attempting to enter fast-growing non-U.S. markets, which remain largely unexploited.
- **Mail Order Sales**—Some manufacturers have created a new niche in the industry by selling electric toothbrushes directly to customers through mail order. Sales for this industry segment are growing at 40% per year.
- **U.S. Market Penetration**—The current penetration rate in the United States is 60% of households and will be difficult to increase.
- **Price Competition**—Manufacturers compete fiercely on the basis of price, and price wars within the industry are common.
- **Niche Markets**—Some manufacturers are able to develop new, unexploited niche markets in the United States based on company reputation, quality, and service.
- **Industry Consolidation**—Several manufacturers have recently merged, and it is expected that consolidation in the Industry will increase.
- **New Entrants**—New manufacturers continue to enter the market.

TABLE 17B

Characteristics of the electric toothbrush manufacturing industry

E-Investments

Economic Indicators

1. Locate the Conference Board's (**www.conference-board.org/economics/bci**) latest monthly release of U.S. Leading Index. The link is located under the heading *Latest Releases*, or on the left-side menu under *Business Cycle Indicators*. Review the latest report. What 10 economic and financial statistics does the Conference Board use in its Leading Indicators series? Which factors contributed positively to the Leading Index; which ones contributed negatively? Why is each of these factors useful when attempting to forecast future economic activity? Answer the same questions for the factors that are coincident indicators and lagging indicators.

2. Is the U.S. economy in a recession or not? Check the "official" opinion at the National Bureau of Economic Research (NBER) at **www.nber.org/data.** Link to the *Official Business Cycle Dates.* How does the NBER select the beginning or end of a recession (follow the available link for a discussion of this topic)? What period in U.S. economic history was the longest expansion? Contraction? Look at the *Announcement Dates* section toward the bottom of the page. How much of a time lag is there between when a peak or a trough occurs and when it is announced? What implication does this have for investors?

SOLUTIONS TO CONCEPT CHECKS

1. The downturn in the auto industry will reduce the demand for the product of this economy. The economy will, at least in the short term, enter a recession. This would suggest that:

   a. GDP will fall.

   b. The unemployment rate will rise.

   c. The government deficit will increase. Income tax receipts will fall, and government expenditures on social welfare programs probably will increase.

   d. Interest rates should fall. The contraction in the economy will reduce the demand for credit. Moreover, the lower inflation rate will reduce nominal interest rates.

2. Expansionary fiscal policy coupled with expansionary monetary policy will stimulate the economy, with the loose monetary policy keeping down interest rates.

3. A traditional demand-side interpretation of the tax cuts is that the resulting increase in after-tax income increased consumption demand and stimulated the economy. A supply-side interpretation is that the reduction in marginal tax rates made it more attractive for businesses to invest and for individuals to work, thereby increasing economic output.

4. Firm C has the lowest fixed cost and highest variable costs. It should be least sensitive to the business cycle. In fact, it is. Its profits are highest of the three firms in recessions but lowest in expansions.

	Recession	Normal	Expansion
Revenue	$10	$12	$14
Fixed cost	2	2	2
Variable cost	7.5	9	10.5
Profits	$ 0.5	$ 1	$ 1.5

5. *a.* Newspapers will do best in an expansion when advertising volume is increasing.

   b. Machine tools are a good investment at the trough of a recession, just as the economy is about to enter an expansion and firms may need to increase capacity.

   c. Beverages are defensive investments, with demand that is relatively insensitive to the business cycle. Therefore, they are relatively attractive investments if a recession is forecast.

   d. Timber is a good investment at a peak period, when natural resource prices are high and the economy is operating at full capacity.

EQUITY VALUATION MODELS

AS OUR DISCUSSION of market efficiency indicated, finding undervalued securities is hardly easy. At the same time, there are enough chinks in the armor of the efficient market hypothesis that the search for such securities should not be dismissed out of hand. Moreover, it is the ongoing search for mispriced securities that maintains a nearly efficient market. Even infrequent discoveries of minor mispricing would justify the salary of a stock market analyst.

This chapter describes the valuation models that stock market analysts use to uncover mispriced securities. The models presented are those used by *fundamental analysts,* those analysts who use information concerning the current and prospective profitability of a company to assess its fair market value. We start with a discussion of alternative measures of the value of a company. From there, we progress to quantitative tools called *dividend discount models,* which security analysts commonly use to measure the value of a firm as an ongoing concern. Next we turn to price–earnings, or P/E, ratios, explaining why they are of such interest to analysts but also highlighting some of their shortcomings. We explain how P/E ratios are tied to dividend valuation models and, more generally, to the growth prospects of the firm.

We close the chapter with a discussion and extended example of free cash flow models used by analysts to value firms based on forecasts of the cash flows that will be generated from the firms' business endeavors. Finally, we apply the several valuation tools covered in the chapter to a real firm and find that there is some disparity in their conclusions—a conundrum that will confront any security analyst—and consider reasons for these discrepancies.

18.1 VALUATION BY COMPARABLES

The purpose of fundamental analysis is to identify stocks that are mispriced relative to some measure of "true" value that can be derived from observable financial data. There are many convenient sources of such data. For U.S. companies, the Securities and Exchange

Commission provides information at its EDGAR Web site, **www.sec.gov/edgar.shtml.** The SEC requires all public companies (except foreign companies and companies with less than $10 million in assets and 500 shareholders) to file registration statements, periodic reports, and other forms electronically through EDGAR. Anyone can access and download this information.

Many Web sites provide analysis of the data. An example is Standard & Poor's Market Insight service, which includes COMPUSTAT.[1] Table 18.1 shows COMPUSTAT's selection of financial highlights for Microsoft Corporation on October 25, 2007.

The price of a share of Microsoft common stock on that day is shown as $31.25, and the total market value of all 9,380 million shares outstanding was $293,125 million. Under the heading Valuation, Table 18.1 reports the ratios of Microsoft's stock price to four different items taken from its latest financial statements (each divided by the number of outstanding shares): operating earnings, book value, sales revenue, and cash flow. Microsoft's price-to-earnings (P/E) ratio is 21.6, the price-to-book value is 9.4, and price-to-sales is 5.7. Such comparative valuation ratios are used to assess the valuation of one firm versus others in the same industry. In the column to the right in Table 18.1 are comparable ratios for the average firm in the PC software industry.

For example, an analyst might compare the price/cash flow ratio for Microsoft—18.9, to the industry average ratio of 19.3. By comparison with this standard, Microsoft appears

TABLE 18.1

Financial highlights for Microsoft Corporation, October 25, 2007

Current Qtr Ended:	Jun. 2007	Current Year Ended:	Jun. 2007
Miscellaneous			
Current price	31.250000	Comn sharehldrs (actual)	148344
Comn shares outstdg (mil)	9380.000	Employees (actual)	79000
Market capitalization (mil)	293125.000	S&P issuer credit rating	
Latest 12 Months	**Company**		**1 Yr Chng (%)**
Sales (mil)	51122.000		15.4
EBITDA (mil)	19964.000		8.0
Net income (mil)	14065.000		11.6
EPS from Ops	1.45		12.4
Dividends/Share	0.390000		14.7
Valuation	**Company**		**Industry Avg**
Price/EPS from Ops	21.6		22.4
Price/Book	9.4		6.3
Price/Sales	5.7		5.2
Price/Cash flow	18.9		19.3
Profitability (%)			
Return on equity	45.2		27.4
Return on assets	22.3		13.8
Oper profit margin	36.2		31.0
Net profit margin	27.5		22.5
Financial Risk			
Debt/Equity	0.0		18.4

[1]A subscription to S&P Market Insight's educational version comes with this textbook.

to be slightly underpriced. The price-to-sales ratio is useful for firms and industries that are in a start-up phase. Earnings figures for start-up firms are often negative and not reported, so analysts shift their focus from earnings per share to sales revenue per share.

The market price of a share of Microsoft stock was 9.4 times its book value. **Book value** is the net worth of a company as reported on its balance sheet. For the average firm in the PC software industry it was 6.3. By comparison with this standard, Microsoft seems a bit overvalued.

Limitations of Book Value

Shareholders in a firm are sometimes called "residual claimants," which means that the value of their stake is what is left over when the liabilities of the firm are subtracted from its assets. Shareholders' equity is this net worth. However, the values of both assets and liabilities recognized in financial statements are based on historical—not current—values. For example, the book value of an asset equals the *original* cost of acquisition less some adjustment for depreciation, even if the market price of that asset has changed over time. Moreover, depreciation allowances are used to allocate the original cost of the asset over several years, but do not reflect loss of actual value.

Whereas book values are based on original cost, market values measure *current* values of assets and liabilities. The market value of the shareholders' equity investment equals the difference between the current values of all assets and liabilities. (The stock price is just the market value of shareholders' equity divided by the number of outstanding shares.) We've emphasized that current values generally will not match historical ones. Equally or even more important, many assets, for example, the value of a good brand name or specialized expertise developed over many years, may not even be included on the financial statements. Market prices therefore reflect the value of the firm as a going concern. It would be unusual if the market price of a stock were exactly equal to its book value.

Can book value represent a "floor" for the stock's price, below which level the market price can never fall? Although Microsoft's book value per share in 2007 was less than its market price, other evidence disproves this notion. While it is not common, there are always some firms selling at a market price below book value. In early 2008, for example, such troubled firms included Northwest Airlines and Countrywide Financial Corp.

A better measure of a floor for the stock price is the firm's **liquidation value** per share. This represents the amount of money that could be realized by breaking up the firm, selling its assets, repaying its debt, and distributing the remainder to the shareholders. The reasoning behind this concept is that if the market price of equity drops below liquidation value, the firm becomes attractive as a takeover target. A corporate raider would find it profitable to buy enough shares to gain control and then actually to liquidate.

Another approach to valuing a firm is the **replacement cost** of its assets less its liabilities. Some analysts believe the market value of the firm cannot remain for long too far above its replacement cost because if it did, competitors would try to replicate the firm. The competitive pressure of other similar firms entering the same industry would drive down the market value of all firms until they came into equality with replacement cost.

This idea is popular among economists, and the ratio of market price to replacement cost is known as **Tobin's q**, after the Nobel Prize–winning economist James Tobin. In the long run, according to this view, the ratio of market price to replacement cost will tend toward 1, but the evidence is that this ratio can differ significantly from 1 for very long periods.

Although focusing on the balance sheet can give some useful information about a firm's liquidation value or its replacement cost, the analyst must usually turn to expected future cash flows for a better estimate of the firm's value as a going concern. We now examine the quantitative models that analysts use to value common stock in terms of the future earnings and dividends the firm will yield.

18.2 INTRINSIC VALUE VERSUS MARKET PRICE

The most popular model for assessing the value of a firm as a going concern starts from the observation that an investor in stock expects a return consisting of cash dividends and capital gains or losses. We begin by assuming a 1-year holding period and supposing that ABC stock has an expected dividend per share, $E(D_1)$, of \$4, the current price of a share, P_0, is \$48, and the expected price at the end of a year, $E(P_1)$, is \$52. For now, don't worry about how you derive your forecast of next year's price. At this point we ask only whether the stock seems attractively priced *today* given your forecast of *next year's* price.

The *expected* holding-period return is $E(D_1)$ plus the expected price appreciation, $E(P_1) - P_0$, all divided by the current price, P_0:

$$\text{Expected HPR} = E(r) = \frac{E(D_1) + [E(P_1) - P_0]}{P_0}$$

$$= \frac{4 + (52 - 48)}{48} = .167, \text{ or } 16.7\%$$

Thus, the stock's expected holding-period return is the sum of the expected dividend yield, $E(D_1)/P_0$, and the expected rate of price appreciation, the capital gains yield, $[E(P_1) - P_0]/P_0$.

But what is the required rate of return for ABC stock? The CAPM states that when stock market prices are at equilibrium levels, the rate of return that investors can expect to earn on a security is $r_f + \beta[E(r_M) - r_f]$. Thus, the CAPM may be viewed as providing the rate of return an investor can expect to earn on a security given its risk as measured by beta. This is the return that investors will require of any other investment with equivalent risk. We will denote this required rate of return as k. If a stock is priced "correctly," it will offer investors a "fair" return, that is, its *expected* return will equal its *required* return. Of course, the goal of a security analyst is to find stocks that are mispriced. For example, an underpriced stock will provide an expected return greater than the required return.

Suppose that $r_f = 6\%$, $E(r_M) - r_f = 5\%$, and the beta of ABC is 1.2. Then the value of k is

$$k = 6\% + 1.2 \times 5\% = 12\%$$

The expected holding period return, 16.7%, therefore exceeds the required rate of return based on ABC's risk by a margin of 4.7%. Naturally, the investor will want to include more of ABC stock in the portfolio than a passive strategy would indicate.

Another way to see this is to compare the intrinsic value of a share of stock to its market price. The **intrinsic value,** denoted V_0, is defined as the present value of all cash payments to the investor in the stock, including dividends as well as the proceeds from the ultimate sale of the stock, discounted at the appropriate risk-adjusted interest rate, k. If the intrinsic value, or the investor's own estimate of what the stock is really worth, exceeds the market price, the stock is considered undervalued and a good investment. In the case of ABC, using a 1-year investment horizon and a forecast that the stock can be sold at the end of the year at price $P_1 = \$52$, the intrinsic value is

$$V_0 = \frac{E(D_1) + E(P_1)}{1 + k} = \frac{\$4 + \$52}{1.12} = \$50$$

Equivalently, at a price of \$50, the investor would derive a 12% rate of return—just equal to the required rate of return—on an investment in the stock. However, at the current price of \$48, the stock is underpriced compared to intrinsic value. At this price, it provides better than a fair rate of return relative to its risk. In other words, using the terminology of the CAPM, it is a positive-alpha stock, and investors will want to buy more of it than they would following a passive strategy.

If the intrinsic value turns out to be lower than the current market price, investors should buy less of it than under the passive strategy. It might even pay to go short on ABC stock, as we discussed in Chapter 3.

In market equilibrium, the current market price will reflect the intrinsic value estimates of all market participants. This means the individual investor whose V_0 estimate differs from the market price, P_0, in effect must disagree with some or all of the market consensus estimates of $E(D_1)$, $E(P_1)$, or k. A common term for the market consensus value of the required rate of return, k, is the **market capitalization rate,** which we use often throughout this chapter.

CONCEPT CHECK 1

You expect the price of IBX stock to be $59.77 per share a year from now. Its current market price is $50, and you expect it to pay a dividend 1 year from now of $2.15 per share.

a. What is the stock's expected dividend yield, rate of price appreciation, and holding-period return?

b. If the stock has a beta of 1.15, the risk-free rate is 6% per year, and the expected rate of return on the market portfolio is 14% per year, what is the required rate of return on IBX stock?

c. What is the intrinsic value of IBX stock, and how does it compare to the current market price?

18.3 DIVIDEND DISCOUNT MODELS

Consider an investor who buys a share of Steady State Electronics stock, planning to hold it for 1 year. The intrinsic value of the share is the present value of the dividend to be received at the end of the first year, D_1, and the expected sales price, P_1. We will henceforth use the simpler notation P_1 instead of $E(P_1)$ to avoid clutter. Keep in mind, though, that future prices and dividends are unknown, and we are dealing with expected values, not certain values. We've already established

$$V_0 = \frac{D_1 + P_1}{1 + k} \tag{18.1}$$

Although this year's dividends are fairly predictable given a company's history, you might ask how we can estimate P_1, the year-end price. According to Equation 18.1, V_1 (the year-end intrinsic value) will be

$$V_1 = \frac{D_2 + P_2}{1 + k}$$

If we assume the stock will be selling for its intrinsic value next year, then $V_1 = P_1$, and we can substitute this value for P_1 into Equation 18.1 to find

$$V_0 = \frac{D_1}{1 + k} + \frac{D_2 + P_2}{(1 + k)^2}$$

This equation may be interpreted as the present value of dividends plus sales price for a 2-year holding period. Of course, now we need to come up with a forecast of P_2. Continuing in the same way, we can replace P_2 by $(D_3 + P_3)/(1 + k)$, which relates P_0 to the value of dividends plus the expected sales price for a 3-year holding period.

More generally, for a holding period of H years, we can write the stock value as the present value of dividends over the H years, plus the ultimate sale price, P_H:

$$V_0 = \frac{D_1}{1 + k} + \frac{D_2}{(1 + k)^2} + \cdots + \frac{D_H + P_H}{(1 + k)^H} \tag{18.2}$$

Note the similarity between this formula and the bond valuation formula developed in Chapter 14. Each relates price to the present value of a stream of payments (coupons in the case of bonds, dividends in the case of stocks) and a final payment (the face value of the bond, or the sales price of the stock). The key differences in the case of stocks are the uncertainty of dividends, the lack of a fixed maturity date, and the unknown sales price at the horizon date. Indeed, one can continue to substitute for price indefinitely, to conclude

$$V_0 = \frac{D_1}{1 + k} + \frac{D_2}{(1 + k)^2} + \frac{D_3}{(1 + k)^3} + \cdots \tag{18.3}$$

Equation 18.3 states that the stock price should equal the present value of all expected future dividends into perpetuity. This formula is called the **dividend discount model (DDM)** of stock prices.

It is tempting, but incorrect, to conclude from Equation 18.3 that the DDM focuses exclusively on dividends and ignores capital gains as a motive for investing in stock. Indeed, we assume explicitly in Equation 18.1 that capital gains (as reflected in the expected sales price, P_1) are part of the stock's value. Our point is that the price at which you can sell a stock in the future depends on dividend forecasts at that time.

The reason only dividends appear in Equation 18.3 is not that investors ignore capital gains. It is instead that those capital gains will be determined by dividend forecasts at the time the stock is sold. That is why in Equation 18.2 we can write the stock price as the present value of dividends plus sales price for *any* horizon date. P_H is the present value at time H of all dividends expected to be paid after the horizon date. That value is then discounted back to today, time 0. The DDM asserts that stock prices are determined ultimately by the cash flows accruing to stockholders, and those are dividends.[2]

The Constant-Growth DDM

Equation 18.3 as it stands is still not very useful in valuing a stock because it requires dividend forecasts for every year into the indefinite future. To make the DDM practical, we need to introduce some simplifying assumptions. A useful and common first pass at the problem is to assume that dividends are trending upward at a stable growth rate that we will call g. Then if $g = .05$, and the most recently paid dividend was $D_0 = 3.81$, expected future dividends are

$$D_1 = D_0(1 + g) \quad = 3.81 \times 1.05 \quad = 4.00$$
$$D_2 = D_0(1 + g)^2 = 3.81 \times (1.05)^2 = 4.20$$
$$D_3 = D_0(1 + g)^3 = 3.81 \times (1.05)^3 = 4.41$$

and so on. Using these dividend forecasts in Equation 18.3, we solve for intrinsic value as

$$V_0 = \frac{D_0(1 + g)}{1 + k} + \frac{D_0(1 + g)^2}{(1 + k)^2} + \frac{D_0(1 + g)^3}{(1 + k)^3} + \cdots$$

[2]If investors never expected a dividend to be paid, then this model implies that the stock would have no value. To reconcile the DDM with the fact that non-dividend-paying stocks do have a market value, one must assume that investors expect that some day it may pay out some cash, even if only a liquidating dividend.

This equation can be simplified to[3]

$$V_0 = \frac{D_0(1 + g)}{k - g} = \frac{D_1}{k - g} \tag{18.4}$$

Note in Equation 18.4 that we divide D_1 (not D_0) by $k - g$ to calculate intrinsic value. If the market capitalization rate for Steady State is 12%, now we can use Equation 18.4 to show that the intrinsic value of a share of Steady State stock is

$$\frac{\$4.00}{.12 - .05} = \$57.14$$

Equation 18.4 is called the **constant-growth DDM,** or the Gordon model, after Myron J. Gordon, who popularized the model. It should remind you of the formula for the present value of a perpetuity. If dividends were expected not to grow, then the dividend stream would be a simple perpetuity, and the valuation formula would be[4] $V_0 = D_1/k$. Equation 18.4 is a generalization of the perpetuity formula to cover the case of a *growing* perpetuity. As g increases (for a given value of D_1), the stock price also rises.

EXAMPLE 18.1   Preferred Stock and the DDM

Preferred stock that pays a fixed dividend can be valued using the constant-growth dividend discount model. The constant-growth rate of dividends is simply zero. For example, to value a preferred stock paying a fixed dividend of $2 per share when the discount rate is 8%, we compute

$$V_0 = \frac{\$2}{.08 - 0} = \$25$$

---

[3]We prove that the intrinsic value, V_0, of a stream of cash dividends growing at a constant rate g is equal to $\dfrac{D_1}{k - g}$ as follows. By definition,

$$V_0 = \frac{D_1}{1 + k} + \frac{D_1(1 + g)}{(1 + k)^2} + \frac{D_1(1 + g)^2}{(1 + k)^3} + \cdots \tag{a}$$

Multiplying through by $(1 + k)/(1 + g)$, we obtain

$$\frac{(1 + k)}{(1 + g)}V_0 = \frac{D_1}{(1 + g)} + \frac{D_1}{(1 + k)} + \frac{D_1(1 + g)}{(1 + k)^2} + \cdots \tag{b}$$

Subtracting equation (a) from equation (b), we find that

$$\frac{1 + k}{1 + g}V_0 - V_0 = \frac{D_1}{(1 + g)}$$

which implies

$$\frac{(k - g)V_0}{(1 + g)} = \frac{D_1}{(1 + g)}$$

$$V_0 = \frac{D_1}{k - g}$$

[4]Recall from introductory finance that the present value of a $1 per year perpetuity is $1/k$. For example, if $k = 10\%$, the value of the perpetuity is $\$1/.10 = \$10$. Notice that if $g = 0$ in Equation 18.4, the constant-growth DDM formula is the same as the perpetuity formula.

EXAMPLE 18.2   The Constant-Growth DDM

High Flyer Industries has just paid its annual dividend of $3 per share. The dividend is expected to grow at a constant rate of 8% indefinitely. The beta of High Flyer stock is 1.0, the risk-free rate is 6%, and the market risk premium is 8%. What is the intrinsic value of the stock? What would be your estimate of intrinsic value if you believed that the stock was riskier, with a beta of 1.25?

Because a $3 dividend has just been paid and the growth rate of dividends is 8%, the forecast for the year-end dividend is $3 \times 1.08 = \$3.24$. The market capitalization rate is $6\% + 1.0 \times 8\% = 14\%$. Therefore, the value of the stock is

$$V_0 = \frac{D_1}{k - g} = \frac{\$3.24}{.14 - .08} = \$54$$

If the stock is perceived to be riskier, its value must be lower. At the higher beta, the market capitalization rate is $6\% \times 1.25 \times 8\% = 16\%$, and the stock is worth only

$$\frac{\$3.24}{.16 - .08} = \$40.50$$

The constant-growth DDM is valid only when g is less than k. If dividends were expected to grow forever at a rate faster than k, the value of the stock would be infinite. If an analyst derives an estimate of g that is greater than k, that growth rate must be unsustainable in the long run. The appropriate valuation model to use in this case is a multistage DDM such as those discussed below.

The constant-growth DDM is so widely used by stock market analysts that it is worth exploring some of its implications and limitations. The constant-growth rate DDM implies that a stock's value will be greater:

1. The larger its expected dividend per share.
2. The lower the market capitalization rate, k.
3. The higher the expected growth rate of dividends.

Another implication of the constant-growth model is that the stock price is expected to grow at the same rate as dividends. To see this, suppose Steady State stock is selling at its intrinsic value of $57.14, so that $V_0 = P_0$. Then

$$P_0 = \frac{D_1}{k - g}$$

Note that price is proportional to dividends. Therefore, next year, when the dividends paid to Steady State stockholders are expected to be higher by $g = 5\%$, price also should increase by 5%. To confirm this, note

$$D_2 = \$4(1.05) = \$4.20$$

$$P_1 = \frac{D_2}{k - g} = \frac{\$4.20}{.12 - .05} = \$60.00$$

which is 5% higher than the current price of $57.14. To generalize,

$$P_1 = \frac{D_2}{k-g} = \frac{D_1(1+g)}{k-g} = \frac{D_1}{k-g}(1+g)$$
$$= P_0(1+g)$$

Therefore, the DDM implies that in the case of constant growth of dividends, the rate of price appreciation in any year will equal that constant-growth rate, g. Note that for a stock whose market price equals its intrinsic value ($V_0 = P_0$), the expected holding-period return will be

$$E(r) = \text{Dividend yield} + \text{Capital gains yield}$$
$$= \frac{D_1}{P_0} + \frac{P_1 - P_0}{P_0} = \frac{D_1}{P_0} + g \qquad (18.5)$$

This formula offers a means to infer the market capitalization rate of a stock, for if the stock is selling at its intrinsic value, then $E(r) = k$, implying that $k = D_1/P_0 + g$. By observing the dividend yield, D_1/P_0, and estimating the growth rate of dividends, we can compute k. This equation is also known as the *discounted cash flow (DCF) formula*.

This is an approach often used in rate hearings for regulated public utilities. The regulatory agency responsible for approving utility pricing decisions is mandated to allow the firms to charge just enough to cover costs plus a "fair" profit, that is, one that allows a competitive return on the investment the firm has made in its productive capacity. In turn, that return is taken to be the expected return investors require on the stock of the firm. The $D_1/P_0 + g$ formula provides a means to infer that required return.

EXAMPLE 18.3   The Constant-Growth Model

Suppose that Steady State Electronics wins a major contract for its new computer chip. The very profitable contract will enable it to increase the growth rate of dividends from 5% to 6% without reducing the current dividend from the projected value of $4.00 per share. What will happen to the stock price? What will happen to future expected rates of return on the stock?

The stock price ought to increase in response to the good news about the contract, and indeed it does. The stock price jumps from its original value of $57.14 to a postannouncement price of

$$\frac{D_1}{k-g} = \frac{\$4.00}{.12 - .06} = \$66.67$$

Investors who are holding the stock when the good news about the contract is announced will receive a substantial windfall.

On the other hand, at the new price the expected rate of return on the stock is 12%, just as it was before the new contract was announced.

$$E(r) = \frac{D_1}{P_0} + g = \frac{\$4.00}{\$66.67} + 0.06 = 0.12, \text{ or } 12\%$$

This result makes sense. Once the news about the contract is reflected in the stock price, the expected rate of return will be consistent with the risk of the stock. Because the risk of the stock has not changed, neither should the expected rate of return.

CONCEPT CHECK 2

a. IBX's stock dividend at the end of this year is expected to be $2.15, and it is expected to grow at 11.2% per year forever. If the required rate of return on IBX stock is 15.2% per year, what is its intrinsic value?

b. If IBX's current market price is equal to this intrinsic value, what is next year's expected price?

c. If an investor were to buy IBX stock now and sell it after receiving the $2.15 dividend a year from now, what is the expected capital gain (i.e., price appreciation) in percentage terms? What is the dividend yield, and what would be the holding-period return?

Convergence of Price to Intrinsic Value

Now suppose that the current market price of ABC stock is only $48 per share and, therefore, that the stock now is undervalued by $2 per share. In this case the expected rate of price appreciation depends on an additional assumption about whether the discrepancy between the intrinsic value and the market price will disappear, and if so, when.

One fairly common assumption is that the discrepancy will never disappear and that the market price will trend upward at rate g forever. This implies that the discrepancy between intrinsic value and market price also will grow at the same rate. In our example:

Now	Next Year
$V_0 = \$50$	$V_1 = \$50 \times 1.04 = \$52$
$P_0 = \$48$	$P_1 = \$48 \times 1.04 = \$49.92$
$V_0 - P_0 = \$2$	$V_1 - P_1 = \$2 \times 1.04 = \$2.08$

Under this assumption the expected HPR will exceed the required rate, because the dividend yield is higher than it would be if P_0 were equal to V_0. In our example the dividend yield would be 8.33% instead of 8%, so that the expected HPR would be 12.33% rather than 12%:

$$E(r) = \frac{D_1}{P_0} + g = \frac{\$4}{\$48} + .04 = .0833 + .04 = .1233$$

An investor who identifies this undervalued stock can get an expected dividend that exceeds the required yield by 33 basis points. This excess return is earned *each year,* and the market price never catches up to intrinsic value.

An alternative assumption is that the gap between market price and intrinsic value will disappear by the end of the year. In that case we would have $P_1 = V_1 = \$52$, and

$$E(r) = \frac{D_1}{P_0} + \frac{P_1 - P_0}{P_0} = \frac{4}{48} + \frac{52 - 48}{48} = .0833 + .0833 = .1667$$

The assumption of complete catch-up to intrinsic value produces a much larger 1-year HPR. In future years, however, the stock is expected to generate only fair rates of return.

Many stock analysts assume that a stock's price will approach its intrinsic value gradually over time—for example, over a 5-year period. This puts their expected 1-year HPR somewhere between the bounds of 12.33% and 16.67%.

is zero. We've seen that following a zero-growth strategy with $b = 0$ and $g = 0$, the value of Cash Cow will be $E_1/k = \$5/.125 = \$40$ per share. Now suppose Cash Cow chooses a plowback ratio of $b = .60$, the same as Growth Prospects's plowback. Then g would increase to

$$g = \text{ROE} \times b = .125 \times .60 = .075$$

but the stock price is still

$$P_0 = \frac{D_1}{k - g} = \frac{\$2}{.125 - .075} = \$40$$

—no different from the no-growth strategy.

In the case of Cash Cow, the dividend reduction used to free funds for reinvestment in the firm generates only enough growth to maintain the stock price at the current level. This is as it should be: If the firm's projects yield only what investors can earn on their own, shareholders cannot be made better off by a high-reinvestment-rate policy. This demonstrates that "growth" is not the same as growth opportunities. To justify reinvestment, the firm must engage in projects with better prospective returns than those shareholders can find elsewhere. Notice also that the PVGO of Cash Cow is zero: $\text{PVGO} = P_0 - E_1/k = 40 - 40 = 0$. With $\text{ROE} = k$, there is no advantage to plowing funds back into the firm; this shows up as PVGO of zero. In fact, this is why firms with considerable cash flow but limited investment prospects are called "cash cows." The cash these firms generate is best taken out of, or "milked from," the firm.

EXAMPLE 18.4   Growth Opportunities

Takeover Target is run by entrenched management that insists on reinvesting 60% of its earnings in projects that provide an ROE of 10%, despite the fact that the firm's capitalization rate is $k = 15\%$. The firm's year-end dividend will be $2 per share, paid out of earnings of $5 per share. At what price will the stock sell? What is the present value of growth opportunities? Why would such a firm be a takeover target for another firm?

Given current management's investment policy, the dividend growth rate will be

$$g = \text{ROE} \times b = 10\% \times .60 = 6\%$$

and the stock price should be

$$P_0 = \frac{\$2}{.15 - .06} = \$22.22$$

The present value of growth opportunities is

$$\text{PVGO} = \text{Price per share} - \text{No-growth value per share}$$
$$= \$22.22 - E_1/k = \$22.22 - \$5/.15 = -\$11.11$$

PVGO is *negative*. This is because the net present value of the firm's projects is negative: The rate of return on those assets is less than the opportunity cost of capital.

Such a firm would be subject to takeover, because another firm could buy the firm for the market price of $22.22 per share and increase the value of the firm by changing its investment policy. For example, if the new management simply paid out all earnings as dividends, the value of the firm would increase to its no-growth value, $E_1/k = \$5/.15 = \$33.33$.

<table>
<tr><td rowspan="3">CONCEPT
CHECK
3</td><td>a. Calculate the price of a firm with a plowback ratio of .60 if its ROE is 20%. Current earnings, E_1, will be $5 per share, and $k = 12.5\%$.</td></tr>
<tr><td>b. What if ROE is 10%, which is less than the market capitalization rate? Compare the firm's price in this instance to that of a firm with the same ROE and E_1, but a plowback ratio of $b = 0$.</td></tr>
</table>

Life Cycles and Multistage Growth Models

As useful as the constant-growth DDM formula is, you need to remember that it is based on a simplifying assumption, namely, that the dividend growth rate will be constant forever. In fact, firms typically pass through life cycles with very different dividend profiles in different phases. In early years, there are ample opportunities for profitable reinvestment in the company. Payout ratios are low, and growth is correspondingly rapid. In later years, the firm matures, production capacity is sufficient to meet market demand, competitors enter the market, and attractive opportunities for reinvestment may become harder to find. In this mature phase, the firm may choose to increase the dividend payout ratio, rather than retain earnings. The dividend level increases, but thereafter it grows at a slower rate because the company has fewer growth opportunities.

Table 18.2 illustrates this pattern. It gives Value Line's forecasts of return on assets, dividend payout ratio, and 3-year growth rate in earnings per share for a sample of the

	Return on Assets (%)	Payout Ratio (%)	Growth Rate 2008–2011
Computer Software			
Adobe Systems	13.5%	0.0%	14.0%
Cognizant	18.0	0.0	20.8
Compuware	14.0	0.0	11.5
Intuit	15.0	0.0	9.5
Microsoft	40.0	30.0	15.9
Oracle	30.0	0.0	17.2
Red Hat	9.5	0.0	17.8
Parametric Tech	15.0	0.0	13.7
SAP	24.0	27.0	12.7
Median	15.0%	0.0%	14.0%
Electric Utilities			
Central Hudson G&E	5.5%	72.0%	4.5%
Central Vermont	5.5	57.0	2.1
Consolidated Edison	6.0	70.0	1.0
Energy East	6.0	76.0	7.7
Northeast Utilities	5.5	49.0	6.8
Nstar	9.5	60.0	10.1
Pennsylvania Power	13.0	50.0	18.6
Public Services Enter.	9.5	43.0	2.2
United Illuminating	6.5	80.0	3.3
Median	6.0%	60.0%	4.5%

TABLE 18.2

Financial ratios in two industries

firms included in the computer software industry versus those of East Coast electric utilities. (We compare return on assets rather than return on equity because the latter is affected by leverage, which tends to be far greater in the electric utility industry than in the software industry. Return on assets measures operating income per dollar of total assets, regardless of whether the source of the capital supplied is debt or equity. We will return to this issue in the next chapter.)

By and large, the software firms have attractive investment opportunities. The median return on assets of these firms is forecast to be 15%, and the firms have responded with high plowback ratios. Most of these firms pay no dividends at all. The high return on assets and high plowback result in rapid growth. The median growth rate of earnings per share in this group is projected at 14%.

In contrast, the electric utilities are more representative of mature firms. Their median return on assets is lower, 6%; dividend payout is higher, 60%; and median growth is lower, 4.5%.

We conclude that the higher payouts of the electric utilities reflect their more limited opportunities to reinvest earnings at attractive rates of return. Consistent with this view, Microsoft's announcement in 2004 that it would sharply increase its dividend and initiate multi-billion-dollar stock buybacks was widely seen as an indication that the firm was maturing into a lower-growth stage. It was generating far more cash than it had the opportunity to invest attractively, and so was paying out that cash to its shareholders.

To value companies with temporarily high growth, analysts use a multistage version of the dividend discount model. Dividends in the early high-growth period are forecast and their combined present value is calculated. Then, once the firm is projected to settle down to a steady-growth phase, the constant-growth DDM is applied to value the remaining stream of dividends.

We can illustrate this with a real-life example. Figure 18.2 is a Value Line Investment Survey report on Honda Motor Co. Some of the relevant information for 2007 is highlighted.

Honda's beta appears at the circled A, its recent stock price at the B, the per-share dividend payments at the C, the ROE (referred to as "return on shareholder equity") at the D, and the dividend payout ratio (referred to as "all dividends to net profits") at the E.[7] The rows ending at C, D, and E are historical time series. The boldfaced, italicized entries under 2008 are estimates for that year. Similarly, the entries in the far right column (labeled 10–12) are forecasts for some time between 2010 and 2012, which we will take to be 2011.

Value Line projects rapid growth in the near term, with dividends rising from $.77 in 2008 to $1.10 in 2011. This rapid growth rate cannot be sustained indefinitely. We can obtain dividend inputs for this initial period by using the explicit forecasts for 2008 and 2011 and linear interpolation for the years between:

2008	$.77		2010	$ .99
2009	$.88		2011	$1.10

Now let us assume the dividend growth rate levels off in 2011. What is a good guess for that steady-state growth rate? Value Line forecasts a dividend payout ratio of .26 and an ROE of 12.5%, implying long-term growth will be

$$g = \text{ROE} \times b = 12.5\% \times (1 - .26) = 9.25\%$$

[7]Because Honda is a Japanese firm, Americans would hold its shares via ADRs, or American depository receipts. ADRs are not shares of the firm, but are *claims* to shares of the underlying foreign stock that are then traded in U.S. security markets. Value Line notes that each Honda ADR is a claim on one common share, but in other cases, each ADR may represent a claim to multiple shares or even fractional shares.

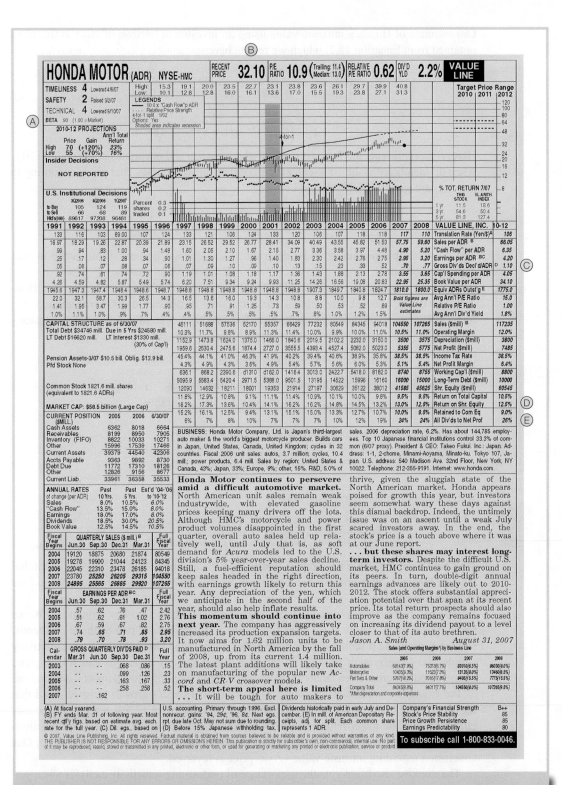

FIGURE 18.2   Value Line Investment Survey report on Honda Motor Co.

Source: Jason A. Smith, Value Line Investment Survey, August 31, 2007. Reprinted with permission of Value Line Investment Survey © 2007 Value Line Publishing, Inc. All rights reserved.

Our estimate of Honda's intrinsic value using an investment horizon of 2011 is therefore obtained from Equation 18.2, which we restate here:

$$V_{2007} = \frac{D_{2008}}{1+k} + \frac{D_{2009}}{(1+k)^2} + \frac{D_{2010}}{(1+k)^3} + \frac{D_{2011}+P_{2011}}{(1+k)^4}$$

$$= \frac{.77}{1+k} + \frac{.88}{(1+k)^2} + \frac{.99}{(1+k)^3} + \frac{1.10+P_{2011}}{(1+k)^4}$$

Here, P_{2011} represents the forecast price at which we can sell our shares at the end of 2011, when dividends are assumed to enter their constant-growth phase. That price, according to the constant-growth DDM, should be

$$P_{2011} = \frac{D_{2012}}{k-g} = \frac{D_{2011}(1+g)}{k-g} = \frac{1.10 \times 1.0925}{k-.0925}$$

The only variable remaining to be determined to calculate intrinsic value is the market capitalization rate, k.

One way to obtain k is from the CAPM. Observe from the Value Line report that Honda's beta is .90. The risk-free rate on Treasury bonds at the end of 2007 was about 4.5%. Suppose that the market risk premium were forecast at 8%, roughly in line with its historical average. This would imply that the forecast for the market return was

$$\text{Risk-free rate} + \text{Market risk premium} = 4.5\% + 8\% = 12.5\%$$

Therefore, we can solve for the market capitalization rate as

$$k = r_f + \beta[E(r_M) - r_f] = 4.5\% + .9(12.5 - 4.5) = 11.7\%$$

Our forecast for the stock price in 2011 is thus

$$P_{2011} = \frac{\$1.10 \times 1.0925}{.117 - .0925} = \$49.05$$

And today's estimate of intrinsic value is

$$V_{2007} = \frac{.77}{1.117} + \frac{.88}{(1.117)^2} + \frac{.99}{(1.117)^3} + \frac{1.10+49.05}{(1.117)^4} = \$34.32$$

We know from the Value Line report that Honda's actual price was $32.10 (at the circled B). Our intrinsic value analysis indicates that the stock was a bit underpriced. Should we increase our holdings?

Perhaps. But before betting the farm, stop to consider how firm our estimate is. We've had to guess at dividends in the near future, the ultimate growth rate of those dividends, and the appropriate discount rate. Moreover, we've assumed Honda will follow a relatively simple two-stage growth process. In practice, the growth of dividends can follow more complicated patterns. Even small errors in these approximations could upset a conclusion.

For example, suppose that we have overestimated Honda's growth prospects and that the actual ROE in the post-2011 period will be 12% rather than 12.5%, a seemingly minor change. Using the lower return on equity in the dividend discount model would result in an intrinsic value in 2007 of $30.09, which is considerably *less* than the stock price. Our conclusion regarding intrinsic value versus price is reversed.

The exercise also highlights the importance of performing sensitivity analysis when you attempt to value stocks. Your estimates of stock values are no better than your assumptions. Sensitivity analysis will highlight the inputs that need to be most carefully examined. For example, even small changes in the estimated ROE for the post-2011 period can result in big changes in intrinsic value. Similarly, small changes in the assumed capitalization rate would change intrinsic value substantially. On the other hand, reasonable changes in the dividends forecast between 2008 and 2011 would have a small impact on intrinsic value.

CONCEPT CHECK 4	Confirm that the intrinsic value of Honda using ROE = 12% is $30.09. (*Hint:* First calculate the stock price in 2011. Then calculate the present value of all interim dividends plus the present value of the 2011 sales price.)

Multistage Growth Models

The two-stage growth model that we just considered for Honda is a good start toward realism, but clearly we could do even better if our valuation model allowed for more flexible patterns of growth. Multistage growth models allow dividends per share to grow at several different rates as the firm matures. Many analysts use three-stage growth models. They may assume an initial period of high dividend growth (or instead make year-by-year forecasts of dividends for the short term), a final period of sustainable growth, and a transition period between, during which dividend growth rates taper off from the initial rapid rate to the ultimate sustainable rate. These models are conceptually no harder to work with than a two-stage model, but they require many more calculations and can be tedious to do by hand. It is easy, however, to build an Excel spreadsheet for such a model.

Spreadsheet 18.1 is an example of such a model. Column B contains the inputs we have used so far for Honda. Column E contains dividend forecasts. In cells E2 through E5 we present the Value Line estimates for the next 4 years. Dividend growth in this period is rapid, about 12.62% annually. Rather than assume a sudden transition to constant dividend growth starting in 2011, we assume instead that the dividend growth rate in 2011 will be 12.62%

	A	B	C	D	E	F	G	H	I
1	Inputs			Year	Dividend	Div growth	Term value	Investor CF	
2	beta	0.9		2008	0.77			0.77	
3	mkt_prem	0.08		2009	0.88			0.88	
4	rf	0.045		2010	0.99			0.99	
5	k_equity	0.117		2011	1.10			1.10	
6	plowback	0.74		2012	1.24	0.1262		1.24	
7	roe	0.125		2013	1.39	0.1229		1.39	
8	term_gwth	0.0925		2014	1.56	0.1195		1.56	
9				2015	1.74	0.1161		1.74	
10				2016	1.93	0.1127		1.93	
11				2017	2.15	0.1094		2.15	
12	Value line			2018	2.37	0.1060		2.37	
13	forecasts of			2019	2.62	0.1026		2.62	
14	annual dividends			2020	2.88	0.0992		2.88	
15				2021	3.15	0.0959		3.15	
16				2022	3.44	0.0925		3.44	
17	Transitional period			2023	3.76	0.0925	167.77	171.53	
18	with slowing dividend								
19	growth							39.71	= PV of CF
20		Beginning of constant-			E17*(1+F17)/(B5–F17)				
21		growth period						NPV(B5,H2:H17)	

SPREADSHEET 18.1

A three-stage growth model for Honda Motor Co.

eXcel

Please visit us at
www.mhhe.com/bkm

One way to summarize these relationships is to say the higher the plowback rate, the higher the growth rate, but a higher plowback rate does not necessarily mean a higher P/E ratio. A higher plowback rate increases P/E only if investments undertaken by the firm offer an expected rate of return higher than the market capitalization rate. Otherwise, higher plowback hurts investors because it means more money is sunk into projects with inadequate rates of return.

Notwithstanding these fine points, P/E ratios commonly are taken as proxies for the expected growth in dividends or earnings. In fact, a common Wall Street rule of thumb is that the growth rate ought to be roughly equal to the P/E ratio. In other words, the ratio of P/E to g, often called the *PEG ratio,* should be about 1.0. Peter Lynch, the famous portfolio manager, puts it this way in his book *One Up on Wall Street:*

> The P/E ratio of any company that's fairly priced will equal its growth rate. I'm talking here about growth rate of earnings here. . . . If the P/E ratio of Coca Cola is 15, you'd expect the company to be growing at about 15% per year, etc. But if the P/E ratio is less than the growth rate, you may have found yourself a bargain.

EXAMPLE 18.5   P/E Ratio versus Growth Rate

Let's try Lynch's rule of thumb. Assume that

$$r_f = 8\% \quad \text{(roughly the value when Peter Lynch was writing)}$$
$$r_M - r_f = 8\% \quad \text{(about the historical average market risk premium)}$$
$$b = .4 \quad \text{(a typical value for the plowback ratio in the United States)}$$

Therefore, $r_M = r_f +$ market risk premium $= 8\% + 8\% = 16\%$, and $k = 16\%$ for an average ($\beta = 1$) company. If we also accept as reasonable that ROE $= 16\%$ (the same value as the expected return on the stock), we conclude that

$$g = \text{ROE} \times b = 16\% \times .4 = 6.4\%$$

and

$$\frac{P}{E} = \frac{1 - .4}{.16 - .064} = 6.26$$

Thus, the P/E ratio and g are about equal using these assumptions, consistent with the rule of thumb.

However, note that this rule of thumb, like almost all others, will not work in all circumstances. For example, the value of r_f today is more like 5%, so a comparable forecast of r_M today would be

$$r_f + \text{Market risk premium} = 5\% + 8\% = 13\%$$

If we continue to focus on a firm with $\beta = 1$, and if ROE still is about the same as k, then

$$g = 13\% \times .4 = 5.2\%$$

while

$$\frac{P}{E} = \frac{1 - .4}{.13 - .052} = 7.69$$

The P/E ratio and g now diverge and the PEG ratio is now 1.5. Nevertheless, lower-than-average PEG ratios are still widely seen as signaling potential underpricing.

The importance of growth opportunities is nowhere more evident than in the valuation of Internet firms. Many companies that had yet to turn a profit were valued by the market in the late 1990s at billions of dollars. The perceived value of these companies was *exclusively* as growth opportunities. For example, the online auction firm eBay had 1998 profits of $2.4 million, far less than the $45 million profit earned by the traditional auctioneer Sotheby's; yet eBay's market value was more than 10 times greater: $22 billion versus $1.9 billion. (As it turns out, the market was quite right to value eBay so much more aggressively than Sotheby's. By 2006, eBay's net income was over $1 billion, more than 10 times that of Sotheby's, and still growing.

Of course, when company valuation is determined primarily by growth opportunities, those values can be very sensitive to reassessments of such prospects. When the market became more skeptical of the business prospects of most Internet retailers at the close of the 1990s, that is, as it revised the estimates of growth opportunities downward, their stock prices plummeted.

As perceptions of future prospects wax and wane, share price can swing wildly. Growth prospects are intrinsically difficult to tie down; ultimately, however, those prospects drive the value of the most dynamic firms in the economy.

CONCEPT CHECK **5**	ABC stock has an expected ROE of 12% per year, expected earnings per share of $2, and expected dividends of $1.50 per share. Its market capitalization rate is 10% per year. *a.* What are its expected growth rate, its price, and its P/E ratio? *b.* If the plowback ratio were .4, what would be the expected dividend per share, the growth rate, price, and the P/E ratio?

P/E Ratios and Stock Risk

One important implication of any stock-valuation model is that (holding all else equal) riskier stocks will have lower P/E multiples. We can see this quite easily in the context of the constant-growth model by examining the formula for the P/E ratio (Equation 18.8):

$$\frac{P}{E} = \frac{1 - b}{k - g}$$

Riskier firms will have higher required rates of return, that is, higher values of *k*. Therefore, the P/E multiple will be lower. This is true even outside the context of the constant-growth model. For *any* expected earnings and dividend stream, the present value of those cash flows will be lower when the stream is perceived to be riskier. Hence the stock price and the ratio of price to earnings will be lower.

Of course, you can find many small, risky, start-up companies with very high P/E multiples. This does not contradict our claim that P/E multiples should fall with risk; instead it is evidence of the market's expectations of high growth rates for those companies. This is why we said that high-risk firms will have lower P/E ratios *holding all else equal.* Given a growth projection, the P/E multiple will be lower when risk is perceived to be higher.

Pitfalls in P/E Analysis

No description of P/E analysis is complete without mentioning some of its pitfalls. First, consider that the denominator in the P/E ratio is accounting earnings, which are influenced by somewhat arbitrary accounting rules such as the use of historical cost in depreciation and inventory valuation. In times of high inflation, historic cost depreciation and inventory

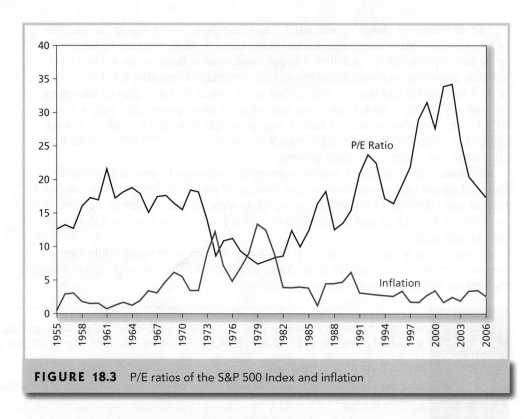

FIGURE 18.3   P/E ratios of the S&P 500 Index and inflation

costs will tend to underrepresent true economic values, because the replacement cost of both goods and capital equipment will rise with the general level of prices. As Figure 18.3 demonstrates, P/E ratios have tended to be lower when inflation has been higher. This reflects the market's assessment that earnings in these periods are of "lower quality," artificially distorted by inflation, and warranting lower P/E ratios.

Earnings management is the practice of using flexibility in accounting rules to improve the apparent profitability of the firm. We will have much to say on this topic in the next chapter on interpreting financial statements. A version of earnings management that became common in the 1990s was the reporting of "pro forma earnings" measures.

Pro forma earnings are calculated ignoring certain expenses, for example, restructuring charges, stock-option expenses, or write-downs of assets from continuing operations. Firms argue that ignoring these expenses gives a clearer picture of the underlying profitability of the firm. Comparisons with earlier periods probably would make more sense if those costs were excluded.

But when there is too much leeway for choosing what to exclude, it becomes hard for investors or analysts to interpret the numbers or to compare them across firms. The lack of standards gives firms considerable leeway to manage earnings.

Even GAAP allows firms considerable discretion to manage earnings. For example, in the late 1990s, Kellogg took restructuring charges, which are supposed to be one-time events, nine quarters in a row. Were these really one-time events, or were they more appropriately treated as ordinary expenses? Given the available leeway in managing earnings, the justified P/E multiple becomes difficult to gauge.

Another confounding factor in the use of P/E ratios is related to the business cycle. We were careful in deriving the DDM to define earnings as being net of *economic* depreciation, that is, the maximum flow of income that the firm could pay out without depleting its productive capacity. But reported earnings are computed in accordance with generally accepted accounting principles and need not correspond to economic earnings. Beyond this, however, notions of a normal or justified P/E ratio, as in Equations 18.7 or 18.8, assume implicitly that earnings rise at a constant rate, or, put another way, on a smooth trend line. In contrast, reported earnings can fluctuate dramatically around a trend line over the course of the business cycle.

Another way to make this point is to note that the "normal" P/E ratio predicted by Equation 18.8 is the ratio of today's price to the *trend value*

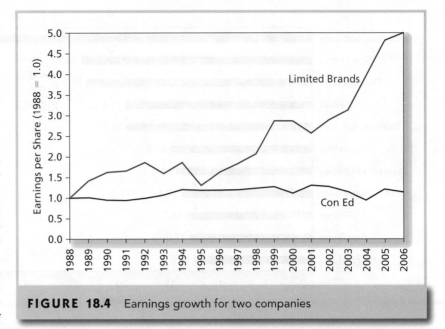

FIGURE 18.4   Earnings growth for two companies

of future earnings, E_1. The P/E ratio reported in the financial pages of the newspaper, by contrast, is the ratio of price to the most recent *past* accounting earnings. Current accounting earnings can differ considerably from future economic earnings. Because ownership of stock conveys the right to future as well as current earnings, the ratio of price to most recent earnings can vary substantially over the business cycle, as accounting earnings and the trend value of economic earnings diverge by greater and lesser amounts.

As an example, Figure 18.4 graphs the earnings per share of Limited Brands and Con Ed since 1988. Note that Limited's EPS fluctuate considerably. This reflects the company's relatively high degree of sensitivity to the business cycle. Value Line estimates its beta at 1.15. Con Ed, by contrast, shows much less variation in earnings per share around a smoother and flatter trend line. Its beta was only .70.

Because the market values the entire stream of future dividends generated by the company, when earnings are temporarily depressed, the P/E ratio should tend to be high—that is, the denominator of the ratio responds more sensitively to the business cycle than the numerator. This pattern is borne out well.

Figure 18.5 graphs the P/E ratios of the two firms. Limited, with the more volatile earnings profile, also has a more volatile

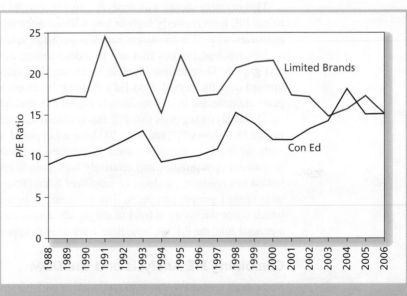

FIGURE 18.5   Price–earnings ratios

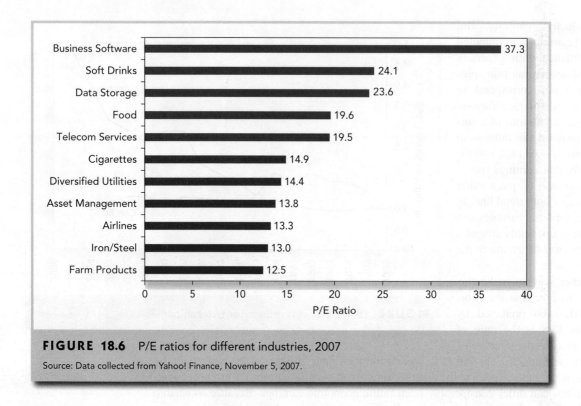

FIGURE 18.6   P/E ratios for different industries, 2007

Source: Data collected from Yahoo! Finance, November 5, 2007.

P/E profile. For example, in 1995, when earnings fell below the trend line (Figure 18.4), the P/E ratio correspondingly jumped (Figure 18.5). The market clearly recognized that earnings were depressed only temporarily. Similarly, the only year in which Con Ed's P/E ratio exceeded Limited's was in 2004, one of the rare years in which Con Ed's earnings fell below its trend line to a meaningful degree.

This example shows why analysts must be careful in using P/E ratios. There is no way to say P/E ratio is overly high or low without referring to the company's long-run growth prospects, as well as to current earnings per share relative to the long-run trend line.

Nevertheless, Figures 18.4 and 18.5 demonstrate a clear relationship between P/E ratios and growth. Despite considerable short-run fluctuations, Limited's EPS clearly trended upward over the period. Con Ed's earnings were essentially flat. Limited's growth prospects are reflected in its consistently higher P/E multiple.

This analysis suggests that P/E ratios should vary across industries, and in fact they do. Figure 18.6 shows P/E ratios in 2007 for a sample of industries. Notice that the industries with the highest multiples—such as business software or data storage—have attractive investment opportunities and relatively high growth rates, whereas the industries with the lowest ratios—farm products or iron/steel manufacturers—are in more mature industries with limited growth prospects. The relationship between P/E and growth is not perfect, which is not surprising in light of the pitfalls discussed in this section, but it appears that as a general rule, the P/E multiple does track growth opportunities.

Combining P/E Analysis and the DDM

Some analysts use P/E ratios in conjunction with earnings forecasts to estimate the price of a stock at an investor's horizon date. The Honda analysis in Figure 18.2 shows that Value Line forecast a P/E ratio for 2011 of 15. EPS for 2011 were forecast at $4.20, implying a price in 2011 of 15 × $4.20 = $63. Given an estimate of $63 for the 2011 sales price, we would compute intrinsic value in 2007 as

$$V_{2007} = \frac{.77}{1.117} + \frac{.88}{(1.117)^2} + \frac{.99}{(1.117)^3} + \frac{1.10 + 63}{(1.117)^4} = \$43.28$$

Other Comparative Valuation Ratios

The price–earnings ratio is an example of a comparative valuation ratio. Such ratios are used to assess the valuation of one firm versus another based on a fundamental indicator such as earnings. For example, an analyst might compare the P/E ratios of two firms in the same industry to test whether the market is valuing one firm "more aggressively" than the other. Other such comparative ratios are commonly used:

Price-to-Book Ratio   This is the ratio of price per share divided by book value per share. As we noted earlier in this chapter, some analysts view book value as a useful measure of value and therefore treat the ratio of price to book value as an indicator of how aggressively the market values the firm.

Price-to-Cash-Flow Ratio   Earnings as reported on the income statement can be affected by the company's choice of accounting practices, and thus are commonly viewed as subject to some imprecision and even manipulation. In contrast, cash flow—which tracks cash actually flowing into or out of the firm—is less affected by accounting decisions. As a result, some analysts prefer to use the ratio of price to cash flow per share rather than price to earnings per share. Some analysts use operating cash flow when calculating this ratio; others prefer "free cash flow," that is, operating cash flow net of new investment.

Price-to-Sales Ratio   Many start-up firms have no earnings. As a result, the price–earnings ratio for these firms is meaningless. The price-to-sales ratio (the ratio of stock price to the annual sales per share) has recently become a popular valuation benchmark for these firms. Of course, price-to-sales ratios can vary markedly across industries, because profit margins vary widely.

Be Creative   Sometimes a standard valuation ratio will simply not be available, and you will have to devise your own. In the 1990s, some analysts valued retail Internet firms based on the number of Web hits their sites received. As it turns out, they valued these firms using too-generous "price-to-hits" ratios. Nevertheless, in a new investment environment, these analysts used the information available to them to devise the best valuation tools they could.

Figure 18.7 presents the behavior of several valuation measures since 1955. While the levels of these ratios differ considerably, for the most part, they track each other fairly closely, with upturns and downturns at the same times.

18.5   FREE CASH FLOW VALUATION APPROACHES

An alternative approach to the dividend discount model values the firm using free cash flow, that is, cash flow available to the firm or its equityholders net of capital expenditures. This approach is particularly useful for firms that pay no dividends, for which the dividend

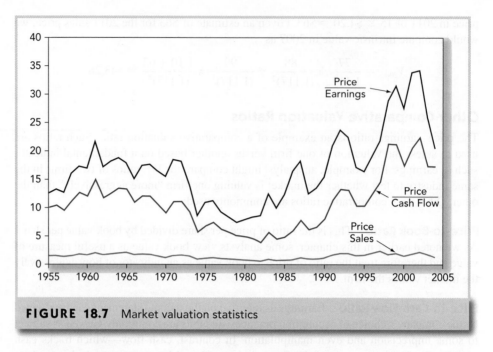

FIGURE 18.7 Market valuation statistics

discount model would be difficult to implement. But free cash flow models may be applied to any firm and can provide useful insights about firm value beyond the DDM.

One approach is to discount the *free cash flow* for the *firm* (FCFF) at the weighted-average cost of capital to obtain the value of the firm, and subtract the then-existing value of debt to find the value of equity. Another is to focus from the start on the free cash flow to *equity holders* (FCFE), discounting those directly at the cost of equity to obtain the market value of equity.

The free cash flow to the firm is the after-tax cash flow that accrues from the firm's operations, net of investments in capital and net working capital. It includes cash flows available to both debt- and equityholders.[9] It is given as follows:

$$\text{FCFF} = \text{EBIT}\,(1 - t_c) + \text{Depreciation} - \text{Capital expenditures} - \text{Increase in NWC}$$
$$\text{(18.9)}$$

where

EBIT = earnings before interest and taxes

t_c = the corporate tax rate

NWC = net working capital

Alternatively, we can focus on cash flow available to equityholders. This will differ from free cash flow to the firm by after-tax interest expenditures, as well as by cash flow associated with net issuance or repurchase of debt (i.e., principal repayments minus proceeds from issuance of new debt).

$$\text{FCFE} = \text{FCFF} - \text{Interest expense} \times (1 - t_c) + \text{Increases in net debt} \quad \text{(18.10)}$$

The free cash flow to the firm approach discounts year-by-year cash flows plus some estimate of terminal value, V_T. In Equation 18.11, we use the constant-growth model to estimate terminal value and discount at the weighted-average cost of capital.

---

[9]This is firm cash flow assuming all-equity financing. Any tax advantage to debt financing is recognized by using an after-tax cost of debt in the computation of weighted-average cost of capital. This issue is discussed in any introductory corporate finance text.

$$\text{Firm value} = \sum_{t=1}^{T} \frac{\text{FCFF}_t}{(1 + \text{WACC})^t} + \frac{V_T}{(1 + \text{WACC})^T}, \quad \text{where } V_T = \frac{\text{FCFF}_{T+1}}{\text{WACC} - g} \quad \textbf{(18.11)}$$

To find equity value, we subtract the existing market value of debt from the derived value of the firm.

Alternatively, we can discount free cash flows to *equity* (FCFE) at the cost of *equity*, k_E.

$$\text{Market value of equity} = \sum_{t=1}^{T} \frac{\text{FCFE}_t}{(1 + k_E)^t} + \frac{V_T}{(1 + k_E)^T}, \quad \text{where } V_T = \frac{\text{FCFE}_{T+1}}{k_E - g} \quad \textbf{(18.12)}$$

As in the dividend discount model, free cash flow models use a terminal value to avoid adding the present values of an infinite sum of cash flows. That terminal value may simply be the present value of a constant-growth perpetuity (as in the formulas above) or it may be based on a multiple of EBIT, book value, earnings, or free cash flow. As a general rule, estimates of intrinsic value depend critically on terminal value.

Spreadsheet 18.2 presents a free cash flow valuation of Honda using the data supplied by Value Line in Figure 18.2. We start with the free cash flow to the firm approach given in Equation 18.9. Panel A of the spreadsheet lays out values supplied by Value Line. Entries

	A	B	C	D	E	F	G	H	I	J	K	L	M
1		2006	2007	2008	2009	2010	2011						
2	A. Value Line data												
3	P/E	12.70	13.16	13.62	14.08	14.54	15.00						
4	Cap spending/shr		3.55	3.65	3.78	3.92	4.05						
5	LT Debt		16000	15000	13333	11667	10000						
6	Shares		1810	1800	1792	1783	1775						
7	EPS		2.95	3.20	3.53	3.87	4.20						
8	Working Capital		8740	8755	8770	8785	8800						
9													
10	B. Cash flow calculations												
11	Profits (after tax)		5355.0	5775.0	6345.0	6915.0	7485.0						
12	Interest (after tax)		560.9	525.8	467.4	409.0	350.6	= r_debt * (1–tax) * LT Debt					
13	Chg Working Cap			15.0	15.0	15.0	15.0						
14	Depreciation			3575.0	3650.0	3725.0	3800.0						
15	Cap Spending			6570.0	6776.3	6982.5	7188.8						
16								Terminal value					
17	FCFF			3290.8	3671.2	4051.5	4431.8	103528.9					
18	FCFE			1765.0	1537.1	1975.8	2414.6	96092.5	assumes fixed debt ratio after 2011				
19													
20	C. Discount rate calculations												
21	Current beta	0.9								from Value Line			
22	Unlevered beta	0.790								current beta/[1+(1–tax)*debt/equity)]			
23	terminal growth	0.06											
24	tax_rate	0.385								from Value Line			
25	r_debt	0.057								YTM in 2007 on A-rated LT debt			
26	risk-free rate	0.045											
27	market risk prem	0.08											
28	MV equity		70472	78656	89338	100544	112275			Row 3 * Row 11			
29	Debt/Value		0.19	0.16	0.13	0.10	0.08			Row 5/(Row 5+Row 28)			
30	Levered beta		0.900	0.882	0.862	0.846	0.833			unlevered beta * [1+(1–tax)*debt/equity]			
31	k_equity		0.117	0.116	0.114	0.113	0.112	0.112	from CAPM and levered beta				
32	WACC		0.102	0.103	0.104	0.105	0.105	0.105	(1–t)*r_debt*D/V+k_equity*(1–D/V)				
33	PV factor for FCFF		1.000	0.907	0.822	0.744	0.673	0.673	Discount each year at WACC				
34	PV factor for FCFE		1.000	0.896	0.805	0.723	0.651	0.651	Discount each year at k_equity				
35													
36	D. Present values									Intrinsic val	Equity val	Intrin/share	
37	PV(FCFF)			2984	3016	3014	2982	69667		81663	65663	36.28	
38	PV(FCFE)			1582	1237	1429	1571	62513		68332	68332	37.75	

SPREADSHEET 18.2

eXcel
Please visit us at
www.mhhe.com/bkm

Free cash flow valuation of Honda Motor Co.

for middle years are interpolated from beginning and final values. Panel B calculates free cash flow. The sum of after-tax profits in row 11 (from Value Line) plus after-tax interest payments in row 12 [i.e., interest expense $\times (1 - t_c)$] equals EBIT$(1 - t_c)$. In row 13 we subtract the change in net working capital, in row 14 we add back depreciation, and in row 15 we subtract capital expenditures. The result in row 17 is the free cash flow to the firm, FCFF, for each year between 2006 and 2009.

To find the present value of these cash flows, we will discount at WACC, which is calculated in panel C. WACC is the weighted average of the after-tax cost of debt and the cost of equity in each year. When computing WACC, we must account for the change in leverage forecast by Value Line. To compute the cost of equity, we will use the CAPM as in our earlier (dividend discount model) valuation exercise, but accounting for the fact that equity beta will decline each year as the firm reduces leverage.[10]

To find Honda's cost of debt, we note that its long-term bonds were rated A in late 2007 and that yields to maturity on A-rated debt at the time were about 5.7%. Honda's debt-to-value ratio is computed in row 29 (assuming that its debt is selling near par value), and WACC is computed in row 32. WACC increases slightly over time as the debt-to-value ratio declines between 2008 and 2011. The present value factor for cash flows accruing in each year is the previous year's factor divided by (1 + WACC) for that year. The present value of each cash flow (row 37) is the free cash flow times the cumulative discount factor.

The terminal value of the firm (cell H17) is computed from the constant-growth model as FCFF$_{2011} \times (1 + g)/($WACC$_{2011} - g)$, where g (cell B23) is the assumed value for the steady growth rate. We assume in the spreadsheet that $g = .06$, which is perhaps a bit higher than the long-run growth rate of the broad economy.[11] Terminal value is also discounted back to 2007 (cell H37), and the intrinsic value of the firm is thus found as the sum of discounted free cash flows between 2008 and 2011 plus the discounted terminal value. Finally, the value of debt in 2007 is subtracted from firm value to arrive at the intrinsic value of equity in 2007 (cell K37), and value per share is calculated in cell L37 as equity value divided by number of shares in 2007.

The free cash flow to equity approach yields a similar intrinsic value for the stock.[12] FCFE (row 18) is obtained from FCFF by subtracting after-tax interest expense and net debt repurchases. The cash flows are then discounted at the equity rate. Like WACC, the

---

[10]Call β_L the firm's equity beta at the initial level of leverage as provided by Value Line. Equity betas reflect both business risk and financial risk. When a firm changes its capital structure (debt/equity mix), it changes financial risk, and therefore equity beta changes. How should we recognize the change in financial risk? As you may remember from an introductory corporate finance class, you must first unleverage beta. This leaves us with business risk. We use the following formula to find unleveraged beta, β_U (where D/E is the firm's current debt-equity ratio):

$$\beta_U = \frac{\beta_L}{1 + (D/E)(1 - t_c)}$$

Then, we re-leverage beta in any particular year using the forecast capital structure for that year (which reintroduces the financial risk associated with that year's capital structure):

$$\beta_L = \beta_U [1 + (D/E)(1 - t_c)]$$

[11]In the long run a firm can't grow forever at a rate higher than the aggregate economy. So by the time we assert that growth is in a stable stage, it seems reasonable that the growth rate should not be significantly greater than that of the overall economy (although it can be less if the firm is in a declining industry).

[12]Over the 2008–2011 period, Value Line predicts that Honda will retire a considerable fraction of its outstanding debt. The implied debt repurchases are a use of cash and reduce the cash flow available to equity. Such repurchases cannot be sustained indefinitely, however, for debt outstanding would soon be run down to zero. Therefore, in our estimate of the terminal value of equity, we compute the final cash flow assuming that starting in 2011 Honda will begin *issuing* enough debt to maintain its debt-to-value ratio. This approach is consistent with the assumption of constant growth and constant discount rates after 2011.

cost of equity changes each period as leverage changes. The present value factor for equity cash flows is presented in row 34. Equity value is reported in cell J38, which is put on a per share basis in cell L38.

Spreadsheet 18.2 is available at the Online Learning Center for this text, **www.mhhe .com/bkm.**

Comparing the Valuation Models

In principle, the free cash flow approach is fully consistent with the dividend discount model and should provide the same estimate of intrinsic value if one can extrapolate to a period in which the firm begins to pay dividends growing at a constant rate. This was demonstrated in two famous papers by Modigliani and Miller.[13] However, in practice, you will find that values from these models may differ, sometimes substantially. This is due to the fact that in practice, analysts are always forced to make simplifying assumptions. For example, how long will it take the firm to enter a constant-growth stage? How should depreciation best be treated? What is the best estimate of ROE? Answers to questions like these can have a big impact on value, and it is not always easy to maintain consistent assumptions across the models.

We have now valued Honda using several approaches, with estimates of intrinsic value as follows:

Model	Intrinsic Value
Two-stage dividend discount model	$34.32
DDM with earnings multiple terminal value	43.28
Three-stage DDM	39.71
Free cash flow to the firm	36.28
Free cash flow to equity	37.75
Market price (from Value Line)	32.10

What should we make of these differences? All of these estimates are somewhat higher than Honda's actual stock price, perhaps indicating that they use an unrealistically high value for the ultimate constant growth rate. In the long run, it seems unlikely that Honda will be able to grow as rapidly as Value Line's forecast for 2011 growth, 9.25%. The two-stage dividend discount model is the most conservative of the estimates, probably because it assumes that Honda's dividend growth rate will fall to its terminal value after only 3 years. In contrast, the three-stage DDM allows growth to taper off over a longer period. The DDM with a terminal value provided by the earnings multiple results in the most extreme estimate of intrinsic value, one that is 35% higher than Honda's actual stock price. Value Line's estimate of the 2011 P/E ratio is higher than recent experience, and its earnings per share estimates also seem on the optimistic side. On the other hand, given the consistency with which these estimates exceed market price, perhaps the stock is indeed underpriced compared to its intrinsic value.

This valuation exercise shows that finding bargains is not as easy as it seems. While these models are easy to apply, establishing proper inputs is more of a challenge. This should not be surprising. In even a moderately efficient market, finding profit opportunities will be more involved than analyzing Value Line data for a few hours. These models are extremely useful to analysts, however, because they provide ballpark estimates of intrinsic value. More than that, they force rigorous thought about underlying assumptions and highlight the variables with the greatest impact on value and the greatest payoff to further analysis.

---

[13]Franco Modigliani and M. Miller, "The Cost of Capital, Corporation Finance, and the Theory of Investment," *American Economic Review,* June 1958, and "Dividend Policy, Growth, and the Valuation of Shares," *Journal of Business,* October 1961.

18.6 THE AGGREGATE STOCK MARKET

Explaining Past Behavior

It has been well documented that the stock market is a leading economic indicator.[14] This means that it tends to fall before a recession and to rise before an economic recovery. However, the relationship is far from perfectly reliable.

Most scholars and serious analysts would agree that, although the stock market sometimes appears to have a substantial life of its own, responding perhaps to bouts of mass euphoria and then panic, economic events and the anticipation of such events do have a substantial effect on stock prices. Perhaps the two factors with the greatest impact are interest rates and corporate profits.

Figure 18.8 shows the behavior of the earnings-to-price ratio (i.e., the earnings yield) of the S&P 500 stock index versus the yield to maturity on long-term Treasury bonds since 1955. Clearly, the two series track each other quite closely. This is to be expected: The two variables that affect a firm's value are earnings (and implicitly the dividends they can support) and the discount rate, which "translates" future income into present value. Thus, it should not be surprising that the ratio of earnings to stock price (the inverse of the P/E ratio) varies with the interest rate.

Forecasting the Stock Market

The most popular approach to forecasting the overall stock market is the earnings multiplier approach applied at the aggregate level. The first step is to forecast corporate profits for the coming period. Then we derive an estimate of the earnings multiplier, the aggregate

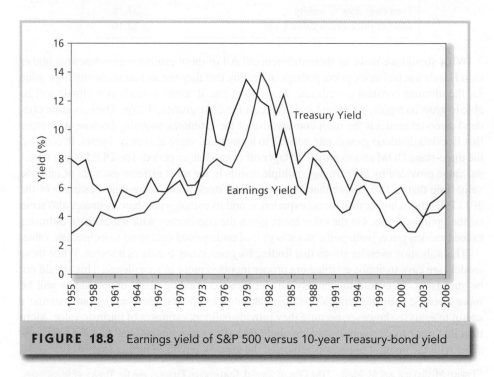

FIGURE 18.8 Earnings yield of S&P 500 versus 10-year Treasury-bond yield

[14]See, for example, Stanley Fischer and Robert C. Merton, "Macroeconomics and Finance: The Role of the Stock Market," *Carnegie-Rochester Conference Series on Public Policy* 21 (1984).

P/E ratio, based on a forecast of long-term interest rates. The product of the two forecasts is the estimate of the end-of-period level of the market.

The forecast of the P/E ratio of the market is sometimes derived from a graph similar to that in Figure 18.8, which plots the *earnings yield* (earnings per share divided by price per share, the reciprocal of the P/E ratio) of the S&P 500 and the yield to maturity on 10-year Treasury bonds. The figure shows that both yields rose dramatically in the 1970s. In the case of Treasury bonds, this was because of an increase in the inflationary expectations built into interest rates. The earnings yield on the S&P 500, however, probably rose because of inflationary distortions that artificially increased reported earnings. We have already seen that P/E ratios tend to fall when inflation rates increase. When inflation moderated in the 1980s, both Treasury and earnings yields fell. For most of the last 30 years, the earnings yield has been within about 1 percentage point of the T-bond rate.

One might use this relationship and the current yield on 10-year Treasury bonds to forecast the earnings yield on the S&P 500. Given that earnings yield, a forecast of earnings could be used to predict the level of the S&P in some future period. Let's consider a simple example of this procedure.

EXAMPLE 18.6   Forecasting the Aggregate Stock Market

A mid-2007 forecast for earnings per share for the S&P 500 portfolio in the coming 12 months was about $97. The 10-year Treasury bond yield was about 4.6%. Because the earnings yield on the S&P 500 has most recently been about 1 percentage point above the 10-year Treasury yield, a first guess for the earnings yield on the S&P 500 might be 5.6%. This would imply a P/E ratio of 1/.056 = 17.86. Our 1-year-ahead forecast for the S&P 500 index would then be 17.86 × 97 = 1,732.

Of course, there is uncertainty regarding all three inputs into this analysis: the actual earnings on the S&P 500 stocks, the level of Treasury yields at year-end, and the spread between the Treasury yield and the earnings yield. One would wish to perform sensitivity or scenario analysis to examine the impact of changes in all of these variables. To illustrate, consider Table 18.4, which shows a simple scenario analysis treating possible effects of variation in the Treasury bond yield. The scenario analysis shows that forecast level of the stock market varies inversely and with dramatic sensitivity to interest rate changes.

Some analysts use an aggregate version of the dividend discount model rather than an earnings multiplier approach. All of these models, however, rely heavily on forecasts of

	Most Likely Scenario	Pessimistic Scenario	Optimistic Scenario	**TABLE 18.4**
Treasury bond yield	4.6%	5.1%	4.1%	S&P 500 price forecasts under various scenarios
Earnings yield	5.6%	6.1%	5.1%	
Resulting P/E ratio	17.9	16.4	19.6	
EPS forecast	97	97	97	
Forecast for S&P 500	1,732	1,590	1,902	

Forecast for the earnings yield on the S&P 500 equals Treasury bond yield plus 1%. The P/E ratio is the reciprocal of the forecast earnings yield.

Factor 4, the ratio of sales to total assets, is known as **total asset turnover** (ATO). It indicates the efficiency of the firm's use of assets in the sense that it measures the annual sales generated by each dollar of assets. In a normal year, ATO for both firms is 1.0 per year, meaning that sales of $1 per year were generated per dollar of assets. In a bad year, this ratio declines to .8 per year, and in a good year, it rises to 1.2 per year.

Comparing Nodett and Somdett, we see that factors 3 and 4 do not depend on a firm's financial leverage. The firms' ratios are equal to each other in all three scenarios.

Similarly, factor 1, the ratio of net income after taxes to pretax profit, is the same for both firms. We call this the *tax-burden ratio*. Its value reflects both the government's tax code and the policies pursued by the firm in trying to minimize its tax burden. In our example it does not change over the business cycle, remaining a constant .6.

Although factors 1, 3, and 4 are not affected by a firm's capital structure, factors 2 and 5 are. Factor 2 is the ratio of pretax profits to EBIT. The firm's pretax profits will be greatest when there are no interest payments to be made to debtholders. In fact, another way to express this ratio is

$$\frac{\text{Pretax profits}}{\text{EBIT}} = \frac{\text{EBIT} - \text{Interest expense}}{\text{EBIT}}$$

We will call this factor the *interest-burden ratio*. It takes on its highest possible value, 1, for Nodett, which has no financial leverage. The higher the degree of financial leverage, the lower the interest burden ratio. Nodett's ratio does not vary over the business cycle. It is fixed at 1.0, reflecting the total absence of interest payments. For Somdett, however, because interest expense is fixed in a dollar amount while EBIT varies, the interest burden ratio varies from a low of .36 in a bad year to a high of .787 in a good year.

A closely related statistic to the interest burden ratio is the **interest coverage ratio,** or **times interest earned.** The ratio is defined as

$$\text{Interest coverage} = \text{EBIT}/\text{Interest expense}$$

A high coverage ratio indicates that the likelihood of bankruptcy is low because annual earnings are significantly greater than annual interest obligations. It is widely used by both lenders and borrowers in determining the firm's debt capacity and is a major determinant of the firm's bond rating.

Factor 5, the ratio of assets to equity, is a measure of the firm's degree of financial leverage. It is called the **leverage ratio** and is equal to 1 plus the total debt-to-equity ratio.[2] In our numerical example in Table 19.6, Nodett has a leverage ratio of 1, while Somdett's is 1.667.

From our discussion in Section 19.2, we know that financial leverage helps boost ROE only if ROA is greater than the interest rate on the firm's debt. How is this fact reflected in the ratios of Table 19.6?

The answer is that to measure the full impact of leverage in this framework, the analyst must take the product of the interest burden and leverage ratios (i.e., factors 2 and 5, shown in Table 19.6 as column 6). For Nodett, factor 6, which we call the *compound leverage factor,* remains a constant 1.0 under all three scenarios. But for Somdett, we see that the compound leverage factor is greater than 1 in normal years (1.134) and in good years (1.311), indicating the positive contribution of financial leverage to ROE. It is less

---

[2] $\dfrac{\text{Assets}}{\text{Equity}} = \dfrac{\text{Equity} + \text{Debt}}{\text{Equity}} = 1 + \dfrac{\text{Debt}}{\text{Equity}}$

than 1 in bad years, reflecting the fact that when ROA falls below the interest rate, ROE falls with increased use of debt.

We can summarize all of these relationships as follows. From Equation 19.2,

$$\text{ROE} = \text{Tax burden} \times \text{Interest burden} \times \text{Margin} \times \text{Turnover} \times \text{Leverage}$$

Because

$$\text{ROA} = \text{Margin} \times \text{Turnover} \qquad (19.3)$$

and

$$\text{Compound leverage factor} = \text{Interest burden} \times \text{Leverage}$$

we can decompose ROE equivalently as follows:

$$\text{ROE} = \text{Tax burden} \times \text{ROA} \times \text{Compound leverage factor} \qquad (19.4)$$

Comparison of profit margin and turnover usually is meaningful only in evaluating firms in the same industry. Cross-industry comparisons of these two ratios are often meaningless and can even be misleading.

EXAMPLE 19.2   Margin versus Turnover

Consider two firms with the same ROA of 10% per year. The first is a discount supermarket chain, the second is a gas and electric utility.

As Table 19.7 shows, the supermarket chain has a "low" profit margin of 2% and achieves a 10% ROA by "turning over" its assets five times per year. The capital-intensive utility, on the other hand, has a "low" asset turnover ratio of only .5 times per year and achieves its 10% ROA through its higher, 20%, profit margin. The point here is that a "low" margin or asset turnover ratio need not indicate a troubled firm. Each ratio must be interpreted in light of industry norms.

Even within an industry, margin and turnover sometimes can differ markedly among firms pursuing different marketing strategies. In the retailing industry, for example, Neiman Marcus pursues a high-margin, low-turnover policy compared to Wal-Mart, which pursues a low-margin, high-turnover policy.

CONCEPT CHECK 2	Do a ratio decomposition analysis for the Mordett corporation of Concept Check 1, preparing a table similar to Table 19.6.

	Margin	× ATO	= ROA
Supermarket chain	2%	5.0	10%
Utility	20%	0.5	10%

TABLE 19.7

Differences between profit margin and asset turnover across industries

Turnover and Other Asset Utilization Ratios

It is often helpful in understanding a firm's ratio of sales to assets to compute comparable efficiency-of-utilization, or turnover, ratios for subcategories of assets. For example, we can think about turnover relative to fixed rather than total assets:

$$\text{Fixed-asset turnover} = \frac{\text{Sales}}{\text{Fixed assets}}$$

This ratio measures sales per dollar of the firm's money tied up in fixed assets.

To illustrate how you can compute this and other ratios from a firm's financial statements, consider Growth Industries, Inc. (GI). GI's historical income statement and opening and closing balance sheets for the years 2005, 2006, and 2007 appear in Table 19.8.

GI's total asset turnover in 2007 was .303, which was below the industry average of .4. To understand better why GI underperformed, we can compute asset utilization ratios separately for fixed assets, inventories, and accounts receivable.

GI's sales in 2007 were $144 million. Its only fixed assets were plant and equipment, which were $216 million at the beginning of the year and $259.2 million at year's end. Average fixed assets for the year were, therefore, $237.6 million [($216 million + $259.2 million)/2]. GI's fixed-asset turnover for 2007 therefore was $144 million

	2004	2005	2006	2007
Income statements				
Sales revenue		$100,000	$120,000	$144,000
Cost of goods sold (including depreciation)		55,000	66,000	79,200
Depreciation		15,000	18,000	21,600
Selling and administrative expenses		15,000	18,000	21,600
Operating income		30,000	36,000	43,200
Interest expense		10,500	19,095	34,391
Taxable income		19,500	16,905	8,809
Income tax (40% rate)		7,800	6,762	3,524
Net income		$ 11,700	$ 10,143	$ 5,285
Balance sheets (end of year)				
Cash and marketable securities	$ 50,000	$ 60,000	$ 72,000	$ 86,400
Accounts receivable	25,000	30,000	36,000	43,200
Inventories	75,000	90,000	108,000	129,600
Net plant and equipment	150,000	180,000	216,000	259,200
Total assets	$300,000	$360,000	$432,000	$518,400
Accounts payable	$ 30,000	$ 36,000	$ 43,200	$ 51,840
Short-term debt	45,000	87,300	141,957	214,432
Long-term debt (8% bonds maturing in 2025)	75,000	75,000	75,000	75,000
Total liabilities	$150,000	$198,300	$260,157	$341,272
Shareholders' equity (1 million shares outstanding)	$150,000	$161,700	$171,843	$177,128
Other data				
Market price per common share at year-end		$ 93.60	$ 61.00	$ 21.00

TABLE 19.8

Growth industries financial statements, 2004–2007 ($ thousand)

per year/$237.6 million = .606 per year. In other words, for every dollar of fixed assets, there were $.606 in sales during the year 2007.

Comparable figures for the fixed-asset turnover ratio for 2005 and 2006 and the 2007 industry average are

2005	2006	2007	2007 Industry Average
.606	.606	.606	.700

GI's fixed asset turnover has been stable over time and below the industry average.

Notice that when a financial ratio includes one item from the income statement, which covers a period of time, and another from a balance sheet, which is a "snapshot" at a particular time, the practice is to take the average of the beginning and end-of-year balance sheet figures. Thus in computing the fixed-asset turnover ratio we divided sales (from the income statement) by average fixed assets (from the balance sheet).

Another widely followed turnover ratio is the **inventory turnover ratio,** which is the ratio of cost of goods sold per dollar of average inventory. The numerator is cost of goods sold instead of sales revenue because inventory is valued at cost. This ratio measures the speed with which inventory is turned over.

In 2005, GI's cost of goods sold (excluding depreciation) was $40 million, and its average inventory was $82.5 million [($75 million + $90 million)/2]. Its inventory turnover was .485 per year ($40 million/$82.5 million). In 2006 and 2007, inventory turnover remained the same, which was below the industry average of .5 per year. In other words, GI was burdened with a higher level of inventories per dollar of sales than its competitors. This higher investment in working capital in turn resulted in a higher level of assets per dollar of sales or profits, and a lower ROA than its competitors.

Another measure of efficiency is the ratio of accounts receivable to sales. The accounts receivable ratio usually is computed as average accounts receivable/sales × 365. The result is a number called the **average collection period,** or **days receivables,** which equals the total credit extended to customers per dollar of daily sales. It is the number of days' worth of sales tied up in accounts receivable. You can also think of it as the average lag between the date of sale and the date payment is received.

For GI in 2007 the average collection period was 100.4 days:

$$\frac{(\$36 \text{ million} + \$43.2 \text{ million})/2}{\$144 \text{ million}} \times 365 = 100.4 \text{ days}$$

The industry average was only 60 days. This statistic tells us that GI's average receivables per dollar of sales exceeds that of its competitors. Again, this implies a higher required investment in working capital, and ultimately a lower ROA.

In summary, these ratios show us that GI's poor total asset turnover relative to the industry is in part caused by lower-than-average fixed-asset turnover and inventory turnover and higher-than-average days receivables. This suggests GI may be having problems with excess plant capacity along with poor inventory and receivables management procedures.

Liquidity Ratios

Liquidity and interest coverage ratios are of great importance in evaluating the riskiness of a firm's securities. They aid in assessing the financial strength of the firm. Liquidity ratios include the current ratio, quick ratio, and interest coverage ratio.

1. **Current ratio:** Current assets/current liabilities. This ratio measures the ability of the firm to pay off its current liabilities by liquidating its current assets (i.e., turning

them into cash). It indicates the firm's ability to avoid insolvency in the short run. GI's current ratio in 2005, for example, was $(60 + 30 + 90)/(36 + 87.3) = 1.46$. In other years, it was

2005	2006	2007	2007 Industry Average
1.46	1.17	.97	2.0

This represents an unfavorable time trend and poor standing relative to the industry. This troublesome pattern is not surprising given the working capital burden resulting from GI's subpar performance with respect to receivables and inventory management.

2. **Quick ratio:** (Cash + marketable securities + receivables)/current liabilities. This ratio is also called the **acid test ratio.** It has the same denominator as the current ratio, but its numerator includes only cash, cash equivalents, and receivables. The quick ratio is a better measure of liquidity than the current ratio for firms whose inventory is not readily convertible into cash. GI's quick ratio shows the same disturbing trends as its current ratio:

2005	2006	2007	2007 Industry Average
.73	.58	.49	1.0

3. **Cash ratio.** A company's receivables are less liquid than its holdings of cash and marketable securities. Therefore, in addition to the quick ratio, analysts also compute a firm's cash ratio, defined as

$$\text{Cash ratio} = \frac{\text{Cash} + \text{marketable securities}}{\text{Current liabilities}}$$

GI's cash ratios are

2005	2006	2007	2007 Industry Average
.487	.389	.324	.70

GI's liquidity ratios have fallen dramatically over this 3-year period, and by 2007, its liquidity measures are far below industry averages. The decline in the liquidity ratios combined with the decline in coverage ratio (you can confirm that times interest earned has also fallen over this period) suggests that its credit rating has been declining as well, and, no doubt, GI is considered a relatively poor credit risk in 2007.

Market Price Ratios: Growth versus Value

Two important market price ratios are the market–book-value ratio and the price–earnings ratio.

The **market–book-value ratio** (P/B) equals the market price of a share of the firm's common stock divided by its *book value,* that is, shareholders' equity per share. Analysts sometimes consider the stock of a firm with a low market–book value to be a "safer" investment, seeing the book value as a "floor" supporting the market price.

Analysts presumably view book value as the level below which market price will not fall because the firm always has the option to liquidate, or sell, its assets for their book values. However, this view is questionable. In fact, the previous chapter provided examples of a few firms selling below book value in 2007. Nevertheless, low market–book-value ratio is seen by some as providing a "margin of safety," and some analysts will screen out or reject high P/B firms in their stock selection process.

In fact, a better interpretation of the market-price-to-book ratio is as a measure of growth opportunities. Recall from the previous chapter that we may view the two components of firm value as assets in place and growth opportunities. As the next example illustrates, firms with greater growth opportunities will tend to exhibit higher multiples of market-price-to-book value.

EXAMPLE 19.3   Price to Book and Growth Options

Consider two firms, both with book value per share of $10, both with a market capitalization rate of 15%, and both with plowback ratios of .60.

Bright Prospects has an ROE of 20%, which is well in excess of the market capitalization rate; this ROE implies that the firm is endowed with ample growth opportunities. With ROE $= .20$, Bright Prospects will earn $2 per share this year. With its plowback ratio of .60, it pays out a dividend of $D_1 = (1 - .6) \times \$2 = \$.80$, has a growth rate of $g = b \times$ ROE $= .60 \times .20 = .12$, and a stock price of $D_1/(k - g) = \$.80/(.15 - .12) = \$26.67$. Its price–book ratio is 26.67/10 = 2.667.

In contrast, Past Glory has an ROE of only 15%, just equal to the market capitalization rate. It therefore will earn $1.50 per share this year and will pay a dividend of $D_1 = .4 \times \$1.50 = \$.60$. Its growth rate is $g = b \times$ ROE $= .60 \times .15 = .09$, and its stock price is $D_1/(k - g) = \$.60/(.15 - .09) = \$10$. Its price–book ratio is $10/$10 = 1.0. Not surprisingly, a firm that earns just the required rate of return on its investments will sell for book value, and no more.

We conclude that the market-price-to-book-value ratio is determined in large part by growth prospects.

Another measure used to place firms along a growth versus value spectrum is the **price–earnings (P/E) ratio.** In fact, we saw in the last chapter that the ratio of the present value of growth options to the value of assets in place largely determines the P/E multiple. While low P/E stocks allow you to pay less per dollar of *current* earnings, the high P/E stock may still be a better bargain if its earnings are expected to grow quickly enough.[3]

Many analysts nevertheless believe that low P/E stocks are more attractive than high P/E stocks. And in fact, low P/E stocks have generally been positive-alpha investments using the CAPM as a benchmark. But an efficient market adherent would discount this track record, arguing that such a simplistic rule could not really generate abnormal returns, and that the CAPM may not be a good benchmark for returns in this case.

In any event, the important points to remember are that ownership of the stock conveys the right to future as well as current earnings and, therefore, that a high P/E ratio may best be interpreted as a signal that the market views the firm as enjoying attractive growth opportunities.

---

[3]Remember, though, P/E ratios reported in the financial pages are based on *past* earnings, while price is determined by the firm's prospects of *future* earnings. Therefore, reported P/E ratios may reflect variation in current earnings around a trend line.

may be more or less rosy presentations of true economic earnings—sustainable cash flow that can be paid to shareholders without impairing the firm's productive capacity. Analysts commonly evaluate the **quality of earnings** reported by a firm. This concept refers to the realism and conservatism of the earnings number, in other words, the extent to which we might expect the reported level of earnings to be sustained.

Examples of the types of factors that influence quality of earnings are:

- *Allowance for bad debt.* Most firms sell goods using trade credit and must make an allowance for bad debt. An unrealistically low allowance reduces the quality of reported earnings.

- *Nonrecurring items.* Some items that affect earnings should not be expected to recur regularly. These include asset sales, effects of accounting changes, effects of exchange rate movements, or unusual investment income. For example, in 2003, which was a banner year for equity returns, some firms enjoyed large investment returns on securities held. These contributed to that year's earnings, but should not be expected to repeat regularly. They would be considered a "low-quality" component of earnings. Similarly, investment gains in corporate pension plans generated large but one-off contributions to reported earnings.

- *Earnings smoothing.* In 2003, Freddie Mac was the subject of a major accounting scandal, when it emerged that it had improperly reclassified mortgages held in its portfolio in an attempt to *reduce* its current earnings. Similarly, in the 1990s, W.R. Grace chose to offset high earnings in one of its subsidiaries by setting aside extra reserves. Why would these firms take such actions? Because later, if earnings turned down, they could "release" earnings by reversing these transactions, and thereby create the appearance of steady earnings growth. Indeed, Freddie Mac's nickname on Wall Street was "Steady Freddie." Wall Street likes strong, steady earnings, but these firms planned to provide such growth only cosmetically, through earnings management.

- *Revenue recognition.* Under GAAP accounting, a firm is allowed to recognize a sale before it is paid. This is why firms have accounts receivable. But sometimes it can be hard to know when to recognize sales. For example, suppose a computer firm signs a contract to provide products and services over a 5-year period. Should the projected revenue be booked immediately or spread out over 5 years? A more extreme version of this problem is called "channel stuffing," in which firms "sell" large quantities of goods to customers, but give them the right to later either refuse delivery or return the product. The revenue from the "sale" is booked now, but the likely returns are not recognized until they occur (in a future accounting period). According to the SEC, Sunbeam, which filed for bankruptcy in 2001, generated $60 million in fraudulent profits in 1999 using this technique. If you see accounts receivable increasing far faster than sales, or becoming a larger percentage of total assets, beware of these practices. Given the wide latitude firms have to manipulate revenue, many analysts choose instead to concentrate on cash flow, which is far harder for a company to manipulate.

- *Off-balance-sheet assets and liabilities.* Suppose that one firm guarantees the outstanding debt of another firm, perhaps a firm in which it has an ownership stake. That obligation ought to be disclosed as a *contingent liability,* because it may require payments down the road. But these obligations may not be reported as part of the firm's outstanding debt. Similarly, leasing may be used to manage off-balance-sheet assets and liabilities. Airlines, for example, may show no aircraft on their balance sheets but have long-term leases that are virtually equivalent to debt-financed ownership. However, if the leases are treated as operating rather than capital leases, they may appear only as footnotes to the financial statements.

International Accounting Conventions

The examples cited above illustrate some of the problems that analysts can encounter when attempting to interpret financial data. Even greater problems arise in the interpretation of the financial statements of foreign firms. This is because these firms do not follow GAAP guidelines. Accounting practices in various countries differ to greater or lesser extents from U.S. standards. Here are some of the major issues that you should be aware of when using the financial statements of foreign firms:

Reserving Practices. Many countries allow firms considerably more discretion in setting aside reserves for future contingencies than is typical in the United States. Because additions to reserves result in a charge against income, reported earnings are far more subject to managerial discretion than in the United States.

Depreciation. In the United States, firms typically maintain separate sets of accounts for tax and reporting purposes. For example, accelerated depreciation is typically used for tax purposes, whereas straight-line depreciation is used for reporting purposes. In contrast, most other countries do not allow dual sets of accounts, and most firms in foreign countries use accelerated depreciation to minimize taxes despite the fact that it results in lower reported earnings. This makes reported earnings of foreign firms lower than they would be if the firms were allowed to use the U.S. practice.

Intangibles. Treatment of intangibles such as goodwill can vary widely. Are they amortized or expensed? If amortized, over what period? Such issues can have a large impact on reported profits.

The effect of different accounting practices can be substantial. Figure 19.2 compares P/E ratios in different countries as reported and restated on a common basis. While P/E multiples have changed considerably since this study was published, these results illustrate how different accounting rules can have a big impact on these ratios.

Such differences in international accounting standards become more of a problem as the drive to globally integrated capital markets progresses. For example, many foreign firms would like to list their shares on the New York Stock Exchange to more easily tap U.S. equity markets, and the NYSE would like to have those firms listed. But the SEC did not

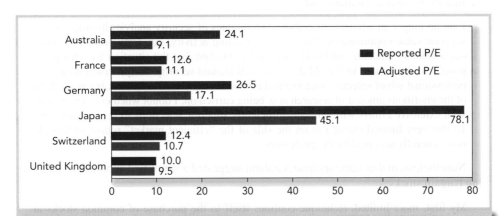

FIGURE 19.2   Adjusted versus reported price–earnings ratios

market–book-value ratio	economic value added	FIFO
price–earnings ratio	residual income	fair value accounting
earnings yield	LIFO	quality of earnings

PROBLEM SETS

Quiz

1. What is the major difference in approach of international financial reporting standards and U.S. GAAP accounting? What are the advantages and disadvantages of each?

2. If markets are truly efficient, does it matter whether firms engage in earnings management? On the other hand, if firms manage earnings, what does that say about management's view on efficient markets?

3. What financial ratios would a credit rating agency such as Moody's or Standard and Poor's be most interested in? Which ratios would be of most interest to a stock market analyst deciding whether to buy a stock for a diversified portfolio?

Problems

4. The Crusty Pie Co., which specializes in apple turnovers, has a return on sales higher than the industry average, yet its ROA is the same as the industry average. How can you explain this?

5. The ABC Corporation has a profit margin on sales below the industry average, yet its ROA is above the industry average. What does this imply about its asset turnover?

6. Firm A and firm B have the same ROA, yet firm A's ROE is higher. How can you explain this?

CFA® PROBLEMS

1. An analyst applies the DuPont system of financial analysis to the following data for a company:

   · Leverage ratio (assets/equity)   2.2
   · Total asset turnover   2.0
   · Net profit margin   5.5%
   · Dividend payout ratio   31.8%

   What is the company's return on equity?

2. The information in the following exhibit comes from the notes to the financial statements of QuickBrush Company and SmileWhite Corporation:

	QuickBrush	SmileWhite
Goodwill	The company amortizes goodwill over 20 years.	The company amortizes goodwill over 5 years.
Property, plant, and equipment	The company uses a straight-line depreciation method over the economic lives of the assets, which range from 5 to 20 years for buildings.	The company uses an accelerated depreciation method over the economic lives of the assets, which range from 5 to 20 years for buildings.
Accounts receivable	The company uses a bad debt allowance of 2% of accounts receivable.	The company uses a bad debt allowance of 5% of accounts receivable.

   Determine which company has the higher quality of earnings by discussing each of the three notes.

3. Scott Kelly is reviewing MasterToy's financial statements in order to estimate its sustainable growth rate. Consider the information presented in the following exhibit.

MasterToy, Inc.: Actual 2003 and estimated 2004 financial statements for fiscal year ending December 31 ($ million, except per-share data)

	2003	2004e	Change (%)
Income Statement			
Revenue	$4,750	$5,140	7.6%
Cost of goods sold	2,400	2,540	
Selling, general, and administrative	1,400	1,550	
Depreciation	180	210	
Goodwill amortization	10	10	
Operating income	$ 760	$ 830	8.4
Interest expense	20	25	
Income before taxes	$ 740	$ 805	
Income taxes	265	295	
Net income	$ 475	$ 510	
Earnings per share	$ 1.79	$ 1.96	8.6
Averages shares outstanding (millions)	265	260	
Balance Sheet			
Cash	$ 400	$ 400	
Accounts receivable	680	700	
Inventories	570	600	
Net property, plant, and equipment	800	870	
Intangibles	500	530	
Total assets	$2,950	$3,100	
Current liabilities	550	600	
Long-term debt	300	300	
Total liabilities	$ 850	$ 900	
Stockholders' equity	2,100	2,200	
Total liabilities and equity	$2,950	$3,100	
Book value per share	$ 7.92	$ 8.46	
Annual dividend per share	$ 0.55	$ 0.60	

a. Identify and calculate the components of the DuPont formula.
b. Calculate the ROE for 2004 using the components of the DuPont formula.
c. Calculate the sustainable growth rate for 2004 from the firm's ROE and plowback ratios.

4. The cash flow data of Palomba Pizza Stores for last year are as follows:

Cash payment of dividends	$ 35,000
Purchase of land	14,000
Cash payments for interest	10,000
Cash payments for salaries	45,000
Sale of equipment	38,000
Retirement of common stock	25,000
Purchase of equipment	30,000
Cash payments to suppliers	85,000
Cash collections from customers	250,000
Cash at beginning of year	50,000

a. Prepare a statement of cash flows for Palomba showing:

- Net cash provided by operating activities.
- Net cash provided by or used in investing activities.
- Net cash provided by or used in financing activities.

b. Discuss, from an analyst's viewpoint, the purpose of classifying cash flows into the three categories listed above.

5. This problem should be solved using the following data:

Cash payments for interest	$(12)
Retirement of common stock	(32)
Cash payments to merchandise suppliers	(85)
Purchase of land	(8)
Sale of equipment	30
Payments of dividends	(37)
Cash payment for salaries	(35)
Cash collection from customers	260
Purchase of equipment	(40)

a. What are cash flows from operating activities?
b. Using the data above, calculate cash flows from investing activities.
c. Using the data above, calculate cash flows from financing activities.

6. Janet Ludlow is a recently hired analyst. After describing the electric toothbrush industry, her first report focuses on two companies, QuickBrush Company and SmileWhite Corporation, and concludes:

QuickBrush is a more profitable company than SmileWhite, as indicated by the 40% sales growth and substantially higher margins it has produced over the last few years. SmileWhite's sales and earnings are growing at a 10% rate and produce much lower margins. We do not think SmileWhite is capable of growing faster than its recent growth rate of 10% whereas QuickBrush can sustain a 30% long-term growth rate.

a. Criticize Ludlow's analysis and conclusion that QuickBrush is more profitable, as defined by return on equity (ROE), than SmileWhite and that it has a higher sustainable growth rate. Use only the information provided in Tables 19A and 19B. Support your criticism by calculating and analyzing:

- The five components that determine ROE.
- The two ratios that determine sustainable growth: ROE and plowback.

b. Explain how QuickBrush has produced an average annual earnings per share (EPS) growth rate of 40% over the last 2 years with an ROE that has been declining. Use only the information provided in Table 19A.

The following case should be used to solve CFA Problems 7–10.

7. Eastover Company (EO) is a large, diversified forest products company. Approximately 75% of its sales are from paper and forest products, with the remainder from financial services and real estate. The company owns 5.6 million acres of timberland, which is carried at very low historical cost on the balance sheet.

Peggy Mulroney, CFA, is an analyst at the investment counseling firm of Centurion Investments. She is assigned the task of assessing the outlook for Eastover, which is being considered for purchase, and comparing it to another forest products company in Centurion's portfolios, Southampton Corporation (SHC). SHC is a major producer of lumber products in the United

Income Statement	December 2005	December 2006	December 2007
Revenue	$3,480	$5,400	$7,760
Cost of goods sold	2,700	4,270	6,050
Selling, general, and admin. expense	500	690	1,000
Depreciation and amortization	30	40	50
Operating income (EBIT)	$ 250	$ 400	$ 660
Interest expense	0	0	0
Income before taxes	$ 250	$ 400	$ 660
Income taxes	60	110	215
Income after taxes	$ 190	$ 290	$ 445
Diluted EPS	$ 0.60	$ 0.84	$ 1.18
Average shares outstanding (000)	317	346	376

Financial Statistics	December 2005	December 2006	December 2007	3-Year Average
COGS as % of sales	77.59%	79.07%	77.96%	78.24%
General & admin. as % of sales	14.37	12.78	12.89	13.16
Operating margin	7.18	7.41	8.51	
Pretax income/EBIT	100.00	100.00	100.00	
Tax rate	24.00	27.50	32.58	

Balance Sheet	December 2005	December 2006	December 2007
Cash and cash equivalents	$ 460	$ 50	$ 480
Accounts receivable	540	720	950
Inventories	300	430	590
Net property, plant, and equipment	760	1,830	3,450
Total assets	$2,060	$3,030	$5,470
Current liabilities	$ 860	$1,110	$1,750
Total liabilities	$ 860	$1,110	$1,750
Stockholders' equity	1,200	1,920	3,720
Total liabilities and equity	$2,060	$3,030	$5,470
Market price per share	$21.00	$30.00	$45.00
Book value per share	$ 3.79	$ 5.55	$ 9.89
Annual dividend per share	$ 0.00	$ 0.00	$ 0.00

TABLE 19A

QuickBrush Company financial statements: yearly data ($000 except per-share data)

States. Building products, primarily lumber and plywood, account for 89% of SHC's sales, with pulp accounting for the remainder. SHC owns 1.4 million acres of timberland, which is also carried at historical cost on the balance sheet. In SHC's case, however, that cost is not as far below current market as Eastover's.

Mulroney began her examination of Eastover and Southampton by looking at the five components of return on equity (ROE) for each company. For her analysis, Mulroney elected to define equity as total shareholders' equity, including preferred stock. She also elected to use year-end data rather than averages for the balance sheet items.

Income Statement	December 2005	December 2006	December 2007
Revenue	$104,000	$110,400	$119,200
Cost of goods sold	72,800	75,100	79,300
Selling, general, and admin. expense	20,300	22,800	23,900
Depreciation and amortization	4,200	5,600	8,300
Operating income	$ 6,700	$ 6,900	$ 7,700
Interest expense	600	350	350
Income before taxes	$ 6,100	$ 6,550	$ 7,350
Income taxes	2,100	2,200	2,500
Income after taxes	$ 4,000	$ 4,350	$ 4,850
Diluted EPS	$ 2.16	$ 2.35	$ 2.62
Average shares outstanding (000)	1,850	1,850	1,850

Financial Statistics	December 2005	December 2006	December 2007	3-Year Average
COGS as % of sales	70.00%	68.00%	66.53%	68.10%
General & admin. as % of sales	19.52	20.64	20.05	20.08
Operating margin	6.44	6.25	6.46	
Pretax income/EBIT	91.04	94.93	95.45	
Tax rate	34.43	33.59	34.01	

Balance Sheet	December 2005	December 2006	December 2007
Cash and cash equivalents	$ 7,900	$ 3,300	$ 1,700
Accounts receivable	7,500	8,000	9,000
Inventories	6,300	6,300	5,900
Net property, plant, and equipment	12,000	14,500	17,000
Total assets	$ 33,700	$ 32,100	$ 33,600
Current liabilities	$ 6,200	$ 7,800	$ 6,600
Long-term debt	9,000	4,300	4,300
Total liabilities	$ 15,200	$ 12,100	$ 10,900
Stockholders' equity	18,500	20,000	22,700
Total liabilities and equity	$ 33,700	$ 32,100	$ 33,600
Market price per share	$ 23.00	$ 26.00	$ 30.00
Book value per share	$ 10.00	$ 10.81	$ 12.27
Annual dividend per share	$ 1.42	$ 1.53	$ 1.72

TABLE 19B

SmileWhite Corporation financial statements: yearly data ($000 except per-share data)

a. Based on the data shown in Tables 19C and 19D, calculate each of the five ROE components for Eastover and Southampton in 2007. Using the five components, calculate ROE for both companies in 2007.

b. Referring to the components calculated in part (a), explain the difference in ROE for Eastover and Southampton in 2007.

c. Using 2007 data, calculate the sustainable growth rate for both Eastover and Southampton. Discuss the appropriateness of using these calculations as a basis for estimating future growth.

	2003	2004	2005	2006	2007
Income Statement Summary					
Sales	$5,652	$6,990	$7,863	$8,281	$7,406
Earnings before interest and taxes (EBIT)	$ 568	$ 901	$1,037	$ 708	$ 795
Interest expense (net)	(147)	(188)	(186)	(194)	(195)
Income before taxes	$ 421	$ 713	$ 851	$ 514	$ 600
Income taxes	(144)	(266)	(286)	(173)	(206)
Tax rate	34%	37%	33%	34%	34%
Net income	$ 277	$ 447	$ 565	$ 341	$ 394
Preferred dividends	(28)	(17)	(17)	(17)	(0)
Net income to common	$ 249	$ 430	$ 548	$ 324	$ 394
Common shares outstanding (millions)	196	204	204	205	201
Balance Sheet Summary					
Current assets	$1,235	$1,491	$1,702	$1,585	$1,367
Timberland assets	649	625	621	612	615
Property, plant, and equipment	4,370	4,571	5,056	5,430	5,854
Other assets	360	555	473	472	429
Total assets	$6,614	$7,242	$7,852	$8,099	$8,265
Current liabilities	$1,226	$1,186	$1,206	$1,606	$1,816
Long-term debt	1,120	1,340	1,585	1,346	1,585
Deferred taxes	1,000	1,000	1,016	1,000	1,000
Equity-preferred	364	350	350	400	0
Equity-common	2,904	3,366	3,695	3,747	3,864
Total liabilities and equity	$6,614	$7,242	$7,852	$8,099	$8,265

TABLE 19C

Eastover Company ($ million, except shares outstanding)

8. *a.* Mulroney (see the previous problem) recalled from her CFA studies that the constant-growth discounted dividend model was one way to arrive at a valuation for a company's common stock. She collected current dividend and stock price data for Eastover and Southampton, shown in Table 19E. Using 11% as the required rate of return (i.e., discount rate) and a projected growth rate of 8%, compute a constant-growth DDM value for Eastover's stock and compare the computed value for Eastover to its stock price indicated in Table 19F.

   b. Mulroney's supervisor commented that a two-stage DDM may be more appropriate for companies such as Eastover and Southampton. Mulroney believes that Eastover and Southampton could grow more rapidly over the next 3 years and then settle in at a lower but sustainable rate of growth beyond 2011. Her estimates are indicated in Table 19G. Using 11% as the required rate of return, compute the two-stage DDM value of Eastover's stock and compare that value to its stock price indicated in Table 19F.

   c. Discuss advantages and disadvantages of using a constant-growth DDM. Briefly discuss how the two-stage DDM improves upon the constant-growth DDM.

9. In addition to the discounted dividend model approach, Mulroney (see previous problem) decided to look at the price–earnings ratio and price–book ratio, relative to the S&P 500, for both Eastover and Southampton. Mulroney elected to perform this analysis using 2004–2008 and current data.

   a. Using the data in Tables 19E and 19F, compute both the current and the 5-year (2004– 2008) average relative price–earnings ratios and relative price–book ratios for Eastover

20.1   THE OPTION CONTRACT

A **call option** gives its holder the right to purchase an asset for a specified price, called the **exercise, or strike, price,** on or before some specified expiration date. For example, an April call option on IBM stock with exercise price $105 entitles its owner to purchase IBM stock for a price of $105 at any time up to and including the expiration date in April. The holder of the call is not required to exercise the option. The holder will choose to exercise only if the market value of the asset to be purchased exceeds the exercise price. When the market price does exceed the exercise price, the option holder may "call away" the asset for the exercise price. Otherwise, the option may be left unexercised. If it is not exercised before the expiration date of the contract, a call option simply expires and no longer has value. Therefore, if the stock price is greater than the exercise price on the expiration date, the value of the call option equals the difference between the stock price and the exercise price; but if the stock price is less than the exercise price at expiration, the call will be worthless. The *net profit* on the call is the value of the option minus the price originally paid to purchase it.

The purchase price of the option is called the **premium.** It represents the compensation the purchaser of the call must pay for the right to exercise the option if exercise becomes profitable.

Sellers of call options, who are said to *write* calls, receive premium income now as payment against the possibility they will be required at some later date to deliver the asset in return for an exercise price lower than the market value of the asset. If the option is left to expire worthless because the exercise price remains above the market price of the asset, then the writer of the call clears a profit equal to the premium income derived from the sale of the option. But if the call is exercised, the profit to the option writer is the premium income derived when the option was initially sold minus the difference between the value of the stock that must be delivered and the exercise price that is paid for those shares. If that difference is larger than the initial premium, the writer will incur a loss.

EXAMPLE 20.1   Profits and Losses on a Call Option

Consider the January expiration call option on a share of IBM with an exercise price of $105 selling on January 2, 2008, for $3.10. Exchange-traded options expire on the third Friday of the expiration month, which for this option was January 18. Until the expiration date, the purchaser of the calls may buy shares of IBM for $105. On January 2, IBM sells for $104.69. Because the stock price is currently less than $105 a share, it clearly would not make sense at the moment to exercise the option to buy at $105. Indeed, if IBM remains below $105 by the expiration date, the call will be left to expire worthless. On the other hand, if IBM is selling above $105 at expiration, the call holder will find it optimal to exercise. For example, if IBM sells for $107 on January 18, the option will be exercised, as it will give its holder the right to pay $105 for a stock worth $107. The value of the option on the expiration date would then be

$$\text{Value at expiration} = \text{Stock price} - \text{Exercise price} = \$107 - \$105 = \$2$$

Despite the $2 payoff at expiration, the call holder still realizes a loss of $1.10 on the investment because the initial purchase price was $3.10:

$$\text{Profit} = \text{Final value} - \text{Original investment} = \$2.00 - \$3.10 = -\$1.10$$

Nevertheless, exercise of the call is optimal at expiration if the stock price exceeds the exercise price because the exercise proceeds will offset at least part of the investment in the option. The investor in the call will clear a profit if IBM is selling above $108.10 at the expiration date. At that stock price, the proceeds from exercise will just cover the original cost of the call.

A **put option** gives its holder the right to *sell* an asset for a specified exercise or strike price on or before some expiration date. An April put on IBM with exercise price $105 entitles its owner to sell IBM stock to the put writer at a price of $105 at any time before expiration in April even if the market price of IBM is less than $105. While profits on call options increase when the asset *increases* in value, profits on put options increase when the asset value *falls*. A put will be exercised only if the exercise price is greater than the price of the underlying asset, that is, only if its holder can deliver for the exercise price an asset with market value less than the exercise price. (One doesn't need to own the shares of IBM to exercise the IBM put option. Upon exercise, the investor's broker purchases the necessary shares of IBM at the market price and immediately delivers, or "puts them," to an option writer for the exercise price. The owner of the put profits by the difference between the exercise price and market price.)

EXAMPLE 20.2   Profits and Losses on a Put Option

Now consider the January 2008 expiration put option on IBM with an exercise price of $105, selling on January 2, 2008, for $3.20. It entitled its owner to sell a share of IBM for $105 at any time until January 18. If the holder of the put buys a share of IBM and immediately exercises the right to sell at $105, net proceeds will be $105 − $104.69 = $.31. Obviously, an investor who pays $3.20 for the put has no intention of exercising it immediately. If, on the other hand, IBM sells for $101 at expiration, the put turns out to be a profitable investment. Its value at expiration would be

$$\text{Value at expiration} = \text{Exercise price} - \text{Stock price} = \$105 - \$101 = \$4$$

and the investor's profit would be $4.00 − $3.20 = $.80. This is a holding-period return of $.80/$3.20 = .25 or 25%—over only 16 days! Obviously, put option sellers on January 2 (who are on the other side of the transaction) did not consider this outcome very likely.

An option is described as **in the money** when its exercise would produce profits for its holder. An option is **out of the money** when exercise would be unprofitable. Therefore, a call option is in the money when the asset price is greater than the exercise price. It is out of the money when the asset price is less than the exercise price; no one would exercise the right to purchase for the strike price an asset worth less than that price. Conversely, put

PRICES AT CLOSE JANUARY 02, 2008

I B M (IBM)   Underlying stock price: 104.69

		Call			Put		
Expiration	Strike	Last	Volume	Open Interest	Last	Volume	Open Interest
Jul	90	...	...	391	3.00	211	1312
Jan	95	10.40	347	16616	0.50	1539	11122
Feb	95	12.70	43	18	1.25	181	854
Apr	95	13.20	12	1183	2.75	59	2016
Jul	95	15.30	2	645	4.35	155	3744
Jan	100	6.00	205	11733	1.25	7860	26999
Feb	100	7.65	85	186	2.53	602	639
Apr	100	9.60	76	1476	4.30	413	9073
Jul	100	11.75	102	621	5.40	115	2554
Jan	105	3.10	1597	11706	3.20	3703	25885
Feb	105	4.40	401	433	4.40	448	692
Apr	105	7.00	152	1718	6.40	79	2361
Jul	105	9.00	33	686	8.10	66	1051
Jan	110	1.10	1775	17423	6.20	700	25999
Feb	110	2.30	472	474	7.40	28	3734
Apr	110	4.50	144	3950	9.10	115	4362
Jul	110	6.60	122	1045	10.50	99	770

FIGURE 20.1 Stock options on IBM

Source: *The Wall Street Journal Online,* January 3, 2008.
Reprinted by permission of *The Wall Street Journal,* © 2008
Dow Jones & Company, Inc. All rights reserved worldwide.

options are in the money when the exercise price exceeds the asset's value, because delivery of the lower-valued asset in exchange for the exercise price is profitable for the holder. Options are **at the money** when the exercise price and asset price are equal.

Options Trading

Some options trade on over-the-counter markets. The OTC market offers the advantage that the terms of the option contract—the exercise price, expiration date, and number of shares committed—can be tailored to the needs of the traders. The costs of establishing an OTC option contract, however, are higher than for exchange-traded options.

Options contracts traded on exchanges are standardized by allowable expiration dates and exercise prices for each listed option. Each stock option contract provides for the right to buy or sell 100 shares of stock (except when stock splits occur after the contract is listed and the contract is adjusted for the terms of the split).

Standardization of the terms of listed option contracts means all market participants trade in a limited and uniform set of securities. This increases the depth of trading in any particular option, which lowers trading costs and results in a more competitive market. Exchanges, therefore, offer two important benefits: ease of trading, which flows from a central marketplace where buyers and sellers or their representatives congregate; and a liquid secondary market where buyers and sellers of options can transact quickly and cheaply.

Until recently, most options trading in the United States took place on the Chicago Board Options Exchange. However, by 2003 the International Securities Exchange, an electronic exchange based in New York, displaced the CBOE as the largest options market. Options trading in Europe is uniformly transacted in electronic exchanges.

Figure 20.1 is a selection of listed stock option quotations for IBM. The last recorded price on the New York Stock Exchange for IBM shares was $104.69 per share.[1] Options are reported on IBM at exercise prices of $90 through $110.

The exercise (or strike) prices bracket the stock price. While exercise prices generally are set at five-point intervals, larger intervals may be set for stocks selling above $100, and intervals of $2.50 may be used for stocks selling below $30. If the stock price moves outside the range of exercise prices of the existing set of options, new options with appropriate exercise prices may be offered. Therefore, at any time, both in-the-money and out-of-the-money options will be listed, as in this example.

Figure 20.1 shows both call and put options listed for each expiration date and exercise price. The three sets of columns for each option report closing price, trading volume in contracts, and open interest (number of outstanding contracts). When we compare prices of call options with the same expiration date but different exercise prices in Figure 20.1,

---

[1]Occasionally, this price may not match the closing price listed for the stock on the stock market page. This is because some NYSE stocks also trade on exchanges that close after the NYSE, and the stock pages may reflect the more recent closing price. The options exchanges, however, close with the NYSE, so the closing NYSE stock price is appropriate for comparison with the closing option price.

we see that the value of a call is lower when the exercise price is higher. This makes sense, because the right to purchase a share at a lower exercise price is more valuable than the right to purchase at a higher price. Thus the January expiration IBM call option with strike price $100 sells for $6.00 whereas the $105 exercise price January call sells for only $3.10. Conversely, put options are worth *more* when the exercise price is higher: You would rather have the right to sell shares for $105 than for $100, and this is reflected in the prices of the puts. The January expiration put option with strike price $105 sells for $3.20, whereas the $100 exercise price January put sells for only $1.25.

If an option does not trade on a given day, three dots will appear in the volume and price columns (see Figure 20.1). Because trading is infrequent, it is not unusual to find option prices that appear out of line with other prices. You might see, for example, two calls with different exercise prices that seem to sell for the same price. This discrepancy arises because the last trades for these options may have occurred at different times during the day. At any moment, the call with the lower exercise price must be worth more than an otherwise-identical call with a higher exercise price.

Expirations of most exchange-traded options tend to be fairly short, ranging up to only several months. For larger firms and several stock indexes, however, longer-term options are traded with expirations ranging up to several years. These options are called LEAPS (for *L*ong-*T*erm *E*quity *A*ntici*P*ation *S*ecurities).

CONCEPT CHECK 1

a. What will be the proceeds and net profits to an investor who purchases the January expiration IBM calls with exercise price $100 if the stock price at expiration is $110? What if the stock price at expiration is $90?

b. Now answer part (a) for an investor who purchases a January expiration IBM put option with exercise price $100.

American and European Options

An **American option** allows its holder to exercise the right to purchase (if a call) or sell (if a put) the underlying asset on *or before* the expiration date. **European options** allow for exercise of the option only on the expiration date. American options, because they allow more leeway than their European counterparts, generally will be more valuable. Virtually all traded options in the United States are American style. Foreign currency options and CBOE stock index options are notable exceptions to this rule, however.

Adjustments in Option Contract Terms

Because options convey the right to buy or sell shares at a stated price, stock splits would radically alter their value if the terms of the options contract were not adjusted to account for the stock split. For example, reconsider the IBM call options in Figure 20.1. If IBM were to announce a 2-for-1 split, its share price would fall from about $105 to about $52.50. A call option with exercise price $105 would be just about worthless, with virtually no possibility that the stock would sell at more than $105 before the options expired.

To account for a stock split, the exercise price is reduced by a factor of the split, and the number of options held is increased by that factor. For example, each original call option with exercise price of $105 would be altered after a 2-for-1 split to 2 new options, with each new option carrying an exercise price of $52.50. A similar adjustment is made for stock dividends of more than 10%; the number of shares covered by each option is increased in proportion to the stock dividend, and the exercise price is reduced by that proportion.

In contrast to stock dividends, cash dividends do not affect the terms of an option contract. Because payment of a cash dividend reduces the selling price of the stock without inducing offsetting adjustments in the option contract, the value of the option is affected by dividend policy. Other things being equal, call option values are lower for high-dividend payout policies, because such policies slow the rate of increase of stock prices; conversely, put values are higher for high-dividend payouts. (Of course, the option values do not necessarily rise or fall on the dividend payment or ex-dividend dates. Dividend payments are anticipated, so the effect of the payment already is built into the original option price.)

CONCEPT CHECK 2	Suppose that IBM's stock price at the exercise date is $110, and the exercise price of the call is $105. What is the payoff on one option contract? After a 2-for-1 split, the stock price is $55, the exercise price is $52.50, and the option holder now can purchase 200 shares. Show that the split leaves the payoff from the option unaffected.

The Options Clearing Corporation

The Options Clearing Corporation (OCC), the clearinghouse for options trading, is jointly owned by the exchanges on which stock options are traded. Buyers and sellers of options who agree on a price will strike a deal. At this point, the OCC steps in. The OCC places itself between the two traders, becoming the effective buyer of the option from the writer and the effective writer of the option to the buyer. All individuals, therefore, deal only with the OCC, which effectively guarantees contract performance.

When an option holder exercises an option, the OCC arranges for a member firm with clients who have written that option to make good on the option obligation. The member firm selects from its clients who have written that option to fulfill the contract. The selected client must deliver 100 shares of stock at a price equal to the exercise price for each call option contract written or must purchase 100 shares at the exercise price for each put option contract written.

Because the OCC guarantees contract performance, option writers are required to post margin to guarantee that they can fulfill their contract obligations. The margin required is determined in part by the amount by which the option is in the money, because that value is an indicator of the potential obligation of the option writer. When the required margin exceeds the posted margin, the writer will receive a margin call. In contrast, the holder of the option need not post margin because the holder will exercise the option only if it is profitable to do so. After purchase of the option, no further money is at risk.

Margin requirements are determined in part by the other securities held in the investor's portfolio. For example, a call option writer owning the stock against which the option is written can satisfy the margin requirement simply by allowing a broker to hold that stock in the brokerage account. The stock is then guaranteed to be available for delivery should the call option be exercised. If the underlying security is not owned, however, the margin requirement is determined by the value of the underlying security as well as by the amount by which the option is in or out of the money. Out-of-the-money options require less margin from the writer, for expected payouts are lower.

Other Listed Options

Options on assets other than stocks are also widely traded. These include options on market indexes and industry indexes, on foreign currency, and even on the futures prices of agricultural products, gold, silver, fixed-income securities, and stock indexes. We will discuss these in turn.

Index Options An index option is a call or put based on a stock market index such as the S&P 500 or the NASDAQ 100. Index options are traded on several broad-based indexes as well as on several industry-specific indexes and even commodity price indexes. We discussed many of these indexes in Chapter 2.

The construction of the indexes can vary across contracts or exchanges. For example, the S&P 100 index is a value-weighted average of the 100 stocks in the Standard & Poor's 100 stock group. The weights are proportional to the market value of outstanding equity for each stock. The Dow Jones Industrial Index, by contrast, is a price-weighted average of 30 stocks.

Option contracts on many foreign stock indexes also trade. For example, options on the (Japanese) Nikkei Stock Index trade on the Chicago Mercantile Exchange, and options on the Eurotop 100, Hong Kong, and Japan indexes trade on the American Stock Exchange. The Chicago Board Options Exchange, as well as the Amex, lists options on industry indexes such as the hightech, pharmaceutical, or banking industries.

In contrast to stock options, index options do not require that the call writer actually "deliver the index" upon exercise or that the put writer "purchase the index." Instead, a cash settlement procedure is used. The payoff that would accrue upon exercise of the option is calculated, and the option writer simply pays that amount to the option holder. The payoff is equal to the difference between the exercise price of the option and the value of the index. For example, if the S&P index is at 1400 when a call option on the index with exercise price 1390 is exercised, the holder of the call receives a cash payment of the difference, 1400–1390, times the contract multiplier of $100, or $1,000 per contract.

Options on the major indexes, that is, the S&P 100 (often called the OEX after its ticker symbol), the S&P 500 (the SPX), the NASDAQ 100 (the NDX), and the Dow Jones Industrials (the DJX), are the most actively traded contracts on the CBOE. Together, these contracts dominate CBOE volume.

Futures Options Futures options give their holders the right to buy or sell a specified futures contract, using as a futures price the exercise price of the option. Although the delivery process is slightly complicated, the terms of futures options contracts are designed in effect to allow the option to be written on the futures price itself. The option holder receives upon exercise a net payoff equal to the difference between the current futures price on the specified asset and the exercise price of the option. Thus if the futures price is, say, $37, and the call has an exercise price of $35, the holder who exercises the call option on the futures gets a payoff of $2.

Foreign Currency Options A currency option offers the right to buy or sell a quantity of foreign currency for a specified amount of domestic currency. Currency option contracts call for purchase or sale of the currency in exchange for a specified number of U.S. dollars. Contracts are quoted in cents or fractions of a cent per unit of foreign currency.

There is an important difference between currency options and currency *futures* options. The former provide payoffs that depend on the difference between the exercise price and the exchange rate at maturity. The latter are foreign exchange futures options that provide payoffs that depend on the difference between the exercise price and the exchange rate *futures price* at maturity. Because exchange rates and exchange rate futures prices generally are not equal, the options and futures-options contracts will have different values, even with identical expiration dates and exercise prices. Trading volume in currency futures options dominates by far trading in currency options.

Interest Rate Options Options are traded on Treasury notes and bonds, Treasury bills, certificates of deposit, GNMA pass-through certificates, and yields on Treasury and Eurodollar securities of various maturities. Options on several interest rate futures also trade.

Among these are contracts on Treasury bond, Treasury note, municipal bond, LIBOR, Euribor,[2] Eurodollar, and German euro-denominated government bond futures.

20.2   VALUES OF OPTIONS AT EXPIRATION

Call Options

Recall that a call option gives the right to purchase a security at the exercise price. Suppose you hold a call option on FinCorp stock with an exercise price of $100, and FinCorp is now selling at $110. You can exercise your option to purchase the stock at $100 and simultaneously sell the shares at the market price of $110, clearing $10 per share. Yet if the shares sell below $100, you can sit on the option and do nothing, realizing no further gain or loss. The value of the call option at expiration equals

$$\text{Payoff to call holder} = \begin{array}{ll} S_T - X & \text{if } S_T > X \\ 0 & \text{if } S_T \leq X \end{array}$$

where S_T is the value of the stock at expiration and X is the exercise price. This formula emphasizes the option property because the payoff cannot be negative. That is, the option is exercised only if S_T exceeds X. If S_T is less than X, exercise does not occur, and the option expires with zero value. The loss to the option holder in this case equals the price originally paid for the option. More generally, the *profit* to the option holder is the value of the option at expiration minus the original purchase price.

The value at expiration of the call with exercise price $100 is given by the schedule:

Stock price:	$90	$100	$110	$120	$130
Option value:	0	0	10	20	30

For stock prices at or below $100, the option is worthless. Above $100, the option is worth the excess of the stock price over $100. The option's value increases by $1 for each dollar increase in the stock price. This relationship can be depicted graphically as in Figure 20.2.

The solid line in Figure 20.2 depicts the value of the call at expiration. The net *profit* to the holder of the call equals the gross payoff less the initial investment in the call. Suppose the call cost $14. Then the profit to the call holder would be given by the dashed (bottom) line of Figure 20.2. At option expiration, the investor suffers a loss of $14 if the stock price is less than or equal to $100.

Profits do not become positive unless the stock price at expiration exceeds $114. The break-even point is $114, because at that price the payoff to the call, $S_T - X = \$114 - \$100 = \$14$, equals the initial cost of the call.

Conversely, the writer of the call incurs losses if the stock price is high. In that scenario, the writer will receive a call and will be obligated to deliver a stock worth S_T for only X dollars:

$$\text{Payoff to call writer} = \begin{array}{ll} -(S_T - X) & \text{if } S_T > X \\ 0 & \text{if } S_T \leq X \end{array}$$

---

[2]The Euribor market is similar to the LIBOR market (see Chapter 2), but the interest rate charged in the Euribor market is the interbank rate for euro-denominated deposits.

The call writer, who is exposed to losses if the stock price increases, is willing to bear this risk in return for the option premium.

Figure 20.3 depicts the payoff and profit diagrams for the call writer. These are the mirror images of the corresponding diagrams for call holders. The break-even point for the option writer also is $114. The (negative) payoff at that point just offsets the premium originally received when the option was written.

Put Options

A put option is the right to sell an asset at the exercise price. In this case, the holder will not exercise the option unless the asset is worth *less* than the exercise price. For example, if FinCorp shares were to fall to $90, a put option with exercise price $100 could be exer-

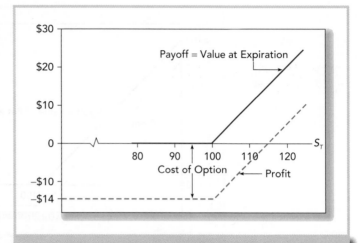

FIGURE 20.2 Payoff and profit to call option at expiration

cised to clear $10 for its holder. The holder would purchase a share for $90 and simultaneously deliver it to the put option writer for the exercise price of $100.

The value of a put option at expiration is

$$\text{Payoff to put holder} = \begin{array}{ll} 0 & \text{if } S_T \geq X \\ X - S_T & \text{if } S_T < X \end{array}$$

The solid line in Figure 20.4 illustrates the payoff at expiration to the holder of a put option on FinCorp stock with an exercise price of $100. If the stock price at expiration is above $100, the put has no value, as the right to sell the shares at $100 would not be exercised. Below a price of $100, the put value at expiration increases by $1 for each dollar the stock price falls. The dashed line in Figure 20.4 is a graph of the put option owner's profit at expiration, net of the initial cost of the put.

Writing puts *naked* (i.e., writing a put without an offsetting short position in the stock for hedging purposes) exposes the writer to losses if the market falls. Writing naked out-of-the-money puts was once considered an attractive way to generate income, as it was believed that as long as the market did not fall sharply before the option expiration, the option premium could be collected without the put holder ever exercising the option against the writer. Because only sharp drops in the market could result in losses to the put writer, the strategy was not viewed as overly risky. However, in the wake of the market crash of October 1987, such put writers suffered huge losses. Participants now perceive much greater risk to this strategy.

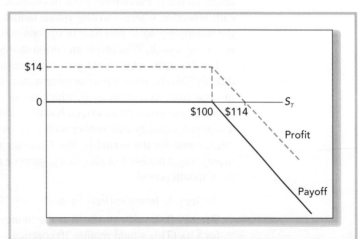

FIGURE 20.3 Payoff and profit to call writers at expiration

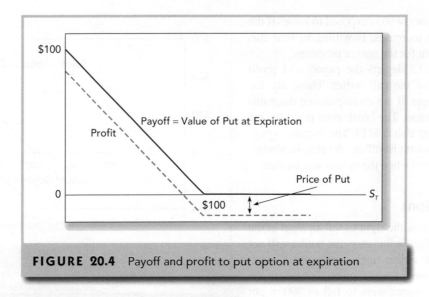

FIGURE 20.4   Payoff and profit to put option at expiration

CONCEPT CHECK 3

Consider these four option strategies: (i) buy a call; (ii) write a call; (iii) buy a put; (iv) write a put.

a. For each strategy, plot both the payoff and profit diagrams as a function of the final stock price.

b. Why might one characterize both buying calls and writing puts as "bullish" strategies? What is the difference between them?

c. Why might one characterize both buying puts and writing calls as "bearish" strategies? What is the difference between them?

Option versus Stock Investments

Purchasing call options is a bullish strategy; that is, the calls provide profits when stock prices increase. Purchasing puts, in contrast, is a bearish strategy. Symmetrically, writing calls is bearish, whereas writing puts is bullish. Because option values depend on the price of the underlying stock, purchase of options may be viewed as a substitute for direct purchase or sale of a stock. Why might an option strategy be preferable to direct stock transactions?

For example, why would you purchase a call option rather than buy shares of stock directly? Maybe you have some information that leads you to believe the stock will increase in value from its current level, which in our examples we will take to be $100. You know your analysis could be incorrect, however, and that shares also could fall in price. Suppose a 6-month maturity call option with exercise price $100 currently sells for $10, and the interest rate for the period is 3%. Consider these three strategies for investing a sum of money, say, $10,000. For simplicity, suppose the firm will not pay any dividends until after the 6-month period.

Strategy A: Invest entirely in stock. Buy 100 shares, each selling for $100.

Strategy B: Invest entirely in at-the-money call options. Buy 1,000 calls, each selling for $10. (This would require 10 contracts, each for 100 shares.)

Strategy C: Purchase 100 call options for $1,000. Invest your remaining $9,000 in 6-month T-bills, to earn 3% interest. The bills will grow in value from $9,000 to $9,000 × 1.03 = $9,270.

Let us trace the possible values of these three portfolios when the options expire in 6 months as a function of the stock price at that time:

	Stock Price					
Portfolio	$95	$100	$105	$110	$115	$120
Portfolio A: All stock	$9,500	$10,000	$10,500	$11,000	$11,500	$12,000
Portfolio B: All options	0	0	5,000	10,000	15,000	20,000
Portfolio C: Call plus bills	9,270	9,270	9,770	10,270	10,770	11,270

Portfolio A will be worth 100 times the share price. Portfolio B is worthless unless shares sell for more than the exercise price of the call. Once that point is reached, the portfolio is worth 1,000 times the excess of the stock price over the exercise price. Finally, portfolio C is worth $9,270 from the investment in T-bills plus any profits from the 100 call options. Remember that each of these portfolios involves the same $10,000 initial investment. The rates of return on these three portfolios are as follows:

	Stock Price					
Portfolio	$95	$100	$105	$110	$115	$120
Portfolio A: All stock	−5.0%	0.0%	5.0%	10.0%	15.0%	20.0%
Portfolio B: All options	−100.0	−100.0	−50.0	0.0	50.0	100.0
Portfolio C: Call plus bills	−7.3	−7.3	−2.3	2.7	7.7	12.7

These rates of return are graphed in Figure 20.5.

Comparing the returns of portfolios B and C to those of the simple investment in stock represented by portfolio A, we see that options offer two interesting features. First, an option offers leverage. Compare the returns of portfolios B and A. Unless the stock increases from its initial value of $100, the value of portfolio B falls precipitously to zero—a rate of return of negative 100%. Conversely, modest increases in the rate of return on the stock result in disproportionate increases in the option rate of return. For example, a 4.3% increase in the stock price from $115 to $120 would increase the rate of return on the call from 50% to 100%. In this sense, calls are a levered investment on the stock. Their values respond more than proportionately to changes in the stock value.

Figure 20.5 vividly illustrates this point. The slope of the all-option portfolio is far steeper than that of the all-stock portfolio, reflecting its greater proportional sensitivity to the value of the underlying security. The leverage factor is the reason investors (illegally) exploiting inside information commonly choose options as their investment vehicle.

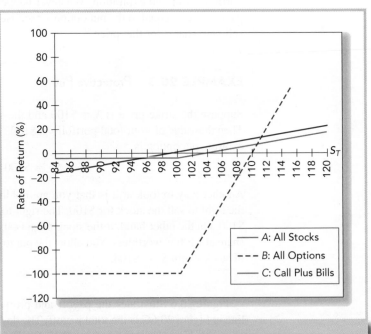

FIGURE 20.5 Rate of return to three strategies

The potential insurance value of options is the second interesting feature, as portfolio C shows. The T-bill-plus-option portfolio cannot be worth less than $9,270 after 6 months, as the option can always be left to expire worthless. The worst possible rate of return on portfolio C is −7.3%, compared to a (theoretically) worst possible rate of return on the stock of −100% if the company were to go bankrupt. Of course, this insurance comes at a price: When the share price increases, portfolio C, the option-plus-bills portfolio, does not perform as well as portfolio A, the all-stock portfolio.

This simple example makes an important point. Although options can be used by speculators as effectively leveraged stock positions, as in portfolio B, they also can be used by investors who desire to tailor their risk exposures in creative ways, as in portfolio C. For example, the call-plus-bills strategy of portfolio C provides a rate of return profile quite unlike that of the stock alone. The absolute limitation on downside risk is a novel and attractive feature of this strategy. We next discuss several option strategies that provide other novel risk profiles that might be attractive to hedgers and other investors.

20.3   OPTION STRATEGIES

An unlimited variety of payoff patterns can be achieved by combining puts and calls with various exercise prices. We explain in this section the motivation and structure of some of the more popular ones.

Protective Put

Imagine you would like to invest in a stock, but you are unwilling to bear potential losses beyond some given level. Investing in the stock alone seems risky to you because in principle you could lose all the money you invest. You might consider instead investing in stock and purchasing a put option on the stock. Table 20.1 shows the total value of your portfolio at option expiration: Whatever happens to the stock price, you are guaranteed a payoff at least equal to the put option's exercise price because the put gives you the right to sell your shares for that price.

EXAMPLE 20.3   Protective Put

Suppose the strike price is $X = \$100$ and the stock is selling at $97 at option expiration. Then the value of your total portfolio is $100. The stock is worth $97 and the value of the expiring put option is

$$X - S_T = \$100 - \$97 = \$3$$

Another way to look at it is that you are holding the stock and a put contract giving you the right to sell the stock for $100. The right to sell locks in a minimum portfolio value of $100. On the other hand, if the stock price is above $100, say, $104, then the right to sell a share at $100 is worthless. You allow the put to expire unexercised, ending up with a share of stock worth $S_T = \$104$.

Figure 20.6 illustrates the payoff and profit to this **protective put** strategy. The solid line in Figure 20.6C is the total payoff. The dashed line is displaced downward by the cost of establishing the position, $S_0 + P$. Notice that potential losses are limited.

	$S_T \leq X$	$S_T > X$
Stock	S_T	S_T
+ Put	$X - S_T$	0
= TOTAL	X	S_T

TABLE 20.1

Value of protective put portfolio at option expiration

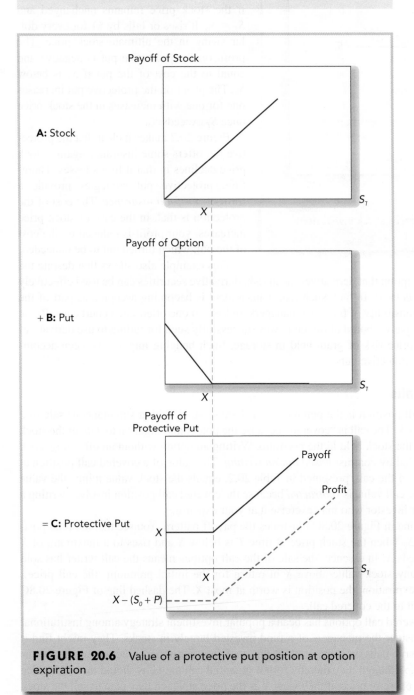

FIGURE 20.6   Value of a protective put position at option expiration

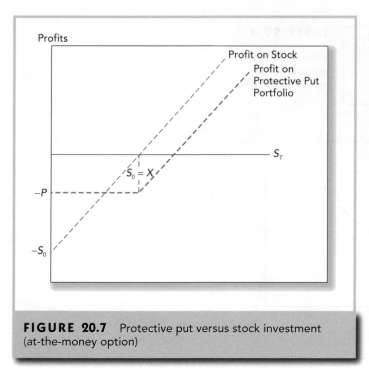

Profits

Profit on Stock

Profit on Protective Put Portfolio

S_T

$S_0 = X$

$-P$

$-S_0$

FIGURE 20.7 Protective put versus stock investment (at-the-money option)

It is instructive to compare the profit on the protective put strategy with that of the stock investment. For simplicity, consider an at-the-money protective put, so that $X = S_0$. Figure 20.7 compares the profits for the two strategies. The profit on the stock is zero if the stock price remains unchanged and $S_T = S_0$. It rises or falls by $1 for every dollar swing in the ultimate stock price. The profit on the protective put is negative and equal to the cost of the put if S_T is below S_0. The profit on the protective put increases one for one with increases in the stock price once S_T exceeds S_0.

Figure 20.7 makes it clear that the protective put offers some insurance against stock price declines in that it limits losses. Therefore, protective put strategies provide a form of *portfolio insurance*. The cost of the protection is that, in the case of stock price increases, your profit is reduced by the cost of the put, which turned out to be unneeded.

This example also shows that despite the common perception that derivatives mean risk, derivative securities can be used effectively for *risk management*. In fact, such risk management is becoming accepted as part of the fiduciary responsibility of financial managers. Indeed, in one often-cited court case, *Brane v. Roth,* a company's board of directors was successfully sued for failing to use derivatives to hedge the price risk of grain held in storage. Such hedging might have been accomplished using protective puts.

Covered Calls

A **covered call** position is the purchase of a share of stock with a simultaneous sale of a call on that stock. The call is "covered" because the potential obligation to deliver the stock is covered by the stock held in the portfolio. Writing an option without an offsetting stock position is called by contrast *naked option writing*. The value of a covered call position at the expiration of the call, presented in Table 20.2, equals the stock value minus the value of the call. The call value is *subtracted* because the covered call position involves writing a call to another investor who may exercise it at your expense.

The solid line in Figure 20.8C illustrates the payoff pattern. You see that the total position is worth S_T when the stock price at time T is below X and rises to a maximum of X when S_T exceeds X. In essence, the sale of the call options means the call writer has sold the claim to any stock value above X in return for the initial premium (the call price). Therefore, at expiration, the position is worth at most X. The dashed line of Figure 20.8C is the net profit to the covered call.

Writing covered call options has been a popular investment strategy among institutional investors. Consider the managers of a fund invested largely in stocks. They might find it appealing to write calls on some or all of the stock in order to boost income by the premiums collected. Although they thereby forfeit potential capital gains should the stock price rise above the exercise price, if they view X as the price at which they plan to sell the stock anyway, then the call may be viewed as a kind of "sell discipline." The written call guarantees the stock sale will occur as planned.

	$S_T \leq X$	$S_T > X$	**TABLE 20.2**
Payoff of stock	S_T	S_T	Value of covered
+ Payoff of written call	-0	$-(S_T - X)$	call position at
= TOTAL	S_T	X	option expiration

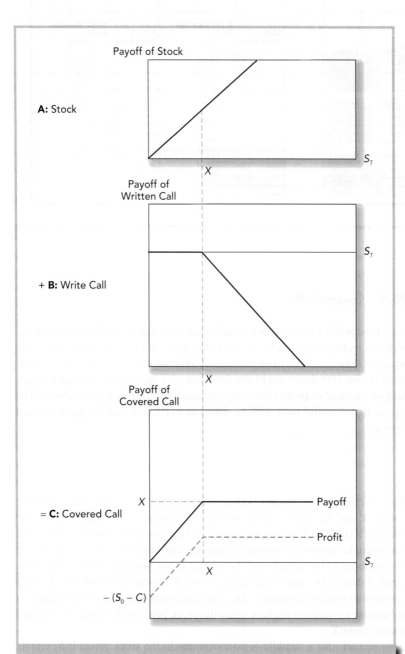

A: Stock

Payoff of Stock

X

S_T

+ B: Write Call

Payoff of Written Call

X

S_T

= C: Covered Call

Payoff of Covered Call

X

Payoff

Profit

X

S_T

$-(S_0 - C)$

FIGURE 20.8   Value of a covered call position at expiration

TABLE 20.3

Value of a straddle position at option expiration

	$S_T < X$	$S_T \geq X$
Payoff of call	0	$S_T - X$
+ Payoff of put	$X - S_T$	0
= TOTAL	$X - S_T$	$S_T - X$

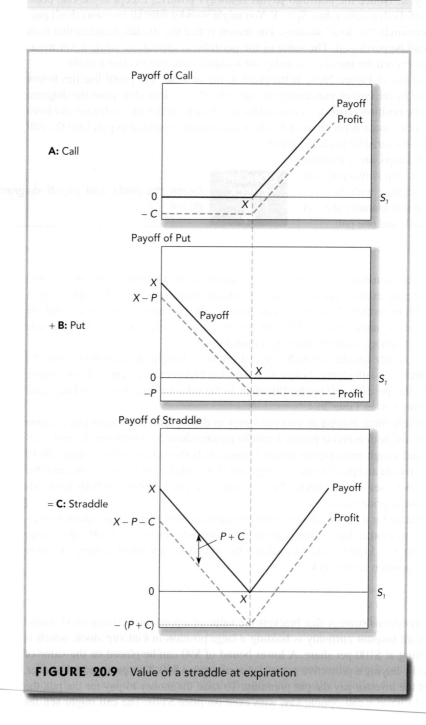

FIGURE 20.9   Value of a straddle at expiration

	$S_T \leq X_1$	$X_1 < S_T \leq X_2$	$S_T \geq X_2$	**TABLE 20.4**
Payoff of purchased call, exercise price $= X_1$	0	$S_T - X_1$	$S_T - X_1$	Value of a bullish spread position at expiration
+ Payoff of written call, exercise price $= X_2$	-0	-0	$-(S_T - X_2)$	
= TOTAL	0	$S_T - X_1$	$X_2 - X_1$	

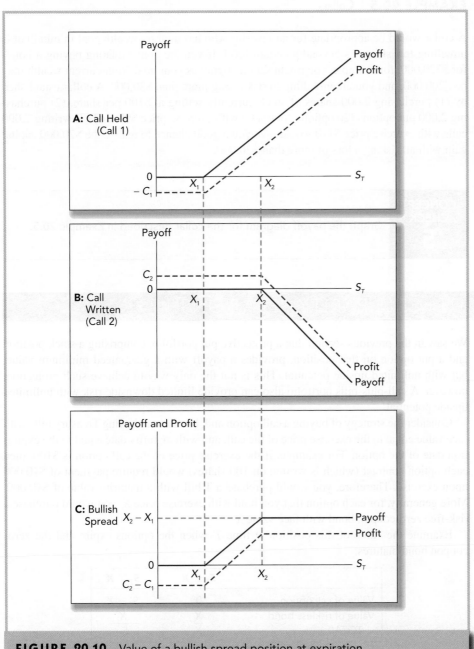

FIGURE 20.10 Value of a bullish spread position at expiration

roughly the same price as the put, meaning that the net outlay for the two options positions is approximately zero. Writing the call limits the portfolio's upside potential. Even if the stock price moves above $110, the investor will do no better than $110, because at a higher price the stock will be called away. Thus the investor obtains the downside protection represented by the exercise price of the put by selling her claim to any upside potential beyond the exercise price of the call.

EXAMPLE 20.5   Collars

A collar would be appropriate for an investor who has a target wealth goal in mind but is unwilling to risk losses beyond a certain level. If you are contemplating buying a house for $220,000, for example, you might set this figure as your goal. Your current wealth may be $200,000, and you are unwilling to risk losing more than $20,000. A collar established by (1) purchasing 2,000 shares of stock currently selling at $100 per share, (2) purchasing 2,000 put options (20 options contracts) with exercise price $90, and (3) writing 2,000 calls with exercise price $110 would give you a good chance to realize the $20,000 capital gain without risking a loss of more than $20,000.

CONCEPT CHECK

5

Graph the payoff diagram for the collar described in Example 20.5.

20.4   THE PUT–CALL PARITY RELATIONSHIP

We saw in the previous section that a protective put portfolio, comprising a stock position and a put option on that position, provides a payoff with a guaranteed minimum value, but with unlimited upside potential. This is not the only way to achieve such protection, however. A call-plus-bills portfolio also can provide limited downside risk with unlimited upside potential.

Consider the strategy of buying a call option and, in addition, buying Treasury bills with face value equal to the exercise price of the call, and with maturity date equal to the expiration date of the option. For example, if the exercise price of the call option is $100, then each option contract (which is written on 100 shares) would require payment of $10,000 upon exercise. Therefore, you would purchase a T-bill with a maturity value of $10,000. More generally, for each option that you hold with exercise price X, you would purchase a risk-free zero-coupon bond with face value X.

Examine the value of this position at time T, when the options expire and the zero-coupon bond matures:

	$S_T \leq X$	$S_T > X$
Value of call option	0	$S_T - X$
Value of riskless bond	X	X
TOTAL	X	S_T

If the stock price is below the exercise price, the call is worthless, but the riskless bond matures to its face value, X. The bond therefore provides a floor value to the portfolio. If the stock price exceeds X, then the payoff to the call, $S_T - X$, is added to the face value of the bond to provide a total payoff of S_T. The payoff to this portfolio is precisely identical to the payoff of the protective put that we derived in Table 20.1.

If two portfolios always provide equal values, then they must cost the same amount to establish. Therefore, the call-plus-bond portfolio must cost the same as the stock-plus-put portfolio. Each call costs C. The riskless zero-coupon bond costs $X/(1 + r_f)^T$. Therefore, the call-plus-bond portfolio costs $C + X/(1 + r_f)^T$ to establish. The stock costs S_0 to purchase now (at time zero), while the put costs P. Therefore, we conclude that

$$C + \frac{X}{(1 + r_f)^T} = S_0 + P \qquad (20.1)$$

Equation 20.1 is called the **put-call parity theorem** because it represents the proper relationship between put and call prices. If the parity relation is ever violated, an arbitrage opportunity arises. For example, suppose you collect these data for a certain stock:

Stock price	$110
Call price (1-year expiration, $X = \$105$)	$ 17
Put price (1-year expiration, $X = \$105$)	$ 5
Risk-free interest rate	5% per year

We can use these data in Equation 20.1 to see if parity is violated:

$$C + \frac{X}{(1 + r_f)^T} \stackrel{?}{=} S_0 + P$$

$$17 + \frac{105}{1.05} \stackrel{?}{=} 110 + 5$$

$$117 \stackrel{?}{=} 115$$

This result, a violation of parity—117 does not equal 115—indicates mispricing. To exploit the mispricing, you buy the relatively cheap portfolio (the stock-plus-put position represented on the right-hand side of the equation) and sell the relatively expensive portfolio (the call-plus-bond position corresponding to the left-hand side). Therefore, if you *buy* the stock, *buy* the put, *write* the call, and *borrow* $100 for 1 year (because borrowing money is the opposite of buying a bond), you should earn arbitrage profits.

Let's examine the payoff to this strategy. In 1 year, the stock will be worth S_T. The $100 borrowed will be paid back with interest, resulting in a cash outflow of $105. The written call will result in a cash outflow of $S_T - \$105$ if S_T exceeds $105. The purchased put pays off $\$105 - S_T$ if the stock price is below $105.

Table 20.5 summarizes the outcome. The immediate cash inflow is $2. In 1 year, the various positions provide exactly offsetting cash flows: The $2 inflow is realized without any offsetting outflows. This is an arbitrage opportunity that investors will pursue on a large scale until buying and selling pressure restores the parity condition expressed in Equation 20.1.

Equation 20.1 actually applies only to options on stocks that pay no dividends before the expiration date of the option. The extension of the parity condition for European call options on dividend-paying stocks is, however, straightforward. Problem 9 at the end of

TABLE 20.5

Arbitrage strategy

Position	Immediate Cash Flow	Cash Flow in 1 year	
		$S_T < 105$	$S_T \geq 105$
Buy stock	−110	S_T	S_T
Borrow $105/1.05 = $100	+100	−105	−105
Sell call	+17	0	$-(S_T - 105)$
Buy put	−5	$105 - S_T$	0
TOTAL	2	0	0

the chapter leads you through the extension of the parity relationship. The more general formulation of the *put-call parity* condition is

$$P = C - S_0 + PV(X) + PV(\text{dividends}) \qquad (20.2)$$

where PV(dividends) is the present value of the dividends that will be paid by the stock during the life of the option. If the stock does not pay dividends, Equation 20.2 becomes identical to Equation 20.1.

Notice that this generalization would apply as well to European options on assets other than stocks. Instead of using dividend income in Equation 20.2, we would let any income paid out by the underlying asset play the role of the stock dividends. For example, European put and call options on bonds would satisfy the same parity relationship, except that the bond's coupon income would replace the stock's dividend payments in the parity formula.

Even this generalization, however, applies only to European options, as the cash flow streams from the two portfolios represented by the two sides of Equation 20.2 will match only if each position is held until expiration. If a call and a put may be optimally exercised at different times before their common expiration date, then the equality of payoffs cannot be assured, or even expected, and the portfolios will have different values.

EXAMPLE 20.6   Put-Call Parity

Let's see how well parity works using real data on the IBM options in Figure 20.1. The January expiration call with exercise price $105 and time to expiration of 16 days cost $3.10 while the corresponding put option cost $3.20. IBM was selling for $104.69, and the annualized short-term interest rate on this date was 3.0%. No dividends will be paid between the date of the listing, January 2, and the option expiration date. According to parity, we should find that

$$P = C + PV(X) - S_0 + PV(\text{dividends})$$

$$3.20 = 3.10 + \frac{105}{(1.030)^{16/365}} - 104.69 + 0$$

$$3.20 = 3.10 + 104.86 - 104.69$$

$$3.20 = 3.27$$

So parity is violated by about $.07 per share, not even close to a big enough difference to exploit. You have to weigh the potential profit against the trading costs of the call, put, and stock. More important, given the fact that options trade relatively infrequently, this deviation from parity might not be "real," but may instead be attributable to "stale" price quotesat which you cannot actually trade.

20.5 OPTION–LIKE SECURITIES

Suppose you never traded an option directly. Why do you need to appreciate the properties of options in formulating an investment plan? Many financial instruments and agreements have features that convey implicit or explicit options to one or more parties. If you are to value and use these securities correctly, you must understand these embedded option attributes.

Callable Bonds

You know from Chapter 14 that many corporate bonds are issued with call provisions entitling the issuer to buy bonds back from bondholders at some time in the future at a specified call price. A call provision conveys a call option to the issuer, where the exercise price is equal to the price at which the bond can be repurchased. A callable bond arrangement is essentially a sale of a *straight bond* (a bond with no option features such as callability or convertibility) to the investor and the concurrent issuance of a call option by the investor to the bond-issuing firm.

There must be some compensation for conveying this implicit call option to the firm. If the callable bond were issued with the same coupon rate as a straight bond, it would sell at a lower price than the straight bond: the price difference would equal the value of the call. To sell callable bonds at par, firms must issue them with coupon rates higher than the coupons on straight debt. The higher coupons are the investor's compensation for the call option retained by the issuer. Coupon rates usually are selected so that the newly issued bond will sell at par value.

Figure 20.11 illustrates this option-like property. The horizontal axis is the value of a straight bond with otherwise identical terms to the callable bond. The dashed 45-degree line represents the value of straight debt. The solid line is the value of the callable bond, and the dotted line is the value of the call option retained by the firm. A callable bond's potential for capital gains is limited by the firm's option to repurchase at the call price.

CONCEPT CHECK 6	How is a callable bond similar to a covered call strategy on a straight bond?

The option inherent in callable bonds actually is more complex than an ordinary call option, because usually it may be exercised only after some initial period of call protection. The price at which the bond is callable may change over time also. Unlike exchange-listed options, these features are defined in the initial bond covenant and will depend on the needs of the issuing firm and its perception of the market's tastes.

CONCEPT CHECK 7	Suppose the period of call protection is extended. How will the coupon rate the company needs to offer on its bonds change to enable the issuer to sell the bonds at par value?

Convertible Securities

Convertible bonds and convertible preferred stock convey options to the holder of the security rather than to the issuing firm. A convertible security typically gives its holder

Bond *A* has a conversion value of only $600. Its value as straight debt, in contrast, is $967. This is the present value of the coupon and principal payments at a market rate for straight debt of 8.5%. The bond's price is $972, so the premium over straight bond value is only $5, reflecting the low probability of conversion. Its reported yield to maturity based on scheduled coupon payments and the market price of $972 is 8.42%, close to that of straight debt.

The conversion option on bond *B* is in the money. Conversion value is $1,250, and the bond's price, $1,255, reflects its value as equity (plus $5 for the protection the bond offers against stock price declines). The bond's reported yield is 4.76%, far below the comparable yield on straight debt. The big yield sacrifice is attributable to the far greater value of the conversion option.

In theory, we could value convertible bonds by treating them as straight debt plus call options. In practice, however, this approach is often impractical for several reasons:

1. The conversion price frequently increases over time, which means the exercise price of the option changes.

2. Stocks may pay several dividends over the life of the bond, further complicating the option-valuation analysis.

3. Most convertibles also are callable at the discretion of the firm. In essence, both the investor and the issuer hold options on each other. If the issuer exercises its call option to repurchase the bond, the bondholders typically have a month during which they still can convert. When issuers use a call option, knowing bondholders will choose to convert, the issuer is said to have *forced a conversion*. These conditions together mean the actual maturity of the bond is indeterminate.

Warrants

Warrants are essentially call options issued by a firm. One important difference between calls and warrants is that exercise of a warrant requires the firm to issue a new share of stock—the total number of shares outstanding increases. Exercise of a call option requires only that the writer of the call deliver an already-issued share of stock to discharge the obligation. In that case, the number of shares outstanding remains fixed. Also unlike call options, warrants result in a cash flow to the firm when the warrant holder pays the exercise price. These differences mean that warrant values will differ somewhat from the values of call options with identical terms.

Like convertible debt, warrant terms may be tailored to meet the needs of the firm. Also like convertible debt, warrants generally are protected against stock splits and dividends in that the exercise price and the number of warrants held are adjusted to offset the effects of the split.

Warrants are often issued in conjunction with another security. Bonds, for example, may be packaged together with a warrant "sweetener," frequently a warrant that may be sold separately. This is called a *detachable warrant*.

Issue of warrants and convertible securities creates the potential for an increase in outstanding shares of stock if exercise occurs. Exercise obviously would affect financial statistics that are computed on a per-share basis, so annual reports must provide earnings per share figures under the assumption that all convertible securities and warrants are exercised. These figures are called *fully diluted earnings per share*.[3]

---

[3] We should note that the exercise of a convertible bond need not reduce EPS. Diluted EPS will be less than undiluted EPS only if interest saved (per share) on the convertible bonds is less than the prior EPS.

THE OPTIONS BACKDATING SCANDAL

ON A SUMMER DAY IN 2002, shares of Affiliated Computer Services Inc. sank to their lowest level in a year. Oddly, that was good news for Chief Executive Jeffrey Rich. His annual grant of stock options was dated that day, entitling him to buy stock at that price for years. Had they been dated a week later, when the stock was 27% higher, they'd have been far less rewarding. It was the same through much of Mr. Rich's tenure: In a striking pattern, all six of his stock-option grants from 1995 to 2002 were dated just before a rise in the stock price, often at the bottom of a steep drop.

Just lucky? A *Wall Street Journal* analysis suggests the odds of this happening by chance are extraordinarily remote—around one in 300 billion. The odds of winning the multistate Powerball lottery with a $1 ticket are one in 146 million. Suspecting such patterns aren't due to chance, the Securities and Exchange Commission is examining whether some option grants carry favorable grant dates for a different reason: They were backdated.

Employee stock options give recipients a right to buy company stock at a set exercise or "strike" price. The exercise price is usually the stock's price on the date of the grant. Naturally, the lower it is, the more valuable is the option.

The *Journal's* analysis raises questions about one of the most lucrative stock-option grants ever. On Oct. 13, 1999, William W. McGuire, CEO of giant insurer United-Health Group Inc., got an enormous grant in three parts that—after adjustment for later stock splits—came to 14.6 million options. So far, he has exercised about 5% of them, for a profit of about $39 million. As of late February he had 13.87 million unexercised options left from the October 1999 tranche. His profit on those, if he exercised them today, would be about $717 million more.

The 1999 grant was dated the very day UnitedHealth stock hit its low for the year. Grants to Dr. McGuire in 1997 and 2000 were also dated on the day with those years' single lowest closing price. A grant in 2001 came near the bottom of a sharp stock dip. In all, the odds of such a favorable pattern occurring by chance would be one in 200 million or greater.

Source: C. Forelle and J. Bandler, "The Perfect Payday; Some CEOs Reap Millions by Landing Stock Options When They Are Most Valuable; Luck—or Something Else? *The Wall Street Journal*, March 18, 2006, p. A1.

The executive and employee stock options that became so popular in the last decade actually were warrants. Some of these grants were huge, with payoffs to top executives in excess of $100 million. Yet firms almost uniformly chose not to acknowledge these grants as expenses on their income statements until new reporting rules that took effect in 2006 required such recognition.

The nearby box reports on the so-called options backdating scandal. Employee option grants are typically issued at the money, i.e., with an exercise price equal to the current stock price. Employee option grants with exercise prices below the stock price are perfectly legal, but would trigger immediate tax liabilities, and their higher values would need to be recognized. However, it appears that many firms *surreptitiously* reduced the exercise price by issuing option grants with the purported grant date chosen *retroactively* on a date at which the stock price was at low ebb. By artificially increasing the value of the option, such backdating of the grant date transfers additional (and unreported) wealth to executives and also skirts tax law. The SEC opened an investigation of several instances in which companies seemed to have backdated executive stock options. One of the biggest recipients of such grants, William W. McGuire of UnitedHealth Group, agreed to return $620 million and was barred from serving as an officer or director of a public company for 10 years.

Collateralized Loans

Many loan arrangements require that the borrower put up collateral to guarantee the loan will be paid back. In the event of default, the lender takes possession of the collateral. A nonrecourse loan gives the lender no recourse beyond the right to the collateral. That is, the lender may not sue the borrower for further payment if the collateral turns out not to be valuable enough to repay the loan.

This arrangement gives an implicit call option to the borrower. Assume the borrower is obligated to pay back L dollars at the maturity of the loan. The collateral will be worth S_T dollars at maturity. (Its value today is S_0.) The borrower has the option to wait until loan maturity and repay the loan only if the collateral is worth more than the L dollars necessary to satisfy the loan. If the collateral is worth less than L, the borrower can default on the loan, discharging the obligation by forfeiting the collateral, which is worth only S_T.[4]

Another way of describing such a loan is to view the borrower as turning over the collateral to the lender but retaining the right to reclaim it by paying off the loan. The transfer of the collateral with the right to reclaim it is equivalent to a payment of S_0 dollars, less a simultaneous recovery of a sum that resembles a call option with exercise price L. In effect, the borrower turns over collateral but keeps an option to "repurchase" it for L dollars at the maturity of the loan if L turns out to be less than S_T. This is a call option.

A third way to look at a collateralized loan is to assume that the borrower will repay the L dollars with certainty but also retain the option to sell the collateral to the lender for L dollars, even if S_T is less than L. In this case, the sale of the collateral would generate the cash necessary to satisfy the loan. The ability to "sell" the collateral for a price of L dollars represents a put option, which guarantees the borrower can raise enough money to satisfy the loan simply by turning over the collateral.

It is perhaps surprising to realize that we can describe the same loan as involving either a put option or a call option, as the payoffs to calls and puts are so different. Yet the equivalence of the two approaches is nothing more than a reflection of the put-call parity relationship. In our call-option description of the loan, the value of the borrower's liability is $S_0 - C$: The borrower turns over the asset, which is a transfer of S_0 dollars, but retains a call worth C dollars. In the put-option description, the borrower is obligated to pay L dollars but retains the put, which is worth P: The present value of this net obligation is $L/(1 + r_f)^T - P$. Because these alternative descriptions are equivalent ways of viewing the same loan, the value of the obligations must be equal:

$$S_0 - C = \frac{L}{(1 + r_f)^T} - P \tag{20.3}$$

Treating L as the exercise price of the option, Equation 20.3 is simply the put-call parity relationship.

Figure 20.13 illustrates this fact. Figure 20.13A is the value of the payment to be received by the lender, which equals the minimum of S_T or L. Panel B shows that this amount can be expressed as S_T minus the payoff of the call implicitly written by the lender and held by the borrower. Panel C shows it also can be viewed as a receipt of L dollars minus the proceeds of a put option.

Levered Equity and Risky Debt

Investors holding stock in incorporated firms are protected by limited liability, which means that if the firm cannot pay its debts, the firm's creditors may attach only the firm's assets, not sue the corporation's equityholders for further payment. In effect, any time the corporation borrows money, the maximum possible collateral for the loan is the total of the firm's assets. If the firm declares bankruptcy, we can interpret this as an admission that

---

[4]In reality, of course, defaulting on a loan is not so simple. There are losses of reputation involved as well as considerations of ethical behavior. This is a description of a pure nonrecourse loan where both parties agree from the outset that only the collateral backs the loan and that default is not to be taken as a sign of bad faith if the collateral is insufficient to repay the loan.

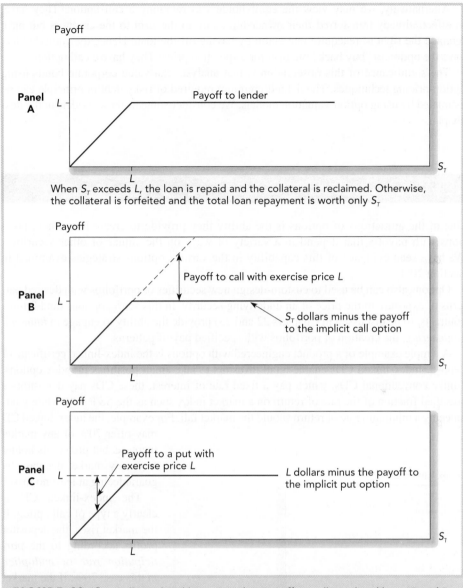

When S_T exceeds L, the loan is repaid and the collateral is reclaimed. Otherwise, the collateral is forfeited and the total loan repayment is worth only S_T

FIGURE 20.13 Collateralized loan. *Panel A*, Payoff to collateralized loan. *Panel B*, Lender can be viewed as collecting the collateral from the borrower, but issuing an option to the borrower to call back the collateral for the face value of the loan. *Panel C*, Lender can be viewed as collecting a risk-free loan from the borrower, but issuing a put to the borrower to sell the collateral for the face value of the loan.

the assets of the firm are insufficient to satisfy the claims against it. The corporation may discharge its obligations by transferring ownership of the firm's assets to the creditors.

Just as is true for nonrecourse collateralized loans, the required payment to the creditors represents the exercise price of the implicit option, while the value of the firm is the underlying asset. The equityholders have a put option to transfer their ownership claims on the firm to the creditors in return for the face value of the firm's debt.

Alternatively, we may view the equityholders as retaining a call option. They have, in effect, already transferred their ownership claim to the firm to the creditors but have retained the right to reacquire that claim by paying off the loan. Hence the equityholders have the option to "buy back" the firm for a specified price: They have a call option.

The significance of this observation is that analysts can value corporate bonds using option-pricing techniques. The default premium required of risky debt in principle can be estimated by using option-valuation models. We consider some of these models in the next chapter.

20.6 FINANCIAL ENGINEERING

One of the attractions of options is the ability they provide to create investment positions with payoffs that depend in a variety of ways on the values of other securities. We have seen evidence of this capability in the various options strategies examined in Section 20.4.

Options also can be used to custom-design new securities or portfolios with desired patterns of exposure to the price of an underlying security. In this sense, options (and futures contracts, to be discussed in Chapters 22 and 23) provide the ability to engage in *financial engineering,* the creation of portfolios with specified payoff patterns.

A simple example of a product engineered with options is the index-linked certificate of deposit. Index-linked CDs enable retail investors to take small positions in index options. Unlike conventional CDs, which pay a fixed rate of interest, these CDs pay depositors a specified fraction of the rate of return on a market index such as the S&P 500, while guaranteeing a minimum rate of return should the market fall. For example, the index-linked CD may offer 70% of any market increase, but protect its holder from any market decrease by guaranteeing at least no loss.

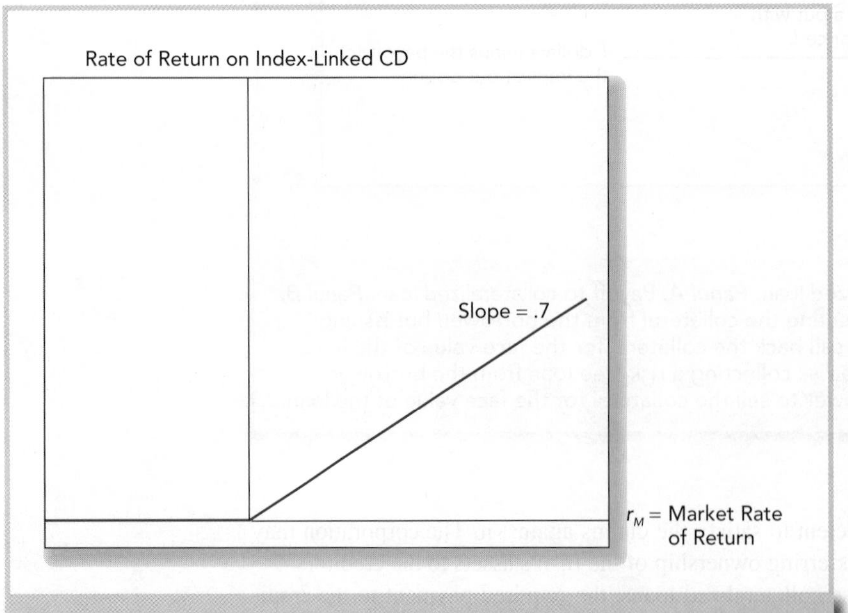

The index-linked CD is clearly a type of call option. If the market rises, the depositor profits according to the *participation rate* or *multiplier,* in this case 70%; if the market falls, the investor is insured against loss. Just as clearly, the bank offering these CDs is in effect writing call options and can hedge its position by buying index calls in the options market. Figure 20.14 shows the nature of the bank's obligation to its depositors.

How might the bank set the appropriate multiplier? To answer this, note various features of the option:

Rate of Return on Index-Linked CD

Slope = .7

r_M = Market Rate of Return

FIGURE 20.14 Return on index-linked CD

1. The price the depositor is paying for the options is the forgone interest on the conventional CD that could be purchased. Because interest is received at the end of the period, the present value of the interest payment on each dollar invested is $r_f/(1 + r_f)$. Therefore, the depositor trades a sure payment with present value per dollar invested of $r_f/(1 + r_f)$ for a return that depends on the market's performance. Conversely, the bank can fund its obligation using the interest that it would have paid on a conventional CD.

2. The option we have described is an at-the-money option, meaning that the exercise price equals the current value of the stock index. The option goes into the money as soon as the market index increases from its level at the inception of the contract.

3. We can analyze the option on a per-dollar-invested basis. For example, the option costs the depositor $r_f/(1 + r_f)$ dollars per dollar placed in the index-linked CD. The market price of the option per dollar invested is C/S_0: The at-the-money option costs C dollars and is written on one unit of the market index, currently at S_0.

Now it is easy to determine the multiplier that the bank can offer on the CDs. It receives from its depositors a "payment" of $r_f/(1 + r_f)$ per dollar invested. It costs the bank C/S_0 to purchase the call option on a \$1 investment in the market index. Therefore, if $r_f/(1 + r_f)$ is, for example, 70% of C/S_0, the bank can purchase at most .7 call option on the \$1 investment and the multiplier will be .7. More generally, the break-even multiplier on an index-linked CD is $r_f/(1 + r_f)$ divided by C/S_0.

EXAMPLE 20.7 Indexed-Linked CDs

Suppose that $r_f = 6\%$ per year, and that 6-month maturity at-the-money calls on the market index currently cost \$50. The index is at 1,000. Then the option costs $50/1,000 = \$.05$ per dollar of market value. The CD rate is 3% per 6 months, meaning that $r_f/(1 + r_f) = .03/1.03 = .0291$. Therefore, the multiplier would be $.0291/.05 = .5825$.

The index-linked CD has several variants. Investors can purchase similar CDs that guarantee a positive minimum return if they are willing to settle for a smaller multiplier. In this case, the option is "purchased" by the depositor for $(r_f - r_{min})/(1 + r_f)$ dollars per dollar invested, where r_{min} is the guaranteed minimum return. Because the purchase price is lower, fewer options can be purchased, which results in a lower multiplier. Another variant of the "bullish" CD we have described is the *bear CD*, which pays depositors a fraction of any *fall* in the market index. For example, a bear CD might offer a rate of return of .6 times any percentage decline in the S&P 500.

CONCEPT CHECK 9

Continue to assume that $r_f = 3\%$ per half-year, that at-the-money calls sell for \$50, and that the market index is at 1,000. What would be the multiplier for 6-month bullish equity-linked CDs offering a guaranteed minimum return of .5% over the term of the CD?

20.7 EXOTIC OPTIONS

Options markets have been tremendously successful. Investors clearly value the portfolio strategies made possible by trading options; this is reflected in the heavy trading volume in these markets. Success breeds imitation, and in recent years we have witnessed

in advance the exchange rate at which an investment in a foreign currency can be converted back into dollars. The right to translate a fixed amount of foreign currency into dollars at a given exchange rate is a simple foreign exchange option. Quantos are more interesting, however, because the amount of currency that will be translated into dollars depends on the investment performance of the foreign security. Therefore, a quanto in effect provides a *random number* of options.

Digital Options

Digital options, also called binary or "bet" options, have fixed payoffs that depend on whether a condition is satisfied by the price of the underlying asset. For example, a digital call option might pay off a fixed amount of $100 if the stock price at maturity exceeds the exercise price.

The Chicago Mercantile Exchange once offered opportunities to trade digital options on various macroeconomic indicators. This gives traders the opportunity to either hedge or tailor their exposure to a variety of economic variables. Digital options (as well as more conventional options) traded on variables including gross domestic product, the U.S. balance of trade, jobless claims, nonfarm payrolls, and inflation. Unfortunately, these contracts were discontinued in 2007. See the nearby box for more discussion of these options.

SUMMARY

1. A call option is the right to buy an asset at an agreed-upon exercise price. A put option is the right to sell an asset at a given exercise price.

2. American-style options allow exercise on or before the expiration date. European options allow exercise only on the expiration date. Most traded options are American in nature.

3. Options are traded on stocks, stock indexes, foreign currencies, fixed-income securities, and several futures contracts.

4. Options can be used either to lever up an investor's exposure to an asset price or to provide insurance against volatility of asset prices. Popular option strategies include covered calls, protective puts, straddles, spreads, and collars.

5. The put-call parity theorem relates the prices of put and call options. If the relationship is violated, arbitrage opportunities will result. Specifically, the relationship that must be satisfied is

$$P = C - S_0 + PV(X) + PV(\text{dividends})$$

where X is the exercise price of both the call and the put options, $PV(X)$ is the present value of a claim to X dollars to be paid at the expiration date of the options, and $PV(\text{dividends})$ is the present value of dividends to be paid before option expiration.

6. Many commonly traded securities embody option characteristics. Examples of these securities are callable bonds, convertible bonds, and warrants. Other arrangements such as collateralized loans and limited-liability borrowing can be analyzed as conveying implicit options to one or more parties.

7. Trading in so-called exotic options now takes place in an active over-the-counter market.

Related Web sites for this chapter are available at **www.mhhe.com/bkm**

KEY TERMS

call option	at the money	straddle
exercise or strike price	American option	spread
premium	European option	collar
put option	protective put	put-call parity theorem
in the money	covered call	warrant
out of the money		

1. We said that options can be used either to scale up or reduce overall portfolio risk. What are some examples of risk-increasing and risk-reducing options strategies? Explain each.

2. What are the trade-offs facing an investor who is considering buying a put option on an existing portfolio?

3. What are the trade-offs facing an investor who is considering writing a call option on an existing portfolio?

4. Why do you think the most actively traded options tend to be the ones that are near the money?

5. Turn back to Figure 20.1, which lists prices of various IBM options. Use the data in the figure to calculate the payoff and the profits for investments in each of the following February maturity options, assuming that the stock price on the maturity date is $105.

   a. Call option, $X = \$100$.
   b. Put option, $X = \$100$.
   c. Call option, $X = \$105$.
   d. Put option, $X = \$105$.
   e. Call option, $X = \$110$.
   f. Put option, $X = \$110$.

6. Suppose you think Wal-Mart stock is going to appreciate substantially in value in the next 6 months. Say the stock's current price, S_0, is $100, and the call option expiring in 6 months has an exercise price, X, of $100 and is selling at a price, C, of $10. With $10,000 to invest, you are considering three alternatives.

   a. Invest all $10,000 in the stock, buying 100 shares.
   b. Invest all $10,000 in 1,000 options (10 contracts).
   c. Buy 100 options (one contract) for $1,000, and invest the remaining $9,000 in a money market fund paying 4% in interest over 6 months (8% per year).

   What is your rate of return for each alternative for the following four stock prices 6 months from now? Summarize your results in the table and diagram below.

	Price of Stock 6 Months from Now			
	$80	$100	$110	$120
a. All stocks (100 shares)				
b. All options (1,000 shares)				
c. Bills + 100 options				

Rate of Return

7. The common stock of the P.U.T.T. Corporation has been trading in a narrow price range for the past month, and you are convinced it is going to break far out of that range in the next 3 months. You do not know whether it will go up or down, however. The current price of the stock is $100 per share, and the price of a 3-month call option at an exercise price of $100 is $10.

   a. If the risk-free interest rate is 10% per year, what must be the price of a 3-month put option on P.U.T.T. stock at an exercise price of $100? (The stock pays no dividends.)

    b. What would be a simple options strategy to exploit your conviction about the stock price's future movements? How far would it have to move in either direction for you to make a profit on your initial investment?

8. The common stock of the C.A.L.L. Corporation has been trading in a narrow range around $50 per share for months, and you believe it is going to stay in that range for the next 3 months. The price of a 3-month put option with an exercise price of $50 is $4.

    a. If the risk-free interest rate is 10% per year, what must be the price of a 3-month call option on C.A.L.L. stock at an exercise price of $50 if it is at the money? (The stock pays no dividends.)

    b. What would be a simple options strategy using a put and a call to exploit your conviction about the stock price's future movement? What is the most money you can make on this position? How far can the stock price move in either direction before you lose money?

    c. How can you create a position involving a put, a call, and riskless lending that would have the same payoff structure as the stock at expiration? What is the net cost of establishing that position now?

9. In this problem, we derive the put-call parity relationship for European options on stocks that pay dividends before option expiration. For simplicity, assume that the stock makes one dividend payment of $D per share at the expiration date of the option.

    a. What is the value of a stock-plus-put position on the expiration date of the option?

    b. Now consider a portfolio comprising a call option and a zero-coupon bond with the same maturity date as the option and with face value $(X + D)$. What is the value of this portfolio on the option expiration date? You should find that its value equals that of the stock-plus-put portfolio regardless of the stock price.

    c. What is the cost of establishing the two portfolios in parts (*a*) and (*b*)? Equate the costs of these portfolios, and you will derive the put-call parity relationship, Equation 20.2.

10. *a.* A butterfly spread is the purchase of one call at exercise price X_1, the sale of two calls at exercise price X_2, and the purchase of one call at exercise price X_3. X_1 is less than X_2, and X_2 is less than X_3 by equal amounts, and all calls have the same expiration date. Graph the payoff diagram to this strategy.

    b. A vertical combination is the purchase of a call with exercise price X_2 and a put with exercise price X_1, with X_2 greater than X_1. Graph the payoff to this strategy.

11. A bearish spread is the purchase of a call with exercise price X_2 and the sale of a call with exercise price X_1, with X_2 greater than X_1. Graph the payoff to this strategy and compare it to Figure 20.10.

12. Joseph Jones, a manager at Computer Science, Inc. (CSI), received 10,000 shares of company stock as part of his compensation package. The stock currently sells at $40 a share. Joseph would like to defer selling the stock until the next tax year. In January, however, he will need to sell all his holdings to provide for a down payment on his new house. Joseph is worried about the price risk involved in keeping his shares. At current prices, he would receive $400,000 for the stock. If the value of his stock holdings falls below $350,000, his ability to come up with the necessary down payment would be jeopardized. On the other hand, if the stock value rises to $450,000, he would be able to maintain a small cash reserve even after making the down payment. Joseph considers three investment strategies:

    a. Strategy A is to write January call options on the CSI shares with strike price $45. These calls are currently selling for $3 each.

    b. Strategy B is to buy January put options on CSI with strike price $35. These options also sell for $3 each.

    c. Strategy C is to establish a zero-cost collar by writing the January calls and buying the January puts.

Evaluate each of these strategies with respect to Joseph's investment goals. What are the advantages and disadvantages of each? Which would you recommend?

13. Use the spreadsheet from the Excel Application boxes on spreads and straddles (available at **www.mhhe.com/bkm;** link to Chapter 20 material) to answer these questions.

a. Plot the payoff and profit diagrams to a straddle position with an exercise (strike) price of $130. Assume the options are priced as they are in the Excel Application.

b. Plot the payoff and profit diagrams to a bullish spread position with exercise (strike) prices of $120 and $130. Assume the options are priced as they are in the Excel Application.

14. The agricultural price support system guarantees farmers a minimum price for their output. Describe the program provisions as an option. What is the asset? The exercise price?

15. In what ways is owning a corporate bond similar to writing a put option? A call option?

16. An executive compensation scheme might provide a manager a bonus of $1,000 for every dollar by which the company's stock price exceeds some cutoff level. In what way is this arrangement equivalent to issuing the manager call options on the firm's stock?

17. Consider the following options portfolio. You write a February expiration call option on IBM with exercise price 105. You write a February IBM put option with exercise price 100.

a. Graph the payoff of this portfolio at option expiration as a function of IBM's stock price at that time.

b. What will be the profit/loss on this position if IBM is selling at 103 on the option expiration date? What if IBM is selling at 110? Use *The Wall Street Journal* listing from Figure 20.1 to answer this question.

c. At what two stock prices will you just break even on your investment?

d. What kind of "bet" is this investor making; that is, what must this investor believe about IBM's stock price to justify this position?

18. Consider the following portfolio. You write a put option with exercise price 90 and buy a put option on the same stock with the same expiration date with exercise price 95.

a. Plot the value of the portfolio at the expiration date of the options.

b. On the same graph, plot the profit of the portfolio. Which option must cost more?

19. A Ford put option with strike price 60 trading on the Acme options exchange sells for $2. To your amazement, a Ford put with the same maturity selling on the Apex options exchange but with strike price 62 also sells for $2. If you plan to hold the options positions to maturity, devise a zero-net-investment arbitrage strategy to exploit the pricing anomaly. Draw the profit diagram at maturity for your position.

20. You buy a share of stock, write a 1-year call option with $X = \$10$, and buy a 1-year put option with $X = \$10$. Your net outlay to establish the entire portfolio is $9.50. What is the risk-free interest rate? The stock pays no dividends.

21. You write a put option with $X = 100$ and buy a put with $X = 110$. The puts are on the same stock and have the same expiration date.

a. Draw the payoff graph for this strategy.

b. Draw the profit graph for this strategy.

c. If the underlying stock has positive beta, does this portfolio have positive or negative beta?

22. Joe Finance has just purchased a stock index fund, currently selling at $400 per share. To protect against losses, Joe also purchased an at-the-money European put option on the fund for $20, with exercise price $400, and 3-month time to expiration. Sally Calm, Joe's financial adviser, points out that Joe is spending a lot of money on the put. She notes that 3-month puts with strike prices of $390 cost only $15, and suggests that Joe use the cheaper put.

a. Analyze Joe's and Sally's strategies by drawing the *profit* diagrams for the stock-plus-put positions for various values of the stock fund in 3 months.

b. When does Sally's strategy do better? When does it do worse?

c. Which strategy entails greater systematic risk?

23. You write a call option with $X = 50$ and buy a call with $X = 60$. The options are on the same stock and have the same expiration date. One of the calls sells for $3; the other sells for $9.

a. Draw the payoff graph for this strategy at the option expiration date.

b. Draw the profit graph for this strategy.

c. What is the break-even point for this strategy? Is the investor bullish or bearish on the stock?

24. Devise a portfolio using only call options and shares of stock with the following value (payoff) at the option expiration date. If the stock price is currently 53, what kind of bet is the investor making?

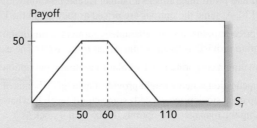

Challenge Problems

25. You are attempting to formulate an investment strategy. On the one hand, you think there is great upward potential in the stock market and would like to participate in the upward move if it materializes. However, you are not able to afford substantial stock market losses and so cannot run the risk of a stock market collapse, which you think is also a possibility. Your investment adviser suggests a protective put position: Buy both shares in a market index stock fund and put options on those shares with 3-month expiration and exercise price of $780. The stock index fund is currently selling for $900. However, your uncle suggests you instead buy a 3-month call option on the index fund with exercise price $840 and buy 3-month T-bills with face value $840.

   a. On the same graph, draw the *payoffs* to each of these strategies as a function of the stock fund value in 3 months. (*Hint:* Think of the options as being on one "share" of the stock index fund, with the current price of each share of the fund equal to $900.)

   b. Which portfolio must require a greater initial outlay to establish? (*Hint:* Does either portfolio provide a final payout that is always at least as great as the payoff of the other portfolio?)

   c. Suppose the market prices of the securities are as follows:

Stock fund	$900
T-bill (face value $840)	$810
Call (exercise price $840)	$120
Put (exercise price $780)	$ 6

   Make a table of the profits realized for each portfolio for the following values of the stock price in 3 months: $S_T = \$700, \$840, \$900, \$960$.
   Graph the profits to each portfolio as a function of S_T on a single graph.

   d. Which strategy is riskier? Which should have a higher beta?

   e. Explain why the data for the securities given in part (c) do *not* violate the put-call parity relationship.

26. Using the IBM option prices in Figure 20.1, calculate the market price of a riskless zero-coupon bond with face value $105 that matures in February on the same date as the listed options.

27. Demonstrate that an at-the-money call option on a given stock must cost more than an at-the-money put option on that stock with the same maturity. The stock will pay no dividends until after the expiration date. (*Hint:* Use put-call parity.)

1. Donna Donie, CFA, has a client who believes the common stock price of TRT Materials (currently $58 per share) could move substantially in either direction in reaction to an expected court decision involving the company. The client currently owns no TRT shares, but asks Donie for advice about implementing a strangle strategy to capitalize on the possible stock price movement. A strangle is a portfolio of a put and a call with different exercise prices but the same expiration date. Donie gathers the TRT option-pricing data:

Characteristic	Call Option	Put Option
Price	$ 5	$ 4
Strike Price	$60	$55
Time to expiration	90 days from now	90 days from now

a. Recommend whether Donie should choose a long strangle strategy or a short strangle strategy to achieve the client's objective.

b. Calculate, at expiration for the appropriate strangle strategy in part (*a*), the:

   i. Maximum possible loss per share.
   ii. Maximum possible gain per share.
   iii. Breakeven stock price(s).

2. Martin Bowman is preparing a report distinguishing traditional debt securities from structured note securities. Discuss how the following structured note securities differ from a traditional debt security with respect to coupon and principal payments:

   i. Equity index-linked notes.
   ii. Commodity-linked bear bond.

3. Suresh Singh, CFA, is analyzing a convertible bond. The characteristics of the bond and the underlying common stock are given in the following exhibit:

Convertible Bond Characteristics	
Par value	$1,000
Annual coupon rate (annual pay)	6.5%
Conversion ratio	22
Market price	105% of par value
Straight value	99% of par value
Underlying Stock Characteristics	
Current market price	$40 per share
Annual cash dividend	$1.20 per share

Compute the bond's:
   i. Conversion value.
   ii. Market conversion price.

4. Rich McDonald, CFA, is evaluating his investment alternatives in Ytel Incorporated by analyzing a Ytel convertible bond and Ytel common equity. Characteristics of the two securities are given in the following exhibit:

Characteristics	Convertible Bond	Common Equity
Par value	$1,000	—
Coupon (annual payment)	4%	—
Current market price	$980	$35 per share
Straight bond value	$925	—
Conversion ratio	25	—
Conversion option	At any time	—
Dividend	—	$0
Expected market price in 1 year	$1,125	$45 per share

a. Calculate, based on the exhibit, the:

   i. Current market conversion price for the Ytel convertible bond.
   ii. Expected 1-year rate of return for the Ytel convertible bond.
   iii. Expected 1-year rate of return for the Ytel common equity.

One year has passed and Ytel's common equity price has increased to $51 per share. Also, over the year, the interest rate on Ytel's nonconvertible bonds of the same maturity increased, while credit spreads remained unchanged.

b. Name the two components of the convertible bond's value. Indicate whether the value of each component should decrease, stay the same, or increase in response to the:

   i. Increase in Ytel's common equity price.
   ii. Increase in interest rates.

5. *a.* Consider a bullish spread option strategy using a call option with a $25 exercise price priced at $4 and a call option with a $40 exercise price priced at $2.50. If the price of the stock increases

for profitable exercise. If not, the worst that can happen is that the option will expire with zero value.

The value $S_0 - X$ is sometimes called the **intrinsic value** of in-the-money call options because it gives the payoff that could be obtained by immediate exercise. Intrinsic value is set equal to zero for out-of-the-money or at-the-money options. The difference between the actual call price and the intrinsic value is commonly called the **time value** of the option.

"Time value" is an unfortunate choice of terminology, because it may confuse the option's time value with the time value of money. Time value in the options context refers simply to the difference between the option's price and the value the option would have if it were expiring immediately. It is the part of the option's value that may be attributed to the fact that it still has positive time to expiration.

Most of an option's time value typically is a type of "volatility value." Because the option holder can choose not to exercise, the payoff cannot be worse than zero. Even if a call option is out of the money now, it still will sell for a positive price because it offers the potential for a profit if the stock price increases, while imposing no risk of additional loss should the stock price fall. The volatility value lies in the value of the right *not* to exercise the call if that action would be unprofitable. The option to exercise, as opposed to the obligation to exercise, provides insurance against poor stock price performance.

As the stock price increases substantially, it becomes likely that the call option will be exercised by expiration. Ultimately, with exercise all but assured, the volatility value becomes minimal. As the stock price gets ever larger, the option value approaches the "adjusted" intrinsic value, the stock price minus the present value of the exercise price, $S_0 - PV(X)$.

Why should this be? If you are virtually certain the option will be exercised and the stock purchased for X dollars, it is as though you own the stock already. The stock certificate, with a value today of S_0, might as well be sitting in your safe-deposit box now, as it will be there in only a few months. You just haven't paid for it yet. The present value of your obligation is the present value of X, so the net value of the call option is $S_0 - PV(X)$.[1]

Figure 21.1 illustrates the call option valuation function. The value curve shows that when the stock price is very low, the option is nearly worthless, because there is almost no chance that it will be exercised. When the stock price is very high, the option value approaches adjusted intrinsic value. In the midrange case, where the option is approximately at the money, the option curve diverges from the straight lines corresponding to adjusted intrinsic value. This is because although exercise today would have a negligible (or negative) payoff, the volatility value of the option is quite high in this region.

The call always increases in value with the stock price. The slope is greatest, however, when the option is deep in the money. In this case, exercise is all but assured, and the option increases in price one-for-one with the stock price.

Determinants of Option Values

We can identify at least six factors that should affect the value of a call option: the stock price, the exercise price, the volatility of the stock price, the time to expiration, the interest rate, and the dividend rate of the stock. The call option should increase in value with the stock price and decrease in value with the exercise price because the payoff to a call,

---

[1]This discussion presumes that the stock pays no dividends until after option expiration. If the stock does pay dividends before expiration, then there *is* a reason you would care about getting the stock now rather than at expiration—getting it now entitles you to the interim dividend payments. In this case, the adjusted intrinsic value of the option must subtract the value of the dividends the stock will pay out before the call is exercised. Adjusted intrinsic value would more generally be defined as $S_0 - PV(X) - PV(D)$, where D is the dividend to be paid before option expiration.

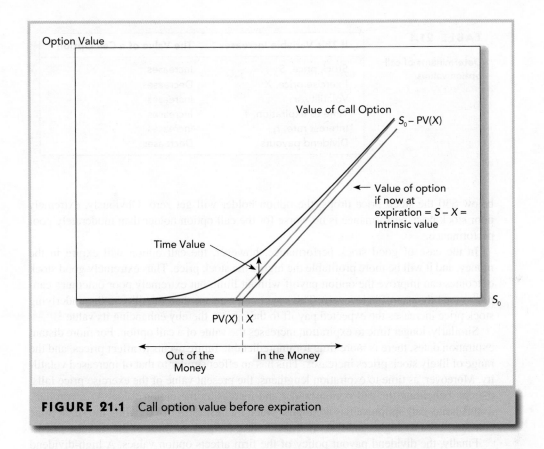

Option Value

Value of Call Option

$S_0 - PV(X)$

Value of option
if now at
expiration = $S - X$ =
Intrinsic value

Time Value

$PV(X)$ | X

S_0

Out of the
Money

In the Money

FIGURE 21.1   Call option value before expiration

if exercised, equals $S_T - X$. The magnitude of the expected payoff from the call increases
with the difference $S_0 - X$.

Call option values also increase with the volatility of the underlying stock price. To see
why, consider circumstances where possible stock prices at expiration may range from
$10 to $50 compared to a situation where stock prices may range only from $20 to $40. In
both cases, the expected, or average, stock price will be $30. Suppose the exercise price on
a call option is also $30. What are the option payoffs?

High-Volatility Scenario					
Stock price	$10	$20	$30	$40	$50
Option payoff	0	0	0	10	20
Low-Volatility Scenario					
Stock price	$20	$25	$30	$35	$40
Option payoff	0	0	0	5	10

If each outcome is equally likely, with probability .2, the expected payoff to the option
under high-volatility conditions will be $6, but under low-volatility conditions the expected
payoff to the call option is half as much, only $3.

Despite the fact that the average stock price in each scenario is $30, the average option
payoff is greater in the high-volatility scenario. The source of this extra value is the limited loss an option holder can suffer, or the volatility value of the call. No matter how far

TABLE 21.1	**If This Variable Increases . . .**	**The Value of a Call Option**
Determinants of call option values	Stock price, S	Increases
	Exercise price, X	Decreases
	Volatility, σ	Increases
	Time to expiration, T	Increases
	Interest rate, r_f	Increases
	Dividend payouts	Decreases

below \$30 the stock price drops, the option holder will get zero. Obviously, extremely poor stock price performance is no worse for the call option holder than moderately poor performance.

In the case of good stock performance, however, the call option will expire in the money, and it will be more profitable the higher the stock price. Thus extremely good stock outcomes can improve the option payoff without limit, but extremely poor outcomes cannot worsen the payoff below zero. This asymmetry means that volatility in the underlying stock price increases the expected payoff to the option, thereby enhancing its value.[2]

Similarly, longer time to expiration increases the value of a call option. For more distant expiration dates, there is more time for unpredictable future events to affect prices, and the range of likely stock prices increases. This has an effect similar to that of increased volatility. Moreover, as time to expiration lengthens, the present value of the exercise price falls, thereby benefiting the call option holder and increasing the option value. As a corollary to this issue, call option values are higher when interest rates rise (holding the stock price constant) because higher interest rates also reduce the present value of the exercise price.

Finally, the dividend payout policy of the firm affects option values. A high-dividend payout policy puts a drag on the rate of growth of the stock price. For any expected total rate of return on the stock, a higher dividend yield must imply a lower expected rate of capital gain. This drag on stock price appreciation decreases the potential payoff from the call option, thereby lowering the call value. Table 21.1 summarizes these relationships.

> **CONCEPT CHECK 1**
>
> Prepare a table like Table 21.1 for the determinants of put option values. How should American put values respond to increases in S, X, σ, T, r_f, and dividend payouts?

21.2 RESTRICTIONS ON OPTION VALUES

Several quantitative models of option pricing have been devised, and we will examine some of them later in this chapter. All models, however, rely on simplifying assumptions. You might wonder which properties of option values are truly general and which depend on the particular simplifications. To start with, we will consider some of the more important

---

[2]You should be careful interpreting the relationship between volatility and option value. Neither the focus of this analysis on total (as opposed to systematic) volatility nor the conclusion that options buyers seem to like volatility contradicts modern portfolio theory. In conventional discounted cash flow analysis, we find the discount rate appropriate for a *given* distribution of future cash flows. Greater risk implies a higher discount rate and lower present value. Here, however, the cash flow from the *option* depends on the volatility of the *stock*. The option value increases not because traders like risk but because the expected cash flow to the option holder increases along with the volatility of the underlying asset.

general properties of option prices. Some of these properties have important implications for the effect of stock dividends on option values and the possible profitability of early exercise of an American option.

Restrictions on the Value of a Call Option

The most obvious restriction on the value of a call option is that its value cannot be negative. Because the option need not be exercised, it cannot impose any liability on its holder; moreover, as long as there is any possibility that at some point the option can be exercised profitably, the option will command a positive price. Its payoff is zero at worst, and possibly positive, so that investors are willing to pay some amount to purchase it.

We can place another lower bound on the value of a call option. Suppose that the stock will pay a dividend of D dollars just before the expiration date of the option, denoted by T (where today is time 0). Now compare two portfolios, one consisting of a call option on one share of stock and the other a leveraged equity position consisting of that share and borrowing of $(X + D)/(1 + r_f)^T$ dollars. The loan repayment is $X + D$ dollars, due on the expiration date of the option. For example, for a half-year maturity option with exercise price $70, dividends to be paid of $5, and effective annual interest of 10%, you would purchase one share of stock and borrow $75/(1.10)^{1/2} = \$71.51$. In 6 months, when the loan matures, the payment due is $75.

At that time, the payoff to the leveraged equity position would be

	In General	Our Numbers
Stock value	$S_T + D$	$S_T + 5$
− Payback of loan	$-(X + D)$	− 75
TOTAL	$S_T - X$	$S_T - 70$

where S_T denotes the stock price at the option expiration date. Notice that the payoff to the stock is the ex-dividend stock value plus dividends received. Whether the total payoff to the stock-plus-borrowing position is positive or negative depends on whether S_T exceeds X. The net cash outlay required to establish this leveraged equity position is $S_0 - \$71.51$, or, more generally, $S_0 - (X + D)/(1 + r_f)^T$, that is, the current price of the stock, S_0, less the initial cash inflow from the borrowing position.

The payoff to the call option will be $S_T - X$ if the option expires in the money and zero otherwise. Thus the option payoff is equal to the leveraged equity payoff when that payoff is positive and is greater when the leveraged equity position has a negative payoff. Because the option payoff is always greater than or equal to that of the leveraged equity position, the option price must exceed the cost of establishing that position.

Therefore, the value of the call must be greater than $S_0 - (X + D)/(1 + r_f)^T$, or, more generally,

$$C \geq S_0 - PV(X) - PV(D)$$

where $PV(X)$ denotes the present value of the exercise price and $PV(D)$ is the present value of the dividends the stock will pay at the option's expiration. More generally, we can interpret $PV(D)$ as the present value of any and all dividends to be paid prior to the option expiration date. Because we know already that the value of a call option must be nonnegative, we may conclude that C is greater than the *maximum* of either 0 or $S_0 - PV(X) - PV(D)$.

We also can place an upper bound on the possible value of the call; this bound is simply the stock price. No one would pay more than S_0 dollars for the right to purchase a stock currently worth S_0 dollars. Thus $C \leq S_0$.

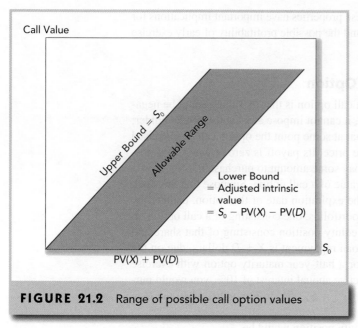

FIGURE 21.2 Range of possible call option values

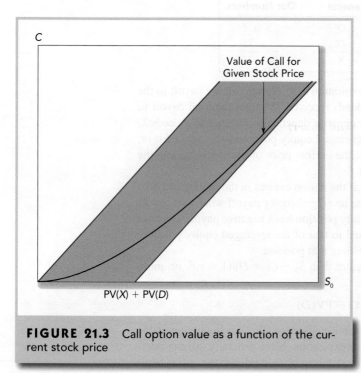

FIGURE 21.3 Call option value as a function of the current stock price

Figure 21.2 demonstrates graphically the range of prices that is ruled out by these upper and lower bounds for the value of a call option. Any option value outside the shaded area is not possible according to the restrictions we have derived. Before expiration, the call option value normally will be *within* the allowable range, touching neither the upper nor lower bound, as in Figure 21.3.

Early Exercise and Dividends

A call option holder who wants to close out that position has two choices: exercise the call or sell it. If the holder exercises at time t, the call will provide a payoff of $S_t - X$, assuming, of course, that the option is in the money. We have just seen that the option can be sold for at least $S_t - PV(X) - PV(D)$. Therefore, for an option on a non-dividend-paying stock, C is greater than $S_t - PV(X)$. Because the present value of X is less than X itself, it follows that

$$C \geq S_t - PV(X) > S_t - X$$

The implication here is that the proceeds from a sale of the option (at price C) must exceed the proceeds from an exercise $(S_t - X)$. It is economically more attractive to sell the call, which keeps it alive, than to exercise and thereby end the option. In other words, calls on non-dividend-paying stocks are "worth more alive than dead."

If it never pays to exercise a call option before expiration, the right to exercise early actually must be valueless. The right to exercise an American call early is irrelevant because it will never pay to exercise early. We therefore conclude that the values of otherwise identical American and European call options on stocks paying no dividends are equal. If we can find the value for the European call, we also will have found the value of the American call. This simplifies matters, because any valuation formula that applies to the European call, for which only one exercise date need be considered, also must apply to an American call.

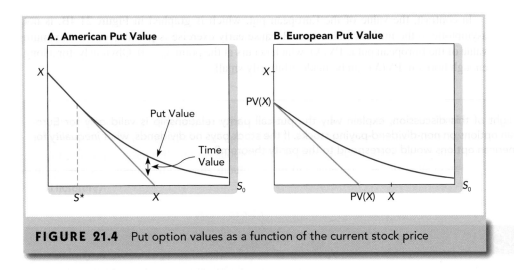

FIGURE 21.4 Put option values as a function of the current stock price

As most stocks do pay dividends, you may wonder whether this result is just a theoretical curiosity. It is not: Reconsider our argument and you will see that all that we really require is that the stock pay no dividends *until the option expires.* This condition will be true for many real-world options.

Early Exercise of American Puts

For American *put options,* the optimality of early exercise is most definitely a possibility. To see why, consider a simple example. Suppose that you purchase a put option on a stock. Soon the firm goes bankrupt, and the stock price falls to zero. Of course you want to exercise now, because the stock price can fall no lower. Immediate exercise gives you immediate receipt of the exercise price, which can be invested to start generating income. Delay in exercise means a time-value-of-money cost. The right to exercise a put option before expiration must have value.

Now suppose instead that the firm is only *nearly* bankrupt, with the stock selling at just a few cents. Immediate exercise may still be optimal. After all, the stock price can fall by only a very small amount, meaning that the proceeds from future exercise cannot be more than a few cents greater than the proceeds from immediate exercise. Against this possibility of a tiny increase in proceeds must be weighed the time-value-of-money cost of deferring exercise. Clearly, there is some stock price below which early exercise is optimal.

This argument also proves that the American put must be worth more than its European counterpart. The American put allows you to exercise anytime before expiration. Because the right to exercise early may be useful in some circumstances, it will command a positive price in the capital market. The American put therefore will sell for a higher price than a European put with otherwise identical terms.

Figure 21.4A illustrates the value of an American put option as a function of the current stock price, S_0. Once the stock price drops below a critical value, denoted S^* in the figure, exercise becomes optimal. At that point the option-pricing curve is tangent to the straight line depicting the intrinsic value of the option. If and when the stock price reaches S^*, the put option is exercised and its payoff equals its intrinsic value.

$C_u = \$10$, whereas if the stock price decreases, the call will be worth $C_d = 0$, for a range of $10. The ratio of ranges, 10/30, is one-third, which is the hedge ratio we have established.

The hedge ratio equals the ratio of ranges because the option and stock are perfectly correlated in this two-state example. When the returns of the option and stock are perfectly correlated, a perfect hedge requires that the option and stock be held in a fraction determined only by relative volatility.

We can generalize the hedge ratio for other two-state option problems as

$$H = \frac{C_u - C_d}{uS_0 - dS_0}$$

where C_u or C_d refers to the call option's value when the stock goes up or down, respectively, and uS_0 and dS_0 are the stock prices in the two states. The hedge ratio, H, is the ratio of the swings in the possible end-of-period values of the option and the stock. If the investor writes one option and holds H shares of stock, the value of the portfolio will be unaffected by the stock price. In this case, option pricing is easy: Simply set the value of the hedged portfolio equal to the present value of the known payoff.

Using our example, the option-pricing technique would proceed as follows:

1. Given the possible end-of-year stock prices, $uS_0 = 120$ and $dS_0 = 90$, and the exercise price of 110, calculate that $C_u = 10$ and $C_d = 0$. The stock price range is 30, while the option price range is 10.
2. Find that the hedge ratio of $10/30 = \frac{1}{3}$.
3. Find that a portfolio made up of $\frac{1}{3}$ share with one written option would have an end-of-year value of $30 with certainty.
4. Show that the present value of $30 with a 1-year interest rate of 10% is $27.27.
5. Set the value of the hedged position to the present value of the certain payoff:

$$\frac{1}{3}S_0 - C_0 = \$27.27$$
$$\$33.33 - C_0 = \$27.27$$

6. Solve for the call's value, $C_0 = \$6.06$.

What if the option is overpriced, perhaps selling for $6.50? Then you can make arbitrage profits. Here is how:

		Cash Flow in 1 Year for Each Possible Stock Price	
	Initial Cash Flow	$S_1 = 90$	$S_1 = 120$
1. Write 3 options	$ 19.50	$ 0	$−30
2. Purchase 1 share	−100	90	120
3. Borrow $80.50 at 10% interest Repay in 1 year	80.50	−88.55	−88.55
TOTAL	$ 0	$ 1.45	$ 1.45

Although the net initial investment is zero, the payoff in 1 year is positive and riskless. If the option were underpriced, one would simply reverse this arbitrage strategy: Buy the option, and sell the stock short to eliminate price risk. Note, by the way, that the present value of the profit to the arbitrage strategy above exactly equals three times the amount by which the option is overpriced. The present value of the risk-free profit of $1.45 at a 10% interest rate is $1.318. With three options written in the strategy above, this translates to a profit of $.44 per option, exactly the amount by which the option was overpriced: $6.50 versus the "fair value" of $6.06.

CONCEPT CHECK 3	Suppose the call option had been underpriced, selling at $5.50. Formulate the arbitrage strategy to exploit the mispricing, and show that it provides a riskless cash flow in 1 year of $.6167 per option purchased. Compare the present value of this cash flow to the option mispricing.

Generalizing the Two-State Approach

Although the two-state stock price model seems simplistic, we can generalize it to incorporate more realistic assumptions. To start, suppose we were to break up the year into two 6-month segments, and then assert that over each half-year segment the stock price could take on two values. We will say it can increase 10% (i.e., $u = 1.10$) or decrease 5% (i.e., $d = .95$). A stock initially selling at 100 could follow these possible paths over the course of the year:

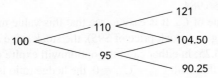

The midrange value of 104.50 can be attained by two paths: an increase of 10% followed by a decrease of 5%, or a decrease of 5% followed by a 10% increase.

There are now three possible end-of-year values for the stock and three for the option:

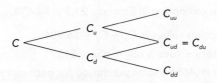

Using methods similar to those we followed above, we could value C_u from knowledge of C_{uu} and C_{ud}, then value C_d from knowledge of C_{du} and C_{dd}, and finally value C from knowledge of C_u and C_d. And there is no reason to stop at 6-month intervals. We could next break the year into four 3-month units, or twelve 1-month units, or 365 1-day units, each of which would be posited to have a two-state process. Although the calculations become quite numerous and correspondingly tedious, they are easy to program into a computer, and such computer programs are used widely by participants in the options market.

EXAMPLE 21.1   Binomial Option Pricing

Suppose that the risk-free interest rate is 5% per 6-month period and we wish to value a call option with exercise price $110 on the stock described in the two-period price tree just above. We start by finding the value of C_u. From this point, the call can rise to an expiration-date value of $C_{uu} = \$11$ (because at this point the stock price is $u \times u \times S_0 = \$121$) or fall to a final value of $C_{ud} = 0$ (because at this point the stock price is $u \times d \times S_0 = \$104.50$, which is less than the $110 exercise price). Therefore the hedge ratio at this point is

$$H = \frac{C_{uu} - C_{ud}}{uuS_0 - udS_0} = \frac{\$11 - 0}{\$121 - 104.50} = \frac{2}{3}$$

Thus, the following portfolio will be worth $209 at option expiration regardless of the ultimate stock price:

	$udS = \$104.50$	$uuS_0 = \$121$
Buy 2 shares at price $uS_0 = \$110$	$209	$242
Write 3 calls at price C_u	0	−33
TOTAL	$209	$209

The portfolio must have a current market value equal to the present value of $209:

$$2 \times 110 - 3C_u = \$209 / 1.05 = \$199.047$$

Solve to find that $C_u = \$6.984$.

Next we find the value of C_d. It is easy to see that this value must be zero. If we reach this point (corresponding to a stock price of $95), the stock price at option expiration will be either $104.50 or $90.25; in either case, the option will expire out of the money. (More formally, we could note that with $C_{ud} = C_{dd} = 0$, the hedge ratio is zero, and a portfolio of *zero* shares will replicate the payoff of the call!)

Finally, we solve for C using the values of C_u and C_d. Concept Check 4 leads you through the calculations that show the option value to be $4.434.

CONCEPT CHECK 4

Show that the initial value of the call option in Example 21.1 is $4.434.

a. Confirm that the spread in option values is $C_u - C_d = \$6.984$.

b. Confirm that the spread in stock values is $uS_0 - dS_0 = \$15$.

c. Confirm that the hedge ratio is .4656 shares purchased for each call written.

d. Demonstrate that the value in one period of a portfolio comprised of .4656 shares and one call written is riskless.

e. Calculate the present value of this payoff.

f. Solve for the option value.

As we break the year into progressively finer subintervals, the range of possible year-end stock prices expands and, in fact, will ultimately take on a familiar bell-shaped distribution. This can be seen from an analysis of the event tree for the stock for a period with three subintervals:

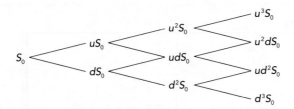

First, notice that as the number of subintervals increases, the number of possible stock prices also increases. Second, notice that extreme events such as u^3S_0 or d^3S_0 are relatively rare, as they require either three consecutive increases or decreases in the three subintervals. More moderate, or midrange, results such as u^2dS_0 can be arrived at by more than one path—any combination of two price increases and one decrease will result in stock price u^2dS_0. Thus the midrange values will be more likely. The probability of each outcome is described by the binomial distribution, and this multiperiod approach to option pricing is therefore called the **binomial model.**

For example, using an initial stock price of $100, equal probability of stock price increases or decreases, and three intervals for which the possible price increase is 5% and decrease is 3%, we can obtain the probability distribution of stock prices from the following calculations. There are eight possible combinations for the stock price movements in the three periods: *uuu, uud, udu, duu, udd, dud, ddu, ddd.* Each has probability of ⅛. Therefore, the probability distribution of stock prices at the end of the last interval would be:

Event	Probability	Final Stock Price	
3 up movements	1/8	100×1.05^3	$= 115.76$
2 up and 1 down	3/8	$100 \times 1.05^2 \times .97$	$= 106.94$
1 up and 2 down	3/8	$100 \times 1.05 \times .97^2$	$= 98.79$
3 down movements	1/8	$100 \times .97^3$	$= 91.27$

The midrange values are three times as likely to occur as the extreme values. Figure 21.5A is a graph of the frequency distribution for this example. The graph approaches the appearance of the familiar bell-shaped curve. In fact, as the number of intervals increases, as in Figure 21.5B, the frequency distribution progressively approaches the lognormal distribution rather than the normal distribution.[3]

Suppose we were to continue subdividing the interval in which stock prices are posited to move up or down. Eventually, each node of the event tree would correspond to an infinitesimally small time interval. The possible stock price movement within that time interval would be correspondingly small. As those many intervals passed, the end-of-period stock price would more and more closely resemble a lognormal distribution. Thus the apparent oversimplification of the two-state model can be overcome by progressively subdividing any period into many subperiods.

---

[3]Actually, more complex considerations enter here. The limit of this process is lognormal only if we assume also that stock prices move continuously, by which we mean that over small time intervals only small price movements can occur. This rules out rare events such as sudden, extreme price moves in response to dramatic information (like a takeover attempt). For a treatment of this type of "jump process," see John C. Cox and Stephen A. Ross, "The Valuation of Options for Alternative Stochastic Processes," *Journal of Financial Economics* 3 (January–March 1976), pp. 145–66, or Robert C. Merton, "Option Pricing when Underlying Stock Returns Are Discontinuous," *Journal of Financial Economics* 3 (January–March 1976), pp. 125–44.

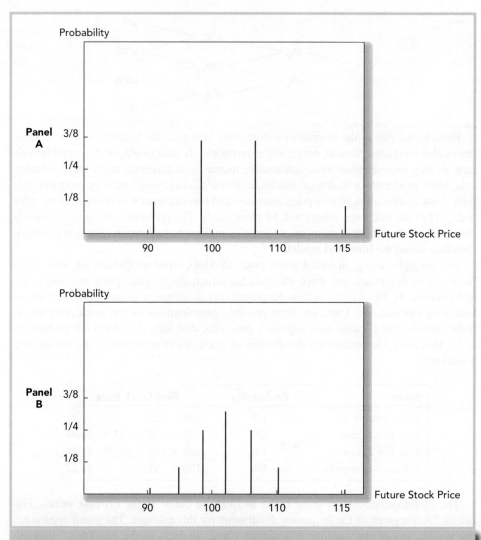

FIGURE 21.5 *Probability distributions. Panel A,* Possible outcomes and associated probabilities for stock prices after three periods. The stock price starts at $100, and in each period it can increase by 5% or decrease by 3%. *Panel B,* Each period is subdivided into two smaller subperiods. Now there are six periods, and in each of these the stock price can increase by 2.5% or fall by 1.5%. As the number of periods increases, the stock price distribution approaches the familiar bell-shaped curve.

At any node, one still could set up a portfolio that would be perfectly hedged over the next tiny time interval. Then, at the end of that interval, on reaching the next node, a new hedge ratio could be computed and the portfolio composition could be revised to remain hedged over the coming small interval. By continuously revising the hedge position, the portfolio would remain hedged and would earn a riskless rate of return over each interval. This is called *dynamic hedging,* the continued updating of the hedge ratio as time passes. As the dynamic hedge becomes ever finer, the resulting option-valuation procedure becomes more precise.

<table>
<tr>
<td>**CONCEPT CHECK**
5</td>
<td>Would you expect the hedge ratio to be higher or lower when the call option is more in the money? (Hint: Remember that the hedge ratio is the change in the option price divided by the change in the stock price. When is the option price most sensitive to the stock price?)</td>
</tr>
</table>

21.4 BLACK–SCHOLES OPTION VALUATION

Although the binomial model we have described is extremely flexible, a computer is needed for it to be useful in actual trading. An option-pricing *formula* would be far easier to use than the complex algorithm involved in the binomial model. It turns out that such a formula can be derived if one is willing to make just two more assumptions: that both the risk-free interest rate and stock price volatility are constant over the life of the option. In this case, as the time to expiration is divided into ever-more subperiods, the distribution of the stock price at expiration progressively approaches the lognormal distribution, as suggested by Figure 21.5. When the stock price distribution is actually lognormal, we can derive an exact option-pricing formula.

The Black-Scholes Formula

Financial economists searched for years for a workable option-pricing model before Black and Scholes[4] and Merton[5] derived a formula for the value of a call option. Scholes and Merton shared the 1997 Nobel Prize in Economics for their accomplishment.[6] Now widely used by options market participants, the **Black-Scholes pricing formula** for a call option is

$$C_0 = S_0 N(d_1) - Xe^{-rT}N(d_2) \qquad (21.1)$$

where

$$d_1 = \frac{\ln(S_0/X) + (r + \sigma^2/2)T}{\sigma\sqrt{T}}$$

$$d_2 = d_1 - \sigma\sqrt{T}$$

and

C_0 = Current call option value.

S_0 = Current stock price.

$N(d)$ = The probability that a random draw from a standard normal distribution will be less than d. This equals the area under the normal curve up to d, as in the shaded area of Figure 21.6. In Excel, this function is called NORMSDIST( ).

X = Exercise price.

e = The base of the natural log function, approximately 2.71828. In Excel, e^x can be evaluated using the function EXP(x).

---

[4]Fischer Black and Myron Scholes, "The Pricing of Options and Corporate Liabilities," *Journal of Political Economy* 81 (May–June 1973).

[5]Robert C. Merton, "Theory of Rational Option Pricing," *Bell Journal of Economics and Management Science* 4 (Spring 1973).

[6]Fischer Black died in 1995.

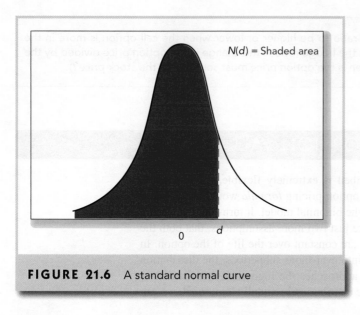

FIGURE 21.6   A standard normal curve

r = Risk-free interest rate (the annualized continuously compounded rate on a safe asset with the same maturity as the expiration date of the option, which is to be distinguished from r_f, the discrete period interest rate).

T = Time to expiration of option, in years.

ln = Natural logarithm function. In Excel, ln(*x*) can be calculated as LN(*x*).

σ = Standard deviation of the annualized continuously compounded rate of return of the stock.

Notice a surprising feature of Equation 21.1: The option value does *not* depend on the expected rate of return on the stock. In a sense, this information is already built into the formula with the inclusion of the stock price, which itself depends on the stock's risk and return characteristics. This version of the Black-Scholes formula is predicated on the assumption that the stock pays no dividends.

Although you may find the Black-Scholes formula intimidating, we can explain it at a somewhat intuitive level. The trick is to view the *N*(*d*) terms (loosely) as risk-adjusted probabilities that the call option will expire in the money. First, look at Equation 21.1 assuming both *N*(*d*) terms are close to 1.0, that is, when there is a very high probability the option will be exercised. Then the call option value is equal to $S_0 - Xe^{-rT}$, which is what we called earlier the adjusted intrinsic value, $S_0 - PV(X)$. This makes sense; if exercise is certain, we have a claim on a stock with current value S_0, and an obligation with present value PV(*X*), or, with continuous compounding, Xe^{-rT}.

Now look at Equation 21.1 assuming the *N*(*d*) terms are close to zero, meaning the option almost certainly will not be exercised. Then the equation confirms that the call is worth nothing. For middle-range values of *N*(*d*) between 0 and 1, Equation 21.1 tells us that the call value can be viewed as the present value of the call's potential payoff adjusting for the probability of in-the-money expiration.

How do the *N*(*d*) terms serve as risk-adjusted probabilities? This question quickly leads us into advanced statistics. Notice, however, that $\ln(S_0/X)$, which appears in the numerator of d_1 and d_2, is approximately the percentage amount by which the option is currently in or out of the money. For example, if $S_0 = 105$ and $X = 100$, the option is 5% in the money, and $\ln(105/100) = .049$. Similarly, if $S_0 = 95$, the option is 5% out of the money, and $\ln(95/100) = -.051$. The denominator, $\sigma\sqrt{T}$, adjusts the amount by which the option is in or out of the money for the volatility of the stock price over the remaining life of the option. An option in the money by a given percent is more likely to stay in the money if both stock price volatility and time to expiration are low. Therefore, $N(d_1)$ and $N(d_2)$ increase with the probability that the option will expire in the money.

EXAMPLE 21.2 Black-Scholes Valuation

You can use the Black-Scholes formula fairly easily. Suppose you want to value a call option under the following circumstances:

Stock price: $S_0 = 100$
Exercise price: $X = 95$
Interest rate: $r = .10$ (10% per year)
Time to expiration: $T = .25$ (3 months or one-quarter of a year)
Standard deviation: $\sigma = .50$ (50% per year)

First calculate

$$d_1 = \frac{\ln(100/95) + (.10 + .5^2/2).25}{.5\sqrt{.25}} = .43$$

$$d_2 = .43 - .5\sqrt{.25} = .18$$

Next find $N(d_1)$ and $N(d_2)$. The values of the normal distribution are tabulated and may be found in many statistics textbooks. A table of $N(d)$ is provided here as Table 21.2. The normal distribution function, $N(d)$, is also provided in any spreadsheet program. In Microsoft Excel, for example, the function name is NORMSDIST. Using either Excel or Table 21.2 we find that

$$N(.43) = .6664$$

$$N(.18) = .5714$$

Thus the value of the call option is

$$C = 100 \times .6664 - 95e^{-.10 \times .25} \times .5714$$

$$= 66.64 - 52.94 = \$13.70$$

CONCEPT CHECK 6

Recalculate the value of the call option in Example 21.2 using a standard deviation of .6 instead of .5. Confirm that the option is worth more using the higher stock-return volatility.

What if the option price in Example 21.2 were $15 rather than $13.70? Is the option mispriced? Maybe, but before betting your fortune on that, you may want to reconsider the valuation analysis. First, like all models, the Black-Scholes formula is based on some simplifying abstractions that make the formula only approximately valid.

Some of the important assumptions underlying the formula are the following:

1. The stock will pay no dividends until after the option expiration date.
2. Both the interest rate, r, and variance rate, σ^2, of the stock are constant (or in slightly more general versions of the formula, both are *known* functions of time—any changes are perfectly predictable).
3. Stock prices are continuous, meaning that sudden extreme jumps such as those in the aftermath of an announcement of a takeover attempt are ruled out.

Variants of the Black-Scholes formula have been developed to deal with many of these limitations.

d	N(d)	d	N(d)	d	N(d)	d	N(d)	d	N(d)	d	N(d)
−3.00	.0013	−1.58	.0571	−0.76	.2236	0.06	.5239	0.86	.8051	1.66	.9515
−2.95	.0016	−1.56	.0594	−0.74	.2297	0.08	.5319	0.88	.8106	1.68	.9535
−2.90	.0019	−1.54	.0618	−0.72	.2358	0.10	.5398	0.90	.8159	1.70	.9554
−2.85	.0022	−1.52	.0643	−0.70	.2420	0.12	.5478	0.92	.8212	1.72	.9573
−2.80	.0026	−1.50	.0668	−0.68	.2483	0.14	.5557	0.94	.8264	1.74	.9591
−2.75	.0030	−1.48	.0694	−0.66	.2546	0.16	.5636	0.96	.8315	1.76	.9608
−2.70	.0035	−1.46	.0721	−0.64	.2611	0.18	.5714	0.98	.8365	1.78	.9625
−2.65	.0040	−1.44	.0749	−0.62	.2676	0.20	.5793	1.00	.8414	1.80	.9641
−2.60	.0047	−1.42	.0778	−0.60	.2743	0.22	.5871	1.02	.8461	1.82	.9656
−2.55	.0054	−1.40	.0808	−0.58	.2810	0.24	.5948	1.04	.8508	1.84	.9671
−2.50	.0062	−1.38	.0838	−0.56	.2877	0.26	.6026	1.06	.8554	1.86	.9686
−2.45	.0071	−1.36	.0869	−0.54	.2946	0.28	.6103	1.08	.8599	1.88	.9699
−2.40	.0082	−1.34	.0901	−0.52	.3015	0.30	.6179	1.10	.8643	1.90	.9713
−2.35	.0094	−1.32	.0934	−0.50	.3085	0.32	.6255	1.12	.8686	1.92	.9726
−2.30	.0107	−1.30	.0968	−0.48	.3156	0.34	.6331	1.14	.8729	1.94	.9738
−2.25	.0122	−1.28	.1003	−0.46	.3228	0.36	.6406	1.16	.8770	1.96	.9750
−2.20	.0139	−1.26	.1038	−0.44	.3300	0.38	.6480	1.18	.8810	1.98	.9761
−2.15	.0158	−1.24	.1075	−0.42	.3373	0.40	.6554	1.20	.8849	2.00	.9772
−2.10	.0179	−1.22	.1112	−0.40	.3446	0.42	.6628	1.22	.8888	2.05	.9798
−2.05	.0202	−1.20	.1151	−0.38	.3520	0.44	.6700	1.24	.8925	2.10	.9821
−2.00	.0228	−1.18	.1190	−0.36	.3594	0.46	.6773	1.26	.8962	2.15	.9842
−1.98	.0239	−1.16	.1230	−0.34	.3669	0.48	.6844	1.28	.8997	2.20	.9861
−1.96	.0250	−1.14	.1271	−0.32	.3745	0.50	.6915	1.30	.9032	2.25	.9878
−1.94	.0262	−1.12	.1314	−0.30	.3821	0.52	.6985	1.32	.9066	2.30	.9893
−1.92	.0274	−1.10	.1357	−0.28	.3897	0.54	.7054	1.34	.9099	2.35	.9906
−1.90	.0287	−1.08	.1401	−0.26	.3974	0.56	.7123	1.36	.9131	2.40	.9918
−1.88	.0301	−1.06	.1446	−0.24	.4052	0.58	.7191	1.38	.9162	2.45	.9929
−1.86	.0314	−1.04	.1492	−0.22	.4129	0.60	.7258	1.40	.9192	2.50	.9938
−1.84	.0329	−1.02	.1539	−0.20	.4207	0.62	.7324	1.42	.9222	2.55	.9946
−1.82	.0344	−1.00	.1587	−0.18	.4286	0.64	.7389	1.44	.9251	2.60	.9953
−1.80	.0359	−0.98	.1635	−0.16	.4365	0.66	.7454	1.46	.9279	2.65	.9960
−1.78	.0375	−0.96	.1685	−0.14	.4443	0.68	.7518	1.48	.9306	2.70	.9965
−1.76	.0392	−0.94	.1736	−0.12	.4523	0.70	.7580	1.50	.9332	2.75	.9970
−1.74	.0409	−0.92	.1788	−0.10	.4602	0.72	.7642	1.52	.9357	2.80	.9974
−1.72	.0427	−0.90	.1841	−0.08	.4681	0.74	.7704	1.54	.9382	2.85	.9978
−1.70	.0446	−0.88	.1894	−0.06	.4761	0.76	.7764	1.56	.9406	2.90	.9981
−1.68	.0465	−0.86	.1949	−0.04	.4841	0.78	.7823	1.58	.9429	2.95	.9984
−1.66	.0485	−0.84	.2005	−0.02	.4920	0.80	.7882	1.60	.9452	3.00	.9986
−1.64	.0505	−0.82	.2061	0.00	.5000	0.82	.7939	1.62	.9474	3.05	.9989
−1.62	.0526	−0.80	.2119	0.02	.5080	0.84	.7996	1.64	.9495		
−1.60	.0548	−0.78	.2177	0.04	.5160						

TABLE 21.2   Cumulative normal distribution

Second, even within the context of the Black-Scholes model, you must be sure of the accuracy of the parameters used in the formula. Four of these—S_0, X, T, and r—are straightforward. The stock price, exercise price, and time to expiration are readily determined. The interest rate used is the money market rate for a maturity equal to that of the option, and the dividend payout is reasonably predictable, at least over short horizons.

	A	B	C	D	E	F	G	H	I	J
1	INPUTS			OUTPUTS			FORMULA FOR OUTPUT IN COLUMN E			
2	Standard deviation (annual)	0.2783		d1	0.0029		(LN(B5/B6)+(B4–B7+.5*B2^2)*B3)/(B2*SQRT(B3))			
3	Maturity (in years)	0.5		d2	–0.1939		E2–B2*SQRT(B3)			
4	Risk-free rate (annual)	0.06		N(d1)	0.5012		NORMSDIST(E2)			
5	Stock price	100		N(d2)	0.4231		NORMSDIST(E3)			
6	Exercise price	105		B/S call value	7.0000		B5*EXP(–B7*B3)*E4–B6*EXP(–B4*B3)*E5			
7	Dividend yield (annual)	0		B/S put value	8.8968		B6*EXP(–B4*B3)*(1–E5)–B5*EXP(–B7*B3)*(1–E4)			

SPREADSHEET 21.1

Spreadsheet to calculate Black-Scholes call option values

eXcel
Please visit us at
www.mhhe.com/bkm

The last input, though, the standard deviation of the stock return, is not directly observable. It must be estimated from historical data, from scenario analysis, or from the prices of other options, as we will describe momentarily.

We saw in Chapter 5 that the historical variance of stock market returns can be calculated from n observations as follows:

$$\sigma^2 = \frac{n}{n-1} \sum_{t=1}^{n} \frac{(r_t - \overline{r})^2}{n}$$

where $\overline{r}$ is the average return over the sample period. The rate of return on day t is defined to be consistent with continuous compounding as $r_t = \ln(S_t/S_{t-1})$. [We note again that the natural logarithm of a ratio is approximately the percentage difference between the numerator and denominator so that $\ln(S_t/S_{t-1})$ is a measure of the rate of return of the stock from time $t-1$ to time t.] Historical variance commonly is computed using daily returns over periods of several months. Because the volatility of stock returns must be estimated, however, it is always possible that discrepancies between an option price and its Black-Scholes value are simply artifacts of error in the estimation of the stock's volatility.

In fact, market participants often give the option-valuation problem a different twist. Rather than calculating a Black-Scholes option value for a given stock's standard deviation, they ask instead: What standard deviation would be necessary for the option price that I observe to be consistent with the Black-Scholes formula? This is called the **implied volatility** of the option, the volatility level for the stock implied by the option price.[7] Investors can then judge whether they think the actual stock standard deviation exceeds the implied volatility. If it does, the option is considered a good buy; if actual volatility seems greater than the implied volatility, its fair price would exceed the observed price.

Another variation is to compare two options on the same stock with equal expiration dates but different exercise prices. The option with the higher implied volatility would be considered relatively expensive, because a higher standard deviation is required to justify its price. The analyst might consider buying the option with the lower implied volatility and writing the option with the higher implied volatility.

The Black-Scholes valuation formula, as well as implied volatilities, are easily calculated using an Excel spreadsheet like Spreadsheet 21.1. The model inputs are provided in column B, and the outputs are given in column E. The formulas for d_1 and d_2 are provided in the spreadsheet, and the Excel formula NORMSDIST(d_1) is used to calculate $N(d_1)$. Cell E6 contains the Black-Scholes formula. (The formula in the spreadsheet actually includes an adjustment for dividends, as described in the next section.)

[7]This concept was introduced in Richard E. Schmalensee and Robert R. Trippi, "Common Stock Volatility Expectations Implied by Option Premia," *Journal of Finance* 33 (March 1978), pp. 129–47.

	A	B	C	D	E	F	G	H	I	J	K
1	INPUTS			OUTPUTS			FORMULA FOR OUTPUT IN COLUMN E				
2	Standard deviation (annual)	0.2783		d1	0.0029		(LN(B5/B6)+(B4−B7+.5*B2^2)*B3)/(B2*SQRT(B3))				
3	Maturity (in years)	0.5		d2	−0.1939		E2−B2*SQRT(B3)				
4	Risk-free rate (annual)	0.06		N(d1)	0.5012		NORMSDIST(E2)				
5	Stock price	100		N(d2)	0.4231		NORMSDIST(E3)				
6	Exercise price	105		B/S call value	7.0000		B5*EXP(−B7*B3)*E4−B6*EXP(−B4*B3)*E5				
7	Dividend yield (annual)	0		B/S put value	8.8968		B6*EXP(−B4*B3)*(1−E5) − B5*EXP(−B7*B3)*(1−E4)				
8											
9											
10											
11											
12											
13											
14											
15											
16											
17											

Goal Seek

Set cell: $E$6

To value: 7

By changing cell: $B$2

OK   Cancel

FIGURE 21.7   Using Goal Seek to find implied volatility   **eXcel**

Please visit us at
www.mhhe.com/bkm

To compute an implied volatility, we can use the Goal Seek command from the Tools menu in Excel. See Figure 21.7 for an illustration. Goal Seek asks us to change the value of one cell to make the value of another cell (called the target cell) equal to a specific value. For example, if we observe a call option selling for $7 with other inputs as given in the spreadsheet, we can use Goal Seek to change the value in cell B2 (the standard deviation of the stock) to set the option value in cell E6 equal to $7. The target cell, E6, is the call price, and the spreadsheet manipulates cell B2. When you click "OK," the spreadsheet finds that a standard deviation equal to .2783 is consistent with a call price of $7; this would be the option's implied volatility if it were selling at $7.

The Chicago Board Options Exchange regularly computes the implied volatility of major stock indexes. Figure 21.8 is a graph of the implied (30-day) volatility of the S&P 500 since 1990. During periods of turmoil, implied volatility can spike quickly. Notice the peaks in January 1991 (Gulf War), August 1998 (collapse of Long-Term Capital Management), September 11, 2001, 2002 (build-up to invasion of Iraq) and August 2007 (subprime mortgage crisis). Because implied volatility correlates with crisis, it is sometimes called an "investor fear gauge."

In March 2004, a futures contract on the 30-day implied volatility of the S&P 500 began trading on the CBOE Futures Exchange. The payoff of the contract depends on market implied volatility at the expiration of the contract. The ticker symbol of the contract is VIX.

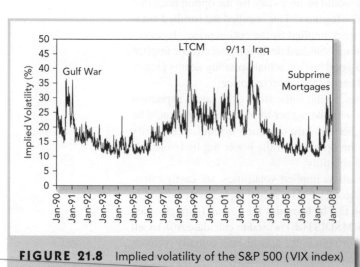

FIGURE 21.8   Implied volatility of the S&P 500 (VIX index)

Source: Chicago Board Options Exchange, **www.cboe.com**.

Figure 21.8 also reveals an awkward empirical fact. While the Black-Scholes formula is derived assuming that stock volatility is constant, the time series of implied volatilities derived from that formula is in fact far from constant. This contradiction reminds us that the Black-Scholes model (like all models) is a simplification that does not capture all aspects of real markets. In this particular context, extensions of the pricing model that allow stock volatility to evolve randomly over time would be desirable, and, in fact, many extensions of the model along these lines have been suggested.[8]

The fact that volatility changes unpredictably means that it can be difficult to choose the proper volatility input to use in any option-pricing model. A considerable amount of recent research has been devoted to techniques to predict changes in volatility. These techniques, which go by the name ARCH and stochastic volatility models, posit that changes in volatility are partially predictable and that by analyzing recent levels and trends in volatility, one can improve predictions of future volatility.[9]

CONCEPT CHECK 7	Suppose the call option in Spreadsheet 21.1 actually is selling for $8. Is its implied volatility more or less than 27.83%? Use the spreadsheet (available at the Online Learning Center) and Goal Seek to find its implied volatility at this price.

Dividends and Call Option Valuation

We noted earlier that the Black-Scholes call option formula applies to stocks that do not pay dividends. When dividends are to be paid before the option expires, we need to adjust the formula. The payment of dividends raises the possibility of early exercise, and for most realistic dividend payout schemes the valuation formula becomes significantly more complex than the Black-Scholes equation.

We can apply some simple rules of thumb to approximate the option value, however. One popular approach, originally suggested by Black, calls for adjusting the stock price downward by the present value of any dividends that are to be paid before option expiration.[10] Therefore, we would simply replace S_0 with $S_0 -$ PV(dividends) in the Black-Scholes formula. Such an adjustment will take dividends into account by reflecting their eventual impact on the stock price. The option value then may be computed as before, assuming that the option will be held to expiration.

In one special case, the dividend adjustment takes a simple form. Suppose the underlying asset pays a continuous flow of income. This might be a reasonable assumption for options on a stock index, where different stocks in the index pay dividends on different days, so that dividend income arrives in a more or less continuous flow. If the dividend yield, denoted δ, is constant, one can show that the present value of that dividend flow accruing until the option expiration date is $S_0(1 - e^{-\delta T})$. (For intuition, notice that $e^{-\delta T}$ approximately equals $1 - \delta T$, so the value of the dividend is approximately $\delta T S_0$.) In this case, $S_0 -$ PV(Div) $= S_0 e^{-\delta T}$, and we can derive a Black-Scholes call option formula on the dividend-paying asset simply by substituting $S_0 e^{-\delta T}$ for S_0 in the original formula. This approach is used in Spreadsheet 21.1.

---

[8]Influential articles on this topic are J. Hull and A. White, "The Pricing of Options on Assets with Stochastic Volatilities," *Journal of Finance* (June 1987), pp. 281–300; J. Wiggins, "Option Values under Stochastic Volatility," *Journal of Financial Economics* (December 1987), pp. 351–72; and S. Heston, "A Closed-Form Solution for Options with Stochastic Volatility with Applications to Bonds and Currency Options," *Review of Financial Studies* 6 (1993), pp. 327–43. For a more recent review, see E. Ghysels, A. Harvey, and E. Renault, "Stochastic Volatility," in *Handbook of Statistics, Vol. 14: Statistical Methods in Finance,* ed. G. S. Maddala (Amsterdam: North Holland, 1996).

[9]For an introduction to these models see C. Alexander, *Market Models* (Chichester, England: Wiley, 2001).

[10]Fischer Black, "Fact and Fantasy in the Use of Options," *Financial Analysts Journal* 31 (July–August 1975).

These procedures yield a very good approximation of option value for European call options that must be held until expiration, but they do not allow for the fact that the holder of an American call option might choose to exercise the option just before a dividend. The current value of a call option, assuming that the option will be exercised just before the ex-dividend date, might be greater than the value of the option assuming it will be held until expiration. Although holding the option until expiration allows greater effective time to expiration, which increases the option value, it also entails more dividend payments, lowering the expected stock price at expiration and thereby lowering the current option value.

For example, suppose that a stock selling at $20 will pay a $1 dividend in 4 months, whereas the call option on the stock does not expire for 6 months. The effective annual interest rate is 10%, so that the present value of the dividend is $1/(1.10)^{1/3} = 0.97. Black suggests that we can compute the option value in one of two ways:

1. Apply the Black-Scholes formula assuming early exercise, thus using the actual stock price of $20 and a time to expiration of 4 months (the time until the dividend payment).

2. Apply the Black-Scholes formula assuming no early exercise, using the dividend-adjusted stock price of $20 − $.97 = 19.03 and a time to expiration of 6 months.

The greater of the two values is the estimate of the option value, recognizing that early exercise might be optimal. In other words, the so-called **pseudo-American call option value** is the maximum of the value derived by assuming that the option will be held until expiration and the value derived by assuming that the option will be exercised just before an ex-dividend date. Even this technique is not exact, however, for it assumes that the option holder makes an irrevocable decision now on when to exercise, when in fact the decision is not binding until exercise notice is given.[11]

Put Option Valuation

We have concentrated so far on call option valuation. We can derive Black-Scholes European put option values from call option values using the put-call parity theorem. To value the put option, we simply calculate the value of the corresponding call option in Equation 21.1 from the Black-Scholes formula, and solve for the put option value as

$$P = C + PV(X) - S_0$$
$$= C + Xe^{-rT} - S_0 \tag{21.2}$$

We must calculate the present value of the exercise price using continuous compounding to be consistent with the Black-Scholes formula.

Sometimes, it is easier to work with a put option valuation formula directly. If we substitute the Black-Scholes formula for a call in Equation 21.2, we obtain the value of a European put option as

$$P = Xe^{-rT}[1 - N(d_2)] - S_0[1 - N(d_1)] \tag{21.3}$$

---

[11]An exact formula for American call valuation on dividend-paying stocks has been developed in Richard Roll, "An Analytic Valuation Formula for Unprotected American Call Options on Stocks with Known Dividends," *Journal of Financial Economics* 5 (November 1977). The technique has been discussed and revised in Robert Geske, "A Note on an Analytical Formula for Unprotected American Call Options on Stocks with Known Dividends," *Journal of Financial Economics* 7 (December 1979), and Robert E. Whaley, "On the Valuation of American Call Options on Stocks with Known Dividends," *Journal of Financial Economics* 9 (June 1981). These are difficult papers, however.

EXAMPLE 21.3   Black-Scholes Put Valuation

Using data from Example 21.2 ($C = \$13.70$, $X = \$95$, $S = \$100$, $r = .10$, $\sigma = .50$, and $T = .25$), Equation 21.3 implies that a European put option on that stock with identical exercise price and time to expiration is worth

$$\$95e^{-.10 \times .25}(1 - .5714) - \$100(1 - .6664) = \$6.35$$

Notice that this value is consistent with put-call parity:

$$P = C + \text{PV}(X) - S_0 = 13.70 + 95e^{-.10 \times .25} - 100 = 6.35$$

As we noted traders can do, we might then compare this formula value to the actual put price as one step in formulating a trading strategy.

Dividends and Put Option Valuation

Equation 21.2 or 21.3 is valid for European puts on non-dividend-paying stocks. As we did for call options, if the underlying asset pays a dividend, we can find European put values by substituting $S_0 - \text{PV}(\text{Div})$ for S_0. Cell E7 in Spreadsheet 21.1 allows for a continuous dividend flow with a dividend yield of δ. In that case $S_0 - \text{PV}(\text{Div}) = S_0 e^{-\delta T}$.

However, listed put options on stocks are American options that offer the opportunity of early exercise, and we have seen that the right to exercise puts early can turn out to be valuable. This means that an American put option must be worth more than the corresponding European option. Therefore, Equation 21.2 or 21.3 describes only the lower bound on the true value of the American put. However, in many applications the approximation is very accurate.[12]

21.5   USING THE BLACK–SCHOLES FORMULA

Hedge Ratios and the Black-Scholes Formula

In the last chapter, we considered two investments in FinCorp stock: 100 shares or 1,000 call options. We saw that the call option position was more sensitive to swings in the stock price than was the all-stock position. To analyze the overall exposure to a stock price more precisely, however, it is necessary to quantify these relative sensitivities. A tool that enables us to summarize the overall exposure of portfolios of options with various exercise prices and times to expiration is the hedge ratio. An option's **hedge ratio** is the change in the price of an option for a $1 increase in the stock price. A call option, therefore, has a positive hedge ratio and a put option a negative hedge ratio. The hedge ratio is commonly called the option's **delta.**

If you were to graph the option value as a function of the stock value, as we have done for a call option in Figure 21.9, the hedge ratio is simply the slope of the value curve evaluated at the current stock price. For example, suppose the slope of the curve at $S_0 = \$120$ equals .60. As the stock increases in value by $1, the option increases by approximately $.60, as the figure shows.

[12]For a more complete treatment of American put valuation, see R. Geske and H. E. Johnson, "The American Put Valued Analytically," *Journal of Finance* 39 (December 1984), pp. 1511–24.

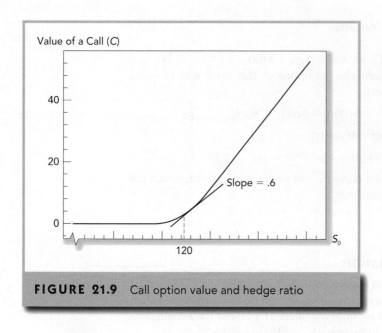

FIGURE 21.9   Call option value and hedge ratio

For every call option written, .60 share of stock would be needed to hedge the investor's portfolio. For example, if one writes 10 options and holds six shares of stock, according to the hedge ratio of .6, a $1 increase in stock price will result in a gain of $6 on the stock holdings, whereas the loss on the 10 options written will be $10 \times \$.60$, an equivalent $6. The stock price movement leaves total wealth unaltered, which is what a hedged position is intended to do. The investor holding the stock and options in proportions dictated by their relative price movements hedges the portfolio.

Black-Scholes hedge ratios are particularly easy to compute. The hedge ratio for a call is $N(d_1)$, whereas the hedge ratio for a put is $N(d_1) - 1$. We defined $N(d_1)$ as part of the Black-Scholes formula in Equation 21.1. Recall that $N(d)$ stands for the area under the standard normal curve up to d. Therefore, the call option hedge ratio must be positive and less than 1.0, whereas the put option hedge ratio is negative and of smaller absolute value than 1.0.

Figure 21.9 verifies the insight that the slope of the call option valuation function is less than 1.0, approaching 1.0 only as the stock price becomes much greater than the exercise price. This tells us that option values change less than one-for-one with changes in stock prices. Why should this be? Suppose an option is so far in the money that you are absolutely certain it will be exercised. In that case, every dollar increase in the stock price would increase the option value by $1. But if there is a reasonable chance the call option will expire out of the money, even after a moderate stock price gain, a $1 increase in the stock price will not necessarily increase the ultimate payoff to the call; therefore, the call price will not respond by a full dollar.

The fact that hedge ratios are less than 1.0 does not contradict our earlier observation that options offer leverage and are sensitive to stock price movements. Although *dollar* movements in option prices are less than dollar movements in the stock price, the *rate of return* volatility of options remains greater than stock return volatility because options sell at lower prices. In our example, with the stock selling at $120, and a hedge ratio of .6, an option with exercise price $120 may sell for $5. If the stock price increases to $121, the call price would be expected to increase by only $.60 to $5.60. The percentage increase in the option value is $\$.60/\$5.00 = 12\%$, however, whereas the stock price increase is only $\$1/\$120 = .83\%$. The ratio of the percentage changes is $12\%/.83\% = 14.4$. For every 1% increase in the stock price, the option price increases by 14.4%. This ratio, the percentage change in option price per percentage change in stock price, is called the **option elasticity.**

The hedge ratio is an essential tool in portfolio management and control. An example will show why.

The spreadsheet below can be used to determine option values using the Black-Scholes model. The inputs are the stock price, standard deviation, expiration of the option, exercise price, risk-free rate, and dividend yield. The call option is valued using Equation 21.1 and the put is valued using Equation 21.3. For both calls and puts, the dividend-adjusted Black-Scholes formula substitutes $Se^{-\delta T}$ for S, as outlined on page 735. The model also calculates the intrinsic and time value for both puts and calls.

Further, the model presents sensitivity analysis using the one-way data table. The first workbook presents the analysis of calls while the second workbook presents similar analysis for puts. You can find these spreadsheets at the Online Learning Center at **www.mhhe.com/bkm.**

	A	B	C	D	E	F	G	H	I	J	K	L	M	N
1	Chapter 21- Black-Scholes Option Pricing						LEGEND:							
2	Call Valuation & Call Time Premiums						Enter data							
3							Value calculated							
4							See comment							
5	Standard deviation (σ)	0.27830												
6	Variance (annual, σ^2)	0.07745			Call			Call			Call			Call
7	Time to expiration (years, T)	0.50		Standard	Option		Standard	Time		Stock	Option		Stock	Time
8	Risk-free rate (annual, r)	6.00%		Deviation	Value		Deviation	Value		Price	Value		Price	Value
9	Current stock price (S_0)	$100.00			7.000			7.000			7.000			7.000
10	Exercise price (X)	$105.00		0.15	3.388		0.150	3.388		$60	0.017		$60	0.017
11	Dividend yield (annual, δ)	0.00%		0.18	4.089		0.175	4.089		$65	0.061		$65	0.061
12				0.20	4.792		0.200	4.792		$70	0.179		$70	0.179
13	d_1	0.0029095		0.23	5.497		0.225	5.497		$75	0.440		$75	0.440
14	d_2	−0.193878		0.25	6.202		0.250	6.202		$80	0.935		$80	0.935
15	$N(d_1)$	0.50116		0.28	6.907		0.275	6.907		$85	1.763		$85	1.763
16	$N(d_2)$	0.42314		0.30	7.612		0.300	7.612		$90	3.014		$90	3.014
17	Black-Scholes call value	$6.99992		0.33	8.317		0.325	8.317		$95	4.750		$95	4.750
18	Black-Scholes put value	$8.89670		0.35	9.022		0.350	9.022		$100	7.000		$100	7.000
19				0.38	9.726		0.375	9.726		$105	9.754		$105	9.754
20				0.40	10.429		0.400	10.429		$110	12.974		$110	7.974
21	Intrinsic value of call	$0.00000		0.43	11.132		0.425	11.132		$115	16.602		$115	6.602
22	Time value of call	6.99992		0.45	11.834		0.450	11.834		$120	20.572		$120	5.572
23				0.48	12.536		0.475	12.536		$125	24.817		$125	4.817
24	Intrinsic value of put	$5.00000		0.50	13.236		0.500	13.236		$130	29.275		$130	4.275
25	Time value of put	3.89670								$135.00	33.893		$135	3.893

EXAMPLE 21.4   Hedge Ratios

Consider two portfolios, one holding 750 IBM calls and 200 shares of IBM and the other holding 800 shares of IBM. Which portfolio has greater dollar exposure to IBM price movements? You can answer this question easily by using the hedge ratio.

Each option changes in value by H dollars for each dollar change in stock price, where H stands for the hedge ratio. Thus, if H equals .6, the 750 options are equivalent to $.6 \times 750 = 450$ shares in terms of the response of their market value to IBM stock price movements. The first portfolio has less dollar sensitivity to stock price change because the 450 share-equivalents of the options plus the 200 shares actually held are less than the 800 shares held in the second portfolio.

This is not to say, however, that the first portfolio is less sensitive to the stock's rate of return. As we noted in discussing option elasticities, the first portfolio may be of lower total value than the second, so despite its lower sensitivity in terms of total market value, it might have greater rate of return sensitivity. Because a call option has a lower market value than the stock, its price changes more than proportionally with stock price changes, even though its hedge ratio is less than 1.0.

CONCEPT CHECK 8

What is the elasticity of a put option currently selling for $4 with exercise price $120 and hedge ratio −.4 if the stock price is currently $122?

Portfolio Insurance

In Chapter 20, we showed that protective put strategies offer a sort of insurance policy on an asset. The protective put has proved to be extremely popular with investors. Even if the asset price falls, the put conveys the right to sell the asset for the exercise price, which is a way to lock in a minimum portfolio value. With an at-the-money put ($X = S_0$), the maximum loss that can be realized is the cost of the put. The asset can be sold for X, which equals its original value, so even if the asset price falls, the investor's net loss over the period is just the cost of the put. If the asset value increases, however, upside potential is unlimited. Figure 21.10 graphs the profit or loss on a protective put position as a function of the change in the value of the underlying asset, P.

While the protective put is a simple and convenient way to achieve **portfolio insurance,** that is, to limit the worst-case portfolio rate of return, there are practical difficulties in trying to insure a portfolio of stocks. First, unless the investor's portfolio corresponds to a standard market index for which puts are traded, a put option on the portfolio will not be available for purchase. And if index puts are used to protect a non-indexed portfolio, tracking error can result. For example, if the portfolio falls in value while the market index rises, the put will fail to provide the intended protection. Tracking error limits the investor's freedom to pursue active stock selection because such error will be greater as the managed portfolio departs more substantially from the market index.

Moreover, the desired horizon of the insurance program must match the maturity of a traded put option in order to establish the appropriate protective put position. Today, long-term options on market indexes and several larger stocks called LEAPS (for *long-term equity anticipation securities*) trade on the CBOE with expirations of several years. However, in the mid-1980s, while most investors pursuing insurance programs had horizons of several years, actively traded puts were limited to expirations of less than a year. Rolling over a sequence of short-term puts, which might be viewed as a response to this problem, introduces new risks because the prices at which successive puts will be available in the future are not known today.

Providers of portfolio insurance who had horizons of several years, therefore, could not rely on the simple expedient of purchasing protective puts for their clients' portfolios. Instead, they followed trading strategies to replicate the payoffs to the protective put position.

Here is the general idea. Even if a put option on the desired portfolio with the desired expiration date does not exist, a theoretical option-pricing model (such as the Black-Scholes model) can be used to determine how that option's price would respond to the portfolio's value if the option did trade. For example, if stock prices were to fall, the put option would increase in value. The option model could quantify this relationship. The net exposure of

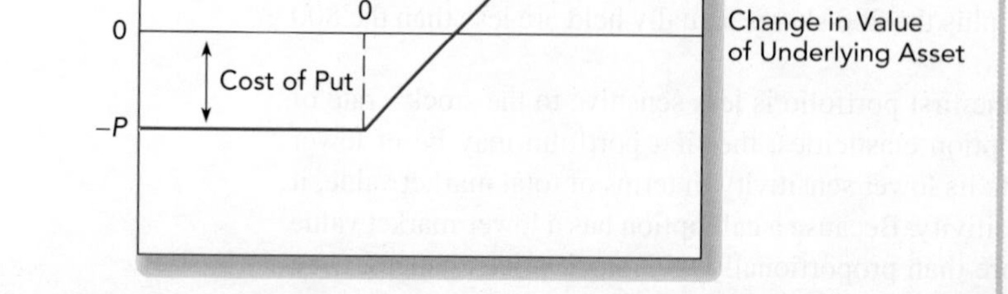

FIGURE 21.10 Profit on a protective put strategy

the (hypothetical) protective put portfolio to swings in stock prices is the sum of the exposures of the two components of the portfolio, the stock and the put. The net exposure of the portfolio equals the equity exposure less the (offsetting) put option exposure.

We can create "synthetic" protective put positions by holding a quantity of stocks with the same net exposure to market swings as the hypothetical protective put position. The key to this strategy is the option delta, or hedge ratio, that is, the change in the price of the protective put option per change in the value of the underlying stock portfolio.

EXAMPLE 21.5 Synthetic Protective Put Options

Suppose a portfolio is currently valued at $100 million. An at-the-money put option on the portfolio might have a hedge ratio or delta of $-.6$, meaning the option's value swings $.60 for every dollar change in portfolio value, but in an opposite direction. Suppose the stock portfolio falls in value by 2%. The profit on a hypothetical protective put position (if the put existed) would be as follows (in millions of dollars):

Loss on stocks:	2% of $100 =	$2.00
Gain on put:	.6 × $2.00 =	1.20
Net loss		= $ .80

We create the synthetic option position by selling a proportion of shares equal to the put option's delta (i.e., selling 60% of the shares) and placing the proceeds in risk-free T-bills. The rationale is that the hypothetical put option would have offset 60% of any change in the stock portfolio's value, so one must reduce portfolio risk directly by selling 60% of the equity and putting the proceeds into a risk-free asset. Total return on a synthetic protective put position with $60 million in risk-free investments such as T-bills and $40 million in equity is

Loss on stocks:	2% of $40 =	$.80
+ Loss on bills:	=	0
Net loss	=	$.80

The synthetic and actual protective put positions have equal returns. We conclude that if you sell a proportion of shares equal to the put option's delta and place the proceeds in cash equivalents, your exposure to the stock market will equal that of the desired protective put position.

The difficulty with this procedure is that deltas constantly change. Figure 21.11 shows that as the stock price falls, the magnitude of the appropriate hedge ratio increases. Therefore, market declines require extra hedging, that is, additional conversion of equity into cash. This constant updating of the hedge ratio is called **dynamic hedging** (alternatively, delta hedging).

Dynamic hedging is one reason portfolio insurance has been said to contribute to market volatility. Market declines trigger additional sales of stock as portfolio insurers strive to increase their hedging. These additional sales are seen as reinforcing or exaggerating market downturns.

In practice, portfolio insurers do not actually buy or sell stocks directly when they update their hedge positions. Instead, they minimize trading costs by buying or selling stock index futures as a substitute for sale of the stocks themselves. As you will see in the next chapter, stock prices and index futures prices usually are very tightly linked by cross-market arbitrageurs so that futures transactions can be used as reliable proxies for stock

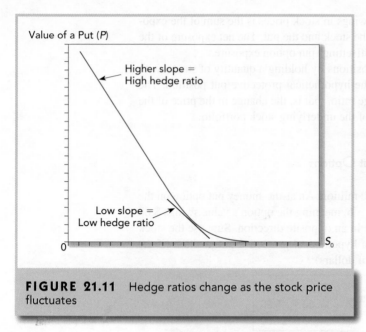

Value of a Put (P)

Higher slope =
High hedge ratio

Low slope =
Low hedge ratio

S_0

FIGURE 21.11   Hedge ratios change as the stock price fluctuates

transactions. Instead of selling equities based on the put option's delta, insurers will sell an equivalent number of futures contracts.[13]

Several portfolio insurers suffered great setbacks during the market crash of October 19, 1987, when the market suffered an unprecedented 1-day loss of about 20%. A description of what happened then should let you appreciate the complexities of applying a seemingly straightforward hedging concept.

1. Market volatility at the crash was much greater than ever encountered before. Put option deltas based on historical experience were too low; insurers underhedged, held too much equity, and suffered excessive losses.

2. Prices moved so fast that insurers could not keep up with the necessary rebalancing. They were "chasing deltas" that kept getting away from them. The futures market also saw a "gap" opening, where the opening price was nearly 10% below the previous day's close. The price dropped before insurers could update their hedge ratios.

3. Execution problems were severe. First, current market prices were unavailable, with trade execution and the price quotation system hours behind, which made computation of correct hedge ratios impossible. Moreover, trading in stocks and stock futures ceased during some periods. The continuous rebalancing capability that is essential for a viable insurance program vanished during the precipitous market collapse.

4. Futures prices traded at steep discounts to their proper levels compared to reported stock prices, thereby making the sale of futures (as a proxy for equity sales) seem expensive. Although you will see in the next chapter that stock index futures prices normally exceed the value of the stock index, Figure 21.12 shows that on October 19, futures sold far below the stock index level. When some insurers gambled that the futures price would recover to its usual premium over the stock index, and chose to defer sales, they remained underhedged. As the market fell farther, their portfolios experienced substantial losses.

Although most observers at the time believed that the portfolio insurance industry would never recover from the market crash, delta hedging is still alive and well on Wall Street. Dynamic hedges are widely used by large firms to hedge potential losses from options positions. For example, the nearby box notes that when Microsoft ended its employee stock option program and J. P. Morgan purchased many already-issued options of Microsoft employees, it was widely expected that Morgan would protect its options position by selling shares in Microsoft in accord with a delta hedging strategy.

---

[13]Notice, however, that the use of index futures reintroduces the problem of tracking error between the portfolio and the market index.

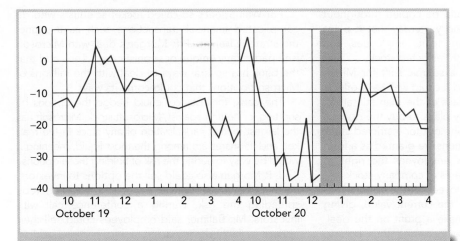

FIGURE 21.12   S&P 500 cash-to-futures spread in points at 15-minute intervals

Note: Trading in futures contracts halted between 12:15 and 1:05.
Source: *The Wall Street Journal*. Reprinted by permission of *The Wall Street Journal*, © 1987 Dow Jones & Company, Inc. All rights reserved worldwide.

Hedging Bets on Mispriced Options

Suppose you believe that the standard deviation of IBM stock returns will be 35% over the next few weeks, but IBM put options are selling at a price consistent with a volatility of 33%. Because the put's implied volatility is less than your forecast of the stock volatility, you believe the option is underpriced. Using your assessment of volatility in an option-pricing model like the Black-Scholes formula, you would estimate that the fair price for the puts exceeds the actual price.

Does this mean that you ought to buy put options? Perhaps it does, but by doing so, you risk losses if IBM stock performs well, *even if* you are correct about the volatility. You would like to separate your bet on volatility from the "attached" bet inherent in purchasing a put that IBM's stock price will fall. In other words, you would like to speculate on the option mispricing by purchasing the put option, but hedge the resulting exposure to the performance of IBM stock.

The option *delta* can be interpreted as a hedge ratio that can be used for this purpose. The delta was defined as

$$\text{Delta} = \frac{\text{Change in value of option}}{\text{Change in value of stock}}$$

Therefore, delta is the slope of the option-pricing curve.

This ratio tells us precisely how many shares of stock we must hold to offset our exposure to IBM. For example, if the delta is $-.6$, then the put will fall by $.60 in value for every one-point increase in IBM stock, and we need to hold .6 share of stock to hedge each put. If we purchase 10 option contracts, each for 100 shares, we would need to buy 600 shares of stock. If the stock price rises by $1, each put option will decrease in value by $.60, resulting in a loss of $600. However, the loss on the puts will be offset by a gain on the stock holdings of $1 per share × 600 shares.

To see how the profits on this strategy might develop, let's use the following example.

J. P. MORGAN ROLLS DICE ON MICROSOFT OPTIONS

Microsoft, in a shift that could be copied throughout the technology business, said yesterday that it plans to stop issuing stock options to its employees, and instead will provide them with restricted stock.

The deal could portend a seismic shift for Microsoft's Silicon Valley rivals, and it could well have effects on Wall Street. Though details of the plan still aren't clear, J. P. Morgan effectively plans to buy the options from Microsoft employees who opt for restricted stock instead. Employee stock options are granted as a form of compensation and allow employees the right to exchange the options for shares of company stock.

The price offered to employees for the options presumably will be lower than the current value, giving J. P. Morgan a chance to make a profit on the deal. Rather than holding the options, and thus betting Microsoft's stock will rise, people familiar with the bank's strategy say J. P. Morgan probably will match each option it buys from the company's employees with a separate trade in the stock market that both hedges the bet and gives itself a margin of profit.

For Wall Street's so-called rocket scientists who do complicated financial transactions such as this one, the strategy behind J. P. Morgan's deal with Microsoft isn't particularly unique or sophisticated. They add that the bank has several ways to deal with the millions of Microsoft options that could come its way.

The bank, for instance, could hedge the options by shorting, or betting against, Microsoft stock. Microsoft has the largest market capitalization of any stock in the market, and its shares are among the most liquid, meaning it would be easy to hedge the risk of holding those options.

J. P. Morgan also could sell the options to investors, much as they would do with a syndicated loan, thereby spreading the risk. During a conference call with investors, Mr. Ballmer said employees could sell their options to "a third party or set of third parties," adding that the company was still working out the details with J. P. Morgan and the SEC.

EXAMPLE 21.6   Speculating on Mispriced Options

Suppose option expiration T is 60 days; put price P is \$4.495; exercise price X is \$90; stock price S is \$90; and the risk-free rate r is 4%. We assume that the stock will not pay a dividend in the next 60 days. Given these data, the implied volatility on the option is 33%, as we posited. However, you believe the true volatility is 35%, implying that the fair put price is \$4.785. Therefore, if the market assessment of volatility is revised to the value you believe is correct, your profit will be \$.29 per put purchased.

Recall that the hedge ratio, or delta, of a put option equals $N(d_1) - 1$, where $N(\bullet)$ is the cumulative normal distribution function and

$$d_1 = \frac{\ln(S/X) + (r + \sigma^2/2)T}{\sigma\sqrt{T}}$$

Using your estimate of $\sigma = .35$, you find that the hedge ratio $N(d_1) - 1 = -.453$.

Suppose, therefore, that you purchase 10 option contracts (1,000 puts) and purchase 453 shares of stock. Once the market "catches up" to your presumably better volatility estimate, the put options purchased will increase in value. If the market assessment of volatility changes as soon as you purchase the options, your profits should equal $1,000 \times \$.29 = \$290$. The option price will be affected as well by any change in the stock price, but this part of your exposure will be eliminated if the hedge ratio is chosen properly. Your profit should be based solely on the effect of the change in the implied volatility of the put, with the impact of the stock price hedged away.

Table 21.3 illustrates your profits as a function of the stock price assuming that the put price changes to reflect *your* estimate of volatility. Panel B shows that the put option alone can provide profits or losses depending on whether the stock price falls or rises. We see in panel C, however, that each *hedged* put option provides profits nearly equal to the original mispricing, regardless of the change in the stock price.

A. Cost to establish hedged position				**TABLE 21.3**
1,000 put options @ $4.495/option	$ 4,495			Profit on hedged
453 shares @ $90/share	40,770			put portfolio
TOTAL outlay	$45,265			

B. Value of put option as a function of the stock price at implied volatility of 35%

Stock Price	89	90	91
Put price	$ 5.254	$ 4.785	$ 4.347
Profit (loss) on each put	0.759	0.290	(0.148)

C. Value of and profit on hedged put portfolio

Stock Price:	89	90	91
Value of 1,000 put options	$ 5,254	$ 4,785	$ 4,347
Value of 453 shares	40,317	40,770	41,223
TOTAL	$45,571	$45,555	$45,570
Profit (= Value − Cost from panel A)	306	290	305

Notice in Example 21.6 that the profit is not exactly independent of the stock price. This is because as the stock price changes, so do the deltas used to calculate the hedge ratio. The hedge ratio in principle

CONCEPT CHECK 9

Suppose you bet on volatility by purchasing calls instead of puts. How would you hedge your exposure to stock-price fluctuations? What is the hedge ratio?

would need to be continually adjusted as deltas evolve. The sensitivity of the delta to the stock price is called the **gamma** of the option. Option gammas are analogous to bond convexity. In both cases, the curvature of the value function means that hedge ratios or durations change with market conditions, making rebalancing a necessary part of hedging strategies.

A variant of the strategy in Example 21.6 involves cross-option speculation. Suppose you observe a 45-day expiration call option on IBM with strike price 95 selling at a price consistent with a volatility of $\sigma = 33\%$ while another 45-day call with strike price 90 has an implied volatility of only 27%. Because the underlying asset and expiration date are identical, you conclude that the call with the higher implied volatility is relatively overpriced. To exploit the mispricing, you might buy the cheap calls (with strike price 90 and implied volatility of 27%) and write the expensive calls (with strike price 95 and implied volatility 33%). If the risk-free rate is 4% and IBM is selling at $90 per share, the calls purchased will be priced at $3.6202 and the calls written will be priced at $2.3735.

Despite the fact that you are long one call and short another, your exposure to IBM stock-price uncertainty will not be hedged using this strategy. This is because calls with different strike prices have different sensitivities to the price of the underlying asset. The lower-strike-price call has a higher delta and therefore greater exposure to the price of IBM. If you take an equal number of positions in these two options, you will inadvertently establish a bullish position in IBM, as the calls you purchase have higher deltas than the calls you write. In fact, you may recall from Chapter 20 that this portfolio (long call with low exercise price and short call with high exercise price) is called a *bullish spread*.

To establish a hedged position, we can use the hedge ratio approach as follows. Consider the 95-strike-price options you write as the asset that hedges your exposure to the 90-strike-price options your purchase. Then the hedge ratio is

$$H = \frac{\text{Change in value of 90-strike-price call for \$1 change in IBM}}{\text{Change in value of 95-strike-price call for \$1 change in IBM}}$$

$$= \frac{\text{Delta of 90-strike-price call}}{\text{Delta of 95-strike-price call}} > 1$$

You need to write *more* than one call with the higher strike price to hedge the purchase of each call with the lower strike price. Because the prices of higher-strike-price calls are less sensitive to IBM prices, more of them are required to offset the exposure.

Suppose the true annual volatility of the stock is midway between the two implied volatilities, so $\sigma = 30\%$. We know that the delta of a call option is $N(d_1)$. Therefore, the deltas of the two options and the hedge ratio are computed as follows:

Option with strike price 90:

$$d_1 = \frac{\ln(90/90) + (.04 + .30^2/2) \times 45/365}{.30\sqrt{45/365}} = .0995$$

$$N(d_1) = .5396$$

Option with strike price 95:

$$d_1 = \frac{\ln(90/95) + (.04 + .30^2/2) \times 45/365}{.30\sqrt{45/365}} = -.4138$$

$$N(d_1) = .3395$$

Hedge ratio:

$$\frac{.5396}{.3395} = 1.589$$

Therefore, for every 1,000 call options purchased with strike price 90, we need to write 1,589 call options with strike price 95. Following this strategy enables us to bet on the relative mispricing of the two options without taking a position on IBM. Panel A of Table 21.4 shows that the position will result in a cash inflow of $151.30. The premium income on the calls written exceeds the cost of the calls purchased.

When you establish a position in stocks and options that is hedged with respect to fluctuations in the price of the underlying asset, your portfolio is said to be **delta neutral,** meaning that the portfolio has no tendency to either increase or decrease in value when the stock price fluctuates.

Let's check that our options position is in fact delta neutral. Suppose that the implied volatilities of the two options come back into alignment just after you establish your position, so that both options are priced at implied volatilities of 30%. You expect to profit from the increase in the value of the call purchased as well as from the decrease in the value of the call written. The option prices at 30% volatility are given in panel B of Table 21.4 and the values of your position for various stock prices are presented in panel C. Although the profit or loss on each option is affected by the stock price, the value of the delta-neutral option portfolio is positive and essentially independent of the price of IBM. Moreover, we saw in panel A that the portfolio would have been established without ever requiring a cash outlay. You would have cash inflows both

A. Cost flow when portfolio Is established			
Purchase 1,000 calls ($X = 90$) @ $3.6202 (option priced at implied volatility of 27%)	$3,620.20 cash outflow		
Write 1,589 calls ($X = 95$) @ $2.3735 (option priced at implied volatility of 33%)	3,771.50 cash inflow		
TOTAL	$ 151.30 net cash inflow		

TABLE 21.4

Profits on delta-neutral options portfolio

B. Option prices at implied volatility of 30%

Stock Price:	89	90	91
90-strike-price calls	$3.478	$3.997	$4.557
95-strike-price calls	1.703	2.023	2.382

C. Value of portfolio after implied volatilities converge to 30%

Stock Price:	89	90	91
Value of 1,000 calls held	$3,478	$3,997	$4,557
− Value of 1,589 calls written	2,705	3,214	3,785
TOTAL	$ 773	$ 782	$ 772

when you establish the portfolio *and* when you liquidate it after the implied volatilities converge to 30%.

This unusual profit opportunity arises because you have identified prices out of alignment. Such opportunities could not arise if prices were at equilibrium levels. By exploiting the pricing discrepancy using a delta-neutral strategy, you should earn profits regardless of the price movement in IBM stock.

Delta-neutral hedging strategies are also subject to practical problems, the most important of which is the difficulty in assessing the proper volatility for the coming period. If the volatility estimate is incorrect, so will be the deltas, and the overall position will not truly be hedged. Moreover, option or option-plus-stock positions generally will not be neutral with respect to changes in volatility. For example, a put option hedged by a stock might be delta neutral, but it is not volatility neutral. Changes in the market assessments of volatility will affect the option price even if the stock price is unchanged.

These problems can be serious, because volatility estimates are never fully reliable. First, volatility cannot be observed directly and must be estimated from past data which imparts measurement error to the forecast. Second, we've seen that both historical and implied volatilities fluctuate over time. Therefore, we are always shooting at a moving target. Although delta-neutral positions are hedged against changes in the price of the underlying asset, they still are subject to **volatility risk,** the risk incurred from unpredictable changes in volatility. Thus, although delta-neutral option hedges might eliminate exposure to risk from fluctuations in the value of the underlying asset, they do not eliminate volatility risk.

21.6   EMPIRICAL EVIDENCE ON OPTION PRICING

There have been an enormous number of empirical tests of the Black-Scholes option-pricing model. For the most part, the results of the studies have been positive in that the Black-Scholes model generates option values fairly close to the actual prices at which options trade. At the same time, some regular empirical failures of the model have been noted.

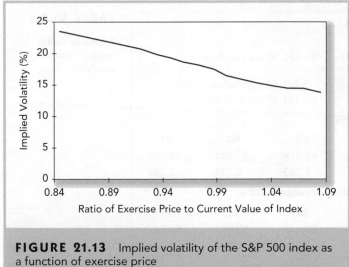

FIGURE 21.13 Implied volatility of the S&P 500 index as a function of exercise price

Source: Mark Rubinstein, "Implied Binomial Trees," *Journal of Finance* (July 1994), pp. 771–818.

Whaley[14] examined the performance of the Black-Scholes formula relative to that of more complicated option formulas that allow for early exercise. His findings indicate that formulas allowing for the possibility of early exercise do better at pricing than the Black-Scholes formula. The Black-Scholes formula seems to perform worst for options on stocks with high dividend payouts. The true American call option formula, on the other hand, seems to fare equally well in the prediction of option prices on stocks with high or low dividend payouts.

Rubinstein has emphasized a more serious problem with the Black-Scholes model.[15] If the model were accurate, the implied volatility of all options on a particular stock with the same expiration date would be equal—after all, the underlying asset and expiration date are the same for each option, so the volatility inferred from each also ought to be the same. But in fact, when one actually plots implied volatility as a function of exercise price, the typical results appear as in Figure 21.13, which treats S&P 500 index options as the underlying asset. Implied volatility steadily falls as the exercise price rises. Clearly, the Black-Scholes model is missing something.

Rubinstein suggests that the problem with the model has to do with fears of a market crash like that of October 1987. The idea is that deep out-of-the-money puts would be nearly worthless if stock prices evolve smoothly, because the probability of the stock falling by a large amount (and the put option thereby moving into the money) in a short time would be very small. But a possibility of a sudden large downward jump that could move the puts into the money, as in a market crash, would impart greater value to these options. Thus, the market might price these options as though there is a bigger chance of a large drop in the stock price than would be suggested by the Black-Scholes assumptions. The result of the higher option price is a greater implied volatility derived from the Black-Scholes model.

Interestingly, Rubinstein points out that prior to the 1987 market crash, plots of implied volatility like the one in Figure 21.13 were relatively flat, consistent with the notion that the market was then less attuned to fears of a crash. However, postcrash plots have been consistently downward sloping, exhibiting a shape often called the *option smirk*. When we use option-pricing models that allow for more general stock price distributions, including jumps and random changes in volatility, they generate downward-sloping implied volatility curves similar to the one observed in Figure 21.13.[16]

[14]Robert E. Whaley, "Valuation of American Call Options on Dividend-Paying Stocks: Empirical Tests," *Journal of Financial Economics* 10 (1982).

[15]Mark Rubinstein, "Implied Binomial Trees," *Journal of Finance* 49 (July 1994), pp. 771–818.

[16]For an extensive discussion of these more general models, see R. L. McDonald, *Derivatives Markets,* 2nd ed. (Boston: Pearson Education [Addison-Wesley], 2006).

1. Option values may be viewed as the sum of intrinsic value plus time or "volatility" value. The volatility value is the right to choose not to exercise if the stock price moves against the holder. Thus the option holder cannot lose more than the cost of the option regardless of stock price performance.

2. Call options are more valuable when the exercise price is lower, when the stock price is higher, when the interest rate is higher, when the time to expiration is greater, when the stock's volatility is greater, and when dividends are lower.

3. Call options must sell for at least the stock price less the present value of the exercise price and dividends to be paid before expiration. This implies that a call option on a non-dividend-paying stock may be sold for more than the proceeds from immediate exercise. Thus European calls are worth as much as American calls on stocks that pay no dividends, because the right to exercise the American call early has no value.

4. Options may be priced relative to the underlying stock price using a simple two-period, two-state pricing model. As the number of periods increases, the binomial model can approximate more realistic stock price distributions. The Black-Scholes formula may be seen as a limiting case of the binomial option model, as the holding period is divided into progressively smaller subperiods when the interest rate and stock volatility are constant.

5. The Black-Scholes formula applies to options on stocks that pay no dividends. Dividend adjustments may be adequate to price European calls on dividend-paying stocks, but the proper treatment of American calls on dividend-paying stocks requires more complex formulas.

6. Put options may be exercised early, whether the stock pays dividends or not. Therefore, American puts generally are worth more than European puts.

7. European put values can be derived from the call value and the put-call parity relationship. This technique cannot be applied to American puts for which early exercise is a possibility.

8. The implied volatility of an option is the standard deviation of stock returns consistent with an option's market price. It can be backed out of an option-pricing model by finding the stock volatility that makes the option's value equal to its observed price.

9. The hedge ratio is the number of shares of stock required to hedge the price risk involved in writing one option. Hedge ratios are near zero for deep out-of-the-money call options and approach 1.0 for deep in-the-money calls.

10. Although hedge ratios are less than 1.0, call options have elasticities greater than 1.0. The rate of return on a call (as opposed to the dollar return) responds more than one-for-one with stock price movements.

11. Portfolio insurance can be obtained by purchasing a protective put option on an equity position. When the appropriate put is not traded, portfolio insurance entails a dynamic hedge strategy where a fraction of the equity portfolio equal to the desired put option's delta is sold and placed in risk-free securities.

12. The option delta is used to determine the hedge ratio for options positions. Delta-neutral portfolios are independent of price changes in the underlying asset. Even delta-neutral option portfolios are subject to volatility risk, however.

13. Empirically, implied volatilities derived from the Black-Scholes formula tend to be lower on options with higher exercise prices. This may be evidence that the option prices reflect the possibility of a sudden dramatic decline in stock prices. Such "crashes" are inconsistent with the Black-Scholes assumptions.

Related Web site for this chapter are available at **www.mhhe.com/bkm**

KEY TERMS

intrinsic value	pseudo-American call option	portfolio insurance
time value	value	dynamic hedging
binomial model	hedge ratio	gamma
Black-Scholes pricing formula	delta	delta neutral
implied volatility	option elasticity	volatility risk

18. If the time to expiration falls and the put price rises, then what has happened to the put option's implied volatility?

19. According to the Black-Scholes formula, what will be the value of the hedge ratio of a call option as the stock price becomes infinitely large? Explain briefly.

20. According to the Black-Scholes formula, what will be the value of the hedge ratio of a put option for a very small exercise price?

21. The hedge ratio of an at-the-money call option on IBM is .4. The hedge ratio of an at-the-money put option is −.6. What is the hedge ratio of an at-the-money straddle position on IBM?

22. Consider a 6-month expiration European call option with exercise price $105. The underlying stock sells for $100 a share and pays no dividends. The risk-free rate is 5%. What is the implied volatility of the option if the option currently sells for $8? Use Spreadsheet 21.1 (available at **www.mhhe.com/bkm;** link to Chapter 21 material) to answer this question.

   a. Go to the Tools menu of the spreadsheet and select Goal Seek. The dialog box will ask you for three pieces of information. In that dialog box, you should *set cell E6 to value 8 by changing cell* B2. In other words, you ask the spreadsheet to find the value of standard deviation (which appears in cell B2) that forces the value of the option (in cell E6) equal to $8. Then click OK, and you should find that the call is now worth $8, and the entry for standard deviation has been changed to a level consistent with this value. This is the call's implied standard deviation at a price of $8.
   b. What happens to implied volatility if the option is selling at $9? Why has implied volatility increased?
   c. What happens to implied volatility if the option price is unchanged at $8, but option expiration is lower, say only 4 months? Why?
   d. What happens to implied volatility if the option price is unchanged at $8, but the exercise price is lower, say, only $100? Why?
   e. What happens to implied volatility if the option price is unchanged at $8, but the stock price is lower, say, only $98? Why?

23. A collar is established by buying a share of stock for $50, buying a 6-month put option with exercise price $45, and writing a 6-month call option with exercise price $55. Based on the volatility of the stock, you calculate that for a strike price of $45 and expiration of 6 months, $N(d_1) = .60$, whereas for the exercise price of $55, $N(d_1) = .35$.

   a. What will be the gain or loss on the collar if the stock price increases by $1?
   b. What happens to the delta of the portfolio if the stock price becomes very large? Very small?

24. These three put options are all written on the same stock. One has a delta of −.9, one a delta of −.5, and one a delta of −.1. Assign deltas to the three puts by filling in this table.

Put	X	Delta
A	10	
B	20	
C	30	

25. You are *very* bullish (optimistic) on stock EFG, much more so than the rest of the market. In each question, choose the portfolio strategy that will give you the biggest dollar profit if your bullish forecast turns out to be correct. Explain your answer.

   a. *Choice A:* $10,000 invested in calls with X = 50.
      Choice B: $10,000 invested in EFG stock.
   b. *Choice A:* 10 call option contracts (for 100 shares each), with X = 50.
      Choice B: 1,000 shares of EFG stock.

26. You would like to be holding a protective put position on the stock of XYZ Co. to lock in a guaranteed minimum value of $100 at year-end. XYZ currently sells for $100. Over the next year the stock price will increase by 10% or decrease by 10%. The T-bill rate is 5%. Unfortunately, no put options are traded on XYZ Co.

a. Suppose the desired put option were traded. How much would it cost to purchase?

b. What would have been the cost of the protective put portfolio?

c. What portfolio position in stock and T-bills will ensure you a payoff equal to the payoff that would be provided by a protective put with $X = 100$? Show that the payoff to this portfolio and the cost of establishing the portfolio matches that of the desired protective put.

27. Return to Example 21.1. Use the binomial model to value a 1-year European put option with exercise price $110 on the stock in that example. Does your solution for the put price satisfy put-call parity?

28. Suppose that the risk-free interest rate is zero. Would an American put option ever be exercised early? Explain.

29. Let $p(S, T, X)$ denote the value of a European put on a stock selling at S dollars, with time to maturity T, and with exercise price X, and let $P(S, T, X)$ be the value of an American put.

a. Evaluate $p(0, T, X)$.

b. Evaluate $P(0, T, X)$.

c. Evaluate $p(S, T, 0)$.

d. Evaluate $P(S, T, 0)$.

e. What does your answer to (*b*) tell you about the possibility that American puts may be exercised early?

30. You are attempting to value a call option with an exercise price of $100 and 1 year to expiration. The underlying stock pays no dividends, its current price is $100, and you believe it has a 50% chance of increasing to $120 and a 50% chance of decreasing to $80. The risk-free rate of interest is 10%. Calculate the call option's value using the two-state stock price model.

31. Consider an increase in the volatility of the stock in the previous problem. Suppose that if the stock increases in price, it will increase to $130, and that if it falls, it will fall to $70. Show that the value of the call option is now higher than the value derived in the previous problem.

32. Calculate the value of a put option with exercise price $100 using the data in Problem 30. Show that put-call parity is satisfied by your solution.

33. XYZ Corp. will pay a $2 per share dividend in 2 months. Its stock price currently is $60 per share. A call option on XYZ has an exercise price of $55 and 3-month time to expiration. The risk-free interest rate is .5% per month, and the stock's volatility (standard deviation) = 7% per month. Find the pseudo-American option value. (Hint: Try defining one "period" as a month, rather than as a year.)

34. "The beta of a call option on General Motors is greater than the beta of a share of General Motors." True or false?

35. "The beta of a call option on the S&P 500 index with an exercise price of 1,330 is greater than the beta of a call on the index with an exercise price of 1,340." True or false?

36. What will happen to the hedge ratio of a convertible bond as the stock price becomes very large?

37. Salomon Brothers believes that market volatility will be 20% annually for the next 3 years. Three-year at-the-money call and put options on the market index sell at an implied volatility of 22%. What options portfolio can Salomon Brothers establish to speculate on its volatility belief without taking a bullish or bearish position on the market? Using Salomon's estimate of volatility, 3-year at-the-money options have $N(d_1) = .6$.

38. You are holding call options on a stock. The stock's beta is .75, and you are concerned that the stock market is about to fall. The stock is currently selling for $5 and you hold 1 million options on the stock (i.e., you hold 10,000 contracts for 100 shares each). The option delta is .8. How much of the market index portfolio must you buy or sell to hedge your market exposure?

39. Imagine you are a provider of portfolio insurance. You are establishing a 4-year program. The portfolio you manage is currently worth $100 million, and you hope to provide a minimum return of 0%. The equity portfolio has a standard deviation of 25% per year, and T-bills pay 5%

Challenge Problems

per year. Assume for simplicity that the portfolio pays no dividends (or that all dividends are reinvested).

   a. How much should be placed in bills? How much in equity?
   b. What should the manager do if the stock portfolio falls by 3% on the first day of trading?

40. Suppose that call options on ExxonMobil stock with time to expiration 3 months and strike price $60 are selling at an implied volatility of 30%. ExxonMobil stock currently is $60 per share, and the risk-free rate is 4%. If you believe the true volatility of the stock is 32%, how can you trade on your belief without taking on exposure to the performance of ExxonMobil? How many shares of stock will you hold for each option contract purchased or sold?

41. Using the data in the previous problem, suppose that 3-month put options with a strike price of $60 are selling at an implied volatility of 34%. Construct a delta-neutral portfolio comprising positions in calls and puts that will profit when the option prices come back into alignment.

42. Suppose that Salomon Brothers sells call options on $1.25 million worth of a stock portfolio with beta = 1.5. The option delta is .8. It wishes to hedge out its resultant exposure to a market advance by buying a market index portfolio.

   a. How many dollars worth of the market index portfolio should Salomon Brothers purchase to hedge its position?
   b. What if Salomon instead uses market index puts to hedge its exposure? Should it buy or sell puts? Each put option is on 100 units of the index, and the index at current prices represents $1,000 worth of stock.

1. The board of directors of Abco Company is concerned about the downside risk of a $100 million equity portfolio in its pension plan. The board's consultant has proposed temporarily (for 1 month) hedging the portfolio with either futures or options. Referring to the following table, the consultant states:

   a. "The $100 million equity portfolio can be fully protected on the downside by selling (shorting) 2,000 futures contracts."
   b. "The cost of this protection is that the portfolio's expected rate of return will be zero percent."

Market, Portfolio, and Contract Data

Equity index level	99.00
Equity futures price	100.00
Futures contract multiplier	$500
Portfolio beta	1.20
Contract expiration (months)	3

Critique the accuracy of each of the consultant's two statements.

2. Michael Weber, CFA, is analyzing several aspects of option valuation, including the determinants of the value of an option, the characteristics of various models used to value options, and the potential for divergence of calculated option values from observed market prices.

   a. What is the expected effect on the value of a call option on common stock if the volatility of the underlying stock price decreases? If the time to expiration of the option increases?
   b. Using the Black-Scholes option-pricing model, Weber calculates the price of a 3-month call option and notices the option's calculated value is different from its market price. With respect to Weber's use of the Black-Scholes option-pricing model,

      i. Discuss why the calculated value of an out-of-the-money European option may differ from its market price.
      ii. Discuss why the calculated value of an American option may differ from its market price.

3. Joel Franklin is a portfolio manager responsible for derivatives. Franklin observes an American-style option and a European-style option with the same strike price, expiration, and underlying stock. Franklin believes that the European-style option will have a higher premium than the American-style option.

   a. Critique Franklin's belief that the European-style option will have a higher premium. Franklin is asked to value a 1-year European-style call option for Abaco Ltd. common stock, which last traded at $43.00. He has collected the information in the following table.

Closing stock price	$43.00
Call and put option exercise price	45.00
1-year put option price	4.00
1-year Treasury bill rate	5.50%
Time to expiration	One year

   b. Calculate, using put-call parity and the information provided in the table, the European-style call option value.

   c. State the effect, if any, of each of the following three variables on the value of a call option. (No calculations required.)

      i. An increase in short-term interest rate.

      ii. An increase in stock price volatility.

      iii. A decrease in time to option expiration.

4. A stock index is currently trading at 50. Paul Tripp, CFA, wants to value 2-year index options using the binomial model. The stock will either increase in value by 20% or fall in value by 20%. The annual risk-free interest rate is 6%. No dividends are paid on any of the underlying securities in the index.

   a. Construct a two-period binomial tree for the value of the stock index.

   b. Calculate the value of a European call option on the index with an exercise price of 60.

   c. Calculate the value of a European put option on the index with an exercise price of 60.

   d. Confirm that your solutions for the values of the call and the put satisfy put-call parity.

5. Ken Webster manages a $200 million equity portfolio benchmarked to the S&P 500 index. Over the past 2 years, the S&P 500 index has appreciated considerably. Webster believes the market is overvalued when measured by several traditional fundamental/economic indicators. He is concerned about maintaining the excellent gains the portfolio has experienced in the past 2 years but recognizes that the S&P 500 index could still move above its current 1336 level.

   Webster is considering the following *option collar* strategy:

   - Protection for the portfolio can be attained by purchasing an S&P 500 index put with a strike price of 1330 (just out of the money).
   - The put can be financed by selling two 1350 calls (farther out-of-the-money) for every put purchased.
   - Because the combined delta of the two calls (see following table) is less than 1 (that is, $2 \times 0.36 = 0.72$) the options will not lose more than the underlying portfolio will gain if the market advances.

   The information in the following table describes the two options used to create the collar.

Characteristics	1350 Call	1330 Put
Option price	$8.60	$16.10
Option implied volatility	11.00%	14.00%
Option's delta	0.36	−0.44
Contracts needed for collar	602	301

   Notes:
   - Ignore transaction costs.
   - S&P 500 historical 30-day volatility = 12.00%.
   - Time to option expiration = 30 days.

a. Describe the potential returns of the combined portfolio (the underlying portfolio plus the option collar) if after 30 days the S&P 500 index has:

   i. risen approximately 5% to 1402.
   ii. remained at 1336 (no change).
   iii. declined by approximately 5% to 1270.
   (No calculations are necessary.)

b. Discuss the effect on the hedge ratio (delta) of *each* option as the S&P 500 approaches the level for *each* of the potential outcomes listed in part (*a*).

c. Evaluate the pricing of *each* of the following in relation to the volatility data provided:

   i. the put
   ii. the call

STANDARD &POOR'S

Option traders love stock volatility. (Why?) From the Market Insight entry page **(www.mhhe.com/edumarketinsight)**, link to *Industry,* then locate the Airlines industry. Review the *Industry Profile* for a measure of high and low stock prices over the last year. Are airline companies' prices more or less volatile than the market in general, as measured by the S&P 500? Next review the S&P Industry Survey for the airlines industry. What factors associated with the industry have produced the recent stock price volatility? Do a similar analysis for the Regional Banks industry. How does its volatility compare to that of the Airlines industry? Are the results what you expected? Why? In the Black-Scholes valuation model, how is volatility associated with option value? What options strategies exploit volatility?

E-Investments

Option Price Differences

Select a stock for which options are listed on the CBOE Web site **(www.cboe.com)**. The price data for captions can be found on the "delayed quotes" menu option. Enter a ticker symbol for a stock of your choice and pull up its option price data.

Using daily price data from **finance.yahoo.com** calculate the annualized standard deviation of the daily percentage change in the stock price. Create a Black-Scholes option-pricing model in a spreadsheet, or use our Spreadsheet 21.1, available at **www.mhhe.com/bkm** with Chapter 21 material. Using the standard deviation and a risk-free rate found at **www.bloomberg.com/markets/rates/index.html,** calculate the value of the call options.

How do the calculated values compare to the market prices of the options? On the basis of the difference between the price you calculated using historical volatility and the actual price of the option, what do you conclude about expected trends in market volatility?

SOLUTIONS TO CONCEPT CHECKS

1.

If This Variable Increases . . .	The Value of a Put Option
S	Decreases
X	Increases
σ	Increases
T	Increases*
r_f	Decreases
Dividend payouts	Increases

*For American puts, increase in time to expiration must increase value. One can always choose to exercise early if this is optimal; the longer expiration date simply expands the range of alternatives open to the option holder which must make the option more valuable. For a European put, where early exercise is not allowed, longer time to expiration can have an indeterminate effect. Longer expiration increases volatility value because the final stock price is more uncertain, but it reduces the present value of the exercise price that will be received if the put is exercised. The net effect on put value is ambiguous.

To understand the impact of higher volatility, consider the same scenarios as for the call. The low volatility scenario yields a lower expected payoff.

High	Stock price	$10	$20	$30	$40	$50
volatility	Put payoff	$20	$10	$ 0	$ 0	$ 0
Low	Stock price	$20	$25	$30	$35	$40
volatility	Put payoff	$10	$ 5	$ 0	$ 0	$ 0

2. The parity relationship assumes that all options are held until expiration and that there are no cash flows until expiration. These assumptions are valid only in the special case of European options on non-dividend-paying stocks. If the stock pays no dividends, the American and European calls are equally valuable, whereas the American put is worth more than the European put. Therefore, although the parity theorem for European options states that

$$P = C - S_0 + PV(X)$$

in fact, P will be *greater* than this value if the put is American.

3. Because the option now is underpriced, we want to reverse our previous strategy.

	Initial Cash Flow	Cash Flow in 1 Year for Each Possible Stock Price	
		$S = 90$	$S = 120$
Buy 3 options	−16.50	0	30
Short-sell 1 share; repay in 1 year	100	−90	−120
Lend $83.50 at 10% interest rate	−83.50	91.85	91.85
TOTAL	0	1.85	1.85

The riskless cash flow in 1 year per option is $1.85/3 = $.6167, and the present value is $.6167/1.10 = $.56, precisely the amount by which the option is underpriced.

4. *a.* $C_u - C_d = \$6.984 - 0$

   b. $uS_0 - dS_0 = \$110 - \$95 = \$15$

   c. $6.984/15 = .4656$

d.

Action Today (time 0)	Value in Next Period As Function of Stock Price	
	$dS_0 = \$95$	$uS_0 = \$110$
Buy .4656 shares at price $S_0 = \$100$	$44.232	$51.216
Write 1 call at price C_0	0	−6.984
TOTAL	$44.232	$44.232

The portfolio must have a market value equal to the present value of $44.232.

e. $\$44.232/1.05 = \$42.126$

f. $.4656 \times \$100 - C_0 = \$42.126$

$C_0 = \$46.56 - \$42.126 = \$4.434$

5. Higher. For deep out-of-the-money call options, an increase in the stock price still leaves the option unlikely to be exercised. Its value increases only fractionally. For deep in-the-money options, exercise is likely, and option holders benefit by a full dollar for each dollar increase in the stock, as though they already own the stock.

6. Because $\sigma = .6$, $\sigma^2 = .36$.

$$d_1 = \frac{\ln(100/95) + (.10 + .36/2).25}{.6\sqrt{.25}} = .4043$$

$$d_2 = d_1 - .6\sqrt{.25} = .1043$$

Using Table 21.2 and interpolation, or from a spreadsheet function:

$$N(d_1) = .6570$$
$$N(d_2) = .5415$$
$$C = 100 \times .6570 - 95e^{-.10 \times .25} \times .5415 = 15.53$$

7. Implied volatility exceeds .2783. Given a standard deviation of .2783, the option value is $7. A higher volatility is needed to justify an $8 price. Using Spreadsheet 21.1 and Goal Seek, you can confirm that implied volatility at an option price of $8 is .3138.

8. A $1 increase in stock price is a percentage increase of $1/122 = .82\%$. The put option will fall by $(.4 \times \$1) = \$.40$, a percentage decrease of $\$.40/\$4 = 10\%$. Elasticity is $-10/.82 = -12.2$.

9. The delta for a call option is $N(d_1)$, which is positive, and in this case is .547. Therefore, for every 10 option contracts purchased, you would need to *short* 547 shares of stock.

CHAPTER TWENTY-TWO

FUTURES MARKETS

FUTURES AND FORWARD contracts are like options in that they specify purchase or sale of some underlying security at some future date. The key difference is that the holder of an option is not compelled to buy or sell, and will not do so if the trade is unprofitable. A futures or forward contract, however, carries the obligation to go through with the agreed-upon transaction.

A forward contract is not an investment in the strict sense that funds are paid for an asset. It is only a commitment today to transact in the future. Forward arrangements are part of our study of investments, however, because they offer powerful means to hedge other investments and generally modify portfolio characteristics.

Forward markets for future delivery of various commodities go back at least to ancient Greece. Organized *futures markets*, though, are a relatively modern development, dating only to the 19th century. Futures markets replace informal forward contracts with highly standardized, exchange-traded securities.

While futures markets have their roots in agricultural products and commodities, the markets today are dominated by trading in financial futures such as those on stock indices, interest-rate-dependent securities such as government bonds, and foreign exchange. The markets themselves also have changed. An ever-greater proportion of futures trading is conducted electronically, and this trend seems sure to continue.

This chapter describes the workings of futures markets and the mechanics of trading in these markets. We show how futures contracts are useful investment vehicles for both hedgers and speculators and how the futures price relates to the spot price of an asset. We also show how futures can be used in several risk-management applications. This chapter deals with general principles of future markets. Chapter 23 describes specific futures markets in greater detail.

22.1   THE FUTURES CONTRACT

To see how futures and forwards work and how they might be useful, consider the portfolio diversification problem facing a farmer growing a single crop, let us say wheat. The entire planting season's revenue depends critically on the highly volatile crop price. The farmer can't easily diversify his position because virtually his entire wealth is tied up in the crop.

The miller who must purchase wheat for processing faces a portfolio problem that is the mirror image of the farmer's. He is subject to profit uncertainty because of the unpredictable future cost of the wheat.

Both parties can reduce this source of risk if they enter into a **forward contract** requiring the farmer to deliver the wheat when harvested at a price agreed upon now, regardless of the market price at harvest time. No money need change hands at this time. A forward contract is simply a deferred-delivery sale of some asset with the sales price agreed on now. All that is required is that each party be willing to lock in the ultimate price to be paid or received for delivery of the commodity. A forward contract protects each party from future price fluctuations.

Futures markets formalize and standardize forward contracting. Buyers and sellers trade in a centralized futures exchange. The exchange standardizes the types of contracts that may be traded: It establishes contract size, the acceptable grade of commodity, contract delivery dates, and so forth. Although standardization eliminates much of the flexibility available in forward contracting, it has the offsetting advantage of liquidity because many traders will concentrate on the same small set of contracts. Futures contracts also differ from forward contracts in that they call for a daily settling up of any gains or losses on the contract. In the case of forward contracts, no money changes hands until the delivery date.

The centralized market, standardization of contracts, and depth of trading in each contract allows futures positions to be liquidated easily through a broker rather than personally renegotiated with the other party to the contract. Because the exchange guarantees the performance of each party to the contract, costly credit checks on other traders are not necessary. Instead, each trader simply posts a good-faith deposit, called the *margin,* in order to guarantee contract performance.

The Basics of Futures Contracts

The futures contract calls for delivery of a commodity at a specified delivery or maturity date, for an agreed-upon price, called the **futures price,** to be paid at contract maturity. The contract specifies precise requirements for the commodity. For agricultural commodities, the exchange sets allowable grades (e.g., No. 2 hard winter wheat or No. 1 soft red wheat). The place or means of delivery of the commodity is specified as well. Delivery of agricultural commodities is made by transfer of warehouse receipts issued by approved warehouses. In the case of financial futures, delivery may be made by wire transfer; in the case of index futures, delivery may be accomplished by a cash settlement procedure such as those for index options. Although the futures contract technically calls for delivery of an asset, delivery rarely occurs. Instead, parties to the contract much more commonly close out their positions before contract maturity, taking gains or losses in cash.

Because the futures exchange specifies all the terms of the contract, the traders need bargain only over the futures price. The trader taking the **long position** commits to purchasing the commodity on the delivery date. The trader who takes the **short position** commits to delivering the commodity at contract maturity. The trader in the long position is said to "buy" a contract; the short-side trader "sells" a contract. The words *buy* and *sell* are figurative only, because a contract is not really bought or sold like a stock or bond; it is entered into by mutual agreement. At the time the contract is entered into, no money changes hands.

Figure 22.1 shows prices for several futures contracts as they appear in *The Wall Street Journal.* The boldface heading lists in each case the commodity, the exchange where the futures contract is traded in parentheses, the contract size, and the pricing unit. The first agricultural contract listed is for corn, traded on the Chicago Board of Trade (CBT). (The CBT merged with the Chicago Mercantile Exchange in 2007, but for now, maintains a separate identity.) Each contract calls for delivery of 5,000 bushels, and prices in the entry are quoted in cents per bushel.

The next several rows detail price data for contracts expiring on various dates. The March 2008 maturity corn contract, for example, opened during the day at a futures price of 450 cents per bushel. The highest futures price during the day was 457, the lowest was 447.75, and the settlement price (a representative trading price during the last few minutes of trading) was 455.50. The settlement price increased by 3.50 cents from the previous trading day. Finally, open interest, or the number of outstanding contracts, was 597,895. Similar information is given for each maturity date.

The trader holding the long position, that is, the person who will purchase the good, profits from price increases. Suppose that when the contract matures in March, the price of corn turns out to be 460.50 cents per bushel. The long-position trader who entered the contract at the futures price of 455.50 cents earns a profit of 5 cents per bushel: The eventual price is 5 cents higher than the originally agreed-to futures price. As each contract calls for delivery of 5,000 bushels, the profit to the long position equals $5,000 \times \$.05 = \$250$ per contract. Conversely, the short position loses 5 cents per bushel. The short position's loss equals the long position's gain.

To summarize, at maturity:

$$\text{Profit to long} = \text{Spot price at maturity} - \text{Original futures price}$$
$$\text{Profit to short} = \text{Original futures price} - \text{Spot price at maturity}$$

where the spot price is the actual market price of the commodity at the time of the delivery.

The futures contract is, therefore, a *zero-sum game,* with losses and gains to all positions netting out to zero. Every long position is offset by a short position. The aggregate profits to futures trading, summing over all investors, also must be zero, as is the net exposure to changes in the commodity price. For this reason, the establishment of a futures market in a commodity should not have a major impact on prices in the spot market for that commodity.

Figure 22.2, panel A, is a plot of the profits realized by an investor who enters the long side of a futures contract as a function of the price of the asset on the maturity date. Notice that profit is zero when the ultimate spot price, P_T, equals the initial futures price, F_0. Profit per unit of the underlying asset rises or falls one-for-one with changes in the final spot price. Unlike the payoff of a call option, the payoff of the long futures position can be negative: This will be the case if the spot price falls below the original futures price. Unlike the holder of a call, who has an *option* to buy, the long futures position trader cannot simply walk away from the contract. Also unlike options, in the case of futures there is no need to distinguish gross payoffs from net profits. This is because the futures contract is not purchased; it is simply a contract that is agreed to by two parties. The futures price adjusts to make the present value of either side of the contract equal to zero.

KEY TO EXCHANGES: **CBT:** Chicago Board of Trade; **CME:** Chicago Mercantile Exchange; **CMX:** Comex; **KC:** Kansas City Board of Trade; **MPLS:** Minneapolis Grain Exchange; **ICE-US:** ICE Futures U.S. **NYM:** New York Mercantile Exchange, or Nymex

Metal & Petroleum Futures

Copper-High (CMX)-25,000 lbs.; cents per lb.

	Open	High hi lo	Low	Settle	Chg	Open interest
Jan	305.00	305.00	301.85	303.05	-2.70	2,196
March	307.35	309.45	302.20	304.10	-3.10	51,193

Gold (CMX)-100 troy oz.; $ per troy oz.

	Open	High hi lo	Low	Settle	Chg	Open interest
Jan	843.20	843.20 ▲	843.20	834.90	-4.70	81
Feb	843.20	847.40	833.00	838.00	-4.70	284,263
April	852.30	853.20	840.20	844.50	-4.80	69,051
June	857.90	858.90	845.50	850.40	-4.90	56,471
Aug	863.30	863.30	856.00	855.90	-5.00	31,030
Dec	871.90	873.00	861.00	865.90	-5.10	29,080

Platinum (NYM)-50 troy oz.; $ per troy oz.

	Open	High hi lo	Low	Settle	Chg	Open interest
Jan	1539.00	1539.00	1513.00	1528.40	-12.10	504
April	1540.00	1542.90	1514.10	1525.40	-14.10	16,644

Silver (CMX)-5,000 troy oz.; cnts per troy oz.

	Open	High hi lo	Low	Settle	Chg	Open interest
Jan	...	...	...	1479.7	2.7	331
March	1489.5	1508.0	1481.0	1492.0	2.5	71,349

Crude Oil, Light Sweet (NYM)-1,000 bbls.; $ per bbl.

	Open	High hi lo	Low	Settle	Chg	Open interest
Feb	96.12	96.78	94.73	95.98	-0.02	319,543
March	96.00	96.50	94.55	95.78	0.02	166,417
April	95.50	95.90	94.12	95.24	0.09	67,090
June	94.17	94.71	93.11	94.03	0.14	77,742
Dec	91.00	91.70	90.16	90.97	0.11	172,840
Dec'09	87.03	87.35	86.00	86.61	-0.11	69,686

Heating Oil No. 2 (NYM)-42,000 gal.; $ per gal.

	Open	High hi lo	Low	Settle	Chg	Open interest
Jan	2.6435	2.6770	2.6284	2.6444	.0074	8,187
Feb	2.6316	2.6704	2.6224	2.6494	.0206	86,285

Gasoline-NY RBOB (NYM)-42,000 gal.; $ per gal.

	Open	High hi lo	Low	Settle	Chg	Open interest
Jan	2.4776	2.4985	2.4580	2.4758	.0161	4,409
Feb	2.4785	2.5165	2.4723	2.4908	.0126	64,835

Natural Gas (NYM)-10,000 MMBtu.; $ per MMBtu.

	Open	High hi lo	Low	Settle	Chg	Open interest
Feb	7.349	7.540	7.283	7.483	.097	115,717
March	7.350	7.569	7.300	7.521	.110	123,381
April	7.371	7.580	7.334	7.546	.110	58,408
May	7.399	7.639	7.399	7.613	.109	47,840
Oct	7.875	8.015	7.874	7.986	.097	41,931
Jan'09	8.945	8.985	8.940	9.021	.060	40,818

Agriculture Futures

Corn (CBT)-5,000 bu.; cents per bu.

	Open	High hi lo	Low	Settle	Chg	Open interest
March	450.00	457.00 ▲	447.75	455.50	3.50	597,895
Dec	470.25	475.00	469.50	473.50	.50	281,042

Ethanol (CBT)-29,000 gal.; $ per gal.

	Open	High hi lo	Low	Settle	Chg	Open interest
Jan	2.350	2.370	2.350	2.368	.033	108

Oats (CBT)-5,000 bu.; cents per bu.

	Open	High hi lo	Low	Settle	Chg	Open interest
March	300.00	308.00	299.25	306.75	3.75	9,595
May	310.50	314.50	309.50	312.00	1.00	875

Soybeans (CBT)-5,000 bu.; cents per bu.

	Open	High hi lo	Low	Settle	Chg	Open interest
Jan	1197.00	1202.00	1180.75	1199.00	-8.75	23,303
March	1210.50	1218.75	1197.00	1214.25	-8.75	280,180

Soybean Meal (CBT)-100 tons; $ per ton.

	Open	High hi lo	Low	Settle	Chg	Open interest
Jan	335.00	335.00	321.00	331.50	5.50	13,218
March	333.40	337.70	327.80	336.70	3.20	107,885

Soybean Oil (CBT)-60,000 lbs.; cents per lb.

	Open	High hi lo	Low	Settle	Chg	Open interest
Jan	49.51	49.51 ▲	48.29	48.85	.02	15,305
March	49.32	49.70	49.16	49.63	-.04	167,262

Rough Rice (CBT)-2,000 cwt.; cents per cwt.

	Open	High hi lo	Low	Settle	Chg	Open interest
Jan	1356.00	1364.00	1355.00	1355.00	-10.00	1,046
March	1396.00	1400.00	1385.00	1386.50	-10.50	14,071

Wheat (CBT)-5,000 bu.; cents per bu.

	Open	High hi lo	Low	Settle	Chg	Open interest
March	883.00	900.00	877.25	885.00	...	203,756
July	778.50	780.00	769.00	775.50	-2.50	98,801

Wheat (KC)-5,000 bu.; cents per bu.

	Open	High hi lo	Low	Settle	Chg	Open interest
March	914.00	920.00	890.00	913.50	-.50	69,712
July	812.00	822.00	800.00	820.25	6.25	29,994

Wheat (MPLS)-5,000 bu.; cents per bu.

	Open	High hi lo	Low	Settle	Chg	Open interest
March	1029.00	1044.00	1024.00	1036.25	6.25	37,129
May	995.00	1006.00	990.00	1006.00	12.00	10.268

Cattle-Feeder (CME)-50,000 lbs.; cents per lb.

	Open	High hi lo	Low	Settle	Chg	Open interest
Jan	104.550	105.650	104.500	105.100	.775	6,027
March	106.000	107.750	105.850	107.100	.750	15,503

Cattle-Live (CME)-40,000 lbs.; cents per lb.

	Open	High hi lo	Low	Settle	Chg	Open interest
Dec	93.600	96.250	93.500	96.250	2.750	132
Feb'08	96.225	96.750	95.700	96.175	.125	117,393

Hogs-Lean (CME)-40,000 lbs.; cents per lb.

	Open	High hi lo	Low	Settle	Chg	Open interest
Feb	57.200	58.100 ▼	57.000	57.875	.575	94,841
April	63.150	64.050	62.950	63.750	.400	50,525

Pork Bellies (CME)-40,000 lbs.; cents per lb.

	Open	High hi lo	Low	Settle	Chg	Open interest
Feb	84.600	87.000	84.100	85.975	1.200	1,200
March	85.000	85.000	85.000	85.500	.700	358

Coffee (ICE-US)-37,500 lbs.; cents per lb.

	Open	High hi lo	Low	Settle	Chg	Open interest
March	133.20	137.00	133.10	136.20	3.10	110,413
May	135.85	139.35	135.85	138.75	3.10	24,312

Sugar-World (ICE-US)-112,000 lbs.; cents per lb.

	Open	High hi lo	Low	Settle	Chg	Open interest
March	10.93	11.02	10.79	10.82	-.12	462,625
May	11.24	11.29	11.11	11.12	-.13	118,502

Sugar-Domestic (ICE-US)-112,000 lbs.; cents per lb.

	Open	High hi lo	Low	Settle	Chg	Open interest
March	...	...	...	20.48	-.01	3,527

Cotton (ICE-US)-50,000 lbs.; cents per lb.

	Open	High hi lo	Low	Settle	Chg	Open interest
March	67.89	68.10	67.35	68.01	.12	133,258
May	75.25	75.35	74.65	75.21	.01	43,843

Orange Juice (ICE-US)-15,000 lbs.; cents per lb.

	Open	High hi lo	Low	Settle	Chg	Open interest
Jan	142.80	150.25	140.50	143.60	.60	1,184
March	144.35	153.00	142.40	144.80	.45	18,650

Interest Rate Futures

Treasury Bonds (CBT)-$100,000; pts 32nds of 100%

	Open	High hi lo	Low	Settle	Chg	Open interest
March	115-27	116-23	115-25	116-12	22	918,180
June	115-16	116-09	115-16	115-24	22	2,437

Treasury Notes (CBT)-$100,000; pts 32nds of 100%

	Open	High hi lo	Low	Settle	Chg	Open interest
March	113-005	113-180	112-310	113-125	15.5	2,116,449
June	112-070	112-070	112-070	112-225	16.0	1,322

5 Yr. Treasury Notes (CBT)-$100,000; pts 32nds of 100%

	Open	High hi lo	Low	Settle	Chg	Open interest
Dec	110-240	110-240	110-135	110-145	8.0	15,471
March'08	110-020	110-120	110-005	110-090	10.5	1,760,240

2 Yr. Treasury Notes (CBT)-$200,000; pts 32nds of 100%

	Open	High hi lo	Low	Settle	Chg	Open interest
Dec	104-300	104-300	104-300	105-000	2.2	9,580
March'08	105-000	105-052	105-000	105-040	5.0	978,735

30 Day Federal Funds (CBT)-$5,000,000; 100 - daily avg.

	Open	High hi lo	Low	Settle	Chg	Open interest
Dec	95.745	95.760	95.745	95.755	.015	119,194
Jan'08	95.835	95.845 ▲	95.825	95.840	.010	141,448

1 Month Libor (CME)-$3,000,000; pts of 100%

	Open	High hi lo	Low	Settle	Chg	Open interest
Jan	95.5300	95.5400	95.5300	95.5350	.0125	21,284
Feb	95.6825	95.7000 ▲	95.6725	95.6825	.0075	9,411

Eurodollar (CME)-$1,000,000; pts of 100%

	Open	High hi lo	Low	Settle	Chg	Open interest
Jan	95.4025	95.4250	95.3975	95.4050	.0075	83,562
March	95.7450	95.7800	95.7300	95.7650	.0350	1,440,884
June	96.2150	96.2850	96.2050	96.2550	.0600	1,446,031
Dec	96.5800	96.6600	96.5700	96.6300	.0650	1,493,832

Currency Futures

Japanese Yen (CME)-¥12,500,000; $ per 100¥

	Open	High hi lo	Low	Settle	Chg	Open interest
March	.8965	.9048	.8945	.9013	.0077	159,034
June	.9100	.9124 ▼	.9100	.9095	.0077	24,489

Canadian Dollar (CME)-CAD 100,000; $ per CAD

	Open	High hi lo	Low	Settle	Chg	Open interest
March	1.0210	1.0247	1.0056	1.0099	-.0101	76,435
June	1.0199	1.0220	1.0064	1.0096	-.0100	3,711

British Pound (CME)-£62,500; $ per £

	Open	High hi lo	Low	Settle	Chg	Open interest
March	1.9911	2.0061	1.9768	1.9785	-.0100	78,699
June	1.9801	1.9999	1.9740	1.9730	-.0100	245

Swiss Franc (CME)-CHF 125,000; $ per CHF

	Open	High hi lo	Low	Settle	Chg	Open interest
March	.8910	.8947	.8832	.8838	-.0078	62,101
June	.8959	.8973	.8885	.8874	-.0078	53

Australian Dollar (CME)-AUD 100,000; $ per AUD

	Open	High hi lo	Low	Settle	Chg	Open interest
March	.8724	.8788	.8711	.8726	.0033	58,255
June	.8735	.8735	.8675	.8665	.0033	434

Mexican Peso (CME)-MXN 500,000; $ per 10MXN

	Open	High hi lo	Low	Settle	Chg	Open interest
Jan	...	...	...	.91500	-.00175	3
March	.91125	.91250	.91025	.91075	-.00175	88,117

Euro (CME)-€125,000; $ per €

	Open	High hi lo	Low	Settle	Chg	Open interest
March	1.4739	1.4759	1.4580	1.4590	-.0136	170,740
June	1.4735	1.4749	1.4580	1.4581	-.0141	1,251

Index Futures

DJ Industrial Average (CBT)-$10 x index

	Open	High hi lo	Low	Settle	Chg	Open interest
March	13424	13452	13310	13328	-99	24,590
June	13425	13425	13390	13404	-99	37

Mini DJ Industrial Average (CBT)-$5 x index

	Open	High hi lo	Low	Settle	Chg	Open interest
March	13423	13454	13301	13328	-99	67,841
June	13370	13435	13370	13404	-99	3

S&P 500 Index (CME)-$250 x index

	Open	High hi lo	Low	Settle	Chg	Open interest
March	1485.20	1488.90	1472.00	1477.20	-8.30	514,454
June	1490.50	1496.00	1481.40	1486.00	-8.40	6.604

Mini S&P 500 (CME)-$50 x index

	Open	High hi lo	Low	Settle	Chg	Open interest
March	1485.25	1489.00	1471.00	1477.25	-8.25	1,751,604
June	1493.50	1497.25	1480.50	1486.00	-8.50	5.119

Nasdaq 100 (CME)-$100 x index

	Open	High hi lo	Low	Settle	Chg	Open interest
March	2125.50	2127.50	2101.00	2104.75	-20.25	38,600

Source: Reuters

FIGURE 22.1　Futures listings

Source: *The Wall Street Journal*, January 2, 2008. Reprinted by permission of *The Wall Street Journal*, © 2008 Dow Jones & Company, Inc. All Rights Reserved Worldwide.

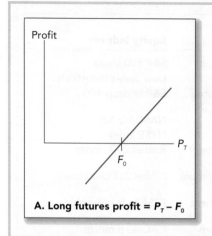
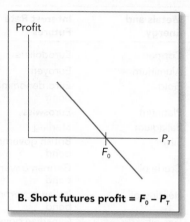
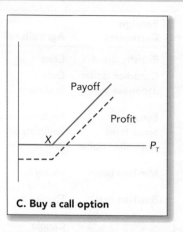

A. Long futures profit = $P_T - F_0$

B. Short futures profit = $F_0 - P_T$

C. Buy a call option

FIGURE 22.2 Profits to buyers and sellers of futures and options contracts

The distinction between futures and options is highlighted by comparing panel A of Figure 22.2 to the payoff and profit diagrams for an investor in a call option with exercise price, X, chosen equal to the futures price F_0 (see panel C). The futures investor is exposed to considerable losses if the asset price falls. In contrast, the investor in the call cannot lose more than the cost of the option.

Figure 22.2, panel B, is a plot of the profits realized by an investor who enters the short side of a futures contract. It is the mirror image of the profit diagram for the long position.

CONCEPT CHECK **1**	a. Compare the profit diagram in Figure 22.2B to the payoff diagram for a long position in a put option. Assume the exercise price of the option equals the initial futures price. b. Compare the profit diagram in Figure 22.2B to the payoff diagram for an investor who writes a call option.

Existing Contracts

Futures and forward contracts are traded on a wide variety of goods in four broad categories: agricultural commodities, metals and minerals (including energy commodities), foreign currencies, and financial futures (fixed-income securities and stock market indexes). In addition to indexes on broad stock indexes, one can now trade **single-stock futures** on individual stocks and narrowly based indexes. OneChicago (a joint venture of the Chicago Board Options Exchange and the Chicago Mercantile Exchange) has operated an entirely electronic market in single-stock futures since 2002. The exchange maintains futures markets in actively traded stocks with the most liquidity. However, trading volume in this market has to date been somewhat disappointing.

Table 22.1 enumerates some of the various contracts trading in 2008. Contracts now trade on items that would not have been considered possible only a few years ago. For example, there are now electricity as well as weather futures and options contracts. Weather derivatives (which trade on the Chicago Mercantile Exchange) have payoffs that depend

Foreign Currencies	Agricultural	Metals and Energy	Interest Rate Futures	Equity Indexes
British pound	Corn	Copper	Eurodollars	S&P 500 index
Canadian dollar	Oats	Aluminum	Euroyen	Dow Jones Industrials
Japanese yen	Soybeans	Gold	Euro-denominated bond	S&P Midcap 400
Euro	Soybean meal	Platinum	Euroswiss	NASDAQ 100
Swiss franc	Soybean oil	Palladium	Sterling	NYSE index
Australian dollar	Wheat	Silver	British government bond	Russell 2000 index
Mexican peso	Barley	Crude oil	German government bond	Nikkei 225 (Japanese)
Brazilian real	Flaxseed	Heating oil	Italian government bond	FTSE index (British)
	Canola	Gas oil	Canadian government bond	CAC-40 (French)
	Rye	Natural gas	Treasury bonds	DAX-30 (German)
	Cattle	Gasoline	Treasury notes	All ordinary (Australian)
	Hogs	Propane	Treasury bills	Toronto 35 (Canadian)
	Pork bellies	Commodity index	LIBOR	Dow Jones Euro STOXX 50
	Cocoa	Electricity	EURIBOR	Industry indexes, e.g.,
	Coffee	Weather	Euroswiss	Banking
	Cotton		Municipal bond index	Telecom
	Milk		Federal funds rate	Utilities
	Orange juice		Bankers' acceptance	Health care
	Sugar		Interest rate swaps	Technology
	Lumber			
	Rice			

TABLE 22.1

Sample of futures contracts

on average weather conditions, for example, the number of degree-days by which the temperature in a region exceeds or falls short of 65 degrees Fahrenheit. The potential use of these derivatives in managing the risk surrounding electricity or oil and natural gas use should be evident.

While Table 22.1 includes many contracts, the large and ever-growing array of markets makes this list necessarily incomplete. The nearby box discusses some comparatively fanciful futures markets, sometimes called *prediction markets,* in which payoffs may be tied to the winner of presidential elections, the box office receipts of a particular movie, or anything else in which participants are willing to take positions.

Outside the futures markets, a well-developed network of banks and brokers has established a forward market in foreign exchange. This forward market is not a formal exchange in the sense that the exchange specifies the terms of the traded contract. Instead, participants in a forward contract may negotiate for delivery of any quantity of goods, whereas in the formal futures markets contract size and delivery dates are set by the exchange. In forward arrangements, banks and brokers simply negotiate contracts for clients (or themselves) as needed.

PRESIDENTIAL AND OTHER PREDICTION FUTURES

If you find S&P 500 or T-bond contracts a bit dry, perhaps you'd be interested in futures contacts with payoffs that depend on the winner of the next presidential election, or the severity of the next influenza season, or the host city of the 2016 Olympics. You can now find "futures markets" in these events and many others.

For example, both Intrade (www.intrade.com) and Iowa Electronic Markets (www.biz.uiowa.edu/iem) maintain presidential futures markets. Contracts pay $1 if the candidate you "purchase" wins the election. The contract price for each candidate therefore may be viewed as the probability of that candidate's success, at least according to the consensus view of the participants in the market.

The accompanying figure reproduces presidential futures prices from Intrade in late December 2007, a date still far in advance of the 2008 election. If you wished to bet on a Hillary Clinton victory, you could have purchased a Clinton contract for the ask price of $.397, which would pay $1 if she were to win in November. Alternatively, if you wanted to bet against her, you could *sell* a Clinton contract for the bid price of $.396. You'd then be on the hook for $1 if she were to win the election. Based on these prices, the odds of a Clinton victory seemed to be just a shade below 40%, making her the favorite at the time. But even her probability was far from 1, indicating the considerable uncertainty at that time concerning the ultimate winner.

Notice that the sum of the bid prices for all of the candidates combined is $.998, slightly below $1.00. Can you explain why this makes sense? Notice also that the sum of the ask prices is $1.026, a bit *above* $1.00. Does this make sense? [The answers appear in the Solutions to Concept Check section at the end of the chapter.]

Source: www.intrade.com, December 22, 2007.

22.2 MECHANICS OF TRADING IN FUTURES MARKETS

The Clearinghouse and Open Interest

Until recently, most futures trades in the United States occurred among floor traders in the "trading pit" for each contract. Participants there use voice or hand signals to signify their desire to buy or sell and locate a trader willing to accept the opposite side of a trade. Today, however, trading is conducted primarily over electronic networks, particularly for financial futures.

The impetus for this shift originated in Europe, where electronic trading is the norm. Eurex, which is jointly owned by the Deutsche Börse and Swiss exchange, is currently the world's largest futures and options exchange. It operates a fully electronic trading and clearing platform and, in 2004, received clearance from regulators to list contracts in the U.S. In response, the Chicago Board of Trade adopted an electronic platform provided by Eurex's European rival Euronext.liffe,[1] and the great majority of the CBOT's Treasury contracts are traded electronically. The Chicago Mercantile Exchange maintains another electronic trading system called Globex.

[1] Euronext.liffe is the international derivatives market of Euronext. It resulted from Euronext's purchase of LIFFE (the London International Financial Futures and Options Exchange) and a merger with the Lisbon exchange in 2002. Euronext was itself the result of a 2000 merger of the exchanges of Amsterdam, Brussels, and Paris.

The CBOT and CME agreed in 2007 to merge into one combined company, named the CME Group, and intend to move all electronic trading from both exchanges onto CME Globex. It seems inevitable that electronic trading will continue to displace floor trading. The combined firm will be the world's largest derivatives exchange as well as a very strong competitor in the over-the-counter derivatives market.

Once a trade is agreed to, the **clearinghouse** enters the picture. Rather than having the long and short traders hold contracts with each other, the clearinghouse becomes the seller of the contract for the long position and the buyer of the contract for the short position. The clearinghouse is obligated to deliver the commodity to the long position and to pay for delivery from the short; consequently, the clearinghouse's position nets to zero. This arrangement makes the clearinghouse the trading partner of each trader, both long and short. The clearinghouse, bound to perform on its side of each contract, is the only party that can be hurt by the failure of any trader to observe the obligations of the futures contract. This arrangement is necessary because a futures contract calls for future performance, which cannot be as easily guaranteed as an immediate stock transaction.

Figure 22.3 illustrates the role of the clearinghouse. Panel A shows what would happen in the absence of the clearinghouse. The trader in the long position would be obligated to pay the futures price to the short-position trader, and the trader in the short position would be obligated to deliver the commodity. Panel B shows how the clearinghouse becomes an intermediary, acting as the trading partner for each side of the contract. The clearinghouse's position is neutral, as it takes a long and a short position for each transaction.

The clearinghouse makes it possible for traders to liquidate positions easily. If you are currently long in a contract and want to undo your position, you simply instruct your broker to enter the short side of a contract to close out your position. This is called a *reversing trade*. The exchange nets out your long and short positions, reducing your net position to zero. Your zero net position with the clearinghouse eliminates the need to fulfill at maturity either the original long or reversing short position.

The **open interest** on the contract is the number of contracts outstanding. (Long and short positions are not counted separately, meaning that open interest can be defined as the number of either long or short contracts outstanding.) The clearinghouse's position nets out to zero, and so is not counted in the computation of open interest. When contracts begin trading, open interest is zero. As time passes, open interest increases as progressively more contracts are entered.

There are many apocryphal stories about futures traders who wake up to discover a small mountain of wheat or corn on their front lawn. But the truth is that futures contracts rarely result in actual delivery of the underlying asset. Traders establish long or short positions in contracts that will benefit from a rise or fall in the futures price and almost always close out, or reverse, those positions before the contract expires. The fraction of contracts that result in actual delivery is estimated to range from less than 1% to 3%, depending on the commodity and activity in the contract. In the unusual case

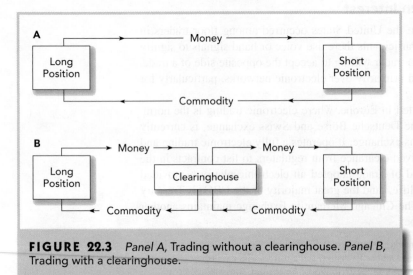

FIGURE 22.3   *Panel A,* Trading without a clearinghouse. *Panel B,* Trading with a clearinghouse.

of actual deliveries of commodities, they occur via regular channels of supply, most often warehouse receipts.

You can see the typical pattern of open interest in Figure 22.1. In the gold contract, for example, the January delivery contract is approaching maturity, and open interest is small; most contracts have been reversed already. The greatest open interest is in the February contract. The more-distant maturity contracts have little open interest, as they have been available only recently, and few participants have yet traded. For other contracts, for example, corn, for which the nearest maturity date isn't until March, open interest is typically highest in the nearest contract.

The Margin Account and Marking to Market

The total profit or loss realized by the long trader who buys a contract at time 0 and closes, or reverses, it at time t is just the change in the futures price over the period, $F_t - F_0$. Symmetrically, the short trader earns $F_0 - F_t$.

The process by which profits or losses accrue to traders is called *marking to market*. At initial execution of a trade, each trader establishes a margin account. The margin is a security account consisting of cash or near-cash securities, such as Treasury bills, that ensures the trader is able to satisfy the obligations of the futures contract. Because both parties to a futures contract are exposed to losses, both must post margin. To illustrate, return to the first corn contract listed in Figure 22.1. If the initial required margin on corn, for example, is 10%, then the trader must post $2,277.50 per contract of the margin account. This is 10% of the value of the contract, $4.555 per bushel $\times$ 5,000 bushels per contract.

Because the initial margin may be satisfied by posting interest-earning securities, the requirement does not impose a significant opportunity cost of funds on the trader. The initial margin is usually set between 5% and 15% of the total value of the contract. Contracts written on assets with more volatile prices require higher margins.

On any day that futures contracts trade, futures prices may rise or may fall. Instead of waiting until the maturity date for traders to realize all gains and losses, the clearinghouse requires all positions to recognize profits as they accrue daily. If the futures price of corn rises from 455.5 to 457.5 cents per bushel, the clearinghouse credits the margin account of the long position for 5,000 bushels times 2 cents per bushel, or $100 per contract. Conversely, for the short position, the clearinghouse takes this amount from the margin account for each contract held.

This daily settling is called **marking to market.** It means the maturity date of the contract does not govern realization of profit or loss. Marking to market ensures that, as futures prices change, the proceeds accrue to the trader's margin account immediately. We will provide a more detailed example of this process shortly.

Marking to market is the major way in which futures and forward contracts differ, besides contract standardization. Futures follow this pay-(or receive-)as-you-go method.

CONCEPT CHECK 2

What must be the net inflow or outlay from marking to market for the clearinghouse?

Forward contracts are simply held until maturity, and no funds are transferred until that date, although the contracts may be traded.

If a trader accrues sustained losses from daily marking to market, the margin account may fall below a critical value called the **maintenance margin.** If the value of the account falls below this value, the trader receives a margin call. Margins and margin calls safeguard the position of the clearinghouse. Positions are closed out before the margin account is exhausted—the trader's losses are covered, and the clearinghouse is not put at risk.

EXAMPLE 22.1   Maintenance Margin

Suppose the maintenance margin is 5% while the initial margin was 10% of the value of the corn, or $2,277.50. Then a margin call will go out when the original margin account has fallen in half, by about $1,139. Each 1-cent decline in the corn price results in a $50 loss to the long position. Therefore, the futures price need only fall by 23 cents to trigger a margin call. Either new funds must be transferred into the margin account or the broker will close out enough of the trader's account to re-establish the required margin for the position.

It is important to note that the futures price on the delivery date will equal the spot price of the commodity on that date. As a maturing contract calls for immediate delivery, the futures price on that day must equal the spot price—the cost of the commodity from the two competing sources is equalized in a competitive market.[2] You may obtain delivery of the commodity either by purchasing it directly in the spot market or by entering the long side of a futures contract.

A commodity available from two sources (spot or futures market) must be priced identically, or else investors will rush to purchase it from the cheap source in order to sell it in the high-priced market. Such arbitrage activity could not persist without prices adjusting to eliminate the arbitrage opportunity. Therefore, the futures price and the spot price must converge at maturity. This is called the **convergence property.**

For an investor who establishes a long position in a contract now (time 0) and holds that position until maturity (time T), the sum of all daily settlements will equal $F_T - F_0$, where F_T stands for the futures price at contract maturity. Because of convergence, however, the futures price at maturity, F_T, equals the spot price, P_T, so total futures profits also may be expressed as $P_T - F_0$. Thus we see that profits on a futures contract held to maturity perfectly track changes in the value of the underlying asset.

EXAMPLE 22.2   Marking to Market

Assume the current futures price for silver for delivery 5 days from today is $14.10 per ounce. Suppose that over the next 5 days, the futures price evolves as follows:

Day	Futures Price
0 (today)	$14.10
1	14.20
2	14.25
3	14.18
4	14.18
5 (delivery)	14.21

The spot price of silver on the delivery date is $14.21: The convergence property implies that the price of silver in the spot market must equal the futures price on the delivery day.

---

[2]Small differences between the spot and futures price at maturity may persist because of transportation costs, but this is a minor factor.

The daily mark-to-market settlements for each contract held by the long position will be as follows:

Day	Profit (Loss) per Ounce × 5,000 Ounces/Contract = Daily Proceeds	
1	14.20 − 14.10 = .10	$500
2	14.25 − 14.20 = .05	250
3	14.18 − 14.25 = −.07	−350
4	14.18 − 14.18 = 0	0
5	14.21 − 14.18 = .03	150
		Sum = $550

The profit on Day 1 is the increase in the futures price from the previous day, or ($14.20 − $14.10) per ounce. Because each silver contract on the Commodity Exchange (CMX) calls for purchase and delivery of 5,000 ounces, the total profit per contract is 5,000 times $.10, or $500. On Day 3, when the futures price falls, the long position's margin account will be debited by $350. By Day 5, the sum of all daily proceeds is $550. This is exactly equal to 5,000 times the difference between the final futures price of $14.21 and original futures price of $14.10. Thus the sum of all the daily proceeds (per ounce of silver held long) equals $P_T − F_0$.

Cash versus Actual Delivery

Most futures contracts call for delivery of an actual commodity such as a particular grade of wheat or a specified amount of foreign currency if the contract is not reversed before maturity. For agricultural commodities, where quality of the delivered good may vary, the exchange sets quality standards as part of the futures contract. In some cases, contracts may be settled with higher- or lower-grade commodities. In these cases, a premium or discount is applied to the delivered commodity to adjust for the quality difference.

Some futures contracts call for **cash settlement.** An example is a stock index futures contract where the underlying asset is an index such as the Standard & Poor's 500 or the New York Stock Exchange Index. Delivery of every stock in the index clearly would be impractical. Hence the contract calls for "delivery" of a cash amount equal to the value that the index attains on the maturity date of the contract. The sum of all the daily settlements from marking to market results in the long position realizing total profits or losses of $S_T − F_0$, where S_T is the value of the stock index on the maturity date T and F_0 is the original futures price. Cash settlement closely mimics actual delivery, except the cash value of the asset rather than the asset itself is delivered by the short position in exchange for the futures price.

More concretely, the S&P 500 index contract calls for delivery of $250 times the value of the index. At maturity, the index might list at 1,300, the market-value-weighted index of the prices of all 500 stocks in the index. The cash settlement contract calls for delivery of $250 × 1,300, or $325,000 cash in return for $250 times the futures price. This yields exactly the same profit as would result from directly purchasing 250 units of the index for $325,000 and then delivering it for $250 times the original futures price.

Regulations

Futures markets are regulated by the Commodities Futures Trading Commission, a federal agency. The CFTC sets capital requirements for member firms of the futures exchanges, authorizes trading in new contracts, and oversees maintenance of daily trading records.

The futures exchange may set limits on the amount by which futures prices may change from one day to the next. For example, if the price limit on silver contracts traded on the Chicago Board of Trade is $1 and silver futures close today at $14.10 per ounce, then trades in silver tomorrow may vary only between $15.10 and $13.10 per ounce. The exchanges may increase or reduce price limits in response to perceived changes in price volatility of the contract. Price limits are often eliminated as contracts approach maturity, usually in the last month of trading.

Price limits traditionally are viewed as a means to limit violent price fluctuations. This reasoning seems dubious. Suppose an international monetary crisis overnight drives up the spot price of silver to $18.00. No one would sell silver futures at prices for future delivery as low as $14.10. Instead, the futures price would rise each day by the $1 limit, although the quoted price would represent only an unfilled bid order—no contracts would trade at the low quoted price. After several days of limit moves of $1 per day, the futures price would finally reach its equilibrium level, and trading would occur again. This process means no one could unload a position until the price reached its equilibrium level. This example shows that price limits offer no real protection against fluctuations in equilibrium prices.

Taxation

Because of the mark-to-market procedure, investors do not have control over the tax year in which they realize gains or losses. Instead, price changes are realized gradually, with each daily settlement. Therefore, taxes are paid at year-end on cumulated profits or losses regardless of whether the position has been closed out.

22.3 FUTURES MARKETS STRATEGIES

Hedging and Speculation

Hedging and speculating are two polar uses of futures markets. A speculator uses a futures contract to profit from movements in futures prices, a hedger to protect against price movement.

If speculators believe prices will increase, they will take a long position for expected profits. Conversely, they exploit expected price declines by taking a short position.

EXAMPLE 22.3   Speculating with Oil Futures

Suppose you believe that crude oil prices are going to increase, and therefore decide to purchase crude oil futures. Each contract calls for delivery of 1,000 barrels of oil. Suppose that the current futures price for delivery in February is $97.15 per barrel. For every dollar increase in the futures price of crude, the long position gains $1,000 and the short position loses that amount.

Conversely, suppose you think that prices are heading lower and therefore sell a contract. If crude oil prices do in fact fall, then you will gain $1,000 per contract for every dollar that prices decline.

If crude oil is selling at the contract maturity date for $99.15, which is $2 more than the initial futures price, the long side will profit by $2,000 per contract purchased. The short side will lose an identical amount on each contract sold. On the other hand, if oil has fallen to $95.15, the long side will lose, and the short side will gain, $2,000 per contract.

Why does a speculator buy a futures contract? Why not buy the underlying asset directly? One reason lies in transaction costs, which are far smaller in futures markets.

Another important reason is the leverage that futures trading provides. Recall that futures contracts require traders to post margin considerably less than the value of the asset underlying the contract. Therefore, they allow speculators to achieve much greater leverage than is available from direct trading in a commodity.

EXAMPLE 22.4 Futures and Leverage

Suppose the initial margin requirement for the oil contract is 10%. At a current futures price of $97.15, and contract size of 1,000 barrels, this would require margin of $.10 \times 97.15 \times 1,000 = \$9,715$. A $2 jump in oil prices represents an increase of 2.06%, and results in a $2,000 gain on the contract for the long position. This is a percentage gain of 20.6% in the $9,715 posted as margin, precisely 10 times the percentage increase in the oil price. The 10-to-1 ratio of percentage changes reflects the leverage inherent in the futures position, because the contract was established with an initial margin of one-tenth the value of the underlying asset.

Hedgers, by contrast, use futures to insulate themselves against price movements. A firm planning to sell oil, for example, might anticipate a period of market volatility and wish to protect its revenue against price fluctuations. To hedge the total revenue derived from the sale, the firm enters a short position in oil futures. As the following example illustrates, this locks in its total proceeds (i.e., revenue from the sale of the oil plus proceeds from its futures position).

EXAMPLE 22.5 Hedging with Oil Futures

Consider an oil distributor planning to sell 100,000 barrels of oil in February that wishes to hedge against a possible decline in oil prices. Because each contract calls for delivery of 1,000 barrels, it would sell 100 contracts that mature in February. Any decrease in prices would then generate a profit on the contracts that would offset the lower sales revenue from the oil.

To illustrate, suppose that the only three possible prices for oil in February are $95.15, $97.15, and $99.15 per barrel. The revenue from the oil sale will be 100,000 times the price per barrel. The profit on each contract sold will be 1,000 times any decline in the futures price. At maturity, the convergence property ensures that the final futures price will equal the spot price of oil. Therefore, the profit on the 100 contracts sold will equal $100,000 \times (F_0 - P_T)$, where P_T is the oil price on the delivery date, and F_0 is the original futures price, $97.15.

Now consider the firm's overall position. The total revenue in February can be computed as follows:

	Oil Price in February, P_T		
	$95.15	**$97.15**	**$99.15**
Revenue from oil sale: $100,000 \times P_T$	$9,515,000	$9,715,000	$9,915,000
+ Profit on futures: $100,000 \times (F_0 - P_T)$	200,000	0	−200,000
TOTAL PROCEEDS	$9,715,000	$9,715,000	$9,715,000

The revenue from the oil sale plus the proceeds from the contracts equals the current futures price, \$97.15 per barrel. The variation in the price of the oil is precisely offset by the profits or losses on the futures position. For example, if oil falls to \$95.15 a barrel, the short futures position generates \$200,000 profit, just enough to bring total revenues to \$9,715,000. The total is the same as if one were to arrange today to sell the oil in February at the futures price.

Figure 22.4 illustrates the nature of the hedge in Example 22.5. The upward-sloping line is the revenue from the sale of oil. The downward-sloping line is the profit on the futures contract. The horizontal line is the sum of sales revenue plus futures profits. This line is flat, as the hedged position is independent of oil prices.

To generalize Example 22.5, note that oil will sell for P_T per barrel at the maturity of the contract. The profit per barrel on the futures will be $F_0 - P_T$. Therefore, total revenue is $P_T + (F_0 - P_T) = F_0$, which is independent of the eventual oil price.

The oil distributor in Example 22.5 engaged in a *short hedge*, taking a short futures position to offset risk in the sales price of a particular asset. A *long hedge* is the analogous hedge for someone who wishes to eliminate the risk of an uncertain purchase price. For example, suppose a power supplier planning to purchase oil is afraid that prices might rise by the time of the purchase. As the following Concept Check illustrates, the supplier might *buy* oil futures to lock in the net purchase price at the time of the transaction.

CONCEPT CHECK 3

Suppose as in Example 22.5 that oil will be selling in February for \$95.15, \$97.15, or \$99.15 per barrel. Consider a firm such as an electric utility that plans to buy 100,000 barrels of oil in February. Show that if the firm buys 100 oil contracts today, its net expenditures in February will be hedged and equal to \$9,715,000.

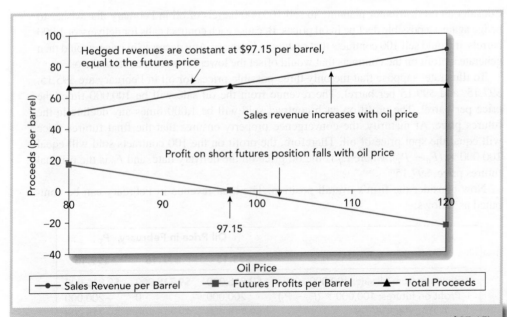

FIGURE 22.4 Hedging revenues using futures, Example 22.5 (Futures price = \$97.15)

Exact futures hedging may be impossible for some goods because the necessary futures contract is not traded. For example, a portfolio manager might want to hedge the value of a diversified, actively managed portfolio for a period of time. However, futures contracts are listed only on indexed portfolios. Nevertheless, because returns on the manager's diversified portfolio will have a high correlation with returns on broad-based indexed portfolios, an effective hedge may be established by selling index futures contracts. Hedging a position using futures on another asset is called *cross-hedging.*

CONCEPT CHECK 4

What are the sources of risk to an investor who uses stock index futures to hedge an actively managed stock portfolio?

Basis Risk and Hedging

The **basis** is the difference between the futures price and the spot price.[3] As we have noted, on the maturity date of a contract, the basis must be zero: The convergence property implies that $F_T - P_T = 0$. Before maturity, however, the futures price for later delivery may differ substantially from the current spot price.

In Example 22.5 we discussed the case of a short hedger who manages risk by entering a short position to deliver oil in the future. If the asset and futures contract are held until maturity, the hedger bears no risk. Risk is eliminated because the futures price and spot price at contract maturity must be equal: Gains and losses on the futures and the commodity position will exactly cancel. However, if the contract and asset are to be liquidated early, before contract maturity, the hedger bears **basis risk,** because the futures price and spot price need not move in perfect lockstep at all times before the delivery date. In this case, gains and losses on the contract and the asset may not exactly offset each other.

Some speculators try to profit from movements in the basis. Rather than betting on the direction of the futures or spot prices per se, they bet on the changes in the difference between the two. A long spot–short futures position will profit when the basis narrows.

EXAMPLE 22.6 Speculating on the Basis

Consider an investor holding 100 ounces of gold, who is short one gold-futures contract. Suppose that gold today sells for $891 an ounce, and the futures price for June delivery is $896 an ounce. Therefore, the basis is currently $5. Tomorrow, the spot price might increase to $895, while the futures price increases to $899, so the basis narrows to $4.

The investor's gains and losses are as follows:

Gain on holdings of gold (per ounce): $895 − $891 = $4

Loss on gold futures position (per ounce): $899 − $896 = $3

The net gain is the decrease in the basis, or $1 per ounce.

A related strategy is a **calendar spread** position, where the investor takes a long position in a futures contract of one maturity and a short position in a contract on the same commodity, but with a different maturity.[4] Profits accrue if the difference in futures prices

---

[3]Usage of the word *basis* is somewhat loose. It sometimes is used to refer to the futures-spot difference $F - P$, and sometimes to the spot-futures difference $P - F$. We will consistently call the basis $F - P$.

[4]Yet another strategy is an *intercommodity spread,* in which the investor buys a contract on one commodity and sells a contract on a different commodity.

between the two contracts changes in the hoped-for direction; that is, if the futures price on the contract held long increases by more (or decreases by less) than the futures price on the contract held short.

EXAMPLE 22.7   Speculating on the Spread

Consider an investor who holds a September maturity contract long and a June contract short. If the September futures price increases by 5 cents while the June futures price increases by 4 cents, the net gain will be 5 cents − 4 cents, or 1 cent. Like basis strategies, spread positions aim to exploit movements in relative price structures rather than to profit from movements in the general level of prices.

22.4   THE DETERMINATION OF FUTURES PRICES

The Spot-Futures Parity Theorem

We have seen that a futures contract can be used to hedge changes in the value of the underlying asset. If the hedge is perfect, meaning that the asset-plus-futures portfolio has no risk, then the hedged position must provide a rate of return equal to the rate on other risk-free investments. Otherwise, there will be arbitrage opportunities that investors will exploit until prices are brought back into line. This insight can be used to derive the theoretical relationship between a futures price and the price of its underlying asset.

Suppose, for example, that the S&P 500 index currently is at 1,500 and an investor who holds $1,500 in a mutual fund indexed to the S&P 500 wishes to temporarily hedge her exposure to market risk. Assume that the indexed portfolio pays dividends totaling $25 over the course of the year, and for simplicity, that all dividends are paid at year-end. Finally, assume that the futures price for year-end delivery of the S&P 500 contract is 1,550.[5] Let's examine the end-of-year proceeds for various values of the stock index if the investor hedges her portfolio by entering the short side of the futures contract.

Final value of stock portfolio, S_T	$ 1,510	$ 1,530	$ 1,550	$ 1,570	$ 1,590	$ 1,610
Payoff from short futures position (equals $F_0 - F_T = \$1,550 - S_T$)	40	20	0	−20	−40	−60
Dividend income	25	25	25	25	25	25
TOTAL	$ 1,575	$1,575	$1,575	$1,575	$1,575	$1,575

The payoff from the short futures position equals the difference between the original futures price, $1,550, and the year-end stock price. This is because of convergence: The futures price at contract maturity will equal the stock price at that time.

Notice that the overall position is perfectly hedged. Any increase in the value of the indexed stock portfolio is offset by an equal decrease in the payoff of the short futures position, resulting in a final value independent of the stock price. The $1,575 total payoff

---

[5]Actually, the futures contract calls for delivery of $250 times the value of the S&P 500 index, so that each contract would be settled for $250 times the index. We will simplify by assuming that you can buy a contract for one unit rather than 250 units of the index. In practice, one contract would hedge about $250 × 1,500 = $375,000 worth of stock. Of course, institutional investors would consider a stock portfolio of this size to be quite small.

is the sum of the current futures price, $F_0 = \$1{,}550$, and the $25 dividend. It is as though the investor arranged to sell the stock at year-end for the current futures price, thereby eliminating price risk and locking in total proceeds equal to the sales price plus dividends paid before the sale.

What rate of return is earned on this riskless position? The stock investment requires an initial outlay of $1,500, whereas the futures position is established without an initial cash outflow. Therefore, the $1,500 portfolio grows to a year-end value of $1,575, providing a rate of return of 5%. More generally, a total investment of S_0, the current stock price, grows to a final value of $F_0 + D$, where D is the dividend payout on the portfolio. The rate of return is therefore

$$\text{Rate of return on perfectly hedged stock portfolio} = \frac{(F_0 + D) - S_0}{S_0}$$

This return is essentially riskless. We observe F_0 at the beginning of the period when we enter the futures contract. While dividend payouts are not perfectly riskless, they are highly predictable over short periods, especially for diversified portfolios. Any uncertainty is *extremely* small compared to the uncertainty in stock prices.

Presumably, 5% must be the rate of return available on other riskless investments. If not, then investors would face two competing risk-free strategies with different rates of return, a situation that could not last. Therefore, we conclude that

$$\frac{(F_0 + D) - S_0}{S_0} = r_f$$

Rearranging, we find that the futures price must be

$$F_0 = S_0(1 + r_f) - D = S_0(1 + r_f - d) \tag{22.1}$$

where d is the dividend yield on the stock portfolio, defined as D/S_0. This result is called the **spot-futures parity theorem.** It gives the normal or theoretically correct relationship between spot and futures prices. Any deviation from parity would give rise to risk-free arbitrage opportunities.

EXAMPLE 22.8 Futures Market Arbitrage

Suppose that parity were violated. For example, suppose the risk-free interest rate in the economy were only 4% so that according to Equation 22.1, the futures price should be $1,500(1.04) - \$25 = \$1{,}535$. The actual futures price, $F_0 = \$1{,}550$, is $15 higher than its "appropriate" value. This implies that an investor can make arbitrage profits by shorting the relatively overpriced futures contract and buying the relatively underpriced stock portfolio using money borrowed at the 4% market interest rate. The proceeds from this strategy would be as follows:

Action	Initial Cash Flow	Cash Flow in 1 Year
Borrow $1,500, repay with interest in 1 year	+1,500	$-1{,}500(1.04) = -\$1{,}560$
Buy stock for $1,500	−1,500	$S_T + \$25$ dividend
Enter short futures position ($F_0 = \$1{,}550$)	0	$\$1{,}550 - S_T$
TOTAL	0	$15

The net initial investment of the strategy is zero. But its cash flow in 1 year is $15 regardless of the stock price. In other words, it is riskless. This payoff is precisely equal to the mispricing of the futures contract relative to its parity value.

When parity is violated, the strategy to exploit the mispricing produces an arbitrage profit—a riskless profit requiring no initial net investment. If such an opportunity existed, all market participants would rush to take advantage of it. The results? The stock price would be bid up, and/or the futures price offered down until Equation 22.1 is satisfied. A similar analysis applies to the possibility that F_0 is less than $1,535. In this case, you simply reverse the strategy above to earn riskless profits. We conclude, therefore, that in a well-functioning market in which arbitrage opportunities are competed away, $F_0 = S_0(1 + r_f) - D$.

CONCEPT CHECK 5

Return to the arbitrage strategy laid out in Example 22.8. What would be the three steps of the strategy if F_0 were too low, say, $1,520? Work out the cash flows of the strategy now and in 1 year in a table like the one in the example.

The arbitrage strategy of Example 22.8 can be represented more generally as follows:

Action	Initial Cash Flow	Cash Flow in 1 Year
1. Borrow S_0 dollars	S_0	$-S_0(1 + r_f)$
2. Buy stock for S_0	$-S_0$	$S_T + D$
3. Enter short futures position	0	$F_0 - S_T$
TOTAL	0	$F_0 - S_0(1 + r_f) + D$

The initial cash flow is zero by construction: The money necessary to purchase the stock in step 1 is borrowed in step 2, and the futures position in step 3, which is used to hedge the value of the stock position, does not require an initial outlay. Moreover, the total cash flow to the strategy at year-end is riskless because it involves only terms that are already known when the contract is entered. If the final cash flow were not zero, all investors would try to cash in on the arbitrage opportunity. Ultimately prices would change until the year-end cash flow is reduced to zero, at which point F_0 would equal $S_0(1 + r_f) - D$.

The parity relationship also is called the **cost-of-carry relationship** because it asserts that the futures price is determined by the relative costs of buying a stock with deferred delivery in the futures market versus buying it in the spot market with immediate delivery and "carrying" it in inventory. If you buy stock now, you tie up your funds and incur a time-value-of-money cost of r_f per period. On the other hand, you receive dividend payments with a current yield of d. The net carrying cost advantage of deferring delivery of the stock is therefore $r_f - d$ per period. This advantage must be offset by a differential between the futures price and the spot price. The price differential just offsets the cost-of-carry advantage when $F_0 = S_0(1 + r_f - d)$.

The parity relationship is easily generalized to multiperiod applications. We simply recognize that the difference between the futures and spot price will be larger as the maturity of the contract is longer. This reflects the longer period to which we apply the net cost of carry. For contract maturity of T periods, the parity relationship is

$$F_0 = S_0(1 + r_f - d)^T \tag{22.2}$$

Although dividends of individual securities may fluctuate unpredictably, the annualized dividend yield of a broad-based index such as the S&P 500 is fairly stable, recently in the neighborhood of about 2% per year. The yield is seasonal, however, with regular peaks and troughs, so the dividend yield for the relevant months must be the one used. Figure 22.5 illustrates the yield pattern for the S&P 500. Some months, such as January or April, have consistently low yields, while others, such as May, have consistently high ones.

We have described parity in terms of stocks and stock index futures, but it should be clear that the logic applies as well to any financial futures contract. For gold futures, for example, we would simply set the dividend yield to zero. For bond contracts, we would let the coupon income on the bond play the role of dividend payments. In both cases, the parity relationship would be essentially the same as Equation 22.2.

The arbitrage strategy described above should convince you that these parity relationships are more than just theoretical results. Any violations of the parity relationship give rise to arbitrage opportunities that can provide large profits to traders. We will see in the next chapter that index arbitrage in the stock market is a tool to exploit violations of the parity relationship for stock index futures contracts.

Spreads

Just as we can predict the relationship between spot and futures prices, there are similar ways to determine the proper relationships among futures prices for contracts of different maturity dates. Equation 22.2 shows that the futures price is in part determined by time to maturity. If the risk-free rate is greater than the dividend yield (i.e., $r_f > d$), then the futures price will be higher on longer-maturity contracts. This has been the common pattern in the last several decades. You can confirm from Figure 22.1 that longer-maturity stock index contracts had higher future prices. For futures on assets like gold, which pay no "dividend yield," we can set $d = 0$ and conclude that F *must* increase as time to maturity increases.

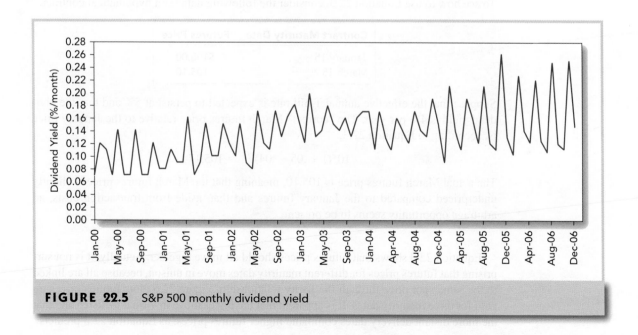

FIGURE 22.5   S&P 500 monthly dividend yield

To be more precise about spread pricing, call $F(T_1)$ the current futures price for delivery at date T_1, and $F(T_2)$ the futures price for delivery at T_2. Let d be the dividend yield of the stock. We know from the parity Equation 22.2 that

$$F(T_1) = S_0(1 + r_f - d)^{T_1}$$
$$F(T_2) = S_0(1 + r_f - d)^{T_2}$$

As a result,

$$F(T_2)/F(T_1) = (1 + r_f - d)^{(T_2 - T_1)}$$

Therefore, the basic parity relationship for spreads is

$$F(T_2) = F(T_1)(1 + r_f - d)^{(T_2 - T_1)} \qquad (22.3)$$

Equation 22.3 should remind you of the spot-futures parity relationship. The major difference is in the substitution of $F(T_1)$ for the current spot price. The intuition is also similar. Delaying delivery from T_1 to T_2 provides the long position the knowledge that the stock will be purchased for $F(T_2)$ dollars at T_2 but does not require that money be tied up in the stock until T_2. The savings realized are the net cost of carry between T_1 and T_2. Delaying delivery from T_1 until T_2 frees up $F(T_1)$ dollars, which earn risk-free interest at r_f. The delayed delivery of the stock also results in the lost dividend yield between T_1 and T_2. The net cost of carry saved by delaying the delivery is thus $r_f - d$. This gives the proportional increase in the futures price that is required to compensate market participants for the delayed delivery of the stock and postponement of the payment of the futures price. If the parity condition for spreads is violated, arbitrage opportunities will arise. (Problem 19 at the end of the chapter explores this possibility.)

EXAMPLE 22.9   Spread Pricing

To see how to use Equation 22.3, consider the following data for a hypothetical contract:

Contract Maturity Data	Futures Price
January 15	$105.00
March 15	105.10

Suppose that the effective annual T-bill rate is expected to persist at 5% and that the dividend yield is 4% per year. The "correct" March futures price relative to the January price is, according to Equation 22.3,

$$105(1 + .05 - .04)^{1/6} = 105.174$$

The actual March futures price is 105.10, meaning that the March futures price is slightly underpriced compared to the January futures and that, aside from transaction costs, an arbitrage opportunity seems to be present.

Equation 22.3 shows that futures prices should all move together. Actually, it is not surprising that futures prices for different maturity dates move in unison, because all are linked to the same spot price through the parity relationship. Figure 22.6 plots futures prices on gold for three maturity dates. It is apparent that the prices move in virtual lockstep and that the more distant delivery dates command higher futures prices, as Equation 22.3 predicts.

The parity spreadsheet allows you to calculate futures prices corresponding to a spot price for different maturities, interest rates, and income yields. You can use the spreadsheet to see how prices of more distant contracts will fluctuate with spot prices and the cost of carry. You can learn more about this spreadsheet by using the version available on our Web site at **www.mhhe.com/bkm.**

Spot Futures Parity and Time Spreads				
Spot price	100			
Income yield (%)	2		Futures prices versus maturity	
Interest rate (%)	4.5			
Today's date	5/14/05		Spot price	100.00
Maturity date 1	11/17/05		Futures 1	101.26
Maturity date 2	1/2/06		Futures 2	101.58
Maturity date 3	6/7/06		Futures 3	102.66
Time to maturity 1	0.51			
Time to maturity 2	0.63			
Time to maturity 3	1.06			

Forward versus Futures Pricing

Until now we have paid little attention to the differing time profile of returns of futures and forward contracts. Instead, we have taken the sum of daily mark-to-market proceeds to the long position as $P_T - F_0$ and assumed for convenience that the entire profit to the futures contract accrues on the delivery date. The parity theorems we have derived apply strictly to forward pricing because they assume that contract proceeds are in fact realized only on delivery. Although this treatment is appropriate for a forward contract, the actual timing of cash flows influences the determination of the futures price.

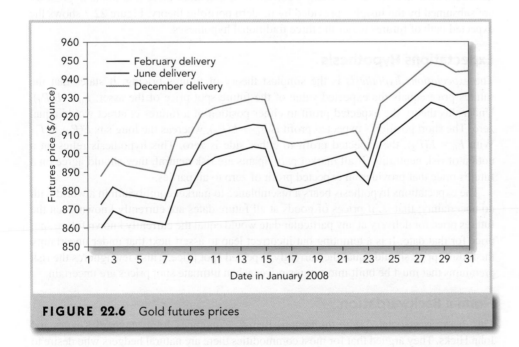

FIGURE 22.6 Gold futures prices

779

Futures prices will deviate from parity values when marking to market gives a systematic advantage to either the long or short position. If marking to market tends to favor the long position, for example, the futures price should exceed the forward price, because the long position will be willing to pay a premium for the advantage of marking to market.

When will marking to market favor either a long or short trader? A trader will benefit if daily settlements are received when the interest rate is high and are paid when the interest rate is low. Receiving payments when the interest rate is high allows investment of proceeds at a high rate; traders therefore prefer a high correlation between the level of the interest rate and the payments received from marking to market. The long position will benefit if futures prices tend to rise when interest rates are high, and therefore will be willing to accept a higher futures price. Whenever there is a positive correlation between interest rates and changes in futures prices, the "fair" futures price will exceed the forward price. Conversely, a negative correlation means that marking to market favors the short position and implies that the equilibrium futures price should be below the forward price.

For most contracts, the covariance between futures prices and interest rates is so low that the difference between futures and forward prices will be negligible. However, contracts on long-term fixed-income securities are an important exception to this rule. In this case, because prices have a high correlation with interest rates, the covariance can be large enough to generate a meaningful spread between forward and future prices.

22.5   FUTURES PRICES VERSUS EXPECTED SPOT PRICES

So far we have considered the relationship between futures prices and the *current* spot price. One of the oldest controversies in the theory of futures pricing concerns the relationship between the futures price and the *expected value* of the spot price of the commodity at some future date. In other words, how well does the futures price forecast the ultimate spot price? Three traditional theories have been put forth: the expectations hypothesis, normal backwardation, and contango. Today's consensus is that all of these traditional hypotheses are subsumed by the insights provided by modern portfolio theory. Figure 22.7 shows the expected path of futures under the three traditional hypotheses.

Expectations Hypothesis

The *expectations hypothesis* is the simplest theory of futures pricing. It states that the futures price equals the expected value of the future spot price of the asset: $F_0 = E(P_T)$. Under this theory the expected profit to either position of a futures contract would equal zero: The short position's expected profit is $F_0 - E(P_T)$, whereas the long's is $E(P_T) - F_0$. With $F_0 = E(P_T)$, the expected profit to either side is zero. This hypothesis relies on a notion of risk neutrality. If all market participants are risk neutral, they should agree on a futures price that provides an expected profit of zero to all parties.

The expectations hypothesis bears a resemblance to market equilibrium in a world with no uncertainty; that is, if prices of goods at all future dates are currently known, then the futures price for delivery at any particular date would equal the currently known future spot price for that date. It is a tempting but incorrect leap to assert next that under uncertainty the futures price should equal the currently expected spot price. This view ignores the risk premiums that must be built into futures prices when ultimate spot prices are uncertain.

Normal Backwardation

This theory is associated with the famous British economists John Maynard Keynes and John Hicks. They argued that for most commodities there are natural hedgers who desire to shed risk. For example, wheat farmers desire to shed the risk of uncertain wheat prices. These farmers will take short positions to deliver wheat in the future at a guaranteed price; they will short hedge. In order to induce speculators to take the corresponding long positions, the farmers need to offer speculators an expectation of profit. Speculators will enter the long side of the contract only if the futures price is below the expected spot price of wheat, for an expected profit of $E(P_T) - F_0$. The speculators' expected profit is the farmers' expected loss, but farmers are willing to bear the expected loss on the contract in order to shed the risk of uncertain wheat prices. The theory of *normal backwardation* thus suggests that the futures price will be bid down to a level below

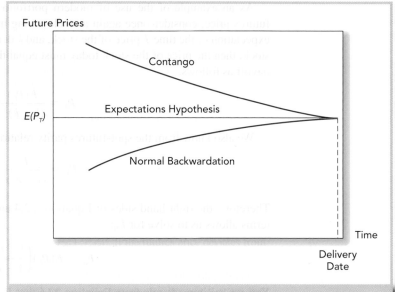

FIGURE 22.7 Futures price over time, in the special case that the expected spot price remains unchanged

the expected spot price and will rise over the life of the contract until the maturity date, at which point $F_T = P_T$.

Although this theory recognizes the important role of risk premiums in futures markets, it is based on total variability rather than on systematic risk. (This is not surprising, as Keynes wrote almost 40 years before the development of modern portfolio theory.) The modern view refines the measure of risk used to determine appropriate risk premiums.

Contango

The polar hypothesis to backwardation holds that the natural hedgers are the purchasers of a commodity, rather than the suppliers. In the case of wheat, for example, we would view grain processors as willing to pay a premium to lock in the price that they must pay for wheat. These processors hedge by taking a long position in the futures market; they are long hedgers, whereas farmers are short hedgers. Because long hedgers will agree to pay high futures prices to shed risk, and because speculators must be paid a premium to enter into the short position, the *contango* theory holds that F_0 must exceed $E(P_T)$.

It is clear that any commodity will have both natural long hedgers and short hedgers. The compromise traditional view, called the "net hedging hypothesis," is that F_0 will be less than $E(P_T)$ when short hedgers outnumber long hedgers and vice versa. The strong side of the market will be the side (short or long) that has more natural hedgers. The strong side must pay a premium to induce speculators to enter into enough contracts to balance the "natural" supply of long and short hedgers.

Modern Portfolio Theory

The three traditional hypotheses all envision a mass of speculators willing to enter either side of the futures market if they are sufficiently compensated for the risk they incur. Modern portfolio theory fine-tunes this approach by refining the notion of risk used in the determination of risk premiums. Simply put, if commodity prices pose positive systematic risk, futures prices must be lower than expected spot prices.

b. If the March futures price were to increase to 1,500, what percentage return would you earn on your net investment if you entered the long side of the contract at the price shown in the figure?

c. If the March futures price falls by 1%, what is your percentage return?

8. a. A single-stock futures contract on a non-dividend-paying stock with current price $150 has a maturity of 1 year. If the T-bill rate is 6%, what should the futures price be?

b. What should the futures price be if the maturity of the contract is 3 years?

c. What if the interest rate is 8% and the maturity of the contract is 3 years?

9. How might a portfolio manager use financial futures to hedge risk in each of the following circumstances:

a. You own a large position in a relatively illiquid bond that you want to sell.

b. You have a large gain on one of your Treasuries and want to sell it, but you would like to defer the gain until the next tax year.

c. You will receive your annual bonus next month that you hope to invest in long-term corporate bonds. You believe that bonds today are selling at quite attractive yields, and you are concerned that bond prices will rise over the next few weeks.

10. Suppose the value of the S&P 500 stock index is currently 1,500. If the 1-year T-bill rate is 5% and the expected dividend yield on the S&P 500 is 2%, what should the 1-year maturity futures price be?

11. Consider a stock that pays no dividends on which a futures contract, a call option, and a put option trade. The maturity date for all three contracts is T, the exercise price of the put and the call are both X, and the futures price is F. Show that if $X = F$, then the call price equals the put price. Use parity conditions to guide your demonstration.

12. It is now January. The current interest rate is 5%. The June futures price for gold is $846.30, whereas the December futures price is $860.00. Is there an arbitrage opportunity here? If so, how would you exploit it?

13. OneChicago has just introduced a single-stock futures contract on Brandex stock, a company that currently pays no dividends. Each contract calls for delivery of 1,000 shares of stock in 1 year. The T-bill rate is 6% per year.

a. If Brandex stock now sells at $120 per share, what should the futures price be?

b. If the Brandex price drops by 3%, what will be the change in the futures price and the change in the investor's margin account?

c. If the margin on the contract is $12,000, what is the percentage return on the investor's position?

14. The multiplier for a futures contract on a stock market index is $250. The maturity of the contract is 1 year, the current level of the index is 1,300, and the risk-free interest rate is .5% per month. The dividend yield on the index is .2% per month. Suppose that after 1 month, the stock index is at 1,320.

a. Find the cash flow from the mark-to-market proceeds on the contract. Assume that the parity condition always holds exactly.

b. Find the holding-period return if the initial margin on the contract is $13,000.

15. You are a corporate treasurer who will purchase $1 million of bonds for the sinking fund in 3 months. You believe rates will soon fall, and you would like to repurchase the company's sinking fund bonds (which currently are selling below par) in advance of requirements. Unfortunately, you must obtain approval from the board of directors for such a purchase, and this can take up to 2 months. What action can you take in the futures market to hedge any adverse movements in bond yields and prices until you can actually buy the bonds? Will you be long or short? Why? A qualitative answer is fine.

16. The S&P portfolio pays a dividend yield of 1% annually. Its current value is 1,300. The T-bill rate is 4%. Suppose the S&P futures price for delivery in 1 year is 1,330. Construct an arbitrage

strategy to exploit the mispricing and show that your profits 1 year hence will equal the mispricing in the futures market.

17. The Excel Application box in the chapter (available at **www.mhhe.com/bkm;** link to Chapter 22 material) shows how to use the spot-futures parity relationship to find a "term structure of futures prices," that is, futures prices for various maturity dates.

Please visit us at www.mhhe.com/bkm

    a. Suppose that today is January 1, 2008. Assume the interest rate is 3% per year and a stock index currently at 1,500 pays a dividend yield of 1.5%. Find the futures price for contract maturity dates of February 14, 2008, May 21, 2008, and November 18, 2008.

    b. What happens to the term structure of futures prices if the dividend yield is higher than the risk-free rate? For example, what if the dividend yield is 4%?

18. a. How should the parity condition (Equation 22.2) for stocks be modified for futures contracts on Treasury bonds? What should play the role of the dividend yield in that equation?

    b. In an environment with an upward-sloping yield curve, should T-bond futures prices on more-distant contracts be higher or lower than those on near-term contracts?

    c. Confirm your intuition by examining Figure 22.1.

Challenge Problems

19. Consider this arbitrage strategy to derive the parity relationship for spreads: (1) enter a long futures position with maturity date T_1 and futures price $F(T_1)$; (2) enter a short position with maturity T_2 and futures price $F(T_2)$; (3) at T_1, when the first contract expires, buy the asset and borrow $F(T_1)$ dollars at rate r_f; (4) pay back the loan with interest at time T_2.

    a. What are the total cash flows to this strategy at times 0, T_1, and T_2?

    b. Why must profits at time T_2 be zero if no arbitrage opportunities are present?

    c. What must the relationship between $F(T_1)$ and $F(T_2)$ be for the profits at T_2 to be equal to zero? This relationship is the parity relationship for spreads.

---

1. Joan Tam, CFA, believes she has identified an arbitrage opportunity for a commodity as indicated by the information given in the following exhibit:

Spot price for commodity	$120
Futures price for commodity expiring in 1 year	$125
Interest rate for 1 year	8%

    a. Describe the transactions necessary to take advantage of this specific arbitrage opportunity.

    b. Calculate the arbitrage profit.

2. Michelle Industries issued a Swiss franc–denominated 5-year discount note for SFr200 million. The proceeds were converted to U.S. dollars to purchase capital equipment in the United States. The company wants to hedge this currency exposure and is considering the following alternatives:

    • At-the-money Swiss franc call options.
    • Swiss franc forwards.
    • Swiss franc futures.

    a. Contrast the essential characteristics of each of these three derivative instruments.

    b. Evaluate the suitability of each in relation to Michelle's hedging objective, including both advantages and disadvantages.

3. Identify the fundamental distinction between a futures contract and an option contract, and briefly explain the difference in the manner that futures and options modify portfolio risk.

4. Maria VanHusen, CFA, suggests that using forward contracts on fixed income securities can be used to protect the value of the Star Hospital Pension Plan's bond portfolio against the possibility

of rising interest rates. VanHusen prepares the following example to illustrate how such protection would work:

- A 10-year bond with a face value of $1,000 is issued today at par value. The bond pays an annual coupon.
- An investor intends to buy this bond today and sell it in 6 months.
- The 6-month risk-free interest rate today is 5% (annualized).
- A 6-month forward contract on this bond is available, with a forward price of $1,024.70.
- In 6 months, the price of the bond, including accrued interest, is forecast to fall to $978.40 as a result of a rise in interest rates.

  a. Should the investor buy or sell the forward contract to protect the value of the bond against rising interest rates during the holding period?
  b. Calculate the value of the forward contract for the investor at the maturity of the forward contract if VanHusen's bond-price forecast turns out to be accurate.
  c. Calculate the change in value of the combined portfolio (the underlying bond and the appropriate forward contract position) 6 months after contract initiation.

5. Sandra Kapple asks Maria VanHusen about using futures contracts to protect the value of the Star Hospital Pension Plan's bond portfolio if interest rates rise. VanHusen states:

  a. "Selling a bond futures contract will generate positive cash flow in a rising interest rate environment prior to the maturity of the futures contract."
  b. "The cost of carry causes bond futures contracts to trade for a higher price than the spot price of the underlying bond prior to the maturity of the futures contract."

  Comment on the accuracy of each of VanHusen's two statements.

STANDARD &POOR'S

From the Market Insight entry page (**www.mhhe.com/edumarketinsight**), link to *Industry*, then locate the Airlines industry. Open the S&P Industry Survey for Airlines and review the *Current Environment* and the *Industry Profile* sections. What futures contracts might this industry use to hedge its risk? Where are these contracts traded? For information on these markets see **www.nymex.com.**

E-Investments

Contract Specifications for Financial Futures and Options

Go to the Chicago Mercantile Exchange site at **www.cme.com.** In the *Quick links* section, select *Contract Specifications*, and follow the link for *CME Equity* futures. Answer the following questions about the CME E-mini Russell 2000 futures contract:

1. What is the trading unit for the futures contract?
2. What is the settlement method for the futures contract?
3. For what months are the futures contracts available?
4. What is the 10% limit for the futures contracts? Click on the *Equity limits* link to find the *Price Limit Guide* and locate the E-mini Russell 2000 contract. Click on the *10% Limit* link at the top of the column for a description of what the limit means.
5. When is the next futures contract scheduled to be added?

SOLUTIONS TO CONCEPT CHECKS

1.

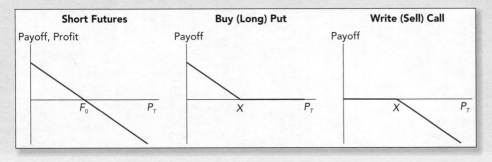

2. The clearinghouse has a zero net position in all contracts. Its long and short positions are offsetting, so that net cash flow from marking to market must be zero.

3.

	Oil Price in February, P_T		
	$95.15	$97.15	$99.15
Cash flow to purchase oil: $-100{,}000 \times P_T$	−$9,515,000	−$9,715,000	−$9,915,000
+ Profit on long futures: $100{,}000 \times (P_T - F_0)$	−200,000	0	+200,000
TOTAL CASH FLOW	−$9,715,000	−$9,715,000	−$9,715,000

4. The risk would be that the index and the portfolio do not move perfectly together. Thus basis risk involving the spread between the futures price and the portfolio value could persist even if the index futures price were set perfectly relative to the index itself.

5.

Action	Initial Cash Flow	Cash Flow in 1 Year
Lend S_0 dollars	−1,500	$1{,}500(1.04) = 1{,}560$
Sell stock short	+1,500	$-S_T - 25$
Long futures	0	$S_T - 1{,}520$
TOTAL	0	$15 risklessly

6. It must have zero beta. If the futures price is an unbiased estimator, then we infer that it has a zero risk premium, which means that beta must be zero.

Solution to question in Words from the Street, "Presidential and Other Prediction Futures"
Suppose you sell a contract on every candidate. No matter which of these candidates wins, your obligation come November will be $1 (and if a yet-unknown candidate happens to enter the race and win, your obligation will be zero). Therefore, if the total proceeds from selling each contract (at the bid price) were more than $1, you would have an arbitrage opportunity: your up-front proceeds would *necessarily* be greater than your future obligation. Such opportunities are not likely to be found in even mildly rational markets. We conclude that the sum of the bid prices *must* be less than $1.

The rationale for why the sum of ask prices is greater than $1 is not as strong. If you *buy* each contract (at the ask price), and if any of the candidates wins, you will receive a payoff of $1. Of course, if a previously unanticipated candidate enters and wins the race, you will end up with nothing. If the possibility of a dark-horse candidate is highly remote, then you should expect to pay approximately the present value of $1 for the portfolio of long positions on each candidate. In this case, we can view the excess of the sum of all ask prices above the present value of a dollar as reflecting bid–ask spreads, which are far higher here than in markets for conventional securities. Note that if the probability of a surprise candidate is not trivial, the expected payoff of the portfolio of long positions on each candidate will be less than $1, so the sum of the ask prices could be *less* than $1.

FUTURES, SWAPS, AND RISK MANAGEMENT

THE PREVIOUS CHAPTER provided a basic introduction to the operation of futures markets and the principles of futures pricing. This chapter explores both pricing and risk management in selected futures markets in more depth. Most of the growth has been in financial futures, which now dominate trading, so we emphasize these contracts.

Hedging refers to techniques that offset *particular* sources of risk, rather than as a more ambitious search for an optimal risk-return profile for an entire portfolio. Because futures contracts are written on particular quantities such as stock index values, foreign exchange rates, commodity prices, and so on, they are ideally suited for these applications. In this chapter we will consider several hedging applications, illustrating general

principles using a variety of contracts. We also show how hedging strategies can be used to isolate bets on perceived profit opportunities.

We begin with foreign exchange futures, where we show how forward exchange rates are determined by interest rate differentials across countries, and examine how firms can use futures to manage exchange rate risk. We then move on to stock-index futures, where we focus on program trading and index arbitrage. Next we turn to the most actively traded markets, those for interest rate futures. We also examine commodity futures pricing. Finally, we turn to swaps markets in foreign exchange and fixed-income securities. We will see that swaps can be interpreted as portfolios of forward contracts and valued accordingly.

23.1 FOREIGN EXCHANGE FUTURES

The Markets

Exchange rates between currencies vary continually and often substantially. This variability can be a source of concern for anyone involved in international business. A U.S. exporter who sells goods in England, for example, will be paid in British pounds, and the dollar value of those pounds depends on the exchange rate at the time payment is made.

Until that date, the U.S. exporter is exposed to foreign exchange rate risk. This risk can be hedged through currency futures or forward markets. For example, if you know you will receive £100,000 in 90 days, you can sell those pounds forward today in the forward market and lock in an exchange rate equal to today's forward price.

The forward market in foreign exchange is fairly informal. It is simply a network of banks and brokers that allows customers to enter forward contracts to purchase or sell currency in the future at a currently agreed-upon rate of exchange. The bank market in currencies is among the largest in the world, and most large traders with sufficient creditworthiness execute their trades here rather than in futures markets. Unlike those in futures markets, contracts in forward markets are not standardized in a formal market setting. Instead, each is negotiated separately. Moreover, there is no marking to market, as would occur in futures markets. Currency forward contracts call for execution only at the maturity date. Participants need to consider *counterparty risk,* the possibility that a trading partner may not be able to make good on its obligations under the contract if prices move against it. For this reason, traders who participate in forward markets must have solid creditworthiness.

For currency *futures,* however, there are formal markets on exchanges such as the Chicago Mercantile Exchange (International Monetary Market) or the London International Financial Futures Exchange. Here contracts are standardized by size, and daily marking to market is observed. Moreover, there are standard clearing arrangements that allow traders to enter or reverse positions easily. Margin positions are used to ensure contract performance, which is in turn guaranteed by the exchange's clearinghouse, so the identity and creditworthiness of the counterparty to a trade are less of a concern.

Figure 23.1 reproduces *The Wall Street Journal* listing of foreign exchange spot and forward rates. The listing gives the number of U.S. dollars required to purchase some unit of foreign currency and then the amount of foreign currency needed to purchase $1. Figure 23.2 reproduces futures listings, which show the number of dollars needed to purchase a given unit of foreign currency. In Figure 23.1, both spot and forward exchange rates are listed for various delivery dates.

The forward quotations listed in Figure 23.1 apply to rolling delivery in 30, 90, or 180 days. Thus tomorrow's forward

Currencies

January 2, 2008

U.S.-dollar foreign-exchange rates in late New York trading

Country/currency	Wed in US$	per US$	US$ vs, YTD chg (%)		Country/currency	Wed in US$	per US$	US$ vs, YTD chg (%)
Americas					**Europe**			
Argentina peso*	.3179	3.1456	-0.1		**Czech Rep.** koruna***	.05586	17.902	-1.5
Brazil real	.5672	1.7630	-1.0		**Denmark** krone	.1976	5.0607	-0.9
Canada dollar	1.0072	.9929	-0.1		**Euro area** euro	1.4729	.6789	-0.9
1-mos forward	1.0075	.9926	-0.1		**Hungary** forint	.005807	172.21	-0.6
3-mos forward	1.0079	.9922	-0.1		**Norway** krone	.1852	5.3996	-0.6
6-mos forward	1.0076	.9925	-0.1		**Poland** zloty	.4076	2.4534	-0.6
Chile peso	.002010	497.51	-0.1		**Russia** ruble‡	.04091	24.444	-0.5
Colombia peso	.0004959	2016.54	-0.1		**Slovak Rep** koruna	.04378	22.842	-0.8
Ecuador US dollar	1	1	unch		**Sweden** krona	.1564	6.3939	-1.1
Mexico peso*	.0916	10.9146	unch		**Switzerland** franc	.8944	1.1181	-1.3
Peru new sol	.3357	2.979	-0.6		1-mos forward	.8961	1.1159	-1.3
Uruguay peso†	.04640	21.55	unch		3-mos forward	.8988	1.1126	-1.3
Venezuela b. fuerte	.466287	2.1446	unch		6-mos forward	.9021	1.1085	-1.3
Asia-Pacific					**Turkey** lira***	.8543	1.1706	0.2
					UK pound	1.9809	.5048	0.3
Australia dollar	.8838	1.1315	-0.8		1-mos forward	1.9792	.5053	0.3
China yuan	.1371	7.2938	-0.1		3-mos forward	1.9758	.5061	0.3
Hong Kong dollar	.1280	7.8119	0.2		6-mos forward	1.9693	.5078	0.3
India rupee	.02544	39.308	-0.2		**Middle East/Africa**			
Indonesia rupiah	.0001066	9381	-0.1					
Japan yen	.009133	109.49	-1.8		**Bahrain** dinar	2.6574	.3763	0.1
1-mos forward	.009164	109.12	-1.7		**Egypt** pound*	.1813	5.5151	-0.3
3-mos forward	.009220	108.46	-1.7		**Israel** shekel	.2606	3.8373	-0.5
6-mos forward	.009295	107.58	-1.7		**Jordan** dinar	1.4139	.7073	-0.2
Malaysia ringgit§	.3021	3.3102	0.1		**Kuwait** dinar	3.6642	.2729	-0.2
New Zealand dollar	.7753	1.2898	-1.2		**Lebanon** pound	.0006616	1511.49	unch
Pakistan rupee	.01616	61.881	0.4		**Saudi Arabia** riyal	.2666	3.7509	unch
Philippines peso	.0243	41.135	-0.2		**South Africa** rand	.1466	6.8213	-0.3
Singapore dollar	.6953	1.4382	-0.2		**UAE** dirham	.2723	3.6724	unch
South Korea won	.0010673	936.94	0.1					
Taiwan dollar	.03083	32.436	unch					
Thailand baht	.03339	29.949	-0.3		**SDR**††	1.5785	.6335	unch

*Floating rate †Financial §Government rate ‡Russian Central Bank rate ***Rebased as of Jan 1, 2005
††Special Drawing Rights (SDR); from the International Monetary Fund; based on exchange rates for U.S., British and Japanese currencies.
Note: Based on trading among banks of $1 million and more, as quoted at 4 p.m. ET by Reuters.

FIGURE 23.1   Spot and forward prices in foreign exchange

Source: *The Wall Street Journal,* January 3, 2008. Reprinted by permission of *The Wall Street Journal,* © 2008 Dow Jones & Company, Inc. All rights reserved worldwide.

United States, and enter a long futures position to eliminate foreign exchange risk. If the value is negative, borrow in the United States, lend in the United Kingdom, and take a short position in pound futures. When prices preclude arbitrage opportunities, the expression must equal zero. This no-arbitrage condition implies that

$$F_0 = \frac{1 + r_{US}}{1 + r_{UK}} E_0 \tag{23.2}$$

which is the interest rate parity theorem for a 1-year horizon.

EXAMPLE 23.2   Covered Interest Arbitrage

Ample empirical evidence bears out the interest rate parity relationship. For example, on December 14, 2007, the dollar-denominated LIBOR interest rate with maturity of 6 months was 4.91%, while the comparable U.K. pound-denominated rate was 6.25%. The spot exchange rate was $2.0398/£. Using these values, we find that interest rate parity implies that the forward exchange rate for delivery in 6 months should have been $2.0398 \times (1.0491/1.0625)^{\frac{1}{2}} = \$2.0269/£$. The actual forward rate was $2.0275/£, which was so close to the parity value that transaction costs would have prevented arbitrageurs from profiting from the discrepancy.

Direct versus Indirect Quotes

The exchange rate in Examples 23.1 and 23.2 is expressed as dollars per pound. This is an example of a *direct* exchange rate quote. The euro-dollar exchange rate is also typically expressed as a direct quote. In contrast, exchange rates for other currencies such as the Japanese yen or Swiss franc are typically expressed as *indirect* quotes, that is, as units of foreign currency per dollar, for example 110 yen per dollar. For currencies expressed as indirect quotes, depreciation of the dollar would result in a *decrease* in the quoted exchange rate ($1 buys fewer yen); in contrast, dollar depreciation versus the pound would show up as a *higher* exchange rate (more dollars are required to buy £1). When the exchange rate is quoted as foreign currency per dollar, the domestic and foreign exchange rates in Equation 23.2 must be switched: in this case the equation becomes

> **CONCEPT CHECK 1**
>
> What would be the arbitrage strategy and associated profits in Example 23.1 if the initial futures price were $F_0 = \$2.01$/pound?

$$F_0(\text{foreign currency} / \$) = \frac{1 + r_{\text{foreign}}}{1 + r_{US}} \times E_0(\text{foreign currency} / \$)$$

If the interest rate in the U.S. is higher than in Japan, the dollar will sell in the forward market at a lower price (will buy fewer yen) than in the spot market.

Using Futures to Manage Exchange Rate Risk

Consider a U.S. firm that exports most of its product to Great Britain. The firm is vulnerable to fluctuations in the dollar/pound exchange rate for several reasons. First, the dollar value of the pound-denominated revenue derived from its customers will fluctuate with the exchange rate. Second, the pound price that the firm can charge its customers in the

United Kingdom will itself be affected by the exchange rate. For example, if the pound depreciates by 10% relative to the dollar, the firm would need to increase the pound price of its goods by 10% in order to maintain the dollar-equivalent price. However, the firm might not be able to raise the price by 10% if it faces competition from British producers, or if it believes the higher pound-denominated price would reduce demand for its product.

To offset its foreign exchange exposure, the firm might engage in transactions that bring it profits when the pound depreciates. The lost profits from business operations resulting from a depreciation will then be offset by gains on its financial transactions. Suppose, for example, that the firm enters a futures contract to deliver pounds for dollars at an exchange rate agreed to today. Therefore, if the pound depreciates, the futures position will yield a profit.

For example, suppose that the futures price is currently $2 per pound for delivery in 3 months. If the firm enters a futures contract with a futures price of $2.00 per pound, and the exchange rate in 3 months is $1.90 per pound, then the profit on the transaction is $.10 per pound. The futures price converges at the maturity date to the spot exchange rate of $1.90 and the profit to the short position is therefore $F_0 - F_T = \$2.00 - \$1.90 = \$.10$ per pound.

How many pounds should be sold in the futures market to most fully offset the exposure to exchange rate fluctuations? Suppose the dollar value of profits in the next quarter will fall by $200,000 for every $.10 depreciation of the pound. To hedge, we need a futures position that provides a $200,000 *profit* for every $.10 that the pound depreciates. Therefore, we need a futures position to deliver £2,000,000. As we have just seen, the profit per pound on the futures contract equals the difference in the current futures price and the ultimate exchange rate; therefore, the foreign exchange profits resulting from a $.10 depreciation[1] will equal $.10 × 2,000,000 = $200,000.

The proper hedge position in pound futures is independent of the actual depreciation in the pound as long as the relationship between profits and exchange rates is approximately linear. For example, if the pound depreciates by only half as much, $.05, the firm would lose only $100,000 in operating profits. The futures position would also return half the profits: $.05 × 2,000,000 = $100,000, again just offsetting the operating exposure. If the pound *appreciates,* the hedge position still (unfortunately in this case) offsets the operating exposure. If the pound appreciates by $.05, the firm might gain $100,000 from the enhanced value of the pound; however, it will lose that amount on its obligation to deliver the pounds for the original futures price.

The hedge ratio is the number of futures positions necessary to hedge the risk of the unprotected portfolio, in this case the firm's export business. In general, we can think of the **hedge ratio** as the number of hedging vehicles (e.g., futures contracts) one would establish to offset the risk of a particular unprotected position. The hedge ratio, H, in this case is

$$H = \frac{\text{Change in value of unprotected position for a given change in exchange rate}}{\text{Profit derived from one futures position for the same change in exchange rate}}$$

$$= \frac{\$200,000 \text{ per } \$.10 \text{ change in } \$/£ \text{ exchange rate}}{\$.10 \text{ profit } per \ pound \text{ delivered per } \$.10 \text{ change in } \$/£ \text{ exchange rate}}$$

$$= 2,000,000 \text{ pounds to be delivered}$$

Because each pound-futures contract on the International Monetary Market (a division of the Chicago Mercantile Exchange) calls for delivery of 62,500 pounds, you would need to sell 2,000,000/62,500 per contract = 32 contracts.

---

[1]Actually, the profit on the contract depends on the changes in the futures price, not the spot exchange rate. For simplicity, we call the decline in the futures price the depreciation in the pound.

One interpretation of the hedge ratio is as a ratio of sensitivities to the underlying source of uncertainty. The sensitivity of operating profits is $200,000 per swing of $.10 in the exchange rate. The sensitivity of futures profits is $.10 per pound to be delivered per swing of $.10 in the exchange rate. Therefore, the hedge ratio is $200,000/.10 = 2,000,000$ pounds.

We could just as easily have defined the hedge ratio in terms of futures contracts. Because each contract calls for delivery of 62,500 pounds, the profit on each contract per swing of $.10 in the exchange rate is $6,250. Therefore, the hedge ratio defined in units of futures contracts is $200,000/\$6,250 = 32$ contracts, as derived above.

CONCEPT CHECK 2	Suppose a multinational firm is harmed when the *dollar* depreciates. Specifically, suppose that its profits decrease by $200,000 for every $.05 rise in the dollar/ pound exchange rate. How many contracts should the firm enter? Should it take the long side or the short side of the contracts?

Given the sensitivity of the unhedged position to changes in the exchange rate, calculating the risk-minimizing hedge position is easy. Far more difficult is the determination of that sensitivity. For the exporting firm, for example, a naive view might hold that one need only estimate the expected pound-denominated revenue, and then contract to deliver that number of pounds in the futures or forward market. This approach, however, fails to recognize that pound revenue is itself a function of the exchange rate because the U.S. firm's competitive position in the United Kingdom is determined in part by the exchange rate.

One approach relies, in part, on historical relationships. Suppose, for example, that the firm prepares a scatter diagram as in Figure 23.3 that relates its business profits (measured in dollars) in each of the last 40 quarters to the dollar/pound exchange rate in that

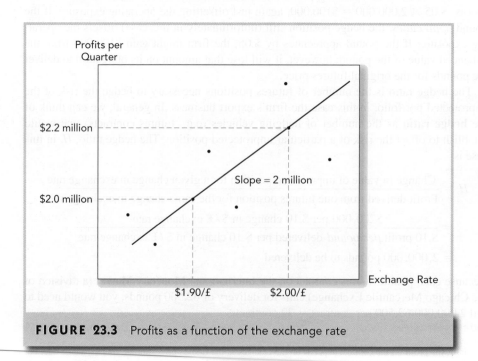

FIGURE 23.3   Profits as a function of the exchange rate

quarter. Profits generally are lower when the exchange rate is lower, that is, when the pound depreciates. To quantify that sensitivity, we might estimate the following regression equation:

$$\text{Profits} = a + b(\$/£ \text{ exchange rate})$$

The slope of the regression, the estimate of *b,* is the sensitivity of quarterly profits to the exchange rate. For example, if the estimate of *b* turns out to be 2,000,000, as in Figure 23.3, then on average, a $1 *increase* in the value of the pound results in a $2,000,000 *increase* in quarterly profits. This, of course, is the sensitivity we posited when we asserted that a $.10 drop in the dollar/pound exchange rate would decrease profits by $200,000.

Of course, one must interpret regression output with care. For example, one would not want to extrapolate the historical relationship between profitability and exchange rates exhibited in a period when the exchange rate hovered between $1.80 and $2.10 per pound to scenarios in which the exchange rate might be forecast at below $1.40 per pound or above $2.50 per pound.

In addition, one always must use care when extrapolating past relationships into the future. We saw in Chapter 8 that regression betas from the index model tend to vary across time; such problems are not unique to the index model. Moreover, regression estimates are just that—estimates. Parameters of a regression equation are sometimes measured with considerable imprecision.

Still, historical relationships are often a good place to start when looking for the average sensitivity of one variable to another. These slope coefficients are not perfect, but they are still useful indicators of hedge ratios.

CONCEPT CHECK 3	United Millers purchases corn to make cornflakes. When the price of corn increases, the cost of making cereal increases, resulting in lower profits. Historically, profits per quarter have been related to the price of corn according to the equation: Profits = $8 million − 1 million × price per bushel. How many bushels of corn should United Millers purchase in the corn futures market to hedge its corn-price risk?

23.2 STOCK–INDEX FUTURES

The Contracts

In contrast to most futures contracts, which call for delivery of a specified commodity, stock-index contracts are settled by a cash amount equal to the value of the stock index in question on the contract maturity date times a multiplier that scales the size of the contract. The total profit to the long position is $S_T - F_0$, where S_T is the value of the stock index on the maturity date. Cash settlement avoids the costs that would be incurred if the short trader had to purchase the stocks in the index and deliver them to the long position, and if the long position then had to sell the stocks for cash. Instead, the long trader receives $S_T - F_0$ dollars, and the short trader $F_0 - S_T$ dollars. These profits duplicate those that would arise with actual delivery.

There are several stock-index futures contracts currently traded. Table 23.1 lists some of the major ones, showing under contract size the multiplier used to calculate contract settlements. An S&P 500 contract, for example, with a futures price of 1,400 and a final index

Contract	Underlying Market Index	Contract Size	Exchange
S&P 500	Standard & Poor's 500 index. A value-weighted arithmetic average of 500 stocks.	$250 times S&P 500 index	Chicago Mercantile Exchange
Dow Jones Industrial Average (DJIA)	Dow Jones Industrial Average. Price-weighted average of 30 firms.	$10 times index	Chicago Board of Trade
Russell 2000	Index of 2,000 smaller firms.	$500 times index	Chicago Mercantile Exchange
S&P Mid-Cap	Index of 400 firms of mid-range market value.	$500 times index	Chicago Mercantile Exchange
NASDAQ 100	Value-weighted arithmetic average of 100 of the largest over-the-counter stocks.	$100 times index	Chicago Mercantile Exchange
Nikkei	Nikkei 225 stock average.	$5 times Nikkei Index	Chicago Mercantile Exchange
FTSE 100	Financial Times Stock Exchange Index of 100 U.K. firms.	£10 times FTSE Index	London International Financial Futures Exchange
DAX-30	Index of 30 German stocks.	25 euros times index	Eurex
CAC-40	Index of 40 French stocks.	10 euros times index	Euronext Paris
DJ Euro Stoxx-50	Index of 50 large stocks in Euro-zone.	10 euros times index	Eurex

TABLE 23.1

Major stock-index futures

value of 1,405 would result in a profit for the long side of $250 \times (1,405 - 1,400) = $1,250$. The S&P contract by far dominates the market in stock index futures.[2]

The broad-based stock market indexes are all highly correlated. Table 23.2 presents a correlation matrix for the major U.S. indexes. Notice that the correlations among the Dow Jones Industrial Average, the New York Stock Exchange Index, and the S&P 500 are all well above .9. The NASDAQ Composite index, which is dominated by technology firms, and the Russell 2000 index of smaller capitalization firms have smaller correlations with the large-cap indexes and with each other, but for the most part, even these are above .8.

Creating Synthetic Stock Positions: An Asset Allocation Tool

One reason stock-index futures are so popular is that they substitute for holdings in the underlying stocks themselves. Index futures let investors participate in broad market movements without actually buying or selling large amounts of stock.

Because of this, we say futures represent "synthetic" holdings of the market portfolio. Instead of holding the market directly, the investor takes a long futures position in the index. Such a strategy is attractive because the transaction costs involved in establishing and liquidating futures positions are much lower than taking actual spot positions. Investors who wish to frequently buy and sell market positions find it much less costly to play the futures market rather than the underlying spot market. "Market timers," who speculate on broad market moves rather than on individual securities, are large players in stock-index futures for this reason.

[2]We should point out that while the multipliers on these contracts may make the resulting positions too large for many small investors, there are effectively equivalent futures contracts with smaller multipliers (typically one-fifth the value of the standard contract) called *E-Minis* that are traded on the Chicago Mercantile Exchange's Globex electronic exchange. The exchange offers E-Mini contracts in several stock indexes as well as foreign currencies.

	DJIA	NYSE	NASDAQ	S&P 500	Russell 2000	TABLE 23.2
DJIA	1.000					Correlations among
NYSE	0.931	1.000				major U.S. stock
NASDAQ	0.839	0.825	1.000			market indexes
S&P 500	0.957	0.973	0.899	1.000		
Russell 2000	0.758	0.837	0.855	0.822	1.000	

Note: Correlations computed using monthly returns for 5 years ending in March 2006.

One means to market time, for example, is to shift between Treasury bills and broad-based stock market holdings. Timers attempt to shift from bills into the market before market upturns, and to shift back into bills to avoid market downturns, thereby profiting from broad market movements. Market timing of this sort, however, can result in huge brokerage fees with the frequent purchase and sale of many stocks. An attractive alternative is to invest in Treasury bills and hold varying amounts of market-index futures contracts.

The strategy works like this. When timers are bullish, they will establish many long futures positions that they can liquidate quickly and cheaply when expectations turn bearish. Rather than shifting back and forth between T-bills and stocks, they buy and hold T-bills and adjust only the futures position. This minimizes transaction costs. An advantage of this technique for timing is that investors can implicitly buy or sell the market index in its entirety, whereas market timing in the spot market would require the simultaneous purchase or sale of all the stocks in the index. This is technically difficult to coordinate and can lead to slippage in execution of a timing strategy.

You can construct a T-bill plus index futures position that duplicates the payoff to holding the stock index itself. Here is how:

1. Purchase as many market-index futures contracts as you need to establish your desired stock position. A desired holding of $1,000 multiplied by the S&P 500 index, for example, would require the purchase of four contracts because each contract calls for delivery of $250 multiplied by the index.

2. Invest enough money in T-bills to cover the payment of the futures price at the contract's maturity date. The necessary investment will equal the present value of the futures price that will be paid to satisfy the contracts. The T-bill holdings will grow by the maturity date to a level equal to the futures price.

EXAMPLE 23.3   Synthetic Positions Using Stock-Index Futures

Suppose that an institutional investor wants to invest $140 million in the market for 1 month and, to minimize trading costs, chooses to buy the S&P 500 futures contracts as a substitute for actual stock holdings. If the index is now at 1,400, the 1-month delivery futures price is 1,414, and the T-bill rate is 1% per month, it would buy 400 contracts. (Each contract controls $250 × 1,400 = $350,000 worth of stock, and $140 million/$350,000 = 400.) The institution thus has a long position on $100,000 times the S&P 500 index (400 contracts times the contract multiplier of $250). To cover payment of the futures price, it must invest 100,000 times the present value of the futures price in T-bills. This equals

$100,000 \times (1,414/1.01) = \$140$ million market value of bills. Notice that the \$140 million outlay in bills is precisely equal to the amount that would have been needed to buy the stock directly. (The face value of the bills will be $100,000 \times 1,414 = \$141.4$ million.)

This is an artificial, or synthetic, stock position. What is the value of this portfolio at the maturity date? Call S_T the value of the stock index on the maturity date T and, as usual, let F_0 be the original futures price:

	In General (Per Unit of the Index)	Our Numbers
1. Profits from contract	$S_T - F_0$	$\$100,000(S_T - 1,414)$
2. Face value of T-bills	F_0	141,400,000
TOTAL	S_T	100,000S_T

The total payoff on the contract maturity date is exactly proportional to the value of the stock index. In other words, adopting this portfolio strategy is equivalent to holding the stock index itself, aside from the issue of interim dividend distributions and tax treatment.

The bills-plus-futures contracts strategy in Example 23.3 may be viewed as a 100% stock strategy. At the other extreme, investing in zero futures results in a 100% bills position. Moreover, a short futures position will result in a portfolio equivalent to that obtained by short-selling the stock market index, because in both cases the investor gains from decreases in the stock price. Bills-plus-futures mixtures clearly allow for a flexible and low-transaction-cost approach to market timing. The futures positions may be established or reversed quickly and cheaply. Also, because the short futures position allows the investor to earn interest on T-bills, it is superior to a conventional short sale of the stock, where the investor may earn little or no interest on the proceeds of the short sale.

The nearby box illustrates that it is now commonplace for money managers to use futures contracts to create synthetic equity positions in stock markets. The article notes that futures positions can be particularly helpful in establishing synthetic positions in foreign equities, where trading costs tend to be greater and markets tend to be less liquid.

CONCEPT CHECK 4

The market timing strategy of Example 23.3 also can be achieved by an investor who holds an indexed stock portfolio and "synthetically exits" the position using futures if and when he turns pessimistic concerning the market. Suppose the investor holds \$140 million of stock. What futures position added to the stock holdings would create a synthetic T-bill exposure when he is bearish on the market? Confirm that the profits are effectively risk-free using a table like that in Example 23.3.

Index Arbitrage

Whenever the actual futures price falls outside the no-arbitrage band, there is an opportunity for profit. This is why the parity relationships are so important. Far from being theoretical academic constructs, they are in fact a guide to trading rules that can generate large profits. One of the most notable developments in trading activity has been the advent of **index arbitrage,** an investment strategy that exploits divergences between the actual futures price and its theoretically correct parity value.

In theory, index arbitrage is simple. If the futures price is too high, short the futures contract and buy the stocks in the index. If it is too low, go long in futures and short the

GOT A BUNDLE TO INVEST FAST?
THINK STOCK-INDEX FUTURES

As investors go increasingly global and market turbulence grows, stock-index futures are emerging as the favorite way for nimble money managers to deploy their funds. Indeed, in most major markets, trading in stock futures now exceeds the buying and selling of actual shares.

What's the big appeal? Speed, ease and cheapness. For most major markets, stock futures not only boast greater liquidity but also lower transaction costs than traditional trading methods.

"When I decide it's time to move into France, Germany or Britain, I don't necessarily want to wait around until I find exactly the right stocks," says Fabrizio Pierallini, manager of New York–based Vontobel Ltd.'s Euro Pacific Fund.

Mr. Pierallini says he later fine-tunes his market picks by gradually shifting out of futures into favorite stocks. To the extent Mr. Pierallini's stocks outperform the market, futures provide a means to preserve those gains, even while hedging against market declines.

For instance, by selling futures equal to the value of the underlying portfolio, a manager can almost completely insulate a portfolio from market moves. Say a manager succeeds in outperforming the market, but still loses 3% while the market as a whole falls 10%. Hedging with

futures would capture that margin of out-performance, transforming the loss into a profit of roughly 7%.

Among futures-intensive strategies is "global tactical asset allocation," which involves trading whole markets worldwide as traditional managers might trade stocks. The growing popularity of such asset-allocation strategies has given futures a big boost in recent years.

To capitalize on global market swings, "futures do the job for us better than stocks, and they're cheaper," said Jarrod Wilcox, director of global investments at PanAgora Asset Management, a Boston-based asset allocator. Even when PanAgora does take positions in individual stocks, it often employs futures to modify its position, such as by hedging part of its exposure to that particular stock market.

When it comes to investing overseas, Mr. Wilcox noted, futures are often the only vehicle that makes sense from a cost standpoint. Abroad, transaction taxes and sky-high commissions can wipe out more than 1% of the money deployed on each trade. By contrast, a comparable trade in futures costs as little as 0.05%.

stocks. You can perfectly hedge your position and should earn arbitrage profits equal to the mispricing of the contract.

In practice, however, index arbitrage is difficult to implement. The problem lies in buying "the stocks in the index." Selling or purchasing shares in all 500 stocks in the S&P 500 is impractical for two reasons. The first is transaction costs, which may outweigh any profits to be made from the arbitrage. Second, it is extremely difficult to buy or sell stock of 500 different firms simultaneously, and any lags in the execution of such a strategy can destroy the effectiveness of a plan to exploit temporary price discrepancies.

Arbitrageurs need to trade an entire portfolio of stocks quickly and simultaneously if they hope to exploit disparities between the futures price and its corresponding stock index. For this they need a coordinated trading program; hence the term **program trading,** which refers to purchases or sales of entire portfolios of stocks. Electronic trading enables traders to submit coordinated buy or sell programs to the stock market at once.

The success of these arbitrage positions and associated program trades depends on only two things: the relative levels of spot and futures prices and synchronized trading in the two markets. Because arbitrageurs exploit disparities in futures and spot prices, absolute price levels are unimportant.

Using Index Futures to Hedge Market Risk

How might a portfolio manager use futures to hedge market exposure? Suppose, for example, that you manage a $30 million portfolio with a beta of .8. You are bullish on the market over the long term, but you are afraid that over the next 2 months, the market is vulnerable to a sharp downturn. If trading were costless, you could sell your portfolio, place the proceeds in T-bills for 2 months, and then reestablish your position after you perceive that the risk of the downturn has passed. In practice, however, this strategy would result in unacceptable trading costs, not to mention tax problems resulting from the realization of capital gains or losses on the portfolio. An alternative approach would be to use stock index futures to hedge your market exposure.

EXAMPLE 23.4   Hedging Market Risk

Suppose that the S&P 500 index currently is at 1,000. A decrease in the index to 975 would represent a drop of 2.5%. With a portfolio beta of .8, you would expect a loss of .8 × 2.5% = 2%, or in dollar terms, .02 × $30 million = $600,000. Therefore, the sensitivity of your portfolio value to market movements is $600,000 per 25-point movement in the S&P 500 index.

To hedge this risk, you could sell stock index futures. When your portfolio falls in value along with declines in the broad market, the futures contract will provide an offsetting profit.

The sensitivity of a futures contract to market movements is easy to determine. With its contract multiplier of $250, the profit on the S&P 500 futures contract varies by $6,250 for every 25-point swing in the index. Therefore, to hedge your market exposure for 2 months, you could calculate the hedge ratio as follows:

$$H = \frac{\text{Change in portfolio value}}{\text{Profit on one futures contract}} = \frac{\$600,000}{\$6,250} = 96 \text{ contracts (short)}$$

You would enter the short side of the contracts, because you want profits from the contract to offset the exposure of your portfolio to the market. Because your portfolio does poorly when the market falls, you need a position that will do well when the market falls.

We also could approach the hedging problem in Example 23.4 using a similar regression procedure as that illustrated in Figure 23.3 for foreign exchange risk. The predicted value of the portfolio is graphed in Figure 23.4 as a function of the value of the S&P 500 index. With a beta of .8, the slope of the relationship is 24,000: A 2.5% increase in the index, from 1,000 to 1,025, results in a capital gain of 2% of $30 million, or $600,000. Therefore, your portfolio will increase in value by $24,000 for each increase of one point in the index. As a result, you should enter a short position on 24,000 units of the S&P 500 index to fully offset your exposure to marketwide movements. Because the contract multiplier is $250 times the index, you need to sell 24,000/250 = 96 contracts.

Notice that when the slope of the regression line relating your unprotected position to the value of an asset is positive, your hedge strategy calls for a *short* position in that asset. The hedge ratio is the negative of the regression slope. This is because the hedge position should offset your initial exposure. If you do poorly when the asset value falls, you need a hedge vehicle that will do well when the asset value falls. This calls for a short position in the asset.

Active managers sometimes believe that a particular asset is underpriced, but that the market as a whole is about to fall. Even if the asset is a good buy relative to other stocks in the market, it still might perform poorly in a broad market downturn. To solve this problem, the manager would like to separate the bet on the firm from the bet on the market: The bet on the company must be offset with a hedge against the market exposure that normally would accompany a purchase of the stock. In other words, the manager seeks a **market-neutral bet** on the stock, by which we mean that a position on the stock is taken to capture

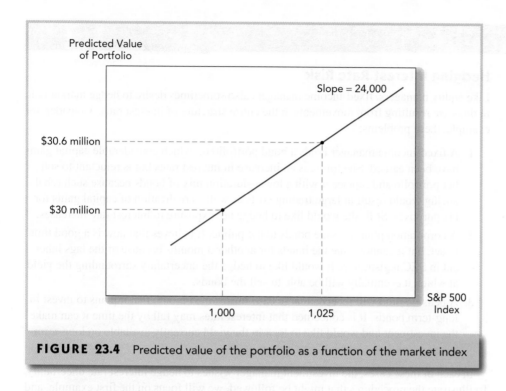

FIGURE 23.4   Predicted value of the portfolio as a function of the market index

its alpha (its abnormal risk-adjusted expected return), but that market exposure is fully hedged, resulting in a position beta of zero.

By allowing investors to hedge market performance, the futures contract allows the portfolio manager to make stock picks without concern for the market exposure of the stocks chosen. After the stocks are chosen, the resulting market risk of the portfolio can be modulated to any degree using the stock futures contracts. Here again, the stock's beta is the key to the hedging strategy. We discuss market-neutral strategies in more detail in Chapter 26.

EXAMPLE 23.5   Market-Neutral Active Stock Selection

Suppose the beta of the stock is ⅔, and the manager purchases $375,000 worth of the stock. For every 3% drop in the broad market, the stock would be expected to respond with a drop of ⅔ × 3% = 2%, or $7,500. The S&P 500 contract will fall by 30 points from a current value of 1,000 if the market drops 3%. With the contract multiplier of $250, this would entail a profit to a short futures position of 30 × $250 = $7,500 per contract. Therefore, the market risk of the stock can be offset by shorting one S&P contract. More formally, we could calculate the hedge ratio as

$$H = \frac{\text{Expected change in stock value per 3\% market drop}}{\text{Profit on one short contract per 3\% market drop}}$$

$$= \frac{\$7,500 \text{ swing in unprotected position}}{\$7,500 \text{ profit per contract}}$$

$$= 1 \text{ contract}$$

Now that market risk is hedged, the only source of variability in the performance of the stock-plus-futures portfolio will be the firm-specific performance of the stock.

23.3 INTEREST RATE FUTURES

Hedging Interest Rate Risk

Like equity managers, fixed-income managers also sometimes desire to hedge market risk, in this case resulting from movements in the entire structure of interest rates. Consider, for example, these problems:

1. A fixed-income manager holds a bond portfolio on which considerable capital gains have been earned. She foresees an increase in interest rates but is reluctant to sell her portfolio and replace it with a lower-duration mix of bonds because such rebalancing would result in large trading costs as well as realization of capital gains for tax purposes. Still, she would like to hedge her exposure to interest rate increases.

2. A corporation plans to issue bonds to the public. It believes that now is a good time to act, but it cannot issue the bonds for another 3 months because of the lags inherent in SEC registration. It would like to hedge the uncertainty surrounding the yield at which it eventually will be able to sell the bonds.

3. A pension fund will receive a large cash inflow next month that it plans to invest in long-term bonds. It is concerned that interest rates may fall by the time it can make the investment and would like to lock in the yield currently available on long-term issues.

In each of these cases, the investment manager wishes to hedge interest rate uncertainty. To illustrate the procedures that might be followed, we will focus on the first example, and suppose that the portfolio manager has a $10 million bond portfolio with a modified duration of 9 years.[3] If, as feared, market interest rates increase and the bond portfolio's yield also rises, say, by 10 basis points (.10%), the fund will suffer a capital loss. Recall from Chapter 16 that the capital loss in percentage terms will be the product of modified duration, D^*, and the change in the portfolio yield. Therefore, the loss will be

$$D^* \times \Delta y = 9 \times .10\% = .90\%$$

or $90,000. This establishes that the sensitivity of the value of the unprotected portfolio to changes in market yields is $9,000 per 1 basis point change in the yield. Market practitioners call this ratio the **price value of a basis point,** or PVBP. The PVBP represents the sensitivity of the dollar value of the portfolio to changes in interest rates. Here, we've shown that

$$\text{PVBP} = \frac{\text{Change in portfolio value}}{\text{Predicted change in yield}} = \frac{\$90,000}{10 \text{ basis points}} = \$9,000 \text{ per basis point}$$

One way to hedge this risk is to take an offsetting position in an interest rate futures contract. The Treasury bond contract is the most widely traded contract. The bond nominally calls for delivery of $100,000 par value T-bonds with 6% coupons and 20-year maturity. In practice, the contract delivery terms are fairly complicated because many bonds with different coupon rates and maturities may be substituted to settle the contract. However, we will assume that the bond to be delivered on the contract already is known and has a modified duration of 10 years. Finally, suppose that the futures price currently is $90 per $100 par value. Because the contract requires delivery of $100,000 par value of bonds, the contract multiplier is $1,000.

---

[3]Recall that modified duration, D^*, is related to duration, D, by the formula $D^* = D/(1 + y)$, where y is the bond's yield to maturity. If the bond pays coupons semiannually, then y should be measured as a semiannual yield. For simplicity, we will assume annual coupon payments, and treat y as the effective annual yield to maturity.

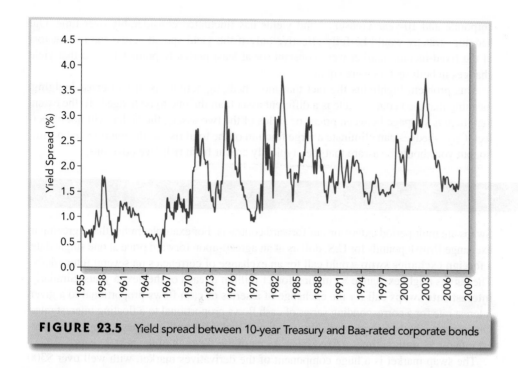

FIGURE 23.5 Yield spread between 10-year Treasury and Baa-rated corporate bonds

Given these data, we can calculate the PVBP for the futures contract. If the yield on the delivery bond increases by 10 basis points, the bond value will fall by $D^* \times .1\% = 10 \times .1\% = 1\%$. The futures price also will decline 1% from 90 to 89.10.[4] Because the contract multiplier is $1,000, the gain on each short contract will be $1,000 \times .90 = 900. Therefore, the PVBP for one futures contract is $900/10-basis-point change, or $90 for a change in yield of 1 basis point.

Now we can easily calculate the hedge ratio as follows:

$$H = \frac{\text{PVBP of portfolio}}{\text{PVBP of hedge vehicle}} = \frac{\$9,000}{\$90 \text{ per contract}} = 100 \text{ contracts}$$

Therefore, 100 T-bond futures contracts will serve to offset the portfolio's exposure to interest rate fluctuations.

Notice that this is another example of a market-neutral strategy. In Example 23.5, which illustrated an equity-hedging strategy, stock-index futures were used to drive a portfolio beta to zero. In this application, we used a T-bond contract to drive the interest

> **CONCEPT CHECK 5**
>
> Suppose the bond portfolio is twice as large, $20 million, but that its modified duration is only 4.5 years. Show that the proper hedge position in T-bond futures is the same as the value just calculated, 100 contracts.

rate exposure of a bond position to zero. The hedged fixed-income position has a duration (or a PVBP) of zero. The source of risk differs, but the hedging strategy is essentially the same.

Although the hedge ratio is easy to compute, the hedging problem in practice is more difficult. We assumed in our example that the yields on the T-bond contract and the bond portfolio would move perfectly in unison. Although interest rates on various fixed-income instruments do tend to vary in tandem, there is considerable slippage across sectors of the fixed-income market. For example, Figure 23.5 shows that the spread between long-term

---

[4]This assumes the futures price will be exactly proportional to the bond price, which ought to be nearly true.

corporate and 10-year Treasury bond yields has fluctuated considerably over time. Our hedging strategy would be fully effective only if the yield spread across the two sectors of the fixed-income market were constant (or at least perfectly predictable) so that yield changes in both sectors were equal.

This problem highlights the fact that most hedging activity is in fact **cross-hedging,** meaning that the hedge vehicle is a different asset than the one to be hedged. To the extent that there is slippage between prices or yields of the two assets, the hedge will not be perfect. Cross-hedges can eliminate a large fraction of the total risk of the unprotected portfolio, but you should be aware that they typically are far from risk-free positions.

23.4 SWAPS

Swaps are multiperiod extensions of forward contracts. For example, rather than agreeing to exchange British pounds for U.S. dollars at an agreed-upon forward price at one single date, a **foreign exchange swap** would call for an exchange of currencies on several future dates. The parties might exchange $2 million for £1 million in each of the next 5 years. Similarly, **interest rate swaps** call for the exchange of a series of cash flows proportional to a given interest rate for a corresponding series of cash flows proportional to a floating interest rate.[5] One party might exchange a variable cash flow equal to $1 million times a short-term interest rate for $1 million times a fixed interest rate of 8% for each of the next 7 years.

The swap market is a huge component of the derivatives market, with well over $300 trillion in swap agreements outstanding. We will illustrate how these contracts work by using a simple interest rate swap as an example.

EXAMPLE 23.6   Interest Rate Swap

Consider the manager of a large portfolio that currently includes $100 million par value of long-term bonds paying an average coupon rate of 7%. The manager believes interest rates are about to rise. As a result, he would like to sell the bonds and replace them with either short-term or floating-rate issues. However, it would be exceedingly expensive in terms of transaction costs to replace the portfolio every time the forecast for interest rates is updated. A cheaper and more flexible way to modify the portfolio is to "swap" the $7 million a year in interest income the portfolio currently generates for an amount of money that is tied to the short-term interest rate. That way, if rates do rise, so will the portfolio's interest income.

A swap dealer might advertise its willingness to exchange, or "swap," a cash flow based on the 6-month LIBOR rate for one based on a fixed rate of 7%. (The LIBOR, or London Interbank Offered Rate, is the interest rate at which banks borrow from each other in the Eurodollar market. It is the most commonly used short-term interest rate in the swap market.) The portfolio manager would then enter into a swap agreement with the dealer to *pay* 7% on **notional principal** of $100 million and *receive* payment of the LIBOR rate on that amount of notional principal.[6] In other words, the manager swaps a payment of .07 × $100 million for a payment of LIBOR × $100 million. The manager's *net* cash flow

---

[5]Interest rate swaps have nothing to do with the Homer-Liebowitz bond swap taxonomy described in Chapter 16.

[6]The participants to the swap do not loan each other money. They agree only to exchange a fixed cash flow for a variable cash flow that depends on the short-term interest rate. This is why the principal is described as *notional.* The notional principal is simply a way to describe the size of the swap agreement. In this example, the parties to the swap exchange a 7% fixed rate for the LIBOR rate; the difference between LIBOR and 7% is multiplied by notional principal to determine the cash flow exchanged by the parties.

from the swap agreement is therefore (LIBOR − .07) × $100 million. Note that the swap arrangement does not mean that a loan has been made. The participants have agreed only to exchange a fixed cash flow for a variable one.

Now consider the net cash flow to the manager's portfolio in three interest rate scenarios:

	LIBOR Rate		
	6.5%	**7.0%**	**7.5%**
Interest income from bond portfolio (= 7% of $100 million bond portfolio)	$7,000,000	$7,000,000	$7,000,000
Cash flow from swap [= (LIBOR − 7%) × notional principal of $100 million]	(500,000)	0	500,000
Total (= LIBOR × $100 million)	$6,500,000	$7,000,000	$7,500,000

Notice that the total income on the overall position—bonds plus swap agreement—is now equal to the LIBOR rate in each scenario times $100 million. The manager has, in effect, converted a fixed-rate bond portfolio into a synthetic floating-rate portfolio.

Swaps and Balance Sheet Restructuring

Example 23.6 illustrates why swaps have tremendous appeal to fixed-income managers. These contracts provide a means to quickly, cheaply, and anonymously restructure the balance sheet. Suppose a corporation that has issued fixed-rate debt believes that interest rates are likely to fall; it might prefer to have issued floating-rate debt. In principle, it could issue floating-rate debt and use the proceeds to buy back the outstanding fixed-rate debt. In practice, however, this would be enormously expensive in terms of transaction costs. Instead, the firm can convert the outstanding fixed-rate debt into synthetic floating-rate debt by entering a swap to receive a fixed interest rate (offsetting its fixed-rate coupon obligation) and paying a floating rate.

Conversely, a bank that pays current market interest rates to its depositors, and thus is exposed to increases in rates, might wish to convert some of its financing to a fixed-rate basis. It would enter a swap to receive a floating rate and pay a fixed rate on some amount of notional principal. This swap position, added to its floating-rate deposit liability, would result in a net liability of a fixed stream of cash. The bank might then be able to invest in long-term fixed-rate loans without encountering interest rate risk.

For another example, consider a fixed-income portfolio manager. Swaps enable the manager to switch back and forth between a fixed- or floating-rate profile quickly and cheaply as forecast for interest rate changes. A manager who holds a fixed-rate portfolio can transform it into a synthetic floating-rate portfolio by entering a pay fixed–receive floating swap and can later transform it back by entering the opposite side of a similar swap.

Foreign exchange swaps also enable the firm to quickly and cheaply restructure its balance sheet. Suppose, for example, that a firm issues $10 million in debt at an 8% coupon rate, but actually prefers that its interest obligations be denominated in British pounds. For example, the issuing firm might be a British corporation that perceives advantageous financing opportunities in the United States but prefers pound-denominated liabilities. Then the firm, whose debt currently obliges it to make dollar-denominated payments of $800,000, can agree to swap a given number of pounds each year for $800,000. By so doing, it effectively covers its dollar obligation and replaces it with a new pound-denominated obligation.

> **CONCEPT CHECK 6**
>
> Show how a firm that has issued a floating-rate bond with a coupon equal to the LIBOR rate can use swaps to convert that bond into synthetic fixed-rate debt. Assume the terms of the swap allow an exchange of LIBOR for a fixed rate of 8%.

The Swap Dealer

What about the swap dealer? Why is the dealer, which is typically a financial intermediary such as a bank, willing to take on the opposite side of the swaps desired by these participants in these hypothetical swaps?

Consider a dealer who takes on one side of a swap, let's say paying LIBOR and receiving a fixed rate. The dealer will search for another trader in the swap market who wishes to receive a fixed rate and pay LIBOR. For example, Company A may have issued a 7% coupon fixed-rate bond that it wishes to convert into synthetic floating-rate debt, while Company B may have issued a floating-rate bond tied to LIBOR that it wishes to convert into synthetic fixed-rate debt. The dealer will enter a swap with Company A in which it pays a fixed rate and receives LIBOR, and will enter another swap with Company B in which it pays LIBOR and receives a fixed rate. When the two swaps are combined, the dealer's position is effectively neutral on interest rates, paying LIBOR on one swap and receiving it on another. Similarly, the dealer pays a fixed rate on one swap and receives it on another. The dealer becomes little more than an intermediary, funneling payments from one party to the other.[7] The dealer finds this activity profitable because it will charge a bid–asked spread on the transaction.

This rearrangement is illustrated in Figure 23.6. Company A has issued 7% fixed-rate debt (the leftmost arrow in the figure) but enters a swap to pay the dealer LIBOR and receive a 6.95% fixed rate. Therefore, the company's net payment is 7% + (LIBOR − 6.95%) = LIBOR + .05%. It has thus transformed its fixed-rate debt into synthetic floating-rate debt. Conversely, Company B has issued floating-rate debt paying LIBOR (the rightmost arrow), but enters a swap to pay a 7.05% fixed rate in return for LIBOR. Therefore, its net payment is LIBOR + (7.05% − LIBOR) = 7.05%. It has thus transformed its floating-rate debt into synthetic fixed-rate debt. The bid–asked spread, the source of the dealer's profit, in the example illustrated in Figure 23.6 is .10% of notional principal each year.

> **CONCEPT CHECK 7**
>
> A pension fund holds a portfolio of money market securities that the manager believes are paying excellent yields compared to other comparable-risk short-term securities. However, the manager believes that interest rates are about to fall. What type of swap will allow the fund to continue to hold its portfolio of short-term securities while at the same time benefiting from a decline in rates?

---

[7]Actually, things are a bit more complicated. The dealer is more than just an intermediary because it bears the credit risk that one or the other of the parties to the swap might default on the obligation. Referring to Figure 23.6, if firm A defaults on its obligation, for example, the swap dealer still must maintain its commitment to firm B. In this sense, the dealer does more than simply pass through cash flows to the other swap participants.

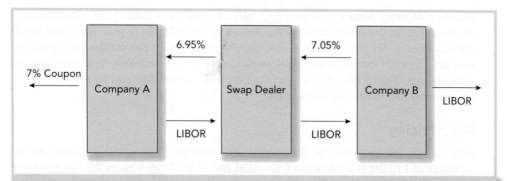

FIGURE 23.6 Interest rate swap. Company B pays a fixed rate of 7.05% to the swap dealer in return for LIBOR. Company A receives 6.95% from the dealer in return for LIBOR. The swap dealer realizes a cash flow each period equal to .10% of notional principal.

Other Interest Rate Contracts

Swaps are multiperiod forward contracts that trade over the counter. There are also exchange-listed contracts that trade on interest rates. The biggest of these in terms of trading activity is the Eurodollar contract, the listing for which we reproduce in Figure 23.7. The profit on this contract is proportional to the difference between the LIBOR rate at contract maturity and the contract rate entered into at contract inception. There are analogous rates on interbank loans in other currencies. For example, one close cousin of LIBOR is EURIBOR, which is the rate at which euro-denominated interbank loans within the euro zone are offered by one prime bank to another.

The listing conventions for the Euro dollar contract are a bit peculiar. Consider, for example, the first contract listed, which matures in January 2008. The settlement price is presented as $F_0 = 95.4525$. However, this value is not really a price. In effect, participants in the contract negotiate over the contract interest rate, and the so-called futures price is actually set equal to $100 -$ contract rate. Because the futures price is listed as 95.4525, the contract rate is $100 - 95.4525$, or 4.5475%. Similarly, the final futures price on contract maturity date will be marked to $F_T = 100 - \text{LIBOR}_T$. Thus, profits to the buyer of the contract will be proportional to

$$F_T - F_0 = (100 - \text{LIBOR}_T) - (100 - \text{Contract rate}) = \text{Contract rate} - \text{LIBOR}_T$$

Thus, the contract design allows participants to trade directly on the LIBOR rate. The contract multiplier is $1 million, but the LIBOR rate on which the contract is written is a 3-month (quarterly) rate; for each basis point that the (annualized) LIBOR increases, the quarterly interest rate increases by only ¼ of a basis point, and the profit to the buyer decreases by

$$.0001 \times \tfrac{1}{4} \times \$1,000,000 = \$25$$

Examine the payoff on the contract, and you will see that, in effect, the Eurodollar contract allows traders to "swap" a fixed interest rate (the contract rate) for a floating rate (LIBOR). Thus, this is in effect a one-period

	Open	High	hi lo	Contract Low	Settle	Chg	Open interest
Eurodollar (CME)-$1,000,000; pts of 100%							
Jan	95.4100	95.4700		95.4100	**95.4525**	.0475	86,478
March	95.7650	95.9200		95.7500	**95.8950**	.1300	1,438,008
June	96.2550	96.4150 ▲		96.2300	**96.4000**	.1450	1,453,627
Dec	96.6350	96.8150 ▲		96.6000	**96.8000**	.1700	1,496,549

FIGURE 23.7 Interest rate futures

Source: *The Wall Street Journal*, January 3, 2008. Reprinted by permission of The Wall Street Journal, © 2008 Dow Jones & Company, Inc. All rights reserved worldwide.

interest rate swap. Notice in Figure 23.7 that the total open interest on this contract is enormous—over 4 million contracts for maturities extending to 1 year. Moreover, while not presented in *The Wall Street Journal,* significant trading in Eurodollars takes place for contract maturities extending out to 10 years. Contracts with such long-term maturities are quite unusual. They reflect the fact that the Eurodollar contract is used by dealers in long-term interest rate swaps as a hedging tool.

Swap Pricing

How can the fair swap rate be determined? For example, how would we know that an exchange of LIBOR is a fair trade for a fixed rate of 8%? Or, what is the fair swap rate between dollars and pounds for a foreign exchange swap? To answer these questions we can exploit the analogy between a swap agreement and forward or futures contract.

Consider a swap agreement to exchange dollars for pounds for one period only. Next year, for example, one might exchange $1 million for £.5 million. This is no more than a simple forward contract in foreign exchange. The dollar-paying party is contracting to buy British pounds in 1 year for a number of dollars agreed to today. The forward exchange rate for 1-year delivery is $F_1 = \$2.00/\text{pound}$. We know from the interest rate parity relationship that this forward price should be related to the spot exchange rate, E_0, by the formula $F_1 = E_0(1 + r_{US})/(1 + r_{UK})$. Because a one-period swap is in fact a forward contract, the fair swap rate is also given by the parity relationship.

Now consider an agreement to trade foreign exchange for two periods. This agreement could be structured as a portfolio of two separate forward contracts. If so, the forward price for the exchange of currencies in 1 year would be $F_1 = E_0(1 + r_{US})/(1 + r_{UK})$, while the forward price for the exchange in the second year would be $F_2 = E_0[(1 + r_{US})/(1 + r_{UK})]^2$. As an example, suppose that $E_0 = \$2.03/\text{pound}$, $r_{US} = 5\%$, and $r_{UK} = 7\%$. Then, using the parity relationship, prices for forward delivery would be $F_1 = \$2.03/£ \times (1.05/1.07) = \$1.992/£$ and $F_2 = \$2.03/£ \times (1.05/1.07)^2 = \$1.955/£$. Figure 23.8A illustrates this sequence of cash exchanges assuming that the swap calls for delivery of one pound in each year. Although the dollars to be paid in each of the 2 years are known today, they differ from year to year.

In contrast, a swap agreement to exchange currency for 2 years would call for a fixed exchange rate to be used for the duration of the swap. This means that the same number of dollars would be paid per pound in each year, as illustrated in Figure 23.8B. Because the forward prices for delivery in each of the next 2 years are $\$1.992/£$ and $\$1.955/£$, the fixed exchange rate that makes the two-period swap a fair deal must be between these two values. Therefore, the dollar payer underpays for the pound in the first year (compared to the forward exchange rate) and overpays in the second year. Thus, the swap can be viewed as a portfolio of forward transactions, but instead of each transaction being priced independently, one forward price is applied to all of the transactions.

Given this insight, it is easy to determine the fair swap price. If we were to purchase one pound per year for 2 years using two independent forward agreements, we would pay F_1 dollars in 1 year and F_2 dollars in 2 years. If instead we enter a swap, we pay a constant rate of F^* dollars per pound. Because both strategies must be equally costly, we conclude that

$$\frac{F_1}{1 + y_1} + \frac{F_2}{(1 + y_2)^2} = \frac{F^*}{1 + y_1} + \frac{F^*}{(1 + y_2)^2}$$

where y_1 and y_2 are the appropriate yields from the yield curve for discounting dollar cash flows of 1- and 2-year maturities, respectively. In our example, where we have assumed a flat U.S. yield curve at 5%, we would solve

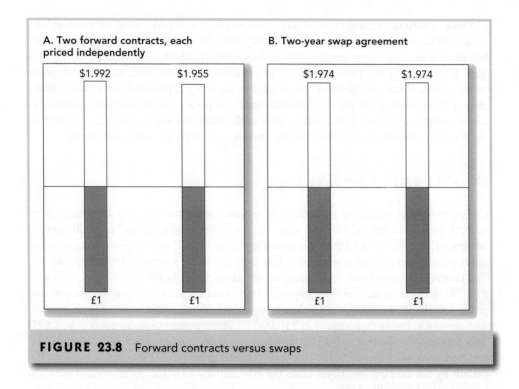

A. Two forward contracts, each priced independently

$1.992 $1.955

£1   £1

B. Two-year swap agreement

$1.974 $1.974

£1   £1

FIGURE 23.8   Forward contracts versus swaps

$$\frac{1.992}{1.05} + \frac{1.955}{1.05^2} = \frac{F^*}{1.05} + \frac{F^*}{1.05^2}$$

which implies that $F^* = 1.974$. The same principle would apply to a foreign exchange swap of any other maturity. In essence, we need to find the level annuity, F^*, with the same present value as the stream of annual cash flows that would be incurred in a sequence of forward rate agreements.

Interest rate swaps can be subjected to precisely the same analysis. Here, the forward contract is on an interest rate. For example, if you swap LIBOR for a 7% fixed rate with notional principal of $100, then you have entered a forward contract for delivery of $100 times LIBOR for a fixed "forward" price of $7. If the swap agreement is for many periods, the fair spread will be determined by the entire sequence of interest rate forward prices over the life of the swap.

Credit Risk in the Swap Market

The rapid growth of the swap market has given rise to increasing concern about credit risk in these markets and the possibility of a default by a major swap trader. Actually, although credit risk in the swap market certainly is not trivial, it is not nearly as large as the magnitude of notional principal in these markets would suggest. To see why, consider a simple interest rate swap of LIBOR for a fixed rate.

At the time the transaction is initiated, it has zero net present value to both parties for the same reason that a futures contract has zero value at inception: Both are simply contracts to exchange cash in the future at terms established today that make both parties willing to enter into the deal. Even if one party were to back out of the deal at this moment, it would not cost the counterparty anything, because another trader could be found to take its place.

Once interest or exchange rates change, however, the situation is not as simple. Suppose, for example, that interest rates increase shortly after an interest-rate swap agreement has begun. The floating-rate payer therefore suffers a loss, while the fixed-rate payer enjoys a gain. If the floating-rate payer reneges on its commitment at this point, the fixed-rate payer suffers a loss. However, that loss is not as large as the notional principal of the swap, for the default of the floating-rate payer relieves the fixed-rate payer from its obligation as well. The loss is only the *difference* between the values of the fixed-rate and floating-rate obligations, not the *total* value of the payments that the floating-rate payer was obligated to make.

EXAMPLE 23.7   Credit Risk in Swaps

Consider a swap written on $1 million of notional principal that calls for exchange of LIBOR for a fixed rate of 8% for 5 years. Suppose, for simplicity, that the yield curve is currently flat at 8%. With LIBOR thus equal to 8%, no cash flows will be exchanged unless interest rates change. But now suppose that the yield curve immediately shifts up to 9%. The floating-rate payer now is obligated to pay a cash flow of $(.09 - .08) \times \$1$ million $= \$10,000$ each year to the fixed-rate payer (as long as rates remain at 9%). If the floating-rate payer defaults on the swap, the fixed-rate payer loses the prospect of that 5-year annuity. The present value of that annuity is $10,000 \times$ Annuity factor(9%, 5 years) $= \$38,897$. This loss may not be trivial, but it is less than 4% of notional principal. We conclude that the credit risk of the swap is far less than notional principal. Again, this is because the default by the floating-rate payer costs the counterparty only the *difference* between the LIBOR rate and the fixed rate.

Credit Default Swaps

Despite the similarity in names, a **credit default swap,** or CDS, is not the same type of instrument as interest rate or currency swaps. Payment on a CDS is tied to the financial status of one or more reference firms; the CDS therefore allows two counterparties to take positions on the credit risk of those firms. When a particular "credit event" is triggered, say, default on an outstanding bond or failure to pay interest, the seller of protection is expected to cover the loss in the market value of the bond. For example, the swap seller may be obligated to pay par value to take delivery of the defaulted bond (in which case the swap is said to entail physical settlement) or may instead pay the swap buyer the difference between the par value and market value of the bond (termed cash settlement). The swap purchaser pays a periodic fee to the seller for this protection against credit events.

Unlike interest rate swaps, credit default swaps do not entail periodic netting of one reference rate against another. They are in fact more like insurance policies written on particular credit events. Bondholders may buy these swaps to transfer their credit risk exposure to the swap seller, effectively enhancing the credit quality of their portfolios. Unlike insurance policies, however, the swap holder need not hold the bonds underlying the CDS contract; therefore, credit default swaps can be used purely to speculate on changes in the credit standing of the reference firms.

More recently, indexes of credit default swaps have been introduced. Unlike actual credit default swaps, which depend on the status of particular firms, CDS indexes can be standardized and therefore more easily traded. Contracts tied to these indexes can be used to take a position on overall credit conditions and may be effective tools to hedge the credit risk of broadly diversified corporate bond portfolios.

23.5 COMMODITY FUTURES PRICING

Commodity futures prices are governed by the same general considerations as stock futures. One difference, however, is that the cost of carrying commodities, especially those subject to spoilage, is greater than the cost of carrying financial assets. The underlying asset for some contracts, such as electricity futures, simply cannot be "carried" or held in portfolio. Finally, spot prices for some commodities demonstrate marked seasonal patterns that can affect futures pricing.

Pricing with Storage Costs

The cost of carrying commodities includes, in addition to interest costs, storage costs, insurance costs, and an allowance for spoilage of goods in storage. To price commodity futures, let us reconsider the earlier arbitrage strategy that calls for holding both the asset and a short position in the futures contract on the asset. In this case we will denote the price of the commodity at time T as P_T, and assume for simplicity that all noninterest carrying costs (C) are paid in one lump sum at time T, the contract maturity. Carrying costs appear in the final cash flow.

Action	Initial Cash Flow	CF at Time T
Buy asset; pay carrying costs at T	$-P_0$	$P_T - C$
Borrow P_0; repay with interest at time T	P_0	$-P_0(1 + r_f)$
Short futures position	0	$F_0 - P_T$
TOTAL	0	$F_0 - P_0(1 + r_f) - C$

Because market prices should not allow for arbitrage opportunities, the terminal cash flow of this zero net investment, risk-free strategy should be zero.

If the cash flow were positive, this strategy would yield guaranteed profits for no investment. If the cash flow were negative, the reverse of this strategy also would yield profits. In practice, the reverse strategy would involve a short sale of the commodity. This is unusual but may be done as long as the short sale contract appropriately accounts for storage costs. Thus,[8] we conclude that

$$F_0 = P_0(1 + r_f) + C$$

Finally, if we define $c = C/P_0$, and interpret c as the percentage "rate" of carrying costs, we may write

$$F_0 = P_0(1 + r_f + c) \tag{23.3}$$

which is a (1-year) parity relationship for futures involving storage costs. Compare Equation 23.3 to the parity relation for stocks, Equation 22.1 from the previous chapter, and you will see that they are extremely similar. In fact, if we think of carrying costs as a "negative dividend," the equations are identical. This result makes intuitive sense because, instead of receiving a dividend yield of d, the storer of the commodity must pay a storage cost of c. Obviously, this parity relationship is simply an extension of those we have seen already.

Although we have called c the carrying cost of the commodity, we may interpret it more generally as the *net* carrying cost, that is, the carrying cost net of the benefits derived from

---

[8]Robert A. Jarrow and George S. Oldfield, "Forward Contracts and Futures Contracts," *Journal of Financial Economics* 9 (1981).

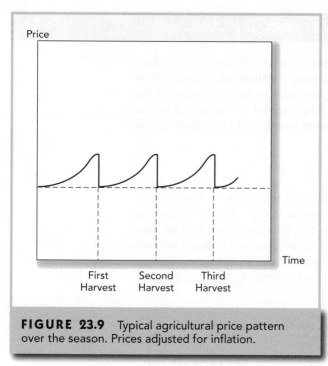

FIGURE 23.9 Typical agricultural price pattern over the season. Prices adjusted for inflation.

holding the commodity in inventory. For example, part of the "convenience yield" of goods held in inventory is the protection against stocking out, which may result in lost production or sales.

It is vital to note that we derive Equation 23.3 assuming that the asset will be bought and stored; it therefore applies only to goods that currently *are* being stored. Two kinds of commodities cannot be expected to be stored. The first kind is commodities for which storage is technologically not feasible, such as electricity. The second includes goods that are not stored for economic reasons. For example, it would be foolish to buy an agricultural commodity now, planning to store it for ultimate use in 3 years. Instead, it is clearly preferable to delay the purchase until after the harvest of the third year, and avoid paying storage costs. Moreover, if the crop in the third year is comparable to this year's, you could obtain it at roughly the same price as you would pay this year. By waiting to purchase, you avoid both interest and storage costs.

Because storage across harvests is costly, Equation 23.3 should not be expected to apply for holding periods that span harvest times, nor should it apply to perishable goods that are available only "in season." You can see that this is so if you look back to the futures listings in Figure 22.1 from the previous chapter. Whereas the futures price for gold, which is a stored commodity, increases steadily with the maturity of the contract, the futures price for wheat is seasonal; its futures price falls across harvests between March and July as new supplies become available.

Figure 23.9 is a stylized version of the seasonal price pattern for an agricultural product. Clearly this pattern differs from financial assets such as stocks or gold for which there is no seasonal price movement. Financial assets are priced so that holding them in portfolio produces a fair expected return. Agricultural prices, in contrast, are subject to steep periodic drops as each crop is harvested, which makes storage across harvests generally unprofitable.

Futures pricing across seasons therefore requires a different approach that is not based on storage across harvest periods. In place of general no-arbitrage restrictions we rely instead on risk premium theory and discounted cash flow (DCF) analysis.

CONCEPT CHECK 8	People are willing to buy and "store" shares of stock despite the fact that their purchase ties up capital. Most people, however, are not willing to buy and store soybeans. What is the difference in the properties of the expected evolution of stock prices versus soybean prices that accounts for this result?

Discounted Cash Flow Analysis for Commodity Futures

Given the current expectation of the spot price of the commodity at some future date and a measure of the risk characteristics of that price, we can measure the present value of a claim to receive the commodity at that future date. We simply calculate the appropriate risk premium from a model such as the CAPM or APT and discount the expected spot price at the appropriate risk-adjusted interest rate, as illustrated in the following example.

EXAMPLE 23.8   Commodity Futures Pricing

Table 23.3, which presents betas on a variety of commodities, shows that the beta of orange juice, for example, was estimated to be .117 over the period. If the T-bill rate is currently 5% and the historical market risk premium is about 8%, the appropriate discount rate for orange juice would be given by the CAPM as

$$5\% + .117 \times 8\% = 5.94\%$$

If the expected spot price for orange juice 6 months from now is $1.45 per pound, the present value of a 6-month deferred claim to a pound of orange juice is simply

$$\$1.45 / (1.0594)^{1/2} = \$1.409$$

What would the proper futures price for orange juice be? The contract calls for the ultimate exchange of orange juice for the futures price. We have just shown that the present value of the juice is $1.409. This should equal the present value of the futures price that will be paid for the juice. A commitment to a payment of F_0 dollars in 6 months has a present value of $F_0/(1.05)^{1/2} = .976 \times F_0$. (Note that the discount rate is the risk-free rate of 5%, because the promised payment is fixed and therefore independent of market conditions.)

To equate the present values of the promised payment of F_0 and the promised receipt of orange juice, we would set

$$.976F_0 = \$1.409$$

or $F_0 = \$1.444$.

Commodity	Beta	Commodity	Beta	
Wheat	−0.370	Orange juice	0.117	**TABLE 23.3**
Corn	−0.429	Propane	−3.851	Commodity betas
Oats	0.000	Cocoa	−0.291	
Soybeans	−0.266	Silver	−0.272	
Soybean oil	−0.650	Copper	0.005	
Soybean meal	0.239	Cattle	0.365	
Broilers	−1.692	Hogs	−0.148	
Plywood	0.660	Pork bellies	−0.062	
Potatoes	−0.610	Egg	−0.293	
Platinum	0.221	Lumber	−0.131	
Wool	0.307	Sugar	−2.403	
Cotton	−0.015			

Source: Zvi Bodie and Victor Rosansky, "Risk and Return in Commodity Futures," *Financial Analysts Journal* 36 (May–June 1980). Copyright 1980, CFA Institute. Reproduced from the *Financial Analysts Journal* with permission from the CFA Institute. All rights reserved.

beyond 1 year. Suppose a firm wishes to use available (short maturity) contracts to hedge commodity prices at a more distant horizon, say, 4 years from now. Do you think the hedge will be more effective for the oil- or the gold-producing firm?

4. You believe that the spread between municipal bond yields and U.S. Treasury bond yields is going to narrow in the coming month. How can you profit from such a change using the municipal bond and T-bond futures contracts?

Problems

5. Consider the futures contract written on the S&P 500 index and maturing in 6 months. The interest rate is 3% per 6-month period, and the future value of dividends expected to be paid over the next 6 months is $15. The current index level is 1,425. Assume that you can short sell the S&P index.

   a. Suppose the expected rate of return on the market is 6% per 6-month period. What is the expected level of the index in 6 months?

   b. What is the theoretical no-arbitrage price for a 6-month futures contract on the S&P 500 stock index?

   c. Suppose the futures price is 1,422. Is there an arbitrage opportunity here? If so, how would you exploit it?

6. Suppose that the value of the S&P 500 stock index is 1,350.

   a. If each futures contract costs $25 to trade with a discount broker, how much is the transaction cost per dollar of stock controlled by the futures contract?

   b. If the average price of a share on the NYSE is about $40, how much is the transaction cost per "typical share" controlled by one futures contract?

   c. For small investors, a typical transaction cost per share in stocks directly is about 15 cents per share. How many times the transactions costs in futures markets is this?

7. You manage a $13.5 million portfolio, currently all invested in equities, and believe that the market is on the verge of a big but short-lived downturn. You would move your portfolio temporarily into T-bills, but you do not want to incur the transaction costs of liquidating and reestablishing your equity position. Instead, you decide to temporarily hedge your equity holdings with S&P 500 index futures contracts.

   a. Should you be long or short the contracts? Why?

   b. If your equity holdings are invested in a market-index fund, into how many contracts should you enter? The S&P 500 index is now at 1,350 and the contract multiplier is $250.

   c. How does your answer to (b) change if the beta of your portfolio is .6?

8. A manager is holding a $1 million stock portfolio with a beta of 1.25. She would like to hedge the risk of the portfolio using the S&P 500 stock index futures contract. How many dollars' worth of the index should she sell in the futures market to minimize the volatility of her position?

9. Suppose that the relationship between the rate of return on IBM stock, the market index, and a computer industry index can be described by the following regression equation: $r_{IBM} = .5r_M + .75r_{Industry}$. If a futures contract on the computer industry is traded, how would you hedge the exposure to the systematic and industry factors affecting the performance of IBM stock? How many dollars' worth of the market and industry index contracts would you buy or sell for each dollar held in IBM?

10. Suppose that the spot price of the euro is currently $1.50. The 1-year futures price is $1.55. Is the interest rate higher in the United States or the euro zone?

11. a. The spot price of the British pound is currently $2.00. If the risk-free interest rate on 1-year government bonds is 4% in the United States and 6% in the United Kingdom, what must be the forward price of the pound for delivery 1 year from now?

   b. How could an investor make risk-free arbitrage profits if the forward price were higher than the price you gave in answer to (a)? Give a numerical example.

12. Consider the following information:

$$r_{US} = 4\%; \qquad r_{UK} = 7\%$$
$$E_0 = 2.00 \text{ dollars per pound}$$
$$F_0 = 1.98 \text{ (1-year delivery)}$$

where the interest rates are annual yields on U.S. or U.K. bills. Given this information:

  a. Where would you lend?
  b. Where would you borrow?
  c. How could you arbitrage?

13. Farmer Brown grows Number 1 red corn and would like to hedge the value of the coming harvest. However, the futures contract is traded on the Number 2 yellow grade of corn. Suppose that yellow corn typically sells for 90% of the price of red corn. If he grows 100,000 bushels, and each futures contract calls for delivery of 5,000 bushels, how many contracts should Farmer Brown buy or sell to hedge his position?

14. Return to Figure 23.7. Suppose the LIBOR rate when the first listed Eurodollar contract matures in January is 4.80%. What will be the profit or loss to each side of the Eurodollar contract?

15. Yields on short-term bonds tend to be more volatile than yields on long-term bonds. Suppose that you have estimated that the yield on 20-year bonds changes by 10 basis points for every 15-basis-point move in the yield on 5-year bonds. You hold a $1 million portfolio of 5-year maturity bonds with modified duration 4 years and desire to hedge your interest rate exposure with T-bond futures, which currently have modified duration 9 years and sell at $F_0 = \$95$. How many futures contracts should you sell?

16. A manager is holding a $1 million bond portfolio with a modified duration of 8 years. She would like to hedge the risk of the portfolio by short-selling Treasury bonds. The modified duration of T-bonds is 10 years. How many dollars' worth of T-bonds should she sell to minimize the variance of her position?

17. A corporation plans to issue $10 million of 10-year bonds in 3 months. At current yields the bonds would have modified duration of 8 years. The T-note futures contract is selling at $F_0 = 100$ and has modified duration of 6 years. How can the firm use this futures contract to hedge the risk surrounding the yield at which it will be able to sell its bonds? Both the bond and the contract are at par value.

18. If the spot price of gold is $880 per troy ounce, the risk-free interest rate is 4%, and storage and insurance costs are zero, what should the forward price of gold be for delivery in 1 year? Use an arbitrage argument to prove your answer. Include a numerical example showing how you could make risk-free arbitrage profits if the forward price exceeded its upper bound value.

19. If the corn harvest today is poor, would you expect this fact to have any effect on today's futures prices for corn to be delivered (postharvest) 2 years from today? Under what circumstances will there be no effect?

20. Suppose that the price of corn is risky, with a beta of .5. The monthly storage cost is $.03, and the current spot price is $2.75, with an expected spot price in 3 months of $2.94. If the expected rate of return on the market is 1.8% per month, with a risk-free rate of 1% per month, would you store corn for 3 months?

21. Suppose the U.S. yield curve is flat at 4% and the euro yield curve is flat at 3%. The current exchange rate is $1.50 per euro. What will be the swap rate on an agreement to exchange currency over a 3-year period? The swap will call for the exchange of 1 million euros for a given number of dollars in each year.

22. Firm ABC enters a 5-year swap with firm XYZ to pay LIBOR in return for a fixed 8% rate on notional principal of $10 million. Two years from now, the market rate on 3-year swaps is LIBOR for 7%; at this time, firm XYZ goes bankrupt and defaults on its swap obligation.

  a. Why is firm ABC harmed by the default?
  b. What is the market value of the loss incurred by ABC as a result of the default?
  c. Suppose instead that ABC had gone bankrupt. How do you think the swap would be treated in the reorganization of the firm?

23. Suppose that at the present time, one can enter 5-year swaps that exchange LIBOR for 8%. An *off-market swap* would then be defined as a swap of LIBOR for a fixed rate other than 8%. For example, a firm with 10% coupon debt outstanding might like to convert to synthetic floating-rate debt by entering a swap in which it pays LIBOR and receives a fixed rate of 10%. What

up-front payment will be required to induce a counterparty to take the other side of this swap? Assume notional principal is $10 million.

Challenge Problems

24. Suppose the 1-year futures price on a stock-index portfolio is 1,218, the stock index currently is 1,200, the 1-year risk-free interest rate is 3%, and the year-end dividend that will be paid on a $1,200 investment in the market index portfolio is $15.

    a. By how much is the contract mispriced?

    b. Formulate a zero-net-investment arbitrage portfolio and show that you can lock in riskless profits equal to the futures mispricing.

    c. Now assume (as is true for small investors) that if you short sell the stocks in the market index, the proceeds of the short sale are kept with the broker, and you do not receive any interest income on the funds. Is there still an arbitrage opportunity (assuming that you don't already own the shares in the index)? Explain.

    d. Given the short-sale rules, what is the no-arbitrage *band* for the stock-futures price relationship? That is, given a stock index of 1,200, how high and how low can the futures price be without giving rise to arbitrage opportunities?

25. Consider these futures market data for the June delivery S&P 500 contract, exactly 6 months hence. The S&P 500 index is at 1,350, and the June maturity contract is at $F_0 = 1,351$.

    a. If the current interest rate is 2.2% semiannually, and the average dividend rate of the stocks in the index is 1.2% semiannually, what fraction of the proceeds of stock short sales would need to be available to you to earn arbitrage profits?

    b. Suppose that you in fact have access to 90% of the proceeds from a short sale. What is the lower bound on the futures price that rules out arbitrage opportunities? By how much does the actual futures price fall below the no-arbitrage bound? Formulate the appropriate arbitrage strategy, and calculate the profits to that strategy.

1. Donna Doni, CFA, wants to explore potential inefficiencies in the futures market. The TOBEC stock index has a spot value of 185. TOBEC futures contracts are settled in cash and underlying contract values are determined by multiplying $100 times the index value. The current annual risk-free interest rate is 6.0%.

    a. Calculate the theoretical price of the futures contract expiring 6 months from now, using the cost-of-carry model. The index pays no dividends.

    The total (round-trip) transaction cost for trading a futures contract is $15.

    b. Calculate the lower bound for the price of the futures contract expiring 6 months from now.

2. Suppose your client says, "I am invested in Japanese stocks but want to eliminate my exposure to this market for a period of time. Can I accomplish this without the cost and inconvenience of selling out and buying back in again if my expectations change?"

    a. Briefly describe a strategy to hedge both the local market risk and the currency risk of investing in Japanese stocks.

    b. Briefly explain why the hedge strategy you described in part (*a*) might not be fully effective.

3. René Michaels, CFA, plans to invest $1 million in U.S. government cash equivalents for the next 90 days. Michaels's client has authorized her to use non–U.S. government cash equivalents, but only if the currency risk is hedged to U.S. dollars by using forward currency contracts.

    a. Calculate the U.S. dollar value of the hedged investment at the end of 90 days for each of the two cash equivalents in the table below. Show all calculations.

    b. Briefly explain the theory that best accounts for your results.

    c. Based on this theory, estimate the implied interest rate for a 90-day U.S. government cash equivalent.

Interest Rates
90-Day Cash Equivalents

Japanese government	7.6%
Swiss government	8.6%

Exchange Rates
Currency Units per U.S. Dollar

	Spot	90-Day Forward
Japanese yen	133.05	133.47
Swiss franc	1.5260	1.5348

4. After studying Iris Hamson's credit analysis, George Davies is considering whether he can increase the holding-period return on Yucatan Resort's excess cash holdings (which are held in pesos) by investing those cash holdings in the Mexican bond market. Although Davies would be investing in a peso-denominated bond, the investment goal is to achieve the highest holding-period return, measured in U.S. dollars, on the investment.

Davies finds the higher yield on the Mexican 1-year bond, which is considered to be free of credit risk, to be attractive, but he is concerned that depreciation of the peso will reduce the holding-period return, measured in U.S. dollars. Hamson has prepared the following selected financial data to help Davies make the decision:

Selected Economic and Financial Data

U.S. 1-year Treasury bond yield	2.5%
Mexican 1-year bond yield	6.5%

Nominal Exchange Rates

Spot	9.5000 Pesos = U.S. $1.00
1-year forward	9.8707 Pesos = U.S. $1.00

Hamson recommends buying the Mexican 1-year bond and hedging the foreign currency exposure using the 1-year forward exchange rate. Calculate the U.S. dollar holding-period return that would result from the transaction recommended by Hamson. Is the U.S. dollar holding-period return resulting from the transaction more or less than that available in the U.S.?

5. *a.* Pamela Itsuji, a currency trader for a Japanese bank, is evaluating the price of a 6-month Japanese yen/U.S. dollar currency futures contract. She gathers the following currency and interest rate data:

Japanese yen/U.S. dollar spot currency exchange rate	¥124.30/$1.00
6-month Japanese interest rate	0.10%
6-month U.S. interest rate	3.80%

Calculate the theoretical price for a 6-month Japanese yen/U.S. dollar currency futures contract, using the data above.

b. Itsuji is also reviewing the price of a 3-month Japanese yen/U.S. dollar currency futures contract, using the currency and interest rate data shown below. Because the 3-month Japanese interest rate has just increased to 0.50%, Itsuji recognizes that an arbitrage opportunity exists and decides to borrow $1 million U.S. dollars to purchase Japanese yen. Calculate the yen arbitrage profit from Itsuji's strategy, using the following data:

Japanese yen/U.S. dollar spot currency exchange rate	¥124.30/$1.00
New 3-month Japanese interest rate	0.50%
3-month U.S. interest rate	3.50%
3-month currency futures contract value	¥123.2605/$1.00

6. Janice Delsing, a U.S.-based portfolio manager, manages an $800 million portfolio ($600 million in stocks and $200 million in bonds). In reaction to anticipated short-term market events, Delsing wishes to adjust the allocation to 50% stock and 50% bonds through the use of futures. Her position will be held only until "the time is right to restore the original asset allocation." Delsing determines a financial futures-based asset allocation strategy is appropriate. The stock futures index multiplier is $250 and the denomination of the bond futures contract is $100,000. Other information relevant to a futures-based strategy is as follows:

Bond portfolio modified duration	5 years
Bond portfolio yield to maturity	7%
Price value of a basis point of bond futures	$97.85
Stock-index futures price	1378
Stock portfolio beta	1.0

   a. Describe the financial futures-based strategy needed and explain how the strategy allows Delsing to implement her allocation adjustment. No calculations are necessary.

   b. Compute the number of *each* of the following needed to implement Delsing's asset allocation strategy:

   i. Bond futures contracts.
   ii. Stock-index futures contracts.

7. You are provided the information outlined as follows to be used in solving this problem.

Issue	Price	Yield to Maturity	Modified Duration*
U.S. Treasury bond 11¾% maturing Nov. 15, 2024	100	11.75%	7.6 years
U.S. Treasury long bond futures contract (contract expiration in 6 months)	63.33	11.85%	8.0 years
XYZ Corporation bond 12½% maturing June 1, 2015 (sinking fund debenture, rated AAA)	93	13.50%	7.2 years
Volatility of AAA corporate bond yields relative to U.S. Treasury bond yields = 1.25 to 1.0 (1.25 times)			
Assume no commission and no margin requirements on U.S. Treasury long bond futures contracts. Assume no taxes.			
One U.S. Treasury bond futures contract is a claim on $100,000 par value long-term U.S. Treasury bonds.			

   *Modified duration = Duration/(1 + y).

   Situation A   A fixed-income manager holding a $20 million market value position of U.S. Treasury 11¾% bonds maturing November 15, 2024, expects the economic growth rate and the inflation rate to be above market expectations in the near future. Institutional rigidities prevent any existing bonds in the portfolio from being sold in the cash market.

   Situation B   The treasurer of XYZ Corporation has recently become convinced that interest rates will decline in the near future. He believes it is an opportune time to purchase his company's sinking fund bonds in advance of requirements because these bonds are trading at a discount from par value. He is preparing to purchase in the open market $20 million par value XYZ Corporation 12½% bonds maturing June 1, 2015. A $20 million par value position of these bonds is currently offered in the open market at 93. Unfortunately, the treasurer must obtain approval from the board of directors for such a purchase, and this approval process can take up to 2 months. The board of directors' approval in this instance is only a formality.

   For each of these two situations, demonstrate how interest rate risk can be hedged using the Treasury bond futures contract. Show all calculations, including the number of futures contracts used.

8. You ran a regression of the yield of KC Company's 10-year bond on the 10-year U.S. Treasury benchmark's yield using month-end data for the past year. You found the following result:

$$\text{Yield}_{KC} = 0.54 + 1.22\ \text{Yield}_{\text{Treasury}}$$

where Yield_{KC} is the yield on the KC bond and $\text{Yield}_{Treasury}$ is the yield on the U.S. Treasury bond. The modified duration on the 10-year U.S. Treasury is 7.0 years, and modified duration on the KC bond is 6.93 years.

a. Calculate the percentage change in the price of the 10-year U.S. Treasury, assuming a 50-basis-point change in the yield on the 10-year U.S. Treasury.

b. Calculate the percentage change in the price of the KC bond, using the regression equation above, assuming a 50-basis-point change in the yield on the 10-year U.S. Treasury.

From the *Market Insight* entry page (**www.mhhe.com/edumarketinsight**), click on the *Company* tab and enter HMC in the *Ticker* box to link to information about Honda Motor Co. Under the EDGAR menu on the left side of the screen, find the latest 20-F report. Where is Honda incorporated? In the 20-F, find the section that shows exchange rate information. In what currency are the numbers shown? In the *Risk Factors* section, locate the *Financial* subsection. Which currency exchange rates are mentioned? Look further into the report to find the *Markets, Sales, and Competition* section. Which countries are listed and what percentages of revenues came from sales in each of the countries? If Honda needs to transfer funds from foreign countries, how might it hedge these transactions with currency futures and options contracts?

E-Investments

Foreign Currency Futures

Go to the Chicago Mercantile Exchange Web site (**www.cme.com**) and link to the tab for *Trade CME Products*, then *Foreign Exchange*. Link to the *Canadian Dollar* contracts and answer the following questions about the futures contract:

What is the size (units of $CD) of each contract?

What is the maximum daily price fluctuation?

What time period during the day is the contract traded?

If the delivery option is exercised, when and where does delivery take place?

SOLUTIONS TO CONCEPT CHECKS

1. According to interest rate parity, F_0 should be $1.981. Because the futures price is too high, we should reverse the arbitrage strategy just considered.

	CF Now ($)	CF in 1 Year
1. Borrow $2.00 in the U.S. Convert to 1 U.K. pound.	+2.00	−2.00(1.04)
2. Lend the 1 pound in the U.K.	−2.00	$1.05E_1$
3. Enter a contract to sell 1.05 pounds at a futures price of $2.01/£.	0	(£1.05)($2.01/£ − E_1)
TOTAL	0	$.0305

2. Because the firm does poorly when the dollar depreciates, it hedges with a futures contract that will provide profits in that scenario. It needs to enter a *long* position in pound futures, which means that it will earn profits on the contract when the futures price increases, that is, when more dollars are required to purchase one pound. The specific hedge ratio is determined by noting that

if the number of dollars required to buy one pound rises by \$.05, profits decrease by \$200,000 at the same time that the profit on a long future contract would be $.05 \times 62,500 = \$3,125$. The hedge ratio is

$$\frac{\$200,000 \text{ per } \$.05 \text{ depreciation in the dollar}}{\$3,125 \text{ per contract per } \$.05 \text{ depreciation}} = 64 \text{ contracts long}$$

3. Each \$1 increase in the price of corn reduces profits by \$1 million. Therefore, the firm needs to enter futures contracts to purchase 1 million bushels at a price stipulated today. The futures position will profit by \$1 million for each increase of \$1 in the price of corn. The profit on the contract will offset the lost profits on operations.

4.

	In General (per unit of index)	Our Numbers
Hold 100,000 units of indexed stock portfolio with $S_0 = 1,400$.	S_T	$100,000\ S_T$
Sell 400 contracts.	$F_0 - S_T$	$400 \times \$250 \times (1,414 - S_T)$
TOTAL	F_0	\$141,400,000

The net cash flow is riskless, and provides a 1% monthly rate of return, equal to the risk-free rate.

5. The price value of a basis point is still \$9,000, as a 1-basis-point change in the interest rate reduces the value of the \$20 million portfolio by $.01\% \times 4.5 = .045\%$. Therefore, the number of futures needed to hedge the interest rate risk is the same as for a portfolio half the size with double the modified duration.

6.

	LIBOR		
	7%	8%	9%
As debt payer (LIBOR × \$10 million)	−700,000	−800,000	−900,000
As fixed payer receives \$10 million × (LIBOR − .08)	−100,000	0	+100,000
Net cash flow	−800,000	−800,000	−800,000

Regardless of the LIBOR rate, the firm's net cash outflow equals $.08 \times$ principal, just as if it had issued a fixed-rate bond with a coupon of 8%.

7. The manager would like to hold on to the money market securities because of their attractive relative pricing compared to other short-term assets. However, there is an expectation that rates will fall. The manager can hold this *particular* portfolio of short-term assets and still benefit from the drop in interest rates by entering a swap to pay a short-term interest rate and receive a fixed interest rate. The resulting synthetic fixed-rate portfolio will increase in value if rates do fall.

8. Stocks offer a total return (capital gain plus dividends) large enough to compensate investors for the time value of the money tied up in the stock. Agricultural prices do not necessarily increase over time. In fact, across a harvest, crop prices will fall. The returns necessary to make storage economically attractive are lacking.

9. If systematic risk were higher, the appropriate discount rate, k, would increase. Referring to Equation 23.4, we conclude that F_0 would fall. Intuitively, the claim to 1 pound of orange juice is worth less today if its expected price is unchanged, but the risk associated with the value of the claim increases. Therefore, the amount investors are willing to pay today for future delivery is lower.

PART VII

CHAPTER TWENTY-FOUR

PORTFOLIO PERFORMANCE EVALUATION

HOW CAN WE evaluate the performance of a portfolio manager? It turns out that even average portfolio return is not as straightforward to measure as it might seem. In addition, adjusting average returns for risk presents a host of other problems. We begin with the measurement of portfolio returns. From there we move on to conventional approaches to risk adjustment. We identify the problems with these approaches when applied in various real-life situations. We then turn to some practical procedures for performance evaluation in the field such as style analysis, the Morningstar Star Ratings, and in-house performance attribution.

24.1 THE CONVENTIONAL THEORY OF PERFORMANCE EVALUATION

Average Rates of Return

We defined the holding-period return (HPR) in Section 5.1 of Chapter 5 and explained the differences between arithmetic and geometric averages. Suppose we evaluate the performance of a portfolio over a period of 5 years from 20 quarterly rates of return. The arithmetic average of this sample of returns would be the best estimate of the expected rate of return of the portfolio for the next quarter. In contrast, the geometric average is the constant quarterly return over the 20 quarters that would yield the same total or cumulative return. Therefore, the geometric average is defined by

$$(1 + r_G)^{20} = (1 + r_1)(1 + r_2) \cdots (1 + r_{20})$$

The right-hand side of this equation is the compounded final value of a $1 investment earning the 20 quarterly rates of return over the 5-year observation period. The left-hand side is the compounded value of a $1 investment earning r_G *each* quarter. We solve for $1 + r_G$ as

$$1 + r_G = [(1 + r_1)(1 + r_2) \cdots (1 + r_{20})]^{1/20}$$

Each return has an equal weight in the geometric average. For this reason, the geometric average is referred to as a **time-weighted average.**

To set the stage for discussing the more subtle issues that follow, let us start with a trivial example. Consider a stock paying a dividend of $2 annually that currently sells for $50. You purchase the stock today, collect the $2 dividend, and then sell the stock for $53 at year-end. Your rate of return is

$$\frac{\text{Total proceeds}}{\text{Initial investment}} = \frac{\text{Income} + \text{Capital gain}}{50} = \frac{2 + 3}{50} = .10, \text{ or } 10\%$$

Another way to derive the rate of return that is useful in the more difficult multiperiod case is to set up the investment as a discounted cash flow problem. Call r the rate of return that equates the present value of all cash flows from the investment with the initial outlay. In our example the stock is purchased for $50 and generates cash flows at year-end of $2 (dividend) plus $53 (sale of stock). Therefore, we solve $50 = (2 + 53)/(1 + r)$ to find again that $r = 10\%$.

Time-Weighted Returns versus Dollar-Weighted Returns

When we consider investments over a period during which cash was added to or withdrawn from the portfolio, measuring the rate of return becomes more difficult. To continue our example, suppose that you were to purchase a second share of the same stock at the end of the first year, and hold both shares until the end of year 2, at which point you sell each share for $54.

Total cash outlays are

Time	Outlay
0	$50 to purchase first share
1	$53 to purchase second share a year later
	Proceeds
1	$2 dividend from initially purchased share
2	$4 dividend from the 2 shares held in the second year, plus $108 received from selling both shares at $54 each

Using the discounted cash flow (DCF) approach, we can solve for the average return over the 2 years by equating the present values of the cash inflows and outflows:

$$50 + \frac{53}{1 + r} = \frac{2}{1 + r} + \frac{112}{(1 + r)^2}$$

resulting in $r = 7.117\%$.

This value is called the internal rate of return, or the **dollar-weighted rate of return** on the investment. It is "dollar weighted" because the stock's performance in the second year, when two shares of stock are held, has a greater influence on the average overall return than the first-year return, when only one share is held.

The time-weighted (geometric average) return is 7.83%:

$$r_1 = \frac{53 + 2 - 50}{50} = .10 = 10\% \qquad r_2 = \frac{54 + 2 - 53}{53} = .0566 = 5.66\%$$

$$r_G = (1.10 \times 1.0566)^{1/2} - 1 = .0783 = 7.83\%$$

The dollar-weighted average is less than the time-weighted average in this example because the return in the second year, when more money was invested, is lower.

> **CONCEPT CHECK 1**
>
> Shares of XYZ Corp. pay a $2 dividend at the end of every year on December 31. An investor buys two shares of the stock on January 1 at a price of $20 each, sells one of those shares for $22 a year later on the next January 1, and sells the second share an additional year later for $19. Find the time- and dollar-weighted rates of return on the 2-year investment.

Adjusting Returns for Risk

Evaluating performance based on average return alone is not very useful. Returns must be adjusted for risk before they can be compared meaningfully. The simplest and most popular way to adjust returns for portfolio risk is to compare rates of return with those of other investment funds with similar risk characteristics. For example, high-yield bond portfolios are grouped into one "universe," growth stock equity funds are grouped into another universe, and so on. Then the (usually time-weighted) average returns of each fund within the universe are ordered, and each portfolio manager receives a percentile ranking depending on relative performance with the **comparison universe.** For example, the manager with the ninth-best performance in a universe of 100 funds would be the 90th percentile manager: Her performance was better than 90% of all competing funds over the evaluation period.[1]

These relative rankings are usually displayed in a chart such as that in Figure 24.1. The chart summarizes performance rankings over four periods: 1 quarter, 1 year, 3 years, and 5 years. The top and bottom lines of each box are drawn at the rate of return of the 95th and 5th percentile managers. The three dashed lines correspond to the rates of return of the 75th, 50th (median), and 25th percentile managers. The diamond is drawn at the average return of a particular fund and the square is drawn at the return of a benchmark index such as the S&P 500. The placement of the diamond within the box is an easy-to-read representation of the performance of the fund relative to the comparison universe.

This comparison of performance with other managers of similar investment style is a useful first step in evaluating performance. However, such rankings can be misleading. Within a particular universe, some managers may concentrate on particular subgroups, so that portfolio characteristics are not truly comparable. For example, within the equity universe, one manager may concentrate on high-beta or aggressive growth stocks. Similarly, within fixed-income universes, durations can vary across managers. These considerations suggest that a more precise means for risk adjustment is desirable.

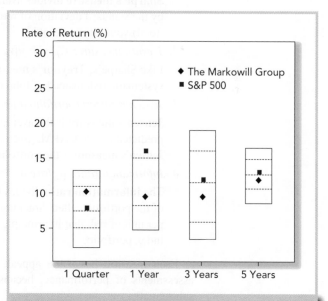

FIGURE 24.1 Universe comparison. Periods ending December 31, 2008

[1]In previous chapters (particularly in Chapter 11 on the efficient market hypothesis), we have examined whether actively managed portfolios can outperform a passive index. For this purpose we looked at the distribution of alpha values for samples of mutual funds. We noted that any conclusion from such samples was subject to error due to survivorship bias if funds that failed during the sample period were excluded from the sample. In this chapter, we are interested in how to assess the performance of individual funds (or other portfolios) of interest. When a particular portfolio is chosen today for inspection of its returns going forward, survivorship bias is not an issue. However, comparison groups must be free of survivorship bias. A sample comprised only of surviving funds will bias upward the return of the benchmark group.

Methods of risk-adjusted performance evaluation using mean-variance criteria came on stage simultaneously with the capital asset pricing model. Jack Treynor,[2] William Sharpe,[3] and Michael Jensen[4] recognized immediately the implications of the CAPM for rating the performance of managers. Within a short time, academicians were in command of a battery of performance measures, and a bounty of scholarly investigation of mutual fund performance was pouring from ivory towers. Shortly thereafter, agents emerged who were willing to supply rating services to portfolio managers and their clients.

But risk-adjusted performance measures have encountered resistance from industry. This may be due in part to the generally negative cast to the performance statistics that have emerged from this analysis. Another reason for the reluctance to adopt mean-variance performance criteria may be related to inherent problems in these measures. We will explore these problems, as well as innovations designed to overcome them, later in the chapter. Finally, reliability of performance measures requires quite a long history of consistent management with a steady level of performance and a representative sample of investment environments, for example, bull as well as bear markets. In practice, we may need to make decisions before the necessary data are available.

For now, however, we start by cataloging some possible risk-adjusted performance measures for a portfolio, P, and examine the circumstances in which each measure might be most relevant.

1. *Sharpe measure:* $(\bar{r}_P - \bar{r}_f)/\sigma_P$

   Sharpe's measure divides average portfolio excess return over the sample period by the standard deviation of returns over that period. It measures the reward to (total) volatility trade-off.[5]

2. *Treynor measure:* $(\bar{r}_P - \bar{r}_f)/\beta_P$

   Like Sharpe's, **Treynor's measure** gives excess return per unit of risk, but it uses systematic risk instead of total risk.

3. *Jensen measure (portfolio alpha):* $\alpha_P = \bar{r}_P - [\bar{r}_f + \beta_P(\bar{r}_M - \bar{r}_f)]$

   Jensen's measure is the average return on the portfolio over and above that predicted by the CAPM, given the portfolio's beta and the average market return. Jensen's measure is the portfolio's alpha value.

4. *Information ratio:* $\alpha_P/\sigma(e_P)$

   The **information ratio** divides the alpha of the portfolio by the nonsystematic risk of the portfolio called "tracking error" in the industry. It measures abnormal return per unit of risk that in principle could be diversified away by holding a market index portfolio.

Each measure has some appeal. But each does not necessarily provide consistent assessments of performance, because the risk measures used to adjust returns differ substantially.

---

[2]Jack L. Treynor, "How to Rate Management Investment Funds," *Harvard Business Review* 43 (January–February 1966).

[3]William F. Sharpe, "Mutual Fund Performance," *Journal of Business* 39 (January 1966).

[4]Michael C. Jensen, "The Performance of Mutual Funds in the Period 1945–1964," *Journal of Finance*, May 1968; and "Risk, the Pricing of Capital Assets, and the Evaluation of Investment Portfolios," *Journal of Business*, April 1969.

[5]We place bars over r_f as well as r_P to denote the fact that because the risk-free rate may not be constant over the measurement period, we are taking a sample average, just as we do for r_P. Equivalently, we may simply compute sample average *excess* returns.

<table>
<tr><td rowspan="7" style="background:black">
CONCEPT
CHECK

2</td><td colspan="3">Consider the following data for a particular sample period:</td></tr>
<tr><td></td><td>Portfolio P</td><td>Market M</td></tr>
<tr><td>Average return</td><td>35%</td><td>28%</td></tr>
<tr><td>Beta</td><td>1.20</td><td>1.00</td></tr>
<tr><td>Standard deviation</td><td>42%</td><td>30%</td></tr>
<tr><td>Tracking error
(nonsystematic risk), $\sigma(e)$</td><td>18%</td><td>0</td></tr>
<tr><td colspan="3">Calculate the following performance measures for portfolio P and the market: Sharpe, Jensen (alpha), Treynor, information ratio. The T-bill rate during the period was 6%. By which measures did portfolio P outperform the market?</td></tr>
</table>

The M^2 Measure of Performance

While the Sharpe ratio can be used to rank portfolio performance, its numerical value is not easy to interpret. Comparing the ratios for portfolios M and P in Concept Check 2, you should have found that $S_P = .69$ and $S_M = .73$. This suggests that portfolio P under-performed the market index. But is a difference of .04 in the Sharpe ratio economically meaningful? We often compare rates of return, but these ratios are pure numbers and hence difficult to interpret.

An equivalent representation of Sharpe's measure was proposed by Graham and Harvey, and later popularized by Leah Modigliani of Morgan Stanley and her grandfather Franco Modigliani, past winner of the Nobel Prize in Economics.[6] Their approach has been dubbed the M^2 measure (for Modigliani-squared). Like the Sharpe ratio, the M^2 measure focuses on total volatility as a measure of risk, but its risk-adjusted measure of performance has the easy interpretation of a differential return relative to the benchmark index.

To compute the M^2 measure, we imagine that a managed portfolio, P, is mixed with a position in T-bills so that the complete, or "adjusted," portfolio matches the volatility of a market index such as the S&P 500. For example, if the managed portfolio has 1.5 times the standard deviation of the index, the adjusted portfolio would be two-thirds invested in the managed portfolio and one-third invested in bills. The adjusted portfolio, which we call P^*, would then have the same standard deviation as the index. (If the managed portfolio had *lower* standard deviation than the index, it would be leveraged by borrowing money and investing the proceeds in the portfolio.) Because the market index and portfolio P^* have the same standard deviation, we may compare their performance simply by comparing returns. This is the M^2 measure:

$$M^2 = r_{P^*} - r_M \qquad (24.1)$$

[6]John R. Graham and Campbell R. Harvey, "Market Timing Ability and Volatility Implied in Investment Advisors' Asset Allocation Recommendations," National Bureau of Economic Research Working Paper 4890, October 1994. The part of this paper dealing with volatility-adjusted returns was ultimately published as "Grading the Performance of Market Timing Newsletters," *Financial Analysts Journal* 53 (November/December 1997), pp. 54–66. Franco Modigliani and Leah Modigliani, "Risk-Adjusted Performance," *Journal of Portfolio Management,* Winter 1997, pp. 45–54.

EXAMPLE 24.1 M^2 Measure

Using the data of Concept Check 2, P has a standard deviation of 42% versus a market standard deviation of 30%. Therefore, the adjusted portfolio P^* would be formed by mixing bills and portfolio P with weights $30/42 = .714$ in P and $1 - .714 = .286$ in bills. The return on this portfolio would be $(.286 \times 6\%) + (.714 \times 35\%) = 26.7\%$, which is 1.3% less than the market return. Thus portfolio P has an M^2 measure of -1.3%.

A graphical representation of the M^2 measure appears in Figure 24.2. We move down the capital allocation line corresponding to portfolio P (by mixing P with T-bills) until we reduce the standard deviation of the adjusted portfolio to match that of the market index. The M^2 measure is then the vertical distance (i.e., the difference in expected returns) between portfolios P^* and M. You can see from Figure 24.2 that P will have a negative M^2 measure when its capital allocation line is less steep than the capital market line, that is, when its Sharpe ratio is less than that of the market index.[7]

Sharpe's Measure as the Criterion for Overall Portfolios

Suppose that Jane Close constructs a portfolio and holds it for a considerable period of time. She makes no changes in portfolio composition during the period. In addition, suppose that the daily rates of return on all securities have constant means, variances, and covariances. This assures that the portfolio rate of return also has a constant mean and variance. These assumptions are unrealistic, but they make it easier to highlight important issues. They are also crucial to understanding the shortcoming of conventional applications of performance measurement.

Now we want to evaluate the performance of Jane's portfolio. Has she made a good choice of securities? This is really a three-pronged question. First, "good choice" compared with what alternatives? Second, in choosing between two distinct alternative portfolios, what are the appropriate criteria to evaluate performance? Finally, the performance criteria, having been identified, is there a rule that will separate basic ability from the random luck of the draw?

Earlier chapters of this text help to determine portfolio choice criteria. If investor preferences can be summarized by a mean-variance utility function such as that introduced in Chapter 6, we can arrive at a relatively simple criterion. The particular utility function that we used is

$$U = E(r_P) - \tfrac{1}{2} A\sigma_P^2$$

where A is the coefficient of risk aversion. With mean-variance preferences, Jane wants to maximize the Sharpe measure (i.e., the reward-to-volatility ratio $[E(r_P) - r_f]/\sigma_P$). Recall that this criterion led to the selection of the tangency portfolio in Chapter 7. Jane's problem reduces to the search for the highest possible Sharpe ratio.

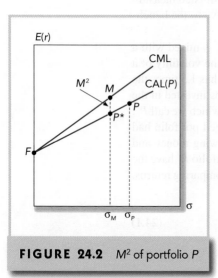

FIGURE 24.2 M^2 of portfolio P

[7]In fact you use Figure 24.2 to show that the M^2 and Sharpe measures are directly related. Letting R denote excess returns and S denote Sharpe measures, the geometry of the figure implies that $R_{P^*} = S_P\sigma_M$, and therefore that

$$M^2 = r_{P^*} - r_M = R_{P^*} - R_M = S_P\sigma_M - S_M\sigma_M = (S_P - S_M)\sigma_M$$

Appropriate Performance Measures in Two Scenarios

To evaluate Jane's portfolio choice, we first ask whether this portfolio is her exclusive investment vehicle. If the answer is no, we need to know her "complementary" portfolio. The appropriate measure of portfolio performance depends critically on whether the portfolio is the entire investment fund or only a portion of the investor's overall wealth.

Jane's Portfolio Represents Her Entire Risky Investment Fund   In this simplest case we need to ascertain only whether Jane's portfolio has the highest Sharpe measure. We can proceed in three steps:

1. Assume that past security performance is representative of expected performance, meaning that realized security returns over Jane's holding period exhibit averages and covariances similar to those that Jane had anticipated.
2. Determine the benchmark (alternative) portfolio that Jane would have held if she had chosen a passive strategy, such as the S&P 500.
3. Compare Jane's Sharpe measure or M^2 to that of the best portfolio.

In sum, when Jane's portfolio represents her entire investment fund, the benchmark is the market index or another specific portfolio. The performance criterion is the Sharpe measure of the actual portfolio versus the benchmark.

Jane's Choice Portfolio Is One of Many Portfolios Combined into a Large Investment Fund   This case might describe a situation where Jane, as a corporate financial officer, manages the corporate pension fund. She parcels out the entire fund to a number of portfolio managers. Then she evaluates the performance of individual managers to reallocate the fund to improve future performance. What is the correct performance measure?

Although alpha is one basis for performance measurement, it alone is not sufficient to determine P's potential contribution to the overall portfolio. The discussion below shows why, and develops the Treynor measure, the appropriate criterion in this case.

Suppose you determine that portfolio P exhibits an alpha value of 2%. "Not bad," you tell Jane. But she pulls out of her desk a report and informs you that another portfolio, Q, has an alpha of 3%. "One hundred basis points is significant," says Jane. "Should I transfer some of my funds from P's manager to Q's?"

You tabulate the relevant data, as in Table 24.1, and graph the results as in Figure 24.3. Note that we plot P and Q in the expected return–beta (rather than the expected return–standard deviation) plane, because we assume that P and Q are two of many subportfolios in the fund, and thus that nonsystematic risk will be largely diversified away, leaving beta as the appropriate risk measure. The security market line (SML) shows the value of α_P and α_Q as the distance of P and Q above the SML.

	Portfolio P	Portfolio Q	Market	
Beta	.90	1.60	1.0	**TABLE 24.1**
Excess return $(\bar{r} - \bar{r}_f)$	11%	19%	10%	Portfolio performance
Alpha*	2%	3%	0	

*Alpha = Excess return − (Beta × Market excess return)

$\quad = (\bar{r} - \bar{r}_f) - \beta(\bar{r}_M - \bar{r}_f) = \bar{r} - [\bar{r}_f + \beta(\bar{r}_M - \bar{r}_f)]$

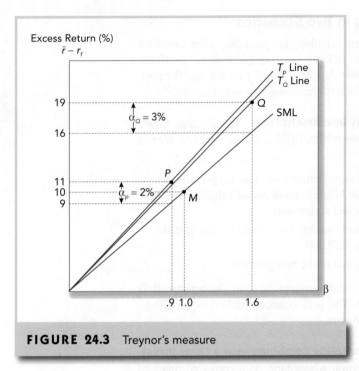

FIGURE 24.3 Treynor's measure

Suppose portfolio Q can be mixed with T-bills. Specifically, if we invest w_Q in Q and $w_F = 1 - w_Q$ in T-bills, the resulting portfolio, Q^*, will have alpha and beta values proportional to Q's alpha and beta scaled down by w_Q:

$$\alpha_{Q^*} = w_Q \alpha_Q$$
$$\beta_{Q^*} = w_Q \beta_Q$$

Thus all portfolios Q^* generated from mixing Q with T-bills plot on a straight line from the origin through Q. We call it the T-line for the Treynor measure, which is the slope of this line.

Figure 24.3 shows the T-line for portfolio P as well. P has a steeper T-line; despite its lower alpha, P is a better portfolio after all. For any *given* beta, a mixture of P with T-bills will give a better alpha than a mixture of Q with T-bills. Consider an example.

EXAMPLE 24.2 Equalizing Beta

Suppose we choose to mix Q with T-bills to create a portfolio Q^* with a beta equal to that of P. We find the necessary proportion by solving for w_Q:

$$\beta_{Q^*} = w_Q \beta_Q = 1.6 w_Q = \beta_P = .9$$
$$w_Q = \%16$$

Portfolio Q^* therefore has an alpha of

$$\alpha_{Q^*} = \%16 \times 3 = 1.69\%$$

which is less than that of P.

In other words, the slope of the T-line is the appropriate performance criterion in this case. The slope of the T-line for P, denoted by T_P, is given by

$$T_P = \frac{\bar{r}_P - \bar{r}_f}{\beta_P}$$

Treynor's performance measure is appealing because when an asset is part of a large investment portfolio, one should weigh its mean excess return against its *systematic* risk rather than against total risk to evaluate contribution to performance.

Like M^2, Treynor's measure is a percentage. If you subtract the market excess return from Treynor's measure, you will obtain the difference between the return on the T_P line in Figure 24.3 and the SML, at the point where $\beta = 1$. We might dub this difference the Treynor-square, or T^2, measure (analogous to M^2). Be aware though that M^2 and T^2 are as different as Sharpe's measure is from Treynor's measure. They may well rank portfolios differently.

The following performance measurement spreadsheet computes all the performance measures discussed in this section. You can see how relative ranking differs according to the criterion selected. This Excel model is available at the Online Learning Center (www.mhhe.com/bkm).

	A	B	C	D	E	F	G	H	I	J	K
1	Performance Measurement							LEGEND			
2								Enter data			
3								Value calculated			
4								See comment			
5											
6					Non-						
7		Average	Standard	Beta	systematic	Sharpe's	Treynor's	Jensen's	M2	T2	Appraisal
8	Fund	Return	Deviation	Coefficient	Risk	Measure	Measure	Measure	Measure	Measure	Ratio
9	Alpha	28.00%	27.00%	1.7000	5.00%	0.8148	0.1294	−0.0180	−0.0015	−0.0106	−0.3600
10	Omega	31.00%	26.00%	1.6200	6.00%	0.9615	0.1543	0.0232	0.0235	0.0143	0.3867
11	Omicron	22.00%	21.00%	0.8500	2.00%	0.7619	0.1882	0.0410	−0.0105	0.0482	2.0500
12	Millennium	40.00%	33.00%	2.5000	27.00%	1.0303	0.1360	−0.0100	0.0352	−0.0040	−0.0370
13	Big Value	15.00%	13.00%	0.9000	3.00%	0.6923	0.1000	−0.0360	−0.0223	−0.0400	−1.2000
14	Momentum Watcher	29.00%	24.00%	1.4000	16.00%	0.9583	0.1643	0.0340	0.0229	0.0243	0.2125
15	Big Potential	15.00%	11.00%	0.5500	1.50%	0.8182	0.1636	0.0130	−0.0009	0.0236	0.8667
16	S & P Index Return	20.00%	17.00%	1.0000	0.00%	0.8235	0.1400	0.0000	0.0000	0.0000	0.0000
17	T-Bill Return	6.00%		0.0000							
18											
19	Ranking By Sharpe's Measure				Non-						
20		Average	Standard	Beta	systematic	Sharpe's	Treynor's	Jensen's	M2	T2	Appraisal
21	Fund	Return	Deviation	Coefficient	Risk	Measure	Measure	Measure	Measure	Measure	Ratio

The Role of Alpha in Performance Measures

With some algebra we can derive the relationship between the various performance measures that we've introduced above. The following table shows some of these relationships.

	Treynor (T_P)	Sharpe* (S_P)
Relation to alpha	$\dfrac{E(r_P) - r_f}{\beta_P} = \dfrac{\alpha_P}{\beta_P} + T_M$	$\dfrac{E(r_P) - r_f}{\sigma_P} = \dfrac{\alpha_P}{\sigma_P} + \rho S_M$
Deviation from market measure	$T_P^2 = T_P - T_M = \dfrac{\alpha_P}{\beta_P}$	$S_P - S_M = \dfrac{\alpha_P}{\sigma_P} + (\rho - 1)S_M$

*ρ denotes the correlation coefficient between portfolio P and the market, and is less than 1.

All of these models are consistent in that superior performance requires a positive alpha. Hence, alpha is the most widely used performance measure. However, the Treynor and Sharpe measures make different uses of alpha and can therefore rank portfolios differently. A positive alpha alone cannot guarantee a better Sharpe measure of a portfolio, because taking advantage of security mispricing means departing from full diversification which entails a cost (notice in the table that $\rho - 1$ is negative, so that the Sharpe measure can actually fall).

Actual Performance Measurement: An Example

Now that we have examined possible criteria for performance evaluation, we need to deal with a statistical issue: Can we assess the quality of ex ante decisions using ex post data? Before we plunge into a discussion of this problem, let us look at the rate of return on Jane's portfolio over the last 12 months. Table 24.2 shows the excess return recorded each month for Jane's portfolio P, one of her alternative portfolios Q, and the benchmark index portfolio M. The last rows in Table 24.2 give sample average and standard deviations. From these, and regressions of P and Q on M, we obtain the necessary performance statistics.

TABLE 24.2

Excess returns for portfolios P and Q and the benchmark M over 12 months

Month	Jane's Portfolio P	Alternative Q	Benchmark M
1	3.58%	2.81%	2.20%
2	−4.91	−1.15	−8.41
3	6.51	2.53	3.27
4	11.13	37.09	14.41
5	8.78	12.88	7.71
6	9.38	39.08	14.36
7	−3.66	−8.84	−6.15
8	5.56	0.83	2.74
9	−7.72	0.85	−15.27
10	7.76	12.09	6.49
11	−4.01	−5.68	−3.13
12	0.78	−1.77	1.41
Average	2.76	7.56	1.63
Standard deviation	6.17	14.89	8.48

TABLE 24.3

Performance statistics

	Portfolio P	Portfolio Q	Portfolio M
Sharpe's measure	0.45	0.51	0.19
M^2	2.19	2.69	0.00
SCL regression statistics			
Alpha	1.63	5.28	0.00
Beta	0.69	1.40	1.00
Treynor	4.00	5.40	1.63
T^2	2.37	3.77	0.00
$\sigma(e)$	1.95	8.98	0.00
Information ratio	0.84	0.59	0.00
R-SQR	0.91	0.64	1.00

The performance statistics in Table 24.3 show that portfolio Q is more aggressive than P, in the sense that its beta is significantly higher (1.40 vs. .69). At the same time, from its residual standard deviation, P appears better diversified (1.95% vs. 8.98%). Both portfolios outperformed the benchmark market index, as is evident from their larger Sharpe measures (and thus positive M^2) as well as their positive alphas.

Which portfolio is more attractive based on reported performance? If P or Q represents the entire investment fund, Q would be preferable on the basis of its higher Sharpe measure (.51 vs. .45) and better M^2 (2.69% vs. 2.19%). For the second scenario, where P and Q are competing for a role as one of a number of subportfolios, Q also dominates because its Treynor measure is higher (5.40 versus 4.00). However, as an active portfolio to be mixed with the index portfolio, P is preferred because its information ratio (IR $= \alpha/\sigma(e)$) is larger (.84 versus .59), as discussed in Chapter 8 and restated in the next section. Thus, the example illustrates that the right way to evaluate a portfolio depends in large part on how the portfolio fits into the investor's overall wealth.

This analysis is based on 12 months of data only, a period too short to lend statistical significance to the conclusions. Even longer observation intervals may not be enough to make the decision clear-cut, which represents a further problem. A model that calculates these performance measures is available on the Online Learning Center (**www.mhhe.com/bkm**).

Realized Returns versus Expected Returns

When evaluating a portfolio, the evaluator knows neither the portfolio manager's original expectations nor whether those expectations made sense. One can only observe performance after the fact and hope that random results are neither taken for, nor hide, true underlying ability. But risky asset returns are "noisy," which complicates the inference problem. To avoid making mistakes, we have to determine the "significance level" of a performance measure to know whether it reliably indicates ability.

Consider Joe Dart, a portfolio manager. Suppose that his portfolio has an alpha of 20 basis points per month, which makes for a hefty 2.4% per year before compounding. Let us assume that the return distribution of Joe's portfolio has constant mean, beta, and alpha, a heroic assumption, but one that is in line with the usual treatment of performance measurement. Suppose that for the measurement period Joe's portfolio beta is 1.2 and the monthly standard deviation of the residual (nonsystematic risk) is .02 (2%). With a market index standard deviation of 6.5% per month (22.5% per year), Joe's portfolio systematic variance is

$$\beta^2 \sigma_M^2 = 1.2^2 \times 6.5^2 = 60.84$$

and hence the correlation coefficient between his portfolio and the market index is

$$\rho = \left[\frac{\beta^2 \sigma_M^2}{\beta^2 \sigma_M^2 + \sigma^2(e)} \right]^{1/2} = \left[\frac{60.84}{60.84 + 4} \right]^{1/2} = .97$$

which shows that his portfolio is quite well diversified.

To estimate Joe's portfolio alpha from the security characteristic line (SCL), we regress the portfolio excess returns on the market index. Suppose that we are in luck and the regression estimates yield precisely the true parameters. That means that our SCL estimates for the N months are

$$\hat{\alpha} = .2\%, \quad \hat{\beta} = 1.2, \quad \hat{\sigma}(e) = 2\%$$

The evaluator who runs such a regression, however, does not know the true values, and hence must compute the t-statistic of the alpha estimate to determine whether to reject the hypothesis that Joe's alpha is zero, that is, that he has no superior ability.

The standard error of the alpha estimate in the SCL regression is approximately

$$\hat{\sigma}(\alpha) = \frac{\hat{\sigma}(e)}{\sqrt{N}}$$

where N is the number of observations and $\hat{\sigma}(e)$ is the sample estimate of nonsystematic risk. The t-statistic for the alpha estimate is then

$$t(\hat{\alpha}) = \frac{\hat{\alpha}}{\hat{\sigma}(\alpha)} = \frac{\hat{\alpha}\sqrt{N}}{\hat{\sigma}(e)} \tag{24.2}$$

Suppose that we require a significance level of 5%. This requires a $t(\hat{\alpha})$ value of 1.96 if N is large. With $\hat{\alpha} = .2$ and $\hat{\sigma}(e) = 2$, we solve Equation 24.2 for N and find that

$$1.96 = \frac{.2\sqrt{N}}{2}$$

$$N = 384 \text{ months}$$

or 32 years!

What have we shown? Here is an analyst who has very substantial ability. The example is biased in his favor in the sense that we have assumed away statistical complications.

Nothing changes in the parameters over a long period of time. Furthermore, the sample period "behaves" perfectly. Regression estimates are all perfect. Still, it will take Joe's entire working career to get to the point where statistics will confirm his true ability. We have to conclude that the problem of statistical inference makes performance evaluation extremely difficult in practice.

CONCEPT CHECK 3	Suppose an analyst has a measured alpha of .2% with a standard error of 2%, as in our example. What is the probability that the positive alpha is due to luck of the draw and that true ability is zero?

24.2 PERFORMANCE MEASUREMENT FOR HEDGE FUNDS

In describing Jane's portfolio performance evaluation we left out one scenario that may well be the most relevant.

Suppose Jane has been satisfied with her well-diversified mutual fund, but now she stumbles upon information on hedge funds. Hedge funds are rarely designed as candidates for an investor's overall portfolio. Rather than focusing on Sharpe ratios, which would entail establishing an attractive trade-off between expected return and overall volatility, these funds tend to concentrate on opportunities offered by temporarily mispriced securities, and show far less concern for broad diversification. In other words, these funds are *alpha driven,* and best thought of as possible *additions* to core positions in more traditional portfolios established with concerns of diversification in mind. For hedge funds, therefore, Sharpe ratios will certainly not be relevant performance measures. The nearby box notes that the industry has moved away from using Sharpe ratios to evaluate hedge funds, recognizing that the ratio was designed to evaluate diversified complete portfolios, not actively managed positions with potentially great exposure to unforeseen shocks.

In Chapter 8, we considered precisely this question, specifically, how best to mix an actively managed portfolio with a broadly diversified core position. We saw that the key statistic for this mixture is the information ratio of the actively managed portfolio; this ratio, therefore, becomes the active fund's appropriate performance measure.

To briefly review, call the active portfolio established by the hedge fund H, and the investor's baseline passive portfolio M. Then the optimal position of H in the overall portfolio, denoted P^*, would be

$$w_H = \frac{w_H^0}{1 + (1 - \beta_H)w_H^0}$$

$$w_H^0 = \frac{\dfrac{\alpha_H}{\sigma^2(e_H)}}{\dfrac{E(R_M)}{\sigma_M^2}} \tag{24.3}$$

As we saw in Chapter 8, when the hedge fund is optimally combined with the baseline portfolio using Equation 24.3, the improvement in the Sharpe measure will be determined by its information ratio $\alpha_H/\sigma(e_H)$, according to

$$S_{P^*}^2 = S_M^2 + \left[\frac{\alpha_H}{\sigma(e_H)}\right]^2 \tag{24.4}$$

SHARPE POINT: RISK GAUGE IS MISUSED

William F. Sharpe was probably the biggest expert in the room when economists from around the world gathered to hash out a pressing problem: How to gauge hedge-fund risk. About 40 years ago, Dr. Sharpe created a simple calculation for measuring the return that investors should expect for the level of volatility they are accepting. In other words: How much money do they stand to make compared with the size of the up-and-down swings they will lose sleep over?

The so-called Sharpe Ratio became a cornerstone of modern finance, as investors used it to help select money managers and mutual funds. But the use of the ratio has been criticized by many prominent academics—including Dr. Sharpe himself.

The ratio is commonly used—"misused," Dr. Sharpe says—for promotional purposes by hedge funds. Hedge funds, loosely regulated private investment pools, often use complex strategies that are vulnerable to surprise events and elude any simple formula for measuring risk. "Past average experience may be a terrible predictor of future performance," Dr. Sharpe says.

Dr. Sharpe designed the ratio to evaluate portfolios of stocks, bonds, and mutual funds. The higher the Sharpe Ratio, the better a fund is expected to perform over the long term. However, at a time when smaller investors and pension funds are pouring money into hedge funds, the ratio can foster a false sense of security.

Dr. Sharpe says the ratio doesn't foreshadow hedge-fund woes because "no number can." The formula can't predict such troubles as the inability to sell off investments quickly if they start to head south, nor can it account for extreme unexpected events. Long-Term Capital Management, a huge hedge fund in Connecticut, had a glowing Sharpe Ratio before it abruptly collapsed in 1998 when Russia devalued its currency and defaulted on debt. Plus, hedge funds are generally secretive about their strategies, making it difficult for investors to get an accurate picture of risk.

Another problem with the Sharpe Ratio is that it is designed to evaluate the risk-reward profile of an investor's entire portfolio, not small pieces of it. This shortcoming is particularly telling for hedge funds.

Equation 24.4 tells us that the appropriate performance measure for the hedge fund is its information ratio (IR).

Looking back at Table 24.3, we can calculate the IR of portfolios P and Q as

$$\text{IR}_P = \frac{\alpha_P}{\sigma(e_P)} = \frac{1.63}{1.95} = .84 \tag{24.5}$$

$$\text{IR}_Q = \frac{5.28}{8.98} = .59$$

If we were to interpret P and Q as hedge funds, the low beta of P, .69, could result from short positions the fund holds in some assets. The relatively high beta of Q, 1.40, might result from leverage that would also increase the firm-specific risk of the fund, $\sigma(e_Q)$. Using these calculations, Jane would favor hedge fund P with the higher information ratio.

In practice, evaluating hedge funds poses considerable practical challenges. We will discuss many of these in Chapter 26, which is devoted to these funds. But for now we can briefly mention a few of the difficulties:

1. The risk profile of hedge funds (both total volatility as well as exposure to relevant systematic factors) may change rapidly. Hedge funds have far greater leeway than

    mutual funds to change investment strategy opportunistically. This instability makes it hard to measure exposure at any given time.

2. Hedge funds tend to invest in illiquid assets. We therefore must disentangle liquidity premiums from true alpha to properly assess their performance. Moreover, it can be difficult to accurately price inactively traded assets, and correspondingly difficult to measure rates of return.

3. Many hedge funds pursue strategies that may provide apparent profits over long periods of time, but expose the fund to infrequent but severe losses. Therefore, very long time periods may be required to formulate a realistic picture of their true risk–return trade-off.

4. When hedge funds are evaluated as a group, survivorship bias can be a major consideration, because turnover in this industry is far higher than for investment companies such as mutual funds.

24.3 PERFORMANCE MEASUREMENT WITH CHANGING PORTFOLIO COMPOSITION

We have seen already that the volatility of stock returns requires a very long observation period to determine performance levels with any precision, even if portfolio returns are distributed with constant mean and variance. Imagine how this problem is compounded when portfolio return distributions are constantly changing.

It is acceptable to assume that the return distributions of passive strategies have constant mean and variance when the measurement interval is not too long. However, under an active strategy return distributions change by design, as the portfolio manager updates the portfolio in accordance with the dictates of financial analysis. In such a case, estimating various statistics from a sample period assuming a constant mean and variance may lead to substantial errors. Let us look at an example.

EXAMPLE 24.3   Changing Portfolio Risk

Suppose that the Sharpe measure of the market index is .4. Over an initial period of 52 weeks, the portfolio manager executes a low-risk strategy with an annualized mean excess return of 1% and standard deviation of 2%. This makes for a Sharpe measure of .5, which beats the passive strategy. Over the next 52-week period this manager finds that a *high*-risk strategy is optimal, with an annual mean excess return of 9% and standard deviation of 18%. Here, again, the Sharpe measure is .5. Over the 2-year period our manager maintains a better-than-passive Sharpe measure.

Figure 24.4 shows a pattern of (annualized) quarterly returns that are consistent with our description of the manager's strategy of 2 years. In the first four quarters the excess returns are −1%, 3%, −1%, and 3%, making for an average of 1% and standard deviation of 2%. In the next four quarters the returns are −9%, 27%, −9%, 27%, making for an average of 9% and standard deviation of 18%. Thus *both* years exhibit a Sharpe measure of .5. However, over the eight-quarter sequence the mean and standard deviation are 5% and 13.42%, respectively, making for a Sharpe measure of only .37, apparently inferior to the passive strategy!

What happened in Example 24.3? The shift of the mean from the first four quarters to the next was not recognized as a shift in strategy. Instead, the difference in mean returns in the 2 years added to the *appearance* of volatility in portfolio returns. The active strategy with shifting means appears riskier than it really is and biases the estimate of the Sharpe measure downward. We conclude that for actively managed portfolios it is helpful to keep track of portfolio composition and changes in portfolio mean and risk. We will see another example of this problem in the next section, which deals with market timing.

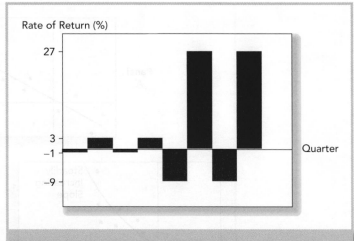

FIGURE 24.4 Portfolio returns. Returns in last four quarters are more variable than in the first four.

24.4 MARKET TIMING

In its pure form, market timing involves shifting funds between a market-index portfolio and a safe asset, such as T-bills or a money market fund, depending on whether the market as a whole is expected to outperform the safe asset. In practice, of course, most managers do not shift fully between T-bills and the market. How can we account for partial shifts into the market when it is expected to perform well?

To simplify, suppose that an investor holds only the market-index portfolio and T-bills. If the weight of the market were constant, say, .6, then portfolio beta would also be constant, and the SCL would plot as a straight line with slope .6, as in Figure 24.5A. If, however, the investor could correctly time the market and shift funds into it in periods when the market does well, the SCL would plot as in Figure 24.5B. If bull and bear markets can be predicted, the investor will shift more into the market when the market is about to go up. The portfolio beta and the slope of the SCL will be higher when r_M is higher, resulting in the curved line that appears in Figure 24.5B.

Treynor and Mazuy[8] were the first to propose that such a line can be estimated by adding a squared term to the usual linear index model:

$$r_P - r_f = a + b(r_M - r_f) + c(r_M - r_f)^2 + e_P$$

where r_P is the portfolio return, and *a, b,* and *c* are estimated by regression analysis. If *c* turns out to be positive, we have evidence of timing ability, because this last term will make the characteristic line steeper as $r_M - r_f$ is larger. Treynor and Mazuy estimated this equation for a number of mutual funds, but found little evidence of timing ability.

A similar and simpler methodology was proposed by Henriksson and Merton.[9] These authors suggested that the beta of the portfolio take only two values: a large value if the

[8]Jack L. Treynor and Kay Mazuy, "Can Mutual Funds Outguess the Market?" *Harvard Business Review* 43 (July–August 1966).

[9]Roy D. Henriksson and R. C. Merton, "On Market Timing and Investment Performance. II. Statistical Procedures for Evaluating Forecast Skills," *Journal of Business* 54 (October 1981).

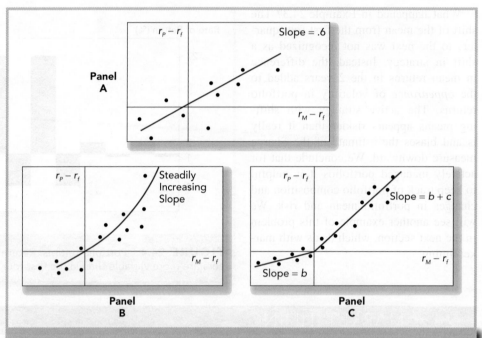

FIGURE 24.5 Characteristic lines. *Panel A:* No market timing, beta is constant. *Panel B:* Market timing, beta increases with expected market excess return. *Panel C:* Market timing with only two values of beta.

market is expected to do well and a small value otherwise. Under this scheme the portfolio characteristic line appears as Figure 24.5C. Such a line appears in regression form as

$$r_P - r_f = a + b(r_M - r_f) + c(r_M - r_f)D + e_P$$

where D is a dummy variable that equals 1 for $r_M > r_f$ and zero otherwise. Hence the beta of the portfolio is b in bear markets and $b + c$ in bull markets. Again, a positive value of c implies market timing ability.

Henriksson[10] estimated this equation for 116 mutual funds. He found that the average value of c for the funds was *negative,* and equal to $-.07$, although the value was not statistically significant at the conventional 5% level. Eleven funds had significantly positive values of c, while eight had significantly negative values. Overall, 62% of the funds had negative point estimates of timing ability. In sum, the results showed little evidence of market timing ability. Perhaps this should be expected; given the tremendous values to be reaped by a successful market timer, it would be surprising in nearly efficient markets to uncover clear-cut evidence of such skills.

To illustrate a test for market timing, return to Table 24.2. Regressing the excess returns of portfolios P and Q on the excess returns of M and the square of these returns,

$$r_P - r_f = a_P + b_P(r_M - r_f) + c_P(r_M - r_f)^2 + e_P$$

$$r_Q - r_f = a_Q + b_Q(r_M - r_f) + c_Q(r_M - r_f)^2 + e_Q$$

[10]Roy D. Henriksson, "Market Timing and Mutual Fund Performance: An Empirical Investigation," *Journal of Business* 57 (January 1984).

we derive the following statistics:

Estimate	Portfolio	
	P	**Q**
Alpha (a)	1.77 (1.63)	–2.29 (5.28)
Beta (b)	0.70 (0.69)	1.10 (1.40)
Timing (c)	0.00	0.10
R-SQR	0.91 (0.91)	0.98 (0.64)

The numbers in parentheses are the regression estimates from the single variable regression reported in Table 24.3. The results reveal that portfolio P shows no timing. It is not clear whether this is a result of Jane's making no attempt at timing or that the effort to time the market was in vain and served only to increase portfolio variance unnecessarily.

The results for portfolio Q, however, reveal that timing has, in all likelihood, successfully been attempted. The timing coefficient, c, is estimated at .10. The evidence thus suggests successful timing (positive c) offset by unsuccessful stock selection (negative a). Note that the alpha estimate, a, is now -2.29% as opposed to the 5.28% estimate derived from the regression equation that did not allow for the possibility of timing activity.

This example illustrates the inadequacy of conventional performance evaluation techniques that assume constant mean returns and constant risk. The market timer constantly shifts beta and mean return, moving into and out of the market. Whereas the expanded regression captures this phenomenon, the simple SCL does not. The relative desirability of portfolios P and Q remains unclear in the sense that the value of the timing success and selectivity failure of Q compared with P has yet to be evaluated. The important point for performance evaluation, however, is that expanded regressions can capture many of the effects of portfolio composition change that would confound the more conventional mean-variance measures.

The Potential Value of Market Timing

Suppose we define perfect market timing as the ability to tell (with certainty) at the beginning of each year whether the S&P 500 portfolio will outperform the strategy of rolling over 1-month T-bills throughout the year. Accordingly, at the beginning of each year, the market timer shifts all funds into either cash equivalents (T-bills) or equities (the S&P 500 portfolio), whichever is predicted to do better. Beginning with $1 on January 1, 1926, how would the perfect timer end the 80-year experiment on December 31, 2005, in comparison with investors who kept their funds in either equity or T-bills for the entire period?

Table 24.4, columns 1–3, presents summary statistics for each of the three strategies, computed from the historical annual returns of bills and the S&P 500. (We first introduced a spreadsheet containing these returns in Chapter 5. You can find the spreadsheet at our Online Learning Center at **www.mhhe.com/bkm;** follow the links for Chapter 5.) From the returns on stocks and bills, we calculate wealth indexes of the all-bills and all-equity investments and show terminal values for these investors at the end of 2005. The return for the perfect timer in each year is the *maximum* of the return on stocks and the return on bills.

The first row in Table 24.4 tells all. The terminal value of investing $1 in bills over the 80 years (1926–2005) is about $18, while the terminal value of the same initial investment in equities is about $2,300. We saw a similar pattern for a 25-year investment in Chapter 5; the much larger terminal values (and difference between them) when extending the horizon from 25 to 80 years is just another manifestation of the power of compounding.

Strategy	Bills	Equities	Perfect Timer	Imperfect Timer*
Terminal value	18.35	2,318.04	172,732.75	3,494.91
Arithmetic average (%)	3.75	12.15	17.04	54.81
Standard deviation (%)	3.15	20.26	13.82	15.77
Geometric average (%)	3.70	10.17	16.27	10.74
LPSD (relative to bills)	0	10.63	0	5.75
Minimum (%)	−.06**	−45.56	−.06	−25.90
Maximum (%)	14.86	54.56	54.56	54.56
Skew	1.03	−.36	.66	.53
Kurtosis	1.10	−.07	−.37	.31
One-period call value ($)	0	0	.1605	.0642
Terminal value of call ($)	0	0	225,330.92	174.19

TABLE 24.4

Performance of bills, equities, and (annual) timers—perfect and imperfect

*The imperfect timer has $P_1 = .7$ and $P_2 = .7$. $P_1 + P_2 - 1 = .4$.

**A negative rate on "bills" of −.06% was observed in 1940. The Treasury security used in the data series for this year actually was not a T-bill, but a T-bond with a short remaining maturity.

We argued in Chapter 5 that as impressive as the difference in terminal values is, it is best interpreted as no more than fair compensation for the risk borne by equity investors. Notice that the standard deviation of the all-equity investor was a hefty 20.26%. This is also why the geometric average of large stocks for the period is "only" 10.17%, compared with the arithmetic average of 12.15%. (Remember that the geometric average is less than the arithmetic average and that the difference between the two increases with the volatility of returns.)

Now observe that the terminal value of the perfect timer is about $173,000, a 70-fold increase over the already large terminal value of the all-equity strategy! In fact, this result is even better than it looks, because the return to the market timer is truly risk-free. This is the classic case where a large standard deviation (13.82%) has nothing to do with risk. Because the timer never delivers a return below the risk-free rate, the standard deviation is a measure of *good* surprises only. The positive skew of the distribution (compared with the small negative skew of equities) is a manifestation of the fact that the extreme values are all positive. Another indication of this stellar performance is the minimum and maximum returns—the minimum return equals the minimum return on bills (in 1940) and the maximum return is that of equities (in 1933)—so that all negative returns on equities (as low as −45.56% in 1931) were avoided by the timer. Finally, the best indication of the performance of the timer is a lower partial standard deviation, LPSD, in which we calculate the (square root of the) average squared deviation below the risk-free rate (rather than below the mean).[11] The LPSD of the all-equity portfolio is only slightly less than the conventional standard deviation (because of the small negative skew), but it is necessarily zero for the perfect timer.

[11]The conventional LPSD is based on the average squared deviation below the mean. Because the threshold performance in this application is the risk-free rate, we modify the LPSD for this discussion by taking squared deviations from that rate.

If we recognize that the terminal value of the all-equity portfolio in excess of the value for the T-bill portfolio is entirely a risk-premium commensurate with investment risk, we must conclude that the risk-adjusted equivalent value of the all-equity terminal value is the same as that of the T-bill portfolio, $18.35.[12] In contrast, the perfect timer's portfolio has no risk, and so receives no discount for risk. Hence, it is fair to say that the forecasting ability of the perfect timer converts an $18.35 final value to a value of $172,732.75 for free.

Valuing Market Timing as a Call Option

The key to valuing market timing ability is to recognize that perfect foresight is equivalent to holding a call option on the equity portfolio. The perfect timer

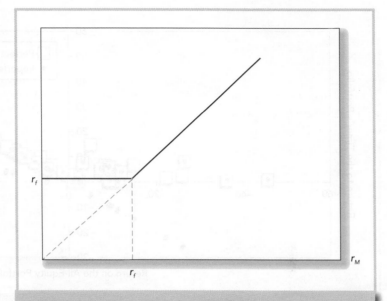

FIGURE 24.6 Rate of return of a perfect market timer as a function of the rate of return on the market index.

invests 100% in either the safe asset or the equity portfolio, whichever will provide the higher return. The rate of return is *at least* the risk-free rate. This is shown in Figure 24.6.

To see the value of information as an option, suppose that the market index currently is at S_0 and that a call option on the index has an exercise price of $X = S_0(1 + r_f)$. If the market outperforms bills over the coming period, S_T will exceed X, whereas it will be less than X otherwise. Now look at the payoff to a portfolio consisting of this option and S_0 dollars invested in bills:

	$S_T < X$	$S_T \geq X$
Bills	$S_0(1 + r_f)$	$S_0(1 + r_f)$
Option	0	$S_T - X$
Total	$S_0(1 + r_f)$	S_T

The portfolio pays the risk-free return when the market is bearish (i.e., the market return is less than the risk-free rate), and it pays the market return when the market is bullish and beats bills. Such a portfolio is a perfect market timer.[13]

Figure 24.7 illustrates the actual pattern of returns to the perfect timer relative to the all-equity investor using historical data. The squares in the scatter diagram show the return to the perfect timer paired with the return in that period on the all-equity portfolio. When the market does well (i.e., when $r_M > r_f$), the return of the perfect timer matches the market's and falls on the 45-degree line. When the market does poorly, the timer earns the T-bill rate. If the risk-free rate were constant, the plot would precisely match that of the payoff to

[12]It may seem hard to attribute such a big difference in final outcome solely to risk aversion. But think of it this way: the final value of the equity position is about 125 times that of the bills position ($2,300 versus $18.35). Over 80 years, this implies a reasonable annualized risk premium of 6.2%: $125^{1/80} = 1.062$.

[13]The analogy between market timing and call options, and the valuation formulas that follow from it, were developed in Robert C. Merton, "On Market Timing and Investment Performance: An Equilibrium Theory of Value for Market Forecasts," *Journal of Business,* July 1981.

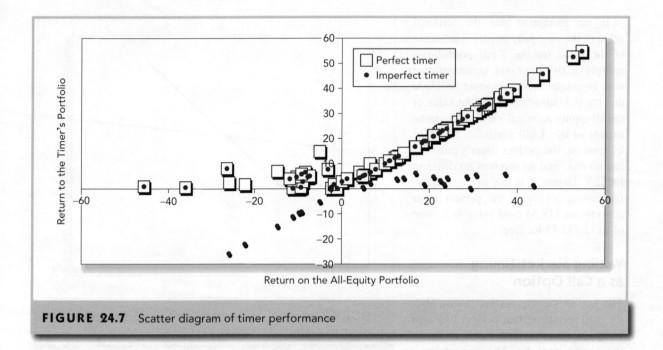

FIGURE 24.7   Scatter diagram of timer performance

a call option as in Figure 24.6, flat when $r_M > r_f$ and with a slope of 1.0 when $r_M > r_f$. The only reason the actual pattern deviates from the simple call-option graph is that the risk-free rate is not constant.

Because the ability to predict the better-performing investment is equivalent to holding a call option on the market, in any given period, when the risk-free rate is known, we can use option-pricing models to assign a dollar value to the potential contribution of perfect timing ability. This contribution would constitute the fair fee that a perfect timer could charge investors for his or her services. Placing a value on perfect timing also enables us to assign value to less-than-perfect timers.

The exercise price of the perfect-timer call option on \$1 of the equity portfolio is the final value of the T-bill investment. Using continuous compounding, this is $\$1 \times e^{rT}$. When you use this exercise price in the Black-Scholes formula for the value of the call option, the formula simplifies considerably to[14]

$$\text{MV(Perfect timer)} = C = 2N(\sigma_M \sqrt{T}) - 1 \qquad \textbf{(24.6)}$$

We have so far assumed annual forecasts, that is, $T = 1$ year. Using the estimate for the standard deviation of the S&P 500 from Table 24.4, 20.26%, we compute the value of this call option in Table 24.4 as 16.05 cents, or 16.05% of the value of the equity portfolio.[15] This is an estimate of the current price of the equivalent call option, and

---

[14]If you substitute $S_0 = \$1$ for the current value of the equity portfolio and $X = \$1 \times e^{rT}$ in Equation 21.1 of Chapter 21, you will obtain Equation 24.6.

[15]Notice that this is a call option with a maturity of 1 year, and hence it is equivalent to shortfall insurance for 1 year. (Recall that shortfall insurance is insurance against underperforming some benchmark, in this case T-bills, and pays off any underperformance over some specified investment horizon.) We can obtain the value of implicit shortfall insurance provided by perfect timing over a 25-year period by multiplying the annual standard deviation by $\sqrt{25}$ to obtain cumulative volatility for the 25-year horizon. The resulting insurance value is 58 cents per dollar invested. Compare this to the value we found in Chapter 5, which was about 30 cents. The larger value here is a result of a larger assumed standard deviation, 20.26%, compared with the 15.4% value we used in Chapter 5. The sensitivity of the insurance premium to volatility is self-evident.

therefore is the *present value* of the service that the perfect timer provides. To compare this value to the historical end-of-period returns shown in Table 24.4, we would have to increase it by the risk-free rate, arriving at 16.65%. This value is larger than the actual annual premium of the perfect timer from Table 24.4 (i.e., $17.04 - 3.75 = 13.29\%$) and implies a terminal value of $225,000, correspondingly larger than the actual $173,000 value. The reason is that the call value formula assumes a lognormal distribution for stock prices while the actual distribution in this period was negatively skewed, meaning that more extreme values were on the negative side.

The value of perfect timing depends on the frequency of the forecast and the always-correct choice to be in equities or T-bills. If the timer could make the correct choice every month instead of every year, the value of the forecasts would dramatically increase. Of course, making perfect forecasts more frequently requires even better powers of prediction. As the frequency of such perfect predictions increases without bound, the value of the services will increase without bound as well.

Suppose the perfect timer could make perfect forecasts every month. In this case, each forecast would be for a shorter interval, and the value of each individual forecast would be lower, but there would be 12 times as many forecasts, each of which could be valued as another call option. The net result is a big increase in total value. With monthly predictions, the value of the call will be $2N(.2026 \times \sqrt{1/12}) - 1 = .0466$. Using a monthly T-bill rate of 3.75%/12, the present value of a 1-year string of such monthly calls, each worth $.0466, is $.550. Thus, the value of the monthly perfect timer is 55.0 cents on the dollar, compared to 16.05 cents for an annual timer. For an investment period of 80 years, the forecast future value of a $1 investment would be a staggering $(1 + .55 \times 1.0375)^{80} = \$4,900$ *trillion!*

The Value of Imperfect Forecasting

Unfortunately, managers are not perfect forecasters. It seems pretty obvious that if managers are right most of the time, they are doing very well. However, when we say "most of the time," we cannot mean merely the percentage of the time a manager is right. The weather forecaster in Tucson, Arizona, who *always* predicts no rain, may be right 90% of the time. But a high success rate for a "stopped-clock" strategy clearly is not evidence of forecasting ability.

Similarly, the appropriate measure of market forecasting ability is not the overall proportion of correct forecasts. If the market is up 2 days out of 3 and a forecaster always predicts market advance, the two-thirds success rate is not a measure of forecasting ability. We need to examine the proportion of bull markets ($r_M > r_f$) correctly forecast *and* the proportion of bear markets ($r_M > r_f$) correctly forecast.

If we call P_1 the proportion of the correct forecasts of bull markets and P_2 the proportion for bear markets, then $P = P_1 + P_2 - 1$ is the correct measure of timing ability. For example, a forecaster who always guesses correctly will have $P_1 = P_2 = 1$, and will show ability of 1 (100%). An analyst who always bets on a bear market will mispredict all bull markets ($P_1 = 0$), will correctly "predict" all bear markets ($P_2 = 1$), and will end up with timing ability of $P = P_1 + P_2 - 1 = 0$.

CONCEPT CHECK 4   What is the market timing score of someone who flips a fair coin to predict the market?

The accuracy of a market timer in terms of probability of guessing correctly bull and bear markets can be estimated from data that include predictions and realizations. When timing is imperfect, Merton shows that if we measure overall accuracy by the statistic $P = P_1 + P_2 - 1$, the market value of the services of an imperfect timer is simply

$$\text{MV(Imperfect timer)} = P \times C = (P_1 + P_2 - 1)[2N(\sigma_M \sqrt{T}) - 1] \qquad \textbf{(24.7)}$$

The last column in Table 24.4 provides an assessment of the imperfect market-timer in two ways. To simulate the performance of an imperfect timer, we drew random numbers for predictions in each year (assuming that both P_1 and $P_2 = .7$) and compiled results for the 80 years of history.[16] The statistics of this exercise resulted in a terminal value for the timer of "only" \$3,495, compared with \$2,318 for the all-equity investments. But the rest of the statistics show that this is not a fair comparison, because the imperfect timer's returns are less risky despite the "noise" created by frequent errors. Notice that the lower partial standard deviation (LPSD) of the imperfect timer is about one-half that of the equity investment! To compare results on a risk-adjusted basis we compute the value of the annual call from Equation 24.7. The table shows this value as \$174.19 compared with the terminal value of the T-bill investment of \$18.35. Thus, with ability of $P = P_1 + P_2 - 1 = .7 + .7 - 1 = .4$, the timer's value is still quite considerable.[17]

A further variation on the valuation of market timing is a case in which the timer does not shift fully from one asset to the other. In particular, if the timer knows her forecasts are imperfect, one would not expect her to shift fully between markets. She presumably would moderate her positions. Suppose that she shifts a fraction ω of the portfolio between T-bills and equities. In that case, Equation 24.7 can be generalized as follows:

$$\text{MV(Imperfect timer)} = \omega \times P \times C = \omega(P_1 + P_2 - 1)[2N(\sigma_M \sqrt{T}) - 1]$$

For example, if the shift is $\omega = .50$ (50% of the portfolio), the timer's value will be one-half of the value we would obtain for full shifting, for which $\omega = 1.0$.

24.5 STYLE ANALYSIS

Style analysis was introduced by Nobel laureate William Sharpe.[18] The popularity of the concept was aided by a well-known study[19] concluding that 91.5% of the variation in returns of 82 mutual funds could be explained by the funds' asset allocation to bills, bonds, and stocks. Later studies that considered asset allocation across a broader range of asset classes found that as much as 97% of fund returns can be explained by asset allocation alone.

[16]In each year, we started with the correct forecast, but then used a random number generator to occasionally change the timer's forecast to an incorrect prediction. We set the probability that the timer's forecast would be correct equal to .70 for both up and down markets.

[17]Notice that Equation 24.7 implies that an investor with a value of $P = 0$ who attempts to time the market would add zero value. The shifts across markets would be no better than a random decision concerning asset allocation. The asset shifts will result in higher standard deviation than an all-bills strategy. That volatility is the standard deviation of excess returns on equity that will arise from the periodic shifts into the stock market. It will be exactly compensated for by the risk premium on equity. The SD of the timer's portfolio will be lower than that of the all-equity portfolio and so will be the average return. (Because the SD is lower, the difference between the average return and geometric return will also be smaller.)

[18]William F. Sharpe, "Asset Allocation: Management Style and Performance Evaluation," *Journal of Portfolio Management,* Winter 1992, pp. 7–19.

[19]Gary Brinson, Brian Singer, and Gilbert Beebower, "Determinants of Portfolio Performance," *Financial Analysts Journal,* May/June 1991.

Style Portfolio	Regression Coefficient
T-Bill	0
Small Cap	0
Medium Cap	35
Large Cap	61
High P/E (growth)	5
Medium P/E	0
Low P/E (value)	0
Total	100
R-square	97.5

TABLE 24.5

Style analysis for Fidelity's Magellan Fund

Source: Authors' calculations. Return data for Magellan obtained from **finance.yahoo.com/funds** and return data for style portfolios obtained from the Web page of Professor Kenneth French: **mba. tuck.dartmouth.edu/pages/faculty/ken.french/ data_library.html.**

Sharpe's idea was to regress fund returns on indexes representing a range of asset classes. The regression coefficient on each index would then measure the fund's implicit allocation to that "style." Because funds are barred from short positions, the regression coefficients are constrained to be either zero or positive and to sum to 100%, so as to represent a complete asset allocation. The R-square of the regression would then measure the percentage of return variability attributable to style or asset allocation, while the remainder of return variability would be attributable either to security selection or to market timing by periodic changes in the asset-class weights.

To illustrate Sharpe's approach, we use monthly returns on Fidelity Magellan's Fund over the five-year period from October 1986 to September 1991, with results shown in Table 24.5. While seven asset classes are included in this analysis (of which six are represented by stock indexes and one is the T-bill alternative), the regression coefficients are positive for only three, namely, large capitalization stocks, medium cap stocks, and high P/E (growth) stocks. These portfolios alone explain 97.5% of the variance of Magellan's returns. In other words, a tracking portfolio made up of the three style portfolios, with weights as given in Table 24.5, would explain the vast majority of Magellan's variation in monthly performance. We conclude that the fund returns are well represented by three style portfolios.

The proportion of return variability *not* explained by asset allocation can be attributed to security selection within asset classes, as well as timing that shows up as periodic changes in allocation. For Magellan, residual variability was $100 - 97.5 = 2.5\%$. This sort of result is commonly used to play down the importance of security selection and timing in fund performance, but such a conclusion misses the important role of the intercept in this regression. (The R-square of the regression can be 100%, and yet the intercept can be nonzero due to a superior risk-adjusted abnormal return.) For Magellan, the intercept was 32 basis points per month, resulting in a cumulative abnormal return over the 5-year period of 19.19%. The superior performance of Magellan is displayed in Figure 24.8, which plots the cumulative impact of the intercept plus monthly residuals relative to the tracking portfolio composed of the style portfolios. Except for the period surrounding the crash of October 1987, Magellan's return consistently increased relative to the benchmark portfolio.

You can do style analysis with Excel's Solver. The strategy is to regress a fund's rate of return on those of a number of style portfolios (as in Table 24.5). The style portfolios are passive (index) funds that represent a style alternative to asset allocation. Suppose you choose three style portfolios, labeled 1–3. Then the coefficients in your style regression are alpha (the intercept that measures abnormal performance) and three slope coefficients, one for each style index. The slope coefficients reveal how sensitively the performance of the fund follows the return of each passive style portfolio. The residuals from this regression, $e(t)$, represent "noise," that is, fund performance at each date, t, that is independent of any of the style portfolios. We cannot use a standard regression package in this analysis, however, because we wish to constrain each coefficient to be nonnegative and sum to 1.0, representing a portfolio of styles.

To do style analysis using Solver, start with arbitrary coefficients (e.g., you can set $\alpha = 0$ and set each $\beta = 1/3$). Use these to compute the time series of residuals from the style regression according to

$$e(t) = R(t) - [\alpha - \beta_1 R_1(t) - \beta_2 R_2(t) - \beta_3 R_3(t)] \qquad \textbf{(24.8)}$$

where

$R(t)$ = Excess return on the measured fund for date t

$R_i(t)$ = Excess return on the ith style portfolio ($i = 1, 2, 3$)

α = Abnormal performance of the fund over the sample period

β_i = Beta of the fund on the ith style portfolio

Equation 24.8 yields the time series of residuals from your "regression equation" with those arbitrary coefficients. Now square each residual and sum the squares. At this point, you call on the Solver to minimize the sum of squares by changing the value of the four coefficients. You will use the "by changing variables" command. You also add four constraints to the optimization: three that force the betas to be nonnegative and one that forces them to sum to 1.0.

Solver's output will give you the three style coefficients, as well as the estimate of the fund's unique, abnormal performance as measured by the intercept. The sum of squares also allows you to calculate the R-square of the regression and p-values as explained in Chapter 8.

24.6 MORNINGSTAR'S RISK–ADJUSTED RATING

The commercial success of Morningstar, Inc., the premier source of information on mutual funds, has made its *Risk Adjusted Rating* (RAR) among the most widely used performance measures. The Morningstar five-star rating is coveted by the managers of the thousands of funds covered by the service. We reviewed the rating system in Chapter 4.

Morningstar calculates a number of RAR performance measures that are similar, although not identical, to the standard mean/variance measures we discussed in this chapter. The best-known measure, the Morningstar Star Rating, is based on comparison of each fund to a peer group. The peer group for each fund is selected on the basis of the fund's investment universe (e.g., international, growth versus value, fixed income, and so on) as well as portfolio characteristics such as average price-to-book value, price–earnings ratio, and market capitalization.

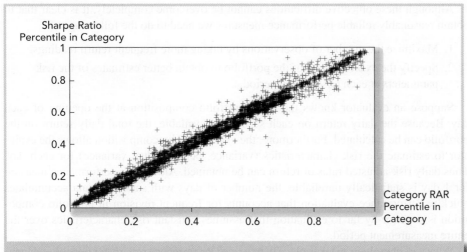

FIGURE 24.10 Rankings based on Morningstar's category RARs and excess return Sharpe ratios

Source: William F. Sharpe, "Morningstar Performance Measures," **www.wsharpe.com.** Used by permission of William F. Sharpe.

Morningstar computes fund returns (adjusted for loads) as well as a risk measure based primarily on fund performance in its worst years. The risk-adjusted performance is ranked across funds in a style group and stars are awarded based on the following table:

Percentile	Stars
0–10	1
10–32.5	2
32.5–67.5	3
67.5–90	4
90–100	5

The Morningstar RAR method produces results that are similar but not identical to that of the mean/variance-based Sharpe ratios. Figure 24.10 demonstrates the fit between ranking by RAR and by Sharpe ratios from the performance of 1,286 diversified equity funds over the period 1994–1996. Sharpe notes that this period is characterized by high returns that contribute to a good fit.

24.7 EVALUATING PERFORMANCE EVALUATION

Performance evaluation has two very basic problems:

1. Many observations are needed for significant results even when portfolio mean and variance are constant.
2. Shifting parameters when portfolios are actively managed makes accurate performance evaluation all the more elusive.

Although these objective difficulties cannot be overcome completely, it is clear that to obtain reasonably reliable performance measures we need to do the following:

1. Maximize the number of observations by taking more frequent return readings.
2. Specify the exact makeup of the portfolio to obtain better estimates of the risk parameters at each observation period.

Suppose an evaluator knows the exact portfolio composition at the opening of each day. Because the daily return on each security is available, the total daily return on the portfolio can be calculated. Furthermore, the exact portfolio composition allows the evaluator to estimate the risk characteristics (variance, beta, residual variance) for each day. Thus daily risk-adjusted rates of return can be obtained. Although a performance measure for 1 day is statistically unreliable, the number of days with such rich data accumulates quickly. Performance evaluation that accounts for frequent revision in portfolio composition is superior by far to evaluation that assumes constant risk characteristics over the entire measurement period.

What sort of evaluation takes place in practice? Performance reports for portfolio managers traditionally have been based on quarterly data over 5 to 10 years. Currently, managers of mutual funds are required to disclose the exact composition of their portfolios only quarterly. Trading activity that immediately precedes the reporting date is known as "window dressing." Window dressing involves changes in portfolio composition to make it look as if the manager chose successful stocks. If IBM performed well over the quarter, for example, a portfolio manager might make sure that his or her portfolio includes a lot of IBM on the reporting date whether or not it did during the quarter and whether or not IBM is expected to perform as well over the next quarter. Of course, portfolio managers deny such activity, and we know of no published evidence to substantiate the allegation. However, if window dressing is quantitatively significant, even the reported quarterly composition data can be misleading. Mutual funds publish portfolio values on a daily basis, which means the rate of return for each day is publicly available, but portfolio composition is not.

Still, even with more data, an insidious problem that will continue to complicate performance evaluation is survivorship bias. Because poorly performing mutual funds are regularly closed down, sample data will include only surviving funds, which correspondingly tend to be the more successful ones. At the same time, survivorship bias also affects broad-market indexes used as bogey portfolios and generates upward-biased returns that are harder to beat. Several providers supply returns for various indexes that are adjusted for survivorship bias. These providers also attempt to adjust returns for cross holdings of shares that can distort the appropriate weights in the index.

24.8 PERFORMANCE ATTRIBUTION PROCEDURES

Rather than focus on risk-adjusted returns, practitioners often want simply to ascertain which decisions resulted in superior or inferior performance. Superior investment performance depends on an ability to be in the "right" securities at the right time. Such timing and selection ability may be considered broadly, such as being in equities as opposed to fixed-income securities when the stock market is performing well. Or it may be defined at a more detailed level, such as choosing the relatively better-performing stocks within a particular industry.

Portfolio managers constantly make broad-brush asset allocation decisions as well as more detailed sector and security allocation decisions within asset class. Performance attribution studies attempt to decompose overall performance into discrete components that may be identified with a particular level of the portfolio selection process.

Attribution studies start from the broadest asset allocation choices and progressively focus on ever-finer details of portfolio choice. The difference between a managed portfolio's performance and that of a benchmark portfolio then may be expressed as the sum of the contributions to performance of a series of decisions made at the various levels of the portfolio construction process. For example, one common attribution system decomposes performance into three components: (1) broad asset market allocation choices across equity, fixed-income, and money markets; (2) industry (sector) choice within each market; and (3) security choice within each sector.

The attribution method explains the difference in returns between a managed portfolio, P, and a selected benchmark portfolio, B, called the **bogey.** Suppose that the universe of assets for P and B includes n asset classes such as equities, bonds, and bills. For each asset class, a benchmark index portfolio is determined. For example, the S&P 500 may be chosen as a benchmark for equities. The bogey portfolio is set to have fixed weights in each asset class, and its rate of return is given by

$$r_B = \sum_{i=1}^{n} w_{Bi} r_{Bi}$$

where w_{Bi} is the weight of the bogey in asset class i, and r_{Bi} is the return on the benchmark portfolio of that class over the evaluation period. The portfolio managers choose weights in each class, w_{Pi}, based on their capital market expectations, and they choose a portfolio of the securities within each class based on their security analysis, which earns r_{Pi} over the evaluation period. Thus the return of the managed portfolio will be

$$r_P = \sum_{i=1}^{n} w_{Pi} r_{Pi}$$

The difference between the two rates of return, therefore, is

$$r_P - r_B = \sum_{i=1}^{n} w_{Pi} r_{Pi} - \sum_{i=1}^{n} w_{Bi} r_{Bi} = \sum_{i=1}^{n} (w_{Pi} r_{Pi} - w_{Bi} r_{Bi}) \qquad \textbf{(24.9)}$$

Each term in the summation of Equation 24.9 can be rewritten in a way that shows how asset allocation decisions versus security selection decisions for each asset class contributed to overall performance. We decompose each term of the summation into a sum of two terms as follows. Note that the two terms we label as contribution from asset allocation and contribution from security selection in the following decomposition do in fact sum to the total contribution of each asset class to overall performance.

Contribution from asset allocation	$(w_{Pi} - w_{Bi}) r_{Bi}$
+ Contribution from security selection	$w_{Pi}(r_{Pi} - r_{Bi})$
= Total contribution from asset class i	$w_{Pi} r_{Pi} - w_{Bi} r_{Bi}$

The first term of the sum measures the impact of asset allocation because it shows how deviations of the actual weight from the benchmark weight for that asset class multiplied by the index return for the asset class added to or subtracted from total performance. The second term of the sum measures the impact of security selection because it shows how the manager's excess return *within* the asset class compared to the benchmark return for that class multiplied by the portfolio weight for that class added to or subtracted from total

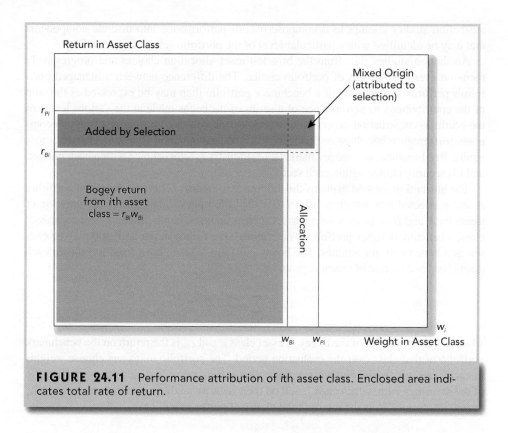

FIGURE 24.11   Performance attribution of ith asset class. Enclosed area indicates total rate of return.

performance. Figure 24.11 presents a graphical interpretation of the attribution of overall performance into security selection versus asset allocation.

To illustrate this method, consider the attribution results for a hypothetical portfolio. The portfolio invests in stocks, bonds, and money market securities. An attribution analysis appears in Tables 24.6 through 24.9. The portfolio return over the month is 5.34%.

The first step is to establish a benchmark level of performance against which performance ought to be compared. This benchmark, again, is called the bogey. It is designed to measure the returns the portfolio manager would earn if he or she were to follow a

TABLE 24.6

Performance of the managed portfolio

Component	Bogey Performance and Excess Return	
	Benchmark Weight	Return of Index during Month (%)
Equity (S&P 500)	.60	5.81
Bonds (Lehman Brothers Index)	.30	1.45
Cash (money market)	.10	0.48
Bogey = (.60 × 5.81) + (.30 × 1.45) + (.10 × 0.48) = 3.97%		
Return of managed portfolio	5.34%	
− Return of bogey portfolio	3.97	
Excess return of managed portfolio	1.37%	

completely passive strategy. "Passive" in this context has two attributes. First, it means that the allocation of funds across broad asset classes is set in accord with a notion of "usual," or neutral, allocation across sectors. This would be considered a passive asset-market allocation. Second, it means that *within* each asset class, the portfolio manager holds an indexed portfolio such as the S&P 500 index for the equity sector. In such a manner, the passive strategy used as a performance benchmark rules out asset allocation as well as security selection decisions. Any departure of the manager's return from the passive benchmark must be due to either asset allocation bets (departures from the neutral allocation across markets) or security selection bets (departures from the passive index within asset classes).

While we have already discussed in earlier chapters the justification for indexing within sectors, it is worth briefly explaining the determination of the neutral allocation of funds across the broad asset classes. Weights that are designated as "neutral" will depend on the risk tolerance of the investor and must be determined in consultation with the client. For example, risk-tolerant clients may place a large fraction of their portfolio in the equity market, perhaps directing the fund manager to set neutral weights of 75% equity, 15% bonds, and 10% cash equivalents. Any deviation from these weights must be justified by a belief that one or another market will either over- or underperform its usual risk–return profile. In contrast, more risk-averse clients may set neutral weights of 45%/35%/20% for the three markets. Therefore, their portfolios in normal circumstances will be exposed to less risk than that of the risk-tolerant client. Only intentional bets on market performance will result in departures from this profile.

In Table 24.6, the neutral weights have been set at 60% equity, 30% fixed income, and 10% cash (money market securities). The bogey portfolio, comprised of investments in each index with the 60/30/10 weights, returned 3.97%. The managed portfolio's measure of performance is positive and equal to its actual return less the return of the bogey: $5.34 - 3.97 = 1.37\%$. The next step is to allocate the 1.37% excess return to the separate decisions that contributed to it.

Asset Allocation Decisions

Our hypothetical managed portfolio is invested in the equity, fixed-income, and money markets with weights of 70%, 7%, and 23%, respectively. The portfolio's performance could have to do with the departure of this weighting scheme from the benchmark 60/30/10 weights and/or to superior or inferior results *within* each of the three broad markets.

To isolate the effect of the manager's asset allocation choice, we measure the performance of a hypothetical portfolio that would have been invested in the indexes for each market with weights 70/7/23. This return measures the effect of the shift away from the benchmark 60/30/10 weights without allowing for any effects attributable to active management of the securities selected within each market.

Superior performance relative to the bogey is achieved by overweighting investments in markets that turn out to perform well and by underweighting those in poorly performing markets. The contribution of asset allocation to superior performance equals the sum over all markets of the excess weight (sometimes called the *active weight* in the industry) in each market times the return of the market index.

Table 24.7A demonstrates that asset allocation contributed 31 basis points to the portfolio's overall excess return of 137 basis points. The major factor contributing to superior performance in this month is the heavy weighting of the equity market in a month when the equity market has an excellent return of 5.81%.

a. What are the arithmetic and geometric average time-weighted rates of return for the investor?

b. What is the dollar-weighted rate of return? (*Hint:* Carefully prepare a chart of cash flows for the *four* dates corresponding to the turns of the year for January 1, 2005, to January 1, 2008. If your calculator cannot calculate internal rate of return, you will have to use trial and error.)

6. A manager buys three shares of stock today, and then sells one of those shares each year for the next 3 years. His actions and the price history of the stock are summarized below. The stock pays no dividends.

Time	Price	Action
0	$ 90	Buy 3 shares
1	100	Sell 1 share
2	100	Sell 1 share
3	100	Sell 1 share

a. Calculate the time-weighted geometric average return on this "portfolio."

b. Calculate the time-weighted arithmetic average return on this portfolio.

c. Calculate the dollar-weighted average return on this portfolio.

7. Based on current dividend yields and expected capital gains, the expected rates of return on portfolios A and B are 12% and 16%, respectively. The beta of A is .7, while that of B is 1.4. The T-bill rate is currently 5%, whereas the expected rate of return of the S&P 500 index is 13%. The standard deviation of portfolio A is 12% annually, that of B is 31%, and that of the S&P 500 index is 18%.

a. If you currently hold a market-index portfolio, would you choose to add either of these portfolios to your holdings? Explain.

b. If instead you could invest *only* in T-bills and *one* of these portfolios, which would you choose?

8. Consider the two (excess return) index-model regression results for stocks A and B. The risk-free rate over the period was 6%, and the market's average return was 14%. Performance is measured using an index model regression on excess returns.

	Stock A	Stock B
Index model regression estimates	$1\% + 1.2(r_M - r_f)$	$2\% + .8(r_M - r_f)$
R-square	.576	.436
Residual standard deviation, $\sigma(e)$	10.3%	19.1%
Standard deviation of excess returns	21.6%	24.9%

a. Calculate the following statistics for each stock:

i. Alpha

ii. Information ratio

iii. Sharpe measure

iv. Treynor measure

b. Which stock is the best choice under the following circumstances?

i. This is the only risky asset to be held by the investor.

ii. This stock will be mixed with the rest of the investor's portfolio, currently composed solely of holdings in the market index fund.

iii. This is one of many stocks that the investor is analyzing to form an actively managed stock portfolio.

9. Evaluate the market timing and security selection abilities of four managers whose performances are plotted in the accompanying diagrams.

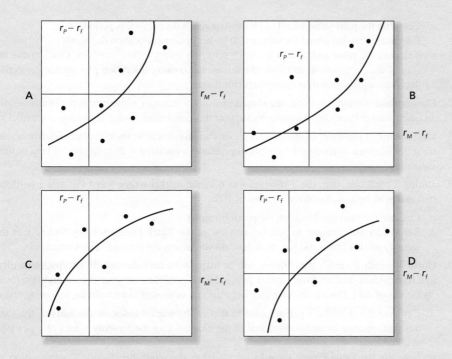

10. Consider the following information regarding the performance of a money manager in a recent month. The table represents the actual return of each sector of the manager's portfolio in column 1, the fraction of the portfolio allocated to each sector in column 2, the benchmark or neutral sector allocations in column 3, and the returns of sector indices in column 4.

	Actual Return	Actual Weight	Benchmark Weight	Index Return
Equity	2%	.70	.60	2.5% (S&P 500)
Bonds	1	.20	.30	1.2 (Salomon Index)
Cash	0.5	.10	.10	0.5

a. What was the manager's return in the month? What was her overperformance or underperformance?

b. What was the contribution of security selection to relative performance?

c. What was the contribution of asset allocation to relative performance? Confirm that the sum of selection and allocation contributions equals her total "excess" return relative to the bogey.

11. A global equity manager is assigned to select stocks from a universe of large stocks throughout the world. The manager will be evaluated by comparing her returns to the return on the MSCI World Market Portfolio, but she is free to hold stocks from various countries in whatever proportions she finds desirable. Results for a given month are contained in the following table:

Country	Weight In MSCI Index	Manager's Weight	Manager's Return in Country	Return of Stock Index for That Country
U.K.	.15	.30	20%	12%
Japan	.30	.10	15	15
U.S.	.45	.40	10	14
Germany	.10	.20	5	12

    a. Calculate the total value added of all the manager's decisions this period.

    b. Calculate the value added (or subtracted) by her *country* allocation decisions.

    c. Calculate the value added from her stock selection ability within countries. Confirm that the sum of the contributions to value added from her country allocation plus security selection decisions equals total over- or underperformance.

12. Conventional wisdom says that one should measure a manager's investment performance over an entire market cycle. What arguments support this convention? What arguments contradict it?

13. Does the use of universes of managers with similar investment styles to evaluate relative investment performance overcome the statistical problems associated with instability of beta or total variability?

14. During a particular year, the T-bill rate was 6%, the market return was 14%, and a portfolio manager with beta of .5 realized a return of 10%.

    a. Evaluate the manager based on the portfolio alpha.

    b. Reconsider your answer to part (*a*) in view of the Black-Jensen-Scholes finding that the security market line is too flat. Now how do you assess the manager's performance?

Challenge Problem

15. Go to Kenneth French's data library site at **http://mba.tuck.dartmouth.edu/pages/faculty/ken.french/data_library.html.** Select two industry portfolios of your choice and download 36 months of data. Download other data from the site as needed to perform the following tasks.

    a. Compare the portfolio's performance to that of the market index on the basis of the various performance measures discussed in the chapter. Plot the monthly values of alpha plus residual return.

    b. Now use the Fama-French three-factor model as the return benchmark. Compute plots of alpha plus residual return using the FF model. How does performance change using this benchmark instead of the market index?

1. You and a prospective client are considering the measurement of investment performance, particularly with respect to international portfolios for the past 5 years. The data you discussed are presented in the following table:

International Manager or Index	Total Return	Country and Security Return	Currency Return
Manager A	–6.0%	2.0%	–8.0%
Manager B	–2.0	–1.0	–1.0
International Index	–5.0	0.2	–5.2

    a. Assume that the data for manager A and manager B accurately reflect their investment skills and that both managers actively manage currency exposure. Briefly describe one strength and one weakness for each manager.

    b. Recommend and justify a strategy that would enable your fund to take advantage of the strengths of each of the two managers while minimizing their weaknesses.

2. Carl Karl, a portfolio manager for the Alpine Trust Company, has been responsible since 2010 for the City of Alpine's Employee Retirement Plan, a municipal pension fund. Alpine is a growing community, and city services and employee payrolls have expanded in each of the past 10 years. Contributions to the plan in fiscal 2015 exceeded benefit payments by a three-to-one ratio.

    The plan board of trustees directed Karl 5 years ago to invest for total return over the long term. However, as trustees of this highly visible public fund, they cautioned him that volatile or erratic results could cause them embarrassment. They also noted a state statute that mandated that not more than 25% of the plan's assets (at cost) be invested in common stocks.

At the annual meeting of the trustees in November 2015, Karl presented the following portfolio and performance report to the board:

Alpine Employee Retirement Plan

Asset Mix as of 9/30/15	At Cost (millions)		At Market (millions)	
Fixed-income assets:				
Short-term securities	$ 4.5	11.0%	$ 4.5	11.4%
Long-term bonds and mortgages	26.5	64.7	23.5	59.5
Common stocks	10.0	24.3	11.5	29.1
	$41.0	100.0%	$39.5	100.0%

Investment Performance

	Annual Rates of Return for Periods Ending 9/30/15	
	5 Years	1 Year
Total Alpine Fund:		
Time-weighted	8.2%	5.2%
Dollar-weighted (internal)	7.7%	4.8%
Assumed actuarial return	6.0%	6.0%
U.S. Treasury bills	7.5%	11.3%
Large sample of pension funds (average 60% equities, 40% fixed income)	10.1%	14.3%
Common stocks—Alpine Fund	13.3%	14.3%
Alpine portfolio beta coefficient	0.90	0.89
Standard & Poor's 500 stock index	13.8%	21.1%
Fixed-income securities—Alpine Fund	6.7%	1.0%
Salomon Brothers' bond index	4.0%	−11.4%

Karl was proud of his performance and was chagrined when a trustee made the following critical observations:

a. "Our 1-year results were terrible, and it's what you've done for us lately that counts most."
b. "Our total fund performance was clearly inferior compared to the large sample of other pension funds for the last 5 years. What else could this reflect except poor management judgment?"
c. "Our common stock performance was especially poor for the 5-year period."
d. "Why bother to compare your returns to the return from Treasury bills and the actuarial assumption rate? What your competition could have earned for us or how we would have fared if invested in a passive index (which doesn't charge a fee) are the only relevant measures of performance."
e. "Who cares about time-weighted return? If it can't pay pensions, what good is it!"

Appraise the merits of each of these statements and give counterarguments that Mr. Karl can use.

3. The Retired Fund is an open-ended mutual fund composed of $500 million in U.S. bonds and U.S. Treasury bills. This fund has had a portfolio duration (including T-bills) of between 3 and 9 years. Retired has shown first-quartile performance over the past 5 years, as measured by an independent fixed-income measurement service. However, the directors of the fund would like to measure the market timing skill of the fund's sole bond investor manager. An external consulting firm has suggested the following three methods:

a. Method I examines the value of the bond portfolio at the beginning of every year, then calculates the return that would have been achieved had that same portfolio been held throughout the year. This return would then be compared with the return actually obtained by the fund.

Average annual rate of return	22.1%
Beta	1.2
Standard deviation of returns	16.8%

TABLE 24A
Williamson capital performance data, 1997–2008

Average annual rate of return	24.2%
Beta	0.8
Standard deviation of returns	20.2%

TABLE 24B
Joyner asset management performance data 1997–2008

Risk-free Asset	
Average annual rate of return	5.0%
Market Index	
Average annual rate of return	18.9%
Standard deviation of returns	13.8%

TABLE 24C
Relevant risk-free asset and market index performance data, 1997–2008

a. Calculate the Sharpe ratio and Treynor measure for both Williamson Capital and Joyner Asset Management.

b. The Investment Committee notices that using the Sharpe ratio versus the Treynor measure produces different performance rankings of Williamson and Joyner. Explain why these criteria may result in different rankings.

Go to the *Market Insight* entry page (**www.mhhe.com/edumarketinsight**) and click on the *Commentary* tab. Follow the current Investment Policy Committee Notes (*USA IPC Notes*) link to open the notes. Answer the following questions based on information provided in the report:

- What recent and upcoming reports are listed in the *Economic Outlook* and the *Upcoming Reports* sections?
- What factors are important for the longer-term outlook?
- What fundamental and technical factors are discussed in the *Market Outlook* section?
- What is the current recommended allocation for each asset class?
- What are the year-end target levels for the S&P 500 index, the Federal Funds rate, real Gross Domestic Product growth, and West Texas Intermediate crude oil prices?
- Which sectors are recommended for overweighting in current portfolios? Which are recommended for underweighting?

How would you evaluate the usefulness of these asset allocation recommendations?

STANDARD
&POOR'S

Performance of Mutual Funds

Several popular finance-related Web sites offer mutual fund screeners. Go to **moneycentral.msn.com** and click on the *Investing* link on the top menu. Choose *Funds* from the submenu, then look for the *Easy Screener* link on the left-side menu. Before you start to specify your preferences using the drop-down boxes, look for the *Show More Options* link toward the bottom of the page and select it. When all of the options are shown, devise a screen for funds that meet the following criteria: 5-star Morningstar Overall Rating, a Minimum Initial Investment as low as possible, Low Morningstar Risk, No Load, Manager Tenure of at least 5 years, Morningstar Overall Return high, 12b-1 fees as low as possible, and Expense Ratio as low as possible. Click on the *Find Funds* link to run the screen.

When you get the list of results, you can sort them according to any one criterion that interests you by clicking on its column heading. Are there any funds you would rule out based on what you see? If you want to rerun the screen with different choices click on the *Change Criteria* link toward the top of the page and make the changes. Click on *Find Funds* again to run the new screen. You can click on any fund symbol to get more information about it.

Are any of these funds of interest to you? How might your screening choices differ if you were choosing funds for various clients?

E-Investments

SOLUTIONS TO CONCEPT CHECKS

1.

Time	Action	Cash Flow
0	Buy two shares	−40
1	Collect dividends; then sell one of the shares	4 + 22
2	Collect dividend on remaining share, then sell it	2 + 19

a. Dollar-weighted return:

$$-40 + \frac{26}{1+r} + \frac{21}{(1+r)^2} = 0$$

$$r = .1191, \text{ or } 11.91\%$$

b. Time-weighted return:

The rates of return on the stock in the 2 years were:

$$r_1 = \frac{2 + (22 - 20)}{20} = .20$$

$$r_2 = \frac{2 + (19 - 22)}{22} = -.045$$

$$(r_1 + r_2)/2 = .077, \text{ or } 7.7\%$$

2. Sharpe: $(\bar{r} - \bar{r}_f)/\sigma$

$$S_P = (35 - 6)/42 = .69$$
$$S_M = (28 - 6)/30 = .733$$

Alpha: $\bar{r} - [\bar{r}_f + \beta(\bar{r}_M - \bar{r}_f)]$

$$\alpha_P = 35 - [6 + 1.2(28 - 6)] = 2.6$$
$$\alpha_M = 0$$

Treynor: $(\bar{r} - \bar{r}_f)/\beta$

$$T_P = (35 - 6)/1.2 = 24.2$$
$$T_M = (28 - 6)/1.0 = 22$$

Information ratio: $\alpha/\sigma(e)$

$$I_P = 2.6/18 = .144$$
$$I_M = 0$$

3. The t-statistic on α is $.2/2 = .1$. The probability that a manager with a true alpha of zero could obtain a sample period alpha with a t-statistic of .1 or better by pure luck depends on the length of the sample period. The smallest probability would occur with a large sample and is found in a table of the normal distribution. That probability is 46%.

4. The timer will guess bear or bull markets completely randomly. One-half of all bull markets will be preceded by a correct forecast, and similarly for bear markets. Hence $P_1 + P_2 - 1 = \frac{1}{2} + \frac{1}{2} - 1 = 0$.

5. Performance Attribution

First compute the new bogey performance as $(.70 \times 5.81) + (.25 \times 1.45) + (.05 \times .48) = 4.45$.

a. Contribution of asset allocation to performance:

Market	(1) Actual Weight in Market	(2) Benchmark Weight in Market	(3) Active or Excess Weight	(4) Market Return (%)	(5) = (3) × (4) Contribution to Performance (%)
Equity	.70	.70	.00	5.81	.00
Fixed-income	.07	.25	−.18	1.45	−.26
Cash	.23	.05	.18	0.48	.09
Contribution of asset allocation					−.17

b. Contribution of selection to total performance:

Market	(1) Portfolio Performance (%)	(2) Index Performance (%)	(3) Excess Performance (%)	(4) Portfolio Weight	(5) = (3) × (4) Contribution (%)
Equity	7.28	5.00	2.28	.70	1.60
Fixed-income	1.89	1.45	0.44	.07	0.03
Contribution of selection within markets					1.63

CHAPTER TWENTY-FIVE

INTERNATIONAL DIVERSIFICATION

ALTHOUGH WE IN the United States customarily use a broad index of U.S. equities as the market-index portfolio, the practice is increasingly inappropriate. U.S. equities represent less than 40% of world equities and a far smaller fraction of total world wealth. In this chapter, we look beyond domestic markets to survey issues of international and extended diversification. In one sense, international investing may be viewed as no more than a straightforward generalization of our earlier treatment of portfolio selection with a larger menu of assets from which to construct a portfolio. Similar issues of diversification, security analysis, security selection, and asset allocation face the investor. On the other hand, international investments pose some problems not encountered in domestic markets. Among these are the presence of exchange rate risk, restrictions on capital flows across national boundaries, an added dimension of political risk and

country-specific regulations, and differing accounting practices in different countries. Therefore, in this chapter we review the major topics covered in the rest of the book, emphasizing their international aspects. We start with the central concept of portfolio theory—diversification. We will see that global diversification offers opportunities for improving portfolio risk–return trade-offs. We also will see how exchange rate fluctuations and political risk affect the risk of international investments. We next turn to passive and active investment styles in the international context. We will consider some of the special problems involved in the interpretation of passive index portfolios, and we will show how active asset allocation can be generalized to incorporate country and currency choices in addition to traditional domestic asset class choices. Finally, we demonstrate performance attribution for international investments.

Developed Countries

To appreciate the myopia of an exclusive investment focus on U.S. stocks and bonds, consider the data in Table 25.1, developed by the authors in a 2006 study. Developed (high-income) countries are defined as those with per capita income exceeding $10,000 (in 2005), and their broad stock indexes are generally less risky than those of emerging markets. The World Bank listed 55 developed countries in 2005, many of them with very small exchanges. Our list includes the 25 countries with the largest equity capitalization, the smallest of which is New Zealand with a capitalization of $39 billion in 2005. These countries made up 76% of world gross domestic product in 2005. Our list also includes 20 emerging markets that make up 8.9% of the market capitalization of the world stock markets.

The first six columns of Table 25.1 show market capitalization over the years 2000–2005 for developed markets. The first line is capitalization for all world exchanges, showing total capitalization of corporate equity in 2005 as $35.6 trillion, of which U.S. stock exchanges made up $13.9 trillion (39%). The next three columns of Table 25.1 show country equity capitalization as a percentage of the world's in 2000 and 2005 and the growth in capitalization over the period. The large volatility of country stock indexes resulted in significant changes in relative size. For example, the U.S. weight in the world equity portfolio decreased from 47% in 2000 to 39.2% in 2005. The weights of the five largest countries behind the U.S. (Japan, U.K., France, Germany, and Canada) added up to 32% in 2005, so that in the universe of these six countries alone, the weight of the U.S. was only 55%. Clearly, U.S. stocks may not comprise a fully diversified portfolio of equities.

The last three columns of Table 25.1 show GDP, per capita GDP, and equity capitalization as a percentage of GDP for the year 2005. As we would expect, per capita GDP in developed countries is not as variable across countries as total GDP, which is determined in part by total population. But market capitalization as a percentage of GDP is quite variable, suggesting widespread differences in economic structure even across developed countries. We return to this issue in the next section.

Emerging Markets

For a passive strategy one could argue that a portfolio of equities of just the six countries with the largest capitalization would make up 71.5% (in 2005) of the world portfolio and may be sufficiently diversified. This argument will not hold for active portfolios that seek to tilt investments toward promising assets. Active portfolios will naturally include many stocks or even indexes of emerging markets.

Table 25.2 makes the point. Surely, active portfolio managers must prudently scour stocks in markets such as China, Colombia, or Russia. Table 25.2 shows data from the 20 largest emerging markets, the most notable of which is China with growth of 1,154% over the 5 years ending in 2005. But managers also would not want to have missed a market like Colombia (0.12% of world capitalization) with a growth of 950% over the same years.

These 20 emerging markets make up 18% of the world GDP and 9% of world market capitalization. Per capita GDP in these countries in 2005 was quite variable, ranging from $714 (India) to $15,120 (Taiwan); still, no active manager would want to ignore India in an international portfolio. Market capitalization as a percent of GDP, which ranges from 7% (China) to 119% (South Africa), suggests that these markets are expected to show significant growth over the coming years, even absent spectacular growth in GDP.

Market Capitalization

| | Market Capitalization | | | | | | Percent of World | | Growth (%) | GDP | GDP per Capita | Market Capitalization as % of GDP |
| | Billions of $ U.S. | | | | | | | | | | | |
	2005	2004	2003	2002	2001	2000	2005	2000	2000–2005	2005	2005	2005
World	35,572	31,514	27,088	20,026	23,842	27,473	100%	100%	29.48	44,433		
Total Developed Countries	32,336	29,124	25,317	18,689	22,792	26,417	90.9	96.2	22.40	33,599	33,599	96
U.S.	13,934	13,225	12,023	9,172	11,850	12,900	39.2	47.0	8.01	12,486	42,101	112
Japan	4,420	3,472	2,934	2,076	2,254	3,140	12.4	11.4	40.76	4,571	35,787	97
U.K.	2,975	2,706	2,363	1,796	2,157	2,566	8.4	9.3	15.94	2,201	36,599	135
France	1,680	1,435	1,238	911	1,068	1,278	4.7	4.7	31.49	2,106	33,734	80
Germany	1,228	1,115	990	633	831	1,061	3.5	3.9	15.66	2,797	33,922	44
Canada	1,207	949	750	488	547	615	3.4	2.2	96.21	1,130	35,064	107
Switzerland	921	814	710	543	604	783	2.6	2.9	17.52	368	50,524	250
Italy	790	773	600	463	508	716	2.2	2.6	10.41	1,766	30,450	45
Hong Kong	778	706	593	402	462	564	2.2	2.1	37.94	178	25,444	438
Australia	721	636	540	360	362	349	2.0	1.3	106.66	708	34,714	102
Spain	655	633	479	312	351	331	1.8	1.2	97.76	1,127	27,226	58
Korea	552	353	265	200	186	123	1.6	0.4	349.23	793	16,422	70
Netherlands	548	612	539	437	551	680	1.5	2.5	-19.46	625	38,333	88
Sweden	367	344	267	170	218	274	1.0	1.0	33.70	359	39,658	102
Belgium	271	269	171	127	146	159	0.8	0.6	70.83	372	35,750	73
Finland	200	173	161	133	183	280	0.6	1.0	-28.77	193	37,014	103
Singapore	183	153	133	92	106	136	0.5	0.5	35.28	118	26,835	156
Norway	177	137	92	65	64	52	0.5	0.2	239.43	296	64,268	60
Denmark	165	143	110	72	80	99	0.5	0.4	66.37	260	48,000	64
Austria	133	87	54	31	22	28	0.4	0.1	381.85	307	37,528	43
Greece	124	105	83	52	63	72	0.3	0.3	72.94	223	20,082	56
Ireland	111	105	76	53	69	82	0.3	0.3	35.54	200	48,351	55
Israel	87	66	54	33	42	46	0.2	0.2	90.12	124	18,266	71
Portugal	70	73	62	46	50	64	0.2	0.2	10.09	183	17,439	38
New Zealand	39	39	31	21	19	20	0.1	0.1	96.97	109	26,441	36

TABLE 25.1

Market capitalization of stock exchanges in developed countries

Sources: Market capitalization, Datastream; GDP, World Bank.

Market Capitalization

	Billions of $ U.S.						Percent of World		Growth (%)	GDP	GDP per Capita	Market Capitalization as % of GDP
	2005	2004	2003	2002	2001	2000	2005	2000	2000–2005	2005	2005	2005
Total Emerging Markets	3,166	2,321	1,737	1,045	1,087	1,067	8.9	3.9	196.72	8,097		39
Russia	458	221	172	101	78	44	1.29	0.16	940.91	766	5,369	60
India	408	319	216	111	157	180	1.15	0.66	126.67	775	714	53
Brazil	408	306	224	101	85	107	1.15	0.39	281.31	793	4,316	51
Taiwan	348	332	281	190	235	177	0.98	0.64	96.61	346	15,120	101
South Africa	284	226	149	102	71	104	0.80	0.38	173.08	239	5,100	119
Mexico	239	171	124	99	121	112	0.67	0.41	113.39	768	7,298	31
China	163	59	48	20	18	13	0.46	0.05	1153.85	2,225	1,703	7
Malaysia	142	137	116	94	90	83	0.40	0.30	71.08	131	5,040	109
Turkey	128	84	59	29	40	50	0.36	0.18	156.00	362	5,062	35
Chile	110	92	74	43	49	44	0.31	0.16	150.00	114	7,040	97
Thailand	97	86	86	33	27	23	0.27	0.08	321.74	169	2,577	57
Poland	78	63	34	27	25	27	0.22	0.10	188.89	301	7,875	26
Indonesia	70	64	43	24	18	21	0.20	0.08	233.33	276	1,259	25
Colombia	42	20	10	6	6	4	0.12	0.01	950.00	122	2,742	34
Czech Rep.	41	26	21	16	17	20	0.12	0.07	105.00	124	12,106	33
Philippines	38	30	17	12	11	12	0.11	0.04	216.67	98	1,159	39
Pakistan	36	21	13	9	4	5	0.10	0.02	620.00	118	769	30
Hungary	33	28	17	13	10	12	0.09	0.04	175.00	109	11,217	30
Argentina	24	21	20	7	19	24	0.07	0.09	0.00	182	4,802	13
Peru	19	15	13	8	6	5	0.05	0.02	280.00	79	2,812	24

TABLE 25.2

Market capitalization of stock exchanges in emerging markets

Sources: Market capitalization (end of year), Datastream; GDP and GDP per capita, World Bank.

The growth of capitalization in emerging markets over 2000–2005 was very large (197%) and much more volatile than growth in developed countries, suggesting that both risk and rewards in this segment of the globe may be substantial.

Market Capitalization and GDP

The contemporary view of economic development (see, for example, deSoto[1]) holds that a major requirement for economic advancement is a developed code of business laws, institutions, and regulation that allows citizens to legally own, capitalize, and trade capital assets. As a corollary, we expect that development of equity markets will serve as catalysts for

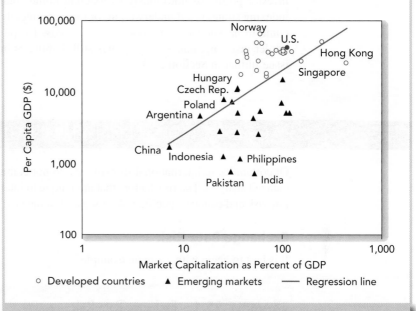

FIGURE 25.1 Per capita GDP and market capitalization as percent of GDP (log scale)

enrichment of the population, that is, that countries with larger relative capitalization of equities will tend to be richer. Work by La Porta, Lopez-De-Silvanes, Shleifer, and Vishny[2] indicates that, other things equal, market value of corporations is higher in countries with better protection of minority shareholders.

Figure 25.1 is a simple (perhaps simplistic, because other relevant explanatory variables are omitted) rendition of the argument that a developed market for corporate equity contributes to the enrichment of the population. The R-square of the regression line shown in Figure 25.1 is 28% and the regression coefficient is .91, suggesting that an increase of 1% in the ratio of market capitalization to GDP is associated with an increase in per capita GDP of 0.91%. It is remarkable that only 2 of the 25 developed countries lie below the regression line; only 4 of 20 low-income emerging markets lie above the line. A country like Norway that lies above the line, that is, exhibits higher per capita GDP than predicted by the regression, enjoys oil wealth that contributes to population income. Countries below the line, such as Indonesia, Philippines, and Pakistan, suffered from deterioration of the business environment due to political strife and/or government policies that restricted the private sector. China's policies of freeing up economic activities contributed to the remarkable growth in market capitalization over 2000–2005 and moved it in recent years toward the predicted relationship.

Home-Country Bias

One would expect that most investors, particularly institutional and professional investors, would be aware of the opportunities offered by international investing. Yet in practice,

[1]Hernando de Soto, *The Mystery of Capital* (New York: Basic Books, 2000).

[2]Rafael La Porta, Florencio Lopez-De-Silvanes, Andrei Shleifer, and Robert Vishny, "Investor Protection and Corporate Valuation," *Journal of Finance* 57 (June 2002).

investor portfolios notoriously overweight home-country stocks compared to a neutral indexing strategy and underweight, or even completely ignore, foreign equities. This has come to be known as the *home-country bias.* Despite a continuous increase in cross-border investing, home-country bias still dominates investor portfolios. We discuss this issue further in Section 25.3.

25.2 RISK FACTORS IN INTERNATIONAL INVESTING

Opportunities in international investments do not come free of risk or of the cost of specialized analysis. The risk factors that are unique to international investments are exchange rate risk and country-specific risk, discussed in the next two sections.

Exchange Rate Risk

It is best to begin with a simple example.

EXAMPLE 25.1   Exchange Rate Risk

Consider an investment in risk-free British government bills paying 10% annual interest in British pounds. While these U.K. bills would be the risk-free asset to a British investor, this is not the case for a U.S. investor. Suppose, for example, the current exchange rate is $2 per pound, and the U.S. investor starts with $20,000. That amount can be exchanged for £10,000 and invested at a riskless 10% rate in the United Kingdom to provide £11,000 in 1 year.

What happens if the dollar–pound exchange rate varies over the year? Say that during the year, the pound depreciates relative to the dollar, so that by year-end only $1.80 is required to purchase £1. The £11,000 can be exchanged at the year-end exchange rate for only $19,800 (= £11,000 × $1.80/£), resulting in a loss of $200 relative to the initial $20,000 investment. Despite the positive 10% pound-denominated return, the dollar-denominated return is a negative 1%.

We can generalize from Example 25.1. The $20,000 is exchanged for $20,000/$E_0$ pounds, where E_0 denotes the original exchange rate ($2/£). The U.K. investment grows to $(20,000/E_0)[1 + r_f(\text{UK})]$ British pounds, where $r_f(\text{UK})$ is the risk-free rate in the United Kingdom. The pound proceeds ultimately are converted back to dollars at the subsequent exchange rate E_1, for total dollar proceeds of $20,000(E_1/E_0)[1 + r_f(\text{UK})]$. The dollar-denominated return on the investment in British bills, therefore, is

$$1 + r(\text{US}) = [1 + r_f(\text{UK})]E_1/E_0 \qquad (25.1)$$

We see in Equation 25.1 that the dollar-denominated return for a U.S. investor equals the pound-denominated return times the exchange rate "return." For a U.S. investor, the investment in British bills is a combination of a safe investment in the United Kingdom and a risky investment in the performance of the pound relative to the dollar. Here, the pound fared poorly, falling from a value of $2.00 to only $1.80. The loss on the pound more than offset the earnings on the British bill.

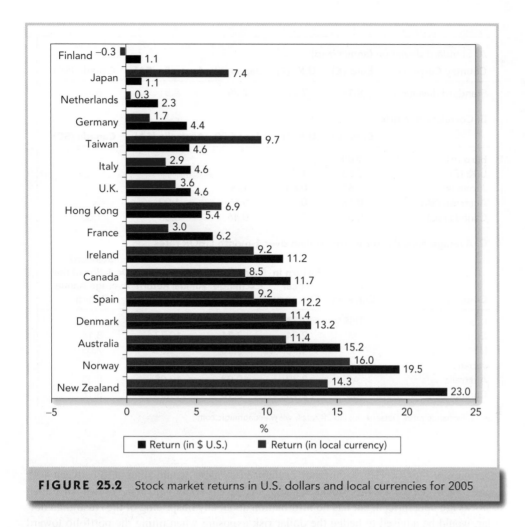

FIGURE 25.2 Stock market returns in U.S. dollars and local currencies for 2005

Figure 25.2 illustrates this point. It presents rates of returns on stock market indexes in several countries for 2005. The colored boxes depict returns in local currencies, while the dark boxes depict returns in dollars, adjusted for exchange rate movements. It's clear that exchange rate fluctuations over this period had large effects on dollar-denominated returns in several countries.

Pure **exchange rate risk** is the risk borne by investments in foreign safe assets. The investor in U.K. bills of Example 25.1 bears only the risk of the U.K./U.S. exchange rate. We can assess the magnitude of exchange rate risk by examining historical rates of change in various exchange rates and their correlations.

Table 25.3A shows historical exchange rate risk measured from monthly percent changes in the exchange rates of major currencies over the period 2001–2005. The data show that currency risk can be quite high. The annualized standard deviation of the percent changes in the exchange rate ranged from 6.12% (Canadian dollar) to 8.31% (Australian dollar). The annualized standard deviation of returns on U.S. large stocks for the same

CONCEPT CHECK 1

Using the data in Example 25.1, calculate the rate of return in dollars to a U.S. investor holding the British bill if the year-end exchange rate is: (a) $E_1 = \$2.00/£$; (b) $E_1 = \$2.20/£$.

TABLE 25.3

Rates of change in the U.S. dollar against major world currencies, 2001–2005 (annualized from monthly data)

A. Standard deviation (annualized)

Country Currency	Euro (€)	U.K. (£)	Japan (¥)	Australia ($A)	Canada ($C)
Standard deviation	8.16	7.06	7.29	8.31	6.12

B. Correlation matrix

	Euro (€)	U.K. (£)	Japan (¥)	Australia ($A)	Canada ($C)
Euro (€)	1.00				
U.K. (£)	0.83	1.00			
Japan (¥)	0.68	0.63	1.00		
Australia ($A)	0.66	0.58	0.55	1.00	
Canada ($C)	0.51	0.29	0.46	0.66	1.00

C. Average annual returns from rolling over 1-month LIBOR rates

Country	Currency	Return in Local Currency	Gains from Exchange Rates	Average Annual Return in U.S. $	Standard Deviation of the Average Annual Return
U.S.	US$	2.34		2.34	
Euro	€	2.84	7.71	10.77	8.14
U.K.	£	4.40	5.18	9.81	7.05
Japan	¥	0.07	2.07	2.14	7.29
Australia	A$	2.79	10.02	13.08	8.33
Canada	C$	2.95	8.16	11.35	6.16

Sources: Exchange rates, Datastream; LIBOR rates, **www.economagic.com.**

period was 14.97%. Hence, currency exchange risk alone would amount to between 40% and 55% of the risk on U.S. stocks. Clearly, an active investor who believes that Australian stocks are underpriced, but has no information about any mispricing of the Australian dollar, would be advised to hedge the dollar risk exposure when tilting the portfolio toward Australian stocks. Exchange rate risk of the major currencies seems fairly stable over time. For example, a study by Solnik[3] for the period 1971–1998 finds similar standard deviations, ranging from 4.8% (Canadian dollar) to 12.0% (Japanese yen).

In the context of international portfolios, exchange rate risk may be partly diversifiable. This is evident from the relatively low correlation coefficients in Table 25.3B. (This observation will be reinforced when we compare the risk of hedged and unhedged country portfolios in a later section.) Thus, passive investors with well-diversified international portfolios may not need to hedge 100% of their exposure to foreign currencies.

The annualized average change in the value of the U.S. dollar against the major currencies over the 5-year period and dollar returns on foreign bills (cash investments) appear in Table 25.3C. The table shows that the value of the U.S. dollar consistently depreciated in this particular period. For example, the average rate of depreciation against the Japanese yen over the 5 years was 2.07% and against the Australian dollar, 10.02%. Had an investor been able to forecast these large exchange rate movements, it would have been a source of great profit. The currency market thus provided attractive opportunities for investors with superior information or analytical ability.

---

[3]B. Solnik, *International Investing*, 4th ed. (Reading, MA: Addison Wesley, 1999).

The investor in Example 25.1 could have hedged the exchange rate risk using a forward or futures contract in foreign exchange. Recall that a forward or futures contract on foreign exchange calls for delivery or acceptance of one currency for another at a stipulated exchange rate. Here, the U.S. investor would agree to deliver pounds for dollars at a fixed exchange rate, thereby eliminating the risk involved with conversion of the pound investment back into dollars.

EXAMPLE 25.2 Hedging Exchange Rate Risk

If the forward exchange rate in Example 25.1 had been $F_0 = \$1.93/\pounds$ when the investment was made, the U.S. investor could have assured a riskless dollar-denominated return by arranging to deliver the £11,000 at the forward exchange rate of $\$1.93/\pounds$. In this case, the riskless U.S. return would then have been 6.15%:

$$[1 + r_f(\text{UK})]F_0 / E_0 = (1.10)1.93 / 2.00 = 1.0615$$

You may recall that the hedge underlying Example 25.2 is the same type of hedging strategy at the heart of the spot-futures parity relationship first discussed in Chapter 22. In both instances, futures or forward markets are used to eliminate the risk of holding another asset. The U.S. investor can lock in a riskless dollar-denominated return either by investing in United Kingdom bills and hedging exchange rate risk or by investing in riskless U.S. assets. Because investments in two riskless strategies must provide equal returns, we conclude that $[1 + r_f(\text{UK})]F_0 /E_0 = 1 + r_f(\text{US})$, which can be rearranged to

$$\frac{F_0}{E_0} = \frac{1 + r_f(\text{US})}{1 + r_f(\text{UK})} \tag{25.2}$$

This relationship is called the **interest rate parity relationship** or **covered interest arbitrage relationship,** which we first encountered in Chapter 23.

Unfortunately, such perfect exchange rate hedging usually is not so easy. In our example, we knew exactly how many pounds to sell in the forward or futures market because the pound-denominated return in the United Kingdom was riskless. If the U.K. investment had not been in bills, but instead had been in risky U.K. equity, we would have known neither the ultimate value in pounds of our U.K. investment nor how many pounds to sell forward. The hedging opportunity offered by foreign exchange forward contracts would thus be imperfect.

To summarize, the generalization of Equation 25.1 for unhedged investments is that

$$1 + r(\text{US}) = [1 + r(\text{foreign})]E_1 / E_0 \tag{25.3}$$

where r (foreign) is the possibly risky return earned in the currency of the foreign investment. You can set up a perfect hedge only in the special case that r(foreign) is itself a known number. In that case, you know you must sell in the forward or futures market an amount of foreign currency equal to $[1 + r(\text{foreign})]$ for each unit of that currency you purchase today.

CONCEPT CHECK 2

How many pounds would the investor in Example 25.2 need to sell forward to hedge exchange rate risk if: (a) r(UK) = 20%; and (b) r(UK) = 30%?

Country-Specific Risk

In principle, security analysis at the macroeconomic, industry, and firm-specific level is similar in all countries. Such analysis aims to provide estimates of expected returns and risk of individual assets and portfolios. To achieve the same quality of information about assets in a foreign country is by nature more difficult and hence more expensive. Moreover, the risk of coming by false or misleading information is greater.

Consider two investors: an American wishing to invest in Indonesian stocks and an Indonesian wishing to invest in U.S. stocks. While each would have to consider macroeconomic analysis of the foreign country, the task would be much more difficult for the American investor. The reason is not that investment in Indonesia is necessarily riskier than investment in the U.S. You can easily find many U.S. stocks that are, in the final analysis, riskier than a number of Indonesian stocks. The difference lies in the fact that the U.S. investment environment is more transparent than that of Indonesia.

In the past, when international investing was novel, the added risk was referred to as **political risk** and its assessment was an art. As cross-border investment has increased and more resources have been utilized, the quality of related analysis has improved. A leading organization in the field (which is quite competitive) is the PRS Group, Inc. (Political Risk Services), which publishes two methodologies, *Political Risk Services* and the one presented here—*International Country Risk Guide (ICRG).*[4]

PRS's country risk analysis results in a country composite risk rating on a scale of 0 (most risky) to 100 (least risky). Countries are then ranked by the composite risk measure and divided into five categories: very low risk (100–80), low risk (79.9–70), moderate risk (69.9–60), high risk (59.9–50), and very high risk (less than 50). To illustrate, Table 25.4 shows the placement of five countries in the October 2004 issue of the PRS *International Country Risk Guide.* It is not surprising to find Norway at the top of the very-low-risk list, and small emerging markets at the bottom, with Zimbabwe (ranked 140) closing the list.

TABLE 25.4

Composite risk ratings for October 2004 and November 2003

Rank in 10/04	Country	Composite Risk Rating 10/04	10/04 minus 11/03	Rank in 11/03
	Very low risk			
1	Norway	92.3	1.75	2
14	Japan	84.5	−1.75	9
15	United Kingdom	84.0	0	17
	Low risk			
42	United States	77.5	1.75	48
44	China, People's Republic	76.8	−0.5	40
55	Mexico	74.8	4.25	65
67	India	71.8	2.75	72
	Moderate risk			
86	Argentina	67.5	3.5	92
109	Indonesia	62.5	1.75	108
	High risk			
119	Lebanon	59.0	3.5	124
125	Sierra Leone	58.3	7.5	133
	Very high risk			
139	Iraq	38.0	−3.5	138
140	Zimbabwe	36.3	2	140

Source: *International Country Risk Guide.* October 2004, Table 1. © The PRS Group, Inc., **www.prsgroup.com/ICRG_methodology.aspx**

---

[4]You can find more information on the Web site: **www.prsgroup.com.**

Political Risk Variables	Financial Risk Variables	Economic Risk Variables
Government stability	Foreign debt (% of GDP)	GDP per capita
Socioeconomic conditions	Foreign debt service (% of GDP)	Real annual GDP growth
Investment profile	Current account (% of exports)	Annual inflation rate
Internal conflicts	Net liquidity in months of imports	Budget balance (% of GDP)
External conflicts	Exchange rate stability	Current account balance (% GDP)
Corruption		
Military in politics		
Religious tensions		
Law and order		
Ethnic tensions		
Democratic accountability		
Bureaucracy quality		

TABLE 25.5

The three ratings that comprise ICRG's composite risk rating

Source: *International Country Risk Guide Methodology* © The PRS Group, Inc., www.prsgroup.com/ICRG_methodology.aspx

What may be surprising is the fairly mediocre ranking of the U.S. (rank 42), comparable to that of China (44) and India (67), all three appearing in the low-risk category.

The composite risk rating is a weighted average of three measures: political risk, financial risk, and economic risk. Political risk is measured on a scale of 100–0, while financial and economic risk are measured on a scale of 50–0. The three measures are added and divided by two to obtain the composite rating. The variables used by ICRG to determine the composite risk rating from the three measures are shown in Table 25.5.

Table 25.6 shows the three risk measures for five of the countries in Table 25.4, in order of the October 2004 ranking of the composite risk ratings. The table shows that by political risk, the five countries ranked in the same order. But in the financial risk measure, the U.S. ranked *last* among these countries. The surprisingly poor performance of the U.S. in this dimension is probably due to its exceedingly large government and balance-of-trade deficits, which have put considerable pressure on its exchange rate. Exchange rate stability, foreign trade imbalance, and foreign indebtedness all enter ICRG's computation of financial risk.

Country risk is captured in greater depth by scenario analysis for the composite measure and each of its components. Table 25.7 (panels A and B) shows 1- and 5-year worst case and best case scenarios for the composite ratings and for the political risk measure.

	Composite Ratings		Current Ratings		
Country	Year Ago Nov. 4	Current Oct. 4	Political Risk Oct. 4	Financial Risk Oct. 4	Economic Risk Oct. 4
Japan	86.3	84.5	82	46.5	40.5
United States	75.8	77.5	82	33.5	39.5
China, People's Rep.	77.3	76.8	70.5	44.5	38.5
India	69	71.8	63.5	44.5	35.5
Indonesia	60.8	62.5	50.5	37.5	37

TABLE 25.6

Current risk ratings and composite risk forecasts

Source: *International Country Risk Guide*, October 2004, Table 2B. © The PRS Group, Inc., E. Syracuse, NY. Used by permission. www.prsgroup.com/ICRG_methodology.aspx

Country	Returns in U.S. Dollars				Returns in Local Currency			
	Average	Standard Dev.	Beta/U.S.	Correlation/ U.S.	Average	Standard Dev.	Beta/U.S.	Correlation/ U.S.
A. Developed countries								
U.K.	3.05	14.83	0.83	0.83	0.26	14.64	0.82	0.83
U.S.	0.63	14.89	1.00	1.00	0.63	14.89	1.00	1.00
Austria	27.65	15.08	0.41	0.40	22.62	12.24	0.48	0.74
Switzerland	4.50	15.82	0.79	0.74	0.41	16.03	0.86	0.80
Australia	14.36	16.10	0.97	0.38	7.93	9.67	0.68	0.23
Canada	12.20	17.19	0.92	0.79	6.50	13.00	0.70	0.81
New Zealand	19.70	17.27	0.63	0.55	10.13	11.33	0.37	0.48
Portugal	5.17	17.90	0.70	0.58	0.13	14.96	0.68	0.67
Singapore	6.88	18.14	0.76	0.62	5.78	16.79	0.73	0.65
Belgium	11.55	18.28	0.69	0.56	6.57	15.87	0.67	0.63
Spain	11.56	18.47	0.97	0.78	6.86	17.77	0.95	0.80
Japan	6.09	18.74	0.54	0.43	6.42	16.84	0.51	0.45
Ireland	11.55	18.99	0.90	0.71	6.93	18.81	0.89	0.70
Hong Kong	3.93	19.27	0.96	0.75	3.80	19.26	0.96	0.74
Italy	4.35	19.28	0.96	0.74	−0.45	17.91	0.94	0.78
Netherlands	1.56	19.64	1.08	0.82	−2.94	19.89	1.06	0.79
France	4.58	20.00	1.12	0.83	−0.09	19.40	1.10	0.84
Denmark	14.39	20.24	0.98	0.72	9.60	19.39	0.97	0.75
Norway	18.44	21.74	1.01	0.69	12.98	21.08	1.03	0.73
Germany	4.20	22.62	1.29	0.85	−0.42	22.21	1.27	0.85
Greece	9.13	23.42	0.85	0.54	4.35	22.50	0.82	0.54
Israel	10.62	24.38	0.87	0.53	12.46	21.05	0.70	0.50
Sweden	7.67	26.71	1.57	0.88	3.63	24.36	1.43	0.88
Korea	29.14	31.11	1.49	0.72	23.85	28.66	1.41	0.73
Finland	0.74	36.09	1.70	0.70	−3.56	36.69	1.68	0.68
B. Emerging markets								
Peru	18.29	16.02	0.16	0.14	17.65	15.54	0.12	0.12
Malaysia	7.79	16.29	0.31	0.28	7.67	16.17	0.30	0.27
Mexico	19.53	19.56	0.99	0.76	21.05	16.51	0.81	0.73
Chile	15.02	20.21	0.87	0.64	11.62	13.84	0.46	0.50
Philippines	7.12	20.85	0.46	0.33	8.01	19.42	0.50	0.38
Czech Rep.	35.19	21.73	0.64	0.44	26.22	19.88	0.56	0.42
South Africa	23.85	25.25	0.80	0.47	18.89	19.17	0.78	0.61
Hungary	23.64	25.41	0.95	0.56	17.36	22.48	0.89	0.59
Poland	16.40	26.88	1.12	0.62	10.83	23.80	0.89	0.55
China	25.55	27.00	0.34	0.19	−9.13	19.94	0.13	0.10
India	24.94	28.17	1.06	0.56	23.88	27.01	1.03	0.57
Russia	45.97	28.92	0.72	0.38	na	na	na	na
Taiwan	7.90	29.51	1.07	0.54	7.34	28.02	1.02	0.54
Thailand	25.16	32.72	0.84	0.38	23.14	29.60	0.77	0.39
Pakistan	32.15	33.60	0.62	0.28	32.61	32.48	0.56	0.26
Brazil	19.76	35.15	1.74	0.74	19.51	21.85	1.03	0.70
Argentina	5.15	38.09	0.97	0.38	28.23	43.38	0.68	0.23
Turkey	28.49	56.15	2.73	0.73	36.37	44.51	1.89	0.63
Colombia	na	na	na	na	39.85	18.62	0.39	0.31
Indonesia	na	na	na	na	20.24	25.02	0.60	0.35

TABLE 25.9

Risk and return across the globe, 2001–2005

and emerging markets in panel B. We use this table to develop insights into the risk and reward in international investing. The equity markets in both panels of Table 25.9 are ordered by standard deviation.

Are Investments in Emerging Markets Riskier?

In Figure 25.3, countries in both developed and emerging markets are ordered from low to high standard deviation. The standard deviations of investments in emerging markets are charted over those in developed countries. The graphs clearly show that investment in emerg-

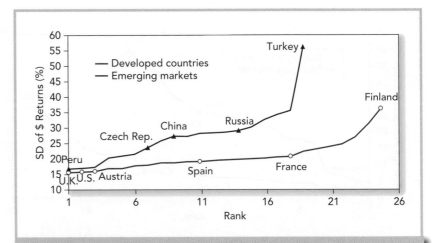

FIGURE 25.3   Annualized standard deviation of investments across the globe ($ returns, 2001–2005)

Note: Developed countries and emerging markets are ranked from low to high standard deviation.

ing markets is largely riskier than in developed countries, at least as measured by total volatility of returns.

Figure 25.4 shows that in terms of systematic risk to a U.S. investor, as measured by beta against the U.S. market, emerging markets are not necessarily riskier. The beta of China, to take one example, is only .13.

Are Average Returns in Emerging Markets Greater?

Figure 25.5 repeats the previous exercises for average returns. The graphs show that investing in emerging markets provided higher average returns than investing in developed countries. Of course these data are far from conclusive because 5-year averages are subject to

considerable imprecision. But regardless of these qualifications, we should not even expect a clear relationship because the higher standard deviation of emerging market equities is not an adequate measure of risk. In the context of a diversified international portfolio, the risk of any single market is measured by its covariance with the overall portfolio. Assessment of the proportion of systematic risk in country portfolios can be gleaned from the graph of beta against the U.S.

Table 25.9 shows that the beta of many countries against the U.S. is practically the same for dollar and local currency returns. However, there are quite a few

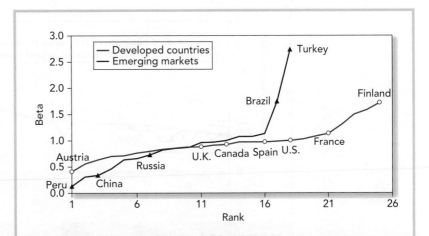

FIGURE 25.4   Beta on U.S. stocks across the globe, 2001–2005

Note: Developed countries and emerging markets are ranked from low to high beta on U.S. stocks.

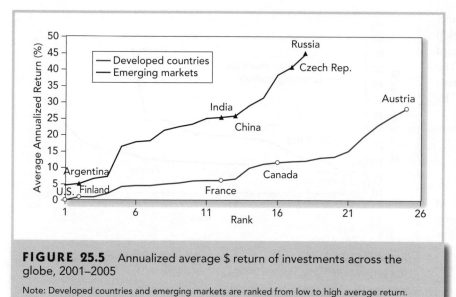

FIGURE 25.5   Annualized average $ return of investments across the globe, 2001–2005

Note: Developed countries and emerging markets are ranked from low to high average return.

countries for which currency fluctuations would add significant risk to a U.S. investor. The standard deviation of dollar-denominated returns will be higher than local currency returns as long as the correlation between currency fluctuation and local stock returns is not negative. Figure 25.6 shows that dollar-denominated returns generally were in fact more volatile. In some cases, when the correlation is highly positive, the difference in volatility was substantial. For this reason, managers of international portfolios commonly hedge a significant fraction of their foreign investments.

Benefits from International Diversification

Table 25.10 presents correlations between returns on stock and long-term bond portfolios in various countries. Panel A shows correlation of returns in U.S. dollars, that is, returns to a U.S. investor when currency risk is not hedged. Panel B shows correlation of returns in local currencies, that is, returns to a U.S. investor when the exchange risk is hedged. As noted earlier, the correlation coefficients of the hedged (local currency) and unhedged (U.S. dollar) returns are very similar, confirming that hedging currencies is not a significant issue in internationally well-diversified portfolios.

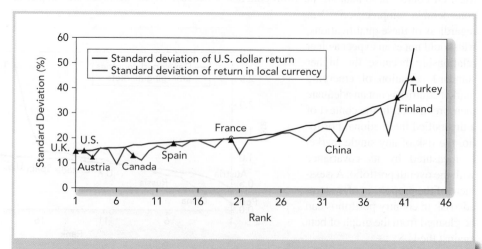

FIGURE 25.6   Standard deviation of investments across the globe in U.S. dollars vs. local currency, 2001–2005

Note: Countries are ranked from low to high standard deviation of $ return.

A. Correlation of monthly asset return 2001–2005 in $U.S. (unhedged currencies)

	Stocks							Bonds						
	U.S.	Germany	U.K.	Japan	Australia	Canada	France	U.S.	Germany	U.K.	Japan	Australia	Canada	France
Stocks														
U.S.	1.00													
Germany	0.85	1.00												
U.K.	0.83	0.88	1.00											
Japan	0.45	0.48	0.48	1.00										
Australia	0.74	0.79	0.79	0.44	1.00									
Canada	0.81	0.76	0.78	0.44	0.75	1.00								
France	0.84	0.96	0.91	0.53	0.76	0.78	1.00							
Bonds														
U.S.	−0.23	−0.40	−0.22	−0.21	−0.22	−0.20	−0.34	1.00						
Germany	−0.16	−0.18	−0.07	−0.16	−0.01	−0.08	−0.14	0.77	1.00					
U.K.	−0.15	−0.21	−0.11	−0.26	−0.10	−0.12	−0.21	0.76	0.88	1.00				
Japan	−0.04	−0.13	−0.04	−0.33	−0.06	−0.13	−0.14	0.28	0.17	0.18	1.00			
Australia	−0.28	−0.42	−0.26	−0.27	−0.24	−0.22	−0.38	0.82	0.72	0.80	0.27	1.00		
Canada	−0.01	−0.13	0.07	−0.12	0.01	0.03	−0.08	0.85	0.82	0.81	0.26	0.79	1.00	
France	−0.18	−0.22	−0.10	−0.17	−0.04	−0.10	−0.18	0.80	1.00	0.88	0.19	0.75	0.83	1.00

B. Correlation of monthly asset return 2001–2005 in $U.S. (hedged currencies)

	Stocks							Bonds						
	U.S.	Germany	U.K.	Japan	Australia	Canada	France	U.S.	Germany	U.K.	Japan	Australia	Canada	France
Stocks														
U.S.	1.00													
Germany	0.85	1.00												
U.K.	0.82	0.88	1.00											
Japan	0.43	0.43	0.44	1.00										
Australia	0.80	0.82	0.84	0.48	1.00									
Canada	0.79	0.78	0.80	0.49	0.84	1.00								
France	0.83	0.96	0.92	0.47	0.80	0.78	1.00							
Bonds														
U.S.	−0.23	−0.25	−0.07	0.00	−0.04	−0.11	−0.18	1.00						
Germany	−0.09	0.10	0.21	0.09	0.21	0.09	0.16	0.69	1.00					
U.K.	−0.10	0.02	0.18	0.01	0.12	0.03	0.07	0.64	0.88	1.00				
Japan	0.00	0.08	0.18	0.20	0.25	0.11	0.11	0.44	0.60	0.53	1.00			
Australia	0.28	0.33	0.47	0.27	0.60	0.44	0.38	0.56	0.73	0.65	0.59	1.00		
Canada	0.30	0.36	0.46	0.31	0.52	0.56	0.39	0.60	0.64	0.53	0.46	0.77	1.00	
France	−0.09	0.09	0.22	0.09	0.21	0.09	0.16	0.67	1.00	0.88	0.61	0.74	0.64	1.00

TABLE 25.10

Correlation for asset returns: Unhedged and hedged currencies

INVESTORS' CHALLENGE: MARKETS SEEM TOO LINKED

It's one of the golden rules of investing: Reduce risk by diversifying your money into a variety of holdings—stock funds, bonds, commodities—that don't move in lockstep with one another. And it's a rule that's getting tougher to obey.

According to recent research, an array of investments whose prices used to rise and fall independently are now increasingly correlated. For an example, look no further than the roller coaster in emerging-markets stocks of recent weeks. The MSCI EAFE index, which measures emerging markets, now shows .96 correlation to the S&P, up from just .32 six years ago.

For investors, that poses a troubling issue: how to maintain a portfolio diversified enough so all the pieces don't tank at once.

The current correlation trend doesn't mean investors should go out and ditch their existing investments. It's just that they may not be "getting the same diversification"

they thought if the investment decisions were made some time ago, says Mr. Ezrati, chief economist at money-management firm Lord Abbett & Co. He adds that over long periods of time, going back decades, sometimes varied asset classes tend to converge.

One explanation for today's higher correlation is increased globalization, which has made the economies of various countries more interdependent. International stocks, even with their higher correlations of present, deserve some allocation in a long-term investor's holdings, says Jeff Tjornehoj, an analyst at data firm Lipper Inc. Mr. Tjornehoj is among those who believe these correlations are a temporary phenomenon, and expects that the diversity will return some time down the line—a year or few years.

Source: Shefali Anand, "Investors Challenge: Markets Seem Too Linked," *The Wall Street Journal*, June 2, 2006, p. C1. © 2006 Dow Jones & Company, Inc. All rights reserved worldwide.

The correlation coefficients between stock indexes of one country and bond portfolios of another are very low, suggesting that income portfolios that are balanced between stocks and bonds would greatly benefit from international diversification. The correlation among stock portfolios of the countries in Table 25.10 is much larger, in the range of .48 (Japan–Germany, panel A) to .96 (France–Germany). These correlation coefficients are much larger than conventional wisdom; they suggest that cross-border correlation of stock indexes has been increasing. For another, independent example, Table 25.11 shows the correlation of various country indexes with U.S. stocks using monthly excess returns over various periods from 1970 to 2005. The marked increase in correlation with 17 stock indexes and the world portfolio is uniform and striking in magnitude.

These results raise the question of whether the increase in correlation is an artifact of the sample period or a result of globalization and increased capital market integration that would be expected to increase cross-border correlation. While there is no question that a 5-year sample period is fairly short and limits precision, the fact that we find the increase in correlation across the board and over extended periods suggests that globalization and market integration are the cause, as discussed in the nearby box.

The observed high correlation across markets calls into question the common claim of large diversification benefits from international investing. This conventional wisdom is depicted in Figure 25.7, which is based on data for the period 1961–1975. Figure 25.7 suggests that international diversification can reduce the standard deviation of a domestic portfolio by as much as half (from about 27% of the standard deviation of a single stock to about 12%). This improvement may well be exaggerated if correlation across markets has markedly increased, as data from recent years suggest. Still, while benefits from international diversification may be significant, we first need to dispose of a misleading, yet widespread, representation of potential benefits from diversification.

Misleading Representation of Diversification Benefits

The baseline technique for constructing efficient portfolios is the efficient frontier. A useful efficient frontier is constructed from *expected* returns and an estimate of the covariance matrix of returns. This frontier combined with cash assets generates the capital

TABLE 25.11

Correlation of U.S. equity returns with country equity returns

	Sample Period (monthly excess return in $U.S.)			
	2001–2005*	**1996–2000***	**1991–1995***	**1970–1989****
World	.95	.92	.64	.86
Sweden	.89	.60	.42	.38
Germany	.85	.66	.33	.33
France	.83	.63	.43	.42
United Kingdom	.82	.77	.56	.49
Netherlands	.82	.63	.50	.56
Australia	.81	.64	.36	.47
Canada	.80	.79	.49	.72
Spain	.78	.59	.51	.25
Hong Kong	.75	.63	.33	.29
Italy	.75	.44	.12	.22
Switzerland	.73	.56	.43	.49
Denmark	.74	.56	.36	.33
Norway	.70	.58	.50	.44
Belgium	.56	.49	.54	.41
Japan	.43	.54	.23	.27
Austria	.40	.53	.19	.12

*Source: Datastream.
**Source: Campbell R. Harvey, "The World Price of Covariance Risk," *Journal of Finance,* March 1991.

allocation line, the set of efficient complete portfolios, as elaborated in Chapter 7. The benefit from this efficient diversification is reflected in the curvature of the efficient frontier. Other things equal, the lower the covariance across stocks, the greater the curvature of the efficient frontier and the greater the risk reduction for any desired *expected* return. So far, so good. But suppose we replace *expected* returns with *realized* average returns from a sample period to construct an efficient frontier; what is the possible use of this graph?

The ex post efficient frontier (derived from realized returns) describes the portfolio of only one investor—the clairvoyant who actually predicted the precise averages of realized returns on all assets and estimated a covariance matrix that materialized, precisely, in the actual realizations of the sample period returns on all assets. Obviously, we are talking about a slim to empty set of investors. For all other, less-than-clairvoyant investors, such a frontier may have value only for purposes of performance evaluation.

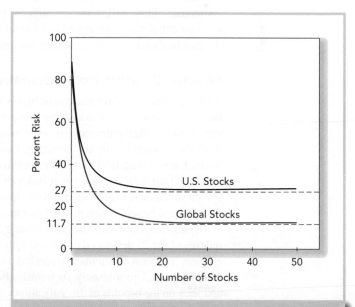

FIGURE 25.7 International diversification. Portfolio standard deviation as a percent of the average standard deviation of a one-stock portfolio

Source: B. Solnik, "Why Not Diversify Internationally Rather Than Domestically." *Financial Analysts Journal,* July/August 1974, pp. 48–54. Copyright 1976, CFA Institute. Reproduced and republished from *Financial Analysts Journal* with permission from the CFA Institute. All rights reserved.

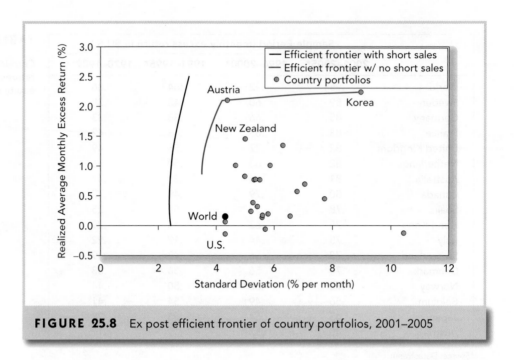

FIGURE 25.8   Ex post efficient frontier of country portfolios, 2001–2005

In the world of volatile stocks, some stocks are bound to realize large, *unexpected* average returns. This will be reflected in ex post efficient frontiers of enormous apparent "potential." They will, however, suggest exaggerated diversification benefits. Such (elusive) potential was enumerated in Chapter 24 on performance evaluation. It has no meaning as a tool to discuss the potential for future investments for real-life investors.

Realistic Benefits from International Diversification

While recent realized returns can be highly misleading estimates of expected future returns, they are more useful for measuring prospective risk. There are two compelling reasons for this. First, market efficiency (or even near efficiency) implies that stock prices will be difficult to predict with any accuracy, but no such implication applies to risk measures. Second, it is a statistical fact that errors in estimates of standard deviation and correlation from realized data are of a lower order of magnitude than estimates of expected returns. For these reasons, using risk estimates from realized returns does not exaggerate as much the potential benefits from diversification.

Figure 25.8 shows the efficient frontier using realized average monthly returns on the stock indexes of the 25 developed countries, with and without short sales. Even when the (ex post) efficient frontier is constrained to preclude short sales, it greatly exaggerates the benefits from diversification. Unfortunately, such misleading efficient frontiers are still presented in articles and texts on the benefits of diversification.

A more reasonable description of diversification is achievable only when we input reasonable equilibrium expected returns. Absent superior information, such expected returns are best based on appropriate risk measures of the assets. The capital asset pricing model (CAPM) suggests using the beta of the stock against the world portfolio. To generate expected excess returns (over the risk-free rate) for all assets, we specify the expected excess return on the world portfolio. We obtain the expected excess return on each asset by multiplying the beta of the asset by the world portfolio expected excess return. This

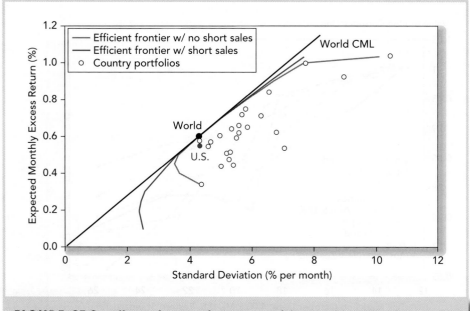

FIGURE 25.9 Efficient frontier of country portfolios (world expected excess return = .6% per month)

procedure presupposes that the world portfolio will lie on the efficient frontier, at the point of tangency with the world capital market line. The curvature of the efficient frontier will not be affected by the estimate of the world portfolio excess return. A higher estimate will simply shift the curve upward.

We perform this procedure with risk measures estimated from actual returns and further impose the likely applicable constraint on short sales. We use the betas to compute the expected return on individual markets, assuming the expected excess return on the world portfolio is .6% per month. This excess return is in line with the average return over the previous 50 years. Varying this estimate would not qualitatively affect the results shown in Figure 25.9 (which is drawn on the same scale as Figure 25.8). The figure shows a realistic assessment that reveals modest but significant benefits from international diversification using only developed markets. Incorporating emerging markets would further increase these benefits.

Are Benefits from International Diversification Preserved in Bear Markets?

Some studies[5] suggest that correlation in country portfolio returns increases during periods of turbulence in capital markets. If so, benefits from diversification would be lost exactly when they are needed the most. For example, a study by Roll[6] of the crash of October 1987 shows that all 23 country indexes studied declined over the crash period of October 12–26.

---

[5]F. Longin and B. Solnik, "Is the Correlation in International Equity Returns Constant: 1960–1990?" *Journal of International Money and Finance* 14 (1995), pp. 3–26; and Eric Jacquier and Alan Marcus, "Asset Allocation Models and Market Volatility," *Financial Analysts Journal* 57 (March/April 2001), pp. 16–30.

[6]Richard Roll, "The International Crash of October 1987," *Financial Analysts Journal,* September/October 1988.

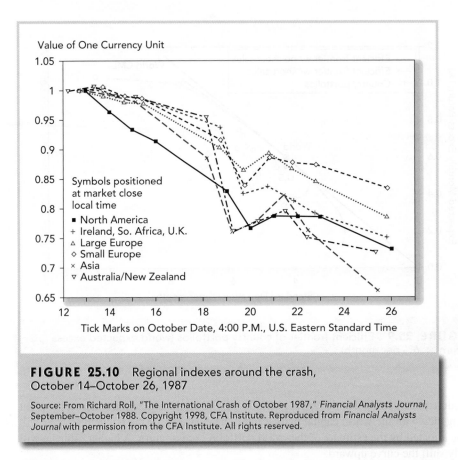

Value of One Currency Unit

Symbols positioned
at market close
local time
- ■ North America
- + Ireland, So. Africa, U.K.
- △ Large Europe
- ◇ Small Europe
- × Asia
- ▽ Australia/New Zealand

Tick Marks on October Date, 4:00 P.M., U.S. Eastern Standard Time

FIGURE 25.10   Regional indexes around the crash,
October 14–October 26, 1987

Source: From Richard Roll, "The International Crash of October 1987," *Financial Analysts Journal*,
September–October 1988. Copyright 1998, CFA Institute. Reproduced from *Financial Analysts
Journal* with permission from the CFA Institute. All rights reserved.

This correlation is reflected in the movements of regional indexes depicted in Figure 25.10.
Roll found that the beta of a country index on the world index (estimated prior to the crash)
was the best predictor of that index's response to the October crash of the U.S. stock market.
This suggests a common factor underlying the movement of stocks around the world. This
model predicts that a macroeconomic shock would affect all countries and that diversification can only mitigate country-specific events. Our best guess, therefore, is that the diversification benefits shown by the world CAPM model are realistic.

25.4 ASSESSING THE POTENTIAL OF INTERNATIONAL DIVERSIFICATION

We focus first on investors who wish to hold largely passive portfolios. Their objective is
to maximize diversification with limited expense and effort.

The Home Bias

Scholars have indirectly questioned passive as well as active investors for the apparent home
bias (i.e., preference for domestic securities) demonstrated in their portfolio choices. A certain degree of home bias may be justified on theoretical grounds. Investor consumption consists in large part of goods and services produced in the home country, and prices of these

goods and services may be correlated with home-country stock prices. To illustrate, consider an investor who lives in Silicon Valley. Prices of homes and other big-ticket items will be correlated with the success of local corporations. These prices therefore can be partially hedged by investing in the equity of local firms.[7] Moreover, "keeping up with the Joneses" of Silicon Valley also calls for tilting your portfolio toward local investment opportunities to keep your wealth aligned with that of your neighbors'.

How exactly does one measure home bias? At first blush the question seems simple. Home bias is the excess weight of your country relative to its weight in the otherwise efficient portfolio. The problem is that we must identify that efficient portfolio. If a world CAPM is in force, then a portfolio weighted by market capitalization would be the efficient portfolio for all investors. There is, however, no evidence that the world portfolio is efficient. Neither is there support for a model in which the expected return–beta equation is based on a beta against the U.S. market. At a minimum, however, we would expect international diversification to reduce portfolio variance.

The Pursuit of Efficient Diversification

Interestingly, the period 2001–2005 is a difficult one to test the potential for U.S. investors to reduce risk through international diversification. The U.S. excess market return was practically tied (with the U.K.) for the lowest standard deviation of all 43 countries. Still, the principle of diversification guarantees that variance still can be reduced because the minimum-variance portfolio must have a lower variance than any asset in the universe of securities. However, this procedure does not promise that the resultant portfolio weights will satisfy practical considerations. This, indeed, turns out to be the problem.

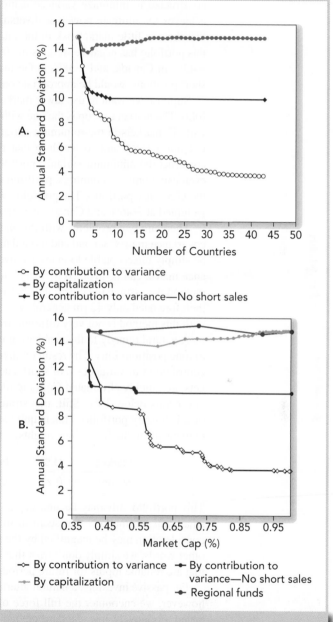

FIGURE 25.11 Efficient diversification by various methods

Figure 25.11 shows the standard deviation of portfolios with various degrees of diversification, with and without short-sale constraints. Figure 25.11A shows the number of countries in the portfolio on the horizontal axis, while Figure 25.11B has market capitalization as percent of world cap on the horizontal axis. Let's begin with the graph in panel A labeled "By contribution to variance." The right-most point on the graph represents the portfolio

---

[7]For a formal analysis of this idea see Peter M. De Marzo, Ron Kaniel, and Ilan Kremer, "Diversification as a Public Good: Community Effects in Portfolio Choice," *Journal of Finance* 59 (August 2004).

constructed to minimize variance using all 43 markets. This minimum-variance portfolio achieves the ultimate power of diversification; its low standard deviation of 3.7% shows that there is little market risk in the international universe. With no short-sale constraints, this portfolio has negative weights in 20 markets, the largest of which are −50% in France, −43% in Canada, and −38% in Germany. Clearly, this portfolio, with its dramatic long/short positions, would be appropriate only for the most aggressive "passive" investors.

Suppose we want to use fewer markets when we construct our minimum-variance portfolio. The market to drop is the one with the smallest weight in the portfolio.[8] For example, with 43 markets in the minimum-variance portfolio, the market with the smallest weight is Chile (.18%) and so we drop that market first. The remaining countries are used to construct the minimum-variance portfolio for 42 markets and so on. The graph shows that even using only six countries, portfolio standard deviation is 8.5%, less than 60% of that of the U.S.-only portfolio. The portfolio assigns the U.S. a weight of 78%, but has Germany weighted at −46% and Canada at −33%.

There are two problems with this method. First, it requires good estimates of the entire covariance matrix; second and more damning, its extreme long/short portfolio weights will be simply unacceptable to many passive investors. The need to estimate the entire covariance matrix can be avoided by using an index model as illustrated in Chapter 8. With this method we assume the covariance between any two markets, j and k, is $\beta_j \beta_k \text{Var(US)}$, and therefore need only 42 (in general, $n-1$) beta estimates. We saw that the efficient frontier with this method is not very different from the one that uses the full covariance matrix.

A natural remedy to the problem of extreme short positions is to constrain the portfolio to long positions only. The resultant diversification graph is labeled in Figure 25.11 as "By contribution to variance—No short sales." With the no short-sales constraint, many markets are quickly eliminated from the minimum-variance portfolio, and standard deviation never falls below 10%. Still, this strategy eliminates one-third of the standard deviation of a U.S.-only portfolio. This is quite an achievement and can be obtained with only five markets using the following weights:

Market:	U.S.	Peru	Malaysia	Japan	Austria
Weights:	0.24	0.27	0.20	0.11	0.18

This portfolio still may be unacceptable because the weight of the U.S. is deemed too small and the markets that seem to minimize variance are deemed too risky. The latter consideration may be magnified by the possible estimation errors in these market betas. In other words, we simply don't trust that our historical sample period is providing estimates that are reliable inputs for future periods.

For passive investors, a natural alternative is to use market capitalization weights. Here, however, we encounter the full force of the fact that the U.S. index portfolio has experienced a relatively low standard deviation over the period 2001–2005. The graph labeled "By capitalization" shows that this approach leads to only a modest gain from diversification. Still, because this approach may be the only feasible one for passive investors, we focus on this approach in Figure 25.12.

Figure 25.12 shows two alternatives for diversifying internationally via market-cap portfolios. The first is by investing in country index funds (dark curve). Here we see that the modest gains that can be achieved with only two large countries: the U.K. and Japan. The standard deviation of this portfolio, 13.7%, betters that of the U.S.-only portfolio

[8]A mathematical property of the minimum-variance portfolio is that all component assets have the same covariance with it (and so, the same contribution to variance). If an asset had a smaller covariance with the minimum-variance portfolio, we could increase its weight to reduce overall variance. Therefore, the asset with the smallest weight has the largest contribution per unit weight and should be dropped first.

by less than 1.5%. The failure of an alternative using regional funds (colored curve) to improve on the risk of the U.S.-only portfolio is both surprising and discouraging.

So far it appears that, for a passive investor, the benefits of international diversification are not what they are commonly purported to be. Perhaps the notorious home bias isn't a bias at all, just a common-sense response to these sorts of results. Yet international diversification wouldn't get as much attention as it does from theory alone. It must have had a better past.

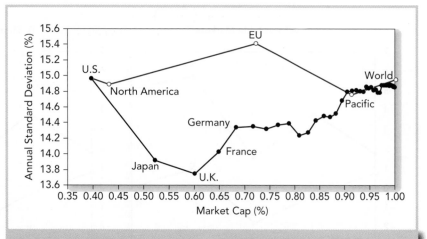

FIGURE 25.12   Diversification by market capitalization: National markets vs. regional funds

Diversification Benefits over Time

Table 25.11 shows why international diversification comes so highly recommended. The right-hand column shows that correlation coefficients with the U.S. over the period 1970–1989 were far lower than in more recent periods. With the low correlations of the earlier years, diversification benefits would be far greater than we have seen in this millennium.

Another issue to consider is the fact that there are more markets today that are acceptable in terms of regulation and transparency. Figure 25.13 shows gains from diversification at 5-year intervals, as measured by the difference in standard deviation between the U.S.-only portfolio and the internationally diversified portfolio. The strategies in Figure 25.13A all use countries for which there is reliable data for the period, and the horizontal axis also shows how many countries are included (the number ranges from 18 to 43). Figure 25.13B restricts the international portfolio to the 18 markets available in 1985.

The two strategies compared in Figure 25.13 are (i) minimum-variance portfolios with no short sales, and (ii) market-capitalization-weighted portfolios. Comparing the minimum-variance strategies across portfolio size, we tentatively conclude that the increase in diversification benefits over time has been due to the increase in the number of markets. Risk reduction from the market-cap portfolio has been small to negative, and larger when confined to the original country list that is more concentrated in large, developed markets.

Active Investors

For active investors, diversification is a small part of the gain from international investing. The chances of finding mispriced, high-information-ratio securities increases with the size of the investable universe. As we discuss in Chapter 27, there are returns to scale in security analysis, allowing active investors to increase the operating leverage of the organization.

Recall from Chapter 24 that the contribution of the active portfolio to the overall Sharpe ratio results from the sum of the information ratio of the covered securities. Expanding the universe of covered securities increases the expected value of the sum of these ratios. The costs to the organization of adding international coverage, however, do not increase at the same rate, because there are returns to scale in security analysis. The advantage from a better-diversified passive portfolio is just icing on the cake.

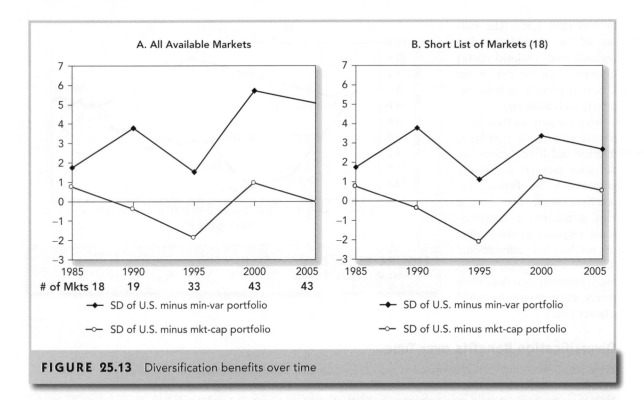

FIGURE 25.13   Diversification benefits over time

25.5   INTERNATIONAL INVESTING AND PERFORMANCE ATTRIBUTION

The benefits from international diversification may be modest for passive investors but for active managers international investing offers greater opportunities. International investing calls for specialization in additional fields of analysis: currency, country and worldwide industry, as well as a greater universe for stock selection.

Constructing a Benchmark Portfolio of Foreign Assets

Active international investing, as well as passive, requires a benchmark portfolio (the bogey). One widely used index of non-U.S. stocks is the **European, Australian, Far East (EAFE) index** computed by Morgan Stanley Capital International. Additional indexes of world equity performance are published by Morgan Stanley Capital International Indices, Salomon Brothers, Credit Suisse First Boston, and Goldman Sachs. Portfolios designed to mirror or even replicate the country, currency, and company representation of these indexes would be the obvious generalization of the purely domestic passive equity strategy.

An issue that sometimes arises in the international context is the appropriateness of market-capitalization weighting schemes in the construction of international indexes. Capitalization weighting is far and away the most common approach. However, some argue that it might not be the best weighting scheme in an international context. This is in part because different countries have differing proportions of their corporate sector organized as publicly traded firms.

Country	2005		2003		1998	
	% of EAFE Market Capitalization	% of EAFE GDP	% of EAFE Market Capitalization	% of EAFE GDP	% of EAFE Market Capitalization	% of EAFE GDP
Japan	27.1	24.0	23.6	26.8	26.8	29.1
United Kingdom	16.8	11.5	20.4	11.1	22.4	10.5
France	10.2	11.0	10.4	10.8	7.2	10.7
Germany	7.5	14.7	7.2	14.9	8.9	15.8
Switzerland	5.7	1.9	6.2	1.9	6.0	1.9
Italy	4.8	9.3	5.3	9.1	3.9	8.8
Hong Kong	4.8	0.9	4.6	1.0	4.0	1.2
Australia	4.4	3.7	4.1	3.2	2.9	2.7
Spain	4.0	5.9	3.6	5.2	2.7	4.3
Netherlands	3.3	3.3	5.0	3.2	5.9	2.9
Sweden	2.2	1.9	1.9	1.9	2.4	1.8
Belgium	1.7	2.0	1.4	1.9	1.4	1.8
Finland	1.2	1.0	1.5	1.0	0.7	1.0
Singapore	1.1	0.6	1.1	0.6	1.1	0.6
Norway	1.1	1.6	0.7	1.4	0.6	1.1
Denmark	1.0	1.4	0.8	1.3	0.9	1.3
Austria	0.8	1.6	0.4	1.6	0.4	1.6
Greece	0.8	1.2	0.6	1.1	0.3	0.9
Ireland	0.7	1.0	0.6	0.9	0.5	0.6
Portugal	0.4	1.0	0.5	0.9	0.6	0.8
New Zealand	0.2	0.6	0.2	0.5	0.4	0.4

TABLE 25.12

Weighting schemes for EAFE countries
Source: Datastream.

Table 25.12 shows data for market capitalization weights versus GDP for countries in the EAFE index for periods between 1998 and 2005. These data reveal substantial disparities between the relative sizes of market capitalization and GDP. Because market capitalization is a stock figure (the value of equity at one point in time), while GDP is a flow figure (production of goods and services during the entire year), we expect capitalization to be more volatile and the relative shares to be more variable over time. Some discrepancies are persistent, however. For example, the U.K.'s share of capitalization is about double its share of GDP, while Germany's share of capitalization is much less than its share of GDP. These disparities indicate that a greater proportion of economic activity is conducted by publicly traded firms in the U.K. than in Germany.

Some argue that it would be more appropriate to weight international indexes by GDP rather than market capitalization. The justification for this view is that an internationally diversified portfolio should purchase shares in proportion to the broad asset base of each country, and GDP might be a better measure of the importance of a country in the international economy than the value of its outstanding stocks. Others have even suggested weights proportional to the import share of various countries. The argument is that investors who wish to hedge the price of imported goods might choose to hold securities in foreign firms in proportion to the goods imported from those countries. The nearby box considers the question of global asset allocation for investors seeking effective international diversification.

INTERNATIONAL INVESTING RAISES QUESTIONS

As Yogi Berra might say, the problem with international investing is that it's so darn foreign.

Currency swings? Hedging? International diversification? What's that?

Here are answers to five questions that I'm often asked:

• Foreign stocks account for some 60% of world stock market value, so shouldn't you have 60% of your stock market money overseas?

The main reason to invest abroad isn't to replicate the global market or to boost returns. Instead, "what we're trying to do by adding foreign stocks is to reduce volatility," explains Robert Ludwig, chief investment officer at money manager SEI Investments.

Foreign stocks don't move in sync with U.S. shares and, thus, they may provide offsetting gains when the U.S. market is falling. But to get the resulting risk reduction, you don't need anything like 60% of your money abroad.

• So, how much foreign exposure do you need to get decent diversification?

"Based on the volatility of foreign markets and the correlation between markets, we think an optimal portfolio is 70% in the U.S., 20% in developed foreign markets, and 10% in emerging markets," Mr. Ludwig says.

Even with a third of your stock market money in foreign issues, you may find that the risk-reduction benefits aren't all that reliable. Unfortunately, when U.S. stocks get really pounded, it seems foreign shares also tend to tumble.

• Can U.S. companies with global operations give you international diversification?

"When you look at these multinationals, the factor that drives their performance is their home market," says Mark Riepe, a vice president with Ibbotson Associates, a Chicago research firm.

How come? U.S. multinationals tend to be owned by U.S. investors, who will be swayed by the ups and downs of the U.S. market. In addition, Mr. Riepe notes that while multinationals may derive substantial profits and revenue abroad, most of their costs—especially labor costs—will be incurred in the U.S.

• Does international diversification come from the foreign stocks or the foreign currency?

"It comes from both in roughly equal pieces," Mr. Riepe says. "Those who choose to hedge their foreign currency raise the correlation with U.S. stocks, and so the diversification benefit won't be nearly as great."

Indeed, you may want to think twice before investing in a foreign-stock fund that frequently hedges its currency exposure in an effort to mute the impact of—and make money from—changes in foreign-exchange rates.

"The studies that we've done show that stock managers have hurt themselves more than they've helped themselves by actively managing currencies," Mr. Ludwig says.

• Should you divvy up your money among foreign countries depending on the size of each national stock market?

At issue is the nagging question of how much to put in Japan. If you replicated the market weightings of Morgan Stanley Capital International's Europe, Australasia and Far East index, you would currently have around a third of your overseas money in Japan.

That's the sort of weighting you find in international funds, which seek to track the performance of the EAFE or similar international indexes. Actively managed foreign-stock funds, by contrast, pay less attention to market weights and on average, these days have just 14% in Japan.

If your focus is risk reduction rather than performance, the index—and the funds that track it—are the clear winners. Japan performs quite unlike the U.S. market, so it provides good diversification for U.S. investors, says Tricia Rothschild, international editor at Morningstar Mutual Funds, a Chicago newsletter.

"But correlations aren't static," she adds. "There's always a problem with taking what happened over the past 20 years and projecting it out over the next 20 years."

Source: Jonathan Clements, "International Investing Raises Questions on Allocation, Diversification, Hedging," *The Wall Street Journal*, July 29, 1997. Excerpted by permission of *The Wall Street Journal*. © 1997 Dow Jones & Company, Inc. All rights reserved worldwide.

Performance Attribution

We can measure the contribution of each of these factors following a manner similar to the performance attribution techniques introduced in Chapter 24.

1. **Currency selection** measures the contribution to total portfolio performance attributable to exchange rate fluctuations relative to the investor's benchmark currency, which we will take to be the U.S. dollar. We might use a benchmark like the EAFE index to compare a portfolio's currency selection for a particular period to a passive

This Excel model provides an efficient frontier analysis similar to that in Chapter 6. In Chapter 6 the frontier was based on individual securities, whereas this model examines the returns on international exchange traded funds and enables us to analyze the benefits of international diversification. Go to the Online Learning Center at **www.mhhe.com/bkm.**

	A	B	C	D	E	F	G	H	I	J
58				Bordered Covariance Matrix for Target Return Portfolio						
59			EWD	EWH	EWI	EWJ	EWL	EWP	EWW	SP 500	
60	Weights		0.00	0.00	0.08	0.38	0.02	0.00	0.00	0.52
61		0.0000	0.00	0.00	0.00	0.00	0.00	0.00	0.00	0.00
62		0.0000	0.00	0.00	0.00	0.00	0.00	0.00	0.00	0.00
63		0.0826	0.00	0.00	4.63	3.21	0.55	0.00	0.00	7.69
64		0.3805	0.00	0.00	3.21	98.41	1.82	0.00	0.00	53.79
65		0.0171	0.00	0.00	0.55	1.82	0.14	0.00	0.00	2.09
66		0.0000	0.00	0.00	0.00	0.00	0.00	0.00	0.00	0.00
67		0.0000	0.00	0.00	0.00	0.00	0.00	0.00	0.00	0.00
68		0.5198	0.00	0.00	7.69	53.79	2.09	0.00	0.00	79.90
69		1.0000	0.00	0.00	16.07	157.23	4.59	0.00	0.00	143.47
70										
71	Port Via	321.36								
72	Port S.D.	17.93								
73	Port Mean	12.00								
74										
75										
76					Weights					
77	Mean	St. Dev	EWD	EWH	EWI	EWJ	EWL	EWP	EWW	SP 500
78	6	21.89	0.02	0.00	0.00	0.71	0.00	0.02	0.00	0.26
79	9	19.66	0.02	0.00	0.02	0.53	0.02	0.00	0.00	0.41
80	12	17.93	0.00	0.00	0.08	0.38	0.02	0.00	0.00	0.52
81	15	16.81	0.00	0.00	0.14	0.22	0.02	0.00	0.00	0.62
82	18	16.46	0.00	0.00	0.19	0.07	0.02	0.00	0.00	0.73
83	21	17.37	0.00	0.00	0.40	0.00	0.00	0.00	0.00	0.60
84	24	21.19	0.00	0.00	0.72	0.00	0.00	0.00	0.00	0.28
85	27	26.05	0.00	0.00	1.00	0.00	0.00	0.00	0.00	0.00
86										
87										

benchmark. EAFE currency selection would be computed as the weighted average of the currency appreciation of the currencies represented in the EAFE portfolio using as weights the fraction of the EAFE portfolio invested in each currency.

2. **Country selection** measures the contribution to performance attributable to investing in the better-performing stock markets of the world. It can be measured as the weighted average of the equity *index* returns of each country using as weights the share of the manager's portfolio in each country. We use index returns to abstract from the effect of security selection within countries. To measure a manager's contribution relative to a passive strategy, we might compare country selection to the weighted average across countries of equity index returns using as weights the share of the EAFE portfolio in each country.

3. **Stock selection** ability may, as in Chapter 24, be measured as the weighted average of equity returns *in excess of the equity index* in each country. Here, we would use local currency returns and use as weights the investments in each country.

4. **Cash/bond selection** may be measured as the excess return derived from weighting bonds and bills differently from some benchmark weights.

Table 25.13 gives an example of how to measure the contribution of the decisions an international portfolio manager might make.

CONCEPT
CHECK
3

Using the data in Table 25.13, compute the manager's country and currency selection if portfolio weights had been 40% in Europe, 20% in Australia, and 40% in the Far East.

TABLE 25.13

Example of performance attribution: international

	EAFE Weight	Return on Equity Index	Currency Appreciation $E_1/E_0 - 1$	Manager's Weight	Manager's Return
Europe	0.30	10%	10%	0.35	8%
Australia	0.10	5	−10	0.10	7
Far East	0.60	15	30	0.55	18

Overall performance (dollar return = return on index + currency appreciation)
EAFE: .30(10 + 10) + .10(5 − 10) + .60(15 + 30) = 32.5%
Manager: .35(8 + 10) + .10(7 − 10) + .55(18 + 30) = 32.4%
Loss of .10% relative to EAFE

Currency selection
EAFE: (0.30 × 10%) + (0.10 × (−10%)) + (0.60 × 30%) = 20% appreciation
Manager: (0.35 × 10%) + (0.10 × (−10%)) + (0.55 × 30%) = 19% appreciation
Loss of 1% relative to EAFE

Country selection
EAFE: (0.30 × 10%) + (0.10 × 5%) + (0.60 × 15%) = 12.5%
Manager: (0.35 × 10%) + (0.10 × 5%) + (0.55 × 15%) = 12.25%
Loss of 0.25% relative to EAFE

Stock selection
        (8% − 10%)0.35 + (7% − 5%)0.10 + (18% − 15%)0.55 = 1.15%
Contribution of 1.15% relative to EAFE

Sum of attributions (equal to overall performance)
Currency (−1%) + country (−.25%) + selection (1.15%) = − .10%

SUMMARY

1. U.S. assets are only a part of the world portfolio. International capital markets offer important opportunities for portfolio diversification with enhanced risk–return characteristics.

2. Exchange rate risk imparts an extra source of uncertainty to investments denominated in foreign currencies. Much of that risk can be hedged in foreign exchange futures or forward markets, but a perfect hedge is not feasible unless the foreign currency rate of return is known.

3. Several world market indexes can form a basis for passive international investing. Active international management can be partitioned into currency selection, country selection, stock selection, and cash/bond selection.

KEY TERMS

exchange rate risk	political risk	country selection
interest rate parity relationship	European, Australian, Far East	stock selection
covered interest arbitrage	(EAFE) index	cash/bond selection
relationship	currency selection	

1. Return to the box "International Investing Raises Questions." The article is excellent, but was written several years ago. Do you agree with its response to the question, "Can U.S. companies with global operations give you international diversification?"

2. In Figure 25.2, we provide stock market returns in both local and dollar-denominated terms. Which of these is more relevant? What does this have to do with whether the foreign exchange risk of an investment has been hedged?

3. Suppose a U.S. investor wishes to invest in a British firm currently selling for £40 per share. The investor has $10,000 to invest, and the current exchange rate is $2/£.

   a. How many shares can the investor purchase?

   b. Fill in the table below for rates of return after 1 year in each of the nine scenarios (three possible prices per share in pounds times three possible exchange rates).

		Dollar-Denominated Return for Year-End Exchange Rate		
Price per Share (£)	Pound-Denominated Return (%)	$1.80/£	$2/£	$2.20/£
£35				
£40				
£45				

   c. When is the dollar-denominated return equal to the pound-denominated return?

4. If each of the nine outcomes in Problem 3 is equally likely, find the standard deviation of both the pound- and dollar-denominated rates of return.

5. Now suppose the investor in Problem 3 also sells forward £5,000 at a forward exchange rate of $2.10/£.

   a. Recalculate the dollar-denominated returns for each scenario.

   b. What happens to the standard deviation of the dollar-denominated return? Compare it to both its old value and the standard deviation of the pound-denominated return.

6. Calculate the contribution to total performance from currency, country, and stock selection for the manager in the example below. All exchange rates are expressed as units of foreign currency that can be purchased with 1 U.S. dollar.

	EAFE Weight	Return on Equity Index	E_1/E_0	Manager's Weight	Manager's Return
Europe	0.30	20%	0.9	0.35	18%
Australia	0.10	15	1.0	0.15	20
Far East	0.60	25	1.1	0.50	20

7. If the current exchange rate is $1.75/£, the 1-year forward exchange rate is $1.85/£, and the interest rate on British government bills is 8% per year, what risk-free dollar-denominated return can be locked in by investing in the British bills?

8. If you were to invest $10,000 in the British bills of Problem 7, how would you lock in the dollar-denominated return?

9. Much of this chapter was written from the perspective of a U.S. investor. But suppose you are advising an investor living in a small country (choose one to be concrete). How might the lessons of this chapter need to be modified for such an investor?

PROBLEM SETS

Quiz

Problems

Challenge Problems

1. You are a U.S. investor who purchased British securities for £2,000 1 year ago when the British pound cost U.S.$1.50. What is your total return (based on U.S. dollars) if the value of the securities is now £2,400 and the pound is worth $1.75? No dividends or interest were paid during this period.

2. The correlation coefficient between the returns on a broad index of U.S. stocks and the returns on indexes of the stocks of other industrialized countries is mostly _____, and the correlation coefficient between the returns on various diversified portfolios of U.S. stocks is mostly _____.

   a. less than .8; greater than .8.
   b. greater than .8; less than .8.
   c. less than 0; greater than 0.
   d. greater than 0; less than 0.

3. An investor in the common stock of companies in a foreign country may wish to hedge against the _____ of the investor's home currency and can do so by _____ the foreign currency in the forward market.

   a. depreciation; selling.
   b. appreciation; purchasing.
   c. appreciation; selling.
   d. depreciation; purchasing.

4. John Irish, CFA, is an independent investment adviser who is assisting Alfred Darwin, the head of the Investment Committee of General Technology Corporation, to establish a new pension fund. Darwin asks Irish about international equities and whether the Investment Committee should consider them as an additional asset for the pension fund.

   a. Explain the rationale for including international equities in General's equity portfolio. Identify and describe three relevant considerations in formulating your answer.
   b. List three possible arguments against international equity investment and briefly discuss the significance of each.
   c. To illustrate several aspects of the performance of international securities over time, Irish shows Darwin the accompanying graph of investment results experienced by a U.S. pension fund in the recent past. Compare the performance of the U.S. dollar and non-U.S. dollar equity and fixed-income asset categories, and explain the significance of the result of the account performance index relative to the results of the four individual asset class indexes.

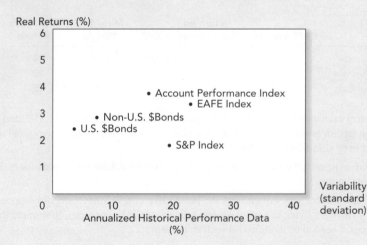

5. You are a U.S. investor considering purchase of one of the following securities. Assume that the currency risk of the Canadian government bond will be hedged, and the 6-month discount on Canadian dollar forward contracts is −.75% versus the U.S. dollar.

Bond	Maturity	Coupon	Price
U.S. government	6 months	6.50%	100.00
Canadian government	6 months	7.50%	100.00

Calculate the expected price change required in the Canadian government bond that would result in the two bonds having equal total returns in U.S. dollars over a 6-month horizon. Assume that the yield on the U.S. bond is expected to remain unchanged.

6. A global manager plans to invest $1 million in U.S. government cash equivalents for the next 90 days. However, she is also authorized to use non-U.S. government cash equivalents, as long as the currency risk is hedged to U.S. dollars using forward currency contracts.

   a. What rate of return will the manager earn if she invests in money market instruments in either Canada or Japan and hedges the dollar value of her investment? Use the data in the following tables.

   b. What must be the approximate value of the 90-day interest rate available on U.S. government securities?

Interest Rates (APR) 90-Day Cash Equivalents	
Japanese government	2.52%
Canadian government	6.74%

Exchange Rates Dollars per Unit of Foreign Currency		
	Spot	90-Day Forward
Japanese yen	.0119	.0120
Canadian dollar	.7284	.7269

7. The Windsor Foundation, a U.S.-based, not-for-profit charitable organization, has a diversified investment portfolio of $100 million. Windsor's board of directors is considering an initial investment in emerging market equities. Robert Houston, treasurer of the foundation, has made the following four comments:

   a. "For an investor holding only developed market equities, the existence of stable emerging market currencies is one of several preconditions necessary for that investor to realize strong emerging market performance."

   b. "Local currency depreciation against the dollar has been a frequent occurrence for U.S. investors in emerging markets. U.S. investors have consistently seen large percentages of their returns erased by currency depreciation. This is true even for long-term investors."

   c. "Historically, the addition of emerging market stocks to a U.S. equity portfolio such as the S&P 500 index has reduced volatility; volatility has also been reduced when emerging market stocks are combined with an international portfolio such as the MSCI EAFE index."

   d. "Although correlations among emerging markets can change over the short term, such correlations show evidence of stability over the long term. Thus, an emerging markets portfolio that lies on the efficient frontier in one period tends to remain close to the frontier in subsequent periods."

   Discuss whether *each* of Houston's four comments is correct or incorrect.

8. After much research on the developing economy and capital markets of the country of Otunia, your firm, GAC, has decided to include an investment in the Otunia stock market in its Emerging

Markets Commingled Fund. However, GAC has not yet decided whether to invest actively or by indexing. Your opinion on the active versus indexing decision has been solicited. The following is a summary of the research findings:

Otunia's economy is fairly well diversified across agricultural and natural resources, manufacturing (both consumer and durable goods), and a growing finance sector. Transaction costs in securities markets are relatively large in Otunia because of high commissions and government "stamp taxes" on securities trades. Accounting standards and disclosure regulations are quite detailed, resulting in wide public availability of reliable information about companies' financial performance.

Capital flows into and out of Otunia, and foreign ownership of Otunia securities is strictly regulated by an agency of the national government. The settlement procedures under these ownership rules often cause long delays in settling trades made by nonresidents. Senior finance officials in the government are working to deregulate capital flows and foreign ownership, but GAC's political consultant believes that isolationist sentiment may prevent much real progress in the short run.

a. Briefly discuss aspects of the Otunia environment that favor investing actively, and aspects that favor indexing.
b. Recommend whether GAC should invest in Otunia actively or by indexing. Justify your recommendation based on the factors identified in part (*a*).

STANDARD &POOR'S

Go to the *Market Insight* entry page (**www.mhhe.com/edumarketinsight**) and click on the *Commentary* tab. Click on the link for the most recent Investment Policy Committee (IPC) Notes. What is the recommended allocation for Foreign Equities? Scan the notes to see what issues are mentioned that might affect international investments.

Return to the *Commentary* page and click on the link for the IPC Notes archive. Open the notes from four other dates and compare the Foreign Equity allocation percentages and the topics discussed that pertain to international issues. Have the percentages changed much over time? Do the notes from different dates have similar comments or is there substantial variation?

E-Investments

International Investing

Go to the Morgon Stanley Global Economic Forum (GEF) archives at **www .morganstanley.com/views/gef.** Look for the link to the GEF archive, and click on a recent date to see the report for that day. Choose a company from those listed and read the section that discusses the country's current economic situation. What factors are cited as significant? How would each of the factors affect your decision about whether to include securities from this country in your portfolio?

Return to the archives page and choose another report approximately 1 year older than the one you just reviewed. Find the report for the same country (you might have to check a few surrounding dates to find the same country). Compare the issues that were listed a year ago to those you found in the recent report. Is there any overlap or are they completely different?

SOLUTIONS TO CONCEPT CHECKS

1. $1 + r(\text{US}) = [1 + r_f(\text{UK})] \times (E_1/E_0)$

   a. $1 + r(\text{US}) = 1.1 \times 1.0 = 1.10$. Therefore, $r(\text{US}) = 10\%$.
   b. $1 + r(\text{US}) = 1.1 \times 1.1 = 1.21$. Therefore, $r(\text{US}) = 21\%$.

2. You must sell forward the number of pounds you will end up with at the end of the year. This value cannot be known with certainty, however, unless the rate of return of the pound-denominated investment is known.

   a. $10,000 \times 1.20 = 12,000$ pounds
   b. $10,000 \times 1.30 = 13,000$ pounds

3. *Country selection:*

$$(0.40 \times 10\%) + (0.20 \times 5\%) + (0.40 \times 15\%) = 11\%$$

   This is a loss of 1.5% (11% versus 12.5%) relative to the EAFE passive benchmark.

   Currency selection:

$$(0.40 \times 10\%) + (0.20 \times (-10\%)) + (0.40 \times 30\%) = 14\%$$

   This is a loss of 6% (14% versus 20%) relative to the EAFE benchmark.

CHAPTER TWENTY-SIX

HEDGE FUNDS

WHILE MUTUAL FUNDS are still the dominant form of investing in securities markets for most individuals, hedge funds have enjoyed far greater growth rates in the last decade, with assets under management increasing from around $200 billion in 1997 to $1.9 trillion in 2008. Like mutual funds, hedge funds allow private investors to pool assets to be invested by a fund manager. Unlike mutual funds, however, they are commonly organized as private partnerships and thus not subject to many SEC regulations. They typically are open only to wealthy or institutional investors.

Hedge funds touch on virtually every issue discussed in the earlier chapters of the text, including liquidity, security analysis, market efficiency, portfolio analysis, hedging, and option pricing. For example, these funds often bet on relative mispricing of specific securities, but hedge broad market exposure. This sort of pure "alpha seeking" behavior requires a procedure for optimally mixing a hedge fund position with a more traditional portfolio. Other funds engage in aggressive market timing; their risk profiles can shift rapidly and substantially, raising difficult questions for performance evaluation. Many hedge funds take extensive derivatives positions. Even those funds that do not trade derivatives charge incentive fees that resemble the payoff to a call option; an option-pricing background therefore is necessary to interpret both hedge fund strategies and costs. In short, hedge funds raise the full range of issues that one might confront in active portfolio management.

We begin with a survey of various hedge fund orientations. We devote considerable attention to the classic "market-neutral" or hedged strategies that historically gave hedge funds their name. We move on to evidence on hedge fund performance, and the difficulties in evaluating that performance. Finally, we consider the implications of their unusual fee structure for investors in and managers of such funds.

26.1 HEDGE FUNDS VERSUS MUTUAL FUNDS

Like mutual funds, the basic idea behind **hedge funds** is investment pooling. Investors buy shares in these funds, which then invest the pooled assets on their behalf. The net asset value of each share represents the value of the investor's stake in the portfolio. In this regard, hedge funds operate much like mutual funds. However, there are important differences between the two.

Transparency   Mutual funds are subject to the Securities Act of 1933 and the Investment Company Act of 1940 (designed to protect unsophisticated investors), which require transparency and predictability of strategy. They periodically must provide the public with information on portfolio composition. In contrast, hedge funds usually are set up as limited liability partnerships, and provide minimal information about portfolio composition and strategy to their investors only.

Investors   Hedge funds traditionally have no more than 100 "sophisticated" investors, in practice usually defined by minimum net worth and income requirements. They do not advertise to the general public, although the recent trend is to market as well to ever-smaller and less sophisticated investors. Minimum investments for some new funds are as low as $25,000, compared to traditional $250,000–$1 million minimums.

Investment Strategies   Mutual funds lay out their general investment approach (e.g., large, value stock orientation versus small-cap growth orientation) in their prospectus. They face pressure to avoid *style drift* (departures from their stated investment orientation), especially given the importance of retirement funds such as 401(k) plans to the industry, and the demand of such plans for predictable strategies. Most mutual funds promise to limit their use of short-selling and leverage, and their use of derivatives is highly restricted. (In recent years, some so-called 130/30 funds have opened, primarily for institutional clients, with prospectuses that explicitly allow for more active short-selling and derivatives positions, but even these have less flexibility than hedge funds. See the nearby box.) In contrast, hedge funds may effectively partake in any investment strategy and may act opportunistically as conditions evolve. For this reason, it would be a mistake to view hedge funds as anything remotely like a uniform asset class. Hedge funds by design are empowered to invest in a wide range of investments, with various funds focusing on derivatives, distressed firms, currency speculation, convertible bonds, emerging markets, merger arbitrage, and so on. Other funds may jump from one asset class to another as perceived investment opportunities shift.

Liquidity   Hedge funds often impose **lock-up periods,** that is, periods as long as several years in which investments cannot be withdrawn. Many also employ redemption notices that require investors to provide notice weeks or months in advance of their desire to redeem funds. These restrictions limit the liquidity of investors but in turn enable the funds to invest in illiquid assets where returns may be higher, without worrying about meeting unanticipated demands for redemptions.

Compensation Structure   Hedge funds also differ from mutual funds in their fee structure. Whereas mutual funds assess management fees equal to a fixed percentage of assets, for example, between 0.5% and 1.5% annually for typical equity funds, hedge funds charge a management fee, usually between 1% and 2% of assets, *plus* a substantial *incentive fee* equal to a fraction of any investment profits beyond some benchmark. The incentive fee

"HEDGEY" MUTUAL FUNDS

Hedge funds and their elaborate strategies—particularly their ability to short sell assets perceived as overpriced—have long been open only to wealthy or institutional clients. The Investment Companies Act of 1940 makes it more difficult for mutual funds to short sell, requiring that they set aside in a separate account liquid securities that can be used to close out short positions. Nevertheless, short-selling has become more common among some funds.

More recently, smaller investors have been able to invest in so-called 130/30 funds that mimic some of the features of hedge funds. These are funds that may sell short up to 30% of the value of their portfolios, using the proceeds of the sale to increase their positions in invested assets. So for every $100 in net

assets, the fund could sell short $30, investing the proceeds to increase its long positions to $130. This gives rise to the 130/30 moniker. These funds have been among the fastest-growing segments of the institutional money management sector. Variations on these funds range from 110/10 funds to 150/50 funds.

These funds are promoted as maintaining full exposure to the market (for example, the net exposure of a 130/30 fund is 130% long minus the 30% short position, or 100%) while still providing the fund manager the opportunity to enhance alpha by selling overpriced securities. In contrast, conventional long-only mutual funds can produce alpha only by identifying and purchasing underpriced securities.

typically is 20%, but is sometimes higher. The threshold return to earn the incentive fee is often a money market rate such as LIBOR. Indeed, some observers only half-jokingly characterize hedge funds as "a compensation scheme masquerading as an asset class."

26.2 HEDGE FUND STRATEGIES

Table 26.1 presents a list of most of the common investment themes found in the hedge fund industry. The list contains a wide diversity of styles and suggests how hard it can be to speak generically about hedge funds as a group. We can, however, divide hedge fund strategies into two general categories: directional and nondirectional.

Directional and Nondirectional Strategies

Directional strategies are easy to understand. They are simply bets that one sector or another will outperform other sectors of the market.

In contrast, **nondirectional strategies** are usually designed to exploit temporary misalignments in security valuations. For example, if the yield on mortgage-backed securities seems abnormally high compared to that on Treasury bonds, the hedge fund would buy mortgage-backed and short sell Treasury securities. Notice that the fund is *not* betting on broad movements in the entire bond market: it buys one type of bond and sells another. By taking a long mortgage-short Treasury position, the fund hedges its interest rate exposure, while making a bet on the *relative* valuation across the two sectors. The idea is that when yield spreads converge back to their "normal" relationship, the fund will profit from the realignment regardless of the general trend in the level of interest rates. In this respect, it strives to be **market neutral,** or hedged with respect to the direction of interest rates, which gives rise to the term "hedge fund."

Nondirectional strategies are sometimes further divided into convergence or relative value positions. The difference between convergence and relative value is a time horizon at which one can say with confidence that any mispricing ought to be resolved. An example of a convergence strategy would entail mispricing of a futures contract that must be corrected by the time the contract matures. In contrast, the mortgage versus Treasury spread we just discussed would be a relative value strategy, because there is no obvious horizon during which the yield spread would "correct" from unusual levels.

Convertible arbitrage	Hedged investing in convertible securities, typically long convertible bonds and short stock.
Dedicated short bias	Net short position, usually in equities, as opposed to pure short exposure.
Emerging markets	Goal is to exploit market inefficiencies in emerging markets. Typically long-only because short-selling is not feasible in many of these markets.
Equity market neutral	Commonly uses long/short hedges. Typically controls for industry, sector, size, and other exposures, and establishes market-neutral positions designed to exploit some market inefficiency. Commonly involves leverage.
Event driven	Attempts to profit from situations such as mergers, acquisitions, restructuring, bankruptcy, or reorganization.
Fixed-income arbitrage	Attempts to profit from price anomalies in related interest-rate securities. Includes interest rate swap arbitrage, U.S. versus non-U.S. government bond arbitrage, yield-curve arbitrage, and mortgage-backed arbitrage.
Global macro	Involves long and short positions in capital or derivative markets across the world. Portfolio positions reflect views on broad market conditions and major economic trends.
Long/Short equity hedge	Equity-oriented positions on either side of the market (i.e., long or short), depending on outlook. *Not* meant to be market neutral. May establish a concentrated focus regionally (e.g., U.S. or Europe) or on a specific sector (e.g., tech or health care stocks). Derivatives may be used to hedge positions.
Managed futures	Uses financial, currency, or commodity futures. May make use of technical trading rules or a less structured judgmental approach.
Multistrategy	Opportunistic choice of strategy depending on outlook.
Fund of funds	Fund allocates its cash to several other hedge funds to be managed.

TABLE 26.1

Hedge fund styles

CS/TASS (Credit Suisse/Tremont Advisors Shareholder Services) maintains one of the most comprehensive databases on hedge fund performance. It categorizes hedge funds into these 11 different investment styles.

EXAMPLE 26.1   Market-Neutral Positions

We can illustrate a market-neutral position with a strategy used extensively by several hedge funds, which have observed that newly issued 30-year on-the-run Treasury bonds regularly sell at higher prices (lower yields) than 29½-year bonds with almost identical duration. The yield spread presumably is a premium due to the greater liquidity of the on-the-run bonds. Hedge funds, which have relatively low liquidity needs, therefore buy the 29½-year bond and sell the 30-year bond. This is a hedged, or market-neutral, position that will generate a profit whenever the yields on the two bonds converge, as typically happens when the 30-year bonds age, are no longer the most liquid on-the-run bond, and are no longer priced at a premium.

Notice that this strategy should generate profits regardless of the general direction of interest rates. The long-short position will return a profit as long as the 30-year bonds underperform the 29½-year bonds, as they should when the liquidity premium dissipates. Because the pricing discrepancies between these two securities almost necessarily *must* disappear at a given date, this strategy is an example of convergence arbitrage. While the convergence date in this application is not quite as definite as the maturity of a futures contract, one can be sure that the currently on-the-run T-bonds will lose that status by the time the Treasury next issues 30-year bonds.

Long-short positions such as in Example 26.1 are characteristic of hedged strategies. They are designed to *isolate* a bet on some mispricing without taking on market exposure. Profits are made regardless of broad market movements once prices "converge" or return to their "proper" levels. Hence, use of short positions and derivatives are part and parcel of the industry.

A more complex long-short strategy is *convertible bond arbitrage,* one of the more prominent sectors of the hedge-fund universe. Noting that a convertible bond may be viewed as a straight bond plus a call option on the underlying stock, the market-neutral strategy in this case involves a position in the bond offset by an opposite position in the stock. For example, if the convertible is viewed as underpriced, the fund will buy it, and offset its resultant exposure to declines in the stock price by shorting the stock.

Although these market-neutral positions are hedged, we emphasize that they are *not* risk-free arbitrage strategies. Rather they should be viewed as **pure plays,** that is, bets on *particular* (perceived) mispricing between two sectors or securities, with extraneous sources of risk such as general market exposure hedged away. Moreover, because the funds often operate with considerable leverage, returns can be quite volatile.

CONCEPT CHECK **1**	Classify each of the following strategies as directional or nondirectional. *a.* The fund buys shares in the India Investment Fund, a closed-end fund that is selling at a discount to net asset value, and sells the MSCI India Index Swap. *b.* The fund buys shares in Petrie Stores and sells Toys "R" Us, which is a major component of Petrie's balance sheet. *c.* The fund buys shares in ABN Amro Holdings, a Dutch bank that in 2007 was the target of a bidding war among several potential acquirers.

Statistical Arbitrage

Statistical arbitrage is a version of a market-neutral strategy, but one that merits its own discussion. It differs from pure arbitrage in that it does not seek out risk-free positions based on unambiguous mispricing (such as index arbitrage). Instead, it uses quantitative and often automated trading systems that seek out many temporary misalignments in prices among securities. By taking relatively small positions in many of these opportunities, the law of averages would make the probability of profiting from the collection of ostensibly positive-value bets very high, ideally almost a "statistical certainty." Of course, this strategy presumes that the fund's modeling techniques can actually identify reliable, if small, market inefficiencies. The law of averages will work for the fund only if the expected return is positive!

Statistical arbitrage often involves trading in hundreds of securities a day with holding periods that can be measured in minutes or less. Such rapid and heavy trading requires extensive use of quantitative tools such as automated trading and mathematical algorithms to identify profit opportunities and efficient diversification across positions. These strategies try to profit from the smallest of perceived mispricing opportunities, and require the fastest trading technology and the lowest possible trading costs. They would not be possible without the electronic communication networks discussed in Chapter 3.

A particular form of statistical arbitrage is **pairs trading,** in which stocks are paired up based on an analysis of either fundamental similarities or market exposures (betas). The general approach is to pair up similar companies whose returns are highly correlated but where one company seems to be priced more aggressively than the other.[1] Market-neutral positions can be formed by buying the relatively cheap firm and selling the expensive one. Many such pairs comprise the hedge fund's overall portfolio. Each pair may have an uncertain outcome, but with many such matched pairs, the presumption is that the large number of long-short bets will provide a very high probability of a positive abnormal return. More general versions of pairs trading allow for positions in clusters of stocks that may be relatively mispriced.

Statistical arbitrage is commonly associated with **data mining,** which refers to sorting through huge amounts of historical data to uncover systematic patterns in returns that can be exploited by traders. The risk of data mining, and statistical arbitrage in general, is that historical relationships may break down when fundamental economic conditions change or, indeed, that the apparent patterns in the data may be due to pure chance. Enough analysis applied to enough data is sure to produce apparent patterns that do not reflect real relationships that can be counted on to persist in the future.

26.3 PORTABLE ALPHA

An important implication of the market-neutral pure play is the notion of **portable alpha.** Suppose that you wish to speculate on a stock that you think is underpriced, but you think that the market is about to fall. Even if you are right about the stock being *relatively* underpriced, you still might lose money investing in it if it falls along with the broad market. You would like to separate the stock-specific bet from the implicit asset allocation bet on market performance that arises because the stock's beta is positive. The solution is to buy the stock and eliminate the resultant market exposure by selling enough index futures to drive beta to zero. This long stock–short futures strategy gives you a pure play or, equivalently, a *market-neutral* position on the stock.

More generally, you might wish to separate asset allocation from security selection. The idea is to invest wherever you can "find alpha." You would then hedge the systematic risk of that investment to isolate its alpha from the asset market where it was found. Finally, you establish exposure to desired market sectors by using passive indexes. In other words, you have created portable alpha that can be mixed with an exposure to whatever sector of the market you choose. This procedure is also called **alpha transfer,** because you transfer alpha from the sector where you find it to the asset class in which you finally establish exposure. Finding alpha requires skill. By contrast, beta, or market exposure, is a "commodity" that can be supplied cheaply through index funds or futures contracts, and offers little value added.

An Example of a Pure Play

Suppose you manage a $1.5 million portfolio. You believe that the alpha of the portfolio is positive, $\alpha > 0$, but also that the market is about to fall, that is, that $r_M < 0$. You would therefore try to establish a pure play on the perceived mispricing.

The return on portfolio over the next month may be described by Equation 26.1, which states that the portfolio return will equal its "fair" CAPM return (the first two terms on the

---

[1] Rules for deciding relative "aggressiveness" of pricing may vary. In one approach, a computer scans for stocks whose prices historically have tracked very closely but have recently diverged. If the differential in cumulative return typically dissipates, the fund will buy the recently underperforming stock and sell the outperforming one. In other variants, pricing aggressiveness may be determined by evaluating the stocks based on some measure of price to intrinsic value.

right-hand side), plus firm-specific risk reflected in the "residual," *e,* plus an alpha that reflects perceived mispricing:

$$r_{\text{portfolio}} = r_f + \beta(r_M - r_f) + e + \alpha \tag{26.1}$$

To be concrete, suppose that $\beta = 1.20$, $\alpha = .02$, $r_f = .01$, the current value of the S&P 500 index is $S_0 = 1{,}440$, and, for simplicity, that the portfolio pays no dividends. You want to capture the positive alpha of 2% per month, but you don't want the positive beta that the stock entails because you are worried about a market decline. So you choose to hedge your exposure by selling S&P 500 futures contracts.

Because the S&P contracts have a multiplier of $250, and the portfolio has a beta of 1.20, your stock position can be hedged for 1 month by selling five futures contracts[2]:

$$\text{Hedge ratio} = \frac{\$1{,}500{,}000}{1{,}440 \times \$250} \times 1.20 = 5 \text{ contracts}$$

The dollar value of your portfolio after 1 month will be

$$\begin{aligned}\$1{,}500{,}000 \times (1 + r_{\text{portfolio}}) &= \$1{,}500{,}000 \,[1 + .01 + 1.20 \,(r_M - .01) + .02 + e] \\ &= \$1{,}527{,}000 + \$1{,}800{,}000 \times r_M + \$1{,}500{,}000 \times e\end{aligned}$$

The dollar proceeds from your futures position will be:

$5 \times \$250 \times (F_0 - F_1)$	Mark to market on 5 contracts sold
$= \$1{,}250 \times [S_0(1.01) - S_1]$	Substitute for futures prices from parity relationship
$= \$1{,}250 \times S_0[1.01 - (1 + r_M)]$	Because $S_1 = S_0(1 + r_M)$ when no dividends are paid
$= \$1{,}250 \times [S_0(.01 - r_M)]$	Simplify
$= \$18{,}000 - \$1{,}800{,}000 \times r_M$	Because $S_0 = 1{,}440$

The total value of the stock plus futures position at month's end will be the sum of the portfolio value plus the futures proceeds, which equals

$$\text{Hedged proceeds} = \$1{,}545{,}000 + \$1{,}500{,}000 \times e \tag{26.2}$$

Notice that the dollar exposure to the market from your futures position precisely offsets your exposure from the stock portfolio. In other words, you have reduced beta to zero. Your investment is $1.5 million, so your total monthly rate of return is 3% plus the remaining nonsystematic risk (the second term of Equation 26.2). The fair or equilibrium expected rate of return on such a zero-beta position is the risk-free rate, 1%, so you have preserved your alpha of 2%, while eliminating the market exposure of the stock portfolio.

This is an idealized example of a pure play. In particular, it simplifies by assuming a known and fixed portfolio beta, but it illustrates that the goal is to speculate on the stock while hedging out the undesired market exposure. Once this is accomplished, you can establish any desired exposure to other sources of systematic risk by buying indexes or entering index futures contracts in those markets. Thus, you have made alpha portable.

Figure 26.1 is a graphical analysis of this pure play. Panel A shows the excess returns to betting on a positive-alpha stock portfolio "naked," that is, unhedged. Your *expected* return is better than an equilibrium return given your risk, but because of your market exposure

---

[2]We simplify here by assuming that the maturity of the futures contract precisely equals the hedging horizon, in this case, 1 month. If the contract maturity were longer, one would have to slightly reduce the hedge ratio in a process called "tailing the hedge."

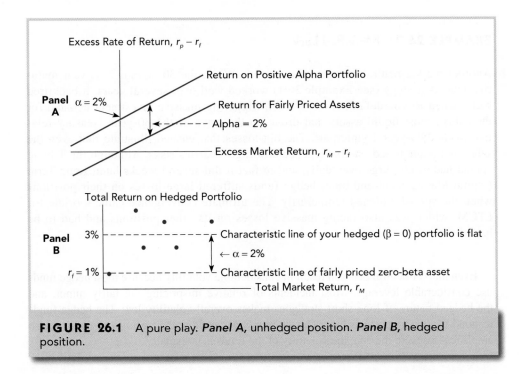

FIGURE 26.1   A pure play. *Panel A*, unhedged position. *Panel B*, hedged position.

you still can lose if the market declines. Panel B shows the characteristic line for the position with systematic risk hedged out. There is no market exposure.

A warning: Even market-neutral positions are still bets, and they can go wrong. This is not true arbitrage because your profits still depend on whether your analysis (your perceived alpha) is correct. Moreover, you can be done in by simple bad luck, that is, your analysis may be correct but a bad realization of idiosyncratic risk (negative values of e in Equation 26.1 or 26.2) can still result in losses.

CONCEPT CHECK 2

What would be the dollar value and rate of return on the market-neutral position if the value of the residual turns out to be −4%? If the market return in that month is 5%, where would the plot of the strategy return lie in each panel of Figure 26.1?

EXAMPLE 26.2   The Risks of Pure Plays

In May 2005, several hedge funds viewed General Motors' debt as underpriced and purchased it either directly or indirectly through credit default swaps. To protect against dramatic deterioration in GM's financial condition, they hedged their exposure by buying GM put options, which would increase in value if GM's stock price declined. In fact, GM ran into trouble and its bonds were downgraded to junk status. But rather than falling, GM's share price actually rose in response to Kirk Kerkorian's nearly simultaneous announcement that he was prepared to pay $31 a share to increase his stake in GM. So the hedge funds lost both on their position in the bonds, which fell in price, and their intended hedge position in puts, which also fell when the share price increased.

EXAMPLE 26.3   More Bad Luck

Another market-neutral bet misfired in 1998. While the 30- versus 29½-year maturity T-bond strategy (see Example 26.1) worked well over several years, it backfired badly when Russia defaulted on its debt, triggering massive investment demand for the safest, most liquid assets that drove up the price of the 30-year Treasury relative to its 29½-year counterpart. The big losses that ensued illustrate that even the safest bet—one based on convergence arbitrage—carries risks. Although the T-bond spread had to converge eventually, and in fact it did several weeks later, Long Term Capital Management and other hedge funds suffered large losses on their positions when the spread widened temporarily. The ultimate convergence came too late for LTCM, which was also facing massive losses on its other positions and had to be bailed out.[3]

Even market-neutral bets can result in considerable volatility because most hedge funds use considerable leverage. Most incidents of relative mispricing are fairly minor, and the hedged nature of long-short strategies makes overall volatility low. The hedge funds respond by scaling up their bets. This amplifies gains when their bets work out, but also amplifies losses. In the end, the volatility of the funds is not small.

26.4   STYLE ANALYSIS FOR HEDGE FUNDS

While the classic hedge fund strategy may have focused on market-neutral opportunities, as the market has evolved, the freedom to use derivatives contracts and short positions means that hedge funds can in effect follow any investment strategy. While many hedge funds pursue market-neutral strategies, a quick glance at the range of investment styles in Table 26.1 should convince you that many, if not most, funds pursue directional strategies. In these cases, the fund makes an outright bet, for example, on currency movements, the outcome of a takeover attempt, or the performance of an investment sector. These funds are most certainly not hedged, despite their name.

In Chapter 24, we introduced you to style analysis, which uses regression analysis to measure the exposure of a portfolio to various factors or asset classes. The analysis thus measures the implicit asset class exposure of a portfolio. The betas on a series of factors measure the fund's exposure to each source of systematic risk. A market-neutral fund will have no sensitivity to an index for that market. In contrast, directional funds will exhibit significant betas, often called *loadings* in this context, on whatever factors the fund tends to bet on. Observers attempting to measure investment style can use these factor loadings to impute exposures to a range of variables.

---

[3]This timing problem is a common one for active managers. We saw other examples of this issue when we discussed limits to arbitrage in Chapter 12. More generally, when security analysts think they have found a mispriced stock, they usually acknowledge that it is hard to know how long it will take for price to converge to intrinsic value.

Fund Classification*	n	Alpha	S&P 500	Long Bond	U.S. Dollar	Credit Premium	Market Volatility	Commodities Index
Convertible arbitrage	82	0.43	−0.02	0.30	−0.02	0.52	0.05	0.02
Dedicated short bias	10	0.67	−0.88	0.25	0.67	−0.19	0.04	−0.12
Emerging markets	102	1.41	0.43	0.01	−0.42	0.59	0.01	0.06
Equity-market neutral	83	0.59	0.05	0.02	−0.04	−0.06	0.03	0.02
Event-driven	169	0.93	0.13	0.04	−0.13	0.33	0.05	0.01
Fixed-income arb	62	0.58	0.02	0.27	0.07	0.19	0.07	0.02
Global macro	54	0.59	0.10	0.34	−0.23	0.18	0.07	0.04
Long/Short equity Hedge	520	0.89	0.38	0.03	−0.09	0.28	0.07	0.06
Managed futures	114	0.42	0.03	0.89	−0.39	−0.35	0.15	0.13
Multistrategy	59	0.71	0.15	0.12	0.01	0.17	0.09	0.04
Fund of funds	355	0.43	0.12	0.18	−0.10	0.17	0.07	0.05
Total	1,610							

TABLE 26.2

Style analysis for a sample of hedge funds

*Fund definitions given in Table 26.1.
Source: J. Hasanhodzic and Andrew Lo, "Can Hedge Fund Returns Be Replicated?: The Linear Case," *Journal of Investment Management* 5 (2007), pp. 5–45.

Fung and Hsieh[4] provided an early version of style analysis for hedge funds. A more recent application appears in Hasanhodzic and Lo[5], who focus on the following six factors:

- Equity market conditions: return on the S&P 500
- Foreign exchange: U.S. dollar index return
- Interest rates: return on Lehman Corporate AA intermediate bond index
- Credit conditions: spread between Lehman BAA index vs. Treasury index return
- Commodity markets: Goldman Sachs commodity index return
- Volatility: change in the CBOE volatility index (VIX)

The returns on hedge fund i in month t may be statistically described by

$$R_{it} = \alpha_i + \beta_{i1}\, \text{Factor1}_t + \cdots + \beta_{i6}\, \text{Factor6}_t + e_{it} \qquad (26.3)$$

The betas (equivalently, factor loadings) measure the sensitivity to each factor. As usual, the residual, e_{it}, measures "fund-specific" risk that is uncorrelated with the set of explanatory factors, and the intercept, α_i, measures average performance of fund i net of the impact of these systematic factors.

Table 26.2 presents factor exposure estimates for a sample of 1,610 hedge funds. The results confirm that most funds are in fact directional with very clear exposures to one or

[4]William Fung and David Hsieh, "Empirical Characteristics of Dynamic Trading Strategies: The Case of Hedge Funds," *Review of Financial Studies* 10 (1997), pp. 275–302.

[5]Jasmina Hasanhodzic and Andrew W. Lo, "Can Hedge Fund Returns Be Replicated?: The Linear Case," *Journal of Investment Management* 5 (2007), pp. 5–45. The analysis in this paper differs in two important respects from style analysis for mutual funds introduced in Chapter 24. First, in this application, factor loadings are not constrained to be non-negative. This is because, unlike mutual funds, hedge funds easily can take on short positions in various asset classes. Second, portfolio weights are not constrained to sum to 1.0. Again, unlike mutual funds, hedge funds can operate with considerable leverage.

more of the six factors. Moreover, the estimated factor betas seem reasonable in terms of the funds' stated style. For example:

- The equity market neutral funds have uniformly low factor betas, as one would expect of a market-neutral posture.
- Dedicated short bias funds exhibit substantial negative betas on the S&P index.
- Convertible arbitrage portfolios show exposure to both bond returns and credit conditions, measured by the return premium on BAA-rated corporate versus Treasury bonds.
- Event-driven funds have notable exposure to credit conditions (more positive credit spreads in this table indicate better economic conditions). This exposure arises because both merger arbitrage and restructuring activities often entail considerable amounts of borrowing.
- Emerging market funds show positive exposure to the S&P 500 and credit conditions, and negative exposure to a stronger U.S. dollar, which would make the dollar value of foreign investments less valuable.

We conclude that, by and large, most hedge funds are making very explicit directional bets on a wide array of economic factors.

CONCEPT CHECK 3	Analyze the betas of the fixed-income arbitrage funds in Table 26.2. Based on these results, are these funds typically market neutral? If not, do their factor exposures make sense in terms of the markets in which they operate?

26.5 PERFORMANCE MEASUREMENT FOR HEDGE FUNDS

Hasanhodzic and Lo also calculate both the alphas and the Sharpe measures of their sample of hedge funds. In this application, the alpha is the excess fund return after controlling for the impact of the systematic factors. Alpha is estimated as the intercept in Equation 26.3. The Sharpe measure is the ratio of average excess return to the standard deviation of returns. Table 26.3 indicates that by either measure hedge funds as a group seem to have outperformed: alphas are positive and large for many of these fund groups and Sharpe ratios consistently are higher than that of the S&P 500. What might be the source of such seemingly impressive performance?

One possibility, of course, is the obvious one: these results may reflect a high degree of skill among hedge fund managers. Another possibility is that funds maintain some exposure to omitted risk factors that convey a positive risk premium, but given the extensive list of included factors, this seems unlikely. However, there are several other factors that make hedge fund performance difficult to evaluate, and these are worth considering.

Liquidity and Hedge Fund Performance

Another explanation for these attractive performance measures is liquidity. Recall from Chapter 9 that one of the more important extensions of the CAPM is a version that allows for the possibility of a return premium for investors willing to hold less liquid assets. Hedge funds tend to hold more illiquid assets than other institutional investors such as mutual funds. They can do so because of restrictions such as the lock-up provisions that

Fund Classification*	n	Alpha	Mean	Std Dev	Monthly Serial Corr.	Annualized Sharpe Ratio
Convertible arbitrage	82	0.43	8.41	6.20	0.422	2.70
Dedicated short bias	10	0.67	4.92	28.75	0.034	0.20
Emerging markets	102	1.41	20.41	22.92	0.180	1.42
Equity-market neutral	83	0.59	8.09	7.78	0.091	1.44
Event-driven	169	0.93	13.03	8.40	0.222	1.99
Fixed-income arb	62	0.58	9.50	6.56	0.221	2.05
Global macro	54	0.59	11.38	11.93	0.058	1.07
Long/Short equity hedge	520	0.89	14.59	15.96	0.128	1.06
Managed futures	114	0.42	13.64	21.46	0.025	0.67
Multistrategy	59	0.71	10.79	8.72	0.210	1.86
Fund of funds	355	0.43	8.25	6.36	0.232	1.66
S&P 500		0.00	13.16	16.65	0.021	0.79

TABLE 26.3

Performance measures for hedge funds

*Fund definitions given in Table 26.1.

Source: J. Hasanhodzic and Andrew Lo, "Can Hedge Fund Returns Be Replicated?: The Linear Case," *Journal of Investment Management* 5 (2007), pp. 5–45.

commit investors to keep their investment in the fund for some period of time. Therefore, it is important to control for liquidity when evaluating performance. If it is ignored, what may be no more than compensation for illiquidity may appear to be true alpha, that is, risk-adjusted abnormal returns.

Aragon[6] demonstrates that hedge funds with lock-up restrictions do tend to hold less liquid portfolios. Moreover, once he controlled for lock-ups or other share restrictions (such as redemption notice periods), the apparently positive average alpha of those funds turned insignificant. Aragon's work suggests that the typical "alpha" exhibited by hedge funds may be better interpreted as an equilibrium liquidity premium rather than a sign of stock-picking ability, in other words a "fair" reward for providing liquidity to other investors.

Notice also the strong suggestion of serial correlation in returns in Table 26.3. Positive serial correlation means that positive returns are more likely to be followed by positive than by negative returns. Such a pattern is often taken as an indicator of less liquid markets for the following reason. When prices are not available because an asset is not actively traded, the hedge fund must estimate its value to calculate net asset value and rates of return. But such procedures are at best imperfect and, as demonstrated by Getmansky, Lo, and Makarov,[7] tend to result in serial correlation in prices as firms either smooth out their value estimates or only gradually mark prices to true market values. Positive serial correlation is therefore often interpreted as evidence of liquidity problems; in nearly efficient markets with frictionless trading, we would expect serial correlation or other predictable patterns in prices to be minimal. Most mutual funds show almost no evidence of such correlation in their returns and, as Table 26.3 documents, the serial correlation of the S&P 500 is just about zero.

[6]George O. Aragon, "Share Restrictions and Asset Pricing: Evidence from the Hedge Fund Industry," *Journal of Financial Economics* 83 (2007), pp. 33–58.

[7]Mila Getmansky, Andrew W. Lo, and Igor Makarov, "An Econometric Model of Serial Correlation and Illiquidity in Hedge Fund Returns," *Journal of Financial Economics* 74 (2004), pp. 529–609.

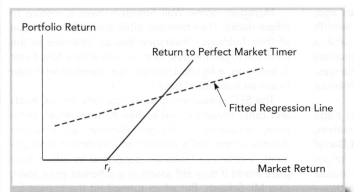

FIGURE 26.3   Characteristic line of a perfect market timer. The true characteristic line is kinked, with a shape like that of a call option. Fitting a straight line to the relationship will result in misestimated slope and intercept.

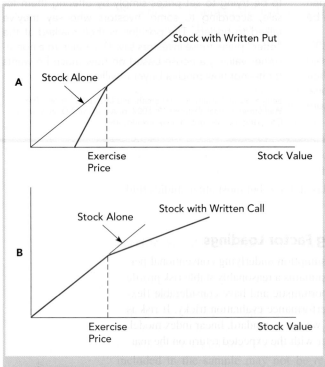

FIGURE 26.4   Characteristic lines of stock portfolio with written options. *Panel A:* Buy stock, write put. Here, the fund writes fewer puts than the number of shares it holds. *Panel B:* Buy stock, write calls. Here, the fund writes fewer calls than the number of shares it holds.

pattern would result in a fitted line with a slope between 0 and 1, and a positive alpha. Neither statistic accurately describes the fund.

As we noted in Chapter 24, and as is evident from Figure 26.3, an ability to conduct perfect market timing is much like obtaining a call option on the underlying portfolio without having to pay for it. Similar nonlinearities would arise if the fund actually buys or writes options. Figure 26.4, panel A, illustrates the case of a fund that holds a stock portfolio and writes put options on it, and panel B illustrates the case of a fund that holds a stock portfolio and writes call options. In both cases, the characteristic line is steeper when portfolio returns are poor—in other words, the fund has greater sensitivity to the market when it is falling than when it is rising. This is the opposite profile that would arise from timing ability, which is much like acquiring rather than writing options, and therefore would give the fund greater sensitivity to market advances.[11]

Lo[12] offers evidence that these sorts of nonlinearities can be empirically significant for hedge funds. He estimates a single-index model, using the S&P 500 as the market index, but allowing for different up-market and down-market betas. The equation describing fund returns therefore distinguishes positive from negative market returns and allows a different beta coefficient against each:

$$R_{it} = \alpha_i + \beta^+ R_{Mt}^+ + \beta^- R_{Mt}^- + e_{it} \quad \textbf{(26.4)}$$

The $+$ and $-$ superscripts in Equation 26.4 denote up and down markets, respectively. Table 26.4 shows the average up- and down-market betas for several types of hedge funds. (The statistical significance of these estimates can be assessed from the t-statistics that appear next to each parameter estimate. Remember that a t-statistic of around 2 is the traditional benchmark for statistical significance.)

Notice that the betas typically differ by substantial margins and, further, that down-market betas tend to be greater than up-market betas.

---

[11]But the fund that writes options would at least receive fair compensation for the unattractive shape of its characteristic line in the form of the premium received when it writes the options.

[12]Andrew Lo, "Risk Management for Hedge Funds: Introduction and Overview," *Financial Analysts Journal,* 57 November/December 2001), pp. 16–33.

Style	α	t(α)	β⁺	t(β⁺)	β⁻	t(β⁻)	R-square
Currencies	0.93	1.97	0.05	0.34	0.13	0.81	0.01
Event-driven (distressed firms)	1.95	7.84	−0.11	−1.50	0.58	6.95	0.36
Event-driven (merger arbitrage)	1.35	7.99	0.04	0.91	0.27	4.78	0.27
Emerging markets (equity)	3.78	2.41	0.16	0.34	1.49	2.84	0.11
Fund of funds	1.07	6.89	0.08	1.84	0.27	5.13	0.33
Futures trading	0.69	1.35	0.18	1.23	0.13	0.76	0.04
Growth	1.49	3.65	0.69	5.80	0.98	7.13	0.62
Macro	0.61	1.09	0.30	1.84	0.05	0.28	0.05
Relative value (convertibles)	1.25	8.44	−0.01	−0.31	0.18	3.55	0.14
Relative value (option arbitrage)	4.48	4.29	−0.78	−2.56	0.33	0.95	0.07
Short-selling	0.04	0.07	−0.67	−3.94	−1.25	−6.41	0.51
Value	1.46	4.49	0.24	2.54	0.69	6.41	0.45

TABLE 26.4

Index model results for hedge funds, allowing for different up- and down-market betas

Source: Andrew W. Lo, "Risk Management for Hedge Funds: Introduction and Overview," *Financial Analysts Journal*, Vol. 57 (November/December 2001), pp. 16–33.

This is precisely what investors presumably do *not* want: higher market sensitivity when the market is weak. This is evidence that funds may be *writing* options, either explicitly or implicitly through dynamic trading strategies (see Chapter 21, Section 21.5, for a discussion of such dynamic strategies). On the other hand, the alphas of these funds are uniformly positive, and many are statistically significant (although the interpretation of these alphas is subject to the caveats discussed in this section, such as liquidity, survivorship bias, and price accuracy).

Tail Events and Hedge Fund Performance

Imagine a hedge fund whose entire investment strategy is to hold an S&P 500 index fund and write deep out-of-the-money put options on the index. Clearly the fund manager brings no skill to his job. But if you knew only his investment results over limited periods, and not his underlying strategy, you might be fooled into thinking that he is extremely talented. For if the put options are written sufficiently out-of-the-money, they will only rarely end up imposing a loss, and such a strategy can appear over long periods—even over many years—to be consistently profitable. In most periods, the strategy brings in a modest premium from the written puts and therefore outperforms the S&P 500, yielding the impression of consistently superior performance. The huge loss that might be incurred in an extreme market decline might not be experienced even over periods as long as years. Every so often, such as in the market crash of October 1987, the strategy may lose multiples of its entire gain over the last decade. But if you are lucky enough to avoid these rare but extreme *tail events* (so named because they fall in the far-left tail of the probability distribution), the strategy might appear to be gilded.

The evidence in Table 26.4 indicating that hedge funds are at least implicitly option writers should make us nervous about taking their measured performance at face value. The problem in interpreting strategies with exposure to extreme tail events (such as short options positions) is that these events by definition occur very infrequently, so it can take *decades* of results to fully appreciate their true risk and reward attributes. In two influential books,[13] Nassim Taleb, who is a hedge fund operator himself, makes the case that many hedge funds are analogous to our hypothetical manager, racking up fame and fortune through strategies that make money *most* of the time, but expose investors to rare but extreme losses.

Taleb uses the metaphor of the black swan to discuss the importance of highly improbable, but highly impactful, events. Until the discovery of Australia, Europeans believed that all swans were white: they had never encountered swans that were not white. In their experience, the black swan was outside the realm of reasonable possibility, in statistical jargon, an extreme outlier relative to their sample of observations. Taleb argues that the world is filled with black swans, deeply important developments that simply could not have been predicted from the range of accumulated experience to date. While we can't predict which black swans to expect, we nevertheless know that some black swan may be making an appearance at any moment. The October 1987 crash, when the market fell by more than 20% in 1 day, might be viewed as a black swan—an event that had never taken place before, one that most market observers would have dismissed as impossible and certainly not worth modeling, but with high impact. These sorts of events seemingly come out of the blue, and they caution us to show great humility when we use past experience to evaluate the future risk of our actions. With this in mind, consider again the example of Long Term Capital Management.

EXAMPLE 26.4 Tail Events and Long-Term Capital Management

In the late 1990s, Long Term Capital Management was widely viewed as the most successful hedge fund in history. It had consistently provided double-digit returns to its investors, and it had earned hundreds of millions of dollars in incentive fees for its managers. The firm used sophisticated computer models to estimate correlations across assets and believed that its capital was almost 10 times the annual standard deviation of its portfolio returns, presumably enough to withstand any "possible" shock to capital (at least, assuming normal distributions!). But in the summer of 1998, things went badly. On August 17, 1998, Russia defaulted on its sovereign debt and threw capital markets into chaos. LTCM's *1-day* loss on August 21 was $550 million (approximately nine times its estimated *monthly* standard deviation). Total losses in August were about $1.3 billion, despite the fact that LTCM believed that the great majority of its positions were market-neutral relative-value trades. Losses accrued on virtually all of its positions, flying in the face of the presumed diversification of the overall portfolio.

How did this happen? The answer lies in the massive flight to quality and, even more so, to liquidity that was set off by the Russian default. LTCM was typically a seller of liquidity (holding less liquid assets, selling more liquid assets with lower yields, and earning the yield spread) and suffered huge losses. This was a different type of shock from those that appeared in its historical sample/modeling period. In the liquidity crisis that engulfed asset markets, the unexpected commonality of liquidity risk across ostensibly uncorrelated asset classes became obvious. Losses that seemed statistically impossible on past experience had in fact come to pass; LTCM fell victim to a black swan.

---

[13]Nassim N. Taleb, *Fooled by Randomness: The Hidden Role of Chance in Life and in the Markets* (New York: TEXERE (Thomson), 2004); Nassim N. Taleb, *The Black Swan: The Impact of the Highly Improbable,* (New York: Random House, 2007).

26.6   FEE STRUCTURE IN HEDGE FUNDS

The typical hedge fund fee structure is a management fee of 1% to 2% of assets plus an **incentive fee** equal to 20% of investment profits beyond a stipulated benchmark performance, annually. Incentive fees are effectively call options on the portfolio with a strike price equal to current portfolio value times 1 + benchmark return. The manager gets the fee if the portfolio value rises sufficiently, but loses nothing if it falls. Figure 26.5 illustrates the incentive fee for a fund with a 20% incentive fee and a hurdle rate equal to the money market rate, r_f. The current value of the portfolio is denoted S_0 and the year-end value is S_T. The incentive fee is equivalent to .20 call options on the portfolio with exercise price $S_0 (1 + r_f)$.

EXAMPLE 26.5   Black-Scholes Valuation of Incentive Fees

Suppose the standard deviation of a hedge fund's annual rate of return is 30% and the incentive fee is 20% of any investment return over the risk-free money market rate. If the portfolio currently has a net asset value of $100 per share, and the effective annual risk-free rate is 5% (or 4.88% expressed as a continuously compounded rate), then the implicit exercise price on the incentive fee is $105. The Black-Scholes value of a call option with $S_0 = 100$, $X = 105$, $\sigma = .30$, $r = .0488$, $T = 1$ year is $11.92, just a shade below 12% of net asset value. Because the incentive fee is worth 20% of the call option, its value is just about 2.4% of net asset value. Together with a typical management fee of 2% of net asset value, the investor in the fund pays fees with a total value of 4.4%.

The major complication to this description of the typical compensation structure is the **high water mark.** If a fund experiences losses, it may not be able to charge an incentive fee unless and until it recovers to its previous higher value. With large losses, this may be difficult. High water marks therefore give managers an incentive to shut down funds that have performed poorly, and likely are a cause of the high attrition rate for funds noted above.

One of the fastest-growing sectors in the hedge fund universe has been in **funds of funds.** These are hedge funds that invest in several other hedge funds. Optionality can have a big impact on expected fees in these funds. This is because the fund of funds pays an incentive fee to each underlying fund that outperforms its benchmark, even if the aggregate performance of the fund of funds is poor. In this case, diversification can hurt you![14]

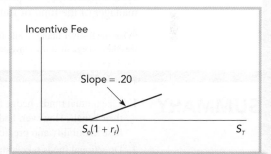

FIGURE 26.5   Incentive fees as a call option. The current value of the portfolio is denoted S_0 and its year-end value is S_T. The incentive fee is equivalent to .20 call options on the portfolio with exercise price $S_0(1 + r_f)$.

EXAMPLE 26.6   Incentive Fees in Funds of Funds

Suppose a fund of funds is established with $1 million invested in each of three hedge funds. For simplicity, we will ignore the asset-value-based portion of fees (the management fee) and focus only on the incentive fee. Suppose that the hurdle rate for the incentive fee is a zero return, so each fund charges an incentive fee of 20% of total return. The following table shows the performance of each underlying fund over a year, the gross rate

[14]S. J. Brown, W. N. Goetzmann, and B. Liang, "Fees on Fees in Funds of Funds," *Journal of Investment Management* 2 (2004), pp. 39–56.

of return, and the return realized by the fund of funds net of the incentive fee. Funds 1 and 2 have positive returns, and therefore earn an incentive fee, but Fund 3 has terrible performance, so its incentive fee is zero.

	Fund 1	Fund 2	Fund 3	Fund of Funds
Start of year (millions)	$1.00	$1.00	$1.00	$3.00
End of year (millions)	$1.20	$1.40	$0.25	$2.85
Gross rate of return	20%	40%	−75%	−5%
Incentive fee (millions)	$0.04	$0.08	$0.00	$0.12
End of year, net of fee	$1.16	$1.32	$.25	$2.73
Net rate of return	16%	32%	−75%	−9%

Even though the return on the aggregate portfolio of the fund of funds is *negative* 5%, it still pays incentive fees of $.12 for every $3 invested, which amounts to 4% of net asset value. As demonstrated in the last column, this reduces the rate of return earned by the fund of funds from −5% to −9%.

The idea behind funds of funds is to spread risk across several different funds. However, investors need to be aware that these funds of funds operate with considerable leverage, on top of the leverage of the primary funds in which they invest, which can make returns highly volatile. Moreover, if the various hedge funds in which these funds of funds invest have similar investment styles, the diversification benefits of spreading investments across several funds may be illusory—but the extra layer of steep management fees paid to the manager of the fund of funds certainly is not.[15]

[15]One small silver lining: while funds of funds pay incentive fees to each of the underlying funds, the incentive fees they charge their own investors tend to be lower, typically around 10% rather than 20%.

SUMMARY

1. Like mutual funds, hedge funds pool the assets of several clients and manage the pooled assets on their behalf. However, hedge funds differ from mutual funds with respect to disclosure, investor base, flexibility and predictability of investment orientation, regulation, and fee structure.

2. Directional funds take a stance on the performance of broad market sectors. Nondirectional funds establish market-neutral positions on relative mispricing. However, even these hedged positions still present idiosyncratic risk.

3. Statistical arbitrage is the use of quantitative systems to uncover many perceived misalignments in relative pricing and ensure profits by averaging over all of these small bets. It often uses data-mining methods to uncover past patterns that form the basis for the established investment positions.

4. Portable alpha is a strategy in which one invests in positive-alpha positions, then hedges the systematic risk of that investment, and, finally, establishes market exposure where desired by using passive indexes or futures contracts.

5. Performance evaluation of hedge funds is complicated by survivorship bias, by the potential instability of risk attributes, by the existence of liquidity premiums, and by unreliable market valuations of infrequently traded assets. Performance evaluation is particularly difficult when the fund engages in option positions. Tail events make it hard to assess the true performance of positions involving options without extremely long histories of returns.

6. Hedge funds typically charge investors both a management fee and an incentive fee equal to a percentage of profits beyond some threshold value. The incentive fee is akin to a call option on the portfolio. Funds of hedge funds pay the incentive fee to each underlying fund that beats its hurdle rate, even if the overall performance of the portfolio is poor.

Related web sites for this chapter are available at www.mhhe.com/bkm

TABLE 27.1

Construction
and properties of
the optimal risky
portfolio

1. Initial position of security i in the active portfolio	$w_i^0 = \dfrac{\alpha_i}{\sigma^2(e_i)}$
2. Scaled initial positions	$w_i = \dfrac{w_i}{\sum\limits_{i=1}^{n} \dfrac{\alpha_i}{\sigma^2(e_i)}}$
3. Alpha of the active portfolio	$\alpha_A = \sum\limits_{i=1}^{n} w_i \alpha_i$
4. Residual variance of the active portfolio	$\sigma^2(e_A) = \sum\limits_{i=1}^{n} w_i^2 \sigma^2(e_i)$
5. Initial position in the active portfolio	$w_A^0 = \dfrac{\dfrac{\alpha_A}{\sigma^2(e_A)}}{\dfrac{E(R_M)}{\sigma_M^2}}$
6. Beta of the active portfolio	$\beta_A = \sum\limits_{i=1}^{n} w_i \beta_i$
7. Adjusted (for beta) position in the active portfolio	$w_A^* = \dfrac{w_A^0}{1 + (1 - \beta_A) w_A^0}$
8. Final weights in passive portfolio and in security i	$w_M^* = 1 - w_A^*; \quad w_i^* = w_A^* w_i$
9. The beta of the optimal risky portfolio and its risk premium	$\beta_P = w_M^* + w_A^* \beta_A = 1 - w_A^*(1 - \beta_A)$ $E(R_P) = \beta_P E(R_M) + w_A^* \alpha_A$
10. The variance of the optimal risky portfolio	$\sigma_P^2 = \beta_P^2 \sigma_M^2 + [w_A^* \sigma(e_A)]^2$
11. Sharpe ratio of the risky portfolio	$S_P^2 = S_M^2 + \sum\limits_{i=1}^{n} \left(\dfrac{\alpha_i}{\sigma(e_i)} \right)^2$

that allows for correlation among residuals. Moreover, we saw that despite the significant correlation between some pairs of residuals in the portfolio construction example we used in Chapter 8, for example, between Shell and BP, the efficient frontiers formed from the index model and the Markowitz model were barely distinguishable (see Figure 8.5 of Chapter 8).

For illustration, in this chapter we continue with the example employed in Chapter 8. Spreadsheet 27.1 recaps the data and results of this exercise. Table D in the spreadsheet shows the improvement in the Sharpe ratio over the **passive market index portfolio** offered by adding the **active portfolio** to the mix. To better appreciate this improvement we have included the M-square measure of performance. M-square is the incremental expected return of the optimized portfolio compared to the passive alternative once the active portfolio is mixed with bills to provide the same total volatility as the index portfolio (for a review, see Chapter 24).

Forecasts of Alpha Values and Extreme Portfolio Weights

The overriding impression from Spreadsheet 27.1 is apparently meager performance improvement: Table D of the spreadsheet shows that M-square increases by only 19 basis points (equivalent to an improvement of .0136 in the Sharpe ratio). Notice that the Sharpe

	A	B	C	D	E	F	G	H	I	J
1										
2										
3	Table A: Risk Parameters of the Investable Universe (annualized)									
4										
5		SD of Excess Return	Beta	SD of Systematic Component	SD of Residual	Correlation with the S&P 500				
6	S&P 500	0.1358	1.00	0.1358	0	1				
7	HP	0.3817	2.03	0.2762	0.2656	0.72				
8	DELL	0.2901	1.23	0.1672	0.2392	0.58				
9	WMT	0.1935	0.62	0.0841	0.1757	0.43				
10	TARGET	0.2611	1.27	0.1720	0.1981	0.66				
11	BP	0.1822	0.47	0.0634	0.1722	0.35				
12	SHELL	0.1988	0.67	0.0914	0.1780	0.46				
13										
14	Table B: The Index Model Covariance Matrix									
15										
16			SP 500	HP	DELL	WMT	TARGET	BP	SHELL	
17		Beta	1.00	2.03	1.23	0.62	1.27	0.47	0.67	
18	S&P 500	1.00	0.0184	0.0375	0.0227	0.0114	0.0234	0.0086	0.0124	
19	HP	2.03	0.0375	0.1457	0.0462	0.0232	0.0475	0.0175	0.0253	
20	DELL	1.23	0.0227	0.0462	0.0842	0.0141	0.0288	0.0106	0.0153	
21	WMT	0.62	0.0114	0.0232	0.0141	0.0374	0.0145	0.0053	0.0077	
22	TARGET	1.27	0.0234	0.0475	0.0288	0.0145	0.0682	0.0109	0.0157	
23	BP	0.47	0.0086	0.0175	0.0106	0.0053	0.0109	0.0332	0.0058	
24	SHELL	0.67	0.0124	0.0253	0.0153	0.0077	0.0157	0.0058	0.0395	
25										
26	Table C: Macro Forecast (S&P 500) and Forecasts of Alpha Values									
27										
28										
29			SP 500	HP	DELL	WMT	TARGET	BP	SHELL	
30	Alpha		0	0.0150	−0.0100	−0.0050	0.0075	0.012	0.0025	
31	Risk premium		0.0600	0.0750	0.1121	0.0689	0.0447	0.0880	0.0305	
32										
33	Table D: Computation of the Optimal Risky Portfolio									
34										
35			S&P 500	Active Pf A		HP	DELL	WMT	TARGET	BP	SHELL
36					$\sigma^2(e)$	0.0705	0.0572	0.0309	0.0392	0.0297	0.0317
37				0.5505	$\alpha/\sigma^2(e)$	0.2126	−0.1748	−0.1619	0.1911	0.4045	0.0789
38				1.0000	$w_0(i)$	0.3863	−0.3176	−0.2941	0.3472	0.7349	0.1433
39					$[w_0(i)]^2$	0.1492	0.1009	0.0865	0.1205	0.5400	0.0205
40	α_A			0.0222							
41	$\sigma^2(e_A)$			0.0404							
42	w_0			0.1691	Overall						
43	w^*		0.8282	0.1718	Portfolio	0.0663	−0.0546	−0.0505	0.0596	0.1262	0.0246
44	Beta		1	1.0922	1.0158	0.0663	−0.0546	−0.0505	0.0596	0.1262	0.0246
45	Risk premium		0.06	0.0878	0.0648	0.0750	0.1121	0.0689	0.0447	0.0880	0.0305
46	SD		0.1358	0.2497	0.1422	0.3817	0.2901	0.1935	0.2611	0.1822	0.1988
47	Sharpe ratio		0.44	0.35	0.4556						
48	M-square		0	−0.0123	0.0019						
49	Benchmark risk				0.0345						

SPREADSHEET 27.1

Active portfolio management with a universe of six stocks

eXcel

Please visit us at
www.mhhe.com/bkm

ratio of the active portfolio is inferior to that of the passive portfolio (due to its large standard deviation) and hence its *M*-square is actually negative. But remember that the active portfolio is mixed with the passive portfolio, so total volatility is not its appropriate measure of risk. When combined with the passive portfolio, it does offer some improvement in performance, although such improvement is quite modest. This is the best that can be had given the **alpha values** uncovered by the security analysts (see Table C). Notice that the position in the active portfolio amounts to 17%, financed in part by a combined short position in Dell and Wal-Mart of about 10%. Because the figures in Spreadsheet 27.1 are annualized, this performance is equivalent to a 1-year HPR.

The alpha values we used in Spreadsheet 27.1 are actually small by the standard of typical analysts' forecasts. On June 1, 2006, we downloaded the current prices of the six stocks in the example, as well as analysts' 1-year target prices for each firm. These data and the

Stock	HP	Dell	WMT	Target	BP	Shell	**TABLE 27.2**
Current price	32.15	25.39	48.14	49.01	70.8	68.7	Stock prices and analysts' target prices for June 1, 2006
Target price	36.88	29.84	57.44	62.8	83.52	71.15	
Implied alpha	0.1471	0.1753	0.1932	0.2814	0.1797	0.0357	

implied annual alpha values are shown in Table 27.2. Notice that all alphas are positive, indicating an optimistic view for this group of stocks. Figure 27.1 shows the graphs of the stock prices, as well as the S&P 500 index (ticker = GSPC), for the previous year, June 2005–May 2006. The graph shows that the optimistic views in Table 27.2 are not a result of extrapolating rates from the past.

Table 27.3 shows the optimal portfolio using the analysts' forecasts rather than the original alpha values in Table D in Spreadsheet 27.1. The difference in performance is striking. The Sharpe ratio of the new optimal portfolio has increased from .44 to 2.32, amounting to a huge risk-adjusted return advantage. This shows up in an *M*-square of 25.53%! However, these results also expose the potential major problem with the Treynor-Black model. The optimal portfolio calls for extreme long/short positions that are simply infeasible for a real-world portfolio manager. For example, the model calls for a position of 5.79 (579%) in the active portfolio, largely financed by a short position of −4.79 in the S&P 500 index. Moreover, the standard deviation of this optimal portfolio is 52.24%, a level of risk that only extremely aggressive hedge funds would be willing to bear. It is important to notice that this risk is largely nonsystematic because the beta of the active portfolio, at .95, is less than 1.0, and the beta of the overall risky portfolio is even lower, only .73, because of the short position in the passive portfolio.

A somewhat common approach to this problem is to restrict extreme portfolio positions, beginning with short sales. When the short position in the S&P 500 index is eliminated, forcing us to constrain the position in the active portfolio to be no more than 1.0, the position in the passive portfolio (the S&P 500) is zero, and the active portfolio comprises the entire risky position. Table 27.4 shows that the active portfolio has a standard deviation of 15.68%, not overwhelmingly greater than the SD of the passive portfolio (13.58%). The

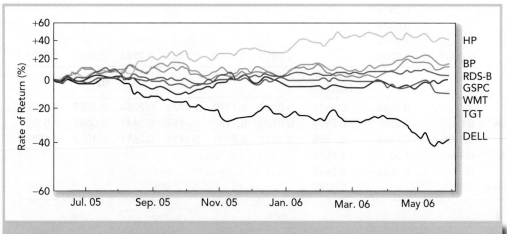

FIGURE 27.1   Rates of return on the S&P 500 (GSPC) and the six stocks, June 2005–May 2006

	S&P 500	Active Pf A		HP	Dell	WMT	Target	BP	Shell
			$\sigma^2(e)$	0.0705	0.0572	0.0309	0.0392	0.0297	0.0317
		25.7562	$\alpha/\sigma^2(e)$	2.0855	3.0641	6.2544	7.1701	6.0566	1.1255
		1.0000	$w_0(i)$	0.0810	0.1190	0.2428	0.2784	0.2352	0.0437
			$[w_0(i)]^2$	0.0066	0.0142	0.0590	0.0775	0.0553	0.0019
α_A		0.2018							
$\sigma^2(e_A)$		0.0078							
w_0		7.9116							
w^*	−4.7937	5.7937		0.4691163	0.6892459	1.4069035	1.6128803	1.3624061	0.2531855
			Overall Portfolio						
Beta	1	0.9538	0.7323	0.4691	0.6892	1.4069	1.6129	1.3624	0.2532
Risk premium	0.06	0.2590	1.2132	0.0750	0.1121	0.0689	0.0447	0.0880	0.0305
SD	0.1358	0.1568	0.5224	0.3817	0.2901	0.1935	0.2611	0.1822	0.1988
Sharpe ratio	0.44	1.65	2.3223						
M-square	0	0.1642	0.2553						
Benchmark risk			0.5146						

TABLE 27.3

The optimal risky portfolio with the analysts' new forecasts

	S&P 500	Active Pf A		HP	Dell	WMT	Target	BP	Shell
			$\sigma^2(e)$	0.0705	0.0572	0.0309	0.0392	0.0297	0.0317
		25.7562	$\alpha/\sigma^2(e)$	2.0855	3.0641	6.2544	7.1701	6.0566	1.1255
		1.0000	$w_0(i)$	0.0810	0.1190	0.2428	0.2784	0.2352	0.0437
			$[w_0(i)]^2$	0.0066	0.0142	0.0590	0.0775	0.0553	0.0019
α_A		0.2018							
$\sigma^2(e_A)$		0.0078							
w_0		7.9116							
w^*	0.0000	1.0000		0.0810	0.1190	0.2428	0.2784	0.2352	0.0437
			Overall Portfolio						
Beta	1	0.9538	0.9538	0.0810	0.1190	0.2428	0.2784	0.2352	0.0437
Risk premium	0.06	0.2590	0.2590	0.0750	0.1121	0.0689	0.0447	0.0880	0.0305
SD	0.1358	0.1568	0.1568	0.3817	0.2901	0.1935	0.2611	0.1822	0.1988
Sharpe ratio	0.44	1.65	1.6515						
M-square	0	0.1642	0.1642						
Benchmark risk			0.0887						

TABLE 27.4

The optimal risky portfolio with constraint on the active portfolio ($w_A \leq 1$)

beta of the overall risky portfolio is now that of the active portfolio (.95), still a slightly defensive portfolio in terms of systematic risk. Despite this severe restriction, the optimization procedure is still powerful, and the *M*-square of the optimal risky portfolio (now the active portfolio) is a very large 16.42%.

Is this a satisfactory solution? This would depend on the organization. For hedge funds, this may be a dream portfolio. For most mutual funds, however, the lack of diversification would rule it out. Notice the positions in the six stocks; the position in Wal-Mart, Target, and British Petroleum alone account for 76% of the portfolio.

Here we have to acknowledge the limitations of our example. Surely, when the investment company covers more securities, the problem of lack of diversification would largely vanish. But it turns out that the problem with extreme long/short positions typically persists even when we consider a larger number of firms, and this can gut the practical value of the optimization model. Consider this conclusion from an important article by Black and Litterman[1] (whose model we will present in Section 27.3):

> the mean-variance optimization used in standard asset allocation models is extremely sensitive to expected return assumptions the investor must provide . . . The optimal portfolio, given its sensitivity to the expected returns, often appears to bear little or no relation to the views the investor wishes to express. In practice, therefore, despite obvious conceptual attractions of a quantitative approach, few global investment managers regularly allow quantitative models to play a major role in their asset allocation decisions.

This statement is more complex than it reads at first blush, and we will analyze it in depth in Section 27.3. We bring it up in this section, however, to point out the general conclusion that ". . . few global investment managers regularly allow quantitative models to play a major role in their asset allocation decisions." In fact, this statement also applies to many portfolio managers who avoid the mean-variance optimization process altogether for other reasons. We return to this issue in Section 27.4.

Restriction of Benchmark Risk

Black and Litterman point out a related important practical issue. Many investment managers are judged against the performance of a **benchmark,** and a benchmark index is provided in the mutual fund prospectus. Implied in our analysis so far is that the passive portfolio, the S&P 500, is that benchmark. Such commitment raises the importance of what is called **tracking error.** Tracking error is defined as the difference between the returns on the overall risky portfolio versus the benchmark return, that is, $T_E = R_P - R_M$. The portfolio manager must be mindful of benchmark risk, that is, the standard deviation of the tracking error.

The tracking error of the optimized risky portfolio can be expressed in terms of the beta of the portfolio and thus reveals the benchmark risk:

$$\text{Tracking error} = T_E = R_P - R_M$$
$$R_P = w_A^* \alpha_A + [1 - w_A^*(1 - \beta_A)]R_M + w_A^* e_A$$
$$T_E = w_A^* \alpha_A - w_A^*(1 - \beta_A)R_M + w_A^* e_A \tag{27.1}$$
$$\text{Var}(T_E) = [w_A^*(1 - \beta_A)]^2 \text{Var}(R_M) + \text{Var}(w_A^* e_A) = [w_A^*(1 - \beta_A)]^2 \sigma_M^2 + [w_A^* \sigma(e_A)]^2$$
$$\text{Benchmark risk} = \sigma(T_E) = w_A^* \sqrt{(1 - \beta_A)^2 \sigma_M^2 + [\sigma(e_A)]^2}$$

---

[1]Fischer Black and Robert Litterman, "Global Portfolio Optimization," *Financial Analysts Journal,* September/October 1992. Originally published by Goldman Sachs Company, © 1991.

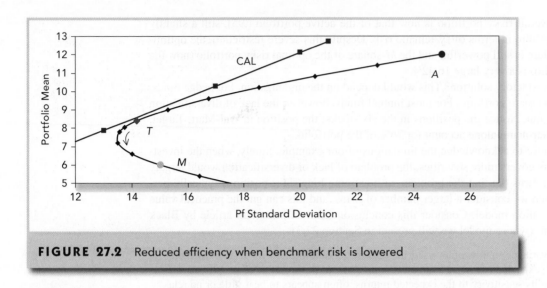

FIGURE 27.2   Reduced efficiency when benchmark risk is lowered

Equation 27.1 shows us how to calculate the volatility of tracking error (i.e., benchmark risk) and how to set the position in the active portfolio, w_A^*, to restrict tracking risk to any desired level. For a unit investment in the active portfolio, that is, for $w_A^* = 1$, benchmark risk is

$$\sigma(T_E; w_A^* = 1) = \sqrt{(1 - \beta_A)^2 \sigma_M^2 + [\sigma(e_A)]^2} \qquad (27.2)$$

For a desired benchmark risk of $\sigma_0 (T_E)$ we would restrict the weight of the active portfolio to

$$w_A(T_E) = \frac{\sigma_0(T_E)}{\sigma(T_E; w_A^* = 1)} \qquad (27.3)$$

Obviously, introducing a constraint on tracking risk entails a cost. We must shift weight from the active to the passive portfolio. Figure 27.2 illustrates the cost. The portfolio optimization would lead us to portfolio *T,* the tangency of the capital allocation line (CAL), which is the ray from the risk-free rate to the efficient frontier formed from *A* and *M.* Reducing risk by shifting weight from *T* to *M* takes us down the efficient frontier, instead of along the CAL, to a lower risk position, reducing the Sharpe ratio and *M*-square of the constrained portfolio.

Notice that the standard deviation of tracking error using the "meager" alpha forecasts in Spreadsheet 27.1 is only 3.45% because the weight in the active portfolio is only 17%. Using the larger alphas based on analysts' forecasts with no restriction on portfolio weights, the standard deviation of tracking error is 51.46% (see Table 27.3), more than any real-life manager who is evaluated against a benchmark would be willing to bear. However, with the constraint on the active portfolio in Equation 27.2, the benchmark risk falls to 8.87% (Table 27.4).

Finally, suppose a manager wishes to restrict benchmark risk to the same level as it was using the original forecasts, that is, to 3.45%. Equations 27.2 and 27.3 instruct us how to set the weight in the active portfolio. Applying these equations to the data in Spreadsheet 27.1, we obtain the results in Table 27.5. This portfolio is moderate, yet superior in performance: (1) its standard deviation is only slightly higher than that of the passive portfolio, 13.85%; (2) its beta is .98; (3) the standard deviation of tracking error that we

	S&P 500	Active Pf A		HP	Dell	WMT	Target	BP	Shell
			$\sigma^2(e)$	0.0705	0.0572	0.0309	0.0392	0.0297	0.0317
		25.7562	$\alpha/\sigma^2(e)$	2.0855	3.0641	6.2544	7.1701	6.0566	1.1255
		1.0000	$w_0(i)$	0.0810	0.1190	0.2428	0.2784	0.2352	0.0437
			$[w_0(i)]^2$	0.0066	0.0142	0.0590	0.0775	0.0553	0.0019
α_A		0.2018							
$\sigma^2(e_A)$		0.0078							
w_0		7.9116							
w^*	0.5661	0.4339		0.0351	0.0516	0.1054	0.1208	0.1020	0.0190
		Overall Portfolio							
Beta	1	0.9538	0.9800	0.0351	0.0516	0.1054	0.1208	0.1020	0.0190
Risk premium	0.06	0.2590	0.1464	0.0750	0.1121	0.0689	0.0447	0.0880	0.0305
Standard deviation	0.1358	0.1568	0.1385	0.3817	0.2901	0.1935	0.2611	0.1822	0.1988
Sharpe ratio	0.44	1.65	1.0569						
M-square	0	0.1642	0.0835						
Benchmark risk			0.0385						

TABLE 27.5

The optimal risky portfolio with the analysts' new forecasts (benchmark risk constrained to 3.85%)

specified is extremely low, 3.45%; (4) given that we have only six securities, the largest position of 12% (in Target) is quite low and would be lower still if more securities were covered; yet (5) the Sharpe ratio is a whopping 1.06, and the M-square is a very impressive 8.35%. Thus, by controlling benchmark risk we can avoid the flaws of the unconstrained portfolio and still maintain superior performance.

27.2 THE TREYNOR–BLACK MODEL AND FORECAST PRECISION

Suppose the risky portfolio of your 401(k) retirement fund is currently in an S&P 500 index fund, and you are pondering whether you should take some extra risk and allocate some funds to Target's stock, the high-performing discounter. You know that, absent research analysis, you should assume the alpha of any stock is zero. Hence, the mean of your **prior distribution** of Target's alpha is zero. Downloading return data for Target and the S&P 500 reveals a residual standard deviation of 19.8%. Given this volatility, the prior mean of zero, and an assumption of normality, you now have the entire prior distribution of Target's alpha.

One can make a decision using a prior distribution, or refine that distribution by expending effort to obtain additional data. In jargon, this effort is called *the experiment*. The experiment as a stand-alone venture would yield a probability distribution of possible outcomes. The optimal statistical procedure is to combine one's prior distribution for alpha with the information derived from the experiment to form a **posterior distribution** that reflects both. This posterior distribution is then used for decision making.

A "tight" prior, that is, a distribution with a small standard deviation, implies a high degree of confidence in the likely range of possible alpha values even before looking at the data. In this case, the experiment may not be sufficiently convincing to affect your beliefs, meaning that the posterior will be little changed from the prior.[2] In the context of the present discussion, an active forecast of alpha and its precision provides the experiment that may induce you to update your prior beliefs about its value. The role of the portfolio manager is to form a posterior distribution of alpha that serves portfolio construction.

Adjusting Forecasts for the Precision of Alpha

Imagine it is June 1, 2006, and you have just downloaded from Yahoo! Finance the analysts' forecasts we used in the previous section, implying that Target's alpha is 28.1%. Should you conclude that the optimal position in Target, before adjusting for beta, is $\alpha/\sigma^2(e) = .281/.198^2 = 7.17$ (717%)? Naturally, before committing to such an extreme position, any reasonable manager would first ask: "How accurate is this forecast?" and "How should I adjust my position to take account of forecast imprecision?"

Treynor and Black[3] asked this question and supplied an answer. The logic of the answer is quite straightforward; you must quantify the uncertainty about this forecast, just as you would the risk of the underlying asset or portfolio. A Web surfer may not have a way to assess the precision of a downloaded forecast, but the employer of the analyst who issued the forecast does. How? By examining the **forecasting record** of previous forecasts issued by the same forecaster.

Suppose that a security analyst provides the portfolio manager with forecasts of alpha at regular intervals, say, the beginning of each month. The investor portfolio is updated using the forecast and held until the update of next month's forecast. At the end of each month, T, the realized abnormal return of Target's stock is the sum of alpha plus a residual:

$$u(T) = R_{TGT}(T) - \beta R_M(T) = \alpha(T) + e(T) \tag{27.4}$$

where beta is estimated from Target's security characteristic line (SCL) using data for periods prior to T,

$$\text{SCL: } R_{TGT}(t) = \alpha + \beta R_M(t) + e(t), \quad t < T \tag{27.5}$$

The 1-month, forward-looking forecast $\alpha^f(T)$ issued by the analyst at the beginning of month T is aimed at the abnormal return, $u(T)$, in Equation 27.4. In order to decide on how to use the forecast for month T, the portfolio manager uses the analyst's forecasting record. The analyst's record is the paired time series of all past forecasts, $\alpha^f(t)$, and realizations, $u(t)$. To assess forecast accuracy, that is, the relationship between forecast and realized alphas, the manager uses this record to estimate the regression:

$$u(t) = a_0 + a_1\alpha^f(t) + \varepsilon(t) \tag{27.6}$$

Our goal is to adjust alpha forecasts to properly account for their imprecision. We will form an **adjusted alpha** forecast $\alpha(T)$ for the coming month by using the original forecasts $\alpha^f(T)$ and applying the estimates from the regression Equation 27.6, that is,

$$\alpha(T) = a_0 + a_1\alpha^f(T) \tag{27.7}$$

---

[2]In application to debates about social issues, you might define a fanatic as one who enters the debate with a prior that is so tight that no argument will influence his posterior, making the debate altogether a waste of time.

[3]Jack Treynor and Fischer Black, "How to Use Security Analysis to Improve Portfolio Selection," *Journal of Business*, January 1973.

The properties of the regression estimates assure us that the adjusted forecast is the "best linear unbiased estimator" of the abnormal return on Target in the coming month, T. "Best" in this context means it has the lowest possible variance among unbiased forecasts that are linear functions of the original forecast. We show in Appendix A that the value we should use for a_1 in Equation 27.7 is the R-square of the regression Equation 27.6. Because R-square is less than 1, this implies that we "shrink" the forecast toward zero. The lower the precision of the original forecast (the lower its R-square), the more we shrink the adjusted alpha back toward zero. The coefficient a_0 adjusts the forecast upward if the forecaster has been consistently pessimistic, and downward for consistent optimism.

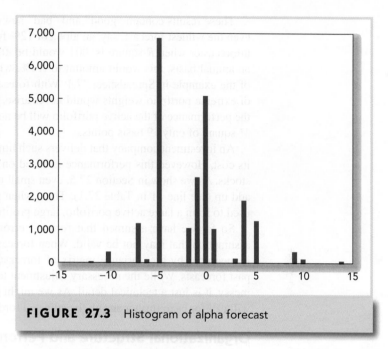

FIGURE 27.3   Histogram of alpha forecast

Distribution of Alpha Values

Equation 27.7 implies that the quality of security analysts' forecasts, as measured by the R-square in regressions of realized abnormal returns on their forecasts, is a critical issue for construction of optimal portfolios and resultant performance. Unfortunately, these numbers are usually impossible to come by.

Kane, Kim, and White[4] obtained a unique database of analysts' forecasts from an investment company specializing in large stocks with the S&P 500 as a benchmark portfolio. Their database includes a set of 37 monthly pairs of forecasts of alpha and beta values for between 646 and 771 stocks over the period December 1992 to December 1995—23,902 forecasts in all. The investment company policy was to truncate alpha forecasts at +14% and −12% per month.[5] The histogram of these forecasts is shown in Figure 27.3. Returns of large stocks over these years were about average, as shown in the following table, including one average year (1993), one bad year (1994), and one good year (1995):

	1993	1994	1995	1926–1999 Average	SD (%)
Rate of return, %	9.87	1.29	37.71	12.50	20.39

The histogram shows that the distribution of alpha forecasts was positively skewed, with a larger number of pessimistic forecasts. The adjusted R-square in a regression of these forecasts with actual alphas was .001134, implying a tiny correlation coefficient of .0337. As it turned out, the optimistic forecasts were of superior quality to the pessimistic ones. When the regression allowed separate coefficients for positive and negative forecasts, the R-square increased to .001536, and the correlation coefficient to .0392.

---

[4]Alex Kane, Tae-Hwan Kim, and Halbert White, "Active Portfolio Management: The Power of the Treynor-Black Model," in *Progress in Financial Market Research,* ed. C. Kyrtsou (New York: Nova, 2004).

[5]These constraints on forecasts make sense because on an annual basis they imply a stock would rise by more than 380% or fall below 22% of its beginning-of-year value.

These results contain "good" and "bad" news. The "good" news is that after adjusting even the wildest forecast, say, an alpha of 12% for the next month, the value to be used by a forecaster when R-square is .001 would be .012%, just 1.2 basis points per month. On an annual basis, this would amount to .14%, which is of the order of the alpha forecasts of the example in Spreadsheet 27.1. With forecasts of this small magnitude, the problem of extreme portfolio weights would never arise. The bad news arises from the same data: the performance of the active portfolio will be no better than in our example—implying an M-square of only 19 basis points.

An investment company that delivers such limited performance will not be able to cover its cost. However, this performance is based on an active portfolio that includes only six stocks. As we show in Section 27.5, even small information ratios of individual stocks can add up (see line 11 in Table 27.1). Thus, when many forecasts of even low precision are used to form a large active portfolio, large profits can be made.

So far we have assumed that forecast errors of various stocks are independent, an assumption that may not be valid. When forecasts are correlated across stocks, precision is measured by a covariance matrix of forecasting errors, which can be estimated from past forecasts. While the necessary adjustment to the forecasts in this case is algebraically messy, it is just a technical detail. As we might guess, correlations among forecast errors will call for us to further shrink the adjusted forecasts toward zero.

Organizational Structure and Performance

The mathematical property of the optimal risky portfolio reveals a central feature of investment companies, namely, economies of scale. From the Sharpe measure of the optimized portfolio shown in Table 27.1, it is evident that performance as measured by the Sharpe ratio and M-square grows monotonically with the squared information ratio of the active portfolio (see Equation 8.22, Chapter 8, for a review), which in turn is the sum of the squared information ratios of the covered securities (see Equation 8.24). Hence, a larger force of security analysts is sure to improve performance, at least before adjustment for cost. Moreover, a larger universe will also improve the diversification of the active portfolio and mitigate the need to hold positions in the neutral passive portfolio, perhaps even allowing a profitable short position in it. Additionally, a larger universe allows for an increase in the size of the fund without the need to trade larger blocks of single securities. Finally, as we will show in some detail in Section 27.5, increasing the universe of securities creates another diversification effect, that of forecasting errors by analysts.

The increases in the universe of the active portfolio in pursuit of better performance naturally come at a cost, because security analysts of quality do not come cheap. However, the other units of the organization can handle increased activity with little increase in cost. All this suggests economies of scale for larger investment companies provided the organizational structure is efficient.

Optimizing the risky portfolio entails a number of tasks of different nature in terms of expertise and need for independence. As a result, the organizational chart of the portfolio management outfit requires a degree of decentralization and proper controls. Figure 27.4 shows an organizational chart designed to achieve these goals. The figure is largely self-explanatory and the structure is consistent with the theoretical considerations worked out in previous chapters. It can go a long way in forging sound underpinnings to the daily work of portfolio management. A few comments are in order, though.

The control units responsible for forecasting records and determining forecast adjustments will directly affect the advancement and bonuses of security analysts and estimation experts. This implies that these units must be independent and insulated from organizational pressures.

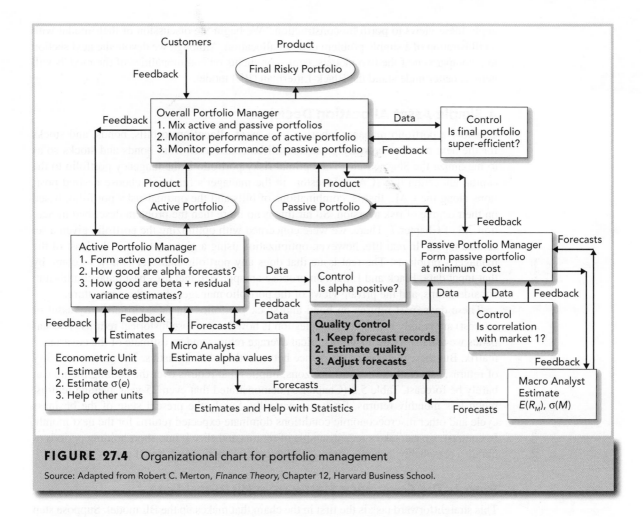

FIGURE 27.4   Organizational chart for portfolio management

Source: Adapted from Robert C. Merton, *Finance Theory*, Chapter 12, Harvard Business School.

An important issue is the conflict between independence of security analysts' opinions and the need for cooperation and coordination in the use of resources and contacts with corporate and government personnel. The relative size of the security analysis unit will further complicate the solution to this conflict. In contrast, the macro forecast unit might become *too* insulated from the security analysis unit. An effort to create an interface and channels of communications between these units is warranted.

Finally, econometric techniques that are invaluable to the organization have seen a quantum leap in sophistication in recent years, and this process seems still to be accelerating. It is critical to keep the units that deal with estimation updated and on top of the latest developments.

27.3   THE BLACK–LITTERMAN MODEL

Fischer Black, famous for both the Treynor-Black model as well as the Black-Scholes option-pricing formula, teamed up with Robert Litterman to produce another useful model that allows portfolio managers to quantify complex forecasts (which they call **views**) and apply these views to portfolio construction.[6] We begin the discussion of their model with an illustration of a simple problem of asset allocation. Although we devote the next section to a comparison of the two models, some comments on commonalities of the models will help us better understand the Black-Litterman (BL) model.

A Simple Asset Allocation Decision

Consider a portfolio manager laboring over **asset allocation** to bills, bonds, and stocks for the next month. The risky portfolio will be constructed from bonds and stocks so as to maximize the Sharpe ratio. The optimal risky portfolio is the tangency portfolio to the capital allocation line (CAL). Investors in the manager's fund will choose desired positions along the CAL, that is, combinations of bills and the optimal risky portfolio, based on their degree of risk aversion. So far this is no more than the problem described in Section 7.3 of Chapter 7. There, we were concerned with optimizing the portfolio given a set of data inputs. In real life, however, optimization using a given data set is the least of the manager's problems. The real issue that dogs any portfolio manager is how to come by that input data. Black and Litterman propose an approach that uses past data, equilibrium considerations, and the private views of the portfolio manager about the near future.

These days, past returns on bond and stock portfolios (in fact, virtually any asset of interest) are readily available. The question is how to use those historical returns. The statistics we usually focus on are historical average returns and an estimate of the covariance matrix. But there is a critical difference between these two statistics. The great variability of returns, especially over short horizons, implies that returns over the coming month can barely be forecast. Table 5.2 (Chapter 5) demonstrated that even 25-year average returns, much less monthly returns, fluctuate markedly. Surely the present state of the business cycle and other macroeconomic conditions dominate expected returns for the next month. In contrast, we can take a recent sample of returns and slice it into short holding periods to obtain a reasonably accurate forecast of the covariance matrix for next month.

Step 1: The Covariance Matrix from Historical Data

This straightforward task is the first in the chain that makes up the BL model. Suppose step 1 results in the following annualized covariance matrix, estimated from recent historical excess returns:

	Bonds (B)	Stocks (S)
Standard deviation	.08	.17
Correlation (bonds/stocks)	.3	
Covariance		
Bonds	.0064	.00408
Stocks	.00408	.0289

Notice that step 1 is common to both the BL and the Treynor-Black (TB) models. This activity appears in the organizational chart in Figure 27.4.

Step 2: Determination of a Baseline Forecast

Because past data are of such limited use in inferring expected returns for the next month, BL propose an alternative approach. They start with a **baseline forecast** derived

---

[6]Fischer Black and Robert Litterman, "Global Portfolio Optimization," *Financial Analysts Journal,* September/October 1992. Originally published by Goldman Sachs Company, © 1991.

from the assumption that the market is in equilibrium where current prices of stocks and bonds reflect all available information and, as a result, the theoretical market portfolio with weights equal to market-value proportions is efficient. Suppose that current market values of outstanding bonds and stocks imply that the weight of bonds in the baseline portfolio is $w_B = .25$, and the weight of stocks is $w_S = .75$. When we apply these portfolio weights to the covariance matrix from step 1, the variance of the baseline portfolio emerges as

$$\text{Var}(R_M) = w_B^2 \text{Var}(R_B) + w_S^2 \text{Var}(R_S) + 2w_B w_S \text{Cov}(R_B, R_S) \qquad (27.8)$$
$$= .25^2 \times .0064 + .75^2 \times .0289 + 2 \times .25 \times .75 \times .00408 = .018186$$

The CAPM equation (Equation 9.2 in Chapter 9) gives the relationship between the market portfolio risk (variance) and its risk premium (expected excess return) as

$$E(R_M) = \bar{A} \times \text{Var}(R_M) \qquad (27.9)$$

where $\bar{A}$ is the average coefficient of risk aversion. Assuming $\bar{A} = 3$ yields the equilibrium risk premium of the baseline portfolio as: $E(R_M) = 3 \times .018186 = .0546 = 5.46\%$. The equilibrium risk premiums on bonds and stocks can be inferred from their betas on the baseline portfolio:

$$E(R_B) = \frac{\text{Cov}(R_B, R_M)}{\text{Var}(R_M)} E(R_M)$$

$$\text{Cov}(R_B, R_M) = \text{Cov}(R_B, w_B R_B + w_S R_S) = .25 \times .0064 + .75 \times .00408 = .00466$$

$$E(R_B) = \frac{.00466}{.018186} \times 5.46\% = 1.40\% \qquad (27.10)$$

$$E(R_S) = \frac{.75 \times .0289 + .25 \times .00408}{.018186} \times 5.46\% = 6.81\%$$

Thus, step 2 ends up with baseline forecasts of a risk premium for bonds of 1.40% and for stocks of 6.81%.

The final element in step 2 is to determine the covariance matrix of the baseline forecasts. This is a statement about the precision of these *forecasts,* which is different from the covariance matrix of realized excess returns on the bond and stock portfolios. We are looking for the precision of the estimate of expected return, as opposed to the volatility of the actual return. A conventional rule of thumb in this application is to use a standard deviation that is 10% of the standard deviation of returns (or equivalently, a variance that is 1% of the return variance). To illustrate, imagine a special circumstance when the economic conditions foreseen for next month are identical to those that prevailed over the most recent 100 months. This implies that the average return over the recent 100 months would provide an unbiased estimate of the expected return for the next month. The variance of the average would then be 1% of the variance of the actual return. Hence in this case it would be correct to use .01 times the covariance matrix of returns for the expected return. Thus step 2 ends with a forecast and covariance matrix:

	Bonds (B)	Stocks (S)
Expected return (%)	.0140	.0681
Covariance		
Bonds	.000064	.0000408
Stocks	.0000408	.000289

Now that we have backed out market expectations, it is time to integrate the manager's private views into our analysis.

Step 3: Integrating the Manager's Private Views

The BL model allows the manager to introduce any number of views about the baseline forecasts into the optimization process. Appended to the views, the manager specifies his degree of confidence in them. Views in the BL model are expressed as values of various linear combinations of excess returns, and confidence in them as a covariance matrix of errors in these values.

EXAMPLE 27.1   Views in the Black-Litterman Model

Suppose the manager takes a contrarian's view concerning the baseline forecasts, that is, he believes that in the next month bonds will outperform stocks by .5%. The following equation expresses this view:

$$1 \times R_B + (-1) \times R_S = .5\%$$

More generally, any view that is a linear combination of the relevant excess returns can be presented as an array (in Excel, an array would be a column of numbers) that multiplies another array (column) of excess returns. In this case, the array of weights is $P = (1, -1)$ and the array of excess returns is (R_B, R_S). (We can perform the multiplication in Excel by applying the SUMPRODUCT function to the two arrays.) The value of this linear combination, denoted Q, reflects the manager's view. In this case, $Q = .5\%$, will be taken into account in optimizing the portfolio.

A view must come with a degree of confidence, that is, a standard deviation to measure the precision of Q. In other words, the manager's view is really $Q + \varepsilon$, where ε represents zero-mean "noise" surrounding the view with a standard deviation that reflects the manager's confidence. Noticing that the variance of the difference between the expected rates on stocks and bonds is 2.7% (calculated below in Equation 27.13), suppose that the manager assigns a value of $\sigma(\varepsilon) = 1.73\%$. To summarize, if we denote the array of returns by $R = (R_B, R_S)$, then the manager's view, P, applied to these returns is

$$PR' = Q + \varepsilon$$
$$P = (1, -1)$$
$$R = (R_B, R_S) \tag{27.11}$$
$$Q = .5\% = .005$$
$$\sigma^2(\varepsilon) = .0173^2 = .0003$$

Step 4: Revised (Posterior) Expectations

The baseline forecasts of expected returns derived from market values and their covariance matrix comprise the prior distribution of the rates of return on bonds and stocks. The manager's view, together with its confidence measure, provides the probability distribution arising from the "experiment," that is, the additional information that must be optimally integrated with the prior distribution. The result is a new set of expected returns, conditioned on the manager's views.

To acquire intuition about the solution, consider what the baseline expected returns imply about the view. The expectations derived from market data were that the expected return on bonds is 1.40% and on stocks 6.81%. Therefore, the baseline view is that $R_B - R_S = -5.41\%$. In contrast, the manager thinks this difference is $Q = R_B - R_S = .5\%$. Using the BL linear-equation notation for market expectations:

$$
\begin{aligned}
Q^E &= PR_E' \\
P &= (1, -1) \\
R_E &= [E(R_B), E(R_S)] = (1.40\%, 6.81\%) \\
Q^E &= 1.40 - 6.81 = -5.41\%
\end{aligned}
\tag{27.12}
$$

Thus, the baseline "view" is -5.41% (i.e., stocks will outperform bonds), which is vastly different from the manager's view. The difference, D, is

$$
\begin{aligned}
D &= Q - Q^E = .005 - (-.0541) = .0591 \\
\sigma^2(D) &= \sigma^2(\varepsilon) + \sigma^2(Q^E) = .0003 + \sigma^2(Q^E) \\
\sigma^2(Q^E) &= \mathrm{Var}[E(R_B) - E(R_S)] = \sigma_{E(R_B)}^2 + \sigma_{E(R_S)}^2 - 2\mathrm{Cov}[E(R_B), E(R_S)] \tag{27.13} \\
&= .000064 + .000289 - 2 \times .0000408 = .0002714 \\
\sigma^2(D) &= .0003 + .0002714 = .0005714
\end{aligned}
$$

Given the large difference between the manager's and the baseline expectations, we expect a significant change in the conditional expectations from those of the baseline and, as result, a very different optimal portfolio.

The change in expected returns is a function of four elements: the baseline expectations, $E(R)$; the difference, D, between the manager's view and the baseline view (see Equation 27.13); the variance of $E(R)$; and the variance of D. Using the BL updating formulas given the baseline and manager's views and their precision, we get

$$
\begin{aligned}
E(R_B \mid P) &= E(R_B) + \frac{D\{\sigma_{E(R_B)}^2 - \mathrm{Cov}[E(R_B), E(R_S)]\}}{\sigma_D^2} \\
&= .0140 + \frac{.0591(.000064 - .0000408)}{.0005714} = .0140 + .0024 = .0164 \\
E(R_S \mid P) &= E(R_S) + \frac{D\{\mathrm{Cov}[E(R_B), E(R_S)] - \sigma_{E(R_S)}^2\}}{\sigma_D^2} \tag{27.14} \\
&= .0681 + \frac{.0591(.0000408 - .000289)}{.0005714} = .0681 - .0257 = .0424
\end{aligned}
$$

We see that the manager increases his expected returns on bonds by .24% to 1.64%, and reduces his expected return on stocks by 2.57% to 4.24%. The difference between the expected returns on stocks and bonds is reduced from 5.41% to 2.60%. While this is a very large change, we also realize that the manager's private view that $Q = .5\%$ has been greatly tempered by the prior distribution to a value roughly halfway between his private view and the baseline view. In general, the degree of compromise between views will depend on the precision assigned to them.

The example we have described contains only two assets and one view. It can easily be generalized to any number of assets with any number of views about future returns. The views can be more complex than a simple difference between a pair of returns. Views can

	A	B	C	D	E	F	G	H	I
1									
2									
3									
4	Table 1: Bordered Covariance Matrix Based on Historical Excess Returns								
5	and Market-Value Weights and Calculation of Baseline Forecasts								
6									
7			Bonds	Stocks					
8		Weights	0.25	0.75					
9	Bonds	0.25	0.006400	0.004080					
10	Stocks	0.75	0.004080	0.028900					
11		sumproduct	0.001165	0.017021					
12	Market portfolio variance V(M) = sum(c11:d11) =					0.018186			
13	Coefficient of risk aversion of representative investor =					3			
14	Baseline market portfolio risk premium = A × V(M) =					0.0546			
15	Covariance with R$_M$		0.00466	0.022695					
16	Baseline risk premiums		0.01	0.07					
17									
18	Proportion of covariance attributed to expected returns:					0.01			
19	Covariance matrix of expected returns								
20			Bonds	Stocks					
21		Bonds	0.000064	0.0000408					
22		Stocks	0.0000408	0.000289					
23									
24	Table 2: Views, Confidence and Revised (Posterior) Expectations								
25									
26	View: Difference between returns on bonds and stocks, Q =					0.0050			
27	View embedded in baseline forecasts Q^E =					−0.0541			
28	Variance of Q^E = Var(R$_B$ − R$_S$)					0.000271			
29	Var[E(R$_B$)] − Cov[E(R$_B$),E(R$_S$)] =					0.000023			
30	Cov[E(R$_B$),E(R$_S$)] − Var[E(R$_B$)] =					−0.000248			
31	Difference between view and baseline data, D =					0.0591			
32	Confidence measured by standard deviation of view Q								
33	Possible SD	0	0.0100	0.0173	0.0300	0.0600			
34	Variance	0	0.0015	0.0003	0.0009	0.0036	Baseline		
35	E(R$_B$|P)	0.0190	0.0148	0.0164	0.0152	0.0143	0.0140		
36	E(R$_S$|P)	0.0140	0.0598	0.0424	0.0556	0.0643	0.0681		

SPREADSHEET 27.2

e X cel

Please visit us at
www.mhhe.com/bkm

Sensitivity of the Black-Litterman portfolio to confidence in views

assign a value to *any* linear combination of the assets in the universe, and the confidence level (the covariance matrix of the set of ε values of the views) can allow for dependence across views. This flexibility gives the model great potential by quantifying a rich set of information that is unique to a portfolio manager. The appendix to the chapter presents the general BL model.

Step 5: Portfolio Optimization

At this point, the portfolio optimization follows the Markowitz procedure of Chapter 7, with an input list that replaces baseline expectations with the conditional expectations arising from the manager's view.

Spreadsheet 27.2 presents the calculations of the BL model. Table 1 of the spreadsheet shows the calculation of the benchmark forecasts and Table 2 incorporates a view to arrive at the revised (conditional) expectations. We show these for various degrees of confidence in the view. Figure 27.5 shows properties of the optimal portfolio for the various levels of confidence on the assumption that the view is correct. Figure 27.6 conducts the same sensitivity analysis when the view is wrong. Figures 27.5 and 27.6 illustrate the important role that confidence plays in the performance of the BL portfolio. In the next section we discuss the implication of these results.

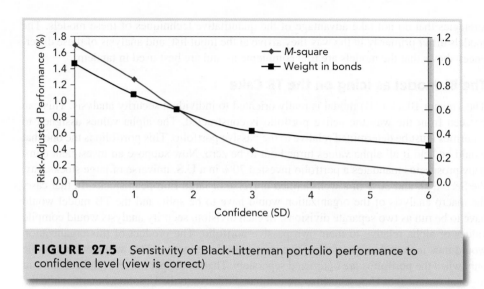

FIGURE 27.5 Sensitivity of Black-Litterman portfolio performance to confidence level (view is correct)

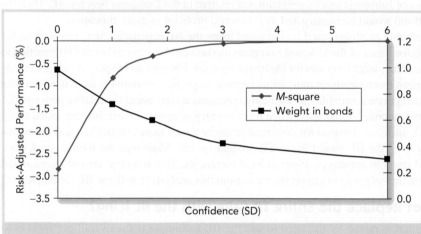

FIGURE 27.6 Sensitivity of Black-Litterman portfolio performance to confidence level (view is false)

27.4 TREYNOR–BLACK VERSUS BLACK–LITTERMAN: COMPLEMENTS, NOT SUBSTITUTES

Treynor, Black, and Litterman have earned a place among the important innovators of the investments industry. Wide implementation of their models could contribute much to the industry. The comparative analysis of their models presented here is not aimed at elevating one at the expense of the other—in any case, we find them complementary—but rather to clarify the relative merits of each.

First and foremost, once you reach the optimization stage, the models are identical. Put differently, if users of either model arrive at identical input lists, they will choose identical portfolios and realize identical performance measures. In Section 27.6, we show that these levels of performance should be far superior to passive strategies, as well as to active strategies that do not take advantage of the quantitative techniques of these models. The models differ primarily in the way they arrive at the input list, and analysis of these differences shows that the models are true complements and are best used in tandem.

The BL Model as Icing on the TB Cake

The Treynor-Black (TB) model is really oriented to individual security analysis. This can be seen from the way the active portfolio is constructed. The alpha values assigned to securities must be determined relative to the passive portfolio. This portfolio is the one that would be held if all alpha values turned out to be zero. Now suppose an investment company prospectus mandates a portfolio invested 70% in a U.S. universe of large stocks, say, the S&P 500, and 30% in a well-defined universe of large European stocks. In that case, the macro analysis of the organization would have to be split, and the TB model would have to be run as two separate divisions. In each division, security analysts would compile values of alpha relative to their own passive portfolio. The product of this organization would thus include four portfolios, two passive and two active. This scheme is workable only when the portfolios are optimized separately. That is, the parameters (alpha, beta, and residual variance) of U.S. securities are estimated relative to the U.S. benchmark, while the parameters of European stocks are estimated relative to the European benchmark. Then the final portfolio would be constructed as a standard problem in asset allocation.

The resulting portfolio could be improved using the BL approach. First, views about the relative performance of the U.S. and European markets can be expected to add information to the independent macro forecasts for the two economies. For reasons of specialization, the U.S. and European macro analysts must focus on their respective economies; there is no way for them to incorporate a variable that explicitly represents a view about the relative performance of the two economies. Obviously, when more country or regional portfolios are added to the company's universe, the need for decentralization becomes more compelling, and the potential of applying the BL model to the TB product greater. Moreover, the foreign-stock portfolios will result in various positions in local currencies. This is a clear area of international finance and the only way to import forecasts from this analysis is with the BL technique.[7]

Why Not Replace the Entire TB Cake with the BL Icing?

This question is raised by the need to use the BL technique if the overall portfolio is to include forecasts from comparative economic and international finance analyses. It is indeed possible to use the BL model for the entire process of constructing the efficient portfolio. The reason is that the alpha compiled for the TB model can be replaced with BL views. To take a simple example, suppose only one security makes up the active portfolio. With the TB model, we have macro forecasts, $E(R_M)$ and σ_M, as well as alpha, beta, and residual variance for the active portfolio. This input list also can be represented in the following form, along the lines of the BL framework:

$$R = [E(R_M), E(R_A) = \beta_A E(R_M)]$$

$$P = \left(0, 1 + \frac{\alpha_A}{\beta_A E(R_M)}\right)$$

$$PR' = Q + \varepsilon = \alpha_A + \varepsilon$$

$$Q^E = 0$$

$$D = \alpha_A$$

$$\sigma^2(\varepsilon) = \text{Var(forecasting error) in Equation 27.6}$$

$$\sigma^2(D) = \sigma^2(\varepsilon) + \sigma^2(e)$$

(27.15)

[7]The BL model can also be used to introduce views about relative performance of various U.S and foreign corporations.

where e is the residual in the SCL regression of Equation 27.5. Calculation of the conditional expectations from Equation 27.15 as in Equation 27.13 will bring us to the same adjusted alpha as in Equation 27.7 of the TB model.

In this light, the BL model can be viewed as a generalization of the TB model. The BL model allows you to adjust expected return from views about alpha values as in the TB model, but it also allows you to express views about *relative* performance that cannot be incorporated in the TB model.

However, this conclusion might produce a false impression that is consequential to investment management. To understand the point, we first discuss the degree of confidence, which is essential to fully represent a view in the BL model. Spreadsheet 27.2 and Figures 27.5 and 27.6 illustrate that the optimal portfolio weights and performance are highly sensitive to the degree of confidence in the BL views. Thus, the validity of the model rests in large part on the way the confidence about views is arrived at.

When a BL view is structured to replace a direct alpha estimate in a TB framework, we must use the variance of the forecasting error taken from Equation 27.7 and applied to Equation 27.15. This is how "confidence" is quantified in the BL model. Whereas in the TB framework one can measure forecast accuracy by computing the correlation between analysts' alpha forecasts and subsequent realizations, such a procedure is not as easily applied to BL views about relative performance. Managers' views may be expressed about different quantities in different time periods, and, therefore, we will not have long forecast histories on a particular variable with which to assess accuracy. To our knowledge, no promotion of any kind of how to quantify "confidence" appears in academic or industry publications about the BL model.

This raises the issue of adjusting forecasts in the TB model. We have never seen evidence that analysts' track records are systematically compiled and used to adjust alpha forecasts, although we cannot assert that such effort is nowhere expended. However, indirect evidence confirms the impression that alphas are usually not adjusted, specifically, the common "complaint" that the TB model is not applied in the field because it results in "wild" portfolio weights. Yet, as we saw in Section 27.3, those wild portfolio weights are a consequence of failing to adjust alpha values to reflect forecast precision. Any realistic R-square that can be obtained even by excellent forecasters will result in moderate portfolio weights. Even when "wild" weights do occasionally materialize, they can be "tamed" by a straightforward restriction on benchmark risk.

It is therefore useful to keep the two models separate and distinct; the TB model for the management of security analysis with proper adjustment of forecasts and the BL model for asset allocation where views about relative performance are useful *despite* the fact that the degree of confidence must in practice be inaccurately estimated.

27.5   THE VALUE OF ACTIVE MANAGEMENT

We showed in Chapter 24 that the value of successful market timing is enormous. Even a forecaster with far-from-perfect predictive power would contribute significant value. Nevertheless, active portfolio management based on security analysis has even far greater potential. Even if each individual security analyst has only modest forecasting power, the power of a *portfolio* of analysts is potentially unbounded.

A Model for the Estimation of Potential Fees

The value of market timing was derived from the value of an equivalent number of call options that mimic the return to the timer's portfolio. Thus, we were able to derive an unambiguous market value to timing ability, that is, we could price the implicit call in the timer's services. We cannot get quite that far with valuation of active portfolio management, but we can do the next best thing, namely, we can calculate what a representative investor would pay for such services.

Kane, Marcus, and Trippi[8] derive an annuitized value of portfolio performance measured as a percent of funds under management. The percentage fee, f, that investors would be willing to pay for active services can be related to the difference between the square of the portfolio Sharpe ratio and that of the passive portfolio as

$$f = (S_P^2 - S_M^2)/2A \tag{27.16}$$

where A is the coefficient of the investor's risk aversion.

The source of the power of the active portfolio is the additive value of the squared **information ratios** (information ratio $= \dfrac{\alpha_i}{\sigma(e_i)}$) and precision of individual analysts. Recall the expression for the square of the Sharpe ratio of the optimized risky portfolio:

$$S_P^2 = S_M^2 + \sum_{i=1}^{n} \left[\frac{\alpha_i}{\sigma(e_i)}\right]^2$$

Therefore,

$$f = \frac{1}{2A} \sum_{i=1}^{n} \left[\frac{\alpha_i}{\sigma(e_i)}\right]^2 \tag{27.17}$$

Thus, the fee that can be charged, f, depends on three factors: (1) the coefficient of risk aversion, (2) the distribution of the squared information ratio in the universe of securities, and (3) the precision of the security analysts. Notice that this fee is in excess of what an index fund would charge. If an index fund charges about 30 basis points, the active manager could charge incremental fees above that level by the percentage given in Equation 27.17.

Results from the Distribution of Actual Information Ratios

Kane, Marcus, and Trippi investigated the distribution of the squared IR for all S&P 500 stocks over two 5-year periods and estimated that this (annualized) expectation, $E(\text{IR}^2)$, is in the range of .845 to 1.122. With a coefficient of risk aversion of 3, a portfolio manager who covers 100 stocks with security analysts whose R-square of forecasts with realized alpha is only .001 would still be able to charge an annual fee that is 4.88% higher than that of an index fund. This fee is based on the lower end of the range of the expected squared information ratio.

One limitation of this study is that it assumes that the portfolio manager knows the quality of the forecasts, however low they may be. As we have seen, portfolio weights are sensitive to forecast quality, and when that quality is estimated with error, performance will be further reduced.

Results from Distribution of Actual Forecasts

A study of actual forecasts by Kane, Kim, and White (see footnote 4) found the distribution of over 11,000 alpha forecasts for over 600 stocks over 37 months presented in Figure 27.3. The average forecast precision from this database of forecasts provided an R-square of .00108 using ordinary least squares (OLS) regressions and .00151 when allowing separate coefficients for positive and negative forecasts. These are only marginally better

---

[8]Alex Kane, Alan Marcus, and Robert R. Trippi, "The Valuation of Security Analysis," *Journal of Portfolio Management* 25 (Spring 1999).

Forecast Adjustment	Diagonal Model	Covariance Model	**TABLE 27.6**
Line*	2.67	3.01	*M*-square for the portfolio, actual forecasts
Kinked**	4.25	6.31	

*Same coefficients for positive and negative forecasts.
**Different coefficients for positive and negative forecasts.

than the precision used to interpret the Kane, Marcus, and Trippi study of the distribution of realized information value. Kane, Kim, and White use these *R*-squares to adjust the forecasts in their database and form optimal portfolios from 105 stocks selected randomly from the 646 covered by the investment company.

Kane, Kim, and White assume that forecast quality is the same each month for all alpha forecasts for the 105 stocks, but act as though they do not know that quality. Thus, the adjustment process is performed each month by using past forecasts. This introduces another source of estimation error that compounds the difficulty of low forecast quality. To dull the impact of this real-life difficulty, the estimation of forecast quality adopts improved econometric technique. They find that least absolute deviation (LAD) regressions perform uniformly better than OLS regressions. The optimization model used both the diagonal index model (as in TB) as well as the full-covariance model (the Markowitz algorithm).

The annualized *M*-square measures of performance are shown in Table 27.6. The *M*-square values, which range from 2.67% to 6.31%, are quite impressive. The results in Table 27.6 also show that using the residual covariance matrix can significantly improve performance when many stocks are covered, contrary to the small difference when only six stocks are covered, as in Spreadsheet 8.1 of Chapter 8.

Results with Reasonable Forecasting Records

To investigate the role of the forecasting record in performance with low-quality forecasts, Kane, Kim, and White simulate a market with the S&P 500 index portfolio as benchmark and 500 stocks with the same characteristics as the S&P 500 universe.[9] Various sizes of active portfolios are constructed by selecting stocks randomly from this universe with available forecasting records of only 36 to 60 months. To avoid estimation techniques that may not be available to portfolio managers, all estimates in this study are obtained from OLS regressions.

The portfolio manager in the simulation must deploy a full-blown "organizational structure" to capture performance under realistic conditions. At any point, the manager uses only past returns and past forecast records to produce forward-looking estimates which include (1) the benchmark risk premium and standard deviation, (2) beta coefficients for the stocks in the active portfolio, and (3) the forecasting quality of each security analyst. At this point, the manager receives a set of alpha forecasts from the security analysts and proceeds to construct the optimal portfolio. The portfolio is optimized on the basis of macro forecasts for the benchmark portfolio, and alpha forecasts adjusted for quality using the past record of performance for each analyst. Finally, the next month returns are simulated and the performance of the portfolio is recorded.

Table 27.7 summarizes the results for portfolios when, unbeknownst to the portfolio manager, security-analyst forecasts are generated with an *R*-square of .001. *M*-square

[9]Alex Kane, Tae-Hwan Kim, and Halbert White, "Forecast Precision and Portfolio Performance," UCSD working paper, University of California–San Diego, April 2006.

TABLE 27.7

M-square of simulated portfolios

Stocks in Portfolio	Forecast Record (months)		
	36	**48**	**60**
100	0.96	3.12	6.36
300	0.60	5.88	12.72
500	3.00	5.88	15.12

clearly increases when performance records are longer. The results also show that, in general, performance improves with the size of the portfolio.

The results of all three studies show that even the smallest forecast ability can result in greatly improved performance. Moreover, with better estimation techniques, performance can be further enhanced. We believe that one reason the proposed procedures are not widely used in the industry is that security analysts believe that low individual correlations imply low aggregate forecasting value and thus wish to avoid the estimation of their abilities. We hope that results of studies of the type discussed here will lure investment companies to adopt these techniques and move the industry to new levels of performance.

27.6   CONCLUDING REMARKS ON ACTIVE MANAGEMENT

A common concern of students of investments, who encounter a heavy dose of theory laced with math and statistics, is whether the analytical approach is necessary or even useful. Here are some observations that should allay any such concern. Investment theory has developed in recent decades at a galloping pace. Yet, perhaps surprisingly, the distance between the basic science of investments and industry practice, one that exists in any field, has actually narrowed in recent years. This satisfying trend is due at least in part to the vigorous growth of the CFA Institute. The CFA designation has become nearly a prerequisite to success in the industry, and the number of individuals seeking it already exceeds that of finance-major MBAs. They continuously contribute to the proximity between investments science and the industry.

Even more important is the zeal of the Institute in advancing and enriching the curriculum of the CFA degree and taking it ever closer to contemporary investment theory. Indeed, finance professors indirectly benefit from this curriculum, because they can argue the practicality of the text material by pointing out that it is part of the body of knowledge required of CFA candidates.

Yet there is one area in which practice still lags far behind theory, and that is the subject of this chapter—this despite the fact that TB and BL models have been around since 1973 and 1992, respectively. Yet, as we have seen, these models have to date failed to materially penetrate the industry. We speculated on the reason for this failure in the previous section. We hope, however, that we will be forced to discard this paragraph from future editions due to obsolescence.

Finally, there is little time in the already dense investments curriculum to discuss the welfare implication of nearly efficient security prices. Prices can reach such levels only when investors optimize portfolios with high-quality analysis and implementation. The value of nearly efficient prices to the welfare of the economy is enormous, competing in importance with advances in technology. High-quality active management therefore can contribute to society even as it enriches its practitioners.

1. Treynor-Black portfolio weights are sensitive to large alpha values, which can result in practically infeasible long/short portfolio positions.

2. Benchmark portfolio risk, the variance of the return difference between the portfolio and the benchmark, can be constrained to keep the TB portfolio within reasonable weights.

3. Alpha forecasts must be shrunk (adjusted toward zero) to account for less-than-perfect forecasting quality. Compiling past analyst forecasts and subsequent realizations allows one to estimate the correlation between realizations and forecasts. Regression analysis can be used to measure the forecast quality and guide the proper adjustment of future forecasts. When alpha forecasts are scaled back to account for forecast imprecision, the resulting portfolio positions become far more moderate.

4. The Black-Litterman model allows the private views of the portfolio manager to be incorporated with market data in the optimization procedure.

5. The Treynor-Black and Black-Litterman models are complementary tools. Both should be used: the TB model is more geared toward security analysis while the BL model more naturally fits asset allocation problems.

6. Even low-quality forecasts are valuable. Imperceptible R-squares of only .001 in regressions of realizations on analysts' forecasts can be used to substantially improve portfolio performance.

SUMMARY

Related Web sites for this chapter are available at www.mhhe.com/bkm

KEY TERMS

passive portfolio	prior distribution	asset allocation
active portfolio	posterior distribution	baseline forecasts
alpha values	forecasting records	information ratio
benchmark portfolio	adjusted alphas	
tracking error	views	

PROBLEM SETS

Quiz

Problems

eXcel

Please visit us at www.mhhe.com/bkm

Challenge Problem

1. How would the application of the BL model to a stock and bond portfolio (as the example in the text) affect security analysis? What does this suggest about the hierarchy of use of the BL and TB models?

2. Figure 27.4 includes a box for the econometrics unit. Item (3) is to "help other units." What sorts of specific tasks might this entail?

3. Make up new alpha forecasts and replace those in Spreadsheet 27.1 in Section 27.2. Find the optimal portfolio and its expected performance.

4. Make up a view and replace the one in Spreadsheet 27.2 in Section 27.3. Recalculate the optimal asset allocation and portfolio expected performance.

5. Suppose that sending an analyst to an executive education program will raise the precision of the analyst's forecasts as measured by R-square by .01. How might you put a dollar value on this improvement? Provide a numerical example.

E-Investments

Tracking Errors

Visit **www.jpmorganfunds.com/pdfs/other/Tracking_Error.pdf** for a discusssion about the measurement of tracking error. What factors are mentioned as possible causes of high tracking error? What is the relationship between high tracking error and a manager's generation of high positive alphas? How can the tracking error measurement and the Sharpe ratio be used to assess a manager's performance?

APPENDIX A: Forecasts and Realizations of Alpha

A linear representation of the process that generates forecasts from the (yet unknown) future values of alpha would be

$$\alpha^f(t) = b_0 + b_1 u(t) + \eta(t) \tag{27A.1}$$

where $\eta(t)$ is the forecasting error and is uncorrelated with the actual $u(t)$. Notice that when the forecast is optimized as in Equation 27.7, the error of the adjusted forecast, $\varepsilon(t)$ in Equation 27.6, is uncorrelated with the optimally adjusted forecast $\alpha(T)$. The coefficients b_0 and b_1 are shift and scale biases in the forecast. Unbiased forecasts would result in $b_0 = 0$ (no shift) and $b_1 = 1$ (no scale bias).

We can derive both the variance of the forecast and the covariance between the forecast and realization from Equation 27A.1:

$$\sigma^2(\alpha^f) = b_1^2 \times \sigma^2(u) + \sigma^2(\eta)$$
$$\text{Cov}(\alpha^f, u) = b_1 \times \sigma^2(u) \tag{27A.2}$$

Therefore the slope coefficient, a_1, in Equation 27.6 is

$$a_1 = \frac{\text{Cov}(u, \alpha^f)}{\sigma^2(\alpha^f)} = \frac{b_1 \times \sigma^2(u)}{b_1^2 \times \sigma^2(u) + \sigma^2(\eta)} \tag{27A.3}$$

When the forecast has no scale bias, that is, when $b_1 = 1$, a_1 equals the R-square of the regression of forecasts on realizations in Equation 27A.1, which also equals the R-square of the regression of realizations on forecasts in Equation 27.6. When b_1 is different from 1.0, we must adjust the coefficient a_1 to account for the scale bias. Notice also that with this adjustment, $a_0 = -b_0$.

APPENDIX B: The General Black-Litterman Model

The BL model is easiest to write using matrix notation. We describe the model according to the steps in Section 27.3.

STEPS 1 and 2: The Covariance Matrix and Baseline Forecasts

A sample of past excess returns of the universe of n assets is used to estimate the $n \times n$ covariance matrix, denoted by Σ. It is assumed that the excess returns are normally distributed.

Market values of the universe assets are obtained and used to compute the $1 \times n$ vector of weights, w_M, in the baseline equilibrium portfolio. The variance of the baseline portfolio is calculated from

$$\sigma_M^2 = w_M \Sigma w_M' \tag{27B.1}$$

A coefficient of risk aversion for the representative investor in the economy, $\bar{A}$, is applied to the CAPM equation to obtain the baseline macro forecast for the market portfolio risk premium,

$$E(R_M) = \bar{A}\sigma_M^2 \qquad \text{(27B.2)}$$

The $1 \times n$ vector of baseline forecasts for the universe securities risk premiums, R, is computed from the macro forecast and the covariance matrix by

$$E(R') = E(R_M) \Sigma\, w'_M \qquad \text{(27B.3)}$$

The data so far describe the prior (baseline) distribution of the rates of return of the asset universe by

$$\tilde{R} \sim N(E(R), \Sigma) \qquad \text{(27B.4)}$$

The $n \times n$ covariance matrix of the baseline *expected* returns, $\tau\Sigma$ is assumed proportional to the covariance matrix, Σ, by the scalar τ.

STEP 3: The Manager's Private Views

The $k \times n$ matrix of views, P, includes k views. The ith view is a $1 \times k$ vector that multiplies the $1 \times n$ vector of returns, $\tilde{R}$, to obtain the value of the view, Q_i, with forecasting error ε_i. The entire vector of view values and their forecasting errors is given by

$$RP = Q + \varepsilon \qquad \text{(27B.5)}$$

The confidence of the manager in the views is given by the $k \times k$ covariance matrix, Ω, of the vector of errors in views, ε. The views embedded in the baseline forecast, R, are given by Q^E,

$$RP = Q^E$$

Thus, the $1 \times k$ vector of deviation of the view from the baseline view (forecasts) and its covariance matrix S_D is

$$D = Q^E - Q \qquad \text{(27B.6)}$$
$$S_D = \tau P \Sigma P' + \Omega$$

STEP 4: Revised (Posterior) Expectations

The $1 \times n$ vector of posterior (revised) expectations conditional on the views is given by

$$R^* = R \mid P = R + \tau D S_D^{-1} \Sigma P' \qquad \text{(27B.7)}$$

STEP 5: Portfolio Optimization

The vector of revised expectations is used in conjunction with the covariance matrix of excess returns to produce the optimal portfolio weights with the Markowitz algorithm.

INVESTMENT POLICY
AND THE FRAMEWORK
OF THE CFA INSTITUTE

TRANSLATING THE ASPIRATIONS and circumstances of diverse households into appropriate investment decisions is a daunting task. The task is equally difficult for institutions, most of which have many stakeholders and often are regulated by various authorities. The investment process is not easily reduced to a simple or mechanical algorithm.

While many principles of investments are quite general and apply to virtually all investors, some issues are peculiar to the specific investor. For example, tax bracket, age, risk tolerance, wealth, job prospects, and uncertainties make each investor's circumstances somewhat unique. In this chapter we focus on the process by which investors systematically review their particular objectives, constraints, and circumstances. Along the way, we survey some of the major classes of institutional investors and examine the special issues they must confront.

Of course, there is no unique "correct" investment process. However, some approaches are better than others, and it can be helpful to take one high-quality approach as a useful case study. For this reason, we will examine the systematic approach suggested by the CFA Institute. Among other things,

the Institute administers examinations to certify investment professionals as Chartered Financial Analysts. Therefore, the approach we outline is also one that a highly respected professional group endorses through the curriculum that it requires investment practitioners to master.

The basic framework involves dividing the investment process into four stages: specifying objectives, specifying constraints, formulating policy, and later monitoring and updating the portfolio as needed. We will treat each of these activities in turn. We start with a description of the major types of investors, both individual and institutional, as well as their special objectives. We turn next to the constraints or circumstances peculiar to each investor class, and we consider some of the investment policies that each can choose.

We will examine how the special circumstances of both individuals as well as institutions such as pension funds affect investment decisions. We also will see how the tax system can impart a substantial effect on investment decisions. In an Appendix, we present a spreadsheet model of the lifetime savings/investment decision that you can adapt to a wide variety of special circumstances as well as tax regimes.

28.1 THE INVESTMENT MANAGEMENT PROCESS

The CFA Institute divides the process of investment management into three main elements that constitute a dynamic feedback loop: planning, execution, and feedback. Figure 28.1 and Table 28.1 describe the steps in that process. As shorthand, you might think of *planning* as focused largely on establishing all the inputs necessary for decision making. These include data about the client as well as the capital market, resulting in very broad policy guidelines (the strategic asset allocation). *Execution* fleshes out the details of optimal asset allocation and security selection. Finally, *feedback* is the process of adapting to changes in expectations and objectives as well as to changes in portfolio composition that result from changes in market prices.

The result of this analysis can be summarized in an Investment Policy Statement addressing the topics specified in Table 28.2. In the next sections we elaborate on the steps leading to such an Investment Policy Statement. We start with the planning phase, panel A of Table 28.1.

Objectives

Table 28.1 indicates that the management planning process starts off by analyzing one's investment clients—in particular, by considering the objectives and constraints that govern their decisions. Portfolio objectives center on the **risk–return trade-off** between the expected return the investors want (*return requirements* in the first column of Table 28.3) and how much risk they are willing to assume (*risk tolerance*). Investment managers must know the level of risk that can be tolerated in the pursuit of a higher expected rate of return.

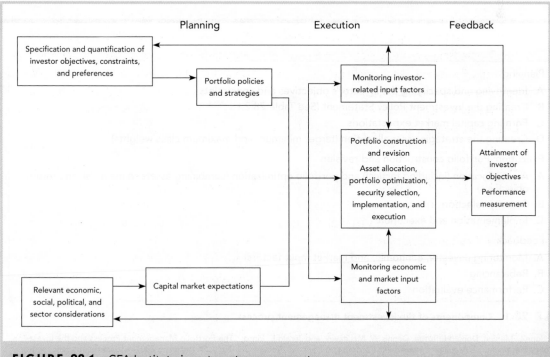

FIGURE 28.1 CFA Institute investment management process

RISK TOLERANCE QUESTIONNAIRE

Here is an example of a short quiz which may be used by financial institutions to help estimate risk tolerance.

Question	1 Point	2 Points	3 Points	4 Points
1. I plan on using the money I am investing:	Within 6 months.	Within the next 3 years.	Between 3 and 6 years.	No sooner than 7 years from now.
2. My investments make up this share of assets (excluding home):	More than 75%.	50% or more but less than 75%.	25% or more but less than 50%.	Less than 25%.
3. I expect my future income to:	Decrease.	Remain the same or grow slowly.	Grow faster than the rate of *inflation*.	Grow quickly.
4. I have emergency savings:	No.	—	Yes, but less than I'd like to have.	Yes.
5. I would risk this share in exchange for the same probability of doubling my money:	Zero.	10%.	25%.	50%.
6. I have invested in stocks and stock mutual funds:	—	Yes, but I was uneasy about it.	No, but I look forward to it.	Yes, and I was comfortable with it.
7. My most important investment goal is to:	Preserve my original investment.	Receive some growth and provide income.	Grow faster than inflation but still provide some income.	Grow as fast as possible. Income is not important today.

Add the number of points for all seven questions. Add one point if you choose the first answer, two if you choose the second answer, and so on. If you score between 25 and 28 points, consider yourself an *aggressive investor*. If you score between 20 and 24 points, your risk tolerance is above average. If you score between 15 and 19 points, consider yourself a *moderate*

investor. This means you are willing to accept some risk in exchange for a potential higher rate of return. If you score fewer than 15 points, consider yourself a *conservative investor*. If you have fewer than 10 points, you may consider yourself a very conservative investor.

Source: Securities Industry and Financial Markets Association.

I. Planning

   A. Identifying and specifying the investor's objectives and constraints

   B. Creating the Investment Policy Statement (See Table 28.2.)

   C. Forming capital market expectations

   D. Creating the strategic asset allocation (target minimum and maximum class weights)

II. Execution: Portfolio construction and revision

   A. Asset allocation (including tactical) and portfolio optimization (combining assets to meet risk and return objectives)

   B. Security selection

   C. Implementation and execution

III. Feedback

   A. Monitoring (investor, economic, and market input factors)

   B. Rebalancing

   C. Performance evaluation

TABLE 28.1 Components of the investment management process

Source: John L. Maginn, Donald L. Tuttle, Dennis W. McLeavey, and Jerald E. Pinto, "The Portfolio Management Process and the Investment Policy Statement," in *Managing Investment Portfolios: A Dynamic Process*, 3rd ed. (CFA Institute, 2007) and correspondence with Tom Robinson, head of educational content.

1. Brief client description
2. Purpose of establishing policies and guidelines
3. Duties and investment responsibilities of parties involved
4. Statement of investment goals, objectives, and constraints
5. Schedule for review of investment performance and the IPS
6. Performance measures and benchmarks
7. Any considerations in developing strategic asset allocation
8. Investment strategies and investment styles
9. Guidelines for rebalancing

TABLE 28.2

Components of the investment policy statement

Objectives	Constraints	Policies
Return requirements	Liquidity	Asset allocation
Risk tolerance	Horizon	Diversification
	Regulations	Risk positioning
	Taxes	Tax positioning
	Unique needs	Income generation

TABLE 28.3

Determination of portfolio policies

The nearby box is an illustration of a questionnaire designed to assess an investor's risk tolerance. Table 28.4 lists factors governing return requirements and risk attitudes for each of the seven major investor categories we will discuss.

Individual Investors

The basic factors affecting individual investor return requirements and risk tolerance are life-cycle stage and individual preferences. A middle-aged tenured professor will have a

Type of Investor	Return Requirement	Risk Tolerance
Individual and personal trusts	Life cycle (education, children, retirement)	Life cycle (younger are more risk tolerant)
Mutual funds	Variable	Variable
Pension funds	Assumed actuarial rate	Depends on proximity of payouts
Endowment funds	Determined by current income needs and need for asset growth to maintain real value	Generally conservative
Life insurance companies	Should exceed new money rate by sufficient margin to meet expenses and profit objectives; also actuarial rates important	Conservative
Non–life insurance companies	No minimum	Conservative
Banks	Interest spread	Variable

TABLE 28.4

Matrix of objectives

different set of needs and preferences from a retired widow, for example. We will have much more to say about individual investors later in this chapter.

Personal Trusts

Personal trusts are established when an individual confers legal title to property to another person or institution (the trustee) to manage that property for one or more beneficiaries. Beneficiaries customarily are divided into **income beneficiaries,** who receive the interest and dividend income from the trust during their lifetimes, and **remaindermen,** who receive the principal of the trust when the income beneficiary dies and the trust is dissolved. The trustee is usually a bank, a savings and loan association, a lawyer, or an investment professional. Investment of a trust is subject to trust laws, as well as "prudent investor" rules that limit the types of allowable trust investment to those that a prudent person would select.

Objectives for personal trusts normally are more limited in scope than those of the individual investor. Because of their fiduciary responsibility, personal trust managers typically are more risk averse than are individual investors. Certain asset classes such as options and futures contracts, for example, and strategies such as short-selling or buying on margin are ruled out.

Mutual Funds

Mutual funds are pools of investors' money. They invest in ways specified in their prospectuses and issue shares to investors entitling them to a pro rata portion of the income generated by the funds. The objectives of a mutual fund are spelled out in its prospectus. We discussed mutual funds in detail in Chapter 4.

Pension Funds

Pension fund objectives depend on the type of pension plan. There are two basic types: **defined contribution plans** and **defined benefit plans.** Defined contribution plans are in effect tax-deferred retirement savings accounts established by the firm in trust for its employees, with the employee bearing all the risk and receiving all the return from the plan's assets.

The largest pension funds, however, are defined benefit plans. In these plans the assets serve as collateral for the liabilities that the firm sponsoring the plan owes to plan beneficiaries. The liabilities are life annuities, earned during the employee's working years, that start at the plan participant's retirement. Thus it is the sponsoring firm's shareholders who bear the risk in a defined benefit pension plan. We discuss pension plans more fully later in this chapter.

Endowment Funds

Endowment funds are organizations chartered to use their money for specific nonprofit purposes. They are financed by gifts from one or more sponsors and are typically managed by educational, cultural, and charitable organizations or by independent foundations established solely to carry out the fund's specific purposes. Generally, the investment objectives of an endowment fund are to produce a steady flow of income subject to only a moderate degree of risk. Trustees of an endowment fund, however, can specify other objectives as dictated by the circumstances of the particular endowment fund.

Life Insurance Companies

Life insurance companies generally try to invest so as to hedge their liabilities, which are defined by the policies they write. Thus there are as many objectives as there are distinct types of policies. Until the 1980s, there were for all practical purposes only two types of life insurance policies available for individuals: whole-life and term.

A **whole-life insurance policy** combines a death benefit with a kind of savings plan that provides for a gradual buildup of cash value that the policyholder can withdraw at a later point in life, usually at age 65. **Term insurance,** on the other hand, provides death benefits only, with no buildup of cash value.

The interest rate that is embedded in the schedule of cash value accumulation promised under a whole-life policy is a fixed rate, and life insurance companies try to hedge this liability by investing in long-term bonds. Often the insured individual has the right to borrow at a prespecified fixed interest rate against the cash value of the policy.

During the inflationary years of the 1970s and early 1980s, when many older whole-life policies carried contractual borrowing rates as low as 4% or 5% per year, policyholders borrowed heavily against the cash value to invest in money market mutual funds paying double-digit yields. In response to these developments the insurance industry came up with two new policy types: **variable life** and **universal life.** Under a variable life policy the insured's premium buys a fixed death benefit plus a cash value that can be invested in a variety of mutual funds from which the policyholder can choose. With a universal life policy, policyholders can increase or reduce the premium or death benefit according to their needs. Furthermore, the interest rate on the cash value component changes with market interest rates. The great advantage of variable and universal life insurance policies is that earnings on the cash value are not taxed until the money is withdrawn.

Non–Life Insurance Companies

Non–life insurance companies such as property and casualty insurers have investable funds primarily because they pay claims *after* they collect policy premiums. Typically, they are conservative in their attitude toward risk. As with life insurers, non–life insurance companies can be either stock companies or mutual companies.

Banks

The defining characteristic of banks is that most of their investments are loans to businesses and consumers and most of their liabilities are accounts of depositors. As investors, the objective of banks is to try to match the risk of assets to liabilities while earning a profitable spread between the lending and borrowing rates.

28.2   CONSTRAINTS

Both individuals and institutional investors restrict their choice of investment assets. These restrictions arise from their specific circumstances. Identifying these restrictions/ constraints will affect the choice of investment policy. Five common types of constraints are described below. Table 28.5 presents a matrix summarizing the main constraints in each category for each of the seven types of investors.

Liquidity

Liquidity is the ease (and speed) with which an asset can be sold and still fetch a fair price. It is a relationship between the time dimension (how long will it take to dispose) and the price dimension (any discount from fair market price) of an investment asset. (See the discussion of liquidity in Chapter 9.)

Type of Investor	Liquidity	Horizon	Regulations	Taxes
Individuals and personal trusts	Variable	Life cycle	None	Variable
Mutual funds	High	Variable	Few	None
Pension funds	Young, low; mature, high	Long	ERISA	None
Endowment funds	Low	Long	Few	None
Life insurance companies	Low	Long	Complex	Yes
Non–life insurance companies	High	Short	Few	Yes
Banks	High	Short	Changing	Yes

TABLE 28.5

Matrix of constraints

When an actual concrete measure of liquidity is necessary, one thinks of the discount when an immediate sale is unavoidable. Cash and money market instruments such as Treasury bills and commercial paper, where the bid–asked spread is a small fraction of 1%, are the most liquid assets, and real estate is among the least liquid. Office buildings and manufacturing structures can potentially experience a 50% liquidity discount.

Both individual and institutional investors must consider how likely they are to dispose of assets at short notice. From this likelihood, they establish the minimum level of liquid assets they want in the investment portfolio.

Investment Horizon

This is the *planned* liquidation date of the investment or substantial part of it. Examples of an individual **investment horizon** could be the time to fund a child's college education or the retirement date for a wage earner. For a university endowment, an investment horizon could relate to the time to fund a major campus construction project. Horizon needs to be considered when investors choose between assets of various maturities, such as bonds, which pay off at specified future dates.

Regulations

Only professional and institutional investors are constrained by regulations. First and foremost is the **prudent investor rule.** That is, professional investors who manage other people's money have a fiduciary responsibility to restrict investment to assets that would have been approved by a prudent investor. The law is purposefully nonspecific. Every professional investor must stand ready to defend an investment policy in a court of law, and interpretation may differ according to the standards of the times.

Also, specific regulations apply to various institutional investors. For instance, U.S. mutual funds (institutions that pool individual investor money under professional management) may not hold more than 5% of the shares of any publicly traded corporation. This regulation keeps professional investors from getting involved in the actual management of corporations.

Tax Considerations

Tax consequences are central to investment decisions. The performance of any investment strategy is measured by how much it yields after taxes. For household and institutional investors who face significant tax rates, tax sheltering and deferral of tax obligations may be pivotal in their investment strategy.

Unique Needs

Virtually every investor faces special circumstances. Imagine husband-and-wife aeronautical engineers holding high-paying jobs in the same aerospace corporation. The entire human capital of that household is tied to a single player in a rather cyclical industry. This couple would need to hedge the risk of a deterioration of the economic well-being of the aerospace industry by investing in assets that will yield more if such deterioration materializes.

Similar issues would confront an executive on Wall Street who owns an apartment near work. Because the value of the home in that part of Manhattan probably depends on the vitality of the securities industry, the individual is doubly exposed to the vagaries of the stock market. Because both job and home already depend on the fortunes of Wall Street, the purchase of a typical diversified stock portfolio would actually increase the exposure to the stock market.

These examples illustrate that the job is often the primary "investment" of an individual, and the unique risk profile that results from employment can play a big role in determining a suitable investment portfolio.

Other unique needs of individuals often center around their stage in the life cycle, as discussed below. Retirement, housing, and children's education constitute three major demands for funds, and investment policy will depend in part on the proximity of these expenditures.

Institutional investors also face unique needs. For example, pension funds will differ in their investment policy, depending on the average age of plan participants. Another example of a unique need for an institutional investor would be a university whose trustees allow the administration to use only cash income from the endowment fund. This constraint would translate into a preference for high-dividend-paying assets.

The nearby box explores some of the issues that interact with an investor's particular situation. We turn next to an examination of the specific objectives and constraints of the major investor types.

28.3 ASSET ALLOCATION

Consideration of their objectives and constraints leads investors to a set of investment policies. The policies column in Table 28.3 lists the various dimensions of portfolio management policymaking—asset allocation, diversification, risk and tax positioning, and income generation. By far the most important part of policy determination is asset allocation, that is, deciding how much of the portfolio to invest in each major asset category.

We can view the process of asset allocation as consisting of the following steps:

1. Specify asset classes to be included in the portfolio. The major classes usually considered are the following:

   a. Money market instruments (usually called *cash*).
   b. Fixed-income securities (usually called *bonds*).
   c. Stocks.
   d. Real estate.
   e. Precious metals.
   f. Other.

LOOKING TO LOWER YOUR RISK? JUST ADD MORE

If you're like a lot of investors these days, you're looking to make your portfolio "less risky."

The way to do that is by adding more risk, or at least more types of risk. That strange twist—adding more to get less—is why risk is one of the hardest elements of investing to understand.

The first rule in risk is the hardest for many investors to accept: There is no such thing as a "risk-free investment."

Avoiding one form of risk means embracing another; the safest of investments generally come with the lowest returns, while the biggest potential gainers bring larger potential losses.

The primary risks in fund investing include the following.

Market risk: This is the big one, also known as principal risk, and it's the chance that downturn chews up your money.

Purchasing power risk: Sometimes called "inflation risk," this is the "risk of avoiding risk," and it's at the opposite end of the spectrum from market risk. In a nutshell, this is the possibility that you are too conservative and your money won't grow fast enough to keep pace with inflation.

Interest-rate risk: This is a key factor in an environment of declining rates, where you face potential income declines when a bond or certificate of deposit matures and you need to reinvest the money.

Goosing returns using higher-yielding, longer-term securities creates the potential to get stuck losing ground to inflation if the rate trend changes again.

Timing risk: This is another highly individual factor, revolving around your personal time horizon. Simply put, the chance of stock mutual funds making money over the next 20 years is high; the prospects for the next 18 months are murky.

If you need money at a certain time, this risk must be factored into your asset allocation.

Liquidity risk: Another risk heightened by current tensions, it affects everything from junk bonds to foreign stocks. If world events were to alter the flow of money in credit markets or to close some foreign stock exchanges for an extended period, your holdings in those areas could be severely hurt.

Political risk: This is the prospect that government decisions will affect the value of your investments. Given the current environment, it is probably a factor in all forms of investing, whether you are looking at stocks or bonds.

Societal risk: Call this "world-event risk." It was evident when the first anthrax scares sent markets reeling briefly. Some businesses are more susceptible (airlines, for example), though virtually all types of investing have some concerns here.

Even after all of those risks, some investments face currency risk, credit risk, and more. Every type of risk deserves some consideration as you build your holdings.

Ultimately, by making sure that your portfolio addresses all types of risk—heavier on the ones you prefer and lighter on those that make you queasy—you ensure that no one type of risk can wipe you out.

That's something that a "less risky" portfolio may not be able to achieve.

Source: Abridged from Charles A. Jaffee's article of the same title, *Boston Sunday Globe*, October 21, 2001. BOSTON SUNDAY GLOBE ("GLOBE STAFF"/"CONTRIBUTING REPORTER" PRODUCED COPY ONLY) by CHARLES A. JAFFEE. Copyright 2001 by GLOBE NEWSPAPER CO (MA). Reproduced with permission of GLOBE NEWSPAPER CO (MA) in the format Textbook via Copyright Clearance Center.

Institutional investors will rarely invest in more than the first four categories, whereas individual investors may include precious metals and other more exotic types of investments in their portfolios.

2. Specify capital market expectations. This step consists of using both historical data and economic analysis to determine your expectations of future rates of return over the relevant holding period on the assets to be considered for inclusion in the portfolio.

3. Derive the efficient portfolio frontier. This step consists of finding portfolios that achieve the maximum expected return for any given degree of risk.

4. Find the optimal asset mix. This step consists of selecting the efficient portfolio that best meets your risk and return objectives while satisfying the constraints you face.

Policy Statements

Institutions such as pension plans and endowment funds are governed by boards that issue official statements of investment policy. These statements often provide information about the objectives and constraints of the investment fund. The following is an example of such a policy statement for a defined benefit pension plan.

> The plan should emphasize production of adequate levels of real return as its primary return objective, giving special attention to the inflation-related aspects of the plan. To the extent consistent with appropriate control of portfolio risk, investment action should seek to maintain or increase the surplus of plan assets relative to benefit liabilities over time. Five-year periods, updated annually, shall be employed in planning for investment decision making; the plan's actuary shall update the benefit liabilities breakdown by country every three years.
>
> The orientation of investment planning shall be long term in nature. In addition, minimal liquidity reserves shall be maintained so long as annual company funding contributions and investment income exceed annual benefit payments to retirees and the operating expenses of the plan. The plan's actuary shall update plan cash flow projections annually. Plan administration shall ensure compliance with all laws and regulations related to maintenance of the plan's tax-exempt status and with all requirements of the Employee Retirement Income Security Act (ERISA).

Taxes and Asset Allocation

Until this point we have glossed over the issue of income taxes in discussing asset allocation. Of course, to the extent that you are a tax-exempt investor such as a pension fund, or if all of your investment portfolio is in a tax-sheltered account such as an individual retirement account (IRA), then taxes are irrelevant to your portfolio decisions.

But let us say that at least some of your investment income is subject to income taxes at the highest rate under current U.S. law. You are interested in the after-tax holding-period return (HPR) on your portfolio. At first glance it might appear to be a simple matter to figure out what the after-tax HPRs on stocks, bonds, and cash are if you know what they are before taxes. However, there are several complicating factors.

The first is the fact that you can choose between tax-exempt and taxable bonds. We discussed this issue in Chapter 2 and concluded there that you will choose to invest in tax-exempt bonds (i.e., municipal bonds) if your personal tax rate is such that the after-tax rate of interest on taxable bonds is less than the interest rate on "munis."

Because we are assuming that you are in the highest tax bracket, it is fair to assume that you will prefer to invest in munis for both the short maturities (cash) and the long maturities (bonds). As a practical matter, this means that cash for you will probably be a tax-exempt money market fund.

The second complication is not quite so easy to deal with. It arises from the fact that part of your HPR is in the form of a capital gain or loss. Under the current tax system you pay income taxes on a capital gain only if you *realize* it by selling the asset during the holding period. This applies to bonds as well as stocks, and it makes the after-tax HPR a function of whether the security will actually be sold at the end of the holding period. Sophisticated investors time the realization of their sales of securities to minimize their tax burden. This often calls for selling securities that are losing money at the end of the tax year and holding on to those that are making money.

Furthermore, because cash dividends on stocks are fully taxable and capital gains taxes can be deferred by not selling stocks that appreciate in value, the after-tax HPR on stocks will depend on the dividend payout policies of the corporations that issued the stock.

These tax complications make the process of portfolio selection for a taxable investor a lot harder than for the tax-exempt investor. There is a whole branch of the money management industry that deals with ways to defer or avoid paying taxes through special investment strategies. Unfortunately, many of these strategies conflict with the principles of efficient diversification.

We will discuss these and related issues in greater detail later in this chapter.

28.4 MANAGING PORTFOLIOS OF INDIVIDUAL INVESTORS

The overriding consideration in individual investor goal-setting is one's stage in the life cycle. Most young people start their adult lives with only one asset—their earning power. In this early stage of the life cycle an individual may not have much interest in investing in stocks and bonds. The needs for liquidity and preserving safety of principal dictate a conservative policy of putting savings in a bank or a money market fund. If and when a person gets married, the purchase of life and disability insurance will be required to protect the value of human capital.

When a married couple's labor income grows to the point at which insurance and housing needs are met, the couple may start to save for any children's college education and their own retirement, especially if the government provides tax incentives for retirement savings. Retirement savings typically constitute a family's first pool of investable funds. This is money that can be invested in stocks, bonds, and real estate (other than the primary home).

Human Capital and Insurance

The first significant investment decision for most individuals concerns education, building up their human capital. The major asset most people have during their early working years is the earning power that draws on their human capital. In these circumstances, the risk of illness or injury is far greater than the risk associated with financial wealth.

The most direct way of hedging human capital risk is to purchase insurance. With the combination of your labor income and a disability insurance policy viewed as a portfolio, the rate of return on this portfolio is less risky than the labor income by itself. Life insurance is a hedge against the complete loss of income as a result of death of any of the family's income earners.

Investment in Residence

The first major economic asset many people acquire is their own house. Deciding to buy rather than rent a residence qualifies as an investment decision.

An important consideration in assessing the risk and return aspects of this investment is the value of a house as a hedge against two kinds of risk. The first kind is the risk of increases in rental rates. If you own a house, any increase in rental rates will increase the return on your investment.

The second kind of risk is that the particular house or apartment where you live may not always be available to you. By buying, you guarantee its availability.

Saving for Retirement and the Assumption of Risk

People save and invest money to provide for future consumption and leave an estate. The primary aim of lifetime savings is to allow maintenance of the customary standard of living after retirement. As Figure 28.2 suggests, your retirement consumption depends on your life expectancy at that time. Life expectancy, when one makes it to retirement at age 65, approximates 85 years, so the average retiree needs to prepare a 20-year nest egg and sufficient savings to cover unexpected health care costs. Investment income may also increase the welfare of one's heirs, favorite charity, or both.

Questionnaires suggest that attitudes shift away from risk tolerance and toward risk aversion as investors near retirement age. With age, individuals lose the potential to recover from a disastrous investment performance. When they are young, investors can respond to a loss by working harder and saving more of their income. But as retirement approaches, investors realize there will be less time to recover. Hence the shift to safe assets.

Retirement Planning Models

In recent years, investment companies and financial advisory firms have created a variety of "user-friendly" interactive tools and models for retirement planning. Although they vary in detail, the essential structure behind most of them can be explained using The American Saving Education Council's "Ballpark Estimate" worksheet (See Figure 28.3). The worksheet assumes you'll need 70% of current income, that you'll live to age 87, and you'll realize a constant real rate of return of 3% after inflation. For example, let's say Jane is a 35-year-old working woman with two children, earning $30,000 per year. Seventy percent of Jane's current annual income ($30,000) is $21,000. Jane would then subtract the income she expects to receive from Social Security ($12,000 in her case) from $21,000, equaling $9,000. This is

FINANCIAL SERVICES

"With your investments, you should enjoy a lifetime of financial security...providing you start drinking, smoking, and eating more fatty foods."

FIGURE 28.2   Long life expectancy is a double-edged sword

Source: **www.glasbergen.com.** Copyright 2000 by Randy Glasbergen. Reprinted by permission of Randy Glasbergen.

how much Jane needs to make up for each retirement year. Jane expects to retire at age 65, so (using panel 3 of the worksheet) she multiplies $9,000 × 16.4 equaling $147,600. Jane has already saved $2,000 in her 401(k) plan. She plans to retire in 30 years so (from panel 4) she multiplies $2,000 × 2.4 equaling $4,800. She subtracts that from her total, making her projected total savings needed at retirement $142,800. Jane then multiplies $142,800 × .020 = $2,856 (panel 6). This is the amount Jane will need to save annually for her retirement. The appendix to this chapter presents an example of a far more sophisticated and flexible planning model using spreadsheets.

CONCEPT CHECK 1	a. Think about the financial circumstances of your closest relative in your parents' generation (preferably your parents' household if you are fortunate enough to have them around). Write down the objectives and constraints for their investment decisions.
	b. Now consider the financial situation of your closest relative who is in his or her 30s. Write down the objectives and constraints that would fit his or her investment decision.
	c. How much of the difference between the two statements is due to the age of the investors?

Manage Your Own Portfolio or Rely on Others?

Lots of people have assets such as Social Security benefits, pension and group insurance plans, and savings components of life insurance policies. Yet they exercise limited control, if any, on the investment decisions of these plans. The funds that secure pension and life insurance plans are managed by institutional investors.

Outside the "forced savings" plans, however, individuals can manage their own investment portfolios. As the population grows richer, more and more people face this decision.

Managing your own portfolio *appears* to be the lowest-cost solution. Conceptually, there is little difference between managing one's own investments and professional financial planning/investment management.

BALLPARK ESTIMATE®

1. How much annual income will you want in retirement? (Figure 70% of your current annual income just to maintain your current standard of living. Really.)   **$ 21,000**

2. Subtract the income you expect to receive annually from:
   - Social Security
     If you make under $25,000, enter $8,000; between $25,000 - $40,000, enter $12,000; over $40,000, enter $14,500   **– $ 12,000**

   - Traditional Employer Pension—a plan that pays a set dollar amount for life, where the dollar amount depends on salary and years of service (in today's dollars)   – $ _____

   - Part-time income   – $ _____

   - Other   – $ _____

   This is how much you need to make up for each retirement year   **= $ 9,000**

   Now you want a ballpark estimate of how much money you'll need in the bank the day you retire. So the accountants went to work and devised this simple formula. For the record, they figure you'll realize a constant real rate of return of 3% after inflation, you'll live to age 87, and you'll begin to receive income from Social Security at age 65.

3. To determine the amount you'll need to save, multiply the amount you need to make up by the factor below.   **$147.600**

Age you expect to retire:	55	Your factor is:	21.0
	60		18.9
	65		**16.4**
	70		13.6

4. If you expect to retire before age 65, multiply your Social Security benefit from line 2 by the factor below.   + $ _____

Age you expect to retire:	55	Your factor is:	8.8
	60		4.7

5. Multiply your savings to date by the factor below (include money accumulated in a 401(k), IRA, or similar retirement plan):   **– $ 4,800**

If you want to retire in:	10 years	Your factor is:	1.3
	15 years		1.6
	20 years		1.8
	25 years		2.1
	30 years		**2.4**
	35 years		2.8
	40 years		3.3

   Total additional savings needed at retirement: **= $142,800**

6. To determine the ANNUAL amount you'll need to save, multiply the TOTAL amount by the factor below.   **$ 2,856**

If you want to retire in :	10 yrs.	Your factor is:	.085
	15 yrs.		.052
	20 yrs.		.036
	25 yrs.		.027
	30 yrs.		**.020**
	35 yrs.		.016
	40 yrs.		.013

   This worksheet simplifies several retirement planning issues such as projected Social Security benefits and earnings assumptions on savings. It also reflects today's dollars; therefore you will need to re-calculate your retirement needs annually and as your salary and circumstances change. You may consider doing further analysis, either yourself using a more detailed worksheet or computer software or with the assistance of a financial professional.

FIGURE 28.3   Sample of American Saving Education Council worksheet

Source: EBRI (Employee Benefit Research Institute)/American Saving Education Council.

Against the fees and charges that financial planners and professional investment managers impose, you will want to offset the value of your time and energy expended on diligent portfolio management. People with a suitable background may even look at investment as recreation. Most of all, you must recognize the *potential* difference in investment results.

Besides the need to deliver better-performing investments, professional managers face two added difficulties. First, getting clients to communicate their objectives and constraints requires considerable skill. This is not a one-time task because objectives and constraints are forever changing. Second, the professional needs to articulate the financial plan and keep the client abreast of outcomes. Professional management of large portfolios is complicated further by the need to set up an efficient organization where decisions can be decentralized and information properly disseminated.

The task of life cycle financial planning is a formidable one for most people. It is not surprising that a whole industry has sprung up to provide personal financial advice.

Tax Sheltering

In this section we explain three important tax sheltering options that can radically affect optimal asset allocation for individual investors. The first is the tax-deferral option, which arises from the fact that you do not have to pay tax on a capital gain until you choose to realize the gain. The second is tax-deferred retirement plans such as individual retirement accounts, and the third is tax-deferred annuities offered by life insurance companies. Not treated here at all is the possibility of investing in the tax-exempt instruments discussed in Chapter 2.

The Tax-Deferral Option   A fundamental feature of the U.S. Internal Revenue Code is that tax on a capital gain on an asset is payable only when the asset is sold; this is its **tax-deferral option.** The investor therefore can control the timing of the tax payment. This conveys a benefit to stock investments.

To see this, compare IBM stock with an IBM bond. Suppose both offer an expected total return of 12%. The stock has a dividend yield of 4% and expected price appreciation of 8%, whereas the bond pays an interest rate of 12%. The bond investor must pay tax on the bond's interest in the year it is earned, whereas the stockholder pays tax only on the dividend and defers paying capital gains tax until the stock is sold.

Suppose one invests $1,000 for 5 years. Although in reality interest is taxed as ordinary income while capital gains and dividends are taxed at a rate of only 15% for most investors, to isolate the benefit of tax deferral, we will assume that all investment income is taxed at 15%. The bond will earn an after-tax return of $12\% \times (1 - .15) = 10.2\%$. The after-tax accumulation at the end of 5 years is

$$\$1,000 \times 1.102^5 = \$1,625.20$$

For the stock, the dividend yield after taxes is $4\% \times (1 - .15) = 3.4\%$. Because no taxes are paid on the 8% annual capital gain until year 5, the before-tax accumulation will be

$$\$1,000 \times (1 + .034 + .08)^5 = 1,000(1.114)^5 = \$1,715.64$$

In year 5, when the stock is sold, the (now-taxable) capital gain is

$$\$1,715.64 - \$1,000(1.034)^5 = 1,715.64 - 1,181.96 = \$533.68$$

Taxes due are $80.05, leaving $1,635.59, which is $10.39 more than the bond investment yields. Deferral of the capital gains tax allows the investment to compound at a faster rate until the tax is actually paid. Note that the more of one's total return that is in the form of price appreciation, the greater the value of the tax-deferral option.

Tax-Deferred Retirement Plans   Recent years have seen increased use of **tax-deferred retirement plans** in which investors can choose how to allocate assets. Such plans include traditional IRAs, Keogh plans, and employer-sponsored "tax-qualified" defined contribution plans such as 401 (k) plans. A feature they have in common is that contributions and earnings are not subject to federal income tax until the individual withdraws them as benefits.

Typically, an individual may have some investment in the form of such qualified retirement accounts and some in the form of ordinary taxable accounts. The basic investment principle that applies is to hold whatever bonds you want to hold in the retirement account while holding equities in the ordinary account. You maximize the tax advantage of the retirement account by holding it in the security that is the least tax advantaged.

To see this point, consider an investor who has $200,000 of wealth, $100,000 of it in a tax-qualified retirement account. She currently invests half of her wealth in bonds and half in stocks, so she allocates half of her retirement account and half of her nonretirement funds to each. She could reduce her tax bill with *no change* in before-tax returns simply by shifting her bonds into the retirement account and holding all her stocks outside the retirement account.

CONCEPT CHECK 2	Suppose our investor earns a 10% per year rate of interest on bonds and 15% per year on stocks, all in the form of price appreciation. In 5 years she will withdraw all her funds and spend them. By how much will she increase her final accumulation if she shifts all bonds into the retirement account and holds all stocks outside the retirement account? She is in a 28% tax bracket for ordinary income, and her capital gains income is taxed at 15%.

Deferred Annuities   **Deferred annuities** are essentially tax-sheltered accounts offered by life insurance companies. They combine deferral of taxes with the option of withdrawing one's funds in the form of a life annuity. Variable annuity contracts offer the additional advantage of mutual fund investing. One major difference between an IRA and a variable annuity contract is that whereas the amount one can contribute to an IRA is tax-deductible and extremely limited as to maximum amount, the amount one can contribute to a deferred annuity is unlimited, but not tax-deductible.

The defining characteristic of a life annuity is that its payments continue as long as the recipient is alive, although virtually all deferred annuity contracts have several withdrawal options, including a lump sum of cash paid out at any time. You need not worry about running out of money before you die. Like Social Security, therefore, life annuities offer longevity insurance and thus would seem to be an ideal asset for someone in the retirement years. Indeed, theory suggests that where there are no bequest motives, it would be optimal for people to invest heavily in actuarially fair life annuities.[1]

There are two types of life annuities, **fixed annuities** and **variable annuities.** A fixed annuity pays a fixed nominal sum of money per period (usually each month), whereas a variable annuity pays a periodic amount linked to the investment performance of some underlying portfolio.

In pricing annuities, insurance companies use **mortality tables** that show the probabilities that individuals of various ages will die within a year. These tables enable the insurer

---

[1] For an elaboration of this point see Laurence J. Kotlikoff and Avia Spivak, "The Family as an Incomplete Annuities Market," *Journal of Political Economy* 89 (April 1981).

to compute with reasonable accuracy how many of a large number of people in a given age group will die in each future year. If it sells life annuities to a large group, the insurance company can estimate fairly accurately the amount of money it will have to pay in each future year to meet its obligations.

Variable annuities are structured so that the investment risk of the underlying asset portfolio is passed through to the recipient, much as shareholders bear the risk of a mutual fund. There are two stages in a variable annuity contract: an accumulation phase and a payout phase. During the *accumulation* phase, the investor contributes money periodically to one or more open-end mutual funds and accumulates shares. The second, or *payout,* stage usually starts at retirement, when the investor typically has several options, including the following:

1. Taking the market value of the shares in a lump sum payment.
2. Receiving a fixed annuity until death.
3. Receiving a variable amount of money each period that depends on the investment performance of the portfolio.

Variable and Universal Life Insurance   Variable life insurance is another tax-deferred investment vehicle offered by the life insurance industry. A variable life insurance policy combines life insurance with the tax-deferred annuities described earlier.

To invest in this product, you pay either a single premium or a series of premiums. In each case there is a stated death benefit, and the policyholder can allocate the money invested to several portfolios, which generally include a money market fund, a bond fund, and at least one common stock fund. The allocation can be changed at any time.

Variable life insurance policies offer a death benefit that is the greater of the stated face value or the market value of the investment base. In other words, the death benefit may rise with favorable investment performance, but it will not go below the guaranteed face value. Furthermore, the surviving beneficiary is not subject to income tax on the death benefit.

The policyholder can choose from a number of income options to convert the policy into a stream of income, either on surrender of the contract or as a partial withdrawal. In all cases income taxes are payable on the part of any distribution representing investment gains.

The insured can gain access to the investment without having to pay income tax by borrowing against the cash surrender value. Policy loans of up to 90% of the cash value are available at any time at a contractually specified interest rate.

A universal life insurance policy is similar to a variable life policy except that, instead of having a choice of portfolios to invest in, the policyholder earns a rate of interest that is set by the insurance company and changed periodically as market conditions change. The disadvantage of universal life insurance is that the company controls the rate of return to the policyholder, and, although companies may change the rate in response to competitive pressures, changes are not automatic. Different companies offer different rates, so it often pays to shop around for the best.

28.5   PENSION FUNDS

By far the most important institution in the retirement income system is the employer-sponsored pension plan. These plans vary in form and complexity, but they all share certain common elements in every country. In general, investment strategy depends on the type of plan.

Pension plans are defined by the terms specifying the "who," "when," and "how much," for both the plan benefits and the plan contributions used to pay for those benefits. The *pension fund* of the plan is the cumulation of assets created from contributions and the investment earnings on those contributions, less any payments of benefits from the fund. In the United States, contributions to the fund by either employer or employee are tax-deductible, and investment income of the fund is not taxed. Distributions from the fund, whether to the employer or the employee, are taxed as ordinary income. There are two "pure" types of pension plans: *defined contribution* and *defined benefit*.

Defined Contribution Plans

In a defined contribution plan, a formula specifies contributions but not benefit payments. Contribution rules usually are specified as a predetermined fraction of salary (e.g., the employer contributes 15% of the employee's annual wages to the plan), although that fraction need not be constant over the course of an employee's career. The pension fund consists of a set of individual investment accounts, one for each employee. Pension benefits are not specified, other than that at retirement the employee may apply that total accumulated value of contributions and earnings on those contributions to purchase an annuity. The employee often has some choice over both the level of contributions and the way the account is invested.

In principle, contributions could be invested in any security, although in practice most plans limit investment choices to bond, stock, and money market funds. The employee bears all the investment risk; the retirement account is, by definition, fully funded by the contributions, and the employer has no legal obligation beyond making its periodic contributions.

For defined contribution plans, investment policy is essentially the same as for a tax-qualified individual retirement account. Indeed, the main providers of investment products for these plans are the same institutions such as mutual funds and insurance companies that serve the general investment needs of individuals. Therefore, in a defined contribution plan much of the task of setting and achieving the income-replacement goal falls on the employee.

<table>
<tr>
<td>**CONCEPT
CHECK**

3</td>
<td>An employee is 45 years old. Her salary is $40,000 per year, and she has $100,000 accumulated in her self-directed defined contribution pension plan. Each year she contributes 5% of her salary to the plan, and her employer matches it with another 5%. She plans to retire at age 65. The plan offers a choice of two funds: a guaranteed return fund that pays a risk-free real interest rate of 3% per year and a stock index fund that has an expected real rate of return of 6% per year and a standard deviation of 20%. Her current asset mix in the plan is $50,000 in the guaranteed fund and $50,000 in the stock index fund. She plans to reinvest all investment earnings in each fund in that same fund and to allocate her annual contribution equally between the two funds. If her salary grows at the same rate as the cost of living, how much can she expect to have at retirement? How much can she be *sure* of having?</td>
</tr>
</table>

Defined Benefit Plans

In a defined benefit plan, a formula specifies benefits, but not the manner, including contributions, in which these benefits are funded. The benefit formula typically takes into account years of service for the employer and level of wages or salary (e.g., an employer might pay an employee for life, beginning at age 65, a yearly amount equal to 1% of his final annual wage for each year of service). The employer (called the "plan sponsor") or an insurance company hired by the sponsor guarantees the benefits and thus absorbs the investment risk. The obligation of the plan sponsor to pay the promised benefits is like a long-term debt liability of the employer.

As measured both by number of plan participants and the value of total pension liabilities, the defined benefit form dominates in most countries around the world. This is so in the United States, although the strong trend since the mid-1970s has been for sponsors to choose the defined contribution form when starting new plans. But the two plan types are not mutually exclusive. Many sponsors adopt defined benefit plans as their primary plan, in which participation is mandatory, and supplement them with voluntary defined contribution plans.

With defined benefit plans, there is an important distinction between the pension *plan* and the pension *fund.* The plan is the contractual arrangement setting out the rights and obligations of all parties; the fund is a separate pool of assets set aside to provide collateral for the promised benefits. In defined contribution plans, by definition, the value of the benefits equals that of the assets, so the plan is always fully funded. But in defined benefit plans, there is a continuum of possibilities. There may be no separate fund, in which case the plan is said to be unfunded. When there is a separate fund with assets worth less than the present value of the promised benefits, the plan is underfunded. And if the plan's assets have a market value that exceeds the present value of the plan's liabilities, it is said to be overfunded.

Alternative Perspectives on Defined Benefit Pension Obligations

As previously described, in a defined benefit plan, the pension benefit is determined by a formula that takes into account the employee's history of service and wages or salary. The plan sponsor provides this benefit regardless of the investment performance of the pension fund assets. The annuity promised to the employee is therefore the employer's liability. What is the nature of this liability?

There is a widespread belief that pension benefits in final-pay formula plans are protected against inflation at least up to the date of retirement. But this is a misperception. Unlike Social Security benefits, whose starting value is indexed to a general index of wages, pension benefits even in final-pay private-sector plans are "indexed" only to the extent that (1) the employee continues to work for the same employer, (2) the employee's own wage or salary keeps pace with the general price index, and (3) the employer continues to maintain the same plan. Very few private corporations in the United States offer pension benefits that are automatically indexed for inflation; thus workers who change jobs wind up with lower pension benefits at retirement than otherwise identical workers who stay with the same employer, even if the employers have defined benefit plans with the same final-pay benefit formula. This is referred to as the *portability problem.*

Both the rule-making body of the accounting profession (the Financial Accounting Standards Board) and Congress have adopted the present value of the nominal benefits as the appropriate measure of a sponsor's pension liability. FASB Statement 87 specifies that the measure of corporate pension liabilities to be used on the corporate balance sheet in external reports is the accumulated benefit obligation (ABO)—that is, the present value of pension benefits owed to employees under the plan's benefit formula absent any salary projections and discounted at a nominal rate of interest. Similarly, in its Omnibus Budget Reconciliation Act (OBRA) of 1987, Congress defined the current liability as the measure of a corporation's pension liability and set limits on the amount of tax-qualified contributions a corporation could make as a proportion of the current liability. OBRA's definition of the current liability is essentially the same as FASB Statement 87's definition of the ABO.

The ABO is thus a key element in a pension fund's investment strategy. It affects a corporation's reported balance sheet liabilities; it also reflects economic reality.

Statement 87, however, recognizes an additional measure of a defined benefit plan's liability: the projected benefit obligation (PBO). The PBO is a measure of the sponsor's pension liability that includes projected increases in salary up to the expected age of retirement. Statement 87 requires corporations to use the PBO in computing pension expense reported in their income statements. This is perhaps useful for financial analysts, in that the amount may help them to derive an appropriate estimate of expected future labor costs for discounted cash flow valuation models of the firm as a going concern. The PBO is not, however, an appropriate measure of the benefits that the employer has explicitly guaranteed. The difference between the PBO and the ABO should not be treated as a liability of the firm, because these additional pension costs will be realized only if the employees continue to work in the future. If these future contingent labor costs are to be treated as a liability of the firm, then why not book the entire future wage bill as a liability? If this is done, then shouldn't one add as an asset the present value of future revenues generated by these labor activities? It is indeed difficult to see either the accounting or economic logic for using the PBO as a measure of pension liabilities.

> **CONCEPT CHECK**
> **4**
>
> An employee is 40 years old and has been working for the firm for 15 years. If normal retirement age is 65, the interest rate is 8%, and the employee's life expectancy is 80, what is the present value of the accrued pension benefit?

Pension Investment Strategies

The special tax status of pension funds creates the same incentive for both defined contribution and defined benefit plans to tilt their asset mix toward assets with the largest spread between pretax and after-tax rates of return. In a defined contribution plan, because the participant bears all the investment risk, the optimal asset mix also depends on the risk tolerance of the participant.

In defined benefit plans, optimal investment policy may be different because the sponsor absorbs the investment risk. If the sponsor has to share some of the upside potential of the pension assets with plan participants, there is an incentive to eliminate all investment risk by investing in securities that match the promised benefits. If, for example, the plan sponsor has to pay $100 per year for the next 5 years, it can provide this stream of benefit payments by buying a set of five zero-coupon bonds each with a face value of $100 and maturing sequentially. By so doing, the sponsor eliminates the risk of a shortfall. This is an example of **immunization** of the pension liability.

If a corporate pension fund has an ABO that exceeds the market value of its assets, FASB Statement 87 requires that the corporation recognize the unfunded liability on its balance sheet. If, however, the pension assets exceed the ABO, the corporation cannot include the surplus on its balance sheet. This asymmetric accounting treatment expresses a deeply held view about defined benefit pension funds. Representatives of organized labor, some politicians, and even a few pension professionals believe that the sponsoring corporation, as guarantor of the accumulated pension benefits, is liable for pension asset shortfalls but does not have a clear right to the entire surplus in case of pension overfunding.

If the pension fund is overfunded, then a 100% fixed-income portfolio is no longer required to minimize the cost of the corporate pension guarantee. Management can invest surplus pension assets in equities, provided it reduces the proportion so invested when the market value of pension assets comes close to the value of the ABO. Such an investment strategy, first introduced in Chapter 16, is known as *contingent immunization.*

Investing in Equities   If the only goal guiding corporate pension policy were shareholder wealth maximization, it is hard to understand why a financially sound pension sponsor would invest in equities at all. A policy of 100% bond investment would minimize the cost of guaranteeing the defined benefits.

In addition to the reasons given for a fully funded pension plan to invest only in fixed income securities, there is a tax reason for doing so too. The tax advantage of a pension fund stems from the ability of the sponsor to earn the pretax interest rate on pension investments. To maximize the value of this tax shelter, it is necessary to invest entirely in assets offering the highest pretax interest rate. Because capital gains on stocks can be deferred and dividends are taxed at a lower rate than interest on bonds, corporate pension funds should invest entirely in taxable bonds and other fixed-income investments.

Yet we know that in general pension funds invest from 40% to 60% of their portfolios in equity securities. Even a casual perusal of the practitioner literature suggests that they do so for a variety of reasons—some right and some wrong. There are three possible correct reasons.

The first is that corporate management views the pension plan as a trust for the employees and manages fund assets as if it were a defined contribution plan. It believes that a successful policy of investment in equities might allow it to pay extra benefits to employees and is therefore worth taking the risk.

The second possible correct reason is that management believes that through superior market timing and security selection it is possible to create value in excess of management fees and expenses. Many executives in nonfinancial corporations are used to creating value in excess of cost in their businesses. They assume that it can also be done in the area of portfolio management. Of course, if that is true, then one must ask why they do not do it on their corporate account rather than in the pension fund. That way they could have their tax shelter "cake" and eat it too. It is important to realize, however, that to accomplish this feat, the plan must beat the market, not merely match it.

Note that a very weak form of the efficient markets hypothesis would imply that management cannot create shareholder value simply by shifting the pension portfolio out of bonds and into stocks. Even when the entire pension surplus belongs to the shareholders, investing in stocks just moves the shareholders along the capital market line (the market trade-off between risk and return for passive investors) and does not create value. When the net cost of providing plan beneficiaries with shortfall risk insurance is taken into account, increasing the pension fund equity exposure reduces shareholder value unless the equity investment can put the firm above the capital market line. This implies that it makes sense for a pension fund to invest in equities only *if* it intends to pursue an active strategy of beating the market either through superior timing or security selection. A completely passive strategy will add no value to shareholders.

For an underfunded plan of a corporation in financial distress there is another possible reason for investing in stocks and other risky assets—federal pension insurance. Firms in financial distress have an incentive to invest pension fund money in the riskiest assets, just as troubled thrift institutions insured by the Federal Savings and Loan Insurance Corporation (FSLIC) in the 1980s had similar motivation with respect to their loan portfolios.

Wrong Reasons to Invest in Equities   The wrong reasons for a pension fund to invest in equities stem from interrelated fallacies. The first is the notion that stocks are not risky in the long run. This fallacy was discussed at length in Chapter 5. Another related fallacy is the notion that stocks are a hedge against inflation. The reasoning behind this fallacy is that stocks are an ownership claim over real physical capital. Real profits are either unaffected or enhanced when there is unanticipated inflation, so owners of real capital should not be hurt by it.

Let us assume that this proposition is true, and that the real rate of return on stocks is uncorrelated or slightly positively correlated with inflation. If stocks are to be a good hedge against inflation risk in the conventional sense, however, the nominal return on stocks has to be *highly* positively correlated with inflation. However, empirical studies show that stock returns have been negatively correlated with inflation in the past with a low R^2. Thus even in the best of circumstances, stocks can offer only a limited hedge against inflation risk.

28.6 INVESTMENTS FOR THE LONG RUN

As the aged population around the world grows more rapidly than any other age group, issues of saving for the long run, for the most part surrounding retirement, have come to the fore of the investments industry. Traditionally, the advice for the long run could be summarized by rules of thumb concerning various rates of gradual, age-determined shifts in asset allocation from risky to safe assets. Implications of "modern" portfolio management, now more than 30 years old, originated from Merton's lifetime consumption/investment model (ICAPM) suggesting that one consider hedge assets to account for extramarket sources of risk, such as inflation, and needs emanating from uncertain longevity.

In previous sections, we presented the CFA Institute process of devising investment programs for individual investments, as well as for concerns of various institutions. Here we emphasize two important aspects of investment for the long run based on insights from recent research, namely, duration matching and the term structure of volatilities.

Advice from the Mutual Fund Industry

Many employees don't know the basics of how to invest wisely, despite the wealth of information on the Internet and countless books and magazines freely available at libraries. The mutual fund industry's list of basic investing rules includes the following:

- Don't try to outguess the market by pulling money out or putting it in just because the market is suddenly up or down. The long-term trend for the market is up (the market risk premium is positive); buying and holding generally pays off.
- Diversify investments to spread risk.
- Put portions of the money into stocks, bonds, and money-market funds. Within these categories there are additional choices to help further diversify, for example, corporate bonds, government bonds, municipal bonds.
- Avoid keeping 401(k) money in a company's default investment scheme. It's usually a low-risk fund with a correspondingly low rate of return.
- Be wary of investing a large percentage of your 401(k) in your company's stock. If your company falters, you could lose your job and your nest egg at once.

As useful as it is, this list neglects some important fundamentals.

Target Investing and the Term Structure of Bonds

Interest rates usually vary by maturity. For example, a person considering investing money in an insured certificate of deposit or a Treasury security will observe that the interest rate she can earn depends on its maturity. Thus, for any given target date there is a different risk-free interest rate. Each investor, with a unique horizon, therefore has his or her own risk-free asset. For Mr. Short it is bills and for Ms. Long it is bonds. Thus, to accommodate investors with different time horizons, there must be a menu of choices that has a term structure of risk-free investments. The principle of duration matching means matching one's assets to one's objectives (liabilities) and is equivalent to the immunization strategy for pension funds that we examined in Chapter 16.

In what unit of account should the risk-free term structure be denominated? This is a critical issue because a bond is risk-free only in terms of a specified numeraire (unit of account), such as dollars, yen, and so on. Thus, if a bond promises to pay $100 two years from now, its payoff in terms of yen depends on the dollar price of the yen 2 years from now, and vice versa. Thus even a zero-coupon bond with no default risk can still be very risky if it is denominated in a unit of account (such as a foreign currency) that does not match the investor's goal. This type of risk is called "basis risk."

To illustrate, assume the goal is retirement. If the goal is specified as a level of real wealth at the retirement date, then the unit of account should be consumption units. The risk-free asset in this case would be a bond with a payoff linked to an index of consumer prices, such as the CPI. However, if the index chosen does not truly reflect the specific investor's future cost of living, there will be some risk. If the goal is to maintain a certain standard of living for the rest of one's life, then instead of a fixed level of retirement wealth in terms of consumption units, a more appropriate unit of account would be a lifetime *flow* of real consumption. This can be computed by dividing dollar amounts by the market price of a lifetime real annuity that starts paying benefits at the target retirement date. The term structure is then given by the prices of lifetime real annuities with different starting dates. Similarly, education bonds that are linked to the cost of college education provide the appropriate unit of account for children's college funds.

Making Simple Investment Choices

A target-date retirement fund (TDRF) is a fund of funds diversified across stocks and bonds with the feature that the proportion invested in stocks is automatically reduced as time passes.[2] TDRFs are often advocated as the simple solution to the complex task of determining the appropriate asset allocation among funds in 401(k) plans, IRAs, and other personal investment accounts. TDRFs are marketed as enabling investors to put their investment plans on autopilot. Once you choose a fund with a target year matching your horizon, the life cycle manager moves some of your money out of stocks and into bonds as your retirement date nears. But this will be optimal only for individuals with "typical" human capital risk and tolerance for market risk.

An improved design for TDRFs would offer at least one additional fund to each age cohort of life cycle investors: a risk-free investment portfolio with a matching investment horizon. Individuals could mix the TDRF and the risk-free fund depending on their personal

---

[2]Vanguard describes its TDRFs as follows: "With Target Retirement Funds, you have only one decision to make: when you plan to retire. Your Target Retirement Fund automatically grows more conservative as your retirement date nears. When you are ready to draw income in your retirement, your Target Retirement Fund has a stable, income-oriented mix of assets." From "Choose a Simple Solution: Vanguard Target Retirement Funds," **www.vanguard.com/jumppage/retire.**

characteristics. Under such a portfolio policy, the individual continues to be exposed to equity risk via human capital risk. Directing individuals based on their personal characteristics to either the TDRF and/or the risk-free fund matching their investment horizon would add an additional degree of freedom that generates economically significant individual welfare gains.[3]

Inflation Risk and Long-Term Investors

While inflation risk is usually low for short horizons, it is a first-order source of risk for retirement planning, where horizons may be extremely long. An inflation "shock" may last for many years, and impart substantial uncertainty to the purchasing power of any dollar you (or your client) have saved for retirement.

A conventional answer to the problem of inflation risk is to invest in price-indexed bonds such as TIPS (see Chapter 14 for a review). This is a good first step but is not a full answer to inflation risk. A zero-coupon priced-indexed bond with maturity equal to an investor's horizon would be a riskless investment in terms of purchasing power. This can be achieved with CPI-indexed savings bonds, but the government limits the amount of such bonds one may buy in any year. Unfortunately, market-traded TIPS bonds are not risk-free. As the (real) interest rate changes, the value of those bonds will fluctuate. Moreover, these bonds pay coupons, so the accumulated (real) value of the portfolio is subject to reinvestment-rate risk. These issues should remind you of our discussion of bond risk in Chapter 16. In this context too, one must balance price risk with reinvestment rate risk by tailoring the duration of the bond portfolio to the investment horizon. But in this case, we need to calculate duration using the real interest rate and focus on real payoffs from our investments.

[3]The model is detailed in Zvi Bodie and Jonathan Treussard, "Making Investment Choices as Simple as Possible but Not Simpler," *Financial Analysts Journal* 63 (May–June 2007).

SUMMARY

1. When the principles of portfolio management are discussed, it is useful to distinguish among seven classes of investors:

   a. Individual investors and personal trusts.
   b. Mutual funds.
   c. Pension funds.
   d. Endowment funds.
   e. Life insurance companies.
   f. Non–life insurance companies.
   g. Banks.

   In general, these groups have somewhat different investment objectives, constraints, and portfolio policies.

2. To some extent, most institutional investors seek to match the risk-and-return characteristics of their investment portfolios to the characteristics of their liabilities.

3. The process of asset allocation consists of the following steps:

   a. Specifying the asset classes to be included.
   b. Defining capital market expectations.
   c. Finding the efficient portfolio frontier.
   d. Determining the optimal mix.

4. People living on money-fixed incomes are vulnerable to inflation risk and may want to hedge against it. The effectiveness of an asset as an inflation hedge is related to its correlation with unanticipated inflation.

5. For investors who must pay taxes on their investment income, the process of asset allocation is complicated by the fact that they pay income taxes only on certain kinds of investment income. Interest income on munis is exempt from tax, and high-tax-bracket investors will prefer to hold them rather than short- and long-term taxable bonds. However, the really difficult part of the tax effect to deal with is the fact that capital gains are taxable only if realized through the sale of an asset during the holding period. Investment strategies designed to avoid taxes may contradict the principles of efficient diversification.

6. The life cycle approach to the management of an individual's investment portfolio views the individual as passing through a series of stages, becoming more risk averse in later years. The rationale underlying this approach is that as we age, we use up our human capital and have less time remaining to recoup possible portfolio losses through increased labor supply.

7. People buy life and disability insurance during their prime earning years to hedge against the risk associated with loss of their human capital, that is, their future earning power.

8. There are three ways to shelter investment income from federal income taxes besides investing in tax-exempt bonds. The first is by investing in assets whose returns take the form of appreciation in value, such as common stocks or real estate. As long as capital gains taxes are not paid until the asset is sold, the tax can be deferred indefinitely.

   The second way of tax sheltering is through investing in tax-deferred retirement plans such as IRAs. The general investment rule is to hold the least tax-advantaged assets in the plan and the most tax-advantaged assets outside of it.

   The third way of sheltering is to invest in the tax-advantaged products offered by the life insurance industry—tax-deferred annuities and variable and universal life insurance. They combine the flexibility of mutual fund investing with the tax advantages of tax deferral.

9. Pension plans are either defined contribution plans or defined benefit plans. Defined contribution plans are in effect retirement funds held in trust for the employee by the employer. The employees in such plans bear all the risk of the plan's assets and often have some choice in the allocation of those assets. Defined benefit plans give the employees a claim to a money-fixed annuity at retirement. The annuity level is determined by a formula that takes into account years of service and the employee's wage or salary history.

10. If the only goal guiding corporate pension policy were shareholder wealth maximization, it would be hard to understand why a financially sound pension sponsor would invest in equities at all. A policy of 100% bond investment would both maximize the tax advantage of funding the pension plan and minimize the costs of guaranteeing the defined benefits.

11. If sponsors viewed their pension liabilities as indexed for inflation, then the appropriate way for them to minimize the cost of providing benefit guarantees would be to hedge using securities whose returns are highly correlated with inflation. Common stocks would not be an appropriate hedge because they have a low correlation with inflation.

Related Web sites for this chapter are available at www.mhhe.com/bkm

KEY TERMS

risk–return trade-off	whole-life insurance policy	tax-deferral option
personal trusts	term insurance	tax-deferred retirement plans
income beneficiaries	variable life	deferred annuities
remaindermen	universal life	fixed annuities
defined contribution plans	liquidity	variable annuities
defined benefit plans	investment horizon	mortality tables
endowment funds	prudent investor rule	immunization

PROBLEM SETS

Quiz

1. Your neighbor has heard that you successfully completed a course in investments and has come to seek your advice. She and her husband are both 50 years old. They just finished making their last payments for their condominium and their children's college education and are planning for retirement. What advice on investing their retirement savings would you give them? If they are very risk averse, what would you advise?

2. What is the least-risky asset for each of the following investors?

   a. A person investing for her 3-year-old child's college tuition.
   b. A defined benefit pension fund with benefit obligations that have an average duration of 10 years. The benefits are not inflation-protected.
   c. A defined benefit pension fund with benefit obligations that have an average duration of 10 years. The benefits are inflation-protected.

Problems

3. George More is a participant in a defined contribution pension plan that offers a fixed-income fund and a common stock fund as investment choices. He is 40 years old and has an accumulation of $100,000 in each of the funds. He currently contributes $1,500 per year to each. He plans to retire at age 65, and his life expectancy is age 80.

   a. Assuming a 3% per year real earnings rate for the fixed-income fund and 6% per year for common stocks, what will be George's expected accumulation in each account at age 65?
   b. What will be the expected real retirement annuity from each account, assuming these same real earnings rates?
   c. If George wanted a retirement annuity of $30,000 per year from the fixed-income fund, by how much would he have to increase his annual contributions?

4. The difference between a Roth IRA and a conventional IRA is that in a Roth IRA taxes are paid on the income that is contributed but the withdrawals at retirement are tax-free. In a conventional IRA, however, the contributions reduce your taxable income, but the withdrawals at retirement are taxable. Try using the Excel spreadsheet introduced in the Appendix to answer these questions.

   a. Which of these two types provides higher after-tax benefits?
   b. Which provides better protection against tax rate uncertainty?

CFA® PROBLEMS

1. Angus Walker, CFA, is reviewing the defined benefit pension plan of Acme Industries. Based in London, Acme has operations in North America, Japan, and several European countries. Next month, the retirement age for full benefits under the plan will be lowered from age 60 to age 55. The median age of Acme's workforce is 49 years. Walker is responsible for the pension plan's investment policy and strategic asset allocation decisions. The goals of the plan include achieving a minimum expected return of 8.4% with expected standard deviation no greater than 16.0%.

   Walker is evaluating the current asset allocation (Table 28A) and selected financial information for the company (Table 28B). There is an ongoing debate within Acme Industries about the pension plan's investment policy statement (IPS). Two investment policy statements under consideration are shown in Table 28C.

International Equities (MSCI World, excluding U.K.)	10%
U.K. bonds	42
U.K. small capitalization equities	13
U.K. large capitalization equities	30
Cash	5

TABLE 28A

Acme pension plan: Current asset allocation

Acme Industries total assets	£ 16,000
Pension plan data:	
Plan assets	6,040
Plan liabilities	9,850

TABLE 28B
Acme Industries selected financial information (in millions)

	IPS X	IPS Y
Return requirement	Plan's objective is to outperform the relevant benchmark return by a substantial margin.	Plan's objective is to match the relevant benchmark return.
Risk tolerance	Plan has a high risk tolerance because of the long-term nature of the plan and its liabilities.	Plan has a low risk tolerance because of its limited ability to assume substantial risk.
Time horizon	Plan has a very long time horizon because of the plan's infinite life.	Plan has a shorter time horizon than in the past because of plan demographics.
Liquidity	Plan needs moderate level of liquidity to fund monthly benefit payments.	Plan has minimal liquidity needs.

TABLE 28C
Investment policy statements

	Current	Graham	Michael
U.K. large capitalization equities	30	20	40
U.K. small capitalization equities	13	8	20
International equities (MSCI World ex-U.K.)	10	10	18
U.K. bonds	42	52	17
Cash	5	10	5
Total	100	100	100
Expected portfolio return (%)	9.1	8.2	10.6
Expected portfolio volatility (standard deviation in %)	16.1	12.8	21.1

TABLE 28D
Asset allocations (in %)

a. Determine, for each of the following components, whether IPS X or IPS Y (see Table 28C) has the appropriate language for the pension plan of Acme Industries. Justify each response with one reason.

    i. Return requirement
    ii. Risk tolerance
    iii. Time horizon
    iv. Liquidity

Note: Some components of IPS X may be appropriate, while other components of IPS Y may be appropriate.

b. To assist Walker, Acme has hired two pension consultants, Lucy Graham and Robert Michael. Graham believes that the pension fund must be invested to reflect a low risk tolerance, but Michael believes the pension fund must be invested to achieve the highest possible returns. The fund's current asset allocation and the allocations recommended by Graham and Michael are shown in Table 28D. Select which of the three asset allocations in Table 28D is most appropriate for Acme's pension plan. Explain how your selection meets each of the following objectives or constraints for the plan:

    i. Return requirement
    ii. Risk tolerance
    iii. Liquidity

2. Your client says, "With the unrealized gains in my portfolio, I have almost saved enough money for my daughter to go to college in 8 years, but educational costs keep going up." Based on this statement alone, which one of the following appears to be least important to your client's investment policy?

    a. Time horizon.
    b. Purchasing power risk.
    c. Liquidity.
    d. Taxes.

3. The aspect least likely to be included in the portfolio management process is

    a. Identifying an investor's objectives, constraints, and preferences.
    b. Organizing the management process itself.
    c. Implementing strategies regarding the choice of assets to be used.
    d. Monitoring market conditions, relative values, and investor circumstances.

4. Sam Short, CFA, has recently joined the investment management firm of Green, Spence, and Smith (GSS). For several years, GSS has worked for a broad array of clients, including employee benefit plans, wealthy individuals, and charitable organizations. Also, the firm expresses expertise in managing stocks, bonds, cash reserves, real estate, venture capital, and international securities. To date, the firm has not utilized a formal asset allocation process but instead has relied on the individual wishes of clients or the particular preferences of its portfolio managers. Short recommends to GSS management that a formal asset allocation process would be beneficial and emphasizes that a large part of a portfolio's ultimate return depends on asset allocation. He is asked to take his conviction an additional step by making a proposal to executive management.

    a. Recommend and justify an approach to asset allocation that could be used by GSS.
    b. Apply the approach to a middle-aged, wealthy individual characterized as a fairly conservative investor (sometimes referred to as a "guardian investor").

5. Jarvis University (JU) is a private, multiprogram U.S. university with a $2 billion endowment fund as of fiscal year-end May 31, 2006. With little government support, JU is heavily dependent on its endowment fund to support ongoing expenditures, especially because the university's enrollment growth and tuition revenue have not met expectations in recent years. The endowment fund must make a $126 million annual contribution, which is indexed to inflation, to JU's general operating budget. The U.S. Consumer Price Index is expected to rise 2.5% annually and the U.S. higher education cost index is anticipated to rise 3% annually. The endowment has also budgeted $200 million due on January 31, 2007, representing the final payment for construction of a new main library.

    In a recent capital campaign, JU only met its fund-raising goal with the help of one very successful alumna, Valerie Bremner, who donated $400 million of Bertocchi Oil and Gas common stock at fiscal year-end May 31, 2006. Bertocchi Oil and Gas is a large-capitalization, publicly traded U.S. company. Bremner donated the stock on the condition that no more than 25% of the initial number of shares may be sold in any fiscal year. No substantial additional donations are expected in the future.

    Given the large contribution to and distributions from the endowment fund, the endowment fund's investment committee has decided to revise the fund's investment policy statement. The investment committee also recognizes that a revised asset allocation may be warranted. The asset allocation in place for the JU endowment fund as of May 31, 2006, is given in Table 28E.

    a. Prepare the components of an appropriate investment policy statement for the Jarvis University endowment fund as of June 1, 2006, based only on the information given.

Asset	Current Allocation (millions)	Current Allocation Percentage	Current Yield	Expected Annual Return	Standard Deviation of Returns
U.S. money market bond fund	$ 40	2%	4.0%	4.0%	2.0%
Intermediate global bond fund	60	3	5.0	5.0	9.0
Global equity fund	300	15	1.0	10.0	15.0
Bertocchi Oil and Gas common stock	400	20	0.1	15.0	25.0
Direct real estate	700	35	3.0	11.5	16.5
Venture capital	500	25	0.0	20.0	35.0
TOTAL	$2,000	100%			

TABLE 28E

Jarvis University endowment fund asset allocation as of May 31, 2006

Note: Each component in your response must specifically address circumstances of the JU endowment fund.

b. Determine the most appropriate revised allocation percentage for each asset in Table 28E as of June 1, 2006. Justify each revised allocation percentage.

6. Susan Fairfax is president of Reston Industries, a U.S.-based company whose sales are entirely domestic and whose shares are listed on the New York Stock Exchange. The following are additional facts concerning her current situation:

- Fairfax is single, aged 58. She has no immediate family, no debts, and does not own a residence. She is in excellent health and covered by Reston-paid health insurance that continues after her expected retirement at age 65.
- Her base salary of $500,000/year, inflation-protected, is sufficient to support her present lifestyle but can no longer generate any excess for savings.
- She has $2,000,000 of savings from prior years held in the form of short-term instruments.
- Reston rewards key employees through a generous stock-bonus incentive plan but provides no pension plan and pays no dividend.
- Fairfax's incentive plan participation has resulted in her ownership of Reston stock worth $10 million (current market value). The stock, received tax-free but subject to tax at a 35% rate (on entire proceeds) if sold, is expected to be held at least until her retirement.
- Her present level of spending and the current annual inflation rate of 4% are expected to continue after her retirement.
- Fairfax is taxed at 35% on all salary, investment income, and realized capital gains. Assume her composite tax rate will continue at this level indefinitely.

Fairfax's orientation is patient, careful, and conservative in all things. She has stated that an annual after-tax real total return of 3% would be completely acceptable to her if it was achieved in a context where an investment portfolio created from her accumulated savings was not subject to a decline of more than 10% in nominal terms in any given 12-month period. To obtain the benefits of professional assistance, she has approached two investment advisory firms—HH Counselors ("HH") and Coastal Advisors ("Coastal")—for recommendations on allocation of the investment portfolio to be created from her existing savings assets (the "Savings Portfolio") as well as for advice concerning investing in general.

a. Create and justify an investment policy statement for Fairfax based only on the information provided thus far. Be specific and complete in presenting objectives and constraints. (An asset allocation is not required in answering this question.)

b. Coastal has proposed the asset allocation shown in Table 28F for investment of Fairfax's $2 million of savings assets. Assume that only the current yield portion of projected total return (comprised of both investment income and realized capital gains) is taxable to Fairfax and that the municipal bond income is entirely tax-exempt.

Visit us at www.mhhe.com/bkm

Asset Class	Proposed Allocation (%)	Current Yield (%)	Projected Total Return (%)
Cash equivalents	15.0	4.5	4.5
Corporate bonds	10.0	7.5	7.5
Municipal bonds	10.0	5.5	5.5
Large-cap U.S. stocks	0.0	3.5	11.0
Small-cap U.S. stocks	0.0	2.5	13.0
International stocks (EAFE)	35.0	2.0	13.5
Real estate investment trusts (REITs)	25.0	9.0	12.0
Venture capital	5.0	0.0	20.0
TOTAL	100.0	4.9	10.7
Inflation (CPI), projected			4.0

TABLE 28F

Susan Fairfax proposed asset allocation, prepared by Coastal Advisors

    Critique the Coastal proposal. Include in your answer three weaknesses in the Coastal proposal from the standpoint of the investment policy statement you created for her in (*a*).

c. HH Counselors has developed five alternative asset allocations (shown in Table 28G) for client portfolios. Answer the following questions based on Table 28G and the investment policy statement you created for Fairfax in (*a*).

  i. Determine which of the asset allocations in Table 28G meet or exceed Fairfax's stated return objective.

  ii. Determine the three asset allocations in Table 28G that meet Fairfax's risk tolerance criterion. Assume a 95% confidence interval is required, with 2 standard deviations serving as an approximation of that requirement.

Asset Class	Projected Total Return	Expected Standard Deviation	Asset Allocation A	Asset Allocation B	Asset Allocation C	Asset Allocation D	Asset Allocation E
Cash equivalents	4.5%	2.5%	10%	20%	25%	5%	10%
Corporate bonds	6.0	11.0	0	25	0	0	0
Municipal bonds	7.2	10.8	40	0	30	0	30
Large-cap U.S. stocks	13.0	17.0	20	15	35	25	5
Small-cap U.S. stocks	15.0	21.0	10	10	0	15	5
International stocks (EAFE)	15.0	21.0	10	10	0	15	10
Real estate investment trusts (REITs)	10.0	15.0	10	10	10	25	35
Venture capital	26.0	64.0	0	10	0	15	5
TOTAL			100	100	100	100	100

Summary Data

	Asset Allocation A	Asset Allocation B	Asset Allocation C	Asset Allocation D	Asset Allocation E
Projected total return	9.9%	11.0%	8.8%	14.4%	10.3%
Projected after-tax total return	7.4%	7.2%	6.5%	9.4%	7.4%
Expected standard deviation	9.4%	12.4%	8.5%	18.1%	10.1%
Sharpe ratio	0.574	0.524	0.506	—	0.574

TABLE 28G

Alternative asset allocations, prepared by HH Counselors

  d. Assume that the risk-free rate is 4.5%.

    i. Calculate the Sharpe ratio for Asset Allocation D.

    ii. Determine the two asset allocations in Table 28G having the best risk-adjusted returns, based only on the Sharpe ratio measure.

  e. Recommend and justify the one asset allocation in Table 28G you believe would be the best model for Fairfax's savings portfolio.

7. John Franklin is a recent widower with some experience in investing for his own account. Following his wife's recent death and settlement of the estate, Mr. Franklin owns a controlling interest in a successful privately held manufacturing company in which Mrs. Franklin was formerly active, a recently completed warehouse property, the family residence, and his personal holdings of stocks and bonds. He has decided to retain the warehouse property as a diversifying investment but intends to sell the private company interest, giving half of the proceeds to a medical research foundation in memory of his deceased wife. Actual transfer of this gift is expected to take place about 3 months from now. You have been engaged to assist him with the valuations, planning, and portfolio building required to structure his investment program appropriately.

  Mr. Franklin has introduced you to the finance committee of the medical research foundation that is to receive his $45 million cash gift 3 months hence (and will eventually receive the assets of his estate). This gift will greatly increase the size of the foundation's endowment (from $10 million to $55 million) as well as enable it to make larger grants to researchers. The foundation's grant-making (spending) policy has been to pay out virtually all of its annual net investment income. As its investment approach has been very conservative, the endowment portfolio now consists almost entirely of fixed-income assets. The finance committee understands that these actions are causing the real value of foundation assets and the real value of future grants to decline due to the effects of inflation. Until now, the finance committee has believed that it had no alternative to these actions, given the large immediate cash needs of the research programs being funded and the small size of the foundation's capital base. The foundation's annual grants must at least equal 5% of its assets' market value to maintain its U.S. tax-exempt status, a requirement that is expected to continue indefinitely. No additional gifts or fund-raising activities are expected over the foreseeable future.

  Given the change in circumstances that Mr. Franklin's gift will make, the finance committee wishes to develop new grant-making and investment policies. Annual spending must at least meet the level of 5% of market value that is required to maintain the foundation's tax-exempt status, but the committee is unsure about how much higher than 5% it can or should be. The committee wants to pay out as much as possible because of the critical nature of the research being funded; however, it understands that preserving the real value of the foundation's assets is equally important in order to preserve its future grant-making capabilities. You have been asked to assist the committee in developing appropriate policies.

  a. Identify and briefly discuss the three key elements that should determine the foundation's grant-making (spending) policy.

  b. Formulate and justify an investment policy statement for the foundation, taking into account the increased size of its assets arising from Mr. Franklin's gift. Your policy statement must encompass all relevant objectives, constraints, and the key elements identified in your answer to part (*a*).

  c. Recommend and justify a long-term asset allocation that is consistent with the investment policy statement you created in part (*b*). Explain how your allocation's expected return meets the requirements of a feasible grant-making (spending) policy for the foundation. (*Hint:* Your allocation must sum to 100% and should use the economic/market data presented in Table 28H and your knowledge of historical asset-class characteristics.)

8. Christopher Maclin, aged 40, is a supervisor at Barnett Co. and earns an annual salary of £80,000 before taxes. Louise Maclin, aged 38, stays home to care for their newborn twins. She recently inherited £900,000 (after wealth-transfer taxes) in cash from her father's estate. In addition, the Maclins have accumulated the following assets (current market value):

- £5,000 in cash.
- £160,000 in stocks and bonds.
- £220,000 in Barnett common stock.

	Historic Averages	Intermediate Term Consensus Forecast
U.S. Treasury bills	3.7%	4.2%
Intermediate-term U.S. T-bonds	5.2	5.8
Long-term U.S. T-bonds	4.8	7.7
U.S. corporate bonds (AAA)	5.5	8.8
Non-U.S. bonds (AAA)	N/A	8.4
U.S. common stocks (all)	10.3	9.0
U.S. common stocks (small-cap)	12.2	12.0
Non-U.S. common stocks (all)	N/A	10.1
U.S. inflation	3.1	3.5

TABLE 28H

Capital markets annnualized return data

The value of their holdings in Barnett stock has appreciated substantially as a result of the company's growth in sales and profits during the past 10 years. Christopher Maclin is confident that the company and its stock will continue to perform well.

The Maclins need £30,000 for a down payment on the purchase of a house and plan to make a £20,000 non–tax deductible donation to a local charity in memory of Louise Maclin's father. The Maclins' annual living expenses are £74,000. After-tax salary increases will offset any future increases in their living expenses.

During their discussions with Grant Webb, the Maclins' express concern about achieving their educational goals for their children and their own retirement goals. The Maclins tell Webb:

- They want to have sufficient funds to retire in 18 years when their children begin their 4 years of university education.
- They have been unhappy with the portfolio volatility they have experienced in recent years and they do not want to experience a loss greater than 12% in any one year.
- They do not want to invest in alcohol and tobacco stocks.
- They will not have any additional children.

After their discussions, Webb calculates that in 18 years the Maclins will need £2 million to meet their educational and retirement goals. Webb suggests that their portfolio be structured to limit shortfall risk (defined as expected total return minus two standard deviations) to no lower than a −12% return in any one year. Maclin's salary and all capital gains and investment income are taxed at 40% and no tax-sheltering strategies are available. Webb's next step is to formulate an investment policy statement for the Maclins.

a. Formulate the risk objective of an investment policy statement for the Maclins.
b. Formulate the return objective of an investment policy statement for the Maclins. Calculate the pretax rate of return that is required to achieve this objective. Show your calculations.
c. Formulate the constraints portion of an investment policy statement for the Maclins, addressing each of the following:

   i. Time horizon
   ii. Liquidity requirements
   iii. Tax concerns
   iv. Unique circumstances

9. Louise and Christopher Maclin have purchased their house and made the donation to the local charity. Now that an investment policy statement has been prepared for the Maclins, Grant Webb recommends that they consider the strategic asset allocation described in Table 28I.

Asset Class	Recommended Allocation	Current Yield	Projected Annualized Pretax Total Return	Expected Standard Deviation
Cash	15.0%	1.0%	1.0%	2.5%
U.K. corporate bonds	55.0	4.0	5.0	11.0
U.K. small-capitalization equities	0.0	0.0	11.0	25.0
U.K. large-capitalization equities	10.0	2.0	9.0	21.0
U.S. equities*	5.0	1.5	10.0	20.0
Barnett Co. common stock	15.0	1.0	16.0	48.0
Total portfolio	100.0	—	6.7	12.4

TABLE 28I

Louise and Christopher Maclin's recommended strategic asset allocation
*U.S. equity data are in British pound terms.

Asset Class	Allocation Ranges		
Cash	0%–3%	5%–10%	15%–20%
U.K. corporate bonds	10%–20%	30%–40%	50%–60%
U.S. equities	0%–5%	10%–15%	20%–25%
Barnett Co. common stock	0%–5%	10%–15%	20%–25%

TABLE 28J

Louise and Christopher Maclin's asset class ranges

a. Identify aspects of the recommended asset allocation in Table 28I that are inconsistent with the Maclins' investment objectives and constraints. Support your responses.

b. After further discussion, Webb and the Maclins agree that any suitable strategic asset allocation will include 5 to 10% in U.K. small-capitalization equities and 10 to 15% in U.K. large-capitalization equities. For the remainder of the portfolio, Webb is considering the asset class ranges described in Table 28J.

Recommend the most appropriate allocation range for each of the asset classes in Table 28J. Justify each appropriate allocation range with a reason based on the Maclins' investment objectives and constraints.

Note: No calculations are required.

E-Investments

Asset Allocation and Financial Planning

Visit the *Asset Allocation Wizard* site, which provides suggestions about portfolio asset proportions based on your time frame and attitude toward risk: **http://cgi. money.cnn.com/tools/assetallocwizard/assetallocwizard.html.** After you run the calculator with your preferences, change your inputs slightly to see what effect that would have on the results.

For a comprehensive retirement planning calculator, go to **http://cgi.money. cnn. com/tools/retirementplanner/retirementplanner.jsp.** After you specify your current income and savings habits, your attitude toward risk, and other relevant information, the calculator will tell you the probability of successfully meeting your goals. It also offers suggestions for future savings plans and a graph of probabilities for several possible outcomes.

SOLUTIONS TO CONCEPT CHECKS

1. Identify the elements that are life cycle–driven in the two schemes of objectives and constraints.

2. If the investor keeps her present asset allocation, she will have the following amounts to spend after taxes 5 years from now:

   Tax-qualified account:

   Bonds: $50,000(1.1)^5 \times .72$ $= \$\ 57,978.36$

   Stocks: $50,000(1.15)^5 \times .72$ $= \$\ 72,408.86$

   Subtotal $\$130,387.22$

   Nonretirement account:

   Bonds: $50,000[1 + (.10 \times .85)]^5$ $= \$\ 75,182.83$

   Stocks: $50,000(1.15)^5 - .15 \times [50,000(1.15)^5 - 50,000]$ $= \$\ 92,982.68$

   Subtotal $\$168,165.51$

   Total $\$298,552.73$

   If she shifts all of the bonds into the retirement account and all of the stock into the nonretirement account, she will have the following amounts to spend after taxes 5 years from now:

   Tax-qualified account:

   Bonds: $100,000(1.1)^5 \times .72$ $= \$115,956.72$

   Nonretirement account:

   Stocks: $100,000(1.15)^5 - .15 \times [100,000(1.15)^5 - 100,000]$ $= \$185,965.36$

   Total $= \$301,922.08$

   Her spending budget will increase by $3,369.35.

3. The contribution to each fund will be $2,000 per year (i.e., 5% of $40,000) in constant dollars. At retirement she will have in her guaranteed return fund:

   $$\$50,000 \times 1.03^{20} + \$2,000 \times \text{Annuity factor}(3\%, 20 \text{ years}) = \$144,046$$

   That is the amount she will have for *sure.*

   In addition the expected future value of her stock account is:

   $$\$50,000 \times 1.06^{20} + \$2,000 \times \text{Annuity factor}(6\%, 20 \text{ years}) = \$233,928$$

4. He has accrued an annuity of $.01 \times 15 \times 15,000 = \$2,250$ per year for 15 years, starting in 25 years. The present value of this annuity is $2,812.13:

   $$\text{PV} = 2,250 \times \text{Annuity factor}(8\%, 15) \times \text{PV factor}(8\%, 25) = 2,812.13$$

APPENDIX: A Spreadsheet Model for Long-Term Investing

Saving for the Long Run

Our objective here is to quantify the essentials of savings/investment plans and adapt them to environments in which investors confront both inflation and taxes. As a first step in the process, we set up a spreadsheet for a simple retirement plan, ignoring for the moment saving for other objectives.

A Hypothetical Household   Imagine you are now 30 years old and have already completed your formal education, accumulated some work experience, and settled down to plan the rest of your economic life. Your plan is to retire at age 65 with a remaining life expectancy of an additional 25 years. Later on, we will further assume that you have two small children and plan to finance their college education.

For starters, we assume you intend to obtain a (level) annuity for your 25-year retirement period. Suppose your gross income this year was $50,000, and you expect annual income to increase at a rate of 7% per year. In this section, we assume that you ignore the impact of inflation and taxes. You intend to steadily save 15% of income and invest in safe government bonds that will yield 6% over the entire period. Proceeds from your investments will be automatically reinvested at the same 6% until retirement. Upon retirement, your funds in the retirement account will be used to purchase a 25-year annuity (using the same 6% interest rate) to finance a steady consumption annuity. Let's examine the consequences of this framework.

The Retirement Annuity   We can easily obtain your *retirement annuity* from Spreadsheet 28A.1, where we have hidden the lines for ages 32–34, 36–44, 46–54, and 56–64. You can obtain all the spreadsheets in this chapter from the Web page for the text available at the Online Learning Center: **www.mhhe.com/bkm.**

Let's first see how this spreadsheet was constructed. To view the formulas of all cells in an Excel spreadsheet, choose "Preferences" under the "Tools" menu, and select the box "Formulas" in the "View" tab. The formula view of Spreadsheet 28A.1 is also shown on the next page (numbers are user inputs).

Inputs in row 2 include: retirement years (cell A2 = 25); income growth (cell B2 = .07); age (column A); and income at age 30 (B4 = 50,000). Column B computes income in future years using the growth rate in cell B2; column C computes annual savings by applying the savings rate (cell C2) to income; and column E computes consumption as the difference between income and savings: column B – column C. Cumulative savings appear in column D. To obtain the value in D6, for example, multiply cell D5 by 1 plus the assumed rate of return in cell D2 (the ROR) and then add current savings from column C. Finally, C40 shows the sum of dollars saved over the lifetime, and E40 converts cumulative

	A	B	C	D	E
1	Retirement Years	Income Growth	Savings Rate	ROR	
2	25	0.07	0.15	0.06	
3	Age	Income	Savings	Cumulative Savings	Consumption
4	30	50,000	7,500	7,500	42,500
5	31	53,500	8,025	15,975	45,475
6	32	57,245	8,587	25,520	48,658
9	35	70,128	10,519	61,658	59,608
19	45	137,952	20,693	308,859	117,259
29	55	271,372	40,706	943,477	230,666
39	65	533,829	80,074	2,457,518	453,755
40	Total	7,445,673	1,116,851	Retirement Annuity	192,244

	A	B	C	D	E
1	Retirement Years	Income Growth	Savings Rate	ROR	
2	25	0.07	0.15	0.06	
3	Age	Income	Savings	Cumulative Savings	Consumption
4	30	50000	=B4*$C$2	=C4	=B4-C4
5	31	=B4*(1+$B$2)	=B5*$C$2	=D4*(1+$D$2)+C5	=B5-C5
39	65	=B38*(1+$B$2)	=B39*$C$2	=D38*(1+$D$2)+C39	=B39-C39
40	Total	=SUM(B4:B39)	=SUM(C4:C39)	Retirement Annuity	=PMT($D$2,$A$2,-$D$39,0,0)

SPREADSHEET 28A.1   e**X**cel

The Savings plan

Please visit us at
www.mhhe.com/bkm

savings (including interest) at age 65 to a 25-year annuity using the financial function PMT from Excel's function menu. Excel provides a function to solve for annuity levels given the values of the interest rate, the number of periods, the present value of the savings account, and the future value of the account: PMT(rate, nper, PV, FV).

We observe that your retirement fund will accumulate approximately $2.5 million (cell D39) by age 65. This hefty sum shows the power of compounding, because your contributions to the savings account were only $1.1 million (C40). This fund will yield an annuity of $192,244 per year (E40) for your 25-year retirement, which seems quite attractive, except that the standard of living you'll have to get accustomed to in your retirement years is much lower than your consumption at age 65 (E39). In fact, if you unhide the hidden lines, you'll see that upon retirement, you'll have to make do with what you used to consume at age 51. This may not worry you much because, with your children having flown the coop and the mortgage paid up, you may be able to maintain the luxury to which you recently became accustomed. But your projected well-being is deceptive: get ready to account for inflation and taxes.

<table><tr><td>CONCEPT CHECK A.1</td><td>If you project an ROR of only 5%, what savings rate would you need to maintain the same retirement annuity?</td></tr></table>

Accounting for Inflation

Inflation puts a damper on your plans in two ways: First, it erodes the purchasing power of the cumulative dollars you have so far saved. Second, the *real* dollars you earn on your portfolio each year depend on the *real* interest rate, which is approximately equal to the nominal rate minus inflation. Because an appropriate savings plan must generate a decent *real* annuity, we must recast the entire plan in real dollars. We will assume your income still is forecast to grow at a 7% rate, but now you recognize that part of income growth is due to inflation, which is running at 3% per year.

A Real Savings Plan   To convert nominal dollars to real dollars we need to calculate the price level in future years relative to today's prices. The "deflator" (or relative price level) for a given year is that year's price level divided by today's. It equals the dollars needed at that future date which provide the same purchasing power as $1 today (at age 30). For an inflation rate of $i = 3\%$, the deflator for age 35 is $(1 + i)^5$, or in Excel notation, $(1 + i)^5 = 1.03^5 = 1.16$. By age 65, the deflator is 2.81. Thus, even with a moderate rate of inflation, nominal dollars will lose a lot of purchasing power over long horizons. We also can compute the *real* rate of return (rROR) from the nominal ROR of 6%: rROR = (ROR − i)/(1 + i) = 3/1.03 = 2.91%.

Spreadsheet 28A.2, with the formula view below it, is the reworked Spreadsheet 28A.1 adjusted for inflation. In addition to the rate of inflation (cell C2) and the real rate of return (F2), the major addition to this sheet is the price level deflator (column C). Instead of nominal consumption, we present *real consumption* (column F), calculated by dividing nominal consumption (column B − column D) by the price deflator, column C.

The numbers have changed considerably. Gone is the luxurious retirement we anticipated earlier. At age 65 and beyond, with a real annuity of $49,668, you will have to revert to a standard of living equal to that you attained at age 34; this is less than a third of your real consumption in your last working year, at age 65. The reason is that the retirement fund of $2.5 million (E39) is worth only $873,631 in today's purchasing power (E39/C39). Such is the effect of inflation. If you wish to do better than this, you must save more.

	A	B	C	D	E	F
1	Retirement Years	Income Growth	Rate of Inflation	Savings Rate	ROR	rROR
2	25	0.07	0.03	0.15	0.06	0.0291
3	Age	Income	Deflator	Saving	Cumulative Savings	rConsumption
4	30	50,000	1.00	7,500	7,500	42,500
5	31	53,500	1.03	8,025	15,975	44,150
9	35	70,128	1.16	10,519	61,658	51,419
19	45	137,952	1.56	20,693	308,859	75,264
29	55	271,372	2.09	40,706	943,477	110,167
39	65	533,829	2.81	80,074	2,457,518	161,257
40	Total	7,445,673		1,116,851	Real Annuity	49,668

	A	B	C	D	E	F
1	Retirement Years	Income Growth	Rate of Inflation	Savings Rate	ROR	rROR
2	25	0.07	0.03	0.15	0.06	=(E2-C2)/(1+C2)
3	Age	Income	Deflator	Savings	Cumulative Savings	rConsumption
4	30	50000	1	=B4*$D$2	=D4	=(B4-D4)/C4
5	31	=B4*(1+$B$2)	=C4*(1+$C$2)	=B5*$D$2	=E4*(1+$E$2)+D5	=(B5-D5)/C5
39	65	=B38*(1+$B$2)	=C38*(1+$C$2)	=B39*$D$2	=E38*(1+$E$2)+D39	=(B39-D39)/C39
40	Total	=SUM(B4:B39)		=SUM(D4:D39)	Real Annuity	=PMT($F$2,$A$2,-$E$39/$C$39,0,0)

SPREADSHEET 28A.2

eXcel

Please visit us at
www.mhhe.com/bkm

A real retirement plan

In our initial plan (Spreadsheet 28A.1), we envisioned consuming a level, nominal annuity for the retirement years. This is an inappropriate goal once we account for inflation, because it would imply a declining standard of living starting at age 65. Its purchasing power at age 65 in terms of current dollars would be $64,542 (i.e., $181,362/2.81), and at age 90 only $30,792. (Check this!)

It is tempting to contemplate solving the problem of an inadequate retirement annuity by increasing the assumed rate of return on investments. However, this can only be accomplished by putting your savings at risk. Much of this text elaborates on how to do so efficiently; yet it also emphasizes that while taking on risk will give you an *expectation* for a better retirement, it implies as well a nonzero probability of doing a lot worse. At the age of 30, you should be able to tolerate some risk to the retirement annuity for the simple reason that if things go wrong, you can change course, increase your savings rate, and work harder. As you get older, this option progressively fades, and increasing risk becomes less of a viable option. If you do choose to increase risk, you can set a "safety-first target" (i.e., a minimum acceptable goal) for the retirement annuity and continuously monitor your risky portfolio. If the portfolio does poorly and approaches the safety-first target, you progressively shift into risk-free bonds—you may recognize this strategy as a version of dynamic hedging.

The difficulty with this strategy is twofold: First it requires monitoring, which is time-consuming and may be nerve-racking as well. Second, when decision time comes, it may be psychologically hard to withdraw. By shifting out of the risky portfolio if and when your portfolio is hammered, you give up any hope of recovery. This is hard to do and many investors fail the test. For these investors, therefore, the right approach is to stick with the safe, lower ROR and make the effort to balance standard of living before and after retirement. Avoiding sleepless nights is ample reward.

Therefore, the only variable we leave under your control in this spreadsheet is the rate of saving. To improve retirement lifestyle relative to the preretirement years, without jeopardizing its safety, you will have to reduce consumption during the saving years—there is no free lunch.

CONCEPT CHECK A.2

If you project a rate of inflation of 4%, what nominal ROR on investments would you need to maintain the same real retirement annuity as in Spreadsheet 28A.2?

Visit us at www.mhhe.com/bkm

	A	B	C	D	E	F
1	Retirement Years	Income Growth	Rate of Inflation	Savings Rate	ROR	rROR
2	25	0.07	0.03	0.1	0.06	0.0291
3	Age	Income	Deflator	Savings	Cumulative Savings	rConsumption
4	30	50,000	1.00	5,000	5,000	45,000
5	31	53,500	1.03	5,511	10,811	46,592
9	35	70,128	1.16	8,130	44,351	53,480
19	45	137,952	1.56	21,492	260,927	74,751
29	55	271,372	2.09	56,819	947,114	102,471
39	65	533,829	2.81	150,212	2,964,669	136,331
40	Total	7,445,673		1,572,466	Real Annuity	59,918

	A	B	C	D	E	F
1	Retirement Years	Income Growth	Rate of Inflation	Savings Rate	ROR	rROR
2	25	0.07	0.03	0.1	0.06	=(E2-C2)/(1+C2)
3	Age	Income	Deflator	Savings	Cumulative Savings	rConsumption
4	30	50000	1	=B4*C4*$D$2	=D4	=(B4-D4)/C4
5	31	=B4*(1+$B$2)	=C4*(1+$C$2)	=B5*C5*$D$2	=E4*(1+$E$2)+D5	=(B5-D5)/C5
39	65	=B38*(1+$B$2)	=C38*(1+$C$2)	=B39*C39*$D$2	=E38*(1+$E$2)+D39	=(B39-D39)/C39
40	Total	=SUM(B4:B39)		=SUM(D4:D39)	Real Annuity	=PMT($F$2,$A$2,-$E$39/$C$39,0,0)

SPREADSHEET 28A.3   eXcel

Saving from real income

Please visit us at www.mhhe.com/bkm

An Alternative Savings Plan   In Spreadsheet 28A.2, we saved a constant fraction of income. But because real income grows over time (nominal income grows at 7% while inflation is only 3%), we might consider deferring our savings toward future years when our real income is higher. By applying a higher savings rate to our future (higher) real income, we can afford to reduce the current savings rate. In Spreadsheet 28A.3, we use a base savings rate of 10% (lower than the savings rate in the previous spreadsheet), but we increase the savings target by 3% per year. Saving in each year t therefore equals a fixed savings rate times annual income (column B), times 1.03^t. By saving a larger fraction of income in later years, when real income is larger, you create a smoother profile of real consumption.

Spreadsheet 28A.3 shows that with an *initial* savings rate of 10%, compared with the unchanging 15% rate in the previous spreadsheet, you can achieve a retirement annuity of $59,918, larger than the $49,668 annuity in the previous plan.

Notice that real consumption in the early years is greater than with the previous plan. What you have done is to postpone saving until your income is much higher. At first blush, this plan is preferable: It allows for a more comfortable consumption of 90% of income at the outset, a consistent increase in standard of living during your earning years, all without significantly affecting the retirement annuity. But this program has one serious downside: By postponing the bulk of your savings to a later age, you come to depend on your health, longevity, and, more ominously (and without possibility of insurance), on a successful future career. Put differently, this plan achieves comfort by increasing risk, making this choice a matter of risk tolerance.

CONCEPT CHECK A.3

Suppose you like the plan of tilting savings toward later years, but worry about the increased risk of postponing the bulk of your savings to later years. Is there anything you can do to mitigate the risk?

Accounting for Taxes

To initiate a discussion of taxes, let's assume that you are subject to a *flat tax* rate of 25% on taxable income less one exemption of $15,000. An important feature of this (and

	A	B	C	D	E	F	G	H
1	Retirement Years	Income Growth	Rate of Inflation	Exemption Now	Tax Rate	Savings Rate	ROR	rROR
2	25	0.07	0.03	15000	0.25	0.15	0.06	0.0291
3	Age	Income	Deflator	Exemption	Taxes	Savings	Cumulative Savings	rConsumption
4	30	50,000	1.00	15,000	8,750	6,188	6,188	35,063
5	31	53,500	1.03	15,450	9,605	6,584	13,143	36,224
9	35	70,128	1.16	17,389	13,775	8,453	50,188	41,319
19	45	137,952	1.56	23,370	31,892	15,909	245,334	57,864
29	55	271,372	2.09	31,407	69,943	30,214	733,467	81,773
39	65	533,829	2.81	42,208	148,611	57,783	1,874,346	116,365
40	Total				1,884,163	834,226	Real Annuity=	37,882
41	**RETIREMENT**							
42	Age	Nom Withdraw	Deflator	Exemption	Taxes		Funds Left	rConsumption
43	66	109,792	2.90	43,474	17,247		1,877,014	31,931
47	70	123,572	3.26	48,931	15,743		1,853,382	33,056
52	75	143,254	3.78	56,724	12,200		1,721,015	34,656
57	80	166,071	4.38	65,759	6,047		1,422,954	36,503
62	85	192,521	5.08	76,232	0		883,895	37,882
67	90	223,185	5.89	88,374	0		0	37,882
68	Total	4,002,944			203,199			

	A	B	C	D	E	F	G	H
1	Retirement Years	Income Growth	Rate of Inflation	Exemption Now	Tax Rate	Savings Rate	ROR	rROR
2	25	0.07	0.03	15000	0.25	0.15	0.06	=(G2-C2)/(1+C2)
3	Age	Income	Deflator	Exemption	Taxes	Savings	Cumulative Savings	rConsumption
4	30	50000	1	=$D$2*C4	=(B4-D4)*$E$2	=(B4-E4)*$F$2	=F4	=(B4-E4-F4)/C4
5	31	=B4*(1+$B$2)	=C4*(1+$C$2)	=$D$2*C5	=(B5-D5+G4*$G$2)*$E$2	=(B5-E5)*$F$2	=G4*(1+$G$2)+F5	=(B5-E5-F5)/C5
39	65	=B38*(1+$B$2)	=C38*(1+$C$2)	=$D$2*C39	=(B39-D39+G38*$G$2)*$E$2	=(B39-E39)*$F$2	=G38*(1+$G$2)+F39	=(B39-E39-F39)/C39
40	Total				=SUM(E4:E39)	=SUM(F4:F39)	Real Annuity	=PMT($H$2,$A$2,-$G$39/$C$39,0,0)
41	**RETIREMENT**							
42	Age	Nom Withdraw	Deflator	Exemption	Taxes		Funds Left	rConsumption
43	66	=$H$40*C43	=C39*(1+$C$2)	=$D$2*C43	=MAX(0,(G39*$G$2-D43)*$E$2)		=G39*(1+$G$2)-B43	=(B43-E43)/C43
44	67	=$H$40*C44	=C43*(1+$C$2)	=$D$2*C44	=MAX(0,(G43*$G$2-D44)*$E$2)		=G43*(1+$G$2)-B44	=(B44-E44)/C44
67	90	=$H$40*C67	=C66*(1+$C$2)	=$D$2*C67	=MAX(0,(G66*$G$2-D67)*$E$2)		=G66*(1+$G$2)-B67	=(B67-E67)/C67
68	Total	=SUM(B43:B67)			=SUM(E43:E67)			

SPREADSHEET 28A.4

eXcel
Please visit us at
www.mhhe.com/bkm

Savings with a simple tax code

the existing) tax code is that the tax rate is levied on nominal income and applies as well to investment income. (This is the concept of double taxation—you pay taxes when you earn income and then you pay taxes again when your savings earn interest.) Some relief from the effect of taxing nominal dollars both in this proposal and the current U.S. code is provided by raising the exemption, annually, by the rate of inflation. To adapt our spreadsheet to this simple tax code, we must add columns for taxes and after-tax income. The tax-adjusted plan is shown in Spreadsheet 28A.4. It adapts the savings plan of Spreadsheet 28A.2.

The top panel of the sheet deals with the earning years. Column D adjusts the exemption (D2) by the price level (column C). Column E applies the tax rate (cell E2) to taxable income (column B – column D). The savings rate (F2) is applied to after-tax income (column B – column E), allowing us to calculate cumulative savings (column G) and real consumption (column H). The formula view shows the detailed construction.

As you might have expected, real consumption is lower in the presence of taxes, as are savings and the retirement fund. The retirement fund provides for a real, before-tax annuity of only $37,882, compared with $49,668 absent taxes in Spreadsheet 28A.2.

The bottom panel of the sheet shows the further reduction in real consumption due to taxes paid during the retirement years. While you do not pay taxes on the cumulative savings in the retirement plan (you did that already as the savings accrued interest), you do pay taxes on interest earned by the fund while you are drawing it down. These taxes are quite significant and further deplete the fund and its net-of-tax earning power. For this reason, your consumption annuity is lower in the early years when your fund has not yet been depleted and earns quite a bit.

In the end, despite a handsome income that grows at a real rate of almost 4%, an aggressive savings rate of 15%, a modest rate of inflation, and a modest tax, you will only be able to achieve a modest (but at least low-risk) real retirement income. This is a reality with which most people must struggle. Whether to sacrifice more of today's standard of living through an increased rate of saving, or take some risk in the form of saving a real annuity and/or invest in a risky portfolio with a higher expected return, is a question of preference and risk tolerance.

Of course, this model is just a beginning. Its description of the tax code is overly simplistic. You probably would want to add a progressive tax feature to the spreadsheet. You would want to add as well opportunities for tax sheltering (e.g., IRAs and 401k plans), Social Security, and large expenditures such as housing purchase and college education. But the model is highly adaptable and lays out a basic framework that can accommodate taxes, inflation, and a variety of institutional features such as tax-sheltered savings plans. We invite you to download the model from this text's Web site (**www.mhhe.com/bkm**) and adapt it to your needs.

SOLUTIONS TO CONCEPT CHECKS

A1. When ROR falls by 1% to 5%, the retirement annuity falls from $192,244 to $149,855 (i.e., by 22.45%). To restore this annuity, the savings rate must rise by 4.24 percentage points to 19.24%. With this savings rate, the entire loss of 1% in ROR falls on consumption during the earning years.

A2. Intuition suggests you need to keep the real rate (2.91%) constant, that is, increase the nominal rate to 7.03% (confirm this). However, this will not be sufficient because the nominal income growth of 7% has a lower real growth when inflation is higher. Result: You must increase the real ROR to compensate for a lower growth in real income, ending with a nominal rate of 7.67%.

A3. There are two components to the risk of relying on future income: disability/death and career failure/unemployment. You can insure the first component, but not the second.

Each end-of-chapter CFA question is reprinted with permission from the CFA Institute, Charlottesville, VA. Following is a list of the CFA questions in the end-of-chapter material and the exams and study guides from which they were taken and updated.

Chapter 2

1–3. 1996 Level I CFA Study Guide, © 1996
4. 1994 Level I CFA Study Guide, © 1994
5. 1994 Level I CFA Study Guide, © 1994

Chapter 3

1. 1986 Level I CFA Study Guide, © 1986
2–3. 1986 Level I CFA Study Guide, © 1986

Chapter 5

1. 1992 Level I CFA Study Guide, © 1992
2. 1992 Level I CFA Study Guide, © 1992
3–7. 1993 Level I CFA Study Guide, © 1993

Chapter 6

1–3. 1991 Level I CFA Study Guide, © 1991
4–5. 1991 Level I CFA Study Guide, © 1991
6. 1991 Level I CFA Study Guide, © 1991
7–9. 1993 Level I CFA Study Guide, © 1993
10. 1991 Level I CFA Study Guide, © 1991

Chapter 7

1–3. 1982 Level III CFA Study Guide, © 1982
4. 1993 Level I CFA Study Guide, © 1993
5. 1993 Level I CFA Study Guide, © 1993
6. 1992 Level I CFA Study Guide, © 1992
7. 1992 Level I CFA Study Guide, © 1992
8–10. 1994 Level I CFA Study Guide, © 1994
11. 2001 Level III CFA Study Guide, © 2001
12. 2001 Level II CFA Study Guide, © 2001
13. 2000 Level II CFA Study Guide, © 2000

Chapter 8

1. 1982 Level I CFA Study Guide, © 1982
2. 1993 Level I CFA Study Guide, © 1993
3. 1993 Level I CFA Study Guide, © 1993
4. 1993 Level I CFA Study Guide, © 1993
5. 1994 Level I CFA Study Guide, © 1994

Chapter 9

1. 2002 Level I CFA Study Guide, © 2002
2. 2002 Level I CFA Study Guide, © 2002
3–5. 1993 Level I CFA Study Guide, © 1993
6. 1992 Level I CFA Study Guide, © 1992
7. 1994 Level I CFA Study Guide, © 1994

8. 1993 Level I CFA Study Guide, © 1993
9. 1994 Level I CFA Study Guide, © 1994
10. 1994 Level I CFA Study Guide, © 1994
11. 2002 Level II CFA Study Guide, © 2002
12. 2000 Level II CFA Study Guide, © 2000

Chapter 10

1. 2001 Level II CFA Study Guide, © 2001
2–8. 1991–1993 Level I CFA Study Guides

Chapter 11

1–5. 1993 Level I CFA Study Guide, © 1993
6. 1992 Level I CFA Study Guide, © 1992
7. 1992 Level I CFA Study Guide, © 1992
8–10. 1996 Level III CFA Study Guide, © 1996

Chapter 12

1. 2000 Level III CFA Study Guide, © 2000
2. 2001 Level III CFA Study Guide, © 2001
3. 2004 Level III CFA Study Guide, © 2004
4. 2003 Level III CFA Study Guide, © 2003
5. 2002 Level III CFA Study Guide, © 2002

Chapter 13

1. 1993 Level I CFA Study Guide, © 1993
2. 1993 Level I CFA Study Guide, © 1993
3. 2002 Level II CFA Study Guide, © 2002

Chapter 14

1. 1993 Level I CFA Study Guide, © 1993
2. 1994 Level I CFA Study Guide, © 1994
3. 1999 Level II CFA Study Guide, © 1999
4. 1992 Level II CFA Study Guide, © 1992
5. 1993 Level I CFA Study Guide, © 1993
6. 1992 Level I CFA Study Guide, © 1992

Chapter 15

1. 1993 Level II CFA Study Guide, © 1993
2. 1993 Level I CFA Study Guide, © 1993
3. 1993 Level II CFA Study Guide, © 1993
4. 1994 Level I CFA Study Guide, © 1994
5. 1994 Level II CFA Study Guide, © 1994
6. 2004 Level II CFA Study Guide, © 2004
7. 1999 Level II CFA Study Guide, © 1999
8. 2000 Level II CFA Study Guide, © 2000
9. 1996 Level II CFA Study Guide, © 1996
10. 2000 Level II CFA Study Guide, © 2000

Chapter 16

1. 1993 Level II CFA Study Guide, © 1993
2. 1992–1994 Level I CFA study guides
3. 1993 Level I CFA Study Guide, © 1993
4. 1993 Level I CFA Study Guide, © 1993
5. 2004 Level II CFA Study Guide, © 2004
6. 1996 Level III CFA Study Guide, © 1996
7. 1998 Level II CFA Study Guide, © 1998
8. From various Level I study guides
9. 1994 Level III CFA Study Guide, © 1994
10. 2000 Level III CFA Study Guide, © 2000
11. 2003 Level II CFA Study Guide, © 2003
12. 2001 Level II CFA Study Guide, © 2001
13. 1992 Level II CFA Study Guide, © 1992

Chapter 17

1. 1993 Level I CFA Study Guide, © 1993
2. 1993 Level I CFA Study Guide, © 1993
3. 1993 Level II CFA Study Guide, © 1993
4. 1993 Level II CFA Study Guide, © 1993
5. 1998 Level II CFA Study Guide, © 1998
6. 1995 Level II CFA Study Guide, © 1995
7. 2004 Level II CFA Study Guide, © 2004
8. 1993 Level I CFA Study Guide, © 1993

Chapter 18

1. 1998 Level II CFA Study Guide, © 1998
2. 1998 Level II CFA Study Guide, © 1998
3. 1995 Level II CFA Study Guide, © 1995
4. 2001 Level II CFA Study Guide, © 2001
5. 2001 Level II CFA Study Guide, © 2001
6. 2001 Level II CFA Study Guide, © 2001
7–8. 2004 Level II CFA Study Guide, © 2004
9. 2001 Level II CFA Study Guide, © 2001
10. 1993 Level I CFA Study Guide, © 1993
11. 2003 Level I CFA Study Guide, © 2003
12. 2003 Level I CFA Study Guide, © 2003
13. 2003 Level II CFA Study Guide, © 2003

Chapter 19

1. 1998 Level II CFA Study Guide, © 1998
2. 1998 Level II CFA Study Guide, © 1998
3. 1999 Level II CFA Study Guide, © 1999
4. 1992 Level I CFA Study Guide, © 1992
5. 1994 Level I CFA Study Guide, © 1994
6. 1998 Level II CFA Study Guide, © 1998

REFERENCES TO CFA QUESTIONS

7–10. 1992 Level I CFA Study Guide, © 1992
11. 1998 Level I CFA Study Guide, © 1998
12. 1994 Level I CFA Study Guide, © 1994
13. 1992 Level I CFA Study Guide, © 1992
14. 1993 Level II CFA Study Guide, © 1993
15. 1993 Level II CFA Study Guide, © 1993
16. 2002 Level II CFA Study Guide, © 2002
17. 1990 Level II CFA Study Guide, © 1990

Chapter 20

1. 2002 Level II CFA Study Guide, © 2002
2. 2000 Level II CFA Study Guide, © 2000
3. 2001 Level II CFA Study Guide, © 2001
4. 2002 Level II CFA Study Guide, © 2002
5. From various Level I study guides

Chapter 21

1. 1998 Level II CFA Study Guide, © 1998
2. 2003 Level II CFA Study Guide, © 2003
3. 1998 Level II CFA Study Guide, © 1998
4. 2000 Level II CFA Study Guide, © 2000
5. 1997 Level III CFA Study Guide, © 1997

Chapter 22

1. 2000 Level II CFA Study Guide, © 2000
2. 1993 Level II CFA Study Guide, © 1993
3. 1986 Level III CFA Study Guide, © 1986
4. 2004 Level II CFA Study Guide, © 2004
5. 2004 Level II CFA Study Guide, © 2004

Chapter 23

1. 2001 Level II CFA Study Guide, © 2001
2. 1995 Level III CFA Study Guide, © 1995
3. 1991 Level III CFA Study Guide, © 1991
4–5. 2003 Level II CFA Study Guide, © 2003
6. 2000 Level III CFA Study Guide, © 2000
7. 1985 Level III CFA Study Guide, © 1985
8. 1996 Level II CFA Study Guide, © 1996

Chapter 24

1. 1995 Level III CFA Study Guide, © 1995
2. 1981 Level I CFA Study Guide, © 1981
3. 1986 Level II CFA Study Guide, © 1986
4–13. From various Level I CFA study guides

14. 2001 Level III CFA Study Guide, © 2001
15. 2000 Level III CFA Study Guide, © 2000
16. 2002 Level III CFA Study Guide, © 2002

Chapter 25

1–3. From various Level I CFA study guides
4. 1986 Level III CFA Study Guide, © 1986
5. 1991 Level II CFA Study Guide, © 1991
6. 1995 Level II CFA Study Guide, © 1995
7. 2003 Level III CFA Study Guide, © 2003
8. 1998 Level II CFA Study Guide, © 1998

Chapter 28

1. 2001 Level III CFA Study Guide, © 2001
2–4. 1988 Level I CFA Study Guide, © 1988
5. 2002 Level III CFA Study Guide, © 2002
6. 1996 Level III CFA Study Guide, © 1996
7. 1993 Level III CFA Study Guide, © 1993
8. 2004 Level III CFA Study Guide, © 2004
9. 2004 Level III CFA Study Guide, © 2004

GLOSSARY

A

abnormal return Return on a stock beyond what would be predicted by market movements alone. Cumulative abnormal return (CAR) is the total abnormal return for the period surrounding an announcement or the release of information.

accounting earnings Earnings of a firm as reported on its income statement.

acid test ratio See quick ratio.

active management Attempts to achieve portfolio returns more than commensurate with risk, either by forecasting broad market trends or by identifying particular mispriced sectors of a market or securities in a market.

active portfolio In the context of the Treynor-Black model, the portfolio formed by mixing analyzed stocks of perceived nonzero alpha values. This portfolio is ultimately mixed with the passive market index portfolio.

adjusted alphas Forecasts for alpha that are modulated to account for statistical imprecision in the analyst's estimate.

agency problem Conflicts of interest among stockholders, bondholders, and managers.

alpha The abnormal rate of return on a security in excess of what would be predicted by an equilibrium model like CAPM or APT.

American depository receipts (ADRs) Domestically traded securities representing claims to shares of foreign stocks.

American option An American option can be exercised before and up to its expiration date. Compare with a *European option*, which can be exercised only on the expiration date.

announcement date Date on which particular news concerning a given company is announced to the public. Used in *event studies*, which researchers use to evaluate the economic impact of events of interest.

annual percentage rate (APR) Interest rate is annualized using simple rather than compound interest.

anomalies Patterns of returns that seem to contradict the efficient market hypothesis.

appraisal ratio The signal-to-noise ratio of an analyst's forecasts. The ratio of alpha to residual standard deviation.

arbitrage A zero-risk, zero-net investment strategy that still generates profits.

arbitrage pricing theory An asset pricing theory that is derived from a factor model, using diversification and arbitrage arguments. The theory describes the relationship between expected returns on securities, given that there are no opportunities to create wealth through risk-free arbitrage investments.

asked price The price at which a dealer will sell a security.

asset allocation Choosing among broad asset classes such as stocks versus bonds.

at the money When the exercise price and asset price of an option are equal.

auction market A market where all traders in a good meet at one place to buy or sell an asset. The NYSE is an example.

average collection period, or days' receivables The ratio of accounts receivable to sales, or the total amount of credit extended per dollar of daily sales (average AR/sales × 365).

B

backfill bias Bias in the average returns of a sample of funds induced by including past returns on funds that entered the sample only if they happened to be successful.

balance sheet An accounting statement of a firm's financial position at a specified time.

bank discount yield An annualized interest rate assuming simple interest, a 360-day year, and using the face value of the security rather than purchase price to compute return per dollar invested.

banker's acceptance A money market asset consisting of an order to a bank by a customer to pay a sum of money at a future date.

baseline forecasts Forecast of security returns derived from the assumption that the market is in equilibrium where current prices reflect all available information.

basis The difference between the futures price and the spot price.

basis risk Risk attributable to uncertain movements in the spread between a futures price and a spot price.

behavioral finance Models of financial markets that emphasize implications of psychological factors affecting investor behavior.

benchmark error Use of an inappropriate proxy for the true market portfolio.

benchmark portfolio Portfolio against which a manager is to be evaluated.

beta The measure of the systematic risk of a security. The tendency of a security's returns to respond to swings in the broad market.

bid–asked spread The difference between a dealer's bid and asked price.

bid price The price at which a dealer is willing to purchase a security.

binomial model An option-valuation model predicated on the assumption that stock prices can move to only two values over any short time period.

Black-Scholes formula An equation to value a call option that uses the stock price, the exercise price, the risk-free interest rate, the time to maturity, and the standard deviation of the stock return.

block sale A transaction of more than 10,000 shares of stock.

block transactions Large transactions in which at least 10,000 shares of stock are bought or sold. Brokers or "block houses" often search directly for other large traders rather than bringing the trade to the stock exchange.

bogey The return an investment manager is compared to for performance evaluation.

bond A security issued by a borrower that obligates the issuer to make specified payments to the holder over a specific period. A *coupon bond* obligates the issuer to make interest payments called coupon payments over the life of the bond, then to repay the *face value* at maturity.

bond equivalent yield Bond yield calculated on an annual percentage rate method. Differs from effective annual yield.

bond indenture The contract between the issuer and the bondholder.

bond reconstitution Combining stripped Treasury securities to re-create the original cash flows of a Treasury bond.

bond stripping Selling bond cash flows (either coupon or principal payments) as stand-alone zero-coupon securities.

book-to-market effect The tendency for stocks of firms with high ratios of book-to-market value to generate abnormal returns.

book value An accounting measure describing the net worth of common equity according to a firm's balance sheet.

breadth The extent to which movements in the broad market index are reflected widely in movements of individual stock prices.

brokered market A market where an intermediary (a broker) offers search services to buyers and sellers.

budget deficit The amount by which government spending exceeds government revenues.

bull CD, bear CD A *bull CD* pays its holder a specified percentage of the increase in return on a specified market index while guaranteeing a minimum rate of return. A *bear CD* pays the holder a fraction of any fall in a given market index.

bullish, bearish Words used to describe investor attitudes. *Bullish* means optimistic; *bearish* means pessimistic. Also used in bull market and bear market.

bundling, unbundling A trend allowing creation of securities either by combining primitive and derivative securities into one composite hybrid or by separating returns on an asset into classes.

business cycle Repetitive cycles of recession and recovery.

C

calendar spread Buy one option, and write another with a different expiration date.

callable bond A bond that the issuer may repurchase at a given price in some specified period.

call option The right to buy an asset at a specified exercise price on or before a specified expiration date.

call protection An initial period during which a callable bond may not be called.

capital allocation decision Allocation of invested funds between risk-free assets versus the risky portfolio.

capital allocation line (CAL) A graph showing all feasible risk–return combinations of a risky and risk-free asset.

capital gains The amount by which the sale price of a security exceeds the purchase price.

capital market line (CML) A capital allocation line provided by the market index portfolio.

capital markets Includes longer-term, relatively riskier securities.

cash/bond selection Asset allocation in which the choice is between short-term cash equivalents and longer-term bonds.

cash equivalents Short-term money-market securities.

cash flow matching A form of immunization, matching cash flows from a bond portfolio with an obligation.

cash ratio Measure of liquidity of a firm. Ratio of cash and marketable securities to current liabilities.

cash settlement The provision of some futures contracts that requires not delivery of the underlying assets (as in agricultural futures) but settlement according to the cash value of the asset.

certainty equivalent rate The certain return providing the same utility as a risky portfolio.

certificate of deposit A bank time deposit.

clearinghouse Established by exchanges to facilitate transfer of securities resulting from trades. For options and futures contracts, the clearinghouse may interpose itself as a middleman between two traders.

closed-end (mutual) fund A fund whose shares are traded through brokers at market prices; the fund will not redeem shares at their net asset value. The market price of the fund can differ from the net asset value.

collar An options strategy that brackets the value of a portfolio between two bounds.

collateral A specific asset pledged against possible default on a bond. *Mortgage bonds* are backed by claims on property. *Collateral trust bonds* are backed by claims on other securities. *Equipment obligation bonds* are backed by claims on equipment.

collateralized debt obligation (CDO) A pool of loans sliced into several tranches with different levels of risk.

collateralized mortgage obligation (CMO) A mortgage pass-through security that partitions cash flows from underlying mortgages into classes called *tranches* that receive principal payments according to stipulated rules.

commercial paper Short-term unsecured debt issued by large corporations.

common stock Equities, or equity securities, issued as ownership shares in a publicly held corporation. Shareholders have voting rights and may receive dividends based on their proportionate ownership.

comparison universe The collection of money managers of similar investment style used for assessing relative performance of a portfolio manager.

complete portfolio The entire portfolio, including risky and risk-free assets.

conditional tail expectation Expectation of a random variable conditional on its falling below some threshold value. Often used as a measure of down-side risk.

confidence index Ratio of the yield of top-rated corporate bonds to the yield on intermediate-grade bonds.

conservatism Notion that investors are too slow to update their beliefs in response to new evidence.

constant-growth model A form of the dividend discount model that assumes dividends will grow at a constant rate.

contango theory Holds that the futures price must exceed the expected future spot price.

contingent claim Claim whose value is directly dependent on or is contingent on the value of some underlying assets.

contingent immunization A mixed passive-active strategy that immunizes a portfolio if necessary to guarantee a minimum acceptable return but otherwise allows active management.

convergence arbitrage A bet that two or more prices are out of alignment and that profits can be made when the prices converge back to proper relationship.

convergence property The convergence of futures prices and spot prices at the maturity of the futures contract.

convertible bond A bond with an option allowing the bondholder to exchange the bond for a specified number of shares of common stock in the firm. A *conversion ratio* specifies the number of shares. The *market conversion price* is the current value of the shares for which the bond may be exchanged. The *conversion premium* is the excess of the bond's value over the conversion price.

convexity The curvature of the price-yield relationship of a bond.

corporate bonds Long-term debt issued by private corporations typically paying semiannual coupons and returning the face value of the bond at maturity.

correlation coefficient A statistic in which the covariance is scaled to a value between -1 (perfect negative correlation) and $+1$ (perfect positive correlation).

cost-of-carry relationship See spot-futures parity theorem.

country selection A type of active international management that measures the contribution to performance attributable to investing in the better-performing stock markets of the world.

coupon rate A bond's interest payments per dollar of par value.

covariance A measure of the degree to which returns on two risky assets move in tandem. A positive covariance means that asset returns move together. A negative covariance means they vary inversely.

covered call A combination of selling a call on a stock together with buying the stock.

covered interest arbitrage relationship See interest rate parity theorem.

credit default swap A derivative contract in which one party sells insurance concerning the credit risk of another firm.

credit enhancement Purchase of the financial guarantee of a large insurance company to raise funds.

credit risk Default risk.

cross hedge Hedging a position in one asset using futures on another commodity.

cumulative abnormal return See abnormal return.

currency selection Asset allocation in which the investor chooses among investments denominated in different currencies.

current ratio A ratio representing the ability of the firm to pay off its current liabilities by liquidating current assets (current assets/current liabilities).

current yield A bond's annual coupon payment divided by its price. Differs from yield to maturity.

cyclical industries Industries with above-average sensitivity to the state of the economy.

D

data mining Sorting through large amounts of historical data to uncover systematic patterns that can be exploited.

day order A buy order or a sell order expiring at the close of the trading day.

days' receivables See average collection period.

dealer market A market where traders specializing in particular commodities buy and sell assets for their own accounts. The OTC market is an example.

debenture or unsecured bond A bond not backed by specific collateral.

debt securities Bonds; also called fixed-income securities.

dedication strategy Refers to multiperiod cash flow matching.

default premium A differential in promised yield that compensates the investor for the risk inherent in purchasing a corporate bond that entails some risk of default.

defensive industries Industries with little sensitivity to the state of the economy.

deferred annuities Tax-advantaged life insurance product. Deferred annuities offer deferral of taxes with the option of withdrawing one's funds in the form of a life annuity.

defined benefit plans Pension plans in which retirement benefits are set according to a fixed formula.

defined contribution plans Pension plans in which the employer is committed to making contributions according to a fixed formula.

degree of operating leverage Percentage change in profits for a 1% change in sales.

delta (of option) See hedge ratio.

delta neutral The value of the portfolio is not affected by changes in the value of the asset on which the options are written.

demand shock An event that affects the demand for goods and services in the economy.

derivative asset/contingent claim Securities providing payoffs that depend on or are contingent on the values of other assets such as commodity prices, bond and stock prices, or market index values. Examples are futures and options.

derivative security See primitive security.

direct search market Buyers and sellers seek each other directly and transact directly.

directional strategy Speculation that one sector or another will outperform other sectors of the market.

discount bonds Bonds selling below par value.

discretionary account An account of a customer who gives a broker the authority to make buy and sell decisions on the customer's behalf.

diversifiable risk Risk attributable to firm-specific risk, or nonmarket risk. *Nondiversifiable* risk refers to systematic or market risk.

diversification Spreading a portfolio over many investments to avoid excessive exposure to any one source of risk.

dividend discount model (DDM) A formula stating that the intrinsic value of a firm is the present value of all expected future dividends.

dividend payout ratio Percentage of earnings paid out as dividends.

dividend yield The percent rate of return provided by a stock's dividend payments.

dollar-weighted rate of return The internal rate of return on an investment.

doubling option A sinking fund provision that may allow repurchase of twice the required number of bonds at the sinking fund call price.

Dow theory A technical analysis technique that seeks to discern long- and short-term trends in security prices.

DuPont system Decomposition of firm profitability measures into the underlying factors that determine such profitability.

duration A measure of the average life of a bond, defined as the weighted average of the times until each payment is made, with weights proportional to the present value of the payment.

dynamic hedging Constant updating of hedge positions as market conditions change.

E

EAFE index The European, Australian, Far East index, computed by Morgan Stanley, is a widely used index of non-U.S. stocks.

earnings management The practice of using flexibility in accounting rules to improve the apparent profitability of the firm.

earnings retention ratio Plowback ratio.

earnings yield The ratio of earnings to price, E/P.

economic earnings The real flow of cash that a firm could pay out forever in the absence of any change in the firm's productive capacity.

economic value added (EVA) The spread between ROA and cost of capital multiplied by the capital invested in the firm. It measures the dollar value of the firm's return in excess of its opportunity cost.

effective annual rate (EAR) Interest rate is annualized using compound rather than simple interest.

effective annual yield Annualized interest rate on a security computed using compound interest techniques.

effective duration Percentage change in bond price per change in the level of market interest rates.

efficient diversification The organizing principle of modern portfolio theory, which maintains that any risk-averse investor will search for the highest expected return for any level of portfolio risk.

efficient frontier Graph representing a set of portfolios that maximize expected return at each level of portfolio risk.

efficient frontier of risky assets The portion of the minimum-variance frontier that lies above the global minimum-variance portfolio.

efficient market hypothesis The prices of securities fully reflect available information. Investors buying securities in an efficient market should expect to obtain an equilibrium rate of return. Weak-form EMH asserts that stock prices already reflect all information contained in the history of past prices. The semistrong-form hypothesis asserts that stock prices already reflect all publicly available information. The strong-form hypothesis asserts that stock prices reflect all relevant information including insider information.

elasticity (of an option) Percentage change in the value of an option accompanying a 1% change in the value of a stock.

electronic communication network (ECN) A computer-operated trading network offering an alternative to formal stock exchanges or dealer markets for trading securities.

endowment funds Organizations chartered to invest money for specific purposes.

equities Ownership shares in a firm.

equity Ownership in a firm. Also, the net worth of a margin account.

equivalent taxable yield The pretax yield on a taxable bond providing an after-tax yield equal to the rate on a tax-exempt municipal bond.

Eurodollars Dollar-denominated deposits at foreign banks or foreign branches of American banks.

European, Australian, Far East (EAFE) index A widely used index of non-U.S. stocks computed by Morgan Stanley.

European option A European option can be exercised only on the expiration date. Compare with an American option, which can be exercised before, up to, and on its expiration date.

event study Research methodology designed to measure the impact of an event of interest on stock returns.

event tree Depicts all possible sequences of events.

excess return Rate of return in excess of the risk-free rate.

exchange rate Price of a unit of one country's currency in terms of another country's currency.

exchange rate risk The uncertainty in asset returns due to movements in the exchange rates between the dollar and foreign currencies.

exchange-traded funds (ETFs) Offshoots of mutual funds that allow investors to trade portfolios of securities just as they do shares of stock.

exchanges National or regional auction markets providing a facility for members to trade securities. A seat is a membership on an exchange.

exercise or strike price Price set for calling (buying) an asset or putting (selling) an asset.

expectations hypothesis (of interest rates) Theory that forward interest rates are unbiased estimates of expected future interest rates.

expected return The probability-weighted average of the possible outcomes.

expected return–beta relationship Implication of the CAPM that security risk premiums (expected excess returns) will be proportional to beta.

F

face value The maturity value of a bond.

factor beta Sensitivity of security returns to changes in a systematic factor. Alternatively, factor loading; factor sensitivity.

factor loading See factor beta.

factor model A way of decomposing the factors that influence a security's rate of return into common and firm-specific influences.

factor portfolio A well-diversified portfolio constructed to have a beta of 1.0 on one factor and a beta of 0 on any other factor.

factor sensitivity See factor beta.

fair game An investment prospect that has a zero risk premium.

fair value accounting Use of current values rather than historic cost in the firm's financial statements.

federal funds Funds in a bank's reserve account.

FIFO The first-in first-out accounting method of inventory valuation.

financial assets Financial assets such as stocks and bonds are claims to the income generated by real assets or claims on income from the government.

financial engineering Creating and designing securities with custom-tailored characteristics.

financial intermediary An institution such as a bank, mutual fund, investment company, or insurance company that serves to connect the household and business sectors so households can invest and businesses can finance production.

firm-specific risk See diversifiable risk.

first-pass regression A time series regression to estimate the betas of securities or portfolios.

fiscal policy The use of government spending and taxing for the specific purpose of stabilizing the economy.

fixed annuities Annuity contracts in which the insurance company pays a fixed dollar amount of money per period.

fixed-charge coverage ratio Ratio of earnings to all fixed cash obligations, including lease payments and sinking fund payments.

fixed-income security A security such as a bond that pays a specified cash flow over a specific period.

flight to quality Describes the tendency of investors to require larger default premiums on investments under uncertain economic conditions.

floating-rate bond A bond whose interest rate is reset periodically according to a specified market rate.

forced conversion Use of a firm's call option on a callable convertible bond when the firm knows that bondholders will exercise their option to convert.

forecasting records The historical record of the forecasting errors of a security analyst.

foreign exchange market An informal network of banks and brokers that allows customers to enter forward contracts to purchase or sell currencies in the future at a rate of exchange agreed upon now.

foreign exchange swap An agreement to exchange stipulated amounts of one currency for another at one or more future dates.

forward contract An agreement calling for future delivery of an asset at an agreed-upon price. Also see futures contract.

forward interest rate Rate of interest for a future period that would equate the total return of a long-term bond with that of a strategy of rolling over shorter-term bonds. The forward rate is inferred from the term structure.

framing Decisions are affected by how choices are described, for example, whether uncertainty is posed as potential gains from a low baseline level, or as losses from a higher baseline value.

fully diluted earnings per share Earnings per share expressed as if all outstanding convertible securities and warrants have been exercised.

fundamental analysis   Research to predict stock value that focuses on such determinants as earnings and dividends prospects, expectations for future interest rates, and risk evaluation of the firm.

fundamental risk   Risk that even if an asset is mispriced, there is still no arbitrage opportunity, because the mispricing can widen before price eventually converges to intrinsic value.

funds of funds   Hedge funds that invest in several other hedge funds.

futures contract   Obliges traders to purchase or sell an asset at an agreed-upon price on a specified future date. The long position is held by the trader who commits to purchase. The short position is held by the trader who commits to sell. Futures differ from forward contracts in their standardization, exchange trading, margin requirements, and daily settling (marking to market).

futures option   The right to enter a specified futures contract at a futures price equal to the stipulated exercise price.

futures price   The price at which a futures trader commits to make or take delivery of the underlying asset.

G

gamma   The curvature of an option pricing function (as a function of the value of the underlying asset).

geometric average   The nth root of the product of n numbers. It is used to measure the compound rate of return over time.

globalization   Tendency toward a worldwide investment environment, and the integration of national capital markets.

gross domestic product (GDP)   The market value of goods and services produced over time including the income of foreign corporations and foreign residents working in the United States, but excluding the income of U.S. residents and corporations overseas.

H

hedge fund   A private investment pool, open to institutional or wealthy investors, that is largely exempt from SEC regulation and can pursue more speculative policies than mutual funds.

hedge ratio (for an option)   The number of stocks required to hedge against the price risk of holding one option. Also called the option's delta.

hedging   Investing in an asset to reduce the overall risk of a portfolio.

hedging demands   Demands for securities to hedge particular sources of consumption risk, beyond the usual mean variance diversification motivation.

high water mark   The previous value of a portfolio that must be reattained before a hedge fund can charge incentive fees.

holding-period return   The rate of return over a given period.

homogenous expectations   The assumption that all investors use the same expected returns and covariance matrix of security returns as inputs in security analysis.

horizon analysis   Forecasting the realized compound yield over various holding periods or investment horizons.

I

illiquidity   Difficulty, cost, and/or delay in selling an asset on short notice without offering substantial price concessions.

illiquidity cost   Costs due to imperfect liquidity of some security.

illiquidity premium   Extra expected return as compensation for limited liquidity.

immunization   A strategy that matches durations of assets and liabilities so as to make net worth unaffected by interest rate movements.

implied volatility   The standard deviation of stock returns that is consistent with an option's market value.

incentive fee   A fee charged by hedge funds equal to a share of any investment returns beyond a stipulated benchmark performance.

in the money   In the money describes an option whose exercise would produce profits. Out of the money describes an option where exercise would not be profitable.

income beneficiary   One who receives income from a trust.

income statement   A financial statement showing a firm's revenues and expenses during a specified period.

indenture   The document defining the contract between the bond issuer and the bondholder.

index arbitrage   An investment strategy that exploits divergences between actual futures prices and their theoretically correct parity values to make a profit.

index fund   A mutual fund holding shares in proportion to their representation in a market index such as the S&P 500.

index model   A model of stock returns using a market index such as the S&P 500 to represent common or systematic risk factors.

index option   A call or put option based on a stock market index.

indifference curve   A curve connecting all portfolios with the same utility according to their means and standard deviations.

industry life cycle   Stages through which firms typically pass as they mature.

inflation   The rate at which the general level of prices for goods and services is rising.

information ratio   Ratio of alpha to the standard deviation of diversifiable risk.

initial public offering   Stock issued to the public for the first time by a formerly privately owned company.

input list List of parameters such as expected returns, variances, and covariances necessary to determine the optimal risky portfolio.

inside information Nonpublic knowledge about a corporation possessed by corporate officers, major owners, or other individuals with privileged access to information about a firm.

insider trading Trading by officers, directors, major stockholders, or others who hold private inside information allowing them to benefit from buying or selling stock.

insurance principle The law of averages. The average outcome for many independent trials of an experiment will approach the expected value of the experiment.

interest coverage ratio Measure of financial leverage. Earnings before interest and taxes as a multiple of interest expense.

interest coverage ratio, or **times interest earned** A financial leverage measure (EBIT divided by interest expense).

interest rate The number of dollars earned per dollar invested per period.

interest rate parity relationship (theorem) The spot-futures exchange rate relationship that prevails in well-functioning markets.

interest rate swaps A method to manage interest rate risk where parties trade the cash flows corresponding to different securities without actually exchanging securities directly.

intermarket spread swap Switching from one segment of the bond market to another (from Treasuries to corporates, for example).

intrinsic value (of a firm) The present value of a firm's expected future net cash flows discounted by the required rate of return.

intrinsic value of an option Stock price minus exercise price, or the profit that could be attained by immediate exercise of an in-the-money option.

inventory turnover ratio Cost of goods sold as a multiple of average inventory.

investment Commitment of current resources in the expectation of deriving greater resources in the future.

investment bankers Firms specializing in the sale of new securities to the public, typically by underwriting the issue.

investment company Firm managing funds for investors. An investment company may manage several mutual funds.

investment-grade bond Bond rated BBB and above or Baa and above. Lower-rated bonds are classified as speculative-grade or junk bonds.

investment horizon Time horizon for purposes of investment decisions.

investment portfolio Set of securities chosen by an investor.

J

Jensen's measure The alpha of an investment.

junk bond See speculative-grade bond.

K

kurtosis Measure of the fatness of the tails of a probability distribution. Indicates probability of observing extreme high or low values.

L

Law of One Price The rule stipulating that equivalent securities or bundles of securities must sell at equal prices to preclude arbitrage opportunities.

leading economic indicators Economic series that tend to rise or fall in advance of the rest of the economy.

leverage ratio Ratio of debt to total capitalization of a firm.

LIFO The last-in first-out accounting method of valuing inventories.

limited liability The fact that shareholders have no personal liability to the creditors of the corporation in the event of bankruptcy.

limit order An order specifying a price at which an investor is willing to buy or sell a security.

liquidation value Net amount that could be realized by selling the assets of a firm after paying the debt.

liquidity Liquidity refers to the speed and ease with which an asset can be converted to cash.

liquidity preference theory Theory that the forward rate exceeds expected future interest rates.

liquidity premium Forward rate minus expected future short interest rate.

load Sales charge on the purchase of some mutual funds.

load fund A mutual fund with a sales commission, or load.

lock-up period Period in which investors cannot redeem investments in the hedge fund.

lognormal distribution The log of the variable has a normal (bell-shaped) distribution.

London Interbank Offered Rate (LIBOR) Rate that most creditworthy banks charge one another for large loans of Eurodollars in the London market.

long position hedge Hedging the future cost of a purchase by taking a long futures position to protect against changes in the price of the asset.

lower partial standard deviation Standard deviation computed using only the portion of the probability distribution below the mean of the variable.

M

Macaulay's duration Effective maturity of bond, equal to weighted average of the times until each payment, with weights proportional to the present value of the payment.

maintenance, or **variation, margin** An established value below which a trader's margin cannot fall. Reaching the maintenance margin triggers a margin call.

margin Describes securities purchased with money borrowed from a broker. Current maximum margin is 50%.

market–book-value ratio Ratio of price per share to book value per share.

market capitalization rate The market-consensus estimate of the appropriate discount rate for a firm's cash flows.

market model Another version of the index model that breaks down return uncertainty into systematic and nonsystematic components.

market neutral A strategy designed to exploit relative mispricing within a market, but which is hedged to avoid taking a stance on the direction of the broad market.

market or systematic risk, firm-specific risk Market risk is risk attributable to common macroeconomic factors. Firm-specific risk reflects risk peculiar to an individual firm that is independent of market risk.

market order A buy or sell order to be executed immediately at current market prices.

market portfolio The portfolio for which each security is held in proportion to its market value.

market price of risk A measure of the extra return, or risk premium, that investors demand to bear risk. The reward-to-risk ratio of the market portfolio.

market risk See systematic risk.

market segmentation or preferred habitat theory The theory that long- and short-maturity bonds are traded in essentially distinct or segmented markets and that prices in one market do not affect those in the other.

market timer An investor who speculates on broad market moves rather than on specific securities.

market timing Asset allocation in which the investment in the market is increased if one forecasts that the market will outperform T-bills.

market-value-weighted index An index of a group of securities computed by calculating a weighted average of the returns of each security in the index, with weights proportional to outstanding market value.

marking to market Describes the daily settlement of obligations on futures positions.

mean-variance analysis Evaluation of risky prospects based on the expected value and variance of possible outcomes.

mean-variance criterion The selection of portfolios based on the means and variances of their returns. The choice of the higher expected return portfolio for a given level of variance or the lower variance portfolio for a given expected return.

mental accounting Individuals mentally segregate assets into independent accounts rather than viewing them as part of a unified portfolio.

minimum-variance frontier Graph of the lowest possible portfolio variance that is attainable for a given portfolio expected return.

minimum-variance portfolio The portfolio of risky assets with lowest variance.

modern portfolio theory (MPT) Principles underlying analysis and evaluation of rational portfolio choices based on risk–return trade-offs and efficient diversification.

modified duration Macaulay's duration divided by 1 + yield to maturity. Measures interest rate sensitivity of bond.

momentum effect The tendency of poorly performing stocks and well-performing stocks in one period to continue that abnormal performance in following periods.

monetary policy Actions taken by the Board of Governors of the Federal Reserve System to influence the money supply or interest rates.

money market Includes short-term, highly liquid, and relatively low-risk debt instruments.

mortality tables Tables of probability that individuals of various ages will die within a year.

mortgage-backed security Ownership claim in a pool of mortgages or an obligation that is secured by such a pool. Also called a *pass-through,* because payments are passed along from the mortgage originator to the purchaser of the mortgage-backed security.

multifactor CAPM Generalization of the basic CAPM that accounts for extra-market hedging demands.

multifactor models Model of security returns positing that returns respond to several systematic factors.

municipal bonds Tax-exempt bonds issued by state and local governments, generally to finance capital improvement projects. General obligation bonds are backed by the general taxing power of the issuer. Revenue bonds are backed by the proceeds from the project or agency they are issued to finance.

mutual fund A firm pooling and managing funds of investors.

mutual fund theorem A result associated with the CAPM, asserting that investors will choose to invest their entire risky portfolio in a market-index mutual fund.

N

NAICS codes North American Industrial Classification System codes that use numerical values to identify industries.

naked option writing Writing an option without an offsetting stock position.

NASDAQ The automated quotation system for the OTC market, showing current bid–asked prices for thousands of stocks.

neglected-firm effect That investments in stock of less well-known firms have generated abnormal returns.

net asset value (NAV) The value of each share expressed as assets minus liabilities on a per-share basis.

nominal interest rate The interest rate in terms of nominal (not adjusted for purchasing power) dollars.

nondirectional strategy A position designed to exploit temporary misalignments in relative pricing. Typically involves a long position in one security hedged with a short position in a related security.

nondiversifiable risk See systematic risk.

nonsystematic risk Nonmarket or firm-specific risk factors that can be eliminated by diversification. Also called unique risk or diversifiable risk. Systematic risk refers to risk factors common to the entire economy.

normal distribution Bell-shaped probability distribution that characterizes many natural phenomena.

notional principal Principal amount used to calculate swap payments.

O

on the run Recently issued bond, selling at or near par value.

on-the-run yield curve Relationship between yield to maturity and time to maturity for newly issued bonds selling at par.

open-end (mutual) fund A fund that issues or redeems its own shares at their net asset value (NAV).

open interest The number of futures contracts outstanding.

optimal risky portfolio An investor's best combination of risky assets to be mixed with safe assets to form the complete portfolio.

option elasticity The percentage increase in an option's value given a 1% change in the value of the underlying security.

original issue discount bond A bond issued with a low coupon rate that sells at a discount from par value.

out of the money Out of the money describes an option where exercise would not be profitable. In the money describes an option where exercise would produce profits.

over-the-counter market An informal network of brokers and dealers who negotiate sales of securities (not a formal exchange).

P

pairs trading Stocks are paired up based on underlying similarities, and longshort positions are established to exploit any relative mispricing between each pair.

par value The face value of the bond.

passive investment strategy See passive management.

passive management Buying a well-diversified portfolio to represent a broad-based market index without attempting to search out mispriced securities.

passive portfolio A market index portfolio.

passive strategy See passive management.

pass-through security Pools of loans (such as home mortgage loans) sold in one package. Owners of pass-throughs receive all principal and interest payments made by the borrowers.

peak The transition from the end of an expansion to the start of a contraction.

P/E effect That portfolios of low P/E stocks have exhibited higher average risk-adjusted returns than high P/E stocks.

personal trust An interest in an asset held by a trustee for the benefit of another person.

plowback ratio The proportion of the firm's earnings that is reinvested in the business (and not paid out as dividends). The plowback ratio equals 1 minus the dividend payout ratio.

political risk Possibility of the expropriation of assets, changes in tax policy, restrictions on the exchange of foreign currency for domestic currency, or other changes in the business climate of a country.

portable alpha; alpha transfer A strategy in which you invest in positive alpha positions, then hedge the systematic risk of that investment, and, finally, establish market exposure where you want it by using passive indexes.

portfolio insurance The practice of using options or dynamic hedge strategies to provide protection against investment losses while maintaining upside potential.

portfolio management Process of combining securities in a portfolio tailored to the investor's preferences and needs, monitoring that portfolio, and evaluating its performance.

portfolio opportunity set The expected return–standard deviation pairs of all portfolios that can be constructed from a given set of assets.

posterior distribution Probability distribution for a variable after adjustment for empirical evidence on its likely value.

preferred habitat theory Holds that investors prefer specific maturity ranges but can be induced to switch if risk premiums are sufficient.

preferred stock Nonvoting shares in a corporation, paying a fixed or variable stream of dividends.

premium The purchase price of an option.

premium bonds Bonds selling above par value.

present value of growth opportunities (PVGO) Net present value of a firm's future investments.

price–earnings multiple See price–earnings ratio.

price–earnings ratio The ratio of a stock's price to its earnings per share. Also referred to as the P/E multiple.

price value of a basis point The change in the value of a fixed-income asset resulting from a 1 basis point change in the asset's yield to maturity.

price-weighted average Weighted average with weights proportional to security prices rather than total capitalization.

primary market New issues of securities are offered to the public here.

primitive security, derivative security A *primitive security* is an instrument such as a stock or bond for which payments depend only on the financial status of its issuer. A *derivative* *security* is created from the set of primitive securities to yield returns that depend on factors beyond the characteristics of the issuer and that may be related to prices of other assets.

principal The outstanding balance on a loan.

prior distribution Probability distribution for a variable before adjusting for empirical evidence on its likely value.

private placement Primary offering in which shares are sold directly to a small group of institutional or wealthy investors.

profit margin See return on sales.

program trading Coordinated buy orders and sell orders of entire portfolios, usually with the aid of computers, often to achieve index arbitrage objectives.

prospect theory Behavioral (as opposed to rational) model of investor utility. Investor utility depends on changes in wealth rather than levels of wealth.

prospectus A final and approved registration statement including the price at which the security issue is offered.

protective covenant A provision specifying requirements of collateral, sinking fund, dividend policy, etc., designed to protect the interests of bondholders.

protective put Purchase of stock combined with a put option that guarantees minimum proceeds equal to the put's exercise price.

proxy An instrument empowering an agent to vote in the name of the shareholder.

prudent investor rule An investment manager must act in accord with the actions of a hypothetical prudent investor.

pseudo-American call option value The maximum of the value derived by assuming that an option will be held until expiration and the value derived by assuming that the option will be exercised just before an ex-dividend date.

public offering, private placement A *public offering* consists of bonds sold in the primary market to the general public; a *private placement* is sold directly to a limited number of institutional investors.

pure plays Bets on particular mispricing across two or more securities, with extraneous sources of risk such as general market exposure hedged away.

pure yield curve Refers to the relationship between yield to maturity and time to maturity for zero-coupon bonds.

pure yield pickup swap Moving to higher-yield bonds.

put bond A bond that the holder may choose either to exchange for par value at some date or to extend for a given number of years.

put/call ratio Ratio of put options to call options outstanding on a stock.

put-call parity theorem An equation representing the proper relationship between put and call prices. Violation of parity allows arbitrage opportunities.

put option The right to sell an asset at a specified exercise price on or before a specified expiration date.

Q

quality of earnings The realism and conservatism of the earnings number and the extent to which we might expect the reported level of earnings to be sustained.

quick ratio A measure of liquidity similar to the current ratio except for exclusion of inventories (cash plus receivables divided by current liabilities).

R

random walk Describes the notion that stock price changes are random and unpredictable.

rate anticipation swap A switch made in response to forecasts of interest rates.

real assets, financial assets *Real assets* are land, buildings, and equipment that are used to produce goods and services. *Financial assets* are claims such as securities to the income generated by real assets.

real interest rate The excess of the interest rate over the inflation rate. The growth rate of purchasing power derived from an investment.

realized compound return Yield assuming that coupon payments are invested at the going market interest rate at the time of their receipt and rolled over until the bond matures.

rebalancing Realigning the proportions of assets in a portfolio as needed.

registered bond A bond whose issuer records ownership and interest payments. Differs from a bearer bond, which is traded without record of ownership and whose possession is its only evidence of ownership.

regression equation An equation that describes the average relationship between a dependent variable and a set of explanatory variables.

regret avoidance Notion from behavioral finance that individuals who make decisions that turn out badly will have more regret when that decision was more unconventional.

reinvestment rate risk The uncertainty surrounding the cumulative future value of reinvested bond coupon payments.

REIT Real estate investment trust, which is similar to a closed-end mutual fund. REITs invest in real estate or loans secured by real estate and issue shares in such investments.

remainderman One who receives the principal of a trust when it is dissolved.

replacement cost Cost to replace a firm's assets. "Reproduction" cost.

representativeness bias People seem to believe that a small sample is just as representative of a broad population as a large one and therefore infer patterns too quickly.

repurchase agreements (repos) Short-term, often overnight, sales of government securities with an agreement to repurchase the securities at a slightly higher price. A *reverse* *repo* is a purchase with an agreement to resell at a specified price on a future date.

residual claim   Refers to the fact that shareholders are at the bottom of the list of claimants to assets of a corporation in the event of failure or bankruptcy.

residual income   See economic value added (EVA).

residuals   Parts of stock returns not explained by the explanatory variable (the market-index return). They measure the impact of firm-specific events during a particular period.

resistance level   A price level above which it is supposedly difficult for a stock or stock index to rise.

return on assets (ROA)   A profitability ratio; earnings before interest and taxes divided by total assets.

return on equity (ROE)   An accounting ratio of net profits divided by equity.

return on sales (ROS), or profit margin   The ratio of operating profits per dollar of sales (EBIT divided by sales).

reversal effect   The tendency of poorly performing stocks and well-performing stocks in one period to experience reversals in following periods.

reversing trade   Entering the opposite side of a currently held futures position to close out the position.

reward-to-volatility ratio   Ratio of excess return to portfolio standard deviation.

riding the yield curve   Buying long-term bonds in anticipation of capital gains as yields fall with the declining maturity of the bonds.

risk arbitrage   Speculation on perceived mispriced securities, usually in connection with merger and acquisition targets.

risk-averse, risk-neutral, risk lover   A *risk-averse* investor will consider risky portfolios only if they provide compensation for risk via a risk premium. A *risk-neutral* investor finds the level of risk irrelevant and considers only the expected return of risk prospects. A *risk lover* is willing to accept lower expected returns on prospects with higher amounts of risk.

risk-free asset   An asset with a certain rate of return; often taken to be short-term T-bills.

risk-free rate   The interest rate that can be earned with certainty.

risk lover   See risk-averse.

risk-neutral   See risk-averse.

risk premium   An expected return in excess of that on risk-free securities. The premium provides compensation for the risk of an investment.

risk–return trade-off   If an investor is willing to take on risk, there is the reward of higher expected returns.

risky asset   An asset with an uncertain rate of return.

S

scatter diagram   Plot of returns of one security versus returns of another security. Each point represents one pair of returns for a given holding period.

seasoned new issue   Stock issued by companies that already have stock on the market.

secondary market   Already existing securities are bought and sold on the exchanges or in the OTC market.

second-pass regression   A cross-sectional regression of portfolio returns on betas. The estimated slope is the measurement of the reward for bearing systematic risk during the period.

sector rotation   An investment strategy which entails shifting the portfolio into industry sectors that are forecast to outperform others based on macroeconomic forecasts.

securitization   Pooling loans for various purposes into standardized securities backed by those loans, which can then be traded like any other security.

security analysis   Determining correct value of a security in the marketplace.

security characteristic line   A plot of the excess return on a security over the risk-free rate as a function of the excess return on the market.

security market line   Graphical representation of the expected return–beta relationship of the CAPM.

security selection   See security selection decision.

security selection decision   Choosing the particular securities to include in a portfolio.

semistrong-form EMH   See efficient market hypothesis.

separation property   The property that portfolio choice can be separated into two independent tasks: (1) determination of the optimal risky portfolio, which is a purely technical problem, and (2) the personal choice of the best mix of the risky portfolio and the risk-free asset.

Sharpe's measure   Reward-to-volatility ratio; ratio of portfolio excess return to standard deviation.

shelf registration   Advance registration of securities with the SEC for sale up to 2 years following initial registration.

short position or hedge   Protecting the value of an asset held by taking a short position in a futures contract.

short rate   A one-period interest rate.

short sale   The sale of shares not owned by the investor but borrowed through a broker and later repurchased to replace the loan. Profit is earned if the initial sale is at a higher price than the repurchase price.

single-factor model   A model of security returns that acknowledges only one common factor. See factor model.

single-index model   A model of stock returns that decomposes influences on returns into a systematic factor, as measured by the return on a broad market index, and firm-specific factors.

single-stock futures   Futures contracts on single stock rather than an index.

sinking fund   A procedure that allows for the repayment of principal at maturity by calling for the bond issuer to repurchase some proportion of the outstanding bonds either in the open market or at a special call price associated with the sinking fund provision.

skew Measure of the asymmetry of a probability distribution.

small-firm effect That investments in stocks of small firms appear to have earned abnormal returns.

soft dollars The value of research services that brokerage houses supply to investment managers "free of charge" in exchange for the investment managers' business.

specialist A trader who makes a market in the shares of one or more firms and who maintains a "fair and orderly market" by dealing personally in the stock.

speculation Undertaking a risky investment with the objective of earning a greater profit than an investment in a risk-free alternative (a risk premium).

speculative-grade bond Bond rated Ba or lower by Moody's, or BB or lower by Standard & Poor's, or an unrated bond.

spot-futures parity theorem, or cost-of-carry relationship Describes the theoretically correct relationship between spot and futures prices. Violation of the parity relationship gives rise to arbitrage opportunities.

spot rate The current interest rate appropriate for discounting a cash flow of some given maturity.

spread (futures) Taking a long position in a futures contract of one maturity and a short position in a contract of different maturity, both on the same commodity.

spread (options) A combination of two or more call options or put options on the same stock with differing exercise prices or times to expiration. A money spread refers to a spread with different exercise price; a time spread refers to differing expiration date.

standard deviation Square root of the variance.

statement of cash flows A financial statement showing a firm's cash receipts and cash payments during a specified period.

statistical arbitrage Use of quantitative systems to uncover many perceived misalignments in relative pricing and ensure profit by averaging over all of these small bets.

stock exchanges Secondary markets where already-issued securities are bought and sold by members.

stock selection An active portfolio management technique that focuses on advantageous selection of particular stocks rather than on broad asset allocation choices.

stock split Issue by a corporation of a given number of shares in exchange for the current number of shares held by stockholders. Splits may go in either direction, either increasing or decreasing the number of shares outstanding. A *reverse split* decreases the number outstanding.

stop-loss order A sell order to be executed if the price of the stock falls below a stipulated level.

stop orders Order to trade contingent on security price designed to limit losses if price moves against the trader.

straddle A combination of buying both a call and a put on the same asset, each with the same exercise price and expiration date. The purpose is to profit from expected volatility.

straight bond A bond with no option features such as callability or convertibility.

street name Describes securities held by a broker on behalf of a client but registered in the name of the firm.

strike price See exercise price.

strip, strap Variants of a straddle. A *strip* is two puts and one call on a stock; a *strap* is two calls and one put, both with the same exercise price and expiration date.

stripped of coupons Describes the practice of some investment banks that sell "synthetic" zero-coupon bonds by marketing the rights to a single payment backed by a coupon-paying Treasury bond.

strong-form EMH See efficient market hypothesis.

subordination clause A provision in a bond indenture that restricts the issuer's future borrowing by subordinating the new leaders' claims on the firm to those of the existing bond holders. Claims of *subordinated* or *junior* debtholders are not paid until the prior debt is paid.

substitution swap Exchange of one bond for a bond with similar attributes but more attractively priced.

supply shock An event that influences production capacity and costs in the economy.

support level A price level below which it is supposedly difficult for a stock or stock index to fall.

survivorship bias Bias in the average returns of a sample of funds induced by excluding past returns on funds that left the sample because they happened to be unsuccessful.

swaption An option on a swap.

systematic risk Risk factors common to the whole economy, nondiversifiable risk; also called market risk.

T

tax anticipation notes Short-term municipal debt to raise funds to pay for expenses before actual collection of taxes.

tax deferral option The feature of the U.S. Internal Revenue Code that the capital gains tax on an asset is payable only when the gain is realized by selling the asset.

tax-deferred retirement plans Employer-sponsored and other plans that allow contributions and earnings to be made and accumulate tax-free until they are paid out as benefits.

tax swap Swapping two similar bonds to receive a tax benefit.

technical analysis Research to identify mispriced securities that focuses on recurrent and predictable stock price patterns and on proxies for buy or sell pressure in the market.

tender offer An offer from an outside investor to shareholders of a company to purchase their shares at a stipulated price, usually substantially above the market price, so that the investor may amass enough shares to obtain control of the company.

term insurance   Provides a death benefit only, no build-up of cash value.

term premiums   Excess of the yields to maturity on long-term bonds over those of short-term bonds.

term structure of interest rates   The pattern of interest rates appropriate for discounting cash flows of various maturities.

times interest earned   Ratio of profits to interest expense.

time value (of an option)   The part of the value of an option that is due to its positive time to expiration. Not to be confused with present value or the time value of money.

time-weighted average   An average of the period-by-period holding-period returns of an investment.

Tobin's q.   Ratio of market value of the firm to replacement cost.

total asset turnover   The annual sales generated by each dollar of assets (sales/assets).

tracking error   The difference between the return on a specified portfolio and that of a benchmark portfolio designed to mimic that portfolio.

tracking portfolio   A portfolio constructed to have returns with the highest possible correlation with a systematic risk factor.

tranche   See collateralized mortgage obligation.

treasury bill   Short-term, highly liquid government securities issued at a discount from the face value and returning the face amount at maturity.

treasury bond or note   Debt obligations of the federal government that make semiannual coupon payments and are issued at or near par value.

Treynor's measure   Ratio of excess return to beta.

trin statistic   Ratio of average trading volume in declining stocks to average volume in advancing stocks. Used in technical analysis.

trough   The transition point between recession and recovery.

turnover   The ratio of the trading activity of a portfolio to the assets of the portfolio.

U

unbundling   See bundling.

underwriters   Investment bankers who help companies issue their securities to the public.

underwriting, underwriting syndicate   Underwriters (investment bankers) purchase securities from the issuing company and resell them. Usually a syndicate of investment bankers is organized behind a lead firm.

unemployment rate   The ratio of the number of people classified as unemployed to the total labor force.

unique risk   See diversifiable risk.

unit investment trust   Money invested in a portfolio whose composition is fixed for the life of the fund. Shares in a unit trust are called redeemable trust certificates, and they are sold at a premium above net asset value.

universal life policy   An insurance policy that allows for a varying death benefit and premium level over the term of the policy, with an interest rate on the cash value that changes with market interest rates.

utility   The measure of the welfare or satisfaction of an investor.

utility value   The welfare a given investor assigns to an investment with a particular return and risk.

V

value at risk   Measure of downside risk. The loss that will be incurred in the event of an extreme adverse price change with some given, typically low, probability.

variable annuities   Annuity contracts in which the insurance company pays a periodic amount linked to the investment performance of an underlying portfolio.

variable life policy   An insurance policy that provides a fixed death benefit plus a cash value that can be invested in a variety of funds from which the policyholder can choose.

variance   A measure of the dispersion of a random variable. Equals the expected value of the squared deviation from the mean.

variation margin   See maintenance margin.

views   An analyst's opinion on the likely performance of a stock or sector compared to the market-consensus expectation.

volatility risk   The risk in the value of options portfolios due to unpredictable changes in the volatility of the underlying asset.

W

warrant   An option issued by the firm to purchase shares of the firm's stock.

weak-form EMH   See efficient market hypothesis.

well-diversified portfolio   A portfolio spread out over many securities in such a way that the weight in any security is close to zero.

whole-life insurance policy   Provides a death benefit and a kind of savings plan that builds up cash value for possible future withdrawal.

workout period   Realignment period of a temporary misaligned yield relationship.

world investable wealth   The part of world wealth that is traded and is therefore accessible to investors.

writing a call   Selling a call option.

GLOSSARY

Y

yield curve   A graph of yield to maturity as a function of time to maturity.

yield to maturity   A measure of the average rate of return that will be earned on a bond if held to maturity.

Z

zero-beta portfolio   The minimum-variance portfolio uncorrelated with a chosen efficient portfolio.

zero-coupon bond   A bond paying no coupons that sells at a discount and provides payment of face value only at maturity.

zero-investment portfolio   A portfolio of zero net value, established by buying and shorting component securities, usually in the context of an arbitrage strategy.

12b-1 fees   Annual fees charged by a mutual fund to pay for marketing and distribution costs.

NAME·INDEX

Page numbers followed by n indicate material found in notes.

NAME INDEX

Useful Formulas

Measures of Risk

Variance of returns: $\sigma^2 = \sum_s p(s)[r(s) - E(r)]^2$

Standard deviation: $\sigma = \sqrt{\sigma^2}$

Covariance between returns: $Cov(r_i, r_j) = \sum_s p(s)[r_i(s) - E(r_i)]\,[r_j(s) - E(r_j)]$

Beta of security i: $\beta_i = \dfrac{Cov(r_i, r_M)}{Var(r_M)}$

Portfolio Theory

Expected rate of return on a portfolio with weights w_i in each security: $E(r_p) = \sum_{i=1}^{n} w_i E(r_i)$

Variance of portfolio rate of return: $\sigma_p^2 = \sum_{j=1}^{n} \sum_{i=1}^{n} w_j w_i\, Cov(r_i, r_j)$

Market Equilibrium

The security market line: $E(r_i) = r_f + \beta_i[E(r_M) - r_f]$

Fixed-Income Analysis

Present value of $1:

Discrete period compounding: $PV = 1/(1 + r)^T$

Continuous compounding: $PV = e^{-rT}$

Forward rate of interest for period T: $f_T = \dfrac{(1 + y_T)^T}{(1 + y_{T-1})^{T-1}} - 1$

Real interest rate: $r = \dfrac{1 + R}{1 + i} - 1$

where R is the nominal interest rate and i is the inflation rate

Duration of a security: $D = \sum_{t=1}^{T} t \times \dfrac{CF_t}{(1 + y)^t}\,/Price$

Modified duration: $D^* = D/(1 + y)$